General International Law in International Investment Law

Foreword

Inaugurating the contemporary field of investment treaty arbitration some thirty-three years ago, the Tribunal in *Asian Agricultural Products Ltd v Sri Lanka* insisted that a bilateral investment treaty '*is not a self-contained closed legal system ... but it has to be envisaged within a wider juridical context in which rules from other sources are integrated*'.[1] Yet a persistent strand in thinking about investment treaty law has been to emphasize its distinctive character as *lex specialis*, providing remedies that the customary international law of diplomatic protection for the property of aliens does not.

The question, then, is not whether there is a relationship between investment treaties and general international law, but rather precisely what that relationship is: when do—or must— states, private parties, and arbitral tribunals look beyond the four corners of the treaty text and take into account the rules of general international law in order to determine the scope and application of their rights and obligations? This question is not susceptible of an abstract answer. Rather, the answer has to be found by disaggregating the issues, examining the particular problems to which the interface between investment treaties and general international law gives rise.

At the same time, we should be in no doubt as to the more general significance of creating a more detailed cartography of the role of general international law in investment law. Investment treaty law is fragmented by the design of states into a patchwork of numerous overlapping treaties. Yet states continue to emphasize the importance that they attach to the coherence of tribunal decisions. Coherence in legal reasoning may be understood as a fundamental attribute of a legal system governed by the rule of law. In the context of international investment law, coherence is best understood as the extent to which the obligations that states have assumed in particular treaties are integrated into the framework of general international law.

Charting the relation between general international law and investment treaties in this way is likely to shed light on two broader issues of both practical and theoretical importance for the international legal system as a whole. In the first place, it provides a key context, helping us to understand better the manner in which, despite its decentralized character, international law operates as a legal system through systemic integration. This issue has only gained importance in the twenty years since the International Court of Justice drew attention to it in *Oil Platforms*.[2] It has taken on a renewed urgency in view of the multiple challenges facing the international community and the disintegrative pressures imposed upon it.

In the second place, it will provide a deeper appreciation of what is meant by 'general international law', a compendious expression that refers not only to custom, but also to general principles *of* international law. The International Law Commission is currently considering the scope of this latter element of general international law. The jurisprudence of investment

---

[1] *Asian Agricultural Products Ltd v Sri Lanka* (Award) ICSID Case No ARB/87/3, 4 ICSID Rep 245, IIC 18 (1990, El-Kosheri P, Goldman & Asante (dissenting)), para 21.
[2] *Oil Platforms (Iran v United States)* (Judgment) [2003] ICJ Rep 161, 130 ILR 323.

tribunals provides a rich material source of the ways in which tribunals have found it necessary to refer to it in deciding cases before them, which, one hopes, may assist the Commission in appreciating its importance.

For all of these reasons, Andreas Kulick and Michael Waibel are to be congratulated for their initiative in conceiving this distinctive 'semi-systematic' Commentary. The editors themselves embody the premise behind the book. They are at one and the same time great specialists in investment law and great general international lawyers. Moreover, they have succeeded in bringing together an array of renowned authors to contribute their wisdom to particular entries.

The result is a fascinating and rigorous review of the interface between general international law and investment law, which will become an indispensable reference tool for scholars and practitioners in the field.

Campbell McLachlan KC
Cambridge, England
17 August 2023

Acknowledgements

This Commentary benefitted from the support and generosity of many people and institutions—intellectually, organizationally, and financially. First ideas for a Commentary on General International Law in International Investment Law ripened in summer 2019 at the Lauterpacht Centre for International Law at the University of Cambridge. It was again at the Centre that these Acknowledgements were written in summer 2023. It is no coincidence that many authors of entries in this Commentary have a connection to Cambridge and the Lauterpacht Centre. The Lauterpacht Centre has been an important constant in the academic lives of both editors—to Andreas, as his academic refuge and place of inspiration during multiple visits, and to Michael, as his academic home for more than a decade. The Centre has also been the anchor for our friendship and collaboration. In addition, the Commentary draws on the Centre's research strengths in public international law and international investment law, inspired by Centre Directors such as Professor Sir Elihu Lauterpacht QC, Judge James Crawford AC SC FBA, Professor Marc Weller, and Professor Eyal Benvenisti. We are delighted that Professor Campbell McLachlan KC contributed such a lucid and generous Foreword to this Commentary during his tenure as the Goodhart Visiting Professor of Legal Science at the University of Cambridge, for which we are equally grateful.

The University of Vienna and its Department for European, International and Comparative Law, led by Professor August Reinisch and another leading institution for research in international investment law and arbitration, also deserve to be singled out. As Michael's academic home since autumn 2019, the University of Vienna hosted the second authors' workshop and granted generous financial support. Professor Christina Binder, Professor Ursula Kriebaum, Professor Irmgard Marboe, Professor Christoph Schreuer, and Professor Stephan Wittich provided intellectual input at the workshop. Special thanks to Martin Baumgartner, Rebecca McMenamin, Nicola Nesi, Nektarios Papadimos, and Brigitte Weidinger for organizing the workshop and helping to review the forty-six entries in this Commentary. Our assistant editor, Andrijana Mišović, did the bulk of the work of reviewing, commenting, and revising several drafts of every entry. Andrijana handled these major tasks with impressive skill, knowledge, energy, and patience. We owe an enormous debt of gratitude to her.

Andreas also thanks the Amsterdam Centre of International Law and the European University Institute for hosting him as visitor in early 2022 and 2023, respectively, where he wrote parts of the entry on Article 31 VCLT and the Introductory entry. We are most grateful to our editors at Oxford University Press for their support of this project, including Merel Alstein, Fay Gibbons, Kathryn Plunkett, and Rebecca Lewis. We thank Kim Harris for preparing the index, and Reyman Joseph and his colleagues at Newgen for the efficient copy-editing, production of the proofs and shepherding of the Commentary through the production process.

A work such as this, spanning almost five years, received numerous ideas, insights, and inspirations from various friends and colleagues from practice and academia who would be too many to list individually here. We are indebted to every single one of them.

Finally, we thank all the authors for their important contributions to this Commentary. Beyond writing their own entries—on schedule despite the pandemic—they also participated in two workshops and provided crucial input on draft entries written by other authors. As a result, this volume is the outcome of a fruitful collaboration between a diverse group of practitioners and academics in public international law and international investment law.

Andreas Kulick and Michael Waibel, Cambridge/Heidelberg and Vienna, July 2023

Contents

Table of Cases   xiii
List of Contributors   lxi
List of Abbreviations   lxiii

General international law in international investment law (*Andreas Kulick and Michael Waibel*)   1

PART I LAW OF TREATIES (VCLT)

Article 18 of the VCLT: Obligation not to defeat the object and purpose of a treaty prior to its entry into force (*Belinda McRae*)   23

Articles 19–23 of the VCLT: Reservations (overview)—flexibility devices in applying treaties in the field of investment (*Alain Pellet and Jean-Baptiste Merlin*)   33

Article 24 of the VCLT: Entry into force (*Tania Voon*)   45

Article 25 of the VCLT: Provisional application (*Tania Voon*)   52

Article 26 of the VCLT: *Pacta sunt servanda* (*Can Yeginsu and Patrick Pearsall*)   64

Article 27 of the VCLT: Internal law and observance of treaties (*Rumiana Yotova*)   74

Article 28 of the VCLT: Non-retroactivity of treaties (*Ben Juratowitch and Jackie McArthur*)   84

Article 29 of the VCLT: Territorial scope (*Emma Lindsay and Philippa Webb*)   100

Article 30 of the VCLT: Application of successive treaties relating to the same subject-matter (*Sean Aughey*)   109

Article 31 of the VCLT: General rule of interpretation (*Andreas Kulick and Panos Merkouris*)   120

Article 32 of the VCLT: Supplementary means of interpretation (*Esmé Shirlow and Michael Waibel*)   146

Article 33 of the VCLT: Interpretation of treaties authenticated in two or more languages (*Peter Tzeng*)   166

Parts IV and V of the VCLT: Amendment, invalidity, termination, and suspension of treaties (*Luke Sobota and Amelia Keene*)   177

Article 59 of the VCLT: Termination or suspension of the operation of a treaty implied by conclusion of a later treaty (*Hélène Ruiz Fabri and Randi Ayman*)   214

Article 60 of the VCLT: Termination or suspension of the operation of a treaty as consequence of its breach (*Hélène Ruiz Fabri and Randi Ayman*) — 225

Article 62 of the VCLT: Fundamental change of circumstances (*Makane Moïse Mbengue*) — 233

PART II RESPONSIBILITY OF STATES AND INTERNATIONAL ORGANIZATIONS

Article 4 of the ARSIWA: Conduct of organs of a State (*Chester Brown*) — 249

Article 5 of the ARSIWA: Conduct of empowered entities (*Jorge E Viñuales and Oliver Hailes*) — 264

Article 6 of the ARSIWA and Article 7 of the ARIO (*Jonathan Bonnitcha and Alisha Mathew*) — 280

Article 7 of the ARSIWA: Excess of authority or contravention of instructions (*Chester Brown*) — 288

Article 8 of the ARSIWA: Attribution of conduct instructed, directed or controlled by a State (*Jorge E Viñuales and Alina Papanastasiou*) — 298

Article 13 of the ARSIWA: International obligation in force for a State (*Claudia Annacker and Enikő Horváth*) — 313

Article 14 of the ARSIWA: Extension in time of the breach of an international obligation (*Claudia Annacker and Enikő Horváth*) — 318

Article 15 of the ARSIWA: Breach consisting of a composite act (*Claudia Annacker and Enikő Horváth*) — 325

Article 20 of the ARSIWA: Consent (*Federica Paddeu*) — 331

Article 21 of the ARSIWA: Self-defence (*Federica Paddeu*) — 336

Article 23 of the ARSIWA: *Force majeure* (*Federica Paddeu*) — 341

Article 24 of the ARSIWA: Distress (*Federica Paddeu*) — 348

Article 25 of the ARSIWA: Necessity (*Federica Paddeu and Michael Waibel*) — 353

Article 26 of the ARSIWA: Compliance with peremptory norms (*Federica Paddeu*) — 365

Article 27 of the ARSIWA: Consequences of invoking a circumstance precluding wrongfulness (*Federica Paddeu*) — 369

Part Two, Chapters I and II of the ARSIWA: Remedies (*Geraldo Vidigal and Stephanie Forrest*) — 375

Articles 49–54 of the ARSIWA: Countermeasures (*Martins Paparinskis*) — 401

Article 55 of the ARSIWA: *Lex specialis* (*Fernando Lusa Bordin*) — 412

PART III STATE SUCCESSION, SOURCES AND STATE IMMUNITY

The procedure for succession to bilateral investment treaties (*Arman Sarvarian*)   423

Succession in respect of cession, unification and separation of States
(*James G Devaney and Christian J Tams*)   435

The protection of foreign investment in the law of State succession
(*Arman Sarvarian*)   450

Article 38 of the ICJ Statute: Sources (*Patrick Dumberry*)   464

State immunity in investment arbitration (*August Reinisch*)   489

PART IV SUBSTANTIVE AND PROCEDURAL ASPECTS OF GENERAL INTERNATIONAL LAW IN INTERNATIONAL INVESTMENT LAW

Cross-cutting substantive aspects: NAFTA standards in light of the decisions of international courts and tribunals (*Jingyuan Zhou and Sergio Puig*)   505

Denial of justice (*Jarrod Hepburn*)   523

The international law minimum standard of treatment (*Robert Howse*)   539

Cross-cutting procedural powers of international courts and tribunals
(*Cameron Miles*)   555

Nationality (*Chiara Giorgetti*)   588

Abuse of process (*Régis Bismuth*)   605

Unjust enrichment (*Kathleen Claussen*)   618

Index   629

Table of Cases

ICSID CONVENTION AND ADDITIONAL FACILITY PROCEEDINGS

A11Y LTD v Czech Republic, ICSID Case No UNCT/15/1, Jurisdiction
 (9 February 2017) 204n.176, 562n.68
AAPL v Sri Lanka, ICSID Case No ARB/87/3, Final Award (27 June 1990) 16, 8–9, 9n.71,
 122–23, 122nn.12–13, 145, 545–46
Abaclat and Others v Argentine Republic, ICSID Case No ARB/07/5,
 Decision on Jurisdiction and Admissibility (4 August 2011) 127, 127n.60, 484n.226,
 563n.69, 573n.161, 609n.47
ABCI Investments N.V v Republic of Tunisia, ICSID Case No ARB/04/12,
 Decision on Jurisdiction (18 February 2011) 322n.47
Abed El Jaouni & Imperial Holding SAL v Lebanon, ICSID Case No ARB/15/3,
 Award (14 January 2021) 574n.170
Accession Mezzanine Capital L.P. and Danubius Kereskedohaz
 Vagyonkezelo v Hungary, ICSID Case No ARB/12/3, Decision on
 Respondents Objection under Arbitration Rule 41(5) (16 January 2013) 467n.21, 477n.141
Adamakopoulos, Theodoros and others v Republic of Cyprus, ICSID Case No ARB/15/49,
 Decision on Jurisdiction (7 February 2020) 115n.44, 117n.70, 204, 204n.177,
 219–20, 219–20nn.25, 30, 224
 Dissenting Opinion of Professor Marcelo Kohen (3 February 2020) 30, 204n.177,
 219–20, 219n.25
ADC Affiliate Limited and ADC & ADMC Management Limited v Republic of
 Hungary, ICSID Case No ARB/03/16, Award (2 October 2006) 127, 127n.59,
 394–95n.144, 396n.162, 467n.21, 625, 625n.43
Addiko Bank AG and Addiko Bank d.d. v Republic of Croatia, ICSID Case No
 ARB/17/37, Decision on Respondent Jurisdictional Objection (12 June 2020) 219–20,
 219n.21, 220n.35, 221n.40, 224, 566, 566n.95
ADF Group v USA, ICSID Case No ARB (AF)/00/1, Award (9 January 2003) 126, 126n.42,
 135n.155, 181, 181n.25, 290n.19, 471n.72, 510n.38, 512–13, 521
ADM v Mexico. See Archer Daniels Midland Company and Tate & Lyle Ingredients
 Americas, Inc v United Mexican States
AES Corporation v Argentina, ICSID Case No ARB/02/17, Jurisdiction (26 April 2005) ... 570n.126
AES Summit Generation Limited v Hungary, ICSID Case No ARB/07/22
 Award (23 September 2010) 54n.15, 286n.47
African Holding Company of America, Inc. and Société Africaine de Construction
 au Congo S.A.R.L. v Democratic Republic of the Congo, ICSID Case No ARB/05/21,
 Award on Objections to Jurisdiction and Admissibility (29 July 2008) 322n.40
AGIP S.p.A. v People's Republic of the Congo, ICSID Case No ARB/77/1,
 Award (30 November 1979) 241, 241n.97, 245, 383n.55, 383n.58
Aguas del Tunari v Bolivia, ICSID Case No ARB/02/03,
 Decision on Respondent's Objections to Jurisdiction (21 October 2005) 124–25, 125n.32,
 130n.92, 132n.109, 142, 142n.222, 145, 151n.34, 162n.129
 Order taking note of the discontinuance issued by the Tribunal, pursuant to
 ICSID Arbitration Rule 44 (28 March 2006) 611n.64
Al Tamimi, Adel A Hamadi v Sultanate of Oman, ICSID Case No ARB/11/33,
 Award (3 November 2015) 11n.103, 262, 262n.112, 321n.35,
 414–16, 414n.14, 416n.21, 419, 578n.208
 Award (27 October 2015) 309n.93, 310, 310n.97

Albaniabeg Ambient Sh.p.k, M. Angelo Novelli and Costruzioni S.r.l. v Republic of Albania,
  ICSID Case No ARB/14/26, Decision on the Applicant's Request for the Continuation
  of the Provisional Stay of Enforcement of the Award (10 August 2021) 499n.65
Almasryia for Operating & Maintaining Touristic Construction Co LLC v Kuwait,
  ICSID Case No ARB/18/2, Rule 41(5) (1 November 2019) 562n.68
Alpha Projektholding GmbH v Ukraine, ICSID Case No ARB/07/16, Award
  (8 November 2010) 573nn.160,63
Ambiente Ufficio v Argentine Republic, ICSID Case No ARB/08/9, Decision on
  Jurisdiction and Admissibility (8 February 2013) 136–37n.170, 139n.188, 140n.201,
                                                              152–53, 152n.44, 153n.53
AMCO Asia Corp. and others v Republic of Indonesia, ICSID Case No ARB/81/1,
  Vol 1, 569, 38–50 (5 June 1993) 624n.37, 628
  Jurisdiction (25 September 1983) 467n.19
Award (20 November 1984) 303n.37, 312, 385n.70, 476n.127, 477–78, 478n.149
Annulment Decision (16 May 1986) 162n.122, 163, 163n.132
  Resubmitted Case, Decision on Jurisdiction (10 May 1988) 482–83n.208
Award on Resubmitted Proceedings (31 May 1990) 530n.58, 531, 535, 535n.99
  Decision on the Application for Annulment of the 1990 Award (17 December 1992) 530n.60
American Manufacturing & Trading, Inc. v Republic of Zaire, ICSID Case No ARB/93/1,
  Award (21 February 1977) 77n.28
Ampal-American Israel Corporation and others v Arab Republic of Egypt,
  ICSID Case No ARB/12/11,
Decision on Jurisdiction (1 February 2016) 611, 611nn.69–72, 617
Decision on Liability and Heads of Loss (21 February 2017) 277n.97, 302n.30, 302nn.31–32,
                        302n.34, 303n.35, 305n.50, 308, 308nn.83–84, 482–83n.208, 580n.232
Anderson v Costa Rica, ICSID Case No ARB(AF)/07/3, Award (19 May 2010) 126n.44
Ansung Housing Co. Ltd v China, ICSID Case No ARB/14/25, Award (9 March 2017) 323n.52
Antin Infrastructure Services Luxembourg S.a.r.l. and Antin Energia Termosolar BV v Kingdom
  of Spain. See Infrastructure Services Luxembourg Sàrl & Anor v Spain
Apotex Holdings Inc & Anor v US, ICSID Case No ARB(AF)/12/1, Award
  (25 August 2014) 480n.172, 483n.212, 510,
                                            510n.39, 510n.42, 521, 573n.163, 580n.231
Archer Daniels Midland Company and Tate & Lyle Ingredients Americas, Inc. v United
  Mexican States, ICSID Case No ARB (AF)/04/5,
  Concurring Opinion of Arbitrator Rovine (20 September 2007) 409n.65
Award (21 November 2007) 13n.126, 376n.5, 407n.55, 408n.63, 409–10,
                        409nn.68–70, 410n.75, 410n.76, 410n.77, 411, 413n.7, 413n.9, 416–17,
                                      417nn.30–32, 419, 467n.21, 473n.98, 507n.11, 507n.12,
                                                    512–13, 512n.58, 521, 560, 560n.48
  Franck Charles Arif v Republic of Moldova, ICSID Case No ARB/11/23,
    Award (8 April 2013) 129–30, 130n.89, 378n.15, 385–86,
                                                  386n.76, 397n.164, 399n.173, 400, 532–33,
                                                  532n.75, 532nn.76–77, 533n.85, 538
AS PNB Banka and others v Republic of Latvia, ICSID Case No ARB/17/47,
  Decision on the Proposal to Disqualify Messrs. James Spigelman, Peter Tomka
    and John M. Townsend (16 June 2020) 610n.62
  Decision on the Intra-EU Objection (14 May 2021) 139n.196, 210nn.206–8,
                                                              220nn.26,31, 221n.38, 224
  Decision on the Intra-EU Objection (14 July 2021) 112n.19, 112n.22, 113n.29,
                                            116nn.52,58, 116n.60, 117–18, 118n.73, 118nn.74,78, 119
Asian Agric. Prods. Ltd v Republic of Sri Lanka, ICSID Case No ARB /87/3,
  4 ICSID Rep 245, IIC 18,
  Award (27 June 1990) vn.1, 573n.163
  Dissenting Opinion of Samuel K.B. Asante (15 June 1990) 4 ICSID Rep 296 .... 546n.23
ATA Construction, Industrial and Trading Company v Jordan,
  ICSID Case No ARB/08/2,
  Award (18 May 2010) 79, 79nn.40–41, 386n.77

TABLE OF CASES XV

Interpretation and Provisional Measures (7 March 2011) 582, 582n.251
Autopista Concesionada de Venezuela v Bolivarian Republic of Venezuela,
    ICSID Case No ARB/00/5, Award (23 September 2003) 13n.124, 344–45, 344n.29,
            345nn.32–34, 345nn.35–36, 346, 347
Ayoub-Farid Michel Saab v United Republic of Thailand, ICSID Case No ARB/19/8 ...... 200n.154
Azinian, Robert, Davitian, Kenneth & Baca, Ellen v United Mexican States,
    ICSID Case No ARB (AF)/97/2,
    Counter Memorial (5 October 1998) 520nn.38–39, 42
    Claimants' Reply to Counter Memorial (19 January 1999)........................... 528n.37
    Award (1 November 1999) 43, 494n.32, 528–29, 528nn.40–41
Azurix Corp v Argentina, ICSID Case No ARB/01/12, Award (14 July 2006) 329n.36, 389n.97,
            396n.162, 570n.128, 625, 625n.41, 628
B3 Croatian Courier Coöperatief U.A. v Republic of Croatia, ICSID Case No ARB/ 15/ 5, Award
    (Excerpts) (5 April 2019) 322–23nn.47–48
Bayindir Insaat Turizm Ticaret Ve Sanayi A.S. v Islamic Republic of Pakistan,
    ICSID Case No ARB/03/29,
    Decision on Jurisdiction (14 November 2005)...................................... 128n.73
    Award (27 August 2009) 20 ICSID Rep 99 .... 269n.28, 274–75, 275n.77, 276n.93,
            279, 299n.5, 302n.31, 303n.40, 308, 308nn.81–82,
            310–11, 310n.99, 315n.16, 570n.129
Bayview Irrigation District & Ors v Mexico, ICSID Case No ARB(AF)/05/1,
    Award (19 June 2007) 571n.141
BayWa r.e. Renewable Energy GmbH and BayWa r.e. Asset Holding GmbH
    v Spain, ICSID Case No ARB/15/16,
    Decision on Jurisdiction, Liability and Directions of Quantum (2 December 2019) 41,
            182–83, 183n.39, 185, 185n.54, 185n.55, 189, 189nn.84–85, 213
    Award (25 January 2021) 139n.196
Bear Creek Mining v Peru, ICSID Case No ARB/14/21, Award
    (30 November 2017) 547–48, 548n.34
Beijing Urban Construction Group Co Ltd v Republic of Yemen,
    ICSID Case No ARB/14/30, Decision on Jurisdiction (31 May 2017) 162n.127, 301n.25
Belenergia SA v Italian Republic, ICSID Case No ARB/15/40, Award (6 August 2019) 117n.72,
            185n.55, 578n.205
Berkowitz, Aaron C., Berkowitz, Brett E. and Berkowitz, Trevor B. (formerly Spence
    International Investments and others) v Republic of Costa Rica,
    ICSID Case No UNCT/13/2
    Interim Award (25 October 2016) 46n.6
    Interim Award (Corrected) (30 May 2017)........................ 316n.25, 323n.48, 323n.52,
            329n.34, 329nn.38–39
Besserglik v Mozambique, ICSID Case No ARB(AF)/14/2, Award (28 October 2019) 49–50,
            50nn.37–40, 51
Biwater Gauff (Tanzania) Limited v Tanzania, ICSID Case No ARB/05/22, 19
    ICSID Rep 183,
    Procedural Order No 1 (31 March 2006) 568n.108
    Procedural Order No 2 (24 May 2006) 77, 77n.31, 78, 83
    Procedural Order No 3 (29 September 2006)................................... 566n.102
    Award (24 July 2008) 275–76n.84, 394n.139, 563n.69
Blue Bank International & Trust Ltd v Venezuela, ICSID Case No ARB/12/20,
    Award (26 April 2017) 578n.209
Blusun SA, Jean-Pierre Lecorcier and Michael Stein v Italian Republic,
    ICSID Case No ARB/14/3, Award (27 December 2016) 118nn.75,77, 118nn.80–81, 119,
            152n.43, 189, 189nn.79–81, 328n.21
Border Timbers et al v Republic of Zimbabwe, ICSID Case No ARB/10/25,
    Award (28 July 2015) 360, 360n.63, 366–67nn.9–10, 368, 373n.30
Bosh International, Inc and B&P Ltd Foreign Investment Enterprise v Ukraine, ICSID Case No
    ARB/08/11, Award (25 October 2012) 252–53n.32, 267n.13, 271n.44,
            273n.58, 277n.103, 302n.30, 564n.75

Brandes Investment Partners LP v Venezuela, ICSID Case No ARB/08/3,
  Award (2 August 2011) 574n.168
Bridgestone Licensing Services Inc v Panama, ICSID Case No ARB/16/34,
  Award (14 August 2020) 532nn.76–77, 538n.112
Bureau Veritas, Inspection, Valuation, Assessment and Control, BIVAC BV v Republic of
  Paraguay, ICSID Case No ARB/07/9,
  Decision on Jurisdiction (29 May 2009) 129, 129n.81, 130n.91, 564n.75, 570n.126
  Further Decision on Objections to Jurisdiction (9 October 2012) 496–97n.50
Burlington Resources Inc. v Republic of Ecuador (formerly Burlington Resources Inc. and
  others v Republic of Ecuador and Empresa Estatal Petróleos del Ecuador (PetroEcuador)),
  ICSID Case No ARB/08/5,
  Procedural Order No 1 (29 June 2009) 382n.45
  Decision on Jurisdiction (14 June 2010) 496–97n.50
  Decision on Reconsideration (7 February 2017) 395n.149, 397n.164, 584n.271
  Decision on Liability (14 December 2012) 328n.29
Cambodia Power Company v Cambodia and Electricité du Cambodge LLC,
  ICSID Case No ARB/09/18, Decision on Jurisdiction (22 March 2011) 467n.22
Çap, Muhammet & Anor v Turkmenistan, ICSID Case No ARB/12/6
  Decision on Jurisdiction (13 February 2015) 9n.73, 124n.29
  Award (4 May 2021) 306n.61, 312, 578n.205
Capital Financial Holdings Luxembourg SA v Republic of Cameroon,
  ICSID Case No ARB/15/18, Award (22 June 2017) 613n.86
Caratube International Oil Company LLP v Kazakhstan (I), ICSID Case No ARB/08/12,
  Decision on Provisional Measures (31 July 2009) 162n.125
  Annulment (21 February 2014) 572n.144
  Decision on the Claimants' Request for Provisional Measures (4 December 2014) 29n.52
Cargill, Inc v Mexico, ICSID Case No ARB(AF)/05/2 (NAFTA), Award
  (18 September 2009) 11n.98, 13n.126, 407n.55, 409n.65,
                       411, 468n.34, 469n.50, 472n.76, 473n.90, 473nn.95,97,
                       507n.11, 507n.12, 510, 510n.40, 512, 512n.58, 512n.62, 521
Cargill, Inc v Poland, ICSID Case No ARB(AF)/04/2, Award (29 February 2008) 570n.126
Carrizosa, Astrida Benita v Republic of Colombia, ICSID Case No ARB/18/5,
  Award (19 April 2021) 323n.48, 323n.49
Casinos Austria International GmbH & Casinos Austria Aktiengesellschaft
  v Argentina, ICSID Case No ARB/14/32,
  Jurisdiction (29 June 2018) 558n.33
  Award (5 November 2021) 254nn.43,46
Cavalum SGPS, SA v Kingdom of Spain, ICISD Case No ARB/15/34,
  Decision on Jurisdiction, Liability and Directions on Quantum (31 August 2020) 121n.4
  Decision on the Kingdom of Spain's Request for Reconsideration
    (10 January 2022) 200–1n.156, 213
CDC Group plc v Republic of the Seychelles, ICSID Case No ARB/02/14, Decision
  on Whether or Not to Continue Stay and Order (14 July 2004) 500n.72
Cementownia "Nowa Huta" SA v Republic of Turkey, ICSID Case No
  ARB(AF)/06/2, Award (17 September 2009) 393, 393n.137, 610n.61
CEMEX Caracas Investments BV & Anor v Venezuela, ICSID Case No ARB/08/15,
  Provisional Measures (3 March 2010) 567n.107
Cervin Investissements SA and Rhone Investissements SA v Republic of Costa Rica,
  ICSID Case No ARB/13/2, Decision on Jurisdiction (15 December 2014) 322n.46
Ceskoslovenska Obchodni Banka, AS v Slovak Republic, ICSID Case No ARB/97/4,
  Decision of the Tribunal on Objections to Jurisdiction (24 May 1999) 49, 49nn.34–36, 50,
                                                                                130n.96
Champion Trading Company and Ameritrade International, Inc. v Arab Republic
  of Egypt, ICSID Case No ARB/02/9, Jurisdiction (21 October 2003) 151–52, 593,
                                                           593n.27, 597, 597n.48, 601, 601n.66, 603
Chevron Bangladesh Block Twelve, Ltd and Chevron Bangladesh Blocks Thirteen
  and Fourteen, Ltd v People's Republic of Bangladesh, ICSID
  Case No ARB/06/10, Award (17 May 2010) 303n.37, 312

Churchill Mining PLC & Planet Mining Pty Ltd v Republic of Indonesia,
    ICSID Case No ARB/12/40 & 12/14,
    Procedural Order No 3 (3 March 2013) 567n.104
    Decision on Jurisdiction (24 February 2014) 161–62n.121
    Award (6 December 2016) 18, 18nn.189–90, 477, 477n.142, 483–85,
                                                       483n.222, 485n.235, 488, 573n.160, 575n.175, 625, 625n.44
CMC Africa Austral, LDA, CMC Muratori Cementisti CMC Di Ravenna SOC.
    Coop., et al v Republic of Mozambique, ICSID Case No ARB/17/23,
    Award (24 October 2019) 115n.46, 200n.155, 625, 625n.45
CMS Gas Transmission Co v Argentine Republic, ICSID Case No ARB/01/8,
    Jurisdiction Award (17 July 2003) 557n.18
    Award (12 May 2005) 206n.186, 353–54n.2, 358n.41, 361–62,
                                                       362n.77, 364, 366, 366n.8, 368n.25, 373, 373n.29, 373n.32, 374,
                                                       374n.40, 383–84, 383n.55, 384n.61, 394, 394n.143, 516n.100, 521
    Decision on the Argentine Republic's Request for a Continued Stay of
        Enforcement of the Award (1 September 2006) 499, 499n.70, 502
    Annulment (25 September 2007) 13n.120, 357, 357nn.33,37, 358–59, 358n.42,
                                                       359nn.46–48, 364, 373n.29, 373n.32, 418nn.38–40
Compagnia del Desarrollo de Santa Elena v Costa Rica, ICSID Case No ARB/96/1,
    Final Award (17 February 2000) 329n.36, 389n.97, 396, 396n.161
Compañiá de Aguas del Aconquija SA and Vivendi Universal SA v Argentine Republic, ICSID
    Case No ARB/97/3 (formerly Compañía de Aguas del Aconquija, SA and Compagnie
    Générale des Eaux v Argentine Republic)
    Decision on the Challenge to the President of the Committee (3 October 2001) 151, 151n.37,
                                                       152nn.38–39
    Decision on Annulment (3 July 2002) 302n.28, 312
    Award (20 August 2007) 327n.18, 394–95n.144
ConocoPhillips v Venezuela, ICSID Case No ARB/07/30, Decision on Jurisdiction
    and the Merits (3 September 2013) 127, 127n.62
Consortium R.F.C.C. v Kingdom of Morocco, ICSID Case No ARB/00/6, Award
    (22 December 2003) 496n.46
Consorzio Groupement LESI-DIPENTA v People's Democratic Republic of Algeria,
    ICSID Case No ARB/03/08, Award (10 January 2005) 301n.26
Continental Casualty Company v Argentine Republic, ICSID Case No ARB/03/9,
    Award (5 September 2008) 128n.70, 358n.44, 396, 396n.163
Corn Products International, Inc v Mexico, ICSID Case No ARB(AF)/04/01,
    Decision on Responsibility (15 January 2008) 13n.126, 407n.55, 409–10,
                                                       409n.65, 410n.74, 411
    Separate Opinion of Arbitrator Lowenfeld. Award (18 August 2009) 407n.56, 507n.11,
                                                       507n.12, 512–13, 512n.58, 521
Corona Materials LLC v Dominican Republic, ICSID Case No ARB(AF)/14/3,
    Submission of the United States of America (11 March 2016) 531n.69
    Award on the Respondent's Expedited Preliminary Objections (31 May 2016) 323n.50, 531,
                                                       531n.72, 534, 534nn.89–90, 537n.109
Cortec Mining Kenya Limited & Ors v Kenya, ICSID Case No ARB/15/29,
    Award (22 October 2018) 578n.208
Crystallex International Corp. v Bolivarian Republic of Venezuela,
    ICSID Case No ARB(AF)/11/2, Award (4 April 2016) 277n.97, 327n.18, 395,
                                                       395nn.151–52, 476–77, 477nn.134–35, 488
Daimler Financial Services v Argentina, ICSID Case No ARB/05/1, Award
    (22 August 2012) 9n.73, 121n.4, 124n.29
Dan Cake (Portugal) SA v Hungary, ICSID Case No ARB/12/9,
    Decision on Applicant's Request for the Continued Stay of Enforcement of the
        Award (25 December 2018) 611n.65
    Jurisdiction and Liability (24 August 2015) 525n.17, 536n.102
Desert Line Projects LLC v Republic of Yemen, ICSID Case No ARB/05/17,
    Award (6 February 2008) 390, 390n.110, 482n.196
Deutsche Bank AG v Democratic Socialist Republic of Sri Lanka,
    ICSID Case No ARB/09/2, Award (31 October 2012) 252–53nn.31,34, 263, 303n.35

xviii   TABLE OF CASES

(DS)2 SA, Peter de Sutter & Anor v Madagascar (II), ICSID
　　Case No ARB/17/18, Award (17 April 2020) 344n.27, 351nn.22–24, 352, 564n.79
Duke Energy Electroquil Partners & Electroquil SA v Republic of Ecuador,
　　ICSID Case No ARB/04/19, Award (18 August 2008) 496–97n.50
Duke Energy International Peru Investments No 1 Ltd v Republic of Peru,
　　ICSID Case No ARB/03/28,
　　Award (18 August 2008) 188, 188n.77, 241, 241n.99, 245
　　Decision on Annulment (1 March 2011) 315–16n.20
Eco Oro Minerals Corp. v Republic of Colombia, ICSID Case No ARB/16/41 Decision on
　　Jurisdiction, Liability and Directions on Quantum (9 September 2021) 316n.27
EDF (Services) Limited v Romania, ICSID Case No ARB/05/13, 20 ICSIDRep118,
　　Award (8 October 2009) 11n.97, 191n.97, 252n.30, 276n.93, 277n.104, 279, 301n.23,
　　　　　　　　　　　　　　　　302n.28, 302n.34, 306–7, 306n.61, 306n.66, 308, 308n.79, 312
EDF International SA, SAUR International SA and Leon Participaciones Argentinas SA v
　　Argentine Republic, ICSID Case ARB/03/23,
　　Award (11 June 2012) 192, 192nn.104–5, 373, 373n.35
　　Annulment (5 February 2016) 143n.237, 373n.36
Edmond Khudyan and Arin Capital & Investment Corp. v Republic of Armenia,
　　ICSID Case No ARB/17/36, Award (15 December 2021) 456n.57, 463, 597n.49, 603
Eiser Infrastructure Limited and Energía Solar Luxembourg S.à r.l. v Kingdom of Spain,
　　ICSID Case No ARB/13/36,
　　Award (4 May 2017) 385n.72, 547n.31
　　Decision on Respondent Application for Annulment (11 June 2020) 137n.171
El Paso Energy International Company v Argentine Republic,
　　ICSID Case No ARB/03/15,
　　Award (27 April 2006) 394–95n.144, 561n.57
　　Award (31 October 2011) 133–34, 134n.137, 151–52, 327n.19, 328n.28,
　　　　　　　　　　　　　　　　　　　　　　　　　　　417–18, 417n.34, 475n.116, 478n.149
Electrabel SA v Republic of Hungary, ICSID Case No ARB/07/19, Decision on
　　Jurisdiction, Applicable Law and Liability (30 November 2012) 12n.114,
　　　　　　　　　　　　　　　　118n.75, 118n.81, 119, 143n.233, 185n.50, 220n.29, 221n.38,
　　　　　　　　　　　　　　　　252n.30, 284–85, 285nn.33–35, 285n.36, 285n.37,
　　　　　　　　　　　　　　　　285nn.40–41, 286–87, 298–99nn.2,5, 301n.23, 312
Eli Lilly and Company v Government of Canada, UNCITRAL,
　　ICSID Case No UNCT/14/2, Award (16 March 2017) 523n.3
Emmis International Holding BV & Ors v Hungary, ICSID Case No ARB/12/2
　　Award (16 April 2014) 560n.46, 571n.143, 573n.161
Empresas Lucchetti, SA and Lucchetti Peru, SA v Republic of Peru, ICSID Case No ARB/03/4
　　(also known as: Industria Nacional de Alimentos, A.S. and Indalsa Perú SA v Republic of
　　Peru), ICSID Case No ARB/03/4, Award (7 February 2005) 98n.60, 163, 163n.130
Enron Corporation and Ponderosa Assets L.P. v Argentine Republic, ICSID Case No ARB/01/3,
　　Decision on Jurisdiction (14 January 2004) 323n.56
　　Award (15 May 2007) 471n.70, 473n.95, 477n.143
　　Award (22 May 2007) 242–43, 243n.117, 245, 359–60, 359n.49, 359n.54, 359n.56, 361,
　　　　　　　　　　　　　　　361n.69, 362, 362n.79, 364, 372n.25, 373, 373n.29, 373n.34, 382n.44, 389n.97
　　Decision on the Argentine Republic's Request for a Continued Stay of Enforcement of the
　　Award (Rule 54 of the ICSID Arbitration Rules) (7 October 2008) 162n.125, 162n.128,
　　　　　　　　　　　　　　　　　　　　　　　　　　　　　　　　　　473n.95, 500, 500n.73
　　Annulment (30 July 2010) 344, 357, 357n.36, 359–60nn.57–58, 362, 362n.80, 364
Eskosol S.p.A. in liquidazione v Italian Republic, ICSID Case No ARB/15/50,
　　Decision on Termination Request and Intra-EU Objection (7 May 2019) 117n.61,
　　　　　　　　　　　　　　　　117nn.71–72, 132n.109, 134n.138, 185n.55, 187,
　　　　　　　　　　　　　　　　187n.67, 189, 189n.83, 199n.150, 213
ESPF Beteiligungs GmbH, ESPF Nr. 2 Austria Beteiligungs GmbH and InfraClass
　　Energie 5 GmbH & Co. KG v Italian Republic, ICSID Case No ARB/16/5,
　　Award (14 September 2020) 221n.37

Europe Cement Investment & Trade SA v Republic of Turkey, ICSID Case No
ARB(AF)/07/2, Award (13 August 2009) 610n.61
Fabrica De Vidrios Los Andes, C.A. and Owens-Illinois De Venezuela, C.A. v Bolivarian
Republic of Venezuela, ICSID Case No ARB/12/21, Award (13 November 2017) 152n.43
Fengzhen Min v Republic of Korea, ICSID Case No ARB/20/26, Decision on the
Respondent's Preliminary Objection (18 June 2021) 328n.23
Fireman's Fund Insurance Company v Mexico, ICSID Case No ARB(AF)/02/1,
Award (17 July 2006) 516n.98, 522, 570n.126
Flughafen Zürich AG v Venezuela, ICSID Case No ARB/10/19, Award
(18 November 2014) 536, 536n.100
Fouad Alghanim & Sons Co for General Trading & Contracting WLL &
Anor v Jordan, ICSID Case No ARB/13/38, Dissenting Opinion of Professor
Marcelo Kohen (24 November 2014) 568n.115
Fraport AG Frankfurt Airport Services Worldwide v Philippines (II), ICSID
Case No ARB/11/12, Award (10 December 2014) 571n.141, 574n.172
Fuchs, Ron v Georgia, ICSID Case No ARB/07/15, Award (3 March 2010) 253n.33
F-W Oil Interests, Inc v Republic of Trinidad and Tobago, ICSID
Case No ARB/01/14, Award (3 March 2006), 16 ICSID Rep 394 ...... 274n.72, 302–3, 303n.36,
309, 309n.90, 497n.55
Garanti Koza LLP v Turkmenistan, ICSID Case No ARB/11/20,
Award (19 December 2016) 270n.38, 273n.57
Dissenting Opinion of Laurence Boisson de Chazournes (3 July 2013) 124n.27
Gas Natural v Argentina, ICSID Case No ARB/03/10, Decision of the Tribunal on
Preliminary Objections to Jurisdiction (17 June 2005) 133n.134
Gavazzi, Marco & Anor v Romania, ICSID Case No ARB/12/25,
Decision on Jurisdiction, Admissibility and Liability (21 April 2015) 200, 200n.154
Award (18 April 2017) 578n.209
Gavrilović, Georg & Anor v Croatia, ICSID Case No ARB/12/39, Award (26 July 2018)
20 ICSID Rep 512 .... 252n.31, 277n.104, 299n.5, 301n.23,
302n.28, 306n.62, 572n.149, 578n.209
Gemplus SA, SLP SA, Gemplus Industrial SA de C.V v United Mexican States,
ICSID Case No ARB(AF)/04/3, Award (16 June 2010) 329n.37, 578n.207
Generation Ukraine, Inc. v Ukraine, ICSID Case No ARB/00/9, Award
(16 September 2003) 161–62n.121, 473n.99
Genin, Alex v Estonia, ICSID Case No ARB/99/2, Award (25 June 2001) 50, 529, 529nn.46–48
Getma International and others v Republic of Guinea, ICSID Case No ARB/11/29,
Award (16 August 2016) 191n.97
Glamis Gold Ltd v United States of America, ICSID Case No ARB(AF)/ 97/ 1
(NAFTA), Award (8 June 2009) 328n.22, 516n.97, 522, 551, 551n.40, 552–53
Glencore International A.G. and C.I. Prodeco SA v Republic of Colombia,
ICSID Case No ARB/16/6, Award (27 August 2019) 378–79n.21, 379n.22, 386n.78, 400
Global Telecom Holding S.A.E. v Canada, ICSID Case No ARB/16/16,
Award (27 March 2020) 328n.24
Goetz, Antoine and Others v Republic of Burundi (I), ICSID Case No ARB/95/3,
Award (10 February 1999) 323n.57
Gold Reserve Inc v Venezuela, ICSID Case No ARB(AF)/09/1,
Award (22 September 2014) 477n.136, 488
Corrections (15 December 2014) 584n.275
Gustav F W Hamester GmbH & Co KG v Ghana, ICSID Case No ARB/07/24,
Award (18 June 2010) 20 ICSID Rep 164 .... 258, 258nn.85–87, 259, 259n.88,
259n.89, 263, 267n.13, 270n.35, 273nn.57–58, 275n.78, 275–76n.84,
276, 276nn.87–91, 279, 284n.32, 302n.28, 302n.34,
303n.40, 306n.61, 307, 307n.72, 312, 573n.161
H&H Enterprises Investments, Inc. v Arab Republic of Egypt,
ICSID Case No ARB/09/15, Award (6 May 2014) 273n.57

xx   TABLE OF CASES

Helnan International Hotels A/S v Arab Republic of Egypt, ICSID Case No ARB/05/19,
    Decision of the Tribunal on Objection to Jurisdiction (17 October 2006)
    17 ICSID Rep 268 .... 97–98, 98n.58, 268n.22, 272n.55
Hochtief Aktiengesellschaft v Argentine Republic, ICSID Case No ARB/07/31,
    Award (9 December 2014) 334, 334n.26, 372–73, 373n.28
Hrvatska elektroprivreda dd v Slovenia, ICSID Case No ARB/05/24,
    Decision on Treaty Interpretation (12 June 2009) 48, 48nn.20–21, 50
    Decision on Treaty Interpretation: Individual Opinion of Jan Paulsson
    (12 June 2009) 48nn.22–23, 124n.30, 126n.47
Hydro Energy 1 S.À.R.L. and Hydroxana Sweden AB v Kingdom of Spain,
    ICSID Case No ARB/15/42, Award (9 March 2020) 200–1n.156
Hydro S.r.l., Costruzioni S.r.l., Francesco Becchetti, Mauro De Renzis, Stefania
    Grigolon, Liliana Condomitti v Republic of Albania, ICSID Case No ARB/15/28,
    Award (24 April 2019) 328–29n.32
Iberdrola Energia SA v Guatemala, ICSID Case No ARB/09/5, Award
    (17 August 2012) 494n.32, 529, 529n.45, 529n.54, 538n.114
Içkale v Turkmenistan, ICSID Case No ARB/10/24, Award (8 March 2016) 128n.70, 140n.202
Impregilo S.p.A. v Argentine Republic, ICSID Case No ARB/07/17,
    Award (21 June 2011) 362n.76
    Decision of the ad hoc Committee on the Application for Annulment
    (24 January 2014) 362n.76
Impregilo SpA v Islamic Republic of Pakistan, ICSID Case No ARB/03/3,
    Decision on Jurisdiction (22 April 2005) 97n.55, 302n.28, 315–16n.20,
                                                                322n.41, 496–97n.50
Inceysa Vallisoletana S.L. v Republic of El Salvador, ICSID Case No ARB/03/26
    Award (2 August 2006) 71, 71nn.70–72, 73, 152–53, 152n.45,
                        161n.120, 191n.99, 468–69, 468n.38, 475n.116, 485, 485n.241
Indian Metals & Ferro Alloys Ltd v Republic of Indonesia, PCA Case No 2015-40,
    Final Award (29 March 2019) 315n.17
Industria Nacional de Alimentos, SA and Indalsa Perú, S.A v Republic of Peru,
    ICSID Case No ARB/03/4,
    Award (7 February 2005) 98n.60
    Annulment Proceeding (5 September 2007) 473n.95, 483nn.211,13
    Dissenting Opinion of Sir Franklin Berman (5 September 2007) 473n.95
Infinito Gold Ltd v Costa Rica, ICSID Case No ARB/14/5, Award (3 June 2021) 131, 131n.106,
                        151n.34, 469n.42, 478, 478n.156, 478n.160, 488, 537n.108
Infracapital F1 Sàrl & Anor v Spain, ICSID Case No ARB/16/18,
    Jurisdiction, Liability and Directions on Quantum (13 September 2021) 573n.162
    Reconsideration (1 February 2022) 579n.220
Infrastructure Services Luxembourg Sàrl & Anor v Spain
    ICSID Case No ARB/13/31,
    Award (15 June 2018) 385n.72, 484n.226
    Annulment (30 July 2021) 570n.126
Interocean Oil Development Company and Interocean Oil Exploration Company
    v Federal Republic of Nigeria, ICSID Case No ARB/13/20, Award (6 October 2020) 276n.86
Itisaluna Iraq LLC, Munir Sukhtian International Investment LLC, VTEL
    Holdings Ltd, VTEL Middle East and Africa Limited v Republic of Iraq,
    ICSID Case No ARB/17/10, Award (3 April 2020) 166n.2, 175
Jan de Nul N.V and Dredging International N.V v Arab Republic of Egypt,
    ICSID Case No ARB/04/13,
    Decision on Jurisdiction (16 June 2006) 95n.48, 98n.60, 265n.5
    Award (6 November 2008) 245, 258, 258nn.79–84, 259, 263, 270, 270n.40,
                                                273n.57, 275–76n.84, 276n.92, 279, 299n.5,
                                                306n.61, 306n.62, 312, 316n.22, 527n.33
Kappes, Daniel W v Guatemala, ICSID Case No ARB/18/43, Decision on Respondent
    Preliminary Objections (13 March 2020) 132n.109, 133–34, 134nn.135,38, 570n.125

Kardassopoulos, Ioannis v Georgia, ICSID Case No ARB/05/18,
    Decision on Jurisdiction (6 July 2007) 10n.87, 52–53, 53n.3, 56, 56nn.29–33, 57, 60, 62,
                            136–37nn.170,72, 140n.200, 294, 294–95nn.51–55, 297, 315n.16
    Award (3 March 2010) 269n.32, 294n.51, 295, 395n.152, 574n.170
Karkey Karadeniz Elektrik Uretim A.S. v Islamic Republic of Pakistan,
    ICSID Case No ARB/13/1, Award (22 August 2017) 191n.97, 302n.30, 305n.49, 305n.51,
                            322n.44, 574n.172, 576n.191, 578n.208
Karpa, Marvin Roy Feldman v Mexico, ICSID Case No ARB(AF)/99/1,
    Interim Decision on Preliminary Jurisdictional Issues (6 December 2000) 316n.24, 321n.34,
                            322nn.46–47, 323n.51
Award (16 December 2002) 126n.43, 475n.119, 480n.171,
                            507n.11, 512–13, 512n.58, 512n.59, 522, 573n.163
    Correction and Interpretation (13 June 2003) 582n.252
Kılıç İnşaat İthalat İhracat Sanayi ve Ticaret Anonim Şirketi v Turkmenistan,
    ICSID Case No ARB/10/1, Decision on Article VII.2 of the Turkey-Turkmenistan
    Bilateral Investment Treaty (7 May 2012) 172, 172nn.44–47, 172n.48, 175
Kimberly-Clark Dutch Holdings, BV, Kimberly-Clark S.L.U., and Kimberly-Clark
    BVBA v Bolivarian Republic of Venezuela, ICSID Case No ARB(AF)/18/3,
    Award (5 November 2021) 162, 162n.124
Klöckner Industrie-Anlagen GmbH and Others v Cameroon and Société Camerounaise
    des Engrais, ICSID Case No ARB/81/2,
    Award (21 October 1983) 229n.37
    Decision of the ad hoc Committee on the Application for Annulment (3 May 1985) 229n.37
Krederi Ltd v Ukraine, ICSID Case No ARB/14/17 Award (2 July 2018) 533, 533n.79,
                            537n.107, 578n.210
Kruck, Mathias & Ors v Spain, ICSID Case No ARB/15/23,
    Jurisdiction and Admissibility (19 April 2021) 557n.19
    Decision on Jurisdiction, Liability and Principles of Quantum (14 September 2022) 200–1n.156
KT Asia v Kazakhstan, ICSID Case No ARB/09/8, Award (17 October 2013) 140n.198,
                            140n.202
Lahoud and Lahoud v Democratic Republic of the Congo, ICSID Case No ARB/10/4,
    Award (7 February 2014) 273n.57
Landesbank Baden-Württemberg and Others v Kingdom of Spain,
    ICSID Case No ARB/15/45, Decision on the Intra-EU Jurisdictional
    Objection (25 February 2019) 140n.198, 185n.55, 301n.26
Lao Holdings N.V v Lao People's Democratic Republic, ICSID Case No ARB(AF)/12/6,
    Decision on Jurisdiction (20 February 2014) 612n.80
    Award (6 August 2019) 191n.98
Lee-Chin, Michael Anthony v Dominican Republic, ICSID Case No UNCT/18/3,
    Partial Award (15 July 2020) 570n.127
Lemire, Joseph Charles v Ukraine, ICSID Case No ARB/06/18, Award (28 March 2011) 390,
                            390n.112
L.E.S.I. S.p.A. and ASTALDI S.p.A. v République Algérienne Démocratique et Populaire,
    ICSID Case No ARB/05/3, Decision (12 November 2008) 270n.38
Levy, Renée Rose and Gremcitel SA v Republic of Peru, ICSID Case No ARB/11/17,
    Award (9 January 2015) 96, 96n.52, 173, 173nn.51–53, 176,
                            315n.17, 316n.21, 610nn.57–58, 612n.80, 614n.90, 617
LG&E Energy Corp, LG&E Capital Corp, LG&E International Inc v Argentine Republic, ICSID
    Case ARB/02/1,
    Decision on Liability (3 October 2006) 13n.120, 80, 80nn.45–46, 83, 357n.35, 360–61,
                            360n.65, 364, 373–74, 373–74nn.38–39
    Award (25 July 2007) 322n.36, 323n.56, 354n.6, 382n.45, 383–84, 384n.60,
                            385nn.70,72, 394–95n.144
Libananco Holdings Co. Limited v Republic of Turkey, ICSID ARB/06/8,
    Decision on Preliminary Issues (23 June 2008) 70n.60
    Award (2 September 2011) 191n.98

Liman Caspian Oil BV and NCL Dutch Investment BV v Republic of Kazakhstan,
    ICSID Case No ARB/07/14, Award (22 June 2010) 81, 81n.53, 83, 191nn.96,99, 475n.119,
                                                                                529n.45, 538n.114
Lion Mexico Consolidated LP v Mexico, ICSID Case No ARB(AF)/15/2,
    Submission of the United States of America (21 June 2019) 507n.11, 533n.83
    Award (20 September 2021) 106, 517–18, 518nn.114,20, 522, 533n.83,
                                                                536, 536n.104, 537, 537n.108, 538
Loewen Group, Inc and Raymond L Loewen v United States of America,
    ICSID Case No ARB(AF)/98/3,
    Decision on Jurisdiction (5 January 2001) 252n.31
    Counter-Memorial of the United States of America, 118–21 (30 March 2001) 512n.67
    Award (26 June 2003) 512–13, 517–18, 518n.116, 522, 528–29, 529n.44,
                                                530–31, 530n.56, 530n.61, 531n.65, 533, 533n.86, 538
LSF-KEB Holdings SCA and others v Republic of Korea, ICSID
    Case No ARB/12/37, Award (30 August 2022) 252n.31, 268n.22, 276n.86
M. Meerapfel Söhne AG v Central African Republic, ICSID Case No ARB/07/10,
    Award (12 May 2012) 477n.141
Maffezini, Emilio Agustín v Spain, ICSID Case No ARB/97/7,
    Procedural Order No 2 (28 October 1999) 568n.112
    Decision on Objections to Jurisdiction (25 January 2000) 98, 98n.59, 260n.96, 269–70,
                                                                    270n.33, 270nn.37,39, 303n.37
    Award (13 November 2000) 5 ICSID Rep 419 .... 39, 270nn.36–37
Magyar Farming Company Ltd and others v Hungary, ICSID Case No ARB/17/27,
    Award (13 November 2019) 113n.27, 117 nn.63–65, 117n.71,
                                        118nn.75–76, 135, 135n.158, 200n.155, 204n.176, 561n.57
Malaysian Historical Salvors v Government of Malaysia, ICSID Case No ARB/05/10,
    Award on Jurisdiction (17 May 2007) 151–52, 152n.40
Malicorp Ltd v Egypt ICSID Case No ARB/08/18, Award (7 February 2011) 71, 71nn.76–77
Mamidoil Jetoil Greek Petroleum Products Societe Anonyme SA v Republic of
    Albania, ICSID Case No ARB/11/24, Award (30 March 2015) 495, 495n.41, 502
Marfin Investment Group Holdings SA, Alexandros Bakatselos and others v
    Republic of Cyprus, ICSID Case No ARB/13/27, Award (redacted) (26 July 2018) 113n.27,
                                        117n.71, 204n.176, 210n.213, 305–6, 306nn.60–61, 306n.64
Maritime International Nominees Establishment ('MINE') v Republic of
    Guinea, ICSID Case No ARB/84/4, Interim Order No 1 on Guinea's Application
    for Stay of Enforcement of the Award (12 August 1988) 500, 500n.71, 500n.72, 502
Masdar Solar & Wind Cooperatief U.A. v Kingdom of Spain, ICSID Case No ARB/14/1,
    Award (16 May 2018) 301n.26, 384–85, 385n.69, 385n.72
M.C.I. Power Group, L.C. and New Turbine, Inc. v Republic of Ecuador,
    ICSID Case No ARB/03/6 31
    Award (31 July 2007) 10, 10n.91, 11n.99, 13n.117, 30, 30nn.57–58,
                                                            30nn.59–61, 32, 97, 97n.56, 316nn.26–27,
                                                            318–19n.1, 326n.2, 328–29n.32, 329n.38
    Decision on Annulment (19 October 2009) 10n.91
Menzies Middle East and Africa SA and Aviation Handling Services International Ltd v
    Republic of Senegal, ICSID Case No ARB/15/21, Award (5 August 2016) 104, 104nn.29–30
Mercer International Inc. v Government of Canada, ICSID Case No ARB(AF)/12/3,
    Award (6 March 2018) 480n.172, 510, 510n.44, 517–18, 518n.119, 522
Mesa Power Group LLC v Canada, UNCITRAL, PCA Case No 2012-17,
    Award (24 March 2016) 41, 41n.37, 42, 42n.47, 44, 271nn.42,45,
                                                                309n.91, 414–16, 415n.15, 416n.22
Metalclad Corporation v United Mexican States, ICSID Case No ARB(AF)/97/1,
    Award (30 August 2000) 77n.26, 322n.42, 380n.32, 507n.11, 515,
                                                                515nn.89–90, 516n.98, 522
Metal-Tech Ltd v Republic of Uzbekistan, ICSID Case No ARB/10/3,
    Award (4 October 2013) 191, 191n.96, 213, 576n.189

Micula, Ioan, Micula, Viorel, S.C. European Food S.A, S.C. Starmill S.R.L. and
  S.C. Multipack S.R.L. v Romania [I], ICSID Case No ARB/05/20,
  Jurisdiction and Admissibility (24 September 2006) 6–7, 7n.47, 597n.49, 603
  Final Award (11 December 2013) 110n.6, 136n.167, 286, 286n.42, 286nn.43–45, 287,
                                                                     323n.56, 560n.47
  Romania's Annulment Request (18 April 2014) 395n.149
Micula, Ioan & Ors v Romania (II), ICSID Case No ARB/14/29, Award (5 March 2020) 570n.126
Middle East Cement Shipping and Handling Co. SA v Arab Republic of Egypt,
  ICSID Case No ARB/99/6, Award (12 April 2002) 79, 79n.44, 83, 477n.140
Millicom International Operations BV and Sentel GSMSA v Republic of Senegal,
  ICSID Case No ARB/08/20, Decision on Jurisdiction of the Arbitral
  Tribunal (16 July 2010) 151n.34, 161–62n.121
Minnotte, David & Anor v Poland, ICSID Case No ARB(AF)/ 10/ 1,
  Interpretation (22 October 2014) 582n.252, 584n.275
MNSS BV and Recupero Credito Acciaio N.V v Montenegro, ICSID Case No
  ARB(AF)/12/8, Award (4 May 2016) 306n.64, 451n.3
Mobil & Murphy v Canada, ICSID Case No ARB(AF)/07/4,
  Decision on Liability and Quantum (22 May 2012) 40, 40n.35, 40n.36, 41, 42, 42nn.45–46,
                                              44, 151n.34, 472, 472n.83, 482–83, 483nn.214–15, 507n.11
  Award (20 February 2015) 377–78, 378n.13, 522
Mobil Investments Canada Inc. v Canada, ICSID Case No ARB/15/6, Decision on Jurisdiction
  and Admissibility (13 July 2018) 71, 71nn.82–83, 73, 323n.52, 565n.80
Mobil Corporation, Venezuela Holdings, BV and Others v Venezuela. *See* Venezuela
  Holdings, BV, et al (case formerly known as Mobil Corporation, Venezuela
  Holdings, BV, et al) v Venezuela
MOL Hungarian Oil and Gas Company Plc v Republic of Croatia,
  ICSID Case No ARB/13/32, Award (5 July 2022) 41–42, 41n.42
Mondev International Ltd v United States of America, ICSID Case No
  ARB(AF)/99/2, Award (11 October 2002) 10n.89, 46n.7,
              162n.126, 315n.16, 323n.48, 323n.49, 471n.72, 472n.85, 473n.90, 473n.99,
                         492–94, 492n.24, 493nn.29–30, 518n.115, 522, 528–29,
                              528nn.34–36, 530–31, 530n.63, 532n.75, 538
MTD Equity Sdn Bhd and MTD Chile SA v Republic of Chile, ICSID Case No ARB/01/17,
  Decision on the Respondent's Request for a Continued Stay of Execution
  (1 June 2005) 499n.70
  Decision on Annulment (21 March 2007) 397, 397n.167, 571n.141
Murphy Exploration and Production Company International v Republic of Ecuador,
  ICSID Case No ARB/08/4, Award on Jurisdiction (15 December 2010) 195–96,
                                                                     195–96nn.124–26
National Gas SAE v Egypt, ICSID Case No ARB/11/7, Award (3 April 2014) 480n.173, 573n.161
Naturgy Energy Group SA & Anor v Colombia ICSID Case No UNCT/18/1,
  Award (12 March 2021) 577n.197
Niko Resources (Bangladesh) Ltd v Bangladesh Oil Gas and Mineral Corporation &
  Anor, ICSID Case No ARB/10/18,
  Decision on Jurisdiction (19 August 2013) 190, 190nn.91–94, 477n.140, 485, 485n.243
  Corruption Claim (25 February 2019) 573n.163
Noble Ventures, Inc. v Romania, ICSID Case No ARB/01/11, Award (12 October 2005)
  16 ICSID Rep 210 .... 11n.97, 265n.5, 272n.55, 273n.57, 279,
                                         293–94, 294nn.46–47, 294n.48, 295, 297, 497n.55
Occidental Petroleum Corporation & Occidental Exploration and Production
  Company v Republic of Ecuador, ICSID Case No ARB/06/11,
  Decision on Provisional Measures (17 August 2007) 382n.45, 385, 385n.71, 568n.108
  Decision on Jurisdiction (9 September 2008) 77n.30
  Award (5 October 2012) 398n.170, 626n.46
  Dissenting Opinion of Professor Brigitte Stern (5 October 2012) 626n.47
  Award (2 November 2015) 395n.149

xxiv TABLE OF CASES

OI European Group BV v Bolivarian Republic of Venezuela,
    ICSID Case No ARB/11/25, Award (10 March 2015) 390, 390n.113
OKO Pankki Oyj and Others v Republic of Estonia, ICSID Case No ARB/04/6,
    Award (19 November 2007) 315n.16, 321n.34, 322n.45
Olguín, Eudoro Armando v Republic of Paraguay, ICSID Case No ARB/98/5,
    Award (26 July 2001) 598, 598n.50, 603
Orascom TMT Investments S.à r.l. v People's Democratic Republic of Algeria,
    ICSID Case No ARB/12/35,
    Final Award (31 May 2017) 136–37n.170, 140n.200, 162n.126,
                        484n.227, 611, 611nn.67–68, 611nn.72–73, 616, 616n.113, 617
    Decision on Annulment (17 September 2020) 557n.19, 610n.55, 611
Ortiz Construcciones y Proyectos SA v People's Democratic Republic of Algeria,
    ICSID Case No ARB/17/1, Award (29 April 2020) 257, 257nn.73–74,
                        263, 269n.24, 270n.35, 273nn.57,59, 275, 275n.78, 275n.81,
                        275–76n.84, 276n.85, 279, 299n.5, 305n.49, 306nn.62,64,
                        307, 307n.74, 307n.76, 308n.79, 310, 310nn.100,2
Pac Rim Cayman LLC v Republic of El Salvador, ICSID Case No ARB/09/12,
    Opinion of Michael Reisman on the International Legal Interpretation of the
        Waiver Provision in CAFTA Chapter 10 (22 March 2010) 141n.216
    Decision on the Respondent's Jurisdictional Objections (1 June 2012) 316n.27, 318–19n.1,
                        321n.34, 322n.38, 326n.2, 328n.28, 609n.47, 610n.51, 612n.80
PACC Offshore Services Holdings Ltd v Mexico, ICSID Case No UNCT/18/5,
    Award (11 January 2022) 252n.31
Pan American v Argentina, ICSID Case No ARB/03/13, Decision on
    Preliminary Objections (27 July 2006) 129n.81, 130n.91, 482nn.196,98
Parkerings v Lithuania, ICSID Case No ARB/05/8, Award (11 September 2007) 141n.215
Pawlowski AG and Project Sever s.r.o. v Czech Republic, ICSID Case No ARB/17/11,
    Award (1 November 2021) 394, 394n.138
Perenco Ecuador Limited v Ecuador, ICSID Case No ARB/08/6,
    Provisional Measures (8 May 2009) 567nn.104,7, 568n.113
    Decision on Stay of Enforcement of the Award (21 February 2020) 499n.68
Pey Casado, Victor and President Allende Foundation v Republic of Chile,
    ICSID Case No ARB/98/2,
    Provisional Measures (25 September 2001) 568, 568n.112
    Jurisdiction (8 May 2002) 151n.34, 598, 598n.51, 604
    Award (8 May 2008) 315n.18, 315–16n.20, 316n.26,
                        322n.42, 324n.58, 328n.23, 391n.116
    Revision (18 November 2009) 584n.271
    Decision on the Republic of Chile's Application for a Stay of Enforcement of the
        Award, (5 May 2010) 499n.70
Pey Casado, Victor and President Allende Foundation v Republic of Chile, ICSID Case No
    ARB/ 98/2204, (Resubmission), Award (13 September 2016) 380n.27, 536n.103
Philip Morris Brands Sarl and others v Oriental Republic of Uruguay, ICSID Case No ARB/10/7,
    Decision on Jurisdiction (2 July 2013) 151, 151n.36
    Award (8 July 2016) 136–37nn.170,72, 140n.201, 546–47, 547nn.27–29, 574n.171
Phoenix Action, Ltd v Czech Republic, ICSID Case No ARB/06/5,
    Award (15 April 2009) 6n.45, 8, 8n.59, 9n.73, 70n.61, 71, 71n.75,
                        121n.4, 145, 485n.242, 606nn.7–10, 609, 609n.47, 612nn.77–79, 617
Ping An Life Insurance Company of China Limited & Anor v Belgium,
    ICSID Case No ARB/12/29 Award (30 April 2015) 10n.79, 125, 125n.35, 315n.16,
                        315–16n.20, 322n.47, 561n.52, 566, 566n.94
Plama Consortium Ltd v Bulgaria, ICSID Case No ARB/03/24,
    Decision on Jurisdiction (8 February 2005) 54n.13, 54n.17, 485n.242, 563n.74
    Provisional Measures (6 September 2005) 567n.105
PNG Sustainable Development Program Ltd v PNG, ICSID Case No ARB/13/33,
    Provisional Measures (21 January 2015) 567nn.106–7
    Award (5 May 2015) 574n.168

Poštová banka and ISTROKAPITAL v Hellenic Republic, ICSID Case No ARB/13/8,
  Award (9 April 2015) 124n.26, 129–30, 129n.80,
                                                                 130n.90, 141n.215, 145, 578n.205
PSEG Global Inc & Anor v Turkey, ICSID Case No ARB/02/5
  Award (19 January 2007) 394–95n.144, 560n.47
Quiborax SA, Non-Metallic Minerals SA v Plurinational State of Bolivia,
  ICSID Case No ARB/06/2,
  Provisional Measures (26 February 2010) 73, 567n.105
  Award (16 September 2015) 70nn.58–59, 393n.136, 394, 394nn.140–42, 568, 568n.114
Rachel S Grynberg & Ors v Grenada, ICSID Case No ARB/10/6,
  Award (10 December 2010) 580, 580n.232
Raiffeisen Bank International AG and Raiffeisenbank Austria d.d. v Republic of
  Croatia, ICSID Case No ARB/17/34, Decision on the Respondent's
  Jurisdictional Objections (30 September 2020) 116n.48, 189n.82, 566, 566n.96
Railroad Development Corporation v Republic of Guatemala, ICSID Case No ARB/07/23,
  Second Decision on Objections to Jurisdiction (18 May 2010) 322n.47
  Award (29 June 2012) 469n.49
Renco Group v Peru, ICSID Case No UNCT/13/1,
  Preliminary Objections (18 December 2014) 558n.29
  Partial Award on Jurisdiction (15 July 2016) 70n.61, 137nn.171,73, 140n.202, 484n.226
RENERGY S.à r.l. v Kingdom of Spain, ICSID Case No ARB/14/18,
  Award (6 May 2022) 140n.198, 200–1n.156, 220n.36, 221n.37, 221n.41
Ríos, Carlos and Ríos, Francisco v Republic of Chile, ICSID Case No ARB/17/16,
  Award (11 January 2021) 323n.52, 328n.31
Rompetrol Group N.V v Romania, ICSID Case No ARB/06/3,
  Decision on Respondent's Preliminary Objections on Jurisdiction
  and Admissibility (18 April 2008) 127n.63, 610n.52
  Award (6 May 2013) 328n.23, 531, 531n.68, 533n.80, 572n.149, 573nn.160,63
RREEF v Spain, ICSID Case No ARB/13/30, Decision on Jurisdiction (6 June 2016) 286n.46
Rumeli Telekom A.S. and Telsim Mobil Telekomunikasyon Hizmetleri A.S. v Republic of
  Kazakhstan, ICSID Case No ARB/05/16 (29 July 2008) 77–78, 77–78nn.32,33,
                                                                 199n.149, 329n.36
Rusoro Mining Ltd v Bolivarian Republic of Venezuela,
  ICSID Case No ARB(AF)/12/5, Award (22 August 2016) 329n.34, 485n.246
RWE Innogy GmbH and RWE Innogy Aersa S.A.U. v Kingdom of Spain,
  ICSID Case No ARB/14/34, Decision on Jurisdiction, Liability, and Certain
  Issues of Quantum (30 December 2019) 115n.47, 384–85, 384–85nn.67–68
Saint-Gobain Performance Plastics Europe v Bolivarian Republic of Venezuela,
  ICSID Case No ARB/12/13, Decision on Liability and Principles of
  Quantum (30 December 2016) 143n.233, 273n.57
Saipem S.p.A. v People's Republic of Bangladesh, ICSID Case No ARB/05/07,
  Decision on Jurisdiction and Recommendation on Provisional Measures
  (21 March 2007) 494, 494nn.35–37, 502
  Award (30 June 2009) 70, 70nn.62–63, 73, 79, 79nn.38–39,
                                                                 252n.31, 484n.226, 570n.129, 573n.160
Salini Costruttori S.p.A. and Italstrade S.p.A. v Hashemite Kingdom of Jordan,
  ICSID Case No ARB/02/13,
  Decision on Jurisdiction (9 November 2004) 166n.2, 176, 315n.16, 315–16n.20
  Award (31 January 2006) 480, 480n.176
Sempra Energy International v Argentine Republic, ICSID Case ARB/02/16,
  Award (28 September 2007) 71, 71nn.73–74, 152n.42, 344, 344n.25,
                                                                 359, 359n.49, 362n.79, 364, 372nn.25–26, 373n.29,
                                                                 373n.34, 417–18, 417nn.35–37, 467n.21
  Annulment (29 June 2010) 357, 357nn.33,36, 359nn.50–52, 359n.53, 359n.55, 364, 374,
                                                                 374n.41, 418nn.38,40, 419
Sevilla Beheer et al. v Spain, ICSID Case No ARB/16/27, Decision on Jurisdiction,
  Liability and the Principles of Quantum (11 February 2022) 220n.36, 221n.41

SGS Société Générale de Surveillance SA v Islamic Republic of Pakistan,
    ICSID Case No ARB/01/13,
    Procedural Order No 2 (16 October 2002) 78n.37
    Jurisdiction (6 August 2003) 260n.101
    Procedural Order No 2 (2006) 83
SGS Société Générale de Surveillance SA v Republic of Philippines,
    ICSID Case No ARB/02/6, Decision of the Tribunal on Objections to Jurisdiction
    (29 January 2004) 322n.40, 334, 334n.25, 496n.46,
                                                557n.21, 563–64, 564n.75, 570n.126
SGS Société Générale de Surveillance SA v Republic of Paraguay,
    ICSID Case No ARB/07/29,
    Decision on Jurisdiction (12 February 2010) 78, 78nn.34–35
    Award (10 February 2012) 395n.145, 564n.79, 573n.160
Siag, Waguih Elie George and Clorinda Vecchi v Arab Republic of
    Egypt, ICSID Case No ARB/05/15,
    Award (1 April 2007) 594, 594n.31, 597n.49, 604
    Award (1 June 2009) 12, 12n.111, 81, 81n.55, 83, 191n.97, 480n.174, 573n.160
Siemens v Argentine Republic, ICSID Case No ARB/02/8,
    Decision on Jurisdiction (3 August 2004) 129n.88
    Award (6 February 2007) 327n.18, 328n.26, 394–95n.144,
                                        495–96nn.42–44, 496, 496n.45, 496nn.47–48, 502
Silver Ridge Power BV v Italian Republic, ICSID Case No ARB/15/37,
    Award (26 February 2021) 116nn.49–50, 139n.196, 185–86, 186nn.56–57, 213
Sistem Mühendislik In aat Sanayi ve Ticaret A.S. v Kyrgyz Republic,
    ICSID Case No ARB(AF)/06/1, Award (9 September 2009) 322n.44
SolEs Badajoz GmbH v Kingdom of Spain, ICSID Case No ARB/15/38,
    Award (31 July 2019) 185n.55
Southern Pacific Properties (Middle East) Limited v Arab Republic of Egypt,
    ICSID Case No ARB/84/3, Decision on Jurisdiction (14 April 1988) 292nn.34–36,
                                        292n.37, 292n.38, 297, 495, 495n.38, 502, 571n.138
Spyridon Roussalis v Romania, ICSID Case No ARB/06/1, Award (7 December 2011) 576n.190
Stadtwerke München GmbH & Ors v Spain, ICSID Case No ARB/15/1, Award
    (2 December 2019) 578n.208
Standard Chartered Bank (Hong Kong) Limited v Tanzania Electric Supply
    Company Limited, ICSID Case No ARB/10/20
    Award (12 September 2016) 579n.220
    Decision on Applicant Request for a Continued Stay on Enforcement of the
        Award (12 April 2017) 499n.68
Staur Eiendom AS, EBO Invest AS and Rox Holding AS v Republic of Latvia,
    ICSID Case No ARB/16/38, Award (28 February 2020) 273n.59, 275n.78,
                                                            275–76n.84, 302n.34
Strabag SE, Raiffeisen Centrobank AG, Syrena Immobilien Holding AG
    v Republic of Poland, ICSID Case No ADHOC/15/1, Partial Award on
    Jurisdiction (4 March 2020) 116n.53, 116n.58, 117n.72, 221n.43
Strabag SE v Libya, ICSID Case No ARB(AF)/15/1, Award (29 June 2020) 277n.103, 295,
                                                    295nn.59–63, 297, 302n.30, 397n.164
Sudapet v South Sudan, ICSID Case No ARB/12/26, Award (30 September 2016) 444n.61,
                                                            455nn.44–46, 463
Suez, Sociedad General de Aguas de Barcelona, SA and Vivendi Universal, SA v Argentine
    Republic, ICSID Case No ARB/03/19 (formerly Aguas Argentinas, SA, Suez, Sociedad
    General de Aguas de Barcelona, S.A. and Vivendi Universal, SA v Argentine Re, ... 362n.78
    Decision on Liability (30 July 2010) 80, 80nn.47–48, 361, 361n.70,
                                                            362n.78, 364, 469n.47
    Decision on Annulment (5 May 2017) 133n.134
    Judgment of the US Court of Appeals for the District of Columbia
        (14 December 2018) 361n.71, 362n.78, 364

Soufraki, Hussein Nauman v United Arab Emirates, ICSID Case No ARB/02/7,
    Award (7 July 2004) 573n.160, 593n.28, 593n.29, 594n.30, 603
Supervision y Control SA v Costa Rica, ICSID Case No ARB/12/4, Award
    (18 January 2017) 562n.68
Swisslion DOO Skopje v Former Yugoslav Republic of Macedonia,
    ICSID Case No ARB/09/16, Award (6 July 2012) 327n.19, 328n.25, 329n.33
Talsud SA v United Mexican States, ICSID Case No ARB(AF)/04/4,
    Award (16 June 2010) 329n.37
Técnicas Medioambientales Techmed SA v United Mexican States,
    ISCID Case No ARB(AF)/00/2, Award (29 May 2003) 29, 29nn.53–54,
                                                                30–31, 30nn.55–56, 32, 96, 96nn.50–51,
                                                                    99, 315n.18, 316n.28, 328n.24
Teinver SA, Transportes de Cercanías SA and Autobuses Urbanos del Sur SA v Argentina,
    ICSID Case No ARB/09/1,
    Decision on Jurisdiction (21 December 2012) 130n.94
    Award (21 July 2017) 306n.62, 312, 328nn.25,27, 380, 380n.33, 383, 383n.57
Telefónica v Argentina, ICSID Case No ARB/03/20, Decision of the Tribunal on
    Objections to Jurisdiction (25 May 2006) 132–34, 132n.118, 133nn.133–34
Tenaris SA and Talta-Trading e Marketing Sociedade Unipessoal LDA v Bolivarian
    Republic of Venezuela, ICSID Case No ARB/11/26,
    Award (29 January 2016) 275n.78
    Annulment (8 August 2018) 570n.126
Tethyan Copper Company Pty Limited v Islamic Republic of Pakistan,
    ICSID Case No ARB/12/1,
    Decision on Jurisdiction and Liability (10 November 2017) 252–53nn.31–32, 253, 253n.37,
                                                                254, 254nn.43–45, 263, 273n.57, 274, 274n.68,
                                                                    295, 295nn.57–58, 297, 577n.197
    Decision on Stay of Enforcement of the Award (17 September 2020) 500, 500n.74, 502
Tidewater Inc. et al. v Bolivarian Republic of Venezuela, ICSID Case No ARB/10/5,
    Decision on Jurisdiction (8 February 2013) 612n.80
Togo Electricité et GDF-Suez Energie Services v La Republique Togolaise,
    ICSID Case No ARB/06/07, Decision on Annulment (6 September 2011) 151, 151nn.34–35
Tokios Tokeles v Ukraine, ICSID Case No ARB/02/18, Decision on Jurisdiction
    (29 April 2004) 130n.94, 561n.57, 601, 601nn.67–68, 604
Total SA v Argentine Republic, ICSID Case No ARB/04/01, Decision on Liability
    (27 December 2010) 29n.52, 81–82, 81–82nn.57–58, 83,
                                                                475n.116, 476nn.129–33, 477–78nn.146–48, 488, 570n.126
Tradex Hellas SA v Republic of Albania, ICSID Case No ARB/94/2,
    Award (29 April 1999) 303n.37, 308n.80, 312, 480n.177, 573n.160
    Jurisdiction (24 December 1999) 97n.54
Transglobal Green Energy, LLC and Transglobal Green Energy de Panama, SA v
    Republic of Panama, ICSID Case No ARB/13/28, Award (2 June 2016) 614n.91
Trans-Global Petroleum Inc v Jordan, ICSID Case No ARB/07/25, Rule 41(5)
    (12 May 2008) 558n.30
Tulip Real Estate and Development Netherlands BV v Republic of Turkey,
    ICSID Case No ARB/11/28,
    Decision on Bifurcated Jurisdictional Issue (5 March 2013) 495, 495nn.39–40, 502, 562n.68,
                                                                                            570n.128
    Award (10 March 2014) 68, 143, 143n.233, 270n.34, 273,
                                                                273n.57, 273n.65, 279, 299n.5, 302n.34, 305n.49, 306–7, 306n.64, 306n.66
    Decision on Annulment (30 December 2015) 136–37nn.170,73, 138n.179, 143n.233
UAB E energija (Lithuania) v Latvia, ICSID Case No ARB/12/33, Award
    (22 December 2017) 252–53n.32, 254n.43, 308–9, 309n.87, 564n.79, 574n.169
Unión Fenosa Gas, SA v Arab Republic of Egypt, ICSID Case No ARB/14/4, Award
    (31 August 2018) 20 ICSID Rep 546 .... 67, 191n.98, 273, 273n.60, 277n.104, 299n.5, 360,
                                                                360nn.60–61, 362, 362n.81, 364, 484n.227,
                                                                    573n.162, 575n.175, 578n.208

xxviii TABLE OF CASES

Uniper SE and others v Netherlands, ICSID Case No ARB/21/22, Procedural
 Order No 2 (9 May 2022) 567n.104
United Parcel Service of America Inc (UPS) v Government of Canada,
 ICSID Case No UNCT/02/1, UNCITRAL (NAFTA),
 Award on Jurisdiction (22 November 2002) 471nn.70,73, 472, 472n.77,
  472n.84, 473n.92, 488
 Counter Memorial (Merit Phase, paras 597–605 (22 June 2005) 512n.67
 Award on the Merits (24 May 2007) 20 ICSID Rep 436 .... 11n.102, 261, 261nn.109–10,
  261n.111, 263, 271n.42, 309n.91, 323n.53,
  323n.54, 329n.35, 513, 513n.69, 522
 Separate Statement of Dean Ronald A. Cass (24 May 2007) 512n.57, 522
United Utilities (Tallinn) BV and Aktsiaselts Tallinna Vesi v Republic of Estonia,
 ICSID Case No ARB/14/24, Award, (21 June 2019) 117n.71, 204n.176, 210n.209,
  221n.37, 496n.49
Urbaser SA and Consorcio de Aguas Bilbao Bizkaia, Bilbao Biskaia Ur Partzuergoa
 v Argentine Republic, ICSID Case No ARB/07/26,
 Jurisdiction (19 December 2012) 562n.68
 Award (8 December 2016) 133n.134, 136n.169, 137n.172, 138–39,
  138n.187, 177–78n.1, 192n.102, 360–61, 360–61nn.66–67,
  362, 362n.82, 364, 577n.198
Vannessa Ventures Ltd v Bolivarian Republic of Venezuela,
 ICSID Case No ARB (AF)/04/6, Jurisdiction (22 August 2008) 154n.60
Vattenfall AB and Others v Federal Republic of Germany (II),
 ICSID Case No ARB/12/12, Decision on the Achmea Issue (31 August 2018) 115n.45,
  115n.47, 116n.50, 119, 139n.192,
  139n.193, 139n.194, 144, 185, 185n.53, 213
Venezuela Holdings, BV and others (case formerly known as Mobil Corporation,
 Venezuela Holdings, BV, et al) v Venezuela, ICSID Case No ARB/07/27,
 Jurisdiction, (10 June 2010) 70n.61, 475, 475n.120, 483–84, 484nn.224–25,
  488, 606n.10, 612nn.74,76, 612n.80, 617
 Award (9 October 2014) 80, 80nn.50–52, 83
 Revision (12 June 2015) 584, 584nn.270–71
 Decision on Annulment (9 March 2017) 469n.42
Vento Motorcycles, Inc. v United Mexican States, ICSID Case No ARB(AF)/17/3,
 Award (6 July 2020) 510, 510n.43, 522
Vestey Group Ltd v Bolivarian Republic of Venezuela, ICSID Case No ARB/06/4,
 Award (15 April 2016) 415, 415nn.17–18, 419
Vigotop Ltd v Hungary, ICSID Case No ARB/11/22, Award (1 October 2014) 71, 71nn.80–81,
  73, 276n.95
von Pezold, Bernhard and Others v Republic of Zimbabwe,
 ICSID Case No ARB/10/15,
 Award (28 July 2015) 55, 55nn.19–23, 136, 136n.165, 143n.233,
  253n.34, 304n.42, 308n.80, 312, 353, 353–54n.2,
  360n.59, 360n.63, 361, 361nn.72–74, 364, 366–67nn.9–10,
  368, 373n.30, 376n.5, 378, 378n.16, 385–86, 385n.75,
  400, 416–17, 417n.32, 592–93, 593n.26, 604
 Decision on Annulment (12 November 2018) 55n.24
Waste Management, Inc. v United Mexican States (No 2),
 ICSID Case No ARB(AF)/00/3,
 Decision as to Mexico's Preliminary Objection (26 June 2002) 482–83n.208
 Award (30 April 2004) 11 ICSID Rep 361 .... 70n.57, 265n.5, 277n.98,
  303n.37, 472, 472n.82, 482–83nn.208,16, 496n.46, 515–16, 528–29, 529n.44, 551, 552
Webuild SpA v Argentine Republic, ICSID Case No ARB/15/39, Jurisdiction and
 Admissibility (23 February 2018) 564n.79
Wena Hotels Limited v Arab Republic of Egypt, ICSID Case No ARB/98/4,
 Award (8 December 2000) 395n.149, 564n.79
 Interpretation (31 October 2005) 582nn.247–50

Westmoreland Mining Holdings LLC v Canada, ICSID
    Case No UNCT/20/3, Award (31 January 2022) 315n.17, 573n.161
Wintershall Aktiengesellschaft v Argentina, ICSID Case No ARB/04/14, Award
    (8 December 2008) 125, 125n.35, 129n.88, 130n.91, 131n.100, 562n.68
World Duty Free v Republic of Kenya, ICSID Case No ARB/007, Award
    (4 October 2006) 190–91, 191n.95
Zhinvali Development Ltd v Republic of Georgia, ICSID Case No ARB/00/1,
    Award (24 January 2003) 625n.39
    Separate Opinion of Andrew J. Jacovides (24 January 2003) 625n.40, 628

ARBITRATIONS UNDER THE UNCITRAL ARBITRATION RULES

Alps Finance and Trade AG v Slovakia, UNCITRAL, Award (5 March 2011) 563n.69
Al-Warraq, Hesham Talaat M v Indonesia, UNCITRAL,
    Award on Respondents' Preliminary Objections to Jurisdiction and Admissibility
        of the Claims (21 June 2012) 9n.73
    Final Award (15 December 2014) 70, 70nn.65–66, 136n.167,
                                        482n.196, 485nn.244–45, 536, 536n.103, 576n.192, 577n.198
Austrian Airlines v Slovak Republic, UNCITRAL,
Award (9 October 2009) 570n.126
    Separate Opinion of Charles N. Brower (20 October 2009) 127n.63
AWG Group Ltd v Argentine Republic, UNCITRAL, Decision on Liability
    (30 July 2010) 80n.49, 570n.129
BG Group Plc. v Republic of Argentina, UNCITRAL, Final Award
    (24 December 2007) 171, 172n.39, 172nn.40–43, 175, 358n.41, 373n.29, 396n.162
Biloune, Antoine & Anor v Ghana, UNCITRAL, Damages and Costs Award
    (30 July 1990) 584n.274
Binder, Rupert Joseph v Czech Republic, UNCITRAL,
    Award on Jurisdiction (6 June 2007) 116n.53
    Final Award (15 July 2011) 451n.3
Canadian Cattlemen for Fair Trade v United States of America, UNCITRAL
    (formerly Consolidated Canadian Claims v United States of America),
    UNCITRAL Award on Jurisdiction (28 January 2008) 132–33, 132n.111, 132n.119,
                                                                 134n.136, 162nn.125,28
Canfor v United States of America, UNCITRAL,
    Procedural Order No 5 (28 May 2004) 161–62nn.120–21, 163, 163n.134
    Order of the Consolidation Tribunal (7 September 2005) 482n.196, 484n.226
    Decision on Preliminary Question (6 June 2006) 70, 70nn.67–69, 78n.36
    Joint Order of the Costs of Arbitration and for the Termination of Certain
        Arbitral Proceedings (19 July 2007) 141n.215
Chemtura Corporation v Government of Canada, UNCITRAL, Award
    (2 August 2010) 510n.45, 521
CME Czech Republic BV v Czech Republic, UNCITRAL,
    Final Award (14 March 2003) 181n.24, 382n.44
    Separate Opinion on the Issues at the Quantum Phase by Arbitrator
        Brownlie (14 March 2003) 392, 392n.124
Energoalians Ltd v Moldova, UNCITRAL, Arbitral Award (23 October 2013) 536, 536n.101
Ethyl v Canada, UNCITRAL, Award on Jurisdiction (24 June 1998) 130n.92, 563n.69
European Media Ventures v Czech Republic, UNCITRAL, Partial Award on
    Liability (8 July 2009) 138n.179
Eureko BV v Poland, UNCITRAL,
    Partial Award (19 June 2005) 252–53n.32
    Partial Award (19 August 2005) 123n.21
Glamis Gold Ltd v United States of America, UNCITRAL, Award (14 May 2009) 101, 469n.48,
                                                       472, 472n.77, 472n.80, 473nn.95,97, 488
Grand River Enterprises Six Nations Ltd and Others v United States of America,
    UNCITRAL/NAFTA,

xxx   TABLE OF CASES

Decision on Jurisdiction (20 July 2006) 323n.52, 564n.79
Award (12 January 2011) 510, 510n.41, 522
International Thunderbird Gaming Corporation v United Mexican States,
    UNCITRAL, Arbitral Award (26 January 2006) 81n.56, 472, 472n.81, 515n.95, 517–18,
                                                        518n.118, 522, 531, 531n.70
Invesmart v Czech Republic, UNCITRAL, Award (26 June 2009) 301n.27
Lauder, Ronald S v Czech Republic, UNCITRAL, Final Award
    (3 September 2001) 444n.59, 563n.69
Manchester Securities Corporation v Poland, UNCITRAL, Award (7 December 2018) 523n.3,
                                    527n.33, 531, 531n.66, 536, 536nn.104–5, 537, 538
Merrill & Ring Forestry L.P. v Canada, UNCITRAL, ICSID Case No UNCT/07/1,
    Award (31 March 2010) 121, 465n.3, 477n.146, 512, 512n.63,
                                                        515n.93, 517–18, 517n.113, 522
Methanex Corporation v United States of America,
    Response of Respondent United States of America to Methanex's Submission
        Concerning the NAFTA Free Trade Commission (31 July 2001) 510n.46
    Interpretation (26 October 2001) 510n.46
    Partial Award (7 August 2002) 118n.73, 125, 125n.37, 130n.92, 522, 557, 557n.18
    Letter on Interpretation (25 September 2002) 582n.254
    Final Award of the Tribunal on Jurisdiction and Merits (3 August 2005) 70n.60,
                                132n.111, 135nn.156–57, 162n.123, 192–93, 193n.106,
                                213, 465n.3, 512–13, 512n.61, 512n.67, 515n.94, 516
National Grid plc v Argentine Republic, UNCITRAL,
    Decision on Jurisdiction (20 June 2006) 132n.118
    Award (3 November 2008) 359, 359n.55, 413, 413n.8, 571n.139
Oostergetel, Jan and Laurentius, Theodora v Slovak Republic,
    UNCITRAL Rules, Ad hoc Arbitration,
    Decision on Jurisdiction (30 April 2010) 117n.65, 117n.71, 199n.146, 203n.168, 204n.176
    Award (23 April 2012) 527n.33
Paushok, Sergei, CJSC Golden East Company and CJSC Vostokneftegaz
    Company v Government of Mongolia, UNCITRAL,
    Interim Measures (2 September 2008) 567–68nn.104–8
    Award on Jurisdiction and Liability (28 April 2011) 315n.18, 322n.43, 328n.25, 497,
                                    497–98nn.56–58, 498, 498n.63, 502, 576n.189, 610n.60
Pope & Talbot Inc. v Government of Canada, UNCITRAL,
    Interim Award (2000) 515, 515nn.92,94, 516n.98, 522
    Award on the Merits of Phase 2 (10 April 2001) 114n.40, 517n.109, 522, 548, 548n.36, 554
    Damages Award (31 May 2002) 135n.154, 145, 181–82, 181n.26, 198n.142, 199–200,
                                468n.34, 471, 471n.71, 506–7, 522, 549, 550, 550n.38, 551, 553, 554
    Final Award, Award in Respect of Costs (26 November 2002) 512–13, 512n.60, 519n.126, 522
Pugachev, Sergei Viktorovich v Russian Federation, UNCITRAL,
    Interim Award (7 July 2017) 611n.63
    Jurisdiction (18 June 2020) 574n.168
S.D. Myers, Inc. v Government of Canada, UNCITRAL,
    Partial Award (13 November 2000) 77n.27, 380n.32, 507n.11, 515n.92, 518n.117
    Final Award (30 December 2002) 512–13, 512n.58, 512n.60, 516n.99, 519n.124, 522
SwemBalt AB, Sweden v Latvia, UNCITRAL, Award (23 October 2000) 12n.110
Tembec Inc et al v United States of America, UNCITRAL (NAFTA) 507n.12
Terminal Forest Products Ltd v United States of America, UNCITRAL, ... 507n.12
    Decision on Preliminary Questions (6 June 2006) 78n.36
Voecklinghaus v Czech Republic, UNCITRAL, Final Award (19 September 2011) 451n.3
Walter Bau AG (in liquidation) v Kingdom of Thailand, UNCITRAL, Award
    (1 July 2009) 97n.55, 200n.154, 322n.37, 322n.47, 323n.55
Werner Schneider, acting in his capacity as insolvency administrator of Walter
    Bau Ag v Kingdom of Thailand (formerly Walter Bau AG (in liquidation)
    v Kingdom of Thailand), UNCITRAL, Partial Award on Jurisdiction
    (5 October 2007) 16n.161, 114n.40

White Industries Australia Limited v Republic of India, UNCITRAL, Final
    Award (30 November 2011) 12n.109, 302n.34, 306n.61, 312
World Wide Minerals v Kazakhstan (2), UNCITRAL, Jurisdiction, unpublished
    (15 October 2015) 428, 428n.59, 428n.60, 428n.66, 433, 434, 446

PERMANENT COURT OF ARBITRATION

Achmea BV (formerly Eureko BV) v Slovak Republic I (Achmea I), PCA Case No 2008-13,
    Award on Jurisdiction, Arbitrability and Suspension (26 October 2010) 10n.78,
                    114–15, 118nn.76–77, 203, 203nn.168–69, 203–4nn.170–71,
                    204, 204nn.172–75, 210, 210n.205, 213, 220n.34, 221n.37
    Final Award (7 December 2012) 451n.3
Aeroport Belbek LLC and Igor Valerievich Kolomoisky v Russian Federation,
    PCA Case No 2017-07, Partial Award (4 February 2019) 103n.23, 107
AES Solar & Ors (PV Investors) v Spain, PCA Case No 2012-14 Jurisdiction
    (14 October 2014) 558n.32
Affaire des boutres de Mascate (France v UK), PCA No 1904-0, Award
    (8 August 1905) XI UNRIAA 83 .... 138n.183
Alcor Holdings Ltd v Czech Republic, PCA Case No 2018-45, Award (2 March 2022) 146n.3
Almås, Mr. Kristian and Almås, Mr. Geir v Republic of Poland, PCA Case No 2015-13,
    Award (27 June 2016) 256–57, 256n.66, 259, 259nn.90–92,
                    259n.93, 263, 270n.34, 273n.57, 276, 276nn.93–96,
                    279, 302n.31, 306n.61, 307n.70
AMF Aircraftleasing Meier & Fischer GmbH & Co. KG v Czech Republic, PCA Case No 2017/
    15, Final Award (11 May 2020) 187n.66, 189n.82, 211n.214, 221n.39, 221n.42, 252n.31
Arbitration between the Republic of Croatia and the Republic of Slovenia, PCA Case No 2012-
    04, Partial Award (30 June 2016) 227n.16, 229nn.34–36
Armas v Venezuela, PCA Case No 2013-3, Jurisdiction (15 December 2014) 598, 598n.52, 603
Armas v Venezuela, PCA Case No 2016-08, Award on Jurisdiction (13 December 2019) 140,
                    140n.205, 145
Bahgat, Mohamed Abdel Raouf v Arab Republic of Egypt (I), PCA Case No 2012-07,
    Decision on Jurisdiction (30 November 2007) 95–96, 95nn.48–49, 97, 97n.57,
                    99, 315n.19, 316n.22
Ballantine, Michael and Ballantine, Lisa v Dominican Republic,
    PCA Case No 2016-17, Award (3 September 2019) 573n.162, 597, 597n.47
Bank Melli Iran and Bank Saderat Iran v Kingdom of Bahrain, PCA Case No 2017-25,
    Award (9 November 2021) 146n.3, 406n.45
Bosca v Lithuania, PCA Case No 2011-04, Award (17 May 2013) 273n.57, 277n.97
British Caribbean Bank Limited v Government of Belize, PCA Case No 2010-18,
    Award (19 December 2014) 379n.22, 415, 415n.19, 419
Cairn Energy PLC and Cairn UK Holdings Limited v Republic of India,
    PCA Case No 2016-07, Final Award (21 December 2020) 114n.39, 162n.123
Canevaro Claim (Italy v Peru), PCA Case No 1910-01, Award of the Tribunal
    (3 May 1912)....................................... 590–91, 590n.16, 595, 595n.35, 603
Carthage Case (France v Italy), PCA 1913, 11 RIAA 449, Award (6 May 1913) 393, 393n.133
CC/Devas (Mauritius) Ltd, Devas Employees Mauritius Private Limited, and Telcom
    Devas Mauritius Limited v Republic of India, PCA Case No 2013-09, Award on
    Jurisdiction and Merits (25 July 2016) 18 ICSID Rep 487 .... 71, 71nn.78–79, 73,
                    143nn.235–36, 277n.103, 301n.22, 301n.27, 302n.31,
                    304, 304nn.45–46, 308, 308n.85, 358n.45
Chagos Marine Protected Area Arbitration (Mauritius v United Kingdom),
    PCA Case No 2011-03, Award (18 March 2015) XXXI RIAA 359 ...... 106n.44, 158nn.84–86,
                    481, 481nn.193–94, 559n.40, 609n.39
Chevron Corporation and Texaco Petroleum Company v Republic of Ecuador,
    PCA Case No 2007-02/AA277, Interim Award (1 December 2008) 322n.39, 323n.49,
                    323n.51, 327–28n.20, 328–29nn.31–32, 573n.162

xxxii   TABLE OF CASES

Chevron Corporation and Texaco Petroleum Company v Republic of Ecuador,
    PCA Case No 34877, Interim Award (1 December 2008) 162n.128, 610n.56
Chevron Corporation and Texaco Petroleum Company v Republic of Ecuador (II),
    PCA Case No 2009-23 537
    Interim Award (1 December 2008) 7n.47
    Third Interim Award (27 February 2012) 566, 566n.93
    Second Partial Award on Track II (30 August 2018) 199, 70, 70n.56, 70n.61, 73, 293,
                              293nn.42–43, 293n.44, 293n.45, 297, 378, 378n.20, 379n.22,
                              400, 480, 480n.181, 482–83, 482n.196, 525n.17, 529, 529n.45,
                              529n.53, 530–31, 531n.64, 536, 536n.102, 537n.110, 538
Clayton, William Ralph, Clayton, William Richard, Clayton, Douglas, Clayton,
    Daniel and Bilcon Delaware Inc v Government of Canada, UNCITRAL (NAFTA),
    PCA Case No 2009-04,
    Award (2 August 2010) 521
    Award on Jurisdiction and Liability (17 March 2015) 12n.105, 321n.35, 329n.34,
                              512n.58, 512nn.64–66, 512n.67, 513n.70, 519n.125,
                              547, 547n.32, 551–52, 551n.41, 552n.42, 552n.43, 554
    Award on Damages (10 January 2019) 379n.23, 380, 380n.28, 507n.11
Consutel Group S.p.A. in liquidazione v People's Democratic Republic of Algeria,
    PCA Case No 2017-33, Final Award (3 February 2020) 277n.104
Copper Mesa Mining Corporation v Republic of Ecuador, PCA Case No 2012-2,
    Award (15 March 2016) 397, 397n.168, 574n.169
Deripaska, Oleg Vladimirovich v Montenegro, PCA Case No 2017-07,
    Award unpublished (15 October 2019) 427–28, 427n.54, 444–45, 444n.60, 446, 449
Deutsche Telekom AG v Republic of India, PCA Case No 2014-10 (13 December 2017) 162n.127
Dispute Concerning Access to Information under Article 9 of the OSPAR Convention
    (Ireland v UK) PCA Case No 2001-03, XXIII RIAA 59
    Final Award (2 July 2003) 27n.31, 137–38, 137n.177, 251n.11, 265n.5, 568n.116
    Dissenting Opinion of Judge Griffith (2 July 2003) 27n.31, 138n.178
Dispute Concerning Coastal State Rights in the Black Sea, Sea of Azov, and
    Kerch Strait (Ukraine v the Russian Federation), PCA Case No 2017-06,
    Preliminary Objections Award (21 February 2020) 559n.40, 563n.73
Doutremepuich, Christian and Doutremepuich, Antonine v Republic of Mauritius,
    PCA Case No 2018-37, Award on Jurisdiction (23 August 2019) 31, 31nn.62–63, 32
Duzgit Integrity Arbitration (Republic of Malta v Democratic Republic of São Tomé
    and Principe), PCA Case No 2014-07,
    Award on Jurisdiction and the Merits (5 September 2016) 326n.8, 396n.159
    Award on Reparation (18 December 2019) 326n.1, 326nn.7–8, 327n.17
ECE Projektmanagement International GmbH and Kommanditgesellschaft PANTA
    Achtungsechzigste Grundstücksgesellschaft mbH & Co v Czech Republic, PCA Case No
    2010-05, Final Award (19 September 2013) 173, 173n.49, 173n.50, 175
Électricité de France (EDF) International SA v Republic of Hungary, PCA Case No 2009-13,
    Arbitral Award (3 December 2014) 41
Elliott Associates LP v Republic of Korea, PCA Case No 2018-51, Statement of
    Defence (27 September 2019) 309n.94, 310n.97
Enrica Lexie Incident (Italy v India), PCA Case No 2015-28, Award (21 May 2020) 150n.24,
                                  158nn.85–86, 251n.13, 559n.40
European American Investment Bank AG (Austria) v Slovak Republic,
    PCA Case No 2010-17, Award on Jurisdiction (22 October 2012) 55, 66, 67,
                             35, 113n.29, 116n.51, 116nn.59–60, 117, 117nn.62,64,
                             117nn.68–69, 118n.76, 119, 130n.92, 204n.176,
                             220nn.29,33, 221n.38, 224, 433n.116, 433n.117
Everest Estate LLC et al. v Russian Federation, PCA Case No 2015-36,
    Award (2 May 2018) 103n.23, 107, 437–38n.16
Flemingo Duty Free Shop Private Limited v Republic of Poland, UNCITRAL,
    PCA Case No 2014-11, Award (12 August 2016) 20 ICSID Rep 326 .... 254n.43, 257,
                             257nn.69–72, 263, 268n.22, 270n.35, 270n.38, 273n.57

TABLE OF CASES   xxxiii

Frontier Petroleum Services Ltd v Czech Republic, PCA Case No 45035,
    UNCITRAL, Final Award (12 November 2010) 451n.3
Fynerdale Holdings BV v Czech Republic, PCA Case No 2018-18, Award
    (29 April 2021) 218n.35
Gallo, Vito G v Canada, PCA Case No 2008-03, Award (15 September 2011) 573n.160
Gente Oil Ecuador v Republic of Ecuador, PCA Case No 2018-12, Award
    (24 May 2022) 390–91, 390n.114
Glencore Finance (Bermuda) Limited v Bolivia, PCA Case No 2016-39, Procedural
    Order No 2: Decision on Bifurcation (31 January 2018) 485n.235
Gold Pool v Kazakhstan, PCA Case No 2016-23, Award unpublished
    (30 July 2020) 425nn.20–21, 425n.24, 428n.60, 433, 433n.117,
                                  434, 444–45, 444n.60, 445n.66, 446, 446nn.71–72
Guyana v Suriname, PCA Case No 2004-04, Award (17 September 2007) 337n.6, 484n.231
HICEE v Slovakia, UNCITRAL, PCA Case No 2009-11,
    Partial Award on Jurisdiction (23 May 2011) 124n.28, 132n.109, 152–53, 153nn.46–48,
                                                          161n.120, 162, 163
    Dissenting Opinion of Judge Charles N Brower (23 May 2011) 127n.63, 153n.48, 163n.133
Hulley Enterprises Limited (Cyprus) v Russia, PCA Case No 2005-03/AA226,
    Interim Award on Jurisdiction and Admissibility (30 November 2009) 56, 56n.35, 63, 82n.59, 83
    Final Award (18 July 2014) 379n.23, 397, 397n.169, 475n.118, 484n.229, 486n.251, 488
ICS Inspection and Control Services Limited (United Kingdom) v Republic of Argentina,
    UNCITRAL, PCA Case No 2010-9, Jurisdiction (10 February 2012) 140n.202
InterTrade Holding GmbH (Germany) v Czech Republic, PCA Case No2009-12,
    Final Award (29 May 2012) 275n.78, 275–76n.84, 309n.95, 451n.3
    Separate Opinion of Henri Álvarez (29 May 2012) 270n.38
Iron Rhine Arbitration (Belgium v The Netherlands), Award PCA Case No 2003-02
    (24 May 2005) 136–37n.170, 137, 137n.174
Korsguard, Haakon v Croatia, UNCITRAL, PCA Case No 2019-02, Award
    (7 November 2022) 455n.46, 463
Larsen, Lance v Hawaiian Kingdom, PCA Case No 1999-01, Award (5 February 2001) 566n.91
Limited Liability Company Lugzor et al. v Russian Federation, PCA Case No 2015-29,
    Award (4 October 2022) 103n.23
Louis Dreyfus Armateurs SAS v India, PCA Case No 2014-26
    Jurisdiction (22 December 2015) 562n.68
    Award (11 September 2018) 277n.98
Luxtona Limited v Russian Federation, PCA Case No 2014-09, Interim Award on the
    Respondent's Objections to the Jurisdiction of the Tribunal (22 March 2017) 29n.52,
                                                                    59nn.68–71, 63
Manouba Case (France v Italy), PCA Case No 1912-01, 11 RIAA 463, Award
    (6 May 1913).. 393n.133
Maritime Boundary between Timor-Leste and Australia (Timor Leste v Australia),
    PCA Case No 2016-10, Report and Recommendations of the Conciliation
    Commission between Timor-Leste and Australia on the Timor Sea (9 May 2018) 158n.84
Merck v Ecuador, PCA Case No 2012-10 .... 530, 536
Murphy Exploration & Production Company International v Republic of Ecuador, PCA Case
    No 2012-16, Partial Final Award (6 May 2016) 379n.22
Muszynianka Spółka z Ograniczoną Odpowiedzialnością (formerly Spółdzielnia
    Pracy Muszynianka) v Slovak Republic, PCA Case No 2017-08,
    Award (7 October 2020) 116n.56, 117nn.65–66, 146n.3, 275n.78
Nissan Motor Co., Ltd v Republic of India, PCA Case No 2017-37,
    Decision on Jurisdiction (29 April 2019) 323n.52, 557n.19, 564n.75
North Atlantic Coast Fisheries Case (Great Britain v United States),
    PCA Case No 1909-01, Award (7 September 1910) XI RIAA 167 .... 65n.6
Norwegian Shipowners' Claims (Norway v USA), PCA Award (13 October 1922)
    1 RIAA 325 .... 514n.75
OAO Tatneft v Ukraine, PCA Case No 2008-8,
    Partial Award on Jurisdiction (28 September 2010) 301n.25

xxxiv   TABLE OF CASES

Award on the Merits (29 July 2014) 327nn.18–19
OOO Manolium Processing v Republic of Belarus, PCA Case No 2018-06,
  Final Award (22 June 2021) 31, 31n.64, 32, 315n.16, 328–29n.32
Oschadbank v Russia, PCA Case No 2016-14, Award (26 November 2018) 103, 103n.23, 108,
                                                                            437–38n.16
Philip Morris Asia Limited v Commonwealth of Australia, PCA Case No 2012-12,
  Award on Jurisdiction and Admissibility (17 December 2015) 162n.129, 316n.21, 601–2,
                                 601–2nn.71–72, 604, 610nn.58–59, 612, 612 nn.81–83, 617
PJSC CB PrivatBank and Finance Company Finilon LLC v Russian Federation,
  PCA Case No 2015-21,
  Interim Award (27 March 2017) 103n.23, 108, 437n.12, 437–38n.16
  Partial Award (4 February 2019) 253n.34, 276n.86
PJSC Ukrnafta v Russian Federation, PCA Case No 2015-34, Award (26 June 2017) 103n.23,
                                                                         108, 437–38n.16
Press Release of the Final Awards (24 April 2019) 437–38n.16
Reineccius, Dr Horst, Claimant v Bank for International Settlements, Respondent
  (Claim No1) First Eagle SoGen Funds, Inc., Claimant v Bank for International
  Settlements, Respondent (Claim No2) Pierre Mathieu and la Societe de Concours
  Hippique de La Chatre v Bank for International Settlements, PCA Case No 2000-04,
  Award (19 September 2003) 396n.159
Renco Group, Inc. v Republic of Peru (II), PCA Case No 2019-46, Decision on
  Expedited Preliminary Objections (30 June 2020) 46n.7, 315n.16
Republic of Ecuador v United States of America, PCA Case No 2012-5, Expert
  Opinion with Respect to Jurisdiction, Prof W Michael Reisman (24 April 2012) 182n.34
Resolute Forest Products Inc. (RFP) v Government of Canada, PCA Case No 2016-13,
  Decision on Jurisdiction and Admissibility (30 January 2018) 162n.129, 321n.35,
                                                                           323n.52, 558n.31
Rhine Chlorides Arbitration concerning the Auditing of Accounts
  (The Netherlands v France), PCA Case No 2000-02, Award (12 March 2004) 129n.77,
                                                                                141n.214
Russian Claim for Interest on Indemnities (Russia v Turkey), PCA Case No 1910-02,
  Award (11 November 1912) 354n.4
Saluka Investments BV (The Netherlands) v Czech Republic, PCA Case No 2001-04,
  Partial Award (17 March 2006) 70n.64, 127n.57, 140n.201, 516,
                                             516n.101, 522, 601nn.69–70, 625, 625n.42
  Counterclaim (7 May 2004) 576n.189, 577, 577nn.195–96
Sanum Investments Limited v Lao People's Democratic Republic, PCA Case No 2013-13 104
  Award on jurisdiction (13 December 2013) 14–15, 15n.143, 104nn.31–33,
                                        108, 181, 181n.27, 198n.142, 426n.39, 430nn.87–88,
                                        433n.115, 434, 438n.19, 439n.29, 439n.31, 439n.32, 449
  Award (6 August 2019) 191n.98, 451n.3, 574n.173
South American Silver v Bolivia, PCA Case No 2013-15, Award of (22 November 2018) 373,
                                             373n.31, 373n.33, 475n.118, 477n.139, 486n.252, 488
South China Sea Arbitration (Republic of Philippines v People's Republic of China),
  PCA Case No 2013-19,
  Award on Jurisdiction and Admissibility (29 October 2015) 559n.40, 563n.73,
                                                                           566n.91, 608n.37
  Award (12 July 2016) 150n.25, 158nn.87–96, 165, 251n.14
Stabil, Crimea-Petrol LLC and others v Russian Federation, PCA Case No 2015-35,
  Final Award (12 April 2019) 103n.23, 108, 267n.13, 277n.99
ST-AD GmbH v Republic of Bulgaria, PCA Case No 2011-06, Award on Jurisdiction
  (18 July 2013) 152nn.41–42, 315n.17, 323n.50, 555n.2
Timor-Leste v Australia Conciliation (Competence), PCA Case No 2016-10,
  Decision on Australia's Objections to Competence (19 September 2016) 114n.35
Trapote, Fernando Fraiz v Venezuela, PCA Case No 2019-11, Award (31 January 2022) 570n.126
Ulysseas, Inc. v Republic of Ecuador, PCA Case No 2009-19, Final Award (12 June 2012) ... 276n.92
Venezuela US, S.R.L. v Bolivarian Republic of Venezuela, PCA Case No 2013-34,
  Partial Award on Jurisdiction and Liability (5 February 2021) 277n.100, 309n.88, 312

Veteran Petroleum Limited (Cyprus) v Russian Federation, PCA Case No 2005-3/AA 228,
  Interim Award on Jurisdiction and Admissibility (30 November 2009) 56n.35, 63
  Final Award (18 July 2014) 379n.23
Windstream Energy LLC v Government of Canada, PCA Case No 2013-22 (NAFTA),
  Award (27 September 2016) 522
Wirtgen, Jürgen, Wirtgen, Stefan, Wirtgen, Gisela and JSW Solar (zwei) GmbH & Co.
  KG v Czech Republic (Wirtgen), PCA Case No 2014-03, Final Award
  (11 October 2017) 220nn.28,34, 557n.20
WNC Factoring Ltd (WNC) v Czech Republic, PCA Case No 2014-34,
  Award (22 February 2017) 116n.54, 116n.60, 277n.98, 571n.142
Yukos Capital Limited (formerly Yukos Capital SARL) v Russian Federation,
  PCA Case No 2013-31,
  Interim Award on Jurisdiction (18 January 2017) 57, 58–59, 58nn.58–63, 63, 560n.45
  Dissenting Opinion of Professor Brigitte Stern (18 January 2017) 58–59nn.64–65
  Final Award (23 July 2021) 59n.67, 161n.120
Yukos Universal Limited (Isle of Man) v Russian Federation,
  PCA Case No 2005-04/AA227
  Interim Award on Jurisdiction and Admissibility (30 November 2009) 56nn.35–36, 57,
                                                     57nn.37–42, 57n.46, 61n.86, 61n.89, 63
  Final Award (18 July 2014) 229n.37, 306n.64, 308, 308n.86,
                                                     379n.23, 380, 397n.169, 475n.118
  Opinion of Advocate General Paul Vlas (23 April 2021) 141n.207

IRAN-US CLAIMS TRIBUNAL

American Bell International Inc. v Islamic Republic of Iran, the Ministry of Defense of the
  Islamic Republic of Iran, the Ministry of Post, Telegraph and Telephone of the Islamic
  Republic of Iran and the Telecommunications Company of Iran, IUSCT Case No 48,
  Award No 255-48-3 (19 September 1986) 481n.190
Amoco International Finance Corporation v Government of the Islamic Republic of Iran,
  National Iranian Oil Company, National Petrochemical Company and Kharg
  Chemical Company Limited, IUSCT Case No 56, Partial Award No 310-56-3
  (14 July 1987) 314n.6, 383n.58, 416n.27, 467n.19, 515n.88, 521
Consortium for International Development ('CID') v Iran, IUSCT Case No 455,
  Award No 512-455-1 (15 May 1991) 623n.29
Federal Reserve Bank of New York v Bank Markazi, IUSCT Case No A 28,
  Decision No DEC 130-A28-FT (19 December 2000) 127, 127n.64
Flexi-Van Leasing, Inc. v Government of the Islamic Republic of Iran, IUSCT
  Case No 36, Award No 259-36-1 (13 October 1986) 623n.28
Ford Aerospace & Communications Corporation, Aeronutronic Overseas, Inc. v
  Air Force of the Islamic Republic of Iran, the Ground Forces of the Islamic Republic
  of Iran and others, IUSCT Case No 159, Award No 236-159-3 (17 Jun 1986) 582n.253
Gabay, Norman v Islamic Republic of Iran, IUSCT Case No 771, Award No 515-771-2
  (10 July 1991) 582n.253
Hyatt International Corporation and others v Islamic Republic of Iran and others, IUSCT
  Case No 134, Interlocutory Award No ITL 54-134-1 (17 September 1985) 267n.15, 279
International Technical Products Corporation v Government of the Islamic
  Republic of Iran and Its Agencies, Case No 302, Final Award No 196-302-3
  (28 October 1985) 327n.16, 389n.97
Islamic Republic of Iran v United States of America, IUSCT Case No A1, Decision No
  DEC 12-A1-FT (3 August 1982) 121n.3
Islamic Republic of Iran v United States of America, IUSCT Case Nos A3, A8, A9,
  A14, B61, Decision (1 July 2011) 583n.261, 584n.273
Islamic Republic of Iran v United States, IUSCT, Award No 601-A3/A8/A9/A14/B61-FT,
  Partial Award (17 July 2009) 482n.205
Islamic Republic of Iran v United States of America, IUSCT Case No A-18, Decision
  No DEC 32-A18-FT (6 April 1984) 596nn.43–44, 603

xxxvi TABLE OF CASES

Islamic Republic of Iran v United States of America, IUSCT Case No A/20, Decision
    No DEC 45-A20-FT (10 July 1986) 573n.156
Islamic Republic of Iran v United States of America, IUSCT Case No B1
    Award (Counterclaim) No ITL No 83-B1-FT (9 September 2004) 132n.116
    Interlocutory Award (2004–2009) 38 IUSCTR 77 .... 132n.116
Lockheed Corporation v Government of Iran, The Ministry of War & The Iranian
    Air Force, IUSCT Case No 829, Award No 367-829-2 (9 June 1988) 623n.33
McCollough & Company Inc v Ministry of Post, Telegraph and Telephone, IUSCT
    Case No 89, Award No 225-89-3 (16 Apr 1986) 394–95n.144, 395n.150, 396n.157
Malek, Reza Said v Iran, IUSCT Case No 193, Award (11 August 1992) 573n.159
Morris v Government of the Islamic Republic of Iran, Bank Mellat (formerly
    Iran-Arab Bank), IUSCT Case No 200, Award No 36-200-1 (30 March 1983) 584n.272
Paul Donin De Rosiere, Panacaviar, SA v Islamic Republic of Iran, Sherkat Sahami Shilat
    Iran, IUSCT Case No 498, Interim Award No ITM 64-498-1 (4 December 1986) 582n.253
PepsiCo, Inc. v Government of the Islamic Republic of Iran, Foundation for the Oppressed,
    Zamzam Bottling Company and others, IUSCT Case No 18, Award No 260-18-1
    (13 October 1986) 582n.253
Petrolane, Inc. and others v Islamic Republic of Iran and others, IUSCT Case No 131,
    Award No 518-131-2 (14 August 1991) 267n.16
Phelps Dodge Corp v Islamic Republic of Iran, IUSCT Case No 99, Award No 217-99-2
    (19 Mar 1986) 516n.98
Phillips Petroleum Company Iran v Islamic Republic of Iran and National Iranian Oil
    Company, IUSCT Case No 39, Award No 425-39-2 (29 June 1989) 267n.16, 515n.87, 522
Picker International Corporation v Islamic Republic of Iran, IUSCT Case No 10173,
    Decision No DEC 48-10173-3 (8 October 1986) 582n.253
Questech, Inc. v Ministry of National Defence of the Islamic Republic of Iran,
    IUSCT Case No 59, Award No 191-59-1 (12 September 1985) 237–38, 237–38nn.51–55,
                                                                               241–42, 242n.102, 245
Ram International Industries, Inc., Universal Electronics, Inc., General Aviation
    Supply, Inc., Galaxy Electronics Corp. v Air Force of the Islamic Republic of Iran,
    IUSCT Case No 148, Award No 67-148-1 (28 August 1983) 584n.272
Sabet, Aram & Ors v Iran & Ors, IUSCT Case Nos 815, 816 & 817, Partial Award
    (30 June 1999) 573n.156
Schlegel Corporation v National Iranian Copper Industries Company,
    IUSCT Case No 834, Award (27 March 1987) 623n.30
Sea-Land Service, Inc. v Islamic Republic of Iran, IUSCT Case No 33,
    Award No 135-33-1 (22 June 1984) 19n.194, 623, 623nn.26–27, 628
Sedco, Inc. v National Iranian Oil Company and the Islamic Republic of Iran,
    IUSCT Case Nos. 128 and 129, Award (27 March 1986) 515n.87, 522
Starrett Housing Corporation, Starrett Systems, Inc. and others v Government of the
    Islamic Republic of Iran, Bank Markazi Iran and others, IUSCT Case No 24,
    Award (19 December 1983) 515n.87, 522
T.C.S.B., Inc. v Islamic Republic of Iran, Ministry of Housing and Urban Development
    and others, IUSCT Case No 140, Award No 114-140-2 (16 March 1984) 623nn.31–32
Tippets, Abbett, McCarthy, Stratton v TAMS-AFFA Consulting Engineers of Iran,
    Award No 141-7-2, 6 Iran-US CTR 219 (1984), IUSCT No.7 .... 515n.87, 522
Yeager, Kenneth P. v Islamic Republic of Iran, IUSCT Case No 10199,
    Award (2 November 1987) 291, 291–92nn.27–32, 292n.30, 292nn.31–32, 297

INTERNATIONAL COURT OF JUSTICE

Aegean Sea Continental Shelf (Greece v Turkey) Judgment (19 December 1978) 126n.50, 157,
                                                                                                   157n.83, 559n.35
Aerial Incident of 3 July 1988 (Islamic Republic of Iran v United States of America)
    Memorial of the Islamic Republic of Iran (24 July 1990) 336n.5
Allegations of Genocide under the Convention on the Prevention and Punishment
    of the Crime of Genocide (Ukraine v Russia), ICJ General List No 182,
    Provisional Measures (16 March 2022) 567n.105

Alleged Violations of Sovereign Rights and Maritime Spaces in the Caribbean Sea
 (Nicaragua v Colombia), ... 575
 Preliminary Objections Judgment (17 March 2016) 157n.76
 Counterclaims (15 November 2017) 575n.179, 576nn.182,84
 Judgment (21 April 2022) 314n.10, 321n.33
 Dissenting Opinion of Ad Hoc Judge McRae 314n.10
 Dissenting Opinion of Judge Abraham 314n.10
 Dissenting Opinion of Judge Nolte 314n.10
 Declaration of Judge Bennouna 314n.10
 Separate Opinion of Judge Yusuf 314n.10
Alleged violations of the 1955 Treaty of Amity, Economic Relations, and Consular
 Rights (Islamic Republic of Iran v United States of America)
 Provisional Measures (16 July 2018) 567nn.104,7, 568n.110
 Preliminary Objections (3 February 2021) 200n.151, 559–60n.42
Ambatielos (Greece v United Kingdom)
 Preliminary Objection, Judgment (1 July 1952) 127n.55, 216n.10, 558n.28
 Rejoinder Submitted by the Government of the United Kingdom (3 January 1953) 620n.13
 Merits Judgment - Obligation to Arbitrate (19 May 1953) 508n.18, 509, 509nn.26–28
 Dissenting Opinion of Judge Basdevant 216n.10
Anglo-Iranian Oil Co. Case (United Kingdom v Iran) 519
 Preliminary Objection Judgment (22 July 1952) 314n.9
 Judgment on Jurisdiction (1952) 508n.16, 508nn.19–22, 521
 Dissenting Opinion of Judge Hackworth 508n.23
 Dissenting Opinion of Judge Levi Carneiro 508n.23
Appeal relating to the Jurisdiction of the ICAO Council (India v Pakistan)
 Judgment (18 August 1972) 121n.1, 228n.26, 557n.20
 Separate Opinion of Judge de Castro 205n.180
 Separate Opinion of Judge Dillard 121n.1
Appeal relating to the Jurisdiction of the ICAO Council under Article 84 of the
 Convention on International Civil Aviation (Bahrain, Egypt, Saudi Arabia and
 United Arab Emirates v Qatar) Judgment (14 July 2020) 339n.25, 402n.4, 559–60n.42
Application for Review of Judgment No 158 of the United Nations Administrative
 Tribunal, Advisory Opinion (12 July 1973) ICJ Rep 1973 .... 526–27, 527n.26
Application of the Convention on the Prevention and Punishment of the Crime of
 Genocide (Bosnia and Herzegovina v Yugoslavia), Application for Revision
 of the Judgment of 11 July 1996 50
 Preliminary Objections (Yugoslavia v Bosnia and Herzegovina), Judgment
 (3 February 2003) 583n.263
Application of the Convention of 1902 Governing the Guardianship of Infants
 (Netherlands v Sweden), Judgment [1958] ICJ Rep 55 .... 571n.133
Application of the Convention on the Prevention and Punishment of the Crime
 of Genocide (Bosnia and Herzegovina v Serbia and Montenegro) 12nn.104–5, 65n.12, 165,
                       442, 442nn.46–47
 Provisional Measures Order (13 September 1993) 608n.27
 Preliminary Objections Judgment (11 July 1996) 449
 Dissenting Opinion Judge ad hoc Mahiou (11 July 1996) 290n.12, 294, 294nn.49–50, 297
 Counter-Claims Order (17 December 1997) 366n.5
 Judgment (26 February 2007) 8, 146n.1, 148–49nn.13–14,
          155nn.65–66, 250n.7, 255, 255n.53, 255–56nn.54–58,
         256n.59, 256n.60, 256nn.61–63, 263, 265n.6, 267n.20,
         269nn.23,26, 281, 281n.3, 281nn.4–5, 281n.6, 287,
         299n.4, 301n.21, 303n.39, 305– nn.56–58,
         306n.63, 307n.70, 310, 310n.102, 312, 318–19n.1,
         319n.14, 379n.22, 380, 380n.26, 380n.32, 393,
         393n.132, 400, 479n.166, 573n.155, 574n.167,
         578n.212, 579n.220, 580n.225, 580n.226, 584
 Separate Opinion of Judge Tomka (26 February 2007) 27n.31

xxxviii TABLE OF CASES

Application of the Convention on the Prevention and Punishment of the Crime
  of Genocide (Bosnia and Herzegovina v Yugoslavia)
  Preliminary Objections (11 July 1996) 47, 47nn.13–14, 47nn.17–19, 87–89,
                    87n.8, 94, 94n.44, 97, 99, 101n.7, 148–49, 155
  Dissenting Opinion of Judge Kreća (11 July 1996) 47nn.17–19, 107
  Counter-Claims Order (1997) 575n.176, 575–76nn.181,83
Application of the Convention on the Prevention and Punishment of the
  Crime of Genocide (The Gambia v Myanmar),
  Provisional Measures Order (23 January 2020) 567nn.106–7, 568n.110
  Preliminary Objections (22 July 2022) 406n.41, 562n.60, 567n.104
Application of the Convention on the Prevention and Punishment of the
  Crime of Genocide (Croatia v Serbia),
  Preliminary Objections Judgment (18 November 2008) 557n.22, 561n.59, 573n.155, 574n.167
  Separate Opinion of Judge Tomka 100n.*,1, 101, 101n.7
  Merits Judgment (3 February 2015) 149n.21
Application of the Interim Accord of 13 September 1995 (Former Yugoslav
  Republic of Macedonia v Greece) 403–4, 404n.17, 411
  Judgment (5 December 2011) 66nn.22–23, 133, 133n.131, 228n.21, 229, 229n.33
  Separate Opinion of Judge Simma 228n.21
  Dissenting Opinion of Judge ad hoc Roucounas 228n.21
  Declaration of Judge Bennouna 405, 405n.33
Application of the International Convention for the Suppression of the Financing of
  Terrorism and of the International Convention for the Elimination of All
  Forms of Racial Discrimination (Ukraine v Russia),
  Provisional Measures (16 January 2017) 567n.106
  Preliminary Objections Judgment (8 November 2019) 149n.22, 562n.66
Application of the International Convention on the Elimination of All Forms of Racial
  Discrimination (Qatar v United Arab Emirates),
  Provisional Measures, Order (14 June 2019) 615n.100
  Preliminary Objections, Judgment (4 February 2021) 148–49n.14, 155n.62, 165, 615n.101
Application of the International Convention on the Elimination of All Forms of
  Racial Discrimination (Georgia v Russia)
  Provisional Measures (15 October 2008) 449, 567n.104
  Preliminary Objections Judgment (1 April 2011) 129n.87, 562nn.61,65
Arbitral Award of 3 October 1899 (Guyana v Venezuela), Judgment
  (18 December 2020) 149n.15, 156, 156n.72
Arbitral Award of 31 July 1989 (Guinea-Bissau v Senegal),
  Order Provisional Measures (2 March 1990) 187nn.69–70, 567n.105
  Judgment (12 November 1991) 121n.2, 156, 156n.73
Armed Activities on the Territory of the Congo (DRC v Uganda)
  Counter-Memorial of Uganda (21 April 2001) 576nn.182,84
  Merits Judgment (19 December 2005) 106, 106nn.40–41, 250n.6, 252, 252n.28, 263,
                   265n.6, 293n.40, 332n.5, 333n.18,
                   333nn.20–21, 335, 338n.20, 564n.77
  Dissenting Opinion Judge ad hoc Kateka 289–90, 290n.13, 293, 293nn.39,41, 297
  Uganda oral statement, CR 2005/7 .... 338n.19
  Reparations Judgment (9 February 2022) 387n.88, 391–92, 392nn.122–23, 394–95
Armed Activities on the Territory of the Congo (New Application: 2002) (Democratic
  Republic of Congo v Rwanda), Decision on Jurisdiction and Admissibility
  (3 February 2006) 209, 209n.201, 562n.63
Arrest Warrant of 11 April 2000 (Democratic Republic of the Congo v Belgium)
  Judgment (14 February 2002) 382n.41, 569n.120
Asylum Case (Colombia v Peru)
  Judgment (20 November 1950) 126n.49
  Request for Interpretation of the Judgment of 20 November 1950, Judgment
  (27 November 1950) 581n.241
Avena and Other Mexican Nationals (Mexico v United States of America)

Judgment (31 March 2004) 146n.1, 148–49, 149nn.16–18, 165, 377n.11,
                                                                                          382n.41, 400, 543, 543n.14
    Request for Interpretation of the Judgment of 31 March 2004 170
    Provisional Measures Order (16 July 2008) 170n.29, 170n.30, 176
    Judgment (19 January 2009) 170, 581n.242
Barcelona Traction, Light and Power Company, Limited (New Application 1962)
    (Belgium v Spain) 35n.9, 520, 524, 526, 528, 532n.74
    Preliminary Objections Judgment (24 July 1964) 579n.217
    Preliminary Objections (1970) 603
    Judgment (5 February 1970) 5n.25, 367n.15, 521, 524nn.4–8, 600, 600nn.59–60
    Separate Opinion of Judge Ammoun 121n.1
    Separate Opinion of Judge Gros 514nn.80–83
    Separate Opinion of Judge Tanaka 517n.107, 525, 525nn.11–13
Border and Transborder Armed Actions (Nicaragua v Honduras), Jurisdiction and
    Admissibility Judgment (20 December 1988) 67, 67nn.25–26, 73, 129, 129n.76,
                                                        148–49n.14, 155n.62, 157n.78, 165, 608n.26
Certain Activities Carried Out by Nicaragua in the Border Area (Costa Rica v Nicaragua)/
    Construction of a Road in Costa Rica along the San Juan River
    (Nicaragua v Costa Rica),
    Judgment (16 December 2015) 577n.202
    Compensation Judgment (2 February 2018) 387n.89, 573nn.155,57
Certain Iranian Assets (Iran v United States),
    Preliminary Objections (13 February 2019) 484n.234
    Judgment (30 March 2023) 67n.24, 546–47, 546n.25, 547n.29
    Separate Opinion of Judge Charlesworth 547n.29
Certain Norwegian Loans (Dissenting Opinion of Judge Read) [1957] ICJ Rep 79 .... 266n.9
Certain Phosphate Lands in Nauru (Nauru v Australia), Judgment (26 June 1992) 564, 564n.77,
                                                                                564n.78, 565n.86, 607n.22
Certain Property (Liechtenstein v Germany),
    Memorial of Lichtenstein (28 March 2002) 620n.13
    Preliminary Objections Judgment (10 February 2005) 88n.10, 93n.35
Certain Questions of Mutual Assistance in Criminal Matters (Djibouti v France)
    Judgment (4 June 2008) 66, 66nn.18–19, 75n.4, 76, 76n.19, 83, 136n.169
Conditions of Admission of a State to Membership in the United Nations, Advisory
    Opinion (28 May 1948) 130n.94, 141nn.213–14, 149n.22
Continental Shelf (Libya v Malta), Judgment (3 June 1985) 467n.25, 468n.32, 471, 471n.65
Continental Shelf (Tunisia v Libya), Application for Revision and Interpretation of
    the Judgment of 24 February 1982, Judgment (10 December 1985) 579n.214, 583–84,
                                                                                 583n.265, 583–84nn.266–67
Corfu Channel (United Kingdom of Great Britain and Northern Ireland v Albania)
    Preliminary Objections Judgment (25 March 1948) 129n.84, 393, 393n.131, 574n.167
Delimitation of the Maritime Boundary between Mauritius and the Maldives in the
    Indian Ocean (Maldives v Mauritius), Preliminary Objections (2021) 565–66, 566n.91
Delimitation of the Maritime Boundary in the Gulf of Maine Area (Canada/ US),
    Judgment [1984] ICJ Rep 246 .... 569n.121
Diallo, Ahmadou Sadio, Case (Guinea v Democratic Republic of the Congo)
    Preliminary Objections Judgment (24 May 2007) 451n.8, 517n.105, 517n.106, 521,
                                                                                      599nn.57–58, 603
    Compensation Judgement (19 June 2012) 388n.92, 389, 389nn.101–2,
                                          389nn.103–4, 391n.118, 397n.166, 457n.62, 541–42,
                            541nn.7–8, 543, 543n.12, 550, 552, 553, 554, 569n.122, 573n.157, 577n.201
    Declaration of Judge Greenwood 388n.92
Difference relating to the Immunity from Legal Process of a Special Rapporteur of the
    Commission on Human Rights, Advisory Opinion (29 April 1999) 250, 250n.5
Dispute over the Status and Use of the Waters of the Silala (Chile v Bolivia),
    Judgment (1 December 2022) 143, 143n.230, 393n.134

Dispute regarding Navigational and Related Rights (Costa Rica v Nicaragua),
    Judgment (13 July 2009) 67n.24, 134–36, 134n.145, 145,
                                                              321n.32, 377, 377n.9, 479n.168
East Timor (Portugal v Australia), Judgment (30 June 1995) 565–66, 566n.89
Effect of Awards of Compensation made by the UN Administrative Tribunal,
    Advisory Opinion (13 July 1954) 583n.259
Elettronica Sicula S.p.A. (ELSI) (United States v Italy) 35n.9, 511, 514, 516–18, 526, 528,
                                                              529nn.51–52, 542, 545, 547–48
    Judgment (20 July 1989) 5n.25, 167n.10, 169nn.21–24, 175, 511nn.49–52,
                                                516, 516nn.102–4, 518nn.116–18, 522, 525, 525nn.14–15,
                                                525nn.16–17, 542n.10, 547n.33, 554, 600nn.62–63, 603
        Separate Opinion of Judge Oda 526, 526n.18
        Dissenting Opinion of Judge Schwebel 526, 526n.19
Fisheries Jurisdiction (Federal Republic of Germany v Iceland),
    Interim Protection Order (17 August 1972) 566n.100
    Judgment on Jurisdiction (2 February 1973) 186n.63, 194n.112, 207n.192
Fisheries Jurisdiction (Spain v Canada) Judgment (4 December 1998) 129n.84, 354n.8
Fisheries Jurisdiction (United Kingdom of Great Britain and Northern Ireland v Iceland),
    Interim Protection (17 August 1972) 566n.100
    Jurisdiction of the Court Judgment (2 February 1973) 149–50, 149n.23, 194n.112, 238–39,
                                                              238nn.66,68, 244n.128, 245
    Merits Judgment (25 July 1974) 66n.23, 468n.28
Frontier Dispute (Burkina Faso v Mali) Judgment (22 December 1986) 443n.55
Gabčíkovo-Nagymaros Project (Hungary v Slovakia), ... 227n.18, 228, 228n.25, 229, 229nn.31–32
    Judgment (25 September 1997) 8n.65, 65n.5, 66nn.14–16, 70, 73, 186n.59,
                                                194n.112, 205, 205n.178, 206n.181, 206n.182, 207–8,
                                                207n.188, 207n.192, 208n.194, 209, 209n.200, 213, 232,
                                                238–39, 238nn.56–58, 240n.84, 243n.127, 245, 319n.2, 343,
                                                343n.13, 347, 353–54n.2, 354–55, 354n.3, 354n.8, 355n.13,
                                                356n.18, 356n.20, 356nn.25–26, 357, 357nn.31–32, 364,
                                                369–70nn.2,3, 372n.23, 383, 383n.54, 402n.6, 403, 403n.13,
                                                404–5, 405n.30, 410n.77, 411, 442, 442n.45, 443n.55, 449
        Dissenting Opinion of Judge Fleischhauer 27n.31
        Separate Opinion of Judge Bedjaoui 135n.146, 140n.197
Immunities and Criminal Proceedings (Equatorial Guinea v France), ... 148–49, 615–16
    CR 2018/3 (20 February 2018) 613n.88, 615n.106, 616n.110
    Preliminary Objections Judgment (6 June 2018) 148–49, 148– 49–nn.14–19,
                                                156n.75, 606n.6, 608, 608nn.28–29, 608nn.31–33, 610,
                                                614n.92, 614nn.93–94, 614nn.95–96, 615n.104, 617
        Dissenting Opinion of Judge Donoghue 614n.95, 615n.104
    Merits Judgment (11 December 2020) 146n.1, 148n.13, 157n.77
Interpretation of Peace Treaties with Bulgaria, Hungary and Romania
    (Advisory Opinion) (30 March 1950 – first phase) (18 July 1950 – second phase) 129n.86,
                                                              561n.54, 566n.92
Jadhav (India v Pakistan) Judgment (17 July 2019) 121n.2, 148–49nn.13–14, 155n.66, 382n.41
Judgment No 2867 of the Administrative Tribunal of the International Labour
    Organization upon a Complaint Filed against the International Fund for
    Agricultural Development, Advisory Opinion (1 February 2012) 578n.213
Jurisdiction of the ICAO Council under Article II, Section 2, of the 1944 International
    Air Services Agreement (Bahrain, Egypt, Saudi Arabia & UAE v Qatar), Judgment
    (14 July 2020) 559–60n.42, 560n.49
Jurisdictional Immunities of the State (Germany v Italy: Greece intervening)
    Judgment (3 February 2012) 313n.2, 381–82, 382n.40, 384,
                                                384n.64, 473n.93, 490n.5, 492, 492nn.18–20, 502
Kasikili/Sedudu Island (Botswana v Namibia), Judgment (13 December 1999) 125nn.39,41,
                                                132, 132nn.110–11, 132n.112, 132n.116, 145, 166n.1, 175

LaGrand (Germany v United States),
  Provisional Measures Order (3 March 1999) 254n.42, 568, 568n.109
  Judgment (27 June 2001) 128, 128n.68, 166n.1, 169–70, 169–70nn.25–28, 175, 377n.11,
                                    382n.41, 397n.166, 400, 564n.77, 568n.110
Land Boundary in the Northern Part of Isla Portillos (Costa Rica v Nicaragua)
  Judgment (2 February 2018) 27n.30
Land and Maritime Boundary between Cameroon and Nigeria (Cameroon v Nigeria) 133
  Preliminary Objections (11 June 1998) 32, 49nn.28–30, 50, 51, 67nn.27–29, 73
  Counterclaims (2002) 187n.69, 188n.71, 188n.74, 189n.87, 213
  Judgment (10 October 2002) 133nn.124,27, 189, 313n.2
  Interpretation of the Judgment of 11 June 1998
    Preliminary Objections (1998) 49n.28
    Judgment (25 March 1999) 577n.200
Land, Island and Maritime Frontier Dispute (El Salvador v Honduras: Nicaragua intervening)
  Judgment (13 September 1990) 126n.51, 129n.84, 141n.213, 574n.165
  Application for Revision of the Judgment of 11 September 1992, Judgment
    (18 December 2003) 583, 583n.263
Legal Consequences for States of the Continued Presence of South Africa in Namibia
  (South-West Africa) notwithstanding Security Council Resolution
  276 (1970), Advisory Opinion (21 June 1971) 101, 101nn.5–6, 107,
                                                   136n.160, 232, 314n.12, 382n.43
Legal Consequences of the Construction of a Wall in the Occupied Palestinian
  Territory, Advisory Opinion (9 July 2004) 102nn.20–21, 136n.160, 155nn.67–68, 157,
                                                 157n.82, 228nn.22–23, 353–54n.2,
                                                 354n.8, 356n.20, 356n.27, 364, 381–82
Legal Consequences of the Separation of the Chagos Archipelago from Mauritius
  in 1965, Advisory Opinion (25 February 2019) 106n.43, 319n.5, 321n.32, 566n.90
Legality of the Use of Force (Federal Republic of Yugoslavia v Belgium),
  Order of Provisional Measures (2 June 1999) 319n.13, 327n.10, 354n.8
  Separate Opinion of Judge R Higgins 319n.13
  Dissenting Opinion of Judge Shi Jiuyong 319n.13, 327n.10
  Dissenting Opinion of Vice-President Weeramantry 327n.10
  Declaration by Judge Koroma 327n.10
Legality of Use of Force (Serbia and Montenegro v Belgium) Preliminary Objections
  Judgment (15 December 2004) 148–49n.14, 156n.71, 165
Legality of Use of Force (Serbia and Montenegro v Portugal) Preliminary Objections
  Judgment (15 December 2004) 27n.30
Maritime Delimitation and Territorial Questions between Qatar and Bahrain
  (Qatar v Bahrain) 157
  Jurisdiction and Admissibility Judgment (15 February 1995) 148–49n.14, 165
  Merits Judgment (16 March 2001) 27n.33
Maritime Delimitation in the Black Sea (Romania v Ukraine) Judgement
  (3 February 2009) 155–56, 155n.66
Maritime Delimitation in the Caribbean Sea and Pacific Ocean and Land Boundary
  in the Northern Part of the Isla Portillos (Costa Rica v Nicaragua), Judgment
  (2 February 2018) 475n.113, 482n.206
Maritime Delimitation in the Indian Ocean (Somalia v Kenya)
  Preliminary Objections Judgment (2 February 2017) 126n.47, 128n.69, 138n.182,
                                                  148–49nn.14–15, 156nn.69–70, 156n.74,
                                                  157nn.79–80, 157n.81, 165
  Judgment (12 October 2021) 569n.122
Maritime Dispute (Peru v Chile), Judgment (27 January 2014) 148–49n.14, 155, 155n.63
Military and Paramilitary Activities In and Against Nicaragua (Nicaragua
  v United States of America) 48–49, 73, 255, 338n.20, 565n.82
  Preliminary Objections (1984) 565n.82, 573n.155
  Provisional Measures (1984) 567n.104

Memorial of Nicaragua (30 June 1984) 338, 338nn.17–18
   Jurisdiction of the Court and Admissibility of the Application (26 November 1984) 5n.25,
                                                                                           48–49nn.25–27, 49n.30, 67n.24
   Judgement on Merits (27 June 1986) 27n.34, 65, 65nn.9–11, 228–29,
                                                                        228–29nn.27–29, 255n.50, 255n.51, 255n.52,
                                                                        300–1, 300nn.13–14, 305–6, 305n.56, 312,
                                                                        321n.33, 336n.4, 479n.166, 484n.233
      Separate Opinion of Judge Ago 300n.15
      Dissenting opinion of Judge Schwebel 484n.233
Monetary Gold Removed from Rome in 1943 (Italy v France, United Kingdom of
   Great Britain and Northern Ireland and United States of America) 565–66
   Preliminary Question Judgment (15 June 1954) 565nn.81,84, 565n.85
Northern Cameroons (Cameroon v United Kingdom)
   Preliminary Objections (1963) 561n.55
   Judgment (2 December 1963) 314n.8
North Sea Continental Shelf (Federal Republic of Germany v Netherlands;
   Federal Republic of Germany v Denmark) 27, 66n.22, 412–13
   Judgment (20 February 1969) 27n.32, 143n.231, 413n.3,
                                                                        468n.31, 475n.114, 476n.125, 481n.192
      Dissenting Opinion of Judge Lachs 27n.33
      Dissenting Opinion of Judge Morelli 143n.231
      Dissenting Opinion of Judge Tanaka 143, 143n.231
      Separate Opinion of Judge Ammoun 475n.114, 476n.125, 481n.192
Nottebohm (Liechtenstein v Guatemala) 18, 199–200, 596
   Preliminary Objections Judgment (18 November 1953) 200n.151, 571n.134
   Judgment (6 April 1955) 18nn.182–83, 595n.39
Nuclear Tests (Australia v France) 70
   Judgment (20 December 1974) 67n.24, 216n.10, 561n.55
   Dissenting Opinion of Judge De Castro 216n.10
   Dissenting Opinion of Judge Barwick 216n.10
Nuclear Tests (New Zealand v France), Judgment (20 December 1974) 70, 473n.93, 561n.55
Obligation to Negotiate Access to the Pacific Ocean (Bolivia v Chile),
   Judgment (1 October 2018) 66n.22, 574n.166
Obligations concerning Negotiations relating to Cessation of the Nuclear Arms
   Race and to Nuclear Disarmament (Marshall Islands v United Kingdom) 561–62
   Preliminary Objections Judgment (5 October 2016) 561n.58
   Dissenting Opinion of Judge Crawford 561n.59
   Dissenting Opinion of Judge Robinson 561n.59
Oil Platforms (Islamic Republic of Iran v United States of America) CR 2003/5 .... 337, 338n.15,
                                                                         338n.16, 340, 572
   Preliminary Objections (12 December 1996) 125nn.39,41, 126n.48, 128n.69, 133, 133n.130,
                                                                      136–37n.170, 145, 337n.11, 558n.25
   Separate Opinion of Judge Higgins (12 December 1996) 138n.184, 558n.26, 574n.164
   Counter-Memorial and Counter-claim by the USA (23 June 1997) 575n.177
   Order (10 March 1998) 327n.10
   US Rejoinder (23 March 2001) 337n.14
   Merits Judgment (6 November 2003) vn.2, 138n.184, 336n.4,
                                                                     557n.15, 572n.154, 574nn.164–65
   Separate opinion of Judge Simma 476n.125
Palestinian Wall. See Legal Consequences of the Construction of a Wall in the
   Occupied Palestinian Territory
Passage through the Great Belt (Finland v Denmark), Provisional Measures
   Order (29 July 1991) 568n.108
Pulp Mills on the River Uruguay (Argentina v Uruguay)
   Judgment (20 April 2010) 66nn.21–22, 73, 135n.149,
                                                                               384nn.65–66, 393n.135
      Separate Opinion of Judge Cançado Trindade 475n.114

Question of the Delimitation of the Continental Shelf Between Nicaragua and
    Colombia Beyond 200 Nautical Miles from the Nicaraguan Coast
    (Nicaragua v Colombia), Preliminary Objections Judgment (17 March 2016) 475n.113,
                                            482n.206, 559–60n.42, 580n.225, 580n.228
Questions relating to the Obligation to Prosecute or Extradite (Belgium v Senegal)
    Judgment (20 July 2012) 75–76, 75n.9, 76n.16, 313n.2, 319n.9, 571n.133
Questions relating to the Seizure and Detention of Certain Documents and Data
    (Timor-Leste v Australia), Provisional Measures Order (3 March 2014) 568n.108
Reparation for Injuries Suffered in the Service of the United Nations, Advisory
    Opinion (11 April 1949) 595, 595n.37
Reservations to the Convention on Genocide, Advisory Opinion (28 May 1951) 26n.29,
                                            34–35nn.2–3, 35, 44, 65n.12
Review of UNAT Judgment No 158, Advisory Opinion (12 July 1973) 577n.199
Rights of Nationals of the United States of America in Morocco (France v
    United States of America) Judgment (27 August 1952) 66n.19, 508–9, 508n.15, 508n.17,
                                            508–9nn.24–25, 522
Right of Passage over Indian Territory (Portugal v India),
    Preliminary Objections Judgment (26 November 1957) 113n.32, 607n.25
    Judgment on Merits (12 April 1960) 86nn.4–5, 88, 99, 320n.17, 476n.126
South West Africa Cases (Ethiopia v South Africa; Liberia v South Africa),
    Preliminary Objections Judgment (21 December 1962) 561n.56
    Judgment (18 July 1966) 478n.151
    Dissenting opinion of Judge Tanaka 478n.151
Sovereignty over Pedra Branca/Pulau Batu Puteh, Middle Rocks and South Ledge
    (Malaysia v Singapore) Judgment (23 May 2008) 479n.167, 573n.155
Sovereignty over Pulau Ligitan and Pulau Sipadan (Indonesia v Malaysia)
    Judgment (17 December 2002) 127n.54
Temple of Preah Vihear (Cambodia v Thailand) 14
    Preliminary Objections of Thailand (23 May 1960) 425n.29, 430n.82
    Judgment on Merits (15 June 1962) 133n.129, 443n.55, 480n.182, 481n.183, 572, 572n.153
    Separate opinion of Judge Alfaro 481n.191
    Dissenting Opinion of Judge Spender 480n.182, 481n.183
    Request for Interpretation of the Judgment of 15 June 1962, Judgment
    (11 November 2013) 581, 581n.243, 581–82nn.244,46
Territorial and Maritime Dispute (Nicaragua v Colombia)
    Judgment Preliminary Objections (13 December 2007) 114n.33
    Reply of Nicaragua (18 September 2009) 620n.13
    Judgment (2012) 569n.122
Territorial and Maritime Dispute between Nicaragua and Honduras in the Caribbean
    Sea (Nicaragua v Honduras), Judgment (8 October 2007) 574n.166
Territorial Dispute between Libya and Chad (Libyan Arab Jamahiriya v Chad)
    Judgment (3 February 1994) 65n.7, 125, 125n.34, 129n.79, 129n.85
    Separate Opinion of Judge Ajibola 27n.31
United States Diplomatic and Consular Staff in Tehran (United States of America v Iran)
    Judgment (24 May 1980) 208n.197, 300, 300n.12, 307, 307n.71,
                                            312, 319n.7, 321n.33, 409–10, 410n.72, 562n.64, 569n.120
Western Sahara, Advisory Opinion [1975] ICJ Rep 12 .... 141n.213
Whaling in the Antarctic (Australia v Japan: New Zealand intervening) Judgment
    (31 March 2014) 131n.107, 145, 376n.3, 377n.10, 381–82, 382n.42, 400

PERMANENT COURT OF INTERNATIONAL JUSTICE

Acquisition of Polish Nationality, PCIJ Ser B No 7, Advisory Opinion
    (15 September 1923) 590n.15, 603
Certain German Interests in Polish Upper Silesia (Germany v Poland),
    PCIJ Series A No 6, Preliminary Objections (25 August 1925) 75n.3, 76n.16,
                                            513–14nn.72–75, 514–15, 559, 559n.38, 570n.130

xliv   TABLE OF CASES

Certain German Interests in Polish Upper Silesia (Germany v Poland),
  PCIJ Series A No 7, Merits Judgment (25 May 1926) 24, 24nn.9–10, 66n.17, 67n.24, 73,
                                                                    521, 536, 608n.30
Certain German Interests in Polish Upper Silesia (Germany v Poland),
  PCIJ Rep Series A No 9, Claim for Indemnity, Jurisdiction Judgment (26 July 1927) 376,
                  376n.6, 379, 379n.24, 380, 380n.28, 400, 516, 516n.98, 520
Certain German Interests in Polish Upper Silesia (Germany v Poland), PCIJ Rep
  Series A No 12, 47, 48, Claim for Indemnity (Merits), Judgment (1928) 380, 380n.30,
                                                               380n.32, 381, 381n.34, 381n.37, 400
Certain German Interests in Polish Upper Silesia (Germany v Poland),
  PCIJ Rep Series A No 17, Merits Judgment (13 September 1928) 13–14, 14n.132, 575n.177,
                                                               621, 621n.15, 621n.16, 624, 626, 628
Competence of the ILO in regard to International Regulation of the Conditions
  of the Labour of Persons Employed in Agriculture, PCIJ Series B No 2,
  Advisory Opinion (12 August 1922) 126n.46, 130n.95, 168, 168nn.15–17, 175
Consistency of Certain Danzig Legislative Decrees with the Constitution of the
  Free City PCIJ Series A/B, No 65, Advisory Opinion (3 December 1935) 76, 76nn.20–21
  Individual Opinion of Judge Anzilotti 76nn.20–21
Denunciation of the Treaty of 2 November 1865 between China and Belgium (Belgium v
  China), PCIJ Series A No 18/19, Order (8 January 1927) 236 nn.28–32, 245, 567n.107
Diversion of Water from the Meuse (Netherlands v Belgium)
  PCIJ Series A/B No 70 25 .... 228nn.20–21, 232
  Judgment (28 Jun 1937)
      Dissenting opinion of Judge Anzilotti..................................... 228n.21, 484n.232
      Individual opinion of Judge Hudson 228n.21, 229n.37, 484n.232
Electricity Company of Sofia and Bulgaria (Belgium v Bulgaria)
  PCIJ Series A/B No 77 .... 224, 566n.101
  Preliminary Objection Judgment (4 April 1939) 216n.8, 218n.19
  Separate Opinion by Judge Dionisio Anzilotti 216, 216nn.9–10, 218n.20
Exchange of Greek and Turkish Populations (Advisory Opinion), (1925)
  PCIJ Series B No 10 .... 75–76, 75n.12
Free Zones of Upper Savoy and the District of Gex, PCIJ Ser A/B No 46 ...... 66n.17, 235n.16, 236,
                                                                    236n.24, 245
Free Zones of Upper Savoy and the District of Gex (France v Switzerland),
  PCIJ Series A No 22 .... 129n.87
Greco-Bulgarian Communities, PCIJ Ser B, No 17, 32, Advisory Opinion (31 July 1930) 75n.4
Interpretation of Judgments No 7 and 8 Concerning the Case of the Factory
  at Chorzów (Germany v Poland) PCIJ Series A No 13,
  Judgment (16 December 1927) 580nn.224–25, 581n.241, 581–82nn.244,46
  Dissenting Opinion by Judge Dionisio Anzilotti 220n.34, 221n.39
Interpretation of the Statute of the Memel Territory, Advisory Opinion (1932)
  PCIJ Series A/ B No 49 .... 571n.135
Judgment of the Hungaro-Czechoslovak Mixed Arbitral Tribunal (Peter Pàzmàny
  University v Czechoslovakia) (Czechoslovakia v Hungary), PCIJ Ser A/B No 61,
  Judgment (15 December 1933) 578n.213
Legal Status of Eastern Greenland (Denmark v Norway) PCIJ Series A/B No 53 .... 141n.213
Judgment (5 April 1933) 479n.165, 569n.121, 577n.200
Legal Status of the South-Eastern Territory of Greenland (Norway v Denmark),
  Interim Measures (1932) PCIJ Series A/B No 48 .... 567n.105
Lighthouses Case between France and Greece (France v Greece),
  PCIJ Series A/B No 62, 22, Judgment (1934) 570–71nn.130–31
Mavrommatis Palestine Concessions (Greece v Great Britain), PCIJ Series A No 2 .... 88–89, 97,
                                                                    169, 319n.4, 320n.16
  Jurisdiction Judgment (13 May 1924) 87nn.6–7, 94–95, 94nn.42–43, 94n.45,
                  99, 167n.9, 168nn.11–13, 168n.14, 175, 314n.9, 558n.28,
                  559n.34, 561n.53, 561n.59, 562n.62, 563n.70
Mavrommatis Jerusalem Concessions, Judgment, PCIJ Series A No 5 .... 479n.165

Nationality Decrees Issues in Tunis and Morocco, PCIJ Series B No 4,
  Advisory Opinion (7 February 1923) 235, 235nn.18–19, 235n.20, 245, 590, 590n.14
Oscar Chinn Case (UK v Belgium) PCIJ Ser A/B, No 63, Judgment
  (12 December 1934) 514nn.76–78, 522
Pajs, Czáky, Esterházy (Hungary v Yugoslavia), PCIJ Series A/B No 68,
  Judgment (16 December 1936) 577n.200
Panevezys-Saldutiskis Railway (Estonia v Lithuania) PCIJ Series A/ B No 76,
  Judgment (1939) 570n.130
Payment of various Brazilian Loans issued in France (France v Brazil)
  PCIJ Series A No 20, Judgment (12 July 1929) 354n.4
Payment of various Serbian Loans issued in France (France v Kingdom of the Serbs,
  Croats and Slovenes) PCIJ Series A No 20, Judgment (12 July 1929) 354n.4, 570n.130
Payment in Gold of Brazilian Federal Loans Contracted in France (France v Brazil),
  PCIJ Series A No 21, Judgment (21 July 1928) 130n.96, 571nn.134,36
Phosphates in Morocco (Italy v France) PCIJ Series A/B No 74 .... 99, 534
  Preliminary Objections Judgment (14 June 1938) 88nn.9–10, 93n.35, 319n.3, 320n.22,
                                                          321n.31, 526, 526n.23, 534n.87
    Dissenting Opinion of Judge van Eysinga 320n.22
    Separate Opinion of Judge Cheng 320n.22
Polish Postal Service in Danzig Case, PCIJ Series B, No 11, Advisory Opinion
  (16 May 1925) 482n.203, 569n.121
Rights of Minorities in Upper Silesia (Minority Schools) (Germany v Poland),
  Judgment (1928) PCIJ Ser A No 15 .... 563n.70
Société Commerciale de Belgique (Belgium v Greece) PCIJ Series A/B No 78,
  Judgment (15 June 1939) 354n.4
SS Lotus (France v Turkey) PCIJ Series A No 10, 13, Judgment
  (7 September 1927) 526nn.21–22, 569n.118
SS 'Wimbledon' (United Kingdom et al. v Germany) PCIJ Series A No 1, Judgment
  (17 August 1923) 394–95, 395n.146
Status of the Eastern Carelia, PCIJ Series B No 5, Advisory Opinion (27 April 1923) 555n.1
Treatment of Polish Nationals and Other Persons of Polish Origin and Speech in the Danzig
  Territory, The, PCIJ Series A/B, No 44, Advisory Opinion (4 February 1932) 74–75,
                                                                      75n.3, 76n.15

INTERNATIONAL TRIBUNAL FOR THE LAW OF THE SEA

Delimitation of the Maritime Boundary between Ghana and Côte d'Ivoire in the
  Atlantic Ocean (Ghana v Côte d'Ivoire) ITLOS Case No 23, Judgment
  (23 September 2017) 569n.123, 574n.166
Dispute Concerning Delimitation of the Maritime Boundary between Bangladesh
  and Myanmar in the Bay of Bengal (Bangladesh v Myanmar) ITLOC Case No 16,
  Judgment (14 March 2012) 481n.189
M/V 'Norstar' Case (Panama v Italy) ITLOS Case No 25 .... 396n.159
  Preliminary Objections Judgment (4 November 2016) 483n.219, 564n.77, 566n.91, 573n.156,
                                                                           574n.165
    Separate opinion of Judge Lucky 483n.219
M/V 'Saiga' (No 2) (St Vincent and the Grenadines v Guinea) ITLOS,
  Judgment (1 July 1999) 353–54n.2, 354n.9, 356n.20, 356n.28,
                                           380n.29, 389, 389n.105, 395n.148, 396n.159, 471n.66
M/V 'Virginia G' (Panama v Guinea-Bissau) ITLOS Case No 19 .... 396n.159
  Order (8 August 2012) ....
    .... 576n.185
  Judgment (14 April 2014) 379n.22, 397n.166
  Separate Opinion Judge Paik 397n.166
Responsibilities and obligations of States sponsoring persons and entities
  with respect to activities in the Area, ITLOS Case No 17, Advisory
  Opinion (1 February 2011) 166n.2, 176, 265n.5, 379n.22

Southern Bluefin Tuna cases (New Zealand and Australia v Japan) ITLOS Rep 280, ... 114
   Provisional Measures (27 August 1999) 138n.178
   Separate Opinion of Judge Treves 138n.178

CASES ADMINISTERED BY OTHER ARBITRAL INSTITUTIONS

Stockholm Chamber of Commerce (SCC)

Al-Bahloul, Mohammad Ammar v Republic of Tajikistan, SCC Case No V
   (064/2008), Final Award (8 June 2010) 383, 383n.56
Anglia Auto Accessories Limited v Czech Republic, SCC Case No 2014/181,
   Final Award (10 March 2017)............................ 117n.69, 210nn.211–12, 220n.29
Berschader v Russia, SCC Case No 080/2004, Award (21 April 2006) 137n.173, 138n.179
Charanne and Construction Investments v Spain, SCC Case No V 062/2012,
   Award (21 January 2016) 547, 547n.30
Eastern Sugar BV v Czech Republic, SCC Case No 088/2004, Partial Award
   (27 March 2007).................... 116n.53, 199n.146, 204n.176, 219, 219nn.22–23, 219n.24
GPF GP S.à.r.l v Poland, SCC Case No 2014/168, Final Award (29 April 2020) 65, 116n.56,
                                  117nn.62–63, 119, 200–1n.156, 220n.32, 579n.219
Green Power K/S and Obton A/S v Spain, SCC Case No V 2016/13,
   Award (16 Jun 2022) 220n.27, 221
Greentech Energy Systems A/S, NovEnergia II Energy & Environment (SCA)
   SICAR, and NovEnergia II Italian Portfolio SA v Italian Republic,
   SCC Case No V 2015/095, Award (23 December 2018) 116n.49, 116n.54, 185n.55
Iurii Bogdanov, Agurdino-Invest Ltd and Agurdino-Chimia JSC v Republic of Moldova,
   SCC Award (22 September 2005) 259–60, 260n.95
Limited Liability Company Amto v Ukraine, SCC Case No 080/2005, Final Award
   (26 March 2008)................ 271n.44, 302n.28, 303n.37, 309n.92, 532n.75, 533nn.83–85
Littop Enterprises Limited, Bridgemont Ventures Limited and Bordo Management
   Limited v Ukraine, SCC Case No V 2015/092, Final Award (4 February 2021)............ 485,
                                                      485n.238, 486, 486n.253
Nagel, William v Czech Republic, SCC Case No 049/2002, Award
   (9 September 2003) 252n.30, 564n.79
Nykomb Synergetics Technology Holding AB v Republic of Latvia, SCC
   Case No 118/2001, Award (16 December 2003) 303n.37, 380n.32
Petrobart Limited v Kyrgyz Republic, SCC Arbitration No 126/2003, Arbitral
   Award (29 March 2005) 61, 61nn.82–83, 482n.198, 483n.211
PL Holdings S.a.r.l. v Poland, SCC Case No V 2014/163, Partial Award
   (28 June 2017) 114–15, 117n.70, 118n.77, 118n.79
RosInvest Co UK Ltd v Russian Federation, SCC Case No V079/2005, Award on
   Jurisdiction (1 October 2007) 131n.106, 138, 138n.180, 138n.184, 140n.202
RosInvest Co UK Ltd v Russian Federation, SCC Case No 075/2009, Final Award
   (12 September 2010) 7n.47
SunReserve Luxco Holdings and others v Italy, SCC Case No V2016/32, Final
   Award (25 March 2020) 137n.175, 138–39, 139n.189

London Court of International Arbitration (LCIA)

EnCana Corporation v Republic of Ecuador, LCIA Case No UN3481,
   Award (3 February 2006) 81n.56, 252n.30, 268n.22, 303n.37
Société Générale in respect of DR Energy Holdings Limited and Empresa
   Distribuidora de Electricidad del Este, SA v Dominican Republic,
   LCIA Case No UN 7927, Award on Preliminary Objections to
   Jurisdiction (19 September 2008) 97, 97n.53, 128, 128n.72, 315n.17, 321n.35,
                                        322nn.46–47, 327–28n.20, 328–29nn.31–32, 329n.33

International Chamber of Commerce (ICC)

Güris and others v Syria, ICC Case No 21845/ZF/AYZ,
   Award (5 April 2016) 344n.30, 345, 345n.31, 345n.38

TABLE OF CASES   xlvii

Final Award (31 August 2020) 208, 208n.196, 211, 211n.217, 213, 344, 566n.97
Olin Holdings Limited v Libya, ICC Case No 20355/MCP, Partial
  Award (28 June 2016) 563n.69
Selmani v Kosovo, ICC Case No 24443/MHM/HBH, Final Award (1 August 2022) 445n.62
Yemen v Compagnie d'Enterprises, ICC Case No 7748/BGD/OLG (unpublished) 461n.109, 463

AD HOC ARBITRATION PROCEEDINGS

Affaire des réparations allemandes selon l'article 260 du Traité de Versailles
  (Allemagne c Commission des Réparations) (1924) I RIAA 429 . . . . 275n.76
Air Services Agreement (United States v France) (1978) 18 RIAA 417 . . . . 405n.29, 407n.50
Alabama Claims of the USA against Great Britain, Award (14 September 1872)
  XXIX UNRIAA 125 . . . . 74n.2, 76n.16, 83, 556n.11
Ambatielos (Greece v United Kingdom) Award (6 March 1956) 12 RIAA 83 . . . . 508n.18, 509,
                                                           509nn.26–28, 519, 521, 527, 527nn.27–28, 564n.76
American Independent Oil Company v Kuwait, Final Award (24 March 1982) 70n.64
Attiliò Regolo and Other Vessels (USA, Great Britain and Italy v Spain) Award
  (1945) XII RIAA 1 . . . . 266n.9
Award in the arbitration regarding the delimitation of the maritime boundary
  between Guyana and Suriname, Award (17 September 2007) XXX RIAA 1 . . . . 568n.116
Battus (France) v Bulgaria, Revision (1929) 9 TAM 284 . . . . 583n.263
BP Exploration Company (Libya) Limited v Government of the Libyan Arab Republic,
  (1979) 53 ILR 297, Award (10 October 1973) 383n.58, 385n.70, 407n.50
China Navigation Co Ltd (GB) v US (1921) VI RIAA 64 . . . . 579n.222
Cotesworth and Powell (Great Britain v Colombia) (1875) 2 Moore Intl
  Arbitrations 2050 . . . . 535n.94
Crawford & Ors v UN Secretary General, Award (1955) 1 UNAT Rep 331 . . . . 581n.239
De Sabla (US v Panama) (1933) 6 RIAA 358 . . . . 535n.95
Delimitation of the Continental Shelf (UK v France) 582
  Decision of 14 March 1978 (1978) XVIII RIAA 271 . . . . 579nn.214–15, 581n.240
Delimitation of the Frontier Line between Boundary Post 62 and Mount
  Fitzroy (Argentina v Chile), Revision and Interpretation (1995) XXII RIAA 151 . . . . . 581n.238,
                                                                                                                         582n.255
Dickson Car Wheel Company (USA) v United Mexican States, Dissenting Opinion of
  Commissioner Nielsen (1931) IV RIAA 682 . . . . 266n.9
Difference between New Zealand and France concerning the interpretation or
  application of two agreements, concluded on 9 July 1986 between the two States
  and which related to the problems arising from the Rainbow Warrior Affair
  (France v New Zealand) Decision (30 April 1990) 313–14nn.4,8, 319n.2, 321n.32,
                                                           342n.9, 347, 349–50, 349n.7, 349n.8, 350n.14, 351,
                                                                          352, 353–54n.2, 354n.9, 364, 369n.2
Dispute between Argentina and Chile concerning the Beagle Channel
  (18 February 1977) XXI UNRIAA 53 . . . . 128n.71, 132n.115
Dubai-Sharjah Border Arbitration, Award (19 October 1981) 91 ILR (1981) 186n.63
Ethiopia–Eritrea Boundary Commission, Interpretation, Correction and
  Consultation (2002) XXV RIAA 196 . . . . 581n.240
Flegenheimer Case, Conciliation Commissions Established Pursuant to Art. 83
  Peace Treaty with Italy, Decision No 182 (20 September 1958) 591n.17, 592n.25, 596n.41,
                                                                                                                           596.42
Forests of Central Rhodope (Greece v Bulgaria) Award Merits (29 March 1933)
  3 RIAA 1405 . . . . 383, 383n.53
Frontier Case (Argentina v Chile), Award (1966) XVI RIAA 109 . . . . 581n.238
Government of Kuwait v American Independent Oil Co (24 March 1982) 21 ILM 976 . . . . . 241n.96,
                                                                                                        242–43, 242n.112, 245
Idler (US v Venezuela) 4 Moore Intl Arbitrations 3491 . . . . 535n.96
Interpretation of the Air Transport Services Agreement between the United
  States of America and France (US v France), Decision on Interpretation
  (1964) XVI RIAA 73 . . . . 581n.237

xlviii   TABLE OF CASES

Island of Palmas (Netherlands v US), Award (1928) 2 RIAA 829 .... 12–13, 13n.116, 84n.1, 572, 572n.150
Island of Palmas (Netherlands v US), Award (1928) II RIAA 845 .... 313–14n.4
Lena Goldfields Co. Ltd v Government of USSR 621–22
   Award (3 September 1930) 621nn.18,20, 622n.21, 622n.22
Libyan American Oil Company (LIAMCO) v Libya 240
   Award (12 April 1977) 20 ILM 57 .... 240n.82, 245, 382n.44, 383n.58, 385n.70, 622n.25
Libyan Arab Foreign Investment Co (LAFICO) v Burundi 345, 345n.37
   Award (4 March 1991) 344n.28, 347
Lighthouses Arbitration (France v Greece), Award (24 July 1956) 12 RIAA 155 .... 622, 622n.24
Martini (Italy v Venezuela), Award (3 May 1930) 2 RIAA 975 .... 526n.25, 535, 535n.92
Mergé Case, Italy-US Conciliation Commission, Decision No 55 of 10 June 1955,
   (1955) 14 RIAA 236 .... 595–96, 595n.38, 596n.40, 604
Montano (Peru v US) (1863) 2 Moore Intl Arbitrations 1630 .... 535n.96
Montano (Peru) v US (1870) II RdAI 583 .... 580n.233
Nordzucker AG v Republic of Poland
   Partial Award, Jurisdiction (17 February 2006) 99
   Partial Award on Jurisdiction (10 December 2008) 95, 95nn.46–47, 316n.23
Opinion in the Lusitania cases (US v Germany) (1 November 1923) 7 RIAA 32 .... 389n.99
Question whether the re-evaluation of the German Mark in 1961 and 1969 constitutes a
   case for application of the clause in article 2 (e) of Annex I A of the 1953 Agreement
   on German External Debts (Belgium, France Switzerland, United Kingdom,
   United States v Germany), Decision (16 May 1980) XIX RIAA 67 .... 166n.2, 167n.8, 171nn.36–38, 176
Revere Copper & Brass, Inc. v Overseas Private Investment Corporation 56 ILR 257
   (24 August 1978) 241, 241n.98, 245
Salvador Commercial Company Case ('El Triunfo'), Award (8 May 1902) XV
   UNRIAA 467 .... 252, 252n.27
Smith v Marianao (Cuba v US) Award (2 May 1929) 535n.95
Southern Bluefin Tuna (New Zealand-Japan, Australia-Japan), Award on Jurisdiction
   and Admissibility (4 August 2000) XXIII RIAA 1 .... 114n.36, 119, 563n.72, 609n.38
Spanish Zone of Morocco Claims (Great Britain v Spain) (1924) 2 UNRIAA 615 .... 396n.156
Texaco Overseas Petroleum Company and California Asiatic Oil Company v Government
   of the Libyan Arab Republic Award (19 January 1979) 241n.93, 245, 378n.15
Trail Smelter (US/Canada) Decision (11 March 1941) (1941) III RIAA 1938 .... 579, 579n.218, 579n.221, 580n.227, 582n.255, 583n.260
Warsaw Electricity Company (France v Poland) (30 November 1929) 3
   UNRIAA 1669 .... 138nn.182–83
Zhongshang Fucheng Industrial Investment v Nigeria, Final Award (26 March 2021) 254n.43

WORLD TRADE ORGANIZATION

Argentina—Definitive Anti-Dumping Duties on Poultry from Brazil, WT/DS241/R
   (22 April 2003) 68n.40
Brazil—Certain Measures concerning Taxation and Charges, WT/DS472/AB/R
   (13 December 2018) 159n.98
Brazil—Export Financing Programme for Aircraft, Report of the Panel (14 April 1999) 27n.35
Brazil—Measures Affecting Desiccated Coconut, WT/DS22/AB/R (20 March 1997) 314n.5
Canada—Civilian Aircraft, WT/DS20/AB/R (2 August 1999) 125n.39
Canada—Measures Affecting the Importation of Milk and the Exportation of Dairy
   Products, WT/DS103/AB/R (adopted 13 October 1999) 150–51, 150nn.28–29, 159n.99, 165
Chile—Taxes on Alcoholic Beverages, Report of the Appellate Body,
   WT/DS110/AB/R (13 December 1999) 511n.56, 521
China—Certain Measures Affecting Electronic Payment Services, WT/DS413/R
   (16 July 2012) 521
EEC—Imposition of Anti-Dumping Duties on Imports of Cotton Yarn from
   Brazil, GATT, Panel Report (4 July 1995) 114n.34

European Communities—Anti-Dumping Duties on Imports of Cotton-Type
  Bed Linen from India—Recourse to Article 21.5 of the DSU by India,
  WT/DS141/RW (29 November 2002) 68n.40
European Communities—Anti-Dumping Duties on Malleable Cast Iron Tube or
  Pipe Fittings from Brazil, WT/DS219/AB/R (22 July 2003) 68n.38
European Communities—Bananas, Second Recourse to Article 21.5 of the DSU,
  WTO Doc WT/DS27/AB/RW2/ECU (27 November 2008) 159, 159n.104
  WT/DS27/AB/RW2/ECU and WT/DS27/AB/RW/USA (11 and 22 December 2008) 135,
                                                                          135n.150
European Communities—Customs Classification of Certain Computer Equipment,
  WT/DS62/AB/R, WT/DS67/AB/R, WR/DS68/AB/R (5 June 1998) 69n.49, 158–59,
                                                             159nn.99–100, 160–61
European Communities—Customs Classification of Frozen Boneless Chicken
  Cuts, WT/DS269/AB/R (12 September 2005) 159–60, 159nn.103–4, 160n.106,
                                           160nn.110–11, 160n.113, 161, 161nn.115–19
  Report of the Appellate Body WTO Doc WT/DS269/AB/R 165
European Communities—Measures Affecting Asbestos and Asbestos-Containing
  Products, Report of the Appellate Body, WT/DS135/AB/R (12 March 2001) 511n.54, 522
European Communities—Measures Concerning Meat and Meat Products (Hormones)
  Appellate Body Report, WT/DS26/AB/R and WT/DS48/AB/R (13 February 1998) 314n.5
  Decision of the Arbitrators, WT/DS26/ARB (12 July 1999) 114n.34
European Communities—Poultry, Panel Report, 1 WT/DS69 (2 March 1998) 110n.5
European Communities—Regime for the Importation, Sale and Distribution of Bananas,
  Complaint by the United States
  Panel Report, WT/DS27/R (22 May 1997) 522
  Panel Report, WT/DS27/R/USA (25 September 1997) 314n.5
European Communities—Trade Description of Sardines, WT/DS231/AB/R
  (26 September 2002) 68n.39
European Communities and Certain Member States—Measures Affecting Trade in
  Large Civil Aircraft, WT/DS316/AB/R (18 May 2011) 138n.184, 319n.2
European Union—Anti-Dumping Measures on Biodiesel from Argentina,
  WT/DS473/AB/R (6 October 2016) 159n.105
India—Patent Protection for Pharmaceutical and Agricultural Chemical Products,
  WT/DS50/R (5 September 1997) 68–69, 68–69nn.46–47, 73
  WT/DS50/AB/R (19 December 1997) 69nn.48–49
India—Quantitative Restrictions on Imports of Agricultural, Textile and Industrial
  Products, WT/DS90/AB/R (adopted 23 August 1999) 160, 160n.107
Japan—Alcoholic Beverages, WT/DS8/AB/R, WT/DS10/AB/R and WT/DS11/AB/R
  (adopted 1 November 1996) 132n.114, 132n.118
Japan—Countervailing Duties on Dynamic Random Access Memories from
  Korea, WT/DS336/R (13 July 2007) 166n.2, 175
Japan—Measures Affecting Consumer Photographic Film and Paper, Report of the
  Panel, WT/DS44/R (31 March 1998) 114n.34
Japan—Taxes on Alcoholic Beverages, WT/DS8/AB/R and WT/DS11/AB/R
  (adopted 4 October 1996) 146n.2, 150n.26, 511nn.53–54, 522
Korea—Measures Affecting Government Procurement, WT/DS163R (1 May 2000) 68n.41
Peru—Additional Duty on Imports of Certain Agricultural Products, Report of the
  Panel (27 November 2014) 27, 27n.36
Russia—Measures Concerning Traffic in Transit, WT/DS512/R (adopted
  5 April 2019) 67–68n.36
Saudi Arabia—Measures Concerning the Protection of Intellectual Property
  Rights, WT/DS567/R (16 June 2020) 208n.197
Thailand—Customs and Fiscal Measures on Cigarettes from the Philippines,
  Final Report of the Panel, WT/DS371/R (15 November 2010) 251n.10
  Report of the Panel—Addendum, WT/DS371/RW (12 November 2018) 251n.10
United States—Anti-Dumping and Countervailing Measures on Certain Coated
  Paper from Indonesia, WT/DS491/R (6 December 2017) 290n.18

l   TABLE OF CASES

United States—Anti-Dumping And Countervailing Measures On Large Residential
    Washers From Korea, WT/DS464/RPT (adopted 13 April 2017) 160n.109
United States—Certain Country of Origin Labelling (Cool) Requirements,
    WT/DS384/R, WT/DS386/R (18 November 2011) 68n.38
United States—Continued Dumping and Subsidy Offset Act of 2000,
    WT/DS217/R, WT/DS234/R (16 September 2002) 68, 68nn.42–43, 73
    WT/DS217/AB/R, WT/DS234/AB/R (16 January 2003) 68nn.44–45
United States—Continued Suspension of Obligations in the EC-Hormones
    Disputes, WT/DS320/AB/R (16 October 2008) 405nn.38–39, 406nn.40–41
United States—Countervailing Duties on Certain Corrosion-Resistant
    Carbon Steel Flat Products from Germany, WT/DS213/AB/R
    (adopted 28 November 2002) 150nn.28–29, 160n.109, 571n.134
United States—Countervailing Measures on Certain Hot-Rolled Steel Flat
    Products from India, WT/DS436/AB/R (19 December 2014) 271n.49
United States—Definitive Anti-Dumping and Countervailing Duties on
    Certain Products from China,
    WT/DS379/AB/R (11 March 2011) 159, 159nn.101–2, 265n.5, 415n.20, 417n.33
    WT/DS379/R (22 October 2010) 415n.20
United States—Definitive Anti-Dumping and Countervailing Duties on Certain
    Products from China—Recourse to Article 21.5 of the DSU,
    WT/DS437/AB/RW (15 August 2019) 46, 271–72, 272n.50
United States—Definitive Safeguard Measures on Imports of Circular Welded Carbon
    Quality Line Pipe from Korea, WT/DS202/AB/R (15 February 2022) 159n.98, 404–5n.26
United States—European Community Measures Concerning Meat and Meat
    Products (Hormones), WT/DS26/R/USA (18 August 1997) 320n.20, 320n.21
United States—Final Anti-Dumping Measures on Stainless Steel from Mexico,
    WT/DS344/AB/R (adopted 30 April 2008) 150n.27, 160–61, 160n.112, 161n.114
United States—Final Countervailing Duty Determination with respect to
    Certain Softwood Lumber from Canada, WT/DS257/AB/R (19 January 2004) 170–71,
                                                                    171nn.34–35, 176
United States—Gasoline, WT/DS2/AB/R (20 May 1996) 121n.3, 145
United States—Import Prohibition of Certain Shrimp and Shrimp Products,
    WT/DS58/AB/R (12 October 1998) 67, 67–68nn.35–36, 73,
                                                                    129n.78, 150n.26, 483n.221
    WT/DS58/R (15 May 1998) 67, 67nn.32–34
United States—Measures Affecting Imports of Woven Wool Shirts and Blouses from
    India, WT/DS33/AB/R (25 April 1997) 472n.164, 479–80nn.169–70, 573nn.156,59
United States—Measures Affecting the Cross-Border Supply of Gambling and Betting Services,
    Panel report, WT/DS285/R (10 November 2004, adopted on 20 April 2005) 251n.10
    Appellate Body Report, WT/DS285/AB/R (7 April 2005, adopted on 20 April 2005) 150–51,
                                                                    150nn.30–31, 160n.108
United States—Measures Affecting Trade in Large Civil Aircraft (Second Complaint),
    WTO Doc WT/DS353/AB/RW (adopted 28 March 2019) 158n.97
United States—Section 211 Omnibus Appropriations Act of 1998,
    WT/DS176/R (6 August 2001) 67–68n.36
    WT/DS176/AB/R (adopted 2 January 2002) 68n.37, 160, 160n.108
United States—Sections 301-310 of the Trade Act 1974, Report of the Panel
    (22 December 1999) 27n.35
United States—Subsidies on Upland Cotton, WT/DS267/AB/R (adopted 3 March 2005) 150n.32
United States—Transitional Safeguard Measure on Combed Cotton Yarn from Pakistan,
    WT/DS192/AB/RW (8 October 2001) 67n.30
United States—Tuna, WT/DS381/AB/R (13 June 2012) 131n.107

HUMAN RIGHTS COURTS AND COMMITTEES

UN Human Rights Committee on Civil and Political Rights

General Comment No 31, The nature of the general legal obligation imposed on States
    Parties to the Covenant, UN Doc CCPR/C/21/Rev1/Add.13 (26 May 2004) 103n.22

E and AK v Hungary, Human Rights Committee, UN Doc CCPR/C/5/D/520/1992
  (7 April 1994) 91, 91n.23, 92n.26
Jegatheeswara Sarma v Sri Lanka, Comm No 950/2000 (31 July 2003) 290n.16
Lovelace, Sandra v Canada, Human Rights Committee, UN Doc CCPR/C/13/
  D/24/1977 (30 July 1981) 90–91n.21, 92n.29
Mariam Sankara et al. v Burkina Faso, Comm No 1159/2003 (28 March 2006) 90–91n.21,
  93n.38, 321n.29
Mario Otilia Vargas Vargas v Chile, Communication no 718/1996 (26 July 1999) 93n.38
MIT v Spain, Human Rights Committee, UN Doc CCPR/C/41/D/310/1998
  (11 April 1991) 90–91n.21
Piandiong et al v The Philippines, Comm No 869/1999 (19 October 2000) 69n.52, 73
SE v Argentina, Human Rights Committee, UN Doc CCPR/C/38/D/275/1988
  (26 March 1990) 90–91n.21
Simunek, Hastings, Tuzilova and Prochazka v Czech Republic, Comm
  No 516/1992 (31 July 1995) 90–91n.21, 92n.26, 320n.25
Somers, Ivan v Hungary, Human Rights Committee, UN Doc CCPR/C/53/
  D/566/1993 (23 July 1996) 91n.23

UN Committee on Economic, Social and Cultural Rights
Marangopoulos Foundation for Human Rights v Greece, Comm No 30/2005,
  Decision on the Merits (6 December 2006) 319n.15
S.C. and G.P. v Italy, Comm No 22/2017, UN Doc E/C.12/65/D/22/2017 (2017) 319n.3

UN Committee against Torture
Cecilia Rosana Núñez Chipana v Venezuela, UN Doc CAT/C/21/D/110/1998
  (16 December 1998) 69n.52

European Court of Human Rights (including European Commission of Human Rights)
Al-Adsani v United Kingdom, Application No 35763/97 Grand Chamber Judgment
  (21 November 2001) 493n.29
Ališić and others v Bosnia and Herzegovina, Croatia, Serbia, Slovenia and the
  Former Yugoslav Republic of Macedonia, App No 60642/08, Judgement
  (16 July 2014) 15n.150, 461, 461n.106, 463
Al-Jedda v United Kingdom, Application No 27021/08, Judgment (7 July 2011) 284nn.27–28,
  389–90, 389n.106
Almeida Garrett, Mascarenhas Falcão and Others v Portugal, Apps nos 29813/96
  and 30229/96 (11 January 2000) 319n.10
Al-Saadoon and Mufdhi v UK, Appl. No 61498/08 (2 March 2010) 136n.163
Al-Skeini and others v United Kingdom, App no 55721/07 (7 July 2011) 102n.15
Anchugov and Gladkov v Russia, Apps nos 11157/04 and 15162/05 (4 July 2013) 321n.30
Assanidze v Georgia, App No 71503/01, Merits and Just Satisfaction (8 April 2004) 377n.10
Bankovic and Others v Belgium and Others, App no 52207/99 (12 December 2001) 102n.15
Behrami and Behrami v France and Saramati v France, Germany and Norway,
  GC-71412/01, Decision on Admissibility (31 May 2007) 282–84, 282n.9, 282n.11,
  282–83nn.14–15, 283nn.16–20, 287
Bergauer and Others v Czech Republic, App no 17120/04, Decision (13 December 2005) 320n.23
Blečić v Croatia, App no 59532/00, Judgment (8 March 2006) 88–89nn.13,15, 93, 93n.34,
  93n.37, 313n.3, 320nn.27–28
Bojlekov v Poland, App no 22819/93, Commission Decision (9 April 1997) 89n.16
Borozinsky v Poland, App no 24086/94 Commission Decision (2 December 1996).......... 89n.16
Bosphorus Hava Yollary Turizm ve Ticaret Anonim Sirketi v Ireland, Application
  No 45036/ 98, Judgment (30 June 2005) 284n.32
Bureš v Czech Republic, No 37679/08 (18 October 2012) 265n.5, 272, 272n.53, 279
Capital Bank AD v Bulgaria, Application No 49429/99, Judgment (24 November 2005) 284n.31
Chiragov v Armenia, App no 13216/05 (16 June 2015) 320n.26
Chrysostomos, Papachrysostomou and Loizidou v Turkey, App nos 15299/89,
  15300/89, 15318/89, Commission Decision (4 March 1991) 89n.16

Crnojević v Croatia, App no 71614/01, Decision (29 April 2003) 320n.18
Cruz Varas v Sweden, App No 15576/89, A/20 (20 March 1991) 179–80n.15
Cyprus v Turkey, App no 25781/94 (10 May 2001) 319n.8, 320n.26, 321n.30
De Napolis Pacheco v Belgium, App no 7775/77 (Commission Decision,
    5 October 1978) 88–89n.13
El Masri v Former Yugoslav Republic of Macedonia, App No 39630/09,
    Grand Chamber, Judgment (13 December 2012) 290n.15, 326n.9
Fogarty v United Kingdom, Application No 37112/97 (2002) 34 EHRR 12 .... 493n.29
Gallo v Slovak Republic, App no 30900/96 Commission Decision (4 September 1996) 88–89n.13
Golder v United Kingdom, App No 4451/70, Judgment (21 February 1975) 125n.39, 137n.171,
                                                                          166n.2, 175, 493n.31
Gravina v Italy, App no 60124/00 (15 November 2005) 320n.24
Harutyunyan v Armenia, App no 36549/03 (28 June 2007) 88, 88n.11
Hassan v United Kingdom, App No 29750/09 (16 September 2014) 179–80n.15
Husayn (Abu Zubaydah) v Poland, App No 7511/13, Judgment (24 July 2014) 69n.53, 290n.15
Ilaşcu and others v Moldova and Russia, App No 48787/99,
    Grand Chamber Judgment (8 July 2004) 102n.19, 290n.15, 319n.2, 326n.9, 327n.14
    Dissenting Opinion of Judge Kovler 327n.14
Ireland v United Kingdom, App No 5310/71 (18 January 1978) 327n.12
Issa and Others v Turkey, App no 31821/96 (16 November 2004) 102n.15
Ivanţoc v Moldova and Russia, App No 23687/05, Merits and Just Satisfaction
    (4 April 2012) 377n.10
Jamaa, Hirsi and Others v Italy, App no 27765/09 (23 February 2012) 102n.15
Janowiec and Others v Russia, Apps nos 55508/07 and 29520/09, Judgement
    (21 October 2013) 88–89n.13, 93n.35, 93n.38, 313n.3, 321n.29
Jonas v Czech Republic, App no 23063/93 Commission Decision
    (13 May 1996) 88–89n.13, 92n.31
Jones v United Kingdom, App Nos 34356/06 and 40528/06, Judgment (14 January 2014) 290n.15
Kasumaj, Ilaz v Greece, Application No 6974/05, Decision on Admissibility (5 July 2007) ... 283n.22
Kefalas and Others v Greece, App no 14726/89 (8 June 1995) 320n.27
Kerojärvi v Finland, App no 17506/90 (19 July 1995) 314n.14
Kholodov and Kholodova v Russia, App no 30651/05, Judgment (14 September 2006) 319n.12
Khoroshenko v Russia, App no 41418/04 (30 June 2015) 88–89n.13
Kotov v Russia, No 54522/00 (3 April 2012) 272nn.51,54
Kovačić and others v Slovenia, App. Nos 44574/98, 45133/98 & 48316/99, Judgement
    (3 October 2008) 460n.97
Kövendi v Hungary, App no 26287/95, Commission Decision (4 September 1996) 88–89n.13
Kurić and Others v Slovenia, App no 26828/06 (13 July 2010) 319n.6
Liseytseva and Maslov v Russia, App nos 39483/05 and 40527/10 (9 October 2014) 272n.54
Litovchenko v Russia, App no 69580/01 (18 April 2002) 93n.35, 321n.31
Loizidou v Turkey, App no 15318/89, ... 93n.34, 324n.58
    Preliminary Objections (23 March 1995) 89n.16, 102n.15, 132n.115
    Grand Chamber Judgment (18 December 1996) 320n.26
Loizidou v Turkey App no 40/1993/435/514 (ECtHR, Merits, 1996) 177–78n.1
Lupulet v Romania, App no 25497/94 Commission Decision (17 May 1996) 88–89n.13, 93n.34
Magyar Helsinki Bizottság v Hungary, App no 18030/11 (8 November 2016) 314n.12
Malhous v Czech Republic, App no 33071/96 (13 December 2000) 93n.34, 320n.23
Marguš v Croatia, App no 4455/10 (27 May 2014) 92n.28
Matthews v United Kingdom, Application No 24833/94, Judgment (18 February 1999) 284n.31
McElhinney v Ireland, Application No 31253/96 (2002) 34 EHRR 13 .... 493n.29
Mirolubovs and others v Latvia, No 798/05, Judgment (15 September 2009) 609n.40
Misson v Slovenia, App no 27337/95, Commission Decision (21 January 1997) 88–89n.13
Öcalan v Turkey, App No 46221/99 (12 May 2005) 136n.163, 179–80n.15
Oleynikov v Russia, No 36703/04 (14 March 2013) 491–92n.17
Ostojić v Croatia, No 16837/02 (26 September 2002) 93n.34
P.M. v Hungary, App no 23636/94 (Commission Decision, 21 May 1997) 93n.33

TABLE OF CASES   liii

Paksas v Lithuania, App No 34932/04 (6 January 2011) 321n.30
Papamichalopoulos and Others v Greece, App no 14556/89
    Judgment (24 June 1993) 26, 93n.34, 320n.24
    Article 50 Judgment (31 October 1995) 380n.32
Petrovic v Serbia, No 56551/11 (18 October 2011) 609n.44
Preussische Treuhand GmbH & Co. KG a.A. v Poland, App no 47550/06
    (7 October 2008) 26, 314n.15, 320n.23
Radio France and Others v France, App no 53984/00 (23 September 2003) 272n.54
Rosiński v Poland, App no 17373/02 (17 July 2007) 320n.24
Sargsyan v Azerbaijan, App no 40167/06 (14 December 2011) 89n.14
Selmouni v France, Appl. No 25803/94 (28 July 1999) 136n.169
Šilih v Slovenia, App no 71463/01 (9 April 2009) 89n.16, 320n.28, 321n.29
Slovenia v Croatia, App. No 54155/16, Decision (16 December 2020) 460n.97
Smoleanu v Romania, App no 30324/96 (3 December 2002) 320n.23
Soering v United Kingdom, Application No 14038/88 (7 July 1989) 179–80n.15
Staiku v Greece; App no 35426/97, Commission Decision (2 July 1997) 88–89n.13
Stamoulakatos v Greece (No 1) Application No 12806/87 (26 October 1993) 93, 93n.36
Teren Aksakal v Turkey, App no 51967/99 (11 September 2007) 93n.38
Ukraine v Russia (re Crimea), App nos 20958/14 and 38334/18 (14 January 2021) 102n.12,
                                                                                                  102nn.16–18, 106n.39, 108
Úri v Hungary, App no 31973/96, Commission Decision (16 October 1996) 88–89n.13
Varbanov v Bulgaria, No 31365/96, Judgment (5 October 2000) 609n.42
Varnava v Turkey, App nos 16064/90, 16065/90, 16066/09, 16068/90, 16069/90, 16070/90,
    16071/90, 16072/90, 16073/90 (18 September 2009) 89n.16, 93n.35, 93n.38, 320n.28
Veeber v Estonia (No 1), App no 37571/97 (7 November 2002) 93n.35
Verein Gegen Tierfabriken Schweiz (VgT) v Switzerland (No 2), App No 32772/02,
    Judgment (30 June 2009) 69n.54
Viikman v Estonia, App no 35086/97, Commission Decision (1 July 1998) 88–89n.13
Vinter and others v United Kingdom, Application nos. 66069/09, 130/10 and 3896/10)
    (9 July 2013) 376n.6
Concurring Opinion of Judge Ziemele 376n.6
Von Maltzan and Others v Germany, Apps nos 71916/01, 71917/01, and 10260/02
    (2 March 2005) 320n.23
Wallishauser v Austria, App no 156/04 (17 July 2012) 491–92n.17
X v Austria, App no 913/60, Commission Decision (19 December 1961) 88–89n.13
X v Belgium, App no 2568/65, Commission Decision (6 February 1968) 92n.31
X v France, App no 13473/87, Commission Decision (13 December 1982) 89, 89n.17
X v Germany, App no 2113/64, Commission Decision (3 April 1967) 88–89n.13
X v Italy, App no 8261/78, Commission Decision (11 October 1979) 89n.16
X v Portugal, App no 9453/81, Commission Decision (13 December 1982) 89n.16, 92n.28, 92n.32
X v Switzerland, App no 7211/75, Commission Decision (6 October 1976) 88–89n.13
X and Y v Portugal, App nos 8560/79, 8613/79, Commission Decision (3 July 1979) 89n.16
X, Y and Z v Switzerland, App no 6916/75, Commission Decision (8 October 1976) 88–89n.13
Yuriy Lobanov v Russia, App no 15578/03 (2 December 2010) 319n.10
Zambrano v France, No 41994/21 (21 September 2021) 609n.44
Zana v Turkey, App No 18954/91 (November 1997) 88, 88n.12
Zhdanov and others v Russia, Nos. 12200/08, 35949/11 and 58282/12,
    Judgment (16 July 2019) 607n.23, 609n.43

Inter-American Court of Human Rights

Advisory Opinion OC-14/94 of 9 December 1995, Series A No 14 .... 69n.54
Aloeboetoe v Suriname, Series C No 11, Reparation and Costs Judgment
    (10 September 1993) 377n.12
Andres Aylwin Azocar and Others v Chile, IACHR No 95/98, Report (9 December 1998) ... 320n.19
Baena-Ricardo et al v Panama, Judgment (2 February 2001) 69n.51
Blake v Guatemala, Judgment (2 July 1996) 90n.20

Cantoral Benavides v Peru, Judgment (3 December 2001) (Reparations and Costs),
  Series C No 88 .... 390n.107
Cantos v Argentina, Series C no 85 (8 September 2001) 320n.24
Gomes Lund et al. ("Guerrilha do Araguaia") v Brazil, Series C No 219,
  Judgment (24 November 2010) 319n.8, 321n.29, 321n.30
Gutiérrez-Soler v Colombia, IACHR Series C No 132, Merits, Reparation
  and Costs Judgment (12 September 2005) 377, 377n.12
Heliodoro Portugal v Panama, Judgment (12 August 2008) 90n.20
Herzog et al. v Brazil, Series C No 353 (15 March 2018) 321n.30
James et al v Trinidad and Tobago, Orders of 25 May 1999, and Order of
  25 September 1999 .... 69n.51
Moiwana Community v Suriname, Series C No 124, Judgment (15 June 2005) 319n.8, 320n.26
Right to Information on Consular Assistance in the Framework of the Guarantees
  of the Due Process of Law, The, Series A No 16, Advisory Opinion, OC-16/99
  (1 October 1999) 101–2, 102n.11
Salvador Chiriboga v Ecuador, Reparation and Costs Judgment (3 March 2011) 380n.32
Serrano-Cruz Sisters v El Salvador, Series C No 118 (23 November 2004) 321n.29
Velásquez Rodríguez v Honduras (Merits), Series C No 4, Judgment (29 July 1988),
  95 ILR 232 .... 290n.17
Villamizar Durán et al. v Colombia (Preliminary Objection, Merits, Reparations
  and Costs), Ser C No 364, Judgment (20 November 2018) 290n.17
Women Victims of Sexual Torture in Atenco v Mexico, Series C No 371,
  Judgment (28 November 2018) 272, 272n.52, 279
Ximenes-Lopes v Brazil, Series C No 149, Judgment (4 July 2006) 265n.5, 272n.51
Yean and Bosico Children v Dominican Republic, Judgment
  (8 September 2005) 22, 90–91, 90n.20

AFRICAN COURT ON HUMAN AND PEOPLE'S RIGHTS

Kazingachire and others v Zimbabwe, Communication 295/04 (2 May 2012) 272n.51
Zongo v Burkina Faso, 013/2011, Judgment on Reparations (5 Jun 2015) 379n.22, 380n.29

African Commission on Human and Peoples' Rights

African Commission on Human and Peoples' Rights v Libya, App no 002/2013
  (3 June 2016) 90n.19
Nganyi, Wilfred Onyango v United Republic of Tanzania, App no 006/2013
  (18 March 2016) 90n.19, 92n.27
Tanganyika Law Society v United Republic of Tanzania, App nos 009/2011
  and 011/2011 (14 June 2013) 90n.18
Urban Mkandawire v Republic of Malawi, App no 003/2011 (21 June 2013) 90n.18
Zitha and Zitha v Mozambique, Comm no 361/08 (1 April 2011) 319n.2

REGIONAL COURTS

Court of Justice of the European Union

Commission of the European Communities v Council of the European Union (C-29/99)
  Opinion of Advocate (13 December 2001) [2002] ECR I-11221 .... 47n.11
Council v Front Polisario (C-104/16 P) Judgment of the Grand Chamber
  (21 December 2016) 101nn.9–10, 105n.38, 107
Front Polisario v Council (T-344/19 and T-356/19) Judgment (29 September 2021) 102nn.13–14
Gennaro Currà and Others v Bundesrepublik Deutschland (C-466/11) Order
  (12 July 2012) 314n.7
Hellenic Republic v Commission of the European Communities (Case T-231/04)
  Judgment (17 January 2007) [2007] ECR II-63 .... 25n.17, 29n.51
Krohn v Commission (Case 175/84) Judgment (26 February 1986) 284n.29

TABLE OF CASES lv

NV Algemene Transporten Expeditie Onderneming van Gend & Loos v Netherlands
    Internal Revenue Administration (Case 26/62) [1963] ECR 1 .... 185n.50
Opinion 2/15 of the CJEU, ECLI:EU:C:2017:376 (16 May 2017) 221–22, 221n.44,
        222n.48, 222n.49
Opinion 2/15, Opinion of Advocate General Sharpston, ECLI:EU:C:2016:992
    (21 December 2017) 221–22nn.45–47
Poland (Latvia and Others, intervening) v Council of the European Union
    (Commission of the European Communities, intervening) [2008]
    1 CMLR 23 (AG Opinion) 29n.51
Racke GmbH & Co. v Hauptzollamt Mainz (C-162/96) Judgment (16 June 1998) 207nn.192–93,
        208n.194, 209n.199
Republic of Moldova v Komstroy LLC (C-741/19) CJEU Grand Chamber
    Judgment (2 September 2021) [2021] ECLI:EU:C:2021:655 .... 114–15, 115n.42, 184–85,
        185 nn.49–51, 200, 200–1n.156, 213, 221, 223n.54
Republic of Moldova v Komstroy LLC (C-741/19) [2021] ECLI:EU:C:2021:164
    (AG Opinion) 223n.54
Republic of Poland v PL Holdings Sàrl (C-109/20) CJEU Grand Chamber Judgment
    (26 October 2021) 115n.42
Slovak Republic v Achmea BV (C-284/16) [2018] ECLI:EU:C:2018:158
    Opinion of Advocate General (19 September 2017) 115n.43
    CJEU Grand Chamber Judgment (6 March 2018) 115n.42, 184–85, 184nn.47–48, 187, 188,
        197, 198, 200, 213, 221, 223, 223nn.51–52
Spain v Council of the European Union (C-36/98) Judgment (30 January 2001) 170,
        170nn.31–33, 175
Weber, Herbert v Universal Ogden Services Ltd (C-37/00) ECR (2002) I-02013,
    Judgment (27 February 2002) 101n.8
Western Sahara Campaign UK v Commissioners for Her Majesty's Revenue and
    Customs and Secretary of State for Environment, Food and Rural Affairs
    (C-266/16) (27 February 2018) 101n.10
Wightman and Others v Secretary of State for Exiting the European Union
    (Case C-621/18), Judgment, Full Court (10 December 2018) 210n.204

Court of First Instance of the European Communities
Opel Austria v EU Council (T-115/94) Judgment (22 January 1997) 29, 29n.49, 30

Eastern African Court of Justice (EACJ)
Union Trade Centre (UTC) v Attorney-General of the Republic of Rwanda, Reference
    No 10 of 2013, Judgment of the Court (26 November 2020) 265n.5, 272n.55, 279
Zziwa v EAC Secretary General, Appeal No 2 of 2017, Judgment (25 May 2018) 376n.5, 380n.29

Economic Community of West African States Court of Justice
Benson Olua Okomba v Republic of Benin, Case No ECW/CCJ/JUD/05/17,
    Judgment (10 October 2017) 251n.15
Dorothy Chioma Njemanze and Others v Federal Republic of Nigeria, Case No
    ECW/CCJ/JUD/08/17, Judgment (12 October 2017) 251n.15
Hembadoon Chia v Federal Republic of Nigeria, Case No ECW/CCJ/JUD/21/18,
    Judgment (3 July 2018) 251n.15
Tidjane Konte v Ghana, Case No ECW/CCJ/JUD/11/14, Judgment (13 May 2014) 251n.15
Wing Commander Danladi A Kwasu v Republic of Nigeria, Case No ECW/CCJ/
    JUD/04/17, Judgment (10 October 2017) 251n.15

Southern African Development Community Tribunal
Campbell and Others v Zimbabwe, SADCT Case No 2/2007, Judgment
    (28 November 2008) 378n.17

Caribbean Court of Justice

Maurice Tomlinson v State of Belize and State of Trinidad and Tobago, CCJ 1 (OJ)
　Judgment (10 June 2016) 251n.16

Association of Southeast Asian Nations (ASEAN) Arbitral Tribunal

Yaung Chi Oo Trading Pte. Ltd v Myanmar, ASEAN Case No ARB/01/1,
　Award (31 March 2003) 473n.100

Mercosur Tribunal

Import Prohibition of Remoulded Tyres from Uruguay (Uruguay v Brazil),
　Award (9 January 2002) 251n.17

MIXED COMMISSIONS

Eritrea-Ethiopia

Civilians Claims, Eritrea's Claims 15, 16, 23 & 27-32, Eritrea-Ethiopia Claims
　Commission, Partial Award, (17 December 2004) 456n.58, 599n.56, 603
Decision Regarding Delimitation of the Border between Eritrea and Ethiopia,
　Eritrea-Ethiopia Boundary Commission Decision (13 April 2002) 136n.162
Ethiopia's Damages Claims (Ethiopia v Eritrea), Eritrea-Ethiopia Claims Commission,
　Award (17 August 2009) 379n.22, 387n.88
Prisoners of War – Eritrea's Claim 17, Eritrea-Ethiopia Claims Commission,
　Partial Award (1 July 2003) 574n.164

France-Mexico

Estate of Jean-Baptiste Caire v Mexico (France v Mexico) (1929) 5 RIAA 516 .... 289nn.6–7
Georges Pinson (France) v Mexico, French-Mexican Claims Commission,
　Decision No 1 (19 October 1928) 5 UNRIAA 327 .... 129n.77, 137n.171

France-Venezuela

Company General of the Orinoco (France) v Venezuela, French-Venezuelan
　Commission (1905) X RIAA 184 .... 240, 240nn.80–81, 245, 579n.217
Fabiani (France v Venezuela) (1905) 10 RIAA 83, 4 Moore Intl Arbitrations 4878 .... 535n.96
French Company of Venezuelan Railroads, French-Venezuelan Commission (1904)
　10 RIAA 285 .... 354n.4

Italy-Venezuela

Gentini (Italy) v Venezuela, Mixed Claims Commission (Italy-Venezuela)
　(1903) X RIAA 564n.76
Giacopini (Italy) v Venezuela, Mixed Claims Commission (Italy-Venezuela)
　(1903) X RIAA 564n.76
Miliani Case, Italian-Venezuela Commission (1903) 10 RIAA 584 .... 595, 595n.36, 604
Oliva Case (of a general nature) Mixed Claims Commission (Italy-Venezuela) (1903)
　2006 Reports of International Arbitral Awards (X) 600-609 .... 240, 240nn.78–79, 245
Tagliaferro (Italy) v Venezuela, Mixed Claims Commission (Italy-Venezuela)
　(1903) X RIAA 564n.76

Turkey-Greece

Megalidis v Turkey, Turkish-Greek Mixed Arbitral Tribunal, Award (26 July 1928)
　(1927–28) Annual Digest of Public International Law Cases (Case No 272) (1928)
　8 Recueil des Décisions des Tribunaux Arbitraux Mixtes 386 .... 24, 24n.8, 30

UK-Italy

Cases of Dual Nationality, UK-Italy Mixed Commission, Decision No 22 (8 May 1954) 595n.36

US-Great Britain

Cayuga Indians (Great Britain) v United States (22 January 1926) VI RIAA 564n.76

US-Mexico

Chattin (USA) v Mexico, General Claims US-Mexico Mixed Commission, Award
    (23 July 1927) 252n.27
Neer, LFH and Neer, Pauline (USA) v United Mexican States, General Claims
    US-Mexico Mixed Commission, Decision (15 October 1926) 517–18, 517n.112, 542,
                                                           542n.9, 543, 545, 550, 551, 552–53
Russell v United Mexican States, Special Claims US-Mexico Commission, Award
    (24 April 1931) 169n.18, 176

US-Panama

Mariposa Development Company and Others (United States) v Panama, Decision
    (27 June 1933) 320n.23

US-Venezuela

Spader (US) v Venezuela, American-Venezuelan Commission (1903–1905) IX RIAA 564n.76

INTERNATIONAL CRIMINAL COURTS

International Criminal Tribunal for Rwanda

Prosecutor v Jean-Baptiste Gatete ICTR-2000-61-T, Decision on Defence Motion
    for Exclusion of Evidence and Delineation of the Defence Case (26 March 2010) 314n.15

International Criminal Tribunal for Yugoslavia (ICTY)

Prosecutor v Kupreškić, ICTY Case No IT-95-16-T (14 January 2000) 471n.67
Prosecutor v Tadić (Appeal Judgment), ICTY IT-94-1-A (15 July 1999) 290n.14, 300–1,
                                                           300n.16, 305–6, 305n.57, 312

Special Court for Sierra Leone

Prosecutor v Charles Ghankay Taylor, SCSL-03-01-T, Judgment (18 May 2012) 326n.4

NATIONAL COURTS

Austria

Dralle v Republic of Czechoslovakia, OGH (Supreme Court of Justice) 1 Ob 171/50
    (10 May 1950) 491n.8
OGH (Supreme Court of Justice) Case No 2Ob69/92 (16 December 1992) 433n.118
Termination of Employment (Austrian Supreme Court) Case (1956) 23 ILR 25n.12

Benin

Legal Opinion of Supreme Court of Benin, Case No 029-C (25 July 2003) ILDC 844
    (BJ 2003) 28n.37

Canada

De Guzman v Canada (Minister of Citizenship and Immigration) 3 FCR 655 (2006) 28n.38
Edwards v The Queen (14 October 2003) [2003] FCA 378 . . . . 427n.44
Mexico v Metalclad Corp, 2001 BCSC 664, Reasons for Judgment (2 May 2001) 515n.91
Russia Federation v Luxtona Limited, 2019 ONSC 4503 (Endorsement,
    13 December 2019) 59n.72

Chile

Sepúlveda (Juan Manuel Contreras), Re and Ors, Action to annul, Rol No 517-2004
(17 December 2004) ILDC 394 (CL 2004) 28n.46

Colombia

García de Borrisow v Embassy of Lebanon, Case No 32096, Colombia Supreme
Court of Justice, Decision on Admissibility (13 December 2007) ILDC 1009
(CO 2007) 491–92n.17, 502

Cyprus

Yemen v Compagnie d'Enterprises CFE SA, Case No 10717, Supreme Court of
Cyprus (28 June 1992) 461n.109, 463

France

Assoc. France Palestine (AFP) and organisation Libre de Palestine (OLP) v Alstom
and Veolia, Versailles Court of Appeal (France), No 11/05331 (22 March 2013) 192n.101
Nurol İnşaat ve Ticaret A.Ş. v Libya, Decision of the Paris Court of Appeal
(28 September 2021) 316n.27
Rusoro Mining Ltd v Bolivarian Republic of Venezuela, Decision of the Paris
Court of Appeal (29 January 2019) 329n.38
Rusoro Mining Ltd v Bolivarian Republic of Venezuela, Decision of the French
Court of Cassation (31 March 2021) 329n.38

Germany

BGH III ZB 20/12, Order of the German Federal Supreme Court (30 January 2013) 16n.161
BVerfG, 2 BvM 1/ 03 (8 May 2007) (Argentina necessity) 357n.38
BVerfG, Order of 3 July 2019, 2 BvR 824/15, 2 BvR 825/15 (Argentina's state bankruptcy) ... 357n.38
Constance Regional Court, Case No 4 O 234/05 H, Judgment (27 July 2006) 280n.1
East German Expropriation Case, 112 BVerfGE 1, 2 BvR 955/00, Federal Constitutional
Court (Germany) (26 October 2004) 192n.101
Empire of Iran Case, BVerfGE 2 BvM 1/62 (30 April 1963) 491n.8
Extradition to India Case, G, 2 BvR 685/03, BVerfGE 108, 129 (24 June 2003)
ILDC 484 (DE 2003) 28n.39

Ghana

Banful v Attorney General, J1/7/2016 [2017] GHASC 10 (10 June 2017) 188n.72
Delmas America Africa Line Incorporated v Kisko Products Ghana Limited,
Civil Appeal No J4/28/2004 (2 March 2005) ILDC 1487 (GH 2005) 28n.45

Hong Kong

FG Hemisphere Associates LLC v Democratic Republic of the Congo (2010) 142 ILR 216,
Hong Kong SAR Court of Appeal (10 February 2010) 28–29, 29n.48
Provisional Judgment (8 June 2011) 29n.48
Final Judgment (8 September 2011) 29n.48
Philippine Admiral (Owners) v Wallem Shipping (Hong Kong) Ltd and Another,
The Supreme Court of Hong Kong Judgment (5 November 1975) 491n.8

India

Director of Income Tax v New Skies Satellite, ITA 473/2012 (High Court of Delhi)
(8 February 2016) 70n.57

Italy

Santoro v Settimo senso srl, No 194/2018 (8 November 2018) ILDC 3034 (IT 2018) 28n.44

Latvia

Cilevičs and Ors v Latvia, Case No 2004-18-0106, Latvian Herald, No 77, 3235,
  13 May 2005, ILDC 190 (LV 2005) 28n.42

Netherlands

Aeroport Belbek LLC and Igor Valerievich Kolomoisky v Russian Federation, Case No
  200.266.443/01, Hague Court of Appeal (19 July 2022) 103n.26
NJSC Naftogaz of Ukraine, et. al. v Russian Federation, Case No 200.274.564/01,
  Hague Court of Appeal (19 July 2022) 103n.25
Russian Federation v Veteran Petroleum Ltd, No C/09/477160; Russian Federation v
  Yukos Universal Ltd, No C/09/477162; Russian Federation v Hulley Enterprises
  Ltd, No C/09/481619, The Hague District Court Judgment (20 April 2016) 47, 57nn.43,45
Veteran Petroleum Ltd v Russian Federation, No C/09/477160; Yukos Universal Ltd v
  Russian Federation, No C/09/477162; Hulley Enterprises Ltd v Russian
  Federation, No C/09/481619, Court of Appeal of the Hague Judgment
  (18 February 2020) 56nn.34–35, 57– nn.44–48, 82, 601n.68

New Zealand

Environmental Defence v Auckland Regional Council, New Zealand Environmental
  Court, [2002] 11 NZRMA 492 .... 28n.40

Poland

Polish State Treasury v Von Bismarck (1923) Supreme Court of Poland, Annual
  Digest of Public International Law Cases (Case No 39) 25n.11
Schrager v Workmen's Accident Insurance Institute for Moravia and Silesia (1927) Supreme
  Court of Poland, Annual Digest of Public International Law Cases (Case No 274) 25n.11

Russia

Government of the Russian Federation, Constitutional proceedings, No 2867-O-P
  (24 December 2020) ILDC 3236 (RU 2020) 28n.47
Judicial Review, N 1344-O-P, SZ RF Vol 48 (19 November 2009) ILDC 1553 (RU 2009) 28n.47

Singapore

Government of the Lao People's Democratic Republic v Sanum Investments
  Ltd SGHC No 2015/15 (20 January 2015) 15n.143, 104n.31, 425n.20, 430n.89, 438n.20,
                                                   439n.25, 439n.29, 439n.31, 439n.32, 449
Sanum Investments Ltd v Government of the Lao People's Democratic Republic, Court of
  Appeal of the Republic of Singapore, No 2016/57 (29 September 2016) 15n.143, 77n.29, 83,
                                            104n.31, 181nn.28–30, 182n.33, 425n.21, 426–27nn.40,42,
                                            430n.90, 434, 438n.21, 439n.26, 439nn.28–29, 439n.31, 439n.32, 449
Swissborough Diamond Mines (Pty) Limited and Others v Lesotho, Case No
  SGCA 2015/81, Singapore Court of Appeal Judgment (27 November 2018)
  [2019] 1 SLR 263 .... 103nn.27–28, 147n.5, 557n.23

South Africa

Democratic Alliance v Minister of International Relations and Cooperation et ors
  (2016) Case No 83145/2016, High Court of South Africa (Gauteng Div Pretoria) 209n.202
Law Society of South Africa and Ors v President of the Republic of South Africa and
  Ors, Case CT67/18, [2018] ZACC 51, ILDC 3179 (ZA 2018) 28n.43

Sweden

Deripaska v Montenegro, Svea Court of Appeal, Judgment (10 November 2022) 445n.62

Switzerland

Federal Court V v Regierungsrat des Kantons St Gallen (1994) ATF 120 Ib 360 .... 188n.73
Russian Federation v Yukos Capital Limited, First Civil Court of the Swiss Federal
    Tribunal Judgment (24 August 2022) 59n.66
Swiss Federal Tribunal, First Court of Civil Law, case 4A_34/2015, Judgment
    (6 October 2015) 41n.40, 44

United Kingdom

AIG Capital Partners Inc. and CJSC Tema Real Estate Company v Republic of
    Kazakhstan (ICSID), English High Court of Justice, Queen's Bench Division,
    Judgment (20 October 2005) 16n.161
Czech Republic v European Media Ventures, 2007 Folio No 974 (High Court of
    Justice Queen's Bench Division) 162n.129, 163, 163n.135
Gold Pool JV Limited v Republic of Kazakhstan (15 December 2021) [2021]
    EWHC 3422 (Comm) 428nn.62–63, 429n.68, 434, 449
GPF GP S.à.r.l v Republic of Poland [2018] EWHC 409 (Comm) 328nn.28,30
Khurts Bat v Investigating Judge of the Federal Court of Germany [2013] QB 349;
    [2011] EWHC 2029 (Admin) 28n.41
KOO Golden East Mongolia and Bank of Nova Scotia and others [2007] EWCA Civ 1443 498,
    498nn.60–62
PAO Tatneft v Ukraine [2018] EWHC 1797 (Comm); [2018] 1 WLR 5947,
    Judgment (13 July 2018) 16n.161, 557n.23
R (on the application of Al-Jedda) v Secretary of State for Defence, Judgment
    (12 December 2007) [2007] UKHL 58 .... 283–84, 283nn.23–25, 287
R (on the application of Corner House Research and Campaign against Arms Trade)
    v Director of the Serious Fraud Office, [2008] EWHC 714 (Admin) 357n.39
R (on the application of Hoareau and Bancoult) v Secretary of State for Foreign and
    Commonwealth Affairs, [2020] EWCA Civ 1010 .... 103n.26
R (on the application of Miller) v Secretary of State for Exiting the European Union
    [2017] UKSC 5 .... 210n.203
R (on the application of Yollari & Ors) v Secretary of State for Transport & Anor
    [2009] EWHC 1918 .... 207, 207nn.189–91
R v M [2011] 1 Cr App R 12; [2010] EWCA Crim 2327 .... 28n.41
South Korea v Dayyani & Ors [2020] Bus LR 884 .... 561n.57
Trendtex Trading Corporation v Central Bank of Nigeria, [1977] 2 WLR 356 (CA Civ) 491n.8,
    498, 498n.59

United States

Casa Express Corp. v Bolivarian Republic of Venezuela, 18 Civ 11940 (AT);
    19 Civ 3123 (AT) (SDNY, September 30, 2020) 358n.40
Chubb v Asiana Airlines, 215 F.3d 301 (2nd Cir. 2000) 184n.45
Extradition of Platko, U.S. Southern District Court for California, 213 F. Supp.
    2d 1229 (26 July 2002) 425n.28, 432n.105
Extradition of Sacirbegovic, U.S. Southern District Court for New York, No 03 Crim.
    Misc. 01 Page 19 (18 January 2005) 425n.28, 432n.105
Sabatier v Dabrowski, U.S. First Circuit Court of Appeals 586 F.2d 866
    (15 November 1978) 432n.107

List of Contributors

Claudia Annacker, Partner, Dechert LLP

Sean Aughey, Barrister, Essex Court Chambers

Randi Ayman, Senior Research Fellow, Max Planck Institute Luxembourg

Régis Bismuth, Professor, Sciences Po Law School

Jonathan Bonnitcha, Associate Professor, University of New South Wales

Fernando Lusa Bordin, College Associate Professor, Sidney Sussex College, University of Cambridge

Chester Brown, Professor, University of Sydney Law School

Kathleen Claussen, Professor, Georgetown University Law Center

James G Devaney, Senior Lecturer, University of Glasgow School of Law

Patrick Dumberry, Professor, University of Ottawa

Stephanie Forrest, Associate, Latham & Watkins

Chiara Giorgetti, Professor, Richmond Law School

Oliver Hailes, Assistant Professor, London School of Economics and Political Science

Jarrod Hepburn, Associate Professor, Melbourne Law School

Enikő Horváth, Partner, Dechert LLP

Robert Howse, Professor, New York University School of Law

Ben Juratowitch, Barrister, Essex Court Chambers

Amelia Keene, Legal Adviser to the President, Iran–United States Claims Tribunal

Andreas Kulick, Senior Research Fellow, Eberhard Karls University Tübingen

Emma Lindsay, Partner, Withersworldwide

Alisha Mathew, Senior lawyer, Office of Amal Clooney

Makane Moïse Mbengue, Professor, University of Geneva

Jackie McArthur, Barrister, Essex Court Chambers

Belinda McRae, Barrister, Twenty Essex

Panos Merkouris, Professor, University of Groningen

Jean-Baptiste Merlin, Legal Adviser (International Economic Law), Foreign Ministry (France)

Cameron Miles, Barrister, 3 Verulam Buildings

Federica Paddeu, Associate Professor, Queens' College, University of Cambridge

Alina Papanastasiou, Associate, Three Crowns LLP

Martins Paparinskis, Professor, University College London

Patrick Pearsall, Partner, Allen & Overy

Alain Pellet, Emeritus Professor, Université Paris Nanterre

Sergio Puig, Professor, European University Institute and University of Arizona

August Reinisch, Professor, University of Vienna

Hélène Ruiz Fabri, Professor, University Paris 1 Panthéon-Sorbonne

Arman Sarvarian, Reader, University of Surrey

Esmé Shirlow, Associate Professor, Australian National University

Luke Sobota, Founding Partner, Three Crowns LLP

Christian J Tams, Professor, University of Glasgow

Peter Tzeng, Associate, Foley Hoag LLP

Geraldo Vidigal, Assistant Professor, University of Amsterdam

Jorge E Viñuales, Professor, University of Cambridge

Tania Voon, Professor, University of Melbourne

Michael Waibel, Professor, University of Vienna

Philippa Webb, Professor, King's College London

Can Yeginsu, Barrister, 3 Verulam Buildings

Rumiana Yotova, Assistant Professor, University of Cambridge

Jingyuan Zhou, Researcher, Chongqing University

All authors wrote their entries in their individual capacity. Their views cannot be attributed to any institution with whom they were or are currently affiliated, or to any of their clients.

List of Abbreviations

ACHPR	African Charter on Human and Peoples' Rights
ACtHPR	African Court on Human and Peoples' Rights
AF	Additional Facility
AFDI	Annuaire Français de Droit International
AJIL	American Journal of International Law
AmJCompL	The American Journal of Comparative Law
App	Application
ArbInt	Arbitration International
ARIO	Articles on the Responsibility of International Organizations
ARSIWA	Articles on the Responsibility of States for Internationally Wrongful Acts
Art(s)	Article(s)
ASIL	American Society of International Law
Aust YBIL	Australian Yearbook of International Law
BIICL	British Institute of International and Comparative Law
BIT(s)	Bilateral Investment Treaty(ies)
BJ	Benin
BVerfG	Bundesverfassungsgericht (German Federal Constitutional Court)
BVerfGE	Amtliche Sammlung des Bundesverfassungsgerichts, cited by volume and page
BvR	Case-numbers of the Bundesverfassungsgericht
BYIL	British Yearbook of International Law
CCJ (OJ)	Caribbean Court of Justice (Original Jurisdiction)
CETA	EU–Canada Comprehensive Economic and Trade Agreement
cf	confer (compare)
CJEU	Court of Justice of the European Union
CL	Chile
CMLR	Common Market Law Reports
Co	Company
Commentary	Commentary on General International Law in International Investment Law
Cornell LRev	Cornell Law Review
CrAppR	Criminal Appeal Reports
Crim	Criminal
CUP	Cambridge University Press
DE	Deutschland (Germany)
DSU	Dispute Settlement Understanding, World Trade Organization
EAC	East African Community
EACJ	East African Court of Justice
ECHR	European Convention on Human Rights
ECmHR	European Commission on Human Rights
ECT	Energy Charter Treaty
ECtHR	European Court of Human Rights
ed(s)	editor(s)
edn	edition

eg	exempli gratia (for example)
EJIL	European Journal of International Law
et seq	et sequens
EU	European Union
EWCA	England and Wales Court of Appeal
F Supp	Federal Supplement
FCR	Canada Federal Court Reports
ff	and following
fn	Footnote(s) (external to the Commentary)
FRY	Federal Republic of Yugoslavia
GH	Ghana
GHASC	Supreme Court of Ghana
GmbH	Gesellschaft mit beschränkter Haftung (Limited Liability Company)
GIL	General International Law
ie	id est (that is)
IAReporter	International Arbitration Reporter
IACHR	Inter-American Court of Human Rights
ibid	ibidem (the same)
ICAO	International Civil Aviation Organization
ICC	International Chamber of Commerce
ICGJ	International Courts of General Jurisdiction
ICJ	International Court of Justice
ICLQ	International & Comparative Law Quarterly
ICSID	International Centre for Settlement of Investment Disputes
IIL	International Investment Law
IILA	International Investment Law and Arbitration
ILA	International Law Association
ILC	International Law Commission
ILDC	International Law in Domestic Courts
ILR	International Law Reports
Intl	International
Intl LJ	International Law Journal
Iran–USCTR	Iran–United States Claims Tribunal Reports
ISDS	Investor–State Dispute Settlement
ITLOS	International Tribunal for the Law of the Sea
IUSCT	Iran–United States Claims Tribunal
JISP	UN Convention on Jurisdictional Immunities of States and their Property
JUFIL	Journal on the Use of Force and International Law
King's Counsel	KC
Loy LAIntl & CompLRev	Loyola of Los Angeles International and Comparative Law
LPICT	The Law and Practice of International Courts and Tribunals
Ltd	Limited
LV	Latvia
MERCOSUR	Mercado Común del Sur (Southern Common Market)
MEX	Mexico
MFN	Most Favoured Nation
MPEPIL	Max Planck Encyclopaedia of Public International Law
MUP	Manchester University Press
n	note

NAFTA	North American Free Trade Agreement
No	Number
OECD	Organisation for Economic Co-operation and Development
OUP	Oxford University Press
p, pp	page(s)
para(s)	paragraph(s)
PCA	Permanent Court of Arbitration
PCIJ	Permanent Court of International Justice
Queen's Counsel	QC
RdC	Recueil des Cours/The Hague Academy Collected Courses
Rep	Reports
Res	Resolution
Rev	Review
RGDIP	Revue générale de droit international public
RU	Russia
s	section
SpA	Società per azioni (company with shares)
SADC	Southern African Development Community
SADCT	Southern African Development Community Tribunal
SAR	Special Administrative Region
SCC	Stockholm Chamber of Commerce
SDNY	United States District Court for the Southern District of New York
SGCA	Singapore Court of Appeal
Suppl	Supplement
TDM	Transnational Dispute Management
TRIPS	Agreement on Trade-Related Aspects of Intellectual Property Rights
UAE	United Arab Emirates
UK	United Kingdom
UKSC	United Kingdom Supreme Court (Reports)
UN	United Nations
UN Doc	United Nations Documents
UNCITRAL	United Nations Commission on International Trade Law
UNCLOS	The United Nations Convention on the Law of the Sea
UNGA	United Nations General Assembly
UNTS	United Nations Treaty Series
UPaLRev	University of Pennsylvania Law Review
US	United States (Reports)
USMCA	United States–Mexico–Canada Agreement
USSR	Union of Soviet Socialist Republics
v	versus (against)
VCLT	Vienna Convention on the Law of Treaties
VCSSPAD	Vienna Convention on Succession of States in respect of State Property, Archives and Debts
VCSST	Vienna Convention on Succession of States in respect of Treaties
Vol(s)	Volume(s)
WTO	World Trade Organization
YBIL	Yearbook of International Law
YILC	Yearbook of International Law Commission (ILC)
ZA	South Africa
ZACC	South Africa: Constitutional Court

General international law in international investment law

Andreas Kulick and Michael Waibel

A. Introduction: Aims and goals	1	I. Law of treaties	17
B. The concept of a semi-systematic commentary	8	II. Responsibility of States and international organizations	23
C. General international law in international investment law	11	III. State succession, sources, and State immunity	34
D. Overview of selected provisions of general international law	16	IV. Substantive and procedural aspects	42
		E. Conclusions: Alignment, deviation, and two-way traffic	50

A. Introduction: Aims and goals

General international law (GIL) permeates international investment law (IIL). In many investment disputes, GIL plays a central role on matters such as interpretation, termination, provisional application of treaties, attribution of conduct, circumstances precluding wrongfulness, and remedies. Beyond treaty law and State responsibility, matters such as state succession and state immunity are equally relevant, especially when enforcing arbitral awards. Additionally, recourse to standards and principles such as the International Minimum Standard (IMS) of treatment is common. Questions about the relationship between GIL and IIL and how the interpretation and application of GIL rules and principles aligns with or deviates from—and should align with or deviate from—their interpretation and application in other areas of international law are important for both theory and practice.

It is now widely accepted that IIL forms part of public international law. Voices that regard IIL as an 'exotic'[1] regime detached from GIL have mostly subsided. Indeed, IIL 'is principally founded on fundamental principles derived from international treaty law, and, to a lesser extent, on customary international law and general principles of law'.[2] Investment

---

[1] See ILC, 'Fragmentation of International Law: Difficulties Arising from the Diversification and Expansion of International Law', Report of the Study Group of the International Law Commission, finalized by Martti Koskenniemi, International Law Commission, Fifty-eighth session Geneva, 1 May–9 June and 3 July–11 August 2006, dated 13 April 2006, UN Doc A/CN.4/L.682, para 8 (hereafter Koskenniemi, 'Fragmentation').

[2] E De Brabandere, *Investment Treaty Arbitration as Public International Law—Procedural Aspects and Implications* (CUP 2014) (hereafter De Brabandere, *Investment Treaty Arbitration*) 17.

tribunals often apply GIL, which perform a systemic function in the international legal order.[3] Fragmentation[4] has lost traction in the 2010s.[5] In Crawford's words 'there cannot be, at the international level, any truly self-contained regime'.[6] As the British–United States Claims Arbitral Tribunal noted in *Eastern Extension*, although international law does not contain express rules decisive of particular cases, 'in default of any specific provision of law, the corollaries of general principles' should be applied to resolve the dispute.[7] GIL informs the content of treaty obligations, and arbitral tribunals' interpretations affect GIL.[8]

3   This *Commentary on General International Law in International Investment Law* ('Commentary') engages in detail with central matters of GIL. Monographs,[9] articles,[10] and edited volumes[11] consider aspects of GIL in IIL. Nonetheless, the following questions have yet to be systemically answered: (a) how GIL rules are interpreted and applied and how they should be interpreted and applied in IIL; and (b) whether and why IIL practice deviates from the practice before other judicial fora. The importance of these questions calls for a more comprehensive and systematic treatment—which this Commentary offers. The entries cover selected GIL rules, principles, and concepts in areas central to IIL—the law of treaties, responsibility, sources, state succession, and immunity, among others.

4   While dedicated commentaries cover matters such as the Vienna Convention on the Law of Treaties (VCLT), the ILC Articles on the Responsibility of States for Internationally Wrongful Acts (ARSIWA) or the UN Convention on Jurisdictional Immunities of States and Their Property,[12] the added value of this Commentary is twofold. First, it systematically and

---

[3] C McLachlan, 'Investment Treaties and General International Law' (2008) 57 ICLQ 361–401, 373 (hereafter McLachlan, 'Investment Treaties').

[4] The *locus classicus* is Koskenniemi, 'Fragmentation' (n 1).

[5] See only the contributions in M Andenas and E Bjorge (eds), *A Farewell to Fragmentation—Reassertion and Convergence in International Law* (CUP 2015) and L Boisson de Chazournes, 'Plurality in the Fabric of International Courts and Tribunals: The Threads of a Managerial Approach' (2017) 28 EJIL 13 (emphasizing the positive effects of a 'plurality' of dispute settlement regimes in public international law).

[6] J Crawford, 'The ILC's Articles on Responsibility of States for Internationally Wrongful Acts: A Retrospect' (2002) 96 AJIL 874, 880. See also McLachlan, 'Investment Treaties' (n 3) 369.

[7] *Eastern Extension, Australasia and China Telegraph Co Ltd Case* (British–United States Claims Arbitral Tribunal) (1923) VI RIAA 112, 114.

[8] McLachlan, 'Investment Treaties' (n 3) 364.

[9] eg JR Weeramantry, *Treaty Interpretation in Investment Arbitration* (OUP 2012) (hereafter Weeramantry, *Treaty*); M Paparinskis, *The International Minimum Standard and Fair and Equitable Treatment* (OUP 2013) (hereafter Paparinskis, *The International Minimum Standard*); De Brabandere, *Investment Treaty Arbitration* (n 2); JW Salacuse, *The Law of Investment Treaties* (2nd edn, OUP 2015); T Gazzini, *Interpretation of International Investment Treaties* (Hart Publishing 2016) (hereafter Gazzini, *Interpretation*); I Marboe, *Calculation of Compensation and Damages in International Investment Law* (2nd edn, OUP 2017); P Dumberry, *A Guide to State Succession in International Investment Law* (Edward Elgar Publishing 2018) (hereafter Dumberry, *A Guide*); R Polanco, *The Return of the Home State to Investor-State Disputes—Bringing Back Diplomatic Protection?* (CUP 2019).

[10] eg M Sornarajah, 'State Responsibility and Bilateral Investment Treaties' (1986) 20 JWT 79; M Waibel, 'Two Worlds of Necessity in ICSID Arbitration: CMS and LG&E' (2007) 20 LJIL 637; C McLachlan, 'Investment Treaties' (n 3); See also the 'Special Focus Issue: The Intersection Between Investment Arbitration and Public International Law' in (2016) 31(2) ICSID Rev 255–503.

[11] eg R Hofmann and C Tams (eds), *International Investment Law and General International Law—From Clinical Isolation to Systemic Integration?* (Nomos 2011); T Gazzini and E De Brabandere (eds), *International Investment Law—The Sources of Rights and Obligations* (Martinus Nijhoff Publishers 2012); A Kulick (ed), *Reassertion of Control over the Investment Treaty Regime* (CUP 2017); A Gattini, A Tanzi and F Fontanelli, *General Principles of Law and International Investment Arbitration* (Martinus Nijhoff Publishers 2018); E Shirlow and KN Gore (eds), *The Vienna Convention on the Law of Treaties in Investor-State Disputes: History, Evolution and Future* (Wolters Kluwer 2022); C Tams, S Schill and R Hofmann (eds), *International Investment Law and General International Law—Radiating Effects?* (Edward Elgar Publishing 2023).

[12] eg O Corten and P Klein (eds), *The Vienna Conventions on the Law of Treaties—A Commentary* (OUP 2011); J Crawford, *The International Law Commission's Articles on State Responsibility: Introduction, Text and Commentaries* (United Nations 2002); R O'Keefe, C Tams and A Tzanakopoulos (eds), *The United Nations Convention on Jurisdictional Immunities of States and Their Property—A Commentary* (OUP 2013).

comprehensively brings together the various areas of GIL relevant to IIL and views them from the perspective of IIL: How do investment tribunals use the rules of attribution, state succession, and treaty interpretation? Does their interpretation and application deviate from the practice of the International Court of Justice (ICJ) or other international courts and tribunals, and if so, why? Second, it engages GIL in the practice of investment arbitration tribunals, unlike Commentaries on the International Centre for Settlement of Investment Disputes (ICSID) Convention that cover the procedural and institutional provisions of the ICSID Convention.[13]

The Commentary's comprehensive and systematic treatment responds to a pressing demand in both practice and scholarship: The amount of literature written on areas of GIL and the practical importance of the law of treaties, responsibility, state succession, and other areas of GIL in investment awards testifies to this. The Commentary serves as a work of reference for scholars and practitioners on how investor–State tribunals apply specific GIL rules, whether such interpretation and application deviates from GIL practice and why, and how a specific rule that has yet to feature in investment arbitration could and should be interpreted and applied, considering judicial decisions on comparable rules.

The structure of the entries reflects the Commentary's specific perspective. The following five questions guide each entry—either explicitly or as 'deep structure',[14] depending on the choice of the author(s).

(1) How do the ICJ and other judicial bodies interpret and apply the rule beyond IIL?
(2) How do arbitral tribunals and domestic courts interpret and apply the rule in investment disputes? Have tribunals diverged? How important is the rule in investment arbitration?
(3) To what extent does investment arbitration practice align with the practice of the ICJ and other tribunals?
(4) What explains (non-)alignment? How has GIL affected (non-)alignment?
(5) Should the specific rule or area align with GIL, and why?

Section B sets out the approach of this Commentary. It responds to the scholarly and practical need for a comprehensive treatment of GIL in IIL. However, it constitutes a semi-systematic Commentary that differs from systematic commentaries in the continental European and particularly in the German tradition.[15] Section C explains our understanding of 'GIL' and discusses the relationship between GIL and IIL from a theoretical perspective. Section D elaborates on the current and potential importance of the areas and rules of GIL included in the Commentary. Section E summarizes central findings across all the entries with respect to alignment and deviation between GIL and IIL, including existing and future instances of IIL practice influencing GIL.

---

[13] C Schreuer, L Malintoppi, A Reinisch and A Sinclair, *The ICSID Convention—A Commentary* (2nd edn, CUP 2009; 3rd edn 2022); J Fouret, R Gerbay and GM Alvarez (eds), *The ICSID Convention, Regulations and Rules—A Practical Commentary* (Edward Elgar Publishing 2019).

[14] On the notion of 'deep structure', see N Chomsky, 'Remarks on Nominalization' in ibid, *Studies on Semantics in Generative Grammar* (Mouton Publishers 1975) 11 at 12 et seq and ibid, 'Deep Structure, Surface Structure and Semantic Interpretation' in ibid 62 et seq.

[15] On the history of the commentary as a legal literary genre, particularly in the European tradition since the Roman empire, see D Kästle-Lamparter, *Welt der Kommentare* (Mohr Siebeck 2016), 19–104.

B. The concept of a semi-systematic commentary

8   This Commentary is not systematic because it does not consider a single treaty or piece of legislation, a single *text*,[16] unlike commentaries in the continental European legal tradition.[17] Instead, as a semi-systematic commentary, it focuses on selected treaty provisions and customary rules that have already been or may become important in investment disputes. At the same time, contributors address these rules and principles one at a time, organized according to their different sources and areas, against the background of other rules originating from the same source or in the same area. The Commentary thus shares with traditional commentaries the characteristic of intertextuality,[18] particularly elements of annotation and structural dependence of several texts.

9   This Commentary does not consider a single text. Instead, it combines select GIL rules and principles and places them in a particular order and context according to their normative or thematic source. Moreover, it differs from a handbook or collection of essays: It engages systematically with specific provisions and their interpretation and application and provides a comprehensive guide to all relevant decisions and scholarship. The five questions above guide the entries, subject to adaptions for specific entries, especially those on the law of state succession, immunity, and cross-cutting substantive and procedural aspects of GIL. As a rule, each provision has a separate entry. In a limited number of cases, authors treat rules jointly in a single entry because they are closely connected or the overall matter is of (potential) significance in IIL. Still, the rules have yet to garner sufficient attention in decisions to justify a separate entry for each of these provisions.[19]

10 GIL rules relevant to IIL are custom, and some are only custom, i.e., no treaty provisions are in force. If a central characteristic of a commentary is the systematic discussion of one or several text(s), this poses the challenge that custom is an unwritten source.[20] However, the lack of textuality of customary rules that must be applied and interpreted[21] is marginal to this Commentary: Most customary rules covered are written and widely accepted (e.g. most of the VCLT and many of the ARSIWA).[22] Where acceptance is less widespread, the text still serves as the point of departure, for example, in state succession.[23] In these cases, contributors highlight where custom differs from the texts of the two Vienna Conventions on state succession. Finally, in the interest of comprehensiveness, the Commentary also includes

---

[16] Kästle-Lamparter identifies the reference to a specific text as the defining characteristic of a commentary, in full awareness that this means excluding works such as Blackstone's famous *Commentaries on the Laws of England* that lack such basic text, cf ibid 10.

[17] eg B Simma, D-E Khan, Georg Nolte and Andreas Paulus (eds), *The Charter of the United Nations—A Commentary* (3rd edn, OUP 2012); R Herzog, R Scholz, M Herdegen and HH Klein (eds), *Dürig/Herzog Scholz, Grundgesetz—Kommentar* (99. Ergänzungslieferung, CH Beck 2022).

[18] That is, the way in which several different texts influence, reflect, or differ from each other, see generally G Allen, *Intertextuality* (2nd edn, Routledge 2011). On intertextuality in law see M Morlok, 'Der Text hinter dem Text: Intertextualität im Recht' in A Blankenagel and others (eds), *Verfassung im Diskurs der Welt—Liber Amicorum für Peter Häberle zum 70. Geburtstag* (Mohr Siebeck 2004) 93 et seq.

[19] See, eg, Alain Pellet and Jean-Baptiste Merlin, 'Articles 19–23 of the VCLT: Reservations (overview)—flexibility devices in applying treaties in the field of investment'; Luke Sobota and Amelia Keene, 'Parts IV and V of the VCLT: Amendment, invalidity, termination and suspension of investment treaties'; Geraldo Vidigal and Stephanie Forrest, 'Part Two Ch. I and II of the ARSIWA: Remedies'.

[20] cf H Thirlway, *The Sources of International Law* (OUP 2014) 12 et seq and 53 et seq.

[21] See on this, eg, P Merkouris, 'Interpreting the Customary Rules on Interpretation' (2017) 19 ICLR 126 with further references.

[22] See Part II—Responsibility of States and international organizations.

[23] See Part III—State succession, sources, and State immunity.

some additional procedural and substantive aspects of GIL that lack a single textual point of reference but still carry weight in IIL.[24] On the substantive side, these include denial of justice and the IMS. On the procedural side: nationality, abuse of rights and unjust enrichment. Moreover, two entries on cross-cutting aspects of substance and procedure examine the GIL pedigree of substantive investment law standards and procedural standards and principles. Their importance in investment arbitration practice justifies their inclusion.

C. General international law in international investment law

International courts such as the ICJ often sweepingly refer to 'general international law' without providing a definition.[25] Famously, ILC Special Rapporteur Koskenniemi, in his Report on Fragmentation in International Law stated that 'there is no well-articulated or uniform understanding of what [GIL] might mean'[26] and recommended further study of the issue. What does the Commentary mean by the ambiguous[27] term 'GIL'? The GIL discussed in this Commentary is 'general' in two ways. First, it denotes law that applies to all states.[28] This encompasses custom—even if some states persistently object[29]—and customary rules enshrined in treaties, such as the VCLT, as well as general principles of law.[30] Second, it primarily includes rules that are 'general' in that they do not pertain to a specific area of international law, such as the law of the sea, international human rights law or IIL. For the most part, customary rules on specific areas of law,[31] such as custom in international humanitarian law, are excluded. Instead, the entries focus mainly on international customary rules and general principles that constitute international law's 'common grammar'.[32]

11

The secondary rules of international law constitute an integral part of such 'grammar', its syntax. The concept of primary vs. secondary rules appears frequently in international law scholarship, albeit usage differs.[33] Here, we regard 'secondary rules of international law'

12

---

[24] See Part IV—Substantive and procedural aspects of general international law in international investment law.
[25] cf, eg, *Case Concerning the Barcelona Traction, Light and Power Company, Limited (Belgium v Spain)* (Judgment) [5 February 1970], ICJ Rep 1979, 3, para 34; *Military and Paramilitary Activities in and Against Nicaragua (Nicaragua v United States)* (Jurisdiction and Admissibility Judgment) [26 November 1984], ICJ Rep 1984, 392, para 73; *Elettronica Sicula S.p.A. (ELSI) (United States of America v Italy)* (Judgment of 20 July 1989), ICJ Rep 1989, 15, para 111.
[26] Koskenniemi, 'Fragmentation' (n 1) 254 et seq.
[27] cf M Wood, 'The International Tribunal for the Law of the Sea and General International Law' (2007) 22 Int'l J Marine and Coastal L 351, at 354 ('certain degree of imprecision').
[28] cf, eg, J Pauwelyn, *Conflict of Norms in Public International Law—How WTO Law Relates to Other Rules of International Law* (CUP 2003) 148, 155 (hereafter Pauwelyn, *Conflict*); A Gourgourinis, 'General/Particular International Law and Primary/Secondary Rules: Unitary Terminology of a Fragmented System' (2011) 22 EJIL 993, 1015 (hereafter Gourgourinis, 'General/Particular').
[29] On the notion of persistent objector see JA Green, *The Persistent Objector Rule in International Law* (OUP 2016).
[30] Whether general principles of international law are a self-standing source is contested in legal theory, see, eg, GP Buzzini, 'La "généralité" du droit international général: réflexions sur la polysémie d'un concept' (2004) 108 RGDIP 381, 391; Koskenniemi, 'Fragmentation'(n 1) 233, para 462; Pauwelyn, *Conflict* (n 28) 148.
[31] For a different approach see, eg, Pauwelyn, *Conflict* (n 28) 148.
[32] P-M Dupuy, 'A Doctrinal Debate in the Globalisation Era: On the "Fragmentation" of International Law' (2007) 1 Eur J Leg Stud 1, 4 (hereafter Dupuy, 'A Doctrinal Debate').
[33] Many employ it mainly in the context of State responsibility, following Roberto Ago's introduction of the terminology of primary vs secondary rules in his 1970 ILC Report on State responsibility (cf ILC, 'The Origin of International Responsibility', second report on State responsibility, by Roberto Ago, Special Rapporteur, YILC 1970, Vol II, pp 177 et seq, A/CN.4/233), referring to rules of State responsibility as 'secondary' as opposed to the 'primary rules' the consequences of whose breaches the rules on State responsibility regulated. See also HP Aust, 'The Rules of Interpretation as Secondary Rules: The Perspective of Domestic Courts' in M Heupel and T Reinhold

as the 'systemic mechanisms'[34] or 'toolbox'[35] for the application of 'primary rules of international law'. This is inspired by Hart's distinction between 'primary rules' as those that set out obligations to do or abstain from doing something and 'secondary rules' as those that are 'about [primary] rules' in the sense that they 'specify the ways in which the primary rules may be conclusively ascertained, introduced, eliminated, varied, and the fact of their violation conclusively determined'.[36] Hence, for our purposes, primary rules regulate what to do or not do.[37] Secondary rules, by contrast, are rules about rules,[38] i.e. rules that 'regulate other norms, that is they may address the creation, application, interplay, suspension, termination, breach of enforcement of other norms of international law'.[39]

13   Secondary rules of international law thus understood pertain to the law of sources,[40] the law of treaties, including the interpretation, application, suspension, and termination of treaties, State responsibility, and state succession, to name a few examples. These constitute most of the GIL rules addressed in this Commentary.[41] To treat GIL and IIL as comprehensively as possible, the Commentary departs from the focus on secondary norms and thematic generality in a few cases. It therefore selected a few primary norms—customary rules and general principles—on substantive and procedural aspects that have been, or can be expected to be, important in IIL. These pertain to the IMS and denial of justice, nationality, unjust enrichment, and abuse of rights.[42] These primary rules, discussed in entries in Part IV of the Commentary and the secondary rules discussed in entries in Parts I–III, are only a selection of the full range of GIL rules—and again arguably only a selection of those rules potentially relevant for IIL. Arbitration practice, scholarship, and policy developments informed this choice.[43]

14   What role does GIL play in IIL? As mentioned above, GIL, first and foremost, provides a common language or 'grammar', an overarching framework which IIL, as one of many areas of international law,[44] shares with other areas.[45] IIL resorts to the customary rules on treaty

---

(eds), *The Rule of Law in Global Governance* (Palgrave 2016), 59 (hereafter Aust, 'The Rules'); G Kajtar, B Cali and M Milanovic, *Secondary Rules of Primary Importance in International Law: Attribution, Causality, Evidence, and Standards of Review in the Practice of International Courts and Tribunals* (OUP 2022).

[34] J d'Aspremont, 'The Idea of "Rules" in the Sources of International Law' (2014) 84 BYIL 103, 107 (hereafter D'Aspremont, 'The Idea').

[35] Pauwelyn, *Conflict* (n 28) 149.

[36] HLA Hart, *The Concept of Law* (3rd edn, OUP 2012) 94 (hereafter Hart, *The Concept*). For an example of explicitly adopting Hart's terminology in international law see, eg, TM Franck, *The Power of Legitimacy Among Nations* (OUP 1990), 183 et seq (hereafter Franck, *The Power*).

[37] For a more elaborate account, see Pauwelyn, *Conflict* (n 28) 158–59, (i)–(iv).

[38] Hart, *The Concept* (n 36) 94; see also Aust, 'The Rules' (n 33) 65.

[39] Pauwelyn, *Conflict* (n 28) 159. See also A Nollkaemper, 'The Power of Secondary Rules of International Law to Connect the International and National Legal Orders' in T Broude and Y Shany (eds), *Multi-Sourced Equivalent Norms in International Law* (Hart Publishing 2011) 45, at 47 seq; Franck, *The Power* (n 36) 183 et seq; Aust, 'The Rules' (n 33) 64 et seq.

[40] However, note the criticism in D'Aspremont, 'The Idea' (n 34) 103 et seq of including sources under the rubric of 'secondary norms'.

[41] See in detail Section D.I–III below, as well as the entries in Parts I–III of this Commentary.

[42] On all this see in detail Section D.IV below, and the entries in Part IV of this Commentary.

[43] For explanations with respect to individual rules see Section D below.

[44] On this see CJ Tams, SW Schill and R Hofmann, 'Radiating Effects: The Gentle Impact of International Investment law on General International Law' in ibid (eds), *International Investment Law and General International Law—Radiating Effects?* (Edward Elgar Publishing 2023) 2, at 6 et seq (hereafter Tams, Schill and Hofmann, 'Radiating Effects').

[45] cf, eg, *Phoenix Action Ltd v Czech Republic*, ICSID Case No ARB/06/5, Award, 15 April 2009, para 78 noting that international investment law 'cannot be read and interpreted in isolation from public international law, and its general principles' (hereafter *Phoenix*). See also, for such notion generally and beyond investment law: Dupuy, 'A Doctrinal Debate' (n 32) 1, 4.

interpretation on questions of attribution of conduct to a state or to the principle of good faith, just like the law of the sea or international human rights law, unless the specific regime provides for special rules on the matter. This already hints at a further, yet connected, function of GIL in IIL, its residual character.[46] GIL serves to fill the gaps left by special regimes such as IIL. As the *Micula* tribunal stated, investment tribunals 'will certainly apply residually international law if the other applicable rules are silent or obscure or are eventually determined not to apply *ratione temporis*'.[47] Finally, GIL may serve as fallback option if the special regime fails or does not function properly.[48] In IIL, this concerns mainly primary rules of GIL such as the IMS or denial of justice. Overall, GIL and IIL engage with each other in a two-way traffic, as Tams, Schill, and Hofmann recently pointed out: norms of GIL influencing IIL doctrine and practice (they refer to this form of interaction as 'inward-flowing') and IIL practice, notably the many decisions of international investment tribunals, impacting upon GIL doctrine and practice ('outward-flowing').[49] While the primary emphasis in the entries of this Commentary is on the 'inward-flow' of GIL into IIL, the entries also reveal considerable 'outward-flow' in certain areas, as Section E shows.

If both GIL and IIL are valid and applicable to the issue at hand,[50] they may, in the words of Joost Pauwelyn, 'accumulate or conflict'.[51] They accumulate if GIL adds to IIL, e.g. provides rules on attribution to determine whether the host state bears responsibility for certain conduct, or if it confirms already existing rules, e.g. if an investment treaty contains a provision on territorial application of treaty in case of change of territory of the host state identical to the 'moving treaty frontiers' principle[52] under customary international law.[53] Conflict denotes 'a situation where one norm breaches, has led to or may lead to breach of, another norm'[54]—thus being incompatible or inconsistent with this other norm.[55] For most of the GIL included in this Commentary, i.e. secondary rules of international law, the interrelationship with IIL is straightforward: GIL fills gaps in IIL, adding to, rather than conflicting with it. In most instances, investment treaties do not contain rules on these secondary issues. However, in the rare case that they do contain such rules and there is indeed a conflict—i.e. incompatibility or inconsistency—between the GIL and the IIL rule, the *lex specialis* principle[56] can help to resolve the conflict in favour of the rule in the investment treaty, given that secondary rules are *ius dispositivum*.[57] Conflicts with the rules in this Commentary are rare, mostly about general principles and the primary rules on procedural and substantive aspects of general principles in IIL. In these instances, such conflict may be addressed, again, by resort to the *lex specialis* principle, by specific agreement among the contracting parties, by

---

[46] See Gourgourinis, 'General/Particular' (n 28) 1004 et seq.
[47] *Micula and others v Romania*, Decision on Jurisdiction and Admissibility of 24 September 2008, ICSID Case No ARB/05/20, para 151. For examples of similar approaches see, instead of many, eg, *Chevron Corporation and Texaco Petroleum Corporation v Ecuador*, Interim Award of 1 December 2008, Ad hoc—UNCITRAL Arbitration Rules, para 118 (hereafter *Chevron*); *RosInvest Co UK Ltd v Russian Federation*, Final Award, 12 September 2010, SCC Case No 075/2009, paras 605–09.
[48] cf Fragmentation of International Law: Difficulties Arising from the Diversification and Expansion of International Law, International Law Commission, Fifty-sixth session, YILC 2004, Vol 2, Part Two, 114, para 319.
[49] Tams, Schill and Hofmann, 'Radiating Effects' (n 44) 2, 4.
[50] cf Koskenniemi, 'Fragmentation' (n 1) 30, para 46.
[51] Pauwelyn, *Conflict* (n 28) 161 et seq.
[52] CJ Tams, 'State Succession to Investment Treaties: Mapping the Issues' (2016) 31 ICSID Rev 314–43, 315 (hereafter Tams, 'State Succession').
[53] cf Pauwelyn, *Conflict* (n 28) 161.
[54] ibid 199.
[55] ibid 169.
[56] Which itself constitutes a secondary norm of general international law.
[57] See Koskenniemi, 'Fragmentation' (n 1) 45, para 79.

interpretation, in particular via Article 31(3)(c) VCLT, or exceptionally by the higher rank of one rule over the other (e.g. in case of *ius cogens*).[58]

D. Overview of selected provisions of general international law

16 Investment tribunals have acknowledged, in the tribunal's words in *Phoenix v Czech Republic*, that IIL 'cannot be read and interpreted in isolation from public international law, and its general principles'.[59] The disputing parties frequently refer to, and arbitral tribunals commonly interpret and apply GIL. This is not least because neither the ICSID Convention, which deals solely with procedure, nor most international investment agreements (IIAs) contain provisions concerning matters such as treaty interpretation, attribution of conduct or circumstances precluding wrongfulness. Investment treaties are typically restricted to a short catalogue of primary investment protection rules, coupled with a provision for dispute resolution through arbitration.[60] However, the frequency with which—usually, albeit not exclusively, secondary—rules of GIL feature in international investment disputes, both in arbitral proceedings and in enforcement proceedings before domestic courts, tells us little about how tribunals interpret and apply them. Furthermore, some rules feature more prominently than others and the interpretation of some rules in investment law practice may adhere more closely to GIL practice than others. Only selected provisions are included in this volume. This section explains why the rules selected are important, presently and in future. Further, this subsection also sets out why some rules are closely related, and others may become important together.

I. Law of treaties

17 International investment arbitration today is primarily investment *treaty* arbitration.[61] Douglas defines investment treaties as 'international instruments between states governed by the public international law of treaties'.[62] Hence, the rules and principles of GIL on treaties are crucial in IIL, and the VCLT is of 'primary importance'.[63] The VCLT has 116 State parties.[64] However, most of its provisions reflect custom,[65] which is why this Commentary limits itself to selected provisions of the VCLT.

18 The question of treaty interpretation features prominently in the Commentary. As treaties, IIAs require interpretation before they can be applied.[66] The importance of the rules and

---

[58] cf Koskenniemi, 'Fragmentation' (n 1) 30 et seq; Pauwelyn, *Conflict* (n 28) 212 et seq.
[59] *Phoenix* (n 45) para 78.
[60] McLachlan, 'Investment Treaties' (n 3) 373.
[61] UNCTAD counts a current number of 1,257 treaty-based investor–State disputes (as of 30 April 2023), see UNCTAD Investment Policy Hub https://investmentpolicy.unctad.org/investment-dispute-settlement, accessed 30 April 2023.
[62] Z Douglas, 'The Hybrid Foundations of Investment Treaty Arbitration' (2004) 74 BYIL 151–289, 152.
[63] K Hobér, 'State Responsibility and Attribution' in P Muchlinski, F Ortino and C Schreuer (eds), *The Oxford Handbook of International Investment Law* (OUP 2008) 549, 550.
[64] United Nations Treaty Collection website https://treaties.un.org/Pages/ViewDetailsIII.aspx?src=TREATY&mtdsg_no=XXIII-1&chapter=23&Temp=mtdsg3&clang=_en, accessed 30 April 2023.
[65] cf *Gabčíkovo-Nagymaros Project* (*Hungary v Slovakia*) (Merits) [1997] ICJ Rep 7, 38.
[66] McLachlan, 'Investment Treaties' (n 3) 371.

principles of interpretation in Articles 31–33 VCLT is hard to overstate, not least because IIAs often contain broad and vague treaty language, particularly those of older vintage.[67] Articles 31[68] and 32[69] VCLT represent rules of customary international law on treaty interpretation and these two provisions guide the interpretation of investment treaties.[70] In contrast with the practice of early investment tribunals, most notably *AAPL v Sri Lanka*,[71] investment tribunals nowadays tend to cite Articles 31–33 VCLT[72] and take them as the point of departure when interpreting investment treaties.[73] Despite the frequent citation of, and references to, the VCLT rules on interpretation, the practice of investor–State tribunals sometimes deviates from them.[74] As Schreuer notes, 'different tribunals, even if they faithfully apply Articles 31-33 of the VCLT, are likely to reach different results', which led him to conclude that 'the usefulness of the VCLT as a tool for the harmonization of practice in the application of investment treaties is limited'.[75]

While many complex and contested matters arise with respect to the application and interpretation of Articles 31–33 VCLT, other rules enshrined in the Convention have also acquired importance in investment arbitration practice. This is most obvious with respect to the rules on amendment, invalidity, termination, and suspension of treaties in Parts IV and V of the VCLT: in a regime that does not rely on one or a handful of multilateral agreements but consists of a web of several thousand mostly bilateral treaties, questions as to these matters frequently arise—and increasingly so considering the backlash IIL and arbitration has been experiencing over the past decade.[76] However, since these provisions on amendment, termination, and so on are interconnected but few have yet been dealt with in arbitral awards, an overview Commentary showcases why Parts IV and V of the VCLT are important.[77] Given their relevance for intra-EU Bilateral Investment Treaties

---

[67] See A Reinisch, 'The Interpretation of International Investment Agreements' in M Bungenberg and others (eds), *International Investment Law—A Handbook* (Beck/Hart/Nomos 2015) 372, 373; M Waibel, 'Demystifying the Art of Interpretation' (2011b) 22 EJIL 571–88.
[68] See entry by Andreas Kulick and Panos Merkouris, 'Article 31 of the VCLT: General rule of interpretation'.
[69] See entry by Esmé Shirlow and Michael Waibel, 'Article 32 of the VCLT: Supplementary means of interpretation'.
[70] McLachlan, 'Investment Treaties' (n 3) 371. Whether Article 33 also represents custom is disputed, see On Article 33 VCLT, see entry by Peter Tzeng, 'Article 33 of the VCLT: Interpretation of Treaties Authenticated in two or more Languages'.
[71] *AAPL v Sri Lanka*, ICSID Case No ARB/87/3, Final Award, 27 June 1990, paras 38–40 (referring to a wide range of authorities ranging back to Vattel).
[72] On Article 33 VCLT, see entry by Peter Tzeng, 'Article 33 of the VCLT: Interpretation of treaties authenticated in two or more languages'.
[73] eg *Phoenix* (n 45) para 75; *Al-Warraq v Republic of Indonesia*, UNCITRAL, Award on Respondents' Preliminary Objections to Jurisdiction and Admissibility of the Claims, 21 June 2012, para 70; *Daimler Financial Services v Argentine Republic*, ICSID Case No ARB/05/1, Award, 22 August 2012, para 46; *Muhammet Cap v Turkmenistan*, ICSID Case No ARB/12/6, Decision on Jurisdiction, 13 February 2015, para 93. See also Weeramantry, *Treaty* (n 9) ch 3; Gazzini, *Interpretation* (n 9) 64 et seq.
[74] See, eg, M Waibel, 'International Investment Law and Treaty Interpretation' in R Hofmann and CJ Tams (eds), *International Investment Law and General International Law: From Clinical Isolation to Systemic Integration?* (Nomos 2011) 29 et seq (hereafter Waibel, 'International Investment Law'); B Boknik and T Gazzini, 'Questions of Treaty Interpretation' in Christian Tams and others (eds), *International Investment Law and General International Law—Radiating Effects?* (Edward Elgar Publishing 2023) 80 et seq.
[75] C Schreuer, 'Comments' in R Hofmann and C J Tams (eds), *International Investment Law and General International Law* (Nomos 2011) 71.
[76] See, eg, M Waibel, A Kaushal, K-H Chung and C Balchin (eds), *The Backlash Against Investment Arbitration* (Wolters Kluwer 2010); A Kulick (ed) *Reassertion of Control over the Investment Treaty Regime* (CUP 2017), in particular FL Bordin, 'Reasserting Control through Withdrawal from Investment Agreements: What Role for the Law of Treaties?', in ibid 209 et seq.
[77] See entry by Amelia Keene and Luke Sobota, 'Parts IV and V of the VCLT: Amendment, invalidity, termination and suspension of investment treaties'.

(BITs)[78] and beyond[79], Articles 59 and 60[80] warrant a separate Commentary contribution, as does the related but separate issue of applying successive treaties concerning the same subject matter, Article 30 VCLT[81].[82] Reservations in Articles 19–23 VCLT,[83] given their limited relevance in a regime that mostly, albeit not exclusively, consists of bilateral treaties, where there is little need for reservations, are treated in a single entry, focusing on reservation matters pertaining to investment agreements with more than two parties, particularly the Energy Charter Treaty (ECT).

20 Intertemporal aspects of treaty application, notably those in Articles 18,[84] 24–25,[85] and 28[86] are highly significant in international investment treaty arbitration practice and thus deserve detailed entries. In particular, matters of provisional application of treaties were prominent feature of the *Yukos* cases and other proceedings under the ECT.[87] Further, many investment tribunals assessed the (non-)retroactivity of treaty provisions in Article 28 VCLT vis-à-vis conduct before the IIA entered into force, a provision that is set to remain highly relevant in the future. As a result of this default rule of non-retroactivity, investment treaties typically only apply to the events after the BIT entered into force, which further means that 'the date of the treaty's entry into force provides the cut-off point for the tribunal's jurisdiction ratione temporis'.[88] However, a breach may be found even if the commencement of the continuous act predates the BIT's entry into force, based on the doctrines of the continuous act and composite acts.[89] Here again, the practice among investment tribunals displays a range of approaches.[90] Awards such as *MCI v Ecuador* are particularly controversial.[91]

21 Further, two fundamentally important principles of treaty law are found in Articles 26[92] and 27[93] VCLT. Article 26 reflects the principle of *pacta sunt servanda* which obliges the State

---

[78] See, eg, *Eureko BV v Slovak Republic*, Award on Jurisdiction, Arbitrability and Suspension, 26 October 2010, paras 231 et seq.
[79] See, eg, *Ping An Life Insurance Company of China, Limited v Kingdom of Belgium*, ICSID Case No ARB/12/29, Award, 30 April 2015, paras 207 et seq.
[80] See entries by Hélène Ruiz-Fabri and Randi Ayman, 'Article 59 of the VCLT: Termination or suspension of the operation of a treaty implied by conclusion of a later treaty' and 'Article 60 of the VCLT: Termination or suspension of the operation of a treaty as consequence of its breach'.
[81] See entry by Sean Aughey, 'Article 30 VCLT: Application of successive treaties relating to the same subject-matter'.
[82] See A Orakhelashvili, 'Article 30 of the 1969 Vienna Convention on the Law of Treaties: Application of the Successive Treaties Relating to the Same Subject-Matter' (2016) 31 ICSID Rev 344 et seq with further references.
[83] See entry by Alain Pellet and Jean-Baptiste Merlin, 'Articles 19–23 of the VCLT: Reservations (overview)—flexibility devices in applying treaties in the field of investment'.
[84] See entry by Belinda McRae, 'Article 18 of the VCLT: Obligation not to defeat the object and purpose of a treaty prior to its entry into force'.
[85] See entries by Tania Voon, 'Article 24 of the VCLT: Entry into force' and 'Article 25 of the VCLT: Provisional application'.
[86] See entry by Ben Juratowitch and Jackie McArthur, 'Article 28 of the VCLT: Non-retroactivity of treaties'.
[87] See only *Yukos Universal Limited (Isle of Man) v Russian Federation*, UNCITRAL, PCA Case No AA 227, paras 244 et seq.; *Ioannis Kardassopoulos v Georgia*, ICSID Case No ARB/05/18, Decision on Jurisdiction, 6 July 2007, paras 202 et seq. However, note that Article 45 of the ECT features a *lex specialis* provision on provisional application.
[88] Waibel, 'International Investment Law' (n 74) 49.
[89] ibid 49—referring to *Mondev International Ltd v United States of America*, ICSID Case No ARB(AF)/99/2, Award, 11 October 2002, para 5.
[90] See N Gallus, 'Article 28 of the Vienna Convention on the Law of Treaties and Investment Treaty Decisions' (2016) 31 ICSID Rev 290, 307 et seq.
[91] See *MCI Power Group LC and New Turbine, Inc v Republic of Ecuador*, ICSID Case No ARB/03/6, Award, 31 July 2007, paras 159 et seq and *MCI Power Group LC and New Turbine, Inc v Republic of Ecuador*, ICSID Case No ARB/03/6, Decision on Annulment, 19 October 2009, paras 45 et seq.
[92] See entry by Patrick Pearsall and Can Yeginsu, 'Article 26 of the VCLT: *Pacta sunt servanda*'.
[93] See entry by Rumiana Yotova, 'Article 27 of the VCLT: Internal law and observance of treaties'.

parties to perform their obligations in good faith. Article 27 stipulates that a country may not invoke the provisions of its internal law as justification for its failure to perform a treaty obligation. These two principles are addressed in two separate contributions.

Finally, this part of the Commentary contains entries on some VCLT provisions that have yet to attract much attention, but which may become important in the future. An example is the default rule on the territorial scope of treaty application in Article 29 VCLT. This topic could attract more interest in future international investment disputes, in particular with respect to disputed zones (the polar regions, continental shelves, or exclusive economic zones). Given that this Article limits the treaty's obligation to the state's territory, the question arises whether exercising sovereignty over the territory is required or effective control suffices.[94] Another provision is *rebus sic stantibus* (Article 62 VCLT).[95] Host states could invoke fundamental changes in circumstances in the future.[96]

II. Responsibility of States and international organizations

With the law of treaties, the law of international responsibility, including circumstances precluding wrongfulness, constitutes the most significant area of GIL in IIL. However, in contrast to the VCLT, very few rules of widespread acceptance are codified in treaty law. Instead, many of the provision of the ARSIWA, the result of decades of work of the International Law Commission, have been accepted as representing customary international law.[97] Entries on selected ARSIWA provisions are important for a systematic treatment. However, as the entries demonstrate, the ARSIWA have not become custom in their entirety. Even though some investment tribunals have noted this important caveat,[98] others have indiscriminately treated the ARSIWA as a whole as custom.[99]

State responsibility in the field of investment treaty arbitration is 'a species of State responsibility, i.e. the responsibility of a State party for breach of the substantive international obligations created by the investment treaty'.[100] However, some international legal regimes provide their own *leges speciales* on (some areas of) responsibility, as the savings clause in Article 55 ARSIWA[101] allows.[102] For example, State parties to a treaty may limit the circumstances under which the acts of an entity are attributed to the State. Such specific provisions diminish the relevance of broader principles of State responsibility (under customary international law or as represented in the ILC Articles).[103]

---

[94] ibid.
[95] See entry by Makane Moïse Mbengue, 'Article 62 of the VCLT: *Rebus sic stantibus*'.
[96] O Bayrak, 'Economic Crises and the Fundamental Change of Circumstances in Investment Arbitration' (2020) 35 ICSID Rev 130.
[97] J Crawford, *State Responsibility—the General Part* (1st edn, CUP 2013) 43; K Hobér (n 63), at 553; *Noble Ventures Inc v Romania*, ICSID Case No ARB/01/11, Award, 12 October 2005, para 69; *EDF (Services) Ltd v Romania*, ICSID Case No ARB/05/13, Award, 8 October 2009, para 187.
[98] eg *Cargill, Inc v Mexico*, ICSID Case No ARB(AF)/05/2 (NAFTA), Award, 18 September 2009, para 381.
[99] eg *MCI Power Group LC and New Turbine, Inc v Republic of Ecuador*, ICSID Case No ARB/03/6, Award, 31 July 2007, para 42.
[100] J Crawford, 'Treaty and Contract in Investment Arbitration' (2008) 24 Arb Int'l 351, at 355.
[101] See entry by Fernando Lusa Bordin, 'Article 55 of the ARSIWA: *Lex specialis*'.
[102] eg *United Parcel Service of America Inc v Canada*, ICSID Case No UNCT/02/1 (NAFTA), Merits, 24 May 2007, paras 59 et seq.
[103] *Adel A Hamadi Al Tamimi v Sultanate of Oman*, ICSID Case No ARB/11/33, Award, 3 November 2015, para 321.

25 Attribution is among the most prominent parts of State responsibility in investment disputes. When attributing conduct, the ICJ applied 'customary international law, as reflected in the ILC Articles on State Responsibility'.[104] Although the ARSIWA address the question of attribution for establishing a State's responsibility towards another State, tribunals routinely apply the general rules of attribution in the ARSIWA by analogy to investor–State relations.[105]

26 The conduct of a range of domestic entities, both public and private, may potentially infringe the rights of foreign investors under investment treaties. The question arises whether their conduct is attributable to the Respondent State. In this Commentary, the customary rules[106] enshrined in Articles 4, 5, 7, and 8 each benefit from a separate entry. However, due to their close interrelation, the same contributors (co-)wrote the entries on Articles 4 and 7 and Articles 5 and 8.[107]

27 Regarding Articles 5 and 8, for example, many tribunals have aligned themselves with ILC Commentary on the ARSIWA,[108] noting that the conduct of non-state organs, even if the Respondent State owns all or most of its shares, is only attributable to the state if the strict requirements set out in Articles 5 and 8 ARSIWA are met.[109] On the other hand, some tribunals have used the ARSIWA rules on attribution for purposes other than attribution of conduct.[110] For example, in *Siag v Egypt* the tribunal applied the ARSIWA to determine whether the State should be held to have been aware of certain bankruptcy proceedings before its courts.[111] Such practice contrasts with the ILC's clear stance, underlining that these rules do not concern any legal matter other than attribution of conduct.[112]

28 Finally, Article 6 ARSIWA receives an entry with its companion rule, Article 7 of the 2011 ILC Articles on the Responsibility of International Organizations.[113] EU measures legally or factually forcing an EU Member State to undertake certain conduct, such as repayment of state aid, could violate the state's IIA obligations and may be regarded as effectively placing state organs 'at the disposal' of the EU.[114]

29 Apart from attribution, intertemporal aspects of responsibility are discussed in entries on Articles 13, 14, and 15 ARSIWA.[115] In particular, the famous *Islands of Palmas*

---

[104] *Application of the Convention on the Prevention and Punishment of the Crime of Genocide (Bosnia and Herzegovina v Serbia and Montenegro)* (Merits) [2007] ICJ Rep 43, 209 (hereafter *Bosnian Genocide*).
[105] *William Ralph Clayton, William Richard Clayton, Douglas Clayton, Daniel Clayton and Bilcon Delaware Inc v Government of Canada*, PCA Case No 2009-04, Award on Jurisdiction and Liability, 17 March 2015, para 307; C Kovács, *Attribution in International Investment Law* (Wolters Kluwer 2018) 49.
[106] cf *Bosnian Genocide* (n 104) 202 et seq.
[107] cf YILC 2001, Vol II, Part Two, 31, 39.
[108] ibid 48.
[109] eg *White Industries Australia Ltd v India*, UNCITRAL, Final Award, 30 November 2011, para 8.1.6. See S Olleson, 'Attribution in Investment Treaty Arbitration' (2016) 31 ICSID Rev 457, 472 et seq (hereafter Olleson, 'Attribution').
[110] eg *SwemBalt AB, Sweden v Latvia*, UNCITRAL, Award, 23 October 2000, para 37 (to argue that a State should be regarded as bound by a particular contractual obligation entered into by a separate entity in the context of claims under an umbrella clause).
[111] *Waguih Elie George Siag and Clorinda Vecchi v The Arab Republic of Egypt*, ICSID Case No ARB/05/15, Award, 1 June 2009, para 194 et seq.
[112] See YILC 2001, Vol II, Part Two, 31, 39; Olleson, 'Attribution' (n 109).
[113] See entry by Jonathan Bonnitcha and Alisha Mathew, 'Article 6 of the ARSIWA and Article 7 of the ARIO'.
[114] See *Electrabel SA v Hungary*, ICSID Case No ARB/07/19, Decision on Jurisdiction, Applicable Law and Admissibility, 30 November 2012, para 6.74.
[115] See entries on Articles 13–15 of the ARSIWA by Claudia Annacker and Enikő Horvath.

rule[116] enshrined in Article 13 has gained traction in investment arbitration practice.[117]

Furthermore, several entries elaborate on circumstances precluding wrongfulness under Articles 20–27 ARSIWA.[118] Here, the focus lies, first and foremost, on issues revolving around the state of necessity, which featured prominently in dozens of arbitral proceedings against Argentina following its financial crisis of 2001–2002.[119] The practice has been inconsistent regarding the interpretation of the requirements of the customary necessity test and the relationship of Article 25 ARSIWA with specific treaty provisions, notably Article XI of the US–Argentina BIT.[120] Although investment tribunals affirmed the customary nature of the relevant ARSIWA provisions and even concurred on some crucial aspects of the necessity defence, applying these principles led to divergent outcomes.[121] Indeed, it is questionable whether the rules codified in Article 25 ARSIWA are fully appropriate in the investment arbitration context.[122] **30**

Although *force majeure* presumably plays a more important role in international commerce and State contracts, it represents a defence 'firmly rooted in [general] international law' and has even been categorized as a general principle of law by the ILC.[123] Even though Article 23 ARSIWA has been recognized in some investment arbitration cases,[124] the threshold for successfully invoking *force majeure*, requiring irresistibility and impossibility, is high.[125] **31**

A prominent circumstance precluding wrongfulness is the law of countermeasures,[126] which is addressed in an entry on the mostly customary rules expressed in Articles 49–54 ARSIWA[127].[128] **32**

Finally, remedies, particularly reparation, including compensation, as set out in Articles 28–31 and 34–39 ARSIWA[129] play an important role in virtually all investment arbitrations. Crawford notes that compensation issues represent (one of) the point(s) of disagreement when it comes to the intersection between investment treaties and the ARSIWA.[130] Marboe, however, explains that this 'disagreement' is not on applying the relevant ARSIWA **33**

---

[116] *Island of Palmas (Netherlands v United States of America)* (1928) II RIAA 829, 845.
[117] eg *MCI Power Group LC and New Turbine, Inc v Republic of Ecuador*, ICSID Case No ARB/03/6, Award, 31 July 2007, paras 90, 135; *Chevron* (n 47) para 282.
[118] See entries by Federica Paddeu and Michael Waibel, 'Article 25 of the ARSIWA: Necessity'.
[119] For a discussion see A Kulick, *Global Public Interest in International Investment Law* (CUP 2012) 133 et seq.
[120] See, on the one hand, eg, *LG&E Energy Corp, LG&E Capital Corp, and LG&E International, Inc v Argentine Republic*, ICSID Case No ARB/02/1, Decision on Liability, 3 October 2006, paras 226 et seq. On the other hand, see, eg, *CMS Gas Transmission Company v Argentine Republic*, ICSID Case No ARB/01/8, Decision of the Ad Hoc Annulment Committee, 25 September 2007, para 134.
[121] A Reinisch, 'Necessity in Investment Arbitration' (2010) 41 NYIL 158, 137.
[122] ibid 153 et seq.
[123] International Law Commission Articles on Responsibility of States for Internationally Wrongful Acts, with commentaries (2001), 'Article 23', para 6.
[124] *Autopista Concesionada de Venezuela, CA ('Aucoven') v Venezuela*, ICSID Case No ARB/00/5, Award, 23 September 2003, para 108.
[125] Binder, 'Circumstances' (n 127) 478.
[126] *Archer Daniels Midland Company and Tate & Lyle Ingredients Americas, Inc v Mexico*, ICSID Case No ARB(AF)/04/05, Award, 21 November 2007; *Corn Products International, Inc v Mexico*, ICSID Case No ARB(AF)/04/01, Decision on Responsibility, 15 January 2008; *Cargill, Incorporated v Mexico*, ICSID Case No ARB(AF)/05/2, Award, 18 September 2009.
[127] See entry by Martins Paparinskis, 'Articles 49–54 of the ARSIWA: Countermeasures'.
[128] See, on the matter, particularly on the Mexican corn disputes, M Paparinskis, 'Investment Arbitration and the Law of Countermeasures' (2008) 79 BYIL 264 et seq; Binder, 'Circumstances' (n 127) 461 et seq.
[129] See entry by Stephanie Forrest and Geraldo Vidigal, 'Part II, Ch. I and II of the ARSIWA: Remedies'.
[130] J Crawford, 'Investment Arbitration and the ILC Articles on State Responsibility' (2010) 25 ICSID Rev 127, 132 (hereafter Crawford, 'Investment Arbitration').

provisions, but lies more in 'the manner and in the details of [their] application'.[131] Investors usually introduce investment arbitration proceedings to receive compensation. The extent to which investment tribunals apply and adhere to the customary rules on matters of reparation, besides casually quoting the *Chorzów Factory* principle,[132] constitutes an important focus of analysis.[133] Since investment treaties do not usually deal with the issue of compensation and damages, tribunals typically rely on the customary international law codified in the ARSIWA.[134]

III. State succession, sources, and State immunity

34 Questions of state succession have thus far arisen less frequently in investment arbitration than questions concerning the law of treaties or State responsibility. The issue of succession regarding treaties remains controversial even in GIL because it raises the fundamental question of the state's legal identity.[135] In the few ICJ cases where the issue of succession to a treaty arose, the Court either left those questions open or ruled that it was not called upon to decide the matter (*Temple of Preah Vihear, Trial of Pakistani Prisoners of War*, and *Legality of the Use of Force*).[136] State succession to investment treaties did not attract much interest until the 2010s. However, the *Sanum v Laos* case 'exposed sharp divisions in applying State succession rules'.[137] In a 2018 study, Patrick Dumberry identified no fewer than forty-six disputes involving questions of state succession.[138] Most of those issues revolve around state succession in respect of treaties.

35 The first contribution in this part of the Commentary surveys succession issues addressed in Articles 8, 9, and 24 of the Vienna Convention on the Succession of States in Respect of Treaties (VCSST).[139]

36 Article 15 VCSST is discussed in a separate contribution.[140] It provides that following the transfer of territory, '(a) treaties of the predecessor State cease to be in force in respect of the territory to which the succession of States relates', whereas '(b) treaties of the successor State are in force in respect of the territory to which the succession of States relates'. The so-called 'moving treaty-frontiers' principle, reflecting custom, also found in Article 29 VCLT.[141] This

---

[131] I Marboe, 'Damages in Investor–State Arbitration: Current Issues and Challenges' (2018) 2 Brill Research Perspectives in International Investment Law and Arbitration 86.
[132] *Case Concerning Certain German Interests in Polish Upper Silesia (Germany v Poland)* (Merits) PCIJ Series A No 17, 21 ('reparation must, as far as possible, wipe out all the consequences of the illegal act and re-establish the situation which would, in all probability, have existed if that act had not been committed').
[133] For an overview of the decisions see Crawford, 'Investment Arbitration' (n 130) 182 et seq.
[134] Z Crespi Reghizzi, 'General Rules and Principles on State Responsibility and Damages in Investment Arbitration: Some Critical Issues' in A Gattini and others (eds), *General Principles of Law and International Investment Arbitration* (Brill-Nijhoff 2018) 59. For list of cases see Crawford, 'Investment Arbitration' (n 130) 182–94.
[135] A Zimmermann, 'The International Court of Justice and State Succession to Treaties: Avoiding Principled Answers to Questions of Principle' in *The Development of International Law by the International Court of Justice* (OUP 2013) 53 (hereafter Zimmermann, 'The ICJ').
[136] ibid 53, 58–59.
[137] Tams, 'State Succession' (n 52) 337–39.
[138] Dumberry, *A Guide* (n 9) 143 et seq.
[139] See entry by Arman Sarvarian, 'The procedure for succession to bilateral investment treaties'.
[140] With Articles 31–38 VCSST, see entry by James Devaney and Christian Tams, 'Succession in respect of cession, unification and separation of States'.
[141] See entry by Emma Lindsay and Philippa Webb, 'Article 29 of the VCLT: Territorial scope'.

'widely accepted default rule'[142] (and its exceptions) attracted considerable attention in IIL. In *Sanum v Laos*, for example, the question was whether the China–Laos BIT of 1993 applied to Macau, which Portugal returned to China in 1999. As the competent court at the place of arbitration, the tribunal and the Singapore High Court disagreed on the moving treaty-frontiers rule.[143]

Apart from this central rule in case of secession, the customary law on uniting and separation of states is also relevant in investment disputes. While the provisions in Articles 31–38 VCSST[144] arguably do not reflect custom,[145] the Commentary entry takes these Articles as the starting point and identifies those instances where they deviate from custom or where it is disputed whether a rule of custom has evolved. The principle of universal succession (enshrined in Article 34 VCSST) which provides that successor states should generally be bound by treaties entered into by their predecessor, is 'the most controversial question within the law of state succession to treaties'.[146] While the succession to multilateral treaties has not been highly relevant thus far, it will likely arise more often.[147] The literature on multilateral treaties has also criticized the continuity principle adopted in the VCSST.[148] Membership in the ICSID Convention could be examined as a question of succession to a multilateral treaty. Still, this treaty established an international organization and thus involves the issue of succession of membership in international organizations.[149] **37**

In addition, despite having not yet featured prominently in investment arbitration, matters of state succession in respect of property and debts could arise in future investment disputes. The entry surveys the relevant standards and decisions in GIL and other areas of international law[150] and discusses how they may play a role in future investment cases. The contribution focuses on Articles 8–12 and 33–36 of the Vienna Convention on Succession of States in respect of State Property, Archives and Debts 1983.[151] **38**

Furthermore, the law of sources is pivotal in both GIL and IIL. Hence, a central entry in this Commentary scrutinizes and evaluates the importance of the different sources in Article 38 of the ICJ Statute, i.e. treaty, custom, general principles, and subsidiary sources such as doctrine and judicial decisions.[152] This contribution assesses treaty and customary law relevant in investment arbitration from a meta-perspective. Particularly, it compares how prominently the various sources feature in the arguments of investment tribunals, notably the use **39**

---

[142] Tams, 'State Succession' (n 52), 337–39.
[143] cf *Sanum Investments Limited v Lao People's Democratic Republic*, UNCITRAL, PCA Case No 2013-13, Award on Jurisdiction, 13 December 2013, and *Government of the Lao People's Democratic Republic v Sanum Investments Ltd*, Singapore High Court, Judgment, 20 January 2015, para 60. See Singapore Court of Appeals, however, reversed the judgment of the High Court, see *Sanum Investments Ltd v Government of the Lao People's Democratic Republic*, Court of Appeal of the Republic of Singapore, 29 September 2016.
[144] See entry by James Devaney and Christian Tams, 'Succession in respect of cession, unification and separation of States'.
[145] cf only Tams, 'State Succession' (n 52) 318.
[146] Zimmermann, 'The ICJ' (n 135) 59.
[147] P Dumberry, 'State Succession to Multilateral Investment Treaties and the ICSID Convention' (2018) 3 European Investment Law and Arbitration Review 3–19 at 5 (hereafter Dumberry, 'State Succession'). See also with respect to the ICSID Convention membership: Tams, 'State Succession' (n 52) 320–21.
[148] Tams, 'State Succession' (n 52) 342.
[149] ibid 321.
[150] cf, eg, *Allšić and others v Bosnia and Herzegovina, Croatia, Serbia, Slovenia and the Former Yugoslav Republic of Macedonia*, ECtHR (GC) Application no 60642/08, Judgment, 14 July 2014, paras 120 et seq.
[151] See entry by Arman Sarvarian, 'The protection of foreign investment in the law of state succession'.
[152] See entry by Patrick Dumberry, 'Article 38 of the ICJ Statute: Sources'.

and development of precedent.[153] The contribution focuses on custom, which plays an important role in contemporary international law despite the proliferation of the treaties.[154] There are three traditional reasons for this phenomenon: first, custom is still the applicable legal regime in the absence of any BIT; second, many BITs explicitly reference custom; and third, custom plays a gap-filling role when a treaty is silent on a given issue.[155] The 'double requirement' (state practice and *opinio juris*) for establishing a customary international rule applies in GIL and IIL. In many situations, GIL and IIL agree on identifying customary international law. However, there are situations in which IIL deviates from GIL on this matter, and the contribution highlights these situations.

40   In addition, the entry on sources deals with general principles of law to which investment tribunals often refer and assesses to what extent their application aligns with or deviates from GIL.[156] General principles of law have recently attracted considerable attention in GIL.[157] The ILC even appointed a Special Rapporteur for this topic.[158] However, although general principles are sometimes perceived as 'a fertile source of inspiration and guidance', they are also described as a 'typically neglected' category of sources.[159]

41   Beyond sources, Part III contains an entry on state immunity relevant to IIL.[160] Matters of state immunity usually arise in enforcement proceedings before domestic courts.[161] Article 55 of the ICSID Convention clarifies that immunity from execution may also be invoked when investors seek to enforce ICSID awards against the Respondent State. The contribution maps the issues and awards, referencing the 2004 United Nations Convention on Jurisdictional Immunities of States and Their Property, which partly reflects custom.[162]

IV. Substantive and procedural aspects

42   Whereas GIL primarily affects IIL through secondary rules,[163] primary rules raise important questions about the relationship between investment treaties and GIL. Therefore, Part IV

---

[153] See, on the matter, RR Chen 'Precedent and Dialogue in Investment Treaty Arbitration' (2019) 60 Harv Int'l L J 47 et seq.
[154] P Dumberry, *The Formation and Identification of Rules of Customary International Law in International Investment Law* (CUP 2018a) 352.
[155] ibid 352–68.
[156] On general principles in general international law see B Cheng, *General Principles of Law as Applied by International Courts and Tribunals* (Stevens Publishing 1953).
[157] P Dumberry, 'The Emergence of the Concept of "General Principle of International Law" in Investment Arbitration Case Law' (2020) 11 JIDS 194, 195 (hereafter Dumberry, 'The Emergence').
[158] ILC, Report of the ILC, 70th Session, 3433rd Meeting, 19 July 2018, UN Doc A/73/10, ch XIII, s A, para 363.
[159] CJ Tams, 'The Sources of International Investment Law: Concluding Thoughts' in T Gazzini and E De Brabandere (eds), *International Investment Law: The Sources of Rights and Obligations*, Vol 1 (Martinus Nijhoff Publishers 2012) 319, 324, 325; SW Schill, 'General Principles of Law and International Investment Law' in T. Gazzini and E De Brabandere (eds), *International Investment Law: The Sources of Rights and Obligations* (Martinus Nijhoff Publishers 2012) 133, 137.
[160] See entry by August Reinisch, 'State immunity in investment arbitration'.
[161] For instance, *Werner Schneider, acting in his capacity as insolvency administrator of Walter Bau AG (In Liquidation) v Kingdom of Thailand (formerly Walter Bau AG (In Liquidation) v Kingdom of Thailand)* (UNCITRAL), Order of the German Federal Supreme Court (30 January 2013) BGH III ZB 20/12; *AIG Capital Partners Inc and CJSC Tema Real Estate Company v Republic of Kazakhstan* (ICSID), English High Court of Justice, Queen's Bench Division, Judgment, 20 October 2005; *PAO Tatneft v Ukraine* [2018] EWHC 1797 (Comm), English High Court of Justice, Judgment, 13 July 2018.
[162] See PT Stoll, 'State Immunity' in R Wolfrum (ed), *Max Planck Encyclopedia of International Law* (online), para 12.
[163] See Section C.

deals with procedural and substantive aspects of GIL in IIL not yet dealt with in the other entries. However, the focus here is not on the content of primary rules that the existing literature already covers in considerable detail.[164] Rather, the entries in this Part investigate when, why, and how reference to GIL is permissible or even required; the relationship between treaty and custom; and the gaps that treaties and arbitration rules do not address.

The first contribution in Part IV of the Commentary provides a general overview of the cross-cutting substantive aspects of GIL in IIL, particularly emphasising those enshrined in the North American Free Trade Agreement (NAFTA).[165] Nearly every substantive standard of investment protection has either its origin or another connection to a corresponding notion in GIL. **43**

A second contribution deals with 'denial of justice'.[166] Enjoying 'a long tradition in international law',[167] denial of justice is often described as a 'customary international law guarantee', arising from the 'law concerning the treatment of foreign nationals'.[168] The expansion of investor–State arbitration created a new generation of international cases asserting denial of justice.[169] McLachlan notes the 'denial of justice' investment cases 'display an explicit debt to custom' since they 'referred back to formulations of the concept developed in earlier doctrine and jurisprudence and codifications', among which the Harvard drafts on the responsibilities of States for injuries to aliens 'proved particularly influential'.[170] **44**

A third entry pertains to the IMS, including relevant issues of diplomatic protection.[171] The customary IMS, derived from the law on diplomatic protection, has major relevance to investment disputes. Whether and how the IMS can be applied to contemporary investment disputes represents a crucial aspect of the fair and equitable treatment (FET) debate.[172] IMS governs the treatment of aliens by imposing obligations on States, independent of any obligations they have under human rights law.[173] Although the IMS initially applied to claims involving injury to a person, it subsequently expanded to include property rights, and today the two most prominent areas of application of the IMS are foreign investment and trade, and in particular expropriations.[174] **45**

A fourth entry discusses cross-cutting procedural aspects of GIL in IIL.[175] De Brabandere identified the following 'procedural aspects of the public international law character of investment treaty arbitration': (1) the role, functions, and qualifications of arbitrators; (2) the **46**

---

[164] eg Z Douglas, *The International Law of Investment Claims* (CUP 2009) (hereafter Douglas, *Investment Claims*); J Commission and R Moloo, *Procedural Issues in International Investment Arbitration* (OUP 2018); A Reinisch and C Schreuer, *International Protection of Investments: The Substantive Standards* (CUP 2020) (hereafter Reinisch and Schreuer, *The Substantive Standards*).
[165] See entry by Sergio Puig and Zhou Jingyuan, 'Cross-cutting substantive aspects: NAFTA standards in light of the decisions of international courts and tribunals'.
[166] See entry by Jarrod Hepburn, 'Denial of justice'.
[167] Reinisch and Schreuer, *The Substantive Standards* (n 164) 379, para 631; J Paulsson, *Denial of Justice in International Law* (CUP 2005).
[168] Reinisch and Schreuer, *The Substantive Standards* (n 164) 379, paras 630–31.
[169] JR Crook, 'Denial of Justice in International Law. By Jan Paulsson. Cambridge, New York: Cambridge University Press, 2005' (2006) 100 AJIL 742–46, 743 (hereafter Crook, 'Denial of Justice').
[170] McLachlan, 'Investment Treaties' (n 3) 375.
[171] See entry by Rob Howse, 'The international law minimum standard of treatment'.
[172] Paparinskis, *The International Minimum Standard* (n 9) 32.
[173] D Hollin, 'Minimum Standards' in R Wolfrum (ed), *Max Planck Encyclopedia of Public International Law* (OUP 2010) para 1.
[174] ibid paras 12–13.
[175] See entry by Cameron Miles, 'Cross-cutting procedural powers of international courts and tribunals'.

applicable law and non-investment considerations; (3) transparency and public access; and (4) public international law remedies.[176] It has been argued that the position of arbitrators in investment treaty arbitrations resembles that of arbitrators in inter-State disputes or judges in international judicial procedures.[177] Regarding the applicable law, given that the main purpose of an international investment dispute is to 'rule upon the international legal responsibility of the host states', it is natural to rely on public international law.[178]

47   A fifth entry tackles nationality.[179] The nationality question 'falls within the reserved domain of states', but there are limits.[180] States must respect the relevant rules of international law and international human rights law.[181] As the ICJ held in *Nottebohm*, the primary purpose of nationality is 'to determine that the person upon whom it is conferred enjoys the rights and is bound by the obligations which the law of the State in question grants to or imposes on its nationals'.[182] The ICJ defined *nationality* as 'a legal bond having as its basis a social fact of attachment, a genuine connection of existence, interest and sentiments, together with the existence of reciprocal rights and duties'.[183] This ruling received considerable attention in investment arbitration practice, given that tribunals routinely deal with questions of nationality of individuals and/or nationality of corporations. However, the tests for nationality in diplomatic protection claims in GIL and investment treaty claims are not identical.[184] Arbitral tribunals have limited the permissible scope of 'nationality planning' or 'treaty shopping'.[185]

48   This part includes a sixth contribution on abuse of rights.[186] Many scholars subscribe to the view that the concept of abuse of rights represents a general principle of international law.[187] Such a view has also received some support among international courts and tribunals.[188] For example, in *Churchill v Indonesia*, the tribunal relied on numerous earlier holdings of investment tribunals that 'fraudulent behavior to breach the principle of good faith' constitutes an abuse of right.[189] That theory, the tribunal held, represents a 'manifestation of the general principle that one does not benefit from treaty protection when underlying conduct is deemed improper'.[190]

49   This part's seventh and final entry is dedicated to unjust enrichment,[191] another general principle of law.[192] However, the concept is sometimes applied based on 'general notions of

---

[176] De Brabandere, *Investment Treaty Arbitration* (n 2) 71–204.
[177] ibid 73..
[178] ibid 125.
[179] See entry by Chiara Giorgetti, 'Nationality'.
[180] A Edwards, 'The Meaning of Nationality in International Law in an Era of Human Rights: Procedural and Substantive Aspects' in Alice Edwards and Laura van Waas (eds), *Nationality and Statelessness under International Law* (CUP 2014) 11, 42.
[181] ibid.
[182] *Nottebohm Case* (second phase) (Judgment) [6 April 1955], ICJ Rep 1955, p 4, 20.
[183] ibid 23.
[184] Douglas, *Investment Claims* (n 164) 20.
[185] R Dolzer and C Schreuer, *Principles of International Investment Law* (2nd edn, OUP 2012) 52.
[186] See entry by Régis Bismuth, 'Abuse of rights'.
[187] Dumberry, 'The Emergence' (n 157) 211.
[188] ibid 212.
[189] *Churchill Mining PLC and Planet Mining Pty Ltd v Republic of Indonesia*, ICSID Case No ARB/12/14 and 12/40, Award, 6 December 2016, para 491.
[190] ibid para 492.
[191] See entry by Kathleen Claussen, 'Unjust enrichment'.
[192] C Binder, 'Unjust Enrichment as a General Principle of Law in Investment Arbitration' in A Tanzi, F Fontanelli and A Gattini (eds), *General Principles of Law and International Investment Arbitration*, Vol 12 (Brill Nijhoff 2018) 269, 270 (hereafter Binder, 'Unjust Enrichment').

justice and equity' (by judges, arbitrators, and academics). *It is* occasionally also described as a principle of customary international law.[193] The Iran–US Claims Tribunal relied on unjust enrichment as a useful concept where there has 'been an enrichment of one party to the detriment of the other as a consequence of the same act or event'.[194] Unjust enrichment is particularly relevant in 'general crisis situations of a political kind in which States are permitted to take unusual measures interfering with individual rights without incurring State responsibility' or 'in the context of government contracts which were invalid or had been terminated'.[195] However, the importance of the principle in IIL has remained limited.[196]

E. Conclusions: Alignment, deviation, and two-way traffic

The over forty entries in this Commentary attest to the prominence of GIL in IIL. Their surveys of the practice of international investment arbitration tribunals and other international courts and tribunals, particularly the ICJ, demonstrate how frequently investment tribunals resort to GIL and consider it intertwined with IIL. IIL as a special regime of public international law relies on and draws from the 'common grammar'[197] that GIL establishes.[198] Indeed, it does so extensively in all three ways identified in Section C, including with respect to GIL's functions of gap-filling and fallback. ICJ and Permanent Court of International Justice (PCIJ) decisions are usually investment tribunals' first resort when applying GIL. However, their reference to GIL practice is not limited to the World Court. They draw on the decisions of many international adjudicatory bodies, from standing institutions such as the European Court of Human Rights, the International Tribunal for the Law of the Sea, the Iran–US Claims Tribunal or the World Trade Organization (WTO) Appellate Body to ad hoc inter-State arbitral tribunals.

Pulling together the insights from the entries in this Commentary, much GIL practice by investment tribunals broadly aligns with how the ICJ and other international courts and tribunals apply GIL rules and principles. This is the case vis-à-vis different secondary and primary rules of GIL. To name but a few: the law of sources,[199] the customary rules of attribution in Articles 4, 7, and 8 ARSIWA,[200] Parts IV and V of the VCLT,[201] relevant matters of state succession to treaties,[202] international procedure,[203] and denial of justice.[204]

While alignment is common in how investment tribunals apply GIL, examples of deviation also exist. This is hardly surprising, considering the variety of GIL norms and the large

---

[193] ibid 273–74.
[194] *Sea-Land Service Inc v Iran et al*, 6 Iran–US Claims Tribunal Reports 149, 169.
[195] Binder, 'Unjust Enrichment' (n 192) 280.
[196] ibid 284.
[197] Dupuy, 'A Doctrinal Debate' (n 32) 1, 4.
[198] See Section C.
[199] See entry by Patrick Dumberry, 'Article 38 of the ICJ Statute: Sources'.
[200] See entries by Chester Brown, 'Article 4 of the ARSIWA: Conduct of organs of a State' and 'Article 7 of the ARSIWA: Excess of authority or contravention of instructions' and Alina Papanastasiou and Jorge Viñulaes, 'Article 8 of the ARSIWA: Attribution of conduct instructed, directed or controlled by a State'.
[201] See entry by Luke Sobota and Amelia Keene, 'Parts IV and V of the VCLT: Amendment, invalidity, termination and suspension of investment treaties'.
[202] See entry by James Devaney and Christian Tams, 'Succession in respect of cession, unification and separation of States'.
[203] See entry by Cameron Miles, 'Cross-cutting procedural procedural powers of international courts and tribunals'.
[204] See entry by Jarrod Hepburn, 'Denial of justice'.

number of investment awards in an adjudicatory regime that relies on ad hoc arbitrations without central appeal mechanisms. However, these deviations mostly concern nuances to specific GIL rules and principles. Treaty interpretation is a case in point.[205] Article 31 VCLT features in almost every investment treaty dispute. Despite broad alignment, GIL practice deviates, for example on treaties concluded with third parties,[206] a restrictive application of 'subsequent practice' in Article 31(3)(b) VCLT[207] or the 'common meaning rule' in applying Article 33 VCLT.[208] Similarly, on remedies, investment tribunals prefer compensation over other forms of reparation while broadly aligned with other GIL practice vis-à-vis the customary rules enshrined in Articles 28–31 and 34–39 ARSIWA. They also more readily grant compound interest and are reluctant to award moral damages.[209] Regarding procedure, practice on counterclaims and costs deviate.[210] Specific features of IIL can partly explain all these deviations: a scattered regime of over two thousand IIAs, mostly bilateral, relying on ad hoc arbitrations in which states are almost exclusively respondents and the lack of an apex appeals facility.

53 Beyond matters of alignment and deviation, some entries in this Commentary have unearthed evidence that the relationship of GIL and IIL is no one-way street. 'Outward-flowing radiating effects'[211] characterize several rules of treaty law or State responsibility. The entries on Articles 30,[212] 59, and 60[213] VCLT as well as on the rules enshrined in Articles 5,[214] 15,[215] and 25[216] ARSIWA demonstrate that it is the decisions of investment tribunals that constitute the bulk or all of the existing practice regarding several prominent provisions of GIL. This way, IIL does not merely receive and incorporate GIL rules and principles but gives shape to GIL's contours. Some of this practice has yet to find its way into the mainstream of GIL scholarship and the decisions of other international courts and tribunals. As editors of this *Commentary on General International Law in International Investment Law*, we hope that the entries in this volume also contribute to the two-way traffic between GIL and IIL: supporting IIL scholarship and practice in their engagement with GIL and informing a broader international law audience, both in practice and academia, on the large universe of decisions by investment tribunals that interpret and apply GIL.

---

[205] See entries by Andreas Kulick and Panos Merkouris, 'Article 31 of the VCLT: General rule of interpretation'; Esmé Shirlow and Michael Waibel, 'Article 32 of the VCLT: Supplementary means of interpretation', and Peter Tzeng, 'Article 33 of the VCLT: Interpretation of treaties authenticated in two or more languages'.
[206] See entry by Andreas Kulick and Panos Merkouris, 'Article 31 of the VCLT: General rule of interpretation'.
[207] See ibid.
[208] See entry by Peter Tzeng, 'Article 33 of the VCLT: Interpretation of treaties authenticated in two or more languages'.
[209] See entry by Stephanie Forrest and Geraldo Vidigal, 'Part II, Ch. I and II of the ARSIWA: Remedies'.
[210] See entry by Cameron Miles, 'Cross-cutting procedural procedural powers of international courts and tribunals'.
[211] Tams, Schill and Hofmann, 'Radiating Effects' (n 44) 2, 4.
[212] See entry by Sean Aughey, 'Article 30 VCLT: Application of successive treaties relating to the same subject-matter'.
[213] See entries by Hélène Ruiz Fabri and Randi Ayman, 'Article 59 of the VCLT: Termination or suspension of the operation of a treaty implied by conclusion of a later treaty' and 'Article 60 of the VCLT: Termination or suspension of the operation of a treaty as consequence of its breach'.
[214] See entry by Oliver Hailes and Jorge E Viñuales, 'Article 5 of the ARSIWA: Conduct of empowered entities'.
[215] See entry by Claudia Annacker and Enikő Horvath, 'Article 13 of the ARSIWA: International obligation in force for a State'.
[216] See entry by Federica Paddeu and Michael Waibel, 'Article 25 of the ARSIWA: Necessity'.

PART I
LAW OF TREATIES (VCLT)

Article 18 of the VCLT

Obligation not to defeat the object and purpose of a treaty prior to its entry into force

Belinda McRae

A State is obliged to refrain from acts which would defeat the object and purpose of a treaty when:

(a) it has signed the treaty or has exchanged instruments constituting the treaty subject to ratification, acceptance or approval, until it shall have made its intention clear not to become a party to the treaty; or

(b) it has expressed its consent to be bound by the treaty, pending the entry into force of the treaty and provided that such entry into force is not unduly delayed.

A. Introduction	1	E. Treatment of Article 18 by investment tribunals	19
B. Origins of Article 18	5		
C. Contours of Article 18	10	F. Conclusion	28
D. Treatment of Article 18 by international and domestic courts/tribunals	11		

A. Introduction

The rule in Article 18 of the Vienna Convention on the Law of Treaties (VCLT) provides that a State must 'refrain from acts which would defeat the object and purpose of a treaty' in two circumstances: first, when a State has signed the treaty but not yet ratified it (or taken equivalent steps); and second, when it has expressed its consent to be bound, but the treaty has not yet entered into force. **1**

The International Law Commission (ILC) observed that the obligation of good faith 'to refrain from acts calculated to frustrate the object of the treaty' reflected in its draft article (then Article 15) 'appears to be generally accepted'.[1] A variation of that text was unanimously adopted at the Vienna Conference.[2] Scholars generally appear to accept that Article 18 reflects customary international law,[3] albeit that its contours may not be precisely defined. **2**

---

[1] ILC, 'Draft Articles on the Law of Treaties with commentaries' YILC 1966, Vol II, 202.
[2] Official Records of the United Nations Conference on the Law of Treaties, Second Session (Committee of the Whole) (29 April 1969) UN Doc A/CONF.39/SR.10, 29.
[3] See, eg, P Palchetti, 'Article 18 of the 1969 Vienna Convention: A Vague and Ineffective Obligation or a Useful Means for Strengthening Legal Cooperation?' in E Cannizzaro (ed), *The Law of Treaties Beyond the Vienna Convention* (2011) 25–26 (hereafter Palchetti, 'Article 18'); L Boisson de Chazournes, AM La Rosa and MM Mbengue, 'Article 18' in O Corten and P Klein (eds), *The Vienna Conventions on the Law of Treaties: A Commentary* (OUP 2011) 382–83 (hereafter Boisson de Chazournes, La Rosa and Mbengue, 'Article 18'); P Gragl

However, cases in which a State has alleged a breach of Article 18 by another State are 'extremely rare'[4] and there is said to be 'virtually no practice'[5] on the implementation of the provision. As a result, the prevailing view is that the deepest analysis of Article 18 of the VCLT is to be found in scholarship, rather than in the decisions of international courts and tribunals.

3   Although there has been very little treatment of Article 18 of the VCLT by international courts and tribunals, some insight into its scope and application is to be gained from the four investment tribunals that have considered it to date. In addition, the provision has been frequently invoked by domestic courts in a range of jurisdictions. Both this investment tribunal and domestic practice provides insight into the proper interpretation of Article 18.

4   Given its origin in the concept of good faith, Article 18 bears a close relationship to Article 26 (*pacta sunt servanda*).[6] It is also related to the provisions that similarly employ the concept of the 'object and purpose' of the treaty.[7]

B. Origins of Article 18

5   The principles underlying Article 18 of the VCLT were shaped by early decisions.

6   Two international decisions are of particular note. The first is the *Megalidis* decision of the Turkish–Greek Mixed Arbitral Tribunal, which was issued in 1928. It concerned Turkey's seizure of the property of a Greek national. This allegedly engaged the Treaty of Lausanne, which Turkey had signed in 1923, but which had not yet entered into force. The tribunal recognized that 'from the time of the signature of the Treaty and before its entry into force the contracting parties were under the duty to do nothing which might impair the operation of its clauses'.[8] The second is the *Certain German Interests in Polish Upper Silesia* case before the Permanent Court of International Justice (PCIJ). Poland contended that before ratification of the Treaty of Versailles, but following signature, Germany was prevented from alienating property that was said to be covered by the treaty. The Court rejected the premise of the argument, finding that Germany would not be so prevented even after ratification.[9] It nonetheless recognized that a misuse of Germany's rights to dispose of its property could potentially give rise to a treaty breach.[10]

---

and M Fitzmaurice, 'The Legal Character of Article 18 of the Vienna Convention on the Law of Treaties' (2019) 68 ICLQ 699, 702 (hereafter Gragl and Fitzmaurice, 'Legal Character').

[4] Palchetti, 'Article 18' (n 3) 26.

[5] A Aust, *Modern Treaty Law and Practice* (3rd edn, CUP 2013) 108 (hereafter Aust, 'Modern Treaty Law').

[6] See in this Commentary: Patrick Pearsall and Can Yeginsu, 'Article 26 of the VCLT: *Pacta sunt servanda*'.

[7] See Articles 19(c), 20(2), 31(1), 33(4), 41(1)(b)(ii), 58(1)(b)(ii), and 60(3)(b) of the VCLT. See in this Commentary: Alain Pellet and Jean-Baptiste Merlin, 'Articles 19–23 of the VCLT: Reservations (overview)—flexibility devices in applying treaties in the field of investment'; Panos Merkouris and Andreas Kulick, 'Article 31 of the VCLT: General rule of interpretation'; Peter Tzeng, 'Article 33 of the VCLT: Interpretation of treaties authenticated in two or more languages'; Luke Sobota and Amelia Keene, 'Parts IV and V of the VCLT: Amendment and invalidity, termination and suspension of treaties'; Hélène Ruiz Fabri and Randi Ayman, 'Article 60 of the VCLT: Termination or suspension of the operation of a treaty as consequence of its breach'.

[8] *Megalidis v Turkey* (1927–28) Annual Digest of Public International Law Cases (Case No 272), 395 (see *Megalidis v Etat turc* (1928) 8 Recueil des Décisions des Tribunaux Arbitraux Mixtes 386 for the French original). See also early treaty provisions that contained an equivalent obligation, eg Article 38 of the Final Act of Berlin, 26 February 1885; Protocol to the Convention for the Control of the Trade in Arms and Ammunition, 10 September 1919.

[9] *Certain German Interests in Polish Upper Silesia* (Merits), PCIJ Series A No 7, 39. The Court stated that it 'need not consider the question of whether, and if so how far, the signatories of a treaty are under an obligation to abstain from any action likely to interfere with its execution when ratification has taken place': 40.

[10] ibid 30.

These cases can be compared to early decisions of domestic courts. In particular, in 1923, the Polish Supreme Court recognized the existence of an obligation not to take steps 'contrary to the stipulations and the spirit' of the relevant treaty (that case also concerned the Treaty of Versailles).[11] Similarly, in 1956, the Austrian Supreme Court dismissed a civil claim brought on the basis of breach of a business's 'directive' which imposed controls that would be removed by the Peace Treaty soon to come into force. The Court had 'regard to the imminence of the coming into operation of the Peace Treaty' and held that the directive 'was contrary to good faith and therefore invalid'.[12]

The text of Article 18 itself had its genesis in Article 9 of the 1935 Harvard Draft Convention on the Law of Treaties. That provision made clear that a State was 'under no duty to perform the obligations stipulated' after mere signature of a treaty and relied instead on the concept of 'good faith', which 'in some circumstances ... may require that pending the coming into force of the treaty the State shall, for a reasonable time after signature, refrain from taking action which would render performance ... impossible or more difficult'. The authors of this draft Convention made clear that they did not 'envisage a legal duty' by these words, drawing a distinction between a duty of good faith and a legal obligation the breach of which may sound in damages.[13]

In the course of preparing the text of Article 18, it evolved from 'moral rather than a legal obligation'[14] in the draft prepared by the first ILC Special Rapporteur (James L. Brierly) to a 'legal, not merely a moral, duty'[15] in the 1953 draft prepared by the second ILC Special Rapporteur (Sir Hersch Lauterpacht), and was accepted as such by States. While an explicit reference to good faith was not included in the text of Article 18,[16] it is plain from the *travaux préparatoires* that Article 18 was intended to be an application of that principle.[17]

C. Contours of Article 18

Article 18 has been repeatedly characterized as 'vague' and 'amorphous'.[18] Perhaps as a result, Article 18 has produced an impressive body of scholarship. A consensus seems to be emerging on several key issues:

(a) <u>Nature of the test</u>: As noted above, the commentary to the original ILC draft referred to acts 'calculated' to frustrate the treaty's object and purpose. As a result,

---

[11] *Polish State Treasury v Von Bismarck* (1923) Annual Digest of Public International Law Cases (Case No 39), 80. See also *Schrager v Workmen's Accident Insurance Institute for Moravia and Silesia* (1927) Annual Digest of Public International Law Cases (Case No 274) 396, 399, which is another Polish Supreme Court decision addressing the effect of a treaty following its signature, and refers to 'principles of equity'.

[12] *Termination of Employment (Austria) Case* (1956) 23 ILR 470, 471.

[13] 'Draft Convention on the Law of Treaties' (1935) 29 AJIL Supplement 657, 781.

[14] ILC Special Rapporteur Mr JL Brierly, 'Second Report on the Law of Treaties' (3rd session of the ILC [1951]), UN Doc A/CN.4/43, 73.

[15] ILC Special Rapporteur Sir Hersh Lauterpacht, 'Report on the Law of Treaties' (5th session of the ILC [1953]), UN Doc A/CN.4/63, 110.

[16] This was proposed by the Netherlands: Official Records of the United Nations Conference on the Law of Treaties, First Session (Committee of the Whole; 19th Meeting), UN Doc A/CONF.39/C.1/SR.19, 99.

[17] See, eg, 'Draft Articles on the Law of Treaties with commentaries' (n 1), 202; Official Records of the United Nations Conference on the Law of Treaties, First Session (Committee of the Whole; 20th Meeting), UN Doc A/CONF.39/C.1/SR.20, 103 (hereafter, 'Official Records, 20th meeting') (observations of Mali, Iraq, and Spain). See also *Hellenic Republic v Commission of the European Communities*, Case T-231/04, [2007] ECR II-63, paras 85–86.

[18] See, eg, JS Charme, 'The Interim Obligation of Article 18 of the Vienna Convention on the Law of Treaties: Making Sense of an Enigma' (1991) 25 G Wash J Int'l L & Econ 71, 74, 104.

there was a lingering question about the relevance of the State's intention to an assessment of a breach of Article 18. The prevailing view is that the test is objective, rather than subjective. What matters is whether the relevant conduct had the effect of defeating the treaty's object and purpose, rather than whether the State intended that it would do so.[19] This is consistent with the plain language of the provision.

(b) Nature of the duty: It is well-accepted that a State is not obliged to adhere to the terms of the treaty; this obligation naturally arises only once the treaty enters into force for the State concerned.[20] Instead, it is required 'merely to refrain from rendering the treaty inoperative'[21] or 'render[ing] [the treaty] meaningless'.[22] The treaty language of 'refrain' strongly suggests that States are only subject to a negative, as opposed to a positive, duty. However, it has been argued that some circumstances may require positive steps to be taken in order to preserve the status quo.[23] This, it is suggested, could only arise in an unusual case where actual or constructive knowledge on the part of the State as to likely disruption of the status quo can be proved.

(c) Qualifying acts: A critical question is what acts or omissions will qualify as 'defeating' the object and purpose of the relevant treaty. It is accepted that this language creates a high threshold.[24] The example is typically given of the permanent destruction or disappearance of a tangible asset indispensable for the treaty's execution (e.g. mineral resources that were intended to be exploited pursuant to the treaty).[25] Several scholars have suggested that conduct that would constitute a material breach of the treaty under Article 60 of the VCLT, or otherwise provide grounds for termination under Articles 61–62, may be required.[26] The former suggestion should not be controversial given the parallel reference to 'object or purpose of the treaty' in Article 60(3)(b).[27]

(d) Meaning of 'object and purpose': This question is explored more fully in other entries.[28] It suffices to say here that the understanding of that concept as expressed long ago by the International Court of Justice (ICJ) in the Reservations Advisory Opinion applies equally in this context.[29]

---

[19] Aust, 'Modern Treaty Law' (n 5) 108; Gragl and Fitzmaurice, 'Legal Character' (n 3) 708; Boisson de Chazournes, La Rosa and Mbengue, 'Article 18' (n 3) fn 74.
[20] ILC, 'Report of the ILC' (59th session, 2007), UN Doc A/62/10, 67.
[21] ILC, 'Report of the ILC' (59th session, 2007), UN Doc A/62/10, 67.
[22] 'Official Records, 20th meeting' (n 17) 104 (observations of Sir Humphrey Waldock as Expert Consultant).
[23] Boisson de Chazournes, La Rosa and Mbengue, 'Article 18' (n 3) 398–99; Gragl and Fitzmaurice, 'Legal Character' (n 3) 712.
[24] Aust, 'Modern Treaty Law' (n 5) 108; Palchetti, 'Article 18' (n 3) 29.
[25] See, eg, 'Official Records, 20th meeting' (n 17) 104 (observations of Sir Humphrey Waldock as Expert Consultant). See further J Klabbers, 'How to Defeat a Treaty's Object and Purpose Pending Entry into Force: Toward Manifest Intent' (2001) 34 Vand J Transnat'l L 238, 239.
[26] Palchetti, 'Article 18' (n 3) 30; Gragl and Fitzmaurice, 'Legal Character' (n 3) 712.
[27] See in this Commentary: Hélène Ruiz Fabri and Randi Ayman, 'Article 60 of the VCLT: Termination or suspension of the operation of a treaty as consequence of its breach'.
[28] See in this Commentary: Alain Pellet and Jean-Baptiste Merlin, 'Articles 19–23 of the VCLT: Reservations (overview)—flexibility devices in applying treaties in the field of investment'; Panos Merkouris and Andreas Kulick, 'Article 31 of the VCLT: General rule of interpretation'.
[29] *Reservations to the Convention on the Prevention and Punishment of the Crime of Genocide* (Advisory Opinion) [1951] ICJ Rep 15, 27 ('... what is essential to the object of the Convention', in the sense that, if the object is not met 'the Convention itself would be impaired both in its principle and its application').

D. Treatment of Article 18 by international and domestic courts/tribunals

Article 18 of the VCLT has received little attention before international courts and tribunals.

Before the ICJ, Article 18 has most typically featured in the pleadings of States[30] and in separate or dissenting opinions of individual judges.[31] In the *North Sea Continental Shelf* cases, both Denmark and the Netherlands argued that the Geneva Convention on the Continental Shelf was binding on Germany (which had signed, but not ratified, that treaty). Reliance was placed on Germany's conduct, by which it was said unilaterally to have assumed certain treaty obligations. This was not accepted by the Court, which required 'the existence of a situation of estoppel' in order for Germany's conduct to have preclusive effect.[32] While the VCLT had not yet been concluded, Judge Lachs referred to the draft of Article 18(a), then Article 15(a), in his dissenting opinion.[33] Nonetheless, the ICJ has considered acts defeating the 'object and purpose' of a treaty on previous occasions, which may be instructive in the Article 18 context.[34]

Article 18 has also been invoked by parties in the dispute resolution processes under the auspices of the World Trade Organization.[35] To date, it has only been considered in any detail in one panel report (in the *Peru—Additional Duty on Imports of Certain Agricultural Products* case). Although the Panel ultimately found it unnecessary to rule on the applicability of Article 18, it observed that 'the provision does not require a signatory to comply with the terms of a treaty which it has not yet ratified, and does not even require the signatory not to act in a manner inconsistent with that treaty'.[36] This statement is accurate, so far as it goes, but should not be understood as suggesting that *any* conduct inconsistent with a treaty that is yet to enter into force is permissible. It is simply that the inconsistency of conduct must rise to the level of defeating the treaty's object and purpose in order to engage Article 18.

Article 18 has, however, been deployed far more readily before domestic and regional courts.

---

[30] See, eg, *Land Boundary in the Northern Part of Isla Portillos (Costa Rica v Nicaragua)* (Judgment) [2018] ICJ Rep 139, para 132, which summarizes Costa Rica's argument relying on Article 18; see also *Legality of Use of Force (Serbia and Montenegro v Portugal)* (Preliminary Objections) [2004] ICJ Rep 1160, para 94, summarizing Portugal's argument relying on Article 18(b).

[31] See, eg, *Territorial Dispute (Libyan Arab Jamahiriya v Chad)* (Judgment) [1994] ICJ Rep 6, Separate Opinion of Judge Ajibola, para 82; *Gabčíkovo-Nagymaros Project (Hungary v Slovakia)* (Judgment) [1997] ICJ Rep 7, Dissenting Opinion of Judge Fleischhauer, p 206; *Application of the Convention on the Prevention and Punishment of the Crime of Genocide (Bosnia and Herzegovina v Serbia and Montenegro)* (Judgment) [2007] ICJ Rep 43, Separate Opinion of Judge Tomka, para 35. In another interstate context, see *Dispute Concerning Access to Information Under Article 9 of the OSPAR Convention (Ireland v United Kingdom)* (Final Award) (2003) XXIII RIAA 59, Dissenting Opinion of Gavan Griffith QC, para 13.

[32] *North Sea Continental Shelf (Federal Republic of Germany v Netherlands; Federal Republic of Germany v Denmark)* (Judgment) [1969] ICJ Rep 3, 26.

[33] *North Sea Continental Shelf (Federal Republic of Germany v Netherlands; Federal Republic of Germany v Denmark)* (Judgment) [1969] ICJ Rep 3, Dissenting Opinion of Judge Lachs, 227. The ICJ has also acknowledged that a signed but unratified treaty may constitute an expression of the understanding of the contracting parties at the time of signature: *Maritime Delimitation and Territorial Questions between Qatar and Bahrain* (Merits) [2001] ICJ Rep 40, para 89.

[34] See, eg, *Military and Paramilitary Activities in and Against Nicaragua (Nicaragua v United States)* (Merits) [1986] ICJ Rep 14, paras 270–76; note, in particular, the ICJ's reference to 'activities which are such as to undermine the whole spirit of [the] bilateral agreement' (the Treaty of Amity).

[35] See, eg, *Brazil—Export Financing Programme for Aircraft*, Panel Report, 14 April 1999, para 4.189; *United States—Sections 301–310 of the Trade Act 1974*, Panel Report, 22 December 1999, para 5.196.

[36] *Peru—Additional Duty on Imports of Certain Agricultural Products*, Panel Report, 27 November 2014, para 7.91.

15 In the domestic sphere, courts have made passing reference to the obligation contained in Article 18 in a range of jurisdictions, including Benin,[37] Canada,[38] Germany,[39] New Zealand,[40] and the UK.[41] Several supreme or constitutional courts have also had occasion to consider the provision in more detail. In a 2005 decision, the Latvian Constitutional Court described Article 18 as 'a guarantee so that ratification of the [treaty] does not become senseless, for example, in case the object of the agreement ceases to exist'. It also correctly observed that States are not obliged by Article 18 to adhere to specific treaty obligations.[42] The South African Constitutional Court has recognized that 'serious consequences flow from a mere signing of an international agreement'. In particular, a State is restrained from 'acting in a manner inconsistent with the treaty'. However, the Court emphasized that a treaty's provisions will not have binding effect until ratification; nor will they constrain the State's discretion as to ratification.[43] The Italian Constitutional Court similarly observed that the 'good faith obligation' in Article 18 'cannot go so far as to exclude the State's discretion in deciding whether to ratify ... a treaty'.[44]

16 Several domestic courts, however, have gone further than the terms of Article 18. In particular, the Supreme Court of Ghana invoked Article 18 of the VCLT to justify its reliance on the UN Convention on the Carriage of Goods by Sea, which had been signed but not ratified by Ghana.[45] Similarly, the Chilean Court of Appeal (in a judgment upheld by the Supreme Court) referenced Article 18 in support of its decision to set aside an amnesty law, finding that its application would have defeated the object and purpose of the 1994 Inter-American Convention on the Forced Disappearance of Persons, a treaty that Chile had signed but was yet to ratify.[46] This is even though the obligation to punish that crime was a substantive obligation that would not have effect until the treaty's entry into force. The Russian Constitutional Court also indicated that the delivery of a death penalty judgment could violate Russia's obligations under Article 18, on the basis of its signature of Protocol 6 to the European Convention on Human Rights concerning the abolition of the death penalty.[47] By reaching that conclusion, the Constitutional Court appeared to assume that the treaty's substantive obligations should be respected from the moment of signature.

17 In contrast, the Hong Kong Court of Appeal in the well-known *FG Hemisphere* case declined to apply Article 18 of the VCLT in considering whether Hong Kong law required the application of the absolute or restrictive doctrine of State immunity. China had signed, but not

---

[37] *Legal Opinion of Supreme Court of Benin*, Case No 029-C, 25 July 2003, ILDC 844 (BJ 2003), para 35.
[38] *de Guzman v Canada (Minister of Citizenship and Immigration)* [2006] 3 FCR 655, para 76.
[39] *Extradition to India Case, G*, 2 BvR 685/03, BVerfGE 108, 129, 24 June 2003, ILDC 484 (DE 2003), para 43(b).
[40] *Environmental Defence v Auckland Regional Council*, New Zealand Environmental Court, 6 September 2002 (unreported), para 27.
[41] *R v M* [2011] 1 Cr App R 12; [2010] EWCA Crim 2327, para 2; *Khurts Bat v Investigating Judge of the Federal Court of Germany* [2013] QB 349; [2011] EWHC 2029 (Admin), para 22.
[42] *Cilevičs and Ors v Latvia*, Case No 2004-18-0106, Latvian Herald, No 77, 3235, 13 May 2005, ILDC 190 (LV 2005), para 8.1 (concluding part).
[43] *Law Society of South Africa and Ors v President of the Republic of South Africa and Ors*, Case CT67/18, [2018] ZACC 51, ILDC 3179 (ZA 2018), paras 40–41. The Court also acknowledged that Article 18 represented customary international law: see para 36.
[44] *Santoro v Settimo senso srl*, No 194/2018, 8 November 2018, ILDC 3034 (IT 2018), para 5.4.
[45] *Delmas America Africa Line Incorporated v Kisko Products Ghana Limited*, Civil Appeal No J4/28/2004, 2 March 2005, ILDC 1487 (GH 2005). The Court notably did not identify acts that could be said to defeat the object and purpose of the treaty.
[46] *Sepúlveda (Juan Manuel Contreras), Re and Ors*, Action to annul, Rol No 517-2004, 17 December 2004, ILDC 394 (CL 2004).
[47] Judicial Review, N 1344-O-P, SZ RF Vol 48, 19 November 2009, ILDC 1553 (RU 2009); cf Government of the Russian Federation, Constitutional proceedings, No 2867-O-P, 24 December 2020, ILDC 3236 (RU 2020).

ratified, the 2004 UN Convention espousing the restrictive doctrine. The Court held that the 'injunction not to defeat the object and purpose of a treaty is to be interpreted realistically in the context of the subject matter ... [i]t is unrealistic, and a misreading of the Vienna Convention, to suggest that pending ratification of a multilateral Convention ... where certain States parties have for long adhered to a principled policy which the multilateral instrument seeks to change, continued adherence to that policy by a State, pending a decision whether to ratify, will have the effect, ultimately, of defeating the object and purpose of the treaty'.[48]

Finally, it is worth noting that Article 18 has also been invoked before European regional courts. In particular, in *Opel Austria v EU Council*, the Court of First Instance of the European Communities referred to the principle of good faith codified in Article 18 of the VCLT as a rule of customary international law, alongside its reference to the EU law principle of legitimate expectations. On that foundation, it held that traders could rely on that principle to challenge 'any measure contrary to the provisions' of a treaty approved by the EU, but not yet entered into force.[49] Like the Chilean and Russian Constitutional Court decisions discussed above, it wrongly assumes that Article 18 requires performance of the treaty's terms. It has been rightly criticized for this reason.[50] The *Opel* case has nonetheless been regularly cited in the EU courts.[51] **18**

E. Treatment of Article 18 by investment tribunals

Several awards have referred to Article 18 of the VCLT in passing,[52] but only four awards to date have addressed the provision in any detail. None of them has found a breach of its terms. **19**

The first and most substantial treatment of Article 18 can be found in *Tecmed v Mexico*,[53] which concerned a claim under the Spain–Mexico Bilateral Investment Treaty (BIT) brought by a Spanish company with two Mexican subsidiaries in respect of the Claimant's investment in a hazardous waste landfill. The Claimant argued that Article 18 governed the Respondent's conduct before the entry into force of that treaty.[54] **20**

As a starting point, the tribunal recognized the relevance of the principle of good faith as manifested in Article 18 to its consideration of the Respondent's conduct before the BIT entered into force. It observed that Article 18 'does not only refer to intentional acts of States, **21**

---

[48] *FG Hemisphere Associates LLC v Democratic Republic of the Congo* (2010) 142 ILR 216 (Hong Kong SAR Court of Appeal, 10 February 2010), paras 103–06. This judgment was appealed to the Court of Final Appeal and was overturned: see (2011) 147 ILR 376 (Provisional Judgment; 8 June 2011) and (2011) 150 ILR 684 (Final Judgment; 8 September 2011). Neither of those judgments addressed Article 18 of the VCLT.
[49] *Opel Austria v EU Council*, Case T-115/94, [1997] 1 CMLR 733, paras 90–94.
[50] See, eg, J Odermatt, 'The Use of International Treaty Law by the Court of Justice of the European Union' (2015) 17 CYELS 121, 127–28.
[51] See, eg, *Hellenic Republic v Commission of the European Communities*, Case T-231/04, [2007] ECR II-63, paras 86–87; *Poland (Latvia and Others, intervening) v Council of the European Union (Commission of the European Communities, intervening)* [2008] 1 CMLR 23 (AG Opinion), para 76.
[52] *Total v Argentine Republic*, ICSID Case No ARB/04/1, Decision on Liability, 27 December 2010, fn 141; *Caratube International Oil Company LLP v Republic of Kazakhstan (II)*, ICSID Case No ARB/13/13, Decision on the Claimants' Request for Provisional Measures, 4 December 2014, para 121; *Luxtona Ltd v The Russian Federation*, PCA Case No 2014-09, Interim Award on the Respondent's Objections to the Jurisdiction of the Tribunal, 22 March 2017, para 167.
[53] *Técnicas Medioambientales Techmed SA v United Mexican States*, ICSID Case No ARB(AF)/00/2, Award, 29 May 2003.
[54] ibid para 53.

but also to conduct which falls within its provisions'. That conduct 'need not be intentional or manifestly damaging or fraudulent ... but merely negligent or in disregard of the provisions of the treaty or its underlying principles, or contradictory or unreasonable in light of such provisions or principles'.[55] This broadly accords with the prevailing academic view (see paragraph 10(a) above) that the test is an objective one.

22 When applying those principles to the facts, the tribunal declined to 'pass judgment' on whether the Respondent's conduct preceding the entry into force of the treaty was a stand-alone breach. However, the tribunal stated that 'it cannot be ignored ... that the conduct of the Respondent between the date of execution of the Agreement ... and the effective date thereof is incompatible with the imperative rules deriving from Article 4(1) of the Agreement as to fair and equitable treatment' (emphasis added). It also observed that the BIT applied to investments made before its entry into force and that the relevant State entity's conduct before the BIT's entry into force was consistent with that which the Claimant faced before its licence to operate the landfill was revoked. For that reason, that conduct was 'added to the prejudicial effects of [the Respondent's] conduct at the last stage' which were found to be in breach of the fair and equitable treatment (FET) standard.[56]

23 It is difficult to understand precisely what the tribunal meant by 'imperative rules' of the FET standard. This language may well have been an attempt on the tribunal's part to identify a higher class of rules capable of engaging the Respondent's negative duty in Article 18. However, it is unclear if that indeed was the tribunal's intention, and if so, what those 'rules' were intended to encompass. It is also not clear why the tribunal declined to decide whether an Article 18 breach was made out.

24 The second case is *MCI Power v Ecuador*.[57] The Claimants alleged that Ecuador breached its obligation under Article 18 after signing the BIT, relying on *Megalidis* and *Opel Austria*. Ecuador, for its part, contended that the Claimants' argument amounted to an attempt to apply the BIT retroactively (contrary to Article 28 of the VCLT).[58]

25 The tribunal confirmed that Article 18 is an application of the principle of good faith and that its terms were 'not aimed at triggering the early application of the clauses of a treaty'.[59] It distinguished the *Megalidis* and *Opel Austria* cases on the facts (the former because Article 65 of the Treaty of Lausanne intended the treaty to apply retroactively, and the latter because of the 'exceptional circumstances' of the case before the European Court).[60] Ultimately, the tribunal held that '[i]t has not been proven in the present case that the actions and omissions prior to the entry into force of the BIT ... had defeated the object and purpose of the Treaty'. It emphasized the 'extraordinary nature of the enforcement of the customary norm set out in Article 18'.[61]

26 This analysis of the application of Article 18 of the VCLT in this case is far more rigorous and consistent with both the precise terms of the provision and the prevailing academic and

---

[55] ibid paras 70–71.
[56] ibid para 172.
[57] *MCI Power Group LC v Republic of Ecuador*, ICSID Case No ARB/03/6, Award, 31 July 2007, paras 98–117 (hereafter *MCI Power*).
[58] ibid paras 98–107. See in this Commentary: Ben Juratowitch and Jackie McArthur, 'Article 28 of the VCLT: Non-retroactivity of treaties'.
[59] *MCI Power* (n 57) para 108.
[60] ibid paras 109–15.
[61] ibid para 116.

ILC consensus on their limits. In particular, the recognition that Article 18 does not seek provisionally to apply the treaty and the tribunal's insistence on proof of conduct defeating the BIT's object and purpose are to be preferred to the *Tecmed* tribunal's vague reference to 'imperative rules'.

The third and fourth awards dismissed arguments based on Article 18 of the VCLT with relative despatch. In *Doutremepuich v Mauritius*, the Claimants relied on Article 18 in an attempt to invoke the dispute settlement clause in a treaty signed and ratified by the Respondent, but which had not yet entered into force. They suggested that the Respondent 'should have accepted the application of the arbitration agreement of the 2010 Treaty by anticipation, before the 2010 Treaty entering into force'.[62] This argument was rejected in a mere footnote.[63] Similarly short shrift was given to the Article 18 argument raised in respect of the application of the EEU Treaty in *OOO Manolium-Processing v Belarus*. The tribunal endorsed the basic statement of the law by the *Tecmed* tribunal and put the standard thus: 'Good faith requires that ... signatory States abstain from acts which are incompatible with the treaty's object and purpose'. It rejected the argument on evidential grounds and regrettably appeared to imply that intention to defeat a treaty's object and purpose must be proved.[64] Neither of these awards provides any particularly useful insight into the interpretation or application of Article 18.

F. Conclusion

The paucity of international awards and judgments addressing Article 18 of the VCLT means that it is difficult to comment on the alignment or divergence between general international law and international investment law. As illustrated above, Article 18 has been most frequently invoked before domestic courts, with varying effect. As is the case before those courts, the above survey suggests that investment claimants have sought to accord Article 18 of the VCLT more significance than its terms can reasonably bear by seeking to use it as a vehicle for the provisional application of the treaty. That attempt certainly failed in the *MCI Power* and *Doutremepuich* cases. It appeared to gain more traction in the *Tecmed* case, albeit that the point was not ultimately decided. It is hoped that, as the jurisprudence on Article 18 becomes more developed, the precise contours and textual limits of Article 18 will be borne firmly in mind, and that the domestic decisions properly recognizing those limits (in particular that set out at paragraphs 15 and 17 above) will be profitably deployed to assist that development.

Selected literature

Anthony A, *Modern Treaty Law and Practice* (3rd edn, CUP 2013).
Boisson de Chazournes LB, La Rosa AM and Mbengue MM, 'Article 18' in Corten O and Klein P (eds), *The Vienna Conventions on the Law of Treaties: A Commentary* (OUP 2011).

---

[62] *Christian Doutremepuich and Antonine Doutremepuich v Republic of Mauritius*, PCA Case No 2018-37, Award on Jurisdiction, 23 August 2019, fn 280.
[63] ibid fn 344.
[64] *OOO Manolium-Processing v The Republic of Belarus*, PCA Case No 2018-06, Final Award, 22 June 2021, paras 294–96; see in particular 'there is no evidence that the EEU Treaty was invoked ... in breach of the principle of good faith, <u>with the purpose</u> of "defeat[ing] the object and purpose" of the EEU Treaty' (emphasis added).

Gragl P and Fitzmaurice M, 'The Legal Character of Article 18 of the Vienna Convention on the Law of Treaties' (2019) 68 ICLQ 699.
Palchetti P, 'Article 18 of the 1969 Vienna Convention: A Vague and Ineffective Obligation or a Useful Means for Strengthening Legal Cooperation?' in Cannizzaro E (ed), *The Law of Treaties Beyond the Vienna Convention* (OUP 2011).

Selected decisions

Christian Doutremepuich and Antonine Doutremepuich v Republic of Mauritius, PCA Case No 2018-37, Award on Jurisdiction, 23 August 2019.

MCI Power Group v Republic of Ecuador, ICSID Case No ARB/03/6, Award, 31 July 2007.

OOO Manolium-Processing v The Republic of Belarus, PCA Case No 2018-06, Final Award, 22 June 2021.

Técnicas Medioambientales Techmed SA v United Mexican States, ISCID Case No ARB(AF)/00/2, Award, 29 May 2003.

Articles 19–23 of the VCLT

Reservations (overview)—flexibility devices in applying treaties in the field of investment

Alain Pellet and Jean-Baptiste Merlin

Section 2. Reservations

Article 19. Formulation of reservations

A State may, when signing, ratifying, accepting, approving, or acceding to a treaty, formulate a reservation unless:

(a) The reservation is prohibited by the treaty;

(b) The treaty provides that only specified reservations, which do not include the reservation in question, may be made; or

(c) In cases not falling under subparagraphs (a) and (b), the reservation is incompatible with the object and purpose of the treaty.

Article 20. Acceptance of and objection to reservations

1. A reservation expressly authorized by a treaty does not require any subsequent acceptance by the other contracting States unless the treaty so provides.

2. When it appears from the limited number of the negotiating States and the object and purpose of a treaty that the application of the treaty in its entirety between all the parties is an essential condition of the consent of each one to be bound by the treaty, a reservation requires acceptance by all the parties.

3. When a treaty is a constituent instrument of an international organization and unless it otherwise provides, a reservation requires the acceptance of the competent organ of that organization.

4. In cases not falling under the preceding paragraphs and unless the treaty otherwise provides:

(a) Acceptance by another contracting State of a reservation constitutes the reserving State a party to the treaty in relation to that other State if or when the treaty is in force for those States;

(b) An objection by another contracting State to a reservation does not preclude the entry into force of the treaty as between the objecting and reserving States unless a contrary intention is definitely expressed by the objecting State;

(c) An act expressing a State's consent to be bound by the treaty and containing a reservation is effective as soon as at least one other contracting State has accepted the reservation.

5. For the purposes of paragraphs 2 and 4 and unless the treaty otherwise provides, a reservation is considered to have been accepted by a State if it shall have raised no objection to the reservation by the end of a period of twelve months after it was notified of the reservation or by the date on which it expressed its consent to be bound by the treaty, whichever is later.

Article 21. Legal effects of reservations and of objections to reservations

1. A reservation established with regard to another party in accordance with articles 19, 20 and 23:

(a) Modifies for the reserving State in its relations with that other party the provisions of the treaty to which the reservation relates to the extent of the reservation; and

(b) Modifies those provisions to the same extent for that other party in its relations with the reserving State.

2. The reservation does not modify the provisions of the treaty for the other parties to the treaty inter se.

3. When a State objecting to a reservation has not opposed the entry into force of the treaty between itself and the reserving State, the provisions to which the reservation relates do not apply as between the two States to the extent of the reservation.

Article 22. Withdrawal of reservations and of objections to reservations

1. Unless the treaty otherwise provides, a reservation may be withdrawn at any time and the consent of a State which has accepted the reservation is not required for its withdrawal.

2. Unless the treaty otherwise provides, an objection to a reservation may be withdrawn at any time.

3. Unless the treaty otherwise provides, or it is otherwise agreed:

(a) The withdrawal of a reservation becomes operative in relation to another contracting State only when notice of it has been received by that State;

(b) The withdrawal of an objection to a reservation becomes operative only when notice of it has been received by the State which formulated the reservation.

Article 23. Procedure regarding reservations

1. A reservation, an express acceptance of a reservation and an objection to a reservation must be formulated in writing and communicated to the contracting States and other States entitled to become parties to the treaty.

2. If formulated when signing the treaty subject to ratification, acceptance or approval, a reservation must be formally confirmed by the reserving State when expressing its consent to be bound by the treaty. In such a case the reservation shall be considered as having been made on the date of its confirmation.

3. An express acceptance of, or an objection to, a reservation made previously to confirmation of the reservation does not itself require confirmation.

4. The withdrawal of a reservation or of an objection to a reservation must be formulated in writing.

A. Introduction	1
B. Reservations in general international law and in ICJ practice	3
C. Devising exceptions in treaty-making practice in the field of international investment law	6
I. Overview of relevant multilateral treaties	9
II. Investment decisions	20
D. Rationale for resorting to flexibility devices	31
E. Conclusion	34

A. Introduction

1   Article 2(1)(d) of the 1969 Vienna Convention on the Law of Treaties (VCLT) defines a 'reservation' as 'a unilateral statement, however phrased or named, made by a State, when signing, ratifying, accepting, approving or acceding to a treaty, whereby it purports to exclude or to modify the legal effect of certain provisions of the treaty in their application to that State'. Articles 19–23, which provide for the legal regime of reservations, now reflect customary international law.[1]

2   As evidenced by the International Law Commission (ILC) Guide to Practice on Reservations to Treaties adopted on second reading in 2011 ('Guide to Practice'), distinguishing between reservations and alternative flexibility devices may at times be a significantly complex task,[2]

---

[1] A Pellet, First report on reservations to treaties, UN Doc A/CN.4/470, in YILC 1995, Vol II, Part One, 152, para 157 (hereafter 'First report on reservations to treaties').

[2] Report of the ILC on the Work of its 63rd session, UN Doc A/66/10/Add.1, in YILC 2011, Vol II, Part Two (hereafter 'Guide to Practice'). See, in particular, para 4 of commentary to Guideline 1.7.1.

and the need for flexibility inherent in treaty practice in international investment law has pushed that complexity a step further.

B. Reservations in general international law and in ICJ practice

The modern legal regime governing reservations was impulsed by the International Court of Justice (ICJ) with its much-commented 1951 Advisory Opinion in the case of *Reservations to the Genocide Convention*. There the Court disregarded strictly mechanical approaches for appreciating the validity, entry into force and legal effects of reservations, favouring instead an objective-subjective system based on the central criterion of conformity of the reservation with the object and purpose of the treaty, each State retaining the right to determine for itself the permissibility of the purported reservation in light of this criterion.[3] This 'flexible system' also posited a presumption in favour of the permissibility of reservations,[4] thus reversing the hitherto general requirement of unanimous acceptance.

The innovative solution retained by the ICJ was later followed by the ILC after several years of hesitation,[5] leading to the adoption of the 1969 VCLT. Yet, such culmination was also the starting point of a further, and still ongoing, process of consolidation of the reservation regime insofar as the VCLT, and the following 1978 and 1986 Vienna Conventions also addressing the topic, left a series of ambiguities and silences.[6] Despite the inevitably subjective part of this notion,[7] compatibility with the object and purpose of the treaty became definitely entrenched as the fundamental and unifying criterion for assessing the validity of reservations.[8] The general legal regime of reservations has been codified and developed by the Guide to Practice.

The regime of reservations established by Articles 19–23 of the VCLT is of general scope and does not establish distinctions between different areas of international law.[9] Similarly, the ICJ's approach to the interpretation of reservations does not vary depending on the area of international law concerned.[10] On the contrary, uniformity appears as one of the central factors in the progressive development of a general reservation regime over time. As the ILC and States themselves have highlighted, the balance struck by this general regime of reservations appears to be sufficiently flexible to espouse various circumstances of multilateral treaties irrespective of their object, rendering special regimes unnecessary and unwarranted.[11]

---

[3] Reservations to the Convention on Genocide (Advisory Opinion) [1951] ICJ Rep 24–26 (hereafter *Reservations* Advisory Opinion). See also A Pellet, 'La C.I.J. et les réserves aux traités—Remarques cursives sur une révolution jurisprudentielle' in N Andō et al (eds), *Liber Amicorum Judge Shigeru Oda* (Kluwer 2002) 487–88, para 6.

[4] *Reservations* Advisory Opinion (n 3).

[5] YILC 1962, Vol II, 60, draft Article 17(2)(a).

[6] First report on reservations to treaties, YILC 1995, Vol II, Part One (n 1) 136, para 61(a) and (b); 141 ff, paras 92 and 95 ff.

[7] Sir H Waldock, First report on the law of treaties, A/CN.4/144, in YILC 1962, Vol II, 65–66. See also A Pellet, '1969 Vienna Convention—Article 19: Formulation of Reservations' in O Corten and P Klein (eds), *The Vienna Conventions on the Law of Treaties—A Commentary*, Vol 1 (OUP, 2011) 414, para 15; 415, para 19.

[8] Guide to Practice (n 2), Guideline 3.1.5 and commentary thereto.

[9] Nor does the Guide to Practice (n 2).

[10] Including in ICJ cases touching upon investment issues such as *Interhandel, Barcelona Traction, Light and Power Company, Limited*, or *Elettronica Sicula SpA (ELSI)*.

[11] A Pellet, Second report on reservations to treaties, A/CN.4/477 and Add.1, in YILC 1996, Vol II, Part One, 67–70, paras 163–76; YILC 1997, Vol II, Part Two, 57; debate at the Sixth Committee on the report of the ILC on the work of its 49th session, 1997, A/C.6/52/SR.17 to 25.

C. Devising exceptions in treaty-making practice in the field of international investment law

6   As the UN Conference on Trade and Development (UNCTAD) highlighted, '[f]or the most part, [international investment agreements] allow general and policy-oriented exceptions (e.g. on taxation policies), as well as country-specific reservations (mostly sector-specific) to be lodged against non-discrimination and liberalization disciplines'.[12] In effect, a closer look at those mechanisms shows that, while reservations within the meaning of Article 2(1)(d) of the VCLT are very frequent in the practice of international law generally, when it comes to investment treaty practice they tend to be more restricted or excluded, and they also coexist with a rich spectrum of alternative mechanisms or 'rival' institutions. This in turn explains the relative paucity of international investment decisions and doctrine relating to reservations proper and referring to Articles 19–23 of the VCLT. At least two reasons account for this.

7   First, the great majority of international investment instruments consists of bilateral investment treaties, which means in effect that the issue of applying or interpreting reservations rarely arises. In its Guide to Practice, the ILC confirmed the distinct effect of a 'reservation' made in a bilateral context, which amounts to a proposal to modify the treaty.[13]

8   Second, it appears as a matter of fact that some of the major multilateral investment instruments tend to exclude or severely restrict the formulation of reservations within the meaning of Article 2(1)(d) of the VCLT,[14] or else no such reservations have been made to them. For example, the Energy Charter Treaty (hereinafter ECT) prohibits reservations.[15] While the Convention on the Settlement of Investment Disputes between States and Nationals of Other States (ICSID Convention) neither authorizes nor prohibits reservations, none has been made to it. It has also been clarified that notifications under Article 25(4) of that Convention—which may be made at any time—do not constitute reservations,[16] and the *travaux* confirm that this provision in fact aimed precisely at preventing reservations.[17] Likewise, since a notice made under Article 70 purports to exclude the Convention *as a*

---

[12] 'Preserving Flexibility in IIAs: The Use of Reservations', UNCTAD Series on International Investment Policies for Development, 2006, UN Doc UNCTAD/ITE/IIT/2005/8, 10–11.

[13] Guide to Practice (n 2), Guideline 1.6.1 and its commentary. See also Third report on reservations to treaties, A/CN.4/491, in YILC 1998, Vol II, Part One, 292–94, paras 467–82.

[14] For a counter-example, the 1981 Agreement for the Promotion, Protection and Guarantee of Investments among Member States of the Organization of the Islamic Conference (entered into force in 1988) is silent on the issue of reservations, which are thus authorized in principle as long as they are not incompatible with the object and purpose of the treaty.

[15] Energy Charter Treaty (ECT), 17 December 1994, entered into force on 16 April 1998, Article 46. See also Article 19 of its protocol on energy efficiency. Prohibitions or strict restrictions of reservations, including the requirement of consent by other parties, are also noticeable for commercial and trade-related instruments: WTO Convention, Marrakesh, 5 April 1994, Article XVI(5); Agreement on Trade-Related Aspects of Intellectual Property Rights (TRIPS), Article 72; Dominican Republic–Central America Free Trade Agreement, 5 August 2004, Article 22.4. The provisions on exceptions contained in Chapter 21 of this instrument, just like those of Article XX of the GATT that is incorporated therein by reference, do not constitute reservations. The 1992 Agreement on Common Effective Preferential Tariff (CEPT) Scheme for the Free Trade Area (AFTA) concluded between ASEAN Member States (Article 10) and the 1998 ASEAN Framework Agreement on the Facilitation of Goods in Transit (Article 33(4)) prohibits reservations thereto.

[16] Report of the Executive Directors, para 31.

[17] *History of ICSID Convention: Documents Concerning the Origin and the Formulation of the Convention*, ICSID publication, 1968 (reprint 2009), Vol II(1), 57–58, 59, 362–63, 377; Vol II(2), 822.

whole to part of the territory of a State party, it presumably does not constitute a true reservation.[18] The United Nations Convention on Transparency in Treaty-based Investor–State Arbitration of 10 December 2014 (Mauritius Convention) prohibits reservations (Article 3.4). In this light, 'reservations' that may be made at any time under Article 4.1 and 4.4 of the Mauritius Convention are in fact not true reservations within the meaning of Article 2(1)(d) of the VCLT.

I. Overview of relevant multilateral treaties

Nevertheless, some plurilateral and multilateral instruments pertaining to investment contain a varied range of mechanisms scheduling the degree of commitment to liberalization and protection to which each State party may be prepared to consent. While such mechanisms of exemption sometimes bear the name of 'reservations', that label is not in itself dispositive of their legal nature and a closer examination thereof is necessary to determine in each case whether they in fact constitute or govern genuine reservations (as specified reservations authorized under the treaty[19]) or alternative devices. The ECT as well as the North American Free Trade Agreement (NAFTA)[20] and its successor, the United States Mexico Canada Agreement (USMCA),[21] constitute interesting examples that are emblematic of how States approach the issue of modulating treaty obligations in the field of international investment law. They also illustrate the fine line that may sometimes be difficult to draw between genuine reservations authorized by a reservation clause or exclusion clause, on the one hand, and alternatives to reservations, on the other, which may appear similar to reservations in many respects. 9

The ECT provides for a system of exceptions that, on balance, suggests alternatives to reservations.[22] Article 10(5) provides that contracting parties shall endeavour to limit the exceptions to the most favourable nation treatment to the minimum and to progressively remove existing restrictions affecting investors of other contracting parties. Crucially, under Article 10(9)(a), each contracting party shall, on the date it signs the ECT or deposits its instrument of accession, submit to the Secretariat a report summarizing all laws, regulations, or other measures relevant to exceptions to the most favourable nation treatment contemplated under Article 10(2). A contracting party shall keep its report up to date by promptly submitting amendments to the Secretariat. The Charter Conference shall review these reports periodically. Article 10(9) also specifies that such reports may designate parts of the energy sector in which a contracting party grants to investors of other contracting parties the most favourable nation treatment. 10

Prima facie exceptions under Article 10(9) that contracting parties include in their reports seem to constitute reservations expressly authorized by an exclusionary clause.[23] They can be seen as specified reservations the form of which, but not the content, is specified by the 11

---

[18] See Guide to Practice (n 2), para 5 of commentary to Guideline 1.1.3. On Article 70, see in this Commentary: Emma Lindsay and Philippa Webb, 'Article 29 of the VCLT: Territorial scope'.
[19] Guide to Practice (n 2), Guidelines 3.1.2 and 3.1.4 and commentaries thereto. See also Guide to Practice (n 2), Guideline 1.1.6 and commentary thereto.
[20] North American Free Trade Agreement (NAFTA), 17 December 1992, entered into force on 1 January 1994.
[21] Agreement between the United States of America, the United Mexican States, and Canada (USMCA), 30 November 2018 (initial version) and 10 December 2019 (revised version), entered into force on 1 July 2020. The USMCA replaced the NAFTA upon its entry into force.
[22] ECT, Articles 10 and 26.
[23] Guide to Practice (n 2), Guideline 1.1.6. See also Fifth report on reservations to treaties, UN Doc A/CN.4/508/Add.1, in YILC 2000, Vol II, Part One, 171–76, paras 148–78.

ECT.[24] Indeed, the formulation of exceptions by a contracting party requires a unilateral act the content of which is not known in advance. This distinguishes Article 10 exceptions from Article 17, which is more akin to a restrictive clause. While there is no express indication whether a State may introduce new non-conforming measures or increase a non-conforming measure when updating its report subsequent to its initial filing, the interpretation of Article 10(9)(a) in the context of Article 10 as a whole—in particular in combination with Article 10(5)—and in light of the object and purpose of the ECT suggests a negative answer. Thus, a modification of an exception in the sense towards increased compliance with the treaty may be equated with a partial withdrawal of a reservation.[25]

12   That said, the rules applicable to those reservations are quite specific. First, the existence of a monitoring system (reports reviewed periodically by the Secretariat) is unusual in the context of reservations. Second, Article 10(9) apparently leaves the choice to contracting parties, when preparing their reports, to signal their exceptions in the form of either a negative list or positive list. Positive list reporting seems not entirely in line with the rationale of reservations. Third, and more crucially, Article 10(5)(b) imposes on States an obligation to endeavour to gradually abandon their exceptions. While this does not seem to amount to an obligation of result, it might nevertheless appear to be in tension with the regime of true reservations, which does not specifically compel reserving States to envisage their withdrawal. Another issue with the qualification of Article 10 exceptions as reservations is the express prohibition of reservations provided under Article 46 of the ECT.

13   The NAFTA and the USMCA, which has replaced it since 1 July 2020, provide in very similar terms for a series of exceptions in the field of investment. Article 1108 (reservations and exceptions) of the NAFTA and Article 14.12 (non-conforming measures) of the USMCA each provide for a complex system of opt out or reservation of rights that are authorized by various treaty clauses and the form of which is specified in relevant Annexes. Article 1108(1) and (2) of the NAFTA and Article 14.12(1) of the USMCA provide for a series of exceptions to the application of specific treaty provisions.[26] The scope of these exceptions depends on the government level of the contracting party that is the author of existing non-conforming measures—whether federal, province/state, or local. Contracting parties list exempted or reserved existing non-conforming measures that have been taken at federal, state, or province level under their respective schedules appended to the relevant Annex. Under the NAFTA, contracting parties could list such existing non-conforming measures taken at state or province level up to two years after entry into force of the treaty. In both treaties, existing non-conforming measures taken by a local government are exempted generally and thus are not subject to listing in an Annex. Exceptions listed under parties' schedules appended to the NAFTA Annex I may also be accompanied by commitments to liberalization, for example providing for a phasing-out of the non-conforming measure.

14   Article 1108(3) and (4) of the NAFTA and Article 14.12(2) and (3) of the USMCA provide that, in respect of the same specific treaty provisions, contracting parties may adopt or maintain new non-conforming measures that fall within sectors, subsectors, or activities as listed by them under the relevant Annex, within defined limits.

---

[24] Guide to Practice (n 2), Guidelines 3.1.2 and 3.1.4.
[25] Guide to Practice (n 2), Guidelines 2.5.1 and 2.5.10.
[26] Namely, Articles 1102, 1103, 1106, and 1107 of the NAFTA and Articles 14.4, 14.5, 14.10, and 14.11 of the USMCA.

Contracting parties include their reservations within Schedules that are appended to the **15** corresponding Annexes. Both the NAFTA and the USMCA provide that Annexes thereto 'constitute an integral part' thereof[27] but they do not mention Schedules in this regard.[28] Annexes themselves do not specify that Schedules should be deemed an integral part thereof. This seems consistent with the distinction between treaty and 'reservations'. It is also in line with the fact that amendments decreasing the level of non-compliance of reservations with the treaty contained in the Schedules could be decided by the 'reserving' State unilaterally and were not subject to the procedure required for amending the treaty.

Insofar as their scope depends in part on the content of the schedules they refer to, exceptions **16** provided under Article 1108(1)(a)(i) and (ii), (2)–(4), and (6) of the NAFTA and Article 14.12(1)(a)(i) and (ii), (2), and (3) of the USMCA may be *prima facie* equated with expressly authorized reservations in the form of specified reservations, the form of which—but not the content—is specified by the treaty.[29] Indeed, the contemplated exceptions aim at modifying or excluding the legal effect of the treaty in respect of the reserving State. Besides, they are only triggered towards a contracting party upon such party having lodged a unilateral statement under its schedule. The fact that such exceptions may not have reciprocal effect is not determinative of their true nature (as reservations or alternatives).[30] Neither are their integration in the treaty (which is more apparent than real given the different status of Annexes and Schedules) or the possibility of subsequent modification (limited to a reduction of the non-compliance level of the exception) dispositive.[31] Under Article 1108(2) of the NAFTA, the fact that exceptions in respect of existing non-conforming measures maintained at province or state level could be made up to two years after entry into force of the treaty is not dispositive either[32] and may be explained by the organizational and logistical burden for contracting parties to coordinate with their sub-state entities and identify the relevant exceptions for each of them. This being said, whether such exceptions affect the entry into force of the treaty in respect of the reserving contracting party appears unclear. On the other hand, when commitments to liberalization accompany a given exception, whether such exception constitutes a reservation would seem even less clear.[33]

As their scope is not dependent upon the content of parties' schedules, exceptions provided **17** for under Article 1108(1)(a)(iii), (5), (7), and (8) of the NAFTA and under Article 14.12(1)(a)(iii), (4), and (5) of the USMCA may be more appropriately qualified as restrictive clauses since their operation is not subject to any unilateral act from contracting parties.

---

[27] Article 2201 of the NAFTA; Article 34.2 of the USMCA. The latter provision provides that appendices and footnotes also form part of the agreement.

[28] Thus, the modifications or additions to the Agreement that may be agreed between the parties ought to be understood as extending to the text and Annexes to the Agreement, but not to the Schedules.

[29] Guide to Practice (n 2), paras 10–11 of commentary to Guideline 3.1.2, and Guideline 3.1.4 and commentary. See also paras 9–10 of commentary to Guideline 4.1.1.

[30] Guide to Practice (n 2), Guidelines 4.2.4 and 4.2.5. Following a different perspective, members of the expert groups within the negotiation process of the draft OECD Multilateral Agreement on Investment seemed to regard the non-reciprocity of country schedules as distinguishing them from 'genuine' reservations. Consequently, they had agreed to replace the expression 'country-specific reservations' by 'country-specific exceptions': see OECD Doc DAFFE/MAI(98)7/REV1, 22 April 1998, at 89, fn 1.

[31] While late reservations are hardly compatible with the definition in Article 2(1)(d) VCLT, they are possible as long as they are expressly provided for in the treaty or do not gather objections from the other contracting parties (Guide to Practice (n 2), Guideline 2.3).

[32] The Vienna rules are of residual nature and may be derogated from in the treaty.

[33] Although the Guide to Practice (n 2) accepts that reservations may include a time-limit for their validity: see para 10 of commentary to Guideline 2.5.2.

18 The NAFTA and the USMCA are also interesting for the mechanism they provide for the purpose of implementing and interpreting the exceptions. Annexes provide for rules applicable to the interpretation of the exceptions or non-conforming measures to be included in country schedules appended thereto. Besides, Article 1132 of the NAFTA and Article 14.D.10 of the USMCA on the interpretation of Annexes provide that an arbitral tribunal may request the Free Trade Commission to provide its interpretation of an exception or non-conforming measure.

19 In its Chapter 8 on investment, the Comprehensive Economic and Trade Agreement between Canada and the European Union and its Member States (hereinafter CETA) that has been provisionally applied since 2017 also provides for a 'reservation' system very similar to those of the NAFTA and the USMCA.[34]

II. Investment decisions

20 The investment decisions are slender on the issue of reservations properly said for reasons explained above. The practice of specified reservations and alternatives essentially makes references to Articles 19–23 of the VCLT in the decisions inapposite since the treaty itself provides for an express and sufficient framework for the interpretation, application, validity, and effect of exceptions. Nevertheless, a few decisions have brought interesting perspectives on the consequences of the formal compilation of NAFTA-type reservations into Schedules attached to Annexes on the legal nature of these exceptions.

21 It is generally accepted that the interpretation of treaties and that of reservations—which follows the rules applicable to the interpretation of unilateral acts—are subject to distinct sets of rules.[35] Yet, the decisions seem to reflect a trend that might be in tension with this, which ultimately questions the legal nature of NAFTA-type reservations as reservations within the meaning of Article 2(1)(d) VCLT.

22 The case of *Mobil & Murphy v Canada* touches upon the core of the complex issue of determining the exact legal nature of NAFTA 'reservations'. The majority of the tribunal opined: 'Each NAFTA Party was free to identify and put forth its own reservations, which represented one Member's binding commitment. That said, it is important to stress that the reservations are an integral part of the NAFTA. The task of ascertaining the meaning of a reservation, like the task of interpreting any other treaty text, involves understanding the intention of the NAFTA Parties, and it is to be achieved by following the customary rules of interpretation of public international law, as reflected in Articles 31 and 32 of the VCLT.'[36]

---

[34] CETA, Article 8.15 and Annexes I and II. The system of reservations and exceptions established under Article 8.15 mirrors those of NAFTA Article 1108 and USMCA Article 14.12. Like for the NAFTA and the USMCA, Annexes provide guidelines governing the interpretation of the reservations they contain; see Annex I, Headnote—Reservations for existing measures and liberalisation commitments, para 4. The provision further provides for rules to resolve conflicts that may arise between distinct elements of reservations, namely, the description and the measure elements. A variation of this provision is contained under paras 4–5 of the Explanatory notes to Annex III (schedule of Canada). See also Regional Comprehensive Economic Partnership Agreement, 15 November 2020, entered into force on 1 January 2022, Article 10.8 and party schedules under Annex III.

[35] The interpretation of treaty provisions is subject to the rules of customary international law reflected in Articles 31–32 of the VCLT while the interpretation of reservations follows the principles articulated under Guideline 4.2.6 of the Guide to Practice (n 2). While distinct, these two sets of interpretative rules admittedly contain strikingly similar elements.

[36] *Mobil & Murphy v Canada*, ICSID Case No ARB(AF)/07/4, Decision on Liability and on Principles of Quantum, 22 May 2012, para 254 (hereafter *Mobil*).

Thus, on its face the 2012 decision in *Mobil* appears to assimilate NAFTA 'reservations' to treaty provisions on grounds that they are contained in schedules appended to the treaty and its annexes. The tribunal continued along those lines: 'In carrying out its task, the Tribunal is therefore guided by the principles of interpretation that are set forth in Articles 31 to 32 of the VCLT. These provisions are recognized by the NAFTA Parties to be applicable, both to the provisions of the NAFTA and to the reservations made by each Party.'[37]

The above-cited passage of the *Mobil* decision was later quoted with approval by the arbitral tribunal in the case of *Mesa v Canada*, in 2016.[38]

This approach has been criticized in the doctrine as overlooking the essentially unilateral character of NAFTA-type reservations, which in principle have not been negotiated between the parties. In particular, applying the rules of treaty interpretation to those reservations would overlook the essential role of the intent of the reserving State and substitute it with the intent of all States parties.[39] The characterization of NAFTA-type reservations as 'commitments' by the *Mobil* tribunal also drew the criticism of incompatibility with the definition of a *reservation*, which precisely aims at the opposite.[40]

The approach in *Mobil* may be contrasted with another decision. In a judgment on a request to set aside an arbitral award rendered on 3 December 2014 in the case of *Electricité de France (EDF) International S.A. v Republic of Hungary* under the ECT and UNCITRAL, the Swiss Federal Tribunal expressly relied on the ILC Guide to Practice to reject the restrictive interpretation of reservations to investment treaties. It observed in particular: 'a reservation must be interpreted in good faith, taking into account its author's intent as reflected by the text of the reservation first and by the object and the purpose of the treaty and the circumstances in which the reservation was formulated [. . .]. The official commentary of the Guide emphasizes, among other points, that with the possible exception of the treaties concerning human rights, there is no reason to take the view that, as a general rule, any reservation should be interpreted restrictively'.[41] The latter part also confirms that the approach to reservation interpretation in the context of international investment law is no different from that in general international law, which provides that no specifically narrow interpretation should be made of reservations.[42]

In the context of the ECT, the decision in the case of *MOL v Croatia* touched upon the issue of whether a listed item in Annex IA to the ECT should be treated as a reservation in the context of a treaty that expressly excludes reservations. In rejecting such approach the tribunal relied in particular on the express prohibition and construed the Annex as forming part of

---

[37] ibid para 255.
[38] *Mesa Power Group LLC v Canada*, PCA Case No 2012-17, Award, 24 March 2016, para 405 (hereafter *Mesa*).
[39] See, eg, EA Vázquez, 'The Energy Overhaul's Effect on Mexico's NAFTA Reservations Concerning Investments in the Oil Sector' (2016) 4(2) LatAm JITL 42 (hereafter Vázquez, 'The Energy Overhaul's Effect').
[40] ibid (n 40) 40–41. See also Third report on reservations to treaties, in (1998) YILC, Vol II, Part One, 250–51, paras 159–62; Guide to Practice (n 2), Guideline 1.5.3 and commentary thereto.
[41] Swiss Federal Tribunal, First Court of Civil Law, Judgment, 6 October 2015, case 4A_34/2015, para 3.5.1 (original in French). The tribunal supported its reasoning by express reference to Guideline 4.2.6 of the Guide to Practice (n 2) and to an article subsequently published by the Special Rapporteur: A Pellet, 'The ILC Guide to Practice on Reservations to Treaties: A General Presentation by the Special Rapporteur' (2013) 24 EJIL 1061 (hereafter Pellet, 'The ILC Guide').
[42] Guide to Practice (n 2), Guideline 4.2.6 and para 13 of commentary thereto.

the treaty provisions.[43] This situation may be contrasted with the practice in respect of reservations to International Labor Organization (ILO) Conventions. As the ILC highlights in the Guide to Practice, the ILO's practice to prohibit reservations that States may attempt to formulate in respect of ILO Conventions does not necessarily bar the exception devices contained in the Conventions (such as declarations making use of permitted exceptions or exclusions) from constituting authorized reservations.[44]

28   While the aforementioned words of the *Mobil* tribunal appear unfortunate, on closer inspection they are not radically antithetical to NAFTA-type reservations constituting genuine reservations. Indeed, the tribunal's considerations were not dispositive of the real issue that was the subject of the tribunal's reasoning. First, this point came up in the course of discussing whether reservations should be narrowly interpreted, which was also the point underlying the tribunal's consideration of the matter in *Mesa*. Both of them rejected claims of restrictive interpretation, thus confirming the general understanding reflected in the Guide to Practice.[45]

29   Second, and more crucially, the heart of the tribunal's reasoning in *Mobil* related not to the interpretation of Canada's reservation, but to the interpretation of treaty provisions, namely, Articles 1106, 1108, and para 2 of Annex I, against which the reservation had to be assessed.[46] These provisions were dispositive in determining the scope of the reservation. The *Mobil* tribunal's statement that Articles 31–32 VCLT 'are recognized by the NAFTA Parties to be applicable, both to the provisions of the NAFTA and to the reservations made by each Party'[47] ought to be read in this perspective. Thus, while the reservation was indeed an element of the tribunal's reasoning, what the tribunal seems to have had in mind with the above quotes was in fact limited to treaty provisions.

30   Likewise, in *Mesa*, the point was to interpret a treaty provision, i.e. the meaning of the term 'procurement' under Article 1108(7) of the NAFTA.[48] In any event, it would be a misleading perspective to exaggerate the—otherwise real—difference between the regimes of interpretation of treaties and of reservations.

D. Rationale for resorting to flexibility devices

31   The clear preference for resorting to expressly authorized reservations or to alternatives to reservations in multilateral international investment treaties may be explained by the greater flexibility they offer, which makes them more adequate to the alleged needs and 'realities' of international investments. Besides, when investment provisions are included in multilateral trade treaties—as is often the case, as shown above—they ought to be read in light of such treaties' object and purpose to foster an ever-increasing degree of liberalization of economic exchanges. This implies a philosophy of continuous evolution of the parties' conventional obligations, which is reflected, for instance, by the regular reconsideration of existing exceptions with a view to their progressive lifting. By contrast, some might be tempted

---

[43] *MOL Hungarian Oil and Gas Company Plc v Republic of Croatia*, ICSID Case No ARB/13/32, Award, 5 July 2022, paras 437–448.
[44] Guide to Practice (n 2), paras 3–4 of commentary to Guideline 1.1.6. Similarly, see also Guideline 1.3.3.
[45] Guide to Practice (n 2), para 13 of commentary to Guideline 4.2.6, relying on ICJ decisions regarding the interpretation of reservations accompanying optional declarations made under Article 36(2) of the ICJ Statute.
[46] *Mobil* (n 36) paras 255–56 and ff.
[47] ibid para 255.
[48] *Mesa* (n 38) para 406.

to object that the reciprocity principle of reservations[49] is not very conducive to the gradual realization of this aim because it would 'freeze' the level of mutual obligations—an argument which is however not fully convincing since reservations can always be lifted.[50] In any event, asymmetric commitments may indeed operate as an incentive for progressive change, for instance when exceptions or specified reservations lack reciprocal effect. Flexibility devices— including specified reservations and alternatives—constitute means to foster liberalization and protection in a context where States have different levels of development and may not be all prepared to grant the same rights to investors at the same pace.

Specified reservations offer a convenient way to this end by fixing rules that govern the way reservations may be made and incentives to their subsequent partial or total withdrawal. Alternatives to reservations enable States to resort to more flexible techniques such as phasing out commitments, rollback regular negotiations, ratchet effect or, to the contrary, modification of exceptions (including their increase) after the entry into force of the treaty, which reservations do not withstand. Moreover, the common feature of authorized reservations and alternatives is to provide for a comprehensive and explicit framework for planning liberalization commitments, by contrast to the 'unplanned' system of traditional reservations in which the validity of a reservation depends to a certain extent on possible objections thereto that might be made by other State parties, which makes it difficult to predict beforehand how a reservation will succeed and be valid. **32**

The appending of authorized reservations and alternatives to the treaty text also enhances the clarity and user-friendly character of investment treaties that are to be routinely used and interpreted not only by States but also by investors. On the other hand, as was shown above the formal appending of specified reservations and alternatives to reservations to the text of the treaty may at times result in some uncertainty in respect of their legal nature and in blurring the line between the distinct sets of rules that govern the interpretation of treaties and of reservations. In particular, where the rules of treaty interpretation endeavour to unveil the common intent of the parties to the treaty, the interpretation of reservations is only concerned with the intent of the reserving State.[51] **33**

E. Conclusion

When it comes to reservations, no special regime applies in the field of international investment law. International investment law practice provides no basis for challenging the ILC's finding of a single legal regime of treaty reservations.[52] Rather than altering the unity of the reservation regime, the object and purpose of investment treaties led treaty makers to favour **34**

---

[49] Guide to Practice (n 2), Guideline 4.2.4.
[50] VCLT, Article 22(1); Guide to Practice (n 2), Guideline 2.5.1. See also Guideline 2.5.3 that encourages States having made reservations to a treaty to 'undertake a periodic review of such reservations and consider withdrawing those which no longer serve their purpose'.
[51] See, eg, Vázquez, 'The Energy Overhaul's Effect' (n 39) 42. The role of the object and purpose of the treaty also differs in each situation. In the case of treaty provisions, the object and purpose of the treaty is one of the criteria for determining the meaning of a given provision (cf Article 31(1) of the VCLT). In the case of reservations, the object and purpose serve as a reference against which the reservation ought to be assessed in order to determine its validity.
[52] Guide to Practice (n 2), Guideline 3.1.5.6 and para 2 of the commentary thereto (in respect of human rights treaties); Second report on reservations to treaties, in YILC 1996, Vol II, Part One, 67, para 163; Pellet, 'The ILC Guide' (n 41) 1077–82.

authorized reservations (often in the form of specified reservations or opting out clauses) and alternative mechanisms as particularly adequate to the peculiar requirements and philosophy of such instruments and to their search for flexibility. Investment lawmakers have taken full advantage of the 'modulation regime' largely modelled on that of the reservations while complementing it with alternative devices, without undermining the general reservation regime. In contrast to the often-claimed singularity of human rights treaties with respect (notably) to the reservation regime, this situation does not entail a threat of fragmentation.

Selected literature

Corten O and Klein P (eds), *The Vienna Conventions on the Law of Treaties—A Commentary*, Vol 1 (OUP 2011) 405–627 (entries on Articles 19–23 of the 1969 and 1986 Vienna Conventions).

Guide to Practice on Reservations to Treaties, adopted by the Commission at its sixty-third session, YILC 2011, Vol II, Part Three.

Pellet A, 'La C.I.J. et les réserves aux traités—Remarques cursives sur une révolution jurisprudentielle' in Andō N et al (eds), *Liber Amicorum Judge Shigeru Oda* (Kluwer 2002).

Pellet A, 'The ILC Guide to Practice on Reservations to Treaties: A General Presentation by the Special Rapporteur' (2013) 24 EJIL 1061.

Potestà M, 'An Appellate Mechanism for ICSID Awards and Modification of the ICSID Convention under Article 41 of the VCLT' in Shirlow E and Gore KN (eds), *The Vienna Convention on the Law of Treaties in Investor–State Disputes: History, Evolution and Future* (Wolters Kluwer 2022).

Vázquez EA, 'The Energy Overhaul's Effect on Mexico's NAFTA Reservations Concerning Investments in the Oil Sector' (2016) 4(2) LatAm JITL 27.

Selected decisions

Reservations to the Convention on Genocide (Advisory Opinion) [1951] ICJ Rep 15.

Mesa Power Group LLC v Canada, PCA Case No 2012-17, Award, 24 March 2016.

Mobil & Murphy v Canada, ICSID Case No ARB(AF)/07/4, Decision on liability and on principles of quantum, 22 May 2012.

Swiss Federal Tribunal, First Court of Civil Law, Judgment, 6 October 2015, case 4A_34/2015.

MOL Hungarian Oil and Gas Company Plc v Republic of Croatia, ICSID Case No ARB/ 13/ 32, Award, 5 July 2022.

Article 24 of the VCLT

Entry into force

Tania Voon

1. A treaty enters into force in such manner and upon such date as it may provide or as the negotiating States may agree.

2. Failing any such provision or agreement, a treaty enters into force as soon as consent to be bound by the treaty has been established for all the negotiating States.

3. When the consent of a State to be bound by a treaty is established on a date after the treaty has come into force, the treaty enters into force for that State on that date, unless the treaty otherwise provides.

4. The provisions of a treaty regulating the authentication of its text, the establishment of the consent of States to be bound by the treaty, the manner or date of its entry into force, reservations, the functions of the depositary and other matters arising necessarily before the entry into force of the treaty apply from the time of the adoption of its text.

A. Introduction	1	C. Consent to be bound through notification or deposit of instrument	11
B. Non-retroactivity of treaties	4	D. Conclusion	17

A. Introduction

Commentary by the International Law Commission (ILC) on its draft articles on the law of treaties (preceding the Vienna Convention on the Law of Treaties (VCLT))[1] suggests that at least some aspects of Article 24 of the VCLT can be regarded as reflecting customary international law or perhaps a general principle of law. The ILC referred to the equivalent of Article 24(2) reflecting a 'general presumption', 'existing practice', and an 'existing general rule', and to the equivalent of Article 24(3) laying down 'an undisputed rule'.[2] Article 24(4) was subsequently introduced with limited discussion and has also therefore been regarded as reflecting customary international law.[3]

1

---

[1] Vienna Convention on the Law of Treaties (opened for signature 23 May 1969, entered into force 27 January 1980) 1155 UNTS 331 (hereafter VCLT).
[2] International Law Commission, *Draft Articles on the Law of Treaties with Commentaries* (1966) 210 (hereafter ILC, *Draft Articles*).
[3] H Krieger, 'Article 24: Entry into Force' in O Dörr and K Schmalenbach (eds), *Vienna Convention on the Law of Treaties: A Commentary* (Springer 2012) 391, 393.

2   Article 24 of the VCLT on entry into force of treaties is closely related to Article 25 of the VCLT on the provisional application of treaties, which is discussed in a separate entry.[4] Article 24(2), (3), and (4) refer to a State's consent to be bound by a treaty, which can be expressed by signature (Article 12), an exchange of instruments constituting a treaty (Article 13), ratification, acceptance, or approval (Article 14) or accession (Article 15). Article 16 VCLT provides the general rule that instruments of ratification, acceptance, approval, or accession establish the consent of a State to be bound by a treaty from a particular point in time. The notion of non-retroactivity of treaties (addressed in Article 28) is also related to the date of entry into force as determined by Article 24.[5]

3   This entry focuses on jurisprudence of the International Court of Justice (ICJ) and investment arbitration tribunals in connection with Article 24. It addresses in turn cases concerning: the principle of non-retroactivity of treaties as it relates to Article 24 (Part B); and a State's consent to be bound through notification or deposit of instruments (Part C). These two areas have given rise to disputes before the ICJ and investment tribunals that together explore the relationship between Article 24 of the VCLT and Articles 28 and 16 of the VCLT, respectively. The cases demonstrate a consistent respect for Article 24 while also revealing the dependence of its effects on the context and wording of the treaty under examination: most commonly the ICJ Statute or a Bilateral Investment Treaty (BIT).

B. Non-retroactivity of treaties

4   The 'general principle of non-retroactivity'[6] of treaties is set out in Article 28 of the VCLT: in general, treaty provisions do not bind parties in relation to acts or facts that took place or situations that ceased to exist before the treaty entered into force for that party. Thus, no treaty breach or international responsibility will generally arise with respect to a State's actions taken before the treaty's entry into force.[7]

5   Certain qualifications apply to the principle of non-retroactivity. Pursuant to Article 18 of the VCLT, a State that has signed or expressed consent to be bound by a treaty generally has an obligation not to defeat the object and purpose of a treaty prior to its entry into force.[8] Article 25 of the VCLT provides circumstances in which a treaty will be applied provisionally pending its entry into force.[9] Under Article 24(4) of the VCLT, certain provisions of a treaty apply from the time the treaty text is adopted, and before its entry into force, such as provisions regarding the establishment of the consent of States to be bound by the treaty and the manner or date of its entry into force. Thus, for example, the Court of Justice of the European Union referred in 2002 to Article 24(4) of the VCLT (as a rule of customary international law) in explaining why Article 30(4)(iii) of the Convention on Nuclear Safety[10] (concerning

---

[4] See in this Commentary: Tania Voon, 'Article 25 VCLT: Provisional Application'.
[5] See in this Commentary: Ben Juratowich and Jackie McArthur, 'Article 28 VCLT: Non-retroactivity'.
[6] See *Spence International Investments, LLC v Republic of Costa Rica*, ICSID Case No UNCT/13/2, Interim Award, 25 October 2016, para 215.
[7] *Mondev International Ltd v United States*, ICSID Case No ARB(AF)/99/2, Award, 11 October 2002 [68] (see also [74]), citing ARSIWA Article 13. See also *Renco Group, Inc v Republic of Peru*, PCA Case No 2019–46, Decision on Expedited Preliminary Objections, 30 June 2020, para 146.
[8] See in this Commentary: Belinda McRae, 'Article 18: Obligation not to defeat the object and purpose of a treaty prior to its entry into force'.
[9] See in this Commentary: Tania Voon, 'Article 25 VCLT: Provisional application'.
[10] Convention on Nuclear Safety (opened for signature 20 September 1994, entered into force 24 October 1996) 1963 UNTS 293.

communications to the depository upon becoming a party) applied to the European Atomic Energy Community before the Convention's entry into force.[11]

While Article 24(4) may be seen as an exception to the general principle of non-retroactivity, the remainder of Article 24 may be seen as a confirmation of that principle: in general, a treaty does not have legal force until after the relevant States have consented to be bound by it. Nevertheless, a treaty itself may modify the default rule against non-retroactivity in Article 28, as well as the default rules that connect entry into force with consent to be bound in Article 24(2) or Article 24(3). Identifying when a treaty allows for retrospective application, by its terms or nature, has created some difficulty in both public international law and international investment law, in some cases with reference to Article 24.

In *Bosnia and Herzegovina v Yugoslavia* (1996), the majority of the ICJ declined to pinpoint the precise date on which the Convention on the Prevention and Punishment of the Crime of Genocide[12] (Genocide Convention) entered into force for Bosnia and Herzegovina, whether on 6 March 1992 or 29 December 1992, since in any case it was a party on the date of its application to the Court.[13] The majority rejected Yugoslavia's position that the Court had jurisdiction to deal with only those events subsequent to the date on which the Genocide Convention applied as between the parties. The majority held that the Genocide Convention, and particularly Article IX on which its jurisdiction was based, does not contain such a limitation on the scope of its jurisdiction *ratione temporis*. One reason for this conclusion appears to be the *erga omnes* nature of obligations in the Geneva Convention.[14] The decision may therefore be understood as falling within the qualification in Article 28 of the VCLT, 'Unless a different intention ... is otherwise established', which the ILC has stated 'allow[s] for cases where the very nature of the treaty ... indicates that it is intended to have certain retroactive effects'.[15] The majority's conclusion may alternatively be understood as reading Article IX of the Genocide Convention as providing for the submission to the ICJ of 'disputes' existing after its entry into force for the relevant parties, even where such disputes concern earlier acts or facts.[16]

In dissent in that case, Judge ad hoc Milenko Kreća referred to the 'rule of general international law' in VCLT Article 24(3) and to the ILC's commentary on what is now VCLT Article 28 (containing a 'general rule of non-retroactivity').[17] He considered that neither the Genocide Convention nor its Article IX has retroactive effect and therefore that the Convention applies only to 'events and situations which took place after ... the Convention became applicable between Bosnia and Herzegovina and Yugoslavia'.[18] He concluded that the conditions of jurisdiction and admissibility had not been met.[19]

---

[11] *Commission of the European Communities v Council of the European Union* (C-29/99) Opinion of Advocate (13 December 2001) [2002] ECR I-11221, 11246, para 84.
[12] Convention on the Prevention and Punishment of the Crime of Genocide (opened for signature 9 December 1948, entered into force 12 January 1951) 78 UNTS 277.
[13] *Application of the Convention on the Prevention and Punishment of the Crime of Genocide (Bosnia and Herzegovina v Yugoslavia)* (Preliminary Objections) [1996] ICJ Rep 595, para 23.
[14] ibid para 34 (referring to para 31).
[15] ILC, *Draft Articles* (n 2) 212–13.
[16] ibid 212.
[17] *Application of the Convention on the Prevention and Punishment of the Crime of Genocide (Bosnia and Herzegovina v Yugoslavia)* (Preliminary Objections: Dissenting Opinion of Judge Kreća) [1996] ICJ Rep 658, para 120.
[18] ibid para 120.
[19] ibid.

9 In *Hrvatska elektroprivreda dd v Slovenia* (2009), the majority of the tribunal (established under the auspices of the International Centre for Settlement of Investment Disputes (ICSID)) agreed with the investor claimant that a 2001 treaty between Croatia and Slovenia, which entered into force on 11 March 2003, had the effect of creating a financial settlement between the two countries in relation to their companies as of 30 June 2002.[20] The majority reached this conclusion despite citing Articles 24 and 28 of the VCLT.[21] In dissent, Jan Paulsson challenged the majority's decision as giving the treaty 'retroactive effect ... when neither its express terms nor its object require retroactivity'.[22] The majority's approach may be understood as a different interpretation of the treaty rather than a challenge to the principle of non-retroactivity, which it characterized as a non-issue in the circumstances of the dispute.[23]

10 These two cases illustrate that, in both public international law and international investment law, the question of whether and when a treaty has entered into force pursuant to Article 24 of the VCLT does not necessarily resolve questions of temporal jurisdiction or retroactive effects. This conclusion arises in part from the flexibility in Article 28 of the VCLT, which requires interpretation of the relevant treaty to determine whether a judicial or arbitral tribunal has jurisdiction over facts existing before entry into force and whether the treaty is otherwise intended to have retroactive effect.

C. Consent to be bound through notification or deposit of instrument

11 In the ICJ, some disputes have arisen regarding when or whether a State has consented to be bound by a treaty through the deposit of an instrument of ratification, acceptance, approval, or accession pursuant to Article 16 of the VCLT. The existence and timing of deposit of such an instrument may in turn affect the date of entry into force of the treaty pursuant to Article 24(2) or (3) of the VCLT. A corresponding question may arise in international investment arbitration, where a BIT provides for its entry into force through exchange of notices between the parties, pursuant to Article 24(1) of the VCLT. These scenarios will be considered in turn.

12 In *Nicaragua v United States of America* (1984), the ICJ had to determine whether Nicaragua had accepted the compulsory jurisdiction of the Court based on Article 36(5) of the ICJ Statute. That provision deems as acceptances of the compulsory jurisdiction of the Court 'Declarations made under Article 36 of the Statute of the Permanent Court of International Justice and which are still in force'.[24] Nicaragua never became a party to the Statute of the Permanent Court because it did not deposit an instrument of ratification of the Protocol of Signature.[25] Nevertheless, the ICJ held that it had jurisdiction on the basis that Nicaragua's

---

[20] *Hrvatska elektroprivreda dd v Slovenia*, ICSID Case No ARB/05/24, Decision on Treaty Interpretation, 12 June 2009, para 202(A)(i).
[21] ibid paras 161–62 (see also reference to Article 24 by Slovenia, para 150).
[22] *Hrvatska elektroprivreda dd v Slovenia*, ICSID Case No ARB/05/24, Decision on Treaty Interpretation: Individual Opinion of Jan Paulsson, 12 June 2009, para 5.
[23] ibid para 195.
[24] ICJ Statute, Article 36(5).
[25] *Military and Paramilitary Activities in and against Nicaragua (Nicaragua v United States of America)*, Jurisdiction of the Court and Admissibility of the Application [1984] ICJ Rep 392, paras 16, 25–26 (hereafter *Military and Paramilitary Activities*, Jurisdiction).

declaration accepting the compulsory jurisdiction of the Permanent Court under Article 36(2) of the Statute of the Permanent Court was 'still in force' within the meaning of Article 36(5) of the ICJ Statute.[26] In dissent, Judge Stephen Schwebel referred to Article 24(2) of the VCLT in maintaining that Nicaragua's declaration could not be binding or in force within the meaning of Article 36(5) of the ICJ Statute given that Nicaragua was not a party to the Statute of the Permanent Court.[27]

In *Cameroon v Nigeria* (1998), the ICJ considered Nigeria's contention that Cameroon's declaration accepting the compulsory jurisdiction of the Court, deposited with the United Nations Secretary-General on 3 March 1994, did not take effect until the Secretary-General transmitted copies of the declaration to the parties to the ICJ Statute (pursuant to its Article 36(4)) nearly a year later.[28] Relying on previous caselaw, the Court determined that such a declaration takes effect on the date of deposit.[29] The Court pointed out that the provisions of the VCLT 'may only be applied to declarations *by analogy*' because 'the regime for depositing and transmitting declarations' under Article 36(4) of the ICJ Statute 'is distinct from the regime envisaged for treaties by the Vienna Convention'.[30] Nevertheless, the Court considered the two regimes consistent (as confirmed by the ILC),[31] in that Articles 16 and 24 of the VCLT reflect the 'general rule' that a treaty enters into force for a State on the day of deposit of the relevant instrument of ratification, acceptance, approval or accession to the treaty.[32]

In *CSOB v The Slovak Republic* (1999), an ICSID tribunal considered as one basis for its jurisdiction the Agreement between the Government of the Slovak Republic and the Government of the Czech Republic regarding the Promotion and Reciprocal Investments (Slovak–Czech BIT), Article 8 of which provides for the settlement of investment disputes under the Convention on the Settlement of Investment Disputes between States and Nationals of Other States[33] or the arbitration rules of the United Nations Commission on International Trade Law (UNCITRAL).[34] The Slovak–Czech BIT was signed on 23 November 1992. According to the Court, in stating that 'each Party shall give notice to the other Party of the completion of the constitutional formalities required for this Agreement to enter into force', Article 12 of the BIT indicated pursuant to Article 24(1) of the VCLT that an exchange of notices (which never took place) was required for the BIT to enter into force.[35] The Court found that 'uncertainties relating to the entry into force of the BIT prevent that instrument from providing a sound basis upon which to found the parties' consent to ICSID jurisdiction'.[36]

A similar situation arose in *Besserglik v Mozambique* (2019), which was brought under ICSID's Additional Facility Rules pursuant to the Agreement Between the Government of the Republic of South Africa and the Government of the Republic of Mozambique for the Promotion and Reciprocal Protection of Investments, signed on 6 May 1997 (South

---

[26] ibid para 42.
[27] ibid paras 16, 20, and 24.
[28] *Case Concerning the Land and Maritime Boundary between Cameroon and Nigeria* (*Cameroon v Nigeria*) Preliminary Objections [1998] ICJ Rep 275 [22] (hereafter *Cameroon v Nigeria*).
[29] ibid paras 25–27.
[30] ibid para 30 (emphasis added) (citing *Military and Paramilitary Activities*, Jurisdiction (n 25) para 63).
[31] ILC, *Draft Articles* (n 2) 201.
[32] *Cameroon v Nigeria* (n 28) para 31.
[33] Convention on the Settlement of Investment Disputes between States and Nationals of Other States, opened for signature 18 March 1965, 575 UNTS 159 (entered into force 14 October 1966).
[34] *Ceskoslovenska Obchodni Banka, AS v The Slovak Republic*, ICSID Case No ARB/97/4, Decision of the Tribunal on Objections to Jurisdiction, 24 May 1999, para 37.
[35] ibid para 39.
[36] ibid para 43.

Africa–Mozambique BIT). The ICSID tribunal in this dispute characterized Article 12(1) of this treaty as a provision identifying the manner and date of entry into force as specified in Article 24(1) of the VCLT.[37] Article 12(1) of the BIT provided for the treaty to 'enter into force on the day following the date of receipt of the last notification' between the parties that 'their respective constitutional requirements for entry into force of this Agreement have been fulfilled'.[38] Noting that both South Africa and Mozambique denied that such notifications were ever issued, the tribunal determined that 'it cannot, on the basis of the evidence on the record, conclude that the BIT is in force'.[39] Although it considered this conclusion sufficient to resolve the case, the tribunal went on to state that the 'requirement of reciprocal notifications' for entry into force pursuant to Article 12(1) of the BIT and Article 24 of the VCLT 'cannot be presumed to be in existence by invoking the doctrine of estoppel'.[40]

16 These cases affirm the importance of the treaty under examination in giving effect to the provisions of Article 24 of the VCLT. According to the ICJ, declarations accepting the compulsory jurisdiction of the ICJ under Article 36 of the ICJ Statute are not treaties and therefore will not necessarily follow the same rules as those set out in the VCLT, although those rules may be relevant by analogy. According to the arbitral awards outlined above, Article 24(1) of the VCLT means that a BIT will not enter into force without complying with formalities required in the BIT for that purpose.

D. Conclusion

17 As Article 24 of the VCLT has been mentioned only occasionally in rulings of the ICJ and investment treaty tribunals, it is difficult to discern general patterns regarding its significance and interpretation in public international law and international investment law. A few observations can nevertheless be made. First, Article 24 interacts with Article 28 of the VCLT to heighten the importance of the date of entry into force, since a treaty will usually not have effects with respect to acts or facts that took place or situations that ceased to exist before that date. However, the cases of *Bosnia and Herzegovina v Yugoslavia* and *Hrvatska elektroprivreda dd v Slovenia* show how the ICJ and investment tribunals may both read specific treaties as having retroactive effects depending on their terms and nature. Second, according to the ICJ in *Cameroon v Nigeria*, Article 24 interacts with Article 16 of the VCLT to impose a general rule that where consent to be bound is expressed through deposit of an instrument of ratification, acceptance, approval, or accession, that consent is established and the treaty enters into force on the day of deposit. Nonetheless, Articles 16 and 24 are both broadly worded such that the terms of the particular treaty may change the general rules. Pursuant to Article 24(1) of the VCLT, as shown in *CSOB v The Slovak Republic* and *Besserglik v Mozambique*, a BIT that requires exchange of notices of ratification before it enters into force cannot do so in the absence of such an exchange.

---

[37] *Besserglik v Mozambique*, ICSID Case No ARB(AF)/14/2, Award, 28 October 2019, paras 328–30.
[38] ibid para 330.
[39] ibid paras 369 and 371.
[40] ibid paras 371 and 421.

Selected literature

Aust A, 'Article 24—1969 Vienna Convention' in Corten O and Klein P (eds), *The Vienna Convention on the Law of Treaties—A Commentary* (OUP 2011) 628.

Krieger H, 'Article 24: Entry into force' in Dörr O and Schmalenbach K (eds), *Vienna Convention on the Law of Treaties: A Commentary* (Springer 2012).

Selected decisions

Besserglik v Mozambique, ICSID Case No ARB(AF)/14/2, Award, 28 October 2019.

Case Concerning the Land and Maritime Boundary between Cameroon and Nigeria (Cameroon v Nigeria) (Preliminary Objections) [1998] ICJ Rep 275.

Article 25 of the VCLT

Provisional application

*Tania Voon**

1. A treaty or a part of a treaty is applied provisionally pending its entry into force if:
(a) the treaty itself so provides; or
(b) the negotiating States have in some other manner so agreed.

2. Unless the treaty otherwise provides or the negotiating States have otherwise agreed, the provisional application of a treaty or a part of a treaty with respect to a State shall be terminated if that State notifies the other States between which the treaty is being applied provisionally of its intention not to become a party to the treaty.

A. Introduction	1	II. Implications of the VCLT and the ILC Guide for Understanding ECT Article 45(1)	24
B. Nature of agreement for provisional application	8		
C. Impact of domestic law	14	D. Impact of ratification and non-ratification: termination of provisional application	28
I. Analysis of ECT Article 45(1) in investment treaty disputes	15		
		E. Conclusion	33

A. Introduction

1 Article 25 of the Vienna Convention on the Law of Treaties (VCLT) on provisional application of treaties is closely related to Article 24 of the VCLT, on entry into force. The provisional application of treaties creates obligations prior to entry into force for a given party, just as Article 18 imposes an obligation not to defeat the object and purpose of a treaty prior to its entry into force.

2 In its 1966 commentary on the relevant draft article, the International Law Commission (ILC) described provisional application as 'a practice which occurs with some frequency to-day'.[1] The ILC also recognized that an agreement for a treaty to apply provisionally (originally described in draft Article 22 as entering into force provisionally) 'ha[s] legal effect'.[2] In 2007, the tribunal in *Kardassopoulos v Georgia* suggested that Article 25 merely shows that 'States may agree to provisional application of a treaty if they so wish … it does not

---

* I thank the Academic Research Service of Melbourne Law School for valuable research assistance. All opinions and any errors are mine.
[1] ILC, *Draft Articles on the Law of Treaties with Commentaries* (1966) 210 (hereafter ILC, *Draft Articles*).
[2] ibid.

establish that there is a general rule of customary international law allowing for provisional application apart from the express agreement of the States concerned'.[3] Nevertheless, several authors suggest that Article 25 of the VCLT (or at least Article 25(1)) reflects customary international law today.[4] Moreover, the provisional application of a treaty can have far-reaching, long-term legal effects, as shown by cases discussed below.

The ILC included the topic 'provisional application of treaties' in its work program in 2012.[5] This work continued for close to a decade, in order to clarify the meaning of VCLT Article 25 in view of 'continuing uncertainty among States' and the use of Article 25 'in an inconsistent and at times even rather confusing manner'.[6] In 2021, the work concluded with the ILC adopting a Guide to Provisional Application of Treaties, which includes an annex of examples of existing provisions on provisional application, as well as commentaries to the Guide.[7] Guideline 6 confirms that the 'provisional application of a treaty or a part of a treaty produces a legally binding obligation ... except to the extent that the treaty otherwise provides or it is otherwise agreed'.[8] Guideline 8 states that '[t]he breach of an obligation arising under a treaty or a part of a treaty that is applied provisionally entails international responsibility in accordance with the applicable rules of international law'.[9]

Despite this long exploration of provisional application of treaties by the ILC, Article 25 of the VCLT does not appear to have been examined in depth in caselaw of the ICJ or other international law contexts beyond international investment law. This entry therefore focuses on consideration of provisional application of treaties in the context of disputes in international investment law.

Part B of this entry explores the nature of the agreement for a treaty to apply provisionally. Such an agreement is found most commonly in the treaty itself (such as in the Energy Charter Treaty (ECT)), but the general terms of VCLT Article 25(1) provide a wide scope for other forms of such agreement. The ILC Guide to Provisional Application provides further clarification, making clear that a unilateral decision by a State to apply a treaty provisionally will not constitute an agreement to do so in the absence of acceptance by the other treaty parties.

Part C of this entry explores the area that has caused the most controversy regarding provisional application in international investment law, particularly under the ECT: the potential for domestic law to limit provisional application of a treaty. While the VCLT (in respect of entry into force of a treaty) and the ILC Guide (in respect of provisional application of a treaty) make clear that internal laws cannot be used to justify performance of treaty obligations, the wording of the ECT provision on provisional application leaves several matters

---

[3] *Kardassopoulos v Georgia*, ICSID Case No ARB/05/18, Decision on Jurisdiction, 6 July 2007 para 216 (see also paras 218 and 244) (hereafter *Kardassopoulos v Georgia*). See generally M Belz, 'Provisional Application of the Energy Charter Treaty: *Kardassopoulos v Georgia* and Improving Provisional Application in Multilateral Treaties' (2008) 22 Emory Int'l L Rev 727.
[4] See, eg, C Brölmann and G Den Dekker, 'Treaties, Provisional Application' in *Max Planck Encyclopedias of International Law* (February 2020) 7; ME Villiger, *Commentary on the 1969 Vienna Convention on the Law of Treaties* (Martinus Nijhoff Publishers 2009) 357; cf T Ishikawa, 'Provisional Application of Treaties at the Crossroads between International and Domestic Law' (2016) 31(2) ICSID Rev 270, 271 (distinguishing the customary status of Article 25(1) from Article 25(2)).
[5] ILC, *Report of the International Law Commission: Sixty-fourth Session* (2012) UN Doc A/67/10, para 141.
[6] ILC, *Sixth Report on the Provisional Application of Treaties by Juan Manuel Gómez-Robledo, Special Rapporteur* (24 February 2020) UN Doc A/CN.4/738, para 18 (hereafter ILC, *Sixth report*).
[7] ILC, *Draft guidelines and draft annex constituting the Guide to Provisional Application of Treaties, with commentaries thereto* (2021) UN Doc A/76/10 (hereafter ILC, *Guide to Provisional Application*).
[8] ibid 78.
[9] ibid 80.

under debate regarding the consistency of provisional application of that treaty with domestic law.

7   As seen in Part D of this entry (which concerns termination of provisional application), these uncertainties concerning provisional application of the ECT are exacerbated by the fact that even following termination of such provisional application on the basis of an intention not to ratify the treaty (as, for example, by Russia), obligations regarding pre-existing investments continue for an additional 20 years under the ECT's survival clause. Termination of provisional application will also most commonly arise through ratification of a treaty by a party that was previously only provisionally applying it.

B. Nature of agreement for provisional application

8   Article 25(1) of the VCLT makes clear that a treaty or part of a treaty applies provisionally if (a) the treaty itself so provides or if (b) the relevant negotiating States have so agreed 'in some other manner'.[10] ILC Guideline 3 is titled 'General rule' and reflects VCLT Article 25(1): 'A treaty or part of a treaty is applied provisionally pending its entry into force between the States ... concerned, if the treaty itself so provides, or if in some other manner it has been so agreed.'[11]

9   The clearest instances of parties agreeing that a treaty is to apply provisionally pending its entry into force are when the treaty itself so provides, in accordance with Article 25(1)(a) of the VCLT. Nevertheless, many of the investment treaty arbitrations including disputes over provisional application relate to the ECT, which states explicitly in Article 45(1) that 'Each signatory agrees to apply this Treaty provisionally pending its entry into force for such signatory …, to the extent that such provisional application is not inconsistent with its constitution, laws or regulations'.[12] As elaborated further in Part C below, several tribunals have indicated that provisional application of the ECT includes provisional application of Article 26 of the ECT,[13] which generally entails unconditional consent to jurisdiction of the International Centre for Settlement of Investment Disputes (ICSID).[14]

10 Under Article 45(2) of the ECT, a signatory may issue a declaration at the time of signing 'that it is not able to accept provisional application',[15] in which case only Part VII (on structure and institutions) applies provisionally pending entry into force for that signatory, 'to the extent that such provisional application is not inconsistent with its laws or regulations'.[16] In the absence of such a declaration, the ECT will generally apply provisionally pending entry into force for the relevant signatory,[17] although debates may arise concerning: the extent to which domestic laws allow for provisional application, as recognized in Article 45(1) and

---

[10] VCLT, Article 25(1)(b).
[11] ILC, *Guide to Provisional Application* (n 7) 72.
[12] Energy Charter Treaty (hereinafter ECT), Article 45(1).
[13] See, eg, *Plama Consortium Ltd v Bulgaria*, ICSID Case No ARB/03/24, Decision on Jurisdiction, 8 February 2005 [140] (hereafter *Plama v Bulgaria*).
[14] ECT, Articles 26(3)(a), 26(4)(a)(i).
[15] ECT, Article 45(2)(a). See, eg, *AES Summit Generation Limited v Hungary*, ICSID Case No ARB/07/22, Award, 17 September 2010 para 6.4.1.
[16] ECT, Article 45(2)(c).
[17] See *Plama v Bulgaria* (n 13) para 140.

discussed in Part C below; or the effect of subsequent ratification or non-ratification on provisional application, as discussed in Part D below.

The potential for agreements made outside the text of a treaty that may result in the treaty applying provisionally is uncertain. The decision in *Von Pezold v Zimbabwe* (2015) suggests that 'diplomatic communications by relatively obscure state actors can suffice as intent to be bound by provisional application'.[18] In that case, an ICSID tribunal determined that it had jurisdiction from 18 September 1996 on the basis of provisional application[19] of the Bilateral Investment Treaty (BIT) between Zimbabwe and Germany that was signed on 29 September 1995 and entered into force on 14 April 2000.[20] This provisional application was important because some of the claims related to alleged breaches taking place in January 2000.[21] The agreement for provisional application was based largely on a note sent by the Zimbabwean Minister of Finance to the German Ambassador, dated 18 September 1996, stating that Zimbabwe would 'apply the Agreement on a preliminary basis, as from the date of this Note, pending the Agreement's formal entry into force'.[22] The tribunal considered that the Note reflected an agreement because of Germany's assistance in drafting it and Germany's 'subsequent conduct', such as evidenced by a letter from the German Ambassador to the German Ministry of Affairs on 19 September 1996 advising that 'the "exchange of notes" regarding provisional application of the ... BIT had been completed'.[23] An application for annulment of this decision (not challenging the provisional application) was dismissed.[24]

The use of the words 'in some other manner' in ILC Guideline 3,[25] as in VCLT Article 25(1), does not provide any further clarity as to the scope or types of ways in which parties may agree to provisional application. However, ILC Guideline 4 clarifies that provisional application could be agreed through the treaty itself, a separate treaty, or:

any other means or arrangements, including:

(i) a resolution ... by an international organization or at an intergovernmental conference ... reflecting the agreement of the States or international organizations concerned;
(ii) a declaration by a State or by an international organization that is accepted by the other States or international organizations concerned.[26]

Application of this guideline could assist in determining whether an exchange of notes such as that in *Von Pezold v Zimbabwe* constitutes an agreement to provisional application. Importantly, such an exchange must reflect acceptance by both parties rather than a unilateral announcement.[27]

---

[18] WJ Simonsick, 'Is Provisional Application on the Rise in International Investment Agreements? The European Union's Recent Treaty Practice and the Curious Case of *Von Pezold*' (2019) 88 Nordic JIL 180, 182.
[19] *Von Pezold v Zimbabwe*, ICSID Case No ARB/10/15, Award, 28 July 2015, paras 338 and 343.
[20] ibid para 85.
[21] ibid para 328.
[22] ibid para 334 (see also para 340).
[23] ibid para 341.
[24] *Von Pezold v Zimbabwe*, ICSID Case No ARB/10/15, Annulment, 12 November 2018, para 316(1).
[25] ILC, *Guide to Provisional Application* (n 7) 72.
[26] ibid 75.
[27] See UNGA, *Report of the International Law Commission: Seventieth session* (2018) UN Doc A/73/10, 213 (hereafter ILC, *Report of the 70th session*).

C. Impact of domestic law

14 As noted above, ECT Article 45(1) provides for '[e]ach signatory ... to apply this Treaty provisionally pending entry into force' for that signatory, 'to the extent that such provisional application is not inconsistent with its constitution, laws or regulations'.[28] This provision therefore creates scope for debate as to the consistency of provisional application of the treaty, or part of the treaty, with a signatory's domestic legal framework.

I. Analysis of ECT Article 45(1) in investment treaty disputes

15 The tribunal in *Kardassopoulos v Georgia* determined that it had jurisdiction under ECT Article 26 on the basis of provisional application of that treaty by Georgia and Greece.[29] Georgia and Greece signed the ECT on 17 December 1994, and the treaty entered into force for these countries on 16 April 1998.[30] The tribunal rejected the claimant's argument that a State cannot rely on the 'proviso' to ECT Article 45(1) regarding inconsistency with domestic laws in the absence of a declaration under ECT Article 45(2).[31] Regarding Georgian law, the tribunal found that Article 20 of the Law on International Treaties (which explicitly addressed provisional application) was inapplicable to the acts in dispute because it was not adopted until 16 October 1997 and lacked retroactive effect.[32] Regarding both Georgian and Greek law, the tribunal considered that provisions not dealing with provisional application but requiring entry into force for treaties to prevail over domestic law do 'not necessarily imply that provisional application of treaties is not permitted'.[33]

16 Similar questions have arisen in a series of cases involving Russia, which signed the ECT on 17 December 1994 but never ratified it. Several arbitral tribunals and domestic courts have therefore examined ECT Article 45(1) in the context of Russian law. The most prominent cases (leading to an award of the largest known amount of damages in investment treaty arbitration) were brought by former Yukos majority shareholders: *Yukos Universal Limited, Veteran Petroleum Limited, and Hulley Enterprises Ltd*.[34] Similar but not identical Interim Awards on Jurisdiction and Admissibility were released in these three cases on 30 November 2009.[35] The tribunals in these cases (composed of the same three arbitrators) found that they had jurisdiction pursuant to ECT Article 26 on the basis of provisional application of the ECT by Russia.[36] The award in *Yukos v Russia* illustrates the reasoning in these awards.

---

[28] ECT, Article 45(1).
[29] *Kardassopoulos v Georgia* (n 3) paras 239, 246 and 248.
[30] ibid paras 201 and 203.
[31] ibid paras 227 and 228.
[32] ibid para 223.
[33] ibid paras 237 and 245.
[34] See V Djanic, 'Looking Back: On Jurisdiction, Tribunals Hearing Trifecta of Yukos Cases Deemed the ECT Provisionally Applicable in its Entirety Despite Russia's Lack of Ratification' (*Investment Arbitration Reporter*, 21 May 2021), <www.iareporter.com/articles/looking-back-on-jurisdiction-tribunals-hearing-trifecta-of-yukos-cases-deemed-the-ect-provisionally-applicable-in-its-entirety-despite-russias-lack-of-ratification/> last accessed 23 October 2023.
[35] ibid; *Yukos Universal Limited (Isle of Man) v Russian Federation*, PCA Case No AA 227 Interim Award on Jurisdiction and Admissibility, 30 November 2009 (hereafter *Yukos v Russia*, Interim Award); *Veteran Petroleum Limited (Cyprus) v Russian Federation*, PCA Case No AA 228, Interim Award on Jurisdiction and Admissibility, 30 November 2009; *Hulley Enterprises Ltd v Russian Federation*, PCA Case No AA226, Interim Award on Jurisdiction, 30 November 2009.
[36] See, eg, *Yukos v Russia*, Interim Award (n 35) paras 395 and 397.

As in *Kardassopoulos v Georgia*, the tribunal in *Yukos v Russia* found no declaration was required under ECT Article 45(1) or 45(2) in order for Russia to invoke the limitation in Article 45(1) regarding inconsistency with domestic laws.[37] The tribunal also found that the question of inconsistency under Article 45(1) applies to the ECT as a whole: 'by signing the ECT, the Russian Federation agreed that the Treaty *as a whole* would be applied provisionally pending its entry into force unless the *principle* of provisional application itself were inconsistent "with its constitution, laws or regulations".'[38] In reaching this conclusion, the tribunal relied on VCLT Article 27 and the *pacta sunt servanda* rule[39] in VCLT Article 26. This conclusion took care of Russia's 'principal argument', which was 'based on the interpretation of Article 45(1), not on the assertion that provisional application *per se* is unknown or unrecognized by Russian law'.[40] As for the consistency of provisional application of treaties with Russian law, the tribunal referred to Article 23(1) of the Federal Law on International Treaties (FLIT) of the 1955 Russian Federation, which states that '[a]n international treaty ... may, prior to its entry into force, be applied by the Russian Federation provisionally if the treaty itself so provides ...'.[41] The tribunal found this allowance of provisional application consistent with Russia's Constitution.[42]

17

The Hague District Court set aside these awards in 2016,[43] but the Court of Appeal of the Hague reinstated them in 2020.[44] The Hague District Court agreed with Russia that ECT Article 45 means that provisional application extends only to those 'treaty provisions reconcilable with Russian law'[45] (contrary to the tribunal's 'all-or-nothing approach').[46] The Hague District Court found that the arbitral provision in ECT Article 26 is inconsistent with Russian law, such that the tribunal lacked jurisdiction.[47] The Court of Appeal of the Hague described provisional application of treaties as 'an accepted concept in international law ... codified in Article 25 VCLT'.[48] While criticizing both the 'all-or-nothing' approach of the tribunal[49] and the piecemeal approach of the District Court,[50] the Court of Appeal said that its own interpretation of ECT Article 45(1) (as follows, based on an 'alternative interpretation' proposed by the claimants)[51] 'corresponds with that of the arbitral tribunal in the Yukos Capital case':[52]

18

> [A] signatory which has not made the declaration referred to in Article 45(2)(a) ECT is obliged to apply the Treaty provisionally except to the extent that provisional application of one or more provisions of the ECT is contrary to national law, in the sense that the laws or

---

[37] ibid paras 264, 284 and 290.
[38] ibid para 301 (original emphasis); see also para 329.
[39] ibid para 313.
[40] ibid para 330.
[41] ibid para 332.
[42] ibid para 338.
[43] *Russian Federation v Veteran Petroleum Ltd*, Case No C/09/477160; *Russian Federation v Yukos Universal Ltd*, No C/09/477162; *Russian Federation v Hulley Enterprises Ltd*, Case No C/09/481619 (The Hague District Court, 20 April 2016), paras 6.1, 6.4 and 6.7 (hereafter *Russia v Yukos*, District Court).
[44] *Veteran Petroleum Ltd v Russian Federation*, Case No C/09/477160; *Yukos Universal Ltd v Russian Federation*, No C/09/477162; *Hulley Enterprises Ltd v Russian Federation*, Case no C/09/481619 (Court of Appeal of the Hague, 18 February 2020, unofficial translation), para 11 (hereafter *Yukos v Russia*, Court of Appeal).
[45] *Russia v Yukos*, District Court (n 43) para 5.23.
[46] *Yukos v Russia*, Interim Award (n 35) para 311.
[47] *Russia v Yukos*, District Court (n 43) paras 5.65, 5.93, 5.95 and 5.96.
[48] *Yukos v Russia*, Court of Appeal (n 44) para 4.3.4.
[49] ibid para 4.5.10.
[50] ibid para 4.5.11.
[51] ibid para 4.5.13.
[52] ibid para 4.5.48.

regulations of that state preclude the provisional application of treaty provisions or types or categories of such provisions.[53]

19   Like the tribunal, the Court of Appeal relied on FLIT Article 23(1), holding that that provision contains no restriction on the types of treaty provisions that may be applied provisionally under Russian law.[54]

20   Russia's appeal of the Court of Appeal's decision to the Supreme Court of the Netherlands failed with respect to the provisional application issue.[55] The appeal succeeded on a different ground, with the matter remanded to the Amsterdam Court of Appeal.[56]

21   Two other related arbitral proceedings in the 'second wave' of Yukos proceedings[57] raise similar issues concerning the limitation clause in ECT Article 45(1) with respect to Russia's provisional application of the treaty.

22   The majority of the tribunal in *Yukos Capital v Russia* in 2017[58] described provisional application as 'a well recognised institution in general international law'[59] and VCLT Article 25 as reflecting 'the extensive practice of states'.[60] The majority identified the relevant question as 'whether the *provisional application* of Article 26 of the ECT is not inconsistent with Russian law'.[61] Based on a ruling of the Constitutional Court, the majority concluded that 'the institution of the provisional application of a treaty ... is constitutionally valid under Russian law and gives rise to rights and duties within the Russian legal system that take precedence over other Russian laws'.[62] As Russian law does not prohibit the provisional application of a treaty that refers investment disputes to international arbitration, the majority determined that the provisional application of the ECT was not inconsistent with Russia's laws.[63] In dissent, Arbitrator Brigitte Stern emphasized that, under ECT Article 45(1), only those parts of the treaty consistent with domestic law are provisionally applied.[64] She found 'the introduction

---

[53] ibid para 4.5.48.
[54] ibid para 4.6.1.
[55] V Djanic, 'Yukos v Russia Saga to Continue, as Dutch Supreme Court Overturns Lower Court's Decision to Uphold the Three Underlying Awards Without Considering Russia's Fraud Arguments—But Remands the Case to the Amsterdam Court of Appeal' (*Investment Arbitration Reporter*, 5 November 2021), <www.iareporter.com/articles/breaking-yukos-v-russia-saga-to-continue-as-dutch-supreme-court-overturns-lower-courts-decision-to-uphold-the-three-underlying-awards-without-considering-russias-fraud-arguments/> last accessed 23 October 2023.
[56] Djanic (n 55). See also G Deepak, 'US Court Rejects Application for Stay of Enforcement of Yukos Shareholders Awards, Emphasising Difficulty for Claimants to Access Russian Assets in the Context of Ukraine War' (*Investment Arbitration Reporter*, 14 April 2022), <www.iareporter.com/articles/us-court-rejects-applicat ion-for-stay-of-enforcement-of-yukos-shareholders-awards-emphasising-difficulty-for-claimants-to-access-russ ian-assets-in-the-context-of-ukraine-war/> last accessed 23 October 2023; 'Enforcement Proceedings Regarding Billion-dollar Awards Against Venezuela and Russia See New Developments' (*Investment Arbitration Reporter*, 12 October 2022), <www.iareporter.com/articles/enforcement-proceedings-regarding-billion-dollar-awards-agai nst-venezuela-and-russia-see-new-developments/> last accessed 23 October 2023.
[57] D Charlotin, 'Breaking: Claimant in Second-wave Yukos Case Against Russia Announces $5 Billion Victory' (*Investment Arbitration Reporter*, 28 July 2021) (online).
[58] See also ibid.
[59] *Yukos Capital SARL (Luxembourg) v Russian Federation*, PCA Case No 2013–31, Interim Award on Jurisdiction, 18 January 2017, para 213 (hereafter *Yukos v Russia*, Interim Award 2017).
[60] ibid para 217.
[61] ibid para 243(a).
[62] ibid para 258.
[63] ibid para 284.
[64] *Yukos Capital SARL (Luxembourg) v Russian Federation*, PCA Case No 2013–31, Interim Award on Jurisdiction: Dissenting Opinion of Professor Brigitte Stern, 22 December 2016, paras 32 and 34 (hereafter *Yukos v Russia*, Interim Award: Stern)

of Article 26, through a mere executive act ... inconsistent with the Russian laws on international investment', so as 'to prevent the provisional application of Article 26'.[65] In 2022, the Swiss Federal Tribunal dismissed Russia's set-aside application[66] regarding the tribunal's interim jurisdictional and final awards.[67]

In *Luxtona v Russia* (2017), the tribunal adopted an 'all' approach to ECT Article 45(1),[68] relying in part on the 'necessary implication' of Article 45(3) (discussed further in Part D below) that provisional application extends to 'key parts of the treaty' including 'Part V on dispute settlement'.[69] The tribunal also suggested that the context of Article 45(2)(a), which allows for a 'declaration that it is not able to accept provisional application' (rather than 'provisional application as specified in paragraph (1)'), 'lends further support for the "all-or-nothing" interpretation'.[70] The tribunal therefore found that it had jurisdiction under ECT Article 26, which applied to Russia upon its agreement to provisional application of the ECT.[71] Russia applied to the Ontario Superior Court of Justice for the tribunal's interim award to be set aside.[72]

II. Implications of the VCLT and the ILC Guide for Understanding ECT Article 45(1)

ECT Article 45(1) may be seen as contrasting somewhat with ILC Guideline 10(1), which provides that 'A State that has agreed to the provisional application of a treaty or a part of a treaty may not invoke the provisions of its internal law as justification for its failure to perform an obligation arising under such provisional application'.[73] This guideline echoes VCLT Article 27, which relates to performance of a treaty rather than provisional application. Similarly, ILC Guideline 11(1) provides that '[a] State may not invoke the fact that its consent to the provisional application of a treaty or a part of a treaty has been expressed in violation of a provision of its internal law ... as invalidating its consent unless that violation was manifest and concerned a rule of its internal law of fundamental importance'.[74] This guideline echoes VCLT Article 46(1), which relates to a State's consent to be bound by a treaty rather than consent to provisional application.

Nevertheless, ILC Guideline 12 states that '[t]he present ... guidelines are without prejudice to the right of States or international organizations to agree in the treaty itself or otherwise to the provisional application of the treaty or a part of the treaty with limitations deriving from the internal law of States or from the rules of international organizations'.[75] These various

---

[65] *Yukos v Russia*, Interim Award: Stern (n 64) para 61.
[66] *Russian Federation v Yukos Capital Limited*, 'First Civil Court of the Swiss Federal Tribunal' (24 August 2022) <www.italaw.com/sites/default/files/case-documents/italaw170768.pdf> last accessed 25 October 2022.
[67] *Yukos Capital Limited v Russian Federation*, PCA Case No 2013–31, Final Award, 23 July 2021.
[68] *Luxtona Limited v Russian Federation*, PCA Case No 2014–09, Interim Award on Respondent's Objections to the Jurisdiction of the Tribunal, 2 March 2017, para 112 (see also para 154).
[69] ibid para 112.
[70] ibid para 117.
[71] ibid para 156.
[72] See, eg, *Russia Federation v Luxtona Limited*, Superior Court of Justice—Ontario, 2019 ONSC 4503 (Endorsement, 13 December 2019).
[73] ILC, *Guide to Provisional Application* (n 7) 83.
[74] ibid 85.
[75] ibid 86.

guidelines therefore do little to clarify the meaning of ECT Article 45(1). The potential for limitation of provisional application of the ECT by virtue of domestic law is contained in Article 45(1) of the treaty itself, and 'States have absolute freedom to negotiate the terms of a treaty and, hence, its provisional application'.[76]

26 Neither VCLT Article 25(1) nor other provisions of the VCLT or the ILC Guide shed much light on the central uncertainties and debates concerning ECT Article 45(1). For example, is a declaration under Article 45(2) required in order to invoke the limitation clause in Article 45(1)? The better view, as found by tribunals in *Kardassopoulos v Georgia* and *Yukos v Russia* as mentioned above, is that no such declaration is required. Nevertheless, issuing a declaration would be preferable for a State to avoid future disputes on the question.

27 Is the consistency with domestic law to be assessed with respect to the principle of provisional application (the all-or-nothing approach), the individual provisions of the ECT (the piecemeal approach), or the provisional application of individual provisions of the ECT (the alternative approach)? VCLT Article 25(1) and the ILC Guide refer explicitly to the possibility of provisional application of 'a part of the treaty'.[77] Although ECT Article 45(1) does not use these words, its reference to provisional application 'to the extent that such provisional application is not inconsistent with' domestic laws has created uncertainty in this regard. Reading ECT Article 45(1) in the light of VCLT Article 25(1) and the ILC Guide suggests that the all-or-nothing approach may be incorrect. The piecemeal and alternative approaches would likely produce similar results in many instances and may not be easily distinguished in the abstract.

D. Impact of ratification and non-ratification: termination of provisional application

28 The words 'pending its entry into force' in VCLT Article 25(1) imply that a State ceases to apply a treaty provisionally when the treaty enters into force for that State. ILC Guideline 9(1) makes this suggestion explicit: 'The provisional application of a treaty or a part of a treaty terminates with the entry into force of that treaty in the relations between the States … concerned.'[78]

29 Under VCLT Article 25(2), provisional application of a treaty by a State will also terminate if the State 'notifies the other States between which the treaty is being applied provisionally' that it does not intend to become a party to the treaty, '[u]nless the treaty otherwise provides or the negotiating States have otherwise agreed'.[79] ILC Guideline 9(2) similarly provides for provisional application of a treaty to terminate when the relevant State 'notifies the other States … concerned' of such an intention ('[u]nless the treaty otherwise provides or it is otherwise agreed').[80] This latter provision recognizes that the treaty may be in force for other States and is not necessarily being provisionally applied by all of them.

---

[76] ILC, *Third Report on the Provisional Application of Treaties by Juan Manuel Gómez-Robledo, Special Rapporteur* (5 June 2015) UN Doc A/CN.4/687, para 66 (hereafter ILC, *Third Report*).
[77] See ILC, *Report of the 70th session* (n 27) 209.
[78] ILC, *Guide to Provisional Application* (n 7) 81.
[79] VCLT, Article 25(2).
[80] ILC, *Guide to Provisional Application* (n 7) 81.

30 The ECT provides a good example of how these various provisions may operate in practice. ECT Article 45(1), like VCLT Article 25(1), provides for provisional application of the ECT 'pending its entry into force'.[81] Usually, provisional application will terminate for an ECT signatory upon entry into force of the treaty for that signatory. However, in *Petrobart Limited v Kyrgyz Republic* (2005), an arbitral tribunal had to consider circumstances where the scope of provisional application appeared to differ from the scope of subsequent ratification. The United Kingdom signed the ECT on 17 December 1994 and declared at that time that its provisional application of the treaty would extend to Gibraltar. However, the United Kingdom's instrument of ratification of the ECT dated 13 December 1996 did not mention Gibraltar.[82] As the United Kingdom had not made clear any intention to terminate the provisional application of the ECT with respect to Gibraltar, the tribunal found that the ECT continued to apply on a provisional basis to Gibraltar.[83] This dispute raises issues concerned with territorial scope, discussed in a separate entry on VCLT Article 29.[84]

31 ECT Article 45(3)(a) indicates that a 'signatory may terminate its provisional application of this Treaty by written notification to the Depository of its intention' not to become a party to the ECT, in which case termination of provisional application takes effect after the expiration of sixty days of the receipt of such written notification.[85] Pursuant to this provision, Russia informed the depository on 20 August 2009 that it did not intend to ratify the treaty, such that Russia's provisional application expired on 19 October 2009.[86]

32 Upon termination of provisional application under ECT Article 45(3)(a), ECT Article 45(3)(b) provides that (except for signatories listed in Annex PA)[87] the investment promotion and protection obligations in Part III and the dispute settlement obligations in Part V (including investor–State dispute settlement) of the ECT 'with respect to any Investments made in its Area during such provisional application by Investors of other signatories shall nevertheless remain in effect with respect to those Investments for twenty years following the effective date of termination'.[88] For Russia, Article 45(3)(b) means that it remains subject to ECT claims (with respect to investments made between 17 December 1994 and 19 October 2009) until 19 October 2029.[89] This provision may be understood as falling within the words '[u]nless the treaty otherwise provides' in VCLT Article 25(2) and ILC Guideline 9(2).

E. Conclusion

33 This review of international investment law on provisional application has demonstrated the breadth and flexibility of Article 25(1) of the VCLT and the many questions it leaves open. VCLT Article 25(2), while more precise, also leaves scope for further questions and

---

[81] ECT, Article 45(1).
[82] *Petrobart Limited v Kyrgyz Republic*, SCC Arbitration No 126/2003, Arbitral Award, 29 March 2005, 62.
[83] ibid 62–63.
[84] See in this Commentary: Philippa Webb and Emma Lindsay. 'Article 29 VCLT: Territorial scope'.
[85] ECT, Article 45(3)(a).
[86] See Energy Charter <www.energycharter.org/who-we-are/members-observers/countries/russian-federation/> accessed 7 August 2021; *Yukos v Russia*, Interim Award (n 35), para 338.
[87] ECT, Article 45(3)(c).
[88] ECT, Article 45(3)(b).
[89] *Yukos v Russia*, Interim Award (n 35) para 339.

elaboration about the circumstances of termination of provisional application of a treaty. The existence of these uncertainties supports the decision of the ILC to undertake work in this area, and its Guide to Provisional Application of Treaties do provide some further clarity and guidance surrounding provisional application with respect to some aspects relevant to international investment law. However, both VCLT Article 25 and the ILC Guide allow for individual treaties to supplant the general rules on provisional application and cannot resolve all ambiguities in such other treaties as regards provisional application. ECT Article 45 provides a clear example of the complexities of interpreting a provisional application clause and the practical difficulties associated with doing so.

34 Although this entry has focused on the provisional application provision in ECT Article 45, provisional application does arise in other contexts related to international investment law. As recognized in several of the investment disputes discussed in this entry, several contracting parties provisionally applied parts of the *General Agreement on Tariffs and Trade 1947* from 1948 to 1994.[90] The European Union also provisionally applies 'mixed agreements' pending their entry into force, being agreements to which the EU and its Member States are party, including most EU trade and investment agreements.[91] Potential exists for the considerations of provisional application under international investment law as discussed in this entry to influence provisional application in the EU and other international contexts. For example, the ILC Special Rapporteur referred to Article 45 of the ECT in his first report on provisional application[92] and to the decisions in *Kardassopoulos v Georgia* and *Yukos v Russia* in his second and third reports.[93] The extensive discussion of provisional application in the context of disputes in international investment law provides scope for more significant influence on public international law in general as and when such issues arise in other areas outside investment.

Selected literature

International Law Commission, *Draft guidelines and draft annex constituting the Guide to Provisional Application of Treaties, with commentaries thereto* (2021) UN Doc A/76/10.
Ishikawa T, 'Provisional Application of Treaties at the Crossroads between International and Domestic Law' (2016) 31(2) ICSID Rev 270.
Krieger H, 'Article 25: Provisional Application' in Oliver Dörr and Kirsten Schmalenbach (eds), *Vienna Convention on the Law of Treaties: A Commentary* (Springer 2012) 407.
Mathy D, 'Article 25—1969 Vienna Convention' in Oliver Corten and Pierre Klein (eds), *The Vienna Convention on the Law of Treaties—A Commentary* (OUP 2011) 639.
Simonsick WJ, 'Is Provisional Application on the Rise in International Investment Agreements? The European Union's Recent Treaty Practice and the Curious Case of *Von Pezold*' (2019) 88 Nord J Int'l L 180.

---

[90] *Protocol of Provisional Application of the General Agreement on Tariffs and Trade* (30 October 1947) para 1.
[91] A Suse and J Wouters, 'Exploring the Boundaries of Provisional Application: The EU's Mixed Trade and Investment Agreements' (2019) 53(3) JWT 395, 395 and 399.
[92] ILC, *First Report on the Provisional Application of Treaties, by Mr Juan Manuel Gómez-Robledo, Special Rapporteur* (3 June 2013) UN Doc A/CN.4/664, paras 46 and 50.
[93] ILC, *Second Report on the Provisional Application of Treaties By Juan Manuel Gómez-Robledo, Special Rapporteur* (9 June 2014) UN Doc A/CN.4/675, para 29; ILC, *Third report* (n 76) paras 62–66 and 68.

Selected decisions

Hulley Enterprises Ltd v Russian Federation, PCA Case No 2005-03/AA226, Interim Award on Jurisdiction, 30 November 2009.

Yukos Universal Ltd v Russia, PCA Case No 2005-03/AA227, Interim Award on Jurisdiction, 30 November 2009.

Veteran Petroleum Ltd v Russia, PCA Case No 2005-03/AA228, Interim Award on Jurisdiction, 30 November 2009.

Luxtona Limited v Russian Federation, PCA Case No 2014–09, Interim Award on Respondent's Objections to the Jurisdiction of the Tribunal, 2 March 2017.

Yukos Capital SARL (Luxembourg) v Russian Federation, PCA Case No 2013–31, Interim Award on Jurisdiction, 18 January 2017.

Article 26 of the VCLT

Pacta sunt servanda

Can Yeginsu and Patrick Pearsall

Every treaty in force is binding upon the parties to it and must be performed by them in good faith.

A. Introduction	1	II. The World Trade Organization Appellate Body	10
B. Application of Article 26 by the International Court of Justice and other international courts and tribunals	4	III. Human rights courts and tribunals	16
		C. Application of Article 26 of the VCLT by investment tribunals	18
I. The International Court of Justice	4	D. Conclusion: Convergence with limited divergence	25

A. Introduction

1 Article 26 of the Vienna Convention on the Law of Treaties (VCLT) codifies the principle of *pacta sunt servanda*, which translates to 'agreements must be kept'.[1] As an elementary principle of fundamental importance to the stability of treaty relations, the customary international law status of *pacta sunt servanda* is beyond doubt.[2]

2 The third preamble to the VCLT establishes *pacta sunt servanda* as a foundational (and 'universally recognized') tenet of international treaty law and Article 26 takes pride of place at the beginning of Part III of the treaty. Eminent scholars have described the Article as central to the VCLT framework,[3] and one that 'calls for no comment other than that it may be said to constitute a definition of the very essence of treaties'.[4]

---

[1] *Pacta sunt servanda* applies, equally, to contract law and its roots are to be found in private law (possibly stretching back as far as the Digest of Justinian): see K Schmalenbach, 'Article 26: *Pacta sunt servanda*' in O Dörr and K Schmalenbach (eds), *Vienna Convention on the Law of Treaties* (Springer 2012) 468–69.

[2] See, eg, affirming such character, J Salmon, 'Article 26' in O Corten and P Klein (eds), *The Vienna Convention on the Law of Treaties* (OUP 2011) 6-43 (hereafter Salmon, 'Article 26'); M Villiger, *Commentary on the 1969 Vienna Convention on the Law of Treaties* (Martinus Nijhoff Publishers 2009) 368.

[3] See C Binder, 'The *Pacta Sunt Servanda* Rule in the Vienna Convention on the Law of Treaties: A Pillar and its Safeguards' in I Buffard, J Crawford, A Pellet and S Wittich (eds), *International Law between Universalism and Fragmentation: Festschrift in Honour of Gerhard Hafner* (Brill 2008) 318–19 (hereafter Binder). See also recognizing its centrality to treaty law: A Aust, *Modern Treaty Law and Practice* (3rd edn, CUP 2013) 160.

[4] YILC 1982, Vol II, Part Two: Report of the Commission to the General Assembly on the work of the thirty-fourth session, A/CN.4/SER.A/1982/Add.1 (pt 2), Document A/37/10: Report of the International Law Commission on the work of its thirty-fourth session (3 May–23 July 1982) 38.

Article 26 includes two elements: first, a declaration that a treaty in force is binding on States **3** which are parties to it; and second, an obligation on treaty parties to perform the treaty in good faith.[5] The contours of what it means to perform a treaty 'in good faith' keep courts and tribunals occupied.[6] This entry provides some context to how an Article 26 analysis serves to assist courts and tribunals in resolving international disputes.

B. Application of Article 26 by the International Court of Justice and other international courts and tribunals

I. The International Court of Justice

The International Court of Justice (ICJ) rarely refers to Article 26 of the VCLT in its judgments.[7] **4** At least four strands are nonetheless identifiable in the Court's jurisprudence, which demonstrate the importance the ICJ attaches to the rule of *pacta sunt servanda*.

First, parties must not frustrate the object and purpose of a treaty after its entry into force.[8] In **5** the *Nicaragua* case,[9] for example, the ICJ cited Nicaragua's submission that the United States was duty-bound to refrain from acts which would impede the performance of the 1956 Treaty of Friendship, Commerce and Navigation between them[10]—despite the instrument containing no express provision to that effect. The Court proceeded on the basis that this obligation arose independently, under customary international law, and was implicit in *pacta sunt servanda* (and that certain acts by the US had, 'undermin[ed] the whole spirit' of the agreement).[11] The same logic is evident in other ICJ cases, despite the language of *pacta sunt servanda* not featuring in the Court's reasoning.[12]

Second, and relatedly, ICJ jurisprudence suggests that, in some cases, a treaty's purpose should **6** prevail over its literal application if the two are in conflict.[13] In the *Gabčíkovo-Nagymaros*

---

[5] *Case Concerning the Gabčíkovo-Nagymaros Project (Hungary/Slovakia)* [1997] ICJ Rep 7, para 142 (hereafter *Gabčíkovo-Nagymaros*).
[6] B Cheng, *General Principles of Law as Applied by International Courts and Tribunals* (CUP 1987) 105 (hereafter Cheng). See also JF O'Connor, *Good Faith in International Law* (Dartmouth Publishing 1991) 107–08, and PCA, *The North Atlantic Coast Fisheries Case (Great Britain, United States)*, Award, 7 September 1910, XI RIAA 167, 188–89.
[7] At the time of writing, a search of ICJ judgments for the phrase *pacta sunt servanda* returns just nine results. However, *pacta sunt servanda* is sometimes considered as a 'general principle of law' in the sense of Article 38(1)(c) of the ICJ Statute; a principle of customary law; or even of natural law: see, eg, Binder (n 3) 321; Salmon, 'Article 26' (n 2) 661; and *Territorial Dispute between Libya and Chad (Libyan Arab Jamahiriya/Chad)* [1994] ICJ Rep 6.
[8] Article 18 of the VCLT contains an obligation not to defeat the object and purpose of the treaty prior to its entry into force.
[9] *Case Concerning Military and Paramilitary Activities in and Against Nicaragua (Nicaragua v United States of America)* (Merits) [1986] ICJ Rep 14 (hereafter *Nicaragua*).
[10] ibid para 270.
[11] ibid paras 275–276 and 280.
[12] See, eg, *Reservations to the Convention on Genocide* (Advisory Opinion) [1951] ICJ Rep 15, 21 (none of the parties to an international convention 'is entitled to frustrate or impair, by means of unilateral decisions or particular agreements, the purpose and *raison d'être* of the convention'); *Application of the Convention on the Prevention and Punishment of the Crime of Genocide (Bosnia and Herzegovina v Serbia and Montenegro)* [2007] ICJ Rep 43, para 166 (finding that it would be paradoxical and undermine the purpose of the Genocide Convention if States were obliged by Article I to prevent genocide but were not also themselves prohibited from committing genocide).
[13] The customary rule on treaty interpretation enshrined in Article 31(1) of the VCLT requires that the ordinary meaning be given to the terms of a treaty, in their context, and in the light of the object and purpose of the treaty. The text therefore, properly interpreted, ordinarily has primacy: see Alexander Orakhelashvili, *The Interpretation of Acts and Rules in Public International Law* (OUP 2008) 309, 318–35.

Case,[14] the ICJ was faced with a treaty that had been breached by both parties. The Court considered that it 'would set a precedent with disturbing implications for treaty relations and the integrity of the rule *pacta sunt servanda*' if the treaty were held to have been terminated owing to such reciprocal non-compliance. Finding the treaty to be valid, recognizing that 'part of the obligations of performance ... have been overtaken by events'[15] and addressing what the parties' obligations were going forward, the ICJ held that the requirement of good faith in Article 26 'implies that, in this case, the purpose of the Treaty, and the intentions of the parties in concluding it ... should prevail over its literal interpretation'.[16]

7 *Third*, parties must not abuse their legal rights to evade their international obligations. This principle emerges first in the pre-VCLT jurisprudence of the Permanent Court of International Justice.[17] More recently, in the *Mutual Assistance Case*[18] the ICJ clarified that the duty of good faith, reflected in VCLT Article 26, applies even where the relevant treaty provision offers 'a very considerable discretion' upon a party.[19]

8 *Fourth*, the *pacta sunt servanda* duty to perform treaty obligations in good faith applies irrespective of the nature of the obligation in question. In the *Case Concerning Pulp Mills on the River Uruguay*,[20] the ICJ noted that Article 26 applies to all treaty obligations, including 'procedural obligations which are essential to co-operation between States' such as obligations to negotiate.[21] With respect to these obligations, the Court has held that States must negotiate in good faith and do so meaningfully, which will not be the case when either State insists upon its own position without contemplating any modification of it.[22] States should also pay reasonable regard to the legal rights of the other State.[23]

9 In addition, the ICJ has taken a consistent position on the scope and application for Article 26, holding that:

(a) There is a presumption of good faith. Although Article 26 imposes an obligation to perform treaty obligations in good faith, the Permanent Court of International Justice

---

[14] See *Gabčíkovo-Nagymaros* (n 5).
[15] ibid para 136.
[16] ibid para 142.
[17] See, eg, *Free Zones of Upper Savoy and the District of Gex* (Merits), PCIJ Series A/B No 46, 167; *Case Concerning Certain German Interests in Polish Upper Silesia* (Merits), PCIJ Series A No 7, 30 (hereafter *Upper Silesia*). See also Cheng (n 6) 121.
[18] *Certain Questions of Mutual Assistance in Criminal Matters (Djibouti v France)*, [2008] ICJ Rep 177 (hereafter *Mutual Assistance*).
[19] *Mutual Assistance* (n 18), para 145. See also *Case Concerning Rights of Nationals of the United States of America in Morocco (France v United States of America)*, [1952] ICJ Rep 176, para 212.
[20] *Case Concerning Pulp Mills on the River Uruguay (Argentina v Uruguay)*, [2010] ICJ Rep 14.
[21] ibid para 145.
[22] ibid para 146. See also *North Sea Continental Shelf Cases (Federal Republic of Germany/Denmark; Federal Republic of Germany/Netherlands)* [1969] ICJ Rep 3, para 85 (in relation to a customary international law obligation to negotiate delimitation of adjacent continental shelves). The duty to negotiate in good faith applies even where the relevant treaty-based obligation to negotiate contains no such express requirement of good faith; the obligation is *implicit* by reason of Article 26: see, eg, *Application of the Interim Accord of 13 September 1995 (The Former Yugoslav Republic of Macedonia v Greece)* [2011] ICJ Rep 644, paras 131–32 (hereafter *Interim Accord*). See also *Obligation to Negotiate Access to the Pacific Ocean (Bolivia v Chile)* [2018] ICJ Rep 507, paras 86–87.
[23] *Fisheries Jurisdiction (United Kingdom v Iceland)* [1974] ICJ Rep 3, paras 74–75 and 78 (in relation to a customary international law obligation to negotiate that arose out of the States' overlapping rights); *Interim Accord* (n 22) para 132 (in relation to a treaty-based obligation to negotiate). For examples of other treaty-based obligations to negotiate, see Article 33(1) of the UN Charter enshrining an obligation to seek to settle certain international disputes by 'negotiation ... or other peaceful means'; UNCLOS, Articles 74(1) and 83(1) (obligation to effect by agreement Exclusive Economic Zone and continental shelf delimitations between States with opposite or adjacent coasts).

(PCIJ) and the ICJ have consistently found that States are presumed to act in good faith.[24] As such, the Court will not lightly find bad faith, and thus a State seeking to assert a lack of good faith on the part of another will consequently have a high evidential burden to bear.

(b) Article 26 does not impose a substantive obligation where there is none. The ICJ does not read Article 26 as permitting a *freestanding* good faith requirement. Instead, *pacta sunt servanda* and the principle of good faith are ancillary obligations, to be applied in conjunction with another legal obligation. In the *Case Concerning Border and Transborder Armed Actions*,[25] the ICJ made clear that the principle of good faith in *pacta sunt servanda* 'is not in itself a source of obligation where none would otherwise exist'.[26] The ICJ reinforced this limit in the *Case Concerning the Land and Maritime Boundary Between Cameroon and Nigeria*,[27] in which it repeated the principle[28] and further stated that *pacta sunt servanda* and good faith 'relate only to the fulfilment of existing obligations'.[29]

II. The World Trade Organization Appellate Body

The World Trade Organization (WTO) Appellate Body has recognized 'the pervasive general principle of *good faith* that underlies all treaties'.[30] Indeed, certain WTO provisions expressly refer to the principle of good faith.[31]   **10**

In *United States—Shrimp*,[32] the WTO Panel found that Members 'must not frustrate or defeat the purposes and objects' of the GATT[33] and recognized 'an application of the international law principle according to which international agreements must be applied in good faith, in light of ... *pacta sunt servanda*'.[34] On appeal in *United States—Shrimp*,[35] the WTO Appellate Body elaborated, finding that this principle of good faith 'prohibits the abusive exercise of a state's rights' and dictates that treaty rights 'must be exercised *bona fide*'.[36]   **11**

---

[24] See, eg, the *Upper Silesia* (n 17) para 30; *Nuclear Tests (Australia v France)* [1974] ICJ Rep 253, para 60 (hereafter *Nuclear Tests*); *Certain Iranian Assets (Islamic Republic of Iran v United States of America)*, Judgment of 30 March 2023, para 92 (hereafter *Certain Iranian Assets*). See also *Case Concerning Military and Paramilitary Activities in and Against Nicaragua (Nicaragua v United States of America)* (Jurisdiction) [1984] ICJ Rep 392, para 101. This is so even where a party's conduct has previously been declared wrongful by the Court: see, for instance, *Dispute Regarding Navigational and Related Rights (Costa Rica v Nicaragua)* [2009] ICJ Rep 213, para 150.
[25] *Case Concerning Border and Transborder Armed Actions (Nicaragua v Honduras)* [1988] ICJ Rep 69 (hereafter *Armed Actions*).
[26] ibid para 94.
[27] *Case Concerning the Land and Maritime Boundary Between Cameroon and Nigeria (Cameroon v Nigeria)* [1998] ICJ Rep 275.
[28] ibid para 39.
[29] ibid para 59.
[30] WTO Appellate Body Report, *United States—Transitional Safeguard Measure on Combed Cotton Yarn from Pakistan*, WT/DS192/AB/RW, adopted 8 October 2001, [81].
[31] See, eg, Articles 3(10) and 4(3) of the Understanding on Rules and Procedures Governing Settlement of Disputes. See also the Understanding on the Interpretation of Article XXIV of the General Agreement on Tariffs and Trade 1994 (the 'GATT'), which requires a Member that is increasing a bound rate of duty, when forming a customs union, to enter into negotiations 'in good faith with a view to achieving mutually satisfactory compensatory adjustment'.
[32] WTO Panel Report, WT/DS58/R, adopted 15 May 1998.
[33] ibid para 7.40.
[34] ibid para 7.41.
[35] WTO Appellate Body Report, WT/DS58/AB/R, adopted 12 October 1998.
[36] ibid para 158. See also WTO Panel Report, *United States Section 211 Omnibus Appropriations Act of 1998*, WT/DS176/R, adopted 6 August 2001, para 8.57 (albeit the relevant WTO instrument in that case—the Agreement

12 At least three further principles emerge from the WTO jurisprudence:

13 *First*, like the ICJ, WTO Panels and the WTO Appellate Body have routinely found that there should be a presumption of good faith.[37] Members should be presumed to abide by their treaty obligations in good faith,[38] 'as required by the principle of *pacta sunt servanda*' in Article 26 of the VCLT.[39]

14 *Second*, WTO Panels and the WTO Appellate Body have consistently rejected the idea that there is any autonomous good faith obligation, i.e., existing independently of substantive WTO obligations.[40]

15 *Third*, emphasis is rightly placed on the primacy of the terms of the treaty, properly interpreted, rather than ascribing overriding force to the treaty's object and purpose.[41]

   (a) In *United States—Continued Dumping and Subsidy Offset Act of 2000*,[42] the WTO Panel had held that the relevant legislation had 'undermined' agreements between the US and the complainants, referring to 'the principle of good faith as a general rule of conduct in international relations' requiring parties to a treaty 'to refrain from acting in a manner which would defeat the object and purpose of the treaty as a whole or the treaty provision in question'.[43] The WTO Appellate Body reversed this decision,[44] holding that the WTO Panel had failed properly to apply the VCLT by discounting 'all too quickly' the textual analysis of the words in the agreements, and their ordinary meaning.[45]

   (b) In *India—Patent Protection for Pharmaceutical and Agricultural Chemical Products*,[46] the WTO Panel had found that India had acted inconsistently with the TRIPS

---

on Trade-Related Aspects of Intellectual Property Rights (the 'TRIPS Agreement')—contained a provision—Article 7—the language of which the WTO Panel interpreted as 'a form of the good faith principle'); WTO Panel Report, *Russia—Measures Concerning Traffic in Transit*, WT/DS512/R, adopted 5 April 2019, paras 7.132–7.134 and 7.138.

[37] See, eg, WTO Appellate Body Report, *United States—Section 211 Omnibus Appropriations Act of 1998*, WT/DS176/AB/R, adopted 2 January 2002, para 259. Again, this is so even in the face of prior impugned conduct.

[38] See, eg, WTO Appellate Body Report, *European Communities—Anti-Dumping Duties on Malleable Cast Iron Tube or Pipe Fittings from Brazil*, WT/DS219/AB/R, adopted 22 July 2003, paras 24, 49, 122–123 and 126–127. To rebut this presumption of good faith, 'solid evidence' is required: see WTO Panel Report, *United States—Certain Country of Origin Labelling (Cool) Requirements*, WT/DS384/R, WT/DS386/R, adopted 18 November 2011, para 7.605.

[39] WTO Appellate Body Report, *European Communities—Trade Description of Sardines*, WT/DS231/AB/R, adopted 26 September 2002, para 278. WTO Panels and the WTO Appellate Body have been slow, also, to question the accuracy of this presumption in practice: see A Mitchell, 'Good Faith in WTO Dispute Settlement' (2006) 7(2) MJIL 339, 362 (hereafter Mitchell).

[40] See, eg, WTO Panel Report, *European Communities—Anti-Dumping Duties on Imports of Cotton-Type Bed Linen from India—Recourse to Article 21.5 of the DSU by India*, WT/DS141/RW, adopted 29 November 2002, para 6.91; WTO Panel Report, *Argentina—Definitive Anti-Dumping Duties on Poultry from Brazil*, WT/DS241/R, adopted 22 April 2003, paras 7.34–7.36.

[41] Although cf WTO Panel Report, *Korea—Measures Affecting Government Procurement*, WT/DS163R, adopted 1 May 2000, in which the WTO Panel, in interpreting the non-violation provisions in Article XXIII(1)(b) of the GATT, appeared to apply the *pacta sunt servanda* principle of customary international law at the expense of the ordinary meaning (and object and purpose) of those provisions: see paras 7.93–7.119. The WTO Panel's decision has been criticized, however, by both Members (including Korea itself) and commentators: see Mitchell (n 39) 368.

[42] WTO Panel Report, WT/DS217/R, WT/DS234/R, adopted 16 September 2002.

[43] ibid paras 7.63–7.64.

[44] WTO Appellate Body Report, *United States—Continued Dumping and Subsidy Offset Act of 2000*, WT/DS217/AB/R, WT/DS234/AB/R, adopted 16 January 2003.

[45] ibid paras 281 and 284–285.

[46] WTO Panel Report, WT/DS50/R, adopted 5 September 1997.

Agreement on the grounds that the measures taken did not 'achieve the object and purpose' of the agreement and therefore did not 'protect the legitimate expectations' of other Members.[47] On appeal,[48] the WTO Appellate Body concluded that any finding of a violation should have been based on the text of the TRIPS Agreement and that the parties' legitimate expectations are also to be found in the language of the treaty itself.[49]

III. Human rights courts and tribunals

International human rights courts and tribunals rarely make reference to Article 26 of the VCLT or the principle of *pacta sunt servanda*.[50]   **16**

Curiously, where references to the principle are made, they rarely relate to the State obligation to comply in good faith with its substantive human rights obligations.[51] Rather the principle is more often invoked to underscore States' procedural duties relating to dispute settlement, such as their obligations to cooperate with the relevant tribunal in 'good faith';[52] to comply with requests for evidence;[53] and to execute judgments binding upon them.[54]   **17**

C. Application of Article 26 of the VCLT by investment tribunals

Article 26 of the VCLT is rarely invoked by investor–State arbitration tribunals.[55] Where the provision, or underlying principle of *pacta sunt servanda*, has been invoked, arbitral tribunals have generally chosen to follow the approach taken by the ICJ and the WTO Appellate Body, as set out above, by reference to the following propositions of law.   **18**

---

[47] ibid paras 7.41–7.43.
[48] WTO Appellate Body Report, *India—Patent Protection for Pharmaceutical and Agricultural Chemical Products*, WT/DS50/AB/R, adopted 19 December 1997 (hereafter *India—Patent Protection* Appeal).
[49] ibid paras 41–45. See, also, WTO Appellate Body Report, *European Communities—Customs Classification of Certain Computer Equipment*, WT/DS62/AB/R, WT/DS67/AB/R, WR/DS68/AB/R, adopted 5 June 1998, paras 83–84.
[50] At time of writing, a search of European Court of Human Rights (ECtHR) jurisprudence for the phrase '*pacta sunt servanda*', for example, returns 133 results, only 27 of which also refer to Article 26 of the VCLT.
[51] For notable exceptions, see Inter-American Court of Human Rights (IACtHR), *James et al v Trinidad and Tobago*, Orders of 25 May 1999, para 2.g and Order of 25 September 1999, para 10; and *Case of Baena-Ricardo et al v Panama*, 2 February 2001, para 98.
[52] See, eg, UN Human Rights Committee, *Piandiong et al v The Philippines*, UN doc CCPR/C/70/D/869/1999, 19 October 2000; see also Committee Against Torture, *Cecilia Rosana Núñez Chipana v Venezuela*, UN Doc CAT/C/21/D/110/1998, 16 December 1998, para 8.
[53] See, eg, ECtHR, *Husayn (Abu Zubaydah) v Poland*, App No 7511/13, Judgment, 24 July 2014 (in which the Court found, at para 358, that—as the Convention is a treaty which, in accordance with *pacta sunt servanda* as codified in Article 26 of the VCLT, is binding and must be performed in good faith—States cannot refuse to comply with the ECtHR's evidential requests by relying upon their national laws).
[54] See, eg, William A Schabas, *The European Convention on Human Rights: A Commentary* (OUP 2015) 866 (referring to the obligation to comply with final judgments of the Court in Article 46(1) as 'a specific formulation of the general principle *pacta sunt servanda*'). See also ECtHR, *Verein Gegen Tierfabriken Schweiz (VgT) v Switzerland (No 2)*, App No 32772/02, Judgment, 30 June 2009, para 87. See also Article 68(1) of the American Convention and the IACtHR's *Advisory Opinion OC-14/94* of 9 December 1995, Series A—No 14, para 35.
[55] For a reading of umbrella clauses as *pacta sunt servanda* clauses, see Thomas W Wälde, 'The "Umbrella" Clause in Investment Arbitration' (2005) 6(2) JWIT 183–236.

19 *First*, a party may not act to defeat the object and purpose of a treaty.

    (a) In *Chevron Corporation v Ecuador*,[56] the tribunal found that the underlying treaty's reference to fair and equitable treatment and to the 'principle of good faith' precluded conduct calculated to defeat the object and purpose of the provision in question.[57]

    (b) The tribunal in *Quiborax v Bolivia*[58]—citing Article 26 and the ICJ's *Nuclear Tests* and *Gabčíkovo-Nagymaros* cases—stated that the duty of good faith involves not 'perform[ing] any act that would defeat the object and purpose of the obligation that has been undertaken … even if the act itself is not expressly prohibited by the … treaty'.[59] In that case, the tribunal held that there was a duty to arbitrate in good faith.[60]

20 *Second*, a party may not act in abuse of its legal rights.[61] In *Saipem v Bangladesh*,[62] the tribunal considered that, by revoking the appointment of arbitrators for reasons 'wholly unrelated' to any alleged misconduct on their part, the Bangladeshi courts had exercised their supervisory jurisdiction over the arbitral process 'for an end which was different from that for which it was instituted', equating to a violation of the prohibition on abuse of rights.[63]

21 *Third*, a party must act in good faith.[64] The tribunal in *Al-Warraq v Indonesia*[65] held that the principle of good faith, inherent in *pacta sunt servanda*, required the State, in application of the underlying treaty provision prohibiting measures that directly or indirectly deprived the Claimant of his 'basic rights', to employ existing mechanisms for international mutual legal assistance and take reasonable steps to ensure that the Claimant was properly and promptly informed that he was a subject of a criminal investigation.[66]

22 Investment tribunals have also generally followed the ICJ's approach of presuming good faith on the part of a State. The tribunal in *Canfor Corporation v USA*[67] stated that States 'would not intentionally take steps that would undermine performance of [their treaty] obligations'[68] and cited 'the presumption of good faith under international law as far as compliance with treaty obligations is concerned'.[69]

---

[56] *Chevron Corporation and Texaco Petroleum Company v Ecuador* PCA Case No 2009-23, Second Partial Award on Track II, 30 August 2018 (hereafter *Chevron II*).

[57] ibid paras 7.86 and 7.112. For a similar conclusion by a domestic court, see High Court of Delhi (ITA 473/2012), *Director of Income Tax v New Skies Satellite*, Judgment of 8 February 2016, para 53. The obligation has sometimes also been characterized as a duty not to 'frustrate' the investment or agreement: see, eg, *Waste Management Inc v Mexico*, ICSID Case No ARB(AF)/00/3, Award, 30 April 2004, para 138.

[58] *Quiborax v Bolivia*, ICSID Case No ARB/06/2, Award, 16 September 2015.

[59] ibid paras 589–593.

[60] For recognition of the same duty in other cases, see *Methanex Corporation v United States of America*, Final Award, 3 August 2005, pt II—ch I, para 54, and *Libananco Holdings Co Ltd v Turkey*, ICSID Case No ARB/06/8, Decision on Preliminary Issues, 23 June 2008, para 79.

[61] See, eg, *Phoenix Action v The Czech Republic*, ICSID Case No ARB/06/5, Award, 15 April 2009 (hereafter *Phoenix*), in which the tribunal quoted Sir Hersch Lauterpacht at para 107: 'There is no right, however well established, which could not, in some circumstances, be refused recognition on the ground that it has been abused'; and referred in para 113, to the need 'to prevent an abuse of the system of international investment protection under the ICSID Convention'. See also *Venezuela Holdings BV and others v Venezuela*, ICSID Case No ARB/07/27, Jurisdiction, 10 June 2010, paras 169–177 and 184; *The Renco Group Inc v Peru*, ICSID Case No UNCT/13/1, Partial Award on Jurisdiction, 15 July 2016, in which the tribunal noted in para 175 the 'numerous occasions' on which the abuse of rights principle had been cited and applied; *Chevron II* (n 56) paras 7.87 and 7.105–7.107.

[62] *Saipem v Bangladesh*, ICSID Case No ARB/05/7, Award, 30 June 2009.

[63] ibid paras 159–161.

[64] See, eg, *The American Independent Oil Company v Kuwait* (ad hoc), Final Award, 24 March 1982, para 70; and *Saluka Investments BV v The Czech Republic*, PCA Case No 2001-04, Partial Award, 17 March 2006, paras 430, 432 and 466–467.

[65] *Al-Warraq v Indonesia* (UNCITRAL), Final Award, 15 December 2014.

[66] ibid paras 205 and 560.

[67] *Canfor Corporation v United States of America*, Decision on Preliminary Question, 6 June 2006.

[68] ibid para 323.

[69] ibid para 328.

In a departure from the ICJ's jurisprudence, investment tribunals have shown a willingness **23**
on occasion to interpret the principle of good faith as a freestanding obligation. For example:

(a) In *Inceysa Vallisoletana v El Salvador*,[70] the tribunal described 'general principles of [international] law' as '*autonomous* or *direct*' sources which 'must always be applied',[71] including good faith which is 'a supreme principle' governing legal relations 'in all of their aspects and content'.[72]

(b) In *Sempra Energy International v Argentina*,[73] the tribunal found that good faith is 'the common guiding beacon that will orient the understanding and interpretation of obligations'; and that it 'permeates the whole approach to the protection granted under treaties and contracts'.[74]

(c) The tribunal in *Phoenix* made clear that it was concerned with, and was applying, 'the international principle of good faith as applied to the international arbitration mechanism of ICSID'.[75]

(d) In *Malicorp Limited v Egypt*,[76] the tribunal suggested the normative autonomy of the 'fundamental' principle of good faith, stating, in terms, that it 'fulfils a complementary function' by 'allow[ing] for lacunae in the applicable laws to be filled, and for that law to be clarified ...'.[77]

(e) The tribunal in *CC/Devas (Mauritius) Ltd v India*[78] was more categorical, referring to the 'general obligation of good faith under international law', as specified in Article 26 of the VCLT, as 'self-standing' *as well as* 'stem[ming] from the concept of FET'.[79]

However, the application of good faith as an autonomous obligation has by no means been **24** universal. In *Vigotop Limited v Hungary*,[80] the tribunal stated that, while good faith *informs* how an obligation is to be performed, it is 'not in itself an independent source of obligations'.[81] Similarly, in *Mobil Investments Canada Inc v Canada*,[82] the tribunal noted that good faith 'does not constitute a separate source of obligation where none would otherwise exist ... it is not put forward as a free-standing obligation'.[83]

---

[70] *Inceysa Vallisoletana v El Salvador*, ICSID Case No ARB/03/26, Award, 2 August 2006 (hereafter *Inceysa*).
[71] ibid paras 226–227.
[72] ibid para 230. The tribunal in *Inceysa* (n 70) further stated, at paras 232–234, that all legal relations stem from the implicit confidence each party has in the other; that this is 'based on the good faith with which the parties must act when entering into the legal relation ... Asserting the contrary would imply supposing that the commitment was assumed to be breached, which is ... obviously contrary to the maxim *Pacta Sunt Servanda*, unanimously accepted in legal systems'; and that the Claimant's investment giving rise to the dispute had been made in violation of this principle of good faith. The tribunal in *Inceysa* was invoking the principle of good faith in both a *domestic* and an *international* sense: see paras 243 and 249.
[73] *Sempra Energy International v Argentina*, ICSID Case No ARB/02/16, Award, 28 September 2007 (hereafter *Sempra*).
[74] ibid paras 297–298.
[75] *Phoenix* (n 61) para 113.
[76] *Malicorp Limited v Egypt*, ICSID Case No ARB/08/18, Award, 7 February 2011.
[77] ibid para 116.
[78] *CC/Devas (Mauritius) Limited v India*, PCA Case No 2013-09, Jurisdiction and Merits, 25 July 2016 (hereafter *CC Devas*).
[79] ibid para 467.
[80] *Vigotop Limited v Hungary*, ICSID Case No ARB/11/22, Award, 1 October 2014.
[81] ibid para 585.
[82] *Mobil Investments Canada Inc v Canada*, ICSID Case No ARB/15/6, Jurisdiction and Admissibility, 13 July 2018.
[83] ibid paras 168–169.

D. Conclusion: Convergence with limited divergence

25 Many of the principles identifiable in the interpretation and application of Article 26 of the VCLT and the principle of *pacta sunt servanda* are common across the international dispute resolution fora.

26 Investment tribunals have exhibited a willingness to construe the good faith requirement, inherent in *pacta sunt servanda*, as an autonomous standard: that is not an approach taken by international courts and other international tribunals.

27 The foundational nature of *pacta sunt servanda* necessarily corresponds to a tendency towards alignment, and investment tribunals have generally sought to place themselves within the wider jurisprudence noted above.

28 Several reasons have been advanced to explain investment tribunals' greater willingness to interpret good faith as a freestanding obligation:

  (a) It has been suggested that investment tribunals have more freedom compared to other international courts and tribunals to explore such an independent principle. This is because of the breadth of the applicable law clauses with which they work.[84]
  (b) It has also been suggested that investors (as non-state actors) are not bound to public international law to the same extent as States,[85] and there is additional flexibility enabling arbitrators to move beyond the 'positivistic treaty language' in favour of external norms better reflecting the evolving regulatory needs of a State.[86] Put another way, some investment tribunals may simply be more inclined to acknowledge a freestanding requirement as a way of ensuring that 'justice is being done'.[87]

Selected literature

Binder C, 'Stability and Change in Times of Fragmentation: The Limits of *Pacta Sunt Servanda* Revisited' (2012) 25 LJIL 909.

Binder C, 'The *Pacta Sunt Servanda* Rule in the Vienna Convention on the Law of Treaties: A Pillar and its Safeguards' in Buffard I, Crawford J, Pellet A and Wittich S (eds), *International Law between Universalism and Fragmentation: Festschrift in Honour of Gerhard Hafner* (Brill 2008).

Harvard Research in International Law, 'Article 20: Pacta Sunt Servanda' (1935) 29 AJIL Spec Supp 977–92.

Kunz JL, 'The Meaning and the Range of the Norm Pacta Sunt Servanda' (1945) 39 AJIL 180.

Lukashuk II, 'The Principle *Pacta sunt servanda* and the Nature of Obligation Under International Law' (1989) 83 AJIL 513.

Mitchell A, 'Good Faith in WTO Dispute Settlement' (2006) 7(2) Melb J Int'l L 339.

Molinuevo M, *Protecting Investment in Services: Investor–State Arbitration versus WTO Dispute Settlement* (Kluwer Law International 2011).

Salmon J, 'Article 26' in Corten O and Klein P (eds), *The Vienna Convention on the Law of Treaties* (OUP 2011).

---

[84] See, eg, Article 42(1) of the ICSID Convention.
[85] E Sipiorski, *Good Faith in International Arbitration* (OUP 2019), para 1.18 (hereafter Sipiorski).
[86] SW Schill and HL Bray, 'Good Faith Limitations on Protected Investments and Corporate Structuring' in A Mitchell, M Sornarajah and T Voon (eds), *Good Faith and International Economic Law* (OUP 2015) 91.
[87] Sipiorski (n 85) para 2.113.

Schmalenbach K, 'Article 26: *Pacta sunt servanda*' in Dörr O and Schmalenbach K (eds), *Vienna Convention on the Law of Treaties* (Springer 2012).

Sipiorski E, *Good Faith in International Arbitration* (OUP 2019).

Ziegler AR and Baumgartner J, 'Good Faith as a General Principle of (International) Law' in Mitchell A, Sornarajah M and Voon T(eds), *Good Faith and International Economic Law* (OUP 2015).

Selected decisions

Case Concerning Border and Transborder Armed Actions (Nicaragua v Honduras) [1988] ICJ Rep 69.

Case Concerning Certain German Interests in Polish Upper Silesia (Merits) PCIJ Series A No 7.

Case Concerning Military and Paramilitary Activities in and Against Nicaragua (Nicaragua v United States of America) [1986] ICJ Rep 14.

Case Concerning Pulp Mills on the River Uruguay (Argentina v Uruguay) [2010] ICJ Rep 14.

Case Concerning the Gabčíkovo-Nagymaros Project (Hungary/Slovakia) [1997] ICJ Rep 7.

Case Concerning the Land and Maritime Boundary Between Cameroon and Nigeria (Cameroon v Nigeria) [1998] ICJ Rep 275.

CC/Devas (Mauritius) Ltd v India, PCA Case No 2013-09, Jurisdiction and Merits, 25 July 2016.

Chevron Corporation v Ecuador, PCA Case No 2009-23, Second Partial Award on Track II of 30 August 2018.

Inceysa Vallisoletana v El Salvador, ICSID Case No ARB/03/26, Award, 2 August 2006.

India—Patent Protection for Pharmaceutical and Agricultural Chemical Products, WTO Panel Report, WT/DS50/R, adopted 5 September 1997.

Mobil Investments Canada Inc v Canada, ICSID Case No ARB/15/6, Jurisdiction and Admissibility, 13 July 2018.

Quiborax v Bolivia, ICSID Case No ARB/06/2, Award, 16 September 2015.

Saipem v Bangladesh, ICSID Case No ARB/05/7, Award, 30 June 2009.

United Nations Human Rights Committee, *Piandiong et al v The Philippines*, UN doc CCPR/C/70/D/869/1999, 19 October 2000.

United States—Continued Dumping and Subsidy Offset Act of 2000, WTO Panel Report, WT/DS217/R, WT/DS234/R, adopted 16 September 2002.

United States—Shrimp, WTO Appellate Body Report, WT/DS58/AB/R, adopted 12 October 1998.

Vigotop Limited v Hungary, ICSID Case No ARB/11/22, Award, 1 October 2014.

Article 27 of the VCLT

Internal law and observance of treaties

Rumiana Yotova

A party may not invoke the provisions of its internal law as justification for its failure to perform a treaty. This rule is without prejudice to article 46.

A. Introduction	1	II. Extension to the actions of State organs and officials	15
B. Article 27 VCLT in general international law	4	III. Establishing a hierarchy of sources within the applicable law clause	20
C. Article 27 VCLT in investment law and arbitration	9	IV. Provisions containing *renvoi* to domestic law	25
I. Overriding objections to investment arbitration	10	D. Conclusion	31

A. Introduction

1 Article 27 of the Vienna Convention on the Law of Treaties (VCLT) provides that '[a] party may not invoke the provisions of its internal law as justification for its failure to perform a treaty'. It is without prejudice to the provisions of internal law regarding the competence to conclude treaties under Article 46 VCLT. Its corollary in the International Law Commission (ILC) Articles on State Responsibility (Article 32) affirms the irrelevance of internal law as justification for the State's failure to comply with its international obligations.

2 The principle set out in Article 27 VCLT has been applied in the practice of States[1] and in international adjudication for a long time.[2] The Permanent Court of International Justice (PCIJ) relied on the principle in *The Treatment of Polish Nationals and Other Persons of Polish Origin and Speech in the Danzig Territory*, affirming that 'a State cannot adduce as against another State its own Constitution with a view to evading obligations incumbent upon it under

---

[1] See, eg, Report by the Queen's Advocate dated 11 August 1845, Doctors' Commons quoted in A McNair, *The Law of Treaties* (OUP 1961) 102–03 (hereafter McNair, *The Law of Treaties*).
[2] *Alabama Claims of the USA against Great Britain*, Award, 14 September 1872, (1871) XXIX UNRIAA 125, 130–31 (hereafter *Alabama Claims*).

international law or treaties in force'.[3] Indeed, it is now well established that the principle in Article 27 VCLT is part of customary international law.[4]

There were some differences with respect to the character and effect of Article 27 during the drafting of the VCLT. Fitzmaurice originally included the principle in his Second Report. He considered it as a ground for the termination of treaties that could not be invoked under international law.[5] During the 1968–69 Vienna Conference, Pakistan proposed it as an amendment to the ILC Draft Convention as part of the provision on *pacta sunt servanda*.[6] In the end, States decided that the principle should be set out in a separate article, while acknowledging its link to *pacta sunt servanda*.[7] Seventy-three States voted in favour of Article 27, two against and twenty-four abstained. Some States hesitated to recognize what they perceived to affirm the supremacy of international law over internal law, particularly their domestic constitutions.[8]

B. Article 27 VCLT in general international law

Despite the long history of the principle, in practice, the interpretation of the content of Article 27 is somewhat varied and often linked to related principles extending its scope by binding States with respect to their acts on the domestic plane. For instance, the International Court of Justice (ICJ) construed as a corollary to Article 27 the principle that a State cannot rely on not having adopted the necessary legislation to give effect to a treaty as a justification for its failure to comply with it in *Questions Relating to the Obligation to Prosecute or Extradite*.[9] McNair extended this further to argue that the rule that a State cannot excuse non-performance of treaties by pleading domestic law gives rise to an obligation to adopt administrative and legislative measures to bring domestic law in conformity with the treaties.[10] UK practice supports this interpretation.[11] In *Exchange of Greek and Turkish Populations*, the PCIJ affirmed as self-evident the principle that States are bound to make the necessary modifications in their domestic legislation to fulfil their international obligations[12] (while not expressly linking it to the principle underlying Article 27). Fitzmaurice argued even more broadly that the principle in Article 27 VCLT gives rise to a duty for States on the domestic plane 'not to take any legislative, administrative or other action, whether at the time of the entry into force of the treaty, or at any subsequent time while it remains in force, that would cause the obligation to cease to be capable of being carried out in the domestic field'.[13]

---

[3] *The Treatment of Polish Nationals and Other Persons of Polish Origin and Speech in the Danzig Territory*(1932) PCIJ Series A/B No 44, 24 (hereafter *Treatment of Polish Nationals*). See also *Certain German Interests in Polish Upper Silesia* (1925) PCIJ Series A No 7, 19.
[4] *Greco–Bulgarian Communities* (Advisory Opinion) (1930) PCIJ Series B No 17, 32 and *Certain Questions of Mutual Assistance in Criminal Matters (Djibouti v France)* (Judgment) [2008] ICJ Rep 177, para 124 (hereafter *Mutual Assistance in Criminal Matters*).
[5] Article 5(2)(ii), YILC 1975, Vol II, 41, para 30 et seq.
[6] M Villiger, *The Vienna Convention on the Law of Treaties: A Commentary* (Brill Nijhoff 2009) 371 (hereafter Villiger, *The Vienna Convention*).
[7] See in this Commentary: Can Yeginsu and Patrick Pearsall, 'Article 26 of the VCLT: *Pacta sunt servanda*'.
[8] Villiger, *The Vienna Convention* (n 6) 371.
[9] *Questions Relating to the Obligation to Prosecute or Extradite (Belgium v Senegal)* [2012] ICJ Rep 422, 460 (hereafter *Belgium v Senegal*).
[10] McNair, *The Law of Treaties* (n 1) 100.
[11] ibid 105.
[12] *Exchange of Greek and Turkish Populations* (Advisory Opinion) (1925) PCIJ Series B No 10.
[13] Sir Gerald Fitzmaurice Fourth Report on the Law of Treaties, YILC 1959, Vol II, 49, 76.

In the *Applicability of the Obligation to Arbitrate under Section 21 of the UN Headquarters Agreement of 26 June 1947* advisory opinion, the ICJ construed Article 27 as broadly as denoting 'the fundamental principle of international law that international law prevails over domestic law'.[14]

5 The concept of 'internal law' in Article 27 has been interpreted as encompassing not merely legislative acts but also administrative acts, domestic constitutions,[15] and decisions of domestic courts.[16] According to commentators, the concept also encompasses provisions of internal law that may be enacted subsequent to the entry into force of the treaty.[17]

6 Article 27 does not create a general hierarchy between international and domestic law, nor does it prescribe how States should give effect domestically to international law or its position in the domestic legal order. The question of whether a State adopts a monist or dualist approach is left to its discretion and falls outside the scope of Article 27.[18] The article also does not apply to treaty provisions containing a renvoi to domestic law, as the ICJ expressly affirmed in *Mutual Assistance in Criminal Matters* in relation to a provision requiring that the execution of letters rogatory accord with domestic law.[19]

7 Indeed, in the *Danzig Legislative Decrees* advisory opinion, Judge Anzilotti affirmed that in cases where the applicable international rule contains a renvoi to domestic law, the Court needs 'to interpret a municipal law ... simply as a law which governs certain facts, the legal import of which the Court is called upon to appraise'.[20] It distinguished those instances from cases where it has 'to examine municipal laws from the standpoint of their consistency with international law'.[21] Typical examples of treaty provisions containing a renvoi to domestic law on incidental issues include rules on nationality,[22] the domestic legal existence of property rights and instances where the international rule makes compliance with domestic law a condition for compliance with the international rule.[23] As the ICJ affirmed, Article 27 does not apply to any of these situations.

8 Overall, Article 27 is best understood as a specification of the principle of *pacta sunt servanda* in relation to domestic law. As commentators observed, Article 27 relates to the binding force of treaties—a matter of international law which prevails over internal law.[24] In accordance with this principle, international law can be used to examine whether or not domestic laws, administrative, and judicial acts comply with international legal obligations. Article 27 does neither provide nor entail that in case of conflict, international law always prevails over domestic law.[25] Resolving such conflicts would depend on the conflict rules in

---

[14] *Applicability of the Obligation to Arbitrate under Section 21 of the United Nations Headquarters Agreement of 26 June 1947* (Advisory Opinion) [1988] ICJ Rep 12, para 57.
[15] *Treatment of Polish Nationals* (n 3) 24.
[16] See, eg, *Alabama Claims* (n 2) 131; *Certain German Interests in Polish Upper Silesia* (n 3) 19; and *Belgium v Senegal* (n 9) 422 and 460.
[17] Villiger, *The Vienna Convention* (n 6) 372.
[18] On the distinction between monism and dualism, see in general J Crawford, 'Chance, Order, Change: The Course of International Law, General Course on Public International Law' (2013) Recueil des Cours, ch VII.
[19] *Mutual Assistance in Criminal Matters* (n 4) para 124.
[20] *Consistency of Certain Danzig Legislative Decrees with the Constitution of the Free City* (1935) PCIJ Series A/B No 65, Individual Opinion of Judge Anzilotti, 60, 63.
[21] ibid.
[22] See in this Commentary: Chiara Giorgetti, 'Nationality'.
[23] J Hepburn, *Domestic Law in International Investment Arbitration* (OUP 2017) chs 3 and 7.
[24] A Schaus 'Article 27' in O Corten and P Klein (eds), *The Vienna Convention on the Law of Treaties* (OUP 2011) 688.
[25] ibid.

the legal order governing the relationship, the place of international law within it, as well as the jurisdiction of the dispute settlement body tasked with answering the question and the law(s) that it can apply.

C. Article 27 VCLT in investment law and arbitration

Investment tribunals rely extensively on Article 27 VCLT. In the majority of awards, it is **9** referred to in passing as a justification to consider the accordance with international law of domestic legislation, judicial, or administrative acts. They use Article 27 regularly when assessing compliance with the substantive standards of investment protection such as unlawful expropriation,[26] fair and equitable treatment,[27] or the standard of full protection and security[28] in order to reject the relevance of domestic law as a justification for the breach. Domestic courts too have relied on Article 27 VCLT in an investment law context. For instance, the Court of Appeal of Singapore invoked the provision to find that the PRC could not rely on not having implemented its constitutional arrangements to contract out of extending the PRC–Laos Bilateral Investment Treaty (BIT) to the territory of Macau.[29] These uses of the principle are fully in line with its interpretation and application in general international law. However, there are four groups of instances where investment tribunals invoke Article 27 in a manner that goes beyond its accepted scope of application in general international law. These are the focus of this entry and will be discussed in turn.

I. Overriding objections to investment arbitration

Tribunals have relied on Article 27 VCLT to prevent States from trying to invoke domestic **10** law to avoid investment arbitrations or to guarantee respect for procedural standards in investment law, such as those relating to admissibility of evidence.[30]

In *Biwater Gauff v Tanzania*, the tribunal rejected the respondent's argument for the non- **11** production of documents based on the public interest immunity under its Constitution as going against the consent to International Centre for Settlement of Investment Disputes (ICSID) arbitration under the BIT based on Article 27 VCLT.[31]

Similarly, in *Rumeli Telecom v Kazakhstan* the consent to ICSID arbitration was set out in **12** domestic law, which the host State later repealed.[32] The tribunal dismissed the respondent's argument that the consent to arbitration was no longer valid. It reasoned that 'it is also well

---

[26] See, eg, *Metalclad Corporation v The United Mexican States*, ICSID Case No ARB(AF)/97/1, Award, 30 August 2007, para 70.
[27] *SD Myers, Inc v Government of Canada*, UNCITRAL, Partial Award, 13 November 2000, para 203.
[28] *American Manufacturing & Trading, Inc v Republic of Zaire*, ICSID Case No ARB/93/1, Award, 21 February 1997, para 6.05.
[29] *Sanum Investments Ltd v Laos I*, Court of Appeal of the Republic of Singapore, 29 September 2016, para 79.
[30] See, eg, *Occidental Petroleum Corporation and Occidental Exploration and Production Company v The Republic of Ecuador*, ICSID Case No ARB/06/11, Jurisdiction, 9 September 2008, para 86. See further examples in nn 31–35.
[31] *Biwater Gauff (Tanzania) Ltd v United Republic of Tanzania*, ICSID Case No ARB/05/22, Procedural Order No 2, 24 May 2006, 8.
[32] *Rumeli Telekom AS and Telsim Mobil Telekomunikasyon Hizmetleri AS v Republic of Kazakhstan*, ICSID Case No ARB/05/16, Award, 29 July 2008, para 333.

established in international law that a State may not take away accrued rights of a foreign investor by domestic legislation abrogating the law granting these rights'.[33]

13 In *SGS v Paraguay*, the tribunal rejected the respondent's argument that an additional act was required by its head of State under domestic law to bestow its consent to arbitration under the BIT.[34] The arbitrators noted that no such requirement was set out in the BIT itself and relied on Article 27 VCLT to conclude that the 'claims that domestic Paraguayan law imposes certain procedural or substantive limitations on its consent cannot change or derogate from the unequivocal consent given ... in the BIT'.[35] Arguably, the tribunal disregarded the second part of Article 27 VCLT, which provides that the provision is without prejudice to the provisions of internal law regarding the competence to conclude treaties. The arbitrators should have applied Article 46 VCLT instead to assess whether the alleged violation of Paraguayan law provisions 'was manifest' and concerned a rule of 'fundamental importance'.

14 While most of these instances are uncontroversial and in line with the application of Article 27 under general international law, there is a danger of an overly broad construction of the potential conflict between the consent to investment arbitration and domestic law, which is arguably what happened in *Biwater Gauff v Tanzania*. The selective application of Article 27 VCLT in *SGS v Paraguay* is also problematic as it is not in accordance with the scope and text of the provision itself. These instances show that applying Article 27 to all instances of potential conflict with investment arbitration clauses could lead to unduly undermining the relevance of domestic law, which is applicable alongside international law in most investment cases. It can also extend the scope of Article 27 VCLT too broadly to incidental or ancillary matters that do not directly arise from an investment arbitration clause and are not necessarily governed by it, such as questions of admissibility of evidence.

II. Extension to the actions of State organs and officials

15 In some cases, tribunals extended Article 27 VCLT, often in conjunction with Article 3 ARSIWA (Articles on the Responsibility of States for Internationally Wrongful Acts), directly to the actions of State organs and officials. For example, in *Canfor Corporation v USA*, the tribunal invoked Article 27 VCLT and Article 3 ARSIWA to impugn the USA's failure to notify an amendment to its Tariff Act to Canada and Mexico as required by North American Free Trade Agreement (NAFTA), reasoning that the US officials' 'ignorance of treaty obligations is no defence'.[36]

16 In *SGS v Pakistan*, the tribunal referred to Article 27 VCLT and Article 3 ARSIWA to uphold the challenge against a constraining order of the Pakistan Supreme Court, ordering Pakistan to 'ensure that no action be taken in respect of its ... application for contempt and that, if any other contempt proceedings are initiated by any party, such proceedings not be acted upon'.[37]

---

[33] ibid para 355.
[34] *Société Générale de Surveillance SA v The Republic of Paraguay*, ICSID Case No ARB/07/29, Decision on Jurisdiction, 12 February 2010, para 72.
[35] ibid.
[36] *Canfor Corporation v United States of America; Terminal Forest Products Ltd v United States of America*, UNCITRAL, Decision on Preliminary Questions, 6 June 2006, para 306.
[37] *SGS Société Générale de Surveillance SA v Islamic Republic of Pakistan*, ICSID Case No ARB/01/13, Procedural Order No 2, 2006, 300–01.

Similarly, in *Saipem v Bangladesh*, the respondent's argument that the New York Convention was not applicable in domestic courts as it had not been implemented in domestic law was rejected on the basis of Article 27 VCLT and Article 3 ARSIWA.[38] The tribunal concluded that the issuing of anti-arbitration injunction by the domestic courts was contrary to international law and the New York Convention, engaging the responsibility of Bangladesh.[39]

In *ATA v Jordan*, the arbitrators relied on Article 27 VCLT to draw the far-reaching consequence that 'State authorities are estopped from undertaking any act that contradicts what they previously accepted as obligations incumbent upon them in a given context'.[40] On this basis, the tribunal ordered that the ongoing Jordanian court proceedings were 'terminated with no possibility to conduct further judicial proceedings in Jordan or elsewhere on the substance of the dispute'.[41]

While offering a broader interpretation of the principle in Article 27 VCLT and at times extending its consequences well beyond the law of treaties into the law of State responsibility, thus conflating it with the rule in Article 3 ARSIWA, this string of cases is broadly in line with the opinions of commentators in general international law[42] and goes with the grain of the broader underlying principle expressed in the two provisions. Some of the consequences drawn by tribunals, particularly with respect to specific performance, arguably go beyond what was intended by the principle.

III. Establishing a hierarchy of sources within the applicable law clause

There is a cluster of investment cases where Article 27 VCLT was used to create a hierarchy of sources within the applicable law clause in the relevant investment agreement, including in instances where the text of the provision itself did not provide basis for this.[43] Such use of Article 27 VCLT is problematic as it deviates from the application of the principle in general international law, as well as because it undermines the autonomy of the States parties to the treaty in their choice of applicable law. Conceptually, it is also not clear whether Article 27 VCLT should apply to an applicable law clause which lists as relevant both international law and domestic law.

An example of such a case is *Middle East Cement v Egypt* where the tribunal concluded on the basis of Article 27 VCLT that 'Egyptian law will be taken into account by the Tribunal when it is not overridden by the application of the provisions of the BIT'.[44] It reached this conclusion despite the applicable law clause in the BIT requiring the application of the treaty, the domestic law of the contracting party and obligations under international law. Moreover, the clause specifically provided for a hierarchy of sources stating that when a domestic regulation entitled the investment to a more favourable treatment than the BIT, the former ought to prevail. The tribunal addressed this with the somewhat circular reasoning that there was no conflict between the two legal orders and thus international law prevailed.

---

[38] *Saipem SpA v The People's Republic of Bangladesh*, ICSID Case No ARB/05/07, Award, 30 June 2009, para 165.
[39] ibid para 170.
[40] *ATA Construction, Industrial and Trading Company v The Hashemite Kingdom of Jordan*, ICSID Case No ARB/08/2, Award, 18 May 2010, para 122.
[41] ibid para 132.
[42] See para 4 above.
[43] See nn 44–52.
[44] *Middle East Cement Shipping and Handling Co SA v Arab Republic of Egypt*, ICSID Case No ARB/99/6, Award, 12 April 2002, para 87.

22 The arbitrators in *LG&E v Argentina* had to interpret Article 42(1) of the ICSID Convention, which provides that in the absence of an agreement between the parties, 'the Tribunal shall apply the law of the Contracting State party to the dispute (including its rules on the conflict of laws) and such rules of international law as may be applicable'. It employed Article 27 VCLT when construing the applicable law clause, to establish an order of precedence of the sources, holding very broadly that '[i]nternational law overrides domestic law when there is a contradiction since a State cannot justify non-compliance of its international obligations by asserting the provisions of its domestic law'.[45] On this basis, the tribunal concluded that it 'shall apply first the Bilateral Treaty; second and in the absence of explicit provisions therein, general international law, and third, the Argentine domestic law'.[46] This construction of hierarchy of sources goes against the letter and spirit of Article 42(1) ICSID Convention and does not obviously follow from Article 27 VCLT.

23 A similar approach was adopted in *Suez v Argentina*, this time with respect to the applicable law clauses in the relevant BITs, both of which provided that the tribunal 'shall' apply the provisions of the BIT, the domestic law of the host State and relevant principles of international law.[47] After observing that the applicable law clauses did not provide for a hierarchy of norms nor defined how the different legal orders relate to each other, the tribunal invoked Article 27 to conclude that it will 'resort primarily to the text of the BITs themselves as well as to any relevant rules of international law' but that 'it may also refer to domestic laws' where relevant for the evaluation of the claims under the BIT, for example as a reflection of the investors' expectations.[48] Through this reasoning, the tribunal essentially redrafted the applicable law clauses in the BITs, ignoring their mandatory language and significantly restricting the relevance of domestic law.[49]

24 The preferable approach is that adopted in *Venezuela Holdings v Venezuela* where the applicable law clause included domestic and international law. The tribunal focused not on the hierarchy between the two legal orders in the provision but rather on the fact that it did not allocate issues to either of them.[50] The arbitrators emphasized that it is for the tribunal to determine whether an issue is subject to international or domestic law and to apply the relevant body accordingly.[51] They went on to apply Article 27 VCLT to reject the respondent's attempt to invoke contractual limitations as a defence against the breach of investment standards after concluding that this issue was indeed governed by international law.[52] This is a better and conceptually coherent approach to interpreting applicable law clauses while respecting the choice of the parties and the distinction between domestic and international law in investment arbitration.

---

[45] *LG&E Energy Corp, LG&E Capital Corp, and LG&E International, Inc v Argentine Republic*, ICSID Case No ARB/02/1, Decision on Liability, 3 October 2006, para 94.
[46] ibid para 99.
[47] *Suez, Sociedad General de Aguas de Barcelona, SA and Vivendi Universal, SA v Argentine Republic*, ICSID Case No ARB/03/19, Liability, 30 July 2010, paras 58–59.
[48] ibid paras 61–63.
[49] For an almost identical approach, see *AWG Group Ltd v The Argentine Republic*, UNCITRAL, Liability, 30 July 2010, paras 60–65.
[50] *Venezuela Holdings, BV, et al v Bolivarian Republic of Venezuela*, ICSID Case No ARB/07/27, Award, 9 October 2014, para 223.
[51] ibid.
[52] ibid para 225.

IV. Provisions containing *renvoi* to domestic law

Another controversial line of investment cases concerns the application of Article 27 VCLT to clauses containing a *renvoi* to domestic law. One example are instances relating to legality clauses in BITs. As noted above, the position under general international law is that Article 27 is not applicable to treaty provisions containing a *renvoi* to domestic law, of which legality clauses in investment treaties are a prime example. However, in *Liman Caspian Oil v Kazakhstan*, the tribunal held that the question of the legality of the investment under the domestic law of the host State was irrelevant to the determination as to whether or not its courts violated the fair and equitable treatment standard on the basis that a State cannot invoke its domestic law as a justification for a failure to perform a treaty under Article 27 VCLT and that '[d]omestic law is only considered to be relevant from the international perspective in so far as domestic court decisions are acts attributable to a state and must be assessed under international law like any other State behaviour'.[53]

While it is true that the applicable Energy Charter Treaty (ECT) does not contain a legality clause, in effect, Article 27 VCLT was used to trump the illegality defence under general international law and the relevance of domestic law was significantly limited if not misconstrued. Even more problematically, international law was used to trump domestic law in an instance where international law itself conditions compliance upon domestic law. Last but not least, Article 27 VCLT was applied to an instance beyond its scope of application.

Within this cluster, there are also investment cases where tribunals applied Article 27 VCLT to override domestic rules determining the existence of property rights. As discussed above, due to the lack of international rules on property law, the existence of rights *in rem* is regulated by domestic law[54] and as such falls outside the scope of application of Article 27.

For example, in *Siag v Egypt*, the respondent argued that the investor lost their right to own land under Egyptian law once they changed their nationality and accordingly, could not recover for the loss of the investment that was not permitted under domestic law. The tribunal dismissed this argument on the basis that a State cannot invoke its domestic law to avoid liability for unlawful expropriation. It never asked the question whether there was a valid property right to be expropriated in the first place and disregarded that the law in question was in force well before the alleged expropriation.[55]

This approach is not only inconsistent with the scope of application of Article 27 in general international law but also with a long line of investment cases where tribunals have applied domestic law to determine the existence of property rights.[56] A good example is *Total v Argentina*, where the tribunal distinguished between the broader role of domestic law in determining the extent and content of the investor's economic rights,[57] on the one side, and the relevance of the domestic emergency clause doctrine as a justification for the failure

---

[53] *Liman Caspian Oil BV and NCL Dutch Investment BV v Republic of Kazakhstan*, ICSID Case No ARB/07/14, Award, 22 June 2010, para 326.

[54] See in general Z Douglas, *The International Law of Investment Claims* (CUP 2009) 52 et seq.

[55] *Waguih Elie George Siag and Clorinda Vecchi v The Arab Republic of Egypt*, ICSID Case No ARB/05/15, Award, 1 June 2009, paras 485–86.

[56] See, eg, *EnCana Corporation v Republic of Ecuador*, LCIA Case No UN3481, UNCITRAL, Award, 3 February 2006, para 184 et seq; and *International Thunderbird Gaming Corporation v The United Mexican States*, UNCITRAL, Arbitral Award, 26 January 2006, para 208.

[57] *Total SA v The Argentine Republic*, ICSID Case No ARB/04/01, Decision on Liability, 27 December 2010, para 39.

to comply with the treaty, on the other, which the tribunal rightly rejected on the basis of Article 27 VCLT.[58]

30 An interesting instance of applying Article 27 VCLT can be seen in the joined cases of *Hulley, Yukos and Veteran Petroleum v Russia* in relation to the provisional application clause in the ECT, containing a limited *renvoi* to domestic law in allowing for provisional application to the extent that it is consistent with the domestic laws of the contracting parties. The tribunal used Article 27 VCLT to reject the respondent's argument that provisional application would be precluded where individual provisions of the ECT were contrary to domestic rules. It held instead that it is the principle of provisional application itself that needs to be consistent with domestic law.[59] This interpretation is in line with the text of Article 45 ECT and respectful of its limited *renvoi* to domestic law.

D. Conclusion

31 While the interpretation and application of Article 27 VCLT in investment law generally accords with international law, as seen above, there are a few key areas in which there are notable divergences, including in the construction of applicable law clauses and in extending the application of the principle to provisions containing a *renvoi* to domestic law, particularly with respect to legality and to the existence of property rights.

32 Some divergences can be explained by their close interconnectedness with the question of applicable law and relatedly, the relevance of domestic law in investment arbitration, which has given rise to significant inconsistencies in both the investment decisions and scholarship. The divergences arise from the broader tendency of giving priority to international law over domestic law despite the hybrid character of investment law and its dependence on domestic law for several issues. A second reason could be the greater familiarity of arbitrators with international law compared to domestic law, as well as the ease of its interpretation and application.

33 From a normative perspective, a greater degree of alignment between general international law and investment law with respect to the interpretation and application of Article 27 VCLT is desirable. This would not only promote greater coherence and predictability of the legal effects of the law of treaties across different regimes of international law but more importantly, would ensure greater respect for the distinct functions of international law and domestic law in the hybrid system of investment law and arbitration.

34 Article 27 VCLT was never intended to operate as a general principle of priority of international law over domestic law. The Vienna Conference rejected a draft provision to this effect. Enforcing such a priority is even more problematic in a specialized regime of international law which interacts closely with domestic law and relies on it to define a number of juridical facts. The distinction between the different ways in which international law interacts with domestic law drawn by Anzilotti is particularly pertinent in investment law where the two legal orders often apply to entirely separate legal issues. Article 27 VCLT is and

---

[58] ibid para 40.
[59] *Hulley Enterprises Limited (Cyprus) v The Russian Federation*, UNCITRAL, PCA Case No 2005-03/AA226, Interim Award on Jurisdiction and Admissibility, 30 November 2009, paras 313–29.

should only be relevant where domestic and international law apply to the same issue and conflict with each other.

Selected literature

Corten O and Klein P (eds), *The Vienna Convention on the Law of Treaties* (OUP 2011).
Douglas Z, *The International Law of Investment Claims* (CUP 2009).
Hepburn J, *Domestic Law in International Investment Arbitration* (OUP 2017).
McNair A, *The Law of Treaties* (OUP 1961).
Villiger M, *The Vienna Convention on the Law of Treaties: A Commentary* (Brill Nijhof 2009).

Selected decisions

Alabama Claims of the USA against Great Britain, Award, 14 September 1872, (1871) XXIX UNRIAA 125.
Biwater Gauff (Tanzania) Ltd v United Republic of Tanzania, ICSID Case No ARB/05/22, Procedural Order No 2, 24 May 2006.
Certain Questions of Mutual Assistance in Criminal Matters (Djibouti v France) (Judgment) [2008] ICJ Rep.
Hulley Enterprises Limited (Cyprus) v The Russian Federation, UNCITRAL, PCA Case No 2005-03/AA226, Interim Award on Jurisdiction and Admissibility, 30 November 2009.
LG&E Energy Corp, LG&E Capital Corp, and LG&E International, Inc v Argentine Republic, ICSID Case No ARB/02/1, Liability, 3 October 2006.
Liman Caspian Oil BV and NCL Dutch Investment BV v Republic of Kazakhstan, ICSID Case No ARB/07/14, Award, 22 June 2010.
Middle East Cement Shipping and Handling Co SA v Arab Republic of Egypt, ICSID Case No ARB/99/6, Award, 12 April 2002.
Sanum v Laos I, Court of Appeal of the Republic of Singapore, 29 September 2016.
SGS Société Générale de Surveillance SA v Islamic Republic of Pakistan, ICSID Case No ARB/01/13, Procedural Order No 2, 2006.
Total SA v The Argentine Republic, ICSID Case No ARB/04/01, Liability, 27 December 2010.
Venezuela Holdings, BV, et al v Bolivarian Republic of Venezuela, ICSID Case No ARB/07/27, Award, 9 October 2014.
Waguih Elie George Siag and Clorinda Vecchi v The Arab Republic of Egypt, ICSID Case No ARB/05/15, Award, 1 June 2009.

Article 28 of the VCLT

Non-retroactivity of treaties

Ben Juratowitch and Jackie McArthur

Unless a different intention appears from the treaty or is otherwise established, its provisions do not bind a party in relation to any act or fact which took place or any situation which ceased to exist before the date of the entry into force of the treaty with respect to that party.

A. Introduction	1	III. Jurisdiction to consider disputes arising before a treaty's entry into force	34
B. The rule and its exceptions	2	D. Article 28 and international tribunals constituted under investment treaties	38
C. Article 28 and international courts and tribunals not constituted under investment treaties	8	I. Jurisdiction to consider acts occurring before a treaty's entry into force	38
I. Jurisdiction to consider acts occurring before a treaty's entry into force	10	II. Jurisdiction to consider disputes arising before the investment treaty's entry into force	44
II. Continuing and composite acts	26	E. Conclusion	48

A. Introduction

1 The rule expressed in Article 28 of the Vienna Convention on the Law of Treaties (VCLT) is long standing and exists at least in some form independently of its inclusion in the Convention. In the *Island of Palmas* arbitration, Max Huber famously recognized the existence in international law of a principle that the law to be applied to facts is the law at the time that the facts occurred, as did both parties to that arbitration.[1] The rule against a treaty binding a party, in relation to any fact taking place before the entry into force of the treaty with respect to that party, is an application of that broader principle. There is no doubt that this rule is widely accepted as a rule of treaty law. Whether the rule reflected in Article 28 represents customary international law or is a general principle of law is less clearly established,[2] but its widespread acceptance means that the question holds little practical importance.

---

[1] *The Island of Palmas Case* (or *Miangas*) (*United States of America v The Netherlands*), Award, PCA (ad hoc), 4 April 1928, (1928) II RIAA 829: 'Both Parties are also agreed that a juridical fact must be appreciated in the light of the law contemporary with it, and not of the law in force at the time when a dispute in regard to it arises or falls to be settled'.

[2] See F Dopagne, 'Article 28: Non-Retroactivity of Treaties' in O Corten and P Klein (eds), *The Vienna Conventions on the Law of Treaties* (OUP 2011).

B. The rule and its exceptions

The general rule stated in Article 28 is that a treaty confers no rights, and imposes no obligations, on a party in relation to:

(a) any act or fact which took place before the date of the entry into force of that treaty for that party; and
(b) any situation which ceased to exist before the date of the entry into force of that treaty.

That general rule is subject to three well-established exceptions, or viewed another way, is inapplicable in three types of situation (to which it might otherwise be thought to apply).

First, a treaty can have retroactive effect when that is the objective intention of the States party. Such an intention may be expressly stated in the treaty, or it may be otherwise established by way of the rules on treaty interpretation.[3]

Second, the content of a treaty provision can apply to facts preceding the treaty's entry into force if the treaty provision codifies pre-existing customary international law. As the substantive rule was in force prior to the treaty's entry into force, strictly speaking this is not retroactive application.

Third, a treaty provision can apply to situations that began before the treaty's entry into force but continued to exist after its entry into force. Where the treaty applies to the situation only insofar as it has continued after the treaty's entry into force, then this is usually treated by courts and tribunals as not constituting retroactive application of the treaty. However, it is in reality sometimes difficult or impossible to distinguish between application of the treaty to a situation only insofar as the period of time following entry into force is concerned and application to the same situation for a period of time straddling entry into force.

Although the rule in Article 28 can be stated in clear terms and is intuitively in accord with common sense and justice, areas of complexity and uncertainty remain in its application to some specific areas. One of these is how, if at all, it applies to a treaty that confers jurisdiction on an international court or tribunal. The second is how it applies to situations of continuing and composite breaches of treaty obligations, where those situations commence before and continue after the entry into force of the treaty creating the primary obligation. Below, the approach to these two issues taken by international courts and tribunals other than those deciding disputes under investment treaties is compared to that taken by tribunals constituted under investment treaties.

C. Article 28 and international courts and tribunals not constituted under investment treaties

The rule against retroactivity of treaties is widely accepted and applied by international courts and tribunals. Outside the context of disputes arising under investment treaties, the rule is sufficiently uncontroversial that it is rarely an issue for decision. The parties to a dispute usually accept that whether they breached any international obligation will not be

---

[3] ME Villiger, *Commentary on the 1969 Vienna Convention on the Law of Treaties* (Martinus Nijhoff Publishers 2008) 480.

determined by reference to the provisions of a treaty entering into force after the conduct in question.

9   More difficult questions arise with respect to treaty provisions that do not establish primary obligations, but rather confer jurisdiction on a court or tribunal. Does the court have jurisdiction to consider acts occurring before the treaty entered into force? Does it have jurisdiction to consider disputes that arose before the treaty entered into force? And is there a relevant distinction between a treaty that confers jurisdiction, and an instrument by which a State submits to that jurisdiction?

I. Jurisdiction to consider acts occurring before a treaty's entry into force

10   In the Article 28 jurisprudence of international courts and tribunals, there is an important distinction between a treaty provision that confers jurisdiction on the court or tribunal, and a treaty provision that concerns a primary obligation constituting the law applicable to the determination of a dispute. The manner in which Article 28 VCLT applies to primary rules is uncontroversial. However, the interaction between Article 28 and treaty provisions that confer jurisdiction is more difficult. The practice of international courts and tribunals is varied, and it is difficult to discern a consistent practice. If the treaty that confers jurisdiction on a court or tribunal itself specifies whether or not that jurisdiction is to extend to past acts, facts, or disputes, then the matter is clear: that specification is to be applied in implementation of the objective intention of the parties to the treaty. However, in the absence of such an express specification, the question is whether Article 28 VCLT is to be read as establishing a general limitation on the temporal jurisdiction of a court or tribunal. The International Court of Justice (ICJ) and the Permanent Court of International Justice (PCIJ) have tended to take an approach that gives the rule in Article 28 a very limited role in relation to questions of their own jurisdiction. However, other international courts and tribunals have taken a different approach.

11   Where facts that precede the conferral of jurisdiction on a court or tribunal provide the general background to a dispute, or go towards establishing a right and are not themselves the basis for the dispute, international courts have found that they have jurisdiction to consider those facts. In the *Right of Passage case*,[4] the Respondent State submitted that the ICJ did not have jurisdiction *ratione temporis* over the dispute, because the claimant State's claim concerned a right of passage said to have arisen prior to the Respondent State's submission to the ICJ's jurisdiction. The Respondent State argued that the ICJ did not have jurisdiction to consider or rule on the legal effect of any facts or matters that pre-dated that submission to jurisdiction, with the consequence that the Court would not be able to rule on whether the right of passage had come into existence. The ICJ rejected that argument. It referred to a 'distinction between the situations or facts which constitute the source of the rights claimed by one of the Parties and the situations or facts which are the source of the dispute', with only the latter acting as a limit on the Court's temporal jurisdiction.[5]

---

[4] *Case Concerning Right of Passage over Indian Territory (Portugal v India)* (Merits) [1960] ICJ Rep 6.
[5] ibid 35.

In other cases, the ICJ and its predecessor court have gone even further in limiting the effect of Article 28 on their own jurisdiction. They have taken the view that even if the facts said to constitute a breach of the right occurred or commenced before the conferral of jurisdiction on the Court, that did not preclude the Court from ruling on the dispute. Rather, the important temporal point is whether a dispute was referred to the Court after the jurisdiction-conferring treaty entered into force.

In the well-known *Mavrommatis Palestine Concessions* case,[6] the PCIJ placed great emphasis on this distinction. The case concerned an allegation that Palestine (and through it the United Kingdom as the international mandate holder) had wrongfully failed to recognize certain concessions, granted by the former Ottoman Empire, to a Greek citizen to carry out public works in Palestine. The wrong was said to have commenced in 1921, when Palestine granted rival concessions to another person. In 1922, the Mandate came into force, containing a clause in Article 26 that conferred jurisdiction on the PCIJ in relation to disputes concerning the Mandate's interpretation and application. The Greek government instituted proceedings in 1924.

The PCIJ ruled that it had jurisdiction under the Mandate:

> It must in the first place be remembered that at the time when the opposing views of the two Governments took definite shape (April 1924), and at the time when proceedings were instituted, the Mandate for Palestine was in force. The Court is of the opinion that, in cases of doubt, jurisdiction based on an international agreement embraces all disputes referred to it after its establishment. In the present case, this interpretation appears to be indicated by the terms of Article 26 itself where it is laid down that 'any dispute whatsoever ... which may arise' shall be submitted to the Court. The reservation made in many arbitration treaties regarding disputes arising out of events previous to the conclusion of the treaty seems to prove the necessity for an explicit limitation of jurisdiction and, consequently, the correctness of the rule of interpretation enunciated above. The fact of a dispute having arisen at a given moment between two States is a sufficient basis for determining whether as regards tests of time, jurisdiction exists, whereas any definition of the events leading up to a dispute is in many cases inextricably bound up with the actual merits of the dispute.[7]

To similar effect is the *Genocide Convention case*, where the ICJ found jurisdiction to rule on a claim brought under the Genocide Convention. Some of the acts alleged to have been genocide took place before the date when the Genocide Convention entered into force between the two States party to the case and thus conferred jurisdiction on the Court pursuant to its Article IX. The ICJ held that in the absence of a clause or reservation limiting the scope of its jurisdiction *ratione temporis*, it could 'give effect to the Genocide Convention with regard to the relevant facts which have occurred'.[8] Although genocide is a 'composite act' and therefore, as explained below, the ICJ might have accepted jurisdiction over acts

---

[6] *Case of the Mavrommatis Palestine Concessions (Greece v United Kingdom)* (Judgment No 2) (1924) PCIJ Series A No 2 (hereafter *Mavrommatis Palestine Concessions*). See further M Waibel, 'Mavrommatis Palestine Concessions (Greece v Great Britain) (1924-1927)' in E Bjorge and C Miles (eds), *Landmark Cases in Public International Law* (Hart 2017), 56-57.

[7] *Mavrommatis Palestine Concessions* (n 6) 35. It is possible on the facts that this decision might have been decided on the basis that the breach in question was a continuing breach—see at 35. However, the reasoning in the paragraph quoted indicates that was not the basis of the Court's decision. As to continuing breaches, see further in Section C.II below.

[8] *Application of the Convention on the Prevention and Punishment of the Crime of Genocide (Bosnia and Herzegovina v Yugoslavia)* (Preliminary Objections) [1996] ICJ Rep 595, para 34 (hereafter *Genocide Convention*).

said to constitute genocide that occurred prior to the conferral of jurisdiction so long as the genocide as a whole continued after such conferral, that does not appear to have been the reasoning adopted by the Court.

16. It is of paramount importance whether the treaty in question itself makes provision for temporal limits on the Court's jurisdiction. This is illustrated by the case concerning *Phosphates in Morocco*.[9] In 1925, the French Mines Department made a decision in respect of phosphate mines in Morocco that resulted in the alleged dispossession of certain Italian nationals. France subsequently, in 1931, accepted the compulsory jurisdiction of the PCIJ over disputes that arose after that date with regard to situations or facts subsequent to that date. The PCIJ held that it did not have jurisdiction. However, the PCIJ's decision arose from the limiting terms used in the French declaration of acceptance of jurisdiction both in relation to the date when the dispute arose and in relation to the date of the relevant situation or facts.[10] There were no such limiting words in the *Mavrommatis Palestine Concessions* case or in the *Genocide Convention* case. Properly interpreted, the *Phosphates in Morocco* case does not represent a different approach to jurisdiction *ratione temporis* from that taken in those other cases. Rather, it shows that the ICJ and the PCIJ will not refuse jurisdiction *ratione temporis* over acts that took place before the grant of jurisdiction, unless the parties to the treaty have excluded such jurisdiction. All of this, however, concerns, or should concern, only the question of the jurisdiction of the Court, not the different question of the law applicable to the dispute.

17. Other international courts and tribunals have to an extent followed the ICJ and the PCIJ on issues of jurisdiction *ratione temporis*.

18. The European Court of Human Rights (ECtHR) has taken the approach of the ICJ in the *Right of Passage* case: it has accepted that it can rule on acts or events occurring prior to the entry into force of the constituent treaty if the breach of the treaty only crystallized after entry into force. For instance, in *Harutyunyan v Armenia*, the ECtHR held that it had temporal jurisdiction to hear a complaint about evidence obtained through ill-treatment, where the ill-treatment had occurred prior to the Convention's entry into force for Armenia, but had been used against the applicant in criminal proceedings after entry into force.[11] Similarly, in *Zana v Turkey*, the applicant made certain public statements before the Convention was ratified by Turkey, and was convicted in relation to those statements after the Convention was ratified—the ECtHR held that it had jurisdiction to hear the applicant's complaint that the conviction interfered with his right to freedom of expression.[12]

19. However, the ECtHR has not followed the more permissive approach to temporal jurisdiction adopted by the PCIJ and the ICJ in the *Mavrommatis Palestine Concessions* case and in the *Genocide Convention* case. Where the acts or events which are said to <u>constitute</u> a breach of rights took place prior to the Convention's entry into force for the Respondent State, the ECtHR and the European Commission on Human Rights (ECmHR) have refused jurisdiction[13] or

---

[9] *Phosphates in Morocco (Italy v France)* (Preliminary Objections) (1938) PCIJ Series A/B No 74 (hereafter *Phosphates in Morocco*).
[10] ibid paras 25–26. See also *Case Concerning Certain Property (Liechtenstein v Germany)* (Preliminary Objections) [2005] ICJ Rep 6, para 52 (hereafter *Certain Property*).
[11] *Harutyunyan v Armenia*, App no 36549/03, 28 June 2007, paras 48–50.
[12] *Zana v Turkey*, App no 18954/91, November 1997, paras 41–42.
[13] See, eg, *Blečić v Croatia*, App no 59532/00, 8 March 2006, para 92 (hereafter *Blečić v Croatia*); *Janowiec v Russia*, App nos 55508/07, 29520/09, 21 October 2013, para 161; *Khoroshenko v Russia*, App no 41418/04, 30 June 2015, para 88; *X v Austria*, App no 913/60, Commission Decision, 19 December 1961; *X v Germany*, App no 2113/64, Commission Decision, 3 April 1967; *X v Switzerland*, App no 7211/75, Commission Decision, 6 October 1976;

said they were not competent to rule on the complaint.[14] This was done on the express basis that the principle of non-retroactivity of treaties 'operates to limit *ratione temporis* the application of the jurisdictional, and not only substantive, provisions of the Convention'.[15] The ECtHR and the ECmHR thus take the view that the assumption of jurisdiction to decide on breaches of the Convention that occurred prior to the Convention's entry into force would constitute retroactive application not only of the substantive protections in the Convention, but also of the jurisdictional provisions. This is accordingly a more restrictive application of the rule against retroactivity than adopted by the PCIJ in the *Mavrommatis Palestine Concessions* case and by the ICJ in the *Genocide Convention* case.

That conclusion is subject to an important qualification, which arises from the fact that the jurisdiction of the ECtHR and the ECmHR depends not just on the Convention, but also on the deposit by Member States of declarations accepting that individual petitions may be brought against them under the Convention. The ECmHR, in particular, has held that unless the declaration by the Respondent State expressly limits jurisdiction to acts which took place after the date of the declaration, then it has jurisdiction to consider alleged breaches that took place after the Convention's entry into force but before the date of the declaration. For example, in *X v France*, the Commission considered an application by a person who had been arrested and detained by the French government from October 1975. France had ratified the European Convention on Human Rights (ECHR) on 3 May 1974, before the arrest, but it had not deposited a declaration accepting the right of individual petition until 2 October 1981, after the applicant's release from detention. France's declaration, unlike that of some other Member States,[16] did not contain a reservation restricting individual petitions to acts or events subsequent to the date of the declaration's deposit. The ECmHR held:

20

> Unlike States which have availed themselves of this possibility, the French declaration contains no definition of the scope of the right of individual petition as regards the past.
>
> In the absence of an express limitation in the French declaration, the Commission considers consequently that it is competent *ratione temporis* to deal with the complaints drawn up by the applicant, as the events in question occurred after the date on which France ratified the Convention (3 May 1974).[17]

X, Y and Z v Switzerland, App no 6916/75, Commission Decision, 8 October 1976, para 2; *De Napolis Pacheco v Belgium*, App no 7775/77, Commission Decision, 5 October 1978, para 2; *Jonas v The Czech Republic*, App no 23063/93, Commission Decision, 13 May 1996; *Lupulet v Romania*, App no 25497/94, Commission Decision, 17 May 1996; *Gallo v The Slovak Republic*, App no 30900/96, Commission Decision, 4 September 1996; *Kövendi v Hungary*, App no 26287/95, Commission Decision, 4 September 1996; *Úri v Hungary*, App no 31973/96, Commission Decision, 16 October 1996; *Misson v Slovenia*, App no 27337/95, Commission Decision, 21 January 1997, para 1; *Staiku v Greece*, App no 35426/97, Commission Decision, 2 July 1997, para 1; *Viikman v Estonia*, App no 35086/97, Commission Decision, 1 July 1998, para 1.

[14] *Sargsyan v Azerbaijan*, App no 40167/06, 14 December 2011, para 81.

[15] *Blečić v Croatia* (n 13) para 68.

[16] Such declarations were upheld as valid and effective in, eg, *Loizidou v Turkey*, App no 15318/89, 23 March 1995, para 102; *Šilih v Slovenia*, App no 71463/01, 9 April 2009; *Varnava v Turkey*, App nos 16064/90, 16065/90, 16066/09, 16068/90, 16069/90, 16070/90, 16071/90, 16072/90, 16073/90, 18 September 2009 (hereafter *Varnava v Turkey*); *X and Y v Portugal*, App nos 8560/79, 8613/79, Commission Decision, 3 July 1979 (hereafter *X and Y v Portugal*); *X v Italy*, App no 8261/78, Commission Decision, 11 October 1979; *X v Portugal*, App no 9453/81, Commission Decision, 13 December 1982, para 6 (hereafter *X v Portugal*); *Chrysostomos, Papachrysostomou and Loizidou v Turkey*, App nos 15299/89, 15300/89, 15318/89, Commission Decision, 4 March 1991, paras 10, 50–53; *Borozinsky v Poland*, App no 24086/94, Commission Decision, 2 December 1996; *Bojlekov v Poland*, App no 22819/93, Commission Decision, 9 April 1997.

[17] *X v France*, App no 13473/87, Commission Decision, 13 December 1982, paras 7–8.

21 The ECtHR and the ECmHR thus take the approach that: if the facts said to constitute a breach of the ECHR precede entry into force of the ECHR for the relevant State, then they have no temporal jurisdiction; but if the facts follow entry into force of the Convention but precede deposit of the declaration allowing individual complaints, then they do have temporal jurisdiction. There is a distinction between these two approaches in the sense that one involves the Convention being in force for the relevant State and the other does not, but it is hard to see how it is a principled distinction in circumstances where there can be no jurisdiction until the declaration has been deposited.

22 The jurisprudence of the African Court on Human and Peoples' Rights (ACtHPR) is even less clear. In at least two cases, the Court has accepted jurisdiction over an alleged violation of rights that occurred after the African Charter on Human and Peoples' Rights had been ratified by the Respondent State, but before the Respondent State had accepted the jurisdiction of the Court.[18] The ACtHPR in both cases appeared to consider only the date of the Charter's ratification by the Respondent State to be relevant. There are some indications in *obiter dicta* in other cases, however, that the ACtHPR would have considered the critical date for establishing its jurisdiction to be the date of the Respondent State's declaration accepting the Court's jurisdiction.[19] If adopted, such an approach would be yet more restrictive than that of the European institutions. However, on the basis of the cases actually decided on this point, it appears that the ACtHPR's approach to determining the temporal limits of its jurisdiction accords broadly with that used by the ECtHR and the ECmHR.

23 The Inter-American Court of Human Rights (IACtHR)[20] and the United Nations Human Rights Committee (the UN Human Rights Committee),[21] by contrast, have adopted an equivalent approach to that entertained by the ACtHPR in *obiter dicta*. Both bodies have held that they do not have jurisdiction over events that are said to constitute a breach of the relevant treaty, where those events took place before the Respondent State accepted the body's jurisdiction. In *Yean and Bosico Children v Dominican Republic*, the IACtHR declared that it 'cannot exercise its contentious jurisdiction to apply the Convention and declare that its norms have been violated when the alleged facts or conduct of the defendant

---

[18] *Urban Mkandawire v The Republic of Malawi*, App no 003/2011, ACtHPR, 21 June 2013, para 32; *Tanganyika Law Society v The United Republic of Tanzania*, App nos 009/2011 and 011/2011, ACtHPR, 14 June 2013, para 84.

[19] In *Nganyi v Tanzania*, the ACtHPR held that the breach in question was a continuing breach, and therefore jurisdiction *ratione temporis* had been made out. However, it appeared to consider the critical date for establishing jurisdiction to be the date of the Respondent State's declaration accepting the Court's jurisdiction: *Wilfred Onyango Nganyi v United Republic of Tanzania* App no 006/2013, ACtHPR, 18 March 2016, para 66 (hereafter *Nganyi v Tanzania*).

In *The African Commission on Human and Peoples' Rights v Libya*, the alleged violation had occurred after ratification of both the Charter and the Protocol giving the Court's jurisdiction. However, the Court's reasoning appeared to treat as the critical date that of the jurisdiction Protocol: *The African Commission on Human and Peoples' Rights v Libya* App no 002/2013, ACtHPR, 3 June 2016, paras 55–57.

[20] *Yean and Bosico Children v Dominican Republic*, IACtHR, 8 September 2005, para 105 (hereafter *Yean and Bosico Children v Dominican Republic*); *Blake v Guatemala*, IACtHR, 2 July 1996, para 33; *Heliodoro Portugal v Panama*, IACtHR, 12 August 2008, para 24.

[21] *MIT v Spain*, Human Rights Committee, UN Doc CCPR/C/41/D/310/1998, 11 April 1991, para 5.2. See also *Sandra Lovelace v Canada*, Human Rights Committee, UN Doc CCPR/C/13/D/24/1977, 30 July 1981, para 10 (hereafter *Lovelace v Canada*); *Simunek, Hastings, Tuzilova and Prochazka v The Czech Republic*, Human Rights Committee, UN Doc CCPR/C/54/D 516/1992, 19 July 1995, para 4.5 (hereafter *Simunek v The Czech Republic*); *Mariam Sankara v Burkina Faso*, Human Rights Committee, UN Doc CCPR/C/86/D/1159/2003, 28 March 2006, para 6.3 (hereafter *Sankara v Burkina Faso*). See also *SE v Argentina*, in which the Human Rights Committee observed that 'the Covenant cannot be applied retroactively and that the Committee is precluded *ratione temporis* from examining alleged violations that occurred prior to the entry into force of the Covenant

State that could involve international responsibility precede acceptance of the court's jurisdiction'.[22]

To like effect, in *E and AK v Hungary*, the UN Human Rights Committee refused jurisdiction to hear a complaint about acts performed after the entry into force of the International Covenant on Civil and Political Rights for Hungary, but before the entry into force of the Optional Protocol by which Hungary conferred jurisdiction on the UN Human Rights Committee. The Committee held:

> the State party's obligations under the Covenant apply as of the date of its entry into force for the State party. There is, however, a different issue as to when the Committee's competence to consider complaints about alleged violations of the Covenant under the Optional Protocol is engaged. In its jurisprudence under the Optional Protocol, the Committee has held that it cannot consider alleged violations of the Covenant which occurred before the entry into force of the Optional Protocol for the State party, unless the violations complained of continue after the entry into force of the Optional Protocol.[23]

The jurisprudence of international courts and tribunals therefore varies in the extent to which the rule against retroactive application is applicable to treaty provisions or other instruments that establish jurisdiction. The ICJ and the PCIJ have taken the most permissive approach, upholding their own jurisdiction to decide even on allegations of a breach of rights that took place before the treaty that confers jurisdiction had entered into force. Other international courts and bodies have, to varying degrees, been more restrictive.

II. Continuing and composite acts

Further complications arise in respect of 'continuing' or 'composite' acts, which may be a basis for an international court or tribunal to assume jurisdiction to consider conduct commencing prior to the existence of jurisdiction, and even prior to the entry into force of a treaty creating the relevant primary obligations.

An act or event has a 'continuing' character where it occurs over the course of a relevant period of time, as opposed to an act that is completed prior to a relevant point in time.[24] The International Law Commission lists as typical examples of a continuing act the following: 'the maintenance in effect of legislative provisions incompatible with treaty obligations of the enacting State, unlawful detention of a foreign official or unlawful occupation of embassy premises, maintenance by force of colonial domination, unlawful occupation of part of the territory of another State or stationing armed forces in another State without its consent'.[25]

---

for the State party concerned': *SE v Argentina*, Human Rights Committee, UN Doc CCPR/C/38/D/275/1988, 26 March 1990, para 5.2.

[22] *Yean and Bosico Children v Dominican Republic* (n 20) para 105.

[23] *E and AK v Hungary*, Human Rights Committee, UN Doc CCPR/C/5/D/520/1992, 7 April 1994, para 6.4 (hereafter *E and AK v Hungary*). See also *Ivan Somers v Hungary*, Human Rights Committee, UN Doc CCPR/C/53/D/566/1993, 23 July 1996, para 6.3.

[24] ILC, Articles on the Responsibility of States for Internationally Wrongful Acts, Article 14, and commentary, paras 1–3 (hereafter ARSIWA and commentary).

[25] ibid Article 14, and commentary, para 3.

28 Where a continuing act straddles the point in time in respect of which jurisdiction commences, jurisdiction *ratione temporis* will extend even to those parts of the continuing breach that precede that point in time. According to the UN Human Rights Committee, the reason for this is that '[a] continuing violation is to be interpreted as an affirmation, after the entry into force of the [relevant treaty], by act or by clear implication, of the previous violations of the State party'.[26] The extension of the court or tribunal's jurisdiction to cover all of the continuing act might involve retroactivity, but it is nonetheless consistent with the terms of Article 28 VCLT, which provides that treaty provisions shall not apply to 'any act or fact which took place or any situation which ceased to exist' before the date of the treaty's entry into force.

29 By way of illustration, courts and tribunals have accepted that they have jurisdiction over the following continuing acts, even though they began before the entry into force of the relevant treaty:

(a) A claim for unlawful detention which continued after the relevant date;[27]
(b) An interference with rights of defence that affected the outcome of the final proceedings, which were held after the relevant date;[28] and
(c) A claim arising out of the complainant having been deprived by domestic law of her indigenous status upon her marriage to someone who was not indigenous, meaning *inter alia* that she lost a right to live on an indigenous reserve. The marriage and the loss of status happened before the UN Human Rights Committee had jurisdiction, and so the Committee said it could not decide whether that had been wrongful. However, it held that there was a continuing interference with her right to access her native culture and language in community with others, and that it had jurisdiction to rule on that breach.[29]

30 International courts and tribunals mostly distinguish between continuing acts, and completed acts that have continuing consequences or effects over time that continue to be felt after the relevant date for jurisdiction.[30] Thus, the following have been held not to constitute continuing breaches, with the result that the court or institution has found that the rule against retroactivity precluded it from accepting jurisdiction:

(a) An applicant was convicted for his writings prior to the ECHR entering into force, and on account of that conviction, after entry into force of the ECHR he was refused permission to join the Bar.[31]
(b) Applicants were assigned to the reserve corps of the Portuguese army before the relevant date for ECmHR jurisdiction, and they complained about this decision as well as its continuing consequences for their prospects of advancement in the military.[32]

---

[26] *E and AK v Hungary* (n 23) para 6.4; *Simunek v The Czech Republic* (n 21) para 4.5.
[27] *Nganyi v Tanzania* (n 19) para 66.
[28] *Marguš v Croatia*, App no 4455/10, 27 May 2014, para 97; *X v Portugal* (n 16) paras 7–8.
[29] *Lovelace v Canada* (n 21) para 15.
[30] ARSIWA (n 24) Article 14, and commentary, para 6.
[31] *X v Belgium* App no 2568/65, Commission Decision, 6 February 1968. See, to similar effect, *Jonas v The Czech Republic* (n 13).
[32] *X v Portugal* (n 16).

(c) An applicant, who was in prison, complained that his state of paralysis was caused in part by the failure of the State to give him adequate medical treatment at the time he was first injured, which happened before that State's ratification of the ECHR.[33]
(d) Applicants who had been deprived of their property prior to the relevant date, the deprivation continuing after that date.[34]

International courts and tribunals have also frequently found that the failure by a State to investigate or to provide remedies is not a continuing part of the initial act.[35] Thus, if the relevant conduct occurred prior to the relevant date, the applicant cannot invoke the Court's jurisdiction by arguing that there has been a continuing failure to investigate or to provide remedies for that earlier conduct. By way of example, in *Stamoulakatos v Greece*, the applicant complained of both an alleged unfairness in proceedings by which he was convicted of a crime, and the fact that domestic courts had upheld his conviction on appeal, with only the latter taking place after the relevant date. The ECtHR found that it did not have jurisdiction over any alleged unfairness in respect of the original proceedings.[36] In *Blečić v Croatia*, the Court provided the following summary of the position: 'the Court's temporal jurisdiction is to be determined in relation to the facts constitutive of the alleged interference. The subsequent failure of remedies aimed at redressing that interference cannot bring it within the Court's temporal jurisdiction'.[37] An application cannot circumvent the temporal limits on the Court's jurisdiction simply by reformulating a claim that conduct occurring at a time beyond the Court's jurisdiction was wrongful as a failure to investigate or to provide remedies for that conduct at a time within the Court's jurisdiction. **31**

An exception may apply where the treaty in question imposes a self-standing obligation on a State party to carry out an investigation into a type of act or event. In such a case, courts have held that they have jurisdiction to rule on a failure to carry out an investigation, even though the subject matter of the required investigation occurred before the relevant date. This is because the non-compliance with the substantive obligation to carry out an investigation has occurred or continued within the period of time in respect of which jurisdiction exists. To date, this approach appears to have been limited to situations where the original conduct has involved a putative breach of either the right to life or the right not to be tortured, both of which may be considered to entail a separate obligation on State authorities to carry out an investigation.[38] **32**

---

[33] *PM v Hungary*, App no 23636/94, Commission Decision, 21 May 1997.
[34] *Lupulet v Romania* (n 13); *Blečić v Croatia* (n 13) para 86; *Malhouse v The Czech Republic*, App no 33071/96, ECtHR GC, 13 December 2000, ECHR 2000-XII; *Ostojić v Croatia*, App no 16837/02, 26 September 2002, ECHR 2002-IX. However, note that in *Papamichalopoulos v Greece*, the ECtHR held that the initial taking of property had not been authorized by domestic law, meaning that what was at issue was not a one-off and completed taking but rather an ongoing occupation of the property, which was capable of being a continuing breach: *Papamichalopoulos v Greece* (1993) ECtHR Series B No 260, para 40; see also *Loizidou v Turkey* 1996-VI 2216.
[35] See, eg, *Phosphates in Morocco* (n 9) 28–29; *Certain Property* (n 10) para 52; *Litovchenko v Russia (dec)*, App no 69580/01, 18 April 2002; *Veeber v Estonia (No 1)*, App no 37571/97, 7 November 2002, para 55; *Varnava v Turkey* (n 16) para 130; *Janowiec v Russia* (n 13) para 129.
[36] *Stamoulakatos v Greece (No 1)*, App no 12806/87, 26 October 1993, Series A No 271.
[37] *Blečić v Croatia* (n 13) para 77.
[38] See *Teren Aksakal v Turkey*, App no 51967/99, 11 September 2007, paras 75–76; *Varnava v Turkey* (n 16) para 130; *Janowiec v Russia* (n 13) para 132; *Sankara v Burkina Faso* (n 21) para 6.3; *Mario Otilia Vargas Vargas v Chile*, Human Rights Committee, UN Doc CCPR/C/66/D/ 718/1996, 26 July 1999, para 6.6.

33 A 'composite act' is an internationally wrongful act made up of a series of actions or omissions which are defined in aggregate as wrongful.[39] The breach of obligation will be held to extend over the entire period in which those actions or omissions took place.[40] Where the composite act straddles the relevant date for jurisdiction *ratione temporis*, courts and tribunals usually consider themselves to have jurisdiction even over those parts of the composite act that took place prior to the treaty's entry into force. The International Law Commission gives as examples of composite acts 'genocide, apartheid or crimes against humanity, systematic acts of racial discrimination prohibited by a trade agreement'.[41]

III. Jurisdiction to consider disputes arising before a treaty's entry into force

34 The more permissive approach of the ICJ and the PCIJ to retroactive application of treaty provisions which confer jurisdiction is further evident in two cases that concern disputes which crystallized before jurisdiction had been conferred on the court. In the *Mavrommatis Palestine Concessions* case, the PCIJ dismissed as a mere 'matter of form'[42] the fact that the jurisdiction-conferring treaty had not yet come into force at the time of the institution of proceedings. It reasoned that the treaty had subsequently been ratified by the relevant States parties and had entered into force, and so to dismiss the application on the basis that it had been brought before that time would just result in the claimant resubmitting the same application a second time.[43] The PCIJ declined to dismiss the claim.

35 The ICJ took the same approach in the *Genocide Convention* case. The ICJ reasoned:[44]

> It is the case that the jurisdiction of the Court must normally be assessed on the date of the filing of the act instituting proceedings. However, the Court, like its predecessor the Permanent Court of International Justice, has always had recourse to the principle according to which it should not penalize a defect in a procedural act which the applicant could easily remedy.

36 Although this reasoning displays a form of practical logic, real questions arise as to whether it can be legally correct. If the jurisdiction of a court or tribunal arises from party consent as expressed in either a treaty or some unilateral instrument such as a declaration, then the jurisdiction must necessarily be bounded by that treaty or other instrument. As explained above, in the *Mavrommatis Palestine Concessions* case, the PCIJ recognized that its jurisdiction extended to disputes referred to it <u>after</u> the time when it had been invested with jurisdiction.[45] As a matter of orthodox analysis, then, it seems difficult to explain how the Court could properly expand its jurisdiction to cover disputes referred to it before

---

[39] ARSIWA (n 24) Article 15(1). See in this Commentary: Claudia Annacker and Enikő Horváth 'Article 15 of the ARSIWA'.
[40] ARSIWA (n 24) Article 15(2).
[41] ibid Article 15, and commentary, para 2.
[42] *Mavrommatis Palestine Concessions* (n 6) 34.
[43] ibid 34.
[44] *Genocide Convention* (n 8) para 26.
[45] *Mavrommatis Palestine Concessions* (n 6) 35. It is possible on the facts that this decision might have been decided on the basis that the breach in question was a continuing breach—see at 35. However, the reasoning in the paragraph quoted indicates that was not the basis of the Court's decision.

reciprocal consent to jurisdiction existed. The Court's recourse to practical considerations as a justification for doing so might be appropriate if the question being considered were one of admissibility or procedure. It is more difficult to see how this could be correct when applied to a question of temporal jurisdiction, which turns on reciprocal consent of the parties.

Other non-investment treaty international courts and tribunals have not adopted this very permissive approach.

D. Article 28 and international tribunals constituted under investment treaties

I. Jurisdiction to consider acts occurring before a treaty's entry into force

Investment treaty tribunals have frequently assumed jurisdiction over claims arising out of facts occurring before the entry into force of the investment treaty that confers jurisdiction, so long as the dispute crystallized after the treaty's entry into force. This was explained in *Nordzucker v Poland*, where the tribunal held that Article 28 of the VCLT applied both to substantive obligations and jurisdictional obligations imposed by a treaty, and that it might have a different effect depending on which type of obligation was at issue.[46] A provision imposing a substantive obligation on the treaty parties could not apply to acts or events preceding its entry into force that are alleged to constitute a breach of that obligation. However, a provision creating a right or obligation to arbitrate would apply so long as the claim had been formally brought after that provision came into force.[47]

The different application of Article 28 to treaty provisions imposing substantive obligations, on the one hand, and those conferring jurisdiction, on the other hand, is shown in sharp relief in cases where there are successive investment treaties between the Respondent State and the State of the claimant's nationality. In such cases, the tribunal has ruled that it has jurisdiction to decide a dispute which arises out of conduct that pre-dates the jurisdiction-conferring investment treaty, and then has looked to the prior investment treaty to supply the substantive rules which determine the lawfulness of that conduct.[48] The tribunal in *Bahgat v Egypt* noted that 'the [later] BIT does not restrict the parties' consent to arbitrate only to disputes that involve the application of the [later] BIT', and absent such a restriction it would have jurisdiction so long as the dispute had crystallized after the entry into force of the later Bilateral Investment Treaty (BIT).[49] Like the ICJ and the PCIJ, then, these investment treaty tribunals have taken the view that a treaty provision conferring jurisdiction can be invoked after its entry into force in respect of conduct preceding its entry into force, unless the treaty expressly precludes doing so. The right or obligation being invoked is jurisdictional, and jurisdiction is invoked after

---

[46] *Nordzucker AG v The Republic of Poland*, UNCITRAL, Partial Award, Jurisdiction, 10 December 2008, para 105(iv).
[47] ibid para 107.
[48] See, eg, *Jan de Nul NV v Arab Republic of Egypt*, Case No ARB/04/13, ICSID, Jurisdiction, 16 June 2006, paras 128–129 (hereafter *Jan de Nul*); *Bahgat v Arab Republic of Egypt (No I)*, PCA Case No 2012-07, Jurisdiction, 30 November 2007, paras 300 and 315 (hereafter *Bahgat v Egypt*).
[49] *Bahgat v Egypt* (n 48) para 308.

the entry into force of the right or obligation providing consent to it. There is thus no retroactivity in respect of the particular right or obligation invoked. What law such a tribunal has temporal jurisdiction to apply to what conduct concerning the substance of the dispute, is a different question.

40   Investment treaty tribunals have similarly relied on the concepts of 'continuing acts' and 'composite acts' in determining the temporal scope of their jurisdiction. Thus, if the tribunal is satisfied that there is a continuing act or course of conduct, or a series of composite acts or omissions which in aggregate can breach an investment treaty, that began before the investment treaty entered into force but continued after the entry into force, then the tribunal may both assume jurisdiction to consider the prior conduct, and also apply the substantive rules set out in the investment treaty to that conduct. It cannot find any conduct prior to the treaty's entry into force in self-standing breach of the investment treaty, but it can take it into account in order to assess and rule on the character of the State's conduct overall.

41   In *Tecmed v Mexico*, the tribunal held that the investment treaty in question could not apply retroactively, such that acts or events prior to the treaty's entry into force could not constitute breaches of the treaty; but it noted that this conclusion did not mean that such acts and events were irrelevant for the purpose of determining whether acts or events after the treaty's entry into force could constitute a violation.[50] The tribunal then continued:[51]

> [C]onduct, acts or omissions of the Respondent which, though they happened before the entry into force, may be considered a constituting part, concurrent factor or aggravating or mitigating element of conduct or acts or omissions of the Respondent which took place after such date do fall within the scope of this Arbitral Tribunal's jurisdiction. This is so, provided such conduct or acts, upon consummation or completion of their consummation after the entry into force of the Agreement constitute a breach of the Agreement, and particularly if the conduct, acts or omissions prior to December 18, 1996, could not reasonably have been fully assessed by the Claimant in their significance and effects when they took place, either because as the Agreement was not in force they could not be considered within the framework of a possible claim under its provisions or because it was not possible to assess them within the general context of conduct attributable to the Respondent in connection with the investment, the key point of which led to violations of the Agreement following its entry into force.

42   In *Renée Rose Levy v Peru*, the tribunal held that whether it had jurisdiction *ratione temporis* over a dispute was to be determined by reference to the date on which the State adopted the measure argued to constitute a breach of the treaty. That was so even if the measure 'represents the culmination of a process or sequence of events which may have started years earlier. It is not uncommon that divergences or disagreements develop over a period of time before they finally "crystallize" in an actual measure affecting the investor's treaty rights'.[52]

---

[50] *Técnicas Medioambientales Tecmed, SA v United Mexican States*, ICSID Case No ARB(AF)/00/2, Award, 29 May 2003, para 66.
[51] ibid para 68.
[52] *Renée Rose Levy and Gremcitel SA v Republic of Peru*, ICSID Case No ARB/11/17, Award, 9 January 2015, para 149.

In *Société Générale v Dominican Republic*, the tribunal noted that it could have regard to acts **43** or events that pre-dated the treaty's entry into force where those were part of a composite act that crystallized into a breach after the entry into force. That would be the case where the two categories of acts 'represented action towards the same result'. The tribunal concluded that '[i]n such a situation, the obligations of the treaty will not be applied retroactively but only to acts that will be the final result of that convergence and which take place when the treaty has come into force'.[53]

II. Jurisdiction to consider disputes arising before the investment treaty's entry into force

The jurisprudence of investment treaty tribunals is mixed on the question of whether dis- **44** putes that arose before the entry into force of an investment treaty can come within the jurisdiction of a tribunal constituted under that treaty. The starting point in answering this question must of course be the terms of the treaty in question: do they confer or exclude jurisdiction in such circumstances? However, the terms of few treaties answer this question. If the treaty is silent, then the question is, what rule are the parties to be assumed to have intended?

There is no consistent answer to this from investment treaty tribunals. On the one hand, **45** some have chosen to follow the permissive approach adopted by the PCIJ and the ICJ in the *Mavrommatis Palestine Concessions* case and the *Genocide Convention* case, discussed above.[54] On the other hand, some tribunals have held that, unless an investment treaty contained terms providing that disputes arising before its entry into force are within jurisdiction, then they are not.[55] For instance, in *MCI Power Group v Ecuador*, the tribunal noted that '[t]he non-retroactivity of the BIT excludes its application to disputes arising prior to its entry into force', including the 'dispute resolution system established by the BIT'.[56] Tribunals have approached the question differently, and no consistent practice can be discerned.

The matter is complicated by the divergence of views expressed by tribunals as to what can **46** constitute a 'dispute'. This is of obvious significance: the time at which a mere disagreement between the parties is determined to have crystallized into a dispute may decide whether that dispute arose before or after a treaty's entry into force. Tribunals have adopted, at various times, the following formulations:

(a) In *Bahgat v Egypt*, it was said to be enough that a disagreement on facts and/or law had been communicated by one party to the other.[57]
(b) *Helnan International Hotels v Egypt* adopted a higher bar. The tribunal said that '[I]n case of a dispute, the difference of views forms the subject of an active exchange between the parties under circumstances which indicate that the parties wish to resolve

---

[53] *Société Générale v Dominican Republic*, LCIA Case No UN7927, Preliminary Objections, 19 September 2008, para 92.
[54] *Tradex Hellas SA v Republic of Albania*, ICSID Case No ARB/94/2, Jurisdiction, 24 December 1999, para 174.
[55] *Impregilo SpA v Pakistan (No II)*, ICSID Case No ARB/03/3, Jurisdiction, 22 April 2005, para 300; *Walter Bau Ag v The Kingdom of Thailand*, UNCITRAL (ad hoc), Award, 1 July 2009, para 9.70.
[56] *MCI Power Group, LC and New Turbine, Inc v Republic of Ecuador*, ICSID Case No ARB/03/6, Award, 31 July 2007, para 61.
[57] *Bahgat v Egypt* (n 48) para 300.

the difference....', as compared to a mere divergence in which 'the parties hold different views but without necessarily pursuing the difference in an active manner'.[58]

(c) In *Maffezini v Spain*, the tribunal described a 'dispute' as follows:

> there tends to be a natural sequence of events that leads to a dispute. It begins with the expression of a disagreement and the statement of a difference of views. In time, those events acquire a precise legal meaning through the formulation of legal claims, their discussion and eventual rejection or lack of response by the other party. The conflict of legal views and interests will only be present in the latter stage, even though the underlying facts predate them... this sequence of events has to be taken into account in establishing the critical date.[59]

(d) A number of tribunals have adopted a common formulation to decide whether a dispute heard before domestic courts was the same dispute subsequently brought to the international arbitral tribunal—the test being whether 'the facts or considerations that gave rise to the earlier dispute continued to be central to the later dispute', such that both disputes have the same origin or source.[60]

47 In cases where a disagreement between the parties was already on foot at the time an investment treaty was concluded, the definition of a 'dispute' adopted by the tribunal has obvious significance. The more permissive definitions of a 'dispute', especially the first in the list above, are more likely to result in the dispute having crystallized prior to a treaty's entry into force. That means the tribunal will need to confront the difficult and contested question of whether the rule against retroactivity precludes it from exercising jurisdiction over that dispute. It may be that some tribunals have preferred to define the 'dispute' in a manner that has avoided the need to grapple with this question.

E. Conclusion

48 The rule in Article 28 of the VCLT is readily applied by international courts and tribunals to treaty provisions that establish primary obligations. There is greater difficulty and divergence when Article 28 is applied to, or considered in connection with, treaty provisions that confer jurisdiction on an international court or tribunal. The approach of the ICJ and the PCIJ to questions of their jurisdiction *ratione temporis* indicates that they consider the rule reflected in Article 28 to have a limited, if any, role to play in relation to treaty provisions conferring jurisdiction. Other courts and tribunals have been less permissive in considering their own jurisdiction *ratione temporis*, applying the rule in Article 28 to varying degrees in order to limit their own jurisdiction in relation to conduct occurring, or disputes crystallizing, before the entry into force of the instrument or treaty conferring jurisdiction. Neither the jurisprudence of investment treaty tribunals, nor that of other international courts and tribunals aside from the ICJ and the PCIJ, is clear or consistent in relation to whether and how Article 28 of the VCLT should be applied to treaty provisions and instruments conferring jurisdiction.

---

[58] *Helnan International Hotels A/S v Arab Republic of Egypt*, ICSID Case No ARB/05/19, Jurisdiction, 17 October 2006, para 52.

[59] *Maffezini v Kingdom of Spain*, ICSID Case No ARB/97/7, Jurisdiction, 25 January 2000, para 96.

[60] *Industria Nacional de Alimentos, SA and Indalsa Perú, SA v Republic of Peru*, ICSID Case No ARB/03/4, Award, 7 February 2005, para 50; *Empresas Lucchetti, SA v The Republic of Peru*, ICSID Case No ARB/03/4, Award, 7 February 2005, para 50; *Jan de Nul* (n 48) paras 126–29.

Selected literature

Dopagne F, 'Article 28: Non-Retroactivity of Treaties' in Corten O and Klein P (eds), *The Vienna Conventions on the Law of Treaties* (OUP 2011).

Villiger ME, *Commentary on the 1969 Vienna Convention on the Law of Treaties* (Martinus Nijhoff Publishers 2008).

Selected decisions

Application of the Convention on the Prevention and Punishment of the Crime of Genocide (Bosnia and Herzegovina v Yugoslavia) (Preliminary Objections) [1996] ICJ Rep 595.

Bahgat v Arab Republic of Egypt (No I), PCA Case No 2012-07, Jurisdiction, 30 November 2007.

Case Concerning Right of Passage over Indian Territory (Portugal v India) (Merits) [1960] ICJ Rep 6.

Case of the Mavrommatis Palestine Concessions (Greece v UK) (Judgment No 2) (1924) PCIJ Series A No 2.

Nordzucker AG v The Republic of Poland, UNCITRAL, Partial Award, Jurisdiction, 17 February 2006.

Phosphates in Morocco (Italy v France) (Preliminary Objections) (1938) PCIJ Series A/B No 74.

Técnicas Medioambientales Tecmed, SA v United Mexican States, ICSID Case No RB(AF)/00/2, Award, 29 May 2003.

Article 29 of the VCLT

Territorial scope

Emma Lindsay and Philippa Webb*

Unless a different intention appears from the treaty or is otherwise established, a treaty is binding upon each party in respect of its entire territory.

A. Introduction		1	I. The rule: 'a treaty is binding upon each party in respect of its entire territory'	9
B. Article 29 interpreted and applied by international courts and tribunals		3	II. The exception: 'Unless a different intention appears from the treaty or is otherwise established'	11
I. The rule: 'A treaty is binding upon each party in respect of its entire territory'		3	D. Conclusions: Comparing practice in investment arbitration and general international law	13
II. The exception: 'Unless a different intention appears from the treaty or is otherwise established'		6	I. Alignment or deviation	13
C. Article 29 interpreted and applied in investment disputes		9	II. Reasons for alignment or deviation	17
			III. Justifications for alignment or deviation	22

A. Introduction

1 Article 29 of the Vienna Convention on the Law of Treaties (VCLT) provides guidance as to which territories of a given State are governed by an international treaty. The provision, which is accepted as customary international law,[1] is composed of two parts: (i) a general rule ('a treaty is binding upon each party in respect of its entire territory'); and (ii) an exception ('[u]nless a different intention appears from the treaty or is otherwise established').

2 The provision does not address related matters such as the succession of State parties to a treaty,[2] the provisional application of a treaty to a dependent territory,[3] or the territorial implications of attributing the conduct of private or non-State entities to States.[4]

---

* The authors thank Tyler Goss for research assistance in the preparation of this entry.
[1] *Application of the Convention on the Prevention and Punishment of the Crime of Genocide (Croatia v Serbia)* (Judge Tomka Separate Opinion) [2008] ICJ Rep 515, para 10 (hereafter *Croatia v Serbia*, Sep Op Tomka).
[2] See in this Commentary: James G Devaney and Christian J Tams, 'Succession in respect of cession, unification and separation of States'.
[3] See in this Commentary: Tania Voon, 'Article 25 of the VCLT: Provisional application'.
[4] See in this Commentary: Jorge E Viñuales and Alina Papanastasiou, 'Article 8 of the ARSIWA: Attribution of conduct instructed, directed or controlled by a State'.

B. Article 29 interpreted and applied by international courts and tribunals

I. The general rule: 'A treaty is binding upon each party in respect of its entire territory'

The International Court of Justice (ICJ) has addressed Article 29 indirectly in the *Namibia* **3** *Advisory Opinion*: '[w]ith respect to existing bilateral treaties, member States must abstain from invoking or applying those treaties … concluded by South Africa on behalf of or concerning Namibia. With respect to multilateral treaties, however, the same rule cannot be applied to certain general conventions such as those of a humanitarian character, the non-performance of which may adversely affect the people of Namibia'.[5] This aligns with the United States' written pleadings on the applicability of multilateral treaties under Article 29: '[t]hose [treaties] concluded since the establishment of the United Nations frequently provide that they will be applicable to all territories for the international relations of which the parties are responsible unless at the time of ratification a party otherwise declares'.[6] In his Separate Opinion in *Croatia v Serbia*, Judge Tomka invoked Article 29 directly: 'There is no doubt that the Genocide Convention was binding on the SFRY [Socialist Federal Republic of Yugoslavia] since 12 January 1951, when it entered into force in accordance with Article XIII, until its dissolution and thus was applicable in respect of its entire territory (Article 29 of the Vienna Convention on the Law of Treaties codifying the relevant rule of customary international law[)].'[7]

The Court of Justice of the European Union (CJEU) has directly invoked and applied Article **4** 29 to determine the territorial scope of treaties. It has determined that the continental shelf was within the 'territory' of The Netherlands for the purposes of the Convention of 27 September 1968 on Jurisdiction and the Enforcement of Judgments in Civil and Commercial Matters (Brussels Convention).[8] By contrast, Western Sahara did not fall under the 'territory' of Morocco for the purposes of a liberalization agreement with the European Union (EU) regarding agricultural products.[9] The Court described its understanding of territory under Article 29 as 'the geographical space over which that State exercises the fullness of the powers granted to sovereign entities by international law, to the exclusion of any other territory, such as a territory likely to be under the sole jurisdiction or the sole international responsibility of that State'.[10]

As regards regional human rights courts, in its *Advisory Opinion on Consular Assistance*, the **5** Inter-American Court of Human Rights (IACtHR) found that human rights provisions, including the right to information on consular assistance, are presumed to apply to the entire

---

[5] *Legal Consequences for States of the Continued Presence of South Africa in Namibia (South West Africa) Notwithstanding Security Council Resolution 276* (Advisory Opinion) [1971] ICJ Rep 16, para 122.
[6] ibid, Written Statements of India, United States of America, and Nigeria, 884.
[7] *Croatia v Serbia*, Sep Op Tomka (n 1) para 10. See also internal references at paras 10–11 to *Application of the Convention on the Prevention and Punishment of the Crime of Genocide (Bosnia and Herzegovina v Yugoslavia)* (Preliminary Objections) [1996] ICJ Rep 595 and the separate opinions of that case.
[8] *Herbert Weber v Universal Ogden Services Ltd*, Case C-37/00, [2002] ECR I-02013 (CJEU, 27 February 2002), para 29.
[9] *Council v Front Polisario*, Case C-104/16 P (CJEU GC, 21 December 2016), paras 94–97 (hereafter *Council v Front Polisario*, 2016).
[10] ibid paras 95–96; see also *Western Sahara Campaign UK v Commissioners for Her Majesty's Revenue and Customs and Secretary of State for Environment, Food and Rural Affairs*, Case C-266/16 (CJEU GC, 27 February 2018), para 85 (finding that international agreements concluded by the EU and Morocco in the fisheries sector did not apply to waters adjacent to the territory of Western Sahara).

territory of a State party regardless of its federal or unitary structure.[11] The European Court of Human Rights (ECtHR) in considering the nature of Russia's jurisdiction over Crimea under the European Convention on Human Rights (ECHR), citing Article 29 of the VCLT, noted that Article 1 of the Convention must be understood to mean that a State's jurisdictional competence is primarily territorial, but also that jurisdiction is presumed to be exercised normally throughout the territory.[12]

II. The exception: 'Unless a different intention appears from the treaty or is otherwise established'

6   In another case addressing Western Sahara, the CJEU invoked the exception in Article 29, noting that 'the rule codified in Article 29 of the Vienna Convention does not preclude a treaty from being binding on a State in regard to a territory other than its own if such an intention is apparent from that treaty'.[13] The CJEU held that such an intention was 'explicitly apparent from' the wording of a Joint Declaration on Western Sahara made by Morocco and the EU in the context of an Association Agreement between them and 'supported by' an EU decision adopted on the conclusion of the Association Agreement.[14]

7   Article 1 of the ECHR refers to 'within their jurisdiction', which has been interpreted to extend to territory where the state is in 'effective control'.[15] In one case, since no change to the sovereign territory of Ukraine has been accepted or declared by Ukraine, the Court assumed that Ukraine's jurisdiction extended to the entirety of its territory, including Crimea.[16] However, for the purposes of the admissibility decision, the Court found that Russia was in effective control over the territory of Crimea,[17] and that it was bound to apply the Convention not only from the moment of Crimea's annexation but also for several weeks prior.[18] The Court has also rejected the argument that a unilateral declaration of a state may exclude certain territories from the scope of the Convention.[19]

8   Article 2 of the International Covenant on Civil and Political Rights (ICCPR) refers to 'within its territory and subject to its jurisdiction'. In the Wall Advisory Opinion, the ICJ concluded that the ICCPR is applicable to the acts of a State acting in the exercise of its jurisdiction outside its own territory.[20] It observed that State jurisdiction is 'primarily territorial' but 'may sometimes be exercised outside the national territory'.[21] Article 29 was not directly invoked.

---

[11] *The Right to Information on Consular Assistance in the Framework of the Guarantees of the Due Process of Law* (Advisory Opinion), IACHR Series A No 16, OC-16/99, 1 October 1999, paras 139–40.

[12] *Ukraine v Russia (re Crimea)* App nos 20958/14 and 38334/18 (ECtHR, 14 January 2021), para 345 (hereafter *Ukraine v Russia*, ECtHR)

[13] *Front Polisario v Council* Joined Cases T-344/19 and T-356/19 (CJEU, 29 September 2021), para 305.

[14] ibid.

[15] See *Loizidou v Turkey* App no 15318/89, Preliminary Objections (ECtHR, 23 February 1995); *Al-Skeini and others v United Kingdom*, App no 55721/07 (ECtHR, 7 July 2011), paras 138–42; *Hirsi Jamaa and Others v Italy*, App no 27765/09 (ECtHR, 23 February 2012), paras 73–74; *Issa and Others v Turkey*, App no 31821/96 (ECtHR, 16 November 2004); cf *Bankovic and Others v Belgium and Others*, App no 52207/99 (ECtHR, 12 December 2001), para 82 (a territory bombed by a State party is not territory under the effective control of that State).

[16] *Ukraine v Russia* (n 12) paras 345–46.

[17] ibid para 349.

[18] ibid para 335.

[19] *Ilaşcu and Others v Moldova and Russia*, App no 48787/99 (ECtHR, 8 July 2004).

[20] *Legal Consequences of the Construction of a Wall in the Occupied Palestinian Territory* (Advisory Opinion) [2004] ICJ Rep 136, para 111.

[21] ibid para 109.

The UN Human Rights Committee has confirmed that 'States Parties are required by article 2, paragraph 1, to respect and to ensure the Covenant rights to all persons who may be within their territory and to all persons subject to their jurisdiction. This means that a State party must respect and ensure the rights laid down in the Covenant to anyone within the power or effective control of that State Party, even if not situated within the territory of that State Party'.[22]

C. Article 29 interpreted and applied in investment disputes

I. The rule: 'A treaty is binding upon each party in respect of its entire territory'

Several investment tribunals have directly applied Article 29 to find that Russia's annexation and *de facto* control of the Crimean Peninsula extended Russia's 'territory' for purposes of the Russia–Ukraine Bilateral Investment Treaty (BIT), regardless of whether the annexation was lawful under international law.[23] For example, the *Oschadbank* tribunal concluded that, according to the BIT, the term 'territory' means 'a geographical area over which a Party exercises jurisdiction or control'.[24] In reviewing investment tribunals' jurisdiction, domestic courts have adopted similar reasoning.[25] The Hague Court of Appeal held that the term 'territory' had been used in accordance with the meaning of that term pursuant to Article 29, which refers to a State's 'entire territory', and therefore encompasses territory for which a State has assumed responsibility in international relations, without it being necessary to decide whether this was also the sovereign territory of that State.[26]

In another investment treaty case, the Singapore Court of Appeal indirectly applied Article 29 in considering an alleged treaty breach consisting of the host State's voting conduct within an international organization.[27] The Court of Appeal held that the investment treaty was concerned with protecting against unlawful exercises of the host State's enforcement jurisdiction and, given the treaty's express statement that investors were to be accorded treatment 'in the territory of the host State', was limited to acts occurring within the State's territory.[28]

---

[22] UN Human Rights Committee, 'General comment No 31 [80]', *The nature of the general legal obligation imposed on States Parties to the Covenant* (26 May 2004) UN Doc CCPR/C/21/Rev.1/Add.13, para 10.

[23] See, eg, *SC CB PrivatBank and Finance Company Finilon LLC v The Russian Federation*, PCA Case No 2015-21, Interim Award, 27 March 2017, para 195. And see *Limited Liability Company Lugzor et al v The Russian Federation*, PCA Case No 2015-29, Award, 4 October 2022; *PJSC Ukrnafta v The Russian Federation*, PCA Case No 2015-34, Award, 26 June 2017; *Stabil LLC et al v The Russian Federation*, PCA Case No 2015-35, Award, 12 April 2019; *Everest Estate LLC et al v The Russian Federation*, PCA Case No 2015-36, Award, 2 May 2018; *Oschadbank v The Russian Federation*, PCA Case No 2016-14, Award, 26 November 2019 (set aside by the Paris Court of Appeal for other reasons); *Aeroport Belbek LLC and Igor Valerievich Kolomoisky v The Russian Federation*, PCA Case No 2017-07, Partial Award, 4 February 2019. None of these awards are public at the time of writing.

[24] J Braun, 'Uncovered: Tribunal in Previously-Unseen Award Against Russia Upheld Jurisdiction Over Crimea-Related Claims, and Awarded Over 1.3 Billion USD in Compensation', *IAR* (13 April 2021), <https://www.iareporter.com/articles/uncovered-tribunal-in-previously-unseen-award-against-russia-upheld-jurisdiction-over-crimea-related-claims-and-awarded-over-1-3-billion-usd-in-compensation/> accessed 7 March 2023 (hereafter Braun, 'Uncovered').

[25] See *NJSC Naftogaz of Ukraine, et al v The Russian Federation*, Case No 200.274.564/01, Hague Court of Appeal, 19 July 2022, para 5.5.20.

[26] See *Aeroport Belbek LLC and Igor Valerievich Kolomoisky v The Russian Federation*, Case No 200.266.443/01, Hague Court of Appeal, 19 July 2022, paras 5.5.21–5.5.24. See also in the context of Article 56 of the ECHR, *R (Hoareau and Bancoult) v The Secretary of State for Foreign and Commonwealth Affairs* [2020] EWCA Civ 1010.

[27] See *Swissbourgh Diamond Mines (Pty) Ltd v Kingdom of Lesotho*, Case No SGCA 2015/81, Judgment, 27 November 2018, para 55(c).

[28] ibid paras 102, 202.

II. The exception: 'Unless a different intention appears from the treaty or is otherwise established'

11 One investment tribunal indirectly applied the exception in Article 29 while considering the exclusion of certain territory from a treaty's application. In *Menzies v Senegal*, one of the claimants was incorporated in the British Virgin Islands.[29] The tribunal observed that the applicable UK–Senegal BIT did not extend to the British Virgin Islands and declined jurisdiction on that basis but did not provide any further reasons in support of this observation.[30]

12 Another investment tribunal expressly ruled out the application of the exception in Article 29 to find the People's Republic of China–Laos BIT applicable to Macao Special Administrative Region, where the claimant was incorporated. In *Sanum Investments Ltd v Lao People's Democratic Republic*, the tribunal reached this conclusion due to the absence of any language in the applicable BIT to this effect,[31] and because it was not otherwise established that the BIT was not applicable to the whole territory.[32] Having excluded the application of the exception, the tribunal relied on the general rule in Article 29 to find that the claimant was a protected investor under the BIT.[33]

D. Conclusions: Comparing practice in investment arbitration and general international law

I. Alignment or deviation

13 Explicit reference to Article 29 in the decisions of international courts and tribunals applying either general international law or investment law has been limited, although the provision implicitly underlies consideration of issues relating to territory of treaties across regimes.

14 Article 29 has seen increased use in recent investment arbitration practice relating to the Russia–Ukraine conflict. These recent developments, which focus on the general rule in Article 29, go some way towards mitigating what Miltner has described as 'the looming functional obsolescence of Article 29 VCLT's general rule of full territorial application in favour of its now dominant exception'.[34] Even the *Sanum* tribunal's focus on the exception in its reasoning is not out of step given that the tribunal ultimately found the general rule to apply.

15 Alignment between the interpretation of international human rights treaties and investment treaties can be seen in the approach to recent cases involving the Russia–Ukraine conflict

---

[29] *Menzies Middle East and Africa SA and Aviation Handling Services International Ltd v Republic of Senegal*, ICSID Case No ARB/15/21, Award, 5 August 2016, paras 152–57.
[30] ibid.
[31] *Sanum Investments Limited v Lao People's Democratic Republic*, PCA Case No 2013-13, Jurisdiction, 13 December 2013, IIC 1420 (2013), paras 270–77 (hereafter *Sanum*, Jurisdiction). The tribunal's award on jurisdiction was the subject of court proceedings in Singapore. See *Government of the Lao People's Democratic Republic v Sanum Investments Ltd*, Decision, SGHC Case No 2015/15, Judgment, 20 January 2015; *Sanum Investments Ltd v Government of the Lao People's Democratic Republic*, SGCA Case No 2016/57, Decision, 29 September 2016. The case also involved the application of Article 15 of the Vienna Convention on the Succession of States in respect of Treaties. See also in this Commentary: James G Devaney and Christian J Tams, 'Succession in respect of cession, unification and separation of States'.
[32] *Sanum*, Jurisdiction (n 31) paras 278–99.
[33] ibid para 300.
[34] B Miltner, 'Territory and Its Relationship to Treaties' in D Kritsiotis and MJ Bowman (eds), *Conceptual and Contextual Perspectives on the Modern Law of Treaties* (CUP 2018) 496.

where courts and tribunals in both regimes have assumed jurisdiction over acts and events alleged to have occurred in Crimea based on Russia's effective control of the region. The application of Article 29, however, is different. In the human rights context, the exercise of jurisdiction stems from the application of the exception in Article 29 due to the presence of 'jurisdiction' clauses. In the investment context, the general rule in Article 29 has been applied to interpret 'territory' as territory under the control of a treaty party irrespective of sovereignty. The effect in both regimes, via different legal reasoning based on differences in treaty language, is to broaden treaty protection.

In the investment context, the concept of territory plays a dual role. Most often, the concept is examined in determining whether an investment has taken place in the territory of the host State to establish jurisdiction *ratione materiae* under an investment treaty such that the investment qualifies for treaty protection.[35] The concept also arises in connection with the territorial scope of a treaty to determine whether a treaty extends to a particular territory for purposes of jurisdiction *ratione loci*. For example, the Convention on the Settlement of Investment Disputes between States and Nationals of Other States (ICSID Convention) provides that it 'shall apply to all territories for whose international relations a Contracting State is responsible, except those which are excluded by such State by written notice to the depositary of this Convention either at the time of ratification, acceptance or approval or subsequently'.[36] Exclusions by Contracting States have limited application of the Convention to territories over which a State has effective control (in the case of Moldova) or removed overseas territories from the scope of Convention (New Zealand and the United Kingdom).[37]

II. Reasons for alignment or deviation

There are four main reasons aligning the analytical approach adopted in both investment arbitration practice and the practice under general international law, which in turn may lead to alignment or deviation in the resulting application of Article 29 VCLT depending on the particular context.

First, specific language in a treaty or related document will evidence 'a different intention' as to the meaning of 'territory'.[38] This is consistent with the cardinal principle in Article 31 VCLT that the 'ordinary meaning' of a treaty provision should be the starting point for interpretation.

Second, a court or tribunal may engage in dynamic interpretation to take account of realities on the ground. These may include effective control over the territory by a certain State,

---

[35] M Waibel, 'Investment Arbitration: Jurisdiction and Admissibility' in M Bungenberg and others (eds), *International Investment Law* (Beck/Hart/Nomos 2015) 1248–49, para 144 ('It is a characteristic feature of "investment" as contemplated in Article 25 of the ICSID Convention, and other instruments of investment protection, that the investment be made in the territory of the ICSID State. Only in such cases does the investment fall directly under the control of the host State's legislative, executive and judicial power and requires the protection afforded by the Convention. In keeping with principles of jurisdiction in international law, States cannot reasonably be expected to protect investments outside their territorial jurisdiction, unless they have expressly undertaken such duties of extending investment protection extraterritorially').

[36] Convention on the Settlement of Investment Disputes Between States and Nationals of Other States (International Centre for Settlement of Investment Disputes) 575 UNTS 159 (opened for signature 18 March 1965, entry into force 14 October 1966), Article 70.

[37] ICSID, 'Exclusion of Territories by Contracting States (ICSID/8-B)', *ICSID World Bank* < https://icsid.worldbank.org/sites/default/files/2020_July_ICSID_8_ENG.pdf > accessed 8 March 2023.

[38] See, eg, *Council v Front Polisario*, 2016 (n 9) paras 94–97.

regardless of the lawfulness of such control. Both human rights courts and investment tribunals have treated Crimea as territory of the Russian Federation due to its effective control.[39]

20   Third, there is a presumption of protection in certain situations so that the concept of 'territory' is stretched to ensure the obligation to protect in human rights treaties. Recent investment arbitration practice relating to the Russia–Ukraine conflict can be seen to follow a similar logic. Although it was not an Article 29 VCLT case, in *Armed Activities on the Territory of the Congo*, the ICJ found that 'Uganda established and exercised authority in Ituri', a province of the Democratic Republic of the Congo, 'as an occupying Power'.[40] Accordingly, it found that 'Uganda's responsibility is engaged both for any acts of its military that violated its international obligations and for any lack of vigilance in preventing violations of human rights and international humanitarian law *by other actors* present in the occupied territory, including rebel groups acting on their own account'.[41]

21   Fourth, another potential source of alignment or deviation is the extent to which a decision-maker takes into account the distinction between the metropolitan State and its non-metropolitan territories, such as in the debate over the 'colonial clause'.[42] The ICJ has recognized the right to self-determination is one of the 'basic principles of international law', with a 'normative character under customary international law'.[43] As colonialism fades from the international stage, the focus of courts and tribunals may shift to other forms of influence over territory, such as through supranational entities like the EU and through the use of the federal clause.

III. Justifications for alignment or deviation

22   Any time that 'territory' becomes a heated issue in a case, the Court or tribunal may face a dilemma of whether to avoid pronouncing on the sovereignty over disputed territories. Milanović argues that pronouncing on sovereignty 'may well advance the cause of one of the disputing states ... and contribute to its overarching narrative regarding a wider dispute, but does little for advancing the cause of human rights. Indeed, doing so may even harm the cause of human rights by provoking political backlash by the losing state against the human rights body, including treaty denunciation'.[44] Costelloe observes that where unlawful occupation, coupled with a claim to sovereignty, endures for so significant a period

---

[39] See *Ukraine v Russia* (n 12) para 345; see also Braun, 'Uncovered' (n 24).

[40] *Armed Activities on the Territory of the Congo (Democratic Republic of the Congo v Uganda)* (Merits) [2005] ICJ Rep 168, para 176.

[41] ibid para 179 (emphasis added).

[42] M Fitzmaurice, 'Treaties' in R Wolfrum (ed), *The Max Planck Encyclopedia of Public International Law* (OUP 2010) (Sir Fitzmaurice: 'The question may arise of whether the expression " its entire territory" only refers to areas fully under a State's sovereignty or *also* to territories with respect to which that State has a certain international responsibility including treaty-making power (eg, protectorates and protected States)').

[43] *Legal Consequences of the Separation of the Chagos Archipelago from Mauritius in 1965* (Advisory Opinion) [2019] ICJ Rep 95, para 155.

[44] M Milanović, 'ECtHR Grand Chamber Declares Admissible the Case of Ukraine v Russia re Crimea', *EJIL: Talk!*, 15 January 2021, <https://www.ejiltalk.org/ecthr-grand-chamber-declares-admissible-the-case-of-ukraine-v-russia-re-crimea/> accessed 8 March 2023; see also M Milanović and T Papić, 'The Applicability of the ECHR in Contested Territories' (2018) 67 ICLQ 779; see, eg, *Chagos Marine Protected Area Arbitration (Mauritius v United Kingdom)*, PCA Case No 2011-03, Award, 18 March 2015, para 219 ('In the Tribunal's view, to read Article 298(1)(a)(i) as a warrant to assume jurisdiction over matters of land sovereignty on the pretext that the Convention makes use of the term "coastal State" would do violence to the intent of the drafters of the Convention to craft a balanced text and to respect the manifest sensitivity of States to the compulsory settlement of disputes relating to sovereign rights and maritime territory.').

of time, a transfer of territory may come to be regarded as a fait accompli by other States. In such circumstances, 'the meaning of "territory" as an element of an international legal rule, or where the word appears in a treaty provision, is less clear'.[45] His view, expressed in 2016, that '[u]nder the default approach, a treaty could arguably apply with respect to territory that a State controls and over which it claims sovereignty, even if unlawfully',[46] has proven prescient with respect to decisions involving Russia and Crimea.

Alignment in the approaches of international courts and investment tribunals may be justified by the increasingly porous boundaries between the subject matter of disputes. The latter are increasingly dealing with human rights, environmental matters, and territorial disputes. These matters may be the core of the dispute, ancillary issues, or part of the legal and factual background. In these circumstances, coherence in the interpretation of the same principles and treaty provisions is to be commended. 23

At the same time, deviation may also be justified given the different mandates, procedures, and identities of courts and tribunals. Investment tribunals are more concerned with an investment's relationship with the host State—a factor that rarely arises in inter-State or human rights disputes. 24

Finally, careful attention should be paid to how the notion of 'territory' arises in the case. Is it in relation to the location of natural resources, the alleged commission of human rights violations, the use of force (physical or cyber), transboundary environmental harm, violations of *jus cogens* or *erga omnes* norms, or the course and consequences of an armed conflict? In each of these scenarios, a broad notion of 'territory' may promote protection but it may also risk exacerbating sovereignty disputes or recognizing an unlawful intervention. 25

Selected literature

Costelloe D, 'Treaty Succession in Annexed Territory' (2016) 65(2) ICLQ 343.
Fitzmaurice M, 'Treaties' in Wolfrum R (ed), *The Max Planck Encyclopedia of Public International Law* (OUP 2010).
Miltner B, 'Territory and Its Relationship to Treaties' in Kritsiotis D and Bowman MJ (eds), *Conceptual and Contextual Perspectives on the Modern Law of Treaties* (CUP 2018).

Selected decisions

Aeroport Belbek LLC and Igor Valerievich Kolomoisky v The Russian Federation, PCA Case No 2017-07, Partial Award, 4 February 2019.
Application of the Convention on the Prevention and Punishment of the Crime of Genocide (Croatia v Serbia) (Judge Tomka Separate Opinion) [2008] ICJ Rep 515.
Council v Front Polisario, Case C-104/16 P (ECtHR GC, 21 December 2016).
Everest Estate LLC et al v The Russian Federation, PCA Case No 2015-36, Award, 2 May 2018.
Legal Consequences for States of the Continued Presence of South Africa in Namibia (South West Africa) Notwithstanding Security Council Resolution 276 (Advisory Opinion) [1971] ICJ Rep 16.

---

[45] D Costelloe, 'Treaty Succession in Annexed Territory' (2016) 65(2) ICLQ 343.
[46] ibid.

Oschadbank v The Russian Federation, PCA Case No 2016-14, Award, 26 November 2019.
PJSC Ukrnafta v The Russian Federation, PCA Case No 2015-34, Award, 26 June 2017.
Sanum Investments Limited v Lao People's Democratic Republic, PCA Case No 2013-13, Jurisdiction, 13 December 2013, IIC 1420.
SC CB PrivatBank and Finance Company Finilon LLC v The Russian Federation, PCA Case No 2015-21, Interim Award, 27 March 2017.
Stabil LLC et al v The Russian Federation, PCA Case No 2015-35, Award, 12 April 2019.
Ukraine v Russia (re Crimea) App nos 20958/14 and 38334/18 (ECtHR, 14 January 2021).

Article 30 of the VCLT

Application of successive treaties relating to the same subject-matter

Sean Aughey

1. Subject to Article 103 of the Charter of the United Nations, the rights and obligations of States Parties to successive treaties relating to the same subject matter shall be determined in accordance with the following paragraphs.

2. When a treaty specifies that it is subject to, or that it is not to be considered as incompatible with, an earlier or later treaty, the provisions of that other treaty prevail.

3. When all the parties to the earlier treaty are parties also to the later treaty but the earlier treaty is not terminated or suspended in operation under Article 59, the earlier treaty applies only to the extent that its provisions are compatible with those of the later treaty.

4. When the parties to the later treaty do not include all the parties to the earlier one:

(a) as between States Parties to both treaties the same rule applies as in paragraph 3;

(b) as between a State party to both treaties and a State party to only one of the treaties, the treaty to which both States are parties governs their mutual rights and obligations.

5. Paragraph 4 is without prejudice to Article 41, or to any question of the termination or suspension of the operation of a treaty under Article 60 or to any question of responsibility which may arise for a State from the conclusion or application of a treaty the provisions of which are incompatible with its obligations towards another State under another treaty.

A. Introduction	1
B. The elements of Article 30 VCLT	3
I. Overview	4
II. Three questions of interpretation	11
1. Which treaty is the 'earlier' or 'later' in time?	12
2. When will two treaties 'relate to the same subject matter'?	13
3. When will two treaties be 'incompatible'?	16
C. Article 30 VCLT in non-investment disputes	17
D. Article 30 VCLT in investment disputes	18
I. Relevance of Article 30 VCLT in investment disputes	18
1. Successive international investment agreements	18
2. The 'intra-EU objection'	19
II. The applicability of Article 30(2) VCLT	22
III. Meaning of 'relating to the same subject matter'	23
IV. Meaning of 'incompatible'	28
E. Conclusion	30

A. Introduction

In 1984, Sir Iain Sinclair described Article 30 of the Vienna Convention on the Law of Treaties (VCLT) as a 'particularly obscure' aspect of the law of treaties.[1] Almost four

---

[1] I Sinclair, *The Vienna Convention on the Law of Treaties* (2nd edn, Manchester University Press 1984) 93 (hereafter Sinclair, *The Vienna Convention*).

decades later, much uncertainty remains,[2] both because the drafters left open key issues of interpretation and because Article 30 must be understood in the context of other elements of the law of treaties (such as interpretation, validity, and termination) and the law of State responsibility.[3]

2   Article 30 was adopted without objection.[4] While it has been suggested that Article 30 codified custom, there are no clear judicial pronouncements to this effect.[5]

B. The elements of Article 30 VCLT

3   Article 30 contains default rules on the priority of *application* of successive treaties relating to the same subject matter. The provision is not concerned with validity; it assumes that both treaties are valid.

I. Overview

4   Article 30 applies where at least one state is a 'party' to both the earlier and later treaty and the other state is a party to at least one of those treaties. As a threshold question, the relevant states must be party to the relevant treaties at the relevant time.[6] Article 2(1)(g) defines 'party' as meaning 'a State which has consented to be bound by the treaty, whether or not the treaty has entered into force'. Article 30 will apply from the date that the relevant states become party to the relevant treaty (or, potentially, where they have accepted the provisional application of the treaty).

5   Where a treaty specifies that it is subject to, or that is not to be considered incompatible with, an earlier or later treaty, the provisions of that other treaty will prevail: Article 30(2).[7] Article 30, paragraphs 3 and 4 contain default rules that apply only in the absence of such express provision.[8]

6   As between parties to an earlier treaty who become parties to a later treaty relating to the same subject matter, provided Article 59 VCLT does not apply, the earlier treaty applies only to the extent that its provisions are compatible with those of the later treaty. This rule effectively codifies the principle of *lex posterior* according to which the later treaty is to be taken

---

[2] See, eg, M Fitzmaurice, 'Treaties' in Wolfrum (ed), *Max Planck Encyclopaedia of Public International Law* (OUP 2012) para 109.
[3] A Orakhelashvili, 'Article 30, 1969 Vienna Convention' in O Corten and P Klein (eds), *The Vienna Conventions on the Law of Treaties* (OUP 2011) 774, para 23 (hereafter Orakhelashvili, 'Article 30').
[4] See Official Records of the United Nations Conference on the Law of Treaties, Second Session, 57 (hereafter Official Records, Second Session). There were fourteen abstentions.
[5] A Aust, *Modern Treaty Law and Practice* (3rd edn, CUP 2013) 202 (hereafter Aust, *Modern Treaty Law*); Orakhelashvili, 'Article 30' (n 3) 774, para 22. See also *EC—Poultry*, WT/DS69, Panel Report, 12 March 1998, para 206 (Article 30(3) codifies custom).
[6] See, eg, *Ioan Micula, Viorel Micula and others v Romania (I)*, ICSID Case No ARB/05/20, Final Award, 11 December 2013, paras 319–20.
[7] Such provisions are known as 'conflict clauses': see, eg, YILC 1966, Vol II, 214. With the exception of Article 53 VCLT, there is no a priori limitation on their content: see Aust, *Modern Treaty Law* (n 5) 196–202.
[8] See Official Records, Second Session (n 4) 253, para 42.

to express the most recent and most accurate reflection of the parties' intentions. It applies irrespective of whether the parties to the later treaty include all the parties to the earlier treaty: Article 30(3) and Article 30(4)(a).

As between a party to both treaties and a party to only one of the treaties, the treaty to which both are parties governs their mutual rights and obligations: Article 30(4)(b). 7

All the above rules are expressly subject to the rule that, in the event of a conflict between a treaty party's obligations under the United Nations Charter and any of their obligations under any other international agreement, their obligations under the Charter prevail: Article 30(1).[9] Article 30 is also without prejudice to the rule in Article 53 VCLT that treaties conflicting with a peremptory norm are invalid. 8

Where the parties to the later treaty include all the parties to the earlier treaty, before considering the rule in Article 30(3), it is first necessary to establish that the earlier treaty has not been impliedly terminated or suspended in accordance with Article 59: see Article 30(3).[10] Since both provisions concern successive treaties relating to the same subject matter, Article 30 and Article 59 are commonly invoked and analysed together.[11] 9

Where the parties to the later treaty do not include all the parties to the earlier treaty, before considering the rules in Article 30(4), it is first necessary to establish that neither treaty has been modified by agreement under Article 41 or terminated or suspended as a consequence of its breach under Article 60: see Article 30(5). Nothing in Article 30 interferes with the operation of those rules. It is also important to note that the rules in Article 30(4) concern the mutual rights and obligations of the treaty parties only as between themselves. These rules are expressly without prejudice to any question of State responsibility which may arise from the conclusion or application of a treaty which is incompatible with a state's other obligations towards 'another state' under 'another treaty': Article 30(5). 10

II. Three questions of interpretation

The VCLT leaves unanswered three key questions of interpretation regarding Article 30. 11

1. Which treaty is the 'earlier' or 'later' in time?

The VCLT does not define the words 'earlier treaty' and 'later treaty'. The reference to the 'conclusion' of a later treaty in Article 59, which is an important part of the context, suggests that the focus is on the date of 'conclusion'.[12] In the absence of a definition, however,[13] it is unclear whether 'conclusion' refers to the date of the adoption or authentication of the treaty text (Articles 9–10) or the date of the relevant state's expression of consent to be bound (Articles 11–17), since both sets of provisions are located within the section headed 12

---

[9] See Charter of the United Nations TS 67 (Cmd 7015) (entered into force 25 June 1945), Article 103.
[10] See also YILC 1966, Vol II, 253.
[11] See in this Commentary: Hélène Ruiz Fabri and Randi Ayman, 'Article 59—Termination or suspension of the operation of a treaty implied by conclusion of a later treaty'.
[12] Aust, *Modern Treaty Law* (n 5) 204.
[13] See E Vierdag, 'The Time of "Conclusion" of a Multilateral Treaty: Article 30 of the Vienna Convention on the Law of Treaties and Related Provisions' (1989) 59 BYIL 75, 75 (hereafter Vierdag, 'The Time of Conclusion').

'conclusion of treaties'.[14] This matters because there is frequently no coincidence between the date of adoption/authentication of a given treaty and the date that a given state became a party to that treaty, especially where consent to be bound is subject to a subsequent step such as ratification. Likewise, it is commonly the case that two states will have become a party to the same multilateral treaty (or two treaties) on different dates.[15] The negotiating history indicates that the relevant date is the date of 'adoption of the treaty', not entry into force, because adoption of the later treaty entails the expression of 'a new legislative intention' that should be taken 'as intended to prevail over the intention expressed in the earlier instrument'.[16] There is, however, no agreement between commentators.[17] Since there is a single date of adoption for any given treaty, this provides a pragmatic solution to the practical difficulties raised by focusing on the date of entry into force or of consent to be bound for a given State party.

2. When will two treaties 'relate to the same subject matter'?

13   The words 'relate to the same subject matter' are presumed to have the same meaning as in Article 59 VCLT but they are not defined in that provision either.[18] Does the word 'same' mean 'identical' (consistent with the dictionary definition[19]) or something broader such as 'similar' or 'overlapping'? What degree of connection is required by the words 'relate to'? Do the words 'subject matter' refer to a treaty's subject, objectives, its provisions, or its applicability to a given set of facts? All that can be said with certainty is that any assessment of whether two treaties relate to the same subject matter must involve interpreting both treaties.[20]

14   The International Law Commission (ILC) Study Group on Fragmentation recognized that the words 'same subject matter' is open to interpretation. A strict interpretation posing the question whether the two treaties deal with 'different subjects'[21] would be consistent with the dictionary definition of 'same' as meaning 'identical'[22] but this was rejected as 'neither a necessary nor a reasonable interpretation'[23] because a given treaty 'may be described from various perspectives' and 'the way a treaty is applied would become crucially dependent on how it would [be] classif[ied] under some (presumably) pre-existing classification scheme

---

[14] While the use of the term 'party', as defined in Article 2(1)(g) VCLT, may appear to suggest a focus on the date of expression of consent to be bound, the preferable view is that this term relates to a condition for the applicability of Article 30 VCLT: see para 3 above. cf Orakhelashvili, 'Article 30' (n 3) 786, para 59.

[15] See Official Records of the United Nations Conference on the Law of Treaties, First Session, 165, para 13 (hereafter Official Records, First Session).

[16] Official Records, Second Session (n 4) 253, para 39 (responding to Official Records, First Session (n 15) 165, para 13 and 222, para 40).

[17] For support for the date of adoption see, eg, Sinclair, *The Vienna Convention* (n 1) 98; Aust, *Modern Treaty Law* (n 5) 204. cf Orakhelashvili, 'Article 30' (n 3) 786, para 59 preferring the date of entry into force.

[18] Since Article 59 VCLT is concerned with invalidity, a narrower interpretation of the same words in that provision could perhaps be defended on the basis that this would facilitate the stability of treaties. cf F Dubuisson, 'Termination and Suspension of the Operation of Treaties, Art 59 1969 Vienna Convention' in O Corten and P Klein (eds), *The Vienna Conventions on the Law of Treaties* (OUP 2011) 1336, supporting a more flexible interpretation. See in this Commentary: Hélène Ruiz Fabri and Randi Ayman, 'Article 59 of the VCLT: Termination or suspension of the operation of a treaty implied by conclusion of a later treaty'.

[19] *AS PNB Banka, Grigory Guselnikov and others v Republic of Latvia*, ICSID Case No ARB/17/47, Decision on the Intra-EU Objection, 14 July 2021, paras 636–39 (hereafter *AS PNB Banka v Latvia*).

[20] ILC Study Group, Fragmentation of International Law: Difficulties Arising from the Diversification and Expansion of International Law (13 April 2006) UN doc A/CN.4/L.682, paras 23–26 (hereafter ILC, 'Fragmentation').

[21] ibid para 21.

[22] *AS PNB Banka v Latvia* (n 19) paras 636–39.

[23] ILC, 'Fragmentation' (n 20) para 253.

of different subjects'. Since no such classification scheme exists, 'everything would be in fact dependent on argumentative success in pigeon-holing legal instruments'.[24] The ILC also suggested that 'the question of the relationship between two treaties cannot be resolved completely in abstraction from any institutional relationship between them' and that one should consider whether there exists 'an institutional connection between "chains" or clusters of treaties that are linked institutionally and that States parties envisage as part of the same concerted effort'.[25] In the ILC's view, where the two treaties are not part of the same treaty regime, the *lex posterior* rule has least application.[26]

If the two treaties do not relate to the same subject matter, that is the end of the inquiry and there is no need to proceed to the next stage of considering whether their provisions are incompatible.[27] Although these two elements of Article 30 are conceptually distinct, confusingly, assessments of whether two treaties relate to the same subject matter often include consideration of whether they are incompatible. This can be seen, for example, in the limited guidance derived from the *travaux*[28] as well as in the ILC's conclusion that 'the test of whether two treaties deal with the "same subject matter" is resolved through the assessment of whether the fulfilment of the obligation under one treaty affects the fulfilment of the obligation of another'.[29] To an extent, such conflation is unsurprising given that the heading of Article 30 places the emphasis on the successive treaties 'relating to the same subject matter' without referring to a further condition of 'incompatibility'.

3. When will two treaties be 'incompatible'?

Whereas Article 59 applies only where the two treaties are 'so far incompatible' that the treaties 'are not capable of being applied at the same time', Article 30 concerns incompatibility between individual provisions of the two treaties.[30] The first step is to interpret the treaties to determine whether there is an incompatibility between the relevant individual provisions. Article 30 is concerned with true incompatibilities with respect to the rights and obligations of the relevant states inter-se that cannot be interpreted harmoniously. Since treaty parties are to be presumed not to have intended to act inconsistently with their pre-existing international obligations,[31] so far as possible (i.e. in the absence of clear evidence to the contrary which is admissible under Articles 31–32 VCLT), a treaty should be interpreted in conformity with the parties' pre-existing international obligations provided that the words are reasonably capable of bearing that meaning.[32]

---

[24] ibid para 22.
[25] ibid para 255.
[26] ibid para 323.
[27] See, eg, *Marfin Investment Group Holdings SA, Alexandros Bakatselos and others v Republic of Cyprus*, ICSID Case No ARB/13/27, Award (redacted), 26 July 2018, para 591 (hereafter *Marfin v Cyprus*); *Magyar Farming Company Ltd, Kintyre Kft and Inicia Zrt v Hungary*, ICSID Case No ARB/17/27, Award, 13 November 2019, para 238 (hereafter *Magyar v Hungary*).
[28] Official Records, Second Session (n 4) 253, para 39 (Waldock): the words 'relating to the same subject-matter' 'should not be held to cover cases where a general treaty impinged indirectly on the content of a particular provision of an earlier treaty; in such cases, the question involved such principles as *generalia specialibus non derogant*'.
[29] ILC, 'Fragmentation' (n 20) paras 254, 23–26. For criticism see *European American Investment Bank AG v The Slovak Republic*, PCA Case No 2010-17, Jurisdiction, 22 October 2012, paras 173 (hereafter *EURAM v Slovakia*); *AS PNB Banka v Latvia* (n 19) para 641.
[30] Sixth Report on the Law of Treaties by Sir Humphrey Waldock YILC 1996, Vol II, 75–76.
[31] R Jennings and A Watts (eds), *Oppenheim's International Law* (9th edn, Longman 1992) 1275.
[32] See, eg, ILC, 'Fragmentation' (n 20) para 39 citing *Case Concerning the Right of Passage over Indian Territory (Portugal v India)* (Preliminary Objections) [1957] ICJ Rep 125, 142.

C. Article 30 VCLT in non-investment disputes

17 It appears that neither the International Court of Justice (ICJ)[33] nor State–State arbitration tribunals have directly considered the interpretation or application of Article 30,[34] although the *lex posterior* principle has sometimes been applied in the latter context.[35] As more general guidance, it is useful to recall the following statement of principle in *Southern Bluefin Tuna*: '[I]t is commonplace of international law and State practice for more than one treaty to bear upon a particular dispute. […] There is frequently a parallelism of treaties, both in their substantive content and in their provisions for settlement of disputes arising thereunder.'[36]

D. Article 30 VCLT in investment disputes

I. Relevance of Article 30 VCLT in investment disputes

1. Successive international investment agreements

18 The need to consider Article 30 may arise, for example, in situations where a protocol to an investment treaty is concluded or where a multilateral investment treaty is revised but not all of the parties to the original treaty are party to the protocol or the revised treaty.[37] A 2017 survey by the UN Conference for Trade and Development of 167 investment treaties found that more than two-thirds co-existed with prior, overlapping investment treaties, and that not all of these treaties contained conflict clauses.[38] In principle, inconsistencies between two investment treaties (or between an investment treaty and an investment chapter in a free trade agreement) may exist with respect to, for example, different definitions of 'investment', the presence/absence of a denial of benefits clause or limitation periods or an essential security interests provision, the scope of substantive protections, or dispute settlement clauses where at least one treaty confers or purports to confer exclusive jurisdiction upon a particular tribunal.[39]

2. The 'intra-EU objection'

19 For many years, investor–State arbitration tribunals had given little consideration to the interpretation and application of Article 30 VCLT.[40] Following the conferral of competences

---

[33] Note *Territorial and Maritime Dispute (Nicaragua v Colombia)* (Preliminary Objections), [2007] ICJ Rep 832, paras 125–36 (Article 30 not considered).

[34] For consideration of Art 30 VCLT in the WTO context see, eg, *EEC—Cotton Yarn*, GATT, Panel Report, 4 July 1995, paras 540–41; *Japan—Film*, WT/DS44/R, Panel Report, 31 March 1998, para 10.65; *EC—Hormones (US)*, WT/DS26/ARB, Decision of the Arbitrators, 12 July 1999, para 51 (Art 30 applied).

[35] See, eg, *Timor-Leste v Australia Conciliation (Competence)*, PCA Case No 2016-10, Decision on Australia's Objections to Competence, 19 September 2016, paras 45 and 84. For criticism see P Tzeng, 'The Peaceful Non-Settlement of Disputes: Article 4 of CMATS in Timor-Leste v Australia' (2017) 18 Melb JIL 349, 364.

[36] *Southern Bluefin Tuna Case between Australia and Japan and between New Zealand and Japan*, Award on Jurisdiction and Admissibility, 4 August 2000, XXIII RIAA 1, para 52.

[37] See also UNCITRAL Working Group III, 'Possible reform of investor–State dispute settlement (ISDS)' (22 July 2022) UN Doc A/CN.9/WG.III/WP.221, paras 36, 44.

[38] UNCTAD, 'Reform of the international investment regime: Phase 2' (31 July 2017) UN Doc TD/B/C.II/MEM.4/14, 31 July 2017, paras 30–34.

[39] See, eg, *Cairn Energy PLC and Cairn UK Holdings Limited v The Republic of India*, PCA Case No 2016-07, Final Award, 21 December 2020, para 801–807 (whether tax measures excluded).

[40] See, eg, *Pope & Talbot v Government of Canada*, Award on the Merits of Phase 2, 10 April 2001, para 115, n 112 (referred to as a rule of interpretation); *Werner Schneider, acting in his capacity as insolvency administrator of Walter Bau Ag v The Kingdom of Thailand (formerly Walter Bau AG (in liquidation)) v The Kingdom of Thailand)*, Partial Award on Jurisdiction, 5 October 2007, paras 5.3, 5.10–5.13 (no conflict between definition of 'investment' in earlier and later investment treaty; presumption against conflict).

related to foreign direct investment under the Lisbon Treaty in 2014,[41] the European Union (EU) decided to terminate Bilateral Investment Treaties (BITs) earlier concluded between its Member States, taking the position that such intra-EU BITs were incompatible with EU law. In its judgments in *Achmea*, *Komstroy* and *PL Holdings*, the Court of Justice of the European Union (CJEU) held that Member States are prohibited by EU law from referring disputes arising between themselves to tribunals constituted under intra-EU BITs or the Energy Charter Treaty (ECT).[42] The reasoning turns on giving effect to EU law and the ultimate review of EU law by the CJEU, not the application (or, indeed, any consideration) of Article 30 (or Article 59) of the VCLT or any other rule of international law.[43]

These developments precipitated a flood of objections (commonly referred to as an 'intra-EU objection') by EU Member State respondents to the jurisdiction of investor–State arbitration tribunals constituted under intra-EU BITs and, where the investor was an EU national, the ECT. Respondent states frequently invoked Article 30(3) together with Article 59, arguing that subsequent EU law prevailed over an earlier investment treaty. Such arguments have consistently (and almost unanimously[44]) been dismissed by tribunals on the basis that Article 30 is inapplicable because: (a) the EU Treaties and the applicable investment treaty do not relate to the same subject matter and, (b) in any event, there is no incompatibility between the provisions of the EU Treaties and the applicable investment treaty because there is no rule or principle of EU law that limits or prohibits disputes under investment treaties from being submitted to international arbitration. Doubts have also been raised over the proposition that provisions of the EU Treaties, which existed in substantially similar form prior to the conclusion of an investment treaty and which were merely renumbered in a later version of the EU Treaties, constitute the 'later treaty' for the purpose of Article 30.[45]

The interpretation and application of Article 30 with respect to treaties concluded by the EU has also occasionally arisen outside of the context of the 'intra-EU objection'.[46]

II. The applicability of Article 30(2) VCLT

Investment tribunals have recognized the default nature of the rules in Article 30(3) and Article 30(4),[47] accepting that under Article 30(2) those rules are inapplicable where the relevant BIT expressly provides for the relationship with successive treaties relating to the

---

[41] Treaty of Lisbon amending the Treaty on European Union and Treaty establishing the European Community, UNTS 2702 (2014) 3.

[42] Case C-284/16, *Slovak Republic v Achmea BV*, CJEU Grand Chamber, Judgment of 6 March 2018; Case C-741/19, *Republic of Moldova v Komstroy LLC*, CJEU Grand Chamber, Judgment of 2 September 2021; Case C-109/20, *Republic of Poland v PL Holdings Sàrl*, CJEU Grand Chamber, Judgment of 26 October 2021.

[43] See, eg, *Strabag SE, Raiffeisen Centrobank AG, Syrena Immobilien Holding AG v The Republic of Poland*, ICSID Case No ADHOC/15/1, Partial Award on Jurisdiction, 4 March 2020, para 8.139 (hereafter *Strabag v Poland*). cf Case C-284/16, *Slovak Republic v Achmea BV*, Opinion of Advocate General, 19 September 2017, para 47, n 51 suggesting that the EU law position is consistent with Article 30 VCLT.

[44] cf *Theodoros Adamakopoulos and others v Republic of Cyprus*, ICSID Case No ARB/15/49, Jurisdiction, 7 February 2020, para 163 (hereafter *Adamakopoulos v Cyprus*).

[45] *Vattenfall AB and Others v Federal Republic of Germany (No II)*, ICSID Case No ARB/12/12, Decision on the Achmea Issue, 31 August 2018, para 218 (hereafter *Vattenfall v Germany (II)*).

[46] See, eg, *CMC Africa Austral, LDA, CMC Muratori Cementisti CMC Di Ravenna SOC. Coop., et al v Republic of Mozambique*, ICSID Case No ARB/17/23, Award, 24 October 2019, paras 267–277, 331.

[47] See, eg, *Vattenfall v Germany (II)* (n 45) para 217; *RWE Innogy GmbH and RWE Innogy Aersa SAU v Kingdom of Spain*, ICSID Case No ARB/14/34, Decision on Jurisdiction, Liability, and Certain Issues of Quantum, 30 December 2019, paras 338–42.

same subject matter.[48] There is a difference of opinion on whether provisions governing in general terms the relationship between an investment treaty and other unspecified agreements fall within the scope of Article 30(2). On its face, Article 16 ECT appears to be a rule of interpretation, rather than a conflict rule regulating the relationship between successive treaties relating to the same subject matter.[49] The distinguished tribunal in *Vattenfall v Germany*, however, held that Article 16 does also contain a conflict rule which is *lex specialis* under Article 30(2) VCLT.[50]

III. Meaning of 'relating to the same subject matter'

23 Tribunals have recognized that the determination of whether two treaties relate to the same subject matter is a 'difficult theoretical question', which may not be easy in practice.[51] It is first necessary to interpret the words 'relating to the same subject matter', which is itself a 'complex matter'.[52] Some tribunals have side-stepped this difficulty by declining to interpret Article 30[53] or by relying on previous decisions finding that investment treaties and the EU Treaties do not relate to the same subject matter.[54] Other tribunals have considered the question in detail.[55] Some tribunals have endorsed the view of particular commentators that the criterion that the treaties relate to the 'same subject matter' should be 'understood broadly'.[56] There is, however, no consensus among the most highly qualified publicists on this point[57] and a 'substantial body' of decisions has been characterized as applying a 'strict interpretation'.[58]

24 The tribunal in *EURAM* made an 'important remark' regarding a 'frequent confusion or conflation between sameness and incompatibility',[59] emphasizing that what is required is a 'two-step inquiry': 'First, do the two treaties "relate to the same subject matter"? Secondly, do the rules in those treaties point in the same direction or in different directions?'[60] The first step is concerned with the type of relationship that must be established between two treaties before

---

[48] See, eg, *Raiffeisen Bank International AG and Raiffeisenbank Austria d.d. v Republic of Croatia*, ICSID Case No ARB/17/34, Decision on the Respondent's Jurisdictional Objections, 30 September 2020, paras 131–33.

[49] *Silver Ridge Power BV v Italian Republic*, ICSID Case No ARB/15/37, Award, 26 February 2021, para 207 (hereafter *Silver Ridge v Italy*). See also *Greentech Energy Systems A/S, NovEnergia II Energy & Environment (SCA) SICAR, and NovEnergia II Italian Portfolio SA v The Italian Republic*, SCC Case No V 2015/095, Award, 23 December 2018, para 348 (hereafter *Greentech v Italy*), characterizing Article 16 ECT as 'a more general mechanism whereby a treaty with more favourable provisions is to apply'.

[50] *Vattenfall v Germany (II)* (n 45) paras 217, 223, 229; *Silver Ridge v Italy* (n 49) para 207.

[51] *EURAM v Slovakia* (n 29) para 157.

[52] *AS PNB Banka v Latvia* (n 19) para 639.

[53] See, eg, *Eastern Sugar BV v The Czech Republic*, SCC Case No 088/2004, Partial Award, 27 March 2007, para 180; *Rupert Joseph Binder v Czech Republic*, Jurisdiction, 6 June 2007, paras 59–67.

[54] See, eg, *WNC Factoring Ltd (WNC) v The Czech Republic*, PCA Case No 2014-34, Award, 22 February 2017, para 308 (hereafter *WNC v Czech Republic*); *Greentech v Italy* (n 49) para 346.

[55] *EURAM v Slovakia* (n 29) paras 174–75.

[56] See, eg, *GPF GP Sàrl v Poland*, SCC Case No 2014/168, Final Award, 29 April 2020, para 364 (hereafter *GPF v Poland*); *Spółdzielnia Pracy Muszynianka v Slovak Republic*, PCA Case No 2017-08, Award, 7 October 2020, para 232 (hereafter *Spółdzielnia v Slovakia*).

[57] cf Aust, *Modern Treaty Law* (n 5) 204 supporting a strict interpretation. See also Official Records, First Session (n 15) 222, para 41 (UK).

[58] *AS PNB Banka v Latvia* (n 19) para 642. For an example of this strict approach see *Strabag v Poland* (n 43) para 8.135.

[59] *EURAM v Slovakia* (n 29) para 173 referring to ILC, 'Fragmentation' (n 20) para 23. cf Vierdag, 'The Time of Conclusion' (n 13) 100; Orakhelashvili, 'Article 30' (n 3) 776, para 30.

[60] *EURAM v Slovakia* (n 29) paras 174–75. See also *AS PNB Banka v Latvia* (n 19) para 641; *WNC v Czech Republic* (n 54) para 296; *Adria Group BV and Adria Group Holding BV v Republic of Croatia*, ICSID Case No ARB/20/6, Decision on Intra-EU Jurisdictional Objection, 31 October 2023, paras 172–74 (hereafter *Adria v Croatia*).

any inference may be drawn (based on temporal considerations) that the Contracting Parties intended for the provisions of the later treaty to prevail over those of the earlier treaty.[61] The second step is concerned with identifying whether an incompatibility exists.

Consistent with the approach of the ILC, various tribunals have reasoned that two treaties do not relate to the same subject matter merely because they may apply simultaneously to the same set of facts.[62] It has been suggested that such a broad interpretation would offend the principle of effectiveness because Article 30 presupposes that both treaties are applicable since no conflict could otherwise arise.[63] The *EURAM* tribunal also found that it is not sufficient for two treaties to have the 'same goal' or the 'same overall purpose'.[64] Some tribunals have reasoned that the two treaties must have the same overall objective *and* 'share a degree of general comparability',[65] which has been understood to mean that 'the subject matter of a treaties is defined by the matters with which the treaty's constituent provisions deal'.[66] This is consistent with the reasoning of the tribunal in *EURAM* that 'the subject matter of a treaty is inherent in the substance of the treaty itself and refers to the issues with which its provisions deal, i.e. its topic or substance'.[67]

25

The question for the tribunal is 'with what issues do the rules of the two treaties deal?'[68] This is a question of interpretation. It is to be answered through an examination, *inter alia*, of the terms and the object and purpose of the one treaty and a comparison with those of the other treaty. Different tribunals have adopted different approaches. Some tribunals have focused on the object and purpose of the two treaties (contrasting the establishment of a common market with investment promotion and protection),[69] some have focused on their substantive terms (emphasizing that the protections are 'by no means congruent', with the investment treaty affording investors 'wider' rights, including fair and equitable treatment (FET) and the 'highly valuable' right to submit claims to international arbitration),[70] and some have considered both factors together.[71] Some tribunals have also sought to apply the ILC's test of whether the relevant investment treaty and the EU Treaties are institutionally linked as part of the same concerted effort, finding that they are not.[72]

26

The tribunal in *AS PNB Banka v Latvia*, criticized earlier decisions for focusing on the question of whether the two treaties were of the 'same subject matter' when Article 30 requires

27

---

[61] *Eskosol S.p.A. in liquidazione v Italian Republic*, ICSID Case No ARB/15/50, Decision on Termination Request and Intra-EU Objection, 7 May 2019, para 141 (hereafter *Eskosol v Italy*).
[62] *EURAM v Slovakia* (n 29) paras 169, 171; *GPF v Poland* (n 56) para 364; *Spółdzielnia v Slovakia* (n 56) para 232.
[63] *GPF v Poland* (n 56) para 364; *Magyar v Hungary* (n 27) para 228. See also Orakhelashvili, 'Article 30' (n 3) 775, para 29.
[64] *EURAM v Slovakia* (n 29) para 170.
[65] *Jan Oostergetel and Theodora Laurentius v The Slovak Republic*, Jurisdiction, 30 April 2010, para 79 (hereafter *Oostergetel v Slovakia*) describing this as the 'dominant view expressed in scholarly writings'. See also *Magyar v Hungary* (n 27) para 230; *GPF v Poland* (n 56) para 365; *Spółdzielnia v Slovakia* (n 56) para 233.
[66] *Magyar v Hungary* (n 27) para 230; *GPF v Poland* (n 56) para 365; *Spółdzielnia v Slovakia* (n 56) para 233.
[67] *EURAM v Slovakia* (n 29) para 172.
[68] *EURAM v Slovakia* (n 29) para 178.
[69] See, eg, *EURAM v Slovakia* (n 29) paras 178, 184. See also, eg, *Anglia Auto Accessories Limited v The Czech Republic*, SCC Case No 2014/181, Final Award, 10 March 2017, para 115.
[70] See, eg, *PL Holdings Sarl v Poland*, SCC Case No V 2014/163, Partial Award, 28 June 2017, para 312 (hereafter *PL Holdings v Poland*); *Adamakopoulos v Cyprus* (n 44) para 168.
[71] See, eg, *Oostergetel v Slovakia* (n 65) paras 75–79, 104; *Marfin v Cyprus* (n 27) para 589; *Eskosol v Italy* (n 61) paras 145–46; *United Utilities (Tallinn) BV and Aktsiaselts Tallinna Vesi v Republic of Estonia*, ICSID Case No ARB/14/24, Award, 21 June 2019, para 543; *Magyar v Hungary* (n 27) paras 232–35; *Adria v Croatia* (n 60) para 175.
[72] See, eg, *Eskosol v Italy* (n 61) para 144; *Belenergia SA v Italian Republic*, ICSID Case No ARB/15/40, Award, 6 August 2019, para 317; *Strabag v Poland* (n 43) para 8.135.

them only to 'relate to' the same subject matter. The tribunal interpreted the words 'relate to' as covering 'a broad set of possible connections' between a given treaty and the relevant subject matter.[73] This does not, however, eliminate the need for the treaties to relate to 'the same subject matter'.

IV. Meaning of 'incompatible'

28 The tribunal in *AS PNB Banka v Latvia* explained that: 'the determination of whether there is a conflict involves two stages. The scope of each of the two treaties in issue must be determined by a process of interpretation. Only after that is done can any relevant incompatibility be identified.'[74] As to the first stage, a number of investor–State tribunals have endorsed the existence of a presumption against incompatibility.[75] As regards the second stage, tribunals have defined 'incompatibility' as meaning that both treaties cannot be complied with because one treaty requires what the other prohibits,[76] not merely that their provisions are broader, complementary or different,[77] or that there is a possibility of future incompatibility.[78]

29 Tribunals have consistently held that there is no 'incompatibility', for the purposes of Article 30(3) VCLT, between intra-EU BITs (or the ECT) and EU law. While the investment protection obligations under investment treaties may be broader than under EU law (e.g. FET and Investor–State Dispute Settlement (ISDS)),[79] or arguably narrower (e.g. discrimination),[80] the successive treaties are complementary because there is no rule or principle of EU law that limits or prohibits the submission to international arbitration of disputes under investment treaties.[81]

E. Conclusion

30 Article 30 VCLT has been considered by many investor–State arbitration tribunals. Given the absence of detailed consideration of Article 30 by the ICJ or interstate arbitration tribunals, it is difficult to assess whether this practice represents any form of departure from the approach under general international law. As a matter of principle, there appears to be nothing to require or justify a special approach in investment disputes. Although the detailed consideration given to the matter by certain investor–State tribunals might shape the approach to be adopted in general international law, it remains to be seen whether the ICJ would find that reasoning persuasive.

---

[73] *AS PNB Banka v Latvia* (n 19) paras 636–43. See also, in a different context, *Methanex Corporation v United States of America*, Partial Award, 7 August 2002, para 147 ('relating to' requires a legally significant connection).
[74] *AS PNB Banka v Latvia* (n 19) para 641.
[75] See, eg, *Electrabel SA v The Republic of Hungary*, ICSID Case No ARB/07/19, Decision on Jurisdiction, Applicable Law and Liability, 30 November 2012, para 4.134 (hereafter *Electrabel v Hungary*); *Blusun SA, Jean-Pierre Lecorcier and Michael Stein v Italian Republic*, ICSID Case No ARB/14/3, Award, 27 December 2016, para 286 (hereafter *Blusun v Italy*); *Magyar v Hungary* (n 27) para 240.
[76] See, eg, *EURAM v Slovakia* (n 29) para 246; *Achmea BV (formerly Eureko BV) v The Slovak Republic (I)*, PCA Case No 2008-13, Award on Jurisdiction, Arbitrability and Suspension, 26 October 2010, para 271 (hereafter *Achmea v Slovakia*); *Magyar v Hungary* (n 27) para 241.
[77] *Blusun v Italy* (n 75) para 286; *PL Holdings v Poland* (n 70) para 311; *Achmea v Slovakia* (n 76) paras 245, 261.
[78] *AS PNB Banka v Latvia* (n 19) para 654.
[79] *PL Holdings v Poland* (n 70) para 311.
[80] *Blusun v Italy* (n 75) para 286.
[81] See, eg, *Electrabel v Hungary* (n 75) paras 4.166 and 4.146, 4.153; *Blusun v Italy* (n 75) paras 286–91.

Selected literature

Aust A, *Modern Treaty Law and Practice* (3rd edn, CUP 2013).

ILC Study Group, Fragmentatioh of International Law: Difficulties Arising from the Diversification and Expansion of International Law (13 April 2006) UN Doc A/CN.4/L.682.

Orakhelashvili A, 'Article 30, 1969 Vienna Convention' in Corten O and Klein P (eds), *The Vienna Conventions on the Law of Treaties* (OUP 2011).

Sinclair I, *The Vienna Convention on the Law of Treaties* (2nd edn, Manchester University Press 1984).

Vierdag E, 'The Time of 'Conclusion' of a Multilateral Treaty: Article 30 of the Vienna Convention on the Law of Treaties and Related Provisions' (1989) 59 BYIL 75.

Selected decisions

Adria Group BV and Adria Group Holding BV v Republic of Croatia, ICSID Case No ARB/20/6, Decision on the Intra-EU Jurisdictional Objection, 31 October 2023.

AS PNB Banka, Grigory Guselnikov and others v Republic of Latvia, ICSID Case No ARB/17/47, Decision on the Intra-EU Objection, 14 July 2021.

Blusun SA, Jean-Pierre Lecorcier and Michael Stein v Italian Republic, ICSID Case No ARB/14/3, Award, 27 December 2016.

Electrabel SA v The Republic of Hungary, ICSID Case No ARB/07/19, Decision on Jurisdiction, Applicable Law and Liability, 30 November 2012.

European American Investment Bank AG v The Slovak Republic, PCA Case No 2010-17, Jurisdiction, 22 October 2012.

GPF GP Sàrl v Poland, SCC Case No 2014/168, Final Award, 29 April 2020.

Southern Bluefin Tuna Case between Australia and Japan and between New Zealand and Japan, Award on Jurisdiction and Admissibility, 4 August 2000, XXIII RIAA 1.

Vattenfall AB and Others v Federal Republic of Germany (No II), ICSID Case No ARB/12/12, Decision on the Achmea Issue, 31 August 2018.

Article 31 of the VCLT

General rule of interpretation

Andreas Kulick and Panos Merkouris[*]

1. A treaty shall be interpreted in good faith in accordance with the ordinary meaning to be given to the terms of the treaty in their context and in the light of its object and purpose.

2. The context for the purpose of the interpretation of a treaty shall comprise, in addition to the text, including its preamble and annexes:

(a) any agreement relating to the treaty which was made between all the parties in connexion with the conclusion of the treaty;

(b) any instrument which was made by one or more parties in connexion with the conclusion of the treaty and accepted by the other parties as an instrument related to the treaty.

3. There shall be taken into account, together with the context:

(a) any subsequent agreement between the parties regarding the interpretation of the treaty or the application of its provisions;

(b) any subsequent practice in the application of the treaty which establishes the agreement of the parties regarding its interpretation;

(c) any relevant rules of international law applicable in the relations between the parties.

4. A special meaning shall be given to a term if it is established that the parties so intended.

A. Introduction	1
B. Sources of the international law on the interpretation of treaties	3
I. Genesis of the VCLT and its relationship to customary international law	3
II. 'Principles' not explicitly mentioned in the VCLT	9
C. Doctrine and practice of the VCLT	11
I. Canons of interpretation: ordinary meaning, context, object and purpose	11
1. Ordinary meaning, Article 31(1)	13
2. Context, Article 31(1) and (2)	17
3. Object and purpose, Article 31(1)	23
II. Maxims of interpretation	26
III. Subsequent agreements and subsequent practice, Article 31(3)(a) and (b)	34
1. General considerations	34
2. Subsequent agreement, Article 31(3)(a): requirements and evidence	37
3. Subsequent practice, Article 31(3)(b): requirements and evidence	39
4. Scope of interpretation: treaty modification through Article 31(3)(a) or (b)?	45
IV. Systemic integration, Article 31(3)(c)	52
1. Rules	54
2. Applicable	57
3. Relevant	60
4. Parties	62
5. Intertemporality	68
V. Special meaning, Article 31(4)	70
VI. Special regimes or one unitary regime?	72
D. Interpretation of customary law	76
E. Conclusions	80

---

[*] As regards Panos Merkouris, this paper is based on research conducted in the context of the project 'The Rules of Interpretation of Customary International Law' ('TRICI-Law'). This project has received funding from the European Research Council (ERC) under the European Union's Horizon 2020 Research and Innovation Programme (Grant Agreement No 759728).

A. Introduction

Articles 31–33 of the Vienna Convention on the Law of Treaties (VCLT) have been indelibly etched in the conscience of judges, practitioners, and academics as a reflection of the rules governing the interpretation of treaties. Article 31 sets out the 'general rule' of interpretation. International courts and tribunals never tire of referring to it, sometimes even before the VCLT had entered into force.[1] The customary status of Article 31 has been confirmed by the International Court of Justice (ICJ)[2] and other international adjudicatory bodies,[3] including in investment arbitration.[4]

Section B presents the sources of the international law on treaty interpretation. In Section C, which will form the central part of this entry, we address doctrine and practice on Article 31 and compare the jurisprudence of the ICJ and other international courts and tribunals with investment arbitration case law. We distinguish between canons and maxims of interpretation. As 'canons' we regard the distinctive methods of interpretation explicitly enshrined in Article 31(1), i.e. ordinary meaning, context, and object and purpose (Section C.I). 'Maxims' of interpretation, by contrast, represent interpretive principles requiring that their precepts are to be pursued to the optimal extent (Section C.II). The ensuing sub-sections of Section C discuss, in turn, subsequent agreements and subsequent practice pursuant to Article 31(3)(a) and (b) (Section C.III), matters of systemic integration according to Article 31(3)(c) (C.IV.), special meaning, Article 31(4) (Section C.V), and the question whether there exist separate special regimes or rather one unitary regime of treaty interpretation (Section C.VI). Finally, Section D briefly inquires issues pertaining to the interpretation of custom, while Section E concludes.

B. Sources of the international law on the interpretation of treaties

I. Genesis of the VCLT and its relationship to customary international law

The fact that international courts and tribunals tirelessly refer to Articles 31–33 may give the false impression that this has always been the *status quo*, but that is far from true.

Early codification attempts of the law of treaties like the 1918 Fiore's Draft Code, the 1933 Interpretation of Treaties, and the 1935 Harvard Research Draft Convention on the Law of Treaties[5] present strikingly differing approaches to interpretation, and the elements to be considered therein.[6] The commentary to the Harvard Draft Convention also viewed the

---

[1] For example, *Barcelona Traction, Light and Power Company Limited (New Application, 1962) (Belgium v Spain)* (Second Phase) [1970] ICJ Rep 3, Separate Opinion of Judge Ammoun, para 11; *Appeal Relating to the Jurisdiction of the ICAO Council (India v Pakistan)* [1972] ICJ Rep 46, Separate Opinion of Judge Dillard, para 90.
[2] *Arbitral Award of 31 July 1989 (Guinea-Bissau v Senegal)* [1991] ICJ Rep 53, para 48; more recently *Jadhav (India v Pakistan)* [2019] ICJ Rep 418, para 71.
[3] eg *United States—Gasoline*, WT/DS2/AB/R, 20 May 1996, 16–17; IUSCT, *Decision No DEC 12-A1-FT*, 3 August 1982, 1 IUSCTR 189, 190–92.
[4] eg *Phoenix Action v Czech Republic*, ICSID Case No ARB/06/5, Award, 15 April 2009, para 75; *Daimler Financial Services v Argentina*, ICSID Case No ARB/05/1, Award, 22 August 2012, para 46 (hereafter *Daimler v Argentina*); *Cavalum v Spain*, ICISD Case No ARB/15/34, Decision on Jurisdiction, Liability and Directions on Quantum, 31 August 2020, para 333.
[5] All reproduced in: J Garner, 'Codification of International Law: Part III—Law of Treaties' (1935) 29 AJIL Supp 653, 1219, 1226 and 661, respectively (hereafter Garner).
[6] Fiore's Draft Code, for instance, opting for elements that fell within either logical or grammatical interpretation, and the Harvard Draft Convention considering that the 'function of interpretation is to discover and effectuate the purpose which a treaty is intended to serve'; Garner (n 5) 938.

proposed rule on interpretation not as a rigid, mechanical rule, but rather as a 'guide' aimed at directing 'the interpreter toward a decision which conforms [...] to the circumstances peculiar to the particular case before him'.[7]

5 Even in the International Law Commission (ILC) its members engaged in lengthy discussions as to whether such articles could and should be included in a convention on the law of treaties, with members expressing views all across the spectrum, of the 'rules' of interpretation, being rules in the strict sense, general principles, and/or maxims of logic.[8] The ILC eventually opted for the inclusion of articles on interpretation and its commentary offered not only an explanation of this choice but also on the rule-ness of these articles. '[T]he Commission confined itself to trying to isolate and codify the comparatively few general principles which appear to constitute general rules for the interpretation of treaties. Admittedly, the task of formulating even these rules is not easy, but the Commission considered that there were cogent reasons why it should be attempted. [...] In addition, the establishment of some measure of agreement in regard to the basic rules of interpretation is important not only for the application but also for the drafting of treaties.'[9]

6 Despite this somewhat turbulent negotiating history, it is now undeniable that the language surrounding interpretation of treaty provisions is heavily influenced by the choices by the drafters of the VCLT. This becomes even more pronounced if one considers the mantra-like invocation by international courts and tribunals that Articles 31–33 enjoy customary status.[10]

7 That is not to say that investment tribunals have never deviated from the structure of the VCLT. Early investment tribunals did not take it as self-evident that they should by default adhere to the choices made in the VCLT,[11] also in light of the fact that the rules to be applied were customary rules given that the parties to the dispute were not VCLT members. The most notable example is the first investment treaty arbitration, the *AAPL v Sri Lanka*. There the tribunal listed first that any interpretative issue must be addressed by using the 'law of nations'[12] and then listed six interpretation rules, which it derived drawing not only from Articles 31–32 VCLT, but also from the ILC's work on the law of treaties, the *Institut de Droit International's* 1956 Granada Session Resolutions on treaty interpretation as well as international case law and the writings of renowned publicists.[13] Those rules were, in sum: (i) *in claris non fit interpretatio*;[14] (ii) ordinary meaning; and when the ordinary meaning left the term ambiguous, then[15] (iii) contextual interpretation; (iv) systemic integration; (v) *ut res*

---

[7] Garner (n 5) 947.
[8] ILC, 'Draft Articles on the Law of Treaties with Commentaries' YILC 1966, Vol II, 187, 218, paras 1–4 (hereafter ILC, *Draft Articles*).
[9] ibid 218–19, para 5 (emphasis added).
[10] See nn 2–4 above.
[11] See also M Waibel, 'International Investment Law and Treaty Interpretation' in R Hofmann and CJ Tams (eds), *International Investment Law and General International Law: From Clinical Isolation to Systemic Integration?* (Nomos 2011) 29 et seq.
[12] *AAPL v Sri Lanka*, ICSID Case No ARB/87/3, Final Award, 27 June 1990, para 39 (hereafter *AAPL v Sri Lanka*).
[13] ibid paras 38–40.
[14] This was intentionally left out of the VCLT, because as put by McDougal, the US representative in the Vienna Conference, this maxim was nothing more than an 'obscurantist tautology': United Nations Conference on the Law of Treaties, '31st Meeting of the Committee of the Whole' (19 April 1968) UN Doc A/CONF.39/C.1/SR.31, 164, para 38.
[15] Again here, a hint at a hierarchy between the rules, which is a departure from the 'holistic' and 'crucible' approach of the ILC and the VCLT, see Section C.I below.

magis valeat quam pereat; and (vi) *in pari materia* interpretation.[16] Evidently, this is a departure from the VCLT.

This, is, however, nowadays more of an outlier. The VCLT has gradually and increasingly **8** made its *gravitas* felt, and led to the emergence of a common vocabulary[17] that has somewhat streamlined, although far from perfected, the interpretative process. Investment tribunals, the disputing parties, and other 'users' of international law,[18] almost without fail, explicitly acknowledge the customary status of the Vienna rules, and function on a presumed identity of the content of the two sets of rules.[19]

II. 'Principles' not explicitly mentioned in the VCLT

Both parties and investment tribunals display a tendency to refer to principles or maxims **9** of interpretation that are not explicitly mentioned in the VCLT. This is addressed in detail below (Section C.II). Of relevance here are the relationship between these 'principles',[20] Articles 31–33 and their customary equivalents. Evolutive interpretation, the principle of contemporaneity, *in dubio mitius*, *effet utile*, *contra* or *pro proferentem*, *in claris non fit interpretatio*, *in pari materia*, and various other principles have been invoked before investment tribunals with various degrees of success. Sometimes this is taken to the extreme when customary rules on the law of treaties that have nothing to do with interpretation are invoked as interpretative principles.[21] The question that inexorably then arises is what is the legal status of said principles? Are they merely logical tools, are they simply descriptive of the outcome of the interpretative process,[22] are they ubiquitous in or at least permeate a variety of elements that are already set down in Articles 31–33,[23] or are they principles shared by states, principles stemming from the international legal order, or rules of customary international law? In the latter cases, i.e. principles and customary law, do they exist *praeter* or even *contra* VCLT?

Investment tribunals do not provide much assistance on this matter, as these principles are **10** usually referred to in an assertive fashion. However, given the aforementioned near-uniform practice of acknowledging the customary nature of Articles 31–33 VCLT, it seems highly unlikely that the tribunals would consider these principles as binding either *praeter* or even less *contra* VCLT. It is more likely that they are either descriptive of the interpretative outcome,

---

[16] *AAPL v Sri Lanka* (n 12) para 39.
[17] M Waibel, 'Uniformity versus Specialisation (2): A Uniform Regime of Treaty Interpretation?' in CJ Tams, A Tzanakopoulos and A Zimmermann (eds), *Research Handbook on the Law of Treaties* (Edgar Elgar Publishing 2014) 381.
[18] On this term: E Roucounas, 'The Users of International Law' in M Arsanjani and others (eds), *Looking to the Future: Essays on International Law in Honor of W Michael Reisman* (Brill/Martinus Nijhoff Publishers 2011) 217.
[19] See nn 2–4 above. See also OK Fauchald, 'The Legal Reasoning of ICSID Tribunals—An Empirical Analysis' (2008) 19 EJIL 301, 313 et seq; R Weeramantry, *Treaty Interpretation in Investment Arbitration* (OUP 2012) ch 3; T Gazzini, *Interpretation of International Investment Treaties* (Hart Publishing 2016) 64 et seq.
[20] For reason of convenience, we will use this term to refer to all these approaches. This should not be construed as an indication that these are to be considered as 'general principles' under Article 38 of the ICJ Statute. On the latter see in this Commentary: P Dumberry, 'Article 38 ICJ Statute: Sources'.
[21] See *Eureko BV v Poland*, Partial Award, 19 August 2005, paras 176–77, where Poland invoked the exception of non-performance (*exceptio non adimpleti contractus*) as a maxim of interpretation.
[22] See contributions in J Klingler, Y Parkhomenko and C Salonidis (eds), *Between the Lines of the Vienna Convention? Canons and Other Principles of Interpretation in Public International Law* (Wolters Kluwer 2019) (hereafter Klingler et al).
[23] See Section C.II.

aimed at lending a bit more *gravitas* to the final conclusion, or even if they are considered as binding that they fall within one or more of the existing elements of Articles 31–33.[24]

C. Doctrine and practice of the VCLT

I. Canons of interpretation: ordinary meaning, context, object and purpose

11 Article 31 is entitled 'general rule of interpretation'. 'Rule' is used in the singular and this is deliberate. As the ILC underlined in its 1966 Commentary to the Draft Articles on the Law of Treaties, it

> intended to indicate that the application of the means of interpretation in the article would be a *single combined operation*. *All the various elements*, as they were present in any given case, would be *thrown into the crucible*, and their *interaction* would give the legally relevant interpretation. Thus, […] the Commission desired to emphasize that the *process of interpretation is a unity* and that the provisions of the article form a *single, closely integrated rule*.[25]

12 Consequently, the canons, or 'elements' of interpretation explicitly enshrined in Article 31(1) are no monoliths. The interpretation of a treaty text emerges from their 'interaction'. The interpreter must bring them to effect via 'a single combined operation', which the ILC describes as a 'process'. Therefore, while discussed separately for the sake of conceptual clarity, ordinary meaning, context, and object and purpose relate to each other and none of them enjoys general primacy over the other. The wording of Article 31 exhibits this most clearly by emphasizing that the ordinary meaning of the treaty's 'terms' must be read 'in their context and in light of [the treaty's] object and purpose'. Investment tribunals have accepted these principles, acknowledging that Article 31 forms a 'single',[26] 'integral'[27] 'all-compassing rule'[28] of interpretation that takes a 'holistic approach',[29] and does not establish a 'hierarchy between the various aides to interpretation outlined in [Article 31 VCLT]'.[30],[31] The tribunal in *Aguas*

---

[24] See, for instance, Villiger who argues that even if everything else fails they could fall under Article 32 VCLT. M Villiger, *Commentary on the 1969 Vienna Convention on the Law of Treaties* (Nijhoff Leiden 2009) 445–46, para 5 (hereafter Villiger).

[25] ILC, *Draft Articles* (n 8) 219–20, para 8 (emphasis added).

[26] *Poštová banka and ISTROKAPITAL v Greece*, ICSID Case No ARB/13/8, Award, 9 April 2015, paras 282–83 (hereafter *Poštová v Greece*).

[27] *Garanti Koza v Turkmenistan*, ICSID Case No ARB/11/20, Dissenting Opinion of Laurence Boisson de Chazournes, 3 July 2013, para 11.

[28] *HICEE v Slovakia*, UNCITRAL, Partial Award on Jurisdiction, 23 May 2011, para 135 (hereafter *HICEE v Slovakia*).

[29] *Daimler v Argentina* (n 4) para 46; *Muhammet Cap v Turkmenistan*, ICSID Case No ARB/12/6, Decision on Jurisdiction, 13 February 2015, para 254.

[30] *Hrvatska v Slovenia*, ICSID Case No ARB/05/24, Decision on the Treaty Interpretation Issue, 12 June 2009, para 164 (hereafter *Hrvatska v Slovenia*).

[31] For a position rejecting the 'crucible' or 'holistic' approach see C Brower, D Bray and P Chhoden Tshering, 'Competing Theories of Treaty Interpretation and the Divided Application by Investor-State Tribunals of Articles 31 and 32 of the VCLT' in E Shirlow and KN Gore (eds), *The Vienna Convention on the Law of Treaties in Investor-State Disputes* (Wolters Kluwer 2022) 109, 118 et seq (hereafter Shirlow and Gore). However, their main point of criticism appears to be directed at establishing no clear hierarchy between Articles 31 and 32, while remaining rather ambiguous regarding the relationship among the three canons.

del Tunari described the interpretive process as one of 'progressive encirclement', whereby the interpreter 'iteratively closes in on the proper interpretation'.[32]

1. Ordinary meaning, Article 31(1)

Despite the absence of hierarchy among the canons, Article 31 takes the text as the point of departure ('in accordance with the ordinary meaning').[33] As stated in *Territorial Dispute*, '[i]nterpretation must be based above all upon the text of the treaty'.[34] The starting point is always the 'terms' of the treaty, i.e. its written text, as Articles 31(4) and 33(3) indicate. Therefore, as was held in *Wintershall* and *Ping An*, among others, the treaty text may not be easily overwritten by mere reference to the parties' alleged intentions.[35] However, 'ordinary meaning' is not identical with literal meaning.[36] Considering the 'integral approach' of Article 31, context and object and purpose may inform interpretation in order to diverge from a literal or common meaning of a text, as was confirmed in *Methanex*.[37]

The 'ordinary meaning' must be derived from a linguistic, grammatical, and semantic analysis of the treaty text. This includes, among others, its individual words, phrases, syntax, and tense.[38] In order to discern the meaning of individual words, international courts and tribunals have taken recourse to dictionaries.[39] But this approach must be exercised with caution, since dictionaries usually list all possible meanings of a word and the definitions also depend on which edition one uses, or whether one selects a general language or a specialized dictionary.[40] The ICJ has mainly used dictionaries to demonstrate that the term has various possible meanings, i.e. to counter the notion of a specific definition.[41] Therefore, if it all, dictionaries may mainly serve to reject, rather than confirm, a particular meaning.

---

[32] *Aguas del Tunari v Bolivia*, ICSID Case No ARB/02/03, Jurisdiction, 21 October 2005, para 91 (hereafter *Aguas del Tunari v Bolivia*).

[33] See YILC 1966, Vol II, 220 ('the text must be presumed to be the authentic expression of the intentions of the parties; and that, in consequence, the starting point of interpretation is the elucidation of the meaning of the text, not an investigation *ab initio* into the intentions of the parties'). This entails 'the wording of a treaty has in the textual approach . . . the prime role in interpretation because it is presumed to be an authentic expression of the intention of the parties'. O Dörr, 'Article 31' in O Dörr and K Schmalenbach (eds), *The Vienna Convention on the Law of Treaties—A Commentary* (2nd edn, Springer 2018) 560, para 3 (hereafter Dörr).

[34] *Territorial Dispute between Libya and Chad (Libyan Arab Jamahiriya/Chad)* [1994] ICJ Rep 6, para 41 (hereafter *Territorial Dispute*).

[35] *Wintershall v Argentina*, ICSID Case No ARB/04/14, Award, 8 December 2008, para 88 (hereafter *Wintershall v Argentina*); *Ping An v Belgium*, ICSID Case No ARB/12/29, Award, 30 April 2015, paras 165–66. See also E Shirlow and M Waibel, 'A Sliding Scale Approach to Travaux in Treaty Interpretation: The Case of Investment Treaties' (2022) 89 BYIL 37.

[36] See the discussion at the Institut de Droit International Law on this matter [1956] AIDI 328–30.

[37] *Methanex v USA*, UNCITRAL, Partial Award, 7 August 2002, para 136 (hereafter *Methanex v USA*, Partial Award).

[38] For a detailed discussion that draws on pragmatic linguistics, see B Pirker and J Smolka, 'Five Shades of Grey—A Linguistic and Pragmatic Approach to Treaty Interpretation' (2022) 82 ZaöRV 121 et seq.

[39] eg *Oil Platforms (Islamic Republic of Iran v United States of America)* (Preliminary Objections) [1996] ICJ Rep 803, para 45 (hereafter *Oil Platforms*); *Kasikili/Sedudu Island (Botswana v Namibia)* [1999] ICJ Rep 1045, para 30 (hereafter *Kasikili/Sedudu*); *Canada—Civilian Aircraft*, WT/DS20/AB/R, 2 August 1999, para 153; *Golder v United Kingdom* App no 4451/70 (ECtHR, 21 February 1975), para 32 (hereafter *Golder v UK*).

[40] See Dörr (n 33) 581, para 40.

[41] For example, in *Oil Platforms* (n 39) 818, para 45, while interpreting the term 'commerce' in Article X(1) of the US–Iranian Friendship and Navigation Treaty of 1955, the Court held that '[t]he word "commerce" is not restricted in ordinary usage to the mere act of purchase and sale; it has connotations that extend beyond mere purchase and sale to include "the whole of the transactions, arrangements, etc., therein involved" (Oxford English Dictionary, 1989, Vol. 3, 552)'. Similarly, in *Kasikili/Sedudu* (n 39) 1064, para 30, the Court employed the dictionary definition of 'main channel' to demonstrate that it could not rely on 'one single criterion in order to identify the main channel of the Chobe around Kasikili/Sedudu Island'.

15 Investment tribunals have been divided in their practice on this matter. In *ADF*, the tribunal employed Webster's Dictionary to determine what the term 'procurement' in Article 1001(5) North American Free Trade Agreement (NAFTA) did *not* include,[42] thus following the ICJ's approach. Others have been more generous, using dictionaries also in affirming a specific meaning, such as 'enterprise' or 'asset' in the definition of 'investment' pursuant to Article 1139 NAFTA[43] or a Bilateral Investment Treaty (BIT).[44]

16 Exceptionally, the 'ordinary meaning' must give way to a 'special meaning', Article 31(4). The burden of proof lies with the party invoking such special meaning.[45]

2. Context, Article 31(1) and (2)

17 As the Permanent Court of International Justice (PCIJ) pointed out, 'it is obvious that the Treaty must be read as a whole, and that its meaning is not to be determined merely upon particular phrases which, if detached from the context, may be interpreted in more than one sense'.[46] Accordingly, Article 31(1) requires reading a treaty's terms 'in their context'. Beyond the treaty text itself, including its preamble and annexes, Article 31(2) extends the context to certain other agreements and instruments under the conditions further specified in (a) and (b).

18 The contextual approach relates to, both, ordinary meaning and object and purpose: On the one hand, it must operate within the confines of how the ordinary meaning may be construed. On the other hand, discerning the relevant context requires identifying the object and purpose of the specific provision as well as the overall treaty.[47]

19 The treaty is to be looked at in its entirety. Context includes its title,[48] its preamble,[49] the structure of a sentence,[50] as well as matters of punctuation and syntax.[51]

20 Beyond all the text intrinsic to the treaty in question, a treaty's context further comprises certain documents extrinsic to it,[52] provided they were 'made […] in connection with the conclusion of the treaty', Article 31(2). The underlying rationale is that such extrinsic documents form part of the context only if the other Party accepted them.[53] Both the 'agreement' in accordance with Article 31(2)(a) and the 'instrument' pursuant to Article 31(2) (b) do not

---

[42] *ADF v United States of America*, ICSID Case No ARB (AF)/00/1, Award, 9 January, 2003, para 161, fn 158 (hereafter *ADF v USA*).
[43] *Feldman v Mexico*, ICSID Case No ARB(AF)/99/1, Award, 16 December 2002, para 96.
[44] *Anderson v Costa Rica*, ICSID Case No ARB(AF)/07/3, Award, 19 May 2010, para 48. Note, however, that in para 57 the same tribunal employed a dictionary definition to exclude a certain conduct from the scope of the word 'own' under the Canada–Costa Rica BIT.
[45] On Article 31(4) see Section C.V below.
[46] *Competence of the ILO in regard to International Regulation of the Conditions of the Labour of Persons Employed in Agriculture* (Advisory Opinion), PCIJ Series B No 2, 23 (hereafter *Competence of the ILO*).
[47] See, eg, *Maritime Delimitation in the Indian Ocean (Somalia v Kenya)* [2017] ICJ Rep 3, paras 64 et seq (hereafter *Maritime Delimitation in the Indian Ocean*). However, note *Hrvatska v Slovenia* (n 30), Individual Opinion of Jan Paulsson, 12 June 2009, para 44, stating that it is merely the context of the treaty's terms, not of the treaty generally, that forms part of the permissible context under Article 31(1).
[48] *Oil Platforms* (n 39) para 47.
[49] *Asylum Case (Colombia v Peru)* [1950] ICJ Rep 266, 282.
[50] *Aegean Sea Continental Shelf (Greece v Turkey)* [1978] ICJ Rep 3, para 53.
[51] *Land, Island and Maritime Frontier Dispute (El Salvador/Honduras: Nicaragua intervening)* [1992] ICJ Rep 351, para 373 (hereafter *Land, Island and Maritime Frontier Dispute*).
[52] Dörr (n 33) 588–89.
[53] Compare ILC, *Draft Articles* (n 8) 221, para 13.

require expression in writing but may be made informally and tacitly.[54] The documents referred to in Article 31(2) do not, however, necessarily become an integral part of the treaty itself. As stipulated in *Ambatielos*, this depends on the parties' intentions in the individual circumstances of each case.[55]

In contrast to the first canon, regarding which investment tribunals have, on the whole, adhered to the work of the ILC and ICJ case law,[56] investment tribunals deviate considerably more with respect to contextual interpretation. Tribunals accept the general premises regarding context, particularly taking into account the treaty in its entirety, including preamble, annexes, title etc.[57] Nevertheless, in contradiction to Article 31(1) and (2),[58] several tribunals drew conclusions from international investment agreements with third parties of one or both of the parties to the investment treaty at hand. The *ADC* tribunal, for instance, sought to interpret 'investor', included in the Cyprus–Hungary BIT, by reference to Hungary's BITs with other states.[59] Similarly, in *Abaclat*, Italian BIT practice with third states served to inform the tribunal's interpretation of 'investment' under the Italy–Argentina BIT.[60] In sharp contrast to the language of Article 31(2),[61] the tribunal in *ConocoPhilipps* went as far as explicitly denoting third-party BITs as 'context'.[62]

Indeed, many treaty terms feature in most, if not all, investment agreements (eg 'investor' and 'investment'). Yet, Article 31(2) is clear. Beyond the actual text of the treaty, extrinsic documents only constitute 'context' if they meet the requirements of Article 31(2)(a)–(b). Third-party BITs do not fulfil these conditions, and some investment tribunals have refused to accept third-party BITs as context as a result.[63]

3. Object and purpose, Article 31(1)

Construing a treaty 'in light of its object and purpose', also relates to the treaty text and its ordinary meaning. As the Iran–US Claims Tribunal confirmed in *Federal Reserve Bank of New York v Bank Markazi*, under Article 31, the treaty provides a frame, in which the object and purpose operates, albeit without providing a hierarchy between the two.[64]

---

[54] This includes acceptance by acquiescence. Still, a mere lack of reaction to a previous assertion does not necessarily entail such acquiescence, cf *Sovereignty over Pulau Ligitan and Pulau Sipadan (Indonesia v Malaysia)* [2002] ICJ Rep 625, para 48.
[55] *Ambatielos Case (Greece v UK)* (Preliminary Objections) [1952] ICJ Rep 28, paras 42–44.
[56] And by extension also Article 31(4); see Section C.V below.
[57] *Saluka Investments BV (The Netherlands) v Czech Republic*, PCA Case No 2001-04, Partial Award, 17 March 2006, para 298 (distinguishing between 'immediate context', and 'broader context', including the preamble of the applicable BIT) (hereafter *Saluka Investments v Czech Republic*).
[58] One may also regard this practice as—equally incorrect, see Section C.III.1 below—reference to 'subsequent practice' pursuant to Article 31(3)(b), see B Boknik and T Gazzini, 'Questions of Treaty Interpretation' in Christian Tams and others (eds), *International Investment Law and General International Law—Radiating Effects?* (Edward Elgar Publishing 2023) 80, 95–96 (hereafter Boknik and Gazzini).
[59] *ADC v Hungary*, ICSID Case No ARB/03/16, Award, 2 October 2006, para 359.
[60] *Abaclat and Others v Argentine Republic*, ICSID Case No ARB/07/5, Jurisdiction and Admissibility, 4 August 2011, para 345.
[61] See also the criticism in T Hai Yen, *The Interpretation of Investment Treaties* (Brill 2014) 73–74.
[62] *ConocoPhillips v Venezuela*, ICSID Case No ARB/07/30, Jurisdiction and Merits, 3 September 2013, paras 310–11.
[63] eg *Rompetrol v Romania*, ICSID Case No ARB/06/3, Preliminary Objections, 18 April 2008, para 108. See also *Austrian Airlines v Slovak Republic*, UNCITRAL, Separate Opinion of Charles N Brower, 20 October 2009, para 4, n 3—however, in a dissent in another case, Judge Brower took the opposite position; *HICEE v Slovakia* (n 28), Dissenting Opinion of Judge Charles N Brower, 23 May 2011, para 40. See also AD Mitchell and J Munro, 'Someone Else's Deal: Interpreting International Investment Agreements in the Light of Third-Party Agreements' (2017) 28 EJIL 669–95.
[64] IUSCT, *Federal Reserve Bank of New York v Bank Markazi* [2000] Case A 28, 36 IUSCTR 5, para 58.

24 'Object and purpose' are generally understood as a single notion, not differentiating between 'object' and 'purpose'.[65] The singular form further indicates that it is first and foremost the treaty's *telos* as a whole that Article 31(1) refers to. Nonetheless, a treaty usually has various provisions—which may serve various distinct purposes, even if sharing an overarching goal with all other provisions of the treaty.[66] Therefore, 'object and purpose' must be read as encompassing both the aim of the whole treaty as well as the specific goal of the individual provision within the confines of the overarching aim.[67] The ICJ in *LaGrand* supported this more flexible notion of 'object and purpose'.[68]

25 Furthermore, as the Court has confirmed, the treaty's object and purpose may be discerned from the entirety of its text, including its title and its preamble.[69] Investment arbitration practice mostly follows this approach.[70] However, as the tribunal in *Société Générale v Dominican Republic* stressed, in line with general international law,[71] the preamble is merely a means to investigate the object and purpose but in itself usually 'cannot add substantive requirements to the provisions of the Treaty'.[72] It is not an operative clause and thus does not form part of the treaty text's 'ordinary meaning'.[73]

II. Maxims of interpretation

26 Section I dealt with canons of interpretation, i.e. distinctive methods focusing on text, context, and object and purpose. Maxims of interpretation, instead, comprise interpretive principles that do not constitute a specific method but rather may concern one, two, or all of them and require that their precepts are to be pursued to the optimal extent.[74]

27 Doubtless the most important of these maxims of interpretation, expressly mentioned in Article 31, is the principle of good faith. Article 31(1) places it at the very beginning, demanding that '[a] treaty shall be interpreted in good faith' and only then listing the three central canons of interpretation. It thus serves as an 'umbrella'[75]: the whole process of interpretation pursuant to Articles 31–33 thus must be conducted in the spirit of good faith and to its attainment.

---

[65] J Klabbers, 'Treaties, Object and Purpose' [2008] MPEPIL para 8 (hereafter Klabbers).
[66] See also D Kritsiotis, 'The Object and Purpose of a Treaty's Object and Purpose' in D Kritsiotis and MJ Bowman (eds), *Conceptual and Contextual Perspectives on the Modern Law of Treaties* (CUP 2018) 237 et seq.
[67] In similar direction Dörr (n 33) 585, para 54; cf Klabbers (n 65) paras 6–7.
[68] *La Grand (Germany v United States of America)* [2001] ICJ Rep 466, para 102.
[69] *Oil Platforms* (n 39) 813–14, para 27; *Maritime Delimitation in the Indian Ocean* (n 47) 29–31, paras 65, 70.
[70] eg *Continental Casualty v Argentina Republic*, ICSID Case No ARB/03/9, Award, 5 September 2008, para 258; *Içkale v Turkmenistan*, ICSID Case No ARB/10/24, Award, 8 March 2016, para 337 (hereafter *Içkale v Turkmenistan*).
[71] For example, *Dispute between Argentina and Chile concerning the Beagle Channel*, XXI UNRIAA 53, 89, para 19 (hereafter *Beagle Channel*): 'Although Preambles to treaties do not usually—nor are they intended to—contain provisions or dispositions of substance—(in short they are not operative clauses)—it is nevertheless generally accepted that they may be relevant and important as guides to the manner in which the Treaty should be interpreted, and in order, as it were, to "situate" it in respect of its object and purpose'. (emphasis added).
[72] *Société Générale v Dominican Republic*, UNCITRAL, Preliminary Objections to Jurisdiction, 19 September 2008, paras 31–32.
[73] Contrarily, for an example of exceeding the ordinary meaning by reading an fair and equitable treatment (FET) clause into a BIT because the preamble mentions that FET is 'desirable', see *Bayindir v Pakistan*, ICSID Case No ARB/03/29, Jurisdiction, 14 November 2005, para 230.
[74] cf R Alexy's notion of principles as optimization precepts, *Theorie der Grundrechte* (Suhrkamp 1985) 75 et seq. Similarly, Ronald Dworkin, *Taking Rights Seriously* (HUP 1977) 14 et seq.
[75] Dörr (n 33) 587, para 59.

28 In *Border and Transborder Armed Actions*, the ICJ observed that good faith 'is one of the basic principles governing the creation and performance of legal obligations' but in the same breath also added 'it is in itself not a source of obligation where none would otherwise exist'.[76] While this judgment did not deal with good faith in interpretation, it indicates the limits of the overall principle. It may demand optimal realization and thereby requires a reasonable application[77] of the elements enshrined in Article 31 and their balancing[78] and may even limit the scope of a right or power.[79] But it may not buttress creation of a right or obligation that otherwise cannot be construed from the treaty text by way of the elements of interpretation in Articles 31–33.

29 Investment tribunals have overall aligned with these approaches. For example, the tribunal in *Poštová banka v Greece* stressed that good faith interpretation 'requires elements of reasonableness that go beyond the mere verbal or purely literal analysis'[80] and the *BIVAC* tribunal underlined that good faith 'point[s] to a balanced approach to treaty interpretation'.[81]

30 Further, the principle of effectiveness (*ut res magis valeat quam pereat* or *effet utile*) is considered an important maxim of interpretation, often linked either to good faith[82] or the object and purpose of a treaty, or both.[83] It features prominently in ICJ jurisprudence.[84] It demands giving effect to the terms of the treaty and thus has two aspects.[85] Generally, it requires the interpreter to employ an interpretation that realizes the goals of the treaty.[86] More specifically, among several possible interpretations of a treaty, one must adopt the interpretation which 'enable[s] the treaty to have appropriate effects'.[87] The principle of effectiveness is in tension with the *ex abundante cautela* maxim, which—in exceptional circumstances—may permit treating certain words or phrases of a treaty as redundant.[88]

31 Before investment tribunals, the discussion to what extent investment treaties do or do not contain a general rule requiring an investment/investor-friendly interpretation has featured

---

[76] *Border and Transborder Armed Actions (Nicaragua v Honduras)* (Jurisdiction and Admissibility) [1988] ICJ Rep 69, para 94.
[77] *The Rhine Chlorides Arbitration concerning the Auditing of Accounts (Netherlands v France)* (2004) 25 UNRIAA 267, paras 73–74 (hereafter *The Rhine Chlorides Arbitration*), quoting from *Georges Pinson (France) v Mexico*, Decision No 1, 19 October 1928, 5 UNRIAA 327, para 50 (hereafter *Georges Pinson v Mexico*).
[78] *US—Shrimp*, WT/DS58/AB/R, 12 October 1998, paras 158–59, referring to reasonableness as requiring a fair balancing of the various treaty elements.
[79] cf *Territorial Dispute* (n 34) 51, paras 79–87. See also R Gardiner, *Treaty Interpretation* (2nd edn, OUP 2015) 177 (hereafter Gardiner).
[80] *Poštová v Greece* (n 26) para 284.
[81] *BIVAC v Paraguay*, ICSID Case No ARB/07/9, Decision on Jurisdiction, 29 May 2009, para 59 (hereafter *BIVAC v Paraguay*); in similar vein *Pan American v Argentina*, ICSID Case No ARB/03/13, Decision on Preliminary Objections, 27 July 2006, para 99 (hereafter *Pan American v Argentina*).
[82] Gardiner (n 79) 179–81.
[83] ILC, *Draft Articles* (n 8) 219, para 6.
[84] *Corfu Channel (Great Britain v Albania)* [1949] ICJ Rep 4, 24; *Land, Island and Maritime Frontier Dispute* (n 51) para 375; *Fisheries Jurisdiction (Spain v Canada)* [1998] ICJ Rep 432, para 52.
[85] *Territorial Dispute* (n 34) para 47.
[86] *Interpretation of Peace Treaties with Bulgaria, Hungary and Romania* (Advisory Opinion) [1950] ICJ Rep 221, 229.
[87] ILC, *Draft Articles* (n 8) 219, para 6. The ICJ has confirmed this aspect of *effet utile* on many occasions, eg *Application of the International Convention on the Elimination of All Forms of Racial Discrimination (Georgia v Russia)* (Preliminary Objections) [2011] ICJ Rep 70, paras 133–34, with additional references. See also already the PCIJ in *Free Zones of Upper Savoy and the District of Gex (France v Switzerland)*, PCIJ Series A No 22, 13.
[88] See A MacDonald, '*Ex abundante cautela*' in Klingler and others (n 22) 115, 121 et seq. In investment arbitration note the opposite views in: *Siemens v Argentine Republic*, ICSID Case No ARB/02/8, Decision on Jurisdiction, 3 August 2004, para 90 (endorsing *ex abundante cautela*) and *Wintershall v Argentina* (n 35) para 185 (rejecting the maxim).

prominently under the rubrics of both the principles of good faith and effectiveness. This is what the tribunal in *Arif v Moldova* asserted, holding that *effet utile* 'ensures that the investment enjoys the most favorable legal regime'.[89] However, most tribunals, at least in the abstract, have rejected such notion. *Poštová* concluded that no *in dubio pro investore* interpretive rule may be gleaned from the text, context, or object and purpose of the applicable BIT.[90] Others have followed suit, stressing that a good faith interpretation requires a reasonable and balanced approach that advocates equally taking into account the interests of the investor and the host state.[91] Therefore, they stressed, there is no general presumption for either a broad or narrow interpretation of the investment treaty,[92] thus also rejecting, at least as a general rule, the *in dubio mitius* principle.[93]

32 Several other maxims may be of further relevance, such as *expressio unius est exclusio alterius*,[94] *ejusdem generis*,[95] and *contra proferentem*.[96]

33 Finally, treaty interpretation also has a temporal dimension.[97] The discussion whether a treaty should be interpreted in light of the circumstances of its conclusion or of its application is much older than the VCLT. However, as the ILC emphasized in 2018, no general rule in favour of a principle of either contemporaneous or evolutive interpretation exists in international doctrine or jurisprudence.[98]

III. Subsequent agreements and subsequent practice, Article 31(3)(a) and (b)

1. General considerations

34 The first two sub-paragraphs of Article 31(3) pertain to matters of treaty interpretation over time.[99] Taking into account the treaty parties' (a) 'subsequent agreement' and (b) 'subsequent

---

[89] *Arif v Moldova*, ICSID Case No ARB/11/23, Award, 8 April 2013, para 391.
[90] *Poštová v Greece* (n 26) para 310.
[91] *BIVAC v Paraguay* (n 81) para 59; *Pan American v Argentina* (n 81) para 99; *Wintershall v Argentina* (n 35) para 84.
[92] *Ethyl v Canada*, UNCITRAL, Award on Jurisdiction, 24 June 1998, paras 55–56. *Methanex v USA*, Partial Award (n 37) para 105; *Aguas del Tunari v Bolivia* (n 32) para 91; *Euram v Slovakia*, PCA Case No 2010-17, Award on Jurisdiction, 22 October 2012, para 166.
[93] On this principle see P Merkouris, '*In Dubio Mitius*' in Klingler and others (n 22) 259 et seq.
[94] *Conditions of Admission of a State to Membership in the United Nations* (Advisory Opinion) [1948] ICJ Rep 57, 62 (albeit only implicitly) (hereafter *Conditions of Admission to the UN*); *Tokios Tokeles v Ukraine*, ICSID Case No ARB/02/18, Decision on Jurisdiction, 29 April 2004, para 30; *Teinver v Argentina*, ICSID Case No ARB/09/1, Decision on Jurisdiction, 21 December 2012, paras 164, 186. See also J Klingler, '*Expressio Unius Est Exclusio Alterius*' in Klingler and others (n 22) 73 et seq.
[95] *Competence of the ILO* (n 46) 57. In the investment context, this maxim has mostly arisen in a *sensu lato* regarding the question as to whether to apply most-favoured nations (MFN) to dispute settlement clauses. For an overview and analysis of the case law see F Baetens, 'Ejusdem Generis and Noscitur a Sociis' in Klingler and others (n 22) 133, 149 et seq.
[96] *Locus classicus: Payment in Gold of Brazilian Federal Loans Contracted in France (France v Brazil)*, PCIJ Series A No 21, 114. See also P d'Argent, 'Contra Proferentem' in Klingler and others (n 22) 241, 254, noting that tribunals have rejected attempts by host states to rely on the *contra proferentem* maxim in case of investment treaties they concluded with the investors' home states based on their Model BIT, see, eg, *Ceskoslovenska Obchodni Banka v Slovak Republic*, ICSID Case No ARB/97/4, Jurisdiction, 24 May 1999, para 51.
[97] eg T O Elias, 'The Doctrine of Intertemporal Law' (1980) 74 AJIL 285.
[98] ILC, 'Draft Conclusions on Subsequent Agreements and Subsequent Practice in Relation to the Interpretation of Treaties, with Commentaries' (2018) UN Doc A/73/10 (hereafter ILC, *Subsequent Agreements*) Conclusion 8 and Commentary thereto with further references to case law and doctrine. On this, see in detail Sections B.II, C.III.1, and C.IV.5.
[99] cf the eponymous ILC Study Group, in YILC 2008, Vol II, Part Two, 148, para 353 and Annex I.

practice' means that interpretation is not necessarily static, but can be evolutionary.[100] At the same time, Article 31(3)(a) and (b) remain firmly within the overarching rationale of the law of treaties, i.e. acknowledging the parties as the masters of the treaty: their conduct after the conclusion of the treaty[101] influences its interpretation.[102]

However, as underlined by the ILC, Article 31(3)(a)–(b) explicitly state that, while authentic means of interpretation, 'subsequent agreement', and 'subsequent practice' are to be 'taken into account' in the interpretation of a treaty and are thus not necessarily 'conclusive in the sense that [they] override all other means of interpretation'.[103] Yet, they need to be distinguished from an agreement on a specific interpretation of a treaty provision or term which the treaty parties reach after the conclusion of the treaty and 'which the parties consider to be binding'.[104] In the latter case, the burden of proof lies with the party claiming bindingness. 35

Furthermore, only such conduct falls under Article 31(3)(a)–(b), which is 'in the application of' the treaty or its provisions or 'regarding its interpretation'. After reviewing international case law, the ILC concluded that this requires careful consideration of 'whether the parties [...] assume a position regarding the interpretation of a treaty or whether they are motivated by other considerations'.[105] The tribunal in *Infinito Gold v Costa Rica* appeared to endorse a similar position, finding that Canada's statements referred to by Costa Rica did not relate to the Canada–Costa Rica BIT, but to the NAFTA, and thus could not qualify as conduct 'in application of the treaty' under Article 31(3)(b).[106] 36

2. Subsequent agreement, Article 31(3)(a): requirements and evidence

A 'subsequent agreement' pursuant to Article 31(3)(a) requires joint conduct, i.e. all parties actively participating together, to conclude a single agreement. In *Whaling in the Antarctic*, the ICJ rejected the contention that the International Whaling Commission (IWC) resolutions constituted subsequent agreement or subsequent practice for the purposes of interpreting Article VIII of the International Convention for the Regulation of Whaling (ICRW). The Court emphasized that 'many IWC resolutions were adopted without the support of *all* States parties to the Convention'.[107] The ILC has also confirmed that '[t]he term "subsequent agreement" under article 31, paragraph 3 (a), is limited to a common act or undertaking *between all the parties*'.[108] In a number of decisions, investment tribunals 37

---

[100] ILC, *Subsequent Agreements* (n 98), Conclusion 8 and Commentary thereto, which notes that while a treaty's interpretation is 'capable of evolving over time', there is no clear evidence in practice or literature for a general rule of evolutionary interpretation (or for contemporaneous interpretation, either). However, note a strand of investment arbitrations, starting from *Wintershall v Argentina* (n 35) paras 129, 174, which promotes contemporaneous interpretations. On this, see J Wyatt, 'Signs of a Subjective Approach to Treaty Interpretation in Investment Arbitration: A Justified Divergence from the VCLT?' in Shirlow and Gore (n 31) 89, 101 et seq (hereafter Wyatt).
[101] ILC, *Subsequent Agreements* (n 98), Commentary to Conclusion 4, para 2: 'This point in time is often earlier than the moment when the treaty enters into force (Article 24 [VCLT])'.
[102] On the quality such conduct must take between Article 31(3)(a) and (b) see Section C.III.2–3.
[103] ILC, *Subsequent Agreements* (n 98), Commentary to Conclusion 4, para 4.
[104] ibid para 5.
[105] ibid, Commentary to Conclusion 6, para 18.
[106] *Infinito Gold v Costa Rica*, ICSID Case No ARB/14/5, Award, 3 June 2021, para 344. Similarly, with respect to third-party BITs: *RosInvest v Russia*, SCC Case No V079/2005, Award on Jurisdiction, 1 October 2007, para 119 (hereafter *RosInvest v Russia*).
[107] *Whaling in the Antarctic (Australia v Japan: New Zealand Intervening)* [2014] ICJ Rep 226, para 83 (emphasis added). See also *United States—Tuna*, WT/DS381/AB/R, 13 June 2012, para 371.
[108] ILC, *Subsequent Agreements* (n 98), Commentary to Conclusion 4, para 12 (emphasis added).

also required that all treaty parties must actively engage in concluding the 'subsequent agreement'.[109]

38 Apart from such joint or common conduct, a 'subsequent agreement' does not need to meet any particular formal requirements. This view, inferred, among others, from *Kasikili/Sedudu Island*,[110] is shared in investment arbitration.[111]

3. Subsequent practice, Article 31(3)(b): requirements and evidence
a. Agreement and Form

39 According to Article 31(3)(b) 'subsequent practice' must 'establish [...] the agreement of the parties regarding its interpretation'. As the ICJ underlined in *Kasikili/Sedudu Island*, to evince such agreement it does not suffice that the parties' position overlap by coincidence. Rather, it is necessary that the 'authorities were fully aware of and accepted' the practice.[112]

40 Which form must the practice, including the said 'agreement', take as regards its density and uniformity? This question has led to divergent views. The World Trade Organization (WTO) Appellate Body in *Japan—Alcoholic Beverages*, quoting Sinclair,[113] insisted on 'a "concordant, common and consistent" sequence of acts or pronouncements which is sufficient to establish a discernible pattern implying the agreement of the parties regarding its interpretation'.[114] Contrarily, the European Court of Human Rights (ECtHR) in *Loizidou v Turkey* characterized the relevant practice as 'uniform and consistent' despite the UK and Cyprus actually being in disaccord.[115] The ICJ and the Iran–US Claims Tribunal endorsed a similar, more flexible approach.[116]

41 Investment arbitration practice so far is inconclusive on the matter.[117] The *Telefónica* tribunal adopted the more restrictive approach, quoting affirmatively *Japan—Alcoholic Beverages*.[118] In *CCFT v Canada*, on the other hand, the tribunal opted for a more flexible approach.[119] The latter is preferable, not only because of its more solid following in international case law but because the Appellate Body's minimum threshold approach is based on a misreading of Sinclair, as ILC Special Rapporteur Nolte pointed out.[120] Indeed, in the passage quoted by

---

[109] eg *Aguas del Tunari v Bolivia* (n 32) para 251; *HICEE v Slovakia* (n 28) para 134; *Eskosol v Italy*, ICSID Case No ARB/15/50, Decision, 7 May 2019, para 220 (hereafter *Eskosol v Italy*); *Kappes v Guatemala*, ICSID Case No ARB/18/43, Preliminary Objections, 13 March 2020, para 156 (hereafter *Kappes v Guatemala*).

[110] *Kasikili/Sedudu* (n 39) 1087, para 63. See also ILC, 'Second Report on Subsequent Agreements and Subsequent Practice in Relation to the Interpretation of Treaties, by Mr Georg Nolte, Special Rapporteur' (26 March 2014) UN Doc A/CN.4/671, para 54 (hereafter ILC, Second Report); Dörr (n 33) 594, para 75.

[111] eg *Methanex v USA*, UNCITRAL, Final Award, 3 August 2005, para 20 (referring explicitly to the *Kasikili/Sedudu Island* case) (hereafter *Methanex v USA*); *CCFT v USA*, UNCITRAL, 28 January, 2008, para 207 (hereafter *CCFT v USA*).

[112] *Kasikili/Sedudu* (n 39) 1094, para 74.

[113] I Sinclair, *The Vienna Convention on the Law of Treaties* (2nd edn, MUP 1984) 137 (hereafter Sinclair).

[114] *Japan—Alcoholic Beverages*, WT/DS8/AB/R, WT/DS10/AB/R and WT/DS11/AB/R, 1 November 1996, 13.

[115] *Loizidou v Turkey* [GC], Preliminary Objections, 23 March 1995, App no 15318/89, paras 80, 82. See also *Beagle Channel* (n 71) 188, para 177.

[116] cf *Kasikili/Sedudu* (n 39) 1075–76, 1087, paras 47–50, 63; *Iran v USA*, No ITL 83-B1-FT (Counterclaim), Interlocutory Award (2004–2009) 38 IUSCTR 77, 116–126, paras 109–33.

[117] See also the conclusion in ILC, Second Report (n 110) para 46 ('ICISD tribunals have rendered divergent awards').

[118] *Telefónica v Argentina*, ICSID Case No ARB/03/20, Decision of the Tribunal on Objections to Jurisdiction, 25 May 2006, para 114 (hereafter *Telefónica v Argentina*). See also the similarly restrictive approach in *National Grid v Argentina*, UNCITRAL, Decision on Jurisdiction, 20 June 2006, para 85.

[119] *CCFT v USA* (n 111) paras 182–89.

[120] ILC, Second Report (n 110) para 47.

the Appellate Body, Sinclair writes that 'the *value* of subsequent practice will naturally depend on the *extent* to which it is concordant, common and consistent',[121] thus not setting a threshold but establishing a matter of degree ('extent'). This finds confirmation in the ILC's work on the draft Convention on the Law of Treaties.[122] That said, since most investment agreements merely have two parties, even under the flexible approach, often it will prove difficult to affirm a 'subsequent practice' if one party frequently strays from such alleged practice.

b. (No) formality, conduct, and engagement

Considering that a 'subsequent agreement' does not require any particular formality,[123] a **42** *fortiori* this is also the case regarding a 'subsequent practice'.[124] By contrast, while 'subsequent agreements' presuppose joint conduct,[125] 'subsequent practice' under Article 31(3)(b) neither generally requires a single common act nor active engagement of all treaty parties. As Special Rapporteur Nolte underscored, '[a] merely parallel conduct may suffice',[126] referring to *Cameroon v Nigeria*.[127] Similarly, whereas a subsequent agreement pursuant to Article 31(3)(a) 'cannot [...] be derived from the mere silence of the parties', the ILC stressed that under Article 31(3)(b) 'not all parties must have engaged in a particular practice [...] if it is "accepted" by those parties not engaged'.[128] This finds confirmation in the *Temple* (1962),[129] *Oil Platforms*,[130] and *Application of the Interim Accord*[131] cases, among others.

Several investment tribunals have strayed far from this and adopted a much more restrictive **43** approach.[132] The *Telefónica* tribunal would not accept parallel conduct but insisted that the conduct must be 'directed toward each other'.[133] Accordingly, in several disputes under the Spain–Argentina BIT, tribunals rejected parties' litigation positions as respondents in separate arbitration proceedings to qualify as 'subsequent practice'.[134] However, the *Kappes v Guatemala* tribunal stated that 'separate submissions in separate cases could be compelling

---

[121] Sinclair (n 113) 137.
[122] ILC, *Draft Articles* (n 8) 221, para 14: 'The value of subsequent practice varies depending on how far it shows the common understanding of the parties as to the meaning of the terms'.
[123] See Section C.III.2.
[124] ILC, Second Report (n 110) para 43, citing *Land and Maritime Boundary between Cameroon and Nigeria* (*Cameroon v Nigeria: Equatorial Guinea intervening*) [2002] ICJ Rep 303, para 304 ('express or tacit') (hereafter *Land and Maritime Boundary*).
[125] See Section C.III.2.
[126] ILC, Second Report (n 110) para 43.
[127] *Land and Maritime Boundary* (n 124) 447–48, para 304. The Court found this not to be the case, because the oil concessions in question were not 'based on express or tacit agreement between the parties'.
[128] ILC, Second Report (n 110) paras 58 and 60.
[129] *Temple of Preah Vihear* (*Cambodia v Thailand*) [1962] ICJ Rep 6, 23.
[130] *Oil Platforms* (n 39) 815, para 30.
[131] *Application of the Interim Accord of 13 September 1995* (*FYROM v Greece*) [2011] ICJ Rep 644, paras 99–101.
[132] See, generally, J Arato and A Kulick, 'Final Report on International Investment Tribunals' (2020) <https://www.ila-hq.org/en_GB/documents/final-report-on-international-investment-tribunals-andreas-kulick-and-jul ian-arato> accessed 27 February 2023 (hereafter Arato and Kulick).
[133] *Telefónica v Argentina* (n 118) para 113.
[134] *Gas Natural v Argentina*, ICSID Case No ARB/03/10, Decision of the Tribunal on Preliminary Objections to Jurisdiction, 17 June 2005, para 47, fn 12: 'We do not believe [...] that an argument made by a party in the context of an arbitration reflects practice establishing agreement between the parties to a treaty within the meaning of Article 31(3)(b)'; *Telefónica v Argentina* (n 118) paras 112–13; *Urbaser v Argentina*, ICSID Case No ARB/07/26, Award, 8 December 2016, para 31 (hereafter *Urbaser v Argentina*); *Suez v Argentina*, ICSID Case No ARB/03/19, Annulment, 5 May 2017, para 258.

evidence of subsequent practice'.[135] Also, in *CCFT v US*, a NAFTA tribunal accepted that several unilateral actions by NAFTA parties satisfied the requirements of Article 31(3)(b).[136] As regards the matter of silence, the *El Paso* tribunal insisted that 'internal exchanges between the organs of one Contracting State, coupled with the silence of the other State, are not sufficient [...]. [A]t least *some* communication must be shown to have occurred'.[137] Similarly, *Kappes* required active participation of all treaty parties in the 'subsequent practice', in parallel[138] with the prevalent view on Article 31(3)(a).[139]

44 The less restrictive approach seems more adequate. The evidence of an 'agreement' among the parties is what both Article 31(3)(a) and (b) share. What distinguishes them is that Article 31(3)(a) requires a 'single common act by the parties' and thus '*ipso facto* has the effect of constituting an authentic means of interpretation [...], whereas a "subsequent practice" only has this effect if its different elements, taken together, show "the common understanding of the parties as to the meaning of the terms"'.[140] Such showing of a common understanding through practice compensates for the lack of express and joint agreement and justifies that Article 31(3) treats 'subsequent agreement' and 'subsequent practice' the same in their effects. Since a 'subsequent agreement' itself does not require any particular form,[141] asking for similar requirements with respect to a 'subsequent practice' would forfeit the differentiation that Article 31(3) establishes. Rather, the 'practice' should be permitted to take any shape, including parallel conduct and silence, as long as it demonstrates the parties' 'common understanding'. In addition, requiring active conduct would be at odds with the fundamental principle that State responsibility may incur from both actions and omissions.[142]

4. Scope of interpretation: treaty modification through Article 31(3)(a) or (b)?

45 Finally, what is the scope of change that Article 31(3)(a) and (b) permits? This touches upon the age-old question of drawing the line between interpretation and modification. Legal theory established that every court's or tribunal's interpretative decision constitutes a norm in itself and therefore, particularly if repeated as a *jurisprudence constante*, may form an abstract and general norm,[143] thus blurring the line between interpretation and modification.[144]

46 Still, the distinction remains important. The ICJ's jurisprudence reflects said ambiguity, emblematically—and enigmatically—stating in *Navigational and Related Rights* that '[Article 31(3)(b)] can result in a departure from the original intent on the basis of a tacit agreement',[145] but never explicitly accepting an actual modification *qua* 'subsequent agreement' or

---

[135] *Kappes v Guatemala* (n 109) para 156.
[136] *CCFT v USA* (n 111) para 189.
[137] *El Paso v Argentina*, ICSID Case No ARB/03/15, Award, 31 October 2011, para 603 (emphasis added).
[138] *Kappes v Guatemala* (n 109) para 156. Note that the tribunal quotes as authority *Eskosol v Italy* (n 109) para 220, which, however, merely discussed Article 31(3)(a).
[139] See Section C.III.1.
[140] ILC, *Subsequent Agreements* (n 98), Commentary to Conclusion 4, para 9, quoting ILC, *Draft Articles* (n 8) 221–22, para 15.
[141] See Section C.III.2.
[142] Article 2 ARSIWA. See also ILC, *Subsequent Agreements* (n 98) Conclusion 5: 'Subsequent practice [...] may consist of any conduct of a party in the application of a treaty, whether in the exercise of its executive, legislative, judicial, or other functions'; Commentary, para 2: '[T]he term "any conduct" encompasses actions and omissions').
[143] See, eg, H Kelsen, *Reine Rechtslehre* (1st edn 1934, reprint 2008, Mohr Siebeck) 79–80.
[144] ILC, Second Report (n 110) paras 116 et seq.
[145] *Navigational and Related Rights* (*Costa Rica v Nicaragua*) [2009] ICJ Rep 213, para 64.

'practice'.[146] As a general rule, it is widely accepted, as the ILC confirmed, that there is a presumption against modification, and that the possibility of amending or modifying a treaty by subsequent practice 'has not been generally recognized'.[147] Distinguishing interpretation from modification in practice is not possible in the abstract but depends on various criteria, four of which the ILC underlined as most relevant: (1) 'the treaty itself'; (2) 'the character of the specific treaty provision at hand'; (3) 'the legal context within which the treaty operates'; (4) 'the specific circumstances of the case'.[148]

More specifically, as regards modification by 'subsequent agreement' pursuant to Article 31(3)(a), the most pertinent question relates to where to draw the line to an 'amendment' for the purposes of Article 39 VCLT. This challenge is exacerbated by the fact that the 'agreement' in Article 39 does not need to meet any specific formal requirements, as noted in *Pulp Mills*.[149] Yet, in *Bananas (II)*, the WTO Appellate Body insisted that 'the term "application" in Article (31)(3)(a) […] does not connote the creation of new or the extension of existing obligations',[150] thus rejecting the possibility of substantive change via 'subsequent agreement'.

In investment arbitration, this question featured famously regarding the infamous 2001 NAFTA Free Trade Commission (FTC) Interpretation Note on Article 1105(1) NAFTA.[151] The case law on this is addressed in more detail in another entry.[152] Suffice it to state here that NAFTA tribunals were divided on the issue and overall took as many as four different approaches, treating the FTC Note as[153]: (1) an impermissible amendment;[154] (2) an authentic interpretation, established via *lex specialis* interpretive procedures;[155] (3) an interpretation justified by 31(3)(a) VCLT;[156] and/or (4) a (permissible) informal modification.[157] More recent decisions tend to reject at least the latter notion, with *Magyar Farming v Hungary* holding that a 'subsequent agreement' 'can only interpret the treaty terms; it cannot change their meaning'.[158]

The case law is not settled. Yet, an important guideline remains the 'presumption', as underlined by the ILC, 'that a subsequent agreement which does not satisfy the procedural requirements of the amendment clause of a treaty should be interpreted narrowly'.[159]

The issue of modification by 'subsequent practice' equally featured in the case law of the ICJ and other international courts and tribunals. In addition to *Navigational and Related Rights*,

---

[146] Note also *Gabčíkovo-Nagymaros Project (Hungary v Slovakia)* [1997] ICJ Rep 7, Separate Opinion of Judge Bedjaoui [1997] ICJ Rep 121, para 5 (hereafter *Gabčíkovo-Nagymaros*), stating that 'the "interpretation" of a treaty must not be confused with its "revision"'.
[147] ILC, *Subsequent Agreements* (n 98) Draft Conclusion 8.
[148] ILC, 'Fifth Report on Subsequent Agreements and Subsequent Practice in Relation to the Interpretation of Treaties, by Mr Georg Nolte, Special Rapporteur' (28 February 2018) UN Doc A/CN.4/715, Draft Conclusion 7(3) and Comments, para 165.
[149] *Pulp Mills on the River Uruguay (Argentina v Uruguay)* [2010] ICJ Rep 14, para 128 ('Whatever its specific designation and in whatever instrument it may have been recorded').
[150] *European Communities—Bananas, Second Recourse to Article 21.5*, WT/DS27/AB/RW2/ECU and WT/DS27/AB/RW/USA, 11 and 22 December 2008, 131, para 391.
[151] Notes of Interpretation of Certain Chapter Eleven Provisions, Free Trade Commission (31 July 2001) http://www.international.gc.ca accessed 13 February 2023. According to Article 1131(2) NAFTA, the FTC may issue authoritative interpretations of the NAFTA.
[152] See in this Commentary: Rob Howse, 'The international law minimum standard of treatment'.
[153] Arato and Kulick (n 132) 9. See also ILC, Second Report (n 110) paras 150–55.
[154] *Pope & Talbot v Canada*, Damages, UNCITRAL, 31 May 2002, paras 46–47.
[155] *ADF v USA* (n 42) para 177.
[156] *Methanex v USA* (n 111) para 23 (suggesting that an authentic subsequent agreement on interpretation would 'override the ordinary principles of interpretation' (meaning, here, ordinary meaning).
[157] ibid para 21.
[158] *Magyar Farming v Hungary*, ICSID Case No ARB/17/27, Award, 13 November 2019, para 218.
[159] ILC, Second Report (n 110) para 164.

the *Namibia* and *Wall* Advisory Opinions are prominent in this regard.[160] However, the Court has never recognized explicitly that a treaty may be modified by way of 'subsequent practice' according to Article 31(3)(b).[161] The same holds true for most other international courts and tribunals, with the arbitral tribunal in *Eritrea v Ethiopia*[162] and a few judgments of the ECtHR[163] being the rare exception.

51 As they primarily prefer a restrictive position on what qualifies as 'subsequent practice', most investment arbitration tribunals have not come as far as to consider whether such practice may permit modifying the treaty.[164] Among the few that did, the *von Pezold* tribunal so far appears to be the only one answering the question in the affirmative.[165]

IV. Systemic integration, Article 31(3)(c)

52 The proliferation of treaties and of international courts and tribunals has led to a 'flowering of case-law'[166] where Article 31(3)(c) has been invoked. This provision is known as the 'principle of systemic integration'.[167]

53 A number of elements need to be considered in the application of Article 31(3)(c) VCLT or the apposite customary rule: what counts as a 'rule' (1); what is meant by an 'applicable' rule (2); which 'parties' (3); how relevance is to be determined (4). In addition to the above, and although not featuring explicitly in the text of Article 31(3)(c), it needs to be addressed whether the rules to be taken into account are the rules at the time of the conclusion of the treaty or at the time of its interpretation (5).[168]

1. Rules

54 International jurisprudence has held consistently that 'rules' includes any rule stemming from the three formal sources of international law, i.e. treaties,[169] custom,[170] and general

---

[160] *Legal Consequences for States of the Continued Presence of South Africa in Namibia (South West Africa) notwithstanding Security Council Resolution 276 (1970)* (Advisory Opinion) [1971] ICJ Rep 16, para 22; *Legal Consequences of the Construction of a Wall in the Occupied Palestinian Territory* (Advisory Opinion) [2004] ICJ Rep 136, paras 27–28.

[161] See also the conclusion in ILC, Second Report (n 110) para 129.

[162] *Decision Regarding Delimitation of the Border between Eritrea and Ethiopia*, 13 April 2002, UNRIAA, Vol XXV, 83, 110–11, paras 3.6–3.10.

[163] *Öcalan v Turkey* [GC] App no 426221/99 (12 May 2005), para 163; *Al-Saadoon and Mufdhi v UK* App no 61498/08 (2 March 2010), paras 119–20.

[164] See Section C.III.3.

[165] *Von Pezold v Zimbabwe*, ICSID Case No ARB/10/15, Award, 28 July 2015, para 409 (hereafter *von Pezold v Zimbabwe*).

[166] Gardiner (n 79) 290.

[167] The term was popularized by Campbell McLachlan, 'The Principle of Systemic Integration and Article 31(3)(c) of the Vienna Convention' (2005) 54(2) ICLQ 279 (hereafter McLachlan). Investment arbitration awards have, on occasion, also used as synonyms 'systemic interpretation' (*Micula v Romania*, Final Award, 11 December 2013, ICSID Case No ARB/05/20, paras 307, 310) or 'principle of systematic integration' (*Al Warraq v Indonesia*, Final Award, Ad hoc Tribunal (UNCITRAL), 15 December 2014, para 519).

[168] McLachlan (n 167); B Simma and T Kill, 'Harmonizing Investment Protection and International Human Rights: First Steps Toward a Methodology' in C Binder and others (eds), *International Investment Law for the 21st Century: Essays in Honor of Christoph Schreuer* (OUP 2009) 680, 698–702.

[169] *Certain Questions of Mutual Assistance in Criminal Matters (Djibouti v France)* [2008] ICJ Rep 177, paras 112–13; *Selmouni v France* App no 25803/94 (28 July 1999), paras 97–98; *Urbaser v Argentina* (n 134) paras 1197–98, 1204–10.

[170] *Oil Platforms* (n 39) para 41; *Arbitration Regarding the Iron Rhine ('Ijzeren Rijn') Railway, Belgium v Netherlands*, Award, 24 May 2005, 17 UNRIAA 35, para 59 (hereafter *Iron Rhine*); *Kardassopoulos v Georgia*,

principles.[171] There have been, though, instances where investment tribunals have resorted to non-binding instruments,[172] or international case law.[173] However, it is unclear whether this is done truly under Article 31(3)(c) or whether recourse to such material occurs through different points of entry, such as 'ordinary meaning' or 'supplementary means' that help clarify the meaning of the provision under interpretation, and/or even as material that demonstrates the existence and content of a customary rule that is relevant under Article 31(3)(c). It is more likely that the latter is the case and, in any event, this is the methodologically more accurate form of interpretative reasoning.

With the increasing participation of international organizations in international regulation, have come questions as to whether certain of their acts could also qualify as 'rules' for the purposes of Article 31(3)(c). Although jurisprudence on the matter is rather limited, the *Iron Rhine* tribunal considered secondary legislation of regional organizations, such as European Union (EU) Directives and Regulations, to fall within Article 31(3)(c).[174] **55**

In investment arbitration, in a recent string of cases relating to the interpretation of the Energy Charter Treaty (ECT), the question that arose was whether EU law was a 'relevant rule'. However, the tribunals did not elaborate on whether such secondary legislation could be considered as a rule, because the argument raised by the European Commission was too vague, as it simply referred to EU law *in toto*, without specifying precisely which rules would allegedly be relevant. For this reason, the tribunals opined that such invocation failed the threshold of 'rule' invocation required by Article 31(3)(c), i.e. that a 'clearly determinable rule' needs to be invoked and not merely a reference to an entire system of law.[175] **56**

2. Applicable

In the VCLT's negotiating history the term 'applicable' received very little attention. This trend is replicated in international jurisprudence. A potential factor to this is that the term 'applicable', as Villiger suggests, refers to the bindingness or not of the 'rules' in question and that an ordinary reading of the term 'applicable' excludes non-binding rules.[176] The *OSPAR Arbitration* supports this. There the tribunal did not consider a principle invoked by the parties as it was still in *statu nascendi*.[177] Consequently, the discussion on 'applicability' tends **57**

ICSID Case No ARB/05/18, Decision on Jurisdiction, 6 July 2007, para 208 (hereafter *Kardassopoulos v Georgia*); *Ambiente v Argentina*, Decision on Jurisdiction and Admissibility, 8 February 2013, ICSID Case No ARB/08/9, paras 603–28 (hereafter *Ambiente v Argentina*); *Tulip Real Estate v Turkey*, ICSID Case No ARB/11/28, Decision on Annulment, 30 December 2015, para 87 (hereafter *Tulip Real Estate*, Annulment); *Philip Morris v Uruguay*, ICSID Case No ARB/10/7, Award, 8 July 2016, para 290 (hereafter *Philip Morris v Uruguay*); *Orascom v Algeria*, ICSID Case No ARB/12/35, Final Award, 31 May 2017, para 293 (hereafter *Orascom v Algeria*).

[171] *Golder v UK* (n 39) para 35; *Georges Pinson v Mexico* (n 77) para 50(4); *Renco v Peru*, UNCT/13/1, Partial Award on Jurisdiction, 15 July 2016, para 144 (hereafter *Renco v Peru*); *Eiser v Spain*, ICSID Case No ARB/13/36, Decision on Respondent Application for Annulment, 11 June 2020, para 177.

[172] Like General Comments, non-binding resolutions of international organizations, non-binding declarations, and draft conventions: *Philip Morris v Uruguay* (n 170) paras 290–301; *Urbaser v Argentina* (n 134) paras 1197–98; *Kardassopoulos v Georgia* (n 170) paras 215, 218–19.

[173] *Berschader v Russia*, SCC Case No 080/2004, Award, 21 April 2006, para 97 (hereafter *Berschader v Russia*) (investment tribunals' case law); *Renco v Peru* (n 171) para 144 (ICJ and PCIJ); *Tulip Real Estate*, Annulment (n 170) paras 91–92 (regional human rights courts).

[174] *Iron Rhine* (n 170) para 58.

[175] eg *SunReserve Luxco Holdings and others v Italy*, SCC Case No V2016/32, Final Award, 25 March 2020, para 394 (hereafter *SunReserve v Italy*).

[176] Villiger (n 24) 433.

[177] *Dispute Concerning Access to Information under Article 9 of the OSPAR Convention (Ireland v UK)*, Final Award, 2 July 2003, XXIII UNRIAA 59, paras 99–105.

to be subsumed in the judicial reasoning on 'rules'. That is not to say that there have not been cases where judges have suggested that non-binding elements should be considered as falling under Article 31(3)(c) or where it is unclear whether they consider such elements under the principle of systemic integration or under another element of Articles 31–33 VCLT, i.e. mainly as supplementary means.[178]

58   In investment arbitration this happens to also be the case. However there have been instances where treaties between non-parties, and cases decided under altogether different investment agreements have been invoked.[179] Once again it is unclear whether such discussion occurred under the term 'applicability' or under other terms such as 'relevant' or 'parties'. Of note is the *RosInvest* tribunal which attempted to tackle the issue of 'applicability':

> '*Applicable* in the relations between the parties' must be taken as a reference to rules of international law that condition the performance of the specific rights and obligations stipulated in the treaty—or else it would amount to a general license to override the treaty terms that would be quite incompatible with the general spirit of the Vienna Convention as a whole.[180]

59   Yet, its immediately following analysis suggests, once again, that the term 'applicable' was somewhat conflated with the issue of whether the rule was indeed 'relevant'.

3. Relevant

60   Given the aforementioned overlaps between 'rules', 'applicable', and 'relevant', it is worth examining whether there has been any meaningful discussion on how relevance is to be determined. In international case law, there is very little dedicated analysis of the term. Some repeated patterns, though, pertain to how close or proximate the two rules are. Particular manifestations of this proximity[181] that often come up are: linguistic identity or proximity,[182] temporal proximity,[183] subject-matter proximity,[184] and actor proximity.[185]

61   Similarly in investment case law, there are mostly assertive statements on whether a rule is relevant or not, and broad approaches have been taken by a number of tribunals.[186] Of the few that have offered some insight as to how relevance is approached, the *Urbaser* tribunal noted that the question of relevance should be handled flexibly, 'in light of the openly framed provision of Article 31§3(c)'.[187] The *Ambiente* tribunal elaborated on the issue of 'subject-matter proximity' when it asserted that a rule would be relevant if after comparing its substance and

---

[178] ibid, Dissenting Opinion of Judge Griffith, paras 7–19; *Southern Bluefin Tuna cases (New Zealand and Australia v Japan)*, Provisional Measures (Separate Opinion of Judge Treves), 27 August 1999, ITLOS Rep 280, para 10; see also Dörr (n 33) 608–09, para 100; Arato and Kulick (n 132).

[179] *Berschader v Russia* (n 173) para 97; *European Media Ventures v Czech Republic*, UNCITRAL, Partial Award on Liability, 8 July 2009, para 49; *Tulip Real Estate*, Annulment (n 170) paras 87, 90–92.

[180] *RosInvest v Russia* (n 106) para 39.

[181] For a detailed analysis of the proximity criterion as utilized to determine relevance under Article 31(3)(c) see P Merkouris, 'Principle of Systemic Integration' [2020] MPEiPro 2866 (hereafter Merkouris, 'Principle of Systemic Integration').

[182] *Warsaw Electricity Company (France v Poland)*, 30 November 1929, 3 UNRIAA 1669, 1675 (hereafter *Warsaw Electricity Company*); *Maritime Delimitation in the Indian Ocean* (n 47) para 91.

[183] *Warsaw Electricity Company* (n 182) 1675; *Affaire des boutres de Mascate (France v UK)*, Award, 8 August 1905, XI UNRIAA 83 et seq.

[184] *Oil Platforms (Islamic Republic of Iran v United States of America)* (Merits) [2003] ICJ Rep 161, Separate Opinion of Judge Higgins, para 46; *European Communities and Certain Member States—Civil Aircraft*, WT/DS316/AB/R, 18 May 2011, para 846; *RosInvest v Russia* (n 106) para 39; Gardiner (n 79) 299.

[185] The latter is connected to the discussion of the term 'parties'.

[186] In detail, Merkouris 'Principle of Systemic Integration' (n 181).

[187] *Urbaser v Argentina* (n 134) para 1204.

function to those of the rule being interpreted, the outcome was that they were 'sufficiently comparable'.[188] On the other hand, the *SunReserve* tribunal, while discussing the term 'parties', made a slight foray into 'relevance'. It was of the view that determining whether a rule is relevant *solely* by who the disputing parties are and whether the rules have a similar subject-matter would lead to incoherent and non-unified interpretations.[189] This is not to say that 'subject-matter' is irrelevant, but rather that a particular reading of the 'parties' combined with a sole focus on the 'subject-matter', in the tribunal's view would lead to incoherent interpretations and would transform Article 31(3)(c) into *in pari materia* interpretation.[190]

4. Parties

This final word in Article 31(3)(c) has been a contested point. Does it mean 'parties to the treaty' or '[any one of the] parties to the dispute'? International courts and tribunals have taken a wide range of approaches, while sometimes also highlighting the number of common parties as a factor of 'relevance'.[191] **62**

Investment tribunals have also adopted this wide range of approaches. Specific mention, however, needs to be made to a recent string of cases that dealt with the interpretation of the ECT. In *Vattenfall*, the tribunal dismissed the European Commission's contention that EU law could be considered a 'relevant rule' for the purposes of interpreting the ECT as unacceptable: '[I]t would potentially allow for different interpretations of the same ECT treaty provision.'[192] **63**

> It would create one set of obligations applicable in at least some 'intra-EU' disputes and another set of different obligations applicable to other disputes. This would bring uncertainty and entail the fragmentation of the meaning and application of treaty provisions and of the obligations of ECT Parties, contrary to the plain and ordinary meaning of the ECT provisions themselves.[193]

The tribunal contends that 'parties to the dispute' would lead to incoherence as the 'relevant rules' would be dependent on the parties to the dispute, whereas 'parties to the treaty' ensures a single unified interpretation of each treaty provision.[194] However, firstly, the term 'relevance' is already designed to prevent incoherence.[195] Second, 'parties to the treaty' does not necessarily lead to greater coherence. Every time a State acceded to or withdrew from the treaty being interpreted, or any other treaty of any of the States parties, the set of potential 'relevant rules' would also change even under the 'parties to the treaty' format. **64**

It is perhaps for this reason, that other investment tribunals dealing with the interpretation of the ECT, although repeating the need for coherence, decided to focus more on the 'non-revision/non-re-writing' limit of Article 31(3)(c), on 'relevance' or on the lack of a clearly defined 'rule' to reject EU law as a 'relevant rule'.[196] **65**

---

[188] *Ambiente v Argentina* (n 170) para 602.
[189] *SunReserve v Italy* (n 175) para 391.
[190] On the distinction see Merkouris 'Principle of Systemic Integration' (n 181).
[191] For a detailed analysis, see ibid.
[192] *Vattenfall v Germany*, ICSID Case No ARB/12/12, Decision on the *Achmea* Issue, 31 August 2018, paras 155–56.
[193] ibid para 158.
[194] ibid para 156.
[195] See Section C.IV.3.
[196] *AS PNB Banka v Latvia*, ICSID Case No ARB/17/47, Decision on the intra-EU objection, 14 May 2021, paras 562–71; *Silver Ridge v Italy*, ICSID Case No ARB/15/37, Award, 26 February 2021, paras 220–23; *BayWa v Spain* ICSID Case No ARB/15/16, Award, 25 January 2021, para 229.

66 Finally, choices regarding 'rules', 'relevance', and 'parties' are sometimes spurred by the overall limits or 'precautions' of the interpretative exercise.[197] Investment tribunals often invoke that any application of Article 31(3)(c) should not lead to either a rewriting/revision of the treaty or to substitute a plain reading of the treaty provision being interpreted.[198] Of course, where such lines are to be drawn is not an easy task.[199]

67 Investment tribunals have not had issues with the application of Article 31(3)(c) when it refers to confirmation of the text.[200] They were divided, however, when utilizing it to read exceptions or additional requirements into the text of a provision. Some tribunals prioritized systemic integration over the principle of *lex specialis*,[201] while others suggested that otherwise this amounts to a revision of the treaty and is contrary to the principle of *pacta sunt servanda*.[202]

5. Intertemporality

68 When drafting Article 31(3)(c), the ILC had a heated debate on whether the rules contemporaneous to the conclusion of the treaty or those contemporaneous to the interpretation of the treaty should be taken into account, or whether to introduce a different wording that would establish the intention of the parties as the decisive criterion for resolving intertemporal issues. Eventually, the topic was considered too complex and that the best strategy was to leave out any such reference.[203] The same reasoning prevailed during the Vienna Conference on the Law of Treaties as well.[204]

69 Investment tribunals have also generally refrained from discussing this issue explicitly. A notable exception to this is *Armas v Venezuela*, where the tribunal came to the conclusion that the intertemporality of Article 31(3)(c) would be dependent on whether the relevant provision should be interpreted by applying the principle of contemporaneity or whether an evolutive interpretation was called for.[205]

V. Special meaning, Article 31(4)

70 Where the contracting parties so intended, a treaty term's special meaning prevails over its ordinary meaning. Article 31(4) thus constitutes an exception to the general rule in

---

[197] *Gabčíkovo-Nagymaros* (n 146) para 5.
[198] *KT Asia v Kazakhstan*, ICSID Case No ARB/09/8, Award, 17 October 2013, para 129 (hereafter *KT Asia v Kazakhstan*); *Landesbank Baden-Württemberg v Spain*, ICSID Case No ARB/15/45, Decision on the Intra-EU Jurisdictional Objection, 25 February 2019, para 164; *RENERGY v Spain*, ICSID Case No ARB/14/18, Award, 06 May 2022, para 369.
[199] M Fitzmaurice and P Merkouris, *Treaties in Motion: The Evolution of Treaties from Formation to Termination* (CUP 2020) chs 4–5.
[200] *Orascom v Algeria* (n 170) para 293; *Kardassopoulos v Georgia* (n 170) para 223.
[201] *Ambiente v Argentina* (n 170) para 602; *Saluka Investments v Czech Republic* (n 57) para 254 and fn 6; *Philip Morris v Uruguay* (n 170) para 290.
[202] *Içkale v Turkmenistan* (n 70) paras 260–61; *KT Asia v Kazakhstan* (n 198) para 129; *ICS v Argentina*, UNCITRAL, Jurisdiction, 10 February 2012, paras 265–68; *RosInvest v Russia* (n 106) paras 39, 42; *Renco v Peru* (n 171) paras 155–57; cf *Içkale v Turkmenistan* (n 70), Partially Dissenting Opinion of Ms Carolyn B Lamm, para 13.
[203] For example, ILC, 'Summary Record of the 872nd Meeting' (17 June 1966) UN Doc A/CN.4/SR.872, para 9.
[204] United Nations Conference on the Law of the Treaties, '33rd Meeting of the Committee of the Whole' (22 April 1968) UN Doc A/CONF.39/C.1/SR.33, 177, paras 53–54, 74.
[205] *Armas v Venezuela*, PCA Case No 2016-08, Jurisdiction, 13 December 2019, para 654; see also paras 650–58. For an earlier detailed analysis of this issue, see P Merkouris, *Article 31(3)(c) VCLT and the Principle of Systemic Integration: Normative Shadows in Plato's Cave* (Brill 2015).

Article 31(1).[206] Contracting parties may agree to a special meaning explicitly, i.e. by defining it in the treaty text. In international investment law this is particularly relevant regarding the frequent definitions of 'investor' or 'investment' in investment agreements.[207] However, they may also implicitly intend to grant a certain treaty term a special meaning. Such implicit intention may accrue (a) from the treaty's overall specific purpose or context (eg as human rights treaty and border treaty);[208] (b) from the special use by the parties in the treaty text;[209] or (c) the *travaux préparatoires*.[210] This again demonstrates the intricate link of the textual, contextual, and teleological elements of interpretation, since discerning a special meaning requires recourse to context and object and purpose of a treaty and its terms.[211]

Article 31(4) allocates the burden of proof. This is its main function intended by the ILC, i.e. 'to emphasize that the burden of proof lies on the party invoking the special meaning of the term'.[212] This is also confirmed by the ICJ's *jurisprudence constante*.[213] The standard of proof is high, as emphasized the *Rhine Chlorides* tribunal, requiring 'the party invoking such a meaning to make a convincing case for it'.[214] Investment tribunals have followed this approach, the contention of a 'special meaning' failing in these cases due to the high standard of proof.[215]

VI. Special regimes or one unitary regime?

Although reference to Articles 31–33 VCLT as reflective of customary international law has become somewhat of a *clause de style*,[216] has investment arbitration led to the emergence of new or divergent specialized rules on interpretation? In essence, are we dealing with a unitary regime, or in the case of investment law a special regime on interpretation? This question is not new. Similar questions have been asked for a variety of issues on the law of treaties[217] with respect to a number of 'special regimes' and the answer always tends to favour uniformity.[218] The fact alone that we can encounter situations where different tribunals,

---

[206] See Section C.I.1.
[207] *Yukos v Russia*, PCA Case No 2005-04/AA227, Opinion of Advocate General Paul Vlas, 23 April 2021, para 3.92, referring to the definition of 'investment' in Article 1(6) ECT.
[208] cf Gardiner (n 79) 291.
[209] Dörr (n 33) 613, para 109.
[210] On the *travaux* see in this Commentary: Esmé Shirlow and Michael Waibel, 'Article 32 of the VCLT: Supplementary means of interpretation'.
[211] See Section C.I.1.
[212] ILC, *Draft Articles* (n 8) 222, para 17.
[213] *Legal Status of Eastern Greenland (Denmark v Norway)* PCIJ Series A/B No 53, 49; *Western Sahara* (Advisory Opinion) [1975] ICJ Rep 12, para 116. See also *Conditions of Admission to the UN* (n 94) 63 and *Land, Island and Maritime Frontier Dispute* (n 51) para 377.
[214] *The Rhine Chlorides Arbitration* (n 77) 267, para 67; similarly, *Conditions of Admission to the UN* (n 94) 63 ('a decisive reason would be required').
[215] For example, *Parkerings v Lithuania*, ICSID Case No ARB/05/8, Award, 11 September 2007, para 277; *Canfor v USA*, UNCITRAL, Joint Order of the Costs of Arbitration and for the Termination of Certain Arbitral Proceedings, 19 July 2007, para 111; *Poštová v Greece* (n 26) paras 278 et seq.
[216] *Pac Rim v El Salvador*, ICSID Case No ARB/09/12, Opinion of Michael Reisman on the International Legal Interpretation of the Waiver Provision in CAFTA Chapter 10, 22 March 2010, para 19.
[217] See C Tams, A Tzanakopoulos and A Zimmermann (eds), *Research Handbook on the Law of Treaties* (Edward Elgar Publishing 2014).
[218] For example, the long debate on whether human rights treaties benefitted from a special regime on reservations, to which the ILC gave an emphatic no as an answer; ILC, 'Guide to Practice on Reservations to Treaties' (2011) UN Doc A/66/10/Add.1, Guideline 4.5.3 and Commentary.

although applying in principle the VCLT methodology 'come to diverging results' despite similar treaty language,[219] is not unique to investment arbitration.

73 Even authors who argue that due to this divergence in interpretative outcomes, States have devised various 'special' or 'bespoke' mechanisms to ensure 'greater consistency and "correctness" of interpretations',[220] eventually arrive at the conclusion that these may be considered somewhat of 'special features' but are not really deviations from the VCLT rules.[221]

74 Of particular note is the recourse to interpretative maxims not explicitly mentioned in the VCLT, which was tackled above (in Section C.II). As the *Aguas del Tunari* tribunal noted, 'the Vienna Convention represents a move away from the canons of interpretation previously common in treaty interpretation and which erroneously persist in various international decisions today'.[222] Hence, such recourse runs counter to the choice made in the VCLT. However, as already noted, not only is such recourse not unique to investment arbitration, but also and perhaps most importantly it is either merely descriptive of the interpretative outcome arrived through a regular application of Articles 31–33 VCLT, or such maxims can often fall within one or more of the interpretative elements provided in those articles.

75 Finally, any remaining perceived departures from the VCLT articles on treaty interpretation are most likely unfortunate misapplications of those rules,[223] do not seem to be evidence of an intentional deviation and should thus 'remain unconvincing departures from the rules contained in the VCLT. Far from influencing other international courts and tribunals, these decisions should serve as a warning for the meticulous application of the VCLT rules on interpretation.'[224]

D. Interpretation of customary law

76 Although treaty interpretation is the dominant form of interpretation in investment arbitration, a brief mention needs to be made of the fact that rules emanating from other sources of international law, notably customary international law, can also be the object of interpretation.

77 This may seem *prima facie* somewhat counterintuitive. After all, customary law emerges as a result of state practice and *opinio juris*, and it is unwritten. Thus, as has been argued, 'the irrelevance of linguistic expression *excludes interpretation as a necessary operation* in order to apply [customary rules]'.[225] However, as Alland notes, 'it is difficult to think of a custom independently

---

[219] A Reinisch, 'The Interpretation of International Investment Agreements' in M Bungenberg and others (eds), *International Investment Law* (Nomos 2015) MN 12.
[220] A Ambast and D Pulkowski, 'The VCLT as a Unifying Force in Treaty Design: How Special Is Investment Law?' in Shirlow and Gore (n 31) 439, 450, 454 (hereafter Ambast and Pulkowski). At 450 and following the authors identify that such 'bespoke' mechanisms are: authoritative or authentic interpretations; elements adopted under supplementary means; investment treaties being interpreted in light of other investment treaties or of model BITs; and various interpretative maxims.
[221] Ambast and Pulkowski (n 220) 458–59.
[222] *Aguas del Tunari v Bolivia* (n 32) para 91.
[223] See, for instance, Wyatt (n 100) 89 who views a perceived emergence of a subjective approach to treaty interpretation in investment arbitration, as a misunderstanding and misapplication of the principle of contemporaneity.
[224] Boknik and Gazzini (n 58) 105.
[225] T Treves, 'Customary International Law' [2006] MPEPIL, para 2 (emphasis added). See also J d' Aspremont, 'Custom-making Moment in Customary International Law' in P Merkouris and others (eds), *The Theory, Practice and Interpretation of Customary International Law* (CUP 2022) ch 2. Why this does not bar the interpretability of custom, see P Merkouris, *Interpretation of Customary International Law: Of Methods and Limits* (Brill 2024) (hereafter Merkouris, *Interpretation of Customary International Law*).

of any linguistic expression, of any "lexical garment" [...]. In fact, even if we do not put the customary rule in a codification convention, it must be formulated and, from this formulation, it may appear that we are interpreting linguistic signs expressing a customary rule.'[226]

Furthermore, the ILC's work is replete with examples and references to interpretation not only of unwritten rules,[227] but specifically customary rules.[228] Most importantly, both international and domestic courts have also on multiple occasions proceeded with interpreting customary law rules utilizing methods that judges are familiar with from treaty interpretation to the degree that they are applicable considering the nature of customary rules.[229] For example, in its recent judgment in the *Silala* case 'the ICJ note[d] that, while both Parties consider that [Article 12 of the 1997 Convention on the Law of the Non-Navigational Uses of International Watercourses] reflects customary international law, *they disagree about its interpretation*'.[230] Earlier, in the landmark *North Sea Continental Shelf* cases, Judge Tanaka in no uncertain terms held that '*[t]he method of logical and teleological interpretation can be applied in the case of customary law as in the case of written law*'.[231]

78

Investment arbitration is no foreigner to this process of interpretation of customary law.[232] Naturally, given the fact that in investment law disputes arise regarding the interpretation of treaty provisions, interpretation of customary international law comes into play usually in the context of interpretation of rules on State responsibility. In *Tulip*, the tribunal relied on the Articles on State Responsibility (ARSIWA) as reflective of customary international law and then proceeded interpreting the terms adopted in Article 8 ARSIWA.[233] This approach of using the text of a codificatory instrument can be viewed as a 'by proxy textual interpretation', which is an expanded version of systemic integration.[234] Other tribunals have relied on a teleological interpretation of the customary rule,[235] the principle of effectiveness[236] and 'necessary implication'-type of reasoning to determine the content of a customary rule,[237] to name but a few.

79

---

[226] D Alland, 'L'interprétation du droit international public' (2013) 362 RdC 1, 83 referring to F Müller, *Discours de la méthode juridique* (O Jouanjan tr, Presses Universitaires de France 1996) 171.
[227] ILC, 'Guiding Principles Applicable to Unilateral Declarations of States Capable of Creating Legal Obligations with Commentaries Thereto' (2006) UN Doc A/61/10, Guiding Principle 7.
[228] For example, the ILC in its work on '*Jus cogens*' adopted Draft Conclusion 20 that provides that *jus cogens* should function as an interpretative limit of any international rule irrespective of its source; ILC, 'Peremptory Norms of General International Law (jus cogens)' (29 May 2019) UN Doc A/CN.4/L.936, Draft Conclusion 20.
[229] For a detailed list of cases: Merkouris, *Interpretation of Customary International Law* (n 225).
[230] *Dispute over the Status and Use of the Waters of the Silala (Chile v Bolivia)* (Merits) [2022] ICJ Rep 614, para 113 (emphasis added).
[231] *North Sea Continental Shelf (Germany/Denmark v the Netherlands)* (Judgment), [1969] ICJ Rep 3, Dissenting Opinion of Judge Tanaka 181 (emphasis added). In the same vein, ibid Dissenting Opinion of Judge Morelli, 200.
[232] For a detailed analysis of instances of customary law interpretation in investment arbitration see F Paddeu, 'Investment Tribunals, the Duty of Compensation in Cases of Necessity: A Customary Law Void?' in P Merkouris and others (eds), *Custom and its Interpretation in International Investment Law* (CUP 2023) ch 7; E Giakoumakis, 'A Riddle Wrapped in a Mystery Inside an Enigma': Equitable Considerations in the Assessment of Damages by Investment Tribunals' in Chapter 8 of that text; and SI Lekkas, 'The Uses of the Work of the International Law Commission on State Responsibility in International Investment Arbitration' in Chapter 5 of that text.
[233] *Tulip v Turkey*, ICSID Case No ARB/11/28, Award, 10 March 2014, paras 303–08; *Tulip Real Estate*, Annulment (n 170) paras 187–88. Similarly *von Pezold v Zimbabwe* (n 165) para 448; *Electrabel v Hungary*, ICSID Case No ARB/07/19, Decision on Jurisdiction and Liability, 30 November 2012, paras 7.109, 7.113; *Saint-Gobain v Venezuela*, ICSID Case No ARB/12/13, Decision on Liability and Quantum, 30 December 2016, para 450.
[234] Merkouris, *Interpretation of Customary International Law* (n 225).
[235] *Devas v India*, PCA Case No 2013-09, Decision on Jurisdiction and Merits, 25 July 2016, paras 278–80.
[236] ibid.
[237] *EDF v Argentina*, ICSID Case No ARB/03/23, Decision on Annulment, 5 February 2016, paras 291, 325, 330.

E. Conclusions

80 The above analysis examined how investment tribunals approach the rule on interpretation enshrined in Article 31 VCLT. Despite some perceived deviations, which are only to be expected, and which can be explained through errors in methodology and misapplication of the rule (see, for instance, *Vattenfall v Germany* in Section C.IV.4 or the (non-)existence of a *dubio pro investore* maxim discussion in Section C.II), the conclusion remains that investment tribunals have remained largely faithful to Article 31 VCLT and its customary law counterpart, a position that holds true for other international courts and tribunals as well.[238] Naturally, as with any legal rule, so are rules of interpretation open not only to confirmation, but also to interpretation, content-clarification, and further development. As shown above, investment tribunals have partaken in this process of 'judicial dialogue', i.e. also considering the judgments of other international courts and tribunals. Of particular note are the approach of investment tribunals regarding the use of dictionaries (Section C.I.1), and of third-party BITs as 'context' (Section C.I.2), the density and uniformity of 'practice' required for the purposes of Article 31(3)(b) (Section C.III.3), the issue of modification by subsequent practice and the 2001 NAFTA FTC Note (Section C.III.4), the principle of systemic integration (Section C.IV), as well as the methods employed in the interpretation of customary rules (Section D).

81 Generally, investment tribunals align with the interpretative approaches adopted by other international courts and tribunals and reflected in Article 31. Deviations and interpretations that may strike one as peculiar are to be expected given the flexible nature of Articles 31–33 VCLT, the open-ended nature of several of the interpretative elements included therein combined with the hybrid nature of investment arbitration and the plethora of awards rendered. However, such deviations should not be considered as an intentional divergence from the VCLT interpretative framework, but rather as off-shoots that are course-corrected by an even larger number of investment cases that remain faithful to the interpretive methodology enshrined in Article 31 VCLT.

Selected literature

Alland D, 'L'interprétation du droit international public' (2013) 362 RdC 1.
Dörr O and Schmalenbach K (eds), *The Vienna Convention on the Law of Treaties—A Commentary* (2nd edn, Springer 2018).
Gardiner R, *Treaty Interpretation* (2nd edn, OUP 2015).
Gazzini T, *Interpretation of International Investment Treaties* (Hart Publishing 2016).
Klingler J, Parkhomenko Y and Salonidis C (eds), *Between the Lines of the Vienna Convention? Canons and Other Principles of Interpretation in Public International Law* (Wolters Kluwer 2019).
Merkouris P, 'Principle of Systemic Integration' [2020] MPEiPro 2866.
Merkouris P, Kulick A, Alvarez Zarate JM and Zenkiewicz M (eds), *Custom and its Interpretation in International Investment Law* (CUP 2023).
Shirlow E and Nasir Gore K (eds), *The Vienna Convention on the Law of Treaties in Investor-State Disputes: History, Evolution and Future* (Wolters Kluwer 2022).
Weeramantry R, *Treaty Interpretation in Investment Arbitration* (OUP 2012).

---

[238] For a partly different conclusion: see Boknik and Gazzini (n 58) 91 et seq.

Selected decisions

AAPL v Sri Lanka, ICSID Case No ARB/87/3, Final Award, 27 June 1990.
Aguas del Tunari v Bolivia, ICSID Case No ARB/02/03, Jurisdiction, 21 October 2005.
Armas v Venezuela, PCA Case No 2016-08, Jurisdiction, 13 December 2019.
Kasikili/Sedudu Island (Botswana v Namibia) [1999] ICJ Rep 1045.
Navigational and Related Rights (Costa Rica v Nicaragua) [2009] ICJ Rep 213.
Oil Platforms (Iran v USA) (Preliminary Objections) [1996] ICJ Rep 803.
Phoenix Action v Czech Republic, ICSID Case No ARB/06/5, Award, 15 April 2009.
Pope & Talbot v Canada, Damages, UNCITRAL, 31 May 2002.
Poštová banka and ISTROKAPITAL v Greece, ICSID Case No ARB/13/8, Award, 9 April 2015.
United States—Standards for Reformulated and Conventional Gasoline, WT/DS2/AB/R, 20 May 1996.
Whaling in the Antarctic (Australia v Japan: New Zealand Intervening) [2014] ICJ Rep 226.

Article 32 of the VCLT

Supplementary means of interpretation

Esmé Shirlow and Michael Waibel

Recourse may be had to supplementary means of interpretation, including the preparatory work of the treaty and the circumstances of its conclusion, in order to confirm the meaning resulting from the application of Article 31, or to determine the meaning when the interpretation according to Article 31: (a) leaves the meaning ambiguous or obscure; or (b) leads to a result which is manifestly absurd or unreasonable.

A. Introduction	1
B. When recourse may be had to 'supplementary means of interpretation'	3
I. Approach of the International Court of Justice	5
II. Other international courts and tribunals	7
III. The approach of investment tribunals	9
IV. Convergences and divergences	13
C. What constitutes 'supplementary means of interpretation'	18
I. Approach of the International Court of Justice	19
II. Other international courts and tribunals	28
III. Approach by investment tribunals	41
IV. Towards convergence in the identification of Article 32 materials	46
D. Conclusions	47

A. Introduction

1 International courts and tribunals—including the International Court of Justice (ICJ),[1] the Appellate Body of the World Trade Organization (WTO AB),[2] and investment treaty tribunals[3] have repeatedly recognized Article 32 of the Vienna Convention on the Law of Treaties (VCLT) to be reflective of customary international law.[4] Domestic courts have similarly recognized Article 32 as reflective of customary international law, including when interpreting

---

[1] See, eg, *Avena and Other Mexican Nationals (Mexico v United States of America)* (Judgment) [2004] ICJ Rep 12, para 83 (hereafter *Avena*); *Immunities and Criminal Proceedings (Equatorial Guinea v France)* (Merits) [2020] ICJ Rep 300, para 61 (hereafter *Immunities*, Merits); *Application of the Convention on the Prevention and Punishment of Genocide (Bosnia and Herzegovina v Serbia and Montenegro)* (Merits) [2007] ICJ Rep 43, para 160 (hereafter *Bosnian Genocide*).
[2] See, eg, *Japan—Taxes on Alcoholic Beverages*, WTO Doc WT/DS8/AB/R, Appellate Body Report, adopted 4 October 1996, 10 (hereafter *Taxes on Alcoholic Beverages*).
[3] See, for example, *Alcor v Czech Republic*, Award, 2 March 2022, para 243; *Bank Melli v Bahrain*, Award, 9 November 2021, para 10; *Muszynianka Spolka v Slovak Republic*, Award, 7 October 2020, para 159.
[4] As such, references throughout this entry to cases engaging with Article 32 include also references by courts and tribunals that refer to supplementary means of interpretation under customary international law (rather than as part of a VCLT interpretation).

investment treaties.[5] Given its importance to treaty interpretation under general international law, this entry considers how Article 32 has been interpreted and applied by the ICJ and other international courts and tribunals[6] in order to assess how approaches to the interpretation and application of Article 32 under general international law compare to the approaches adopted towards Article 32 by investment treaty tribunals.

The entry focuses on two particular components of Article 32's interpretive framework. Section B addresses when international adjudicators have had recourse to supplementary means of interpretation under Article 32. That Section introduces the four 'triggers' for recourse to supplementary means of interpretation under Article 32. It highlights that one trigger—which permits recourse to supplementary means of interpretation in order to 'confirm' the meaning reached under application of Article 31 of the VCLT—has been the dominant trigger invoked by international courts and tribunals, including investment treaty tribunals, when justifying recourse to supplementary means of interpretation in international disputes. Section C addresses how adjudicators in each of these settings have identified what constitutes 'supplementary means of interpretation' under Article 32. The Section examines the practice of the ICJ, other international courts and tribunals, and investment treaty tribunals in order to highlight the categories of materials considered as supplementary means of interpretation under Article 32 in each of those settings. This practice supports the view that materials are not typically categorized under Article 32 in binary terms (as supplementary means of interpretation or not), but are rather assessed according to a sliding scale of relevance such as to be accorded more or less relevance in the interpretive process according to various qualitative criteria.[7] To this end, the Section highlights the various criteria identified by different international courts and tribunals as relevant to assessing the role for, and weight to be given to, supplementary means of interpretation under Article 32. This analysis illuminates that Article 32 materials are identified by reference to common qualitative criteria in different adjudicative settings. These criteria in essence seek to give weight to materials under Article 32 according to how capable they are of indicating what the treaty parties intended by their treaty bargain.

B. When recourse may be had to 'supplementary means of interpretation'

Articles 31, 32, and 33 of the VCLT provide a framework to guide the interpretation of treaties. Article 31 requires that treaties be interpreted in good faith in accordance with the ordinary meaning to be given to the terms of the treaty in their context and in light of the treaty's object and purpose.[8] Under Article 32, 'supplementary means of interpretation' may also be referred to in order to (i) 'confirm' a meaning reached on the basis of Article 31, or to 'determine' a meaning where the application of Article 31 produces (ii) an 'ambiguous

---

[5] See, for example, *Swissborough Diamond Mines (Pty) Limited and Others v Lesotho*, Singapore Court of Appeal Judgment, 27 November 2018, paras 60–61.

[6] We selected two fora—UNCLOS Annex VII and WTO AB—because disputes in both take place under treaties for which there are fairly well-developed/extensive negotiating records (and well-publicized circumstances of conclusion).

[7] See generally E Shirlow and M Waibel, 'A Sliding Scale Approach to *Travaux* in Treaty Interpretation: The Case of Investment Treaties' (2021) BYIL (hereafter Shirlow and Waibel, 'A Sliding Scale').

[8] See further in this Commentary: Andreas Kulick and Panos Merkouris, 'Article 31 of the VCLT: General rule of interpretation'.

or obscure' meaning, or (iii) a result which is 'manifestly absurd or unreasonable'.[9] As the terms of Article 32 VCLT itself suggest ('[r]ecourse may be had'), in each of these three situations treaty interpreters have broad discretion to determine whether to have recourse to supplementary means of interpretation. Indeed, the International Law Commission (ILC) noted in developing what became Article 32 that reference to supplementary means would not be 'automatic but depends on the conviction of the interpreter that it is appropriate in the particular circumstances of the case [to refer to them]'.[10] ILC Special Rapporteurs also noted in their reports the subjectivity inherent in identifying whether one of the triggers for recourse to supplementary means of interpretation under Article 32 was present in a given case. Waldock, for instance, observed that the triggers for recourse to supplementary means to 'determine' meaning were 'inherently flexible, since the question whether the text can be said to be "clear" is in some degree subjective'.[11]

4   This Section highlights that international courts and tribunals have made most use of supplementary means of interpretation by reference to the first 'trigger' (to confirm meaning), though some have also referred to supplementary means of interpretation after finding that the meaning of a provision was ambiguous or obscure following an Article 31 interpretation. The approaches of investment treaty tribunals are broadly in line with the practice of other international dispute settlement bodies as to when recourse may be had to supplementary means of interpretation when interpreting a treaty. However, the sheer number of investment arbitration decisions engaging with Article 32 makes this a key body of practice relevant to understanding how international courts and tribunals interpret and apply the VCLT's Article 32 triggers and the complexities that emerge in doing so.[12]

I. Approach of the International Court of Justice

5   The ICJ has accepted in principle the existence of the triggers for recourse to supplementary means of interpretation under Article 32.[13] It has most regularly referred to supplementary means of interpretation under Article 32—including preparatory work[14] and the

---

[9] Supplementary means of interpretation may also play a role in the treaty interpretation process under Article 31 (eg to establish a special meaning) and Article 33 (where the treaty has been authenticated in more than one language). See further J Mortenson, 'The *Travaux* of *Travaux*: Is the Vienna Convention Hostile to Drafting History?' (2013) 107 AJIL 780 (hereafter Mortenson, 'Vienna Convention').
[10] International Law Commission, UN Doc A/CN.4/SER.A/1966, Add.1, YILC 1966, Vol II, 218.
[11] cf also Mortenson, 'Vienna Convention' (n 9) 787, fn 28 (noting varying views about how much uncertainty was required).
[12] See further E Shirlow, 'Applications of the VCLT in Investor-State Arbitration with Accompanying Table Recording References to the VCLT in Some 361 Different Procedural Orders, Decisions and Awards of Investor-State Arbitral Tribunals' in E Shirlow and K Gore (eds), *The Vienna Convention on the Law of Treaties in Investor-State Disputes: History, Evolution, and Future* (Kluwer 2022).
[13] *Immunities*, Merits (n 1) 300, para 61. See, similarly, *Bosnian Genocide* (n 1) 43, para 160; *Jadhav (India v Pakistan)* (Merits) [2019] ICJ Rep 418, para 71 (hereafter *Jadhav*).
[14] *Bosnian Genocide* (n 1) 43, para 163 ('The conclusion is confirmed by two aspects of the preparatory work of the Convention and the circumstances of its conclusion as referred to in Article 32 of the Vienna Convention'); *Immunities and Criminal Proceedings (Equatorial Guinea v France)* (Preliminary Objections) [2018] ICJ Rep 282, para 96 (hereafter *Immunities*, Preliminary Objections); *Jadhav* (n 13), paras 86 and 108; *Border and Transborder Armed Actions (Nicaragua v Honduras)*, Jurisdiction and Admissibility (Judgment) [1988] ICJ Rep 69, para 37 (hereafter *Border and Transborder Armed Actions*); *Maritime Dispute (Peru v Chile)* [2014] ICJ Rep 3, paras 66–68 (hereafter *Peru v Chile*); *Maritime Delimitation and Territorial Questions between Qatar and Bahrain (Qatar v Bahrain)* (Jurisdiction and Admissibility) [1995] ICJ Rep 6, para 40 (hereafter *Maritime Delimitation—Qatar and Bahrain*); *Application of the International Convention on the Elimination of All Forms of Racial Discrimination (Qatar v United Arab Emirates)* (Preliminary Objections) [2021] ICJ Rep 71, paras 89–97 (hereafter *Qatar v UAE*); *Legality of Use of Force (Serbia and Montenegro v Belgium)* (Preliminary Objections) [2004] ICJ Rep 279, para 103

circumstances of a treaty's conclusion[15]—in order to confirm its interpretation of a treaty under Article 31. In *Avena*, for example, the Court rejected that the text and object and purpose of the *Vienna Convention on Consular Relations* (VCCR) supported an interpretation of the term 'without delay' to mean 'immediately upon arrest and before interrogation'.[16] The Court noted that there were 'uncertainties in the *travaux préparatoires*', but concluded that they 'support[ed]' its interpretation.[17] It explained, for instance, that during the negotiations there had been 'an extended discussion by many different delegates as to what such outer time-limit would be acceptable', however '[d]uring that debate no delegate proposed "immediately"'; instead the 'shortest specific period suggested was ... "promptly"'.[18] Similarly, in *Immunities and Criminal Proceedings*, the Court noted that its interpretation of a provision of the Palermo Convention—to the effect that it did not incorporate customary international law rules on the immunities of States and State officials—was 'confirmed by the *travaux préparatoires* of the Palermo Convention'.[19] Specifically, the Court noted that 'the record shows ... no reference was made to immunities of States and State officials in relation to the drafting of Article 4'.[20] So, too, in *Application of the Genocide Convention*, the Court noted that the rule against retroactivity in Article 28 of the VCLT meant that the Genocide Convention could only apply to acts occurring after its entry into force, and confirmed this conclusion by noting that: 'Nothing in the text of the Genocide Convention or the *travaux préparatoires* suggests a different conclusion'.[21]

The ICJ has adopted the view that there will be no need to refer to supplementary means to confirm its interpretation where the meaning reached through application of Article 31 yields a sufficiently clear interpretation.[22] It has, nevertheless, indicated that there may be situations in which, despite a clear interpretation under Article 31, it would still be appropriate to refer to supplementary means of interpretation. In *Fisheries Jurisdiction*, in particular, the Court having interpreted the clauses at issue pursuant to Article 31 noted that it would usually apply the principle 'according to which there is no occasion to resort to preparatory work if the text of a convention is sufficiently clear in itself'. It held, however, that in the absence of an appearance from one of the disputing parties, a 'brief review of the negotiations' was desirable.[23] The Court has not expressly characterized an interpretation as

(hereafter *Use of Force*); *Maritime Delimitation in the Indian Ocean (Somalia v Kenya)* (Preliminary Objections) [2017] ICJ Rep 3, para 99 (hereafter *Delimitation in the Indian Ocean*).

[15] *Arbitral Award of 3 October 1899 (Guyana v Venezuela)* (Jurisdiction) [2020] ICJ Rep 455, para 76 (hereafter *Guyana v Venezuela*) ('as in other cases, it may have recourse to these supplementary means, such as the circumstances in which the Geneva Agreement was concluded, in order to seek a possible confirmation of its interpretation of the text of the Geneva Agreement'); *Delimitation in the Indian Ocean* (n 14) para 99.
[16] *Avena* (n 1) para 85.
[17] ibid paras 86–87.
[18] ibid para 86.
[19] *Immunities*, Preliminary Objections (n 14) para 96.
[20] ibid 282, para 96.
[21] *Application of the Convention on the Prevention and Punishment of the Crime of Genocide (Croatia v Serbia)* (Merits) [2015] ICJ Rep 3, para 95.
[22] eg *Admission of a State to Membership in the United Nations (Charter, Article 4)* (Advisory Opinion) [1948] ICJ Rep 57, 63. See similarly, eg, *Application of the International Convention for the Suppression of the Financing of Terrorism and of the International Convention on the Elimination of All Forms of Racial Discrimination (Ukraine v Russian Federation)* (Preliminary Objections) [2019] ICJ Rep 558, para 112 ('Since the alternative character of the procedural preconditions is sufficiently clear from an interpretation of the ordinary meaning of the terms of Article 22 in their context, and in light of the object and purpose of the Convention, the Court is of the view that there is no need for it to examine the travaux préparatoires of CERD').
[23] *Fisheries Jurisdiction (United Kingdom v Ireland)* (Jurisdiction) [1973] ICJ Rep 3.

ambiguous or obscure, or as leading to a manifestly absurd or unreasonable result, and so has not had reason to engage with the interpretation of these triggers under Article 32.

II. Other international courts and tribunals

7   Other international courts and tribunals have similarly restricted their analysis of supplementary means of interpretation to situations in which one of the triggers specified in Article 32 are present. Several United Nations Convention on the Law of the Sea (UNCLOS) Annex VII tribunals have, for instance, referred to supplementary means of interpretation to 'support' their interpretation under Article 31.[24] Similarly to the ICJ, the tribunal in *South China Sea Arbitration* indicated that it would not have recourse to supplementary means of interpretation in circumstances where the 'text and context of the Convention' were 'clear' and disclosed 'no ambiguity'.[25] The WTO AB has similarly referred to supplementary means of interpretation to 'confirm' its interpretations.[26] The WTO AB has also referred to supplementary means of interpretation to confirm its conclusion despite noting that such reference was not 'strictly necessary' in light of its Article 31 interpretation.[27]

8   Unlike both Annex VII tribunals and the ICJ, the WTO AB has had occasion to engage the other triggers in Article 32 to use supplementary means of interpretation to determine meaning. In *Canada—Milk and Dairy*, for example, the AB held that 'Canada's Schedule is not clear on its face' and was instead 'general and ambiguous'.[28] The AB held '[f]or this reason, it is appropriate, indeed necessary, in this case to turn to "supplementary means of interpretation" pursuant to Article 32 of the Vienna Convention'.[29] Similarly, in *US—Gambling and Betting*, the AB held that recourse could be had to supplementary means of interpretation under Article 32 given that the use of Article 31 to interpret the meaning of the phrase at issue—'other recreational services (except sporting)'—led to an 'ambiguous' result, it being unclear whether the phrase encompassed a commitment in respect of gambling and betting services.[30] The AB in that case found additional ambiguities when interpreting other terms in the General Agreement on Trade in Services, noting that this was therefore 'an appropriate case in which to have recourse to supplementary means of interpretation, such as preparatory work'.[31] The AB has also on occasion expressly rejected a party's view that a given interpretation leads to a 'manifestly absurd or unreasonable' result, such as to open scope to refer to supplementary means to *determine* the meaning of a provision.[32] These WTO cases

---

[24] *The 'Enrica Lexie' Incident (Italy v India)*, PCA Case No 2015-28, Award, 21 May 2020, para 648 (hereafter *Enrica Lexie*).
[25] *South China Sea Arbitration (Philippines v China)*, PCA Case No 2013-19, Award, 12 July 2016, para 247 (hereafter *South China Sea Arbitration*).
[26] See, eg, *Taxes on Alcoholic Beverages* (n 2) s F, fn 52; *United States—Import Prohibition of Certain Shrimp and Shrimp Products*, WTO Doc WT/DS58/AB/R, Appellate Body Report, adopted 12 October 1998, para 157.
[27] *United States—Final Anti-Dumping Measures on Stainless Steel from Mexico*, WTO Doc WT/DS344/AB/R, Appellate Body Report, adopted 30 April 2008, para 128 (hereafter *Stainless Steel from Mexico*).
[28] *Canada—Measures Affecting the Importation of Milk and the Exportation of Dairy Products*, WTO Doc WT/DS103/AB/R, Appellate Body Report, adopted 13 October 1999, para 138 (hereafter *Dairy Products*); *United States—Countervailing Duties on Certain Corrosion-Resistant Carbon Steel Flat Products from Germany*, WTO Doc WT/DS213/AB/R, Appellate Body Report, adopted 28 November 2002, para 90 (hereafter *Carbon Steel*).
[29] *Dairy Products* (n 28) para 138; *Carbon Steel* (n 28) para 90.
[30] *United States—Measures Affecting the Cross-Border Supply of Gambling and Betting Services*, WTO Doc WT/DS285/AB/R, Appellate Body Report, 7 April 2005, para 195 (hereafter *Gambling and Betting*).
[31] ibid paras 236 and 248.
[32] *United States—Subsidies on Upland Cotton*, WTO Doc WT/DS267/AB/R, Appellate Body Report, adopted 3 March 2005, paras 624–25.

show how the AB defines 'ambiguity': the AB tends to apply Article 31 first, and then if more than two meanings are possible after that process, it refers to Article 32 materials. This approach differs from that of some investment tribunals, which have treated the relationship between Articles 31 and 32 in a more fluid and less structured way.

III. The approach of investment tribunals

Investment tribunals have also frequently endorsed the view that one of the triggers specified in Article 32 must be present in order for them to refer to supplementary means of interpretation under Article 32.[33] Like other international courts and tribunals, numerous investment tribunals have referred to supplementary means of interpretation in order to confirm the meaning of a treaty following an Article 31 interpretation.[34] The Annulment Committee in *Togo Electricité*, for example, interpreted the term 'manifest' in the Convention on the Settlement of Investment Disputes between States and Nationals of Other States (ICSID Convention) 'in light of the text and context' of that treaty, and subsequently 'confirmed' that interpretation by reference to the *travaux préparatoires*.[35] To similar effect, the tribunal in *Philip Morris v Uruguay* referred to the treaty's negotiation history to confirm its interpretation of a domestic litigation requirement.[36]

A first divergence between the practice of investment tribunals and that of other international courts and tribunals—and particularly the ICJ—arises from the frequency with which investment tribunals have been asked by disputing parties to engage with the other triggers for recourse to supplementary means of interpretation under Article 32. Several investment tribunals have, for instance, held that an interpretation under Article 31 had yielded an ambiguous meaning, such that reference could be made to supplementary means of interpretation to determine the correct meaning. The understanding animating most such analyses of what constitutes an 'ambiguous' meaning appears to accord with the WTO AB's understanding of that trigger. The Annulment Committee in *Vivendi*, for example, held that there were 'indications both ways', and hence ambiguity, in the text of the ICSID Convention as to whether annulment proceedings were 'arbitration proceedings'. The Committee there referred to the ICSID Convention's *travaux* to resolve this ambiguity.[37]

Investment tribunals have nevertheless at times exhibited willingness to interpret the triggers under Article 32 flexibly to justify recourse to supplementary means of interpretation. Similarly to the decisions referred to above, many investment tribunals have indicated that reference to supplementary means of interpretation may not be necessary where the

---

[33] Rarely have investment tribunals referred to supplementary means of interpretation without referencing Article 32 of the VCLT. See further Shirlow and Waibel, 'A Sliding Scale' (n 7).

[34] See, for example, *Aguas del Tunari v Republic of Bolivia*, ICSID Case No ARB/02/3, Jurisdiction, 21 October 2005, paras 266 and 283 (hereafter *Aguas del Tunari*); *Togo Electricité et GDF-Suez Energie Services v La République Togolaise*, ICSID Case No ARB/06/07, Annulment, 6 September 2011, paras 45–46 (hereafter *Togo* Annulment); *Millicom v Republic of Senegal*, paras 70–72; *Victor Pey Casado, Foundation President Allende v Republic of Chile*, ICSID Case No ARB/98/2, Jurisdiction, 8 May 2002, para 109; *Infinito Gold v Republic of Costa Rica*, ICSID Case No ARB/14/5, Award, 3 June 2021, para 296; *Mobil Investments Canada Inc & Murphy Oil Corporation v Canada*, ICSID Case No ARB(AF)/07/4, Decision on Liability and Quantum, 22 May 2012, para 296.

[35] *Togo* Annulment (n 34) paras 56–57.

[36] *Philip Morris Brands Sarl and others v Oriental Republic of Uruguay*, ICSID Case No ARB/10/7, Jurisdiction, 2 July 2013, paras 34, 44.

[37] *Compañia de Aguas v Argentine Republic*, ICSID Case No ARB/97/3, Decision on the Challenge to the President of the Committee, 3 October 2001, paras 7–24.

interpretation of the treaty under Article 31 produces a clear result. In *Champion Trading*, for example, the tribunal held that the ICSID Convention's approach to dual nationality was 'clear and specific' such that there was no need to refer to the Convention's *travaux*.[38] Other tribunals have nevertheless endorsed a broader approach. In *El Paso*, for example, the tribunal considered that the triggers specified in Article 32 mean that 'in practice it is always possible to have recourse' to supplementary means of interpretation.[39] In *Malaysian Historical Salvors*, the Annulment Committee similarly noted that 'courts and tribunals interpreting treaties regularly review the *travaux préparatoires* whenever they are brought to their attention; it is mythological to pretend that they do so only when they first conclude that the term requiring interpretation is ambiguous or obscure'.[40] So, too, some investment tribunals have appeared more willing than other international courts and tribunals to acknowledge possible ambiguities following an Article 31 interpretation. The tribunal in *ST-AD*, for example, reached an interpretation on the basis of Article 31,[41] but then considered the *travaux* '[f]or the sake of prudence and an abundance of caution ... considering that some might consider that there remains an ambiguity'.[42] Other tribunals have declined recourse to *travaux* due to a lack of ambiguity but nevertheless referred to them to support their interpretation since the parties had made extensive reference to the *travaux* in their pleadings.[43]

12 A second divergence has arisen in relation to the order of analysis between Articles 31 and 32. While most investment tribunals have followed the approach of considering Article 32 materials *after* completing an Article 31 analysis, several have approached interpretation more flexibly. In *Ambiente Ufficio*, for example, the majority noted the structure of the VCLT approach to interpretation, but, '[h]aving made this proviso', observed that it would be 'preferable ... to first turn its attention to the drafting process of the ICSID Convention' in order to 'enlighten the background against which the provision was adopted and to prepare the ground for a proper analysis of the term "investment" according to the rules of interpretation enshrined in Article 31 of the VCLT'.[44] The tribunal in *Inceysa* similarly inverted the order of analysis, beginning its interpretation by reference to the *travaux* to the treaty, before interpreting the treaty on its 'own terms' under Article 31.[45] It concluded its analysis by noting that its interpretation of the terms of the treaty was 'consistent with what Spain indicated [in the *travaux*]'. The tribunal in *HICEE* similarly held that a phrase in the treaty could be interpreted in two ways, and was ambiguous because an Article 31 analysis offered 'virtually nothing by way of authentic guidance as to which of these two "ordinary meanings"

---

[38] ibid para 16.
[39] ibid para 607.
[40] *Malaysian Historical Salvors v Government of Malaysia*, ICSID Case No ARB/05/10, Jurisdiction, 17 May 2007, para 57. See also C Schreuer, 'Diversity and Harmonization of Treaty Interpretation in Investment Arbitration' in M Fitzmaurice, O Elias and P Merkouris (eds), *Treaty Interpretation and the Vienna Convention on the Law of Treaties: 30 Years On* (Martinus Nijhoff Publishers 2012) 137 (noting that the use of *travaux* is determined 'less by their position among the canons of interpretation than by their availability').
[41] *ST-AD GmbH (Germany) v Republic of Bulgaria*, Jurisdiction, 18 July 2013, paras 392–99.
[42] ibid para 401. For a similar approach see *Sempra v The Argentine Republic*.
[43] *Fabrica De Vidrios Los Andes, CA and Owens-Illinois De Venezuela, CA v Bolivarian Republic of Venezuela*, ICSID Case No ARB/12/21, Award, 13 November 2017, paras 291–96; *Blusun SA, Jean Pierre Lecorcier and Michael Stein v Italian Republic*, ICSID Case No ARB/14/3, Award, 27 December 2016, para 280.
[44] *Ambiente Ufficio v Argentine Republic*, ICSID Case No ARB/08/9, Jurisdiction and Admissibility, 8 February 2013, paras 445–47 (hereafter *Ambiente Ufficio*).
[45] *Inceysa Vallisoletana S.L. v Republic of El Salvador*, ICSID Case No ARB/03/26, Award, 2 August 2006, paras 192, 195–96 and 200 (hereafter *Inceysa*).

is to be preferred'.[46] The tribunal subsequently referred, under Article 32, to the *travaux* to the treaty in order to resolve this 'ambiguity'.[47] The *HICEE* tribunal, however, noted that the *travaux* themselves pointed to the ambiguity in the text of the treaty. In his dissenting opinion, Arbitrator Brower criticized the majority for having 'reverse-engineered ambiguity' by reference to the *travaux*.[48]

IV. Convergences and divergences

International courts and tribunals frequently refer to supplementary means of interpretation where one of the triggers specified in Article 32 is present. Investment arbitration decisions conform to this practice, with tribunals referring to supplementary means of interpretation to confirm Article 31 interpretations, or to determine meaning where the application of Article 31 produces an ambiguous or obscure meaning, or leads to a manifestly unreasonable or absurd result. Such use of the triggers—and recourse to supplementary means of interpretation *after* reaching an Article 31 interpretation—has for the most part produced a common, structured, approach to interpretation across different international dispute settlement fora. As noted above, however, several investment tribunals adopted more flexible approaches vis-à-vis both the triggers for recourse to supplementary means of interpretation under Article 32, and the order of analysis when applying Articles 31 and 32. **13**

These decisions illustrate that treaty interpretation is 'a recursive and inelegant process that [spirals] in toward the meaning of a treaty, rather than as a rigidly linear algorithm tied to a particular hierarchical sequence'.[49] Nevertheless, the order of analysis between Articles 31 and 32 was designed to 'filter' the use of Article 32 materials,[50] such as to permit recourse to such materials only 'once the interpreter's mindset was appropriately focused on text'.[51] Admittedly, this is a fine line. At least some members of the ILC during the drafting of what became Article 32 contemplated the approach of the majority in *HICEE*.[52] **14**

The artificiality of separating the interpretive process under Articles 31 and 32 of the VCLT is brought into relief by the differing approaches adopted by the majority and dissenting arbitrator in *Ambiente Ufficio*.[53] The majority in that case partly inverted its analysis, considering the *travaux* twice: once prior to considering the text of the treaty, and then a second time after looking at the text, in keeping with the VCLT methodology.[54] The majority's approach illustrates a recursive use of the means of interpretation listed in the VCLT, reflecting that the separation between the Article 31 and 32 means of interpretation is blurred in practice. **15**

---

[46] *HICEE v Slovakia*, UNCITRAL, PCA Case No 2009-11, Partial Award, 23 May 2011, para 116 (hereafter *HICEE v Slovakia*).
[47] ibid para 117.
[48] ibid, Dissenting Opinion of Judge Charles N Brower, para 38 (hereafter *HICEE v Slovakia*, Diss Op Brower).
[49] Mortenson, 'Vienna Convention' (n 9) 781. See, similarly, T Gazzini, *Interpretation of Investment Treaties* (Hart Publishing 2016) 247 (hereafter Gazzini, *Interpretation*).
[50] YILC 1966, Vol II, 26; Mortenson, 'Vienna Convention' (n 9) 802.
[51] Mortenson, 'Vienna Convention' (n 9) 132.
[52] YILC 1964, Vol I, 283, para 17 (Yasseen); Summary of Records of the 766th Meeting of the International Law Commission, YILC 1964, UN Doc A/CN.4/167/Add.3 (Rosenne). Rosenne's intuition that the notion that travaux serve only to confirm the Article 31 interpretation is a fiction received some support in an experiment, Y Shereshevsky and T Noah, 'Does Exposure to Preparatory Work Affect Treaty Interpretation? An Experimental Study on International Law Students and Experts' (2017) EJIL 1287–316.
[53] *Ambiente Ufficio* (n 44).
[54] Arbitrator Torres Bernárdez criticized the majority's interpretative methodology as 'erratic': ibid, Dissenting Opinion of Santiago Torres Bernárdez, 2 May 2013, para 328.

16 The differences in approach between investment tribunals and other international courts and tribunals link to the frequency with which supplementary materials have been placed before these adjudicators. Like other international courts and tribunals, investment tribunals have tended to rely on supplementary means of interpretation where they are made available to them (in virtually all cases).[55] Broadly speaking, this means that supplementary means of interpretation appear to have a *quasi* 'automatic admissibility' in investment disputes;[56] once brought 'to the tribunal's attention [they] will almost invariably be considered'.[57] Such liberal recourse to supplementary means of interpretation may be justified by reference to other interpretative principles enshrined in general international law.[58] Supplementary means ought to be used to verify whether an Article 31 interpretation is correct and, if not, to correct that interpretation by reference to supplementary means of interpretation.[59] The more flexible approaches to Article 32 seen in investment decisions are therefore potentially consistent with at least the spirit of the VCLT.

17 A further difference between investment arbitration and adjudication before the ICJ and other international courts and tribunals is worth noting at this juncture. In State-to-State disputes, both disputing parties are likely to have access to at least some of the preparatory documents for the treaty at issue (insofar as they were both involved in its negotiation). The same is not true, however, for private entities filing claims against States. In investment treaty arbitration, a particular challenge for investors arises because recourse to *travaux préparatoires* (and possibly other supplementary means of interpretation) almost always relies upon provision of those materials by the State party to the proceedings or a non-disputing third party.[60] Where the respondent State does not itself voluntarily disclose such materials, arbitral approaches to discovery take centre stage in defining the role that *travaux* might play in the arbitral proceedings. It is only if such discovery is successful that the uses that may be made of such materials in interpretation becomes a live issue.

C. What constitutes 'supplementary means of interpretation'

18 The VCLT does not define the concept of 'supplementary means of interpretation' with an exhaustive list, but instead refers to two forms of supplementary means by way of

---

[55] See, in respect of the practice of international courts more generally, J Wouters, C Ryngaert, T Ruys, and G De Baere, *International Law: A European Perspective* (Hart Publishing 2019) 105.
[56] MH Arsanjani and WM Reisman, 'Interpreting Treaties for the Benefit of Third Parties: The "Salvors' Doctrine" and the Use of Legislative History in Investment Treaties' (2010) 104 AJIL 597, 603 (hereafter Arsanjani and Reisman, 'Interpreting Treaties').
[57] Shirlow and Waibel, 'A Sliding Scale' (n 7).
[58] cf A Aust, *Modern Treaty Law and Practice* (3rd edn, CUP 2018) 197, citing S Schwebel, 'May Preparatory Work Be Used to Correct Rather than Confirm the 'Clear' Meaning of a Treaty Provision?' in J Makarczyk (ed), *Theory of International Law at the Threshold of the 21st Century: Essays in Honour of Krzysztof Skubiszewski* (1996) 541–47. A different view is that 'the interpreter must dismiss the supplementary means conflicting with an otherwise sufficiently clear interpretation based on Article 31' because the result produced by recourse to Article 32, in such a situation, 'undermines—rather than confirms—the meaning attached to the treaty under Article 31'. See Gazzini, *Interpretation* (n 49) 251.
[59] Mortenson, 'Vienna Convention' (n 9) 787.
[60] See, for example, *Vanessa Ventures Ltd v Bolivarian Republic of Venezuela*, ICSID Case No ARB (AF)/04/6, Jurisdiction, 22 August 2008, para 3.2.4 (the claimant stated that '[w]e have asked Venezuela if there are any *travaux préparatoires* but we have not been given any'). See further Arsanjani and Reisman, 'Interpreting Treaties' (n 56) 603–04.

illustration: 'the preparatory work of the treaty and the circumstances of its conclusion'. These two concepts are themselves left undefined. This was a conscious drafting decision on the part of the ILC, which was concerned not to define the terms in Article 32 in such a way as 'might only lead to the exclusion of relevant evidence'.[61] This Section considers how different international courts and tribunals have interpreted the concept of 'supplementary means', 'preparatory work', and 'circumstances of conclusion' when applying Article 32.

I. Approach of the International Court of Justice

The ICJ has most frequently referred to Article 32 of the VCLT when considering the role of preparatory work in treaty interpretation. The ICJ's decisions indicate that the Court understands the concept of 'preparatory work' to encompass records of discussions between States during the negotiation and drafting of a treaty.[62] In *Maritime Dispute (Peru v Chile)*, for example, the Court noted that a document which 'summarize[s] the discussions leading to the adoption of [a treaty]' was 'appropriately characterized as *travaux préparatoires* which constitute supplementary means of interpretation within the meaning of Article 32 of the Vienna Convention on the Law of Treaties'.[63]

The Court has also characterized as *travaux* documents prepared by international organizations and their secretariats as part of multilateral treaty negotiations. In *Application of the Genocide Convention*, for instance, the Court confirmed its interpretation of the Genocide Convention by reference to General Assembly resolutions specifying the proposed contents and focus of a draft genocide convention,[64] and the draft text of such a convention prepared by an ad hoc committee of the Assembly.[65] Similarly, in *Jadhav* the ICJ referred to the records of ILC discussions when interpreting Article 36 of the VCCR.[66] So, too, in the *Wall* Advisory Opinion, the Court referred to records of the discussions of the 'Conference of Government Experts convened by the International Committee of the Red Cross ... for the purpose of preparing the new Geneva Convention' as relevant *travaux*.[67] The Court there specifically noted that 'the States parties to the Fourth Geneva Convention approved that interpretation at their Conference on 15 July 1995'.[68]

Despite this recognized 'core', the ICJ's approach to identifying *travaux* has nevertheless been rather wide and inclusive. The Court has not tended, for instance, to require *travaux* to meet particularly rigid requirements in order to be considered as potentially relevant under Article 32. In *Maritime Delimitation in the Indian Ocean*, for example, the Court noted that

---

[61] ILC 1966, Vol II, at 223, para 20. Various scholars have nonetheless identified a 'core' to certain of the terms in Article 32, particularly 'preparatory work', see, for example, R Jennings and A Watts (eds), *Oppenheim's International Law: Volume 1 Peace* (Longman 1992) 1277; A McNair, *Law of Treaties* (2nd edn, Clarendon Press 1961) 411 ('all the documents, such as memoranda, minutes of conferences, and drafts of the treaty under negotiation').
[62] See, for example, *Border and Transborder Armed Actions* (n 14) paras 37 and 46; *Qatar v UAE* (n 14) paras 89–97.
[63] *Peru v Chile* (n 14) para 65.
[64] *Bosnian Genocide* (n 1) para 163.
[65] ibid para 164.
[66] *Jadhav* (n 13) paras 77–86, 108. See, similarly, in relation to the interpretation of UNCLOS: *Maritime Delimitation in the Black Sea (Romania v Ukraine)*, Judgment, 3 February 2009, para 134.
[67] *Legal Consequences of the Construction of a Wall in the Occupied Palestinian Territory* (Advisory Opinion) [2004] ICJ Rep 136, para 95 (hereafter *Wall*).
[68] ibid para 96.

its interpretation of UNCLOS was 'confirmed by the *travaux préparatoires*'.[69] In addition to noting various traditional forms of *travaux* (including reports presented to the plenary conference by the drafting committee's chairman), the ICJ also referred to a 'Working paper' that it observed had resulted 'from informal consultations held between representatives of Australia, Belgium, Bolivia, Colombia, El Salvador, Luxembourg, the Netherlands, Singapore and the United States of America', and an 'Informal single negotiating text'.[70] The ICJ has also referred to the *travaux* of instruments closely linked to the instrument being interpreted as a relevant supplementary means of interpretation. When interpreting Article 35 of the ICJ Statute in *Legality of the Use of Force*, for instance, the Court noted that the '*travaux préparatoires* of the Statute of the present Court are less illuminating' than were those accompanying Article 35(2) of the Statute of the Permanent Court of International Justice.[71]

22 The ICJ has also had recourse—though less frequently—to the circumstances of a treaty's conclusion under Article 32. In *Arbitral Award of 3 October 1899*, for example, the ICJ referred to a statement made by the Venezuelan Foreign Affairs Minister before the National Congress 'on the occasion of the ratification' of the treaty at issue as relevant circumstances of conclusion under Article 32.[72] So, too, in *Arbitral Award of 31 July 1989* the Court noted that it was 'useful to recall ... the circumstances in which the Arbitration Agreement was drawn up' in order to assess what it covered (albeit then seeming to refer to such circumstances as '*travaux préparatoires*').[73] The Court similarly referred to the circumstances of a memorandum of understanding's conclusion in *Maritime Delimitation in the Indian Ocean* to confirm that it was 'not intended to establish a procedure for the settlement of the maritime boundary dispute between the Parties'.[74]

23 Finally, the Court has appeared to accept that supplementary means of interpretation under Article 32 need not be limited to the circumstances of a treaty's conclusion or preparatory work. In *Immunities and Criminal Proceedings*, for instance, the Court—having examined the treaty's drafting history—further noted that certain other documents were 'relevant' to its analysis (without specifying how under the VCLT framework).[75]

24 The ICJ's approach has therefore not been to exclude materials as relevant/irrelevant based upon a binary distinction between 'supplementary means' of interpretation and other materials. Instead, the ICJ has taken an inclusive approach to identifying supplementary means of interpretation, such that the analysis of the weight to be placed upon them then becomes a separate enquiry related to their qualitative features.

25 While indicating that there may be features of supplementary means of interpretation that would warrant placing less weight on them as part of the interpretive process, the Court has not clearly developed a statement as to what those features might be, instead developing this approach on a case-by-case basis. Several features nevertheless emerge from the ICJ's decisions. One key criterion relates to the substance of the supplementary material, and extent to which it can be said to shed light on the issue raised for interpretation. In *Alleged Violations of Sovereign Rights and Maritime Spaces in the Caribbean Sea*, for example, the Court noted

---

[69] *Delimitation in the Indian Ocean* (n 14) para 127.
[70] ibid para 127.
[71] *Use of Force* (n 14) para 113.
[72] *Guyana v Venezuela* (n 15) paras 76–78.
[73] *Arbitral Award of 31 July 1989 (Guinea-Bissau v Senegal)* [1991] ICJ Rep 53, paras 53–54.
[74] *Maritime Delimitation in the Indian Ocean (Somalia v Kenya)* (Preliminary Objections) [2017] ICJ Rep 3, paras 104–05.
[75] *Immunities*, Preliminary Objections (n 14) para 99.

that while the *travaux* demonstrated the origins of a provision, they were of limited utility in interpreting the provision because they 'give no indication as to the precise purpose behind the addition of what became the second paragraph of [the provision]', and moreover did not support Colombia's interpretation because 'there is no indication anywhere in the *travaux préparatoires* that anyone considered that incorporating this new paragraph would bring about such an important change'.[76] In *Immunities and Criminal Proceedings*, the ICJ similarly explained that it had not placed weight on supplementary means of interpretation where they 'provided no clear indication' in favour of a particular interpretation.[77] Other factors have also been highlighted as relevant by the Court. In *Border and Transborder Armed Actions*, for example, the ICJ noted that the relevant *travaux* 'must of course be resorted to only with caution, as not all the stages of the drafting of the texts ... were the subject of detailed records'.[78] In *Maritime Delimitation and Territorial Questions between Qatar and Bahrain*, the Court noted that the *travaux* 'must be used with caution in the present case, on account of their fragmentary nature'.[79] In that case, the Court ultimately concluded that 'the *travaux préparatoires*, in the form in which they have been submitted to it' could not 'provide it with conclusive supplementary elements for the interpretation of the text adopted'.[80]

Other factors have also been hinted at, though left undeveloped, by the ICJ. In *Maritime Delimitation and Territorial Questions between Qatar and Bahrain*, for instance, Qatar disputed whether a particular draft text 'can be regarded as an element of the *travaux préparatoires*, since it says that it was never sent the draft in question'.[81] The Court noted this submission without expressly resolving it. In the *Wall* Advisory Opinion, as noted above, the Court appeared to imply that particular weight could be placed on drafting materials in circumstances in which the treaty parties had specifically approved in their own discussions the interpretation of the provision set forth.[82]

Finally, in interpreting treaty reservations, where determining a party's intention is crucial, the ICJ was willing to consider 'internal' documents or domestic materials. In *Aegean Sea Continental Shelf*, the Court interpreted a Greek reservation. Greece introduced a document as 'the *travaux préparatoires* of the reservation', which the Court accepted as evidence of the intent of the Greek Government in introducing this reservation. The reservation was thus interpreted in accordance with 'the explanations given in the exposé des motifs'.[83]

II. Other international courts and tribunals

Other international courts and tribunals have similarly adopted flexible understandings as to which materials will constitute 'supplementary means of interpretation' under Article 32. This Section considers references to supplementary means of interpretation in disputes under the UNCLOS and in WTO disputes. Some of these tribunals have developed a clearer view of the sliding scale approach to determining the relevance of supplementary means of

---

[76] *Alleged Violations of Sovereign Rights and Maritime Spaces in the Caribbean Sea (Nicaragua v Colombia)* (Preliminary Objections) [2016] ICJ Rep 3, para 45.
[77] *Immunities*, Merits (n 1) para 70.
[78] *Border and Transborder Armed Actions* (n 14) para 37.
[79] *Maritime Delimitation—Qatar and Bahrain* (n 14) para 41.
[80] ibid para 41.
[81] ibid.
[82] *Wall* (n 67) para 96.
[83] *Aegean Sea Continental Shelf (Greece v Turkey)* [1978] ICJ Rep 3, paras 63–68.

interpretation than the ICJ. The WTO AB, in particular, has developed a body of jurisprudence building a nuanced 'sliding scale' approach to identifying potentially relevant means of interpretation under Article 32.

29 UNCLOS Annex VII tribunals have regularly referred to the *travaux préparatoires* for UNCLOS, including records of negotiations between States at the various conferences which led to the adoption of UNCLOS.[84] Akin to ICJ practice, Annex VII tribunals have referred to various documents preceding State-to-State negotiations of UNCLOS as part of the relevant *travaux* for that treaty. This includes references to records of ILC discussions, the ILC's Draft Articles Concerning the Law of the Sea,[85] and the commentary to those articles.[86] Annex VII tribunals have also referred to the negotiating records of related instruments. This has given rise to a rather flexible approach to supplementary means of interpretation in disputes under UNCLOS. In *South China Sea*, for instance, the Annex VII tribunal noted that 'further examination of the circumstances that led to the adoption of Article 121 is warranted for the light it sheds on the purpose of the provision itself'.[87] The tribunal thereafter referred to '[a]n early predecessor definition of "island" [which] was introduced at the Imperial Conference of 1923 in order to harmonise marine policy across the British Empire'.[88] The tribunal further referred to the discussions of States and draft text proposed by a preparatory committee ('although never adopted into any formal instrument') at the 1930 League of Nations Hague Codification Conference,[89] the ILC's definition of the term in the 1956 Articles Concerning the Law of the Sea (as well as the UK's proposal—which was rejected—that an island be 'capable of effective occupation and control'),[90] a modified version of the ILC's definition in the 1958 Convention on the Territorial Sea and the Contiguous Zone,[91] positions of States at the 1971 Seabed Committee meeting prior to the Third UN Conference,[92] and discussions at the Third UN Conference in 1974, 1975, and 1982.[93] The tribunal noted that these documents 'are an imperfect guide in interpreting the meaning of paragraph (3) of [Article 121]',[94] given '[i]n particular, [that] the key compromise that produced the ultimate formulation for that text was reached through informal consultations in 1975, for which no records were kept'.[95] The tribunal nevertheless drew 'a number of general conclusions ... from the negotiating history'.[96]

30 The WTO AB has also regularly referred to records from the negotiations of the WTO Agreements to interpret those treaties. This has included, for instance, draft texts of the treaties,[97] as well as the negotiating records of precursor treaties (such as the Havana

---

[84] See, for example, *Maritime Boundary between Timor-Leste and Australia (The 'Timor Sea Conciliation') (Timor-Leste v Australia)*, PCA Case No 2016-10, Report and Recommendations of the Conciliation Commission between Timor-Leste and Australia on the Timor Sea, 9 May 2018, para 52; *Chagos Marine Protected Area Arbitration (Mauritius v United Kingdom)*, Award, 18 March 2015, para 513 (hereafter *Chagos*).
[85] See, for example, *Enrica Lexie* (n 24) para 649; *Chagos* (n 84) paras 507–13.
[86] See, for example, *Enrica Lexie* (n 24) para 649; *Chagos* (n 84) paras 515–16.
[87] *South China Sea Arbitration* (n 25) para 521 (this was under a heading referring to '*travaux préparatoires*')
[88] ibid para 522.
[89] ibid para 523.
[90] ibid para 524.
[91] ibid para 525.
[92] ibid paras 526–27.
[93] ibid paras 528–33.
[94] ibid para 534.
[95] ibid.
[96] ibid.
[97] *United States—Measures Affecting Trade in Large Civil Aircraft* (Second Complaint), WTO Doc WT/DS353/AB/RW, Appellate Body Report, adopted 28 March 2019, para 530.

Charter).⁹⁸ The WTO AB has also categorized various materials as relevant 'circumstances of [a treaty's] conclusion' under Article 32. The AB in *EC—Computer Equipment*, for instance, noted that reference to the 'circumstances of [a treaty's] conclusion' would entail 'the examination of the historical background against which the treaty was negotiated'.⁹⁹ The AB in that case specifically considered 'the classification practice of the European Communities during the Uruguay Round' to be part of the circumstances of conclusion of the General Agreement on Tariffs and Trade 1994 under Article 32.¹⁰⁰ In *US—Definitive Anti-Dumping on Products from China*, the AB held that 'the Tokyo Round Subsidies Code cannot be considered as context within the meaning of Article 31 of the Vienna Convention',¹⁰¹ holding instead that 'a provision in a predecessor agreement may, at most, form part of the circumstances of the conclusion of a treaty under Article 32 of the Vienna Convention and thus be considered as supplementary means of interpretation'.¹⁰²

31 The WTO AB has also acknowledged the open-ended nature of the reference to 'supplementary means' in Article 32.¹⁰³ To this effect, panels and the AB have held that various materials—other than *travaux* and the circumstances of a treaty's conclusion—may be relevant under Article 32. In *EC—Bananas (Article 21.5)*, for example, the AB observed that, although the Doha Article 1 Waiver was not a 'subsequent agreement' within the meaning of Article 31(3)(a), it 'could be argued ... that the Doha Article I Waiver could qualify as supplementary means of interpretation to confirm the meaning of the European Communities' Schedule of Concessions'.¹⁰⁴

32 The WTO AB has thus tended to adopt a relatively flexible approach to determining whether materials constitute 'supplementary means of interpretation' under Article 32 or not. Where the AB has held that a given material could *not* constitute a supplementary means of interpretation under Article 32, it has tended to be for the reason that such material would be better referred to under Article 31 instead. In *EU—Biodiesel*, for example, the AB noted that it 'would be incorrect to treat the object and purpose of an agreement as a supplementary means of interpretation'.¹⁰⁵

33 Although the WTO AB does not tend, therefore, to exclude materials a priori as not a 'supplementary means' of interpretation under Article 32, it has indicated that different types of materials will be given differing interpretative weight according to their qualitative features. The clearest statement to this effect was made by the AB in *EC—Chicken Cuts*. There, the AB

---

⁹⁸ *United States—Definitive Safeguard Measures on Imports of Circular Welded Carbon Quality Line Pipe from Korea*, WTO Doc WT/DS202/AB/R, Appellate Body Report, adopted 15 February 2022, para 175; *Brazil—Certain Measures concerning Taxation and Charges*, WTO Doc WT/DS472/AB/R, Appellate Body Report, adopted 13 December 2018, para 5.91.
⁹⁹ *European Communities—Customs Classification of Certain Computer Equipment*, WTO Doc WT/DS62/AB/R, Appellate Body Report, adopted 5 June 1998, para 86 (hereafter *Computer Equipment*). Cited also in *Dairy Products* (n 28) para 132.
¹⁰⁰ *Computer Equipment* (n 99) para 92.
¹⁰¹ *United States—Definitive Anti-Dumping and Countervailing Duties on Certain Products from China*, WTO Doc WT/DS379/AB/R, Appellate Body Report, adopted 11 March 2011, para 579.
¹⁰² ibid para 579.
¹⁰³ *European Communities—Customs Classification of Frozen Boneless Chicken Cuts*, WTO Doc WT/DS269/AB/R, Appellate Body Report, adopted 12 September 2005, para 283 (hereafter *Chicken Cuts*).
¹⁰⁴ *European Communities—Regime for the Importation, Sale and Distribution of Bananas, Second Recourse to Article 21.5 of the DSU by Ecuador and Recourse to Article 21.5 of the DSU by the United States*, WTO Doc WT/DS27/AB/RW2/ECU, Appellate Body Report, adopted 27 November 2008, para 445. cf also *Chicken Cuts* (n 103) para 309.
¹⁰⁵ *European Union—Anti-Dumping Measures on Biodiesel from Argentina*, WTO Doc WT/DS473/AB/R, Appellate Body Report, adopted 6 October 2016, para 6.53.

noted several 'objective factors' to assist in identifying the interpretative weight that could be placed upon particular circumstances and events related to the conclusion of a treaty.[106]

34 WTO panels and the AB have expanded upon and applied these various factors in several other proceedings.

35 First, the AB has emphasized that the relevance of a given source will depend upon the extent to which it substantively addresses the provision of the treaty at issue in the dispute. In *India—QR*, for example, the AB noted India's submissions in relation to the negotiating history of the Balance of Payments (BOP) Understanding, but held that: 'in the absence of a record of the negotiations on footnote 1 to the BOP Understanding, we find it difficult to give weight to these arguments'.[107] The AB has appeared to require quite a close connection between the supplementary means of interpretation and the terms or phrase at issue. In *US—Section 211*, for example, the AB considered that the negotiating history for the Agreement on Trade-Related Aspects of Intellectual Property Rights (TRIPS Agreement) could not be 'in any way decisive to the issue before us'.[108]

36 Related to this criterion of connection, the AB has also indicated that it will seek to avoid relying upon a supplementary means of interpretation where to do so it would need to interpret and draw assumptions as to the intent underpinning the supplementary means. This includes, for instance, reliance upon *travaux* recording that a particular approach or provision has been removed from the text, but without further explanation.[109]

37 Second, the AB has also emphasized the need for a temporal connection between the supplementary means of interpretation being referred to and the conclusion of the treaty. This is particularly relevant in relation to materials generated and events occurring *prior* to the conclusion of a treaty,[110] but applies to materials and events occurring *subsequent* to the conclusion of a treaty too.[111] Applying such a criterion, the AB in *US—Stainless Steel from Mexico* held that certain historical materials could not reliably influence its interpretation of the Anti-Dumping Agreement.[112]

38 However, the AB has not required—in assessing the connection between a supplementary means of interpretation and a treaty—a substantive, causative, link between the two. In *EC—Chicken Cuts*, for example, the AB rejected the submission that—to be relevant under Article 32—a circumstance related to a treaty's conclusion must have 'directly influenced the common intentions of parties'.[113]

39 Third, the AB has also emphasized that the weight to be given to a supplementary means of interpretation will depend upon the extent to which it can be taken to be reflective of the intent of *all* the parties to the treaty at issue. For *travaux*, this will typically entail an assessment

---

[106] *Chicken Cuts* (n 103) para 291.
[107] *India—Quantitative Restrictions on Imports of Agricultural, Textile and Industrial Products*, WTO Doc WT/DS90/AB/R, Appellate Body Report, adopted 23 August 1999, para 94.
[108] *United States—Section 211 Omnibus Appropriations Act of 1998*, WTO Doc WT/DS176/AB/R, Appellate Body Report, adopted 2 January 2002, para 339. See, similarly, *Gambling and Betting* (n 30) paras 204–05.
[109] *Carbon Steel* (n 28) para 4.396. See, similarly, *United States—Anti-Dumping And Countervailing Measures On Large Residential Washers From Korea*, WTO Doc WT/DS464/RPT, Appellate Body Report, adopted 13 April 2017, paras 5.167–5.169.
[110] *Chicken Cuts* (n 103) para 293.
[111] ibid para 305.
[112] *Stainless Steel from Mexico* (n 27) para 132.
[113] *Chicken Cuts* (n 103) para 288.

as to the extent to which a given documentary record reflects the views of all negotiating parties. In *US—Stainless Steel from Mexico*, for example, the AB considered that the historical materials cited under Article 32 did not 'provide guidance' for its interpretation of the Anti-Dumping Agreement for several reasons, including because 'the negotiating proposals referred to by the United States reflect the positions of only some of the negotiating parties'.[114] This factor has also underpinned the analysis of other supplementary means of interpretation by the AB. In *EC—Computer Equipment*, for instance, the AB noted that 'the value of the classification practice as a supplementary means of interpretation is subject to certain qualifications'.[115] It thereafter specifically focused upon 'the *consistency* of prior practice', noting that '[i]nconsistent classification practice ... *cannot* be relevant in interpreting the meaning of a tariff concession'.[116] The AB considered that the practice cited by the panel was inconsistent, as the panel had referred to 'evidence relating to *only* five out of the then 12 Member States' and, moreover, that the practice of the five members that was cited was not uniform.[117] The AB subsequently, in *EC—Chicken Cuts* referred to the analysis of consistency in *EC—Computer Equipment* as 'setting a benchmark for determining whether a particular classification practice may qualify at all as "circumstance of the conclusion"'.[118] The AB in *EC—Chicken Cuts* further emphasized the requirement that the treaty parties have 'knowledge' of the supplementary means of interpretation.[119]

This approach of the AB differs from that of the ICJ: while it is similar insofar as it entails not adopting a binary relevant/not relevant approach towards supplementary means of interpretation, it is more detailed in developing *how* different materials might be more or less relevant.

III. Approach by investment tribunals

Like other international courts and tribunals, investment treaty tribunals have most frequently engaged with Article 32 when assessing the interpretive relevance of *travaux préparatoires* in investment disputes. Investment treaty tribunals have tended to regard documents comprising the official negotiating record—including draft treaty texts, and proposals tabled by parties during the negotiations—to be *travaux* for the purposes of treaty interpretation.[120] At least some investment treaty tribunals, however, have been more restrictive in how they have defined 'preparatory work' when compared to the other dispute settlement bodies considered in this Section. In particular, several tribunals have held that documents produced by one party for its own internal purposes, especially where not shared between the negotiating parties, cannot constitute *travaux*.[121] So, too, tribunals have rejected reliance upon the negotiating records of treaties concluded between one of the treaty parties

---

[114] Stainless Steel from Mexico (n 27) para 130.
[115] *Chicken Cuts* (n 103) para 92.
[116] ibid para 95 (emphasis in original).
[117] ibid (emphasis in original).
[118] ibid para 307.
[119] ibid para 297.
[120] See, for example, *Canfor Corporation v United States of America*, Procedural Order No 5, 28 May 2004, paras 4, 7, 18, 20 (hereafter *Canfor*); *Yukos Capital Limited (formerly Yukos Capital SARL) v Russian Federation*, UNCITRAL (Geneva Tribunal), PCA Case No 2013-31, Final Award, 23 July 2021, para 227; *Inceysa* (n 45) para 192; *HICEE v Slovakia* (n 46).
[121] *Canfor* (n 120) para 19. Compare the contention of the Claimant that 'preparatory works' had 'a wide ambit and that even unilateral communications could be of relevance to the Tribunal': ibid para 6. cf also *Generation Ukraine, Inc v Ukraine*, ICSID Case No ARB/00/9, Award, 16 September 2003, paras 15.3–15.6; *Churchill Mining PLC and Planet Mining Pty Ltd v Republic of Indonesia*, ICSID Case No ARB/12/14 and 12/40, Jurisdiction, 24

and third States. Tribunals have also focused upon the timing of a document's creation to determine whether it should be considered part of the 'preparatory work' under Article 32.[122] Investment treaty tribunals have justified this approach based on a caution that documents not available to both sides—or otherwise unrelated directly to the treaty at issue—are not capable of evidencing the common intentions of the treaty parties.[123]

42 Investment treaty tribunals have also referred to the circumstances of a treaty's conclusion under Article 32. In *Kimberly-Clark*, for example, the tribunal noted that: '[w]hile the Tribunal does not have the benefit of *travaux préparatoires*, the historical context at the time of the conclusion of the Dutch BIT buttresses the interpretation reached earlier'.[124] Investment tribunals have also recognized the open-ended nature of Article 32, such as to justify recourse to materials other than just the treaty's preparatory work and circumstances of conclusion.[125] The wide net includes, for instance, documents prepared by one of the treaty parties in connection with the domestic implementation or ratification of an investment treaty;[126] the comparative treaty practice of the home and host State;[127] and even arbitral decisions and awards.[128]

43 These decisions of investment tribunals indicate that tribunals have been open to considering a range of different materials under Article 32, assessing their relevance according to the extent to which they evidence the common intention of the treaty parties. Through these decisions, tribunals have identified various qualitative criteria to guide their analysis of the weight that should be placed on materials under Article 32. Such criteria aim to allow for an inclusive approach while balancing the risks associated with relying on the types of materials typically referred to under Article 32.[129] In *HICEE*, for example, documents prepared to support a domestic ratification process were considered not to fall within the notion of 'preparatory work', but nonetheless within the ambit of the types of 'supplementary means' contemplated by Article 32.

February 2014, para 212; *Millicom International Operations BV and Sentel GSMSA v Republic of Senegal*, ICSID Case No ARB/08/20, Jurisdiction, 16 July 2010, para 72.

[122] eg *Amco v Indonesia*, 89 ILR 514, Annulment, 16 May 1986, para 33 (hereafter *Amco*).

[123] eg *Methanex Corp v United States of America*, Final Award, 3 August 2005, para 25; and *Cairn Energy v India*, Award, 21 December 2020, para 812.

[124] *Kimberly-Clark v Venezuela*, ICSID Case No ARB(AF)/18/3, Award, 5 November 2021, para 157.

[125] eg *The Canadian Cattlemen for Fair Trade v United States of America*, UNCITRAL, Jurisdiction, 28 January 2008, para 50 (hereafter *Canadian Cattlemen*); *Caratube International Oil Company LLP v Kazakhstan*, ICSID Case No ARB/13/13, Provisional Measures, 31 July 2009, para 71: *Enron Corporation and Ponderosa Assets LP v Argentine Republic*, ICSID Case No ARB/01/3, Stay of Enforcement of the Award (Rule 54 of the ICSID Arbitration Rules), 7 October 2008, para 32 (hereafter *Enron*).

[126] See, for example, *Mondev International Ltd v United States of America*, ICSID Case No ARB(AF)/99/2, Award, 11 October 2002, para 111; *Orascom TMT Investments Sàrl v People's Democratic Republic of Algeria*, ICSID Case No ARB/12/35, Final Award, 31 May 2017, fn 339.

[127] See, eg, *Deutsche Telekom AG v The Republic of India*, PCA Case No 2014-10, 13 December 2017, para 146 and *Beijing Urban Construction Group Co Ltd v Republic of Yemen*, ICSID Case No ARB/14/30, Jurisdiction, 31 May 2017, paras 54, 93–97.

[128] See, especially, *Canadian Cattlemen* (n 125) para 49; *Chevron Corporation (USA) and Texaco Petroleum Company (USA) v The Republic of Ecuador*, PCA Case No 34877, Interim Award, 1 December 2008; *Enron* (n 125) para 32.

[129] See, for articulations of such concerns, *Aguas del Tunari* (n 34) para 274; *Czech Republic v European Media Ventures* 2007 Folio No 974 (High Court of Justice Queen's Bench Division—England), paras 30–31 (hereafter *European Media Ventures*); *Philip Morris Asia Limited v Commonwealth of Australia*, PCA Case No 2012-12, Jurisdiction and Admissibility, 17 December 2015, paras 497–506; *Resolute Forest Products Inc v Government of Canada*, PCA Case No 2016-13, Jurisdiction and Admissibility, 30 January 2018, paras 223–25.

Such an approach entails casting a wide net under Article 32, but nonetheless using qualitative criteria to give more weight to materials that are capable of manifesting the joint intent of the parties. While a unilateral internal document might therefore not be excluded *ex ante* it might nonetheless be given lesser weight than, for instance, a joint report on the negotiations signed by all treaty parties. As Arbitrator Berman noted in his Dissent to the Committee's Decision on Annulment in *Lucchetti*, tribunals referring to supplementary means of interpretation must continue to exercise a 'particular duty of caution', given that such materials may be incomplete, inconclusive, silent, or even misleading on key matters.[130]

In determining how much weight should be given to a certain preparatory work, four qualities are of particular relevance: timing vis-à-vis conclusion of a treaty, availability, authorship or awareness, and quality.[131] In *Amco*, for example, the tribunal relied on temporal factors when deciding whether a certain material constituted *travaux*. It held that certain deliberations after the provision at issue 'had already been approved and adopted' were irrelevant to interpretation of the provision.[132] As for the second criterion, availability, Brower's dissenting opinion in *HICEE* is particularly interesting. He argued that it would be inappropriate to give a determinative value to a document which neither of the parties could obtain without 'substantial difficulties'.[133] The third criterion, authorship or awareness, conveys the idea that documents exchanged between the negotiating parties or otherwise known to them will carry more weight than internal documents. The *Canfor* tribunal's analysis is illustrative on this point.[134] Finally, the fourth criterion, quality of the document, refers to the authenticity, completeness, and availability of *travaux*. For example, in *Czech Republic v European Media Ventures*, an English court rejected certain materials as irrelevant due to their ambiguity and inconclusiveness.[135]

IV. Towards convergence in the identification of Article 32 materials

Investment tribunals, like other international courts and tribunals, have interpreted the reference to 'supplementary means of interpretation' in Article 32 as open-ended. This implies that various materials—other than just *travaux* and the circumstances of a treaty's conclusion—may fall within the ambit of Article 32.[136] Cutting across the practice detailed in the Sections above are various indicia that international courts and tribunals have used to determine the weight to be given to materials once referred to under Article 32. These criteria link closely

---

[130] *Empresas Lucchetti, SA and Lucchetti Peru, SA v The Republic of Peru*, ICSID Case No ARB/03/4 (also known as: *Industria Nacional de Alimentos, AS and Indalsa Perú SA v The Republic of Peru*), ICSID Case No ARB/03/4, Award, 7 February 2005, para 9.
[131] Shirlow and Waibel, 'A Sliding Scale' (n 7) 18–21.
[132] *Amco* (n 122) para 33.
[133] *HICEE v Slovakia*, Diss Op Brower (n 48) para 33.
[134] *Canfor Corporation v United States of America*, Procedural Order No 5, 28 May 2004, paras 4, 7 and 18–20.
[135] *European Media Ventures* (n 129).
[136] See, similarly, R Gardiner, *Treaty Interpretation* (OUP 2008) 106–07 (hereafter Gardiner, *Treaty*); I Van Damme, *Treaty Interpretation by the WTO Appellate Body* (OUP 2009) 310 (hereafter Van Damme, *Treaty*); M Fitzmaurice and P Merkouris, 'Canons of Treaty Interpretation: Selected Case Studies from the World Trade Organization and the North American Free Trade Agreement' in M Fitzmaurice, O Elias and P Merkouris (eds), *Treaty Interpretation and the Vienna Convention on the Law of Treaties: 30 Years On* (Brill 2010) 225 (hereafter Fitzmaurice and Merkouris, 'Canons'); ME Villiger, *Commentary on the 1969 Vienna Convention on the Law of Treaties* (Martinus Nijhoff Publishers 2009) 445–46 (hereafter Villiger, *Commentary*); E Shirlow and M Waibel, Article 32 of the VCLT and Precedent in Investor-State Arbitration: A Sliding Scale Approach to Interpretation in Esmé Shirlow and Kiran Nasir Gore (eds), *The Vienna Convention on the Law of Treaties in Investor-State Disputes: History, Evolution, and Future* (Kluwer 2022).

to the text of Article 32 and its purpose, which envisages the use of supplementary means of interpretation to uncover the treaty parties' intention(s). The criteria focus on the quality of the material and its connection with the substance of the treaty provision at issue, the temporal qualities of the supplementary means, their availability of the materials to the treaty parties and the disputing parties, the authors of the materials, and the awareness of the treaty parties of their existence and support for the interpretations advanced therein. All such criteria interrelate insofar as they all seek to determine how closely the documents reflect the collective efforts of the parties in negotiating the treaty.[137]

D. Conclusions

47 International courts and tribunals frequently have reference to supplementary means of interpretation where one of the triggers specified in Article 32 is present. That said, several investment tribunals have adopted more flexible approaches vis-à-vis both the triggers for recourse to supplementary means of interpretation under Article 32, and the order of analysis when applying Articles 31 and 32. Such approaches highlight the discretion inherent in the application of Article 32, and the resulting leeway that international courts and tribunals have when determining the role to be played by supplementary means of interpretation under the VCLT's interpretive framework.

48 Supplementary materials have been placed before investment tribunals more frequently than other international courts and tribunals and, like other international courts and tribunals, investment tribunals have tended to rely on supplementary means of interpretation where they are made available to them. The different approaches of investment tribunals to *travaux préparatoires* may also be explained by the unique context of individual-to-State as compared to State-to-State disputes: parties to investment disputes refer very frequently to supplementary means of interpretation.[138]

49 Investment tribunals, like other international courts and tribunals, have interpreted the reference to 'supplementary means of interpretation' in Article 32 as open-ended, such that the specific forms of supplementary material listed therein are not treated as exhaustive. This approach fits both the terms and purpose of Article 32 as well as its drafting history.[139] This nuanced approach treats these materials as 'supplementary' but allows for differing weight to be given to them in the interpretive process. While investment tribunals, alongside other international courts and tribunals, have therefore adopted an inclusive approach to identifying materials relevant under Article 32, they share the view that some such materials may be more relevant in the interpretive process than others.

Selected literature

Arsanjani MH and Reisman MW, 'Interpreting Treaties for the Benefit of Third Parties: The "Salvors' Doctrine" and the Use of Legislative History in Investment Treaties' (2010) 104 AJIL 597.

---

[137] cf Waldock, Third Report on the Law of Treaties YILC 1964, Vol II, 58, para 21.
[138] See further Shirlow and Waibel, 'A Sliding Scale' (n 7); OK Fauchald, 'The Legal Reasoning of ICSID Tribunals—An Empirical Analysis' (2008) 19 EJIL 301.
[139] See, similarly, Gardiner, *Treaty* (n 136) 302; Van Damme, *Treaty* (n 136) 310; Fitzmaurice and Merkouris, 'Canons' (n 136) 225; Villiger, *Commentary* (n 136) 445–46.

Mortenson J, 'Is the Vienna Convention Hostile to Drafting History?' (2013) 107 AJIL 780.

Shirlow E and Waibel M, 'A Sliding Scale Approach to Travaux in Treaty Interpretation: The Case of Investment Treaties' (2021) BYIL.

Van Damme I, *Treaty Interpretation by the WTO Appellate Body* (OUP 2009).

Selected decisions

Appellate Body Report, *Canada—Measures Affecting the Importation of Milk and the Exportation of Dairy Products*, WTO Doc WT/DS103/AB/R, adopted 13 October 1999.

Appellate Body Report, *European Communities—Customs Classification of Frozen Boneless Chicken Cuts*, WTO Doc WT/DS269/AB/R, adopted 12 September 2005.

Application of the Convention on the Prevention and Punishment of Genocide (*Bosnia and Herzegovina v Serbia and Montenegro*) (Merits) [2007] ICJ Rep 43.

Application of the International Convention on the Elimination of All Forms of Racial Discrimination (*Qatar v United Arab Emirates*) (Preliminary Objections) [2021] ICJ Rep 71.

Avena and Other Mexican Nationals (*Mexico v United States of America*) (Merits) [2004] ICJ Rep 300.

Case Concerning Border and Transborder Armed Actions (*Nicaragua v Honduras*) (Jurisdiction and Admissibility) [1988] ICJ Rep 69.

Legality of Use of Force (*Serbia and Montenegro v Belgium*) (Preliminary Objections) [2004] ICJ Rep 279.

Maritime Delimitation and Territorial Questions between Qatar and Bahrain (*Qatar v Bahrain*) (Jurisdiction and Admissibility) [1995] ICJ Rep 6.

Maritime Delimitation in the Indian Ocean (*Somalia v Kenya*) (Preliminary Objections) [2017] ICJ Rep 3.

South China Sea Arbitration (*Philippines v China*), PCA Case No 2013-19, Award, 12 July 2016.

Article 33 of the VCLT

Interpretation of treaties authenticated in two or more languages

Peter Tzeng

1. When a treaty has been authenticated in two or more languages, the text is equally authoritative in each language, unless the treaty provides or the parties agree that, in case of divergence, a particular text shall prevail.

2. A version of the treaty in a language other than one of those in which the text was authenticated shall be considered an authentic text only if the treaty so provides or the parties so agree.

3. The terms of the treaty are presumed to have the same meaning in each authentic text.

4. Except where a particular text prevails in accordance with paragraph 1, when a comparison of the authentic texts discloses a difference of meaning which the application of Articles 31 and 32 does not remove, the meaning which best reconciles the texts, having regard to the object and purpose of the treaty, shall be adopted.

A. Introduction	1	C. International investment law		17
B. General international law	7	D. Conclusion		27

A. Introduction

1 Article 33 of the Vienna Convention on the Law of Treaties (VCLT) concerns the interpretation of treaties authenticated in two or more languages ('multilingual treaties'). Although the International Court of Justice (ICJ) has expressly recognized only the article's fourth paragraph as custom,[1] many international adjudicatory bodies[2] and

---

[1] *LaGrand (Germany v United States)*, Judgment, 27 June 2001, para 101 ('In the absence of agreement between the parties in this respect, it is appropriate to refer to paragraph 4 of Article 33 of the Vienna Convention on the Law of Treaties, which in the view of the Court again reflects customary international law'). The ICJ has also referred to Article 33(3) of the VCLT in the context of a case where neither party was a party to the VCLT. See *Kasikili/Sedudu Island (Botswana v Namibia)* [1999] ICJ Rep 1045, para 25.

[2] *Golder v The United Kingdom*, ECtHR App no 4451/70, Judgment, 21 February 1975, para 29; *Responsibilities and obligations of States sponsoring persons and entities with respect to activities in the Area*, ITLOS Case No 17, Advisory Opinion, 1 February 2011, para 57; *Japan—Countervailing Duties on Dynamic Random Access Memories from Korea*, WTO Doc WT/DS336/R, Panel Report, 13 July 2007, para 7.45; *Question whether the re-evaluation of the German Mark in 1961 and 1969 constitutes a case for application of the clause in article 2 (e) of Annex I A of the 1953 Agreement on German External Debts (Belgium, France Switzerland, United Kingdom, United States v Germany)*, Decision, 16 May 1980, XIX RIAA 67, 92 (hereafter *Young Loans Arbitration*); *Itisaluna Iraq LLC, Munir Sukhtian International Investment LLC, VTEL Holdings Ltd, VTEL Middle East and Africa Limited v Republic of Iraq*, ICSID Case No ARB/17/10, Award, 3 April 2020, para 61; *Salini Costruttori SpA and Italstrade SpA v The Hashemite Kingdom of Jordan*, ICSID Case No ARB/02/13, Jurisdiction, 9 November 2004, para 75.

commentators³ have considered the totality of Article 33 as reflecting customary international law.

The first two paragraphs of Article 33 are straightforward, and not much commentary need be made on them. The third and fourth paragraphs, however, are worth closer examination. Although they have been accepted as custom by many,[4] considerable uncertainty remains surrounding their application in practice. The fact that '[t]he terms of the treaty are presumed to have the same meaning in each authentic text'[5] does not say much as to how a single meaning is to be derived when different authentic texts appear to have different meanings. And identifying 'the meaning which best reconciles the texts, having regard to the object and purpose of the treaty'[6] can be a very subjective exercise. As a result, the interpreter is left with a significant margin of discretion in applying these two paragraphs.

There has, however, been agitation for a more concrete rule for interpreting seemingly divergent authentic texts—a rule that the present entry refers to as 'the common meaning rule'. An articulation of this rule can be found in Sir Humphrey Waldock's Third Report on the Law of Treaties, where he proposed:

> If in each of two or more authentic texts a term is capable of being given more than one meaning compatible with the objects and purposes of the treaty, a meaning which is common to both or all the texts is to be adopted.[7]

The common meaning rule has elsewhere been described as favouring 'the lowest common denominator'.[8] In addition, in circumstances where the scope of a term in one authentic language is entirely subsumed within the broader scope of the term in another authentic language, the rule has been described as one favouring the more 'limited'[9] or 'restrictive'[10] interpretation. This is because, in such circumstances, the common meaning is the narrower meaning of the term in the first language, that is, the more limited or restrictive interpretation of the term.

---

[3] See O Dörr, 'Article 33' in O Dörr and K Schmalenbach (eds), *Vienna Convention on the Law of Treaties: A Commentary* (2nd edn, Springer 2018) 636 (hereafter Dörr, 'Article 33'); M Villiger, *Commentary on the 1969 Vienna Convention on the Law of Treaties* (Martinus Nijhoff Publishers 2009) 461 (hereafter Villiger, *Commentary*). For less certain views, see A Papaux and R Samson, '1969 Vienna Convention: Article 33' in Olivier Corten and Pierre Klein (eds), *The Vienna Conventions on the Law of Treaties: A Commentary* (OUP 2011) 872–73; ILC, *Report of the Commission to the General Assembly on the Work of its Sixty-fifth Session*, UN Doc A/68/10 (2013), 15–16.

[4] See nn 2 and 3.

[5] VCLT, Article 33(3).

[6] ibid Article 33(4).

[7] ILC, *Third Report on the Law of Treaties, by Sir Humphrey Waldock, Special Rapporteur*, UN Doc A/CN.4/167 and Add.1-3 (3 March, 9 June, 12 June, and 17 July 1964) reproduced in YILC 1964, Vol II, UN Doc A/CN.4/SER.A/1964/Add.1, 62.

[8] See, eg, Villiger, *Commentary* (n 3) 454; Dörr, 'Article 33' (n 3) 637; *Young Loans Arbitration* (n 2) 110.

[9] See, eg, *Mavrommatis Palestine Concessions (Greece v Great Britain)* (Jurisdiction) PCIJ Series A No 2, 13 May 1924, 19 (hereafter *Mavrommatis*).

[10] See, eg, ILC, *Draft Articles on the Law of Treaties with commentaries* (1966) reproduced in YILC 1966, Vol II, UN Doc A/CN.4/SER.A/1966/Add.1 (1967), 225; *Elettronica Sicula SpA (ELSI) (United States of America v Italy)* [1989] ICJ Rep 15, para 118 (hereafter *ELSI*). Despite the use of the word 'restrictive', the common meaning rule must not be confused with the treaty interpretation principle *in dubio mitius*, which is sometimes described as a principle of 'restrictive interpretation'. The principle *in dubio mitius* provides that treaties should be interpreted 'in deference to the sovereignty of states', such that '[i]f the meaning of a term is ambiguous, that meaning is to be preferred which is less onerous to the party assuming an obligation, or which interferes less with the territorial and personal supremacy of a party, or involves less general restrictions upon the parties'. R Jennings and A Watts (eds), *Oppenheim's International Law: Volume I Peace* (9th edn, OUP 2008) 1278.

5   One could consider the common meaning rule to derive from the third and fourth paragraphs of Article 33. After all, adopting the common meaning appears to accord with the presumption in Article 33(3) of terms having 'the same meaning in each authentic text', as well as the objective in Article 33(4) of identifying 'the meaning which best reconciles the texts'. One can, however, question whether the application of the common meaning rule *always* conforms to the result that would be obtained through an application of the third and fourth paragraphs of Article 33.

6   Today, most international adjudicatory bodies do not apply the common meaning rule, preferring instead to strictly adhere to the directive in the fourth paragraph of Article 33 to have regard to the object and purpose of the treaty in reconciling disparities in different authentic texts (Section B). By contrast, investor–State tribunals appear to be more open to following the common meaning rule when applying Article 33 (Section C). This apparent divergence, if it can be said to exist, is difficult to explain, but provides some food for thought on the role and authority of investor–State tribunals in treaty interpretation (Section D).

B. General international law

7   One of the earliest authoritative articulations of the common meaning rule arguably comes from the judgment of the Permanent Court of International Justice (PCIJ) on jurisdiction in the *Mavrommatis Palestine Concessions* case.[11] There, the Court had to interpret Article 11 of the Mandate for Palestine, which referred to the term 'public control' in English and '*contrôle public*' in French.[12] After acknowledging that the English term had 'a more restricted meaning',[13] the Court concluded that the narrower scope of the English term 'public control' should apply:

> The Court is of opinion that, where two versions possessing equal authority exist one of which appears to have a wider bearing than the other, it is bound to adopt the more limited interpretation which can be made to harmonise with both versions and which, as far as it goes, is doubtless in accordance with the common intention of the Parties.[14]

8   The PCIJ, however, was not consistent in applying the common meaning rule. Just two years earlier, in its *ILO Agriculture* advisory opinion, the Court chose not to do so. In that case, it was asked whether the competence of the International Labour Organization (ILO) extended to agricultural labour.[15] It thus had to interpret the provisions of the Treaty of Versailles that established the ILO, which contained the terms 'industrial' in English and '*industriel*' in French. The Court recognized that the French term had a narrower scope, as it normally excluded agriculture.[16] As a result, an application of the common meaning rule would have led to the conclusion that the narrower meaning of the French term should be adopted. Nevertheless, the Court held that 'the context is the final test', and concluded after examining the context that the term 'industrial' or '*industriel*' did in fact extend to agriculture.[17]

---

[11] *Mavrommatis* (n 9).
[12] ibid 18.
[13] ibid.
[14] ibid 19.
[15] *Competence of the ILO in regard to International Regulation of the Conditions of the Labour of Persons Employed in Agriculture* (Advisory Opinion) PCIJ Series B No 2, 12 August 1922, 9.
[16] ibid 34–35.
[17] ibid 39.

The common meaning rule was applied in at least one other case in the following years.[18] **9**
And as mentioned above, Sir Humphrey Waldock proposed the rule in his Third Report on the Law of Treaties.[19] The International Law Commission (ILC), however, expressly rejected the rule. In its commentaries to the Draft Articles on the Law of Treaties, the Commission stated:

> In the *Mavrommatis Palestine Concessions* case, the Permanent Court was thought by some jurists to lay down a general rule of restrictive interpretation in cases of divergence between authentic texts .... But the Court does not appear necessarily to have intended ... to lay down as a general rule that the more limited interpretation which can be made to harmonize with both texts is the one which must be adopted. Restrictive interpretation was appropriate in that case. But the question whether in case of ambiguity a restrictive interpretation ought to be adopted is a more general one the answer to which hinges on the nature of the treaty and the particular context in which the ambiguous term occurs. ... Accordingly, while the *Mavrommatis* case gives strong support to the principle of conciliating—i.e. harmonizing—the texts, it is not thought to call for a general rule laying down a presumption in favour of restrictive interpretation in the case of an ambiguity in plurilingual texts.[20]

Consistent with the ILC, the ICJ has shied away from applying the common meaning rule. **10**
In the *ELSI* case, for example, a Chamber of the Court was asked to interpret the Italy–US Friendship, Commerce and Navigation Treaty and its Protocol, and resolve the discrepancies between the terms 'taken' in English and '*espropriati*' (expropriated) in Italian, and between the terms 'interests' in English and '*diritti*' (rights) in Italian.[21] As for the first pair of terms, the Chamber observed that '[t]he word "taking" is wider and looser than "*espropriazione*"'.[22] And as for the second, Italy argued that the term 'interests' was broader than the term '*diritti*', such that 'on the basis of the principle expressed in Article 33, paragraph 4, of the VCLT, the correct interpretation of the Protocol must be in the more restrictive sense of the Italian text'.[23] The Chamber could have reached the same conclusion that it ultimately reached—that Italy had not breached the treaty—by applying the common meaning rule with respect to either of these discrepancies. Instead, however, it held that these discrepancies did not have to be resolved, and reached its conclusion on the basis of other considerations.[24]

The Court similarly refrained from applying the common meaning rule in the *LaGrand* case. **11**
There, the Court had to determine whether provisional measures indicated under Article 41 of its Statute were binding. The Court noted that the French term '*doivent être prises*' suggested the 'mandatory character' of provisional measures,[25] whereas the English term 'ought to be taken' could arguably have either a mandatory or an optional connotation.[26] In light

---

[18] *Russell v United Mexican States*, Award, 24 April 1931, XIX RIAA 805, 867.
[19] ILC, *Third Report on the Law of Treaties, by Sir Humphrey Waldock, Special Rapporteur*, UN Doc A/CN.4/167 and Add.1-3 (3 March, 9 June, 12 June, and 17 July 1964) reproduced in YILC 1964, Vol II, UN Doc A/CN.4/SER.A/1964/Add.1 (1965), 62.
[20] ILC, *Draft Articles on the Law of Treaties with commentaries* (1966) reproduced in YILC 1966, Vol II, UN Doc A/CN.4/SER.A/1966/Add.1 (1967), 225.
[21] *ELSI* (n 10) paras 113, 118.
[22] ibid para 113.
[23] ibid para 118.
[24] ibid para 119.
[25] *LaGrand (Germany v United States of America)* [2001] ICJ Rep 466, para 100.
[26] See ibid (noting that the United States argued that the term 'ought' suggested that provisional measures 'lack mandatory effect', but that the term could be interpreted to 'have a meaning equivalent to ... "must" or "shall"').

of this, the Court could have simply applied the common meaning rule to conclude that the phrase should be interpreted to mean that provisional measures are mandatory. Instead, the Court proceeded to apply Article 33(4) by assessing the object and purpose of its Statute,[27] and ultimately reached the same conclusion.[28]

12   More recently in the *Avena Interpretation* case, the Court interpreted its Statute in a manner contrary to the common meaning rule. In that case, the Court had to consider whether, pursuant to Article 60 of its Statute, there was a 'dispute as to the meaning or scope' of the original *Avena* judgment. In this respect, the Court observed in its order on provisional measures:

> Whereas the French and English versions of Article 60 of the Statute are not in total harmony; whereas the French text uses the term 'contestation' while the English text refers to a 'dispute'; whereas the term 'contestation' in the French text has a wider meaning than the term used in the English text;[29]

13   Had the Court applied the common meaning rule, it would have found in favour of the English text. Instead, however, the Court held that 'in the present circumstances, a meaning shall be given that best reconciles the French and English texts of Article 60 of its Statute, bearing in mind its object', and concluded that the term should have a more flexible meaning, not unlike the French text.[30]

14   Other international adjudicatory bodies have similarly avoided applying the common meaning rule. The European Court of Justice in *Spain v Council*, for example, did not rely on the rule in reaching the same conclusion that would have resulted through the rule's application. There, the Court was tasked with interpreting the term 'management of water resources' in what was then Article 130 of the Treaty establishing the European Community. The Court observed that in most authentic language texts of the treaty the term included both quantitative and qualitative aspects, but in some texts the equivalent term included only quantitative aspects.[31] The common meaning rule thus would have dictated in favour of the term encompassing only quantitative aspects. Rather than applying the rule, however, the Court recalled that '[i]n the case of divergence between the language versions of a Community measure, the provision in question must be interpreted by reference to the purpose and general scheme of the rules of which it forms part'.[32] Only after examining the purpose and general scheme of the rules did the Court conclude that the term should be interpreted to cover only quantitative aspects of water management.[33]

15   The Appellate Body of the World Trade Organization (WTO) has also refrained from applying the common meaning rule. In *United States—Softwood Lumber*, the Appellate Body had to reconcile the terms 'goods' in English, '*biens*' in French, and '*bienes*' in Spanish in the Agreement on Subsidies and Countervailing Measures. The Appellate Body recognized that the ordinary meaning of the English term 'includes items that are tangible and capable of being possessed', whereas the ordinary meaning of the French and Spanish terms 'include

---

[27] ibid paras 101–03.
[28] ibid para 109.
[29] *Request for Interpretation of the Judgment of 31 March 2004 in the Case concerning Avena and Other Mexican Nationals (Mexico v United States of America)*, Provisional Measures, Order, 16 July 2008, para 53.
[30] ibid.
[31] *Kingdom of Spain v Council of the European Union*, Case C-36/98, Judgment, 30 January 2001, ECR 2001 I-00779, para 48.
[32] ibid para 49.
[33] ibid para 57.

a wide range of property, including immovable property'.³⁴ The application of the common meaning rule would have favoured a narrower meaning. But after invoking Article 33(3) of the VCLT, the Appellate Body concluded that a relatively broad understanding of the term should apply.³⁵

Arbitral tribunals have also followed suit. In fact, the tribunal in the *Young Loans* arbitration **16** remains one of the few adjudicatory bodies, if not the only one, that has expressly rejected the common meaning rule. In that case, the tribunal had to interpret the words 'depreciation' (in English), '*dépréciation*' (in French), and '*Abwertung*' (in German) in the Agreement on German External Debts.³⁶ The tribunal acknowledged that 'depreciation' and '*dépréciation*' had a broader scope than '*Abwertung*', since the German term normally refers to 'the devaluation of a currency by governmental act', whereas the English and French terms could be used to describe both such devaluation, as well as 'the economic phenomenon of depreciation of a currency'.³⁷ On this basis alone, the tribunal could have applied the common meaning rule to adopt the narrower German meaning. But instead, the tribunal expressly objected to 'the principle[] of the "lowest common denominator"', as it considered that this principle 'for more or less formal reasons favour[s] a particular version of the treaty without ... even touching on its "object and purpose", yet under Article 33 (4) of the [VCLT] this is the decisive yardstick'.³⁸

C. International investment law

Compared to other international adjudicatory bodies, investor–State tribunals appear **17** to be more open to applying the common meaning rule in the context of Article 33. A word of caution, though, is necessary at the outset. The reality is that the large majority of investor–State arbitral tribunals do not confront issues relating to Article 33 of the VCLT, and those that do rarely face the situation where there is a discrepancy in authentic texts with a clear common meaning. The present author has been able to identify only four cases where a tribunal did face such a situation, and as a result it is difficult to assert with any certainty that these cases are representative of the broader population of investor–State cases. In the first case, the tribunal did not apply the common meaning rule, but in the remaining three it effectively did.

The first case is *BG v Argentina*. There, the parties disputed whether certain of the claimant's **18** claims to money qualified as 'investments' under Article 1(a)(iii) of the Argentina–UK Bilateral Investment Treaty (BIT). The issue lied in the fact that the authentic English text of the article expressly refers to 'claims to money', but the authentic Spanish text instead employs the term '*título de crédito*'. The tribunal noted in this respect:

> For Argentina, Article 1(a)(iii) of the BIT only extends protection to investors where their 'Investment' takes the form of a '*título de crédito*' (i.e., a 'negotiable instrument'). Conversely, BG believes that the English term 'claims to money' is broader in scope and

---

³⁴ *United States—Final Countervailing Duty Determination with respect to Certain Softwood Lumber from Canada*, WTO Doc WT/DS257/AB/R, Appellate Body Report, 19 January 2004, para 59.
³⁵ ibid.
³⁶ *Young Loans Arbitration* (n 2) 92.
³⁷ ibid 93.
³⁸ ibid 110.

includes claims to money under contracts entered into by MetroGAS. Simply put, the divergence of the Spanish '*título de crédito*' and the English 'claims to money' is semantically irreconcilable.[39]

19 The tribunal thus could have applied the common meaning rule to find in favour of the Spanish text. Instead, however, it recalled that '[p]aragraph 3 of Article 33 [of the VCLT] directs the interpreter to consider the object and purpose of the treaty',[40] and observed that '[a]doption of the Spanish term of the BIT as advocated by Argentina would considerably restrict the coverage of the treaty, discourage "greater investment" and defeat the shared aspiration expressed by Argentina and the U.K. in executing [the BIT] in 1993'.[41] The tribunal thus adopted the English text of Article 1(a)(iii),[42] and held that certain claims to money qualified as 'investments'.[43]

20 In the remaining three cases where an investor–State tribunal faced a discrepancy in authentic texts with a clear common meaning, the tribunal opted in favour of the common meaning rule. The first example is *Kılıç v Turkmenistan*. The tribunal there had to decide whether, under Article VII(2) of the Turkey–Turkmenistan BIT, recourse to local courts was optional or mandatory prior to initiating arbitration.[44] In the tribunal's view, the authentic Russian text made recourse to local courts clearly mandatory,[45] but the authentic English text was 'ambiguous or obscure'.[46] After applying Article 32 of the VCLT to the English text, the tribunal concluded that recourse to local courts was a mandatory precondition to arbitration.[47] Nevertheless, it went on to say:

> To the extent that it might not be possible to resolve the possible difference in meaning of the English and Russian text through the application of Articles 31 and 32, the Tribunal can, in accordance with the principles reflected in Article 33(4) of the VCLT, adopt the meaning which would best reconcile the two texts.
>
> To the extent that this had been necessary—and the Tribunal concludes that it is not—the Tribunal would have had no hesitation in concluding that the ambiguity of the English text could only be reconciled with the clearly mandatory Russian text by the determination that the English text also required a mandatory recourse to the local courts. This follows, because what is plainly mandatory cannot be optional, but what may either be mandatory or optional, can be seen as mandatory.[48]

21 Although this passage was *obiter dictum*, the logic applied by the tribunal in the last sentence of the passage quoted above corresponds to the common meaning rule. That is, the tribunal considered that, in applying Article 33(4) of the VCLT, the narrower meaning of the Russian text should prevail because it expressed the meaning in common between the English and Russian texts.

---

[39] *BG Group Plc v The Republic of Argentina*, Final Award, 24 December 2007, para 130.
[40] ibid para 132.
[41] ibid para 134.
[42] ibid para 137.
[43] ibid para 139.
[44] *Kılıç İnşaat İthalat İhracat Sanayi ve Ticaret Anonim Şirketi v Turkmenistan*, ICSID Case No ARB/10/1, Decision on Article VII.2 of the Turkey–Turkmenistan Bilateral Investment Treaty, 7 May 2012, para 9.1.
[45] ibid para 9.2.
[46] ibid paras 9.14–9.17. For the English text of Article VII(2), see ibid para 2.10.
[47] ibid paras 9.18–9.21.
[48] ibid para 9.23.

The next example is *ECE v Czech Republic*. There, the tribunal had to determine whether the assets in question constituted 'investments' for the purposes of Article 1(1) of the Czech–German BIT. Article 1(1) defined 'investments' as 'every kind of asset invested/contributed in conformity with domestic law', with the parties disputing whether the term 'invested' or 'contributed' was the more appropriate understanding of the authentic German text '*anglegt*' and the authentic Czech text '*vloženě*'.[49] After recalling Article 33 of the VCLT, the tribunal held:

> Approaching the question on [the basis of Article 33 of the VCLT], the two terms are to be presumed to have the same meaning. In light of the fact that, in the end, the Respondent did not dispute that the German word '*angelegt*' can only properly be translated as 'invested', whilst the Parties appear to be in agreement that the Czech-language term '*vloženě*' can bear the meaning either of 'invested' or 'contributed', in application of the presumption contained in Article 33(3) VCLT, and in the context of the surrounding provisions of Article 1(1), the Tribunal concludes that the appropriate translation into English is that, in order to constitute an 'investment', an asset must have been 'invested' in the ordinary sense of that term.[50]

The tribunal thus applied the logic of the common meaning rule, going so far as to refer to it as a 'presumption contained in Article 33(3) VCLT'.

The final example is *Levy and Gremcitel v Peru*. There, the tribunal had to determine the critical date for identifying the nationality of the investor under the France–Peru BIT.[51] The authentic Spanish text provided the critical date to be '*antes surgimiento de la controversia*', whereas the authentic French text provided it to be '*avant que le différend ne soit soulevé*'.[52] After reciting Articles 31–33 of the VCLT, the tribunal held:

> The Spanish version of the BIT ('*antes del surgimiento de la controversia*') has only one possible meaning, which is 'before the emergence of the dispute'. By contrast, the French version of the Treaty ('*avant que le différend ne soit soulevé*') could have two meanings, that is, either 'before the dispute is brought before an international arbitral tribunal' or 'before the dispute is raised with the other side'. The Tribunal agrees with the Respondent that the only harmonious interpretation of the two authentic texts is to say that the locally incorporated company must be under foreign control 'before the dispute is raised with the other side'. Indeed, this understanding coincides with the Spanish wording and with one of the two meanings of the French formula.[53]

The tribunal here thus also applied the common meaning rule, supposedly as an application of Article 33. It considered the Spanish text to reflect the meaning in common between the Spanish and French texts, and thus adopted that meaning as the correct interpretation of the treaty.

---

[49] *ECE Projektmanagement International GmbH and Kommanditgesellschaft PANTA Achtungsechzigste Grundstücksgesellschaft mbH & Co v The Czech Republic*, PCA Case No 2010-05, Final Award, 19 September 2013, paras 3.141, 3.143.
[50] ibid para 3.156.
[51] *Renée Rose Levy and Gremcitel S.A. v Republic of Peru*, ICSID Case No ARB/11/17, Award, 9 January 2015, para 164.
[52] ibid.
[53] ibid para 166.

26 It would be difficult, of course, to assert a clear trend on the basis of just four cases. But it is notable that three out of the four tribunals opted to apply the common meaning rule, even though the rule is no longer in vogue among other international adjudicatory bodies.

D. Conclusion

27 The two previous sections make clear that most international adjudicatory bodies normally do not apply the common meaning rule, even though some investor–State tribunals have done so. These examples, of course, cannot be assumed to be representative of the broader population of cases. It is possible that there may be more investor–State tribunals that have rejected the common meaning rule, just as there may be some other adjudicatory bodies that have applied it. But based on the cases that the present author has been able to find, there does appear to be a slight divergence between investor–State tribunals and other international adjudicatory bodies on the question of the application of the common meaning rule.

28 Assuming that this divergence is real, then one might wonder why investor–State tribunals are more inclined to apply the rule than other international adjudicatory bodies. There is no clear answer to this question, but some thoughts below are perhaps worth consideration.

29 One potential reason for this divergence is that the utility of Article 33's reconciliation rules are particularly limited for investment treaties. For many other treaties, one can ascertain a clear object and purpose that can shed light on how the treaty's provisions should be interpreted. But with investment treaties, which share the common object and purpose of promoting and protecting investment, it is not so clear that this object and purpose should be blindly relied on to reconcile inconsistencies in equally authentic texts of the treaty. Indeed, if one were to do so, then one might be compelled to always adopt a pro-investor interpretation of the treaty. This does not appear to be the correct solution, as investment treaties are largely drafted to strike a balance between the investor's interests and those of the State.

30 Another potential reason explaining the divergence, related to the previous one, is that investor–State tribunals might feel more compelled to provide concrete justifications for their conclusions because their awards are subject to set aside or annulment. Perhaps there is a feeling among investment arbitrators that vaguely assessing the object and purpose of an investment treaty is simply insufficient to justify an interpretation of the treaty's text, thereby risking the possibility of set aside or annulment on grounds of insufficient reasoning. This sort of pressure normally does not exist for many other international adjudicatory bodies, whose decisions are not subject to a compulsory control mechanism.

31 A third and final possible reason relates to the nature of investor–State arbitral tribunals as dispute settlement bodies tasked with resolving investment disputes. In this investment context, there might be a greater importance attached to predictability. And undoubtedly a clear rule like the common meaning rule is much more predictable than an unguided application of Article 33(3) and 33(4) of the VCLT.

32 All this said, even if any of these reasons could help *explain* the divergence, they would not help *justify* it. That is, it does not seem sensible for investor–State tribunals to take a different approach to treaty interpretation compared to other international adjudicatory bodies. There are, of course, many aspects of investor–State arbitration that make it fundamentally

different from other forms of international adjudication. But these aspects probably do not justify differential application of something as core to international law as the interpretation of multilingual treaties.

It should nonetheless be recalled that, in the grand scheme of things, the similarities between investor–State tribunals and other adjudicatory bodies in applying Article 33 are far greater than the differences. That is, the article is in practice universally accepted and applied, even if the means of applying it are not always exactly the same.

Selected literature

Dörr O, 'Article 33' in Dörr O and Schmalenbach K (eds), *Vienna Convention on the Law of Treaties: A Commentary* (2nd edn, Springer 2018).

Hahn JH, 'Value maintenance in the Young Loan Arbitration: History and analysis' (1983) 14 NYIL 3.

Hardy J, 'The Interpretation of Plurilingual Treaties by International Courts and Tribunals' (1961) 37 BYIL 72.

Jennings R and Watts A (eds), *Oppenheim's International Law: Volume I Peace* (9th edn, OUP 2008).

Papaux A and Samson R, '1969 Vienna Convention: Article 33' in Corten O and Klein P (eds), *The Vienna Conventions on the Law of Treaties: A Commentary* (OUP 2011).

Thirlway H, 'The Law and Procedure of The International Court of Justice 1960–1989: Supplement, 2006: Part Three' (2007) 77 BYIL 1.

Van Damme I, *Treaty interpretation by the WTO Appellate Body* (OUP 2009).

Villiger M, *Commentary on the 1969 Vienna Convention on the Law of Treaties* (Martinus Nijhoff Publishers 2009).

Selected decisions

BG Group Plc v The Republic of Argentina, Final Award, 24 December 2007.

Competence of the ILO in regard to International Regulation of the Conditions of the Labour of Persons Employed in Agriculture (Advisory Opinion) PCIJ Series B No 2, 12 August 1922.

ECE Projektmanagement International GmbH and Kommanditgesellschaft PANTA Achtungsechzigste Grundstücksgesellschaft mbH & Co v The Czech Republic, PCA Case No 2010-05, Final Award, 19 September 2013.

Elettronica Sicula SpA (ELSI) (United States of America v Italy) [1989] ICJ Rep 15.

Golder v The United Kingdom, ECtHR App no 4451/70, Judgment, 21 February 1975.

Itisaluna Iraq LLC, Munir Sukhtian International Investment LLC, VTEL Holdings Ltd, VTEL Middle East and Africa Limited v Republic of Iraq, ICSID Case No ARB/17/10, Award, 3 April 2020.

Japan—Countervailing Duties on Dynamic Random Access Memories from Korea, WTO Doc WT/DS336/R, Panel Report, 13 July 2007.

Kasikili/Sedudu Island (Botswana v Namibia) [1999] ICJ Rep 1045.

Kılıç İnşaat İthalat İhracat Sanayi ve Ticaret Anonim Şirketi v Turkmenistan, ICSID Case No ARB/10/1, Decision on Article VII.2 of the Turkey–Turkmenistan Bilateral Investment Treaty, 7 May 2012.

Kingdom of Spain v Council of the European Union, Case C-36/98, Judgment, 30 January 2001, European Court Reports 2001 I-00779.

LaGrand (Germany v United States of America) [2001] ICJ Rep 466.

Mavrommatis Palestine Concessions (Greece v Great Britain) (Jurisdiction) PCIJ Series A No 2, 13 May 1924.

Question whether the re-evaluation of the German Mark in 1961 and 1969 constitutes a case for application of the clause in article 2 (e) of Annex I A of the 1953 Agreement on German External Debts (Belgium, France Switzerland, United Kingdom, United States v Germany), Decision, 16 May 1980, XIX RIAA 67.

Renée Rose Levy and Gremcitel SA v Republic of Peru, ICSID Case No ARB/11/17, Award, 9 January 2015.

Request for Interpretation of the Judgment of 31 March 2004 in the Case concerning Avena and Other Mexican Nationals (Mexico v United States of America) (Mexico v United States of America), Provisional Measures, 16 July 2008.

Responsibilities and obligations of States sponsoring persons and entities with respect to activities in the Area, ITLOS Case No 17, Advisory Opinion, 1 February 2011.

Russell v United Mexican States, Award, 24 April 1931, XIX RIAA 805.

Salini Costruttori S.p.A. and Italstrade S.p.A. v The Hashemite Kingdom of Jordan, ICSID Case No ARB/02/13, Decision on Jurisdiction, 9 November 2004.

United States—Final Countervailing Duty Determination with respect to Certain Softwood Lumber from Canada, Report of the Appellate Body, WTO Doc WT/DS257/AB/R, 19 January 2004.

Parts IV and V of the VCLT

Amendment, invalidity, termination, and suspension of treaties

Luke Sobota and Amelia Keene[*]

A. Introduction	1	II. Article 54(a): Termination by the terms of the treaty (unilateral termination)	46
B. Amendment and modification of investment treaties	3	III. Article 54(b): Termination by consent (mutual termination)	50
I. Article 39: General rule and amendment of bilateral treaties	3	IV. Article 56: Withdrawal in the absence of treaty provisions or consent	63
II. Articles 40–41: Amendment and modification of multilateral treaties	12	V. Articles 57 and 58: Suspension of a treaty	64
C. Invalidity of investment treaties	21	VI. Article 59: Termination or suspension implied by conclusion of a later treaty	66
I. General rules	21		
II. Article 46: Provisions of internal law regarding competence to conclude treaties	25	VII. Articles 60–63: Other grounds for termination or suspension	74
II. Article 50: Corruption of a representative of a State	33	VIII. Articles 65–68: Procedures for invalidity, termination, withdrawal, or suspension	83
IV. Article 53: Treaties conflicting with peremptory norms of general international law	39	E. Conclusion	93
D. Termination and suspension of investment treaties	42		
I. General rules	42		

A. Introduction

Parts IV and V of the 1969 Vienna Convention on the Law of Treaties (VCLT) establish the principles of international law governing the amendment, invalidity, termination, and suspension of treaties. This entry provides an overview of how those provisions have been applied in the investment context, also noting the extent to which they reflect customary international law. As Article 31(3)(c) of the VCLT envisages, investment treaties operate within general international law, not in isolation from it.[1]

---

[*] The authors wish to thank Zara Desai, Laure Dupain, Nayomi Goonesekere, Isha Jain, Srinath Reddy Kethireddy, Vanessa Tsang, Yannick Radi, and Zaid Wahidi for research and editing assistance.
[1] See, eg, *Loizidou v Turkey* App no 40/1993/435/514 (ECtHR, Merits, 1996) 108 ILR 443, para 43; *Urbaser v Argentina*, ICSID Case No ARB/07/26, Award, 8 December 2016, para 1200 ('The BIT cannot be interpreted and

2 The entry is focused on those areas of amendment, invalidity, termination, and suspension where there is some extant investment jurisprudence. This jurisprudence is not evenly distributed. There are, for instance, relatively few cases of invalidity being raised in investment arbitration, and none where termination for breach under Article 60 has been argued, while many awards address Article 59. Accordingly, there is not an entry for every article of the VCLT. Overall, few significant divergences were identified between investment tribunals and international courts and tribunals on the interpretation and application of Parts IV and V of the VCLT. For the most part, investment tribunals apply the language of the investment treaty when dealing with termination, suspension, and amendment. This is consistent with the scheme of the VCLT, which sets out only default rules.

B. Amendment and modification of investment treaties

I. Article 39: General rule and amendment of bilateral treaties

Article 39. General Rule regarding the amendment of treaties
A treaty may be amended by agreement between the parties. The rules laid down in Part II apply to such an agreement except insofar as the treaty may otherwise provide.

3 The general rule on the amendment of treaties set out in Article 39 is that a treaty may be amended by the agreement between the parties, unless the treaty otherwise provides. This is of particular salience for bilateral treaties, since there is no applicable procedure other than Part II of the VCLT, which refers to the general rules on conclusion and entry into force of treaties.[2] By contrast, a specific notification, negotiation, and agreement process is provided for the amendment or modification of a multilateral treaty in Article 40, again subject to the treaty's terms.[3] While the general rule that treaties can be amended reflects customary international law, the particular procedural mechanisms by which amendments are adopted are not recognized as having customary status.[4]

4 According to the United Nations Conference on Trade and Development (UNCTAD) International Investment Agreements Mapping Project,[5] nearly 25 per cent of all Bilateral Investment Treaties (BITs) include a clause expressly permitting the amendment or renegotiation of the treaty, and such clauses have appeared in investment treaties with increasing

---

applied in a vacuum.... The BIT has to be construed in harmony with other rules of international law, of which it forms part.').
[2] K von der Decken, 'Article 39' in O Dörr and K Schmalenbach (eds), *Vienna Convention on the Law of Treaties* (Springer 2012) 757–58 (hereafter von der Decken, 'Article 39').
[3] The term 'modification' is used to refer to an agreement among some of the States parties to vary the terms of a treaty, whereas the term 'amendment' refers to an agreement among all of the States parties. The distinction is otherwise of little import. See von der Decken, 'Article 39' (n 2) 757.
[4] P Sands, 'Article 39 Convention of 1969' in O Corten and P Klein (eds), *The Vienna Conventions on the Law of Treaties—A Commentary* (OUP 2011) 963.
[5] The International Investment Agreement (IIA) Mapping Project is a collaborative initiative between UNCTAD and a number of universities to map the content of IIAs. To date, approximately 2,584 bilateral investment treaties (including treaties that have been signed but have not yet come into force) have been mapped. The project excludes Free Trade Agreements containing investment clauses. The results of the mapping project are helpful to give an indication of trends, but should not be relied on for exact numbers, since not all BITs have been mapped accurately. See <https://investmentpolicy.unctad.org/pages/1031/mapping-of-iia-clauses> accessed 28 September 2022.

frequency over time.[6] While these clauses are strictly unnecessary to the extent that they simply reflect the default rule reflected in Article 39 (and customary international law) that a treaty may be amended by party agreement, some States have also used them to place conditions on how a treaty may be amended. For instance, the Hong Kong and the Association of South East Asian Nations BIT requires that 'this Agreement may be amended by the Parties by agreement *in writing*',[7] a requirement not specified in the VCLT; while the Israel–Japan BIT specifies that any amendment shall come into force once it is approved by the contracting parties in accordance with their internal procedures.[8] In practice, however, investment treaties are not frequently amended.[9] States generally prefer to negotiate a new treaty to replace the former, rather than merely amending the existing treaty.[10] For example, the North American Free Trade Agreement 1994 (NAFTA) was replaced with a wholly new treaty, the United States–Mexico–Canada Agreement (USMCA) on 1 July 2020.[11] However, amendment may be preferred for more limited changes. For instance, in 2018, the United States and Korea agreed to an amendment of their free trade agreement (which includes an investment chapter), which clarified the minimum standard of treatment and excluded investor–State dispute settlement procedures from the scope of the most-favoured nation clause.[12]

It is not always easy to discern the dividing line between interpretation, subsequent practice, and amendment.[13] The VCLT provides that subsequent practice can be used as a tool of interpretation,[14] but it does not deal with the possibility that subsequent practice may also modify a treaty. This is a significant distinction, since subsequent practice and interpretation are constrained by the original terms of the treaty. Whereas an amendment is more commonly seen as a formal modification to the treaty itself, subsequent practice may—at least theoretically—nevertheless offer a possibility for more informal modification where the terms of the treaty leave scope for interpretation. Indeed, the European Court of Human Rights has recognized the possibility of subsequent practice amounting to an outright amendment, stating that 'an established practice within the member States could give rise to *an amendment* of the [European] Convention [on Human Rights]'.[15]

---

[6] K Gordon and J Pohl, 'Investment Treaties Over Time—Treaty Practice and Interpretation in a Changing World' in *OECD Working Papers on International Investment* (OECD Publishing 2015/02) 3 (hereafter Gordon and Pohl).

[7] Agreement on Investment between Hong Kong and the Association of South East Asian Nations, Article 25.

[8] Agreement between the State of Israel and Japan for the Liberalization, Promotion and Protection of Investments, Article 28(3) ('Upon the request of either Contracting Party, the Contracting Parties may agree on any amendment to this Agreement. Any amendment shall be approved by the Contracting Parties in accordance with their respective internal procedures and shall enter into force on such date as the Contracting Parties may agree, and shall thereafter constitute an integral part of this Agreement').

[9] The OECD's 2015 Study found that only 3 per cent of the treaties included (60 out of 2,061 treaties) had been amended or otherwise complemented by protocols or exchanges of letters, some treaties more than once. At the same time, it recognized that the real number may be higher since this information may not always be publicly available. See Gordon and Pohl (n 6) 34.

[10] The OECD's 2015 Study found that around 8 per cent of the treaties (160 out of 2,061 treaties) had been renegotiated. This trend has increased over time and the true number today is likely to be higher. See ibid 35.

[11] See U.S.–Mexico–Canada Agreement (USMCA), 'U.S. Customs and Border Protection' <https://www.cbp.gov/trade/priority-issues/trade-agreements/free-trade-agreements/USMCA> accessed 28 September 2022.

[12] UNCTAD, 'Recent Developments in the International Investment Regime: Taking Stock of Phase 2 Reform Actions' *TD/B/C.II/42* (2 September 2019) <https://unctad.org/system/files/official-document/ciid42_en.pdf> accessed 28 September 2022, 6.

[13] See I Buga, 'Subsequent Practice and Treaty Modification' in MJ Bowman and D Kritsiotis (eds), *Conceptual and Contextual Perspectives on the Modern Law of Treaties* (CUP 2018) ch 12.

[14] VCLT, Article 31(3)(b).

[15] *Öcalan v Turkey*, App no 46221/99 (ECtHR GC, 12 May 2005), para 163 (emphasis added); citing *Soering v United Kingdom* 161 (ECtHR, 7 July 1989) Ser A, 40–41, paras 102–03; see also *Hassan v United Kingdom* App no

6 By contrast, the International Law Commission (ILC)'s 'Draft Report on subsequent agreements and subsequent practice' presumes that parties to a treaty that engage in subsequent practice or subsequent agreements intend to *interpret* the treaty, not to amend it,[16] noting that 'the possibility of amending or modifying a treaty by subsequent practice of the parties has not been generally recognised'. However, it also states that the draft conclusions are 'without prejudice' to the rules on the amendment or modification of treaties set out in the VCLT and customary international law, implicitly acknowledging the difficulty of drawing bright line distinctions.[17]

7 One complication with amendment in the context of investment treaties is that States may participate in the system in different capacities—as treaty-makers, treaty-reformers, and as respondents in an international arbitration.[18] A further complication is the decentralized nature of investment treaties, which makes it harder to identify changing treaty practices over time. To take one example, the 2012 US Model BIT includes specific annexes on the minimum standard of treatment and expropriation standards which have subsequently been incorporated in many US investment treaties,[19] but it is not clear whether these clarifications constitute 'subsequent practice' in respect of earlier US treaties without such clarifications. Also unresolved is the effect of a State party to a BIT having previously taken a position on an issue now in dispute in the arbitration, such as through publicly available submissions as a Respondent elsewhere or as a non-disputing third party. It is increasingly common for parties in an investment arbitration to put such sources forward as evidence of subsequent practice in relation to the meaning of contested issues of treaty interpretation.[20]

8 A further issue arises from interpretative notes or statements jointly issued by all States parties, or by a binding, treaty-mandated interpretative process such as the NAFTA Free Trade Commission (FTC).[21] For instance, in 2017, India and Bangladesh issued a joint interpretive statement, stated to form an 'integral part' of their BIT, providing that:[22]

> Interpretation of this Agreement shall be done in accordance with the high level of deference international law accords to states with regard to their development and implementation of domestic policies. Interpretation and application of the Agreement shall also reflect

---

29750/09 (ECtHR GC), para 101 (holding that subsequent practice 'could be taken as establishing [the Contracting Parties'] agreement not only as regards interpretation but even to modify the text of the Convention'); cf *Cruz Varas v Sweden* 201 (ECtHR, 20 March 1991) Ser A, para 100 ('Subsequent practice could be taken as establishing the agreement of Contracting States regarding the interpretation of a Convention provision [...] but not to create new rights and obligations which were not included in the Convention at the outset').

[16] ILC, 'Subsequent agreements and subsequent practice in relation to the interpretation of treaties: Text of the draft conclusions adopted by the Drafting Committee on Second Reading', UN Doc A/CN/4/L.907 (11 May 2018), Conclusion 7(3).

[17] ibid.

[18] A Roberts, 'Power and Persuasion in Investment Treaty Interpretation: The Dual Role of States' (2010) 104 AJIL 179 (hereafter Roberts, 'Power and Persuasion').

[19] US Model Bilateral Investment Treaty 2012, Annexes I and II.

[20] K Magraw, 'Investor–State Disputes and the Rise of Recourse to State Party Pleadings as Subsequent Agreements or Subsequent Practice under the Vienna Convention on the Law of Treaties' (2015) 30(1) ICSID Review – FILJ 142.

[21] NAFTA, Article 1131(2); see also USMCA, Article 14.D.9(2) ('A decision of the Commission on the interpretation of a provision of this Agreement under Article 30.2 (Functions of the Commission) shall be binding on a tribunal, and any decision or award issued by a tribunal must be consistent with that decision').

[22] Joint Interpretive Notes on the Agreement between the Government of the Republic of India and the Government of the People's Republic of Bangladesh for the Promotion and Protection of Investments, 4 October 2017.

the strong presumption of legitimacy and regularity international law provides to domestic legislative, administrative and judicial determinations made by the Contracting States.

The question is at what point the practice of issuing such statements diverges from interpretation into amendment.[23] In the instance above, applying a presumption of legitimacy could materially impact on the scope of the protections in the treaty. The decisions on interpretive statements are mixed. In *CME v Czech Republic*, the tribunal gave effect to statements issued by the Dutch and Czech governments concerning the application and interpretation of the BIT, even though such statements were issued after—and in direct response to—the Partial Award.[24] Similarly, the tribunal in *ADF Group v United States* accepted the aforementioned NAFTA FTC's interpretation as 'authoritative', and found that it was not authorized to distinguish between interpretations and amendments.[25]

By comparison, as Roberts has described, the *Pope & Talbot* tribunal viewed an 'interpretation' by the FTC as amounting to an 'illegitimate attempt to amend the treaty retroactively in order to interfere with an ongoing case'.[26] Similar concerns were expressed by the Singapore Court of Appeal in the case of *Sanum v Laos*. An arbitral tribunal seated in Singapore determined that it had jurisdiction over an investment dispute arising in the Special Administrative Region of Macau under the BIT between China and Laos.[27] Subsequently, these two States exchanged *notes verbales* purporting to exclude Macau from the scope of that BIT. The question for the Singapore Court of Appeal was whether the tribunal's holding on jurisdiction was correct.[28] The Court rejected Laos' argument that the *notes verbales* confirmed the pre-existing position of both States as to the scope of the treaty, finding that there was no evidence supporting this proposition prior to the 'critical date' on which the arbitration was brought.[29] Nor could the *notes verbales* be treated as evidence of a subsequent agreement or subsequent practice, since this would impermissibly 'amount to effecting a retroactive amendment of the BIT' and would also 'adversely affect a third party which has already brought proceedings', namely, the investor.[30] The Court therefore refused to give primacy to the views of the treaty parties that the BIT did not extend to Macau. It confirmed the investment tribunal's decision that the territorial scope of its jurisdiction extended to Macau.

As these cases illustrate, the issue of amendments or interpretative statements of investment treaties also raises thorny questions about the place of the investor as a third-party beneficiary with access to the dispute resolution mechanisms.[31] Due process issues may

---

[23] CH Brower II, 'Why the FTC Notes of Interpretation Constitute a Partial Amendment of NAFTA Article 1105' (2006) 46 Va J Int'l L 347.

[24] *CME Czech Republic BV v Czech Republic*, UNCITRAL, Final Award, 14 March 2003, paras 87–93, 400, 437, 504; see also UNCTAD IIA Issues Note No 3 December 2011, 11.

[25] Roberts, 'Power and Persuasion' (n 18) 179, 181 citing *ADF Group Inc v United States*, ICSID No ARB(AF)/00/1, 9 January 2003, para 177.

[26] ibid 180–81; *Pope & Talbot Inc v Canada*, NAFTA, Damages Award, 31 May 2002, (2002) 41 ILM 1347, paras 11–16 and 47 (hereafter *Pope & Talbot*) ('… were the Tribunal required to make a determination whether the Commission's action is an interpretation or an amendment, it would choose the latter').

[27] *Sanum Investments Ltd v Government of the Lao People's Democratic Republic*, PCA Case No 2013-13, Jurisdiction, 13 December 2013, para 300 (hereafter *Sanum Investments* PCA Jurisdiction). The tribunal reached this conclusion applying the rules of State succession, since Macau was not administered by China at the time that the BIT was concluded.

[28] *Sanum Investments Ltd v Government of the Lao People's Democratic Republic* [2016] SGCA 57 (hereafter *Sanum Investments* SGCA), para 101.

[29] ibid para 112.

[30] ibid para 116.

[31] See Roberts, 'Power and Persuasion' (n 18) 202 noting the possible analogy between investment treaties and human rights obligations, since investment treaties grant rights or at least privileges to individual investors.

arise acutely where an 'amendment' occurs partway through a dispute with one of the treaty parties, and touches on the substance of that dispute, particularly if it purports to apply retrospectively. That concern appears to have been what motivated the *Pope & Talbot* tribunal's protest against the FTC's 'interpretation' of the minimum standard of treatment,[32] as too the Singapore Court of Appeal's decision in *Sanum v Laos*.[33] It may also be relevant to consider whether the investor has been put on notice of the possibility of such a statement being issued, for instance through the inclusion of an FTC mechanism in the BIT.[34]

II. Articles 40–41: Amendment and modification of multilateral treaties

Article 40. Amendment of multilateral treaties

1. Unless the treaty otherwise provides, the amendment of multilateral treaties shall be governed by the following paragraphs.
2. Any proposal to amend a multilateral treaty as between all the parties must be notified to all the contracting States, each one of which shall have the right to take part in:
   (a) The decision as to the action to be taken in regard to such proposal;
   (b) The negotiation and conclusion of any agreement for the amendment of the treaty.

...

Article 41. Agreements to Modify Multilateral Treaties between Certain of the Parties only

1. Two or more of the parties to a multilateral treaty may conclude an agreement to modify the treaty as between themselves alone if:
   (a) The possibility of such a modification is provided for by the treaty; or
   (b) The modification in question is not prohibited by the treaty and:
      (i) Does not affect the enjoyment by the other parties of their rights under the treaty or the performance of their obligations;
      (ii) Does not relate to a provision, derogation from which is incompatible with the effective execution of the object and purpose of the treaty as a whole.
2. Unless in a case falling under paragraph l(a) the treaty otherwise provides, the parties in question shall notify the other parties of their intention to conclude the agreement and of the modification to the treaty for which it provides.

12   Under the rules of amendment set out in Articles 40 and 41 of the VCLT, an amended treaty applies only among those parties that agreed to the modification. Article 41 expressly contemplates that two or more parties can agree to modify the treaty *inter se*, but only where this possibility is provided for by the treaty, or where the modification is not prohibited and does

---

[32] *Pope & Talbot* (n 26) paras 11–16 (the tribunal expressed particular concern about the 'rule of international law that no-one shall be judge in his own cause').
[33] *Sanum Investments* SGCA (n 28) para 116.
[34] See, eg, *Republic of Ecuador v United States of America*, PCA Case No 2012-5, Expert Opinion with Respect to Jurisdiction, Prof W Michael Reisman, 24 April 2012, para 29 ('where the States-parties decide *ex ante* to reserve to themselves the power to change the rights they are creating for the benefit of third parties, they put the universe of potential third party beneficiaries on express notice that the State-parties have retained this power').

not affect the rights of other State parties or a non-derogable treaty provision.[35] As a consequence, it is possible for a multilateral treaty to apply differently among different States, with the original terms applying unless all relevant States have agreed to the amendment.[36] As noted above, it is not clear that the procedural mechanisms set out in Article 40 have customary status.[37] Moreover, while some commentators have expressed the view that Article 41 reflects customary international law at least in part,[38] no State has formally pronounced on its recognition as such. In the *BayWa re Renewable Energy GmbH v Spain* investment award, the tribunal noted that the conditions in Article 41 applied 'to the extent that they reflect the customary international law of treaty modification'.[39] It went on to find that the Commentary to the Vienna Convention[40] supports a conclusion that Article 41.2 'reflects general international law'.[41] Notably, however, nothing in the Commentary states that it was intended to reflect existing customary international law.

Since the majority of investment agreements are bilateral, the issue of *inter se* modifications does not arise frequently. Nevertheless, Articles 40 and 41 have potentially important ramifications in the context of attempts to amend or reform multilateral investment treaties such as the ICSID Convention, the EU–Canada Comprehensive Economic and Trade Agreement (CETA), the Dominican Republic–Central America Free Trade Agreement (DR-CAFTA), or the Comprehensive and Progressive Agreement for Trans-Pacific Partnership (CPTPP). Indeed, having regard to the reform efforts currently underway with respect to the Energy Charter Treaty (ECT), some commentators have suggested that an *inter se* modification might be agreed among some States parties to the ECT, such as the EU States, even if not all States parties agree.[42] Pursuant to Article 41(1)(b)(i), such a modification would be permitted only if it does not affect the rights and obligations of the other State parties.

---

[35] VCLT, Article 41 ('(a) The possibility of such a modification is provided for by the treaty; or (b) The modification in question is not prohibited by the treaty and: (i) Does not affect the enjoyment by the other parties of their rights under the treaty or the performance of their obligations; (ii) Does not relate to a provision, derogation from which is incompatible with the effective execution of the object and purpose of the treaty as a whole. 2. Unless in a case falling under paragraph l(a) the treaty otherwise provides, the parties in question shall notify the other parties of their intention to conclude the agreement and of the modification to the treaty for which it provides').

[36] See also VCLT, Article 30(4).

[37] See above, para 3; see also K Ardault and D Dormoy, 'Article 40 Convention of 1969' in O Corten and P Klein (eds), *The Vienna Conventions on the Law of Treaties—A Commentary* (OUP 2011) 978, 981 (noting that 'there is no generally admitted State practice aimed at governing the modification of multilateral treaties' and that 'nothing prevents the parties to a multilateral treaty that have not included clauses concerning its amendment at the outset to later come to an agreement on a different procedure than the one provided for in Article 40 of the 1969 Convention'); cf ME Villiger, *Commentary on the 1969 Vienna Convention on the Law of Treaties* (Martinus Nijhoff Publishers 2009) 526 (noting that the provisions reflected progressive development of international law, but appear to have crystallized into custom) (hereafter Villiger).

[38] K Ardault and D Dormoy, 'Article 41 Convention of 1969' in O Corten and P Klein (eds), *The Vienna Conventions on the Law of Treaties—A Commentary* (OUP 2011) 986, 994; Villiger (n 38) 538; cf K von der Decken, 'Article 41' in O Dörr and K Schmalenbach (eds), *Vienna Convention on the Law of Treaties* (Springer 2012) 777, 781 ('the principle embodied in Art 41 reflects customary law', but not the Article in its entirety).

[39] *BayWa re Renewable Energy GmbH and BayWa re Asset Holding GmbH v Spain*, ICSID Case No ARB/15/16, Decision on Jurisdiction, Liability and Directions of Quantum, 2 December 2019, para 276 (hereafter *BayWa re v Spain*).

[40] ILC, Draft Articles on the Law of Treaties with Commentaries YILC 1966, Vol II, 187, 235 ('*Paragraph 2* seeks to add a further protection to the parties against illegitimate modifications of the treaty by some of the parties through an *inter se* agreement by requiring them to notify the other parties in advance of their intention to conclude the agreement of the modifications for which it provides').

[41] *BayWa re v Spain* (n 39) para 278 (noting that 'the commentary stresses its importance as a means of notifying states parties to the prior treaty of the intention to modify it, and thus supports the conclusion that the requirement reflects general international law').

[42] C Verburg, 'Modernising the Energy Charter Treaty: An Opportunity to Enhance Legal Certainty in Investor–State Dispute Settlement' (2019) 20 JWIT 425, 446–48; see also M Fitzmaurice and P Merkouris,

14 An example of the application of Articles 40 and 41 in the investment context is the Mauritius Convention, which promulgated new United Nations Commission on International Trade Law (UNCITRAL) Rules on Transparency in Treaty-based Investor–State Arbitration.[43] Those transparency requirements apply to investor–State arbitrations under the UNCITRAL Rules where both States party to the investment treaty are also party to the Mauritius Convention.[44] The result is that if one State party to an investment treaty on which an investor seeks to rely is party to the Mauritius Convention and the other is not, then the relevant earlier UNCITRAL Rules apply without amendment.

15 Although rarely invoked by investment tribunals, Article 40 has been considered by the US Court of Appeals for the Second Circuit, which found that a State could become 'a party to the treaty' within the meaning of Article 40(5) by adhering to an amending agreement, even if it did not adhere to the original treaty. In that case, the State would not be bound by the original agreement, and the amending agreement would constitute a standalone treaty, meaning that the State was not in privity of treaty with another State that had acceded only to the original agreement.[45]

16 Article 41 also enables States to enter into bilateral arrangements in relation to multilateral investment agreements. For instance, in connection with the conclusion of the Trans-Pacific Partnership (TPP), Australia entered into a side agreement with New Zealand agreeing that the investors of each State could not have recourse to the dispute settlement provisions to bring an action against the other State.[46]

17 Investment tribunals have mainly invoked Article 41 in rejecting the argument that Articles 267 and 344 of the Treaty on the Functioning of the European Union (TFEU) concerning the *inter se* relations of Member States of the EU are incompatible with the provisions of intra-EU BITs. A contrary conclusion was reached by the European Court of Justice (ECJ) in *Slovak Republic v Achmea BV*,[47] where the ECJ ruled that the investor–State arbitration clause in Article 8 of the 1991 Netherlands–Slovakia BIT was incompatible with EU law.[48] Its successor judgment, *Moldova v Komstroy LLC*, confirmed that this decision also applied

---

'Re-Shaping Treaties While Balancing Interests of Stability and Change: Critical Issues in the Amendment/Modification/Revision of Treaties' (2018) 20 ARIEL 41, 44.

[43] United Nations Convention on Transparency in Treaty-based Investor–State Arbitration, UNTS No 54749 (no UNTS volume number yet exists), signed New York, 10 December 2014, entry into force 18 October 2017.

[44] Mauritius Convention, Article 2 ('The UNCITRAL Rules on Transparency shall apply to any investor–State arbitration, whether or not initiated under the UNCITRAL Arbitration Rules, in which the respondent is a Party that has not made a relevant reservation ... and the claimant is of a State that is a Party that has not made a relevant reservation').

[45] *Chubb v Asiana Airlines*, 215 F.3d 301 (2nd Cir 2000) (holding that Korea became a party to the Hague Protocol but not the Original Warsaw Convention).

[46] See Letter from Australia's Minister for Trade, Tourism and Investment to New Zealand's Minister for Trade and Export Growth (8 March 2018) <https://www.dfat.gov.au/sites/default/files/sl15-australia-new-zealand-isds.pdf> accessed 3 October 2022, agreeing that 'No investor of New Zealand shall have recourse to dispute settlement against Australia under Chapter 9, Section B (Investor–State Dispute Settlement) of the Agreement' and vice versa with respect to Australian investors. The TPP ultimately did not come into force, while the CPTPP, which did come into force, does not contain an investor–State dispute resolution clause.

[47] *Slovak Republic v Achmea BV*, Case C-284/16 (CJEU CG, 6 March 2018).

[48] ibid paras 58–60 ('Articles 267 and 344 TFEU must be interpreted as precluding a provision in an international agreement concluded between Member States, such as Article 8 of the BIT, under which an investor from one of those Member States may, in the event of a dispute concerning investments in the other Member State, bring proceedings against the latter Member State before an arbitral tribunal whose jurisdiction that Member State has undertaken to accept').

to the ECT.[49] The divergence between the ECJ and the investor–State tribunals stems not from a disagreement on the VCLT, but rather over whether EU law operates on the same plane as public international law (as investment tribunals have concluded),[50] or is part of an autonomous European 'constitutional framework' (as the ECJ has found).[51] Notably, neither *Achmea* nor *Komstroy* even reference the VCLT provisions.[52]

In *Vattenfall AB and others v Federal Republic of Germany*, an investment tribunal was faced with the European Commission's contention that EU law must prevail over investment law. The EC relied on Article 41(1) to argue that EU law, including in particular the investment protection rules and the system of judicial protection, could be interpreted as an *inter se* modification of the ECT. The tribunal rejected this argument, stating that:[53] **18**

> It is unclear what precise modification of the ECT is alleged to have taken place. Moreover, the Tribunal considers that the modification proposed by the EC would be 'prohibited by the treaty', contrary to Article 41(1)(b) VCLT. Specifically, Article 16 ECT prevents the EU Treaties from being construed so as to derogate from more favourable rights of the Investor in Parts III and V ECT, including the right to dispute resolution.

In *BayWa re Renewable Energy GmbH v Spain*, the tribunal emphasized that the EU States never notified the other non-EU members of the ECT of their intention to modify the ECT, as Article 41(2) requires.[54] **19**

Other investment tribunals faced with the same issue have consistently reached the same conclusion, on the basis that EU law does not expressly indicate an intention to modify or amend intra-EU investment treaties.[55] Generally, tribunals have been reluctant to rely only on an alleged inconsistency with a later treaty to indicate an implicit agreement to modify or amend. Instead, the intention to amend must be made more explicit. Thus, the tribunal in *Silver Ridge v Italy* held, in terms recalling Article 41(1)(b)(ii) of the VCLT, that it would be incompatible with the effective execution of the object and purpose of the ECT to allow it to be modified by the EU Treaty. According to the tribunal, the dispute settlement provision in the ECT was the 'most essential element of an investment treaty' and this was decisive to its **20**

---

[49] Case C-2021-655 *Republic of Moldova v Komstroy LLC* (2 September 2021) European Court of Justice (Grand Chamber) (hereafter *Moldova v Komstroy*).

[50] See *Electrabel SA v Hungary*, ICSID Case No ARB/07/19, Decision on Jurisdiction, Applicable Law and Liability, 30 November 2012, paras 4.120–4.122 ('EU law is international law because it is rooted in international treaties; and both Parties accepted, of course, that the EU Treaties are legal instruments under public international law…. Moreover, the Tribunal considers that EU law as a whole is part of the international legal order … all EU legal rules are part of a regional system of international law and therefore have an international legal character'); citing Case 26/62 *NV Algemene Transporten Expeditie Onderneming van Gend & Loos v Netherlands Internal Revenue Administration* [1963] ECR 1, at s B ('The Community constitutes a new legal order of international law for the benefit of which the states have limited their sovereign rights').

[51] *Moldova v Komstroy* (n 49) para 44.

[52] ibid.

[53] *Vattenfall AB and others v Federal Republic of Germany*, ICSID Case No ARB/12/12, Decision on the Achmea Issue, 31 August 2018, para 221.

[54] *BayWa re v Spain* (n 39) para 278.

[55] ibid para 274; *Belenergia SA v Italian Republic*, ICSID Case No ARB/15/40, Award, 6 August 2019, para 335; *Eskosol SpA in liquidazione v Italian Republic*, ICSID Case No ARB/15/50, Decision on Italy's Request for Immediate Termination, 7 May 2019, para 148 (hereafter *Eskosol v Italy*); *Greentech Energy Systems AS et al v Italian Republic*, SCC Case No V 2015/095, Final Award, 23 December 2018, para 353; *Landesbank Baden-Württemberg and others v Kingdom of Spain*, ICSID Case No ARB/15/45, Decision on the 'Intra-EU' Jurisdictional Objection, 25 February 2019, para 185; *SolEs Badajoz GmbH v Kingdom of Spain*, ICSID Case No ARB/15/38, Award, 31 July 2019, para 251.

conclusion that the ECT was more favourable than EU law.[56] It bolstered its conclusion by reference to the non-derogation provision in Article 16 of the ECT.[57]

C. Invalidity of investment treaties

I. General rules

21   This section will provide an overview of the VCLT rules of invalidity, before considering their application in the investment context in three respects. The basic scheme on invalidity is introduced in Article 42 of the VCLT, which provides that the validity of a treaty 'may be impeached only through the application of the present Convention'.[58] This provision, which most likely reflects customary international law,[59] creates a presumption of validity that may only be displaced by reference to the grounds of invalidity exhaustively listed in the VCLT.[60] Pursuant to Article 69, where a treaty is found to be invalid, it is voided and therefore has no legal force.

22   Articles 46–53—together comprising Section 2 of Part V of the VCLT, entitled 'Invalidity of Treaties'—list the grounds upon which a treaty may be invalidated. In brief, these grounds are: manifest violations of provisions of internal law regarding competence to conclude treaties (Article 46); omission to observe specific restrictions on authority to express the consent of a State (Article 47); error (Article 48); fraud (Article 49); corruption of a representative of a State (Article 50); coercion of a representative of a State (Article 51); coercion of a State by the threat or use of force (Article 52);[61] and conflict with a peremptory norm of general international law ('jus cogens') (Article 53).[62] Broadly, these grounds may be classified as involving violations of domestic law (Articles 46 and 47), imperfect consent (Articles 48–52), and improper substance (Article 53). Some but not all of these articles have been recognized as reflecting customary international law,[63] while others crystallize general principles of law, such as defects in consent (or *vices de consentement*) in civil law.[64]

---

[56] *Silver Ridge Power BV v Italian Republic*, ICSID Case No ARB/15/37, Award, 26 February 2021, para 229.
[57] ibid.
[58] Art 42(1) (emphasis added).
[59] MG Kohen and S Heathcote, 'Article 42 Convention of 1969' in O Corten and P Klein (eds), *The Vienna Conventions on the Law of Treaties—A Commentary* (OUP 2011) 1015, 1018; see also *Gabčíkovo-Nagymaros Project (Hungary v Slovakia)* [1997] ICJ Rep 7, para 100 (hereafter *Gabčíkovo-Nagymaros*).
[60] M Schröder, 'Treaties, Validity' in *Max Planck Encyclopedia of Public International Law* (2015), para 3 (hereafter Schröder, 'Treaties'); J Klabbers, 'Part VI Avoiding or Exiting Treaty Commitments: 23 The Validity and Invalidity of Treaties' in DB Hollis (ed), *The Oxford Guide to Treaties* (2nd edn, OUP 2021) 551 (hereafter Klabbers, 'Part VI').
[61] While Articles 51 and 52 refer only to coercion by physical force, in many domestic legal systems, economic coercion is increasingly recognized as a ground for invalidating a contract (eg a situation of economic duress, unconscionable bargain, dependence, or necessity). Nevertheless, this possibility is not expressly recognized in the text of the VCLT. See J Verhoeven, 'Invalidity of Treaties: Anything New in/under the Vienna Conventions?' in E Cannizzaro (ed), *The Law of Treaties Beyond the Vienna Convention* (OUP 2011) 304–05 (hereafter Verhoeven, 'Invalidity of Treaties'); L Caflisch, 'Unequal Treaties' (1992) 35 German YB Int'l L 52, 71–73, (outlining the negotiation history and concluding that 'the yardstick for defining the concept of coercion as used in Article 52 is the "threat or use of force" prohibited by Article 2, paragraph 4, of the Charter, the content of the latter notion being possibly subject to change over time').
[62] In addition, Article 64 provides that '[i]f a new peremptory norm of general international law emerges, any existing treaty which is in conflict with that norm becomes void and terminates'.
[63] For example, Articles 51 and 52 reflect customary international law, see *Fisheries Jurisdiction (Federal Republic of Germany v Iceland)* (Jurisdiction and Admissibility) [1973] ICJ Rep 49, para 24 ('There can be little doubt ... that under contemporary international law an agreement concluded under the threat or use of force is void'); *Dubai-Sharjah Border Arbitration,* Award, 19 October 1981, 91 ILR (1981) 543, 569 ('Articles 51 and 52 of the Vienna Convention of 1969 reflect [...] customary rules of international law which are binding upon States even in the absence of any ratification of that Convention'). See also S Forlati, 'Coercion as a Ground Affecting the Validity of Peace Treaties' in E Cannizzaro (ed), *The Law of Treaties Beyond the Vienna Convention* (OUP 2011) 322–23.
[64] Verhoeven, 'Invalidity of Treaties' (n 61) 301.

Not all of the grounds of invalidity will automatically invalidate the treaty. While certain grounds result in 'absolute' invalidity, rendering the treaty void *ab initio* (Articles 51–53), others result in 'relative' invalidity or voidability, preserving the validity of the treaty until invalidity is invoked (Articles 46–50).[65] The only ground of invalidity that gives rise to automatic termination is where the treaty is deemed to be contrary to a newly emerged *jus cogens* norm.[66] Otherwise, under Article 69, the invalidation of a treaty based on the absence of consent operates retroactively, with the effect that the provisions of that treaty are 'void' and 'have no legal force'. However, acts that have been performed 'in good faith before the invalidity was invoked' are not considered unlawful simply due to the invalidity of the treaty. Thus, the tribunal in *Eskosol S.p.A v Italy* held that an offer to arbitrate in an intra-EU BIT that was accepted prior to the *Achmea* judgment should be considered valid, since any invalidity was not 'manifest' until that date.[67]

Despite the detailed VCLT provisions on invalidity, they have received only limited treatment in State practice, judicial and arbitral decisions, and academic writing. It remains relatively rare not only for treaties to be declared invalid, but even for parties to argue that they should be.[68] The same holds true in the investment context, where there is also a dearth of jurisprudence on invalidity. To date, only three of the provisions on invalidity have received any meaningful treatment by tribunals: Articles 46, 50, and 53. These are addressed below.

II. Article 46: Provisions of internal law regarding competence to conclude treaties

Article 46. Provisions of internal law regarding competence to conclude treaties

1. A State may not invoke the fact that its consent to be bound by a treaty has been expressed in violation of a provision of its internal law regarding competence to conclude treaties as invalidating its consent unless that violation was manifest and concerned a rule of its internal law of fundamental importance.
2. A violation is manifest if it would be objectively evident to any State conducting itself in the matter in accordance with normal practice and in good faith.

Article 46 reflects customary law.[69] It establishes two pre-requisites for a treaty to be invalidated on the basis of a violation of internal law. First, the violation must be 'manifest', and second, the rule of internal law must be of 'fundamental importance'.[70]

---

[65] Schröder, 'Treaties' (n 60) para 4.
[66] VCLT, Article 64; see also *AMF Aircraftleasing Meier & Fischer GmbH & Co. KG v Czech Republic*, PCA Case No 2017/15, Final Award, 11 May 2020, para 385.
[67] See *Eskosol v Italy* (n 55) para 206.
[68] Klabbers, 'Part VI' (n 60) 545.
[69] *Case Concerning the Arbitral Award of 31 July 1989 (Guinea-Bissau v Senegal)*, (1990) 83 ILR 1, para 55 (hereafter *Guinea-Bissau v Senegal*) (noting that this rule reflects the principle of good faith); *Land and Maritime Boundary between Cameroon and Nigeria (Cameroon v Nigeria)* (Counter-claims) [2002] ICJ Rep 103, para 258 (hereafter *Cameroon v Nigeria*) (impliedly recognizing its customary status); see also M Bothe, 'Article 46 Convention of 1969' in O Corten and P Klein (eds), *The Vienna Conventions on the Law of Treaties—A Commentary* (OUP 2011) 1090, 1092.
[70] See also, ibid, articulating the same two-part test, finding that only 'une violation grave et evidente du droit interne' (a serious and obvious violation of domestic law) justified a declaration of invalidity of a treaty: *Guinea-Bissau v Senegal* (n 69) para 55.

26 Article 46(2) defines 'manifest', grounding its meaning in 'normal practice' and 'good faith'. The International Court of Justice (ICJ) in *Cameroon v Nigeria* has suggested that a manifest violation may exist only if a rule has been 'properly publicized', since 'there is no general legal obligation for States to keep themselves informed of legislative and constitutional developments in other States which are or may become important for the international relations of these States'.[71] Some domestic courts have suggested that there is a 'basic due diligence' obligation on the domestic treaty-making procedures of prospective treaty partners.[72] At the same time, the Swiss Federal Court has confirmed that the 'manifest' test under Article 46 requires that the incompatibility must be 'objectively recognisable', not only from the point of view of the particular legal system allegedly violated.[73]

27 There is no clear test to determine when a rule will be of 'fundamental importance', though it is often presumed that such rules must be constitutional.[74] Crucially, the rules must be *substantively* constitutional rather than merely being designated as such.[75] At the same time, Klabbers has observed that it would be 'untenable' to limit Article 46 only to violations of constitutional provisions, particularly for countries such as the United Kingdom that do not have written constitutions, because it would wrongly compel States to articulate treaty-making procedures in their constitutions.[76]

28 Investment tribunals have relied on Article 46 for the principle that actions by State actors in violation of their domestic law should be treated as binding where third parties would reasonably perceive such acts as being binding. For example, in *Duke Energy v Peru*, an ICSID tribunal referred to Article 46 to determine whether the Respondent State was estopped from denying—in other words, was bound by—representations made by a sub-division of that State in violation of internal law. Using the language of Article 46(2), the tribunal found that a State would be bound by a representation that, '*in accordance with normal practice and good faith*, is perceived by third parties as an expression of the State's position, and as being incompatible with the possibility of being contradicted in the future'.[77]

29 The rule in Article 46 has attained special importance in the investment context in the aftermath of the ECJ's *Achmea* decision.[78] Per *Achmea*, EU law, which operates as internal law for each Member State, prohibits EU Member States from entering into investment arbitration agreements *inter se*. This gives rise to the question of whether intra-EU investment arbitration clauses—contained in bilateral agreements such as BITs as well as multilateral agreements such as the ECT—are invalid for having been concluded in violation of 'internal law regarding competence to conclude treaties' in the language of Article 46(1) of the VCLT. Thus far, investment arbitration tribunals have uniformly answered this question in the negative.

---

[71] *Cameroon v Nigeria* (n 69) para 266.
[72] *Banful v Attorney General*, J1/7/2016 [2017] GHASC 10 (Ghana, 10 June 2017); Klabbers, 'Part VI' (n 60) 556.
[73] *Federal Court V v Regierungsrat des Kantons St Gallen* (1994) ATF 120 Ib 360, 365–66.
[74] See, eg, *Cameroon v Nigeria* (n 69) para 265 ('The rules concerning the authority to sign treaties for a State are constitutional rules of fundamental importance').
[75] Schröder, 'Treaties' (n 60) para 7.
[76] Klabbers, 'Part VI' (n 60) 555.
[77] *Duke Energy v Peru*, ICSID Case No ARB/03/28, Award, 18 August 2008, para 249 (emphasis in original).
[78] See above, para 11.

In *Blusun S.A. et ors v Italian Republic*, the ICSID tribunal relied on Article 46 to reject **30** the argument of the respondent, Italy, that the ECT was invalid as Italy was not competent under EU law to enter into it. The tribunal read a temporal limitation into Article 46, observing that '[n]o limitation on the competence of the EU Member States was communicated *at the time that the ECT was signed*'.[79] Accordingly, objections to violations of internal law may be considered waived if they are not discovered or communicated at the time a treaty is signed. Further, the tribunal remarked that '[n]othing in the text of the ECT' suggested that Member States lacked competence to individually enter into the treaty,[80] and that 'an allocation of competence that the EC says can be *inferred* from a set of EU laws and regulations' was insufficient to invalidate a treaty.[81] By highlighting the absence of clear rules and discounting mere inferences, the tribunal emphasized the requirement of a 'manifest' violation. Furthermore, as a number of subsequent tribunals have emphasized, per the terms of Article 46(2), any incompatibility with EU law was not 'objectively evident' at the time most intra-EU Treaties were concluded, given the wide-ranging debate on the issue.[82]

In *Eskosol S.p.A. in liquidazione v Italian Republic*, Italy filed a request to immediately ter- **31** minate the arbitration in light of the *Achmea* decision. The tribunal dismissed the request. Referring to Article 46, the tribunal noted that the alleged violation of EU law 'could not be considered as "manifest" *before* the Achmea Judgment'.[83] As in *Blusun*, the tribunal focused on the temporal element of capacity in Article 46. A similar approach was applied in *BayWa r.e. Renewable Energy GmbH v Spain*.[84] Consistent with Article 6 of the VCLT, Spain's capacity was to be presumed in the absence of any communication to the contrary at the time of signature. The tribunal also noted that the majority of the EU laws and regulations said to allocate responsibility away from the EU Member States came into force after the conclusion of the ECT. As such, the tribunal held that, at the time the ECT was signed, the competence to enter into investment treaties was a shared one.[85]

Two conclusions may be drawn from these investment cases. First, the critical moment for **32** assessing whether a State has capacity pursuant to both Articles 6 and 46 of the VCLT is at the time that the agreement was entered into. Second, tribunals will be less likely to infer from complex arrangements (such as those that govern the allocation of the investment competence under EU law) the presence of a 'manifest' violation necessary to invalidate a treaty under Article 46.[86] These considerations appear to be in keeping with—and a further development of—general international law on the competence to conclude treaties, including the aforementioned ICJ judgment in *Cameroon v Nigeria*.[87]

---

[79] *Blusun S.A., Jean-Pierre Lecorcier and Michael Stein v Italian Republic*, ICSID Case No ARB/14/3, Award, 27 December 2016, para 283 (emphasis added).
[80] ibid para 282.
[81] ibid para 283 (emphasis added).
[82] See, eg, *AMF v Czech Republic*, PCA Case No 2017-15, Final Award, 11 May 2020, paras 383–84; *Raiffeisen Bank International AG and Raiffeisenbank Austria D.D. v Republic of Croatia*, ICSID Case No ARB/17/34, Decision on the Respondent's Jurisdictional Objections, 30 September 2020, paras 246–48.
[83] *Eskosol v Italy* (n 55) para 191 (emphasis added).
[84] *BayWa r.e v Spain* (n 39) para 249.
[85] ibid.
[86] See Schröder, 'Treaties' (n 60) para 8, arriving at the same conclusion in the general international law context ('Given the complexity of EC internal rules, if the EC enters into a treaty in breach of those rules any internal irregularity is most unlikely to be manifest').
[87] See above, para 25; citing *Cameroon v Nigeria* (n 69) para 266.

III. Article 50: Corruption of a representative of a State

Article 50. Corruption of a representative of a State

If the expression of a State's consent to be bound by a treaty has been procured through the corruption of its representative directly or indirectly by another negotiating State, the State may invoke such corruption as invalidating its consent to be bound by the treaty.

33 Article 50 permits the invalidation of treaties procured by acts of corruption committed by any of the State parties. The use of the term 'corruption' (as opposed to 'fraud', already included in Article 49) implies that only acts of a substantial gravity are covered by Article 50.[88] Whether or not Article 50 reflects customary international law,[89] it may in any case be said to reflect general principles of law based on domestic practice, as recognized in the *World Duty Free v Kenya* case discussed below.[90]

34 In investor–State disputes, corruption is most commonly alleged to have been committed by investors in the procurement of contracts with the Government. To account for this reality, some tribunals have transplanted the principles underlying Article 50 of the VCLT to the contractual context.

35 In *Niko Resources v Bangladesh*, the Respondent State alleged that the claimant had procured through corrupt means another Government contract (called the 'JVA'), which was not the contract at issue in the dispute.[91] Though the Respondent State did not seek to invalidate the JVA on this basis, it argued that the claimant's claim was barred in accordance with the 'clean hands' principle. The tribunal relied on Article 50 of the VCLT, observing that the principle that 'a treaty may be avoided by invalidating the consent of the victim of corruption … may be taken as a general principle not only of public international law but as a general principle of law and as such applicable to contracts'.[92] However, the tribunal noted that since the alleged bribery did not procure the JVA on which the claimant's claims were based, 'there is no link of causation between the established acts of corruption and the conclusion of the agreements'.[93] Furthermore, the tribunal observed that the respondents had not even sought the invalidation of the agreement, seeking only that the investor's claims be ruled inadmissible.[94]

36 As this case highlights, Article 50 of the VCLT requires that a causal link be identified between the corruption and the conclusion of the treaty or contract, allowing a State to vitiate its consent to be bound if it 'has been procured through the corruption of its representative'.

37 A notorious example of this is found in the *World Duty Free v Republic of Kenya* case. There, the claimant's sole witness admitted to paying a US $2 million bribe to the President of Kenya

---

[88] SE Nahlik, 'The Grounds of Invalidity and Termination of Treaties' (1971) 65 AJIL 736, 743.
[89] Klabbers, 'Part VI' (n 60) 11 (of PDF) ('… it is difficult to maintain that the provisions on error, fraud, and corruption have crystallized into customary international law. Useful as such provisions no doubt are, practice would simply seem to be too scarce to meaningfully speak of customary international law'); cf J-P Cot, 'Article 50 Convention of 1969' in O Corten and P Klein (eds), *The Vienna Conventions on the Law of Treaties—A Commentary* (OUP 2011) 1169, 1173 ('One would consequently consider the rule of Article 50 as a rule of customary law, made more specific and shaped by the Vienna Convention').
[90] But see Verhoeven, 'Invalidity of Treaties' (n 61) 303 ('It would … be hazardous to affirm the declaratory character of Article 48 and Article 50 if it is allegedly based on the existence of a general practice accepted as law.… Domestic laws … do not clearly confirm that the contract or at least most of the contracts reached through corruption are void').
[91] *Niko Resources v Bangladesh*, ICSID Case No ARB/10/11 and ICSID Case No ARB/10/18, Jurisdiction, 19 August 2013.
[92] ibid para 445.
[93] ibid paras 454–55.
[94] ibid para 456.

in order to obtain the investment contract at issue.[95] The tribunal held that as a matter of 'transnational public policy' and domestic law, claims based on contracts obtained by corruption cannot be upheld. The tribunal did not refer to the VCLT to support its conclusion, perhaps because it was constituted under an investment contract governed by English and Kenyan law, not an investment treaty governed by international law.

As the tribunal in *Metal-Tech v Uzbekistan* recognized 'corruption is by essence difficult to establish [and] … it is thus generally admitted that it can be shown through circumstantial evidence'.[96] While some tribunals have insisted on a more stringent standard of proof, requiring 'clear and convincing' evidence of fraud or corruption,[97] the emerging view is that some flexibility is necessary given the efforts taken to conceal fraud or corruption, which may thus be established on the balance of probabilities.[98] Moreover, many investment tribunals do not even get to the question of whether the investment contract is vitiated by fraud or corruption, instead finding that the threshold jurisdictional requirement for an 'investment' complying with domestic legal requirements has not been satisfied.[99]

IV. Article 53: Treaties conflicting with peremptory norms of general international law

Article 53. Treaties conflicting with a peremptory norm of general international law ('jus cogens')

A treaty is void if, at the time of its conclusion, it conflicts with a peremptory norm of general international law. For the purposes of the present Convention, a peremptory

---

[95] *World Duty Free v Republic of Kenya*, ICSID Case No ARB/007, Award, 4 October 2006; see also Constantine Partasides, 'Proving Corruption in International Arbitration: A Balanced Standard for the Real World' (2010) 25(1) ICSID Review – FILJ 47.

[96] *Metal-Tech Ltd v Republic of Uzbekistan*, ICSID Case No ARB/10/3, Award, 4 October 2013, para 243; see also *Liman Caspian Oil BV and NCL Dutch Investment BV v Republic of Kazakhstan*, ICSID Case No ARB/07/14, 22 June 2010, para 422 ('The Tribunal is aware that it is very difficult to prove corruption because secrecy is inherent in such cases. Corruption can take various forms but in very few cases can reliable and valid proof of it be brought which is sufficient as a basis for a resulting award declaring liability').

[97] *Waguih Elie George Siag and Clorinda Vecchi v The Arab Republic of Egypt*, ICSID Case No ARB/05/15, Award, 1 June 2009, para 326; *Getma International and others v Republic of Guinea*, ICSID Case No ARB/11/29, Award, 16 August 2016, para 184; *Karkey Karadeniz Elektrik Uretim A.S. v Islamic Republic of Pakistan*, ICSID Case No ARB/13/1, Award, 22 August 2017, para 492 ('the seriousness of the accusation of corruption in the present case, including the fact that it involves officials at the highest level of the Pakistani Government at the time, requires clear and convincing evidence. There is indeed a large consensus among international tribunals regarding the need for a high standard of proof of corruption'); *EDF (Services) Ltd v Romania*, ICSID Case No ARB/05/13, Award, 8 October 2009, para 221 ('[t]he evidence before the Tribunal in the instant case concerning the alleged solicitation of a bribe is far from being clear and convincing').

[98] *Unión Fenosa Gas, S.A. v Arab Republic of Egypt*, ICSID Case No ARB/14/4, Award, 31 August 2018, para 7.52 ('although th[e] allegations [of corruption] amount to serious criminal misconduct, the Tribunal considers that the standard of proof remains "the balance of probabilities"'); see also *Libananco Holdings Co. Limited v the Republic of Turkey*, ICSID ARB/06/8, Award, 2 September 2011, para 125; *Sanum Investments Limited v Lao People's Democratic Republic*, PCA Case No 2013-13, Award, 6 August 2019, paras 138, 147, and 156; *Lao Holdings NV v Lao People's Democratic Republic*, ICSID Case No ARB(AF)/12/6, Award, 6 August 2019, paras 139, 148, and 157.

[99] See *Inceysa Vallisoletana S.L. v Republic of El Salvador*, ICSID Case No ARB/03/26 Award, 2 August 2006, para 244 ('The clear and obvious evidence of the violations committed by Inceysa during the bidding process lead this Tribunal to decide that Inceysa's investment cannot, under any circumstances, enjoy the protection of the BIT. … No legal system based on rational grounds allows the party that committed a chain of clearly illegal acts to benefit from them'). Cf *Liman Caspian Oil BV and NCL Dutch Investment BV v Republic of Kazakhstan*, ICSID Case No ARB/07/14, 22 June 2010, para 187 ('the question of legality might well be relevant to the merits, but it would not have preclusive effect at the level of jurisdiction').

norm of general international law is a norm accepted and recognized by the international community of States as a whole as a norm from which no derogation is permitted and which can be modified only by a subsequent norm of general international law having the same character.

39 Article 53 is not universally recognized as reflecting customary international law.[100] Notably, France declined to sign the VCLT on the basis that Article 53 was imprecise and did not reflect custom.[101] Nevertheless, a number of cases have confirmed the (theoretical) relevance of *jus cogens* norms in the investment treaty context. While tribunals routinely recognize that such norms must take precedence over any conflicting treaty provisions,[102] none have declared a BIT invalid on this basis. *Jus cogens* norms have traditionally been viewed as a narrow and finite set of prohibitions, such as prohibitions on aggression, genocide, slavery, torture, and apartheid.[103] It is unlikely that provisions contrary to these prohibitions will find a place in modern investment treaties. Nevertheless, some tribunals have shown a willingness to expand the otherwise bounded set of peremptory norms to encompass contemporary developments in international law, including the expansion and elevation of international human rights law.

40 The investment award of *EDF v Argentina* is illustrative. EDF, a French company, invested in electricity distribution in Argentina. Subsequently, Argentina introduced 'emergency tariff measures', reducing the tariffs that EDF could collect. When EDF initiated arbitration alleging violation of the France–Argentina BIT, Argentina invoked Article 53 of the VCLT as a defence. Argentina argued that its reduction of tariffs was necessary to guarantee the free enjoyment of basic human right for Argentinian citizens, including the right to life.[104] Argentina further claimed that these human rights were *jus cogens* norms, and that the tribunal could not enforce the BIT in a manner inconsistent with such norms. The tribunal readily accepted its duty to 'be sensitive to international *jus cogens* norms, *including basic principles of human rights*'.[105] But it was unable to accept that Argentina's measures were necessary to guarantee human rights. This case thus seemingly included 'basic principles of human rights' within the traditionally narrow set of *jus cogens* norms, potentially opening the door for respondent States to argue in future for more forceful applications of Article 53 in the investment context.

41 Tribunals have also shown a willingness to apply Article 53 to questions other than the invalidity of treaties. In *Methanex v USA*, the tribunal applied Article 53 to determine the validity not of a treaty, but of a domestic interpretation of a treaty. Here, too, the tribunal looked beyond the traditional category of *jus cogens* norms in its analysis. The issue was whether the US FTC had issued an interpretation excluding the principle of non-discrimination from the North Atlantic

---

[100] But see E Suy, 'Article 53 Convention of 1969' in O Corten and P Klein (eds), *The Vienna Conventions on the Law of Treaties—A Commentary* (OUP 2011) 1224, 1226 (stating that it has, over time, acquired the status of customary international law).

[101] See *Assoc. France Palestine (AFP) and organisation Libre de Palestine (OLP) v Alstom and Veolia*, Versailles Court of Appeal (France), 22 March 2013, No 11/05331; cf 'East German Expropriation Case' 112 BVerfGE 1, 26 October 2004, 2 BvR 955/00, Federal Constitutional Court (Germany), paras 118 and 120–21 (recognizing the rules on peremptory norms set out in the VCLT).

[102] See *Urbaser v Argentina*, ICSID Case No ARB/07/26, Award, 8 December 2016, para 1203 ('[jus cogens] norms must certainly prevail over any contrary provisions in the BIT, as per the express statement in Article 53 of the Vienna Convention').

[103] Klabbers, 'Part VI' (n 60) 562–63.

[104] *EDF International SA, SAUR International S.A. and Leon Participaciones Argentinas SA v Argentine Republic*, ICSID Case No ARB/03/23, Award, 11 June 2012, para 192.

[105] ibid para 909.

Free Trade Agreement (NAFTA), and, if so, whether such interpretation would be valid. The tribunal noted that *if* the FTC interpretation had excluded non-discrimination from NAFTA, such decision 'would, arguably, violate a *jus cogens* and thus be void under Article 53 of the Vienna Convention on the Law of Treaties'.[106] Ultimately, however, the tribunal found that the FTC had not issued such an interpretation.

D. Termination and suspension of investment treaties

I. General rules

Termination and unilateral withdrawal have gained particular salience in recent years. In 2019, one commentator described the issue of unilateral withdrawal as 'omnipresent' in international law, heralded by the United Kingdom's exit from the European Union and the (now reversed) withdrawal of the United States from the Paris Agreement on climate change.[107] But unilateral withdrawal has long been a hot topic in the context of investment treaties, following the so-called 'backlash' against the legitimacy of the international investment regime.[108]

The VCLT has a largely residual role in regulating the termination and suspension of treaties, since most already contain their own specific rules. States remain the 'masters' of their treaties.[109] This is certainly true in the investment context.[110] The VCLT provisions reinforce the primacy of the treaty language in this regard. Articles 54 and 57 of the VCLT provide that termination, withdrawal, or suspension of a treaty may take place 'in conformity with the terms of the treaty' or with the express consent of all parties. Similarly, the rules in Articles 70 and 72 providing that termination and suspension 'release[] the parties from any obligation further to perform the treaty' (as long as the treaty remains suspended), are also expressly subject to the terms of the treaty.

The VCLT nevertheless sets out default termination and suspension rules, as well as a written notification and dispute resolution process to be followed with respect to invalidity,

---

[106] *Methanex Corporation v United States of America*, Final Award, 3 August 2005, pt IV—ch C, para 24.
[107] C McLachlan, 'The Assault on International Adjudication and the Limits of Withdrawal' (2019) 68 ICLQ 499, 501; see also LR Helfer, 'Terminating Treaties' in Duncan B Hollis (ed), *The Oxford Guide to Treaties* (2nd edn, OUP 2021) 624, 635.
[108] See, eg, SD Frankl, 'The Legitimacy Crisis in Investment Arbitration: Privatizing Public International Law through Inconsistent Decisions' (2005) 73(3) Fordham L Rev 1521; M Waibel and others (eds), *The Backlash Against Investment Arbitration* (Kluwer 2010); CH Brower II and JK Sharpe, 'The Coming Crisis in the Global Adjudicatory System' (2003) 19 Arb Int'l L 415. The susceptibility of the investment regime to such backlash was first identified by J Paulsson, 'Arbitration without Privity' (1995) 10 ICSID Rev 232, 257 ('Arbitration without privity is a delicate mechanism. A single incident of an adventurist arbitrator going beyond the proper scope of his jurisdiction in a sensitive case may be sufficient to generate a backlash').
[109] J Tropper and A Reinisch, 'The 2020 Termination Agreement of Intra-EU BITs and Its Effect on Investment Arbitration in the EU-A Public International Law Analysis of the Termination Agreement' (2022) 16 Austrian YB Int'l Arb 301, 316 (hereafter Tropper and Reinisch, 'The 2020 Termination Agreement') ('As a starting point, the principle that the states remain "masters of the treaty" particularly affects the termination of treaties as "the VCLT establishes party autonomy as the central principle for the termination of a treaty and the legal consequences arising therefrom"'); citing C Binder, 'A Treaty Law Perspective on Intra-EU BITs' (2016) 17 JWIT 964, 977.
[110] See A Tzanakopoulos, 'Denunciation of the ICSID Convention under the General International Law of Treaties' in R Hofmann and CJ Tams (eds), *International Investment Law and General International Law—From Clinical Isolation to Systemic Integration?* (Nomos 2010) 3, 10 ('General rules on treaty termination cannot, however, be the starting point of the debate. In fact, on the face of it, they might add little to the special rules found in the ICSID Convention itself, which addresses questions of withdrawal and its effect'; 'residual fallback' to general international law 'seems ... required.... the provisions of Article 70 of VCLT may apply as customary law, and may indeed not be superseded by the relevant special provisions of the ICSID Convention'); see also T Voon and

termination, withdrawal, or suspension under the provisions of the VCLT.[111] Under Article 56(1) of the VCLT, a treaty that is silent on the topic may not be subject to denunciation or withdrawal unless '(a) it is established that the parties intended to admit the possibility of denunciation or withdrawal; or (b) a right of denunciation or withdrawal may be implied by the nature of the treaty'. Termination may also occur by way of a later, incompatible treaty relating to the same subject matter (Article 59); in response to a material breach by one party (Article 60); or due to the supervening impossibility of performance (i.e. *force majeure*) or a fundamental change in circumstances (Articles 61, 62). In this respect, the VCLT largely reflects customary international law.[112]

45 This entry focuses on Articles 54, 56, and 59, which have received the most attention in the investment context to date, while going on briefly to discuss Articles 58, and 60 through 68 for completeness.

II. Article 54(a): Termination by the terms of the treaty (unilateral termination)

Article 54. Termination of or withdrawal from a treaty under its provisions or by consent of the parties

The termination of a treaty or the withdrawal of a party may take place:
(a) in conformity with the provisions of the treaty; or
(b) at any time by consent of all the parties after consultation with the other contracting States.

46 Although is not clear whether Article 54 has customary status, it has been applied by investment tribunals.[113] Article 54 provides for termination of or withdrawal from a treaty under its provisions or by consent of both the parties. Accordingly, it affirms that unilateral termination or withdrawal is permitted, where carried out under the terms of the treaty. But the VCLT does not itself permit unilateral termination, reflecting the general reticence of international law to allow unilateral action to bring treaty obligations to an end.[114]

47 Almost every investment treaty accords its States parties the right to terminate unilaterally after a mandated notice period.[115] For instance, the Turkey–Bangladesh BIT, which entered

---

AD Mitchell, 'Denunciation, Termination and Survival: The Interplay of Treaty Law and International Investment Law' (2016) 31(2) ICSID Rev 413, 414 (hereafter Voon and Mitchell, 'Denunciation') ('International investment agreements (IIAs) represent a more specific law pertaining to two (or more) countries. Accordingly, to the extent of any inconsistency (and assuming no violation of a *jus cogens* (non-derogable) norm of international law), IIAs prevail as *lex specialis* over the *lex generalis* of treaty law'); see generally J Pauwelyn, *Conflict of Norms in Public International Law: How WTO Law Relates to Other Rules of International Law* (CUP 2003) 391–92.

[111] VCLT, Articles 56(2), 57.
[112] *Gabčíkovo* (n 59) para 46; *Fisheries Jurisdiction (United Kingdom and Northern Ireland v Iceland)* (Jurisdiction) [1973] ICJ Rep 3, para 36; *Fisheries Jurisdiction (Germany v Iceland)* (n 63) para 36; SI Lekkas and A Tzanakopoulos, '*Pacta sunt servanda* Versus Flexibility in the Suspension and Termination of Treaties' in CJ. Tams, A Tzanakopoulos and A Zimmermann (eds), *Research Handbook on the Law of Treaties* (Edward Elgar 2014) 317 (hereafter Lekkas and Tzanakopoulos, '*Pacta sunt servanda*').
[113] V Chapaux, 'Article 54 Convention of 1969' in O Corten and P Klein (eds), *The Vienna Conventions on the Law of Treaties—A Commentary* (OUP 2011) 1236, 1238.
[114] Lekkas and Tzanakopoulos, '*Pacta sunt servanda*' (n 112) 314; A McNair, *The Law of Treaties* (OUP 1961) 493.
[115] According to the UNCTAD IIA Mapping Project, 98 per cent of the 2,575 treaties surveyed include a unilateral termination clause, all of which mandate a notice period before the treaty can be terminated. The real number

into force in 2019, permits either Contracting Party to terminate unilaterally by giving one year's written notice, but only after the treaty has been in force for ten years.[116] The few treaties that do not include termination clauses are mainly older treaties that have minimalist drafting and tend to omit any provisions on termination, suspension, or withdrawal altogether.[117]

A handful of States have embarked on a programme to terminate unilaterally some or all of their investment treaties,[118] including Ecuador,[119] India,[120] Indonesia,[121] South Africa, and Venezuela.[122] All of these States subsequently began renegotiating new investment treaties with more State-centric terms. The termination of intra-EU BITs by EU countries is another example, dealt with further below. **48**

Three States, Bolivia, Venezuela, and Ecuador, have also withdrawn from the ICSID Convention, although Ecuador rejoined in 2021.[123] In the case of Ecuador, its 2009 withdrawal from ICSID also included a purported withdrawal from consent for any ICSID arbitrations commenced henceforth.[124] But this attempt to unilaterally terminate the consent **49**

---

may be even higher, since the authors identified a number of other treaties that were not included in this list, but which contain a unilateral termination clause, such as the Ethiopia–Yemen BIT, art 11(2); or the Finland–Mongolia BIT, Article 17(2).

[116] Agreement between the Government of the Republic of Turkey and the Government of the People's Republic of Bangladesh concerning the Reciprocal Promotion and Protection of Investments (signed in 2012, entered into force 2019), Article 13(3).

[117] See, for instance, the Treaty between the United States of America and the Republic of Belarus Concerning the Encouragement and Reciprocal Protection of Investment (Belarus–United States BIT 1994, signed but not in force); Accord Entre La Republique du Burundi et La Republique Federale Islamique des Comores Concernant la Promotion et la Protection Reciproques des Investissement (Comoros–Burundi BIT 2001, signed but not in force); Agreement between the Government of the Socialist Republic of Vietnam and the Government of the Republic of Latvia for the Promotion and Protection of Investments (Vietnam–Latvia BIT 1995, in force).

[118] Notably, Brazil is not included in this list since the investment treaties it entered into in the 1990s were never ratified, following opposition in parliament. See D Campello and LB Lemos, 'The Non-Ratification of Bilateral Investment Treaties in Brazil: A Story of Conflict in a Land of Cooperation' (2015) 22 Rev Int'l Pol Econ 1055; see also H Choer Moraes and F Hees, 'Breaking the BIT Mold: Brazil's Pioneering Approach to Investment Agreements' (2018) 112 AJIL Unbound 197, noting that Brazil has since entered into three international investment agreements in the form of 'Cooperation and Facilitation Investment Agreements', which provide only for inter-State (not investor–State) arbitration

[119] Between 2008 and 2017, Ecuador withdrew from all twenty-six of its bilateral investment treaties. See IISD, 'Ecuador Denounces its Remaining 16 BITs and Publishes CAITISA Audit Report' (12 June 2017) <https://www.iisd.org/itn/2017/06/12/ecuador-denounces-its-remaining-16-bits-and-publishes-caitisa-audit-report/> accessed 14 April 2021. Many of these BITs remain in effect due to the sunset period in the treaties. In 2018, Ecuador began negotiating new BITs with sixteen countries, see 'Ecuador Begins Talks Over New BITs' *GAR* (23 February 2018) <https://globalarbitrationreview.com/ecuador-begins-talks-over-new-bits> accessed 14 April 2021. In 2019, it concluded a new BIT with Brazil in 2019, which has not yet come into force.

[120] In 2016, India terminated BITs with fifty-seven States, where the initial treaty term had or was soon to expire, sending 'joint interpretative statements' to the remaining twenty-five States with whom it had BITs. See K Singh and B Ilge, 'Remodeling India's Investment Treaty Regime' *The Wire* (16 July 2016) <https://thewire.in/trade/remodeling-indias-investment-treaty-regime> accessed 14 April 2021. India is seeking to promote the terms of its new model BIT, rather than renouncing the investment regime altogether. It has since signed BITs with Brazil (2020), Kyrgyzstan (2019), and Belarus (2018), none of which are yet in force.

[121] Between 2014 and 2017, Indonesia unilaterally terminated BITs with twenty-five States. See N Bernasconi-Osterwalder and S Brewin, 'Terminating a Bilateral Investment Treaty', *IISD Best Practices Series*, March 2020, 8.

[122] LR Helfer, 'Terminating Treaties' in DB Hollis (ed), *The Oxford Guide to Treaties* (2nd edn, OUP 2021) 624, 635.

[123] ICSID, 'Database of ICSID Member States' <https://icsid.worldbank.org/en/Pages/about/Database-of-Member-States.aspx> accessed 23 February 2022. Ecuador ratified the Convention again effective 3 September 2021.

[124] *Murphy Exploration and Production Company International v Republic of Ecuador*, ICSID Case No ARB/08/4, Jurisdiction, 15 December 2010, para 82 ('Any instrument containing the Republic of Ecuador's previously expressed will to submit that class of disputes to the jurisdiction of the Centre, which has not been perfected by the express and explicit consent of the other party given prior to the date of submission of the present notification, is hereby withdrawn by the Republic of Ecuador with immediate effect as of this date').

to arbitration already granted in its BITs was given short shrift by the tribunal in *Murphy v Ecuador*, which considered that Ecuador was 'pretend[ing] to achieve legal effects not falling under the scope of [Article 54]'.[125] The tribunal stated by reference to Article 54 that: 'the withdrawal, termination or amendment of the BIT must be governed by the provisions contained in that treaty, and in a suppletory manner, by general International Law, as codified in the Vienna Convention on the Law of Treaties'.[126] The tribunal then gave priority to the provisions on termination in the particular BIT, which required a one-year notice period for unilateral termination and provided a ten-year sunset period. Ecuador could therefore not avoid ICSID jurisdiction to which it had already consented under the BIT merely by withdrawing from the ICSID Convention.[127]

III. Article 54(b): Termination by consent (mutual termination)

50 Although many investment treaties contain a unilateral termination clause, most do not provide for a mutual termination clause (i.e. termination by consent). Such a clause might appear to be superfluous since Article 54(b) of the VCLT already confirms that termination or withdrawal may occur 'at any time' by consent of all parties. But the Convention does not resolve the question whether mutual termination can override a sunset or survival clause already set out in the treaty. The purpose of a sunset clause is to provide a 'counterbalance' to the automaticity of termination or withdrawal, particularly in the context of third-party beneficiaries (such as investors), providing that effects of the treaty shall endure for a period after termination.[128] By contrast, the VCLT fails to grapple with the issue of rights acquired by third-party, non-State beneficiaries of an investment treaty, such as investors.

51 Some commentators have proposed that such a sunset clause can be circumvented by first amending the treaty to delete it, and then terminating the treaty, the 'two-step' approach.[129] The Czech Republic purported to take this approach in 2009 and 2010, agreeing to first modify the sunset clause and then terminate its BITs with each of Malta, Denmark, Italy, and Slovenia, with immediate effect.[130] In other cases, States have agreed to amend the BIT to shorten (but not override altogether) the applicable sunset period, as occurred in the case of Australia's termination of its BITs with Vietnam, Peru, and Mexico following the entry into force of the CPTPP.[131] Some commentators have suggested that if the parties agree to

---

[125] ibid para 84.
[126] ibid para 86.
[127] VCLT, Article 54(1)(a) provides that termination or withdrawal from a treaty may take place 'in conformity with the provisions of the treaty'; see also CP Evans, 'Going, Going, Gone? Assessing Iran's Possible Grounds for Withdrawal from the Treaty on the Non-Proliferation of Nuclear Weapons' (2021) 26 JCSL 309, 316–17.
[128] Lekkas and Tzanakopoulos, '*Pacta sunt servanda*' (n 112) 338.
[129] Voon and Mitchell, 'Denunciation' (n 110) 414; T Voon, A Mitchell and J Munro, 'Parting Ways: The Impact of Mutual Termination of Investment Treaties on Investor Rights' (2014) 29(2) ICSID Rev 451 (hereafter Voon, Mitchell and Munro, 'Parting Ways').
[130] C Titi, 'Most-Favoured Nation Treatment: Survival Clauses and Reform of International Investment Law' (2016) (33)(5) J Int'l Arb 425, 436; see also N Lavranos, 'The End of Intra-EU BITs is Nearing' *Prac L Arb Blog* (13 May 2016) <http://arbitrationblog.practicallaw.com/the-end-of-intra-eu-bits-is-nearing/> accessed 14 April 2021; LE Peterson, 'Czech Republic Terminates Investment Treaties in Such a Way As to Cast Doubt on Residual Legal Protection for Existing Investments' (*Investment Arbitration Reporter*, 1 February 2011)<https://www.iareporter.com/articles/czech-republic-terminates-investment-treaties-in-such-a-way-as-to-cast-doubt-on-residual-legal-protection-for-existing-investments/> accessed 16 April 2021.
[131] Voon and Mitchell, 'Denunciation' (n 110) 427.

terminate a treaty by consent then the survival clause is automatically extinguished without the need for an express agreement to that effect.[132]

There are also cases in which States have mutually agreed to immediate termination, purporting to override a sunset clause. Argentina and Indonesia purported to do so in 2015.[133] But perhaps the most striking example is the Agreement for the Termination of BITs between the Member States of the European Union (*EU Termination Agreement*),[134] which entered into force on 29 August 2020.[135] The EU Termination Agreement is the consequence of the *Achmea* decision, which provides that investor–State arbitration clauses in intra-EU BITs are incompatible with EU law. The Agreement provides for the immediate termination of 277 BITs between the signatories, along with their sunset clauses.[136] It defines a sunset clause as meaning 'any provision in a Bilateral Investment Treaty which extends the protection of investments made prior to the date of termination of that Treaty for a further period of time'.

Much can be said about the EU Termination Agreement and its compliance (or not) with international law.[137] But here the focus is on the provisions concerning sunset clauses, which state:

Article 2 (Termination of Bilateral Investment Treaties)

1. Bilateral Investment Treaties listed in Annex A are terminated according to the terms set out in this Agreement.
2. For greater certainty, Sunset Clauses of Bilateral Investment Treaties listed in Annex A are terminated in accordance with paragraph 1 of this Article and shall not produce legal effects.

Article 3 (Termination of possible effects of Sunset Clauses)

Sunset Clauses of Bilateral Investment Treaties listed in Annex B are terminated by this Agreement and shall not produce legal effects, in accordance with the terms set out in this Agreement.

Annex A refers to BITs that are being terminated by the EU Termination Agreement, whereas Annex B refers to BITs that have already been terminated, but where a sunset clause

---

[132] C Titi, 'Most-Favoured Nation Treatment: Survival Clauses and Reform of International Investment Law' (2016) (33)(5) J Int'l Arb 425, 437 ('The treaty's mutual termination could be perceived as a "renegotiation" that ends with termination of the entire investment agreement'); cf Voon, Mitchell and Munro, 'Parting Ways' (n 129) 468 ('Nothing in the law of treaties necessitates the operation of survival clauses following the termination of IIAs by consent. Nevertheless, parties need to make clear their intentions regarding the survival clause when terminating an IIA').

[133] LE Petersen, 'Indonesia Ramps Up Termination of BITs—and Kills Survival Clause in One Such Treaty—But Faces New $600 mil. Claim from Indian Mining Investor' *Investment Arbitration Reporter* (20 November 2015) <https://www.iareporter.com/articles/indonesia-ramps-up-termination-of-bits-and-kills-survival-clause-in-one-such-treaty-but-faces-new-600-mil-claim-from-indian-mining-investor/> accessed 6 October 2022. The survival clause provided that the investment treaty would remain in force for a period of 10 years. See Indonesia–Argentina BIT, Article 13. There are no reports that the two States first amended this article before terminating the treaty.

[134] With the exceptions of Ireland, Finland, Austria, and Sweden.

[135] Agreement for the Termination of Bilateral Investment Treaties between the Member States of the European Union (2021) 60(1) ILM 99.

[136] Agreement for the Termination of Bilateral Investment Treaties between the Member States of the European Union (2021) 60(1) ILM 99, Articles 2(2) and 3.

[137] See further CA Moarbes, 'Introductory Note to Agreement for the Termination of Bilateral Investment Treaties between the Member States of the European Union' (2021) 60(1) ILM 99; U Kriebaum, 'The Fate of Intra-EU BITs from an Investment Law and Public International Law Perspective' (2015) 1 ELTE LJ 27.

may still be in effect. No distinction is drawn between sunset clauses that may be formulated differently; they are treated as a homogenous group.

55 The intended result of the EU Termination Agreement is that 'New Arbitration Proceedings' may not be initiated by an investor of a signatory State after 6 March 2018 (i.e. the date of the *Achmea* judgment), even where the BIT expressly provides (in its sunset clause) that an investor may initiate such arbitration proceedings.[138] Arbitral proceedings which were pending as at 6 March 2018 are also impacted. The parties may either seek to amicably agree to a settlement, or the investor shall have access to judicial remedies before national courts and under domestic law, but they are not permitted to continue the arbitral proceedings.[139] Instead, the State parties to the BIT shall inform the arbitral tribunal about the legal consequences of the *Achmea* judgment.[140] The result is that investors with a pending claim under an intra-EU BIT covered by the Agreement would no longer be able to continue to prosecute that claim before an international tribunal.

56 The EU Termination Agreement recognizes that 'certain intra-EU bilateral treaties, *including their sunset clauses*, ha[d] already been terminated bilaterally'.[141] This is indeed the case. However, prior to the EU Termination Agreement, the more common practice was to apply the two-step approach explained above, in which the sunset clause would first be removed by amendment, prior to termination. The legality of either approach seeking to avoid sunset clauses is yet to be tested. However, there are several reasons investment tribunals may be hesitant to defer to the States parties' subsequent agreement to remove the jurisdiction granted by the BITs.

57 *First*, tribunals may be concerned about the retroactive effect of the EU Termination Agreement, particularly for claims that were already pending prior to the coming into force of the EU Termination Agreement in August 2020.[142] The EU Termination Agreement claims to have 'in mind the rules of customary international law as codified in the Vienna Convention on the Law of Treaties'.[143] This necessarily includes Article 70 of the VCLT, which is widely recognized as reflecting customary international law.[144] It sets out a general presumption of prospectivity, providing that: 'unless the treaty otherwise provides or the parties otherwise agree, the termination of a treaty ... does not affect any right, obligation or legal situation of the parties created through the execution of the treaty prior to its termination'. However, it does not refer to third-party, non-State beneficiaries under investment

---

[138] Agreement for the Termination of Bilateral Investment Treaties between the Member States of the European Union (2021) 60(1) ILM 99, Article 5 ('Arbitration Clauses shall not serve as legal basis for New Arbitration Proceedings').
[139] M Waibel, 'Symposium on Treaty Exit at the Interface of Domestic and International Law: Brexit and Acquired Rights' (2017) 111 AJIL Unbound 440, 441 (hereafter Waibel, 'Brexit').
[140] Agreement for the Termination of Bilateral Investment Treaties between the Member States of the European Union (2021) 60(1) ILM 99, Article 7 (The applicable text is set out in Annex C, which reads: 'The Parties hereby confirm that Arbitration Clauses are contrary to the EU Treaties and thus inapplicable. As a result of this incompatibility between Arbitration Clauses and the EU Treaties, as of the date on which the last of the parties to a Bilateral Investment Treaty became a Member State of the European Union, the Arbitration Clause in such a Bilateral Investment Treaty cannot serve as legal basis for Arbitration Proceedings').
[141] ibid, Preamble, para VIII.
[142] See above, paras 9–11; referring to *Pope & Talbot* (n 26) paras 11–16 and 47; *Sanum Investments* PCA Jurisdiction (n 27) para 300.
[143] Agreement for the Termination of Bilateral Investment Treaties between the Member States of the European Union, Preamble, para II.
[144] Waibel, 'Brexit' (n 139) 440-441.

agreements, such as investors. Indeed, the Commentary to the VCLT states that Article 70 was intended only to apply to the rights of the State parties to the treaty and is not 'in any way concerned with the question of "vested interests" of individuals'.[145] Nevertheless, several arbitral tribunals have been prepared to interpret Article 70 as also referring to the rights of investors.[146]

In addition, pursuant to Articles 35–37 of the VCLT, 'third States' (i.e. States that are not parties to the treaty) that are treaty beneficiaries must ordinarily consent before their rights can be revoked or modified. Again, the VCLT is silent on the rights of non-State entities. But some commentators have argued that similar reasoning should be extended to investors, who must therefore consent before their rights can be revoked or modified, at least where those rights had been revoked retrospectively.[147]

Another angle is to examine the issue of investor rights in light of Article 43 of the VCLT, which provides that withdrawal of a party from a treaty (i.e. the termination by the EU States of intra-EU BITs) 'shall not in any way impair the duty of any State to fulfil any obligation embodied in the treaty to which it would be subject under international law independently of the treaty'. Some commentators have contended, in the context of Brexit, that the doctrine of 'acquired rights' under customary international law is one such obligation that might survive the termination of a treaty.[148] Similarly, it could be argued that investors under the intra-EU BITs have acquired rights that cannot be abolished by the EU States' termination of those treaties. But this is far from straightforward. It is controversial whether a doctrine of acquired rights, if such a doctrine exists, can be said to extend to investors.[149] Although some tribunals appear to have recognized this as a possibility,[150] there remains the question whether the right to initiate arbitration is fairly considered an obligation to which States would be subject *independently* of the treaty, as Article 43 of the VCLT requires. An investor's right to bring arbitration proceedings will generally only exist because of the existence of the investment treaty.

Second, an investment tribunal may be hesitant to find that its jurisdiction has been usurped where the claim was already pending before it prior to the coming into effect of the EU Termination Agreement. Such a result would be inconsistent with the ICJ's decision in *Nottebohm* that jurisdiction of a tribunal, once seized, does not cease retrospectively simply

---

[145] Draft Articles on the Law of Treaties with Commentaries' (n 40) 265, Article 66.

[146] *Eastern Sugar BV v The Czech Republic*, SCC No 088/2004, Partial Award, 27 March 2007, paras 176–77; *Oostergetel v The Slovak Republic*, UNCITRAL Arbitration, Jurisdiction, 30 April 2010, para 90 ('since the dispute between the Parties arose before Slovakia's accession to the EU, the Claimants' rights under the BIT have remained unchanged, in line with Article 70(1)(b) of the Vienna Convention').

[147] J Harrison, 'The Life and Death of BITs: Legal Issues concerning Survival Clauses and the Termination of Investment Treaties' (2012) 13 JWIT 928, 944 (contending that Article 36 of the VCLT reflects a 'general principle which is applicable to all third party right holders'); cf Y Zhang, 'Mutual Termination of Sunset Clauses in Intra-EU BITs: The Search for Investor Protections' (2019) 29(2) Am Rev Int'l Arb 173, 182.

[148] Waibel, 'Brexit' (n 139) 440.

[149] Voon, Mitchell and Munro, 'Parting Ways' (n 129) 470–71; M Sornarajah, *The International Law on Foreign Investment* (3rd edn, CUP 2010) 419; S Wittich, 'Article 70—Consequences of the Termination of a Treaty' in Dörr and Schmalenbach (n 2) 1208, para 32, fn 72; but see *Rumeli Telekom AS and Telsim Mobil Telekomunikasyon Hizmelteri AS v Republic of Kazakhstan*, ICSID Case No ARB/05/16, Award, 21 July 2008, para 355 (it is 'well established in international law that a State may not take away accrued rights of a foreign investor by domestic legislation abrogating the law granting these rights').

[150] *Eskosol v Italy* (n 55) para 226 ('In the Tribunal's view, it would be inconsistent with general notions of acquired rights under international law to permit States effectively to non-suit an investor part-way through a pending case, simply by issuing a joint document purporting to interpret longstanding treaty text so as to undermine the tribunal's jurisdiction to proceed').

because the underlying treaty is terminated.[151] An arbitral tribunal may also inquire whether the alternatives offered by the EU Termination Agreement would ensure the investor an adequate remedy. At least for pending claims, the EU Termination Agreement raises issues of due process similar to those discussed in the *Pope & Talbot* award above.[152]

61 *Third,* tribunals have routinely applied BITs after termination on the basis of sunset clauses.[153] In *Gavazzi v Romania,* the parties did not even dispute the tribunal's jurisdiction under the sunset clause, notwithstanding the mutual termination of the treaty two years prior to the arbitration being filed.[154]

62 Ultimately, it remains to be seen whether investment tribunals will be willing to accept the legality of the EU Termination Agreement under international law, given the potential prejudice for investors. Many tribunals have already pointed out that mutual termination cannot affect pending proceedings.[155] Meanwhile, arbitral tribunals appear to be willing to exercise jurisdiction in intra-EU claims under the ECT, treating it as unaffected by *Achmea*, *Komstroy*, and the EU Termination Agreement.[156]

IV. Article 56: Withdrawal in the absence of treaty provisions or consent

Article 56. Denunciation of or withdrawal from a treaty containing no provision regarding termination, denunciation or withdrawal

1. A treaty which contains no provision regarding its termination and which does not provide for denunciation or withdrawal is not subject to denunciation or withdrawal unless:
    (a) it is established that the parties intended to admit the possibility of denunciation or withdrawal; or
    (b) a right of denunciation or withdrawal may be implied by the nature of the treaty.

---

[151] *Nottebohm Case (Liechtenstein v Guatemala)* (Preliminary Objections) [1953] ICJ Rep 111, 123 ('An extrinsic fact such as the subsequent lapse of the Declaration, by reason of the expiry of the period or by denunciation, cannot deprive the Court of the jurisdiction already established'); reaffirmed in *Alleged violations of the 1955 Treaty of Amity, Economic Relations, and Consular Rights (Islamic Republic of Iran v United States of America)* (Preliminary Objections) [2021] ICJ Rep 9, paras 24, 94; see also Zhang (n 147) 179–80.

[152] See above, para 9.

[153] Zhang (n 147) 175.

[154] *Marco Gavazzi et ors v Romania*, ICSID Case No ARB/12/25, Decision on Jurisdiction, Admissibility and Liability, 21 April 2015, para 1, fn 1 (noting that the case was brought pursuant to the 'Agreement between the Government of the Italian Republic and the Government of Romania on the Mutual Promotion and Protection of Investments, entered into force 14 March 1995 and terminated on 14 March 2010, subject to the "sunset provision" in Article 11(3) (C-4)'); and para 5 (noting that the case was filed on 2 August 2012); see also *Walter Bau AG v Thailand*, UNCITRAL Award, 1 July 2009, para 9.5, 9.69. On 16 April 2019, ICSID also accepted a filing for arbitration on the basis of a sunset clause in The Netherlands–Tanzania BIT (*Ayoub-Farid Mihel Saab v United Republic of Thailand*, ICSID Case No ARB/19/8), but the proceedings were discontinued due to non-payment of the required advances.

[155] *CMC Africa Austral, LDA, et ors v Republic of Mozambique*, ICSID Case No ARB/17/23, Award, 24 October 2019, para 326 ('An offer to arbitrate the present dispute has thus been made and accepted before the decision in *Achmea* was issued or the member states issued their declaration. A valid and binding agreement to arbitrate has thus been formed'); *Magyar Farming Company Ltd et ors v Hungary*, ICSID Case No ARB/17/27, Award, 13 November 2019, para 214; see also A Reinisch and SM Fallah, 'Post-Termination Responsibility of States?—The Impact of Amendment/Modification, Suspension and Termination of Investment Treaties on (Vested) Rights of Investors' (2022) 37 ICSID Rev 101, 110.

[156] For decisions following *Achmea*, see, eg, *Hydro Energy 1 Sàrl and Hydroxana Sweden AB v Kingdom of Spain*, ICSID Case No ARB/15/42, Award, 9 March 2020, para 502; *GPF GP Sàrl v The Republic of Poland*, SCC Arbitration V 2014/168, 24 April 2020, paras 384–85; for decisions following *Komstroy*, see, eg, *Cavalum SGPS, SA v Kingdom of Spain*, ICSID Case No ARB/15/34, Decision on the Kingdom of Spain's Request for Reconsideration, 10 January 2022, para 97(5)–(6) ('The ruling in *Komstroy* does not affect the jurisdiction of the Tribunal under the applicable international law, namely the ECT and the ICSID Convention. There is nothing in the *Achmea* and *Komstroy* rulings which could deprive a Tribunal so constituted of jurisdiction, or suggest that Member States have no capacity to enter into agreements such as the ECT'); *RENERGY Sàrl. v Kingdom of Spain*, ICSID Case No

2. A party shall give not less than twelve months' notice of its intention to denounce or withdraw from a treaty under paragraph 1.

While Article 56 is at least partially reflective of customary international law,[157] it is rarely applied, since almost all investment treaties, and indeed most treaties, contain provisions regarding termination, denunciation or withdrawal. As Article 56 applies only in the absence of such a provision, it is unsurprising that there are no investment decisions concerning Article 56. Indeed, the Organization for Economic Co-operation and Development (OECD) in its study identified only two investment agreements that do not specify the conditions for their temporal validity.[158]

V. Articles 57 and 58: Suspension of a treaty

Article 57. Suspension of the operation of a treaty under its provisions or by consent of the parties

1. The operation of a treaty in regard to all the parties or to a particular party may be suspended:
   (a) in conformity with the provisions of the treaty; or
   (b) at any time by consent of all the parties after consultation with the other contracting States.

...

Article 58. Suspension of the operation of a multilateral treaty by agreement between certain of the parties only

1. Two or more parties to a multilateral treaty may conclude an agreement to suspend the operation of provisions of the treaty, temporarily and as between themselves alone, if:
   (a) the possibility of such a suspension is provided for by the treaty; or
   (b) the suspension in question is not prohibited by the treaty and: (i) not affect the enjoyment by the other parties of their rights under the treaty or the performance of their obligations; (ii) is not incompatible with the object and purpose of the treaty.
2. Unless in a case falling under paragraph 1(a) the treaty otherwise provides, the parties in question shall notify the other parties of their intention to conclude the agreement and of those provisions of the treaty the operation of which they intend to suspend.

ARB/14/18, Award, 6 May 2022, para 360; *Mathias Kruck et ors v Kingdom of Spain*, ICSID Case No ARB/15/23, Decision on Jurisdiction, Liability and Principles of Quantum, 14 September 2022, para 15.

[157] D Goldsworthy and M Longo, 'Reconceptualising Executive Power to Denounce Treaties in the Twenty-First Century' (2021) 47 Monash ULRev 1, 9; cf T Christakis, 'Article 56 Convention of 1969' in O Corten and P Klein (eds), *The Vienna Conventions on the Law of Treaties—A Commentary* (OUP 2011) 1251, 1255–57 (stating that 'the customary character of the ban on unilateral denunciation ... is beyond doubt', as is Article 56(1)(a) reference to the intention of the parties, however 'serious doubts exist regarding the customary status of paragraph 1(b) which introduces the second exception to the principle of the prohibition of unilateral denunciation, by referring to the "nature" of certain treaties' and further, that the 12-month notice period does not reflect custom, but may generally reflect a reasonable time period, in accordance with the principle of good faith).

[158] These are the 1996 India–Korea BIT, which was terminated by unilateral denunciation by India in 2016; and the 1996 Indonesia–Uzbekistan BIT, which remains in force. Both treaties make a reference to termination, but do not regulate it.

64 There is little to say regarding Articles 57 and 58 of the VCLT in the context of investment law. For the most part, States parties tend to prefer termination over suspension. Moreover, most investment treaties do not allow for unilateral suspension.[159] The result is that suspension of an investment treaty can usually only take place where all of the parties have consented, pursuant to Article 57(1)(b). This sometimes occurs where the parties renegotiate an investment treaty. For example, the 2010 Canada–Panama FTA suspends the 1996 Canada–Panama BIT.[160] A similar approach was adopted when EFTA, which includes Switzerland, negotiated the 2005 EFTA–Korea Agreement on Investment. The 2005 Agreement suspends the 1971 Switzerland–Korea BIT.[161] A further example is the CPTPP, which replaced the TPP when the United States withdrew. It incorporates the TPP *mutatis mutandis* but suspends certain of its provisions.[162] For instance, provisions are suspended to narrow the scope of the Investor–State Dispute Settlement (ISDS) provisions in the CPTPP so that foreign investors can no longer make investor–State claims for a violation of a private investment with the Government, or in relation to investment authorizations. The suspension will be lifted only if the CPTPP countries decide to do so by consensus.[163] This suspension mechanism allows the flexibility of retaining the text provisions that have already been negotiated (when the United States was still at the table), so that these can be revived if necessary.

65 Article 58 deals with the slightly different situation of *inter se* suspension, as between only some of the parties to a treaty. It is not clear whether Article 58 reflects customary international law.[164] An investment treaty has rarely been subject to *inter se* suspension and there is no relevant investor–State jurisprudence.

VI. Article 59: Termination or suspension implied by conclusion of a later treaty

Article 59. Termination or suspension of the operation of a treaty implied by conclusion of a later treaty

(1) A treaty shall be considered as terminated if all the parties to it conclude a later treaty relating to the same subject-matter and:
   (a) It appears from the later treaty or is otherwise established that the parties intended that the matter should be governed by that treaty; or
   (b) The provisions of the later treaty are so far incompatible with those of the earlier one that the two treaties are not capable of being applied at the same time.
(2) The earlier treaty shall be considered as only suspended in operation if it appears from the later treaty or is otherwise established that such was the intention of the parties.

---

[159] Dörr and Schmalenbach (n 2) Article 57, 1061 ('treaty provisions on termination or withdrawal cannot easily be interpreted as also permitting suspension').

[160] Canada–Panama FTA, Article 9.38.

[161] EFTA–Switzerland Agreement on Investment, Article 27. For further examples, see Joachim Pohl, 'Temporal Validity of International Investment Agreements—A Large Sample Survey of Treaty Provisions', *OECD Working Papers on International Investment* (OECD Publishing, 2013/04) 15, n 32.

[162] See Australian Department of Foreign Affairs, 'CPTPP Suspensions Explained' *Fact Sheet* (4 February 2019) (https://www.dfat.gov.au/trade/agreements/in-force/cptpp/outcomes-documents/Pages/cptpp-suspensions-explained accessed 6 October 2022).

[163] CPTPPA, Article 2.

[164] MP Lanfranchi, 'Article 58 Convention of 1969' in O Corten and P Klein (eds), *The Vienna Conventions on the Law of Treaties—A Commentary* (OUP 2011) 1313–14 (concluding that it is 'more likely to reflect a progressive development than a pure codification').

Article 59 of the VCLT establishes the rule that a later investment treaty may have the effect 66
of implicitly terminating an earlier treaty. It reflects customary international law.[165] It is relevant only where other more straightforward means of establishing termination or suspension, such as under the express terms of the treaty, or by consent, cannot be established.

One set of issues concerns multilateral investment treaties (or FTAs with an investment 67
chapter) where some of the parties to that treaty are already party to BITs. The relationship between the new multilateral treaty and any bilateral investment agreements may not always be clear. For example, potential uncertainties arise in relation to the TPP.[166] In a series of side letters, Australia agreed to terminate its existing BITs with Mexico, Peru, and Vietnam once the CPTPP came into force. But not all CPTPP parties terminated their existing BITs. The Vietnam–Malaysia BIT, which came into force in 1992, has provisions that substantively overlap with the investment chapter in the CPTPP. It seems likely that this remains in force however, since Article 1.2 of the TPP (incorporated *mutatis mutandis* into the CPTPP) makes clear that the parties intend that the prior BITs continue and that any inconsistencies shall be resolved by consultations. Moreover, the very fact that at least four of the States parties to the CPTPP entered into a separate agreement to terminate their BITs suggests that the TPP did not otherwise terminate earlier treaties. So Article 59 of the VCLT (termination) would likely not apply, but Article 30 (partial amendment) could.

A related issue that has repeatedly vexed investment tribunals and dominates the jurisprudential landscape is whether intra-EU BITs can be said to have been terminated by subsequent EU law. The cases dealing with this issue are discussed below since they may also have implications outside of the EU context, even if the issue has now practically been superseded within the EU by the EU Termination Treaty.[167] 68

One of the earlier tribunals to consider this issue was *Eureko BV v the Slovak Republic*.[168] 69
The respondent, Slovakia, had argued that the BIT with The Netherlands had been terminated upon Slovakia's accession to the EC Treaty. The European Commission intervened and agreed with the claimant that it could not discern in Slovakia's 2003 Act of Accession any intention to abrogate earlier intra-EU BITs, and thus agreed that the BIT 'has not been implicitly terminated or suspended by virtue of Article 59(1) of the Vienna Convention'.[169]

The tribunal rejected Slovakia's argument that the BIT had been implicitly or tacitly terminated.[170] It reasoned that Article 59 'does not provide for the automatic termination of treaties by 70

---

[165] F Dubuisson, 'Article 59 Convention of 1959' in Olivier Corten and Pierre Klein (eds), *The Vienna Conventions on the Law of Treaties—A Commentary* (OUP 2011) 1325, 1331, para 14.
[166] Voon and Mitchell, 'Denunciation' (n 110) 427.
[167] At least with respect to those EU Member States that are party to the EU Termination Agreement, and to the extent that the sunset clauses in their BITs are held to be ineffective.
[168] *Eureko BV v Slovak Republic*, PCA Case No 2008-13, UNCITRAL Rules, Jurisdiction, 26 October 2010 (hereafter *Eureko v Slovakia*); see also an earlier version to similar effect, *Oostergetel v Slovak Republic*, UNCITRAL (ad hoc), Jurisdiction, 30 April 2010, paras 73–74 ('The Tribunal is not persuaded by the Respondent's argument that the Dutch-Slovak BIT has been terminated in accordance with Article 59 of the Vienna Convention. First, the Tribunal does not consider that the two treaties cover the same subject matter. Second, there is no indication that the Parties would have intended for the BIT to be superseded by the EC Treaty. Third, the Tribunal does not see any direct conflict between the BIT and the relevant EU law provisions that would impede it from applying the two sets of legal norms simultaneously, should such a need arise').
[169] *Eureko v Slovakia* (n 168) para 187.
[170] ibid para 265.

operation of law' and that it was necessary for Slovakia to notify The Netherlands formally if it intended to terminate the BIT under the process set out in Article 65(1) of the VCLT,[171] which provides:

> A party which, under the provisions of the present Convention, invokes either a defect in its consent to be bound by a treaty or a ground for impeaching the validity of a treaty, terminating it, withdrawing from it or suspending its operation, *must notify the other parties of its claim*. The notification shall indicate the measure proposed to be taken with respect to the treaty and the reasons therefor.

71 The tribunal also considered the relationship between Article 30 (partial amendment) and Article 59 (termination), reasoning that 'the very fact that these situations are treated separately in the Vienna Convention points to the need under Article 59 for a broader overlap between the earlier and later treaties than would be needed to trigger the application of Article 30'.[172] The language of Article 59(1)(b), requiring that the provisions of the later treaty must be 'so far incompatible with those of the earlier one that the two treaties are not capable of being applied at the same time', is accordingly a high threshold that will not be easy to meet.[173] The tribunal considered that there was nothing in EU law or any of the extrinsic evidence supporting an intention to terminate the BIT.[174] It placed particular reliance on the fact that a number of the BIT provisions are not duplicated in EU law, such as fair and equitable treatment, and that 'an essential characteristic of an investor's rights under the BIT', namely, its right to initiate neutral arbitration, is not replicated in EU law.[175]

72 The *Eureko* tribunal's conclusion that accession to the EU does not implicitly terminate intra-EU BITs has been unanimously followed by subsequent tribunals, with particular emphasis on the fact that the subject matter of the EU Treaties do not overlap with investment treaties and there is thus no conflict.[176] Even Professor Marcelo Kohen, dissenting in *Theodoros Adamakopoulos et ors v Cyprus*, accepted that the accession of Cyprus to the EU could not have had the consequence of tacitly terminating all of Cyprus' BITs under Article 59.[177]

73 Overall, Article 59 has been the subject of significant development and application by investment tribunals. The investment jurisprudence thus offers a useful contribution to the general body of public international law.

---

[171] ibid para 235.
[172] ibid para 240.
[173] ibid para 241.
[174] ibid paras 244–45.
[175] ibid para 264.
[176] *Oostergetel v Slovak Republic*, UNCITRAL Rules, Ad hoc Arbitration, Jurisdiction, 30 April 2010, paras 73–74; *European American Investment Bank AG (Austria) v Slovak Republic*, PCA Case No 2010-17, Jurisdiction, 22 October 2012, paras 178–85; *Eastern Sugar BV v The Czech Republic*, Partial Award, SCC No 088/2004, 27 March 2007, paras 159–172; *A11Y Ltd v Czech Republic*, ICSID Case No UNCT/15/1, Jurisdiction, 9 February 2017, para 177; *Marfin Investment Group v The Republic of Cyprus*, ICSID Case No ARB/13/27, Award, 26 July 2018, paras 587–88 (hereafter *Marfin v Cyprus*); *Magyar Farming Company Ltd, Kintyre Kft and Inicia Zrt v Hungary*, ICSID Case No ARB/17/27, Award, 13 November 2019, para 239; *United Utilities (Tallinn) BV and Aktsiaselts Tallinna Vesi v Republic of Estonia*, ICSID Case No ARB/14/24, Award, 21 June 2019, para 531.
[177] *Theodoros Adamakopoulos and others v Republic of Cyprus*, ICSID Case No ARB/15/49, Jurisdiction, 7 February 2020, para 163; cf Dissenting Opinion of Professor Marcelo Kohen, paras 10 and 51.

VII. Articles 60–63: Other grounds for termination or suspension

1. Article 60: Termination or suspension as a consequence of breach

Article 60. Termination or suspension of the operation of a treaty as a consequence of its breach

1. A material breach of a bilateral treaty by one of the parties entitles the other to invoke the breach as a ground for terminating the treaty or suspending its operation in whole or in part.
2. A material breach of a multilateral treaty by one of the parties entitles:
   (a) the other parties by unanimous agreement to suspend the operation of the treaty in whole or in part or to terminate it either:(i) in the relations between themselves and the defaulting State, or (ii) as between all the parties;
   (b) a party specially affected by the breach to invoke it as a ground for suspending the operation of the treaty in whole or in part in the relations between itself and the defaulting State;
   (c) any party other than the defaulting State to invoke the breach as a ground for suspending the operation of the treaty in whole or in part with respect to itself if the treaty is of such a character that a material breach of its provisions by one party radically changes the position of every party with respect to the further performance of its obligations under the treaty.
3. A material breach of a treaty, for the purposes of this article, consists in:
   (a) a repudiation of the treaty not sanctioned by the present Convention; or
   (b) the violation of a provision essential to the accomplishment of the object or purpose of the treaty.
4. The foregoing paragraphs are without prejudice to any provision in the treaty applicable in the event of a breach.
5. Paragraphs 1–3 do not apply to provisions relating to the protection of the human person contained in treaties of a humanitarian character, in particular to provisions prohibiting any form of reprisals against persons protected by such treaties.

Article 60 is concerned only with the narrow question of when a treaty may be terminated or suspended as a consequence of a material breach. According to the ICJ, Articles 60–62 of the Vienna Convention reflect customary international law.[178] But in practice, Article 60 is rarely invoked.[179] While an injured party may invoke a material breach in order to terminate or suspend the operation of the treaty, a mere allegation that one party had committed a material breach does not allow the injured party to consider that treaty as terminated or suspended under Article 60.[180] As the ICJ explained in *Gabčíkovo-Nagymaros*:

> it is only a material breach of the treaty itself, by a State party to that treaty, which entitles the other party to rely on it as a ground for terminating the treaty. The violation of other treaty rules or of rules of general international law may justify the taking of certain

---
[178] *Gabčíkovo-Nagymaros* (n 59) paras 46 and 99.
[179] C Binder, 'The VCLT over the Last 50 Years: Developments in the Law of Treaties with a Special Focus on the VCLT's Rules on Treaty Termination' (2021) 24(1) ARIEL , 89, 97 (hereafter Binder, 'The VCLT over the Last 50 Years').
[180] *Appeal Relating to the Jurisdiction of the ICAO Council* [1972] ICJ Rep 46, Separate Opinion of Judge de Castro, 129.

measures, including countermeasures, by the injured State, but it does not constitute a ground for termination under the law of treaties.[181]

75 It went on to note the conceptual distinction between treaty law and the law of State responsibility, which reflect 'two branches of international law' with distinct scopes.[182] According to the Court, a finding of termination or suspension of a treaty does not entail a finding that such termination or suspension was wrongful. But this distinction is not clear cut. The Court proceeds on the basis that non-performance of a treaty, adopted in response to a prior breach of that treaty, could be justified as countermeasures under customary international law (State responsibility), quite apart from the provisions on suspension in Article 60 of the VCLT (treaty law).[183]

76 In any case, Article 60 is rarely invoked in the investment context. The reasons for this are obvious. Almost all breaches of investment treaties are found against a State in a case brought by an investor. The other contracting State would have little incentive in such a case to then terminate the very investment treaty that had just compensated its national investor for the wrong by the host State, even if such a breach could be said to be material. Moreover, if States wish to terminate an investment treaty, they commonly do so by other, more straightforward means that do not first require establishing a material breach (such as unilateral or mutual termination in accordance with the terms of the treaty).

2. Article 61: Supervening impossibility of performance

Article 61. Supervening impossibility of performance

1. A party may invoke the impossibility of performing a treaty as a ground for terminating or withdrawing from it if the impossibility results from the permanent disappearance or destruction of an object indispensable for the execution of the treaty. If the impossibility is temporary, it may be invoked only as a ground for suspending the operation of the treaty.
2. Impossibility of performance may not be invoked by a party as a ground for terminating, withdrawing from or suspending the operation of a treaty if the impossibility is the result of a breach by that party either of an obligation under the treaty or of any other international obligation owed to any other party to the treaty.

77 The interplay between State responsibility and the law of treaties is even more pronounced in the context of Articles 61 and 62 of the VCLT. These have to some extent been overshadowed by the ILC Articles on the Responsibility of States for Internationally Wrongful Acts (ARSIWA), which set out circumstances precluding wrongfulness, including wrongful breach of a treaty, such as necessity or *force majeure*.[184] In the investment context, one may find many investment cases in which the Respondent State has invoked countermeasures,[185] or necessity,[186] but these

---

[181] *Gabčíkovo-Nagymaros* (n 59) para 47.
[182] ibid.
[183] See further J Crawford and S Olleson, 'The Exception of Non-Performance: Links between the Law of Treaties and the Law of State Responsibility' (2000) 21 AYIL 55.
[184] See in this Commentary: F Paddeu, 'Article 23 ARSIWA: *Force majeure*' and F Paddeu and M Waibel, 'Article 25 ARSIWA: Necessity'.
[185] M Paparinskis, 'Investment Arbitration and the Law of Countermeasures' (2008) 79(1) BYIL 264.
[186] See *CMS v Argentina*, ICSID Case No ARB/01/8, Award, 12 May 2005, paras 359–60 and the series of cases in which Argentina invoked necessity as a result of its financial crisis.

are invoked in terms of the ILC articles or of the relevant BIT itself, rather than by reference to the VCLT.

Article 61 is phrased restrictively,[187] and it largely reflects customary international law.[188] Applying Article 61, the English High Court in *Yollari v Secretary of State for Transport* rejected an argument that the provisions of the Chicago Convention had been suspended in respect of Northern Cyprus because the Republic of Cyprus did not have effective control over the territory.[189] The Court held on the facts that this did not amount to a situation of impossibility because the rights under the Convention, while not 'fully effective and enforceable', were able to be exercised effectively in a number of ways.[190] The Court also observed that the formal requirements for suspension under the VCLT had not been invoked.[191]

3. Article 62: Fundamental change of circumstances

Article 62. Fundamental change of circumstances

1. A fundamental change of circumstances which has occurred with regard to those existing at the time of the conclusion of a treaty, and which was not foreseen by the parties, may not be invoked as a ground for terminating or withdrawing from the treaty unless: *(a)* The existence of those circumstances constituted an essential basis of the consent of the parties to be bound by the treaty; and *(b)* The effect of the change is radically to transform the extent of obligations still to be performed under the treaty.
2. A fundamental change of circumstances may not be invoked as a ground for terminating or withdrawing from a treaty: *(a)* If the treaty establishes a boundary; or *(b)* If the fundamental change is the result of a breach by the party invoking it either of an obligation under the treaty or of any other international obligation owed to any other party to the treaty.
3. If, under the foregoing paragraphs, a party may invoke a fundamental change of circumstances as a ground for terminating or withdrawing from a treaty it may also invoke the change as a ground for suspending the operation of the treaty.

The ICJ has recognized that, in many respects, Article 62 reflects customary international law on the 'subject of the termination of a treaty relationship on account of change of circumstances'.[192] The ECJ has also recognized Article 62(1) of the VCLT as constituting customary international law.[193] Article 62 is most commonly invoked in circumstances in which there is an outbreak of hostilities.

There have been a number of international cases considering these provisions. For instance, the ICJ in *Gabčíkovo-Nagymaros* held that the threshold required for a change of circumstances was that they would 'radically transform the extent of the obligations still to be

---

[187] Binder, 'The VCLT over the Last 50 Years' (n 179) 89, 97.
[188] *Gabčíkovo-Nagymaros* (n 59) paras 46, 99, 104.
[189] *Yollari & Ors, R (on the application of) v Secretary of State for Transport & Anor* [2009] EWHC 1918 (Admin), para 38.
[190] ibid para 38.
[191] ibid para 39.
[192] *Fisheries Jurisdiction (Germany v Iceland)* (n 63) para 36; see also *Racke GmbH & Co v Hauptzollamt Mainz*, Judgment, CJEU, 16 June 1998, para 53 (hereafter *Racke*); *Gabčíkovo-Nagymaros* (n 59) paras 46 and 99.
[193] *Racke* (n 192) para 53; cf W Heintschel von Heinegg, 'Treaties, Fundamental Change of Circumstances' in A Peters (ed), *The Max Planck Encyclopedia of Public International Law* (OUP 2021) suggesting that Article 62(2)(a) does not reflect customary international law.

fulfilled' and that this would arise 'only in exceptional cases', where such a change was 'completely unforeseen'.[194] Given the apparent stringency of the test, it is perhaps no surprise that it is not the subject of investment decisions. Nevertheless, some commentators have argued that there is greater scope for its invocation before investment tribunals as a defence for economic emergency measures.[195]

4. Article 63: Severance of diplomatic or consular relations

Article 63. Severance of diplomatic or consular relations

The severance of diplomatic or consular relations between parties to a treaty does not affect the legal relations established between them by the treaty except in so far as the existence of diplomatic or consular relations is indispensable for the application of the treaty.

81   Article 63 sets a very high threshold for suspension or termination of a treaty due to the severance of diplomatic relations. It will have an effect only where the existence of diplomatic or consular relations is 'indispensable'. This threshold could be met in cases of mutual legal assistance, for example.

82   In *Guris v Syria*, Syria argued that the Turkey–Syria BIT was suspended since Syria had severed diplomatic or consular relations. But the tribunal held that in the context of an investment treaty, the suspension of such ties was irrelevant.[196] Similar conclusions have also been reached in the context of the World Trade Organization (WTO) Agreements, as well as under friendship treaties such as the now defunct Iran–US Treaty of Amity, Economic Relations and Consular Rights.[197]

VIII.   Articles 65–68: Procedures for invalidity, termination, withdrawal, or suspension

Article 65. Procedure to be followed with respect to Invalidity, Termination, Withdrawal from or Suspension of the Operation of a Treaty

1. A party which, under the provisions of the present Convention, invokes either a defect in its consent to be bound by a treaty or a ground for impeaching the validity of a treaty, terminating it, withdrawing from it or suspending its operation, must notify the other parties of its claim. The notification shall indicate the measure proposed to be taken with respect to the treaty and the reasons therefor.

...

---

[194] *Gabčíkovo-Nagymaros* (n 59) para 104; see also *Racke* (n 192) para 50.
[195] O Bayrak, 'Economic Crises and the Fundamental Change of Circumstances in Investment Arbitration' (2020) 35(1) ICSID Review–FILJ 130.
[196] *Guris Construction and Engineering Inc and ors v Arab Republic of Syria*, ICC Case No 21845/ZF/AYF, Final Award, 31 August 2020, paras 152–53.
[197] See *Saudi Arabia—Measures Concerning the Protection of Intellectual Property Rights*, WTO, Panel Report, WT/DS567/R, 16 June 2020, para 7.22 (confirming that Saudi Arabia's severance of diplomatic relations with Qatar had no impact on the operation of the applicable WTO agreements as between Qatar and Saudi Arabia.); *United States Diplomatic and Consular Staff in Tehran* (Judgment) [1980] ICJ Rep 3, 28, para 54 ('although the machinery for the effective operation of the 1955 Treaty has, no doubt, now been impaired by reason of diplomatic relations between the two countries having been broken off by the United States, its provisions remain part of the corpus of law applicable between the United States and Iran').

Article 67. Instruments for Declaring Invalid, Terminating, Withdrawing from or Suspending the Operation of a Treaty

1. The notification provided for under article 65, paragraph 1 must be made in writing.
2. Any act declaring invalid, terminating, withdrawing from or suspending the operation of a treaty pursuant to the provisions of the treaty or of paragraphs 2 or 3 of article 65 shall be carried out through an instrument communicated to the other parties. If the instrument is not signed by the Head of State, Head of Government or Minister for Foreign Affairs, the representative of the State communicating it may be called upon to produce full powers.

Article 68. Revocation of Notifications and Instruments provided for in Articles 65 and 67

A notification or instrument provided for in article 65 or 67 may be revoked at any time before it takes effect.

83 It is widely acknowledged that the procedural requirements under the Vienna Convention did not comprise a codification of existing customary international law, reflecting instead a 'progressive development at the time, introducing an innovation in the law of treaties'.[198] However, it is less clear whether the provisions reflect customary international law today.[199] The ICJ in *Gabčíkovo-Nagymaros* demurred from finding that Articles 65–67 of the VCLT reflected customary international law, instead relying on the parties' position that those provisions 'if not codifying customary international law, at least generally reflect customary international law and contain certain procedural principles which are based on an obligation to act in good faith'.[200] The Court went further in *Armed Activities on the Territory of the Congo*, stating that Article 67 did not reflect customary international law.[201]

84 The Convention imposes few conditions on how invalidity, termination, or suspension must be given effect, particularly at a domestic level. Pursuant to Article 67, any such notice made under the provisions of the Convention must be signed by someone with full powers and it must be made in writing with reasons. However, this does not displace internal legal or constitutional requirements for a State to withdraw, as several domestic courts have recently affirmed.

85 The South African High Court held that South Africa's decision to withdraw from the Rome Statute was unconstitutional since no parliamentary approval had been sought, rejecting the Government's argument that neither the Rome Statute nor Article 56 includes such a requirement. It held that these provisions do not 'seek to dictate to the member states ... how and by whom the decision to withdraw must be taken'.[202] Furthermore, the United Kingdom Supreme Court concluded that the United Kingdom could withdraw unilaterally from the

---

[198] A Tzanakopoulos, 'Article 67 Convention of 1969' in O Corten and P Klein (eds), *The Vienna Conventions on the Law of Treaties—A Commentary* (OUP 2011) 1546, 1548; M Prost, 'Article 65 Convention of 1969' in O Corten and P Klein (eds), *The Vienna Conventions on the Law of Treaties—A Commentary* (OUP 2011) 1486; I Sinclair, *The Vienna Convention on the Law of Treaties* (2nd edn, MUP 1984) 10–22.
[199] See *Racke* (n 192) para 59 ('it should be noted that the specific procedural requirements [laid down by Article 65 of the Vienna Convention] do not form part of customary international law').
[200] *Gabčíkovo-Nagymaros* (n 59) para 109.
[201] *Armed Activities on the Territory of the Congo (New Application: 2002) (Democratic Republic of Congo v Rwanda)* (Jurisdiction and Admissibility) [2006] ICJ Rep 6, para 125.
[202] *Democratic Alliance v Minister of International Relations and Cooperation et ors* (2016) Case No 83145/2016, High Court of South Africa (Gauteng Div Pretoria), para 40.

European Union, but only through an act of parliament, not through an executive act as was originally proposed.[203] This was consistent with Article 50 of the Treaty on European Union, which provides that any member may decide to withdraw 'in accordance with its own constitutional requirements'.

86 At the same time, the CJEU relied on Article 68 of the VCLT to confirm—again in the context of Brexit—that a unilateral notice of withdrawal can be revoked within the notice period without any effect, as long as no withdrawal agreement has been reached.[204]

87 These procedural provisions rarely excite commentary in the investment context, except in the context of Articles 59 and 65. The issue is whether Article 65 of the VCLT incorporates a formal notification requirement when termination or suspension under Article 59 is invoked. The *Eureko* tribunal found that it did, rejecting the argument that the entry by Slovakia into the European Union implicitly terminated its intra-EU investment treaties.[205] Similarly, in *AS PNV Banka v Latvia*, the tribunal concluded that 'in the interests of legal certainty with respect to objections undertaken by a State in a treaty, these procedural steps are mandatory'.[206] Latvia's failure to follow these procedures was fatal. But the tribunal then went on to apply Article 59(2) without having regard to the notification requirement. It noted that the terms of Article 59(2) required that 'it must "appear" from the later treaty, or be otherwise established, that the parties actually intended that the earlier treaty should stand suspended'.[207] The tribunal found that the no such intention was apparent in the circumstances and did not appear from the EU Treaties themselves.[208]

88 Some tribunals deciding the intra-EU BIT issue have also not placed as much emphasis on the formal notification requirement in Article 65.[209] Instead, most tribunals considering the impact of the EU Treaties have emphasized that the EU Treaties did not cover the same subject matter, as discussed above, not the notification requirement.[210] Even where a claimant has raised the notification issue,[211] some tribunals avoid relying on Article 65 in their reasoning.[212]

89 The issue is that the notification provision in Article 65 is not easily reconciled with implicit termination or suspension under Article 59. Article 59 does not itself include a notification requirement. Instead, it appears from the heading of Article 59 ('Termination or Suspension of the Operation of a Treaty Implied by Conclusion of a Later Treaty') that termination may be '*implied*' by the very act of concluding a later treaty.[213] Further, Article 59(1) contemplates that a treaty 'shall be considered as terminated' either from the text of

---

[203] *R (ex parte Miller) v Secretary of State for Exiting the European Union* [2017] UKSC 5.
[204] *Wightman and Others v Secretary of State for Exiting the European Union*, Case C-621/18, Judgment, CJEU Full Court, 10 December 2018.
[205] See above, para 68; *Eureko v Slovakia* (n 168) para 235.
[206] *AS PNB Banka and ors v Republic of Latvia*, ICSID Case No ARB/17/47, Decision on the Intra-EU Objection, 14 May 2021, para 632.
[207] ibid para 633.
[208] ibid paras 633–34.
[209] See *United Utilities (Tallinn) BV and Aktsiaselts Tallinna Vesi v Republic of Estonia*, ICSID Case No ARB/14/24, Award, 21 June 2019, para 538, where the lack of formal notification was merely a supporting factor for the tribunal's decision.
[210] See above, para 70.
[211] *Anglia Auto Accessories Ltd v Czech Republic*, SCC Case No V 2014/181, Award, 10 March 2017, para 104.
[212] ibid, paras 116–18. The tribunal instead placed significance on the failure of the parties to exercise the termination provisions already included in the BIT itself, including the fifteen-year survival clause, stating that the 'treaty law safeguards and mechanisms' could not simply vanish by means of a later treaty.
[213] The fact that Article 59 provides for implied termination is recognized in *Marfin v Cyprus* (n 176) paras 594 ('there can be no *implied termination* or invalidation of the Treaty to the detriment of investors who legitimately relied upon the Treaty's protections').

the treaty itself *or from the surrounding circumstances.* If the analysis were to stop merely at the absence of any formal notification per Article 65, it might render Article 59 dead letter.

Some tribunals have reasoned that the inclusion of Article 64 (providing for automatic termination of a treaty in the rare case of a new emergence of a *jus cogens* norm) means that this is the only situation in which automatic termination can occur, without notification.[214] The contrary argument is that the very existence of Article 64 confirms that Article 65 is overbroad and not applicable in every case.

One way to harmonize these provisions could be to read Article 65 as applying unless the ground of suspension, invalidity or termination itself implicitly or explicitly precludes a notification requirement. If a subsequent treaty itself provides for the termination of the earlier treaty, no separate notification is required (Article 59(1)(a), Article 54(b)).[215] Likewise, if it is clear from the circumstances that such termination is intended, as where the provisions are incompatible, this intention should be given effect to without any formal notification requirement (Article 59(1)(b)). Tropper and Reinisch argue that '[c]onsensual termination does not require a specific form' as long as all the parties to the BIT have consented 'in some form'.[216] At the same time, the absence of any notification or exchange of diplomatic notes may be relevant, as a matter of fact, to concluding that there was no intention to suspend or terminate the treaty.

The notification requirements in Article 65(1) and 67(1) of the VCLT were treated as being decisive in *Guris et al v Syria*.[217] In that case, Syria pleaded that the Turkey–Syria BIT had been suspended due to Turkey's hostility towards Syria. The tribunal noted that there was nothing in the BIT concerning suspension, and so applied the VCLT rules. Turkey is not party to the VCLT, but the parties agreed to the application of the VCLT rules as reflecting customary international law. Although the tribunal had no difficulty in concluding that there was an armed conflict, it held that the BIT had not been suspended since no notification of the suspension had been made by Syria. It further supported this conclusion by reference to the draft ILC articles on the Effect of Armed Conflict on Treaties, which provides that the mere existence of an armed conflict does not *ipso facto* terminate or suspend the operation of treaties.[218] It is noted, however, that the draft Articles are not yet widely recognized as customary international law, particularly in respect of the notification provision,[219] which one commentator has described as 'a product of progressive development of law by the ILC'.[220]

---

[214] *AMF Aircraftleasing Meier & Fischer GmbH & Co KG v Czech Republic*, PCA Case No 2017/15, Final Award, 11 May 2020, para 385.

[215] Tropper and Reinisch, 'The 2020 Termination Agreement' (n 109) 314 (arguing that '... "there is no distinct border-line between Article 54, para (b) and Article 59 [...] on the termination of a treaty be means of a later treaty", and in practice the effect is the same'); citing Villiger (n 38) 688.

[216] Tropper and Reinisch, 'The 2020 Termination Agreement' (n 109) 313; furthermore, commentators have historically been divided on how broadly the notification requirement in Article 65 applies. See B Conforti and A Labella, 'Invalidity and Termination of Treaties: the Role of National Courts' (1990) 1 EJIL 44, 44 ('A problem the legal literature does not so far seem to provide much clarity about is whether, and when, the causes of invalidity or termination of a treaty operate automatically'); T Hui-Yi, *Revolution, State Succession, International Treaties and the Diaoyu/Diaoyutai Islands* (Cambridge 2017) 185 ('Articles 65 to 68 raise some questions about whether the automaticity of treaty termination and invalidity is excluded in every case').

[217] *Guris Construction and Engineering Inc and ors v Arab Republic of Syria*, ICC Case No 21845/ZF/AYF, Final Award, 31 August 2020, paras 152–53.

[218] ILC, Draft Articles on the Effect of Armed Conflict on Treaties with Commentaries, YILC 2011, Vol II, Part II, UN Doc A/66/10, Article 3.

[219] ibid Article 9(1) ('1. A State intending to terminate or withdraw from a treaty to which it is a party, or to suspend the operation of that treaty, as a consequence of an armed conflict shall notify the other State party or States parties to the treaty, or its depositary, of such intention').

[220] J Ostřanský, 'The Termination and Suspension of Bilateral Investment Treaties due to an Armed Conflict' (2015) 6 JIDS 136, 142.

E. Conclusion

93   This entry has traversed the most significant investment jurisprudence concerning Parts IV and V of the VCLT. It identified few significant divergences between investment tribunals and international courts and tribunals concerning the provisions dealing with termination, amendment, and invalidity. However, in many cases, specific provisions on termination or amendment are set out in the investment treaty, meaning that it may not be necessary to rely on the VCLT. This is wholly consistent with the scheme of the Convention.

94   The main contribution of investor–State arbitration jurisprudence to the general international law on amendment and modification relates to the dividing line between interpretation and subsequent practice, as well as the application of Article 41. In the main, tribunals have hewed closely to the language of the VCLT and there are no obvious departures from general international law. Any divergence between investment tribunals and the post-*Achmea* ECJ can be said to reflect different paradigms about whether EU law operates on the same plane as public international law, not a disagreement on the VCLT provisions.

95   As to invalidity, the VCLT rules have rarely been considered by investment tribunals to date. The main exception is Article 46 in the intra-EU context, where investment law may ultimately influence the development of public international law in giving meaning to the term 'manifest'. Given the paucity of other jurisprudence on Article 50, the investment jurisprudence may also be of relevance for its interpretation, particularly regarding questions such as the burden and standard of proof for corruption allegations and the necessary degree of causality.

96   Finally, in the context of termination and suspension, the most significant body of investment jurisprudence relates to Article 59, where termination is implied by the terms of a later treaty. In this respect, it is questionable whether the notification procedure in Article 65 ought strictly to apply to Article 59. Furthermore, there are a number of investment cases dealing with the retrospective effects of termination that may also have application where treaties are terminated or suspended in the sphere of general international law.

Selected literature

Aust A, 'Treaties, Termination' in *The Max Planck Encyclopedia of Public International Law* (2006).
Aust A, *Modern Treaty Law and Practice* (3rd edn, CUP 2012).
Binder C, 'A Treaty Law Perspective on Intra-EU BITs' (2016) 17 JWIT 964.
Cannizzaro E (ed), *The Law of Treaties Beyond the Vienna Convention* (OUP 2011).
Cameron I, 'Treaties, Suspension' in *The Max Planck Encyclopedia of Public International Law* (2006).
Conforti B and Labella A, 'Invalidity and Termination of Treaties: the Role of National Courts' (1990) 1 EJIL 44.
Corten O and Klein P (eds), *The Vienna Conventions on the Law of Treaties—A Commentary* (OUP 2011).
Dörr O and Schmalenbach K (eds), *Vienna Convention on the Law of Treaties: A Commentary* (2nd edn, Springer 2018).
Harrison J, 'The Life and Death of BITs: Legal Issues concerning Survival Clauses and the Termination of Investment Treaties' (2012) 13 JWIT 928.
Hollis DB (ed), *The Oxford Guide to Treaties* (2nd edn, OUP 2021).
Nahlik SE, 'The Grounds of Invalidity and Termination of Treaties' (1971) 65 AJIL 736.

Reinisch A and Fallah SM, 'Post-Termination Responsibility of States?—The Impact of Amendment/Modification, Suspension and Termination of Investment Treaties on (Vested) Rights of Investors' (2022) 37 ICSID Rev 101.

Sinclair I, *The Vienna Convention on the Law of Treaties* (2nd edn, MUP 1984).

Tropper J and Reinisch A, 'The 2020 Termination Agreement of intra-EU BITs and Its Effect on Investment Arbitration in the EU-A Public International Law Analysis of the Termination Agreement' (2022) 16 Austrian YB Int'l Arb 301.

Villiger ME, *Commentary on the 1969 Vienna Convention on the Law of Treaties* (Martinus Nijhoff Publishers 2009).

Voon T and Mitchell AD, 'Denunciation, Termination and Survival: The Interplay of Treaty Law and International Investment Law' (2016) 31(2) ICSID Rev 413.

Zhang Y, 'Mutual Termination of Sunset Clauses in Intra-EU BITs: The Search for Investor Protections' (2019) 29(2) Am Rev of Int'l Arb 173.

Selected decisions

BayWa re Renewable Energy GmbH and BayWa r.e. Asset Holding GmbH v Kingdom of Spain, ICSID Case No ARB/15/16, Decision on Jurisdiction, Liability and Directions on Quantum, 2 December 2019.

Cavalum SGPS, SA v Kingdom of Spain, ICSID Case No ARB/15/34, Decision on the Kingdom of Spain's Request for Reconsideration, 10 January 2022.

Eureko BV v Slovak Republic, PCA Case No 2008-13, UNCITRAL Rules, Jurisdiction, 26 October 2010.

Eskosol SpA in liquidazione v Italian Republic, ICSID Case No ARB/15/50, Decision on Italy's Request for Immediate Termination and Italy's Jurisdictional Objection Based on Inapplicability of the ECT to Intra-EU Disputes, 7 May 2019.

Gabčíkovo-Nagymaros Project (Hungary v Slovakia) (Judgment) [1997] ICJ Rep 7.

Guris Construction and Engineering Inc and ors v Arab Republic of Syria, ICC Case No 21845/ZF/AYF, Final Award, 31 August 2020, paras 152–53.

Metal-Tech Ltd v Republic of Uzbekistan, ICSID Case No ARB/10/3, Award, 4 October 2013.

Methanex Corporation v United States of America, Final Award, 3 August 2005.

Republic of Moldova v Komstroy LLC, Case C-741/19 (CJEU GC, 2 September 2021).

Slovak Republic v Achmea BV, Case C-284/16, (CJEU GC, 6 March 2018).

Silver Ridge Power BV v Italian Republic, ICSID Case No ARB/15/37, Award, 26 February 2021.

Vattenfall AB and others v Federal Republic of Germany, ICSID Case No ARB/12/12, Decision on the Achmea Issue, 31 August 2018, para 219.

Land and Maritime Boundary between Cameroon and Nigeria (Cameroon v Nigeria) (Counter-claims) [2002] ICJ Rep 303.

Article 59 of the VCLT

Termination or suspension of the operation of a treaty implied by conclusion of a later treaty

Hélène Ruiz Fabri and Randi Ayman

1. A treaty shall be considered as terminated if all the parties to it conclude a later treaty relating to the same subject-matter and:

(a) it appears from the later treaty or is otherwise established that the parties intended that the matter should be governed by that treaty; or

(b) the provisions of the later treaty are so far incompatible with those of the earlier one that the two treaties are not capable of being applied at the same time.

2. The earlier treaty shall be considered as only suspended in operation if it appears from the later treaty or is otherwise established that such was the intention of the parties.

A. Introduction	1
B. Application in general international law	5
I. Conditions relating to the parties to the treaties and their intention	8
II. Conditions relating to the subject matter and content of the treaties	11
III. Temporal considerations	13
IV. Consequences: Termination or suspension	16
C. Application in international investment law	18
I. Investor–States dispute settlement (ISDS) tribunals	19
II. CJEU (as a regional court ruling on international investment–related matters)	24
D. Alignment of general international law and international investment law	29
E. Conclusion	30

A. Introduction

1 Article 59 of the Vienna Convention on the Law of Treaties (VCLT) provides for the resolution of a conflict between successive treaties concluded by the same parties on the same subject matter by envisaging the termination (or suspension) of the earlier treaty. It reflects customary international law, and has long been present in legal literature,[1] in previous

---

[1] See Q Wright, 'Conflicts Between International Law and Treaties' (1917) 11 AJIL 576; AD Mc Nair, 'La terminaison et la dissolution des traités' (1928) 22 RCADI 517; J Dehaussy, 'Sources du droit international: extinction, suspension, révision' (1960) Jurisclasseur de droit international fasc 12-D 9; P Guggenheim, *Traité de droit International Public* (Book 1, 2nd edn, Librairie de l'Université 1967) 220; C Rousseau, *Droit International Public* (Book 1, Sirey 1970) 207; RD Kearney and RE Dalton, 'The Treaty on Treaties' (1970) 64 AJIL 539; F Capotorti, 'L'extinction et la suspension des traités' (1971) 134 RCADI 496–500; ME Villiger, 'Article 59' in *Commentary on the 1969 Vienna Convention on the Law of Treaties* (Martinus Nijhoff Publishers 2009) 728; F Dubuisson, 'Termination and Suspension of the Operation of Treaties, Art. 59 1969 Vienna Convention' in O Corten and P Klein (eds), *The Vienna Conventions on the Law of Treaties* (OUP 2011) 1325 (hereafter Dubuisson, 'Termination

codification works,[2] in works of the *Institut de Droit International*,[3] and in practice, although the International Law Commission (ILC) cited no example drawn from State practice.[4]

Adopted unanimously at the Vienna Conference on the Law of Treaties, Article 59 belongs to the VCLT section on 'Termination and Suspension of the Operation of Treaties'. This section is criticized for incorporating flexible mechanisms the use of which is, nonetheless, hindered by unattainably strict requirements. This is usually justified by the ultimate objective of the drafters to protect and guarantee treaties' stability. However, like most other provisions of the VCLT, Article 59 is a default rule, ie it applies when the parties to the successive treaties have not provided for a specific solution. Nevertheless, there are examples of treaties that include an express clause referring to Article 59 (rather than termination by the terms of the treaty in Article 54(b)), which is at odds with the implied character of the termination or suspension.[5]

Within the VCLT, Article 59 is closely linked to Article 30 on *Application of successive treaties relating to the same subject matter* (which expressly refers to Article 59).[6] Despite the ILC's efforts to avoid overlaps, 'the division made by the ILC between the respective regimes of Articles 30 and 59 proves to be unclear in practice and fixed in a fairly artificial manner'.[7] Both provisions are commonly invoked and analysed together, given the similarity of their main elements. In addition, Article 59 supplements Articles 54 (on *Termination of or withdrawal from a treaty under its provisions or by consent of the parties*) and 57 (on *Suspension of the operation of a treaty under its provisions or by consent of the parties*). Finally, the dispute settlement procedure of Articles 65–68 VCLT are applicable to Article 59.

Against this brief introduction, this entry will first review the application of Article 59 and how its conditions have been considered under general international law (Section B). The application of Article 59 will then be examined in the context of international investment law, particularly through the lens of investor–State arbitration tribunals (Section C). In light of the findings of these sections, the entry will proceed with some reflections on how aligned

---

and Suspension of the Operation of Treaties'); T Giegerich, 'Article 59' in O Dörr and K Schmalenbach (eds), *Vienna Convention on the Law of Treaties, A Commentary* (2nd edn, Springer 2018) 1083 (hereafter Giegerich, 'Article 59').

[2] It was codified in 1935 in the Draft Convention on the Law of Treaties of Harvard Law School, 'Law of Treaties, Draft Convention, with commentary, prepared by the Research in International Law of the Harvard Law School' (1935) 29 AJIL 1009.

[3] S Rosenne, 'Modification et terminaison des traités' (1967) 1 Ann IDI session de Nice 167: 'l'idée fondamentale qu'un traité subséquent peut implicitement mettre fin ou suspendre l'application d'un traité précédent est une cause de terminaison ou de suspension de l'application ... bien établie en droit international.' See also Resolution by the Institute of International Law relative to 'Problems Arising from a Succession of Codification Conventions on a Particular Subject', adopted at the session of Lisbon, 1995, conclusion no 5.

[4] For an example of State practice before the adoption of the VCLT, see, in reference to the France-Ecuador commercial conventions of 1938 and 1959, Court of Appeal of Paris, 15e ch, 30 January 1967, S.I.M.A.B. c./Sté Calvet et Martinez, in Jean-François Lachaume, 'Jurisprudence française concernant le droit international— Année 1968' (1969) 15 AFDI 837.

[5] The latter is illustrated by Article XXXI of the Convention for the strengthening of the Inter-American Tropical Tuna Commission established by the 1949 Convention between the United States of America and the Republic of Costa Rica (Antigua Convention) (with four annexes), signed in Washington 14 November 2003, according to which '[...] 6. Upon entry into force of this Convention for all Parties to the 1949 Convention, the 1949 Convention shall be considered as terminated in accordance with the relevant rules of international law as reflected in Article 59 of the Vienna Convention on the Law of Treaties'. On termination by mutual consent see in this Commentary: Luke Sobota and Amelia Keene 'Parts IV and V—Amendment, Invalidity, Termination and Suspension of Investment Treaties', para 49 et seq.

[6] See in this Commentary: Sean Aughey, 'Article 30 VCLT: Application of successive treaties relating to the same subject-matter'.

[7] Dubuisson, 'Termination and Suspension of the Operation of Treaties' (n 1) 1327.

the perception of Article 59 is under both general international law and investment law (Section D), before providing some concluding remarks (Section E).

B. Application in general international law

5   Generally, the discussion of Article 59 has been limited to international scholarship and commentaries of the VCLT. In fact, there are no International Court of Justice (ICJ) decisions to date addressing this Article. Nonetheless, the separate opinion of Judge Anzilotti in *Electricity Company of Sofia and Bulgaria*[8] (in the Permanent Court of International Justice (PCIJ) in 1939) was the main inspiration of the drafters of Article 59. In this opinion, Judge Anzilotti noted that, beside express abrogation, 'there is also tacit abrogation'[9] of successive treaties dealing with the 'same thing'.[10]

6   Judge Anzilotti's view in this regard is immediately noticed in the title of Article 59, which specifies an 'implied' termination or suspension of a treaty by the conclusion of a subsequent treaty. However, there is a wide consensus (including by investment arbitration tribunals, discussed below) that an 'implied' termination/suspension does not mean an 'automatic' termination/suspension,[11] which is further supported by the importance granted to the parties' intentions.

7   Indeed, the treaty parties' intentions are an essential part of the cumulative conditions set out in Article 59 (Subsection A). These conditions also refer to the subject matter and content of the treaties (Subsection B). In addition, although Article 59 does not mention them, some temporal circumstances must be considered (Subsection C) as well as their consequences (Subsection D).

I. Conditions relating to the parties to the treaties and their intention

8   With respect to its *ratione personae* element, Article 59(1) states that all parties to the first treaty must also be parties to the second treaty, although the latter could have more parties. Otherwise, Article 30 applies.

9   Although Article 59 does not deal with State succession, the 'all the parties' criterion extends to the replacements of States resulting from a succession, keeping in mind that succession is

---

[8] *The Electricity Company of Sofia and Bulgaria* (*Belgium v Bulgaria*) (Preliminary Objection) PCIJ Series A/B No 77, 64–85.
[9] ibid 92, para 5 (hereafter Separate Opinion by Judge Dionisio Anzilotti). We omit in this entry the discussion whether the declarations at stake in the case were a 'treaty'.
[10] ibid 90, para 3. In the same paragraph, Judge Anzilotti states: 'It is clear that, in the same legal system, there cannot at the same time exist two rules relating to the same facts and attaching to these facts contradictory consequences. ... In cases of this kind, either the contradiction is only apparent and the two rules are really coordinated so that each has its own sphere of application and does not encroach on the sphere of application of the other, or else one prevails over the other, ie, is applicable to the exclusion of the other. I know of no clearer, more certain, or more universally accepted principle than this.' Tacit abrogation is also mentioned in the Dissenting Opinion of Judge Basdevant in *Ambatielos* (*Greece v United Kingdom*) (Preliminary Objections) [1952] ICJ Rep 66, 71, and by Judges De Castro and Barwick in *Nuclear Tests* (*Australia v France*) [1974] ICJ Rep 372, 383 and [1974] ICJ Rep 391, 405 respectively, both mentioning Article 59.
[11] In addition to the interpretation exercise that the operation of Article 59 involves, termination/suspension is subject to the mandatory notification required by Article 65 of the VCLT.

not automatic, except for treaties dealing with borders.[12] This renders even more complex situations such as the European Union (EU) replacing its Member States as party to investment treaties[13] and/or concluding and/or terminating treaties on the latter's behalf.

Since the Article deals with implied termination, it must be established that such was the intention of the parties as 'it appears from the later treaty or is otherwise established' (a subjective test which also applies to suspension, as Article 59(2) states). Such broad wording allows for evidence by any means, if the text of the treaty is insufficiently clear, and, according to some views, even if the two treaties include a compatibility clause.[14] This subjective test refers to the same means used for interpretation, which is further confirmed when considering the other conditions. **10**

II. Conditions relating to the subject matter and content of the treaties

Article 59 primarily requires that the two treaties in question deal with 'the same subject matter'. This, in itself, can raise delicate problems of assessment as shown by the European Commission's unsuccessful efforts, at least until 2022 (see below paragraph 21), to show that European law had replaced the Energy Charter Treaty (ECT) in relations between EU members (see below Section C). In fact, there is a great deal of uncertainty when it comes to the required degree of sameness: identical, similar, overlapping, same objectives, dealing with same situations or circumstances, etc. It is of course impossible to answer such questions in general terms but the wording 'relating to the same subject-matter' seems to imply some flexibility, ie that overall the two treaties 'intend to govern the same object at the same time'.[15] This interpretation is consistent with Article 59 only contemplating termination (or suspension) of the earlier treaty as a whole (see below Subsection D). It is nevertheless agreed that the second treaty could have a broader scope than the first (eg many new free trade agreements (FTAs) are broader than international investment agreements (IIAs), but include provisions pertaining to investment protections and dispute resolution), but not vice versa.[16] Otherwise, Article 30 applies. **11**

Again, as this is a case of tacit termination, which means that the two treaties have formally survived until tacit abrogation is invoked, Article 59 requires that their provisions are 'so far incompatible' that they cannot be applied simultaneously.[17] Thus, the purpose is conflict avoidance. The test of incompatibility looks like an objective one. However, the text of the treaties might not be so clear that the incompatibility is obvious at first glance. Therefore, interpretation may be in order. In one way or another, it brings back the intention of the parties and shows that the two circumstances that Article 59 presents as alternative ('or') are in **12**

---

[12] See the customary rule codified in Article 11 of the 1978 Vienna Convention on Succession of States in Respect of Treaties.
[13] A situation considered by some authors as 'functional succession'. See Giegerich, 'Article 59' (n 1) 1088, para 16.
[14] Dubuisson, 'Termination and Suspension of the Operation of Treaties' (n 1) 1340.
[15] ibid 1336.
[16] See, eg, Robin Churchill's opinion that the European Fisheries Convention (EFC) has been terminated by the conclusion of UNCLOS in accordance with Article 59 of the VCLT. R Churchill, 'Possible EU Fisheries Rights in UK Waters and Possible UK Fishery Rights in EU Waters Post-Brexit' (*Opinion prepared for the Scottish Fishermen's Federation*, November 2016) paras 7–10 www.sff.co.uk/wp-content/uploads/2017/03/Opinion-for-SFF-2016.pdf, last accessed 23 October 2023.
[17] This is the second most discussed criterion by ISDS tribunals, see below Section C.

fact tied together. Indeed, is it plausible that States conclude on the same subject matter two treaties whose terms overall are incompatible without States being aware of it? In this perspective, 'ultimately, [paragraph 1(b) of Article 59] would only constitute a variation of the case provided in paragraph 1(a) of Article 59'.[18] In any event, the question is whether paragraph 1(b) could apply independently. Even if Judge Anzilotti's opinion is the intellectual matrix of Article 59, it was a dissent whereas the Permanent Court of International Justice (PCIJ) focused on the Parties' intentions.[19]

III. Temporal considerations

13   In addition to the above conditions, Article 59 involves two types of temporal considerations: (i) which treaty preceded the other; and (ii) the duration of the treaties. Nonetheless, Article 59's silence on both points only increases the complexity of the situation.

14   First, there is the issue of which is the 'earlier treaty' and which is the 'later treaty'. Article 59 refers to States 'concluding' the later treaty, the debates in the ILC having led to the dominant view that it was at this point (adoption) that the States expressed their intention. However, although meaningful in terms of providing for a single term of reference for the expression of States' intention, this approach does not solve the further issue of fixing the date of the termination. In this respect, the entry into force of the subsequent treaty, provided it concerns all parties to the previous treaty, is decisive. Nevertheless, the conclusion remains relevant in case of provisional application of the later treaty, but it falls under Article 59(2) on suspension.

15   Second, Article 59 does not consider the issue of the duration of the treaties in question, more precisely the case where the later treaty is concluded for a fixed period. The question was addressed by Judge Anzilotti in his dissenting opinion and his view was that the earlier treaty is revived once the later treaty ends.[20] In terms of Article 59, it means that such situation more plausibly falls under Article 59(2) on suspension. In investment law, the question of the possibility to 'revive' the first treaty might be raised in the context of the United Kingdom–European Union Trade and Cooperation Agreement and its potential conflict with the United Kingdom's Bilateral Investment Treaties (BITs).

IV. Consequences: Termination or suspension

16   In order to avoid as much overlap as possible with Article 30, the authors of Article 59 have limited its effect to a total termination (or suspension) of the earlier treaty. In this regard, interpreting the incompatibility referred to in paragraph 1(b) as being an overall or global one is consistent. However, it might explain why Article 59 is not much used in practice. In any event, it does not mean that partial termination or suspension is not possible, as Article

---

[18] Dubuisson, 'Termination and Suspension of the Operation of Treaties' (n 1) 1342. Reaching the same conclusion, see D Costelloe, 'Compatibility in the Law of Treaties and Stability in International Law' (2022) 1 BYIL 35.
[19] 'The Court shares the view of the Parties. In its opinion, the multiplicity of agreements concluded accepting the compulsory jurisdiction is evidence that the contracting Parties intended to open up new ways of access to the Court rather than to close old ways or to allow them to cancel each other out with the ultimate result that no jurisdiction would remain': *The Electricity Company of Sofia and Bulgaria (Belgium v Bulgaria)* (Preliminary Objection) PCIJ Series A/B No 77, 76.
[20] Separate Opinion by Judge Dionisio Anzilotti (n 9) para 5.

59 is subsidiary and States always have the possibility to opt for a special regime the terms of which they decide freely. Otherwise, Article 30 applies.

Thus, the will of the parties remains key, not only to envisage an implicit termination but also to distinguish between cases where adoption of the later treaty results in a suspension of the earlier treaty or in its termination.

C. Application in international investment law

Article 59, along with Article 30, is at the heart of the intra-EU arbitration objection saga that has started a little less than two decades ago. This is mainly through a twofold issue of whether the EU can terminate BITs concluded by its Member States, as a consequence of it acquiring the competences previously held by the Member States, and of the incompatibility of Multilateral Investment Treaties (MITs)/BITs and EU Law. Arbitral tribunals and the Court of Justice of the European Union (CJEU) developed opposing views on the issue. They will be examined in turn.

I. Investor–States dispute settlement (ISDS) tribunals

Article 59 has been invoked multiple times before ISDS tribunals, some of which noted that termination under Article 59 is 'implicit' and not automatic or retroactive.[21]

The first tribunal to consider the intra-EU objection issue was *Eastern Sugar v Czech Republic* in a partial award rendered in 2007, where the Czech Republic argued that its BIT with the Netherlands should be considered as terminated following the Czech Republic's accession to the EU, in accordance with Article 59 (note the question was raised, and the award was rendered before the entry into force of the Treaty on the Functioning of the European Union (TFEU)). The tribunal concluded that the two treaties do not cover the same subject matter (hence 'are not incompatible'[22]), that the parties to the BIT had no common intention that the EU Treaty would supersede the BIT.[23]

Since then, the intra-EU objection invoking Article 59 (and 30) has regularly been raised before ISDS tribunals in arbitration proceedings based on an intra-EU BIT or on the ECT. As put 'frankly' by the tribunal in *Addiko Bank AG and Addiko Bank dd v Republic of Croatia*, the consideration that 'implicit termination [of a BIT] occur[s] from the moment of [a State's] accession to the EU' is 'a non-starter'.[24] Except for the isolated dissenting opinion of Professor Kohen in *Theodoros Adamakopoulos and others v Republic of Cyprus*,[25] ISDS

---

[21] Some referred to the use of the future tense in the 2019 Termination Declarations as being indicative of the Signatories States' recognition that their intra-EU BITs had not already been terminated. *Addiko Bank AG and Addiko Bank dd v Republic of Croatia (Addiko Bank)*, ICSID Case No ARB/17/37, Decision on Respondent Jurisdictional Objection Related to the Alleged Incompatibility of the BIT with the EU Acquis, 12 June 2020, para 296 (hereafter *Addiko Bank*).
[22] *Eastern Sugar BV (Netherlands) v The Czech Republic*, SCC Case No 088/2004, Partial Award, 27 March 2007, para 168.
[23] ibid paras 159ff.
[24] ibid para 294.
[25] *Theodoros Adamakopoulos and others v Republic of Cyprus (Adamakopoulos)*, ICSID Case No ARB/15/49, Jurisdiction, Dissenting Opinion of Professor Marcelo Kohen, 7 February 2020, para 7 (hereafter *Adamakopoulos*, Jurisdiction).

tribunals have consistently rejected the termination or suspension[26] argument based on the incompatibility of the BIT or ECT and the TFEU.[27] Although tribunals have adopted different levels of analysis of the elements of Article 59 (ranging from a brief analysis[28] to a detailed examination of the Article's conditions[29]), they tend to apply a high threshold: they stress that the mere fact that both treaties deal with investment and dispute settlement is not enough to conclude that they have the same subject matter and that the analysis should go to a more specific level.[30] Indeed, tribunals have consistently found that similar objectives,[31] facts,[32] or situations[33] do not mean 'the same subject matter' as required in Article 59(1) VCLT. Some tribunals even considered that sameness under Article 59 shares common features with the notion of 'identity' applied in the context of the doctrine of *res judicata*.[34] It is less frequent that tribunals addressed the 'intention' element,[35] or compare the parties to the treaties, although there are examples of the latter case in the context of ECT.[36]

---

[26] There is one known instance where the Respondent State argued that the BIT was suspended in accordance with Article 59 to avoid the operation of the BIT's sunset clause: *AS PNB Banka and others v Republic of Latvia (AS PNB)*, ICSID Case No ARB/17/47, Decision on the Intra-EU Objection, 14 May 2021, para 629 (hereafter *AS PNB*).

[27] On this point, we note that, on 16 June 2022, the SCC Tribunal in *Green Power K/S and Obton A/S v Spain*, SCC Case No V 2016/13, Award, 16 June 2022 declined jurisdiction upholding the intra-EU objection, on the basis that EU law applied to jurisdiction and that it prevailed over the ECT (*lex superior*). However, there were no arguments related to implicit termination, nor has Article 59 VCLT been invoked or mentioned in the award (Article 30 VCLT was briefly invoked by the Claimant but not addressed by the tribunal). For a further analysis, see F Paddeu and C Tams, 'Interpreting Away Treaty Conflicts? Green Power, ISDS and the Primacy of EU Law' (*Kluwer Arbitration Blog*, 23 August 2022) <http://arbitrationblog.kluwerarbitration.com/2022/08/23/interpreting-away-treaty-conflicts-green-power-isds-and-the-primacy-of-eu-law/> accessed 12 September 2022. It is also worth noting that divergent conclusions have been reached by the German courts. On 1 September 2022, the Higher Regional Court of Cologne held that ECT intra-EU arbitrations are not compatible with EU law despite being ICSID cases, whereas the Higher Regional Court of Berlin dismissed a few months earlier Germany's request of inadmissibility of the ICSID arbitration case *Mainstream v Germany*, stressing that the ICSID Convention was 'a closed legal system'. See the press release summarizing the Higher Regional Court of Cologne's decision (Cologne Higher Regional Court, 1 September 2022, 19 SchH 14/2 and 19 SchH 15/21) <https://www.olg-koeln.nrw.de/behoerde/presse/004_zt_letzte-pm_archiv_zwangs/001_letzte_pressemitteilung/index.php> accessed 10 September 2022. The full decision will be published at <www.nrwe.de>. See also L Bohmer, 'German Court Declares ECT/ICSID Arbitrations Against The Netherlands to Be Inadmissible Due to Their Intra-EU Nature' *IAR* (8 September 2022). With respect to the decision of the Berlin High Court No 12 SchH 6/21 of 28 April 2022. See L Bohmer 'Berlin Court Dismisses Germany's Request for Anti-Arbitration Declaration Directed at ICSID Case' *IAR* (24 May 2022). See also L Halonen and S Eichhorn, 'Berlin Court Finds that ICSID Arbitrations Are Immune from Achmea and Komstroy—At Least While They Are Ongoing' (*Kluwer Arbitration Blog*, 21 July 2022).

[28] See, eg, *Jürgen Wirtgen, Stefan Wirtgen, Gisela Wirtgen and JSW Solar (zwei) GmbH & Co KG v Czech Republic (Wirtgen)*, PCA Case No 2014-03, Final Award, 11 October 2017 (hereafter *Wirtgen*).

[29] See, eg, *Euram v Slovak Republic*, UNCITRAL, Jurisdiction, 22 October 2012; *Electrabel v Hungary*, ICSID Case No ARB/07/19, Decision on Jurisdiction, Applicable Law and Liability, 30 November 2012, paras 2.12–2.16 (hereafter *Electrabel v Hungary*); *Anglia Auto Accessories Ltd v Czech Republic*, SCC Case No V2014/181, Final Award, 10 March 2017 (hereafter *Euram v Slovak Republic*).

[30] *Adamakopoulos*, Jurisdiction (n 25) para 168.

[31] *AS PNB* (n 26) para 628.

[32] *GPF GP Sàrl v Republic of Poland*, SCC Case No V2014/168, Final Award, 29 April 2020, para 364.

[33] *Euram v Slovak Republic* (n 29) para 169.

[34] *Achmea BV (fohrmerly Eureko BV) v Slovak Republic I (Achmea I)*, PCA Case No 2008-13, Award on Jurisdiction, Arbitrability and Suspension, 26 October 2010, para 258 (hereafter *Achmea I*). See also *Wirtgen* (n 28) para 253, fn 152. On this point, it is interesting to note that the seminal statement on the elements of *res judicata* was also mentioned in another dissenting opinion of Judge Anzilotti, namely, in the case of the Chorzow Factory. *Interpretation of Judgments No 7 and 8 Concerning the Case of the Factory at Chorzow* (Dissenting Opinion by Judge Dionisio Anzilotti) PCIJ Series A No 13, 23.

[35] See, eg, *Fynerdale Holdings BV v The Czech Republic*, PCA Case No 2018-18, Award, 29 April 2021, para 314; *Addiko Bank* (n 21) para 296; *Euram v Slovak Republic* (n 29) para 280.

[36] *RENERGY Sàrl v Kingdom of Spain*, ICSID Case No ARB/14/18, Award, 6 May 2022, para 394 (hereafter *RENERGY v Spain*); *Sevilla Beheer et al v Spain*, ICSID Case No ARB/16/27, Decision on Jurisdiction, Liability and the Principles of Quantum, 11 February 2022, para 651 (hereafter *Sevilla Beheer et al v Spain*): 'At least one of the conditions of the application of Article 59 is clearly unmet in the present case, as the ECT's Contracting Parties include both EU and non-EU countries. This argument is therefore dismissed.'

Where relevant, tribunals made a distinction between Articles 30 and 59.[37] Most of them, however, referred to previous decisions by ISDS tribunals. Some of them expressly referred to ILC works,[38] Judge Anzilotti's dissenting opinion,[39] or the 'recognized meaning (of incompatibility) in public international law'.[40]

Apart from the decision in *Green Power v Spain* (which dealt with the ECT and not a BIT), ISDS tribunals that dealt with this issue have followed the same jurisprudence, before and after the CJEU's judgments on *Achmea* and *Komstroy* (see below Section C.II). They consistently noted that they were not bound by the CJEU's decisions,[41] and expressly rejected the argument that the principle of primacy of EU law is the primary conflict rule to be relied upon when it comes to the relationship between a BIT and the TFEU, stating on the contrary that 'the relationship between successive treaties is exclusively governed by international law'[42] and/or that the '*Achmea* Judgment did not make any findings on "public international law relationship between intra-EU BITs and the TFEU"'.[43]

II. CJEU (as a regional court ruling on international investment–related matters)

The issue of (implied) termination was only discussed in Opinion 2/15.[44] The Commission's request of an Opinion from the CJEU on whether the EU had the requisite competence to sign and conclude alone the EU–Singapore Free Trade Agreement (EUSFTA) also covered the question of Article 9.10 according to which the EU and Singapore terminated BITs concluded by EU Member States and Singapore. In their views, '[t]he Council and a significant number of Member States argued that the European Union cannot, acting alone, agree with a third State to terminate and replace international agreements concluded by that State with one or several Member States and to which the European Union itself is not a party'.[45] The intervening Member States further argued that the underlying EUSFTA provision does not respect the general principle, expressed in Article 59(1)(a) of the VCLT.[46] Advocate General Sharpston went in the same direction, considering that there was no basis in international law (as it currently stands) for concluding that the EU may automatically succeed to an international agreement concluded by the Member States, to which it is not a party, and then terminate that agreement. Such a rule would constitute an exception to the fundamental rule of consent in international law-making. Accepting the Commission's position would mean that, as a result of changes in EU law and (possibly) the EU's exercise of its external competences, a Member State

---

[37] See, eg, *RENERGY v Spain* (n 36) para 385; *ESPF Beteiligungs GmbH, ESPF Nr 2 Austria Beteiligungs GmbH and InfraClass Energie 5 GmbH & Co KG v Italian Republic*, ICSID Case No ARB/16/5, Award, 14 September 2020, para 314; *United Utilities (Tallinn) B.V. and Aktsiaselts Tallinna Vesi v Republic of Estonia*, ICSID Case No ARB/14/24, Award, 21 June 2019, para 549; *Achmea I* (n 34) paras 240–41.
[38] *AS PNB* (n 26) para 639; *Euram v Slovak Republic* (n 29) para 95; *Electrabel v Hungary* (n 29) para 175.
[39] *AMF Aircraftleasing Meier & Fischer GmbH & Co KG v Czech Republic*, PCA Case No 2017-15, Final Award, 11 May 2020, para 347 (hereafter *AMF Aircraftleasing Meier & Fischer GmbH & Co KG v Czech Republic*): 'Judge Anzilotti's Dissenting Opinion supports the Arbitral Tribunal's interpretation of Article 59 of the VCLT ....'
[40] *Addiko Bank* (n 21) para 207.
[41] See, eg, *RENERGY v Spain* (n 36) paras 342–57 and 361; and *Sevilla Beheer et al v Spain* (n 36) paras 655–76.
[42] *AMF Aircraftleasing Meier & Fischer GmbH & Co KG v Czech Republic* (n 39) para 363.
[43] *Strabag SE, Raiffeisen Centrobank AG and Syrena Immobilien Holding AG v Republic of Poland*, ICSID Case No ADHOC/15/1, Partial Award on Jurisdiction, 4 March 2020, para 8.139.
[44] CJEU, Opinion 2/15 of the CJEU [2017] ECLI:EU:C:2017:376, 16 May 2017, paras 245–56 (hereafter Opinion 2/15).
[45] CJEU, Opinion 2/15, Opinion of AG Sharpston, [2016] ECLI:EU:C:2016:992, para 373.
[46] ibid para 303.

might cease to be a party to an international agreement, even though it was a State which had consented to be bound by that agreement and for which that agreement was in force (…). I therefore conclude that the Member States enjoy exclusive competence to terminate bilateral investment agreements which they previously concluded with third States. As a result, the EU has no competence to agree to Article 9.10 of the EUSFTA.[47]

25 The CJEU carefully circumvented Article 59. Without referring to it, and after underlining that 'the European Union and the Republic of Singapore have inserted in the envisaged agreement a provision making expressly clear that bilateral investment agreements between Member States and that third State are terminated', the Court considered that 'when the European Union negotiates and concludes with a third State an agreement relating to a field in respect of which it has acquired exclusive competence, it takes the place of its Member States'.[48] Therefore, from the entry into force of the TFEU,

> the European Union has competence to approve, by itself, a provision of an agreement concluded by it with a third State which stipulates that the commitments concerning direct investment contained in bilateral agreements previously concluded between Member States of the European Union and that third State must, upon the entry into force of that agreement concluded by the European Union, be regarded as replaced by the latter.[49]

Such wording remains ambiguous, as the use of the passive voice does not clarify who has the formal power to terminate BITs (the Member States or the EU) nor does the term 'replaced'.

26 Two remarks can be made here, both converging on the fact that the questions asked were outside the scope of Article 59:

1 The first is that Article 59 is not applicable because the 'same parties' condition is not met. Article 59 requires a formal parallelism[50] between those who conclude the treaty and those who tacitly terminate the treaty (the same is true for both VCLT of 1969 and 1986).

2 The second is Article 59 is only a default rule and leaves room for solutions chosen by the parties to the later treaty. In this regard, the initial Article 9.10 of the EUSFTA had expressly disposed of the issue by stating that 'Upon the entry into force of this Agreement, the [bilateral investment] agreements between Member States of the Union and Singapore … including the rights and obligations derived therefrom, shall cease to have effect and shall be replaced and superseded by this Agreement'. In other words, it was express termination, which falls outside the scope of Article 59. The remaining issue is whether formal parallelism would be a mandatory principle beyond Article 59, preventing the EU from having the competence to proceed to the termination of agreements concluded by its Member States. Only a very strict approach of the principle of consent as including such a formal dimension would support such a position. If all Member States and Singapore had consented to the termination of BITs, it seems

---

[47] ibid paras 396 and 398.
[48] Opinion 2/15 (n 44) para 248.
[49] ibid para 249. Such clause is not included in the UK–EU Trade and Cooperation Agreement (TCA) of 24 December 2020. However, UK BITs were not denounced, and it is for the UK and its counterparts to decide the future of their agreements. See also Guido Carducci, 'A State's Capacity and the EU's Competence to Conclude a Treaty, Invalidate, Terminate—and "Preclude" in *Achmea*—a Treaty or BIT of Member States, a State's Consent to be Bound by a Treaty or to Arbitration, under the Law of Treaties and EU Law, and the CJEU's Decisions on EUSFTA and *Achmea*. Their Roles and Interactions in Treaty and Investment Arbitration' (2018) 33 ICSID Rev 604–05.
[50] This principle means that the amendment or termination of an act must follow the same formal process of its conclusion, unless otherwise provided. In the present example, the treaty in question should only be terminated by the States that concluded it.

difficult to contend it was nevertheless contrary to international law because inscribed in a treaty to which the Member States were not supposed to be parties. However, the issue was drowned in the larger problem of shared competences between the EU and its Member States, the outcome of which is a specific agreement devoted to the protection of investments to which both the EU and its Member States are parties.

The following decisions essentially focused on the incompatibility between EU law and investment arbitration as included in BITs or the ECT, without going so far as to claim that this incompatibility led to termination. Thus, in *Slovak Republic v Achmea BV*, the Court did not discuss Article 59 of the VCLT. While considering that 'an international agreement providing for the establishment of a court responsible for the interpretation of its provisions and whose decisions are binding on the institutions, including the Court of Justice, is not in principle incompatible with EU law',[51] the Court found that the arbitration clause whereby disputes between an investor of a Member State and another Member State are referred to an external dispute settlement body (arbitral tribunal) is not compatible with the principles of EU law and has an 'adverse effect on the autonomy of EU law'.[52] However, the Declaration of the Member States of 15 January 2019 on the legal consequences of the *Achmea* judgment and on investment protection,[53] which states that '[i]n light of the *Achmea* judgment, Member States will terminate all bilateral investment treaties concluded between them by means of a plurilateral treaty or, where that is mutually recognised as more expedient, bilaterally', shows that tacit termination of BITs was not considered as an option.

In *Republic of Moldova v Komstroy LLC*[54] as well, the Court followed Advocate General Szpunar's opinion[55] and ruled that ECT based intra-EU arbitration proceedings are not compatible with EU law, but without addressing Article 59 of the VCLT.

D. Alignment of general international law and international investment law

In light of the above, ISDS tribunals' approach seems to align with the general international law rules and principles as well as the VCLT drafters' approach. By contrast, the CJEU and more generally the EU insist that a 'possible incompatibility is sufficient' to terminate the earlier treaty. However, the issue of tacit termination has been cut short as from Opinion 2/15, even if the European Commission and some Member States went on pleading it before arbitral tribunals. In the same spirit, the Termination Agreement concluded in 2020 expressly indicates that the intra-EU BITs 'are contrary to the EU Treaties and as a result of this incompatibility cannot be applied' from the date on which the last of the two parties to the BIT accessed the EU, without any further analysis or justification.[56] However, the conclusion of this agreement only proves that Article 59 was not at stake.

---

[51] Case C-284/16 *Slovak Republic v Achmea BV*, Case C-284/16, [2018] ECLI:EU:C:2018:158, para 57.
[52] ibid paras 56–58.
[53] At: https://commission.europa.eu/system/files/2019-01/190117-bilateral-investment-treaties_en.pdf, last accessed 23 October 2023; see also Commitments of Finland, Malta, Luxembourg, Slovenia, and Sweden, and Commitments of Hungary, at: https://commission.europa.eu/system/files/2021-09/190116-bilateral-investment-treaties-hungary_en.pdf, last accessed on 23 October 2023.
[54] Case C-741/19 *Republic of Moldova v Komstroy LLC* [2021] ECLI:EU:C:2021:655.
[55] Case C-741/19 *Republic of Moldova v Komstroy LLC* [2021] ECLI:EU:C:2021:164, Opinion of AG Szpunar.
[56] See Preamble and Article 4 of the Agreement for the termination of Bilateral Investment Treaties between the Member States of the European Union [2020] OJ L169/1.

E. Conclusion

30 Despite being widely accepted as a rule of treaty law, besides in investment arbitration, no international court or tribunal has ever given effect to the rule enshrined in Article 59 VCLT. In fact, Article 59 has rarely been examined by general international law courts or inter-states arbitration tribunals. It is only less than two decades ago that Article 59 slipped into investor–State proceedings, particularly those dealing with the intra-EU ISDS objection. As such, the practice of investment tribunals constitutes to date the primary corpus on the application of Article 59 and, therefore, the main source of practice informing general international law, all the more so as it does not deviate from the prevailing analyses in this area.

31 Indeed, investment tribunals have meticulously analysed the provision, but none has accepted the alleged termination or suspension of the treaty in question pursuant to Article 59. Therefore, from a comparative standpoint, it appears that, despite the turbulences provoked by the intra-EU objection, international investment decisions confirm the general approach of the ILC and international scholarship on the topic of termination or suspension of treaties implied by the conclusion of later treaties. Indeed, the EU practice—beyond discourses aimed mostly at internal, ie European, audiences and constituencies—has aligned itself with the classical principles of treaty law. Yet, the decisions on Article 59 that was triggered by the intra-EU objection tell us little about the issue that has been the focus of attention, ie what the 'same subject-matter' is.

Selected literature

Dubuisson F, 'Termination and Suspension of the Operation of Treaties, Art. 59 1969 Vienna Convention' in Corten O and Klein P (eds), *The Vienna Conventions on the Law of Treaties* (OUP 2011).

Giegerich T, 'Article 59' in Dörr O and Schmalenbach K (eds), *Vienna Convention on the Law of Treaties, A Commentary* (2nd edn, Springer 2018).

Selected decisions

Addiko Bank AG and Addiko Bank dd v Republic of Croatia, ICSID Case No ARB/17/37, Decision on Respondent Jurisdictional Objection Related to the Alleged Incompatibility of the BIT with the EU Acquis, 12 June 2020.

AS PNB Banka and others v Republic of Latvia, ICSID Case No ARB/17/47, Decision on the Intra-EU Objection, 14 May 2021.

Electricity Company of Sofia and Bulgaria (*Belgium v Bulgaria*) (Preliminary Objection) PCIJ Series A/B No 77.

Euram v Slovak Republic, UNCITRAL, Jurisdiction, 22 October 2012.

Theodoros Adamakopoulos and others v Republic of Cyprus, ICSID Case No ARB/15/49, Jurisdiction, 7 February 2020.

Article 60 of the VCLT

Termination or suspension of the operation of a treaty as consequence of its breach

Hélène Ruiz Fabri and Randi Ayman

1. A material breach of a bilateral treaty by one of the parties entitles the other to invoke the breach as a ground for terminating the treaty or suspending its operation in whole or in part.
2. A material breach of a multilateral treaty by one of the parties entitles:
(a) the other parties by unanimous agreement to suspend the operation of the treaty in whole or in part or to terminate it either:
   (i) in the relations between themselves and the defaulting State, or
   (ii) as between all the parties;
(b) a party specially affected by the breach to invoke it as a ground for suspending the operation of the treaty in whole or in part in the relations between itself and the defaulting State;
(c) any party other than the defaulting State to invoke the breach as a ground for suspending the operation of the treaty in whole or in part with respect to itself if the treaty is of such a character that a material breach of its provisions by one party radically changes the position of every party with respect to the further performance of its obligations under the treaty.
3. A material breach of a treaty, for the purposes of this article, consists in:
(a) a repudiation of the treaty not sanctioned by the present Convention; or
(b) the violation of a provision essential to the accomplishment of the object or purpose of the treaty.
4. The foregoing paragraphs are without prejudice to any provision in the treaty applicable in the event of a breach.
5. Paragraphs 1 to 3 do not apply to provisions relating to the protection of the human person contained in treaties of a humanitarian character, in particular to provisions prohibiting any form of reprisals against persons protected by such treaties.

A. Introduction: Background and status of Article 60 — 1	C. Potential relevance for international investment practice — 15
B. Article 60 as received by international courts and tribunals — 7	D. Conclusion — 23

A. Introduction: Background and status of Article 60

Article 60 of the Vienna Convention on the Law of Treaties (VCLT) entitles a treaty party to seek suspension or termination of the treaty due to its material breach by another party. As such, it is the only provision of the VCLT, at least under the treaty termination section, that deals with the performance of the parties.[1] It is also one of the few provisions that draws near to the sphere of the Law on State Responsibility, namely, the regime of countermeasures.[2] Unlike other responses to a breach of a treaty obligation, Article 60 is not concerned with reparation or compensation. Rather, it alludes to the principle of *inadimplenti non est adimplendum*,[3] according to which a party to a treaty is entitled to no longer honour its obligations as a consequence of the breach of that treaty by another party,[4] and is also referred to as the 'negative reciprocity'.[5] In this specific regard, it is commonly accepted that the rule enshrined in Article 60(1) is reflective of customary international law.[6] However, the status of the other paragraphs of the provision appears to be less clear. They seem to be mostly considered as part of the International Law Commission (ILC)'s efforts to develop international law.[7]

2   Article 60 has been abundantly discussed by international literature.[8] Despite some divergent views, particularly concerning its status, it is a complex provision.[9] Indeed, in line with the drafters' objectives of treaty stability, the requirements for Article 60 are restrictive.[10] And like other termination provisions of the VCLT, Article 60 is considered a cramped 'flexibility' tool[11] to exit or suspend international agreements.[12] The complexity of the provision is further compounded by the establishment of different consequences and regimes depending on whether the treaty is bilateral or multilateral. In a bilateral context, a State is only entitled to invoke the breach as a ground to terminate or suspend the treaty, whereas in a multilateral setting, the provision allows a double-fold response: individual and collective. Individually,

---

[1] Besides Article 26 on Good Faith. See J Crawford and S Olleson, 'The Exception of Non-performance: Links Between the Law of Treaties and the Law of State Responsibility' [2000] 51 Aust YBIL 59. See also JDH Karton, *The Culture of International Arbitration and the Evolution of Contract Law* (OUP 2013) 166, on the roots of the principle in the general principle of good faith. See in this Commentary: Can Yeginsu and Patrick Pearsall, Article 26 of the VCLT.

[2] The rule of Article 60 differs from countermeasures, which cover a broader scope of international obligations and require different conditions to come into play. See B Simma and C Tams, 'Article 60' in O Corten and P Klein (eds), *The Vienna Convention on the Law of Treaties: A Commentary* (OUP 2011) 1354 (hereinafter Simma and Tams, 'Article 60'); J Crawford, *State Responsibility: The General Part* (CUP 2013) 676 and 678ff. See further discussion of this matter below. On countermeasures see in this Commentary: Martins Paparinskis, 'Articles 49–54 of the ARSIWA'.

[3] On the distinction between the rule of Article 60 VCLT, the principle of *inadimplenti non est adimplendum* from which Article 60 stems, and *exceptio non adimpleti contractus*, see M Xiouri, *The Breach of a Treaty. State Responses in International Law* (Brill 2021) 53–54, 226–29 (hereafter Xiouri, *The Breach of a Treaty*).

[4] Simma and Tams, 'Article 60' (n 2) 1353. See also CJ Tams, 'Regulating Treaty Breaches' in MJ Bowman and D Kritsiotis (eds), *Conceptual and Contextual Perspectives on the Modern Law of Treaties* (CUP 2018) 445–46, para 2.2.1 (hereafter Tams, 'Regulating Treaty Breaches').

[5] Simma and Tams, 'Article 60' (n 2) 1353. R Provost, *International Human Rights and Humanitarian Law* (CUP 2002) 163ff.

[6] Simma and Tams, 'Article 60' (n 2) 1353.

[7] Simma and Tams, 'Article 60' (n 2) 1355–57.

[8] See among others, B Simma, 'Reflections on Article 60 of the Vienna Convention on the Law of Treaties and its Background in General International Law' (1970) 20 Österreichische Zeitschrift für öffentliches Recht 5; M Gomaa, *Suspension or Termination of Treaties on Grounds of Breach* (Brill 1996); Simma and Tams, 'Article 60' (n 2); CJ Tams, 'Regulating Treaty Breaches' in MJ Bowman and D Kritsiotis (eds), *Conceptual and Contextual Perspectives on the Modern Law of Treaties* (CUP 2018); Xiouri, *The Breach of a Treaty* (n 3).

[9] See, for example, Simma and Tams, 'Article 60' (n 2) 1353; C Binder, 'The VCLT over the Last 50 Years: Developments in the Law of Treaties with a Special Focus on the VCLT's Rules on Treaty Termination' (2019) 24 ARIEL 91 (hereafter Binder, 'The VCLT over the Last 50 Years').

[10] On the narrow and cautious approach followed in Article 60, see also Tams, 'Regulating Treaty Breaches' (n 4) 445–46.

[11] Binder, 'The VCLT over the Last 50 Years' (n 9) 100.

[12] ibid.

a State could only invoke the breach to suspend its relationship vis-à-vis the defaulting party, and collectively, States could either suspend or end the treaty towards the defaulting party (exclusion) or among all parties.

Article 60 narrowly defines the notion of 'material breach', a *sine qua non* to trigger the operation of the provision, and thereby excludes its application to any other treaty breach.[13] It is worth noting the choice of terms to characterize the breach from 'fundamental' to 'material'. The latter was ultimately elected to encompass provisions that are essential to the effective execution of the underlying treaty or were determinant for a party to conclude the treaty, despite their secondary character.[14] The dispute resolution clauses were the main example given for such provisions by the ILC.[15]

Two alternative circumstances could amount to a material breach: either through a 'repudiation of the treaty not sanctioned'[16] by the VCLT or 'a violation of a provision essential to the accomplishment of the object or purpose of the treaty'.[17]

Although the VCLT provides for a definition of what could amount to a material breach, it does not provide guidance as to what constitutes a repudiation.[18] The concept is broad enough to cover a wide range of possibilities. Nonetheless, it remains rarely invoked, let alone confirmed, in international decisions or arbitral awards.

The second circumstance calls attention to the qualification of the provision instead of the violation itself: requiring a violation of a provision deemed significant to the fulfilment of the object and purpose of the treaty. As such, the provision shifted the traditional focus from nature of violation to the nature of the provision in question, which appears to have deliberately expanded the scope of Article 60.[19]

B. Article 60 as received by international courts and tribunals

Article 60 has been invoked in a handful of cases before the International Court of Justice (ICJ) and State–State arbitrations but has been seldom applied.

---

[13] See among others, Tams, 'Regulating Treaty Breaches' (n 4) 446–47, para 2.2.2.
[14] 'Reports of the Commission to the General Assembly' YILC 1966, Vol II, 255, para 9.
[15] 'Documents of the fifteenth session including the report of the Commission to the General Assembly' YILC 1963, Vol II, Doc A/CN.4/156 and Add1–3, 175, para 11: '[f]or example, a clause providing for compulsory arbitration in the event of a dispute as to the interpretation or application of the treaty is purely ancillary to the main purposes of the treaty, but it may well be regarded by some parties as an essential condition for agreeing to be bound by the treaty'.
[16] On the meaning and scope of repudiation, see ME Villiger, 'Article 60' in *Commentary on the 1969 Vienna Convention on the Law of Treaties* (Brill 2009) 742. See also *Arbitration between the Republic of Croatia and the Republic of Slovenia*, PCA Case No 2012-04, Partial Award, 30 June 2016, para 213 (hereafter *Arbitration between Croatia and Slovenia*). The tribunal noted that in its view 'the right of a party to seek the termination of a treaty on the ground that the other party has repudiated it is closely related to the principle *inadimplenti non est adimplendum*. To safeguard expectations of reciprocity underlying a treaty relationship, a party should not be required to perform a treaty that the other party has clearly and definitively rejected'.
[17] Article 60(3). On the use of 'or' instead of 'and' for object and purpose in this provision as compared to Articles 18, 19(c), 20(2), 31(3), 33(4), 41(1)(b)(ii), and 58(1)(b)(ii), see D Kritsiotis, 'The Object and Purpose of a Treaty's Object and Purpose' in MJ Bowman and D Kritsiotis (eds), *Conceptual and Contextual Perspectives on the Modern Law of Treaties* (CUP 2018) 296ff.
[18] On this point, see J Crawford's analysis of what could constitute a repudiation in his pleadings before the ICJ in *Gabčíkovo-Nagymaros Project (Hungary v Slovakia)* (Verbatim Record, 7 March 1997 at the Peace Palace) [1997] ICJ CR 97/13, para 19.
[19] Simma and Tams, 'Article 60' (n 2) 1360.

8 Prior to the adoption of the VCLT, the exception of non-performance was invoked before the Permanent Court of International Justice (PCIJ) where the Court had to rule on whether construction works by Belgium on the river Meuse were in breach of its treaty with the Netherlands, and similarly for the homologous works done by the latter. Although the Court found no treaty breach by Belgium[20] and therefore did not decide on the exception of non-performance, Judges Anzilotti and Hudson strongly confirmed that in their view the principle *inadimplenti non est adimplendum* was recognized as a general principle of international law.[21]

9 The rule codified in Article 60 was expressly endorsed as a general principle of international law in the *South West Africa* advisory opinion of 1971, rendered only two years after the adoption of the VCLT.[22] The Court even stated that this principle should be presumed existent in all treaties, even if unexpressed, except for humanitarian treaties.[23] This position has been strongly criticized by scholars.[24] Nevertheless, nearly thirty years later, the Court confirmed its position in the *Gabčíkovo-Nagymaros* case discussed below.[25]

10 Article 60 was also invoked in the *ICAO Council* case. Although the Court did not rule on the issue of material breach, it stressed that the allegation by a treaty party of a material breach by another party did not entitle it to unilaterally terminate or suspend said treaty. Rather, the Court recalled that the treaty provisions must be examined to determine whether there has been a material breach (and not only to assess whether there was a violation of an essential provision within the meaning of Article 60(3)(a) but also for a case of repudiation).[26]

11 The same position was followed in the case of *Military and Paramilitary Activities in and against Nicaragua* 1986 where the Court assessed the existence of a material breach through the determination of the object and purpose of the treaty of friendship, commerce, and navigation between the United States and Nicaragua according to Article 60.[27] After analysing the provisions of the treaty in light of the object and purpose of 'friendship', the Court held that the United States had breached the treaty by mining and conducting direct attacks on the Nicaraguan ports which 'undermined the whole spirit of the agreement'.[28] On the other hand, the Court decided that certain acts of economic pressure were 'less flagrantly in contradiction with the purpose of the Treaty' and therefore did not defeat the object and

---

[20] *Diversion of Water from the Meuse (Netherlands v Belgium)* PCIJ Ser A/B No 70, 25.
[21] ibid, dissenting and individual opinions of Judges Anzilotti and Hudson, 50 and 77, respectively. On the principle *inadimplenti non est adimplendum*, see also *Application of the Interim Accord of 13 September 1995 (The Former Yugoslav Republic of Macedonia v Greece)* [2011] ICJ Rep 644 (hereafter *Interim Accord*), Separate Opinion of Judge Simma, paras 115–17, and Dissenting Opinion of Judge ad hoc Roucounas, para 161. Expressing doubt about its quality as general principle, see Roger O'Keefe, *The Protection of Cultural Property in Armed Conflict* (CUP 2006), 30.
[22] In this proceeding, the ICJ found that South Africa had 'deliberate[ly] and persistent[ly]' breached obligations destroying 'the very object and purpose' of the Mandate and that the General Assembly had the right to terminate the Mandate on that basis. While the Court applied the rule of Article 60, it did not seem to have clearly distinguished between the case of repudiation and violations of an essential provision. It did however refer to the General Assembly's declaration of 'repudiation' of the Mandate by South Africa. See *Legal Consequences for States of the Continued Presence of South Africa in Namibia (South West Africa) notwithstanding Security Council Resolution 276* (Advisory Opinion) [1971] ICJ Rep 16, paras 94–95.
[23] ibid paras 94–96.
[24] See among others, HW Briggs, 'Unilateral Denunciation of Treaties: The Vienna Convention and the International Court of Justice' (1974) 68 AJIL 55–56.
[25] *Gabčíkovo-Nagymaros Project (Hungary v Slovakia)* [1997] ICJ Rep 7 (hereafter *Gabčíkovo-Nagymaros*).
[26] *Appeal Relating to the Jurisdiction of the ICAO Council (India v Pakistan)* [1972] ICJ Rep 46, para 38.
[27] *Military and Paramilitary Activities in and against Nicaragua (Nicaragua v United States of America)* (Merits) [1986] ICJ Rep 14, paras 273–75.
[28] ibid para 275.

purpose of the treaty.[29] From the analysis of the Court in this case, 'it may be inferred that flagrant violations of a generally formulated treaty obligation are likely to be seen as "material breaches" in the sense of Article 60(3)'.[30]

In *Gabčíkovo-Nagymaros*, Article 60 was invoked along with other VCLT termination provisions. In this case, the Court expressly drew a line between the regime of Article 60 under the law of treaties and the countermeasures under the law of States responsibility and noted that 'only a material breach of the treaty itself, by a State party to that treaty, ... entitles the other party to rely on it as a ground for terminating the treaty. The violation of other treaty rules or of rules of general international law may justify the taking of certain measures, including countermeasures, by the injured State, but it does not constitute a ground for termination under the law of treaties'.[31] The Court rejected the application of Article 60 in this case as both countries breached the terms of the treaty.[32]

More recently, the Court had to deal with the invocation of three different responses to an alleged treaty breach in the *Interim Accord* case: *exceptio non adimpleti contractus*, material breach under Article 60, and countermeasures. Dealing with each possibility separately and thus avoiding addressing their relationship (and/or any potential overlap), the Court rejected the application of Article 60 for lack of a material breach.[33]

Article 60 has also been invoked before State–State arbitral tribunals. In an arbitration between Croatia and Slovenia, Croatia sought to terminate its arbitration agreement with Slovenia as a result of the latter's alleged material breach. Deciding on Croatia's invocation of Article 60, a five-member tribunal provided a thorough analysis of each element of the Article, including both scenarios: repudiation and violation of an essential provision. Similar to the approach adopted by the ICJ, the tribunal based its analysis on the definition of the object and purpose of an arbitration agreement,[34] and the determination of the object and purpose of the underlying arbitration agreement in this case.[35] Concluding that the conditions of Article 60 were not met in this case, the tribunal ruled out its application.[36]

C. Potential relevance for international investment practice

There seems to be no decisions expressly addressing Article 60 in the international investment context.[37] Hence, no particular pattern or comparison can be drawn with the application or interpretation of this provision under general international law and investment law.

---

[29] ibid paras 270–76.
[30] Simma and Tams, 'Article 60' (n 2) 1360.
[31] *Gabčíkovo-Nagymaros* (n 25) para 106.
[32] ibid paras 99, 105–10.
[33] *Interim Accord* (n 21) para 163. For a further analysis of this aspect, see Xiouri, *The Breach of a Treaty* (n 3) 228–30.
[34] *Arbitration Between Croatia and Slovenia* (n 16) paras 218–19.
[35] ibid paras 220ff.
[36] ibid para 225.
[37] However, a few cases have addressed the concept of *exceptio non adimpleti contractus*. See for example *Klöckner Industrie-Anlagen GmbH and Others v Cameroon and Société Camerounaise des Engrais*, ICSID Case No ARB/81/2, Award, 21 October 1983, paras 114ff. Note that the Award was later annulled: *Klöckner Industrie-Anlagen GmbH and Others v Cameroon and Société Camerounaise des Engrais*, ICSID Case No ARB/81/2, Annulment, 3 May 1985, paras 170–71. We note that this case was based on a contract, not a treaty. For a further analysis, see among others, Xiouri, *The Breach of a Treaty* (n 3) 231–32. See also *Yukos Universal Limited (Isle of Man) v The Russian Federation*, UNCITRAL, PCA Case No 2005-04/AA227, Final Award, 18 July 2014, para 1360, citing *Diversion of Water from the Meuse* (n 21) Individual Opinion of Judge Hudson.

Nonetheless, the application of Article 60 may become relevant, or at least debated, in some specific situations pertaining to the investment practice.

16   A first scenario where the rule of Article 60 could be raised by a State is non-compliance with arbitral awards. In such an instance, the question would be: is a failure to comply with an International Centre for Settlement of Investment Disputes (ICSID) Convention award a material breach of the international investment agreement (IIA) invoked and/or of the ICSID Convention?[38]

17   With respect to the IIAs, it is widely accepted that their main objective is to promote and protect foreign investments. They are also based on the idea that States might breach certain substantive protections accorded to foreign investments and investors. In such case, one of the investment treaty solutions to remedy a potential breach is to resort to investment arbitration. The IIAs however have not necessarily provided for an express remedy in case of breach of procedural provisions, including non-compliance with arbitral awards. One could reasonably consider that a failure to comply with an arbitral award based on an investment treaty amounts to a material breach that defeats the accomplishment of the object and purpose of that treaty within the meaning of Article 60.

18   As to the ICSID Convention, Article 27(1) of the Convention governs the situation of 'failure to abide or comply with an award' without referring to any 'breach' or 'violation' of the Convention. In such an event, the Convention allows the States to either use diplomatic protection or initiate an international claim. In our view, Article 27(1) of the ICSID Convention is a perfect example of the *lex specialis* rule envisaged in Article 60(4) of the VCLT.[39] Moreover, Article 64 of the ICSID Convention provides that any dispute between ICSID Contracting States regarding the interpretation or application of the Convention should be referred to the ICJ (unless they agree to another method of dispute settlement).

19   Assuming that the application of Article 60 is possible in theory, it begs the question of whether the termination or suspension of the ICSID Convention and/or the underlying consent treaty would be effective in practice. If a material breach of the ICSID Convention within the meaning of Article 60 VCLT is established, the exclusion of the defaulting party by the unanimous vote of all 157 ICSID Contracting States is unlikely. Alternatively, if the Convention is only partially suspended between one State and the defaulting State, what provisions could be suspended?

20   In that regard, one author stressed that in the context of international investment law, the application of Article 60 of the VCLT does not seem to provide an 'adequate remedy' to the failure to comply with the duty to enforce arbitral awards. He further noted that

> [t]erminating or suspending the treaty does not contribute to repair the original source of the dispute, i.e. the need to compensate the damages caused by the host State to the foreign investor. Second, terminating or suspending the operation of an IIA may in fact be counterproductive as other investors of the home State remaining in the host State could be left unprotected.[40]

---

[38]   See also the question being raised by the WTO Working Group on the Relationship between Trade and Investment, WTO Doc WT/WGTI/W/134, 7 August 2002, (02-4350), para 67.

[39]   Simma and Tams, 'Article 60' (n 2) 1357.

[40]   R Echandi, 'Non-Compliance with Awards: The Remedies of Customary International Law' [2012] Proceedings of the ASIL Annual Meeting 119.

In the same vein, Article 60 of the VCLT could come into play in investment law with respect to the appeal of ICSID Convention awards. Article 53 of the Convention sets forth the binding character of ICSID awards and expressly excludes appeal from the post-award remedies available thereunder. With that in mind, one could assume that Article 53 of the ICSID Convention is a provision essential to the fulfilment of its object and purpose.[41] If so, would appealing ICSID awards amount to a material breach of the ICSID Convention within the meaning of Article 60?

Some authors have already expressed their view on this matter considering that, in light of the 'self-contained' feature of the ICSID system provided for in Article 53 and its close link to the object and purpose of the ICSID Convention, an appeal of an ICSID award would go against the latter.[42] So far the answer seems to hinge on the determination of whether an *inter se* modification of the ICSID Convention is possible, which has proved a stark contrast of views.[43]

D. Conclusion

The rule on the termination or suspension of a treaty due to its material breach by one of the parties has been invoked before international courts and tribunals, except those dealing with investor–State disputes, but it remains rarely applied as most other VCLT treaty termination provisions. By contrast, Article 60 has garnered little to no attention in the pleadings or rulings addressing international investment disputes. Therefore, no comparative findings could be drawn in this regard. Nonetheless, since the international investment law field is built on a massive network of treaties, Article 60 could elicit discussion about its applicability to these treaties. Theoretically, it seems plausible to terminate or suspend an investment treaty due to its material breach by one of the parties according to Article 60 once the conditions are met, particularly when it comes to compliance with key procedural provisions such as the enforcement of awards. However, the question that remains open is whether, in practice, the application of Article 60 would be adequate to the particularities of this field.

---

[41] The purpose of ICSID could be read in Article 1(2) of the Convention which states that '[t]he purpose of the Centre shall be to provide facilities for conciliation and arbitration of investment disputes between Contracting States and nationals of other Contracting States in accordance with the provisions of this Convention'. However, the object of purpose of the Convention has usually been interpreted to include the finality of ICSID awards and the preservation of the self-contained system established by the ICSID Convention.

[42] See J Calamita, 'The (In)Compatibility of Appellate Mechanisms with Existing Instruments of the Investment Treaty Regime' (2017) 18 JWIT 585–627, 611ff (hereafter J Calamita). See also A Rigaux and D Simon, 'Article 41: Agreement to Modify Multilateral Treaties Between Certain Parties Only' in O Corten and P Klein (eds), *The Vienna Conventions on the Law of Treaties: A Commentary* (OUP 2011) 1001.

[43] For those who view a possible *inter se* modification, see, for example, A Reinisch, 'Will the EU's Proposal Concerning an Investment Court System for CETA and TTIP Lead to Enforceable Awards?—The Limits of Modifying the ICSID Convention and the Nature of Investment Arbitration' (2016) 19 JIEL 761–86; M Potesta, 'An Appellate Mechanism for ICSID Awards and Modification of the ICSID Convention Under Article 41 of the VCLT' in E Shirlow and K Nasir Gore (eds), *The Vienna Convention on the Law of Treaties in Investor-State Disputes: History, Evolution, and Future* (Kluwer 2022) 349–84; and AJ van den Berg, 'Appeal Mechanism for ISDS Awards: Interaction with the New York and ICSID Conventions' (2019) 34 ICSID Rev–FILJ 156–89. As to the opposite views, see among others, J Calamita (n 42) and R Castro de Figueiredo, 'Fragmentation and Harmonization in the ICSID Decision Making Process' in J Kalici and A Joubin-Bret (eds), *Reshaping the Investor–State Dispute Settlement System* (Brill 2015) 506–30.

Selected literature

Simma B and Tams C, 'Article 60' in Corten O and Klein P (eds), *The Vienna Convention on the Law of Treaties: A Commentary* (OUP 2011).

Tams CJ, 'Regulating Treaty Breaches' in Bowman MJ and Kritsiotis D (eds), *Conceptual and Contextual Perspectives on the Modern Law of Treaties* (CUP 2018).

Maria X, *The Breach of a Treaty. State Responses in International Law* (Brill 2021).

Selected decisions

Diversion of Water from the Meuse (Netherlands v Belgium) PCIJ Ser A/B No 70.
Gabčíkovo-Nagymaros Project (Hungary v Slovakia) (Judgment) [1997] ICJ Rep 7.
Legal Consequences for States of the Continued Presence of South Africa in Namibia (South West Africa) notwithstanding Security Council Resolution 276 (Advisory Opinion) [1971] ICJ Rep 16.

Article 62 of the VCLT

Fundamental change of circumstances

Makane Moïse Mbengue

1. A fundamental change of circumstances which has occurred with regard to those existing at the time of the conclusion of a treaty, and which was not foreseen by the parties, may not be invoked as a ground for terminating or withdrawing from the treaty unless:
 (a) the existence of those circumstances constituted an essential basis of the consent of the parties to be bound by the treaty; and
 (b) the effect of the change is radically to transform the extent of obligations still to be performed under the treaty.

2. A fundamental change of circumstances may not be invoked as a ground for terminating or withdrawing from a treaty:
 (a) if the treaty establishes a boundary; or if the fundamental change is the result of a breach by the party invoking it either of an obligation under the treaty or
 (b) of any other international obligation owed to any other party to the treaty.

3. If, under the foregoing paragraphs, a party may invoke a fundamental change of circumstances as a ground for terminating or withdrawing from a treaty it may also invoke the change as a ground for suspending the operation of the treaty.

A. Introduction — 1	C. *Rebus sic stantibus*: from the perspective of investment arbitration — 18
B. *Rebus sic stantibus*: from the perspective of the ICJ, other international judicial bodies, and State practice — 5	I. *Rebus sic stantibus* through the prism of State interest — 19
I. Non-correspondence of the treaty with existing circumstances — 6	II. Stabilization clauses and renegotiation clauses — 22
II. Change in circumstances leading to breach of shared expectations — 12	D. Investigating the applicability of *rebus sic stantibus* to investment arbitration — 28
III. Vital State interests — 16	E. Conclusion — 32

A. Introduction

Pacta sunt servanda is a fundamental legal principle dictating that agreements must be kept.[1] It is based on the notion that a society or legal regime cannot exist peacefully without

---

[1] The author would like to express his gratitude to Ms Nikita Panse for her invaluable assistance in the course of the preparation and drafting of the present contribution.
 Article 26 of the Vienna Convention on the Law of Treaties (entered into force 27 January 1980) 1155 UNTS 331 (hereafter VCLT). See in this Commentary: Can Yeginsu and Patrick Pearsall, 'Article 26 of the VCLT: *Pacta sunt servanda*'.

certainty that commitments will be respected.[2] Importing this notion to the international context provides stability and security to treaty relationships between states. However, the obligation to uphold commitments is not absolute, and *pacta sunt servanda* has certain limitations[3] which permit a state to derogate from treaty obligations in exceptional situations.[4] The principle of *rebus sic stantibus*, codified in Article 62 of the Vienna Convention on the Law of Treaties (VCLT) describes one of those exceptional situations.[5] This principle permits states to terminate, suspend, or alter treaties in case of a fundamental change in circumstances.[6]

2 Originating from canon law, *rebus sic stantibus* has inspired serious debate since its first usage in sixteenth century England.[7] Even today, State practice, international jurisprudence, and provisions of international treaties point to several ways in which the principle has been interpreted and invoked.[8] Due to these discrepancies, it has attracted much controversy, primarily since it can be misused by states to evade their treaty obligations. In spite of this notoriety, *rebus sic stantibus* is as essential to peace and stability as *pacta sunt servanda*.

3 Several jurists contend that the issue of change in circumstances is, essentially, a question of interpretation of a treaty.[9] They believe that *rebus sic stantibus* is an interpretative tool used in ascertaining the conditions that motivated the consent of the parties while concluding the treaty.[10] If these conditions no longer exist, then the parties should have the option to reconsider their commitment to the treaty obligations.[11] Therefore, *rebus sic stantibus* respects the consent of parties and does not derogate from the principle of *pacta sunt servanda*. Brierly captures it well: 'Not every important change of circumstances will put an end to the obligations of a treaty. What puts an end to a treaty is the disappearance of the foundation upon which it rests.'[12]

4 The *rebus sic stantibus* principle is part of customary international law,[13] given that states have frequently invoked it to justify the termination and modification of treaties.[14]

---

[2] In his book *De Jure Belli ac Pacis*, Grotius said that 'Fidelity to promises was the foundation not only of every particular State also of that greater society of States which embraces all nations'. H Grotius, *On the Law of War and Peace* (Clarendon Press 1925) 860.

[3] C Binder, 'Stability and Change in Times of Fragmentation: the Limits of Pacta Sunt Servanda Revisited' (2012) 25 LJIL 909 (hereafter Binder, Stability and Change); M Fitzmaurice, 'Exceptional Circumstances and Treaty Commitments' in DB Hollis (ed), *The Oxford Guide to Treaties* (OUP 2020) 595 (hereafter Fitzmaurice, Exceptional Circumstances).

[4] Fitzmaurice, Exceptional Circumstances (n 3) 595–96.

[5] For a detailed analysis of the principle, see A Vamvoukos, *Termination of Treaties in International Law: The Doctrines of Rebus Sic Stantibus and Desuetude* (Clarendon Press 1985) (hereafter Vamvoukos, Termination).

[6] See J Kulaga, 'A Renaissance of the Doctrine of *Rebus Sic Stantibus*?' (2020) 69 ICLQ 477–78 (hereafter Kulaga, Renaissance).

[7] G Haraszti, 'Treaties and the Fundamental Change of Circumstances' (1977) 146 Recueil des Cours 10–13 (hereafter Haraszti, Treaties and Fundamental Change).

[8] Kulaga, Renaissance (n 6) 477–97.

[9] OJ Lissitzyn, 'Treaties and Changed Circumstances (*Rebus Sic Stantibus*)' (1967) 61 AJIL 895–992 (hereafter Lissitzyn, Treaties and Changed Circumstances); Haraszti, Treaties and Fundamental Change (n 7) 10.

[10] Lissitzyn, Treaties and Changed Circumstances (n 9) 895–96.

[11] ibid.

[12] JL Brierly, *The Law of Nations, An Introduction to the International Law of Peace* (4th edn, Clarendon Press 1949) 245 (hereafter Brierly, Law of Nations).

[13] International Law Commission, 'Draft Articles on the Law of Treaties with Commentaries' YILC 1966, Vol II, 257 (hereafter ILC, Draft Articles on the Law of Treaties); Fitzmaurice, Exceptional Circumstances (n 3) 602.

[14] JW Garner, 'The Doctrine of *Rebus Sic Stantibus* and the Termination of Treaties' (1927) 21 AJIL 509–11 (hereafter Garner, *Rebus Sic Stantibus*); Fitzmaurice, Exceptional Circumstances (n 3) 602.

Considering its importance in general international law, a study of its role, effect, and influence in investment law and arbitration becomes essential. The objective of this entry is thus, threefold. The first objective is to understand the treatment accorded to the principle by the International Court of Justice (ICJ), other judicial bodies and in State practice. While studying this treatment, the entry analyses the history of the evolution in the interpretation of the principle and explores the reasons behind such evolution. The second objective is to examine how investment arbitration tribunals have interpreted and applied the principle. This analysis is based on adaptations of *rebus sic stantibus* in international investment law, and how investment arbitration tribunals have treated these adaptations. The third objective is to investigate whether the principle can be applied without adaptation in investment arbitration. The entry concludes by observing the principle's potential in investor–State disputes.

B. *Rebus sic stantibus*: From the perspective of the ICJ, other international judicial bodies, and State practice

Since the inception of its usage, *rebus sic stantibus* has evolved considerably.[15] This evolution is the result of several factors. First among these is the International Law Commission (ILC)'s work in codifying the principle, but ICJ judgments have also helped to define its scope. Section B observes how states and the ICJ have treated the principle, while surveying the principle's evolution. Such a dual study will allow contextual understanding of the principle's importance in inter-State relations.

I. Non-correspondence of the treaty with existing circumstances

The earliest interpretation of the principle was based on the rule of non-correspondence of the treaty with existing circumstances.[16] States terminated treaties if the circumstances that existed during the conclusion of the treaty had materially altered over the course of time.[17] The first noteworthy instance was France's arguments before the Permanent Court of International Justice (PCIJ) in the *Nationality Decrees* case.[18] France argued that certain capitulation treaties that existed between France and Great Britain had lapsed due to the creation of a new situation.[19] The advisory opinion records as follows:

> [A]ccording to the French contention, as developed in the course of the oral statements, these Treaties, which were concluded for an indefinite period, that is to say, in perpetuity, have lapsed by virtue of the principle known as the *clausula rebus sic stantibus* because the establishment of a legal and judicial regime in conformity with French legislation has created a new situation which deprives the capitulatory regime of its *raison d'être*.[20]

---

[15] Kulaga, Renaissance (n 6) 477–97.
[16] Garner, *Rebus Sic Stantibus* (n 14) 509–16. *Case of Free Zones of Upper Savoy and the District of Gex (Switzerland v France)* PCIJ Series A/B No 46 (hereafter *Free Zones*).
[17] Garner, *Rebus Sic Stantibus* (n 14) 509–16.
[18] *Nationality Decrees Issued in Tunis and Morocco (French Zone)* (Advisory Opinion) PCIJ Series B No 4.
[19] ibid 29.
[20] ibid.

7 The PCIJ did not opine on France's invocation of *rebus sic stantibus*.[21] Yet, three important characteristics emerge from the invocation. First, France applied the principle to capitulation treaties, based on the assumption that the principle is a recognized rule of international law. Second, France associated the clause with perpetual treaties.[22] Third, reliance on the principle was primarily due to *the creation of a new situation*,[23] signifying non-correspondence of the treaty with existing circumstances.

8 France invoked the *rebus sic stantibus* principle again in a similar manner in the *Free Zones* case.[24] In 1815, certain free and neutral zones were established in Upper Savoy and the District of Gex.[25] By referring to Article 435 of the Treaty of Versailles of 1919, France unilaterally denounced the free zones.[26] It argued that since the conclusion of the Treaty of Paris in 1815, there had been material changes in circumstances due to which the treaty was not binding on it.[27] Relying heavily on *rebus sic stantibus*, France argued that it was '… *une règle générale de la clause rebus sic stantibus, clause que l'on peut considérer comme une règle générale et constante du droit international public* …'.

9 State practice thereafter shows a similar tendency to unilaterally terminate treaties when existing circumstances did not align with the treaty. Such a mode of interpretation, for instance, can be seen in China's unilateral termination of the Sino-Belgian Treaty of 1865.[28] China terminated the treaty in 1926 by invoking *rebus sic stantibus*.[29] According to China, the principle was a tacit condition recognized by international law as being a part of all treaties.[30] China stated that this tacit condition ensured that a treaty was no longer binding when the factual circumstances it was based on have materially altered.[31] Belgium brought the issue before the PCIJ,[32] but the parties settled.[33]

10 A noteworthy characteristic of this manner of invocation is the assumption of an unquestioned right and privilege to declare a treaty inoperative in case of change in circumstances.[34] Such an assumption was the basis for the US's withdrawal from the International Load Lines Convention of 1930.[35] Despite the convention containing no provision permitting suspension, President Roosevelt announced that the convention 'has ceased to be binding under *the well-established principle of international law*,[36] rebus sic stantibus'.[37] The change in circumstances was the unlimited national emergency proclaimed in the United States in 1941

---

[21] Haraszti, Treaties and Fundamental Change (n 7) 38–39.
[22] ILC, Draft Articles on the Law of Treaties (n 13) 257.
[23] Emphasis added.
[24] *Free Zones* (n 16).
[25] F Llewellyn Jones, 'Upper Savoy and the Free Zones around Geneva, and Article 435 of the Treaty of Versailles' (1924) 10 Trans Grot Soc 173–88; Haraszti, Treaties and Fundamental Change (n 7) 39.
[26] ibid; Garner, *Rebus Sic Stantibus* (n 14) 510.
[27] Haraszti, Treaties and Fundamental Change (n 7) 39.
[28] *Denunciation of the Treaty of November 2nd, 1865, between China and Belgium (Belgium v China)* (Order) PCIJ Series A No 18/19 (hereafter *Denunciation of the Sino-Belgian Treaty*); Garner, *Rebus Sic Stantibus* (n 14) 509.
[29] Garner, *Rebus Sic Stantibus* (n 14) 509.
[30] ibid.
[31] ibid.
[32] *Denunciation of the Sino-Belgian Treaty* (n 28).
[33] ibid.
[34] HW Briggs, 'The Attorney General Invokes *Rebus Sic Stantibus*' (1942) 36 AJIL 89.
[35] ibid.
[36] Emphasis added.
[37] ibid 93.

in response to Nazi Germany's threats of war.[38] A similar understanding of the principle can be seen in Egypt's denunciation of the Anglo-Egyptian treaty of 1936.[39] The basis for the denunciation was the non-compatibility of the treaty with the United Nations Charter, which represented evolved current circumstances.[40] *Rebus sic stantibus* also found recognition in Article 19 of the Covenant of the League of Nations.[41]

At this stage of the evolution of the principle, four certain salient features become apparent. First, states assumed that *rebus sic stantibus* was an established principle in international law. Second, building on this assumption, they invoked the principle even if the treaties in question did not contain clauses expressly permitting the use of such principle. Third, the termination of treaties was done in a unilateral and definitive manner. Fourth, there were no defined parameters for the invocation of the principle.

II. Change in circumstances leading to breach of shared expectations

The ILC's codification of the principle into Article 62 of the VCLT was an important step in defining its nature, scope, and the parameters for invocation.[42] In its draft articles, the ILC made several important observations.[43] Primarily, the ILC concluded that a *delimited and regulated*[44] application of the principle should find a place in the modern law of treaties.[45] Importantly, it focused on the need to codify and define the principle instead of allowing it to exist as a legal fiction that could be misused.[46] It rejected the notion of *implied applicability*[47] of the principle and formulated it into an objective rule of law.[48] In order to stress its objective character, the ILC also refrained from using the term '*rebus sic stantibus*' in the provision.[49] The codified provision emphasizes on the shared expectations and common intentions of the parties while concluding the treaty.[50]

An example of this type of interpretation is evident in the *Questech* case decided by the Iran–US Claims Tribunal (IUSCT).[51] The Iranian defence ministry terminated the Claimant's contract due to transformations arising from the Islamic revolution in Iran. Interestingly, the tribunal seemingly *proprio motu* examined the applicability of *rebus sic stantibus*, without

---

[38] History, 'FDR Proclaims an Unlimited National Emergency in Response to Nazi Threats' <www.history.com/this-day-in-history/fdr-proclaims-an-unlimited-national-emergency> accessed 17 January 2022.
[39] HW Briggs, '*Rebus Sic Stantibus* before the Security Council: The Anglo-Egyptian Question' (1949) 43 AJIL 762–69.
[40] ibid 763.
[41] Q Wright, H Tobin and Chesney Hill, 'Article 19 of the League Covenant and the Principle "*Rebus Sic Stantibus*"' (1936) 30 Proceedings of the American Society of International Law at its Annual Meeting (1921–1969) 55–86.
[42] Kulaga, Renaissance (n 6) 478–79.
[43] ILC, Draft Articles on the Law of Treaties (n 13) 258.
[44] Emphasis added.
[45] ILC, Draft Articles on the Law of Treaties (n 13) 258.
[46] ibid.
[47] ibid 258–59.
[48] Kulaga, Renaissance (n 6) 478.
[49] ILC, Draft Articles on the Law of Treaties (n 13) 258.
[50] Kulaga, Renaissance (n 6) 478.
[51] *Questech, Inc v The Ministry of National Defence of Iran* (1985) 59 IUSCTR (hereafter *Questech*); M Leigh, 'Decisions of the Iran-United States Claims Tribunal' (1986) 80 AJIL 362 (hereafter Leigh, Decisions of the Tribunal).

it being expressly invoked by the respondent.[52] The tribunal noted that the fundamental changes in Iran's political landscape were such that had they existed during the conclusion of the contract, the parties would have never consented to it.[53] Focusing on shared expectations, it interpreted the contract, and the surrounding circumstances, and tried to ascertain what the causes that motivated the parties' consent were.[54] It ruled that the termination of the contract was valid.[55] Arguably, the IUSCT's invocation of *rebus sic stantibus* was not purely *proprio motu*, since it was following the mandate set out in the Claims Declaration. Nevertheless, it is noteworthy for its application of the principle to a contract between a state entity and a private party.

14 *Gabčíkovo-Nagymaros* is the first case where the ICJ dealt with the *rebus sic stantibus* principle.[56] In 1977, Hungary and Slovakia entered into a bilateral treaty production of hydroelectricity.[57] Following the collapse of the Soviet Union and revolutionary changes in Eastern Europe, Hungary terminated the treaty invoking, *inter alia*, the ground of fundamental change of circumstances.[58] Czechoslovakia rejected Hungary's purported termination.[59] The two states jointly referred the dispute to the ICJ in 1993.[60] Hungary relied on Article 62 VCLT.[61] It identified a number of substantive elements that existed when the treaty had been concluded that had changed fundamentally.[62] The Court refused to accept Hungary's arguments and ruled that the changed circumstances were not of such a nature to radically transform the parties' obligations.[63] It also held that the circumstances identified by Hungary did not constitute the essential basis for the parties' consent.[64] Thus, it applied the common intention of parties approach to ascertain whether the circumstances referred to were fundamental in nature. It is important to note that the ICJ construed the principle in extremely narrow term, reinforcing the idea that 'stability of treaty relations requires that the plea of fundamental change of circumstances be applied only in exceptional cases'.[65] It clarified this interpretation in the *Fisheries Jurisdiction* case.[66] Focusing on the *object and purpose*[67] of the treaty, it ruled that the test does not ask whether the obligations to be performed under the treaty have become unduly burdensome.[68] Rather, the increased burden of obligations (due to the change in circumstances) should be such that it transforms the obligation into

---

[52] ibid 10–11. The tribunal invoked the *rebus sic stantibus* doctrine by referring to Article V of the IUSCT's Claims Settlement Declaration which mandated the tribunal to take into account relevant usages of the trade, contract provisions, *and changed circumstances* when deciding all cases.
[53] ibid 12.
[54] ibid 12–13.
[55] ibid 11; Leigh, Decisions of the Tribunal (n 51) 362–63.
[56] *Case Concerning the Gabčíkovo-Nagymaros Project (Hungary v Slovakia)* [1997] ICJ Rep 7 (hereafter *Gabčíkovo-Nagymaros*).
[57] ibid 17–18; PN Okowa and MD Evans, 'Case Concerning the Gabčíkovo—Nagymaros Project (Hungary/Slovakia)' (1998) 47 ICLQ 689.
[58] *Gabčíkovo-Nagymaros* (n 56), para 92; D Reichert-Facilides, 'Down the Danube: The Vienna Convention on the Law of Treaties and the Case concerning the Gabčíkovo-Nagymaros Project' (1998) 47 ICLQ 839–40 (hereafter Reichert-Facilides, Down the Danube).
[59] Reichert-Facilides, Down the Danube (n 58) 840.
[60] ibid.
[61] *Gabčíkovo-Nagymaros* (n 56) 59–60.
[62] ibid, para 95.
[63] ibid, para 104.
[64] ibid.
[65] ibid.
[66] *Fisheries Jurisdiction Case (United Kingdom of Great Britain and Northern Ireland v Iceland)* (Jurisdiction of the Court: Judgment) [1973] ICJ Rep 3 (hereafter *Fisheries Jurisdiction*).
[67] Emphasis added.
[68] *Fisheries Jurisdiction* (n 66) para 43; Kulaga, Renaissance (n 6) 480.

something essentially different from what was originally undertaken.[69] Thus, yet again, it focused on the common intention, as reflected in the original obligations undertaken by the parties prior to the change in circumstances.

15 The second phase in the evolution of the *rebus sic stantibus* principle denotes coherence, clarity, and consistency in its interpretation. The scope of the principle was narrowed, and invocation was permissible only in exceptional circumstances. The focus would be on the common intention of the parties at the time the relevant treaty was concluded.

III. Vital State interests

16 Despite the consistency in interpretation by judicial bodies, a new method of interpretation has recently evolved in State practice.[70] This method justifies termination by arguing that the continuance of the treaty is harmful to vital State interests due to a change in circumstances.[71] The 1972 Anti-Ballistic Missile (ABM) Treaty between the USA and the Soviet Union contains a modified version of the *rebus sic stantibus* clause.[72] Article XV(2) allows each party in exercising its national sovereignty to withdraw from the Treaty if it decides that extraordinary events related to the subject matter of this Treaty have jeopardized its national interests. In 2001, President Bush terminated the ABM treaty by declaring that conditions affecting US national security had been materially altered by the end of the Cold War and that the United States faced different types of threats than those it faced during the Cold War.[73] The crux of the justification thus lay in a threat to vital State interests.[74]

17 Russia also raised this defence when it suspended the Agreement Concerning the Management and Disposition of Plutonium Designated as No Longer Required for Defense Purposes and Related Cooperation (PMDA).[75] It justified the termination by invoking 'a fundamental change of circumstances, or more precisely, aggressive anti-Russia tendencies'.[76] An emphasis on threat to vital State interests while terminating a treaty is yet to be analysed by international tribunals. It constitutes an evolution of the principle and may be a slight departure from Article 62 VCLT.

C. *Rebus sic stantibus*: from the perspective of investment arbitration

18 Despite a growing trend in State practice to invoke *rebus sic stantibus* to justify termination, thus far, the principle has rarely been used in investment arbitration.[77] Nevertheless, variations of the principle can be observed in investor–State jurisprudence.

---

[69] ibid.
[70] Kulaga, Renaissance (n 6) 484–85.
[71] ibid 485.
[72] Fitzmaurice, Exceptional Circumstances (n 3) 609.
[73] ibid.
[74] Kulaga, Renaissance (n 6) 485.
[75] ibid 486.
[76] K Daugirdas and JD Mortenson, 'Russia Suspends Bilateral Agreement with United States Disposal of Weapons-Grade Plutonium' (2017) 111 AJIL 181.
[77] O Bayrak, 'Economic Crises and the Fundamental Change of Circumstances in Investment Arbitration' (2020) 35 ICSID Rev 132–33 (hereafter Bayrak, Economic Crisis).

I. *Rebus sic stantibus* through the prism of State interest

19 A state's power to interfere with investor–State contracts has been accepted under State practice and jurisprudence of international courts. In the *Oliva* case, the Italian–Venezuelan Claims Commission held that the termination of an investment contract by the state in public interest was justified.[78] The investor was suspected of cooperating with revolutionary factions, and this was the primary motive of public interest that obliged the state to terminate the contract.[79] In the *Company General of Orinoco* case, the French–Venezuelan Claims Commission accepted the unilateral termination of a mining concession, since the concession had given rise to political tensions with a neighbouring state.[80] The Commission stated as follows:

> [A]s the Government of Venezuela, whose duty of self-preservation rose superior to any question of contract, it had the power to abrogate the contract in whole or in part. It exercised that power and cancelled the provision of unrestricted assignment. It considered the peril superior to the obligation and substituted therefor the duty of compensation.[81]

20 Acceptance of a state's power to interfere in investor–State contracts leads one to conclude that the principle can play a key role in investment arbitration. In the *Liamco v Libya* case, the tribunal recognized the importance of *rebus sic stantibus* by stating that:

> [T]he binding force is subject to the continuance of circumstances under which a treaty was concluded. If such circumstances change substantially, then its modification or cancellation may be claimed or resorted to.[82]

21 Despite the success of the principle in international relations, there is little evidence of its usage in investment arbitration.[83] Perhaps the reason for this is the *Gabčíkovo-Nagymaros* judgment of the ICJ. The ICJ rejected Hungary's reliance on Article 62 VCLT because economic viability of a project or political circumstances did not constitute an essential basis for the treaty.[84] This interpretation has restricted the scope of the principle greatly and perhaps is the reason why it has not been invoked in investment arbitration directly. However, two adaptations of the principle exist, and they form a key part of international investment law.

II. Stabilization clauses and renegotiation clauses

22 While analysing changes in circumstances in investment arbitration, the two most frequently invoked clauses are stabilization clauses and renegotiation clauses.[85] Stabilization clauses share a similar rationale with a part of the *rebus sic stantibus* principle, i.e. the need to ensure that the original conditions that motivated party consent are not hampered by a change in circumstances. Stabilization clauses are tools used to freeze the law at the moment

---

[78] *Oliva Case (of a general nature)* Italian–Venezuelan Commission (1903) X RIAA 600–09, 1903.
[79] ibid 608–09.
[80] *Company General of the Orinoco (France v Venezuela)*, French–Venezuelan Commission (1905) X RIAA 184.
[81] ibid 280.
[82] *Libyan American Oil Company (Liamco) v The Government of the Libyan Arab Republic* (Award), 12 April 1977, 20 ILM 57.
[83] Bayrak, Economic Crisis (n 77) 133–35.
[84] *Gabčíkovo-Nagymaros* (n 56) 64–65.
[85] Panel Discussion, 'Panel: Expect the Unexpected: Adjudicating Changed Circumstances in Commercial and Treaty Arbitration' (2020) 2 ITA in Rev 113.

a contract is signed between a state or state entity and an investor[86]: 'A stabilization clause is a way to achieve the parties' common objective to allocate between them the risk inherent in a long-term transaction'.[87] These clauses seek to freeze the agreement between the parties in order to ensure that a change in circumstances does not result in frustration of the original intention of the parties.[88] The necessity for these clauses arises from an economic angle, and the need to provide economic stability to an investor in making a substantial investment.[89] Such clauses are more prevalent in the energy and oil sectors which tend to have long-term investments.[90] They aim at guaranteeing the stability of essential conditions of the agreement that may influence the investment, such as fiscal regimes, labour legislations, and exchange control regulations.[91]

A state's right and ability to enter into contracts containing stabilization clauses have been confirmed by international law and practice.[92] An arbitral tribunal in the *Texaco Overseas Petroleum Company v Libya (TOPCO)* case held that 'in entering into such a contract with the plaintiffs, the Libyan State did not alienate but exercised its sovereignty'.[93] In the *TOPCO* case, Libya nullified the property rights of several oil companies in violation of the terms of a concession agreement due to a change in circumstances.[94] The concession agreement contained a stabilization clause, and this clause played an important role in the tribunal's ruling that the taking was illegal.[95] Subsequent tribunals in *Kuwait v Aminoil*,[96] *AGIP v Congo*,[97] and *Revere Copper v OPIC*[98] endorsed this view. In *Duke Energy v Peru*,[99] the tribunal expanded the scope of the stabilization clause to include not just amendments to the law, but also interpretations of existing law that would breach the stabilization clause.[100] 23

Even though a stabilization clause does not permit the termination or alteration of a contract, several aspects of *rebus sic stantibus* can be noticed in its operation. For instance, the clause maintains those conditions that motivated party consent. In the case of energy and natural resources sectors, those conditions may relate to fiscal regimes and labour law regulations.[101] As held by the IUSCT in *Questech*, a party has certain rights if the conditions that 24

---

[86] WM Reisman, James Richard Crawford, and Raymond Doak Bishop (eds), *Foreign Investment Disputes: Cases, Materials and Commentary* (2nd edn, Kluwer Law International 2014) 214–15 (hereafter Reisman, Crawford, and Bishop, Foreign Investment Disputes).
[87] P Bernardini, 'Stabilization and adaptation in oil and gas investments' (2008) 1 J World Energy L Bus 98 (hereafter Bernardini, Stabilization).
[88] Reisman, Crawford, and Bishop, Foreign Investment Disputes (n 86) 214.
[89] ibid.
[90] J Nwaokoro, ' Enforcing Stabilization of International Energy Contracts' (2010) 3 J World Energy L Bus 103–06.
[91] Bernardini, Stabilization (n 87) 100.
[92] N Rubins and N Stephen Kinsella, *International Investment, Political Risk, and Dispute Resolution: A Practitioner's Guide* (Oceana Publications 2005) 53–57 (hereafter Rubins and Kinsella, International Investment).
[93] *Texaco Overseas Petroleum Company and California Asiatic Oil Company v The Government of the Libyan Arab Republic*, 19 January 1977, 53 ILR 389.
[94] Rubins and Kinsella, International Investment (n 92) 53–57.
[95] ibid.
[96] *Government of Kuwait v American Independent Oil Co*, 24 March 1982, 21 ILM 976 (hereafter *Aminoil*).
[97] *AGIP Company v People's Republic of the Congo*, 30 November 1979, 21 ILM 726.
[98] *Revere Copper & Brass, Inc v Overseas Private Investment Corporation*, 24 August 1978, 56 ILR 257; Lorenzo Cotula, 'Pushing the Boundaries vs. Striking a Balance: The Scope and Interpretation of Stabilization Clauses in Light of the *Duke v. Peru* Award' (2010) 11 JWIT 29 (hereafter Cotula, Pushing the Boundaries).
[99] *Duke Energy International Peru Investments No 1 Ltd v Republic of Peru*, ICSID Case No ARB/03/28, Merits, 18 August 2008, (hereafter *Duke v Peru*).
[100] Cotula, Pushing the Boundaries (n 98) 37.
[101] Bernardini, Stabilization (n 87) 100.

motivated consent to the contract have been materially altered.[102] In other contexts, these rights include termination of the contract. In the stabilization clause context, these rights are adapted, and the investor can demand to be excluded from the change in regulations.

25 The use of stabilization clauses has incurred some criticism as they are deemed to be an obstacle to a state's right to regulate sensitive issues.[103] These clauses are most prevalent in the energy and natural resources sectors, where the potential for harm to the environment or human rights is substantial.[104] It is thus essential that states have the right to regulate in these sectors. At the same time, these sectors can expose investors to extensive political and financial risks, thus requiring a higher degree of protection.[105] A solution is the replacement of stabilization clauses with renegotiation or adaptation clauses.[106]

26 A renegotiation clause is more akin to *rebus sic stantibus* than a stabilization clause. Renegotiation or adaptation is a way for both parties to maintain the benefits of the contractual relationship by adapting the contractual document.[107] This clause balances investor and state rights in the event of a change in circumstances. It allows a state the flexibility to reconsider its obligations in case of a material alteration of conditions.[108] It also guarantees protection to the investor against unilateral termination by the state.[109] A typical renegotiation clause will state that an undetermined future event can trigger renegotiation.[110]

27 There are several instances in State practice where a drastic change of circumstances has triggered the renegotiation clause in investment contracts.[111] For example, consider the renegotiation clause contained in the relevant 1948 concession agreement between Kuwait and Aminoil in the *Aminoil* case.[112] The concession agreement was concluded when Kuwait was still under British control.[113] When Kuwait achieved independence in 1961, an additional agreement was concluded containing a renegotiation clause.[114] In the years thereafter, the international oil industry underwent immense changes due to the formation of OPEC, and OPEC's product pricing policies.[115] The change in circumstances resulted in several rounds of renegotiations between the parties.[116] The legal importance of renegotiation was also accepted by the *Enron* tribunal when it recognized the necessity to renegotiate, but subjected

---

[102] *Questech* (n 51) 12.
[103] A Crockett, 'Stabilisation Clauses and Sustainable Development: Drafting for the Future' in C Brown and K Miles (eds), *Evolution in Investment Treaty Law and Arbitration* (CUP 2011) 516.
[104] ibid 517.
[105] ibid.
[106] Bernardini, Stabilization (n 87) 98.
[107] A Kolo, 'Renegotiation and Contract Adaptation in the International Investment Projects: Applicable Legal Principles & Industry Practices' (2004) 1 TDM <https://www-transnational-dispute-management-com.acces-distant.sciencespo.fr/article.asp?key=30> accessed 19 January 2021.
[108] P Bernardini, 'The Renegotiation of the Investment Contract' (1998) 13 ICSID Rev–FILJ 415 (hereafter Bernardini, Renegotiation).
[109] ibid.
[110] P Wolfgang, 'Arbitration and Renegotiation Clauses' (1986) 3(2) J Int'l Arb 33 (hereafter Wolfgang, Renegotiation Clauses).
[111] P Wolfgang, *Arbitration and Renegotiation of International Investment Agreements* (Kluwer Law International 1995) 51–124.
[112] *Aminoil* (n 96).
[113] Muthucumaraswamy Sornarajah, 'Supremacy of the Renegotiation Clause in International Contracts' (1988) 5(2) J Int'l Arb 105.
[114] ibid.
[115] ibid.
[116] PY Tschanz, 'The Contributions of the Aminoil Award to the Law of State Contracts' (1984) 18 Int'l Law 247 (hereafter Tschanz, Aminoil).

it to the condition that it should be conducted in an orderly manner.[117] The renegotiation clause captures the *rebus sic stantibus* principle more clearly.[118] It allows parties to realign themselves if fundamental conditions have changed over time, changing the nature of the parties' obligations.

D. Investigating the applicability of *rebus sic stantibus* to investment arbitration

Outside the investment context, *rebus sic stantibus* has been invoked frequently by states for terminating treaties due to a change in circumstances.[119] State practice reflects that most terminations based on a change in circumstances have been accepted, without a challenge before a judicial authority.[120]

As stated, in investment arbitration practice, the principle has rarely been invoked directly.[121] Article 1 of the VCLT states that the convention applies to *treaties between states*.[122] Therefore, some academics believe that Article 62 cannot be invoked by states against an investor.[123] However, many provisions of the VCLT are frequently applied in investment arbitration, as many entries in this Commentary testify. Moreover, treaties granting investment protection to foreign investors are essentially third-party beneficiary contracts.[124] Such 'contract' is the basis upon which the third party's (i.e. the investor's) rights rest, despite the fact that it may enforce these rights separately.[125] The investment treaty remains the focal point of the relation between a state and an investor.[126] Investor–State arbitration necessarily involves interpretation and application of the treaty in question for resolution of the dispute and thus of application of the rules enshrined in the VCLT, including Article 62. Article 8.31 of the Comprehensive Economic and Trade Agreement (CETA), for instance, explicitly stipulates that an arbitral tribunal shall apply the VCLT and other rules and principles of international law applicable between the disputing parties. A similar provision can be found in Article 13(2) of the EU Transatlantic Trade and Investment Partnership Text Proposal.

A significant barrier to its invocation in investment arbitration, however, seems the extremely narrow way in which Article 62 has been construed by the ICJ. A state relying on the provision will have to prove that since the investment in the host state, there has been a change in circumstances that has radically transformed the parties' obligations.[127] The state will also have to prove that the effect of the change has led to a complete transformation

---

[117] *Enron Corporation Ponderosa LP v The Argentine Republic*, ICSID Case No ARB/01/3, Award, 22 May 2007, para 143 (hereafter *Enron*); A Florou, *Contractual Renegotiations and International Investment Arbitration* (Brill Nijhoff 2020) 190–201 (hereafter Florou, Contractual Renegotiations).
[118] Wolfgang, Renegotiation Clauses (n 110) 29; Bernardini, Stabilization (n 87) 98.
[119] Garner, *Rebus Sic Stantibus* (n 14) 509–11; ILC, Draft Articles on the Law of Treaties (n 13) 257.
[120] Garner, *Rebus Sic Stantibus* (n 14) 509–11.
[121] Bayrak, Economic Crisis (n 77) 132.
[122] Emphasis added.
[123] Bayrak, Economic Crisis (n 77) 137.
[124] A Van Aaken, 'International Investment Law Between Commitment and Flexibility: A Contract Theory Analysis' (2009) 12 JIEL 507–20 (hereafter Aaken, Investment Law); J Hallebeek and H Dondorp, *Contracts for a Third-Party Beneficiary. A Historical and Comparative Account* (Brill 2008) 138 (hereafter Hallebeek and Dondorp, Contracts for Third-Party Beneficiary).
[125] Bayrak, Economic Crisis (n 77) 138.
[126] ibid 138–39.
[127] *Gabčíkovo-Nagymaros* (n 56).

of the obligations.[128] This means that a state can invoke Article 62 only in rare and exceptional cases.

31 Notwithstanding the above, it can be concluded that there is adequate basis for future invocation of *rebus sic stantibus*. Investment arbitration has seen cases arising out of severe change in circumstances, such as the Argentine crisis of 2000–01, or the recent Spanish renewable energy crisis.[129] Perhaps in the future, states will resort to using this principle to defend termination or breach of contracts in such circumstances.

E. Conclusion

32 Regardless of the lack of popularity in investment arbitration, *rebus sic stantibus* remains an important principle in general international law. Its significance and continuing relevance are evident in State practice. It constitutes an important exception to the *pacta sunt servanda* rule. Codification by the ILC has transformed the principle from being a legal fiction to a well-defined provision with restricted applicability. ICJ judgments have further defined the applicability of the principle.

33 From an investment arbitration perspective, usage of the principle has been rare and if so, only indirectly. However, it ought to be remembered that like *pacta sunt servanda*, *rebus sic stantibus* is essential for peace and stability. It ensures that the original intention of the parties is safeguarded and is to be used as an interpretative tool while adjudging breach of contracts or treaties. Its restricted character is essential for ensuring that there is no misuse, and states do not rely on it to escape their obligations. Thus, albeit only in exceptional circumstances, the principle can be invoked to defend a state's sovereign right to terminate, suspend, or alter contracts that do not conform to the parties' original intention. *Rebus sic stantibus* can act as a guiding principle for investment arbitration tribunals while analysing a state's breach of obligations.

Selected literature

Bayrak O, 'Economic Crises and the Fundamental Change of Circumstances in Investment Arbitration' (2020) 35 ICSID Rev 132.
Bernardini P, 'Stabilization and Adaptation in Oil and Gas Investments' (2008) 1 JWELB 98.
Bernardini P, 'The Renegotiation of the Investment Contract' (1998) 13 ICSID Rev–FILJ 415.
Binder C, 'Stability and Change in Times of Fragmentation: the Limits of *Pacta Sunt Servanda* Revisited' (2012) 25 LJIL 909.
Briggs HW, '*Rebus Sic Stantibus* before the Security Council: The Anglo-Egyptian Question' (1949) 43 AJIL 762.
Fitzmaurice M, 'Exceptional Circumstances and Treaty Commitments' in DB Hollis (ed), *The Oxford Guide to Treaties* (OUP 2020) 595.
Florou A, *Contractual Renegotiations and International Investment Arbitration* (Brill Nijhoff 2020).
Garner JW, 'The Doctrine of *Rebus Sic Stantibus* and the Termination of Treaties' (1927) 21 AJIL 509.
Haraszti G, 'Treaties and the Fundamental Change of Circumstances' (1977) 146 RdC 10.

---

[128] *Fisheries Jurisdiction* (n 66).
[129] Bayrak, Economic Crisis (n 77) 130.

International Law Commission, 'Draft Articles on the Law of Treaties with Commentaries' YILC 1966, Vol II.
Kulaga J, 'A Renaissance of the Doctrine of *Rebus Sic Stantibus*?' (2020) 69 ICLQ 477.
Lissitzyn OJ, 'Treaties and Changed Circumstances (*Rebus Sic Stantibus*)' (1967) 61 AJIL 895.
Reisman WM, Crawford WM and Bishop RD (eds), *Foreign Investment Disputes: Cases, Materials and Commentary* (2nd edn, Kluwer Law International 2014) 214.
Sornarajah M, 'Supremacy of the Renegotiation Clause in International Contracts' (1988) 5(2) J Int'l Arb 105.
Vamvoukos A, *Termination of Treaties in International Law: The Doctrines of Rebus Sic Stantibus and Desuetude* (Clarendon Press 1985).
Wolfgang P, 'Arbitration and Renegotiation Clauses' (1986) 3(2) J Int'l Arb 33.
Wright Q, Tobin H and Hill C, 'Article 19 of the League Covenant and the Principle "*Rebus Sic Stantibus*"' (1936) 30 Proceedings of the American Society of International Law at its Annual Meeting (1921–1969) 55.

Selected decisions

AGIP Company v People's Republic of the Congo, 30 November 1979, 21 ILM 726.
Case of Free Zones of Upper Savoy and the District of Gex (Switzerland v France) PCIJ Series A/B No 46.
Company General of the Orinoco Case (France) v Venezuela, French–Venezuelan Commission (1905) X RIAA 184.
Denunciation of the Treaty of November 2nd, 1865, between China and Belgium (Belgium v China) (Order) PCIJ Series A No 18/19.
Duke Energy International Peru Investments No 1 Ltd v Republic of Peru, ICSID Case No ARB/03/28, Merits, 18 August 2008.
Enron Corporation Ponderosa LP v The Argentine Republic, ICSID Case No ARB/01/3, Award, 22 May 2007.
Fisheries Jurisdiction Case (United Kingdom of Great Britain and Northern Ireland v Iceland) (Jurisdiction) [1973] ICJ Rep 3.
Gabčíkovo-Nagymaros Project (Hungary v Slovakia) [1997] ICJ Rep 7.
Government of Kuwait v American Independent Oil Co, 24 March 1982, 21 ILM 976.
Jan de Nul NV Dredging International NV v Arab Republic of Egypt (Award) ICSID Case No ARB/04/13.
Libyan American Oil Company (Liamco) v The Government of the Libyan Arab Republic, Award, 12 April 1977, 20 ILM 57.
Nationality Decrees Issued in Tunis and Morocco (French Zone) (Advisory Opinion) PCIJ Series B No 4.
Oliva Case (of a general nature), Italian–Venezuelan Commission, X RIAA 600, 1903.
Questech, Inc v The Ministry of National Defence of Iran (1985) 59 IUSCTR.
Revere Copper & Brass, Inc v Overseas Private Investment Corporation, 24 August 1978, 56 ILR 257.
Texaco Overseas Petroleum Company and California Asiatic Oil Company v The Government of the Libyan Arab Republic, 19 January 1977, 53 ILR 389.

PART II
RESPONSIBILITY OF STATES AND INTERNATIONAL ORGANIZATIONS

Article 4 of the ARSIWA

Conduct of organs of a State

*Chester Brown**

1. The conduct of any State organ shall be considered an act of that State under international law, whether the organ exercises legislative, executive, judicial or any other functions, whatever position it holds in the organization of the State, and whatever its character as an organ of the central Government or of a territorial unit of the State.

2. An organ includes any person or entity which has that status in accordance with the internal law of the State.

A. Introduction	1	C. Specific doctrinal issues discussed in investment arbitration	24
B. Definition and scope of 'State organ'	6	I. Reliance on domestic law	25
I. Irrelevance of branch or sub-branch of government	7	II. Conflation of tests for attribution	29
II. Irrelevance of *acta iure imperii* vs. *gestionis* distinction	9	II. Relationship between rules of attribution and issues of contractual liability	31
III. Irrelevance of rank	10	IV. Rules of attribution as residual in character	33
IV. Irrelevance of federal, regional, or local subdivisions	11		
V. '*De facto*' organs of the State	13	D. Conclusion	37

A. Introduction

Article 4 is located in Chapter II of Part One of the International Law Commission's (ILC) **1** Articles on the Responsibility of States for Internationally Wrongful Acts (ARSIWA), which concerns the attribution of conduct to a State. The proposition that the State is responsible for the conduct of its organs when acting in that capacity is largely uncontroversial, and it has long been recognized as a rule of custom in international judicial and arbitral practice.[1] States responding to the League of Nations Preparatory Committee for the 1930 Hague Conference for the Codification of International Law were 'unanimous' in their support for the proposition that 'actions and omissions of organs of the State must be attributed to it'.[2]

---

* I am grateful to Calida Tang for her excellent research assistance.
[1] eg, ILC, 'Draft Articles on Responsibility of States for Internationally Wrongful Acts, with Commentaries' YILC 2001, Vol II, Part Two, 31, Article 4 paras 1–4 (hereafter ARSIWA Commentaries); J Crawford, *State Responsibility: The General Part* (CUP 2013) 116–17 (hereafter Crawford, *State Responsibility*).
[2] ARSIWA Commentaries (n 1) Article 4 para 4, citing League of Nations, *Conference for the Codification of International Law: Bases of Discussion for the Conference drawn up by the Preparatory Committee*, Vol III:

The Third Committee of the Hague Conference proceeded to adopt draft Article 1, which provided that States would be internationally responsible as a consequence of 'any failure on the part of its organs to carry out the international obligations of the State'.[3]

2 Even before the United Nations General Assembly 'took note' of the ARSIWA and 'commended them to the attention of Governments' on 12 December 2001,[4] international courts and tribunals had referred with approval to the ILC's draft articles on issues of attribution. For instance, the International Court of Justice (ICJ) expressed the view in its 1999 advisory opinion concerning the *Difference relating to Immunity from Legal Process of a Special Rapporteur of the Commission on Human Rights* that there was 'a well-established rule of international law', according to which 'the conduct of any organ of a State must be regarded as an act of that State. This rule ... is of a customary character'.[5] It said this with reference to the (then) Draft Article 6. Since the adoption of the ARSIWA, the ICJ has considered and applied Article 4, including in *Armed Activities on the Territory of the Congo* ('*Armed Activities*'), in which it confirmed the customary status of Article 4.[6] It also applied Article 4 in *Application of the Convention on the Prevention and Punishment of the Crime of Genocide* ('*Bosnian Genocide*'), and stated that the rule in Article 4 was one of 'customary international law'.[7]

3 Given its customary status, it is unsurprising that Article 4 of the ARSIWA has been considered and applied by multiple other international courts and tribunals. This practice has been the subject of regular review. In this regard, the United Nations General Assembly has requested the Secretary-General to compile a report of the use by international adjudicatory bodies of the ARSIWA, and the Secretary-General has submitted such a report every three years, beginning in 2007.[8] In the most recent of these reports, published in April 2019, the Secretary-General noted that twenty-two international decisions had in the previous three years referred to and applied Article 4.[9]

'Responsibility of States for Damage caused in their Territory to the Person or Property of Foreigners' (LN Doc C.75.M.69.1929.V), 25, 41, 52; see also C de Stefano, 'Attribution of Conduct to a State' (2022) 37 ICSID Rev 20, 21 (hereafter De Stefano, 'Attribution').

[3] ARSIWA Commentaries (n 1) Article 4 para 4, reproduced in YILC 1956, Vol II, 225, UN Doc A/CN.4/96, Annex 3. As is well known, the Hague Conference ultimately failed to adopt an instrument on State responsibility for damage done in their territory to the person or property of foreigners, which had been one of the first three topics given to the Committee of Experts: see, eg, A Watts, M Wood and O Sender, 'Codification and Progressive Development of International Law' in *Max Planck Encyclopedia of Public International Law* (2021) paras 7–10; United Nations, 'About the Commission: League of Nations Codification Conference' https://legal.un.org/ilc/league.shtml accessed 10 September 2022.

[4] UNGA Res 59/35 (12 December 2001) UN Doc A/RES/59/35.

[5] *Difference relating to the Immunity from Legal Process of a Special Rapporteur of the Commission on Human Rights* (Advisory Opinion) [1999] ICJ Rep 62, para 62.

[6] *Armed Activities on the Territory of the Congo (Democratic Republic of the Congo v Uganda)* (Judgment) [2005] ICJ Rep 168, para 213 (hereafter *Armed Activities*).

[7] *Application of the Convention on the Prevention and Punishment of the Crime of Genocide (Bosnia and Herzegovina v Serbia and Montenegro)* (Judgment) [2007] ICJ Rep 43, para 385 (hereafter *Bosnian Genocide*).

[8] Report of the Secretary-General, 'Responsibility of States for internationally wrongful acts: Compilation of Decisions of International Courts, Tribunals, and Other Bodies', UN Doc A/62/62, 1 February 2007; UN Doc A/62/62/Add.1, 17 April 2007; UN Doc A/65/76, 30 April 2010; UN Doc A/68/72, 30 April 2013; UN Doc A/71/80, 21 April 2016; and UN Doc A/74/83, 23 April 2019.

[9] Report of the Secretary-General, 'Responsibility of States for internationally wrongful acts: Compilation of Decisions of International Courts, Tribunals, and Other Bodies', UN Doc A/74/83, 23 April 2019.

This practice includes decisions of World Trade Organization (WTO) Panels,[10] ad hoc **4** inter-State arbitral tribunals,[11] as well as tribunals constituted under Annex VII of the United Nations Convention on the Law of the Sea (UNCLOS).[12] The UNCLOS tribunal in *The Enrica Lexie Incident (Italy v India)* specifically relied on Article 4 of the ARSIWA in its consideration of whether the conduct of members of the Italian marines was attributable to Italy.[13] It held that the Italian marines were, 'as members of Italy's armed forces, fulfilling a State function'; it went on to hold that their conduct was attributable to Italy as they were 'not only acting as officers of the Italian Navy but also as officers and agents of the judicial police in respect of crimes related to piracy'.[14] Other relevant practice can be found in the decisions and judgments of regional international courts and tribunals, including the Economic Community of West African States Court of Justice,[15] the Caribbean Court of Justice,[16] and a MERCOSUR tribunal established under the Protocol of Brasilia.[17]

Article 4 has also been widely referred to in the context of investment disputes, and it has **5** largely been applied consistently with the practice of the ICJ and other international courts and tribunals. In 2010, James Crawford observed that the rules of attribution in the ARSIWA 'have been comprehensively applied by investment treaty tribunals and, generally speaking, without too much difficulty'.[18] There is indeed much arbitral practice: Crawford's article[19] noted twenty-four investment cases in the period 2001–09 in which the tribunals had referred to Article 4 of the ARSIWA. In 2022,[20] Esmé Shirlow and Kabir Duggal noted a further forty-six investment treaty cases in the period 2010–20 in which the tribunals had discussed Article 4 of the ARSIWA.[21] They observed that the ARSIWA's provisions on attribution 'remain among the most frequently invoked by parties, and the most frequently referred to by tribunals'.[22]

---

[10] *Thailand—Customs and Fiscal Measures on Cigarettes from the Philippines*, WTO Panel Report, WT/DS371/RW, 12 November 2018, paras 7.636 and 7.771; see also *Thailand—Customs and Fiscal Measures on Cigarettes from the Philippines*, WTO Panel Report, WT/DS371/R, 15 November 2010, para 7.120; and see *United States—Measures Affecting the Cross-Border Supply of Gambling and Betting Services*, WTO Panel Report, WT/DS285/R, 10 November 2004, para 6.128.

[11] *Dispute concerning Access to Information under Article 9 of the OSPAR Convention (Ireland v United Kingdom)*, Final Award, 2 July 2003, XXIII RIAA 59, paras 144–45.

[12] United Nations Convention on the Law of the Sea, (adopted 10 December 1982, entered into force 16 November 1994) 1833 UNTS 3.

[13] *The 'Enrica Lexie' Incident (Italy v India)*, PCA Case No 2015-28, Award (21 May 2020).

[14] ibid paras 858–59 (footnotes omitted). See also *The South China Sea Arbitration (Republic of the Philippines v People's Republic of China)*, PCA Case No 2013-19, Award (12 July 2016) paras 703, 755, 810, 1091, although the tribunal did not expressly refer to Article 4.

[15] *Tidjane Konte v Ghana*, Case No ECW/CCJ/JUD/11/14, Judgment 13 May 2014, paras 30–34; see also *Benson Olua Okomba v Republic of Benin*, Case No ECW/CCJ/JUD/05/17, Judgment, 10 October 2017, 21–22; and *Wing Commander Danladi A Kwasu v Republic of Nigeria*, Case No ECW/CCJ/JUD/04/17, Judgment, 10 October 2017, 25; *Dorothy Chioma Njemanze and Others v Federal Republic of Nigeria*, Case No ECW/CCJ/JUD/08/17, Judgment, 12 October 2017, 39–40; and *Hembadoon Chia v Federal Republic of Nigeria*, Case No ECW/CCJ/JUD/21/18, Judgment, 3 July 2018, 15.

[16] *Maurice Tomlinson v The State of Belize and The State of Trinidad and Tobago*, CCJ 1 (OJ) Judgment, 10 June 2016, para 22.

[17] *Import Prohibition of Remoulded Tyres from Uruguay (Uruguay v Brazil)*, MERCOSUR Tribunal Award, 9 January 2002, 39.

[18] J Crawford, 'Investment Arbitration and the ILC Articles on State Responsibility' (2010) 25 ICSID Rev 127, 133 (hereafter Crawford, 'Investment Arbitration').

[19] ibid 143–52.

[20] E Shirlow and K Duggal, 'The ILC Articles on State Responsibility in Investment Treaty Arbitration' (2022) 37 ICSID Rev 378 (hereafter Shirlow and Duggal).

[21] ibid 392, 400–18.

[22] ibid 383.

B. Definition and scope of 'State organ'

6 The term 'State organ' includes 'all the individual or collective entities which make up the organisation of the State and act on its behalf'.[23] There are a number of prefatory observations to make on the concept of 'State organs'.

I. Irrelevance of branch or sub-branch of government

7 First, the rule in Article 4 is broad. It applies to conduct of organs which have 'legislative, executive, judicial or any other functions'. There is no exclusive category of organs which is specially designated for the purposes of Article 4; as the ILC puts it, 'virtually any State organ may be the author of [an internationally wrongful act]'.[24] The reference to State organs in Article 4 is therefore intended 'in the most general sense'.[25] It therefore reflects the principle of the unity of the State, which 'entails that the acts or omissions of all its organs should be regarded as acts or omissions of the State for the purposes of international responsibility'.[26] This is consistent with arbitral practice which informed the content of Article 4, such as the award in the *Salvador Commercial Company Case ('El Triunfo')*, in which the tribunal agreed with the statement that: 'a State is responsible for the acts of its rulers, whether they belong to the legislative, executive, or judicial department of the Government, so far as the acts are done in their official capacity'.[27] In the relatively recent practice of the ICJ, it held in *Armed Activities* that the conduct of the Ugandan People's Defence Forces and its officers and soldiers was attributable to Uganda, 'being the conduct of a State organ'.[28]

8 The abundant practice of investment tribunals is largely consistent with that of the ICJ and other international courts and tribunals in this regard.[29] Thus, arbitral tribunals have variously confirmed that a State is responsible for the conduct of its legislature,[30] its judiciary,[31] and entities forming part of the executive, such as government ministries, the police service, government officials, and regulatory bodies.[32] Tribunals have also found that State-owned

---

[23] ARSIWA Commentaries (n 1) Article 4 para 1.
[24] ibid para 5.
[25] ibid para 6.
[26] ibid para 5; see also Crawford, 'Investment Arbitration' (n 18) 133.
[27] *Salvador Commercial Company Case ('El Triunfo')*, XV UNRIAA 467, 477 (1902); see also *Chattin v Mexico*, IV UNRIAA 282, 285–86 (1927).
[28] *Armed Activities* (n 6) 168, 242, para 213.
[29] The practice is considered by De Stefano, 'Attribution' (n 2) 31–36.
[30] *William Nagel v Czech Republic*, SCC Case No 049/2002, Final Award, 9 September 2003, para 109; *EnCana Corporation v Ecuador*, LCIA Case No UN3481, Award, 3 February 2006, para 157(a); *EDF (Services) Limited v Romania*, ICSID Case No ARB/05/13, Award, 8 October 2009, para 186; *Electrabel SA v Hungary*, ICSID Case No ARB/07/19, Decision on Applicable Law, Jurisdiction and Liability, 30 November 2012, para 7.89.
[31] *Loewen Group, Inc and Raymond L Loewen v United States of America*, ICSID Case No ARB(AF)/98/3, Decision on Jurisdiction, 5 January 2001, paras 70–74; *Saipem SpA v Bangladesh*, ICSID Case No ARB/05/7, Award, 30 June 2009, paras 189–90; *Deutsche Bank AG v Sri Lanka*, ICSID Case No ARB/09/2, Award, 31 October 2012, para 402 (hereafter *Deutsche Bank*); *Tethyan Copper Company Pty Ltd v Pakistan*, ICSID Case No ARB/12/1, Decision on Jurisdiction and Liability, 10 November 2017, para 725 (hereafter *Tethyan*); *Gavrilovic v Croatia*, ICSID Case No ARB/12/39, Award, 26 July 2018, para 803; *AMF Aircraftleasing Meier & Fischer GmbH & Co KG v Czech Republic*, Final Award, 11 May 2020, para 530; *PACC Offshore Services Holdings Ltd v Mexico*, ICSID Case No UNCT/18/5, Award, 11 January 2022, paras 223–27; *LSF-KEB Holdings, Inc v Korea*, ICSID Case No ARB/12/27, Award, 30 August 2022, para 677.
[32] eg, *Eureko BV v Poland*, UNCITRAL, Partial Award, 19 June 2005, para 129; *Gustav F W Hamester GmbH & Co KG v Ghana*, ICSID Case No ARB/07/24, Award, 18 June 2010, para 182; *Bosh International, Inc and B&P Ltd Foreign*

and controlled enterprises were 'State organs' due to their incorporation within the State's Ministry of Fuel;[33] and that a State's central bank is a 'State organ'.[34]

II. Irrelevance of *acta iure imperii* vs. *gestionis* distinction

A second observation on the rule in Article 4 is that it is 'irrelevant for the purposes of attribution that the conduct of a State organ may be classified as "commercial" or as *acta iure gestionis*'.[35] Thus, 'the entry into or breach of a contract by a State organ is nonetheless an act of the State' within the meaning of Article 4,[36] although whether a contract has been breached is a matter of the governing law of the contract (usually a system of domestic law), rather than international law. This can be contrasted with the position under Article 5 of the ARSIWA, where purely commercial conduct (*acta jure gestionis*) of such a person or entity cannot be attributed to the State. The International Centre for Settlement of Investment Disputes (ICSID) tribunal in *Tethyan Copper Company Pty Ltd v Pakistan* confirmed the irrelevance of whether the conduct of State organs was *acta jure imperii* or *acta jure gestionis*, stating that the acts of the Government of Balochistan (which had, by novation, entered into a joint venture agreement with the claimant) and its officials were attributable to Pakistan 'even if they were carried out in performance of the [joint venture agreement] rather than in an executive function'.[37]

III. Irrelevance of rank

A third issue concerning Article 4 is that it does not matter whether the conduct of the State organ in question is that of 'superior' or 'subordinate' officials, provided they are acting in their official capacity.[38] Naturally, subordinate or lower-ranking officials are likely to have 'a more restricted scope of activity', but their conduct in their official capacity 'is nonetheless attributable to the State for the purposes of article 4'.[39]

IV. Irrelevance of federal, regional, or local subdivisions

In a fourth observation, the rule in Article 4 'applies equally to organs of the central government and to those of regional or local units'.[40] It is of no moment for the purposes of

---

Investment Enterprise v Ukraine, ICSID Case No ARB/08/11, Award, 25 October 2012, paras 145–46; *Tethyan* (n 31) para 725; and *UAB E energia (Lithuania) v Latvia*, ICSID Case No ARB/12/33, Award, 22 December 2017, para 804.

[33] eg, *Ron Fuchs v Georgia*, ICSID Case No ARB/07/15, Award, 3 March 2010, paras 274–80.

[34] eg, *Deutsche Bank* (n 31) para 402; *Von Pezold v Zimbabwe*, ICSID Case No ARB/10/15, Award, 28 July 2015, para 443; and *PJSC CB Privatbank and Finance Company Finilon LLC v Russia*, Partial Award, 4 February 2019, para 237. On the relationship and differences with Articles 5 and 8 of the ARSIWA see in this Commentary Jorge E Viñuales and Alina Papanastasiou, 'Article 8 of the ARSIWA' and also in this chapter at Section C.II regarding Article 5 of the ARSIWA.

[35] ARSIWA Commentaries (n 1) Article 4 para 6; J Ho, *State Responsibility for Breaches of Investment Contracts* (CUP 2018) 45; C de Stefano, *Attribution in International Law and Arbitration* (OUP 2020) 61.

[36] ARSIWA Commentaries (n 1) Article 4 para 6.

[37] *Tethyan* (n 31) para 729. See also JE Viñuales, 'Attribution of Conduct to States in Investment Arbitration' (2022) 20 ICSID Rep 13, 41–42, 43 (hereafter Viñuales, 'Attribution').

[38] ARSIWA Commentaries (n 1) Article 4 para 7; De Stefano, 'Attribution' (n 2) 42–44.

[39] ARSIWA Commentaries (n 1) Article 4 para 7.

[40] ibid para 8.

this inquiry whether the territorial unit in question is part of a federal State, or 'a specific autonomous area' within a unitary State.[41] Relevantly, the ICJ had stated in its provisional measures order in *LaGrand* (albeit without referring to the relevant provision of the ILC's then Draft Articles) that 'the international responsibility of a State is engaged by the action of the competent organs and authorities acting in that State, wherever they may be', and that in that case, 'implementation of the measures indicated in the present Order falls within the jurisdiction of the Governor of Arizona', who was 'under the obligation to act in conformity with the international undertakings of the United States'.[42]

12 Investment tribunals have confirmed that provincial governments of territorial units of a State, and agencies of those provisional governments, are 'State organs'.[43] For instance, in *Tethyan Copper Company Pty Ltd v Pakistan*, the ICSID tribunal held that the conduct of the Government of Balochistan and its officials was attributable to Pakistan, 'because a Federal State may not use its internal organization to escape liability under international law'.[44] The tribunal also held that conduct of agencies of the Government of Balochistan, such as the Mines and Mineral Development Department of the Government of Balochistan's Licensing Authority, was also attributable to Pakistan under Article 4.[45] In another example, the ICSID tribunal in *Casinos Austria International GmbH v Argentine Republic* confirmed that the conduct of a regulatory authority of the Province of Salta, a territorial unit of the Argentine Republic, was attributable to it under Article 4 of the ARSIWA.[46]

V. 'De facto' organs of the State

13 A fifth comment concerns the provisions of Article 4(2), which provides that State organs include those entities which have that status under the law of the State, although it is not a requirement that relevant entities be so regarded under the law of the State. The upshot of this is that '[w]here the law of a State characterizes an entity as an organ, no difficulty will arise'.[47] On the other hand, an entity's characterization as a matter of domestic law is not determinative, as the word 'includes' in Article 4(2) indicates. It is not open to a State to 'avoid responsibility' for the conduct of an entity which is in fact one of its organs 'merely by denying it that status under its own law'.[48] In this respect, it is possible for the conduct of entities which are *not* State organs according to domestic law nonetheless to be attributed to a State if it can be said that those entities are '*de facto*' organs of the State. This will only arise in exceptional circumstances, however, because the question whether an entity is a '*de facto*' State organ will be assessed by reference to substance, rather than form.[49]

---

[41] eg, Crawford, *State Responsibility* (n 1) 123–24.
[42] *LaGrand (Germany v United States)* (Provisional Measures) [1999] ICJ Rep 9, 16, para 28.
[43] eg, *Flemingo DutyFree v Poland*, UNCITRAL, Award, 12 August 2016, para 424 (hereafter *Flemingo*); *Tethyan* (n 31) paras 726–29; *UAB E energia (Lithuania) v Latvia*, ICSID Case No ARB/12/33, Award, 22 December 2017, paras 799–801; *Zhongshang Fucheng Industrial Investment v Nigeria*, Final Award of 26 March 2021, para 72; *Casinos Austria International GmbH v Argentine Republic*, ICSID Case No ARB/14/32, Award, 5 November 2021, para 305.
[44] *Tethyan* (n 31) para 726.
[45] ibid para 729.
[46] *Casinos Austria International GmbH v Argentine Republic*, ICSID Case No ARB/14/32, Award, 5 November 2021, para 305.
[47] ARSIWA Commentaries (n 1) Article 4 para 11.
[48] ibid para 11.
[49] Crawford, *State Responsibility* (n 1) 124–26; see also Viñuales, 'Attribution' (n 37) 44–49.

This issue had arisen in *Military and Paramilitary Activities in and against Nicaragua* **14** ('*Nicaragua*'), in which the ICJ had entertained the possibility that the conduct of the *contra* rebels might be imputable to the United States on this basis:

> What the Court has to determine at this point is whether or not the relationship of the *contras* to the United States Government was so much one of dependence on the one side and control on the other that it would be right to equate the *contras,* for legal purposes, with an organ of the United States Government, or as acting on behalf of that Government.[50]

In order for the conduct of such an entity to be considered a *de facto* organ of the State, **15** the ICJ indicated that it was necessary to demonstrate a relationship of 'complete dependence'.[51] The ICJ found that in the initial years of United States providing assistance (including financial, military, and humanitarian assistance), the *contras* were completely dependent on the United States. However, this did not remain the case, for the US military assistance ceased after 1 October 1984, while the activities of the *contras* had continued. The ICJ concluded that:

> In sum, the evidence available to the Court indicates that the various forms of assistance provided to the *contras* by the United States have been crucial to the pursuit of their activities, but is insufficient to demonstrate their complete dependence on United States aid.[52]

Although the ICJ did not refer to the ILC's ongoing work on State responsibility in its judg- **16** ment in *Nicaragua*, Article 4 was considered by the ICJ in its later judgment in *Bosnian Genocide*. In that case, the ICJ had to consider whether the Federal Republic of Yugoslavia (which later became Serbia and Montenegro) was responsible for the conduct of certain entities and persons, including the Republika Srpska, the VRS (the Army of the Republika Srpska), and certain paramilitary groups (namely, the 'Scorpions', the 'Red Berets', the 'Tigers', and the 'White Eagles').[53]

The ICJ first considered whether the Republika Srpska and the VRS were State organs of the **17** Federal Republic of Yugoslavia within the meaning of Article 4.[54] It concluded that there was no evidence to support the conclusion that these entities were State organs of the Federal Republic of Yugoslavia, and added that 'neither the Republika Srpska, nor the VRS were *de jure* organs of the FRY, since none of them had the status of organ of that State under its internal law'.[55] In response to Bosnia and Herzegovina's arguments that certain senior officers of the VRS (including General Mladić) remained officers of the Army of the Federal Republic of Yugoslav (the 'VJ'), and that their salaries, promotions, and pensions were administered by the VJ, the ICJ held that even if this could be conclusively established, this alone would not make them a 'State organ' of the FRY within the meaning of Article 4.[56] The ICJ then considered whether the 'Scorpions' could be considered to be a 'State organ'. This group was incorporated into the Army of the FRY, although it was disputed as to when that

---

[50] *Military and Paramilitary Activities in and against Nicaragua (Nicaragua v United States of America)* Merits (Judgment) [1986] ICJ Rep 14, para 109.
[51] ibid para 110.
[52] ibid para 110.
[53] *Bosnian Genocide* (n 7) para 384, para 390.
[54] ibid para 385.
[55] ibid para 386.
[56] ibid para 388.

occurred, and for what purpose.[57] On the basis of the available (limited) evidence, the ICJ was not satisfied that the Scorpions were *de jure* organs of the FRY.[58]

18 The ICJ then noted that Bosnia and Herzegovina had argued that the relevant entities must be considered to have been '"*de facto* organs" of the FRY ... so that all of their acts, and specifically the massacres at Srebrenica, must be considered attributable to the FRY, just as if they had been organs of that State under its internal law'.[59] The ICJ agreed that it was possible in principle, for the conduct of persons which did not have the status of State organs nonetheless to be attributable to the State. Citing its earlier judgment in *Nicaragua*, it explained that it had previously decided that:

> [P]ersons, groups of persons or entities may, for purposes of international responsibility, be equated with State organs even if that status does not follow from internal law, provided that in fact the persons, groups or entities act in 'complete dependence' on the State, of which they are ultimately merely the instrument. In such a case, it is appropriate to look beyond legal status alone, in order to grasp the reality of the relationship between the person taking action, and the State to which he is so closely attached as to appear to be nothing more than its agent: any other solution would allow States to escape their international responsibility by choosing to act through persons or entities whose supposed independence would be purely fictitious.[60]

19 The ICJ added that the characterization of a person or entity as a *de facto* State organ would 'be exceptional, for it requires proof of a particularly great degree of State control over them'.[61] The ICJ then proceeded to examine whether 'the persons or entities that committed the acts of genocide at Srebrenica had such ties with the FRY that they can be deemed to have been completely dependent on it'.[62] It ultimately concluded that the question had to be answered in the negative: none of the persons or entities in question could be said to have been in such a relationship with the FRY.[63]

20 Tribunals have also applied the concept of *de facto* State organs in the attribution of conduct to the State, and they have generally sought to apply an approach consistent with the ICJ's test of 'complete dependence', which involves a factual analysis of various matters.[64] These include whether there is State ownership of a separate legal entity (which is not sufficient in and of itself to demonstrate 'complete dependence') and 'the particular circumstances of the legal relationship between the legal entity and the State'.[65]

21 In *Almås v Poland*, the tribunal had to consider whether acts of the Polish Agricultural Property Agency (ANR) were attributable to Poland.[66] The tribunal (which was chaired by James Crawford) observed that it was relevant to look at the status of ANR as a matter of Polish law, but that an entity's status under domestic law did 'not necessarily imply that an

---

[57] ibid para 389.
[58] ibid para 389.
[59] ibid para 390. Simon Olleson refers to this as being a 'gloss' put on Article 4 by the ICJ: S Olleson, 'Attribution in Investment Arbitration' (2016) 31 ICSID Rev 457, 460–61.
[60] *Bosnian Genocide* (n 7) para 392.
[61] ibid para 393.
[62] ibid para 393.
[63] ibid paras 394–95.
[64] Viñuales, 'Attribution' (n 37) 47–49.
[65] ibid 47.
[66] *Mr Kristian Almås and Mr Geir Almås v The Republic of Poland*, PCA Case No 2015-13, Award, 27 June 2016 (hereafter *Almås v Poland*).

entity is not a State organ if other factors, such as the performance of core governmental functions, direct day-to-day subordination to central government, or lack of all operational autonomy, point the other way'.[67] The *Almås* tribunal thus identified three factors which would assist in the determination whether the entity was a *de facto* State organ. On reviewing the facts, the tribunal concluded that ANR was not a *de facto* State organ, in light of 'its autonomous management and financial status'.[68]

At issue in *Flemingo DutyFree Shop Private Ltd v Poland* was whether the conduct of the Polish State Airports Enterprise (PPL) was attributable to Poland. The tribunal held that PPL was a *de facto* State organ, with the tribunal taking into account that it was owned and controlled by Poland,[69] that it operated under a statute, the PPL Act, and under the auspices of the Ministry of Transport, whose control over PPL was 'structural' and 'very substantial';[70] that it performed 'strategic functions for the existence of the State',[71] and the tribunal placed 'much importance' on the evidence of the Secretary of State in the Ministry of Transport which emphasized that PPL operated 'within the structure of the Ministry' and that the Ministry was 'also responsible for all issues connected with the functioning of the enterprise'.[72]

In a more recent award, the tribunal in *Ortiz v Algeria* referred to the ICJ's test of 'complete dependence' and applied the three criteria identified by the *Almås* tribunal,[73] after which it concluded that none of the three entities in question were *de facto* State entities.[74]

C. Specific doctrinal issues discussed in investment arbitration

In addition to the general issues regarding Article 4 which have been noted above, certain issues have arisen in the particular context of investment arbitration which have occasionally given rise to some difficulty.[75] These concern (A) the approaches of the tribunals to determining whether or not an entity is a State organ by reference to the applicable domestic law; (B) the occasional practice of tribunals in failing to distinguish between the separate tests of attribution in Articles 4 and 5 of the ARSIWA and conflating them into what Carlo de Stefano terms a 'super-test' of attribution;[76] (C) the application of rules of attribution in connection with claims for breach of contract which are presented under a treaty's 'umbrella clause';[77] and (D) the recognition that the rules of attribution in the ARSIWA are residual in character, with the result that the treaty in question may contain a *lex specialis* on attribution of conduct.[78]

---

[67] ibid para 207.
[68] ibid para 213; Viñuales, 'Attribution' (n 37) 48–49.
[69] *Flemingo* (n 43) para 427.
[70] ibid paras 427–31.
[71] ibid para 429.
[72] ibid para 434.
[73] *Ortiz v Algeria*, ICSID Case No ARB/17/1, Award, 29 April 2020, paras 167–70.
[74] ibid paras 171–88; see also Viñuales, 'Attribution' (n 37) 49.
[75] eg, De Stefano, 'Attribution' (n 2) 25.
[76] ibid.
[77] ibid; Shirlow and Duggal (n 20) 384; Crawford, 'Investment Arbitration' (n 18) 134.
[78] eg, Crawford, 'Investment Arbitration' (n 18) 130–31, 132–33.

I. Reliance on domestic law

25 Turning to the first category, in some cases, the status of the entity in question is unclear (such as State-owned enterprises or regulatory bodies). In assessing whether the entity is a State organ, tribunals have typically begun by examining the domestic law under which the entity is established, which is consistent with Article 4(2), which states that a State organ 'includes any person or entity which has that status in accordance with the internal law of the State'. For instance, in *Jan de Nul NV and Dredging International NV v Egypt*, the claimant argued that Egypt was responsible for the conduct of the Suez Canal Authority.[79] The tribunal referred to Article 4 of the ARSIWA, and observed that '[i]n order for an act to be attributed to a State, it must have a close link to the State. Such a link can result from the fact that the person performing the act is part of the State's organic structure (Article 4 of the ILC Articles)'.[80] The tribunal held that in carrying out this analysis, it must 'look first to domestic law'.[81] In the event, the tribunal looked exclusively to domestic law, and carried out an analysis of the Law No. 35 of 1975, which embodied the Suez Canal Authority Statutes. This made it clear that, even though the Suez Canal Authority generally carried out public duties, in that it was created to 'the management and utilisation of a nationalised activity', it was structurally separate from the State.[82] In this respect, the Suez Canal Authority had an independent legal personality; its management systems were to be consistent with those followed in the private sector, rather than be influenced by government practices; and it had its own independent budget, with its funds being regarded as 'private funds'.[83] The tribunal concluded that the Suez Canal Authority was not an 'organ of the State', thus appearing to treat its characterization under Egyptian domestic law as conclusive.[84]

26 In another case—*Gustav FW Hamester GmbH & Co KG v Ghana*—at issue was the status of 'Cocobod' which was the Ghana Cocoa Board. The tribunal first looked at Ghanaian law, and noted that Cocobod was created by the Ghana Cocoa Board Law of 3 May 1984.[85] It was a corporate body, could sue and be sued in its own name, and could hold assets and open bank accounts.[86] The claimant had also argued that Cocobod was a *de facto* State organ, having regard to the ability of the Provisional National Defence Council to give 'directions of a general character' to Cocobod.[87] But the tribunal did not accept that Cocobod was a *de facto* State organ:

> First, Article 32 [of the Cocoa Board Law] provides that the Government can only give 'directions of a general character' and not specific instructions to Cocobod. Second, these general policy directions can only be made 'after consultation with the Board of Directors or the Management' of Cocobod. Third, these directions of a general character cannot be 'inconsistent with the contractual and other obligations' of Cocobod, which means that the

---

[79] *Jan de Nul NV and Dredging International NV v Egypt*, ICSID Case No ARB/04/13, Award, 6 November 2008.
[80] ibid para 157.
[81] ibid para 160.
[82] ibid para 161.
[83] ibid para 162.
[84] ibid paras 160–62.
[85] *Gustav FW Hamester GmbH & Co KG v Ghana*, ICSID Case No ARB/07/24, Award, 18 June 2010, paras 22, 184.
[86] ibid paras 22, 184–85.
[87] ibid para 187, citing Ghana Cocoa Board Law of 3 May 1984, Article 32.

commitments of Cocobod, accepted in contracts and dealings with other economic actors, prevail over the Government's directions.[88]

27 The *Hamester* tribunal ultimately concluded that Cocobod was neither a *de jure* nor *de facto* organ of the State, but its consideration did (like the *Jan de Nul* tribunal) not appear to go beyond Ghanaian domestic law.[89]

28 Other tribunals have recognized (consistently with the ILC's commentaries on Article 4) that an entity's status under domestic law is not determinative. Thus, in *Almås v Poland*, as noted above, the tribunal considered the status of 'ANR', the Polish Agricultural Property Agency.[90] Under the relevant Polish statute, ANR was not a State organ, but rather a 'State legal entity' which was 'supervised by the minister for rural development', and it had the authority 'to perform on its own behalf the rights and obligations relating to State agricultural property'.[91] The tribunal considered whether ANR might nonetheless be a *de facto* State organ, and the claimants argued that it should be so considered because it exercised executive functions of the State, namely, in managing, selling, and leasing State agricultural property.[92] The tribunal concluded that:

> In the present case, ANR shares features with the entities under consideration in *Hamester* and *Jan de Nul*. While ANR is supervised by the Minister for Rural Development, Poland's control over ANR's Board is limited to the appointment and removal of its president and vice-president. Poland may direct ANR through regulations. The Council of Ministers additionally must approve sales of shares held by ANR of stock in companies of strategic importance to agriculture, a limited category of holdings. These facts suggest that overall, like the Cocoa Board in Hamester, ANR enjoys a level of autonomy not consistent with its being considered a de facto organ. This is confirmed by the financial factors which were considered as relevant in Jan de Nul. In accordance with Articles 20(b)(1)(e) and 55 of the 1991 Act, ANR has its own bank account. It holds property in its own name. In other words, it has financial autonomy similar to that enjoyed by the Suez Canal Authority. In light of its autonomous management and financial status, ANR is not a de facto organ of the Polish State.[93]

II. Conflation of tests for attribution

29 A number of arbitral tribunals have appeared to conflate the tests for attribution of the conduct of State organs (Article 4) with that which applies to State entities which have been empowered to exercise elements of governmental authority, when they are acting in that capacity (Article 5). De Stefano argues that some tribunals have reasoned 'on the basis of the commonality relating to the exercise of governmental authority and functions'.[94] An example can be found in *Bogdanov v Moldova*, in which the tribunal

---

[88] ibid para 187.
[89] ibid para 188.
[90] *Almås v Poland* (n 66).
[91] ibid para 209.
[92] ibid para 212.
[93] ibid para 213 (footnotes omitted).
[94] De Stefano, 'Attribution' (n 2) 26–27.

referred to Article 4 of the ARSIWA, but also discussed the delegation of sovereign functions as follows:

> The Department of Privatisation is ... a central government body of the Republic of Moldova, delegated by Governmental regulations to carry out state functions, and the effects of its conduct may be attributed to the State. It is generally recognised, in international law, that States are responsible for the acts of their bodies or agencies that carry out State functions.[95]

30 As De Stefano explains, it would be preferable for tribunals to assess the separate tests for attribution individually 'in order to preserve the functioning and legal consequences' of each rule.[96] This issue should not be overstated, however. James Crawford observed in 2010 that, on the whole, tribunals had been 'rather good at drawing the distinction between cases governed by Article 4 (dealing with organs of the State) and those governed by Article 5'.[97]

III. Relationship between rules of attribution and issues of contractual liability

31 The third issue concerns the error occasionally fallen into by tribunals which seek to apply rules of attribution in connection with claims for breach of contract.[98] This had already been noted as an area of confusion by James Crawford in 2010.[99] In this respect, some arbitral decisions have applied the rules on attribution in the context of claims for breach of the umbrella clause, in circumstances where the relevant contract had been entered into with a separate entity. More particularly, tribunals have 'assumed that because a State organ has entered into a contract, the State is therefore responsible for compliance with the contract'.[100] To take an example, the ICSID tribunal in *SGS v Pakistan*—albeit in a rhetorical statement that should be characterized as *obiter dictum*—posited that the 'commitments' embraced by the umbrella clause in the Switzerland—Pakistan Bilateral Investment Treaty could 'be commitments of the State itself as a legal person, or of any office, entity or subdivision (local government units) or legal representative thereof whose acts are, under the law on State responsibility, attributable to the State itself'.[101] But the question of contractual liability is a question of the applicable law of the contract, not public international law, and there is 'no conception of the unity of the State in domestic law'.[102] As James Crawford explains:

> When international investment tribunals deal with questions of contractual liability, those questions are governed by the proper law of the contract. The international legal rules on attribution have nothing to do with this inquiry.[103]

---

[95] *Iurii Bogdanov, Agurdino-Invest Ltd and Agurdino-Chimia JSC v Republic of Moldova*, SCC Award, 22 September 2005, para 2.2.2.

[96] De Stefano, 'Attribution' (n 2) 27. Another case in point is *Maffezini v Spain*, ICSID Case No ARB/97/7, Decision on Jurisdiction, 25 January 2000, in which the tribunal appeared to considered the status of the *Sociedad para el Desarrollo Industrial de Galicia* (SODIGA) through the prism of both Articles 4 and 5, applying a 'structural' and 'functional' test (paras 77–79).

[97] Crawford, 'Investment Arbitration' (n 18) 133. This assessment was not revisited by Shirlow and Duggal in their 2022 study (n 20).

[98] De Stefano, 'Attribution' (n 2) 25; Shirlow and Duggal (n 20) 384; Crawford, 'Investment Arbitration' (n 18) 134.

[99] Crawford, 'Investment Arbitration' (n 18) 134.

[100] ibid.

[101] *SGS v Pakistan*, ICSID Case No ARB/01/13, Decision on Jurisdiction, 6 August 2003, para 166.

[102] Crawford, 'Investment Arbitration' (n 18) 134.

[103] ibid.

Shirlow and Duggal have also noted this confusion as a 'constant',[104] and Viñuales also writes that the arbitral practice has created 'significant uncertainty' regarding the operation of the rules of attribution, and 'even their very application'.[105] However De Stefano suggests that this may be overstating the position, arguing that 'the preponderant majority of tribunals' have approached this issue correctly, finding that 'foreign investors may not claim the breach of the umbrella clause in relation to undertakings entered into with parastatal entities, notably based on the latter's separate juristic personality'.[106]

IV. Rules of attribution as residual in character

On the fourth, and final issue, investment tribunals have recognized that the rules of attribution in the ARSIWA are residual in character, with the result that the treaty in question may contain a *lex specialis* on attribution of conduct.[107] The possibility of the treaty containing a special rule is envisaged in Article 55 of the ARSIWA, which states that the Articles 'do not apply where and to the extent that the conditions for the existence of an internationally wrongful act or the content or implementation of the international responsibility of a State are governed by special rules of international law'.[108]

This arose in *UPS v Canada*, where the tribunal had to determine whether Canada was responsible for the conduct of Canada Post. Noting the terms of Article 55 of the ARSIWA, the tribunal held that the provisions of ARSIWA on attribution of conduct did not apply given the content of Article 1502 of the North American Free Trade Agreement (NAFTA) (which generally required the States parties to NAFTA to ensure, 'through regulatory control, administrative supervision, or the application of other measures' that any privately-owned or government monopolies acted in a manner that was not inconsistent with the Party's obligation under NAFTA), and Article 1503 of NAFTA (which generally required the States parties to likewise ensure that any State enterprises acted in a way that was not inconsistent with the Party's obligations under Chapters 11 and 14 of NAFTA).[109] These provisions created 'distinctions between the State and the identified entities', and had the effect of 'the precise placing of limits on investor arbitration when it is the actions of the monopoly or the enterprise that are principally being questioned'.[110] The tribunal rightly held that:

> […] actions of Canada Post are not in general actions of Canada which can be attributed to Canada as a 'Party' within the meaning of articles 1102 to 1105 or for that matter in articles IS02(3)(a) and 1503(2). Chapter 15 provides for a *lex specialis* regime in relation to the attribution of acts of monopolies and state enterprises, to the content of the obligations and to the method of implementation. It follows that the customary international law rules reflected in article 4 of the ILC text do not apply in this case.[111]

---

[104] Shirlow and Duggal (n 20) 384.
[105] Viñuales, 'Attribution' (n 37) 80.
[106] De Stefano, 'Attribution' (n 2) 28.
[107] eg, Crawford, 'Investment Arbitration' (n 18) 130–31, 132–33. Further on *lex specialis* see in this Commentary: Fernando Lusa Bordin, 'Article 55 of the ARSIWA'.
[108] Article 55 of the ARSIWA.
[109] *United Parcel Service of America, Inc v Canada*, ICSID Case No UNCT/02/1, Award, 24 May 2007, paras 58–59.
[110] ibid para 60.
[111] ibid para 62.

35 The residual character of the rules on attribution in the ARSIWA was also acknowledged by the ICSID tribunal in *Al Tamimi v Oman*, which observed that 'State parties to a treaty may by specific provision (*lex specialis*), limit the circumstances under which the acts of an entity will be attributed to the State'.[112]

36 This review of the arbitral practice on these issues should not be seen as detracting from the general correctness with which investment tribunals have interpreted and applied Article 4 of the ARSIWA. Indeed, the arbitral practice on the latter issue merely reflects the reality that treaties can provide for specific rules which apply instead of the ARSIWA, which are residual.

D. Conclusion

37 It can be seen from the foregoing analysis that the practice of investment tribunals is broadly aligned with that of the ICJ and other international courts and tribunals. As demonstrated in Part II.A, investment tribunals have applied Article 4 of the ARSIWA to a broad range of State organs, including organs which have 'legislative, executive, judicial or any other functions'. Investment tribunals have attributed the conduct of State organs to the State irrespective of whether the conduct could be characterized as sovereign or commercial. Tribunals have also held that the conduct of provincial, regional, or local governments is attributable to the State, in addition to the conduct of the central government. Further, investment tribunals have held that it does not matter whether the entity in question has the status of a State organ under the relevant domestic law, but that the conduct of *de facto* State organs is also attributable to the State. In these respects, investment tribunals have largely interpreted and applied Article 4 consistently with other international adjudicatory bodies.

38 The broad consistency of approach with respect to Article 4 reflects that the rules of attribution in Chapter II of Part One of the ARSIWA are general in nature. In this respect, Part One 'sets out the conditions under which the State is responsible for breach of an obligation incumbent on the State'.[113] Thus, '[i]n the context of investment treaty arbitration … general questions surrounding breach of an international obligation contained in an investment treaty is a matter in principle covered by Part One of the ILC Articles'.[114] Because Article 4 is accepted as reflecting customary international law, it is to be expected (absent any *lex specialis*) that investment tribunals would apply Article 4 as one of the applicable rules of attribution. This contrasts with the provisions of (for instance) Part Three of the ARSIWA, which deals with the implementation of international responsibility, and only applies in the context of inter-State relations.[115]

39 Despite the general alignment in the interpretation and application of Article 4, there have been some notable instances of inconsistency (as identified in Part III), although these cases should not be regarded as a systemic difference in the practice of investment tribunals. In particular, they concern the inconsistent approach of the tribunals in relying exhaustively on relevant domestic law to determine whether or not an entity is a *de jure* or *de facto* State organ; the practice of some tribunals in failing to distinguish between the separate tests of

---

[112] *Al Tamimi v Oman*, ICSID Case No ARB/11/33, Award, 3 November 2015, para 321.
[113] Crawford, 'Investment Arbitration' (n 18) 129.
[114] ibid.
[115] C McLachlan, 'James Crawford AC SC FBA (1948–2021): The General Law of State Responsibility and the Specific Case of Investment Claims' (2022) 37 ICSID Rev 1, 7; Crawford, 'Investment Arbitration' (n 18) 130.

attribution in Articles 4 and 5 of the ARSIWA and conflating them in a single test; the application of rules of attribution in connection with claims for breach of contract; and the recognition by tribunals that the rules of attribution in the ARSIWA are residual in character, with the result that the applicable treaty (such as the NAFTA) may contain a *lex specialis* with respect to the conduct of certain State entities. But the arbitral practice (on the first three of these issues) does not detract from the generally sound and correct manner in which investment tribunals have interpreted and applied Article 4 of the ARSIWA.

Selected literature

Crawford J, *The International Law Commission's Articles on State Responsibility: Introduction, Text and Commentaries* (CUP 2002).
Crawford J, *State Responsibility: The General Part* (CUP 2013).
Crawford J, 'Investment Arbitration and the ILC Articles on State Responsibility' (2010) 25 ICSID Rev 127.
Crawford J and Baetens F, 'The ILC's Articles on State Responsibility: More than a 'Plank in a Shipwreck'?' (2022) 37 ICSID Rev 13.
De Stefano C, *Attribution in International Law and Arbitration* (OUP 2020).
De Stefano C, 'Attribution of Conduct to a State' (2022) 37 ICSID Rev 20.
Ho J, *State Responsibility for Breaches of Investment Contracts* (CUP 2018).
Olleson S, 'Attribution in Investment Arbitration' (2016) 31 ICSID Rev 457.
Shirlow E and Duggal K, 'The ILC Articles on State Responsibility in Investment Treaty Arbitration' (2022) 37 ICSID Rev 378.
Viñuales JE, 'Attribution of Conduct to States in Investment Arbitration' (2022) 20 ICSID Rep 13.

Selected decisions

Application of the Convention on the Prevention and Punishment of the Crime of Genocide (*Bosnia and Herzegovina v Serbia and Montenegro*) (Judgment) [2007] ICJ Rep.
Armed Activities on the Territory of the Congo (*Democratic Republic of the Congo v Uganda*) (Judgment) [2005] ICJ Rep.
Deutsche Bank AG v Sri Lanka, ICSID Case No ARB/09/2, Award, 31 October 2012.
Flemingo DutyFree v Poland, UNCITRAL, Award, 12 August 2016.
Gustav FW Hamester GmbH & Co KG v Ghana, ICSID Case No ARB/07/24, Award, 18 June 2010.
Jan de Nul NV and Dredging International NV v Egypt, ICSID Case No ARB/04/13, Award, 6 November 2008.
Mr Kristian Almås and Mr Geir Almås v The Republic of Poland, PCA Case No 2015-13, Award, 27 June 2016.
Ortiz v Algeria, ICSID Case No ARB/17/1, Award, 29 April 2020.
Tethyan Copper Company Pty Ltd v Pakistan, ICSID Case No ARB/12/1, Decision on Jurisdiction and Liability, 10 November 2017.
United Parcel Service of America, Inc v Canada, ICSID Case No UNCT/02/1, Award, 24 May 2007.

Article 5 of the ARSIWA

Conduct of empowered entities

Jorge E Viñuales and Oliver Hailes

The conduct of a person or entity which is not an organ of the State under article 4 but which is empowered by the law of that State to exercise elements of the governmental authority shall be considered an act of the State under international law, provided the person or entity is acting in that capacity in the particular instance.

A. Introduction	1	D. Clarifying the core components through investment arbitration	18
B. Codifying an exceptional rule of attribution	4	I. Form of empowerment: 'By the law of that State'	19
C. Distinguishing Article 5 from other rules of attribution	6	II. Content of empowerment: 'elements of the governmental authority'	21
I. Other customary rules	7	III. Exercise of empowerment: 'In the particular instance'	25
II. Tests developed in arbitral jurisprudence	11	IV. Summary of core components	29
III. Special attribution rules	14	E. Conclusion	30

A. Introduction

1 Investment agreements are generally supplemented by rules of customary international law on attribution of conduct. One such rule delimits the attributable conduct of private or independent entities that are empowered to exercise elements of governmental authority, which may give rise to State responsibility, from their commercial or other non-public activities. Following the International Law Commission's (ILC) second reading of the Articles on Responsibility of States for Internationally Wrongful Acts (ARSIWA),[1] many commentators thought that the principal application of Article 5 would concern attribution to States of the conduct of private military and security companies.[2] But two decades on, following a 'generation of privatization of public sector entities and activities',[3] the growing body of arbitral decisions rendered by investment tribunals provides the most relevant practice on

---

[1] ILC, 'Draft Articles on Responsibility of States for Internationally Wrongful Acts, with Commentaries' YILC 2001, Vol II, Part Two, 31 (hereafter ARSIWA Commentaries).

[2] J Crawford, *State Responsibility: The General Part* (CUP 2013) 127 (hereafter Crawford, *State Responsibility*).

[3] J Crawford, *Brownlie's Principles of Public International Law* (9th edn, OUP 2019) 551.

the application of this rule.[4] Article 5 is widely recognized as the codification of a customary rule of attribution,[5] although the International Court of Justice (ICJ) has not yet taken an explicit stance on it.[6] For this reason, the detailed practice of investment tribunals is particularly useful to determine the contours of custom on the attribution of conduct by hybrid entities operating across a range of commercial sectors, whether in mixed, market, or planned economies.[7]

This entry organizes the body of practice on Article 5 around the decisive requirement of an entity's specific authorization to exercise an impugned instance of public power—its empowerment—which informs both steps of a test commonly applied in investment arbitration. First, an entity must be 'empowered' by internal law to exercise 'elements of the governmental authority' ('*prérogatives de puissance publique*', '*atribuciones del poder público*'). Second, the entity must be exercising such power 'in the particular instance'. This test provides an intuitive framework by splitting the English text at its comma, but the cumulative steps are far from watertight. To underscore the form ('by the law of that State'), content ('elements of the governmental authority'), and exercise ('in the particular instance') of an entity's empowerment as the core components of Article 5—often elided by focusing on an entity's public functions—this entry refers to 'empowered entities' (which are inconsistently called 'State instrumentalities', 'parastatal entities', or 'entities exercising governmental authority') and their specifically 'attributable powers' (in contrast to the attribution of all conduct by State organs).

First, we review the historical backdrop to the ILC's formulation of Article 5 as an exceptional rule of attribution. Second, we distinguish the basis and scope of Article 5 from customary rules that are often pleaded in the alternative, namely, Article 4 on State organs and Article 8 on controlled conduct. We also distinguish Article 5 from tests developed in arbitral jurisprudence before the second reading of the ARSIWA and special attribution rules in

---

[4] This commentary builds upon JE Viñuales, 'Attribution of Conduct to States in Investment Arbitration' (2022) 20 ICSID Rep 13, paras 87–97 (hereafter Viñuales, 'Attribution of Conduct') and JE Viñuales and O Hailes, 'Article 5: Conduct of Persons or Entities Exercising Elements of Governmental Authority' in P Galvão Teles and P Bodeau-Livinec (eds), *The Articles on Responsibility of States for Internationally Wrongful Acts. A Commentary* (OUP forthcoming).

[5] Early cases did not explain the formal status of Article 5: *Dispute Concerning Access to Information Under Article 9 of the OSPAR Convention between Ireland and the United Kingdom of Great Britain and Northern Ireland*, Final Award (2 July 2003) XXIII RIAA 59 para 145; *Waste Management, Inc v United Mexican States (No 2)*, ICSID Case No ARB(AF)/00/3, Award, 30 April 2004, 11 ICSID Rep 361 para 75 (hereafter *Waste Management v Mexico*); *Ximenes-Lopes v Brazil*, Judgment of 4 July 2006, IACtHR Series C No 149 para 86. Investment tribunals were first to acknowledge Article 5 as a codification of customary international law: *Noble Ventures, Inc v Romania*, ICSID Case No ARB/01/11, Award, 12 October 2005, 16 ICSID Rep 210, para 70 (hereafter *Noble Ventures v Romania*); *Jan de Nul N.V. and Dredging International N.V. v Arab Republic of Egypt*, ICSID Case No ARB/04/13, Decision on Jurisdiction, 16 June 2006, 15 ICSID Rep 406, para 89. These cases have been relied upon in different contexts: eg *Union Trade Centre (UTC) v Attorney-General of the Republic of Rwanda*, EACJ Reference No 10 of 2013, Judgment of the Court, 26 November 2020, paras 51–82 (hereafter *UTC v Rwanda*). Some bodies have declined to determine whether Article 5 qualifies as custom: WTO, *United States—Definitive Anti-Dumping and Countervailing Duties on Certain Products from China—Report of the Appellate Body* (adopted 25 March 2011) WT/DS379/AB/R (hereafter *US—Anti-Dumping and Countervailing Duties (China)* AB Report) paras 308–11. Other courts and tribunals have reaffirmed that Article 5 is a customary rule: *Responsibilities and Obligations of States sponsoring Persons and Entities with respect to Activities in the Area* (Advisory Opinion) [2011] ITLOS Rep 10, para 182; *Bureš v Czech Republic* App no 37679/08 (ECtHR, 18 October 2012) para 54.

[6] cf *Application of the Convention on the Prevention and Punishment of the Crime of Genocide (Bosnia and Herzegovina v Serbia and Montenegro)* (Judgment) [2007] ICJ Rep 43 (hereafter *Bosnian Genocide* case) para 414; *Armed Activities on the Territory of the Congo (Democratic Republic of the Congo v Uganda)* (Judgment) [2005] ICJ Rep 168, paras 160, 213.

[7] M Kinnear, 'ARSIWA, ISDS, and the Process of Developing an Investor-State Jurisprudence' (2022) 20 ICSID Rep 3, 5.

investment, trade, and human rights law. Finally, we examine the contribution of investment arbitration to clarifying the core components of Article 5. Tribunals have notably consolidated the content of an entity's empowerment through a positive inquiry into four criteria of governmental authority. The foremost criterion reflects a well-known distinction between sovereign or public powers (*acta jure imperii*) and private acts of a State in its commercial capacity (*acta jure gestionis*), calling for a negative inquiry into whether the impugned conduct fell within the economic liberties of ordinary contractors.[8]

B. Codifying an exceptional rule of attribution

4 The conduct of independent entities was seldom attributable to the State under international law until governments began to authorize private or State-owned corporations to exercise powers of a regulatory or coercive character, alongside their commercial competition with ordinary market participants.[9] This phenomenon expanded in the late twentieth century through corporate restructuring of government monopolies and a turn towards privatization.[10] Yet, despite this recent practice, the ILC mainly based its codification of Article 5 on Germany's reply to a questionnaire on 'Responsibility of States for Damage Caused in Their Territory to the Person or Property of Foreigners' before The Hague Codification Conference in 1930.[11] Affirming that the law of State responsibility continues to apply 'when, by delegation of powers, bodies act in a public capacity, e.g. police an area or exercise sovereign rights as in the case when they levy taxes for their own needs', Germany reasoned that such conduct was similarly attributable when the State, 'as an exceptional measure, invests private organizations with public powers and duties or authorizes them to exercise sovereign rights, as in the case of private railway companies permitted to maintain a police force'.[12] Often recalled

---

[8] This distinction is relevant across a range of other issues: State immunities before domestic courts; application of primary norms (such as investment treaty standards) that do not engage responsibility for commercial conduct (alleged breaches of contract, for example); the jurisdiction *ratione personae* of tribunals constituted by the International Centre for Settlement of Investment Disputes (ICSID) over claims brought by investors acting as an agent of their home State or discharging an essentially governmental function; and the jurisdiction *ratione materiae* of the Iran-United States Claims Tribunal (IUSCT) over conduct of agencies, instrumentalities, or entities controlled by the two governments. On possible interactions with the law of attribution, see C de Stefano, *Attribution in International Law and Arbitration* (OUP 2020) 16–25 (hereafter de Stefano, *Attribution*); Viñuales, 'Attribution of Conduct' (n 4) paras 139–46.

[9] D Momtaz, 'Attribution of Conduct to the State: State Organs and Entities Empowered to Exercise Elements of Governmental Authority' in J Crawford, A Pellet and S Olleson (eds), *The Law of International Responsibility* (OUP 2010) 237, 244; de Stefano, *Attribution* (n 8) 53–56. Older decisions suffered from lack of legal clarity: *Dickson Car Wheel Company (USA) v United Mexican States*, Dissenting Opinion of Commissioner Nielsen (1931) IV RIAA 682, 688; *The Attiliò Regolo and Other Vessels (USA, Great Britain and Italy v Spain)* Award (1945) XII RIAA 1, 10; *Case of Certain Norwegian Loans* (Dissenting Opinion of Judge Read) [1957] ICJ Rep 79, 96.

[10] J Chalmers, 'State Responsibility for Acts of Parastatals Organized in Corporate Form' (1990) 84 ASIL Proceedings 60; ARSIWA Commentaries (n 1) Article 5, para 1.

[11] See 'Third Report on State Responsibility, by Mr. Roberto Ago, Special Rapporteur: The Internationally Wrongful Act of the State, Source of International Responsibility' YILC 1971, Vol II, Part One, 199 paras 163–71. For initial formulations of Article 5, see ibid para 185, Article 7; 'Draft Articles on State Responsibility' YILC 1974, Vol II, Part One, 276, 277, Article 7 para 2.

[12] 'Draft Articles on State Responsibility' (n 11) 281–82. Germany's reply was reflected in a conclusion of the Preparatory Committee for The Hague Codification Conference (acknowledging that States could be responsible for conduct of 'autonomous institutions as exercise public functions of a legislative or administrative character') and the ILC's commentary (contrasting a railway company's police power to non-attributable conduct such as 'the sale of tickets or the purchase of rolling stock'): ARSIWA Commentaries (n 1) Article 5, paras 4–5. Germany's effort to determine the parameters of State responsibility for conduct by empowered entities may reflect that the State-owned *Deutsche Reichsbahn-Gesellschaft* (German National Railway Company)—the world's largest enterprise in the interwar period—had its own police force and Allied representatives on its independent board,

by investment tribunals,[13] the enduring salience of Germany's railway example may be explained by its emphasis on the delegation of a power that is otherwise elemental to the governmental authority of States as responsible subjects of international law, whereas alternative formulations referred ambiguously to the exercise of 'public functions'.[14]

The rule of attribution inferred from Germany's reply was supported by the decisions of the Iran–United States Claims Tribunal (IUSCT), including the attribution of conduct by the Foundation of the Oppressed, a religious charity that played 'an investigative or prosecutorial role in the discovery and seizure of properties eligible for confiscation' and was 'empowered to call upon governmental agencies and institutions for aid in this pursuit'.[15] Conduct of the National Iranian Oil Company (NIOC) was also attributable when there was 'evidence that the corporation was exercising public powers', although activities of State-owned corporations were presumptively unrelated to those of the State.[16] Crawford identified other possible examples: security firms exercising 'powers of detention and discipline pursuant to a judicial sentence or to prison regulations'; airlines that are delegated 'certain powers in relation to immigration control or quarantine';[17] and 'central banks and stock exchanges' that 'exercise regulatory authority'.[18] These examples illustrate the 'decisive' requirement or 'true common feature' for attribution under Article 5: such entities must be 'empowered, if only to a limited extent or in a specific context, to exercise specified elements of governmental authority'.[19]

C. Distinguishing Article 5 from other rules of attribution

Although the ICJ has played a major role in the recognition of the customary law character of attribution rules, notably Article 4 on State organs and Article 8 on conduct instructed, directed, or controlled by a State,[20] it has not taken a position on Article 5. The rules in Articles

---

whereas the German cabinet believed that 'the railway should be the tool of government economic policy and a source of revenue, not a profitable enterprise in its own right': AC Mierzejewski, 'The Dorpmüller Controversy of 1926: Cabinet Politics, Reparations, and Railways in the Weimar Republic' (1992) 14 Int Hist Rev 701, 715.

[13] See, eg, *Gustav F W Hamester GmbH & Co KG v Republic of Ghana*, ICSID Case No ARB/07/24, Award (18 June 2010) 20 ICSID Rep 164, para 177 (hereafter *Hamester v Ghana*); *Bosh International, Inc and B&P, LTD Foreign Investments Enterprise v Ukraine*, ICSID Case No ARB/08/11, Award (25 October 2012) para 175 (hereafter *Bosh v Ukraine*); *Stabil, Crimea-Petrol LLC and others v Russian Federation*, PCA Case No 2015-35, Final Award (12 April 2019) para 178 (hereafter *Stabil v Russia*).

[14] cf 'Draft Articles on State Responsibility' (n 11) 282, fn 583. Germany's example was echoed in discussion of the Japanese national railway company, which 'exercised a part of the State authority by delegation', including powers of law enforcement, unlike 'the hundred or so other private railway companies in Japan or of the telecommunication companies, although they were regarded as public': '1258th Meeting: State Responsibility' YILC 1974, Vol I, 31, para 33 (Tsuruoka). On the Drafting Committee's insertion of the key phrase 'elements of the governmental authority', see '1278th Meeting: State Responsibility' YILC 1974, Vol I, 151, paras 9 (Hambro), 11 (Yasseen), 35 (Bilge), and 36 (Ago).

[15] *Hyatt International Corporation and others v Islamic Republic of Iran and others*, IUSCT Case No 134, Interlocutory Award (Award No ITL 54-134-1) (17 September 1985) para 66.

[16] ARSIWA Commentaries (n 1) Article 8 para 6. The 1974 Petroleum Law vested in NIOC 'the exercise and ownership right of the Iranian nation on the Iranian Petroleum Resources', being a 'governmental capacity granted to it under the internal law': *Phillips Petroleum Company Iran v Islamic Republic of Iran and National Iranian Oil Company*, IUSCT Case No 39, Award (Award No 425-39-2) (29 June 1989) para 89, fn 22; *Petrolane, Inc and others v Islamic Republic of Iran and others*, IUSCT Case No 131, Award (Award No 518-131-2) (14 August 1991) para 97, fn 9.

[17] ARSIWA Commentaries (n 1) Article 5 para 2.

[18] Crawford, *State Responsibility* (n 2) 128.

[19] ARSIWA Commentaries (n 1) Article 5 para 3.

[20] *Bosnian Genocide* case (n 6) paras 385, 406. See in this Commentary: Chester Brown, 'Article 4 of the ARSIWA'.

4, 5, and 8 ARSIWA are liable to conflation, as they are often pleaded in the alternative. It is thus important to clarify their distinct bases and scopes. It is likewise important to distinguish Article 5 from tests developed in investment arbitration before the second reading of ARSIWA. Finally, this section distinguishes Article 5 from special attribution rules in investment, trade, and human rights law.

I. Other customary rules

7 Article 5 makes plain that an empowered entity must not be 'an organ of the State' under Article 4, whether *de jure* or *de facto*.[21] It is thus impossible for a central bank or a national oil company—two perennial examples—to qualify as a State organ and simultaneously fall within the scope of Article 5, despite ambiguities in some arbitral reasoning.[22] Such entities perform important public functions—maintaining price stability, exploiting natural resources—but there is no uniform rule that their conduct is attributable to States. Instead, the conduct of a particular bank or oil company may be relevant under one of several rules in ARSIWA, which differ in their bases for attribution—internal law or a factual relationship—and the general or specific scope of attributable conduct (summarized in Figure 1).

		Basis for attribution	
		Internal law	**Factual relationship**
Scope of attributable conduct	**General**	*De jure* organ 'which has that status in accordance with the internal law of the State' (Article 4)	*De facto* organ in a relationship of complete dependence on the State (Article 4)
	Specific	Entities 'empowered by the law of that State to exercise elements of the governmental authority… acting in that capacity in the particular instance' (Article 5)	Persons or groups 'in fact acting on the instructions of, or under the direction or control of, that State in carrying out the conduct' (Article 8)

Figure 1. Distinct bases and scopes of attribution under Articles 4, 5, and 8

---

[21] On State organs, see Viñuales, 'Attribution of Conduct' (n 4) paras 70–86.
[22] For cases that blur the boundaries, see, eg, *EnCana Corporation v Republic of Ecuador*, LCIA Case No UN3481, Award (3 February 2006) 12 ICSID Rep 427, para 154; *Helnan International Hotels A/S v Arab Republic of Egypt*, ICSID Case No ARB/05/19, Decision of the Tribunal on Objection to Jurisdiction (17 October 2006) 17 ICSID Rep 268, para 93 (hereafter *Helnan v Egypt*); *Flemingo DutyFree Shop Private Limited v Republic of Poland*, PCA Case No 2014-11, Award (12 August 2016) 20 ICSID Rep 326, para 440 (hereafter *Flemingo DutyFree v Poland*). Arbitrators may disagree on which attribution rule applies or ground attribution on alternative rules: *LSF-KEB Holdings SCA and others v Republic of Korea*, ICSID Case No ARB/12/37, Award (30 August 2022) paras 676–77.

De jure organs and empowered entities are defined, respectively, by their status (Article 4) or powers (Article 5) under the internal law of the State. For an entity to qualify as a *de facto* organ, however, the ICJ applied a test of 'complete dependence' on the State.[23] Such dependence may be evidenced by the performance of core State functions, daily subordination to the central government, or the absence of any operational autonomy.[24] The legal form of empowerment also distinguishes the scope of Article 5 from Article 8, the latter attributing the conduct of persons or groups acting under the instruction, direction, or control of the State as a matter of fact, without any 'formal delegation' of governmental authority.[25] Yet, both rules are limited to specific conduct whereby an entity is exercising its attributable powers (Article 5) or acting under the 'effective control' of the State (Article 8).[26] These types of specific conduct are not the same, given the distinct legal or factual basis of each rule: under Article 5, only specific *acta jure imperii* are attributable; whereas, under Article 8, any specific act or omission effectively controlled by the State, whether governmental or commercial, is attributable. Regarding State organs, once they have been characterized as such (whether *de jure* or *de facto*), the entirety of their conduct (whether governmental or commercial) is attributable under Article 4. The only exclusion from Article 4 concerns conduct which is not in an 'official capacity', a concept different from the distinction between *acta jure imperii* and *acta jure gestionis*.[27]

These legal and factual bases for attribution, and the consequent scope of attributable conduct, are summarized in Figure 1. As underlined, attribution according to Article 5 is based on internal law ('empowered by the law of that State to exercise elements of the governmental authority') and specific in scope ('acting in that capacity in the particular instance').

For clarity, because attribution under Articles 4 or 8 does not depend upon an entity's empowerment to exercise elements of governmental authority, these rules make no distinction between *acta jure imperii* and *acta jure gestionis*.[28] Like Article 5, however, the rules in Articles 6 and 9 also require the exercise of governmental authority.[29] Article 7 deals with an entity that exceeds its governmental authority.[30] There are less decisions on these attribution rules, so future cases may well rely on the meaning given to governmental authority in the growing practice on Article 5.[31]

II. Tests developed in arbitral jurisprudence

Prior to the second reading of Article 5, investment tribunals began attributing conduct to the State according to 'tests developed in arbitral jurisprudence'.[32] Notably, the tribunal

---

[23] *Bosnian Genocide* case (n 6) paras 385–97.
[24] *Ortiz Construcciones y Proyectos SA v People's Democratic Republic of Algeria*, ICSID Case No ARB/17/1, Award (29 April 2020) 20 ICSID Rep 571, paras 159–70 (hereafter *Ortiz v Algeria*).
[25] Crawford, *State Responsibility* (n 2) 126–27.
[26] *Bosnian Genocide* case (n 6) para 400.
[27] On this distinction between official capacity and private acts, see Viñuales, 'Attribution of Conduct' (n 4) paras 147–51.
[28] ARSIWA Commentaries (n 1) Article 4 para 6; *Bayindir Insaat Turizm Ticaret Ve Sanayi AŞ v Islamic Republic of Pakistan*, ICSID Case No ARB/03/29, Award (27 August 2009) 20 ICSID Rep 99, para 129 (hereafter *Bayindir v Pakistan*).
[29] See in this Commentary: Jonathan Bonnitcha, 'Article 6 of the ARSIWA'.
[30] See in this Commentary: Chester Brown, 'Article 7 of the ARSIWA'.
[31] On arts 6 and 7, see also Viñuales, 'Attribution of Conduct' (n 4) paras 135–36, 152–55.
[32] *Kardassopoulos v Republic of Georgia*, ICSID Case No ARB/05/18, Award (3 March 2010) para 280. See further Viñuales, 'Attribution of Conduct' (n 4) paras 44–49.

in *Maffezini v Spain* held that conduct of a regional development agency could be attributed to Spain by way of a 'structural test' (whereby the State's direct or indirect ownership or control of the corporation gave rise to 'a rebuttable presumption that it is a State entity') or a 'functional test', based on whether the entity's 'purpose or objectives is the carrying out of functions which are governmental in nature or which are otherwise normally reserved to the State' and 'by their nature are not usually carried out by private businesses or individuals'.[33]

12 The 'presumption' reflected in the structural test has been rejected by subsequent tribunals, which have instead examined whether a State-owned entity is a *de facto* organ according to Article 4.[34] Once such presumption is removed, it is possible to equate this modified test with the customary rule on attribution of conduct by entities that are structurally part of the State apparatus. As for *Maffezini*'s 'functional test', some tribunals have tried to reconcile it with Article 5.[35] Again, this equation requires conceptual clarity to avoid implications that do not arise from custom.

13 The *Maffezini* tribunal rightly draws a 'dividing line' between 'specific acts or omissions' that are 'essentially governmental', and thus attributable, and those that are 'essentially commercial', hence non-attributable.[36] By drawing that line on the basis of an entity's purpose or function, however, the tribunal elided the decisive requirement of an entity's empowerment.[37] The assumption that an entity's public function is coextensive with an element of governmental authority has led to some anomalous results, including the attribution of contractual or lease terminations by independent entities concerning water management, forestry, civil aviation, or road construction—all areas of commercial activity.[38] It is important not to conflate the inchoate 'functional test' in *Maffezini* with the customary rule of attribution codified by Article 5.[39] As noted by the tribunal in *Jan de Nul v Egypt*, '[w]hat matters is not the "*service public*" element' of functions performed by critical entities such as the Suez Canal Authority, but their 'use of "*prérogatives de puissance publique*" or governmental authority'.[40]

---

[33] *Maffezini v Kingdom of Spain*, ICSID Case No ARB/97/7, Decision on Objections to Jurisdiction (25 January 2000) 5 ICSID Rep 396 (hereafter *Maffezini* Jurisdiction) paras 77–79.

[34] *Tulip Real Estate Investment and Development Netherlands BV v Republic of Turkey*, ICSID Case No ARB/11/28, Award (10 March 2014) 20 ICSID Rep 220, para 289 (hereafter *Tulip Real Estate v Turkey*). See also *Almås and Almås v Republic of Poland*, PCA Case No 2015-13, Award (27 June 2016) 20 ICSID Rep 294, paras 207–13 (hereafter *Almås v Poland*).

[35] See, eg, *Hamester v Ghana* (n 13) para 196; *Flemingo DutyFree v Poland* (n 22) para 426; *Ortiz v Algeria* (n 24) para 194. See also de Stefano, *Attribution* (n 8) 152–65.

[36] *Maffezini v Kingdom of Spain*, ICSID Case No ARB/97/7, Award (13 November 2000) 5 ICSID Rep 419 (hereafter *Maffezini* Award) para 57.

[37] The tribunal arguably identified an empowerment by noting that the entity was 'charged with providing subsidies and offering other inducements for the development of industries': *Maffezini* Jurisdiction (n 33) para 86. But the attributed act was its unauthorized transfer of funds from the claimant's account, which was 'not normally open to ordinary commercial companies': *Maffezini* Award (n 36) para 78.

[38] See, eg, *L.E.S.I. S.p.A. and ASTALDI S.p.A. v République Algérienne Démocratique et Populaire*, ICSID Case No ARB/05/3, Decision (12 November 2008) paras 102–18; *InterTrade Holding GmbH v Czech Republic*, PCA Case No 2009-12, Separate Opinion of Henri Álvarez (29 May 2012) para 15; *Flemingo DutyFree v Poland* (n 22) paras 441–42; *Garanti Koza LLP v Turkmenistan*, ICSID Case No ARB/11/20, Award (19 December 2016) para 335 (hereafter *Garanti Koza v Turkmenistan*).

[39] Despite paying lip service to the ILC's work, the *Maffezini* tribunal derived its functional test from I Brownlie, *System of the Law of Nations: State Responsibility, Part I* (Clarendon Press 1983) 135–36. See *Maffezini* Jurisdiction (n 33) paras 76–82. Brownlie's writing on State responsibility 'showed little to no engagement with the ILC's work on the topic': F Paddeu and C Tams, 'Encoding the Law of State Responsibility with Courage and Resolve: James Crawford and the 2001 Articles on State Responsibility' (2022) 11 CILJ 6, 15.

[40] *Jan de Nul N.V. and Dredging International N.V. v Arab Republic of Egypt*, ICSID Case No ARB/04/13, Award (6 November 2008) 15 ICSID Rep 437 (hereafter *Jan de Nul v Egypt* Award) para 170.

III. Special attribution rules

Like all secondary rules of State responsibility, Article 5 has a residual character and therefore **14** does not apply to the extent that the attribution of conduct is regulated by a *lex specialis*.[41] This point has been noted by investment tribunals applying the North American Free Trade Agreement (NAFTA),[42] which obliges a State to 'ensure ... that any state enterprise ... acts in a manner that is not inconsistent' with the chapters on investment and finance 'wherever such enterprise exercises any regulatory, administrative or other governmental authority that the Party has delegated to it'.[43] Doubts may be raised whether this provision constitutes a secondary rule of attribution; tribunals applying similar provisions have framed them as primary rules.[44] In any event, tribunals have referred to Article 5 to determine the content of governmental authority under such provisions.[45] Article 5 has also been cited by other international courts and tribunals applying special rules of attribution or analogous primary rules, including the World Trade Organization (WTO) Appellate Body and human rights courts. On closer inspection, however, Article 5 has limited influence in these fora, which have developed their own approaches to attribution or applied primary rules that require a State to supervise certain types of entities.

In *US—Anti-Dumping and Countervailing Duties (China)*, the WTO Appellate Body held **15** that the 'essence of Article 5' coincided with its interpretation of the term 'public body' under Article 1.1(a)(i) of the Agreement on Subsidies and Countervailing Measures (SCM Agreement), namely, 'an entity that possesses, exercises or is vested with governmental authority'.[46] Whereas WTO panels had interpreted that term to mean 'any entity controlled by a government', the Appellate Body held that Article 5 may be taken into account as a relevant rule of international law in the interpretation of a *lex specialis*, pursuant to Article 31(3)(c) of the Vienna Convention on the Law of Treaties.[47] But while 'similarities in the core principles and functions' served by Article 1.1(a)(i) of the SCM Agreement and the customary rule of attribution lent 'further support' to its interpretation, the result '[did] not turn on Article 5'.[48] Subsequent reports of the WTO Appellate Body have applied the notion of governmental authority without referring to Article 5, shifting their focus from an entity's empowerment towards the functions performed by the relevant entity.[49] The clearest point of divergence from custom was the WTO Appellate Body's rejection of China's submission that a 'public body' is defined by whether a particular instance of impugned conduct was an exercise of

---

[41] See in this Commentary: Fernando Bordin, 'Article 55 of the ARSIWA'.
[42] *United Parcel Service of America Inc v Canada*, UNCITRAL, Award (24 May 2007) 17 ICSID Rep 436 paras 62–63; *Mesa Power Group, LLC v Government of Canada*, PCA Case No 2012-17, Award (24 March 2016) 20 ICSID Rep 267 para 362–63 (hereafter *Mesa Power v Canada*).
[43] Examples include 'the power to expropriate, grant licenses, approve commercial transactions or impose quotas, fees or other charges': North American Free Trade Agreement (adopted 17 December 1992, entered into force 1 January 1994) 32 ILM 289 and 605, Article 1503(2).
[44] *Limited Liability Company Amto v Ukraine*, SCC Case No 080/2005, Final Award (26 March 2008) para 112; *Bosh v Ukraine* (n 13) para 183. Such provisions arguably create 'a State obligation to regulate, monitor and if necessary sanction private economic behaviour' rather than attribution of 'direct State responsibility': TW Waelde and PK Wouters, 'State Responsibility in a Liberalised World Economy: "State, Privileged and Subnational Authorities" under the 1994 Energy Charter Treaty: An Analysis of Articles 22 and 23' (1996) 27 NYIL 143, 165–66. See further Viñuales, 'Attribution of Conduct' (n 4) para 30–34.
[45] See, eg, *Mesa Power v Canada* (n 42) para 367.
[46] *US—Anti-Dumping and Countervailing Duties (China)* AB Report (n 5) paras 304–22.
[47] ibid paras 316, 320.
[48] ibid para 311.
[49] WTO, *United States—Countervailing Measures on Certain Hot-Rolled Steel Flat Products from India—Report of the Appellate Body* (adopted 19 December 2014) WT/DS436/AB/R para 4.29.

governmental authority, finding instead that the 'central question' is 'whether the *entity itself* possesses the core characteristics and functions that would qualify it as a public body'.[50]

16 Some decisions of the Inter-American Court of Human Rights (IACtHR) and the European Court of Human Rights (ECtHR) have cited Article 5, but they have then applied their own approach to attribution or focused on whether the State had a positive obligation to protect human rights from the conduct of private and public entities under a primary rule.[51] In *Women Victims of Sexual Torture in Atenco v Mexico*, however, the IACtHR applied Article 5 to attribute the conduct of prison doctors to the State, whose medical examination of several women in the course of police investigations constituted cruel and degrading treatment as well as gender-based discrimination.[52] A similar finding was reached by the ECtHR in *Bureš v Czech Republic*, wherein the use of restraints by medical staff was attributable under Article 5 because the psychiatric facility was empowered to 'perform governmental authority of detention'.[53] But the ECtHR has largely applied a special approach to attribution, which blurs the boundary between *de facto* organs and empowered entities under customary international law.[54]

17 References to Article 5 by the WTO Appellate Body and human rights courts are mostly ornamental so long as they do not engage with the core components of the customary rule, as clarified below by reference to two decades of investment arbitration. A judgment of the East African Court of Justice, by contrast, was guided by two investment decisions in its application of Article 5 to attribute the seizure and auction of a shopping mall by the national revenue authority and a municipal commission established to oversee the management of abandoned property.[55] This emerging jurisprudence of a regional economic community illustrates how the clarification of Article 5 through investment arbitration has potential to influence a wide range of disputes concerning the conduct of empowered entities, and regardless of the primary rules applied in prominent fora such as the WTO Appellate Body, the ECtHR, or indeed the ICJ.

D. Clarifying the core components through investment arbitration

18 Given the origin of Article 5 in an interwar effort to codify the primary rules of investment protection, followed by recent decades of privatization and the surge in investment treaty claims shortly after the second reading of ARSIWA, it is unsurprising that investment

---

[50] WTO, *United States—Definitive Anti-Dumping and Countervailing Duties on Certain Products from China—Recourse to Article 21.5 of the DSU—Report of the Appellate Body* (adopted 15 August 2019) WT/DS437/AB/RW paras 5.99–5.101 (emphasis in original).

[51] See, eg, *Ximenes-Lopes v Brazil* (n 5) paras 86–89; *Kotov v Russia*, App no 54522/00 (ECtHR, 3 April 2012) paras 31–32, 89–133. While ARSIWA has sometimes been cited in the application of the African Charter on Human and Peoples' Rights, Article 5 does not appear to have been mentioned. cf *Kazingachire and others v Zimbabwe*, ACHPR Communication 295/04 (2 May 2012) para 132 (relying on Brownlie's 1983 text on State responsibility rather than the ILC's work). See also n 39 above.

[52] *Women Victims of Sexual Torture in Atenco v Mexico*, Judgment of 28 November 2018, IACtHR Series C No 371 paras 205–07, 222–23.

[53] *Bureš v Czech Republic* (n 5) paras 54, 76–79.

[54] Combining two lines of decisions—on attributable acts of entities that are not formally considered a 'public authority' and on the *locus standi* of a 'governmental organisation'—the Court focused on the 'legal status' of the liquidator, taking account of 'the rights that status gives it, the nature of the activity it carries out and the context in which it is carried out, and the degree of its independence from the political authorities': *Kotov v Russia* (n 51) para 93 quoting *Radio France and Others v France* App no 53984/00 (ECtHR, 23 September 2003) para 26. See also *Liseytseva and Maslov v Russia*, App nos 39483/05 and 40527/10 (ECtHR, 9 October 2014) paras 184–92.

[55] *UTC v Rwanda* (n 5) paras 51–82 citing *Noble Ventures v Romania* (n 5) and *Helnan v Egypt* (n 22).

arbitration has generated most of the decisions on this customary rule of attribution.[56] Tribunals have tended to apply a two-step test: first, whether an entity has been empowered to exercise an element of governmental authority and, second, whether the entity thus empowered was exercising its governmental authority in an impugned instance.[57] Some tribunals have addressed the first step as a general inquiry into an entity's empowerment with any element of governmental authority, then separately addressed the particular instances of its attributable powers.[58] Yet the steps need not be sequential. Other tribunals have recited the two-step test, then assessed the core components in unison.[59] Such components include the form ('by the law of that State'), content ('elements of the governmental authority'), and exercise ('in the particular instance') of an entity's empowerment, which have been mainly clarified by cases concerning the contracts of statutory or State-owned entities.

I. Form of empowerment: 'By the law of that State'

In *Unión Fenosa v Egypt*, the claimant failed to identify any provision 'specifically authorising' the national oil and gas companies to conclude a sale and purchase agreement 'in the exercise of the Respondent's public authority'.[60] As discussed, the formal requirement that an entity be empowered by internal law distinguishes the 'narrow category' of attribution under Article 5 from other customary rules based on factual relationships.[61] It is not 'necessary that the empowering law should define the roles and responsibilities of the entity exhaustively'.[62] The empowering law may also include 'an independent discretion or power to act'.[63] But the law of the State 'must specifically authorize the conduct as involving the exercise of public authority', in contrast to activities that are permitted 'as part of the general regulation of the affairs of the community' or conferred upon 'citizens or residents generally'.[64] In *Tulip Real Estate v Turkey*, the tribunal held that a zoning law, which granted special privileges to public institutions regarding construction permits and land acquisition, in no way empowered a State-owned investment vehicle to 'exercise' elements of governmental authority 'vis-à-vis any particular object or person'.[65]

---

[56] For tabulated decisions, J Crawford, 'Investment Arbitration and the ILC Articles on State Responsibility' (2010) 25 ICSID Rev 127, 152–57; E Shirlow and K Duggal, 'The Articles on State Responsibility in Investment Treaty Arbitration' (2022) 37 ICSID Rev 378, 419–30. For recent monographs, C Kovács, *Attribution in International Investment Law* (Wolters Kluwer 2018) 129–86; de Stefano, *Attribution* (n 8) 149–67.

[57] See, eg, *Noble Ventures v Romania* (n 5) para 70; *Jan de Nul v Egypt* Award (n 40) paras 163–64; *Hamester v Ghana* (n 13) para 176; *Bosca v Lithuania*, PCA Case No 2011-04, Award (17 May 2013) para 127 (hereafter *Bosca v Lithuania*); *Lahoud and Lahoud v Democratic Republic of the Congo*, ICSID Case No ARB/10/4, Award (7 February 2014) para 378; *Tulip Real Estate v Turkey* (n 34) para 292; *H&H Enterprises Investments, Inc v Arab Republic of Egypt*, ICSID Case No ARB/09/15, Award (6 May 2014) para 387; *Almås v Poland* (n 34) para 215; *Flemingo DutyFree v Poland* (n 22) para 436; *Garanti Koza v Turkmenistan* (n 38) para 335; *Saint-Gobain Performance Plastics Europe v Bolivarian Republic of Venezuela*, ICSID Case No ARB/12/13, Decision on Liability and Principles of Quantum (30 December 2016) 20 ICSID Rep 360, para 458; *Tethyan Copper Company Pty Limited v Islamic Republic of Pakistan*, ICSID Case No ARB/12/1, Decision on Jurisdiction and Liability (10 November 2017) 20 ICSID Rep 453, para 731 (hereafter *Tethyan Copper v Pakistan*); *Ortiz v Algeria* (n 24) para 194.

[58] See, eg, *Bosh v Ukraine* (n 13) paras 164–78; *Hamester v Ghana* (n 13) paras 189–268.

[59] See, eg, *EBO Invest AS and others v Republic of Latvia*, ICSID Case No ARB/16/38, Award (28 February 2020) paras 337–53 (hereafter *EBO v Latvia*); *Ortiz v Algeria* (n 24) paras 193–234.

[60] *Unión Fenosa Gas, S.A. v Arab Republic of Egypt*, ICSID Case No ARB/14/4, Award (31 August 2018) 20 ICSID Rep 546, para 9.114 (hereafter *Unión Fenosa v Egypt*).

[61] ARSIWA Commentaries (n 1) Article 5 para 7.

[62] Crawford, *State Responsibility* (n 2) 132.

[63] ARSIWA Commentaries (n 1) Article 5 para 7.

[64] ibid.

[65] *Tulip Real Estate v Turkey* (n 34) paras 293–94.

20 Empowerment is typically evidenced by statute or decree, but the ILC recognized that States may, for example, authorize security firms to exercise 'powers of detention and discipline' when 'contracted to act as prison guards'.[66] Care must be taken not to assume that every contractual authorization indicates a form of empowerment under Article 5, given that the international law of attribution is distinct from any relevant domestic law of agency.[67] In *Tethyan Copper v Pakistan*, the tribunal examined the contractual and regulatory framework to find that a statutory development entity 'acted as agent' of a regional government in entering a resource exploration agreement and serving on the joint venture's operating committee, which was treated as conclusive that the entity's assurances to the claimant through the committee were attributable to the State under Article 5.[68] While the regional government was exclusively authorized by the federal constitution to enter such agreements, the tribunal did not specify how the entity's participation in the operating committee—a body that commissioned feasibility studies and directed mining activities—exercised any element of governmental authority.[69]

II. Content of empowerment: 'elements of the governmental authority'

21 Governmental authority (*puissance publique, poder público*) offers a 'general standard' for determining whether an entity has been empowered to 'exercise functions of a public character normally exercised by State organs' in light of the 'varied circumstances' of a 'particular society, its history and traditions'.[70] The latter phrase should not be taken as licence for parochial applications of Article 5, but rather a recognition that elements of governmental authority may be variously distributed by internal law among State organs and empowered entities, in accordance with the freedom of every State to organize itself as it sees fit.[71] While the notion of governmental authority is widely considered to be 'a flexible one, not amenable to general definition in advance',[72] its elemental content may be derived from the competence of States under international law. Without doubt, Article 5 covers the delegation of any powers of a State that accrue by virtue of its territorial sovereignty, whether these are framed in broad terms of legislative, executive, and judicial powers,[73] or more granular powers (of police, taxation, investigation, prosecution, confiscation, imprisonment, quarantine, monetary, or financial regulation) that were reflected in the past practice underpinning its codification.[74]

22 As discussed earlier, some tribunals and commentators suggest that an entity also exercises an element of governmental authority when it performs a function that benefits the public

---

[66] ARSIWA Commentaries (n 1) Article 5 para 2.
[67] Viñuales, 'Attribution of Conduct' (n 4) paras 21–26.
[68] *Tethyan Copper v Pakistan* (n 57) paras 730–46, 943–50.
[69] Nor did the tribunal address the claimant's attribution arguments based on Articles 4 and 8: ibid paras 702–05, 730.
[70] ARSIWA Commentaries (n 1) Article 5 paras 2, 6.
[71] '2555th Meeting: State Responsibility' YILC 1998, Vol I, 241 paras 7, 11 (Pellet).
[72] *F-W Oil Interests, Inc v Republic of Trinidad and Tobago*, ICSID Case No ARB/01/14, Award (3 March 2006) 16 ICSID Rep 394, para 203.
[73] cf ARSIWA Commentaries (n 1) Article 4 para 6 (explaining that 'legislative, executive, judicial or any other functions' include 'some combination of public powers' and 'other functions' such as 'the giving of administrative guidance to the private sector'); 'Fourth Report on the Immunity of State Officials from Foreign Criminal Jurisdiction, by Ms. Concepción Escobar Hernández, Special Rapporteur' YILC 2015, Vol II, Part One, 3, para 83 ('there is no doubt that the concept of "elements of the governmental authority" must be understood in a broad sense to include the exercise of legislative, judicial and executive prerogatives').
[74] See Section B above.

and could be fulfilled by State organs, such as provision of water, security, infrastructure, energy, healthcare, sanitation, telecommunications, or education.[75] That is to conflate the mere utility of an entity's activities with a specific authorization of public power, which is why the present emphasis on empowerment is preferable to the ambiguity of a functional test.[76] What was decisive in *Bayindir v Pakistan*, for instance, was not the National Highway Authority's functions in the transport sector but rather its statutory powers of police, revenue, and inspection.[77] Subsequent tribunals have reaffirmed that an entity's engagement in commercial activities of public interest—even those typically linked to sovereignty, such as management of natural resources—is not enough to meet the condition of being specifically authorized to exercise elements of governmental authority.[78]

23 Investment tribunals have consolidated the meaning of governmental authority through four criteria of 'particular importance' identified by the ILC: (1) 'the content of the powers'; (2) 'the way they are conferred on an entity'; (3) 'the purposes for which they are to be exercised'; and (4) 'the extent to which the entity is accountable to government for their exercise'.[79] Various markers of State ownership or control, on the other hand, are 'not decisive criteria'.[80] The fourfold inquiry into positive criteria of governmental authority was fleshed out by Crawford and endorsed by the tribunal in *Ortiz v Algeria*: the first criterion relates essentially to the distinction between *acta jure imperii* and *acta jure gestionis*; the second criterion refers to the mode of delegation of the powers, namely, by law, decree, or even contract; the third criterion seeks to determine if the powers were entrusted in support of State purposes of a typically sovereign nature; and the final criterion relates to the level of supervision of the State over the entity at stake.[81]

24 Of these four criteria, the first criterion has been decisive in arbitral practice due to its binary operation. A tribunal may find that an entity cannot have been empowered to exercise any element of governmental authority because 'a private person can perform the function without the government's permission'.[82] This negative inquiry into the content of empowerment has been called a 'private contractor' test,[83] given the frequency with which tribunals address whether an entity's conduct could have been exercised by an ordinary contractor or shareholder in pursuit of profit or other commercial considerations.[84]

---

[75] G Petrochilos, 'Attribution: State Organs and Entities Exercising Elements of Governmental Authority' in K Yannaca-Small (ed), *Arbitration under International Investment Agreements: A Guide to the Key Issues* (2nd edn, OUP 2018) 332, 348–52.

[76] For an early effort to distinguish public utility companies from delegations of public power, see *Affaire des réparations allemandes selon l'article 260 du Traité de Versailles (Allemagne c Commission des Réparations)* (1924) I RIAA 429, 459–68.

[77] *Bayindir v Pakistan* (n 28) para 121. The tribunal concluded that the NHA's contractual termination was not an exercise of its attributable powers: ibid para 123.

[78] *Hamester v Ghana* (n 13) para 202; *InterTrade Holding GmbH v Czech Republic*, PCA Case No 2009-12, Final Award (29 May 2012) paras 180–88 (hereafter *InterTrade v Czech Republic*); *Tenaris S.A. and Talta-Trading e Marketing Sociedade Unipessoal LDA v Bolivarian Republic of Venezuela*, ICSID Case No ARB/11/26, Award (29 January 2016) para 416; *EBO v Latvia* (n 59) para 342; *Ortiz v Algeria* (n 24) para 232. cf *Muszynianka Spółka z Ograniczoną Odpowiedzialnością v Slovak Republic*, PCA Case No 2017-08, Award (7 October 2020) para 551 ('regulation of the use of natural resources is a self-standing sovereign prerogative').

[79] ARSIWA Commentaries (n 1) Article 5 para 6.

[80] ibid para 3.

[81] *Ortiz v Algeria* (n 24) paras 202–03. See also Crawford, *State Responsibility* (n 2) 133–39.

[82] Crawford, *State Responsibility* (n 2) 130.

[83] de Stefano, *Attribution* (n 8) 161.

[84] See, eg, *Jan de Nul v Egypt* Award (n 40) paras 169–70; *Hamester v Ghana* (n 13) para 202; *InterTrade v Czech Republic* (n 78) para 183; *EBO v Latvia* (n 59) paras 343, 349; *Ortiz v Algeria* (n 24) para 214. Similar inquiries have been undertaken to determine whether a State organ has breached a primary rule. See, eg, *Biwater Gauff*

III. Exercise of empowerment: 'In the particular instance'

25 An entity's empowerment is irrelevant to State responsibility if the delegated governmental authority was not exercised in an instance alleged to breach international law.[85] This core component, commonly described as the second step under Article 5, may be difficult to analyse when claimants refer to a series of acts, conduct in general, or even an omission to act.[86] Yet, the tribunal in *Hamester v Ghana* reaffirmed that Article 5 mandates 'an inquiry into the nature of each and every act'.[87] The tribunal considered that 'tough commercial negotiations' regarding the price of an agricultural commodity showed 'beyond doubt' that a statutory entity was acting *de jure gestionis* in the modification of a joint venture agreement, despite being empowered with monopoly rights and regulatory powers in the relevant sector.[88] The ultimate pricing method accorded with a change in government policy, which 'economic actors had to try to implement through agreements reached in different contexts'.[89] But that policy had not been imposed by any coercive powers of the statutory entity.[90] Similarly, the tribunal considered that neither a corporate dispute among shareholders in a joint venture vehicle nor the violation of a contractual term involved any exercise of attributable powers.[91]

26 Contracts are indeed the quintessence of commercial activity, whether they are governed solely by private law or characterized as administrative contracts.[92] Breaches or termination of contracts entered 'in the exercise of statutory powers', as in *Almås v Poland*, are often alleged to be instances of attributable conduct under Article 5.[93] In this case, the tribunal found that the termination of a lease agreement was 'not an exercise of public power but of a purported contractual right', which could be exercised by any property owner under 'general law'.[94] For completeness, the tribunal also considered (and dismissed) the claimants' argument that the contract had been terminated pursuant to a 'hidden political agenda', namely, 'a desire to distribute land to Polish farmers and a desire to sell State assets'.[95] This inquiry was clearly distinct from the issue of attribution under Article 5 as a secondary rule of State responsibility, dealing instead with whether contractual termination may breach a primary rule of unlawful expropriation.[96]

(Tanzania) Limited v United Republic of Tanzania, ICSID Case No ARB/05/22, Award (24 July 2008) 19 ICSID Rep 183, para 460.

[85] *Ortiz v Algeria* (n 24) para 210.

[86] See, eg, *PJSC CB PrivatBank and Finance Company Finilon LLC v Russian Federation*, PCA Case No 2015-21, Partial Award (4 February 2019) para 240–49 (on circumstantial evidence); *Interocean Oil Development Company and Interocean Oil Exploration Company v Federal Republic of Nigeria*, ICSID Case No ARB/13/20, Award (6 October 2020) paras 297–302 (on omissions); *LSF-KEB Holdings SCA and others v Republic of Korea*, ICSID Case No ARB/12/37, Dissenting Opinion of Brigitte Stern (30 August 2022) paras 5–62 (on the burden and standard of proof).

[87] *Hamester v Ghana* (n 13) para 197.

[88] ibid paras 219–50.

[89] ibid para 238.

[90] ibid para 231.

[91] ibid para 266.

[92] *Jan de Nul v Egypt* Award (n 40) para 170; *Ulysseas, Inc v Republic of Ecuador*, PCA Case No 2009-19, Final Award (12 June 2012) para 139.

[93] *Almås v Poland* (n 34) para 219. See also *Bayindir v Pakistan* (n 28) para 120–23; *EDF (Services) Limited v Romania*, ICSID Case No ARB/05/13, Award (8 October 2009) 20 ICSID Rep 118, para 197 (hereafter *EDF v Romania*).

[94] *Almås v Poland* (n 34) para 219].

[95] ibid paras 252–67 applying a test in *Vigotop Limited v Hungary*, ICSID Case No ARB/11/22, Award (1 October 2014) paras 327–31 (concerning a State organ).

[96] *Almås v Poland* (n 34) paras 253, 267.

Other cases that are sometimes cited in support of extending Article 5 to cover the use of private rights for public purposes were also concerned with breaches of primary rules or largely based on a rule of attribution that is not limited to *acta jure imperii*.[97] Tribunals that were willing to assume *arguendo* that an entity was empowered in terms of Article 5 have proceeded to dismiss alleged breaches that reflected commercial activity or were defensible as *bona fide* regulation under the customary doctrine of police powers.[98] In short, the coincidence of an empowered entity's exercise of contractual or proprietary rights and a relevant government policy does not transform that private conduct into an instance of attributable power.[99] Any contractor can breach a term or exercise its private rights for a range of motives beyond the pursuit of profit, without implying its exercise of public power.[100]

Confusion may be caused by umbrella clauses, wherein a State party to an investment treaty undertakes to respect all commitments entered with investors of the other contracting party.[101] Such clauses create an obligation under international law that is triggered upon breach of domestic commitments created by any agreement between the host State and a foreign investor. An entity may be authorized under domestic law to enter contracts on behalf of the State, creating a relationship governed by rules of agency.[102] But the international law of attribution, including Article 5, has no bearing on the applicable law of agency. Hence, it is legally incorrect to rely on attribution rules to argue that the entity was acting on behalf of the State when it entered into a contract with an investor or that the entity's commitments can otherwise be extended to the State as third party. Despite incorrect or ambiguous statements to the contrary,[103] Article 5 can neither create agency between the entity and the State nor privity of contract between the State and the investor, which are threshold requirements for any umbrella clause.[104]

IV. Summary of core components

The practice of investment arbitration has consolidated the form, content, and exercise of empowerment that is required under the customary rule codified in Article 5. Whereas

---

[97] See, eg, *Crystallex International Corporation v Bolivarian Republic of Venezuela*, ICSID Case No ARB(AF)/11/2, Award (4 April 2016) paras 700–01; *Ampal-American Israel Corporation and others v Arab Republic of Egypt*, ICSID Case No ARB/12/11, Decision on Liability and Heads of Loss (21 February 2017) 20 ICSID Rep 406, para 146; *Bosca v Lithuania* (n 57) para 128.

[98] See, eg, *Waste Management v Mexico* (n 5) paras 75, 102–04; *WNC Factoring Ltd (WNC) v Czech Republic*, PCA Case No 2014-34, Award (22 February 2017) paras 376–400; *Louis Dreyfus Armateurs SAS v Republic of India*, PCA Case No 2014-26, Award (11 September 2018) para 348. On the police powers doctrine, a distinct inquiry from whether an entity was authorized to exercise any attributable power of law enforcement, see Jorge E Viñuales, 'Defence Arguments in Investment Arbitration' (2020) 18 ICSID Rep 9, paras 83–93.

[99] Some policy developments, however, may serve as circumstantial evidence to confirm that an empowered entity was exercising an element of governmental authority in the impugned instance. See, eg, *Stabil v Russia* (n 13) para 197.

[100] *Venezuela US, S.R.L. v Bolivarian Republic of Venezuela*, PCA Case No 2013-34, Partial Award (Jurisdiction and Liability) (5 February 2021) para 200.

[101] See Viñuales, 'Attribution of Conduct' (n 4) paras 163–73.

[102] See also para 20 above.

[103] See, eg, *Bosh v Ukraine* (n 13) para 246; *CC/Devas (Mauritius) Ltd and others v Republic of India*, PCA Case No 2013-09, Award on Jurisdiction and Merits (25 July 2016) 18 ICSID Rep 487, para 281; *Strabag SE v Libya*, ICSID Case No ARB(AF)/15/1, Award (29 June 2020) 20 ICSID Rep 611 paras 167–87.

[104] *EDF v Romania* (n 93) paras 317–19; *Gavrilović and Gavrilović d.o.o. v Republic of Croatia*, ICSID Case No ARB/12/39, Award (26 July 2018) 20 ICSID Rep 512 para 857; *Consutel Group S.p.A. in liquidazione v People's Democratic Republic of Algeria*, PCA Case No 2017-33, Final Award (3 February 2020) paras 364–65; *Unión Fenosa v Egypt* (n 60) paras 9.110–9.111.

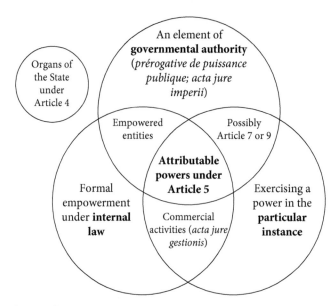

Figure 2. Overlapping form, content, and exercise of empowerment under Article 5

tribunals often articulate their approach in terms of a two-step test, Figure 2 summarizes the overlapping components that inform both steps and thereby distinguishes the unique operation of Article 5 from other categories of conduct.

E. Conclusion

30 It is unsurprising that the main historical context in which the international law of State responsibility was conceptualized—injuries to aliens and their property—has also been the modern context in which attribution rules have been distilled. This is particularly the case of the customary rule codified by Article 5, which concerns the attribution of conduct to the State when it has empowered separate entities to exercise public powers. As noted in this entry, commercial activities that serve a public function must be clearly distinguished from attributable elements of governmental authority. A State's freedom to organize the delivery of a public service through an independent or private entity may involve the specific authorization of some element of governmental authority, such as regulatory power over third parties. But an entity's empowerment cannot be inferred from the public utility of its functions, whether to meet the first step or, even less so, the second step of a commonly applied test. Yet, the investment decisions on Article 5 have faults that go with its qualities. The diversity of situations and of tribunals has led both to clarification and to some confusion. As for Articles 4 and 8, an authoritative clarification of Article 5 by the ICJ would provide welcome bounds to these burgeoning decisions and greater legal certainty on the operation of this rule.

Selected literature

Caron DD, 'The Basis of Responsibility: Attribution and Other Transubstantive Rules of State Responsibility' in Lillich RB and McGraw DB (eds), *The Iran–United States Claims Tribunal: Its Contribution to the Law of State Responsibility* (Transnational Publishers 1998).

Crawford J, 'Investment Arbitration and the ILC Articles on State Responsibility' (2010) 25 ICSID Rev/FILJ 127.

Crawford J, *State Responsibility: The General Part* (CUP 2013).

de Stefano C, *Attribution in International Law and Arbitration* (OUP 2020).

Kovács C, *Attribution in International Investment Law* (Wolters Kluwer 2018).

Lillich RB, Christenson GA, Chalmers J, Caron D and Dupuy PM, 'Attribution Issues in State Responsibility' (1990) 84 Proceedings of the ASIL Annual Meeting 51.

Momtaz D, 'Attribution of Conduct to the State: State Organs and Entities Empowered to Exercise Elements of Governmental Authority' in Crawford J, Pellet A and Olleson S (eds), *The Law of International Responsibility* (OUP 2010).

Petrochilos G, 'Attribution: State Organs and Entities Exercising Elements of Governmental Authority' in Yannaca-Small K (ed), *Arbitration under International Investment Agreements: A Guide to the Key Issues* (2nd edn, OUP 2018).

Shirlow E and Duggal K, 'The Articles on State Responsibility in Investment Treaty Arbitration' (2022) 37 ICSID Rev/FILJ 378.

Tonkin H, *State Control over Private Military and Security Companies in Armed Conflict* (CUP 2011).

Viñuales JE and Waibel M (eds), *ICSID Reports, Volume 20: Attribution of Conduct to the State* (CUP 2022).

Selected decisions

Hyatt International Corporation and others v Islamic Republic of Iran and others, IUSCT Case No 134, Interlocutory Award (Award No ITL 54-134-1), 17 September 1985.

Noble Ventures, Inc v Romania, ICSID Case No ARB/01/11, Award (12 October 2005), 16 ICSID Rep 210.

Jan de Nul N.V. and Dredging International N.V. v Arab Republic of Egypt, ICSID Case No ARB/04/13, Award (6 November 2008), 15 ICSID Rep 437.

Bayindir Insaat Turizm Ticaret Ve Sanayi AŞ v Islamic Republic of Pakistan, ICSID Case No ARB/03/29, Award (27 August 2009), 20 ICSID Rep 99.

EDF (Services) Limited v Romania, ICSID Case No ARB/05/13, Award (8 October 2009), 20 ICSID Rep 118.

Gustav F W Hamester GmbH & Co KG v Republic of Ghana, ICSID Case No ARB/07/24, Award (18 June 2010), 20 ICSID Rep 164.

Bureš v Czech Republic, App no 37679/08) (ECtHR, 18 October 2012).

Tulip Real Estate Investment and Development Netherlands BV v Republic of Turkey, ICSID Case No ARB/11/28, Award (10 March 2014), 20 ICSID Rep 220.

Almås and Almås v Republic of Poland, PCA Case No 2015-13, Award (27 June 2016), 20 ICSID Rep 294.

Women Victims of Sexual Torture in Atenco v Mexico, Judgment of 28 November 2018, IACtHR Series C No 371.

Ortiz Construcciones y Proyectos SA v People's Democratic Republic of Algeria, ICSID Case No ARB/17/1, Award (29 April 2020), 20 ICSID Rep 571.

Union Trade Centre (UTC) v Attorney-General of the Republic of Rwanda, EACJ Reference No 10 of 2013, Judgment of the Court, 26 November 2020.

Article 6 of the ARSIWA and Article 7 of the ARIO

Jonathan Bonnitcha and Alisha Mathew

Article 6 ARSIWA: Conduct of organs placed at the disposal of a State by another State

The conduct of an organ placed at the disposal of a State by another State shall be considered an act of the former State under international law if the organ is acting in the exercise of elements of the governmental authority of the State at whose disposal it is placed.

Article 7 ARIO: Conduct of organs of a State or organs or agents of an international organization placed at the disposal of another international organization

The conduct of an organ of a State or an organ or agent of an international organization that is placed at the disposal of another international organization shall be considered under international law an act of the latter organization if the organization exercises effective control over that conduct.

A. Introduction	1	C. Interpretation in investment disputes	17
B. General interpretation under public international law	5	D. Conclusion	24

A. Introduction

1 The rules enshrined in Article 6 of the Articles on the Responsibility of States for Internationally Wrongful Acts (ARSIWA) and Article 7 of the Articles on the Responsibility of International Organizations (ARIO) both provide for attribution of conduct where an organ of a State is placed at the disposal of another State or an international organization.

2 Overall, there has been little consideration of Article 6 of the ARSIWA and Article 7 of the ARIO by international courts and tribunals. The lack of consistent state practice in support of these rules, and the apparent lack of *opinio juris* attesting to their customary status, raises doubt about whether either is established as a rule of customary international law.[1] The diverse policy considerations at stake in scenarios where an organ of one state is arguably

---

[1] Similarly, Constance Regional Court, Case No 4 O 234/05 H, Judgment of 27 July 2006; partial English translation cited in 'Responsibility of States for internationally wrongful acts; Comments and information received from Governments, Report of the Secretary General', 9 March 2007, UN Doc A/62/63, at paras 18–22.

placed at the disposal of another entity may go some way to explaining why a consistent state practice is yet to emerge.[2]

Insofar as these articles have been considered by international courts, it has been primarily in the context of multinational peacekeeping forces. In investment disputes, these articles may also become relevant in cases where an international organization requires a state to enact economic policies that then become the subject of claims by foreign investors. Examples include changes to subsidy or pricing regimes that a State is required to implement on account of its membership of the European Union (EU), and sovereign debt restructuring arrangements that a state must implement as a condition of receiving the assistance of an international financial organization.

One cross-cutting doctrinal issue is whether a 'factual' or 'legal' approach should be used to determine whether an organ of a State has been placed under the direction and control of another State or international organization. A factual approach to attribution is easier to reconcile with the International Court of Justice's (ICJ) approach to attribution under other articles of the ARSIWA and also reduces the risk that a State can evade international responsibility on account of international obligations it has voluntarily assumed through membership of an international organization.

B. General interpretation under public international law

Neither Article 6 of the ARSIWA nor Article 7 of the ARIO have been explicitly considered by the ICJ. The only reference to these articles by the ICJ seems to be in the case of *Bosnia and Herzegovina v Serbia and Montenegro*,[3] where the ICJ used language that echoed Article 6 of the ARSIWA but did not refer to it specifically.

In those proceedings, one of the questions that the ICJ addressed was whether the Federal Republic of Yugoslavia (FRY) bore any responsibility for the acts of the Scorpions, one of the paramilitary groups involved in the Srebrenica genocide.[4] The issue centred on whether the Scorpions could be considered *de jure* organs of FRY for the purposes of Article 4 of the ARSIWA. At issue was when the Scorpions became incorporated into the armed forces of FRY. Given the lack of evidentiary support for the applicant's position, the ICJ concluded that there was insufficient evidence to find that, in mid-1995, the Scorpions were *de jure* organs of the Respondent.[5]

While the ICJ's application of Article 4 of the ARSIWA was decisive, it also stated in *dicta* that 'in any event the act of an organ placed by a State at the disposal of another public authority shall not be considered an act of that State if the organ was acting on behalf of the public authority at whose disposal it had been placed'.[6] As such, the Court suggested that, even if the

---

[2] eg, the analysis in subsequent paragraphs points to different underlying views about the appropriate structure of accountability in multinational peacekeeping forces, as compared to the appropriate structure of accountability in the context of regional economic integration. It may be that views about the appropriate structure of accountability in specific contexts play a greater role in shaping state practice than commitment to general rules of attribution.

[3] Application of the Convention on the Prevention and Punishment of the Crime of Genocide (*Bosnia and Herzegovina v Serbia and Montenegro*) (Judgment) [2007] ICJ Rep 43 (hereafter *Bosnian Genocide*).

[4] ibid para 389.
[5] ibid.
[6] ibid.

Scorpions were an organ of FRY, it would have found on the facts that they had been placed at the disposal of the Republika Srpska, implying that FRY was not responsible for their conduct at the relevant time.[7] The use of the term 'public authority' reflects the fact that the Republika Srpska was not recognized as a State. In this *dictum*, the ICJ seemingly accepts the overall rationale of Article 6 of the ARSIWA and Article 7 of the ARIO. However, the Court declined to explicitly endorse Article 6 as reflecting customary international law, finding that it was unnecessary to decide the question.[8]

8 The jurisprudence from the European Court of Human Rights similarly does not offer much guidance on Article 6 of the ARSIWA. While the article was raised in the joint cases of *Behrami and Behrami v France* and *Saramati v France, Germany and Norway* ('*Behrami*'),[9] the Court did not consider it in a substantive way.

9 These cases concerned the conduct of French, German, and Norwegian contingents making up part of the United Nations security presence in Kosovo (KFOR), and the United Nations interim administration for Kosovo (UNMIK). The first claim related to a failure to de-mine a municipality, resulting in the death of a boy and injury to his brother, while the second claim related to an alleged deprivation of liberty. The Respondent States denied responsibility on several bases, including the fact that their contingents were under the command of the United Nations, and accordingly the United Nations, not the States, bore responsibility.[10]

10 In laying out the relevant law and practice, the Court extracted Article 6 of the ARSIWA noting that it 'addresses the situation in which an organ of a State is put at the disposal of another, so that the organ may act temporarily for the latter's benefit and under its authority. In such a case the organ, originally that of one State, acts exclusively for the purposes of and on behalf of another State and its conduct is attributed to the latter State alone'.[11]

11 Article 7 of the ARIO has been considered in slightly more depth than Article 6 of the ARSIWA, notably by the European Court of Human Rights in the same joint cases discussed above.[12] In *Behrami*, the Respondent States argued that the United Nations was responsible for the wrongful acts committed by their national contingents.[13] The analysis in respect of UNMIK was straightforward, given that UNMIK was a subsidiary organ of the United Nations created under Chapter VII of the United Nations Charter.[14] The analysis in respect

---

[7] See also S Olleson, 'The Impact of the ILC's Articles on Responsibility of States for Internationally Wrongful Acts' (2007) BIICL [preliminary draft]. See in this Commentary: Chester Brown, 'Article 4 of the ARSIWA'.
[8] *Bosnian Genocide* (n 3) para 414.
[9] *Behrami and Behrami v France; Saramati v France, Germany and Norway*, European Court of Human Rights Grand Chamber, Decision on Admissibility, 31 May 2007 (hereafter *Behrami*).
[10] See paras 82–84 outlining the position of the French government; paras 85–90 outlining the position of the Norwegian government; and paras 91–95 setting out the respondents' joint submissions.
[11] *Behrami* (n 9) para 34.
[12] Note that the Court was relying on an earlier iteration of the Draft Articles, where the relevant article was numbered Article 5, instead of Article 7. The wording of the article remains the same in both iterations.
[13] See n 8 above. Specifically, the French government argued that 'the criterion by which the responsibility of an international organisation was engaged in respect of acts of agents at its disposal was the overall effective, as opposed to exclusive, control of the agent by the organisation' (para 82). Accordingly, because the French contingents acts and omissions were carried out under the authority of NATO and on behalf of KFOR, they were not imputable to France (para 84). Note that Article 7 ARIO was also raised in third-party submissions in the proceedings. The Government of Denmark argued that the ILC's work 'had demonstrated no basis for holding a State responsible for peacekeeping forces placed at the disposal of the UNSC acting under Chapter VII, under unified command and control, within the mandate outlined and in execution of orders from that command structure' (para 100). The Government of Estonia argued that the articles provided that 'any damage caused by UN peacekeeping forces acting within their mandate would be attributable to the UN' (para 107).
[14] *Behrami* (n 9) paras 142–43.

of KFOR was more complicated. In considering whether attribution should fall to the United Nations or to the troop contributing nations (TCNs), the Court noted that 'the key question is whether the United Nations Security Council (UNSC) retained ultimate authority and control so that operational command only was delegated'.[15]

In finding that it did, the Court took into account that UNSC Resolution 1244 allowed the UNSC to delegate to Member States and relevant international organizations, but the leadership of any military presence was required under the Resolution to report to the UNSC (meaning the UNSC remained actively seized of the matter).[16] Accordingly, the Court found that Resolution 1244 gave rise to a chain of command such that the UNSC retained ultimate authority and control over the security mission, thought it delegated to North Atlantic Treaty Organization (NATO) the power to establish KFOR, and operate operational command over it.[17] While the TCNs retained some authority over their troops, the Court noted that NATO's command did not need to be 'exclusive', rather, the relevant question was whether NATO had 'effective' command despite the involvement of the TCNs.[18] Ultimately, the Court found that NATO did have such effective command,[19] and that KFOR was exercising lawfully delegated powers of the UNSC, such that the impugned action was, in principle, attributable to the United Nations.[20]

While the International Law Commission (ILC) endorsed the Court's decision in *Behrami* for considering the relevant question to be one of 'effective' command, the decision has been criticized for its overreliance on the concept of 'ultimate authority' in establishing effective command, as opposed to engaging in a more factually intensive analysis of operational command.[21]

The holding in *Behrami* was applied in the later decision of *Kasumaj v Greece*[22]—though with no further discussion of the application or scope of ARIO. Relevantly, however, some national courts have since provided further guidance on the scope of Article 7 of the ARIO, engaging in a more factual analysis of command and control to determine the criterion of effective control.[23] Notably, the Commentary to ARIO highlights the House of Lords decision in *R (on the application of Al-Jedda) v Secretary of State for Defence*[24] where the Court adopted the reasoning of *Behrami*, but distinguished on the facts—finding that even though the Security Council had authorized the presence of multinational forces in Iraq, the UK and US forces could not realistically be seen as being under the effective control of the United Nations.[25] This sort of analysis, the Commentary notes, seems to be more in line with the way in which the test of effective control was intended to be applied.[26] As noted in the

---

[15] ibid para 133.
[16] ibid para 134.
[17] ibid para 135.
[18] ibid para 138.
[19] ibid paras 139–40.
[20] ibid para 141.
[21] ILC, 'Draft Articles on the Responsibility of International Organizations, with Commentaries' YILC 2011, Vol II, Part Two, 46, Article 7 para 10 (hereafter ARIO Commentaries); M Möldner, 'Responsibility of International Organizations—Introducing the ILC's DARIO' (2012) 16 Max Planck UNYB 282, 294.
[22] *Ilaz Kasumaj v Greece*, European Court of Human Rights (First Section), Decision on Admissibility, 5 July 2007.
[23] See *R (on the application of Al-Jedda) v Secretary of State for Defence*, Judgment of 12 December 2007, House of Lords, [2007] UKHL 58; *State of the Netherlands v Nuhanović*, Hoge Raad [Supreme Court of the Netherlands], 12/03324, 6 September 2013.
[24] Judgment of 12 December 2007, House of Lords, [2007] UHKL, 58.
[25] ibid 136.
[26] ARIO Commentaries (n 21) Article 7 para 12.

Commentary, the European Court of Human Rights seems to have later adopted this method of analysis in subsequent jurisprudence, including the latter case brought by Mr. Al-Jedda.[27] In those proceedings, even though the United Nations *prima facie* had effective control over the multinational forces, the Court engaged in a factual analysis of the actual circumstances to conclude that the United Nations had 'neither effective control nor ultimate authority and control over the acts and omissions of foreign troops within the Multinational Force and that the applicant's detention was not, therefore, attributable to the United Nations'.[28]

15 EU law also addresses the allocation of responsibility between the EU and its organs (i.e. an international organization) and its Member States. As a matter of EU law, where an instruction of the European Commission is binding and Member States are not given discretion as to its implementation, then responsibility for carrying out those instructions lies with the Commission, rather than Member States.[29] Emphasis is therefore placed on the division of competences between the EU organs and the Member States, removing the need for a detailed analysis of the EU's degree of 'control' over the conduct of the Member States.[30]

16 In contrast to the position under EU law, the Strasbourg Court has held that, where a EU Member State is legally obliged to take certain actions by virtue of its EU membership, that State remains responsible for taking those actions.[31] The European Convention on Human Rights (ECHR)'s doctrine of 'equivalent protection' partially mitigates the tension between the two approaches by establishing a presumption that a State that carries out its obligations arising from membership of an international organization does not breach Convention rights provided that the international organization establishes a framework for equivalent protection of those rights.[32] (Note, however, that the doctrine of 'equivalent protection' does *not* attribute conduct solely to the international organization. The conduct in question remains attributable to the State.) This tension between the principles governing the allocation of responsibility under EU law and those under international law also plays out in investment disputes.

C. Interpretation in investment disputes

17 *Electrabel v Hungary* is the only decision of an investment tribunal to have engaged with Article 6 of the ARSIWA. The case arose out of Hungary's termination of a long-term power purchasing agreement (PPA) with an electricity generator. Hungary entered into the PPA with the generator in 1995. In 2004, Hungary acceded to the EU. In June 2008, following an extended investigation, the European Commission issued a decision that the PPA

---

[27] See *Al-Jedda v the United Kingdom* App no 27021/08, Judgment of 7 July 2011 (Grand Chamber), European Court of Human Rights, Reports of Judgments and Decisions 2011. After pursuing his claim in front of the House of Lords, Mr Al-Jedda later brought an application to the European Court of Human Rights.

[28] ibid para 84.

[29] See, eg, *Krohn v Commission*, Case No 175/84, Judgment of 26 February 1986, para 23 (finding that because the Bundesanstalt was obligated to comply with the European Commission's instructions, responsibility for unlawful conduct alleged by the Bundesanstalt fell not to the Bundesanstalt, but to the European Commission).

[30] E Leinarte, 'The Principle of Independent Responsibility of the European Union and its Member States in the International Economic Context' (2018) 21 JIEL 171, 172.

[31] See, eg, *Matthews v the United Kingdom* App no 24833/94, Judgment of 18 February 1999, para 32; similarly in relation to international obligations arising from states' membership of other international organizations, *Capital Bank AD v Bulgaria* App no 49429/99, Judgment of 24 November 2005, para 111.

[32] *Bosphorus Hava Yollary Turizm ve Ticaret Anonim Sirketi v Ireland* App no 45036/98, Judgment of 30 June 2005, para 157.

constituted illegal state aid under European law.[33] The necessary implication of the decision was that Hungary was required to terminate the PPA as a matter of EU law.[34] In November 2008, Hungary's Parliament passed legislation mandating the early termination of the PPA, effective as of 1 January 2009.[35] The investor/claimant in *Electrabel* was a foreign shareholder that owned the majority of shares in the generator and commenced arbitration proceedings pursuant to Article 26 of the Energy Charter Treaty (ECT). Both the EU and Hungary are party to the ECT.

One question raised by the case was whether Hungary was responsible for the termination **18** of the PPA as a matter of international law. While the PPA was, formally speaking, terminated by Hungarian legislation, the tribunal took the view that the EU, not Hungary, was responsible:

> Where Hungary is required to act in compliance with a legally binding decision of an EU institution, recognized as such under the ECT, it cannot (by itself) entail international responsibility for Hungary. Under international law, Hungary can be responsible only for its own wrongful acts. The Tribunal considers that it would be absurd if Hungary could be liable under the ECT for doing precisely that which it was ordered to do by a supranational authority whose decisions the ECT itself recognises as legally binding on Hungary.[36]

The tribunal justified this conclusion by reference to Article 6 of the ARSIWA, applied to **19** these facts by way of analogy, given that the EU is not a state.[37] The hearing on the merits in the proceedings took place in 2010, whereas ARIO were adopted by the ILC in 2011. This chronology may explain why the tribunal did not engage directly with Article 7 of the ARIO, even though the decision on the merits was rendered in 2012.

The tribunal cited the text of Article 6 of the ARSIWA but did not engage with some of the **20** more difficult questions posed by the Commentary to Article 6—for example, whether, in passing legislation terminating the PPA, Hungary's Parliament was acting 'under [the] exclusive direction and control' of the EU, as opposed to engaging in a more ordinary situation of 'inter-State cooperation or collaboration, pursuant to a treaty or otherwise'.[38] The tribunal also did not consider the possibility of joint responsibility of both Hungary and the EU.[39]

Subsequent sections of the tribunal's decision make it clear that the EU's responsibility for **21** the termination of the PPA was engaged only insofar as Hungary was *required* to act in a particular way under EU law.[40] For example, the tribunal recognized that Hungary remained responsible for the scheme that it had set up to account for the generator's 'stranded costs', to the extent it retained discretion in the design of such a scheme under EU law.[41]

---

[33] *Electrabel v Hungary*, ICSID Case No ARB/07/19, Decision on Jurisdiction, Applicable Law and Liability, 30 November 2012, para 6.5 (hereafter *Electrabel v Hungary*).
[34] ibid para 6.77–6.89.
[35] ibid para 6.7.
[36] ibid para 6.72.
[37] ibid para 6.74.
[38] ILC, 'Draft Articles on Responsibility of States for Internationally Wrongful Acts, with Commentaries' YILC 2001, Vol II, Part Two, 31, Article 6 para 2.
[39] ibid para 3. A Delgado Casteleiro, *The International Responsibility of the European Union: From Competence to Normative Control* (CUP 2016) 205 makes similar criticisms of the decision (hereafter Casteleiro, *The International Responsibility*).
[40] For example, *Electrabel v Hungary*, para 6.76
[41] ibid para 6.97.

22 The tribunal's decision in *Electrabel* stands in marked contrast to the decisions of other tribunals in cases arising from states that have terminated financial/fiscal arrangements in order to comply with EU law on state aid. *Micula v Romania*, for example, concerned the termination of a set of tax incentives intended to promote investment in disfavoured regions. During the negotiations for Romania's accession to the EU, EU institutions clearly indicated that the incentives constituted illegal state aid under European law and would need to be brought into line with European law as part of the accession process.[42] Romania terminated the incentives.

23 Romania argued that the 'revocation was necessary to comply with EU state aid obligations, which in turn was necessary for Romania to complete its accession to the EU'.[43] While the tribunal accepted that this argument was factually correct,[44] it held that it had limited legal relevance for the disposition of the investor's claims. The *Micula* tribunal thus did not understand this argument as raising a question of attribution. Instead, the tribunal appears to have characterized Romania's argument that it was *necessary* for it to revoke the incentives as either a general assertion that EU law should be considered as part of the factual background to the dispute or as a suggestion that EU law could be considered as a circumstance precluding wrongfulness.[45]

D. Conclusion

24 The limited practice of international courts and investment tribunals on Article 6 of the ARSIWA and Article 7 of the ARIO makes comparison difficult. Many investment disputes have raised questions of whether a host State is liable for action taken to comply with EU law, yet only one decision has approached this as a question of attribution—*Electrabel v Hungary*. This lack of attention presumably results from the way cases are argued. Respondents seeking to defend claims relating to conduct required by EU law have other arguments available to them, including: that EU law has primacy over investment law, at least insofar as intra-EU legal relationships are concerned;[46] and that EU law delimits an investor's rights in investment and the scope and extent of legitimate expectations the investor may have in relation to it.[47]

25 As to the decision in *Electrabel v Hungary*—it is not clear that the tribunal's approach is consistent with Article 7 of the ARIO. The tribunal did not explicitly consider whether Hungary's legislature had been 'placed at the disposal of the EU' or whether it was under the EU's 'effective control'. The decision seems to deny the relevance of any distinction between situations where a state is required to take measures on account of its membership of an IO, and situations where an IO directly exercises authority over a state organ that acts 'under [the IO's] exclusive direction'. The decision does, however, accord with the European Commission's view,[48] and internal principles of European law that seek to align responsibility of the EU with the extent of its 'normative control' over the Member States.[49]

---

[42] *Micula v Romania*, ICSID Case No ARB/05/20, Award, 11 December 2013, paras 229, 234–35, 788.
[43] ibid para 132.
[44] ibid paras 788–89.
[45] ibid paras 328, 691, 707, and 717.
[46] *RREEF v Spain*, ICSID Case No ARB/13/30, Decision on Jurisdiction, 6 June 2016, paras 48–49.
[47] *AES v Hungary*, ICSID Case No ARB/07/22, Award, 23 September 2010, para 7.4.1.
[48] Casteleiro, *The International Responsibility* (n 39) 197.
[49] Regulation (EU) No 912/2014 of 23 July 2014, Art. 3(1)(c); see also F Hoffmeister, 'Litigating against the European Union and Its Member States—Who Responds under the ILC's Draft Articles on International Responsibility of International Organizations?' (2010) 21 EJIL 723, 741–43 and 746.

One wider doctrinal issue that emerges from this analysis is the distinction between 'factual' **26** and 'legal' approaches to control; another is the distinction between different conceptions of 'legal' control. In its discussion in *Bosnia and Herzegovina v Serbia and Montenegro*, the ICJ hints at an understanding of Article 6 of the ARSIWA that requires a close factual examination of the extent of operational control to determine attribution. This would be consistent with the Court's own jurisprudence on Article 8 of the ARSIWA,[50] and was also the approach adopted by the UK House of Lord in *Al-Jedda*. In contrast, in *Behrami*, the ECHR approached Article 7 of the ARIO as requiring a primarily legal inquiry into the ultimate source of authority over the troops. In *Electrabel v Hungary*, the tribunal also approached the question as one of legal control, but conceived of the requisite control in a different way. Hungary's conduct could be attributed to the EU if it was required under EU law, even if the EU lacked the authority to compel the passage of legislation through the Hungarian parliament.

In our view, a more factual approach to control should be preferred. The factual approach **27** is easier to reconcile with the ICJ's approach to attribution under other articles of ARSIWA, and also reduces the risk that a State can evade international responsibility on account of international obligations it has voluntarily assumed through membership of an international organization.

Selected literature

Delgado Casteleiro A, *The International Responsibility of the European Union: From Competence to Normative Control* (CUP 2016).

Leinarte E, 'The Principle of Independent Responsibility of the European Union and its Member States in the International Economic Context' (2018) 21 JIEL 171.

Möldner M, 'Responsibility of International Organizations—Introducing the ILC's DARIO' (2012) 16 Max Planck UNYB 281.

Olleson S, 'The Impact of the ILC's Articles on Responsibility of States for Internationally Wrongful Acts' (2007) BIICL [preliminary draft].

Selected decisions

Application of the Convention on the Prevention and Punishment of the Crime of Genocide (Bosnia and Herzegovina v Serbia and Montenegro) (Judgment) [2007] ICJ Rep.

Behrami and Behrami v France; Saramati v France, Germany and Norway, European Court of Human Rights Grand Chamber, Decision on Admissibility, 31 May 2007.

Electrabel v Hungary, ICSID Case No ARB/07/19, Decision on Jurisdiction, Applicable Law and Liability, 30 November 2012.

Micula v Romania, ICSID Case No ARB/05/20, Award, 11 December 2013.

---

[50] See in this Commentary: Jorge E Viñuales and Alina Papanastasiou 'Article 8 of the ARSIWA'.

Article 7 of the ARSIWA

Excess of authority or contravention of instructions

*Chester Brown**

The conduct of an organ of a State or of a person or entity empowered to exercise elements of the governmental authority shall be considered an act of the State under international law if the organ, person or entity acts in that capacity, even if it exceeds its authority or contravenes instructions.

A. Introduction	1	II. Acting in an official capacity	10
B. Specific doctrinal issues relevant in investment arbitration	9	III. Excess of authority or contravention of instructions	18
I. Scope of application	9	IV. Irrelevant whether there has been a breach	24
		C. Conclusion	25

A. Introduction

1 Article 7 of the ARSIWA (Articles on the Responsibility of States for Internationally Wrongful Acts) deals with the issue of 'unauthorised or *ultra vires*' acts or omissions of State organs and persons or entities empowered to exercise elements of governmental authority, and clarifies that the acts and omissions of such an organ, person, or entity, if acting in its official capacity, is 'attributable to the State even if it has acted in excess of authority or contrary to instructions'.[1] It therefore operates to prevent a State from denying responsibility for acts on the basis of their characterization under domestic law. The International Law Commission (ILC) elaborated in its commentaries on Article 7:

> The State cannot take refuge behind the notion that, according to the provisions of its internal law or to instructions which may have been given to its organs or agents, their actions or omissions ought not to have occurred or ought to have taken a different form.[2]

2 If it were possible for a State to 'take refuge behind' its own domestic law and argue that the conduct of a State organ, or of a person or entity empowered to exercise elements of governmental authority was not attributable, on the basis that the conduct was in violation of

---

* I am grateful to Calida Tang for her excellent research assistance.
[1] ILC, 'Draft Articles on Responsibility of States for Internationally Wrongful Acts, with Commentaries' YILC 2001, Vol II, Part Two, 31, Article 7 para 1 (hereafter ARSIWA Commentaries).
[2] ibid para 2.

internal law, an inconsistency with Article 3 of the ARSIWA would arise.[3] Article 3 provides that the characterization of an act as internationally wrongful is governed by international law, rather than by internal law.[4]

Following some diplomatic practice consistent with the rule,[5] the award of the French– Mexican Claims Commission in *Estate of Jean-Baptiste Caire v Mexico* is an early arbitral authority.[6] In this 1929 case, a Mexican soldier had attempted to extort money from a French national who owned the boarding house in which the soldier was staying. After the attempt failed, the Mexican soldier, along with another soldier from the same brigade, shot and killed the French national. In a well-known passage, the French–Mexican Claims Commission held that:

> the two officers, even if they are deemed to have acted outside their competence ... and even if their superiors countermanded an order, have involved the responsibility of the State, since they acted under cover of their status as officers and used means placed at their disposal on account of that status.[7]

By the time of the Hague Conference for the Codification of International Law in 1930, a majority of States supported a broad formulation of this rule, which provided that States would be responsible for '[a]cts of officials in the national territory in their public capacity (*actes de fonction*) but exceeding their authority'.[8] The Third Committee of the Hague Conference adopted the following provision:

> International responsibility is ... incurred by a State if damage is sustained by a foreigner as a result of unauthorised acts of its officials performed under cover of their official character, if the acts contravene the international obligations of the State.[9]

This reflects the modern rule that has developed in customary international law, as it has been confirmed in the writings of publicists.[10] It can be regarded as 'a well-established rule of international law'.[11]

The International Court of Justice (ICJ) has not applied Article 7 ARSIWA, although it has been considered in the dissenting opinions of two judges: that of Judge ad hoc Mahiou in

---

[3] ibid.
[4] Article 3 of the ARSIWA.
[5] eg, the view articulated by the British government in the late 1890s that that 'all Governments should always be held responsible for all acts committed by their agents by virtue of their official capacity': ARSIWA Commentaries (n 1) Article 7 para 3.
[6] *Estate of Jean-Baptiste Caire v Mexico* (*France v Mexico*) (1929) 5 RIAA 516 (hereafter *Jean-Baptiste Caire*); ARSIWA Commentaries (n 1) Article 7 para 5; see also J Crawford, *State Responsibility: The General Part* (CUP 2013) 137.
[7] *Jean-Baptiste Caire* (n 6) 529.
[8] League of Nations, *Conference for the Codification of International Law: Bases of Discussion for the Conference drawn up by the Preparatory Committee*, Vol III: 'Responsibility of States for Damage caused in their Territory to the Person or Property of Foreigners' (LN Doc C.75.M.69.1929.V), point V, No 2 (*b*), 74, cited in ARSIWA Commentaries (n 1) Article 7 para 3.
[9] League of Nations, *Conference for the Codification of International Law: Bases of Discussion Bases of Discussion for the Conference drawn up by the Preparatory Committee* (LN Doc C.351(c)M.145(c).1930) V, 237, cited in ARSIWA Commentaries (n 1) Article 7 para 3.
[10] ARSIWA Commentaries (n 1) Article 7 paras 2–4; see also O de Frouville, 'Attribution of Conduct to the State: Private Individuals' in J Crawford, A Pellet, S Olleson and K Parlett (eds), *The Law of International Responsibility* (OUP 2010) 257, 263 (hereafter De Frouville, 'Attribution').
[11] De Frouville, 'Attribution' (n 10) 263.

Application of the Convention on the Prevention and Punishment of the Crime of Genocide,[12] and that of Judge ad hoc Kateka in *Armed Activities on the Territory of the Congo*.[13] It has however been discussed by the Appeals Chamber of the International Criminal Tribunal for the former Yugoslavia, which observed that:

> a State is internationally accountable for *ultra vires* acts or transactions of its organs. In other words it incurs responsibility even for acts committed by its officials outside their remit or contrary to its behest. The rationale behind this provision is that a State must be held accountable for acts of its organs whether or not these organs complied with instructions, if any, from the higher authorities.[14]

7 Other international courts and tribunals to have referred to Article 7 of the ARSIWA include the European Court of Human Rights,[15] the Human Rights Committee,[16] the Inter-American Court of Human Rights,[17] and a panel of the World Trade Organization (WTO). The WTO panel affirmed that:

> it is well established under international law that an action or conduct of a government official or entity is attributable to the State even where that action or conduct is contrary to national law.[18]

8 Article 7 has also been considered and applied by a number of investment tribunals, although the practice is not abundant. In the Appendix to James Crawford's 2010 article on investment arbitration decisions dealing with the ARSIWA, he noted three investment cases in the period 2001–09 in which the tribunals had referred to Article 7,[19] and in an article published by Esmé Shirlow and Kabir Duggal in 2022, they noted a further eight investment treaty cases in the period 2010–20 in which the tribunals had discussed Article 7 of the ARSIWA.[20] In many of these cases, the tribunal did not actually apply Article 7, but merely noted that its findings on attribution (under either Article 4 or 5) were supported by the fact that even if the relevant conduct was *ultra vires*, the conduct would still be attributable to the State under Article 7.

---

[12] *Application of the Convention on the Prevention and Punishment of the Crime of Genocide (Bosnia and Herzegovina v Serbia and Montenegro)* (Judgment, Dissenting Opinion of Judge ad hoc Mahiou) [2007] ICJ Rep 381 (hereafter *Bosnian Genocide*, Diss Op Mahiou).

[13] *Armed Activities on the Territory of the Congo (Democratic Republic of the Congo v Uganda)* (Judgment, Dissenting Opinion of Judge ad hoc Kateka) [2005] ICJ Rep 361 (hereafter *Armed Activities*, Diss Op Kateka).

[14] *Prosecutor v Tadić*, ICTY Appeals Chamber, Case No IT-94-1-A, Judgment, 15 July 1999, para 121.

[15] *Ilaşcu and others v Moldova and Russia* App no 48787/99 (Grand Chamber), Judgment, 8 July 2004, para 319; see also *El Masri v Former Yugoslav Republic of Macedonia* App no 39630/09 (Grand Chamber), Judgment, 13 December 2012, para 97; *Jones v United Kingdom* App nos 34356/06 and 40528/06, Judgment, 14 January 2014, para 108; *Husayn (Abu Zubaydah) v Poland* App no 7511/13, Judgment, 24 July 2014, para 201.

[16] Human Rights Committee, Communication No 950/2000 (Sri Lanka), UN Doc CCPR/C/78/D/950/2000, 31 July 2003, paras 9.2–9.3.

[17] eg, *Velásquez Rodríguez v Honduras (Merits)*, Ser C, No 4, Judgment of 29 July 1988, 95 ILR 232, 296; *Villamizar Durán et al v Colombia (Preliminary Objection, Merits, Reparations and Costs)*, Ser C, No 364, Judgment of 20 November 2018, para 139.

[18] *United States—Anti-Dumping and Countervailing Measures on Certain Coated Paper from Indonesia*, Panel Report, WT/DS491/R, 6 December 2017, para 7.179.

[19] J Crawford, 'Investment Arbitration and the ILC Articles on State Responsibility' (2010) 25 ICSID Rev/FILJ 127, 158 (hereafter Crawford, 'Investment Arbitration'). For example, *ADF Group, Inc v United States*, ICSID Case No ARB(AF)/00/1, Award, 9 January 2003, para 190.

[20] E Shirlow and K Duggal, 'The ILC Articles on State Responsibility in Investment Treaty Arbitration' (2022) 37 ICSID Rev/FILJ 378, 431–33.

B. Specific doctrinal issues relevant in investment arbitration

I. Scope of application

The *ultra vires* rule contained in Article 7 applies to the conduct of State organs or of persons or entities 'empowered to exercise elements of the governmental authority',[21] i.e. conduct which is attributed to the State under Articles 4, 5, and 6 of the ARSIWA. Article 7 does not apply to conduct which is attributed to States under other provisions of the ARSIWA, such as Articles 8 and 11. As Jorge Viñuales explains, 'this is because the very reason for attribution is that the conduct is effectively controlled or specifically acknowledged and adopted. The only exception to this exclusion concerns acts which are incidental to the acts effectively controlled or acknowledged and adopted.'[22]

II. Acting in an official capacity

The principal issue that gives rise to difficulty in applying Article 7 in practice is the need to determine whether the unauthorized acts were performed in an official capacity. This characterization concerns whether the acts were so far removed from the scope of official functions that they are appropriately characterized as acts of private individuals.[23] The distinction is drawn by applying a so-called 'theory of appearance'.[24] Article 7 only captures conduct of organs 'purportedly or apparently carrying out their official functions' or exercising 'apparent authority', and not the 'private actions or omissions of individuals who happen to be organs or agents of the State'.[25] However, conduct which is 'systematic or recurrent, such that the State knew or ought to have known of it and should have taken steps to prevent it' may suggest that the unauthorized acts were 'official' in nature.[26]

This distinction was considered in *Yeager v Iran*, an award of the Iran–United States Claims Tribunal of 1987 which pre-dates the adoption of the ARSIWA.[27] In that case, the claimant brought various complaints against Iran, two of which are relevant for present purposes: first, that he had unlawfully been required to pay an additional fee to an Iran Air agent to secure the travel out of Iran of his daughter, who already held a prepaid air ticket; and second, that uniformed and armed officers of the Revolutionary Guard had seized money from him and his wife prior to their forced departure from Iran.[28] With respect to the complaint regarding the agent, the Iran–United States Claims Tribunal held that the evidence was 'insufficient to demonstrate that the agent was acting in his official capacity as an "organ" of Iran Air on this occasion'.[29] As it explained:

> The critical question here ... is whether the Iran Air agent was acting in his official capacity as an organ of Iran Air when he demanded the extra payment. There is no indication in this

---

[21] Article 7 of the ARSIWA.
[22] J Viñuales, 'Attribution of Conduct to States in Investment Arbitration' (2022) 20 ICSID Rep 13, 76, para 154.
[23] ARSIWA Commentaries (n 1) Article 7 para 7.
[24] De Frouville, 'Attribution' (n 10) 263–64.
[25] ARSIWA Commentaries (n 1) Article 7 para 8.
[26] ibid.
[27] *Kenneth P. Yeager v The Islamic Republic of Iran*, IUSCT Case No 10199, Award No 324-10199-1, 2 November 1987, 82 ILR 178.
[28] ibid 184, para 9, re the Iran Air incident, 184–85, para 12, re the conduct of the Revolutionary Guard in demanding money.
[29] ibid 200–01, para 64.

case that the Iran Air agent was acting for any other reason than personal profit, or that he had passed on the payment to Iran Air. He evidently did not act on behalf or in the interest of Iran Air. The Tribunal finds, therefore, that this agent acted in a private capacity and not in his official capacity as an organ of Iran Air.[30]

12 In contrast, the Iran–United States Claims Tribunal held that the conduct of the members of the Revolutionary Guard in seizing money from the claimant and his wife at the airport was attributable to Iran. As it explained, the members of the Revolutionary Guard were 'performing the functions of customs, immigration and security officers', and that they were therefore 'obviously acting in their capacity as "organs" of the new Government or, at least, on its behalf'.[31] The respondent had not demonstrated that it had 'made at least an attempt to enjoin their activity or to exercise adequate control in order to hinder such seizure of cash', and it followed that these acts were attributable to Iran.[32]

13 In another arbitral decision which pre-dates the adoption by the ILC of the ARSIWA, and the United Nations General Assembly's Resolution which 'took note' of them and 'commended them to the attention of Governments' on 12 December 2001,[33] an International Centre for Settlement of Investment Disputes (ICSID) tribunal confirmed the rule of international law which is encapsulated in Article 7, albeit without referring to the ILC's then draft provision. This ICSID tribunal, in *Southern Pacific Properties (Middle East) Ltd v Egypt*, did not have jurisdiction under a bilateral or multilateral investment treaty, but rather under Egypt's foreign investment law.[34] In this case, Egypt sought to argue that certain acts of Egyptian State officials (including the decrees on the basis of which the claimant had made its investment) were 'legally non-existent or null and void or susceptible to invalidation'.[35] But the tribunal rejected this argument, finding that those acts were nevertheless acts of Egyptian authorities which were 'cloaked with the mantle of Governmental authority and communicated as such to foreign investors who relied on them in making their investments'.[36] The ICSID tribunal further observed that:

> Whether legal under Egyptian law or not, the acts in question were the acts of Egyptian authorities, including the highest executive authority of the Government. These acts, which are now alleged to have been in violation of the Egyptian municipal legal system, created expectations protected by established principles of international law.[37]

14 The ICSID tribunal held that it was 'bound to apply' the rule of international law:

> which establishes the international responsibility of States when unauthorized or *ultra vires* acts of officials have been performed by State agents under cover of their official character. If such unauthorized or *ultra vires* acts could not be ascribed to the State, all State responsibility would be rendered illusory.[38]

---

[30] ibid 201, para 65.
[31] ibid 200, para 61.
[32] ibid.
[33] UNGA Res 59/35 (12 December 2001) UN Doc A/RES/59/35.
[34] *Southern Pacific Properties (Middle East) Ltd v Egypt*, ICSID Case No ARB/84/3, Decision on Jurisdiction, 14 April 1988.
[35] ibid para 82.
[36] ibid.
[37] ibid para 83.
[38] ibid para 85.

In *Armed Activities*, Judge *ad hoc* Kateka discussed Article 7 in his dissenting opinion.[39] In that case, the ICJ had held that Uganda was responsible for the acts of its military forces in the Democratic Republic of the Congo, including its actions in looting, plundering, and exploitation of natural resources, regardless of whether it was an occupying Power in the particular regions.[40] For his part, Judge ad hoc Kateka considered that the Ugandan soldiers who committed such acts did so in violation of orders from Ugandan authorities and characterized the acts as being committed in those soldiers' 'private capacity', with the result that they could not be attributed to the respondent.[41]

In *Chevron v Ecuador (II)*, a claim brought under the United States–Ecuador Bilateral Investment Treaty (BIT), the claimants alleged that the Ecuadorian court judgment in the 'Lago Agrio' litigation (a representative proceedings against Chevron brought by members of the Lago Agrio community before the Ecuador courts) constituted a breach of Ecuador's treaty obligations in that the judge, Judge Zambrano, had corruptly accepted bribes from the legal representatives of the plaintiffs in that case, and that he had permitted them to 'ghostwrite' part of the Lago Agrio judgment.[42] Ecuador argued that his conduct could not be attributed to it, because Judge Zambrano had been motivated by personal gain. The tribunal noted that Judge Zambrano's conduct had not been directed by the respondent, and that his misconduct 'was not authorised under Ecuadorian law'.[43] Nevertheless, the tribunal held that Judge Zambrano's conduct was attributable to Ecuador:

> the Lago Agrio Judgment was issued by Judge Zambrano in his capacity as a judge of the Lago Agrio Court, itself part of the Respondent's judicial branch; the Lago Agrio Judgment was accorded the status of a court judgment under Ecuadorian law; and it was (and remains) subject to enforcement and execution by the Respondent's judicial branch within the Respondent's national legal system.[44]

Referring to Article 7 ARSIWA, the tribunal addressed the distinction between conduct which is attributable even though it is unauthorized, and that which cannot be attributed because it was not done by the State organ, person, or entity in their official capacity. The tribunal explained that:

> In the present case, the conduct of Judge Zambrano in issuing the Lago Agrio Judgment (as with all other judges of the Lago Agrio Court acting in the Lago Agrio Litigation) was manifestly done 'cloaked with governmental authority', as members of the Respondent's judicial branch. Judge Zambrano was held out by the Respondent and also held himself out as a judge acting in the name of the Respondent.[45]

III. Excess of authority or contravention of instructions

In a number of cases, international courts and tribunals have referred to Article 7 of the ARSIWA, and the possibility that the State organ or person or entity exercising elements

---
[39] *Armed Activities*, Diss Op Kateka (n 13).
[40] *Armed Activities on the Territory of the Congo (Democratic Republic of the Congo v Uganda)* (Judgment) [2005] ICJ Rep 168, paras 180, 245.
[41] *Armed Activities*, Diss Op Kateka (n 13) para 54.
[42] *Chevron Corporation and Texaco Petroleum v Ecuador*, PCA Case No 2009-23, Second Partial Award on Track II, 30 August 2018, para 5.85.
[43] ibid paras 8.43–8.44.
[44] ibid para 8.46.
[45] ibid para 8.50.

of governmental authority was acting in excess of their authority, or in contravention of their instructions, in order to fortify their conclusions on attribution. One such case is *Noble Ventures v Romania*.[46] In this case, the ICSID tribunal found that Romania's State privatization agencies, the State Ownership Fund (SOF) and the Authority for Privatisation and Management of State Ownership (APAPS), had been empowered by Romanian law to exercise elements of governmental authority in relation to privatization within the meaning of Article 5 ARSIWA.[47] The tribunal further noted that:

> Even if one were to regard some of the acts of SOF or APAPS as being *ultra vires*, the result would be the same. This is because of the generally recognized rule recorded in Art. 7 2001 ILC Draft according to which the conduct of an organ of a State or of a person or entity empowered to exercise elements of governmental authority shall be considered an act of the State under international law if the organ, person or entity acts in that capacity, even if it exceeds its authority or contravenes instructions. Since, from the Claimant's perspective, SOF and APAPS always acted as if they were entities entitled by the Respondent to do so, their acts would still have to be attributed to the Respondent, even if an excess of competence had been shown.[48]

19 In *Bosnian Genocide*, Judge ad hoc Mahiou considered Article 7 in his dissenting opinion, in which he held (contrary to the ICJ) that Serbia and Montenegro was responsible for acts of genocide committed by State organs and armed groups in Republika Srpska, the Serbian entity within Bosnia and Herzegovina.[49] Judge ad hoc Mahiou observed that such acts were attributable even if the persons were in fact acting under the control of a separate military group, because 'Article 7 of the ILC's Articles provides for the responsibility of a State even when its organs have not followed its instructions or have followed the instructions of another authority'.[50]

20 In another case, *Kardassopoulos v Georgia*, the entities in question were 'SakNavtobi', the Georgian State-owned oil company, and 'Transneft', the entity which held the rights over Georgia's oil pipelines, which were both incorporated as a department of the Georgian Ministry of Fuel and Energy.[51] The tribunal appeared to accept that SakNavtobi did not have the authority to grant to GTI, the joint venture vehicle, the rights which were conferred under the terms of the joint venture agreement.[52] The respondent further argued that Transneft had also exceeded its authority.[53] The tribunal held that, irrespective of the position under Georgian law, it had to apply international law to resolve the dispute.[54] It went on to find that SakNavtobi and Transneft had made representations which gave rise to legitimate expectations which were attributable to Georgia even if they were made *ultra vires*:

> The principle of attribution, in principle, applies to Georgia by virtue of its status as a sovereign State and is not contingent on the timing of its adherence to a treaty. It is also

---

[46] *Noble Ventures Ltd v Romania*, ICSID Case No ARB/01/11, Award, 12 October 2005.
[47] ibid paras 68–80.
[48] ibid paras 81, 86.
[49] *Bosnian Genocide*, Diss Op Mahiou (n 12).
[50] ibid para 95. See also in this Commentary: Chester Brown, 'Article 4 of the ARSIWA', paras 16–19.
[51] *Kardassopoulos v Georgia*, ICSID Case No ARB/05/18, Decision on Jurisdiction, 6 July 2007, paras 15, 24, 189–94 (hereafter *Kardassopoulos*, Jurisdiction); see also *Kardassopoulos v Georgia*, ICSID Case No ARB/05/18, Award, 3 March 2010, paras 273–74.
[52] *Kardassopoulos*, Jurisdiction(n 51) paras 152–56.
[53] ibid paras 166–70.
[54] ibid para 157.

immaterial whether or not SakNavtobi and Transneft were authorized to grant the rights contemplated by the JVA and the Concession or whether or not they otherwise acted beyond their authority under Georgian law. Article 7 of the Articles on State Responsibility provides that even in cases where an entity empowered to exercise governmental authority acts *ultra vires* of it, the conduct in question is nevertheless attributable to the State.

In the Tribunal's view, Respondent cannot simply avoid the legal effect of the representations and warranties set forth in the JVA and the Concession by arguing that they are contained in agreements which are void *ab initio* under Georgian law.[55]

21 This approach of the *Kardassopoulos* tribunal is correct. The question of whether the State has breached its treaty obligations is a matter of public international law, which means that the rule in Article 7 ARSIWA is relevant 'so as to render attributable to the State the conduct of representation and assurance performed by its agents or by its parastatals for the purposes of State responsibility for internationally wrongful acts'.[56]

22 In *Tethyan Copper Company Pty Ltd v Pakistan*, the ICSID tribunal held that the conduct of the Balochistan Government and its officials was attributable to the Respondent, referring to Article 4(1) ARSIWA.[57] The tribunal then took the same belt-and-braces approach to attribution as the *Noble Ventures* tribunal. Citing Article 7 ARSIWA, it held that the conduct in question would be attributable even if the acts of Balochistan officials, such as the Licensing Authority and the Secretary of the Balochistan Mines and Minerals Development Department, were in excess of authority or contravened instructions.[58]

23 In another case, *Strabag v Libya*,[59] the dispute concerned a construction project which was affected by armed conflict in the context of the Arab Spring of early 2011. The claimant alleged that Libyan armed forces loyal to an earlier regime had caused physical damage to the investment, in breach of the Austria–Libya BIT. The respondent argued, *inter alia*, that it was not responsible for any damage caused because such damage resulted from unauthorized conduct by forces acting outside their orders. The tribunal rejected Libya's argument, here referring to Article 91 of the Geneva Protocol 1 and Article 7 of the ARSIWA, noting that a State is responsible 'for all acts by persons forming part of its armed forces', including 'acts committed contrary to orders or instructions'.[60] The tribunal further found that the regiment in question, the 32nd Reinforced Brigade, was 'an elite regular force that acted under the chain of command'.[61] The tribunal nonetheless accepted that some of the damage to the property and facilities in question was not caused by the 32nd Reinforced Brigade, but that these 'were also damaged or looted by others including rebels, NATO, looters, and Al Han i's own employees'.[62] Libya was not responsible for damage caused by these others, and the tribunal had to make its best assessment as to how much damage was actually attributable to the Libyan armed forces. In the end it decided that one-third of the damage was attributable to Libya.[63]

---

[55] ibid paras 190–91.
[56] C de Stefano, 'Attribution of Conduct to a State' (2022) 37 ICSID Rev/FILJ 20, 37.
[57] *Tethyan Copper Company Pty Ltd v Pakistan*, ICSID Case No ARB/12/1, Decision on Jurisdiction and Liability, 10 November 2017, para 726.
[58] ibid para 729.
[59] *Strabag v Libya*, ICSID Case No ARB(AF)/15/1, Award, 29 June 2020.
[60] ibid para 319.
[61] ibid para 320.
[62] ibid.
[63] ibid paras 320–21.

IV. Irrelevant whether there has been a breach

24 A final issue to note is that Article 7 is not concerned with the question whether the relevant conduct which is in excess of authority or in contravention of instructions constitutes a breach of an international obligation. As the ILC has explained, '[t]he fact that instructions given to an organ or entity were ignored, or that its actions were ultra vires, may be relevant in determining whether or not the obligation has been breached, but that is a separate issue'.[64]

C. Conclusion

25 It can be seen from the preceding that, on the whole, the practice of investment tribunals is consistent with general international practice, even though there are comparatively few examples of Article 7 having being considered and applied by other international courts and tribunals. De Stefano also concludes that 'the practice of investment tribunals generally reproduces the customary interpretation of the *ultra vires* rule, with unprecedented applications with regard to the activities of State instrumentalities under [Article 5 ARSIWA], which nevertheless confirm the content of the conventional rule'.[65] Indeed, a considerable part of the relevant practice comes from the field of investment arbitration, with the result that the decisions and awards of investment tribunals are likely to be influential.

26 As is the case with the other rules on attribution, the consistency of approach reflects the fact that the provisions of Chapter II of Part One of the ARSIWA are general in nature.[66] Because Article 7 is accepted as reflecting customary international law, it is to be expected (in the absence of any *lex specialis*) that investment tribunals would apply Article 7 as an applicable rule of attribution.[67]

Selected literature

Crawford J, *The International Law Commission's Articles on State Responsibility: Introduction, Text and Commentaries* (CUP 2002).
Crawford J, *State Responsibility: The General Part* (CUP 2013).
Crawford J, 'Investment Arbitration and the ILC Articles on State Responsibility' (2010) 25 ICSID Review/FILJ 127.
De Frouville O, 'Attribution of Conduct to the State: Private Individuals', in Crawford J, Pellet A, Olleson S and Parlett K (eds), *The Law of International Responsibility* (OUP 2010) 257.
De Stefano C, *Attribution in International Law and Arbitration* (OUP 2020).
De Stefano C, 'Attribution of Conduct to a State' (2022) 37 ICSID Rev/FILJ 20.
Shirlow E and Duggal K, 'The ILC Articles on State Responsibility in Investment Treaty Arbitration' (2022) 37 ICSID Rev/FILJ 378.
Viñuales J, 'Attribution of Conduct to States in Investment Arbitration' (2022) 20 ICSID Rep 13.

---

[64] ARSIWA Commentaries (n 1) Article 7 para 10.
[65] C de Stefano, *Attribution in International Law and Arbitration* (OUP 2020) 147.
[66] Crawford, 'Investment Arbitration' (n 19) 127, 129.
[67] See in this Commentary: Fernando Lusa Bordin, 'Article 55 of the ARSIWA'.

Selected decisions

Application of the Convention on the Prevention and Punishment of the Crime of Genocide (*Bosnia and Herzegovina v Serbia and Montenegro*) (Judgment, Dissenting Opinion of Judge ad hoc Mahiou) [2007] ICJ Rep 381.

Armed Activities on the Territory of the Congo (*Democratic Republic of the Congo v Uganda*) (Judgment, Dissenting Opinion of Judge ad hoc Kateka) [2005] ICJ Rep 361.

Chevron Corporation and Texaco Petroleum v Ecuador, PCA Case No 2009-23, Second Partial Award on Track II, 30 August 2018.

Kardassopoulos v Georgia, ICSID Case No ARB/05/18, Decision on Jurisdiction, 6 July 2007.

Kenneth P. Yeager v The Islamic Republic of Iran, IUSCT Case No 10199, Award No 324-10199-1, 2 November 1987, 82 ILR 178.

Noble Ventures Ltd v Romania, ICSID Case No ARB/01/11, Award, 12 October 2005.

Southern Pacific Properties (Middle East) Ltd v Egypt, ICSID Case No ARB/84/3, Decision on Jurisdiction, 14 April 1988.

Strabag v Libya, ICSID Case No ARB(AF)/15/1, Award, 29 June 2020.

Tethyan Copper Company Pty Ltd v Pakistan, ICSID Case No ARB/12/1, Decision on Jurisdiction and Liability, 10 November 2017.

Article 8 of the ARSIWA

Attribution of conduct instructed, directed or controlled by a State

Jorge E Viñuales and Alina Papanastasiou

The conduct of a person or group of persons shall be considered an act of a State under international law if the person or group of persons is in fact acting on the instructions of, or under the direction or control of, that State in carrying out the conduct.

A. Introduction	1	II. 'In fact acting on the instructions of, or under the direction or control of, that State'	22
B. Codification of a control-based attribution rule	3	1. Disjunctive nature of the test	22
C. Scope and operation of the rule—analytical distinctions	8	2. Acting under the direction or control of the State	25
I. Article 8 and non-ARSIWA rules governing attribution-related questions	8	3. Acting on the instructions of the State	29
II. Article 8 and other attribution rules under ARSIWA	12	E. General and special rules of attribution of conduct under direction or control	37
D. Components of the rule through the lens of investment tribunals	19	F. Concluding observations: confined or general contribution?	42
I. 'Person or a group of persons'	19		

A. Introduction

1 'States, lacking bodies of their own, must act through the agency of others.'[1] These 'others' are not always State organs or public officials, but may also include private entities, individuals, and companies. Acts or omissions of private entities are not normally considered State conduct, for the purposes of State responsibility for internationally wrongful acts. Private conduct may however be attributable to a State when 'there exists a specific factual relationship between the person or entity engaging in the conduct and the State.'[2] Article 8 of the Articles

---

[1] J Crawford and J Watkins, 'International Responsibility' in S Besson and J Tasioulas (eds), *The Philosophy of International Law* (OUP 2010) 283, 287.

[2] ILC, 'Draft Articles on Responsibility of States for Internationally Wrongful Acts, with Commentaries' YILC 2001, Vol II, Part Two, 31, Article 8 para 1 (hereafter ARSIWA Commentaries). See also *Electrabel SA v Republic of Hungary*, ICSID Case No ARB/07/19, Decision on Jurisdiction, Applicable Law and Liability, 30 November 2012, para 7.71 (hereafter *Electrabel v Hungary*).

on the Responsibility of States for Internationally Wrongful Acts (ARSIWA)[3] codifies a rule defining certain situations that establish such a special relationship. Article 8 of the ARSIWA codifies customary international law,[4] as also consistently confirmed by investment tribunals.[5] Investment tribunals have produced extensive jurisprudence applying this rule in a variety of different factual scenarios.

There is a rich body of literature discussing Article 8 of the ARSIWA in general,[6] as well as extensive analysis of the interpretation and application of international attribution rules by investment tribunals.[7] This entry takes up the practical relevance and theoretical importance of the attribution rule codified in Article 8 for investment dispute settlement, and the latter's contribution to the development and clarification of this rule.[8] Section B briefly presents the development of the rule and the process of codifying it in Article 8 of the ARSIWA. Section C discusses the scope and operation of the rule, distinguishing it from other ARSIWA attribution rules, as well as other domestic and international rules governing attribution-related questions. Section D analyses the components of Article 8, as clarified through investment practice, and Section E considers its interaction with special rules of attribution in the context of investment disputes. Section F concludes, offering some thoughts on the wider relevance of that investment arbitration practice. 2

B. Codification of a control-based attribution rule

In the early 1970s, then Special Rapporteur Roberto Ago proposed the predecessor to today's Article 8 providing that the conduct of a person or group of persons would be attributable to a State if 'it is established that such person or group of persons was *in fact acting on behalf of that State*'.[9] Ago sought to limit the application of this rule to cases where 'the person or 3

---

[3] ARSIWA Commentaries (n 2) Article 8.
[4] *Application of the Convention on the Prevention and Punishment of the Crime of Genocide (Bosnia and Herzegovina v Serbia and Montenegro)* (Judgment) [2007] ICJ Rep 43, para 398 (hereafter *Bosnian Genocide*).
[5] *Ortiz Construcciones y Proyectos SA v People's Democratic Republic of Algeria*, ICSID Case No ARB/17/1, Award, 29 April 2020, para 155 (hereafter *Ortiz v Algeria*); *Jan de Nul NV and Dredging International NV v Arab Republic of Egypt*, ICSID Case No ARB/04/13, Award, 6 November 2008, para 156 (hereafter *Jan de Nul v Egypt*); *Bayindir Insaat Turizm Ticaret Ve Sanayi AŞ v Islamic Republic of Pakistan*, ICSID Case No ARB/03/29, Award, 27 August 2009, para 113 (hereafter *Bayindir v Pakistan*); *Tulip Real Estate and Development Netherlands BV v Republic of Turkey*, ICSID Case No ARB/11/28, Award, 10 March 2014, para 281 (hereafter *Tulip v Turkey*); *Georg Gavrilović and Gavrilović doo v Republic of Croatia*, ICSID Case No ARB/12/39, Award, 25 July 2018, para 779 (hereafter *Gavrilović v Croatia*); *Unión Fenosa Gas, SA v Arab Republic of Egypt*, ICSID Case No ARB/14/4, Award, 31 August 2018, para 9.90 (hereafter *UFG v Egypt*); *Electrabel v Hungary* (n 2) para 7.60.
[6] See, eg, O de Frouville, 'Attribution of Conduct to the State: Private Individuals' in J Crawford, A Pellet and S Olleson (eds), *The Law of International Responsibility* (OUP 2010) 257; C Tomuschat, 'Attribution of International Responsibility: Direction and Control' in M Evans and P Koutrakos (eds), *The International Responsibility of the European Union: European and International Perspectives* (Hart Publishing 2013) 7; K Mačák, 'Decoding Article 8 of the International Law Commission's Articles on State Responsibility: Attribution of Cyber Operations by Non-State Actors' (2016) 21(3) J Confl Secur Law 405.
[7] See, eg, C Kovács, *Attribution in International Investment Law* (Kluwer Law International 2018); C de Stefano, *Attribution in International Law and Arbitration* (OUP 2020); E Shirlow and K Duggal, 'The ILC Articles on State Responsibility in Investment Treaty Arbitration' (2022) 37 ICSID Rev 378 (hereafter Shirlow and Duggal); J Crawford and P Mertenskötter, 'The Use of the ILC's Attribution Rules in Investment Arbitration' in M Kinnear and others (eds), *Building International Investment Law—The First 50 Years of ICSID* (Kluwer 2016) (hereafter Crawford and Mertenskötter); J Crawford, 'Investment Arbitration and the ILC Articles on State Responsibility' (2010) 25 ICSID Rev 127.
[8] Some sections of this entry build upon previous analysis in JE Viñuales, 'Attribution of Conduct to States in Investment Arbitration' (2022) 20 ICSID Rep 13 (hereafter *Viñuales*).
[9] ILC, 'Report of the International Law Commission on the Work of its 26th Session' (6 May–26 July 1974) UN Doc A/9610/Rev.1, 277 (draft Article 8(a)) (emphasis added). See also first formulation in Roberto Ago, 'Third Report on State Responsibility' (1971) UN Doc A/CN.4/246 and Add 1–3, 267.

group of persons were actually appointed by organs of the State to discharge a particular function or to carry out a particular duty, that they performed a given task at the instigation of those organs', i.e. cases of 'actual agency'.[10] This draft provision was retained as part of the 1996 draft, adopted by the International Law Commission (ILC) on first reading.[11]

4   In the same period, the International Court of Justice (ICJ) clarified the operation of the rule attributing private conduct to the State. In 1980, in the *Tehran Hostages* case, the ICJ held that the attack and seizure of the US Embassy in Tehran by militants 'might be considered as itself directly imputable to the Iranian State only if it were established that, in fact, on the occasion in question the militants acted *on behalf o[f] the State*, having been charged by some competent organ of the Iranian State to carry out a specific operation'.[12] The ICJ did not find 'such a link between the militants and any competent organ of the State'.

5   Six years later, in *Nicaragua*, the ICJ held that the conduct of *contras* (rebel groups fighting against the Nicaraguan government) could trigger the international responsibility of the United States if the United States had itself '*effective control* of the military or paramilitary operations in the course of which the alleged violations were committed'.[13] The ICJ did not find evidence of such level of control.[14] Roberto Ago, then an ICJ Judge, agreed with the majority's conclusion, but criticized the use of the notion of 'control' as a criterion for attributing the conduct of private entities to the State.[15]

6   In 1999, the International Criminal Tribunal for the Former Yugoslavia (ICTY) Appeals Chamber in the *Tadić* case also adopted the notion of 'control' to determine whether conduct by a 'military organization' consisting of Bosnian Serb armed forces could be attributed to the Yugoslavian State. In doing so, however, ICTY diverged from ICJ's high 'effective control' threshold and held that the requisite degree of control by the Yugoslavian authorities 'was *overall control* going beyond the mere financing and equipping of such forces and involving also participation in the planning and supervision of military operations'.[16]

7   The 'control' criterion made it to the next iteration of Article 8, after James Crawford became ILC Special Rapporteur. The revised formulation provided that the conduct shall be considered an act of a State under international law if '[t]he person or group of persons was *in fact acting on the instructions of, or under the direction and control* of, that State in carrying out the conduct'.[17] As Crawford later wrote, '[th]e ILC had the advantage of a number of decisions concerning direction and control between the first and second readings of the Articles [and] [a]s a result, it felt sufficiently confident to expand Draft Article 8 beyond attribution through instruction alone'.[18] The requisite degree of control was not included in

---

[10] ILC, 'Report of the International Law Commission on the Work of its 26th Session' (6 May–26 July 1974) UN Doc A/9610/Rev.1, 284–85; James Crawford, 'First report on State responsibility' (1998) UN Doc A.CN.4/490 and Add 1–7, 40.
[11] Draft Articles on State Responsibility with Commentaries thereto adopted by the International Law Commission on First Reading, YILC 1996, Vol II, Part Two.
[12] *United States Diplomatic and Consular Staff in Tehran (USA v Iran)* (Merits) [1980] ICJ Rep 3, para 58 (emphasis added) (hereafter *Tehran Hostages*).
[13] *Military and Paramilitary Activities in und against Nicaragua (Nicaragua v USA)* (Merits) [1986] ICJ Rep 14 para 115 (emphasis added) (hereafter *Nicaragua*).
[14] ibid para 116.
[15] *Military and Paramilitary Activities in und against Nicaragua (Nicaragua v USA)* (Merits, Separate Opinion of Judge Ago) [1986] ICJ Rep 181, paras 17–18, fn 1.
[16] *Prosecutor v Tadić* (Appeal Judgment), ICTY IT-94-1-A, 15 July 1999, para 145 (emphasis added) (hereafter *Tadić*).
[17] J Crawford, 'First report on State responsibility' (1998) UN Doc A.CN.4/490 and Add 1–7, 56 (emphasis added).
[18] J Crawford, *State Responsibility: The General Part* (CUP 2013) 147 (hereafter Crawford, *State Responsibility*).

the text of the article.[19] Before the final adoption of the Articles in 2001, the ILC Drafting Committee replaced the conjunction 'and' between 'direction and control' with the disjunction 'or', leading to the final iteration of Article 8[20]—whose core components will be discussed below. Six years later, in the *Bosnian Genocide* case, the ICJ reaffirmed the position it had held in *Nicaragua*, emphasizing the criterion of effective control over the broader general control used in *Tadić*.[21]

C. Scope and operation of the rule—analytical distinctions

I. Article 8 and non-ARSIWA rules governing attribution-related questions

Article 8, as all attribution rules formulated in the ARSIWA, is limited to the attribution **8** of conduct for the purposes of State responsibility for internationally wrongful acts.[22] This means that: (i) it cannot in itself create a primary obligation for the State;[23] and (ii) its scope is limited to the attribution of conduct which may constitute a violation of international law.

Thus, the scope of Article 8 must be distinguished from attribution-related matters governed **9** by domestic law, or by international law for purposes other than State responsibility.[24] While seemingly clear-cut in theory, this distinction is not always easily drawn in practice, mainly because the concepts and facts underlying the question of attribution of wrongful conduct may be largely the same as those relevant for answering other questions, e.g. whether non-wrongful conduct by entities (such as representations or the conclusion of a contract) is attributable to the State, whether a claimant's links to a State are such that they preclude the tribunal's jurisdiction (e.g. under Article 25 of the International Centre for Settlement of Investment Disputes (ICSID) Convention), etc.[25] Those questions may be governed by international law, but they fall outside the ARSIWA's ambit of application. That notwithstanding, tribunals have sometimes applied—questionably—the ARSIWA 'by analogy' in such cases.[26]

Moreover, the attribution rules codified in the ARSIWA are not relevant for the extension of **10** contractual obligations and should be distinguished from rules on agency under domestic law.[27] Article 8 'does not change the extent and content of the obligations arising under […]

---

[19] See further discussion on the notion of 'control' at Section D.II.2 below.
[20] ILC, 2562nd Meeting (13 August 1998) YILC1998, Vol I, 282, 289, para 79.
[21] *Bosnian Genocide* (n 4) paras 400–07.
[22] *CC/Devas (Mauritius) Ltd, Devas Employees Mauritius Private Limited, and Telcom Devas Mauritius Limited v Republic of India*, PCA Case No 2013-09, Award on Jurisdiction and Merits, 25 July 2016, para 276 (hereafter *CC/Devas v India*). See also in this Commentary: Chester Brown, 'Article 4 of the ARSIWA' and Jorge E Viñuales and Oliver Hailes, 'Article 5 of the ARSIWA'.
[23] See, eg, *Gavrilović v Croatia* (n 5) paras 779, 856; *Electrabel v Hungary* (n 2) para 7.61; *EDF (Services) Limited v Romania*, ICSID Case No ARB/05/13, Award, 8 October 2009, para 319 (hereafter *EDF v Romania*).
[24] On the law applicable to attribution-related issues, see Viñuales (n 8) paras 16–26.
[25] *Beijing Urban Construction Group Co Ltd v Republic of Yemen*, ICSID Case No ARB/14/30, Decision on Jurisdiction, 31 May 2017, para 34; *OAO Tatneft v Ukraine*, PCA Case No 2008–8, Partial Award on Jurisdiction, 28 September 2010, para 138.
[26] *Masdar Solar & Wind Cooperatief UA v Kingdom of Spain*, ICSID Case No ARB/14/1, Award, 16 May 2018, paras 166–77. See also *Landesbank Baden-Württemberg and Others v Kingdom of Spain*, ICSID Case No ARB/15/45, Decision on the Intra-EU Jurisdictional Objection, 25 February 2019, para 98; *Consorzio Groupement LESI-DIPENTA v People's Democratic Republic of Algeria*, ICSID Case No ARB/03/08, Award, 10 January 2005, s II, para 19.
[27] *Invesmart v Czech Republic*, UNCITRAL, Award, 26 June 2009, para 258. See also *CC/Devas v India* (n 22) paras 284–85, quoting J Crawford and S Olleson, 'The Application of the Rules of State Responsibility' in M Bungenberg and others (eds), *International Investment Law* (Nomos 2015), 414–15.

[c]ontract[s] […], that remain contractual, nor does it make [the State] party to such contracts'.[28] Hence, the question of whether a contract was entered into by the State, for the purposes of an umbrella clause, is not governed by the international rules of attribution codified in the ARSIWA.[29] Some tribunals, however, have misguidedly invoked international rules of attribution to address issues governed by domestic law, such as the creation of privity of contract with the State.[30]

11 As regards contractual conduct, however, it can be assessed pursuant to Article 8 of the ARSIWA.[31] The exercise of a contractual right (whether in breach of that contract or not)[32] may follow the instructions, direction, or control of the host State. The specific act (as clearly distinct from the contract itself) could therefore be attributed to the State under the international rules of attribution and, if in breach of a primary rule of international law, trigger the responsibility of the State for internationally wrongful acts.

II. Article 8 and other attribution rules under ARSIWA

12 Article 8 is one of the attribution rules most frequently invoked and applied by investor–State tribunals, along with Articles 4 and 5.[33] Claimants often invoke Article 8 as an alternative attribution argument in case recourse to Articles 4 and/or 5 fails.[34]

13 While Article 8 of the ARSIWA may cover the conduct of a range of different entities, including individuals and private entities such as unions, most cases where Article 8 has been invoked involve the conduct of State-owned companies or enterprises. Yet the conduct of

---

[28] *EDF v Romania* (n 23) paras 318–19. See also *Gavrilović v Croatia* (n 5) para 856; *Compañia de Aguas del Aconquija SA and Vivendi Universal v Argentine Republic*, ICSID Case No ARB/97/3, Decision on Annulment, 3 July 2002, para 96; *Impregilo SpA v Islamic Republic of Pakistan*, ICSID Case No ARB/03/3, Decision on Jurisdiction, 22 April 2005, para 216; *Gustav FW Hamester GmbH & Co KG v Republic of Ghana*, ICSID Case No ARB/07/24, Award, 18 June 2010, para 347 (hereafter *Hamester v Ghana*); *Limited Liability Company Amto v Ukraine*, SCC Case No 080/2005, Award, 26 March 2008, paras 110–12 (hereafter *Amto v Ukraine*).
[29] See also Crawford and Mertenskötter (n 7) 30–35 (discussing the different positions on this issue taken by academic commentary and practice, and supporting the position also taken in this entry).
[30] See, eg, *Ampal-American Israel Corporation and others v Arab Republic of Egypt*, ICSID Case No ARB/12/11, Decision on Liability and Heads of Loss, 21 February 2017, para 146 (hereafter *Ampal v Egypt*); *Strabag SE v Libya*, ICSID Case No ARB(AF)/15/1, Award, 29 June 2020, paras 176–87; *Bosh International, Inc and B&P Ltd Foreign Investments Enterprise v Ukraine*, ICSID Case No ARB/08/11, Award, 25 October 2012, para 246 (hereafter *Bosh v Ukraine*); *Karkey Karadeniz Elektrik Uretim AS v Islamic Republic of Pakistan*, ICSID Case No ARB/13/1, Award, 22 August 2017, para 593 (hereafter *Karkey v Pakistan*). This is not to say that the conclusions reached by these tribunals to 'attribute' the contractual obligations to the State were unjustified on the facts of the case (eg in *Ampal v Egypt*, the relevant contract stated that the Egyptian General Petroleum Corporation (EGPC) 'represented' the Ministry of Petroleum in the negotiation and conclusion of the agreement), but rather that it was questionable to do so on the basis of the ARSIWA. See also Viñuales (n 8) para 172.
[31] See, eg, *Bayindir v Pakistan* (n 5) paras 125–28; *CC/Devas v India* (n 22) paras 282–90; *Ampal v Egypt* (n 30) paras 142–46; *Mr Kristian Almås and Mr Geir Almås v The Republic of Poland*, PCA Case No 2015-13, Award, 27 June 2016, para 268 (hereafter *Almås v Poland*).
[32] The existence of a contractual breach will be determined under the law governing the contract. See, eg, *Ampal v Egypt* (n 30) para 81.
[33] See M Kinnear, 'ARSIWA, ISDS, and the Process of Developing an Investor–State Jurisprudence' (2022) 20 ICSID Rep 3, 7.
[34] See, eg, *Tulip v Turkey* (n 5) para 233; *White Industries Australia Limited v Republic of India*, UNCITRAL, Final Award, 30 November 2011, paras 8.1.2–8.1.7 (hereafter *White Industries v India*); *Staur Eiendom AS, EBO Invest AS and Rox Holding AS v Republic of Latvia*, ICSID Case No ARB/16/38, Award, 28 February 2020, para 271; *Ampal v Egypt* (n 30) para 168; *EDF v Romania* (n 23) para 187; *Hamester v Ghana* (n 28) para 158.

such instrumentalities may also fall under Article 4 (as *de facto* organs)[35] or, more likely, Article 5 of the ARSIWA, when the companies are formally exercising elements of governmental authority. That was reiterated by the *F-W Oil Interests v Trinidad and Tobago* tribunal, which added that:

> ... it is not the case that the same answer would necessarily emerge on every occasion; in some of its activities a State enterprise might fall on one side of the line, in others on the other. Considerations of a very similar kind would apply to the case lying on the outer edge of the spectrum of possibilities described above, that in which the State enterprise was not exercising 'governmental authority' as such, but has to be regarded as acting in fact on State instructions, or under State direction, or under State control.[36]

That may indeed be the case and may explain certain tribunals' reluctance to choose between the different attribution routes when determining the attribution of an instrumentality's conduct (especially in earlier investment awards).[37] **14**

Yet, the requirements for attribution under these rules remain distinct. These distinctions have already been drawn in previous entries of this volume.[38] With respect to Article 4, it bears recalling that the characterization of an entity as a *de facto* organ is subject to a more demanding test of 'complete dependence'[39] and has a wider scope of application, making all conduct (rather than specific acts) attributable. By contrast, attribution under Article 8 is governed by a test of 'effective control' (further discussed below) and can only lead to the attribution of specific conduct. Conduct of a person or entity which is not a *de facto* organ (i.e. which is not attributable under Article 4) may still be attributed through the Article 8 route. **15**

Both Articles 5 and 8 are limited to attribution of specific acts. Under Article 5, such acts must be performed in the exercise of elements of governmental authority (*prérogatives de la puissance publique*), formally empowered by law—thus excluding commercial acts. By contrast, commercial acts (or *acta jure gestionis*) may be attributed under Article 8 as long as they were performed in the particular instance under the instructions, direction, or control of the State.[40] **16**

Article 8 may operate in parallel to Article 4 or 5, to the extent that an organ, or a State instrumentality enjoying governmental authority and using it in a specific case, may exercise **17**

---

[35] See, eg, *Ampal v Egypt* (n 30) para 138; *Deutsche Bank AG v Democratic Socialist Republic of Sri Lanka*, ICSID Case No ARB/09/2, Award, 31 October 2012, para 405.

[36] *F-W Oil Interests, Inc v Republic of Trinidad and Tobago*, ICSID Case No ARB/01/14, Award, 3 March 2006, para 203 (hereafter *F-W Oil Interests v Trinidad and Tobago*).

[37] See, eg, *EnCana Corporation v Republic of Ecuador*, LCIA Case No UN3481, Award, 3 February 2006, para 154; *Waste Management v United Mexican States (II)*, ICSID Case No ARB(AF)/00/3, Award, 30 April 2004, para 75; *Chevron Bangladesh Block Twelve, Ltd and Chevron Bangladesh Blocks Thirteen and Fourteen, Ltd v People's Republic of Bangladesh*, ICSID Case No ARB/06/10, Award, 17 May 2010, para 171; *Amto v Ukraine* (n 28) para 102; *Nykomb Synergetics Technology Holding AB v The Republic of Latvia*, SCC Case No 118/2001, Award, 16 December 2003, 31. See also R Dolzer, C Schreuer and U Kriebaum, *Principles of International Investment Law* (2nd edn, OUP 2022) 315. For relevant tribunal decisions before the adoption of the ARSIWA, see *Amco Asia Corporation and Others v Republic of Indonesia*, ICSID Case No ARB/81/1, Award, 20 November 1984, paras 9, 158–62; *Tradex Hellas SA v Republic of Albania*, ICSID Case No ARB/94/2, Award, 29 April 1999, para 165 (hereafter *Tradex v Albania*); *Emilio Agustín Maffezini v The Kingdom of Spain*, ICSID Case No ARB/97/7, Decision of the Tribunal on Objections to Jurisdiction, 25 January 2000, paras 77–78.

[38] See in this Commentary: Chester Brown, 'Article 4 of the ARSIWA' and Jorge E Viñuales and Oliver Hailes, 'Article 5 of the ARSIWA'.

[39] *Bosnian Genocide* (n 4) paras 390–93.

[40] ARSIWA Commentaries (n 2) Article 8 para 2; *Bayindir v Pakistan* (n 5) para 129; *Hamester v Ghana* (n 28) para 203.

effective control over another entity.[41] Articles 5 and 8 may also apply simultaneously with regard to different acts of the same instrumentality, in the sense that an entity empowered to exercise elements of governmental authority would have any acts performed within the limits of that authority attributed under Article 5, but could also perform other acts, falling outside its governmental purview, under State instructions, direction, or control and, therefore, attributable under Article 8.

18 Like most attribution routes under Chapter II of the ARSIWA, the attribution requirements under Article 8 of the ARSIWA need to be met at the time of the alleged wrongful act. In particular, under Article 8 the relevant instructions must have been given or the direction or control must have been exercised before the impugned conduct.[42] In contrast, Article 11 'provides for the attribution to a State of conduct that was not or may not have been attributable to it at the time of commission, but which is subsequently acknowledged and adopted by the State as its own'.[43]

D. Components of the rule through the lens of investment tribunals

I. 'Person or a group of persons'

19 Article 8 uses the term 'person or group of persons'. This broad formulation covers conduct by natural persons, legal entities such as corporations (State-owned or not), as well as groups of individuals that do not have separate legal personality but are nonetheless acting as a collective.[44]

20 This wording of Article 8 could be contrasted with Article 5 of the ARSIWA, which refers to 'conduct of a person or entity' rather than 'persons or group of persons'. However, this divergence should not be construed as excluding the attribution of acts of corporations from Article 8 of the ARSIWA, given that 'person' is widely recognized in modern legal systems, including investment treaties, as including both natural and legal persons.[45] Such was the view of the *CC/Devas v India* tribunal which—through an implied but clear application of the principle of effectiveness (*effet utile*)—found that, 'it would make no sense to impose a restrictive interpretation that would allow a State to circumvent the rules of attribution by sending its direction or instruction to a corporate entity rather than a physical person or group of physical persons'.[46]

21 In addition, the Commentary to Article 8 of the ARSIWA clarifies that 'it does not matter that the person or persons involved are private individuals'.[47] It follows that acts performed in a private capacity (as opposed to 'official capacity', i.e. 'carried out by persons cloaked with governmental authority') are also attributable under Article 8.[48]

---

[41] ARSIWA Commentaries (n 2) Article 4 para 2.
[42] See, eg, *Bernhard von Pezold and Others v Republic of Zimbabwe*, ICSID Case No ARB/10/15, Award, 28 July 2015, para 448 (hereafter *Pezold v Zimbabwe*).
[43] ARSIWA Commentaries (n 2) Article 11 para 1.
[44] ibid Article 8 para 9.
[45] *CC/Devas v India* (n 22) para 278.
[46] ibid para 280.
[47] ARSIWA Commentaries (n 2) Article 8 para 2.
[48] In contrast Articles 4 and 5 only cover conduct performed in the entity's official capacity; See in this Commentary: Chester Brown, 'Article 4 of the ARSIWA' and Jorge E Viñuales and Oliver Hailes, 'Article 5 of the ARSIWA'.

II. 'In fact acting on the instructions of, or under the direction or control of, that State'

1. Disjunctive nature of the test

Article 8 includes three disjunctive criteria: 'instructions', 'direction', or 'control'. As affirmed by the ARSIWA Commentary and investment tribunals, their disjunctive character means that only one of these elements needs to be satisfied for the purposes of attribution under Article 8.[49]

While these terms are intended to function disjunctively, tribunals often refer to and apply the provision *en bloc*, without distinguishing between the existence of instruction, direction, or control.[50] This is not particularly surprising or problematic as such, considering that the respective notions are semantically very close, not always easily distinguishable and often converge on the facts of the case. The disjunctive listing of criteria appears to be a pragmatic approach fit to cover all relevant factual manifestations, and capture situations where 'instructions', 'direction', or 'control' do not fully converge.[51]

This does not mean however that the standard of attribution is different under each of these prongs. The 'effective control' standard is the umbrella test, some elements of which include 'control' but also 'instructions' and 'direction'.[52] Put simply, mere instructions without a showing of effective control over the specific conduct are insufficient for attribution under Article 8—as further discussed below.

2. Acting under the direction or control of the State

Direction of persons or groups of persons 'involves ordering or commanding those persons to undertake a certain conduct'[53] or 'implies a continuing period of instruction, or a relationship between the state and a non-state entity such that suggestion or innuendo may give rise to responsibility'.[54] Those remarks aside, little has been written on the notion of direction and how it differs from the notion of 'control'.[55]

Conversely, the concept of 'control', and specifically the level of control required for attribution under Article 8, has been subject to extensive debate, which led to a division into two interpretative camps: the higher threshold of 'effective control' over the specific conduct in question, originally developed by the ICJ in *Nicaragua* and further refined in *Bosnia Genocide*, on the one hand;[56] and the less-demanding 'overall control' over the entity, introduced by the ICTY Appeals Chamber in *Tadić* and reaffirmed in the tribunal's later decisions, on the other hand.[57] In the *Bosnian Genocide* case, the ICJ noted that the 'overall control' test was unpersuasive in the context of State responsibility, regardless of the particular factual context,[58] 'for it stretches too far, almost to breaking point, the connection

---

[49] ARSIWA Commentaries (n 2) Article 8 para 7; *Tulip v Turkey* (n 5) para 303; *Karkey v Pakistan* (n 30) para 569; *Ortiz v Algeria* (n 5) para 239.
[50] *Ampal v Egypt* (n 30) para 146; Crawford, *State Responsibility* (n 18) 146.
[51] See, eg, *Karkey v Pakistan* (n 30) para 593. See also Viñuales (n 8) para 103.
[52] See also Viñuales (n 8) para 103.
[53] A Cassese, 'The Nicaragua and Tadić Tests Revisited in Light of the ICJ Judgment on Genocide in Bosnia' (2007) 18 EJIL 649, 663.
[54] Crawford, *State Responsibility* (n 18) 146.
[55] ibid.
[56] *Nicaragua* (n 13) 64 para 115; *Bosnian Genocide* (n 4) paras 404–07.
[57] *Tadić* (n 16) para 145.
[58] *Bosnian Genocide* (n 4) para 404.

which must exist between the conduct of a State's organs and its international responsibility'.[59] This debate has largely subsided in favour of the 'effective control' test. As confirmed in 2018 by the *Marfin v Cyprus* tribunal, 'arbitral jurisprudence has consistently upheld the standard set by the ICJ' forming a '*jurisprudence constante*'.[60] Tribunals have considered this 'very demanding threshold' to be in consonance with the exceptional nature of attribution under Article 8.[61]

27 This 'effective control' test involves two aspects: (i) determining whether the entity in question is under the general control of the State, and (ii) determining whether the State has exercised specific control during the act whose attribution to the State is claimed.[62] The effective control, which must extend to the conduct challenged before the tribunal, needs to be established regardless of whether the 'special factual relationship' between the State and the public or private entity in question is subsumed under the 'direction' or 'control' criteria of Article 8. As confirmed by the ARSIWA Commentary, '[s]uch conduct will be attributable to the State only if it directed or controlled the specific operation and the conduct complained of was an integral part of that operation'.[63] For the conduct of an entity, this means, in practice, that the fact that the State initially established a corporate entity or that the State owns the majority or the entirety of the shares of the company is not sufficient to show effective control and therefore establish attribution under Article 8.[64]

28 The answer to the question of what is actually required to prove effective control is case-specific. The ARSIWA Commentary contemplates the possibility that a State may use 'its ownership interest in or control of a corporation specifically in order to achieve a particular result'.[65] The tribunals in *Tulip v Turkey* and *EDF v Romania* interpreted that reference as establishing a subjective test, i.e. a mismatch between what the addressee of the instruction or direction perceives to be its commercial interest and the course of action imposed by the State.[66] That mismatch between the political benefits and the commercial interests from the conduct at stake was also taken into account by the *UFG v Egypt* tribunal, which found that the curtailment in the supply of natural gas to the claimant by the Egyptian Natural Gas Holding Company (EGAS) in favour of other users was under the direction of the Egyptian Ministry of Petroleum.[67] While such a mismatch may provide evidence that the State exercised political control and drove the decision eventually taken (as opposed to 'the ordinary control exercised by a majority shareholder acting in the company's perceived commercial

---

[59] ibid para 406.
[60] *Marfin Investment Group Holdings SA, Alexandros Bakatselos and others v Republic of Cyprus*, ICSID Case No ARB/13/27, Award, 26 July 2018, para 675 (hereafter *Marfin v Cyprus*). See also Shirlow and Duggal (n 7) 384.
[61] *Hamester v Ghana* (n 28) para 179; *Marfin v Cyprus* (n 60) para 674; *Jan de Nul v Egypt* (n 5) para 173; *Almås v Poland* (n 31) para 269; *Muhammet Cap & Sehil Insaat Endustri ve Ticaret Ltd Sti v Turkmenistan*, ICSID Case No ARB/12/6, Award, 4 May 2021, para 774 (hereafter *Muhammet v Turkmenistan*); *EDF v Romania* (n 23) paras 318–19; *White Industries v India* (n 34) paras 8.1.4 and 8.1.10.
[62] *Ortiz v Algeria* (n 5) para 247. See also *Gavrilović v Croatia* (n 5) para 828; *Jan de Nul v Egypt* (n 5) para 173; *Teinver SA, Transportes de Cercanías SA and Autobuses Urbanos del Sur SA v Argentine Republic*, ICSID Case No ARB/09/1, Award, 21 July 2017, paras 723–24.
[63] ARSIWA Commentaries (n 2) Article 8 para 4. See also *Bosnian Genocide* (n 4) para 400.
[64] ARSIWA Commentaries (n 2) Article 8 para 6; *Ortiz v Algeria* (n 5) para 254; *Marfin v Cyprus* (n 60) para 691; *Tulip v Turkey* (n 5) paras 306–09; *Muhammet v Turkmenistan* (n 61) paras 775–77; *Yukos Universal Limited (Isle of Man) v The Russian Federation*, PCA Case No 2005-04/AA227, Final Award, 18 July 2014, para 1468 (hereafter *Yukos v Russia*); *MNSS BV and Recupero Credito Acciaio NV v Montenegro*, ICSID Case No ARB(AF)/12/8, Award, 4 May 2016, para 299.
[65] ARSIWA Commentaries (n 2) Article 8 para 6.
[66] *EDF v Romania* (n 23) paras 201–13; *Tulip v Turkey* (n 5) para 309.
[67] *UFG v Egypt* (n 5) paras 9.118, 9.137–9.138.

best interests'[68]), it is not a requirement under Article 8. In fact, a State may direct an entity to act in a certain way which is also advantageous commercially.[69]

3. Acting on the instructions of the State

While the 'instructions' criterion is often treated as the more straightforward of the elements under Article 8, its application is not without difficulties. Article 8 does not require any specific form or way in which the instructions are given to satisfy the requisite attribution threshold. However, questions often arise in practice concerning the required level of specificity and the level of command involved in the exhortation to act, i.e. the impulsion/imperativeness of the instruction. **29**

The instructions must be specific. To satisfy this test, State instructions must have been given 'in respect of each operation in which the alleged violations occurred, not generally in respect of the overall actions taken by the persons or groups of persons having committed the violation'.[70] Therefore, general declarations or policies would not meet this test. In the *Tehran Hostages* case, the ICJ did not regard the 'general declarations of the Ayatollah Khomeini to the people or students of Iran as amounting to an authorization from the State to undertake the specific operation of invading and seizing the United States Embassy'.[71] In a similar vein, in *Hamester v Ghana*, a general policy on equitable cocoa distribution was deemed to be insufficient to convey an instruction or direction to the relevant entity, Cocobod, regarding the non-delivery of cocoa beans to the claimant.[72] **30**

It is not enough for the instructions to be specific. They also need to lead to a particular result.[73] This means that if a person receives the instruction to perform certain act and they do not perform it or perform a different one, the mere issuance of an instruction would not make the divergent part of the act attributable.[74] **31**

By its very focus, which requires specific instructions to be followed by a private person or group, *ultra vires* conduct is in principle not attributable under Article 8.[75] In *Ortiz v Algeria*, the tribunal held that the fact that the National Company for Real Estate Promotion did not follow an instruction from the Ministry of Housing meant that the specific action could not be attributed under Article 8.[76] There is one exception, according to the ARSIWA Commentary, when the *ultra vires* act 'was really incidental to the mission' as opposed to 'clearly [going] beyond it'.[77] The same test applies in cases where a person or group of persons carrying out lawful instructions or directions, engage in some activity which contravenes both the instructions or directions given and the international obligations of the instructing State. In case that 'unlawful or unauthorized conduct was really incidental to the mission' it will fall under the instructions of the State and will thus be attributable under Article 8.[78] **32**

---

[68] *Tulip v Turkey* (n 5) para 309.
[69] See also Viñuales (n 8) para 105.
[70] *Almås v Poland* (n 31) para 268; *Bosnian Genocide* (n 4) para 400.
[71] *Tehran Hostages* (n 12) para 59.
[72] *Hamester v Ghana* (n 28) para 267.
[73] ARSIWA Commentaries (n 2) Article 8 para 6.
[74] *Ortiz v Algeria* (n 5) para 252.
[75] See Viñuales (n 8) paras 117 and 154. See in this Commentary: Chester Brown, 'Article 7 of the ARSIWA'.
[76] *Ortiz v Algeria* (n 5) para 252.
[77] ARSIWA Commentaries (n 2) Article 8 para 8. See also Viñuales (n 8) para 117.
[78] ARSIWA Commentaries (n 2) Article 8 para 8.

33 The instruction must also be imperative. This does not mean that it needs to be legally binding; rather, what is imperative will largely depend on the specific political and administrative context. Recommendations, suggestions, or exhortations, which leave the recipient margin for their own decision-making, would typically not be considered instructions under Article 8. By the same token, an invitation to negotiation could not constitute an instruction—as confirmed by *the EDF v Romania* tribunal.[79] Mere encouragement by the State would not meet the test under Article 8 either.[80]

34 Relatedly, instruction requires a form of impulsion coming from the State organ in question. This means that mere permission or passive assent to act in a certain way is not equivalent to an instruction. At first, the conclusion of the *Bayindir* tribunal may seem to contradict this proposition. To recall, the *Bayindir* tribunal concluded that 'express clearance' from the then military ruler of Pakistan was sufficient to consider the decision of the National Highway Authority (NHA) to terminate the contract in question as attributable to the State.[81] But, aside from the fact that the *Bayindir* test is not representative of the operation of attribution under Article 8, the sufficiency of express clearance can only be understood in the specific circumstances of the case, i.e. a highly concentrated political authority in the hands of the leader (often found in authoritarian regimes) where certain actions would not be expected to proceed without at least passive approval from the leader.[82] In *Ampal v Egypt*, the tribunal found that the relevant conduct had 'the *blessing* of the highest levels of the Egyptian Government' and was 'attributable to the Respondent pursuant to Article 8' ARSIWA.[83] While the use of the term 'blessing' may appear as if the tribunal considered the government's permission or mere encouragement as sufficient for the purposes of attribution, the tribunal's factual reasoning reveals that it considered, *inter alia*, that the termination of the contract in question by EGAS was discussed and confirmed by the Egyptian Minister of Petroleum and several other Ministers, as chair and members of the Board of Directors of the Egyptian General Petroleum Corporation (EGPC) already found to be an organ of the State.[84]

35 Proof of instruction may be difficult to provide. In *CC/Devas v India*, there was a paper trail from the government of India authorizing the Department of Space to 'instruct Antrix [a State-owned company] to annul the Antrix-Devas contract'.[85] In *Yukos v Russia*, the tribunal found Rosneft's purchase of Yuganskneftegaz shares attributable under Article 8, noting that 'it would be difficult, if not impossible, to prove that Rosneft in so acting, did so at the instructions or direction, or under the control of the Russian State—but for one remarkable fortuity': President Putin's public acceptance that the relevant conduct was an action in the State's 'own interest'.[86]

36 The specific context and the way political authority operates in the State in question plays an important role not only in determining whether the exhortation in question is imperative enough, but also in ascertaining the very existence of said exhortation. The *UAB v Latvia*

---

[79] *EDF v Romania* (n 23) paras 204–720; *Ortiz v Algeria* (n 5) para 242.
[80] *Pezold v Zimbabwe* (n 42) para 448; *Tradex v Albania* (n 37) para 165.
[81] *Bayindir v Pakistan* (n 5) paras 125 and 128.
[82] Pakistan was under military rule at the relevant time, and it became apparent during the hearing on merits that General Musharraf gave clearance to the National Highway Authority (NHA) chairman to resort to contractual termination; *Bayindir v Pakistan* (n 5) para 128.
[83] *Ampal v Egypt* (n 30) para 146 (emphasis added).
[84] ibid paras 142–46.
[85] *CC/Devas v India* (n 22) para 289.
[86] *Yukos v Russia* (n 64) paras 1469–72.

tribunal held that there was 'a dearth of direct evidence as to any such instruction, direction or control in this case', but that there was 'a body of circumstantial evidence which, taken as a whole, permits the inference that the Municipality (as an organ of the Respondent) must have instructed Rēzeknes Siltumtīkli and Rēzeknes Enerģija [two Municipality-owned companies] to bring the claims against Latgales Enerģija [claimant's subsidiary] and must have instructed Rēzeknes Siltumtīkli not to comply with the October 2007 Agreement'.[87] In *Venezuela US v Venezuela*, the tribunal considered that, for attribution purposes, it would be 'too much to ask from [the claimant] to adduce direct proof that this payment [to Petrobras] was carried out under the instruction of the Venezuelan Government'. Noting the temporal 'coincidence' between said payment to Petrobras and a visit from Venezuela's President to Brazil, the tribunal considered that it could operate under a 'presumption that the payment was made under the instruction of the Government of Venezuela'.[88]

E. General and special rules of attribution of conduct under direction or control

All rules codified in ARSIWA are 'residual' in their operation. Article 55 ARSIWA expressly stipulates that States are free to agree to special international law rules regarding State responsibility—including on the attribution of State conduct.[89] Indeed, as the tribunal in *F-W Oil Interests v Trinidad & Tobago* observed, 'particular standards of attributability may apply, as *lex specialis*, in substitute for or supplementation of the general rules of State responsibility'.[90] **37**

Investment tribunals have often been asked to interpret and apply special attribution rules in treaties, such as North American Free Trade Agreement (NAFTA),[91] the Energy Charter Treaty (ECT),[92] the US–Oman Free Trade Agreement (FTA),[93] the US–Korea FTA,[94] or EU secondary legislation[95] among others. Most of these purported special attribution rules refer to 'State enterprises' or 'non-governmental bodies'. These provisions do not specifically address conduct performed under State direction or control. Yet, one relevant and important question that arises is whether such special provisions governing the attributability of conduct of State entities and/or non-governmental bodies, would not only displace the application of Article 5 ARSIWA, but would also preclude the application of the 'additional' attribution route under Article 8. **38**

---

[87] *UAB E energija v Republic of Latvia*, ICSID Case No ARB/12/33, Award, 22 December 2017, paras 826–27.
[88] *Venezuela US, SRL v Bolivarian Republic of Venezuela*, PCA Case No 2013-34, Partial Award, Jurisdiction and Liability, 5 February 2021, paras 220–22.
[89] See also in this Commentary: Fernando Bordin, 'Article 55 of the ARSIWA'; Chester Brown, 'Article 4 of the ARSIWA'; Jorge E Viñuales and Oliver Hailes, 'Article 5 of the ARSIWA'.
[90] *F-W Oil Interests v Trinidad and Tobago* (n 36) para 206.
[91] *United Parcel Service of America, Inc v Government of Canada*, ICSID Case No UNCT/02/1, Award on the Merits, 24 May 2007, para 62; *Mesa Power Group, LLC v Government of Canada*, UNCITRAL, PCA Case No 2012-17, Award, 24 March 2016, paras 362–64.
[92] *Amto v Ukraine* (n 28) para 112 (discussing Article 22(1) ECT).
[93] *Al Tamimi v Sultanate of Oman*, ICSID Case No ARB/11/33, Award, 27 October 2015, paras 318–21 (hereafter *Al Tamimi v Oman*).
[94] *Elliott Associates LP v Republic of Korea*, PCA Case No 2018-51, Award, 20 June 2023, paras 439–40, 446 (hereafter *Elliott v ROK*).
[95] See, eg, *InterTrade Holding GmbH v Czech Republic*, PCA Case No 2009-12, Final Award, 29 May 2012, para 189.

39 An example is *Al Tamimi v Oman*, where the tribunal found that Article 10.1.2 of the US–Oman FTA[96] set out a 'relatively narrow test for the circumstances under which the actions of a state enterprise may be attributed to the State', and decided that it applied as *lex specialis* with regard to the attribution of conduct of State enterprises, substituting the general attribution rules under ARSIWA 5 and 8 alike.[97] The *Al Tamimi* tribunal's approach has been questioned on the grounds that the substance of the rule under Article 10.1.2 of the US–Oman FTA does not appear to differ from Article 5 ARSIWA, and 'the express inclusion of such an attribution rule by converse implication does not, as a matter of some kind of logical necessity, exclude the applicability of other ASR attribution rules' (such as Article 8 of the ARSIWA).[98]

40 One separate but relevant sub-question is whether there are any special attribution rules arising not from a treaty provision but from the specific context of investment law. The tribunal in *Bayindir v Pakistan* alluded to this possibility. To recall, the tribunal found that the exercise of a contractual right (the termination of a construction contract) by a Pakistani instrumentality had been under the direction or control of the government (due to government 'clearance') and was therefore attributable under Article 8. In reaching this conclusion, the tribunal appeared to suggest that the 'realities of international economic law' may call for a different approach to the standard under Article 8 in the investment context.[99]

41 Yet, a systematic review of the now mature body of investment cases dealing with attribution, as recently summarized in *Ortiz v Algeria*,[100] makes it clear that the applicable rules are those of general international law as codified in the ARSIWA, and there is no clear investment-specific test for the operation of Article 8.[101] Indicatively, the *Ortiz* tribunal readily rejected the claimant's argument that '[t]he effective control … should be adjusted to take into account economic realities', and applied the 'effective control' test, reiterating the ICJ's conclusion in *Bosnia Genocide*.[102]

F. Concluding observations: confined or general contribution?

42 Investment tribunals are 'the most prolific users' of the ARSIWA.[103] This holds especially true for the attribution rules enshrined therein. Over the years, the body of investment cases

---

[96] This provision reads in relevant part as follows: '[a] Party's obligations … shall apply to a state enterprise or other person when it exercises any regulatory, administrative, or other governmental authority delegated to it by that Party'.

[97] *Al Tamimi v Oman* (n 93) paras 318–22. The respondent in *Elliott v Republic of Korea* made a similar argument, based on Article 11.1.3 of the US–Korea FTA, providing that 'measures adopted or maintained by a Party means measures adopted or maintained by: (a) central, regional, or local governments or authorities; and (b) non-governmental bodies in the exercise of powers delegated by central, regional, or local governments or authorities'; *Elliott v ROK* (n 94) paras 364–67, 438–46. The tribunal eventually found attribution under Article 11.1.3 and did not address the availability of the Article 8 attribution route under the US–Korea FTA.

[98] M Milanovic, 'Special Rules of Attribution of Conduct in International Law' (2020) 96 Int Law Stud 295, 308–09. For further analysis of special treaty-based rules in investment cases (and potential issues with the tribunals' decisions), see Viñuales (n 8) paras 30–43.

[99] *Bayindir v Pakistan* (n 5) para 130.

[100] *Ortiz v Algeria* (n 5) paras 159–70 on Article 4, paras 193–204 on Article 5, paras 238–48 on Article 8.

[101] See also Shirlow and Duggal (n 7) 383–84.

[102] *Ortiz v Algeria* (n 5) para 244, citing *Bosnian Genocide* (n 4) para 406 (English translation of *Ortiz v Algeria* published in 20 ICSID Rep 571).

[103] J Crawford and F Baetens, 'The ILC Articles on State Responsibility: More than a "Plank in a Shipwreck"?' (2022) 37 ICSID Rev 13.

dealing with attribution has matured. Despite some 'confused debate[s]'[104] and 'less fortunate tendencies',[105] the jurisprudence of investment tribunals has gradually become an important vector in the consolidation of the general international law of attribution. Article 8 is a case in point. As aptly observed by two commentators, '[t]he references to article 8 over the last 10 years also indicate a *qualitative shift* away from the suggestion of the *Bayindir v Pakistan* [tribunal] in 2009 that the levels of control required for attribution under article 8 in other areas of international law were "not always adapted to the realities of international economic law and that they should not prevent a finding of attribution if the specific facts of an investment dispute so warrant"'.[106] It is now well-established that, in the absence of express *lex specialis* rules, international adjudicators must interpret and apply the same international attribution rules based on the same standards.

The question that arises is whether the investment jurisprudence could be extrapolated to other types of disputes. In theory, we see no cogent reason why international adjudicators could not benefit from investment tribunals' analysis of attribution rules as codified in ARSIWA. International investment law is no longer an 'exotic and highly specialised' domain.[107] Investment arbitration 'is essentially a public international law dispute settlement mechanism' regularly addressing questions of general international law.[108] In practice, however, the areas of divergence or confusion across investment decisions significantly reduce their ability to provide a unified authoritative view like the one emerging from ICJ decisions.

For the rule codified in Article 8 of the ARSIWA, the body of ICJ practice is solid and detailed enough to settle the principle. However, given the wide variety of circumstances in which the principle is called to operate, the understanding of Article 8 can greatly benefit from the frequent stress-testing provided by the investment jurisprudence. Whether other international courts are willing or not to explicitly refer to investment cases, the conceptual testing and refining can follow a range of other channels, including through references to legal commentary, pleadings of parties and, of course, the possibility that judges may sit as arbitrators (or that arbitrators may become judges). At that level, the investment jurisprudence is likely to play a growing role in clarifying the operation of the rule codified in Article 8 of the ARSIWA.

Selected literature

Crawford J, *State Responsibility: The General Part* (CUP 2013).

Crawford J, 'Investment Arbitration and the ILC Articles on State Responsibility' (2010) 25 ICSID Rev 127.

Crawford J and Baetens F, 'The ILC Articles on State Responsibility: More than a "Plank in a Shipwreck"?' (2022) 37 ICSID Rev 13.

---

[104] Crawford and Mertenskötter (n 7) 30.

[105] S Wittich, 'Investment Arbitration as an Engine of Development of the Rules of Attribution–With Particular Focus on Lex Specialis and de Facto State Organs' in CJ Tams, S Schill and R Hofmann (eds), *International Investment Law and General International Law* (Edward Elgar Publishing 2023) 186–88.

[106] Shirlow and Duggal (n 7) 383–84 (emphasis added).

[107] ILC, 'Fragmentation of International Law: Difficulties Arising from the Diversification and Expansion of International Law, Report of the Study Group (Martti Koskenniemi)' (13 April 2006) UN Doc A/CN.4/L.682, para 8.

[108] E De Brabandere, *Investment Treaty Arbitration as Public International Law: Procedural Aspects and Implications* (CUP 2014) 202.

Crawford J and Mertenskötter P, 'The Use of the ILC's Attribution Rules in Investment Arbitration' in Kinnear M and others (eds), *Building International Investment Law—The First 50 Years of ICSID* (Kluwer 2016).

De Stefano C, *Attribution in International Law and Arbitration* (OUP 2020).

Kinnear M, 'ARSIWA, ISDS, and the Process of Developing an Investor–State Jurisprudence' (2022) 20 ICSID Rep 3.

Kovács C, *Attribution in International Investment Law* (Kluwer Law International 2018).

Shirlow E and Duggal K, 'The ILC Articles on State Responsibility in Investment Treaty Arbitration' (2022) 37 ICSID Rev 378.

Viñuales JE and Waibel M (eds), *ICSID Reports: Attribution of Conduct to States in Investment Arbitration*, Vol 20 (CUP 2022).

Selected decisions

Amco Asia Corporation and Others v Republic of Indonesia, ICSID Case No ARB/81/1, Award, 20 November 1984.

Application of the Convention on the Prevention and Punishment of the Crime of Genocide (Bosnia and Herzegovina v Serbia and Montenegro) (Judgment) [2007] ICJ Rep 43.

Bernhard von Pezold and Others v Republic of Zimbabwe, ICSID Case No ARB/10/15, Award, 28 July 2015.

Chevron Bangladesh Block Twelve, Ltd and Chevron Bangladesh Blocks Thirteen and Fourteen, Ltd v People's Republic of Bangladesh, ICSID Case No ARB/06/10, Award, 17 May 2010.

Compañia de Aguas del Aconquija S.A. and Vivendi Universal v Argentine Republic, ICSID Case No ARB/97/3, Decision on Annulment, 3 July 2002.

EDF (Services) Limited v Romania, ICSID Case No ARB/05/13, Award, 8 October 2009.

Electrabel SA v Republic of Hungary, ICSID Case No ARB/07/19, Decision on Jurisdiction, Applicable Law and Liability, 30 November 2012.

Gustav FW Hamester GmbH & Co KG v Republic of Ghana, ICSID Case No ARB/07/24, Award, 18 June 2010.

Jan de Nul NV and Dredging International NV v Arab Republic of Egypt, ICSID Case No ARB/04/13, Award, 6 November 2008.

Military and Paramilitary Activities in und against Nicaragua (Nicaragua v USA) (Merits) [1986] ICJ Rep 14.

Muhammet Cap & Sehil Insaat Endustri ve Ticaret Ltd Sti v Turkmenistan, ICSID Case No ARB/12/6, Award, 4 May 2021.

Prosecutor v Tadić (Appeal Judgment), ICTY IT-94-1-A, 15 July 1999.

Teinver SA, Transportes de Cercanías SA and Autobuses Urbanos del Sur SA v Argentine Republic, ICSID Case No ARB/09/1, Award, 21 July 2017.

Tradex Hellas SA v Republic of Albania, ICSID Case No ARB/94/2, Award, 29 April 1999.

United States Diplomatic and Consular Staff in Tehran (USA v Iran) (Merits) [1980] ICJ Rep 3.

Venezuela US, SRL v Bolivarian Republic of Venezuela, PCA Case No 2013-34, Partial Award, Jurisdiction and Liability, 5 February 2021.

White Industries Australia Limited v Republic of India, UNCITRAL, Final Award, 30 November 2011.

Article 13 of the ARSIWA

International obligation in force for a State

Claudia Annacker and Enikő Horváth

An act of a State does not constitute a breach of an international obligation unless the State is bound by the obligation in question at the time the act occurs.

A. Introduction	1	D. Conclusion: Alignment of general international law and international investment law	12
B. Application in general international law	2		
C. Application in international investment law	5		

A. Introduction

Article 13 applies the basic principle of non-retroactivity in the field of State responsibility: a State can only be responsible for breach of an international obligation if the obligation is in force for the State at the time of the alleged breach. The principle is well established and considered to be part of customary international law and/or a general principle of law.[1] Article 28 Vienna Convention on the Law of Treaties (VCLT) codifies the corresponding rule in the field of the law of treaties. **1**

B. Application in general international law

International courts and tribunals—including the International Court of Justice (ICJ),[2] the European Court of Human Rights (ECtHR),[3] ad hoc tribunals,[4] World Trade Organization **2**

---

[1] ILC, 'Draft Articles on Responsibility of States for Internationally Wrongful Acts, with Commentaries' YILC 2001, Vol II, Part Two, 31, Article 13 para 9 (hereafter ARSIWA Commentaries); M Kotzur, 'Intertemporal Law', in *Max Planck Encyclopedia of Public International Law* (OUP 2008), para 5; Institut de Droit International, 'The Intertemporal Problem in Public International Law' (11 August 1975), Article 1.

[2] eg, *Jurisdictional Immunities of the State (Germany v Italy: Greece intervening)* (Judgment) [2012] ICJ Rep 99, para 58. See also *Land and Maritime Boundary between Cameroon and Nigeria (Cameroon v Nigeria: Equatorial Guinea intervening)* (Judgment) [2002] ICJ Rep 303, para 205; *Questions relating to the Obligation to Prosecute or Extradite (Belgium v Senegal)* (Judgment) [2012] ICJ Rep 422, paras 100, 102.

[3] eg, *Janowiec and Others v Russia* App nos 55508/07 and 29520/09 (ECtHR, 21 October 2013), para 128; *Blečić v Croatia* App no 59532/00 (ECtHR, 8 March 2006), para 90.

[4] *Island of Palmas Case (Netherlands v United States of America)* (1928) II RIAA 845, 4 April 1928; *Case concerning the difference between New Zealand and France concerning the interpretation or application of two*

(WTO) panels,[5] the Iran–United States Claims Tribunal (IUSCT),[6] and the Court of Justice of the European Union (CJEU)[7]—consistently affirm that State conduct only constitutes a breach of an international obligation if the obligation is in force at the time of the State conduct. Conversely, once State responsibility has accrued, it is not affected by the termination of the international obligation.[8]

3   International courts and tribunals most frequently refer to Article 13 in ruling on their temporal jurisdiction. Jurisdiction *ratione temporis* is distinct from the temporal applicability of the obligation(s) for breach of which the State may incur responsibility, and may extend to disputes that arose, or concern facts that arose, before the entry into force of the jurisdictional clause. The Permanent Court of International Justice (PCIJ) and ICJ have taken the position that their jurisdiction covers all disputes referred to them after their establishment, unless this is specifically excluded by the jurisdictional title.[9] The ICJ has also assumed jurisdiction over conduct that occurred after the jurisdictional title ceased to be in force where the relevant conduct arose directly out of the subject-matter of the application, was connected to prior conduct already found to fall within its jurisdiction, and did not transform the nature of the dispute.[10] However, if a dispute resolution provision in a treaty is limited to claims alleging a violation of that treaty, the principle of non-retroactivity reflected in Article 13 also operates to limit the application of the dispute settlement clause *ratione temporis*.[11]

4   The principle of non-retroactivity does not rule out the evolutionary interpretation of treaty provisions,[12] which is a question of treaty interpretation.[13] Nor does it prevent an international court or tribunal from considering State conduct prior to the entry into force of the obligation for the State for certain purposes. Such conduct may be taken into account as general background,[14] including to place into context acts or omissions occurring after the entry into force of the obligation.[15]

---

agreements, concluded on 9 July 1986 between the two States and which related to the problems arising from the Rainbow Warrior Affair (1990), XX RIAA 215, 30 April 1990, paras 105–06 (hereafter *Rainbow Warrior*).

[5] eg, WTO, *Brazil—Measures Affecting Desiccated Coconut—Appellate Body Report* (20 March 1997) WT/DS22/AB/R, 15; WTO, *European Communities—Regime for the Importation, Sale and Distribution of Bananas, Complaint by the United States—Panel Report* (25 September 1997) WT/DS27/R/USA, para 7.308, fn 486; WTO, *EC Measures Concerning Meat and Meat Products (Hormones)—Appellate Body Report* (13 February 1998) WT/DS26/AB/R and WT/DS48/AB/R, para 128.

[6] eg, *Amoco International Finance Corp v Government of the Islamic Republic of Iran, et al* (1987) 15 IUSCT 189, para 90.

[7] eg, CJEU Case C-466/11, *Gennaro Currà and Others v Bundesrepublik Deutschland* [2012], paras 22–24.

[8] eg, *Case concerning the Northern Cameroons (Cameroon v United Kingdom)* (Judgment) [1963] ICJ Rep 15, 35; *Rainbow Warrior* (n 4) para 106.

[9] *Mavrommatis Palestine Concessions (United Kingdom v Greece)* (Judgment No 2) [1924] PCIJ Rep Series A No 2, 35; *Anglo-Iranian Oil Co Case (United Kingdom v Iran)* (Judgment) [1952] ICJ Rep 93, 106.

[10] *Alleged Violations of Sovereign Rights and Maritime Spaces in the Caribbean Sea (Nicaragua v Colombia)* (Judgment) [2022] ICJ Rep 266, paras 39–47 (hereafter *Nicaragua v Colombia*). See, however, Dissenting Opinion of Judge Abraham, paras 2–12; Declaration of Judge Bennouna; Separate Opinion of Judge Yusuf, paras 2–14; Dissenting Opinion of Judge Nolte; Dissenting Opinion of Ad Hoc Judge McRae, paras 4–17.

[11] ILC, 'Draft Articles on the Law of Treaties with Commentaries' YILC 1966, Vol II, 187, Article 24 para 2.

[12] eg, *Legal Consequences for States of the Continued Presence of South Africa in Namibia (South-West Africa) notwithstanding Security Council Resolution 276 (1970)* (Advisory Opinion) [1971] ICJ Rep 16, para 53; *Magyar Helsinki Bizottság v Hungary* App no 18030/11 (ECtHR, 8 November 2016), paras 149–56.

[13] ARSIWA Commentaries (n 1) Article 13 para 9. See in this Commentary: Merkouris Panos and Andreas Kulick, 'Article 31 of the VCLT'.

[14] eg, *Kerojärvi v Finland*, App no 17506/90 (ECtHR, 19 July 1995), para 41.

[15] eg, *Preussische Treuhand GmbH & Co. KG a.A. v Poland* App no 47550/06 (ECtHR, 7 October 2008), para 55; *Prosecutor v Jean-Baptiste Gatete* (Decision on Defence Motion for Exclusion of Evidence and Delineation of the Defence Case) ICTR-2000-61-T (26 March 2010), para 25.

C. Application in international investment law

Investment tribunals consistently affirm that, in accordance with Article 13, a State can only be responsible for breach of an investment treaty if the treaty is in force at the time of the alleged breach.[16]

Entry into force of an investment treaty is necessary, but not sufficient for a State to incur responsibility for breach of an investment treaty. Contracting States to an investment treaty are required to accord treaty protection only to eligible investors and investments. Accordingly, conduct otherwise not in conformity with the obligations imposed under an investment treaty does not amount to an internationally wrongful act unless and until the natural or legal person that claims treaty protection qualifies as a protected investor of the other contracting State and acquires an investment protected under the treaty.[17]

While investment treaties typically accord protection to investments made prior to their entry into force, this does not affect the operation of the non-retroactivity rule. Treatment of pre-existing investments that occurred before the investment treaty entered into force does not constitute a treaty violation.[18]

Sunset clauses extending the application of treaty protections for a specified period after the treaty's termination with respect to investments made before such termination likewise do not affect the operation of the non-retroactivity rule. Because the contracting States remain bound by their treaty obligations until the sunset period expires, they may incur responsibility for breach of the treaty, consistent with the non-retroactivity principle.[19]

Investment tribunals distinguish between the temporal scope of an investor–State arbitration clause and the temporal applicability of an investment treaty's substantive provisions.[20]

---

[16] eg, *Mondev International Ltd v United States of America*, ICSID Case No ARB(AF)/99/2, Award, 11 October 2002, para 68; *Salini Costruttori S.p.A. and Italstrade S.p.A. v Hashemite Kingdom of Jordan*, ICSID Case No ARB/02/13, Decision on Jurisdiction, 29 November 2004, paras 177–78 (hereafter *Salini* Decision); *OKO Pankki Oyj and Others v Republic of Estonia*, ICSID Case No ARB/04/6, Award, 19 November 2007, paras 191–93 (hereafter *OKO Pankki* Award); *Ioannis Kardassopoulos v Republic of Georgia*, ICSID Case No ARB/05/18, Decision on Jurisdiction, 6 July 2007, paras 253–55; *Bayindir Insaat Turizm Ticaret Ve Sanayi A.S. v Islamic Republic of Pakistan*, ICSID Case No ARB/03/29, Award, 27 August 2009, para 132; *Ping An Life Insurance Company of China, Limited and Ping An Insurance (Group) Company of China, Limited v Kingdom of Belgium*, ICSID Case No ARB/12/29, Award, 30 April 2015, paras 167–69 (hereafter *Ping* Award); *The Renco Group, Inc v The Republic of Peru (II)*, PCA Case No 2019-46, Decision on Expedited Preliminary Objections, 30 June 2020, paras 141–42; *OOO Manolium Processing v Republic of Belarus*, PCA Case No 2018-06, Final Award, 22 June 2021, para 269 (hereafter *Manolium Processing* Award).

[17] eg, *Renée Rose Levy and Gremcitel S.A. v Republic of Peru*, ICSID Case No ARB/11/17, Award, 9 January 2015, paras 146–47 (hereafter *Levy* Award); *Société Générale in respect of DR Energy Holdings Limited and Empresa Distribuidora de Electricidad del Este, S.A. v Dominican Republic*, LCIA Case No UN 7927, Award on Preliminary Objections to Jurisdiction, 19 September 2008, para 105; *ST-AD GmbH v Republic of Bulgaria*, PCA Case No 2011-06, Award on Jurisdiction, 18 July 2013, para 300 (hereafter *ST-AD* Award); *Indian Metals & Ferro Alloys Ltd v Republic of Indonesia*, PCA Case No 2015-40, Final Award, 29 March 2019, paras 108, 112; *Westmoreland Mining Holdings, LLC v Government of Canada*, ICSID Case No UNCT/20/3, Final Award, 31 January 2022, paras 194–231.

[18] eg, *Sergei Paushok, CJSC Golden East Company and CJSC Vostokneftegaz Company v Government of Mongolia*, Award on Jurisdiction and Liability, 28 April 2011, paras 429–42 (hereafter *Paushok* Award); *Técnicas Medioambientales Tecmed S.A. v United Mexican States*, ICSID Case No ARB(AF)/00/2, Award, 29 May 2003, paras 63–65 (hereafter *Tecmed* Award); *Víctor Pey Casado and President Allende Foundation v Republic of Chile*, ICSID Case No ARB/98/2, Award, 8 May 2008, para 579 (hereafter *Víctor Pey Casado* Award).

[19] eg, *Mohamed Abdel Raouf Bahgat v Arab Republic of Egypt (I)*, PCA Case No 2012-07, Decision on Jurisdiction, 30 November 2017, paras 313, 315 (hereafter *Bahgat* Decision on Jurisdiction).

[20] eg, *Ping* Award (n 16) paras 167–73; *Salini* Decision (n 16) para 176; *Impregilo S.p.A. v Islamic Republic of Pakistan (II)*, ICSID Case No ARB/03/3, Decision on Jurisdiction, 22 April 2005, para 309; *Víctor Pey Casado*

This distinction, however, has less practical relevance in international investment law than in general international law. Investment treaty tribunals are generally seized with claims for breaches of the treaty that confers jurisdiction on them. In most cases, the entry into force of the investment treaty is therefore also the critical date for purposes of jurisdiction *ratione temporis*. Accordingly, some investment tribunals have noted that it is not necessary to distinguish between jurisdiction *ratione temporis* and the temporal application of substantive obligations when the claim is founded on breach of the investment treaty that contains the investor–State arbitration clause.[21]

10 This distinction remains relevant, however, for claims involving successive investment treaties. Depending on the terms of the investor–State arbitration clause of the later treaty, a claim for breach of the earlier treaty may be brought under the later treaty, even if the breach occurred before its entry into force.[22] The distinction may also be relevant in case of amendments to investment treaties.[23] As many investment treaties have recently been, or are currently in the process of being, replaced or renegotiated, the distinction between jurisdiction *ratione temporis* and the temporal application of obligations imposed under an investment treaty may gain significance in international investment law.

11 Investment tribunals have held that conduct occurring before an investment treaty enters into force may be taken into account for certain purposes, but no uniform practice exists. At least one tribunal concluded that it 'may not deal with acts or omissions that occurred before' the treaty's entry into force.[24] Several tribunals have held that prior acts may constitute 'circumstantial evidence that confirms or vitiates an apparent post-entry into force breach',[25] or be considered 'solely in order to understand and determine precisely the scope and effects of the breaches of the BIT after [the entry into force of the investment treaty]',[26] i.e. as 'background, causal link, or the basis of circumstances surrounding the occurrence of a dispute'.[27] At least one tribunal has considered (in the context of a composite act) that State conduct preceding entry into force of the investment treaty 'may be considered a constituting part, concurrent factor or aggravating or mitigating element' of conduct occurring after the treaty's entry into force.[28]

Award (n 18) para 585; *Duke Energy International Peru Investments No 1 Ltd v Republic of Peru*, ICSID Case No ARB/03/28, Decision on Annulment, 1 March 2011, paras 171–72.

[21] *Philip Morris Asia Limited v Commonwealth of Australia*, PCA Case No 2012-12, Award on Jurisdiction and Admissibility, 17 December 2015, paras 528–29; *Levy* Award, paras 146–47.

[22] *Jan de Nul N. V. and Dredging International N. V. v Arab Republic of Egypt*, ICSID Case No ARB/04/13, Award, 6 November 2008, paras 134–35; *Bahgat* Decision on Jurisdiction (n 19) paras 307, 315.

[23] *Nordzucker AG v Republic of Poland*, Partial Award (Jurisdiction), 10 December 2008, paras 106–10.

[24] *Marvin Roy Feldman Karpa v United Mexican States*, ICSID Case No ARB(AF)/99/1, Interim Decision on Preliminary Jurisdictional Issues, 6 December 2000, para 62 (hereafter *Feldman* Interim Decision on Jurisdiction).

[25] *Aaron C. Berkowitz, Brett E. Berkowitz and Trevor B. Berkowitz (formerly Spence International Investments and others) v Republic of Costa Rica*, ICSID Case No UNCT/13/2, Interim Award (Corrected), 30 May 2017, para 217.

[26] *M.C.I. Power Group, L.C. and New Turbine, Inc v Republic of Ecuador*, ICSID Case No ARB/03/6, Award, 31 July 2007, para 135 (hereafter *M.C.I.* Award); *Victor Pey Casado* Award (n 18) paras 611–12.

[27] *M.C.I.* Award (n 26) para 136; *Pac Rim Cayman LLC v Republic of El Salvador*, ICSID Case No ARB/09/12, Decision on the Respondent's Jurisdictional Objections, 1 June 2012, para 2.105 (hereafter *Pac Rim* Decision on Jurisdiction); *Eco Oro Minerals Corp v Republic Colombia*, Decision on Jurisdiction, Liability and Directions on Quantum, 9 September 2021, para 360; *Nurol İnşaat ve Ticaret A.Ş. v Libya*, Decision of the Paris Court of Appeal, 28 September 2021, paras 90–96.

[28] *Tecmed* Award (n 18) para 68.

D. Conclusion: Alignment of general international law and international investment law

The non-retroactivity principle set forth in Article 13 is uncontroversial and its application by investment tribunals generally aligns with that of other international judicial bodies. However, the distinction between jurisdiction *ratione temporis* and the temporal applicability of an investment treaty's substantive obligations has so far been of less practical relevance in investment arbitration than before other international courts or tribunals. **12**

Although the principle of non-retroactivity is firmly established, its application by both investment tribunals and other international courts and tribunals has sometimes been inconsistent, particularly in the treatment of pre-entry into force conduct in the context of continuing and composite acts. **13**

Selected literature

Buyse A, 'A Lifeline in Time—Non-retroactivity and Continuing Violations under the ECHR', 75 Nord J Int'l L 63 (2006).

Crawford J, 'Breach: The Temporal Element' in Crawford J (ed), *State Responsibility: The General Part* (CUP 2013).

Distefano G, 'Fait Continu, Fait Composé et Fait Complexe dans le Droit de la Responsabilité' (2006) 52 AFDI 1.

Douglas Z, *The International Law of Investment Claims*, ch 8 (CUP 2009).

Elias TO, 'The Doctrine of Intertemporal Law' (1980) 74(2) AJIL 285.

Gallus N, *The Temporal Jurisdiction of International Tribunals* (OUP 2017).

Heiskanen V, '*Entretemps*: Is There a Distinction Between Jurisdiction *Ratione Temporis* and Substantive Protection *Ratione Temporis*?' in Banifatemi Y (ed), *Jurisdiction in Investment Treaty Arbitration* (Juris Publishing 2018).

Higgins R, 'Time and Law: International Perspectives on an Old Problem' (1997) 46 ICLQ 501.

Kotzur M, 'Intertemporal Law' in *Max Planck Encyclopedia of Public International Law* (2008).

Pauwelyn, J, 'The Concept of a "Continuing Violation" of an International Obligation: Selected Problems' (1995) 66 BYIL 415.

Salmon J, 'Duration of the Breach' in Crawford J, Pellet A and Olleson S (eds), *The Law of International Responsibility* (OUP 2010).

Van Pachtenbeke A, Haeck Y and Cooper J, 'From De Becker to Varnava: The State of Continuing Situations in the Strasbourg Case Law' (2010) 1 EHRLR 47.

Article 14 of the ARSIWA

Extension in time of the breach of an international obligation

Claudia Annacker and Enikő Horváth

1. The breach of an international obligation by an act of a State not having a continuing character occurs at the moment when the act is performed, even if its effects continue.

2. The breach of an international obligation by an act of a State having a continuing character extends over the entire period during which the act continues and remains not in conformity with the international obligation.

3. The breach of an international obligation requiring a State to prevent a given event occurs when the event occurs and extends over the entire period during which the event continues and remains not in conformity with that obligation.

A. Introduction	1	D. Conclusion: Broad alignment of general international law and international investment law, with some divergences	25
B. Application in general international law	5		
C. Application in international investment law	15		

A. Introduction

1 Article 14 specifies the time of the occurrence of an internationally wrongful act and its duration. Paragraphs 1 and 2 distinguish between (i) instantaneous breaches, which occur when the conduct is undertaken, and (ii) continuing breaches, which extend for as long as the conduct continues and end when the conduct ceases or when the international obligation is no longer in force for the State. Paragraph 3 applies this distinction to breaches of obligations to prevent a given event.

2 In accordance with Article 13, regardless of the continuing character of a wrongful act or omission, the breach only continues as long as the State is bound by and its conduct remains not in conformity with the international obligation.

3 As discussed in paragraphs 4 and 11 of the entry on Article 13 of the ARSIWA, conduct predating the entry into force of the obligation for the State may be taken into account as background or context.

4 Article 14 has been held to reflect customary international law.[1]

---

[1] *M.C.I. Power Group, L.C. and New Turbine, Inc v Republic of Ecuador*, ICSID Case No ARB/03/6, Award, 31 July 2007, paras 85–86 (hereafter *M.C.I.* Award); *Pac Rim Cayman LLC v Republic of El Salvador*, ICSID Case

B. Application in general international law

The distinction in Article 14 between instantaneous and continuing acts is widely adopted 5
by international courts and tribunals.[2] It is also commonly acknowledged that a distinction must be drawn between continuing acts and acts with enduring effects. A breach is not of a continuing character if only its adverse effects continue.[3]

State conduct that has been held to amount to a continuing breach encompasses acts (such 6
as the grant of a concession conflicting with a prior concession,[4] the administration of a territory following decolonization[5] or the erasure of persons from a register of permanent residents[6]) and omissions (such as failure to protect an embassy and its personnel,[7] failure to conduct an effective investigation into forced disappearances,[8] failure to try or extradite persons,[9] or failure to pay sums due[10]). Conduct that has been held to constitute a non-continuing breach includes *de iure* expropriation,[11] assassination,[12] and aerial bombings.[13] Examples of a State's failure to prevent a given event include failure to prevent genocide[14] and failure to prevent air pollution.[15]

No ARB/09/12, Decision on the Respondent's Jurisdictional Objections, 1 June 2012, para 2.67 (hereafter *Pac Rim* Decision on Jurisdiction); with respect to Article 14(3): *Application of the Convention on the Prevention and Punishment of the Crime of Genocide (Bosnia and Herzegovina v Serbia and Montenegro)* (Judgment) [2007] ICJ Rep 43, para 431 (hereafter *Genocide Case*).

[2] eg, *Case concerning the difference between New Zealand and France concerning the interpretation or application of two agreements, concluded on 9 July 1986 between the two States and which related to the problems arising from the Rainbow Warrior Affair (1990)*, XX RIAA 215, 30 April 1990, paras 101, 105 (hereafter *Rainbow Warrior*); WTO, *European Communities and Certain Member States—Measures Affecting Trade in Large Civil Aircraft— Report of the Appellate Body* (18 May 2011) WT/DS316/AB/R, para 685; Zitha and Zitha v Mozambique, ACHPR, Comm No 361/08 (1 April 2011), para 94. See also *Gabčíkovo-Nagymaros Project (Hungary/Slovakia)* (Judgment) [1997] ICJ Rep 7, para 79; *Ilaşcu and Others v Russia and Moldova*, App no 48787/99 (ECtHR, 8 July 2004), para 321 (hereafter *Ilaşcu v Russia and Moldova*).

[3] eg, *Phosphates in Morocco (Preliminary Objections)* (Judgment) [1938] PCIJ Rep Series A/B No 74, 26 (hereafter *Phosphates in Morocco*); S.C. and G.P. v Italy, Committee on Economic, Social and Cultural Rights Comm No 22/2017, UN Doc E/C.12/65/D/22/2017, para 6.5.

[4] *Mavrommatis Palestine Concessions (United Kingdom v Greece)* (Judgment No 2) [1924] PCIJ Rep Series A No 2, 35 (hereafter *Mavrommatis Palestine Concessions*).

[5] *Legal Consequences of the Separation of the Chagos Archipelago from Mauritius in 1965* (Advisory Opinion) [2019] ICJ Rep 95, paras 177–78 (hereafter *Chagos Archipelago*).

[6] *Kurić and Others v Slovenia* App no 26828/06 (ECtHR, 13 July 2010), para 305.

[7] *United States Diplomatic and Consular Staff in Tehran (United States of America v Iran)* (Judgment) [1980] ICJ Rep 3, paras 74, 77–78, 80 (hereafter *United States of America v Iran*).

[8] eg, *Cyprus v Turkey*, App no 25781/94 (ECtHR, 10 May 2001), para 136 (hereafter *Cyprus v Turkey*); *Case of Gomes Lund et al ('Guerrilha do Araguaia') v Brazil* (IACtHR, 24 November 2010), paras 16–17, 110, 121, 179 (hereafter *Guerrilha do Araguaia*); *Case of Moiwana Community v Suriname* (IACtHR, 15 June 2005), para 43 (hereafter *Moiwana Community*).

[9] *Questions relating to the Obligation to Prosecute or Extradite (Belgium v Senegal)* (Judgment) [2012] ICJ Rep 422, paras 71–117.

[10] eg, *Yuriy Lobanov v Russia* App no 15578/03 (ECtHR, 2 December 2010), paras 28–30; *Almeida Garrett, Mascarenhas Falcão and Others v Portugal*, App nos 29813/96 and 30229/96 (ECtHR, 11 January 2000), paras 43, 48.

[11] See para 9 below.

[12] eg, *Kholodov and Kholodova v Russia* App no 30651/05 (ECtHR, 14 September 2006), para 1.

[13] *Legality of Use of Force (Yugoslavia v Belgium)* (Order of Provisional Measures) [1999] ICJ Rep 124, para 29 (hereafter *Yugoslavia v Belgium*). See, however, Separate Opinion of Judge R Higgins, paras 4–8; Dissenting Opinion of Judge Shi Jiuyong, 206–07.

[14] *Genocide Case* (n 1) paras 431–32.

[15] *Marangopoulos Foundation for Human Rights v Greece*, European Committee of Social Rights, Complaint No 30/2005, Decision on the Merits, 6 December 2006, para 193.

7 The distinction between instantaneous and continuing acts may have important consequences for temporal jurisdiction. International courts and tribunals—including the Permanent Court of International Justice (PCIJ),[16] International Court of Justice (ICJ),[17] European Court of Human Rights (ECtHR),[18] Inter-American Court of Human Rights (IACtHR),[19] and World Trade Organization (WTO) panels,[20]—consistently affirm that they have jurisdiction over conduct after the critical date for jurisdiction even if that conduct began before the critical date.

8 Whether conduct is of a continuing nature depends both on the specific circumstances of a given case and the content of the obligation at issue. For example, WTO panels interpret the substantive provisions of the Agreement on the Application of Sanitary and Phytosanitary Measures and the Agreement on Technical Barriers to Trade as applying to sanitary and technical measures adopted before but maintained after the entry into force of the Agreement.[21] The PCIJ, by contrast, treated the enactment of decrees that monopolized the exploitation of phosphate deposits as an instantaneous act.[22] Certain basic elements can be identified nonetheless.

9 First, an expropriation depriving the owner of title is generally treated as an instantaneous act, not a continuous deprivation of property.[23] However, a continuing breach of the right to property may arise from restrictions on the exercise of property rights,[24] discriminatory property legislation,[25] or denial of access to or interference with the control, use, or enjoyment of property,[26] even where such denial amounts to a *de facto* expropriation.

10 Second, a State's failure to remedy or redress unlawful conduct does not give rise to a continuing act.[27] Judicial or other proceedings to redress conduct predating the critical date for jurisdiction therefore only fall within the jurisdiction of an international court or tribunal to the extent that the proceedings themselves may constitute internationally wrongful acts.[28]

---

[16] *Mavrommatis Palestine Concessions* (n 4) 35.
[17] *Right of Passage over Indian Territory (Portugal v India)* (Judgment) [1960] ICJ Rep 6, 35–36.
[18] eg, *Crnojević v Croatia* App no 71614/01 (ECtHR, 29 April 2003), para 1.
[19] eg, *Andres Aylwin Azocar and Others v Chile*, Report, IACHR No 95/98 (9 December 1998), para 26.
[20] eg, WTO, *EC Measures Concerning Meat and Meat Products (Hormones), Complaint by the United States—Report of the Panel* (18 August 1997) WT/DS26/R/USA, paras 8.25–8.26.
[21] ibid.
[22] *Phosphates in Morocco* (n 3) 25–26, 28. See, however, Dissenting Opinion of Judge van Eysinga, 33–35; Separate Opinion of Judge Cheng, 36–37.
[23] eg, *Mariposa Development Company and Others (United States) v Panama* (1933) UNRIAA Vol VI, 27 June 1933, 338; *Bergauer and Others v Czech Republic* App no 17120/04 (ECtHR, 13 December 2005), 10; *Preussische Treuhand GmbH & Co KG a.A. v Poland* App no 47550/06 (ECtHR, 7 October 2008), para 56 (hereafter *Preussische Treuhand*); *Malhous v Czech Republic* App no 33071/96 (ECtHR, 13 December 2000), 16, para (c); *Smoleanu v Romania* App no 30324/96 (ECtHR, 3 December 2002), para 46; *Von Maltzan and Others v Germany* App nos 71916/01, 71917/01, and 10260/02 (ECtHR, 2 March 2005), para 74.
[24] eg, *Rosiński v Poland* App no 17373/02 (ECtHR, 17 July 2007), paras 40, 43; *Papamichalopoulos and Others v Greece* App no 14556/89 (ECtHR, 24 June 1993), para 40 (hereafter *Papamichalopoulos v Greece*); *Case of Cantos v Argentina* (IACtHR, 8 September 2001), para 39; *Gravina v Italy* App no 60124/00 (ECtHR, 15 November 2005), para 85.
[25] eg, *Simunek, Hastings, Tuzilova and Prochazka v Czech Republic* (1995), Human Rights Committee Comm no 516/1992, UN Doc CCPR/C/54/D/516/1992, paras 11.3–11.8.
[26] eg, *Papamichalopoulos v Greece* (n 24) paras 40–41; *Loizidou v Turkey* App no 15318/89 (ECtHR, 18 December 1996), para 63; *Cyprus v Turkey* (n 8) paras 185–89; *Preussische Treuhand* (n 23) para 57; *Chiragov v Armenia* App no 13216/05 (ECtHR, 16 June 2015), paras 193, 196; *Moiwana Community* (n 8) para 43.
[27] eg, *Blečić v Croatia* App no 59532/00 (ECtHR, 8 March 2006) paras 77–81, 85–91 (hereafter *Blečić v Croatia*); *Kefalas and Others v Greece* App no 14726/89 (ECtHR, 8 June 1995), para 45.
[28] eg, *Varnava v Turkey* App no 16064/90 (ECtHR, 18 September 2009), paras 130, 138; *Šilih v Slovenia* App no 71463/01 (ECtHR, 9 April 2009), para 159 (hereafter *Šilih v Slovenia*); *Blečić v Croatia* (n 27) paras 77–79.

11 Third, the occurrence of a particular event may trigger certain obligations, regardless of whether the event occurred prior to the entry into force of the international obligation. For example, human rights courts and treaty bodies consistently treat the obligation to investigate forced disappearances and deaths as an independent obligation, separate from the underlying obligations to protect the right to life and personal integrity. They therefore assume jurisdiction over alleged breaches of this obligation even when the disappearance or death occurred before the relevant human rights treaty entered into force for the State.[29]

12 International courts and tribunals also deal with the concept of continuing acts to decide on the application of limitation periods. Human rights courts commonly disregard limitation periods when a breach is of a continuing nature, as they deem the limitation period to be triggered only when the continuing breach ceases.[30]

13 Because a State's failure to remedy or redress unlawful conduct does not amount to a continuing act, judicial proceedings challenging State conduct do not prevent the expiration of a limitation period with respect to the conduct that is challenged.[31]

14 Finally, the classification of a breach as instantaneous or continuing affects the remedies available to the injured party. While both types of breaches require reparation, the State responsible for a continuing wrongful act is also obliged to cease the wrongful conduct,[32] and international courts and tribunals have occasionally issued orders of cessation.[33]

C. Application in international investment law

15 Investment tribunals endorse the notion of continuing acts. In accordance with the International Law Commission (ILC)'s Commentary on Article 14, they regularly affirm that to constitute a continuing breach, the same wrongful conduct must extend over a period of time,[34] and the conduct itself (not just its effects) must be continuing.[35]

---

[29] eg, *Šilih v Slovenia* (n 28) paras 159–63; *Guerrilha do Araguaia* (n 8) paras 16–17, 110, 121, 179. See also *Janowiec and Others v Russia* App nos 55508/07 and 29520/09 (ECtHR, 21 October 2013), paras 131–35, 140–51; *Mariam Sankara et al v Burkina Faso* (28 March 2006), UN Human Rights Commission Comm No 1159/2003, para 6.3; *Case of the Serrano-Cruz Sisters v El Salvador* (IACtHR, 23 November 2004), paras 77–94.

[30] eg, *Cyprus v Turkey* (n 8) para 104; *Paksas v Lithuania* App no 34932/04 (ECtHR, 6 January 2011), para 83; *Anchugov and Gladkov v Russia* App nos 11157/04 and 15162/05 (ECtHR, 4 July 2013), paras 73–79; *Guerrilha do Araguaia* (n 8) para 171; *Herzog et al v Brazil* (IACtHR, 15 March 2018), para 269.

[31] eg, *Phosphates in Morocco* (n 3) 27–29; *Litovchenko v Russia* App no 69580/01 (ECtHR, 18 April 2002).

[32] ILC, 'Draft Articles on the Responsibility of States for Internationally Wrongful Acts, with Commentaries' YILC 2001, Vol II, Part Two, 31, Article 30; *Dispute Regarding Navigational and Related Rights (Costa Rica v Nicaragua)* (Judgment) [2009] ICJ Rep 213, para 148; *Rainbow Warrior* (n 2) para 114; *Chagos Archipelago* (n 5) paras 177–78.

[33] eg, *United States of America v Iran* (n 7) para 95(3); *Military and Paramilitary Activities in and Against Nicaragua (Nicaragua v United States of America)* (Merits) [1986] ICJ Rep 14, para 292(12); *Alleged Violations of Sovereign Rights and Maritime Spaces in the Caribbean Sea (Nicaragua v Colombia)* (Judgment) [2022] ICJ Rep 266, para 261(4) (hereafter *Nicaragua v Colombia*).

[34] eg, *Pac Rim* Decision on Jurisdiction (n 1) paras 2.69, 2.92–2.94; *OKO Pankki Oyj and Others v Republic of Estonia*, ICSID Case No ARB/04/6, Award, 19 November 2007, para 194 (hereafter *OKO Pankki* Award); *Marvin Roy Feldman Karpa v United Mexican States*, ICSID Case No ARB(AF)/99/1, Interim Decision on Preliminary Jurisdictional Issues, 6 December 2000, para 62 (hereafter *Feldman* Interim Decision on Jurisdiction).

[35] eg, *Adel A Hamadi Al Tamimi v Sultanate of Oman*, ICSID Case No ARB/11/33, Award, 3 November 2015, paras 396–402, 417; *William Ralph Clayton and Others v Government of Canada*, PCA Case No 2009-04, Award on Jurisdiction and Liability, 17 March 2015, paras 268–69 (hereafter *Clayton* Award on Jurisdiction); *Resolute Forest Products Inc v Government of Canada*, PCA Case No 2016-13, Decision on Jurisdiction and Admissibility, 30 January 2018, para 157 (hereafter *RFP* Decision); *Société Générale in respect of DR Energy Holdings Limited and Empresa Distribuidora de Electricidad del Este, S.A. v Dominican Republic*, LCIA Case No UN 7927, Award on Preliminary Objections to Jurisdiction, 19 September 2008, para 88 (hereafter *Société Générale* Award).

16 Examples of continuing investment treaty violations include the host State's abrogation of basic guarantees for a gas tariff regime,[36] refusal to increase highway tolls,[37] continued failure to grant an environmental permit and mining concession,[38] and undue delay in domestic court proceedings.[39] Most investment tribunals also classify failure to pay under a contract as a continuing act,[40] although at least one tribunal has treated such failure as an instantaneous act where the State did not recognize the payment obligation.[41]

17 By contrast, investment tribunals commonly treat (*de iure* and *de facto*) expropriations other than creeping expropriation as instantaneous acts.[42] More generally, discrete acts in the context of ongoing relations between an investor and the host State that do not converge toward a specific result are unlikely to qualify as continuing acts.[43]

18 No established practice exists with respect to acts of the judiciary. Although court decisions are generally deemed instantaneous acts,[44] 'extensive litigation' by a State-owned entity to terminate contracts with an investor, which culminated in a court decision terminating the contracts, was treated as a continuing breach by one tribunal.[45]

19 Investment tribunals frequently resort to the concept of continuing acts to establish jurisdiction *ratione temporis*.[46] They consistently affirm that continuing acts or omissions may give rise to State responsibility even where the conduct began before the critical date, i.e. the entry into force of the investment treaty, the investor's acquisition of the requisite nationality, or the making of a qualifying investment.[47] However, even if an investment tribunal has

---

[36] *LG&E Energy Corp, LG&E Capital Corp and LG&E International Inc v Argentine Republic*, ICSID Case No ARB/02/1, Award, 25 July 2007, para 85 (hereafter *LG&E* Award).

[37] *Walter Bau AG (in liquidation) v Kingdom of Thailand*, UNCITRAL, Award, 1 July 2009, para 12.37 (hereafter *Walter Bau* Award).

[38] *Pac Rim* Decision on Jurisdiction (n 1) para 2.92.

[39] *Chevron Corporation and Texaco Petroleum Company v Republic of Ecuador*, PCA Case No 2007-02/AA277, Interim Award, 1 December 2008, para 298 (hereafter *Chevron* Interim Award).

[40] *SGS Société Générale de Surveillance S.A. v Republic of Philippines*, ICSID Case No ARB/02/6, Decision of the Tribunal on Objections to Jurisdiction, 29 January 2004, para 167; *African Holding Company of America, Inc and Société Africaine de Construction au Congo S.A.R.L. v Democratic Republic of the Congo*, ICSID Case No ARB/05/21, Award on Objections to Jurisdiction and Admissibility, 29 July 2008, para 121.

[41] *Impregilo S.p.A. v Republic of Pakistan*, ICSID Case No ARB/03/3, Decision on Jurisdiction, 22 April 2005, paras 312–13.

[42] eg, *Víctor Pey Casado and President Allende Foundation v Republic of Chile*, ICSID Case No ARB/98/2, Award, 8 May 2008, para 606 (hereafter *Víctor Pey Casado* Award); *Metalclad Corporation v United Mexican States*, ICSID Case No ARB(AF)/97/1, Award, 30 August 2000, paras 102–04, 107.

[43] *Sergei Paushok, CJSC Golden East Company and CJSC Vostokneftegaz Company v. Mongolia*, Award on Jurisdiction and Liability, 28 April 2011, UNCITRAL, para 498.

[44] eg, *Sistem Mühendislik In aat Sanayi ve Ticaret A.S. v Kyrgyz Republic*, ICSID Case No ARB(AF)/06/1, Award, 9 September 2009, paras 117–19, 128; *Karkey Karadeniz Elektrik Uretim A.S. v Islamic Republic of Pakistan*, ICSID Case No ARB/13/1, Award, 22 August 2017, paras 648–50.

[45] *OKO Pankki* Award (n 34) paras 195–96.

[46] eg, *Société Générale* Award (n 35) para 88; *Cervin Investissements S.A. and Rhone Investissements S.A. v Republic of Costa Rica*, ICSID Case No ARB/13/2, Decision on Jurisdiction, 15 December 2014, para 278, fn 296; *Feldman* Interim Decision on Jurisdiction (n 34) para 62.

[47] eg, *ABCI Investments N.V. v Republic of Tunisia*, ICSID Case No ARB/04/12, Decision on Jurisdiction, 18 February 2011, paras 178–79; *Feldman* Interim Decision on Jurisdiction (n 34) para 62; *B3 Croatian Courier Coöperatief U.A. v Republic of Croatia*, ICSID Case No ARB/15/5, Award (Excerpts), 5 April 2019, para 616 (hereafter *B3* Award); *Société Générale* Award (n 35) para 80. In the context of successive investment treaties, see *Walter Bau* Award (n 37) paras 9.83–9.93; *Ping An Life Insurance Company of China, Limited and Ping An Insurance (Group) Company of China, Limited v. Kingdom of Belgium*, ICSID Case No ARB/12/29, Award, 30 April 2015, paras 172, 183; *Railroad Development Corporation v Republic of Guatemala*, ICSID Case No ARB/07/23, Second Decision on Objections to Jurisdiction, 18 May 2010, paras 116, 123–25.

jurisdiction over conduct that continues after the critical date, the subsequent conduct must itself amount to a treaty violation in order to give rise to State responsibility.[48]

The mere fact that conduct has not been remedied does not convert the conduct into a continuing act or constitute a separate breach of an investment treaty.[49] Similarly, an unsuccessful motion for reconsideration of a measure before an administrative or judicial body will generally not give rise to a continuing breach of an investment treaty (or constitute a new cause of action).[50] 20

Prior conduct can be decisive in the context of claims for denial of justice due to delays in domestic court proceedings. At least one tribunal has taken into account delays prior to the entry into force of an investment treaty to find a continuing breach.[51] 21

The continuing nature of a breach may also be decisive if an investment treaty imposes a limitation period on claims. While most tribunals have ruled that the continuing nature of a breach cannot extend the limitation period,[52] one North American Free Trade Agreement (NAFTA) tribunal has held that continuing breaches 'renew' that period.[53] 22

Finally, the distinction between instantaneous and continuing acts may be relevant to determine the compensation due. At least one investment tribunal has stated that any loss suffered before the entry into force of the investment treaty may not be taken into account,[54] while another took the position that prior acts or omissions may 'be taken into consideration if they have had a continuing impact after [the investment treaty's entry into force] and they were not remedied'.[55] 23

Only a few investment tribunals have claimed the power to order cessation of continuing wrongful acts.[56] One tribunal is reported to have actually ordered cessation, but solely as an alternative to the payment of compensation on the basis of party agreement.[57] 24

---

[48] eg, *Mondev International Ltd v United States of America*, ICSID Case No ARB(AF)/99/2, Award, 11 October 2002, para 70 (hereafter *Mondev* Award); *Astrida Benita Carrizosa v Republic of Colombia*, ICSID Case No ARB/18/5, Award, 19 April 2021, para 149 (hereafter *Carrizosa* Award); B3 Award (n 47) para 616; *Aaron C Berkowitz, Brett E Berkowitz, and Trevor B Berkowitz (formerly Spence International Investments and others) v Republic of Costa Rica*, ICSID Case No UNCT/13/2, Interim Award (Corrected), 30 May 2017, para 217 (hereafter *Berkowitz* Interim Award).

[49] eg, *Mondev* Award (n 48) para 70; *Carrizosa* Award (n 48) para 157; *Chevron* Interim Award (n 39) para 282.

[50] *Corona Materials LLC v Dominican Republic*, ICSID Case No ARB(AF)/14/3, Award on the Respondent's Expedited Preliminary Objections in Accordance with Article 10.20.5 of the DR-CAFTA, 31 May 2016, paras 210–11; *ST-AD GmbH v Republic of Bulgaria*, PCA Case No 2011-06, Award on Jurisdiction, 18 July 2013, paras 317, 332 (hereafter *ST-AD* Award).

[51] *Chevron* Interim Award (n 39) paras 284, 298. By contrast, see *Feldman* Interim Decision on Jurisdiction (n 34) paras 62–63.

[52] *Berkowitz* Interim Award (n 48) para 208; *Nissan Motor Co, Ltd v Republic of India*, PCA Case No 2017-37, Decision on Jurisdiction, 29 April 2019, para 325; *Mobil Investments Canada Inc v Canada*, ICSID Case No ARB/15/6, Decision on Jurisdiction and Admissibility, 13 July 2018, para 156–73; RFP Decision (n 35) paras 158–63; *Grand River Enterprises Six Nations Ltd and Others v United States of America*, UNCITRAL, Decision on Objections to Jurisdiction, 20 July 2006, para 81. See also *Ansung Housing Co Ltd v China*, ICSID Case No ARB/14/25, Award, 9 March 2017, paras 108–14; *Carlos Ríos and Francisco Ríos v Republic of Chile*, ICSID Case No ARB/17/16, Award, 11 January 2021, paras 202–05 (hereafter *Ríos* Award).

[53] *Parcel Service of America Inc (UPS) v Government of Canada*, ICSID Case No UNCT/02/1, Award on the Merits, 24 May 2007, para 28 (hereafter *UPS* Award).

[54] *UPS* Award (n 53) para 30.

[55] *Walter Bau* Award (n 37) para 13.1(f).

[56] *Enron Corporation and Ponderosa Assets, L.P. v Argentine Republic*, ICSID Case No ARB/01/3, Decision on Jurisdiction, 14 January 2004, paras 79–81; *Ioan Micula, Viorel Micula and Others v Romania (I)*, ICSID Case No ARB/05/20, Final Award, 11 December 2013, paras 1309–13. But see LG&E Award (n 36) paras 85–87.

[57] *Antoine Goetz and Others v Republic of Burundi (I)*, ICSID Case No ARB/95/3, Award (Embodying the Parties' Settlement Agreement), 10 February 1999, paras 135–36.

D. Conclusion: Broad alignment of general international law and international investment law, with some divergences

25 While the rules set forth in Article 14 to identify when an internationally wrongful act occurs are uncontroversial, neither general international law, nor investment law has an entirely consistent response to when an internationally wrongful act occurs. There is general agreement among international courts and tribunals, including investment tribunals, on the basic concept of a continuing act and the non-continuing nature of unremedied conduct. However, there are divergences in the approach to the application of the concept of continuing act in the context of undue delay and limitation periods.

26 Certain investment tribunals also appear to take a more restrictive approach than human rights courts in qualifying breaches of the right to property as continuing wrongful acts.[58]

Selected literature

Buyse A, 'A Lifeline in Time—Non-retroactivity and Continuing Violations under the ECHR' (2006) 75 Nord J Int'l L 63.

Crawford J, 'Breach: The Temporal Element' in Crawford J (ed), *State Responsibility: The General Part* (CUP 2013).

Distefano G, 'Fait Continu, Fait Composé et Fait Complexe dans le Droit de la Responsabilité' (2006) 52 AFDI 1.

Douglas Z, *The International Law of Investment Claims*, ch 8 (CUP 2009).

Elias TO, 'The Doctrine of Intertemporal Law' (1980) 74(2) AJIL 285.

Gallus N, *The Temporal Jurisdiction of International Tribunals* (OUP 2017).

Heiskanen V, '*Entretemps*: Is There a Distinction Between Jurisdiction *Ratione Temporis* and Substantive Protection *Ratione Temporis*?' in Banifatemi Y (ed), *Jurisdiction in Investment Treaty Arbitration* (Juris Publishing 2018).

Higgins R, 'Time and Law: International Perspectives on an Old Problem' (1997) 46 ICLQ 501.

Kotzur M, 'Intertemporal Law' in *Max Planck Encyclopedia of Public International Law* (2008).

Pauwelyn J, 'The Concept of a "Continuing Violation" of an International Obligation: Selected Problems' (1995) 66 BYIL 415.

Salmon J, 'Duration of the Breach' in Crawford J, Pellet A and Olleson S (eds), *The Law of International Responsibility* (OUP 2010).

Van Pachtenbeke A, Haeck Y and Cooper J, 'From De Becker to Varnava: The. State of Continuing Situations in the Strasbourg Case Law' (2010) 1 EHRLR 47.

---

[58] *Victor Pey Casado* Award (n 42) paras 604–606 (criticizing the ECtHR's approach in the *Loizidou* case for treating the applicant's denial of access to property in Northern Cyprus due to the Turkish invasion as a continuing interference with the applicant's peaceful enjoyment of a possession).

Article 15 of the ARSIWA

Breach consisting of a composite act

Claudia Annacker and Enikő Horváth

1. The breach of an international obligation by a State through a series of actions or omissions defined in aggregate as wrongful occurs when the action or omission occurs which, taken with the other actions or omissions, is sufficient to constitute the wrongful act.

2. In such a case, the breach extends over the entire period starting with the first of the actions or omissions of the series and lasts for as long as these actions or omissions are repeated and remain not in conformity with the international obligation.

A. Introduction	1	D. Conclusion: International investment law potentially influencing general international law	23
B. Application in general international law	5		
C. Application in international investment law	14		

A. Introduction

Following the basic distinction between completed and continuing acts in Article 14, Article 15 introduces a further refinement, the concept of a composite breach—i.e. a series of actions or omissions defined in aggregate as wrongful. Paragraph 1 provides that a composite breach occurs when the last act or omission has occurred which, together with the previous ones, suffices to amount to a breach of the international obligation. Pursuant to paragraph 2, composite acts give rise to continuing wrongs which extend over the entire period during which the relevant acts or omissions continue and remain not in conformity with the international obligation. **1**

In accordance with Article 13, regardless of the continuing character of a composite breach, the breach only continues as long as the State is bound by and its conduct remains not in conformity with its international obligations. **2**

As discussed in paragraphs 4 and 11 of the entry on Article 13 of the ARSIWA, conduct predating the entry into force of the obligation of the State may be taken into account as background or context. **3**

4 International courts and tribunals occasionally refer to Article 15 in defining a series of measures in aggregate as wrongful.[1] Investment tribunals reference the provision more frequently and have held that Article 15 reflects customary international law.[2]

B. Application in general international law

5 Composite acts are composed of distinct, individual acts or omissions that in aggregate amount to an internationally wrongful act. They must be distinguished from repeated acts or omissions which are individual breaches of the same nature.

6 Some international obligations, for example the prohibitions of genocide and apartheid,[3] can only be breached through composite acts. Most obligations however can be breached by individual acts or omissions.[4]

7 General international law has not developed a consistent approach to identify the factors necessary to transform a series of acts or omissions into a composite act.

8 Article 15 does not require any connecting factor between the acts or omissions constituting a composite act. But such a connecting factor, an element of intent implied by the notion of policy or plan, has sometimes been considered a requisite element of a composite act.[5]

9 Special Rapporteur James Crawford was in favour of limiting the notion of composite breaches to violations of systematic obligations, i.e. obligations that define the wrongful conduct in composite or systematic terms.[6] The text of Article 15 does not appear to reflect such a limitation, however. A United Nations Convention on the Law of the Sea (UNCLOS) tribunal has adopted this broader view of composite acts,[7] holding that the respondent State violated a non-systematic obligation—the obligation to exercise its sovereignty in its archipelagic waters in a reasonable and proportionate manner—through a composite act.[8]

10 The European Court of Human Rights (ECtHR) also qualifies acts and omissions as composite breaches even where the European Convention on Human Rights (ECHR) does not define the underlying obligation in systematic terms.[9] The International Court of Justice

---

[1] eg, *The Duzgit Integrity Arbitration (Republic of Malta v Democratic Republic of São Tomé and Principe)*, Award on Reparation, PCA Case No 2014-07, 18 December 2019, paras 85–86 (hereafter *Duzgit Integrity* Reparation Award).

[2] eg, *M.C.I. Power Group, L.C. and New Turbine, Inc v Republic of Ecuador*, ICSID Case No ARB/03/6, Award, 31 July 2007, paras 82, 85, 88 (hereafter *M.C.I.* Award); *Pac Rim Cayman LLC v Republic of El Salvador*, ICSID Case No ARB/09/12, Decision on the Respondent's Jurisdictional Objections, 1 June 2012, para 2.67 (hereafter *Pac Rim* Decision on Jurisdiction).

[3] ILC, 'Draft Articles on Responsibility of States for Internationally Wrongful Acts with Commentaries' YILC 2001, Vol II Part Two, 31, Article 15 para 2. See also, Rome Statute of the International Criminal Court, Articles 7(1)–7(2).

[4] eg, *Prosecutor v Charles Ghankay Taylor* (Judgment) [2012] SCSL-03-01-T Special Court for Sierra Leone, para 453.

[5] eg, Roberto Ago, 'Seventh Report on State Responsibility: The Internationally Wrongful Act of the State, Source of International Responsibility' (1978) UN Doc A/CN.4/307, para 38.

[6] J Crawford, 'Second Report on State Responsibility' (1999) UN Doc A/CN.4/498, para 126.

[7] *Duzgit Integrity* Reparation Award (n 1) paras 85–86.

[8] *The Duzgit Integrity Arbitration (Republic of Malta v Democratic Republic of São Tomé and Principe)*, Award on Jurisdiction and the Merits, 5 September 2016, paras 255–61; *Duzgit Integrity* Reparation Award (n 1) para 85.

[9] eg, *Ilaşcu and Others v Russia and Moldova* App no 48787/99 (ECtHR, 8 July 2004), para 321 (hereafter *Ilaşcu v Russia and Moldova*); *El-Masri v Former Yugoslav Republic of Macedonia* App no 39630/09 ECtHR, 13 December 2012, paras 97, 240–41.

(ICJ), by contrast, has been reluctant to characterize a series of acts or omissions as composite acts but has not taken an explicit position.[10]

Human rights law recognizes a concept related to composite acts—a 'practice' or 'pattern' of wrongful conduct, which is treated as a distinct category. The UN Human Rights Council, for instance, is empowered to examine only complaints concerning 'consistent patterns of gross and reliably attested violations of all human rights and all fundamental freedoms'.[11] The ECtHR, in turn, dispenses with the general requirement to exhaust local remedies where an applicant complains of a 'practice', defined as 'an accumulation of identical or analogous breaches which are sufficiently numerous and inter-connected to amount not merely to isolated incidents or exceptions but to a pattern or system'.[12]

The qualification of conduct as a composite act may have important consequences for temporal jurisdiction. Because composite acts give rise to continuing breaches,[13] conduct after the critical date for jurisdiction may be subject to the temporal jurisdiction of an international court or tribunal even if the composite act began before the critical date.[14]

Composite acts, like other continuing wrongful acts, entail an obligation of cessation, as well as reparation for the injury caused.[15] The classification of a breach as a composite breach may also impact on compensation, and specifically the date of valuation. The Iran–US Claims Tribunal has frequently relied on the date an interference ripened into an irreversible deprivation of relevant property,[16] while an UNCLOS tribunal has used the date of the first act in the series.[17]

C. Application in international investment law

Investment tribunals readily rely on the concept of composite breach, in particular in the context of creeping expropriations,[18] creeping breaches of the fair and equitable treatment standard,[19] or denial of justice.[20] Only one tribunal, chaired by James Crawford, has expressed reservations about the applicability of Article 15 in the context of the fair and

---

[10] eg, *Legality of Use of Force (Yugoslavia v Belgium)* (Order of Provisional Measures) [1999] ICJ Rep 124, paras 28–29 (hereafter *Yugoslavia v Belgium*); Dissenting Opinion of Vice-President Weeramantry, 188; Declaration by Judge Koroma, 142–43; Dissenting Opinion of Judge Shi, 206–07. See also *Oil Platforms (Islamic Republic of Iran v United States of America)* (Order) [1998] ICJ Rep 190, paras 25, 35–36, 38.
[11] UN Human Rights Council, Resolution 5/1 (18 June 2007) UN Doc A/HRC/RES/5/1, para 85.
[12] eg, *Ireland v United Kingdom* App no 5310/71 (ECtHR, 18 January 1978), para 159.
[13] ILC, 'Articles on the Responsibility of States for Internationally Wrongful Acts' YILC 2001, Vol II, Part Two, Article 15(2) (hereafter ARSIWA).
[14] *Ilaşcu v Russia and Moldova* (n 9) paras 321, 399. But see Dissenting Opinion of Judge Kovler, 155.
[15] ARSIWA (n 13) Articles 30–31.
[16] eg, *International Technical Products Corporation v Government of the Islamic Republic of Iran and Its Agencies*, IUSCT Case No 302, Final Award (Award no 196-302-3), 28 October 1985, paras 118–20.
[17] *Duzgit Integrity* Reparation Award (n 1) para 86.
[18] eg, *Siemens A.G. v Argentine Republic*, ICSID Case No ARB/02/8, Award, 6 February 2007, paras 263–66 (hereafter *Siemens* Award); *OAO Tatneft v Ukraine*, PCA Case No 2008-8, Award on the Merits, 29 July 2014, paras 461–66 (hereafter *Tatneft* Award); *Crystallex International Corporation v Bolivarian Republic of Venezuela*, ICSID Case No ARB(AF)/11/2, Award, 4 April 2016, paras 667–72; *Compañía de Aguas del Aconquija S.A. and Vivendi Universal S.A. v Argentine Republic*, ICSID Case No ARB/97/3, Award, 20 August 2007, paras 7.5.31–7.5.34.
[19] eg, *El Paso Energy International Company v Argentine Republic*, ICSID Case No ARB/03/15, Award, 31 October 2011, paras 515–19 (hereafter *El Paso* Award); *Tatneft* Award (n 18) para 412; *Swisslion DOO Skopje v Former Yugoslav Republic of Macedonia*, ICSID Case No ARB/09/16, Award, 6 July 2012, para 275 (hereafter *Swisslion* Award).
[20] *Chevron Corporation and Texaco Petroleum Company v Republic of Ecuador*, PCA Case No 2007-02/AA277, Interim Award, 1 December 2008, paras 284, 300–01 (hereafter *Chevron* Interim Award); *Société Générale in respect of DR Energy Holdings Limited and Empresa Distribuidora de Electricidad del Este, S.A. v Dominican Republic*,

equitable treatment standard since the obligations imposed under this standard are not systematic.[21]

15 There is, however, no consensus concerning the requisite elements of a composite breach. Investment tribunals typically require a connecting factor between acts and omissions to constitute a composite act. Some require a showing of intent,[22] or a link of underlying pattern or common and coordinated purpose between the relevant acts or omissions,[23] others that the conduct constitute 'converging action towards the same result'.[24]

16 Investment tribunals commonly assess each individual act or omission at issue to determine whether it forms part of a series of events constituting a composite act.[25] Certain tribunals require that each step of a composite act have an adverse impact on the investment,[26] others only that the acts form part of a chain that eventually has an adverse impact.[27]

17 Several tribunals have confirmed that the acts or omissions constituting a composite act may include acts or omissions that by themselves are lawful or breach norms different from the legal norm breached by the composite act.[28] However, in the specific context of expropriation, some tribunals consider that there can be no creeping expropriation when one of the acts in the series separately constitutes an expropriation.[29] English courts appear to disagree and have set aside an award that took this position.[30]

18 Investment tribunals frequently resort to the concept of composite acts to establish jurisdiction *ratione temporis*.[31] They consistently affirm that a composite act may give rise to State responsibility for breach of an investment treaty even if the conduct began before the critical date for jurisdiction, so long as the portion of the composite act that occurred after that date by itself constitutes a treaty violation.[32]

LCIA Case No UN 7927, Award on Preliminary Objections to Jurisdiction, 19 September 2008, para 91 (hereafter *Société Générale* Award).

[21] *Blusun S.A., Jean-Pierre Lecorcier and Michael Stein v Italian Republic*, ICSID Case No ARB/14/3, Award, 27 December 2016, para 361.

[22] *Glamis Gold Ltd v United States of America*, UNCITRAL, Award, 8 June 2009, para 826.

[23] eg, *The Rompetrol Group N.V. v Romania*, ICSID Case No ARB/06/3, Award, 6 May 2013, paras 271–73; *Victor Pey Casado and President Allende Foundation v Republic of Chile*, ICSID Case No ARB/98/2, Award, 8 May 2008, para 619 (hereafter *Victor Pey Casado* Award); *Fengzhen Min v Republic of Korea*, ICSID Case No ARB/20/26, Decision on the Respondent's Preliminary Objection Pursuant to Rule 41(5) of the ICSID Arbitration Rules, 18 June 2021, paras 93–94.

[24] *Técnicas Medioambientales Tecmed, S.A. v. United Mexican States*, ICSID Case No. ARB(AF)/00/2, Award, 29 May 2003, para 62; *Global Telecom Holding S.A.E. v Canada*, ICSID Case No ARB/16/16, Award, 27 March 2020, paras 641–42.

[25] eg, *Teinver S.A., Transportes de Cercanías S.A. and Autobuses Urbanos del Sur S.A. v Argentina*, ICSID Case No ARB/09/1, Award, 21 July 2017, para 949 (hereafter *Teinver* Award); *Swisslion* Award (n 19) paras 275–300; *Sergei Paushok, CJSC Golden East Company and CJSC Vostokneftegaz Company v. Mongolia*, Award on Jurisdiction and Liability, 28 April 2011, UNCITRAL, paras 499–500.

[26] eg, *Siemens* Award (n 18) para 263.

[27] eg, *Teinver* Award (n 25) paras 949–50.

[28] *Pac Rim* Decision on Jurisdiction (n 2) para 2.71; *El Paso* Award (n 19) paras 515–16. See also *GPF GP S.à.r.l v Republic of Poland* [2018] EWHC 409 (Comm), paras 120–21.

[29] eg, *Burlington Resources, Inc v Republic of Ecuador*, ICSID Case No ARB/08/5, Decision on Liability, 14 December 2012, para 538.

[30] *GPF GP S.à.r.l v Republic of Poland* [2018] EWHC 409 (Comm), paras 119–25, 130.

[31] eg, *Carlos Ríos and Francisco Ríos v Republic of Chile*, ICSID Case No ARB/17/16, Award, 11 January 2021, para 198 (hereafter *Ríos* Award); *Chevron* Interim Award (n 20) paras 284, 300–01; *Société Générale* Award (n 20) paras 91–92, 94.

[32] *OOO Manolium Processing v Republic of Belarus*, PCA Case No 2018-06, Final Award, 22 June 2021, paras 304, 309 (hereafter *Manolium Processing* Award); *Société Générale* Award (n 20) paras 91, 94; *Chevron* Interim Award (n 20) paras 300–01; *M.C.I.* Award (n 2) para 136; *Hydro S.r.l., Costruzioni S.r.l., Francesco Becchetti, Mauro*

Where a composite breach of an investment treaty is found, the entire series of acts and omissions constituting the composite breach is unlawful, in accordance with Article 15(2).[33] **19**

The composite nature of a breach may also be decisive where an investment treaty imposes a limitation period on claims. While several tribunals have broken down composite claims into individual breaches for this purpose—each referring to a specific act or omission—and applied the limitation period to the individual breaches,[34] one North American Free Trade Agreement (NAFTA) tribunal has determined that the continuing character of the underlying measures 'renew[s]' that period.[35] **20**

Finally, the composite nature of a breach may impact on the compensation due, particularly through the valuation date. Some investment tribunals have looked to the date of irreversible harm to set the valuation date for creeping breaches of investment treaty obligations.[36] Others have established the valuation date by reference to Article 15(2), as of the date of the first act in the composite wrongful act.[37] **21**

Investment tribunals have also confirmed that no damages are due for acts or omissions that occurred prior to the entry into force of the treaty,[38] although they may still have regard to such conduct for purposes of assessing whether compensation is due.[39] **22**

D. Conclusion: International investment law potentially influencing general international law

There is little jurisprudence in general international law on Article 15, and no clear consensus concerning the concept of a composite act. Investment tribunals, by contrast, rely on the concept when assessing acts and omissions that, in aggregate, impact on an investment. **23**

Moreover, while virtually all discussion of composite acts in general international law has been based on breaches of systematic obligations, investment tribunals routinely consider composite breaches of non-systematic obligations. **24**

De Renzis, Stefania Grigolon, Liliana Condomitti v Republic of Albania, ICSID Case No ARB/15/28, Award, 24 April 2019, para 558.

[33] eg, *Société Générale* Award (n 20) para 91; *Swisslion* Award (n 19) paras 275–76.

[34] *Rusoro Mining Ltd v Bolivarian Republic of Venezuela*, ICSID Case No ARB(AF)/12/5, Award, 22 August 2016, paras 227–33; *William Ralph Clayton and Others v Government of Canada*, PCA Case No 2009-04, Award on Jurisdiction and Liability, 17 March 2015, para 266; *Aaron C Berkowitz, Brett E Berkowitz, and Trevor B. Berkowitz (formerly Spence International Investments and others) v Republic of Costa Rica*, ICSID Case No UNCT/13/2, Interim Award (Corrected), 30 May 2017, paras 208–10 (hereafter *Berkowitz* Interim Award).

[35] *Parcel Service of America Inc (UPS) v Government of Canada*, ICSID Case No UNCT/02/1, Award on the Merits, 24 May 2007, para 28.

[36] eg, *Compañia del Desarrollo de Santa Elena, S.A. v Republic of Costa Rica*, ICSID Case ARB/96/1, Final Award, 17 February 2000, paras 76–78; *Azurix Corp v Argentine Republic*, ICSID Case ARB/01/12, Award, 14 July 2006, paras 417–18; *Rumeli Telekom A.S. and Telsim Mobil Telekomunikasyon Hizmetleri A.S. v Republic of Kazakhstan*, ICSID Case No ARB/05/16, 29 July 2008, paras 795–96.

[37] *Gemplus S.A., SLP S.A., Gemplus Industrial S.A. de C.V. v United Mexican States*, ICSID Case No ARB(AF)/04/3, Award, 16 June 2010, paras 12.43–12.45; *Talsud S.A. v United Mexican States*, ICSID Case No ARB(AF)/04/4, Award, 16 June 2010, paras 12.43–12.45.

[38] *M.C.I.* Award (n 2) para 136; *Berkowitz* Interim Award (n 34) para 218. But see *Rusoro Mining Ltd v Bolivarian Republic of Venezuela*, Decision of the Paris Court of Appeal, 29 January 2019, para 41; *Rusoro Mining Ltd v Bolivarian Republic of Venezuela*, Decision of the French Court of Cassation, 31 March 2021, para 8.

[39] *Berkowitz* Interim Award (n 34) para 218.

25 In view of the relative paucity of decisions from international courts and tribunals, international investment law is in the process of crystallizing the elements of composite acts, which may impact on general international law.

Selected literature

Buyse A, 'A Lifeline in Time—Non-retroactivity and Continuing Violations under the ECHR' (2006) 75 Nord J Int'l L 63.
Crawford J, 'Breach: The Temporal Element' in Crawford J (ed), *State Responsibility: The General Part* (CUP 2013).
Distefano G, 'Fait Continu, Fait Composé et Fait Complexe dans le Droit de la Responsabilité' (2006) 52 AFDI 1.
Douglas Z, *The International Law of Investment Claims*, ch 8 (CUP 2009).
Elias TO, 'The Doctrine of Intertemporal Law' (1980) 74(2) AJIL 285.
Gallus N, *The Temporal Jurisdiction of International Tribunals* (OUP 2017).
Heiskanen V, '*Entretemps*: Is There a Distinction Between Jurisdiction *Ratione Temporis* and Substantive Protection *Ratione Temporis*?' in Banifatemi Y (ed), *Jurisdiction in Investment Treaty Arbitration* (Juris Publishing 2018).
Higgins R, 'Time and Law: International Perspectives on an Old Problem' (1997) 46 ICLQ 501.
Kotzur M, 'Intertemporal Law' in *Max Planck Encyclopedia of Public International Law* (2008).
Pauwelyn J, 'The Concept of a "Continuing Violation" of an International Obligation: Selected Problems' (1995) 66 BYIL 415.
Salmon J, 'Duration of the Breach' in Crawford J, Pellet A and Olleson S (eds), *The Law of International Responsibility* (OUP 2010).
Van Pachtenbeke A, Haeck Y and Cooper J, 'From De Becker to Varnava: The State of Continuing Situations in the Strasbourg Case Law' (2010) 1 EHRLR 47.

Article 20 of the ARSIWA

Consent

Federica Paddeu

Valid consent by a State to the commission of a given act by another State precludes the wrongfulness of that act in relation to the former State to the extent that the act remains within the limits of that consent.

A. Introduction	1	D. Conclusion: Alignment of general international law and international investment law	17
B. Application in general international law	4		
C. Application in international investment law	12		

A. Introduction

Consent to non-performance of obligations between States is a regular—and usually uneventful—occurrence. Thus, States consent to overflight by foreign (civil and, less frequently, military) aircraft, to the exercise of extraterritorial jurisdiction, and so on.[1] Article 20 reflects the basic principle of consent in the context of State responsibility: *volenti non fit injuria*.[2]

Consent to the non-performance of an obligation must be distinguished from the consent given to the underlying obligation. States can, for example, agree to terminate or suspend a bilateral treaty, thereby terminating or suspending obligations arising under that treaty: this involves the consent to the underlying obligation. But a State can consent to the non-performance of an obligation arising under that treaty, without suspending or terminating the treaty itself.[3] The distinction may be difficult to draw where consent to the non-performance of an obligation is given by way of agreement, especially written agreement. Such cases would likely not involve Article 20 at all, but rather be resolved by reference to principles and rules concerning conflict of norms.

---

[1] ILC, 'Draft Articles on Responsibility of States for Internationally Wrongful Acts, with Commentaries' YILC 2001, Vol II, Part Two, 31, Article 20 para 2 (hereafter ARSIWA Commentaries).
[2] ibid para 1.
[3] ibid para 3. cf M Paparinskis, writing in the context of investment law, frames the issue as one concerning the suspension of treaty provisions under the law of treaties: M Paparinskis, 'Circumstances Precluding Wrongfulness in International Investment Law' (2016) 31 ICSID Rev 484, 489. The approach is unduly narrow: it is not required as a matter of Article 20 of the ARSIWA.

3 There remain some doubts as to whether consent operates *as a defence*, or whether it is a negative element of the definition of all (dispositive) State obligations.[4] And while this is a conceptual and doctrinal question, it is one that nevertheless can have significant practical consequences—most prominently with respect to the burden of proof.[5] The International Law Commission (ILC) debated this question at length but inconclusively. Ultimately agreeing to disagree on the conceptual point, the Commission opted to retain Article 20 as it counted with broad State support.[6] Most scholars addressing this question have leaned towards the negative rule-element approach.[7] But others have argued that, consent can be either a defence or a negative element of the rule and this depends on the specific rule in question.[8]

B. Application in general international law

4 A State's consent to a specific conduct by another State precludes the wrongfulness of that conduct in relation to the consenting State, so long as this consent is valid and the conduct remains within the limits of the consent given.[9]

5 Consent must be given prior to, or at the time of, the otherwise wrongful conduct. Consent given *after* the occurrence of the wrongful conduct is a form of acquiescence or waiver. If the act is continuing, consent given after its commencement can only preclude wrongfulness from the time when it is given.[10]

6 Consent must also be valid, that is given by a person authorized to do so on behalf of the State, and be free from defects. The Commentary to the International Law Commission (ILC) Articles on the Responsibility of States for Internationally Wrongful Acts (ARSIWA) states that the validity of consent is determined by rules of international law outside the law of responsibility.[11]

7 Authority to consent to the non-performance of obligations is not a question of attribution: whereas the conduct of all State organs acting in an official capacity is attributable to the State, not all State organs can consent for the purposes of Article 20.[12] Who is authorized to consent depends on the specific substantive rule: '[d]ifferent officials or agencies may have authority in different contexts, in accordance with the arrangements made by each State and

---

[4] Peremptory rules cannot be set aside unilaterally, by means of defences in the law of responsibility. See Article 26 of the ARSIWA.
[5] See, eg, the parties' arguments on burden of proof in the context of consent to the use of force in *Case Concerning Armed Activities on the Territory of the Congo (DRC v Uganda)* [2005] ICJ Rep 168 (hereafter *DRC v Uganda*). The DRC, claimant in the case, argued in its Reply of 29 May 2002 that it fell on Uganda to prove that the DRC had given consent to the presence of its troops in DRC territory, at 256. In its Rejoinder, Uganda simply notes that DRC presented 'no evidence to refute the existence of such consent' but does not deny the assertion of principle made by the DRC, see Rejoinder of 6 December 2002, 128.
[6] ILC, 'Report of the Commission on the Work of its Fifty-first Session' YILC 1999, Vol II, Part Two, 76. See also B Mansour, 'Consent' in J Crawford, A Pellet and S Olleson (eds), *The Law of International Responsibility* (OUP 2010) 447.
[7] See, eg, K Bannelier and T Christakis, '*Volenti non fit injuria*? Les effets du consentement à l'intervention militaire' (2004) 50 AFDI 102, 288–89; J Crawford, *State Responsibility: The General Part* (CUP 2013) (hereafter Crawford, *General Part*).
[8] See F Paddeu, 'Military Assistance on Request and General Reasons Against Force: Consent as a Defence to the Prohibition of Force' (2020) 7 JUFIL 227.
[9] ARSIWA Commentaries (n 1) Article 20 para 1. On the scope of consent, see ibid para 9.
[10] Commentary to draft Article 29, adopted on first reading: ILC, 'Report of the Commission on the Work of its Thirty-first Session' YILC 1979, Vol II, Part Two, 113, para 16.
[11] ARSIWA Commentaries (n 1) Article 20 para 4.
[12] ibid para 5. See also Crawford, *General Part* (n 7) 285.

general principles of actual and ostensible authority.'[13] Crawford lists a variety of factors relevant to the issue of authorization, including:

> whether the legitimacy of an authority ostensibly consenting has been called into question; the state's domestic law, which might authorize different persons or authorities to consent in different situations; the international law rules on the will of the state; and, if a person or authority who ostensibly consented was not authorized to do so, whether the state whose act they ostensibly consented to knew or ought to have known that.[14]

Consent must be freely given and be clearly established. Consent may be vitiated by error, fraud, corruption, or coercion. The Commentary refers to the 'principles concerning the validity of consent to treaties' for guidance on these matters.[15]

Consent is not subject to any requirements of form.[16] It can be express or implied, but it cannot be presumed. That consent can be implicit or tacit is recognized in the *jus ad bellum*,[17] as acknowledged by the ICJ in *DRC v Uganda*.[18] There is no reason why this should not also be the case more broadly, after all, international law recognizes informal or tacit agreements, as well as informal unilateral acts and waivers.

The Commentary does not address the termination or withdrawal of consent, leaving open whether it can be effected unilaterally or whether any formalities may be necessary. In *DRC v Uganda*, the ICJ gave effect to the DRC's unilateral and informal withdrawal of consent to the presence of Uganda's troops in its territory. Some scholars have read the Court's holding to mean that regardless of how consent is given, whether formally or informally, unilaterally or by agreement, it can be revoked informally and unilaterally—at least in the *jus ad bellum* context.[19] Two observations can be made on this point. First, it is not clear whether the Court's decision is one applicable generally to all instances of consent to non-performance of obligations, or whether it is limited to the *jus ad bellum* context. Second, the Court's judgment can also be read differently: as reflecting the principle of '*parallelisme des formes*'. Indeed, it is worth noting that in that case, the Court emphasized that the *source* of the DRC's consent had been informal and unilateral (inferred from its silence and inaction). This informal consent antedated an agreement between the parties concerning the presence of Uganda's troops in DRC territory, which the Court held had only 'formalised' the prior and informal consent given by the DRC.[20] In addressing the withdrawal of the DRC consent, the Court made specific reference to the circumstances in which consent had been given to begin with, stating that 'this prior authorization or consent ... could be withdrawn at any time ... without further formalities being necessary'.[21]

Lastly, under Article 20, consent is an inter-State defence only. However, in certain circumstances, international law can take into account the consent of non-State actors for the purposes of disapplying certain international law rules. For example, under the International Centre for Settlement of Investment Disputes (ICSID) Convention, an investor's consent to arbitration has the effect of suspending diplomatic protection.[22]

---

[13] ARSIWA Commentaries (n 1) Article 20 para 6.
[14] Crawford, *General Part* (n 7) 286.
[15] ARSIWA Commentaries (n 1) Article 20 para 6.
[16] Crawford, *General Part* (n 7) 284.
[17] E de Wet, *Military Assistance on Request and the Use of Force* (OUP 2020) 161 (hereafter de Wet, *Military Assistance*).
[18] *DRC v Uganda* (n 5) paras 45–46.
[19] de Wet, *Military Assistance* (n 17) 165.
[20] *DRC v Uganda* (n 5) para 47.
[21] ibid.
[22] Article 27(1) ICSID Convention.

C. Application in international investment law

12 To date, consent has not been invoked as a defence in investment arbitration.

13 To the extent that consent is an inter-State defence, an important question is whether the consent of the home State to non-performance of obligations under investment treaties by the host State is effective against an investor. A similar question has arisen in the context of countermeasures, concerning the effect of countermeasures adopted by the host State against the home State on foreign investors.[23] While the situations are analogous, to the extent that both involve the (potential) effects of an inter-State defence as against investors, there are two key differences between consent and countermeasures, that may justify a different answer to this question than that reached in the context of countermeasures:

14 First, the taking of countermeasures is an act of the host State; whereas the giving of consent is an act of an investor's *own* home State. Investment treaties are usually adopted for the purpose of protecting investors from the actions of host States, and not of their home States.

15 Second, however one chooses to characterize the rights of investors (substantive or procedural), it is undeniable that they derive from the investment treaty. The home State, just as it could enter into the treaty, also retains the power to modify, suspend, or terminate such treaty commitments. If the home State can modify, suspend, and even terminate the investment treaty, with the consequent modification, suspension, or termination of the protections afforded to investors, it seems logical that the home State can agree to the temporary non-performance of one of the obligations in that same treaty: *qui peut le plus, peut le moins*.[24]

16 A different, but connected, question is whether investors can consent to the host-State's non-performance of its investment treaty obligations—to the extent that they affect the investor in question. Two investment tribunals have addressed this question, reaching inconsistent conclusions. In *SGS*, the tribunal said that it was 'doubtful that a private party can by contract waive rights or dispense with the performance of obligations imposed on the States parties to those treaties under international law'.[25] By contrast, the *Hochtief* tribunal held that 'there is no legal reason why effect should not be given to an agreement between an investor and a host State either to limit the rights of the investor or to oblige the investor not to pursue any remedies, including its BIT remedies, in certain circumstances'.[26]

D. Conclusion: Alignment of general international law and international investment law

17 There has been no practice involving consent in investment law, so it is not possible to say whether it aligns with general international law. Consent of the home State is not likely to

---

[23] See in this Commentary: Martins Paparinskis, 'Articles 49–54 of the ARSIWA'.

[24] On the termination of investment treaties, and refuting arguments that investor consent is necessary, see F Bordin, 'Reasserting Control through Withdrawal from Investment Agreements: What Role for the Law of Treaties?' in A Kulick (ed), *Reassertion of Control over the Investment Treaty Regime* (CUP 2015) 214–17. See further T Voon and others, 'Parting Ways: The Impact of Mutual Termination of Investment Treaties on Investor Rights' (2014) 29 ICSID Rev 451.

[25] *SGS Société Générale de Surveillance SA v Philippines*, ICSID Case No ARB/02/6, Decision on Objections to Jurisdiction, 29 January 2004, para 154.

[26] *Hochtief Aktiengesellschaft v Argentine Republic*, ICSID Case No ARB/07/31, Award, 9 December 2014, para 191.

arise often in investment arbitration.[27] Given the flexible requirements and conditions of the regulation of consent to non-performance of obligations under Article 20, as well as the extensive *renvoi* to the specific substantive rules at issue (which would include those regulating investment law on matters such as authorization to give consent, and the validity of home State consent as against investors), it does not seem likely that investment law will need to deviate from general international law in respect of the defence of consent.

Selected literature

Abass A, 'Consent Precluding State Responsibility: A Critical Analysis' (2004) 53 ICLQ 211.

Armed Activities on the Territory of the Congo (DRC v Uganda) (2005) ICJ Rep 168.

Crawford J, *State Responsibility: The General Part* (CUP 2013).

Mansour B, 'Consent' in Crawford J, Pellet A and Olleson S (eds), *The Law of International Responsibility* (OUP 2010) 439.

Paddeu F, 'Military Assistance on Request and General Reasons Against Force: Consent as a Defence to the Prohibition of Force' (2020) 7 JUFIL 227.

Paddeu F, *Justification and Excuse in International Law: Concept and Theory of General Defences* (CUP 2018).

Paparinskis M, 'Circumstances Precluding Wrongfulness in International Investment Law' (2016) 31 ICSID Rev 484.

---

[27] For a potential example of how consent might arise in investment arbitration, see G Ruse-Khan and F Paddeu, 'A TRIPS-COVID Waiver and Overlapping Commitments to Protect Intellectual Property Rights Under International IP and Investment Agreements', *South Centre* Research Paper 144, 44–53 (27 January 2022) https://www.southcentre.int/research-paper-144-27-january-2022/ last accessed 23 October 2023.

Article 21 of the ARSIWA

Self-defence

Federica Paddeu

The wrongfulness of an act of a State is precluded if the act constitutes a lawful measure of self-defence taken in conformity with the Charter of the United Nations.

A. Introduction	1	D. Conclusion: Alignment of general international law and international investment law	13
B. Application in general international law	3		
C. Application in international investment law	8		

A. Introduction

1 The right of self-defence, codified in Article 51 of the UN Charter, provides a justification for the use of force such that, when a State resorts to force in self-defence, it is (all things considered) not a breach of the prohibition of force codified in Article 2(4) of the Charter.[1] Article 21 extends the justificatory effect of self-defence beyond the *jus ad bellum*, to violations of international legal obligations caused by lawful measures of self-defence,[2] that is by defensive force which is compatible with Article 51 of the UN Charter.[3] Indeed, a use of force can infringe many other obligations owed to the State against which it is exercised. For example, States have claimed the following obligations to be breached by uses of force: territorial sovereignty and non-intervention which are often attendant to uses of force in self-defence in the territory of the aggressor State, as well as (potentially) commercial obligations under bilateral treaties,[4] aviation agreements,[5] and the obligation to settle disputes

---

[1] ILC, 'Draft Articles on Responsibility of States for Internationally Wrongful Acts, with Commentaries' YILC 2001, Vol II, Part Two, 31, Article 21 para 1 (hereafter ARSIWA Commentaries).

[2] What may be termed 'collateral impairments' caused by defensive force: JM Thouvenin, 'Self-Defence' in J Crawford, A Pellet and S Olleson (eds), *The Law of International Responsibility* (OUP 2010) 464; F Paddeu, 'Self-Defence as a Circumstance Precluding Wrongfulness: Understanding Article 21 of the Articles on State Responsibility' (2014) 85 BYIL 90 (hereafter Paddeu, 'Self-Defence').

[3] ARSIWA Commentaries (n 1) Article 21 para 1.

[4] See, eg, *Military and Paramilitary Activities in and Against Nicaragua (Nicaragua v United States of America)* (Merits) [1986] ICJ Rep 14; *Oil Platforms (Islamic Republic of Iran v United States of America)* (Judgment) [2003] ICJ Rep 161.

[5] See, eg, Memorial of Iran, *Aerial Incident of 3 July 1988 (Iran v USA)*, 146 (breach of the Chicago Convention), 182 (breach of the Treaty of Amity), 238 (both).

peacefully.[6] Such obligations could potentially be infringed also when a State uses force in self-defence. Article 21 is aimed at providing a justification for these, so-to-speak, 'collateral' breaches caused by lawful measures of self-defence. But while Article 21 is intended to justify these 'collateral' breaches of obligations caused by self-defensive force, it *cannot* justify the breach of any and all obligations of the defending State: obligations of so-called 'total restraint' are excluded from its scope. Obligations of 'total restraint' are those which are intended as definitive constraints on State conduct even in armed conflict, such as humanitarian law, and non-derogable human rights.[7]

Article 21 is made necessary by the decline in importance—at least in practice—of the formal **2** state of war. Historically, the existence of a state war defined the scope of belligerent rights and suspended the normal, peace-time relations, between the States in conflict.[8] As such, the use of force could not infringe the peace-time obligations existing between belligerents. In practice, formal states of war are nowadays rare, even when States are engaged in armed conflict.[9] When States engage in armed conflict, they do so while formally 'at peace'. All of their legal relations remain in force,[10] such that they may be infringed by forcible measures.[11] The question thus arises whether these violations can be justified when the State acts in self-defence. While normatively this may appear desirable,[12] the status of Article 21 as a matter of customary law remains uncertain.[13]

B. Application in general international law

There are, to date, no decisions of international tribunals applying Article 21. Nevertheless, **3** States have had occasion to rely on self-defence to justify the violation of obligations *other* than the prohibition of force, when such violations were caused by what they claimed were lawful measures of self-defence.

In *Oil Platforms*, the Unites States relied on Article 21 as a justification for the breach of the **4** 1955 Treaty of Amity by its destruction of Iranian oil platforms. The United States invoked self-defence as a justification for the use of force, and maintained that '[a]ny actions of the US deemed incompatible with Article X of the Treaty would not be wrongful by the operation of this principle [self-defence] of customary international law'.[14] Iran also accepted this proposition, stating that:

---

[6] See, eg, *Guyana v Suriname*, Award, 17 September 2007, UNCLOS Annex VII Tribunal, at 147, para 445 and dispositif at 165, para 2, on the obligation to solve disputes peacefully contained in Article 279 of the 1982 United Nations Convention on the Law of the Sea (adopted 10 December 1982, entered into force 16 November 1994) 1833 UNTS 397 (UNCLOS).
[7] ARSIWA Commentaries (n 1) Article 21 paras 3–4. Distinguishing three sets of legal relations, and explaining the impact of self-defence in relation to each, see F Paddeu, *Justification and Excuse in International Law: Concept and Theory of General Defences* (CUP 2018) 193–99.
[8] SC Neff, *War and the Law of Nations* (CUP 2005) 177.
[9] For an exhaustive review of practice, see generally M Mancini, *Stato di guerra e conflitto armato nel diritto internazionale* (Giappichelli 2009).
[10] States can suspend or terminate treaties during armed conflict, though it is unclear whether the existence of armed conflict is on its own an accepted ground for suspension or termination. The ILC adopted articles on the Effects of Armed Conflict on Treaties in 2011, UN Doc A/RES/66/99. For a review, and critique, of the ILC's articles, see Y Ronen, 'Treaties and Armed Conflict' in CJ Tams and others (eds), *Research Handbook on the Law of Treaties* (2014) 541.
[11] As clarified by the ICJ '[a] violation of the rights of one party under the Treaty by means of the use of force is as unlawful as would be a violation by administrative decision or by any other means': *Oil Platforms (Islamic Republic of Iran v United States of America)* (Preliminary Objections) [1996] ICJ Rep 803, para 21.
[12] J Crawford, *State Responsibility: The General Part* (CUP 2013) 291; Paddeu, 'Self-Defence' (n 2).
[13] See, eg, M Paparinskis, 'Circumstances Precluding Wrongfulness in International Investment Law' (2016) 31 ICSID Rev 484, 493 (hereafter Paparinskis, 'Circumstances Precluding Wrongfulness').
[14] *Oil Platforms (Islamic Republic of Iran v United States of America)*, US Rejoinder (23 March 2001), 141, para 5.02.

[A]ction otherwise lawfully taken in self-defence could constitute a circumstance precluding wrongfulness in relation to Article X, paragraph 1, of the Treaty. In other words, it accepts the proposition contained in Article 21 of the ILC Articles on the Responsibility of States.[15]

5 Iran later added that if made out, self-defence would 'exonerate the United States entirely; it would provide a complete justification for their conduct, in accordance with Article 21 of the ILC's Articles'.[16]

6 Similar arguments can be found in the *Nicaragua* case, where Nicaragua raised, in counter-argument, whether self-defence could provide a defence for the US bombing of Nicaraguan ports, in violation of the 1956 Treaty of Friendship,[17] and the principles of territorial sovereignty and non-intervention.[18] Likewise, in *DRC v Uganda*, Uganda raised self-defence in response to claims that its use of force in the DRC's territory had infringed the latter's territorial sovereignty and right to non-intervention, and it specifically referred to Article 21 in its oral pleadings before the Court.[19]

7 In all these cases, the Court found that the State was not acting lawfully in self-defence: accordingly, it could not find that lawful self-defence could justify the collateral violation of other obligations. This said, the Court seemed to have accepted in principle that self-defence could have provided a justification for the impairment of these obligations.[20]

C. Application in international investment law

8 Article 21 has not been invoked in investment treaty arbitration.

9 It is nevertheless plausible that a State acting in self-defence harms a foreign investment within its territory in breach of, for example, its full protection and security obligation.[21] Whether self-defence could serve as a defence in these circumstances is unclear. Three observations can be made.

10 First, self-defence is an inter-State defence, operative between the State victim of an armed attack for its forcible response against the author of the armed attack ('aggressor State').[22] Article 21 could serve as a defence in an inter-State claim under an investment treaty between

---

[15] Iran statement, *Oil Platforms*, CR 2003/5, 41, para 29. (references omitted)
[16] ibid para 3.
[17] Memorial of Nicaragua, *Nicaragua*, ICJ Pleadings, Vol IV, 112, para 427.
[18] Memorial of Nicaragua, *Nicaragua*, ICJ Pleadings, Vol IV, 115 (territorial sovereignty), 120 (non-intervention). As explained in the memorial: 'although the claim based upon violations of sovereignty overlap[ped] with other causes of action relating to the use of force' it did not 'simply coincide with those other causes of action and consequently plays a significant independent role': ibid 116, para 441.
[19] Uganda oral statement, *DRC v Uganda*, CR 2005/7, 30, para 78.
[20] In both cases, the Court denied that the defence was met on the facts, thus implicitly accepting the principle that self-defence could have justified the breach of these obligations: *Military and Paramilitary Activities in and Against Nicaragua (Nicaragua v United States of America)* [1986] ICJ Rep 14, para 252; *Armed Activities on the Territory of the Congo (DRC v Uganda)* [2005] ICJ Rep 168, paras 165, 345.1 (note that the Court only refers to the principle of non-use of force and the principle of non-intervention in the dispositif, even though the DRC had claimed also a breach of its territorial sovereignty and the Court had addressed it in its reasoning. For the DRC's prayer for relief, see Memorial of the DRC, 273).
[21] Paparinskis, 'Circumstances Precluding Wrongfulness' (n 13) 492.
[22] ARSIWA Commentaries (n 1) Article 21 para 5. Possibly, though still controversially, a State may rely on self-defence against non-State actors to the extent that they are authors of armed attacks. But the matter remains contentious. For a recent review of practice, see O Corten, *The Law Against War* (Hart Publishing 2021), ch 3; A Haque, 'The Use of Force Against Non-State Actors: All Over the Map' (2021) 8 JUFIL 278.

the aggressor and the defending State: the defending State could rely on self-defence to justify potential violations of the treaty vis-à-vis the aggressor State. It is less clear to what extent Article 21 could be relied upon to justify the breach of rights of third States, and by implication of nationals of third States.[23]

Second, it may be queried whether self-defence could be invoked to justify the breach of obligations owed to private parties. The issue is analogous to that which arises in the context of countermeasures affecting obligations under investment treaties—that is, whether a countermeasure taken by a host State against a home State can be invoked against affected investors. Similar considerations are likely to be relevant in both contexts.[24]

Third, there may be jurisdictional difficulties since the invocation of self-defence requires a tribunal to assess the legality of conduct which falls outside the scope of an investment treaty (namely, the legality of a use of force) and, in the case of investor–State arbitration, the conduct of a third party (to the proceedings namely, the legality of the use of force by the alleged aggressor State). A similar question was addressed by the International Court of Justice (ICJ) in the appeal of the International Civil Aviation Organization (ICAO) jurisdiction judgments in the context of countermeasures. The Court held that the ICAO had incidental jurisdiction to determine the legality of the prior wrongful act triggering countermeasures affecting ICAO obligations, to the extent that this was necessary to solve a dispute under the ICAO treaties—even if the prior wrongful act affected obligations over which the ICAO had no subject-matter jurisdiction.[25] Applying the same reasoning, an investment tribunal could find it has incidental jurisdiction to determine the legality of a use of force to the extent that this has a bearing on the resolution of a dispute under an investment treaty. Nevertheless, the ICJ's reasoning may not assist in overcoming the third-party hurdle: in the ICAO cases, the countermeasures had been taken as between the parties to the dispute before the ICAO and the Court; but an investment tribunal would need to pass judgment on the conduct of a State not party to the proceedings.

D. Conclusion: Alignment of general international law and international investment law

While investment arbitration tribunals have often dealt with alleged breaches of investment treaties in the context of armed conflict, no tribunal to date has addressed a defence based on self-defence. If and when invocations of self-defence are made before investment tribunals,

---

[23] ARSIWA Commentaries (n 1) Article 21 para 5. On Article 21 and third parties, see T Christakis and K Bannelier, 'La légitime défense en tant que "circonstance excluant l'illicéité"' in R Kherad (ed), *Légitimes défenses* (LGDJ 2007) 233–56 (arguing that Article 21 would only be useful to justify breaches of third-party rights); F Paddeu, 'Use of Force against Non-State Actors and the Circumstance Precluding Wrongfulness of Self-Defence' (2017) 30 LJIL 93 (suggesting a way of extending Article 21 to third-party rights).
[24] For more on this question see in this Commentary: Martins Paparinskis, 'Articles 49–54 of the ARSIWA'.
[25] The ICJ considered that the ICAO could consider a defence of countermeasures, involving the breach of obligations other than the Chicago Convention, so long as this was necessary for the resolution of a dispute falling within its jurisdiction: *Appeal Relating to the Jurisdiction of the ICAO Council Under Article 84 of the Convention on International Civil Aviation (Bahrain, Egypt, Saudi Arabia and United Arab Emirates v Qatar)* (Judgment) [2020] ICJ Rep 81, para 61.

it is key that in this important area of international law, investment tribunals do not deviate from general international law.

Selected literature

Crawford J, *State Responsibility: The General Part* (CUP 2013).

Henckels C, 'Investment Treaty Security Exceptions, Necessity and Self-Defence in the Context of Armed Conflict' in Fach Gómez K, Gourgourinis A and Titi C (eds), *International Investment Law and the Law of Armed Conflict* (Springer 2019).

Paddeu F, 'Self-Defence as a Circumstance Precluding Wrongfulness: Understanding Article 21 of the Articles on State Responsibility' (2014) 85 BYIL 90.

Thouvenin JM, 'Self-Defence' in Crawford J, Pellet A and Olleson S (eds), *The Law of International Responsibility* (OUP 2010).

Selected decision

Oil Platforms (Islamic Republic of Iran v United States of America) [2003] ICJ Rep 161.

Article 23 of the ARSIWA

Force majeure

Federica Paddeu

1. The wrongfulness of an act of a State not in conformity with an international obligation of that State is precluded if the act is due to force majeure, that is the occurrence of an irresistible force or of an unforeseen event, beyond the control of the State, making it materially impossible in the circumstances to perform the obligation.

2. Paragraph 1 does not apply if:
   (a) the situation of force majeure is due, either alone or in combination with other factors, to the conduct of the State invoking it; or
   (b) the State has assumed the risk of that situation occurring.

A. Introduction	1	C. Application in international investment law	13
B. Application in general international law	2	D. Conclusion: Some deviation from general international law	22

A. Introduction

The defence of *force majeure* is largely accepted as part of customary international law.[1] Article 23 sets a very high standard that is almost never met. A successful claim of *force majeure* must fulfil five conditions: (i) there must be an unforeseen event or an irresistible force (the 'triggering event'); (ii) the event or force must be beyond the control of the State; (iii) the event must make it 'materially' impossible to perform an obligation; (iv) the State must not have contributed to the situation; and (v) the State must not have assumed the risk of the situation occurring. Each of these will be assessed in turn, except for (v) which is likely to depend on the specific language of particular treaty commitments.

B. Application in general international law

The circumstances giving rise to *force majeure* are exceptional, so that the defence is rarely invoked in practice. Each of the requirements that need to be met are addressed in turn, before considering the classification of this defence as a justification or an excuse.

---

[1] For a review of the practice and *opinio juris* in relation to the defence of *force majeure*, see F Paddeu, 'A Genealogy of *Force Majeure* in International Law' (2011) 82 BYIL 381, 480–93.

3 Triggering event: The triggering event refers to the factual conditions giving rise to the material impossibility to perform the obligation. The triggering event can be of natural or anthropogenic origins, or be the result of a combination of the two.[2] There are two types of triggering events. The event can be an unforeseen one, in the sense that it is 'neither foreseen nor of an easily foreseeable kind'.[3] The Commentary on the International Law Commission (ILC) Articles on the Responsibility of States for Internationally Wrongful Acts (ARSIWA) does not describe what is required to prove foreseeability: to the extent that we can only assign probabilities to the occurrence of future events, beyond what degree of probability (and with what confidence) is the defence excluded? Is *any* probability of an event occurring enough to make it foreseeable and, as such, to dismiss the plea? The point is not settled.

4 *Force majeure* can also be triggered by an 'irresistible force'. Presumably, whether the 'force' was foreseen is irrelevant: Article 23 speaks of an 'unforeseen event or an irresistible force'. The ARSIWA Commentary (hereafter: Commentary) does not clarify the meaning of the term 'force', but it is plausible that 'force' here does not imply an event having a certain physical strength (such as an earthquake), but rather any event which can cause some constraint or coercion. Indeed, as the Commentary clarifies, the adjective 'irresistible' is intended to emphasize 'that there must be an element of constraint which the State was unable to avoid or oppose by its own means'.[4]

5 The State's non-performance of the obligation at issue must be 'due' to the triggering event, implying that the triggering event must be the cause of the material impossibility to perform.[5] But it need not be the sole cause: good-faith contributions to the situation of impossibility by the invoking State will not exclude the plea.

6 Beyond control of the State: This requirement was included in the text of Article 23 'in order to further stress the element of impossibility' at the heart of this defence.[6] The event is beyond State control if it overpowers the State. This element is closely linked to the unforeseen or irresistible nature of the event, as well as to the requirement of non-contribution (addressed below).

7 Material impossibility: To give rise to *force majeure*, the triggering event must have caused a 'material impossibility to perform' the obligation in question. The Commentary indicates that this must be an 'actual impossibility', and that it requires more than an increased difficulty of performance.[7] Furthermore, this impossibility is different from that envisaged in Article 61 of the Vienna Convention on the Law of Treaties (VCLT): as the Commentary indicates, impossibility for *force majeure* is 'less than that' required under Article 61.[8]

8 There are disagreements in the literature as to what this element requires, in particular whether it must be an absolute *and* material impossibility as held in *Rainbow Warrior*.[9]

---

[2] ILC, 'Draft Articles on Responsibility of States for Internationally Wrongful Acts, with Commentaries' YILC 2001, Vol II, Part Two, 31, Article 23 para 3 (hereafter ARSIWA Commentaries). Indeed, it can originate in pressures from another State; see ibid Article 18 para 4.
[3] ibid Article 23 para 2.
[4] ibid.
[5] ibid.
[6] Drafting Committee Chairman, 1579th Meeting, YILC 1979, Vol I, 234, para 3.
[7] ARSIWA Commentaries (n 2) Article 23 para 3.
[8] ibid para 4.
[9] *Rainbow Warrior (New Zealand v France)* (1990) XX RIAA 215, para 77.

On one view, the standard of impossibility in Article 23 need not be 'absolute'.[10] At least **9** one scholar has argued that *force majeure* in Article 23 covers cases of 'relative impossibility of performance'.[11] This understanding of the standard of impossibility relies on the differences between Article 23 of the ARSIWA and Article 61 of the VCLT, highlighted in the Commentary to Article 23, and in particular on the *travaux préparatoires* of the VCLT. The *travaux* show that an amendment to equate the concept of impossibility in Article 61 with *force majeure* was unsuccessful as States desired to keep Article 61 within strict bounds. The implication of this unsuccessful amendment and the reasons behind it, so the argument goes, show that the impossibility required for force majeure is less demanding than that required by Article 61 of the VCLT. This view also finds support on the International Court of Justice (ICJ)'s observation in *Gabčíkovo-Nagymaros*, picked up by Special Rapporteur Crawford in his report to the International Law Commission (ILC),[12] that the standard in Article 61 of the VCLT was narrower than that required under *force majeure*.[13]

On the other view, impossibility under Article 23 must be absolute *as well as* material.[14] This **10** understanding relies on a number of factors. First, the record shows that the ILC Drafting Committee's replacement of the adjective 'absolute' with 'material' was intended to 'convey the idea of an objective rather than a subjective criterion for determining the situation of impossibility',[15] it was not intended to make the standard less stringent. Second, the terms 'material' and 'absolute' refer to different qualities of the impossibility. 'Material' refers to the *kind* of impossibility at issue: it must be a physical inability to perform the obligation, as opposed to, say, a moral or legal impossibility.[16] Whereas 'absolute' refers to the *degree* of this impossibility: the State must have *no way* to perform the obligation in question, it must have no choice in the matter. This is confirmed by the rationale of the defence of *force majeure* which, as explained in the ILC Commentary, lies in the fact that the non-performance of the obligation is 'involuntary or involves no element of free choice'.[17] Cases of relative impossibility, in which the State can comply with the obligation but only at an exceedingly high cost, initially covered under Special Rapporteur Ago's draft provision on *force majeure* (draft Article 31),[18] were excised from this provision and included in a different one (draft Article 32, now Article 24) *precisely because* they involved a lower degree of impossibility.[19] Lastly,

---

[10] See, eg, J Crawford, *State Responsibility: The General Part* (CUP 2013) 299 (hereafter Crawford, *General Part*); A Tzanakopoulos and SI Lekkas, '*Pacta Sunt Servanda* versus Flexibility in the Suspension and Termination of Treaties' in CJ Tams and others (eds), *Research Handbook on the Law of Treaties* (Edward Elgar Publishing 2014) 329–30.

[11] A Gourgourinis, 'Financial crisis as *force majeure* under international law and EU law: Defending emergency measures, *à l'européenne*, in investment arbitration under intra-EU BITs' in CJ Tams and others (eds), *International Investment Law and the Global Financial Architecture* (Edward Elgar Publishing 2017) 293 (hereafter Gourgourinis, 'Financial crisis'). See also L Wang and W Shan, 'Force Majeure and Investment Arbitration' (2022) 37 ICSID Rev 138, 145–46 (who seem to accept that force majeure does not require absolute impossibility, and suggesting that impossibility must be 'insurmountable').

[12] J Crawford, 'Second Report on State Responsibility' YILC 1999 Vol II, Part One, para 259.

[13] *Gabčíkovo-Nagymaros Project (Hungary v Slovakia)* [1997] ICJ Rep 7.

[14] See G Scalese, *La rilevanza delle scusanti nella teoria dell'illecito internazionale* (Editoriale Scientifica 2008) 69; S Szurek, 'Force Majeure' in J Crawford, A Pellet and S Olleson (eds), *The Law of International Responsibility* (OUP 2010) 479–80; F Paddeu, *Justification and Excuse in International Law: Concept and Theory of General Defences* (CUP 2018) 320–23 (hereafter Paddeu, *Justification and Excuse*).

[15] Drafting Committee Chairman, 1579th Meeting, YILC 1979, Vol I, 234, para 3. On which see Paddeu, *Justification and Excuse* (n 14) 309–11, 313–14.

[16] Paddeu, *Justification and Excuse* (n 14) 322–23.

[17] ARRSIWA Commentaries (n 2) Article 23 para 1.

[18] R Ago, 'Eighth Report on State Responsibility' YILC 1979, Vol II, Part One, para 106.

[19] Paddeu, *Justification and Excuse* (n 14) 446–47.

even if it were absolute, impossibility under Article 61 would still be narrower than impossibility under Article 23: the former requires the 'destruction' of an 'object essential to the execution of the treaty', neither of which are necessary under Article 23.[20]

11 Non-contribution: The plea is excluded if the situation of *force majeure* 'is due, either alone or in combination with other factors, to the conduct of the State invoking it'. A State is barred from relying on the defence if it has caused or induced the situation of *force majeure*.[21] However, the Commentary clarifies that it is not enough for the State to have contributed to the situation: the plea will be barred only when the situation is 'due' to the conduct of the invoking State. Furthermore, unwitting contributions done 'in good faith' and which did not themselves make 'the event any less unforeseen' will not preclude reliance on the plea.[22] The standard is somewhat vague. There is no indication, for example, of any temporal proximity required or how to assess the contribution in cases in which the situation is caused by State conduct 'in combination' with other factors. No further clarification has come from international decisions: since force majeure is invoked relatively rarely, international courts and tribunals have not yet had an opportunity to flesh out this requirement.

12 Justification or excuse? The Commentary to the ILC does not settle this question. Scholars have argued that *force majeure* operates as an excuse, insofar as it is concerned with the situation of the State in conditions where its free will is nullified by an external event.[23]

C. Application in international investment law

13 *Force majeure* is often raised as a defence in investment-treaty arbitration, commonly under contract law (either the domestic law of the contract, or under a contract clause) and, though more sporadically, under customary law.[24] However, the defence is rarely invoked in respect of claims for breach of standards of investment protection. Article 23 was referred to, and endorsed in, *Enron*,[25] *Sempra*,[26] and *De Sutter v Madagascar (II)*.[27] The tribunals in *LAFICO*,[28] *Aucoven*,[29] and *Güris*[30] addressed some of the defence's requirements in more detail.

14 Triggering event: The *Aucoven* and *Güris* tribunals accepted, in principle, that *force majeure* could arise from human action (civil unrest and armed conflict, respectively), and both endorsed the need for a causal link between the triggering event and the material impossibility.

---

[20] For an in-depth assessment of the relations between these two rules, see S Forlati, *Diritto dei trattati e responsabilità internazionale* (Giuffrè 2005) 159–62.
[21] ARSIWA Commentaries (n 2) Article 23 para 9.
[22] ibid.
[23] Crawford, *General Part* (n 10) 319; Paddeu, *Justification and Excuse* (n 14) 328–33.
[24] See C Binder, 'Circumstances Precluding Wrongfulness' in M Bungenberg and others (eds), *International Investment Law: A Handbook* (Hart Publishing 2015) 458; Wang and Shan, 'Force Majeure', 152–57.
[25] *Enron Corporation and Ponderosa Assets LP v Argentine Republic*, ICSID Case ARB/01/3, Award, 22 May 2007, para 217.
[26] *Sempra Energy International v Argentine Republic*, ICSID Case ARB/02/16, Award, 29 September 2007, para 246.
[27] *Peter de Sutter and Kristof de Sutter v Madagascar (II)*, ICSID Case ARB/17/18, Award, 17 April 2020, para 347.
[28] *Libyan Arab Foreign Investment Company (LAFICO) v Burundi* (1991) 96 ILR 279 (hereafter *LAFICO v Burundi*).
[29] *Autopista Concesionada de Venezuela v Bolivarian Republic of Venezuela*, ICSID Case No ARB/00/5, Award, 23 September 2003 (hereafter *Aucoven*).
[30] *Güris and others v Syria*, ICC Case No 21845/ZF/AYZ, Award, 5 April 2016 (hereafter *Güris v Syria*).

On this last point in particular, the *Güris* tribunal held that 'war or armed conflict, on its own, does not excuse non-compliance with monetary obligations'.[31]

The *Aucoven* tribunal dismissed the plea on the ground that the triggering event was foreseeable, even if it had not been foreseen by the respondent. It found that given recent historical events, it could not reasonably be 'argue[d] that Venezuelan officials negotiating the Agreement <u>could ignore</u> that the increase in transportation price resulting from the contractual mechanism of toll rate increase <u>could at least potentially</u> lead to violent popular protest similar to the one of 1989'.[32] This was supported by testimony confirming 'that the Ministry wanted to avoid protests of the kind of the Caracazo'.[33] Furthermore, the tribunal was unconvinced that the strong public resistance that became evident after the agreement had been signed would have not have been evident during its negotiation. Likewise, on Venezuela's argument that it had not foreseen the *magnitude* of the unrest, the tribunal held that: 'if popular protest could be foreseen, then the possibility of very violent protest <u>could not be ruled out</u>.'[34]

<u>Material impossibility</u>: The *Aucoven* tribunal applied the standard of impossibility under Venezuelan law, pursuant to which 'it suffices that by all reasonable judgment the event impedes the normal performance of the contract'.[35] The tribunal further held that this standard was not different from that applicable under international law.[36]

<u>Non-contribution</u>: The *LAFICO* tribunal dismissed the defence on the ground that Burundi had contributed to the situation: the material impossibility which prevented the company from operating had been the result of Burundi's unilateral decision to expel the company's board members, without which the company could not function.[37]

<u>Assumption of risk</u>: In *Güris*, the tribunal was concerned with a so-called 'war clause' which required the payment of damages to the investor. The tribunal dismissed Syria's defence of *force majeure* due to lack of evidence, and added that:

> By virtue of Article 4 of the Syria–Italy BIT, the Contracting Parties assumed the risk that 'war, other forms of armed conflict, a state of emergency, civil strife or other similar events' might occur and cause 'losses or damages' to investors. To insure against the occurrence of such harm, the Contracting Parties undertook to 'offer adequate compensation'. It is not open to the Respondent to invoke as force majeure the very risk against which it has undertaken to offer an indemnity.[38]

Force majeure is likely to be invoked in investment disputes arising out of the Covid-19 pandemic-management measures adopted by States.[39] The defence could be raised both as a matter of contract law (in accordance with the contractual terms, or the law applicable to the contract), and as a matter of international law (as a defence against alleged investment-treaty breaches).

---

[31] ibid para 320.
[32] *Aucoven* (n 29) para 115. (emphasis added)
[33] ibid.
[34] ibid para 117.
[35] ibid para 121.
[36] ibid para 123.
[37] *LAFICO v Burundi* (n 28) para 55.
[38] *Güris v Syria* (n 30) para 322.
[39] For an early assessment, see F Paddeu and F Jephcott, 'COVID-19 and Defences in the Law of State Responsibility: Parts I and II' (*EJIL:Talk!*, 17 March 2020) https://www.ejiltalk.org/covid-19-and-defences-in-the-law-of-state-responsibility-part-i/ and https://www.ejiltalk.org/covid-19-and-defences-in-the-law-of-state-responsibility-part-ii/ last accessed 23 October 2023.

20 In respect of the international law defence, much will turn on (i) the obligation allegedly breached and (ii) the point in time during the pandemic when the breach is alleged to have occurred. Indeed, the unforeseen, unforseeable, or irresistible character of the initial outbreak, and of subsequent waves of infection, may differ depending on the point in the pandemic timeline when the State is said to have breached its obligations. The unforeseen, unforeseeable, or irresistible nature of the initial outbreak of the virus may not be too difficult to prove, but matters may differ with respect to subsequent waves of infection.

21 The most difficult hurdle will be proof of 'material impossibility of performance'. A key issue here will be the standard of impossibility applied. The stricter standard of 'absolute and material' impossibility will be hard to meet: it requires the absence of choice for the State in question. States had a choice whether to impose restrictive measures. To be sure, these were often lamentable choices as failure to act could have led to grave risks to the health and life of the State's population and to the continued maintenance of health services. But to the extent that States had some choice whether to adopt restrictive measures (they could have avoided all restrictions, as indeed some did), then this strict standard will not be met. The lower standard endorsed by some scholars (involving some high degree of difficulty of performance) or the *Aucoven* tribunal (whether the event could reasonably be said to have impeded the normal performance of the treaty) would be easier to meet, at least in the earlier phases of the pandemic but possibly also later on.

D. Conclusion: Some deviation from general international law

22 Investor–State tribunals have, for the most part, interpreted and applied the defence of *force majeure* in line with general international law.

23 They have differed, however, in one crucial respect: the standard of material impossibility. There is some disagreement in the literature as to what this standard requires as a matter of general international law. Most investment tribunals have not engaged with this standard in any depth. In *Aucoven*, however, the tribunal accepted a lower standard of disruption to normal performance—that of Venezuelan law—which it considered not to differ from that under international law. The *Aucoven* award seems to support the view that the impossibility required under Article 23 need not be absolute.

24 Whether such deviation is justified by general international law, or is desirable, remains an open question. If impossibility required under Article 23 is not absolute, but is higher than an increased difficulty of performance, the question arises as to the relevant threshold. Anastasios Gourgourinis suggests that a threshold might be found in cases where 'performance of the obligation in question would be an unreasonable sacrifice', such as 'compliance [that] would jeopardise the very existence of the State or the fulfilment of its essential governmental functions'.[40] This risks sliding the defence of *force majeure* into the defence of necessity, which is concerned precisely with situations where performance would impair essential interest of the State, such as its existence and the maintenance of essential governmental functions, but without the safeguards and strict conditions imposed on the invocation of necessity.[41]

---

[40] Gourgourinis, 'Financial crisis' (n 11) 294.
[41] On which see Paddeu, *Justification and Excuse* (n 14) 322–23.

Selected literature

Binder C, 'Circumstances Precluding Wrongfulness' in Bungenberg M and others (eds), *International Investment Law: A Handbook* (Hart Publishing 2015).

Binder C and Janig P, 'The Effect of Armed Hostilities on Investment Treaty Obligations: A Case of *Force Majeure*?' in Ackermann T and Wuschka S (eds), *Investments in Conflict Zones: The Role of International Investment Law in Armed Conflicts, Disputed Territories, and 'Frozen' Conflicts* (Brill/Nijhoff 2021) 112.

Crawford J, *State Responsibility: The General Part* (CUP 2013).

Paddeu F, 'A Genealogy of *Force Majeure* in International Law' (2011) 82 BYIL 381.

Paddeu F, *Justification and Excuse in International Law: Concept and Theory of General Defences* (CUP 2018).

Szurek S, 'Force Majeure' in Crawford J, Pellet A and Olleson S (eds), *The Law of International Responsibility* (OUP 2010).

Wang L and Shan W, '*Force Majeure* and Investment Arbitration' (2022) 37 ICSID Rev 138.

Selected decisions

Autopista Concesionada de Venezuela v Bolivarian Republic of Venezuela, ICSID Case No ARB/00/5, Award, 23 September 2003.

Gabčíkovo-Nagymaros Project (Hungary v Slovakia) [1997] ICJ Rep 7.

Libyan Arab Foreign Investment Company (LAFICO) v Burundi (1991) 96 ILR 279.

Rainbow Warrior (New Zealand v France) (1990) XX RIAA 215.

Article 24 of the ARSIWA

Distress

Federica Paddeu

1. The wrongfulness of an act of a State not in conformity with an international obligation of that State is precluded if the author of the act in question has no other reasonable way, in a situation of distress, of saving the author's life or the lives of other persons entrusted to the author's care.

2. Paragraph 1 does not apply if:

(a) the situation of distress is due, either alone or in combination with other factors, to the conduct of the State invoking it; or

(b) the act in question is likely to create a comparable or greater peril.

A. Introduction	1	D. Conclusion: Unnecessary (and undesirable) restriction from general international law	13
B. Application in general international law	3		
C. Application in international investment law	10		

A. Introduction

1 Distress concerns the situation where a State organ disregards an international obligation of the State with a view to preserving her own life, or the lives of individuals entrusted to her care. The defence was formulated by the International Law Commission (ILC) in 1979, by analogy with the right of refuge historically recognized in the law of the sea and, subsequently, the law of aviation.[1] The ILC expressly stated that the defence of distress was a 'case of progressive development', though one that had received generally favourable responses from States.[2] The practice on this defence is still relatively limited, and so assessments as to its customary character vary.[3]

2 One characteristic feature of distress is its so-called 'human dimension'. The defence seeks to protect life, including that of the State's organs. It thus regards State organs not in their

---

[1] See ILC, 'Draft Articles on Responsibility of States for Internationally Wrongful Acts, with Commentaries' YILC 2001, Vol II, Part Two, 31, Article 24 paras 2 and 3, for some examples of practice (hereafter ARSIWA Commentaries).

[2] J Crawford, 'Second Report on State Responsibility' YILC 1999, Vol II, Part One, paras 271–72.

[3] cf G Scalese, *La rilevanza delle scusanti nella teoria dell'illecito internazionale* (Editoriale Scientifica 2008) 152–53 (asserting customary status) (hereafter Scalese, *Scusanti*); F Paddeu, *Justification and Excuse in International Law: Concept and Theory of General Defences* (CUP 2018) 431 (expressing doubts) (hereafter Paddeu, *Justification and Excuse*).

quality as representatives of the State, but '*qua* human beings'.[4] The fact that a human being was at the centre of the situation of distress was one which, Special Rapporteur Ago noted, 'could not be disregarded'.[5]

B. Application in general international law

To successfully plead this defence, States need to meet five conditions: (i) existence of a threat to life; (ii) a special relationship between the State organ and the individuals whose life is in danger; (iii) no other reasonable way to avert the threat; (iv) non-contribution to the situation; and (v) not create a comparable or greater peril. The ILC Commentary on the Responsibility of States for Internationally Wrongful Acts (ARSIWA) adds that '[i]n situations in which a State agent is in distress and has to act to save lives, there should ... be a certain degree of flexibility in the assessment of the conditions of distress'.[6] To date, distress has been discussed and applied in only one international decision: the *Rainbow Warrior* award.[7] Each of the requirements will be addressed in turn.

<u>Threat to life</u>: The defence of distress is limited to situations where there exist threats to the life of State organs or individuals entrusted to the State organ's care. The threat to life can result from either natural or man-made hazards, or a combination thereof, and it must affect either the State organ herself, or individuals entrusted to her care. The *Rainbow Warrior* award accepted that the defence could operate in circumstances involving a serious health risk.[8] The ILC, however, subsequently restricted the plea to life threats only, due to the difficulty of drawing a line as to the seriousness of the health threat required.[9] It is not clear whether this requires the actual existence of a threat to life, or if the State organ's reasonable belief in the existence of a threat to life will be enough. The language in the Commentary suggests that there must be an actual threat to life, but given the ILC's favouring of a flexible interpretation of the requirements of the defence it may be queried whether reasonable beliefs will suffice.[10]

<u>Special relationship</u>: Where the threats involve individuals other than the State organ, the ILC Commentary requires the existence of a 'special relationship' between the State agent and the individuals in danger.[11] The nationality of the individuals in question is irrelevant.[12] This requirement is intended to exclude the application of the plea to situations of 'more general emergencies' which, according to the Commentary, are 'more a matter of necessity than distress'.[13] The requirement of 'special relationship' is vague. Individuals must be 'entrusted' to the care of the organ, raising the question whether the existence of a legal duty of

---

[4] R Ago, '1573rd Meeting' YILC 1979, Vol I, 207, para 9.
[5] ibid 206–07, para 8.
[6] ARSIWA Commentaries (n 1) Article 24 para 6.
[7] *Rainbow Warrior (New Zealand v France)* (1990) XX RIAA 215 (hereafter *Rainbow Warrior*). Note too that there are doubts as to whether the tribunal actually applied the defence or whether, having cast the obligation at issue as one of best efforts, the situation of distress was accounted for in establishing whether the State had employed best efforts in the circumstances. See Paddeu, *Justification and Excuse* (n 3) 449–53.
[8] *Rainbow Warrior* (n 7) for agent Mafart at 254–59.
[9] ARSIWA Commentaries (n 1) Article 24 para 9.
[10] On which see S Szurek, 'Distress' in Crawford and others (eds), *The Law of International Responsibility* (OUP 2010) 482–83; Crawford J, *State Responsibility: The General Part* (CUP 2013) 303–04.
[11] ARSIWA Commentaries, Article 24 para 6.
[12] ibid para 1.
[13] ibid para 7.

care (possibly as a matter of domestic law *or* international law) is required. Physical proximity does not seem necessary, as evidenced by the *Rainbow Warrior* award: the decision as to repatriation of the French agents confined in Hao was taken by State organs in mainland France.[14]

6 'Reasonable way': This criterion is intended to strike a balance between providing some 'flexibility regarding the choice of action' for the saving of life, acknowledging that there may be no time or personnel available to assess the situation and that urgent action might be needed, while still strictly confining the scope of the defence.[15] This is an objective standard, and one that is lower than that in the case of necessity (which requires that the act be 'the only way' to safeguard the essential interest). But it is not clear what exactly it entails. In particular, it is unclear whether the test concerns what a reasonable person, in the State organ's shoes, would have done, or whether it concerns a standard of reasonableness. In either case, the assessment must be performed from the point of view of the organ at the time of acting. Here, too, however, there are uncertainties: the text of Article 24, the Commentary, or its drafting history do not specify whether the assessment should be performed in light of what the State organ actually knew at the time (about the risk, and the means available to avoid it), or what it should have (reasonably) known.

7 Non-contribution: The non-contribution requirement is here less strict than in the case of necessity: good faith policies that contributed to the life-threatening situation do not exclude reliance on the plea. The standard is the same as in *force majeure*, but the Commentary adds that 'priority should be given to necessary life-saving measures'.[16] This seems reasonable as it would be illogical to prevent the saving of lives *because* the State had contributed to the situation.

8 No comparable or greater peril: The life-saving measures must not create a comparable or greater peril. Fasoli illustrates this requirement with a hypothetical example of a nuclear vessel in distress which 'might threaten the health and safety of the port in which it sought refuge'.[17] The interest protected, as well as the means chosen to protect it, must 'clearly outweigh the other interests at stake in the circumstances'.[18]

9 Justification or Excuse? It is not clear whether distress operates as a justification (precluding the wrongfulness of the act) or an excuse (precluding responsibility for a wrongful act). On the one hand, it operates on a similar consequentialist logic as necessity: to protect life over other less urgent or weighty interests. This could militate in favour of its classification as a justification. On the other, the Commentary and drafting of this Article place emphasis on the pressures placed by the situation of distress on the free will of the State organ: when the latter chooses to act incompatibly with the international obligations of the State, it does so in circumstances in which his ability and freedom to choose how to act have been constrained by the circumstances. Her choice is, therefore, to some extent involuntary.[19] This could militate in favour of its classification as an excuse.[20] The matter remains open.[21]

---

[14] *Rainbow Warrior* (n 7) para 17 (Agent Mafart), para 55 (Captain Prieur).
[15] ARSIWA Commentaries (n 1) Article 24 para 6.
[16] ibid para 10.
[17] E Fasoli, 'Distress' in *Max Planck Encyclopaedia of Public International Law* (2013) para 7.
[18] ARSIWA Commentaries (n 1) Article 24 para 10.
[19] ARSIWA Commentaries (n 1) Article 24 para 1.
[20] Arguing that distress operates as an excuse, see Scalese, *Scusanti* (n 3) 147–55.
[21] See Paddeu, *Justification and Excuse* (n 3) 456–64.

C. Application in international investment law

Distress was invoked by Madagascar in investment-treaty arbitration.[22] The claim concerned the destruction of the claimant's factory during social unrest in the country, and the State's failure to protect the investor's property. Madagascar argued that the reaction of its forces to the events, including their withdrawal from the area of the factory, was proportionate, legitimate, and reasonable, and that a stronger intervention would have led to bloodshed.[23] In short: the inaction of its forces was a reasonable way to save lives. The tribunal rejected the plea *because* inaction was not the 'only way' to save lives.[24]

The defence of distress could could be invoked in response to investment claims arising out of the Covid-19 pandemic-management measures.[25] The SARS-Cov-2 virus poses a threat to the lives of individuals, and it might be argued that in the absence of any pharmaceutical interventions such as vaccinations or treatments, it was reasonable for States to resort to non-pharmaceutical measures such as lockdowns and restrictions on indoor gatherings to prevent the spread of the disease. One potential difficulty of its invocation will be—as in the case of necessity—that of the focus of analysis, that is, whether tribunals will examine the reasonableness of discrete life-saving measures, or of the package of measures adopted by the respondent State.

The most difficult element to satisfy will be, however, that of the 'special relationship'. The existence of this relationship must be a relative question: it will depend on the specific circumstances. It could be argued that the characteristic feature of this relationship is the control that the State organ has over the fate of the individuals in question. This aspect can readily be perceived in situations involving ships or aircraft in distress, the precedents upon which the defence was built: only a decision by the captain can avert the threat to the passengers' lives. Further, physical proximity between the State organ in question and the individuals whose life is in peril may not be necessary, as evidenced in *Rainbow Warrior*. Distress could thus be invoked whenever the measure is adopted by the State organ who is the one capable of, metaphorically, 'turning the ship' so as to bring everyone to safety. And who this person is will depend on the threat, and the measures needed to avert the danger. In respect of the pandemic, the public health measures required are ones that can *only* be adopted by central authorities (either of the State, or of units within the State when this power is devolved): it is only these authorities that can turn the ship away from the impending threat. To be sure, the pandemic may be closer to a situation of 'general emergency' which the ILC thought was 'more a matter of necessity than distress'.[26] But while it may be '*more* a matter of necessity' (emphasis added), this does not mean that it is entirely or solely a matter of necessity: some space is seemingly left for addressing these matters as cases of distress.

---

[22] *Peter de Sutter and Kristof de Sutter v Madagascar (II)*, ICSID Case ARB/17/18, Award, 17 April 2020.
[23] ibid para 335.
[24] ibid para 349.
[25] See further F Paddeu and F Jephcott, 'COVID-19 and Defences in the Law of State Responsibility: Parts I and II' (*EJIL:Talk!*, 17 March 2020) https://www.ejiltalk.org/covid-19-and-defences-in-the-law-of-state-respons ibility-part-i/ and https://www.ejiltalk.org/covid-19-and-defences-in-the-law-of-state-responsibility-part-ii/ last accessed 23 October 2023.
[26] ARSIWA Commentaries (n 1) Article 24 para 7.

D. Conclusion: Unnecessary (and undesirable) restriction from general international law

13 Distress is rarely invoked in investment-treaty arbitration. In the only case in which it has been raised so far, *de Sutter v Madagascar*, the tribunal imposed a stricter standard than that required under GIL: to be justified by distress, according to the tribunal, the act needed to be the 'only way' to save lives. The tribunal thus equated the standard in Article 24, on distress, to that in Article 25, on necessity. But this is inconsistent with the clear language of Article 24 which, as noted, was adopted specifically so as to leave some elbow-room to the State organ in the circumstances. Moreover, the imposition of the stricter standard of the defence of necessity ('only way') to the defence of distress is incompatible with the overall aim of the defence to safeguard human life, and in particular with the 'human dimension' of this defence.

Selected literature

Crawford J, *State Responsibility: The General Part* (CUP 2013).
Paddeu F, *Justification and Excuse in International Law: Concept and Theory of General Defences* (CUP 2018).
Scalese G, *La rilevanza delle scusanti nella teoria dell'illecito internazionale* (Editoriale Scientifica 2008) 147–55.
Szurek S, 'Distress' in Crawford J, Pellet A and Olleson S (eds), *The Law of International Responsibility* (OUP 2010).

Selected decisions

Peter de Sutter and Kristof de Sutter v Madagascar (II), ICSID Case ARB/17/18, Award, 17 April 2020.
Rainbow Warrior (New Zealand v France) (1990) XX RIAA 215.

Article 25 of the ARSIWA

Necessity

Federica Paddeu and Michael Waibel

1. Necessity may not be invoked by a State as a ground for precluding the wrongfulness of an act not in conformity with an international obligation of that State unless the act:
   (a) is the only way for the State to safeguard an essential interest against a grave and imminent peril; and
   (b) does not seriously impair an essential interest of the State or States towards which the obligation exists, or of the international community as a whole.
2. In any case, necessity may not be invoked by a State as a ground for precluding wrongfulness if:
   (a) the international obligation in question excludes the possibility of invoking necessity; or
   (b) the State has contributed to the situation of necessity.

A. Introduction 1	C. Application in international investment law 13
B. Application in general international law 4	I. Relation between treaty exceptions and necessity 16
I. Exclusion by primary rule 5	II. Essential interests 21
II. Grave and imminent peril 6	III. Only way 27
III. Essential interest 7	IV. Non-contribution 32
IV. Only way 11	D. Conclusion: International investment law leading the way for general international law 37
V. Non-contribution 12	

A. Introduction

The defence of necessity permits a State to act in a manner incompatible with its international 1
obligations, provided the relevant primary rule does not exclude it. The defence of necessity is a lesser-evils based justification.[1] It precludes the wrongfulness of a State's conduct aimed at reducing net harm, by protecting an essential interest from grave harm at the cost of impairing an obligation of lesser weight or urgency. The International Law Commission (ILC) and the case-law of international tribunals corroborate the customary status of the defence of necessity.[2]

---

[1] F Paddeu, *Justification and Excuse in International Law: Concept and Theory of General Defences* (CUP 2018), ch 8 (hereafter Paddeu, *Justification and Excuse*).
[2] *Gabčíkovo-Nagymaros Project* (*Hungary v Slovakia*) [1997] ICJ Rep 7, para 51 (hereafter *Gabčíkovo-Nagymaros*); *M/V Saiga (No 2)* (*St Vincent and the Grenadines v Guinea*) ITLOS, Judgment, 1 July 1999, paras 133–34 (hereafter *M/V Saiga*); *Legal Consequences of the Construction of a Wall in the Occupied Palestinian Territory*

2 The double negative in the chapeau ('necessity *may not* be invoked *unless ...*') indicates that necessity is a strict defence. Tribunals have interpreted it as such.[3] Because of the exceptional circumstances that give rise to the defence of necessity, it has featured infrequently in dispute settlement.[4] Indeed, despite several invocations in recent (but also earlier) times,[5] this defence has almost never succeeded.[6] Most States have so far classified this defence as a justification rather than an excuse (they invoke the defence to argue that their conduct is, all things considered, permissible).[7]

3 The defence requires fulfilment of five conditions: (i) no exclusion by relevant primary rule; (ii) a grave and imminent peril; (iii) the identification and weighing of essential interests; (iv) the 'only way' to safeguard the interest in peril; and (v) non-contribution to the situation of necessity. Each will be discussed below.

B. Application in general international law

4 To date, States have only invoked necessity in a handful of disputes before the International Court of Justice (ICJ),[8] the International Tribunal for the Law of the Sea (ITLOS), and inter-State arbitral tribunals.[9] *Gabčíkovo-Nagymaros* is the most important and influential of these decisions, because of the ICJ's in-depth engagement with the defence.[10] Most of these cases

---

[2004] ICJ Rep 136, para 140 (hereafter *Palestinian Wall*); *CMS Gas Transmission Company v The Republic of Argentina*, ICSID Case No ARB/01/8, Award (12 May 2005), para 315 (hereafter *CMS v Argentina*, Award); *Bernhard von Pezold and Others v Republic of Zimbabwe*, ICSID Case No ARB/10/15, Award (28 July 2015), paras 624–68 (hereafter *von Pezold v Zimbabwe*). For a different assessment, see *Rainbow Warrior (New Zealand v France)* (1990) XX RIAA 215, 254 (hereafter *Rainbow Warrior*); T Yamada, 'State of Necessity in International Law: A Study of International Judicial Cases' (2005) 34 Kobe Gakuin LJ 107; S Heathcote, 'Est-ce que l'état de nécessité est un principe de droit international coutumier?' (2007) 1 RBDI 53.

[3] *Gabčíkovo-Nagymaros* (n 2) para 51.

[4] In some cases in the first half of the twentieth century, States did not invoke *necessity* as a discrete defence, but rather raised necessity-like arguments in the context of invocations of *force majeure* (relating to difficulty of performance in the face of threats to the State's self-preservation). See, among others, *French Company of Venezuelan Railroads* (1904) 10 RIAA 285; *Russian Indemnity Case (Russia v Turkey)* (1912) Scott Hague Court Rep 297. Before the PCIJ, see also *Case Concerning the Payment of various Serbian Loans issued in France (France v Kingdom of the Serbs, Croats and Slovenes)* (1929) PCIJ, Series A No 20, 5; *Case Concerning the Payment of various Brazilian Loans issued in France (France v Brazil)* (1929) PCIJ, Series A No 20, 93; *Société Commerciale de Belgique* (1939) PCIJ Series A/B No 78, 160. For a contextual analysis of these cases, and their relation with the defence of necessity, see Paddeu, *Justification and Excuse* (n 1) 378–86. The historical background of these cases is explored in M Waibel, *Sovereign Defaults Before International Courts and Tribunals* (CUP 2011).

[5] For a historical overview, see Paddeu, *Justification and Excuse* (n 1) ch 8.

[6] For a rare example of success, see *LG&E Energy Corp, LG&E Capital Corp, LG&E International Inc v Argentine Republic*, ICSID Case ARB/02/1, Award, 25 July 2007. On which see D Foster, 'Necessity Knows No Law! LG&E v Argentina' (2006) 9 Int'l Arb LR 149; J Fouret, '"CMS c/ LG&E" ou l'état de nécessité en question' (2007) 2 Rev de l'Arbitrage 249; M Waibel, 'Two Worlds of Necessity in ICSID Arbitration: CMS and LG&E' (2007) 20 LJIL 637 (hereafter Waibel, 'Two Worlds of Necessity'). G Bücheler, *Proportionality in Investor-State Arbitration* (OUP 2015) 265.

[7] On which see F Paddeu and M Waibel, 'Necessity 20 Years On: The Limits of Article 25 ARSIWA' (2022) 37 ICSID Rev 160, 162–63 (hereafter Paddeu and Waibel, 'Necessity 20 Years On').

[8] *Gabčíkovo-Nagymaros* (n 2). The defence was also invoked, though only briefly mentioned in the decisions, in *Legality of the Use of Force (Federal Republic of Yugoslavia v Belgium)*, Provisional Measures, Order of 2 June 1999 [1999] ICJ Rep 124 (the defence was raised by Belgium, but not addressed in the Court's decision); *Palestinian Wall* (n 2); Canada invoked a necessity-based argument in *Fisheries Jurisdiction Case (Spain v Canada)* [1998] ICJ Rep 432 (but the Court did not address the defence, as it found it had no jurisdiction over the dispute).

[9] *Rainbow Warrior* (n 2) and *M/V Saiga* (n 2).

[10] On the impact of this judgment, see J D'Aspremont, 'Canonical Cross-Referencing in the Making of the Law of International Responsibility' in S Forlati, MM Mbengue and Brian McGarry (eds), *The Gabčíkovo-Nagymaros Judgment and its Contribution to the Development of International Law* (Brill 2020) 23ff.

pre-date the adoption of the ILC Articles in 2001, and influenced the work of the ILC on this defence. Post-Articles cases have in turn been influenced by the ILC's work.

I. Exclusion by primary rule

The relevant primary rule can exclude the defence by seeking to regulate the situation. By way of example, the ILC refers to the law on the use of force and military necessity.[11]   **5**

II. Grave and imminent peril

The existence of a 'grave and imminent peril' to an essential interest triggers the defence. **6** This requires the existence of a risk of harm to an essential interest of the State, the objective establishment of such risk, and the gravity of the threatened harm. By definition, the harm to the essential interest has not (fully) materialized by the time the State acts in necessity: the State acts precisely to prevent (or minimize the effect of) the harm. Grave means that the harm must be serious. Further, 'imminent' has been understood as 'proximate': it is not a temporal connection, but a causal one.[12] According to the ICJ, the State must be able to establish 'at the relevant point in time, that the realization of the peril, however far off it might be, is not thereby any less certain and inevitable'.[13] This is a very strict—if not impossible—condition to meet: one can never establish future events with certainty, at most we can assign probabilities about their occurrence.[14] Moreover, the farther the event is into the future, the harder it will be to assign probabilities with confidence. The ILC modified this standard by indicating that 'a measure of uncertainty about the future does not necessarily disqualify a State from invoking necessity, if the peril is clearly established on the basis of the evidence reasonably available at the time'.[15] This is a better standard, but still a fuzzy one—is proof on the balance of probabilities enough to meet this requirement?

III. Essential interest

At the heart of this defence is a comparison of the relative importance or weight of the **7** interests at stake: conduct incompatible with an obligation of the State is permitted so long as it safeguards an essential interest and the interest it harms is of lesser weight or urgency.

Interest safeguarded: The ILC Commentary does not define 'essential interest', stating instead that whether an interest is essential depends on 'all the circumstances'.[16] Essential interests are neither limited to the survival of the State, nor must they be of the invoking State itself: arguably, they could be essential interests of the international community as a   **8**

---

[11] ILC, 'Draft Articles on Responsibility of States for Internationally Wrongful Acts, with Commentaries' YILC 2001, Vol II, Part Two, 31, Article 25 para 21 (hereafter ARSIWA Commentaries).
[12] Contrast the meaning of 'imminence' in the law on the use of force. Paddeu and Waibel, 'Necessity 20 Years On' (n 7) 166, fn 45.
[13] *Gabčíkovo-Nagymaros* (n 2) para 54.
[14] On this question, see Paddeu and Waibel, 'Necessity 20 Years On' (n 7) 169.
[15] ARSIWA Commentaries (n 11) Article 25 para 16.
[16] ibid para 15.

whole.[17] Among others, the following have been accepted as essential interests: ecological interests,[18] the preservation of the State's existence, and the wellbeing and safety of its people in time of public emergency.[19]

9 *Interest impaired*: the act in necessity must not impair an essential interest of the other State, or of the international community as a whole. Tribunals have not considered this element, having found that the defence failed on other grounds.[20] Presumably, the same considerations apply to determining the essential character of the interest impaired as for the interest safeguarded.

10 *Weighing*: necessity permits conduct which reduces overall net harm. For the plea to be successful, the interest safeguarded must be more important than the impaired one: it must be one 'outweighing all other considerations'.[21] This requires weighing the interests in conflict. The ILC Commentary provides little guidance on the parameters of this weighting exercise, other than to indicate that it involves an objective reasonableness test (a 'reasonable assessment of the competing interests'). Tribunals have not needed to engage in this exercise, as they have found that the plea failed on other grounds. This is a difficult comparison, which has been at the heart of criticisms of this defence in international law.[22]

IV. Only way

11 As Crawford explained, '[h]ere "only" means "only"'.[23] The 'only way' standard is strict. The plea fails if there are any other lawful means, even if they are more costly. Furthermore, 'way' is not limited to unilateral action but can include 'other forms of conduct available through cooperative action with other States or through international organizations'.[24] In *Gabčíkovo-Nagymaros*, the ICJ held that Hungary had other means available than the suspension and abandonment of the works:[25] Hungary's concern for the quality and movement of water could have been addressed by controlling the distribution of water, and regulating the flows on its side of the dam.[26] Tribunals do not always consider alternatives, but just dismiss that the conduct was the 'only way'.[27] In *M/V Saiga No 2*, the tribunal simply held that it could 'not be suggested that the only means of safeguarding' Guinea's interest in the maximization of tax revenue 'was to extend its customs laws to parts of the exclusive economic zone'.[28]

---

[17] Article 25 speaks of the protection of 'an essential interest' (emphasis added). On which see G Gaja, 'La possibilité d'invoquer l'état de nécessité pour protéger les intérêts de la communauté internationale' in O Corten and others (eds), *Droit du pouvoir, pouvoir du droit: Mélanges offerts à Jean Salmon* (Bruylant 2007) 417.

[18] *Gabčíkovo-Nagymaros* (n 2) para 53.

[19] ARSIWA Commentaries (n 11) Article 25 para 14.

[20] *Gabčíkovo-Nagymaros* (n 2) para 58; *M/V Saiga* (n 2) 56; *Palestinian Wall* (n 2) 195.

[21] ARSIWA Commentaries (n 11) Article 25 para 17.

[22] For example, V Jeutner, *Irresolvable Norm Conflicts in International Law: The Concept of a Legal Dilemma* (OUP 2017) 80 (necessity cannot be invoked when interests involved are equal or unknown); Paddeu and Waibel, 'Necessity 20 Years On' (n 7) 173.

[23] J Crawford, *State Responsibility: The General Part* (CUP 2013) 311.

[24] ARSIWA Commentaries (n 11) Article 25 para 15.

[25] *Gabčíkovo-Nagymaros* (n 2) para 57.

[26] ibid 42–43.

[27] Similarly, in *Palestinian Wall* (n 2) the Court simply noted that the construction of a wall was not the only way to safeguard Israel's interest, para 140.

[28] *M/V Saiga* (n 2) para 135.

V. Non-contribution

12 The defence is unavailable if a State's contribution to the situation is 'sufficiently substantial and not merely incidental or peripheral'.[29] The Commentary indicates that this is a stricter standard than that applicable to *force majeure*. This suggests that unlike for that defence, necessity fails where a State has 'unwittingly contributed' to the situation 'by something which, in hindsight, might have been done differently but which was done in good faith and did not itself make the event any less unforeseen'.[30] In *Gabčíkovo-Nagymaros*, Hungary had commissioned scientific reports, initially slowed down the works in its sectors, and then, responding to new environmental reports, sped them up until it abandoned them. The Court also noted that political changes in Hungary might have made it difficult to 'coordinate the different points of view prevailing from time to time'.[31] It concluded that through its conduct Hungary had 'helped to bring about' the situation of necessity.[32]

C. Application in international investment law

13 The practice of investor–State tribunals, which arose mostly in response to Argentina's financial crisis in the early 2000s, is important and yet inconsistent.[33] Most tribunals rejected Argentina's necessity defence alongside its treaty-based defence.[34] Only one tribunal upheld the defence,[35] though two ad hoc annulment committees (*Enron* and *Sempra*) annulled awards that denied that the defence of necessity applied on the facts,[36] and a third (*CMS*) was highly critical of how the tribunal applied the necessity defence.[37]

14 There is little practice by domestic courts. The German Federal Constitutional Court rejected that necessity applied vis-à-vis private persons (rather than vis-à-vis another State) in a dispute concerning sovereign bonds.[38] The English Divisional Court considered but did not apply the defence in a case relating to the Organization for Economic Co-operation and Development (OECD) Anti-Bribery Convention.[39] In 2020, the Southern District Court

---

[29] ARSIWA Commentaries (n 11) Article 25 para 20.
[30] ibid, in connection with Article 23 para 9.
[31] *Gabčíkovo-Nagymaros* (n 2) para 57.
[32] ibid.
[33] P von Staden, 'Towards Greater Doctrinal Clarity in Investor-State Arbitration: Treaty Exceptions, Necessity, and the CMS, Sempra, and Enron Annulment Decisions' (2011) 2 CYIL 208 ('uneven and partly contradictory'); Waibel, 'Two Worlds of Necessity' (n 6).
[34] The non-precluded measures provision in Argentina's investment treaties.
[35] *LG&E Argentine Republic*, ICSID Case No ARB/02/1, Decision on Liability, 3 October 2006 (hereafter *LG&E v Argentina*, Liability).
[36] *Enron Corporation and Ponderosa Assets, L.P. v Argentine Republic*, ICSID Case No ARB/01/3, Decision on the Application for Annulment of the Argentine Republic, 30 July 2010 (hereafter *Enron v Argentina*, Annulment); *Sempra Energy International v The Argentine Republic*, ICSID Case No ARB/02/16, Decision on the Argentine Republic's Application for Annulment of the Award, 29 June 2010 (hereafter *Sempra v Argentina*, Annulment).
[37] *CMS Gas Transmission Company v The Republic of Argentina*, ICSID Case No ARB/01/8, Decision of the ad hoc Committee on the Application for Annulment of the Argentine Republic, 25 September 2007 (hereafter *CMS v Argentina*, Annulment).
[38] BVerfG, 2 BvM 1/03, 8 May 2007 (Argentina necessity). cf also BVerfG, Order of 3 July 2019, 2 BvR 824/15, 2 BvR 825/15 (Argentina's state bankruptcy).
[39] *R (on the Application of Corner House Research and Campaign against Arms Trade) v Director of the Serious Fraud Office*, [2008] EWHC 714 (Admin), discussed in S Olleson, 'Internationally Wrongful Acts in the Domestic Courts: The Contribution of Domestic Courts to the Development of Customary International Law Relating to the Engagement of International Responsibility' (2013) 26 LJIL 615, 635–37.

of New York declined to apply necessity to the economic and humanitarian situation in Venezuela.[40]

15 Investor–State tribunals have dealt with two main questions concerning the necessity defence, namely: (1) the relationship between treaty-based exception clauses and the necessity defence under customary law, including whether the treaty-based exceptions exclude the general defence; and (2) the conditions of the defence, in particular, (i) essential interests; (ii) the 'only way'; (iii) non-contribution. These cumulative conditions ensure that States can invoke the defence only in exceptional circumstances. Without some degree of deference to the invoking State, however, it would become virtually impossible for the State to successfully invoke necessity.

I. Relation between treaty exceptions and necessity

16 How treaty exception clauses relate to the customary necessity defence is an important question. Some tribunals and authors have considered that the object and purpose of the Bilateral Investment Treaty (BIT) of protecting private property rights not only in times of macroeconomic stability, but also in times of crisis has implications for the defence of necessity: namely, that the invocation of the defence of necessity is excluded, irrespective of whether the applicable investment treaty contains an exception clause.[41]

17 Understanding this relationship is crucial for two reasons. First, exception clauses operate at a different stage than necessity under customary international law. As explained by the *CMS* Annulment Committee: exception clauses exclude that conduct is incompatible with the investment treaty.[42] When they apply, there is no *prima facie* internationally wrongful act.[43] By contrast, the plea of necessity is relevant once a *prima facie* breach of the treaty is established. For this reason, an exception clause in an investment treaty does not amount to 'exclusion of necessity by the primary rule', and a Respondent State may rely on both.

18 Second, the conditions for necessity are strict, whereas the conditions for treaty exception clauses may be considerably more flexible, may include elements of self-judgment,[44] and a different burden of proof (*prima facie* for treaty exceptions versus full burden of proof on the host state as to the conditions for necessity).[45]

19 In *CMS*, the tribunal failed to distinguish between the non-precluded measures provision concerned with essential security interests in the applicable investment treaty and necessity

---

[40] *Casa Express Corp v Bolivarian Republic of Venezuela*, 18 Civ. 11940 (AT); 19 Civ. 3123 (AT) (SDNY, 30 September 2020).

[41] *CMS v Argentina*, Award (n 2) para 354; *BG Group Plc v Argentina*, UNCITRAL Award on the merits (24 December 2007); A Reinisch, 'Necessity in International Investment Arbitration—An Unnecessary Split of Opinions in Recent ICSID Cases? Comments on CMS v. Argentina and LG&E v. Argentina' (2010) JWIT 191, 205; A Bjorklund, 'Emergency Exceptions' in PT Muchlinski, F Ortino and C Schreuer (eds), *The Oxford Handbook of International Investment Law* (OUP 2008) 490.

[42] *CMS v Argentina*, Annulment (n 37) para 129 ('threshold requirement: if it applies, the substantive obligations of the Treaty do not apply').

[43] J Viñuales, 'Defence Arguments in Investment Arbitration' (2020) 18 ICSID Rep 9, 17 (hereafter Viñuales, 'Defence').

[44] *Continental Casualty Company v Argentine Republic*, ICSID Case No ARB/03/9, Award, 5 September 2008, para 187; Viñuales, 'Defence' (n 43) 27–28.

[45] *Devas (Mauritius) Ltd, Devas Employees Mauritius Private Limited, and Telcom Devas Mauritius Limited v Republic of India*, PCA Case No 2013-09, Award, 25 July 2016, para 245.

in customary international law.[46] The ad hoc Committee emphasized that these were two fundamentally different provisions. Equating them represented a manifest error of law.[47] However, the committee still did not annul the award since it considered that the tribunal had not manifestly exceeded its powers.[48]

The *Enron* and *Sempra* tribunals both concluded that the treaty-based exception clause **20** 'does not set out conditions different from customary law',[49] thus incorporating the stricter standard of the customary plea to the treaty-based exception. The *Sempra* ad hoc committee annulled the award in full on the ground of the tribunal's manifest excess of powers due to its failure to apply the non-precluded measures provision, and thus part of the applicable law.[50] By reading the conditions of Article 25 into the non-precluded measures provision, the tribunal had made a fundamental error in identifying and applying the applicable law.[51] The *Enron* ad hoc committee similarly concluded that 'the Tribunal's decision that Argentina is precluded from relying on Article XI, and the Tribunal's decision that Argentina is precluded from relying on the principle of necessity under customary international law, are tainted by annullable error'.[52]

II. Essential interests

Tribunals have shown some flexibility in defining essential interests. They have not limited **21** essential interests to preserving the State's existence, and have accepted that the protection of economic stability and public safety could qualify.

A severe economic crisis can affect an essential interest.[53] The *CMS* tribunal held that the **22** 'need to prevent a major breakdown, with all its social and political implications, might have entailed an essential interest of the State'.[54] The *National Grid* tribunal linked this essential condition to international human rights law. It accepted that 'protection of social stability and the maintenance of essential services vital to the health and welfare of the population represents an objective which is recognized in the framework of the international law of human rights'.[55]

By contrast, the *Enron* tribunal cast doubt on whether Argentina's severe economic crisis af- **23** fected an essential interest. It found that 'business could have continued as usual', because the crisis did not compromise 'the very existence of the State and its independence'.[56] In response to Argentina's arguments on annulment that essential interests were not limited to the State's existence, and that the State was entitled to a 'margin of appreciation' in their protection,[57] the Annulment Committee considered that 'the Tribunal, while rejecting the argument that

---

[46] *CMS v Argentina*, Annulment (n 37) paras 353, 357, 374, and 379.
[47] ibid para 130.
[48] ibid para 136.
[49] *Enron Corporation and Ponderosa Assets, L.P. v Argentine Republic*, ICSID Case No ARB/01/3, Award, 22 May 2007, para 339 (hereafter *CMS v Argentina*, Award); *Sempra Energy International v The Argentine Republic*, ICSID Case No ARB/02/16, Award, 28 September 207, para 388 (hereafter *Sempra v Argentina*, Award).
[50] *Sempra v Argentina*, Annulment (n 36) 159.
[51] ibid para 208.
[52] ibid para 405
[53] ibid para 320.
[54] *CMS v Argentina*, Award (n 49) para 319.
[55] *National Grid plc v The Argentine Republic*, UNCITRAL, Award, 3 November 2008, para 245.
[56] *CMS v Argentina*, Award (n 49) para 306. Same wording used by *Sempra* tribunal, para 347, et seq.
[57] *Enron v Argentina*, Annulment (n 36) para 353(k).

the existence of Argentina was threatened, nonetheless accepted that an "essential interest" of Argentina may have been affected'.[58]

24 In *von Pezold*, the tribunal held that 'to ensure the survival of the incumbent Government and its President at a political level' did not mean that there was a 'threat to the existence of a State and therefore an essential interest that [it] is necessary to protect at all costs'.[59] In *Unión Fenosa*, Egypt argued that its 'essential interest in maintaining stability, security and international peace was threatened'.[60] The tribunal held that Egypt's relevant interest was not the maintenance of public safety but rather its gas shortage (which did not qualify).[61]

25 Tribunals have had more difficulty identifying the holder of the impaired interests than the essential interest themselves—whether investors or their home States. For the most part, however, tribunals have not seriously engaged in the weighing exercise,[62] simply assuming that the invoking State's interests were more important in the circumstances. This seems to be the right result, but it is not clear what parameters tribunals used to reach this conclusion.

26 In at least two decisions (*von Pezold* and *Border Timbers*), tribunals found that the host State's measures were racially discriminatory. They were thus in breach of an *erga omnes* obligation and, as such, affected an essential interest of the international community as a whole.[63]

III. Only way

27 Like in general international law, the defence has usually failed due to this condition. Invoking States have been unable to show the lack of alternative measures that were more favourable to investors. The burden of proof is on the invoking state, but a showing by investors that in theory the State had alternatives at its disposal should be insufficient. The Argentine crisis tribunals relied heavily on expert reports and comparative analyses with crisis management in other States to find that Argentina had alternative means to tackle the crisis, and thus did not fulfil this condition.[64]

28 This condition has been inconsistently applied. Some tribunals have approached this criterion flexibly. In *LG&E*, the tribunal accepted that Argentina's mix of policies was the 'only way' to respond to the grave economic crisis, despite 'a number of ways to draft the economic recovery plan'.[65] Similarly, the *Urbaser* tribunal underscored the significance of two perspectives, 'the wide one, taking into account the needs of Argentina and its population nationwide, and the narrower one of the situation of investors engaged in performing contracts protected by the international obligations arising out of one of the many BITs'.[66] The tribunal accepted that Argentina had shown more than *prima facie* that 'the emergency measures taken were the only ones available to the Argentine Government at the time, taking into

---

[58] ibid para 359.
[59] *von Pezold v Zimbabwe* (n 2) paras 631–32.
[60] *Unión Fenosa Gas, S.A. v Arab Republic of Egypt*, ICSID Case No ARB/14/4, Award, 31 August 2018, para 8.9 (hereafter *Unión Fenosa v Egypt*).
[61] ibid paras 8.49 and 8.58.
[62] Paddeu and Waibel, 'Necessity 20 Years On' (n 7) 173.
[63] *von Pezold v Zimbabwe* (n 2) para 657; *Border Timbers et al v Republic of Zimbabwe*, ICSID Case No ARB/10/25, Award, 28 July 2015, para 656.
[64] Paddeu and Waibel, 'Necessity 20 Years On' (n 7) 174.
[65] *LG&E v Argentina*, Liability (n 35) para 257.
[66] *Urbaser S.A. and Consorcio de Aguas Bilbao Bizkaia, Bilbao Biskaia Ur Partzuergoa v The Argentine Republic*, ICSID Case No ARB/07/26, Award, 8 December 2016, para 716 (hereafter *Urbaser v Argentina*).

account the extreme economic, institutional and social disturbances suffered by the country and its population'. Based on this showing, coupled with the investor's failure to 'offer at least a serious indication as to the nature of other measures that had been available to the Government at that time', the tribunal concluded that the only way condition was met.[67]

By contrast, most tribunals have adopted a rigid approach to this condition, according to **29** which investors only needed to show that the State theoretically had other options available. Such a restrictive approach renders the defence illusory.[68] The *Enron* tribunal accepted the investor's position that the State could have reacted differently to the economic crisis: 'A rather sad world comparative experience in the handling of economic crises, shows that there are always many approaches to address and correct such critical events, and it is difficult to justify that none of them were available.'[69] The Annulment Committee found that the tribunal failed to apply the applicable law (customary international law as reflected in Article 25), since it merely analysed whether alternatives were open to Argentina from an economic perspective.

In *Suez*, Argentina argued that its measures intended to safeguard its population's human **30** right to water. For the tribunal, these measures were not the 'only way' of safeguarding the interest involved.[70] The Annulment Committee, finding no failure to articulate the applicable law or any other manifest excess of power, held that the tribunal 'found on the facts that there were other and more flexible means that could have been resorted to'.[71]

Beyond the Argentine cases, in *von Pezold*, the question was whether the Fast Track Land **31** Reformation Programme (FTLRP) was the only way to stabilize the country by preventing the occupation of farmland. For the tribunal, Zimbabwe 'failed to offer any evidence of the specific measures that could have been explored as possible methods of addressing the Invasions and the reasons why those specific measures were dismissed'.[72] Furthermore, Zimbabwe failed to show that 'it carried out a rigorous process of assessing all possible alternatives'.[73] The tribunal concluded that the FTLRP was not the only means available to stop the occupations.[74]

IV. Non-contribution

Tribunals have interpreted this element in two ways: as a causal contribution, or as requiring **32** some degree of (subjective) fault.[75] The former interpretation renders the defence illusory, especially in the economic context.

For most tribunals, it suffices that State measures causally contributed to the state of neces- **33** sity, often based on the mere presence of 'endogenous' factors. For instance, the *Impregilo*

---

[67] ibid para 717.
[68] A Kent and A Harrington, 'The Plea of Necessity under Customary International Law: A Critical Review in Light of the Argentine Cases' in C Brown and K Miles (eds), *Evolution in Investment Treaty Arbitration* (CUP 2011) 254; Waibel, 'Two Worlds of Necessity' (n 6) 637, 638; Viñuales, 'Defence' (n 43) 84, para 117.
[69] *CMS v Argentina*, Award (n 49) para 309.
[70] *Suez Sociedad General de Aguas de Barcelona SA and InterAgua Servicios Integrales del Agua SA v Argentine Republic*, ICSID Case No ARB/03/17, Decision on Liability, 30 July 2010, para 238 (hereafter *Suez v Argentina*, Liability)
[71] *Suez Sociedad General de Aguas de Barcelona SA and InterAgua Servicios Integrales del Agua SA v Argentine Republic*, Decision on Annulment, 14 December 2018, para 183 (hereafter *Suez v Argentina*, Annulment).
[72] *von Pezold v Zimbabwe* (n 2) para 645.
[73] ibid.
[74] ibid para 646.
[75] Paddeu and Waibel, 'Necessity 20 Years On' (n 7) 178 et seq.

tribunal held that the 'State's contribution to its necessity situation need not be specifically intended or planned—it can be the consequence, *inter alia*, of well-intended but ill-conceived policies'.[76] Similarly, the *CMS* tribunal emphasized that 'government policies and their shortcomings significantly contributed to the crisis and the emergency and while exogenous factors did fuel additional difficulties they do not exempt the Respondent from its responsibility in the matter'.[77] The *Suez-InterAgua* and *Suez-Vivendi* tribunals found that Argentina contributed to its situation of emergency while acknowledging 'the substantial external forces that were buffeting the Argentine economy'.[78]

34 The *Enron* tribunal considered that both endogenous and exogenous factors intervened, meaning that Argentina's crisis depended not 'entirely on exogenous factors'.[79] However, the Annulment Committee found that the tribunal failed to apply the non-contribution condition because it relied on an expert opinion by an economist. The Committee held that '[w]hile an economist might regard a State's economic policies as misguided, and might conclude that such policies led to or amplified the effects of an economic crisis, that would not of itself necessarily mean that as a matter of law, the State had "contributed to the situation of necessity"'.[80] This is the only annulment based on a failure to apply the applicable law as regards the non-contribution condition.

35 A minority of tribunals held instead that only faulty contributions (either negligent or intended) could meet this condition. For example, the *Unión Fenosa* tribunal considered that it was not necessary to decide the question of non-contribution for three reasons: (i) Egypt did not intend social unrest; (ii) Egypt did not cause or foresee the consequences of the global financial crisis; (iii) independently of these two events, Egypt did not intend a shortage of electricity and gas.[81]

36 Similarly, the *Urbaser* tribunal considered that contributions excluding the plea must be intended or reckless. That internal factors contributed to Argentina's crisis was insufficient to exclude the plea: it was necessary to show 'that the Government's acts were such that they either were directed towards a crisis resulting in the emergency situation that the country experienced in early 2002, or at least of such a nature that the Government must have known that such crisis and emergency must have been the outcome of its economic and financial policy'.[82]

D. Conclusion: International investment law leading the way for general international law

37 There are few inter-State cases applying the defence of necessity in international law, but for the most part these are consistent with the codification of the plea in Article 25.

---

[76] *Impregilo S.p.A. v Argentine Republic*, ICSID Case No ARB/07/17, Award, 21 June 2011, para 356. The Annulment Committee upheld the award. See *Impregilo v Argentina*, ICSID Case No ARB/07/1, Decision of the ad hoc Committee on the Application for Annulment, 24 January 2014, para 203.
[77] *CMS v Argentina*, Award (n 2) para 329.
[78] *Suez v Argentina*, Liability (n 70) para 242. *Suez, Sociedad General de Aguas de Barcelona, S.A. and Vivendi Universal, S.A. v Argentine Republic*, ICSID Case No ARB/03/19, Decision in Liability, 30 July 2010, para 264. The Annulment Committee upheld the award on this point—see Decision on Annulment, 14 December 2018, para 184.
[79] *CMS v Argentina*, Award (n 49) paras 311, 312. cf also *Sempra v Argentina*, Award (n 49) paras 353–54. The Annulment Committee did not deal with the 'non-contribution' condition in any detail, as the Committee annulled the award on a different ground.
[80] *Enron v Argentina*, Annulment (n 36) para 393.
[81] *Unión Fenosa v Egypt* (n 60) para 8.61
[82] *Urbaser v Argentina* (n 66) para 711.

Investment tribunals purported to apply general international law, and there is no evidence **38** that investment tribunals consciously or expressly intended to modify the defence of necessity for its application to investment disputes.

However, there is evidence of some deviation from the customary defence: **39**

Essential interests: Some tribunals took investor interests into account as the interest impaired **40** by the measure of necessity. This is in contrast to Article 25 which speaks of interests of another State/international community. Nevertheless, no tribunal held investor interests to be superior to essential interests of the invoking State.

'Only way': Article 25 seems to focus on a specific 'act', assuming a 'single act' is the measure **41** adopted to avert the impending risk. Some investor–State tribunals have taken a broader perspective, and assessed the impugned measure in light of its context (ie package of measures) adopted by the State. This is justified, especially when dealing with multifaceted crises which require multiple measures by the State.

Non-contribution: The causal standard implied by the ILC Commentary to Article 25 **42** has proven too strict, especially since in most multifaceted crises there will be both exogenous and endogenous factors at play—sometimes temporally remote from the situation of necessity. As such, the plea would almost always be excluded. Some tribunals have opted for a fault-based standard (also endorsed by the ILC on first reading), thus requiring that the State either know or intend, or be reckless as to, the contribution of its actions to the defence of necessity. A non-contribution requirement is important to curb moral hazard, especially in circumstances in which States unilaterally invoke the plea of necessity and there is no mandatory third-party review of such invocations. However, it is difficult to see how some past action of the State, adopted in good faith, should exclude invocation of the plea. After all, if the point is to protect essential interests, why put the bar that high? A standard based on fault (perhaps based on negligence) seems preferable.

Investment tribunals have augmented the practice on the defence, especially on how **43** to construe the conditions that apply to it.[83] Indeed, most of the practice and serious engagement with necessity since 2001 has taken place in investor–State dispute settlement.[84] The practice has, to be sure, been inconsistent. But this should not mean that it is to be wholly ignored. The ILC drafted this defence based on few instances of practice, and it should thus not be surprising if the inconsistency arose in respect of matters that needed refining and finessing—like the application of the defence in respect of non-State actors, what is meant by 'only way' in the context of macro-crises, or what degree of contribution should be enough to exclude the plea. The way in which investment tribunals have applied the defence of necessity could have some relevance for the interpretation and application of this defence by other international courts and tribunals in the future.

---

[83] Viñuales, 'Defence' (n 43) 83, para 116.

[84] See further F Paddeu, 'The Impact of Investment Arbitration in the Development of State Responsibility Defences', in R Hofmann, S Schill and CJ Tams (eds), *ICSID at 50: Investment Arbitration as a Motor of General International Law* (Edward Elgar Publishing 2022).

Selected literature

Bjorklund A, 'Emergency Exceptions: State of Necessity and Force Majeure' in Muchlinski P, Ortino F and Schreuer C (eds), *The Oxford Handbook of International Investment Law* (OUP 2008).
Foster CE, 'Necessity and Precaution in International Law: Responding to Oblique Forms of Urgency' (2008) 23 NZULR 265.
Heathcote S, 'Est-ce que l'Etat de nécessité est un principe de droit international coutumier' (2007) RBDI 53
Heathcote S, 'State of Necessity and International Law' (PhD thesis, Université de Genève 2005).
Manton R, 'Necessity in International Law' (DPhil thesis, University of Oxford 2016).
Paddeu F and Waibel M, 'Necessity 20 Years On: The Limits of Article 25 ARSIWA' (2021) 36 ICSID Rev 160.
Paddeu F, *Justification and Excuse in International Law: Concept and Theory of General Defences* (CUP 2018).
Sloane RD, 'On the Use and Abuse of Necessity in the Law of State Responsibility' (2012) 106 AJIL 447.
Sykes AO, 'Economic Necessity in International Law' (2015) 109 AJIL 296.
Viñuales J, 'Defence Arguments in Investment Arbitration' (2020) 18 ICSID Rep 9.
Waibel M, 'Two Worlds of Necessity in ICSID Arbitration: CMS vs. LG&E' (2007) 20 LJIL 637.

Selected decisions

Bernhard von Pezold and Others v Republic of Zimbabwe, ICSID Case No ARB/10/15, Award, 28 July 2015.
CMS Gas Transmission Company v The Republic of Argentina, ICSID Case No ARB/01/8, Award (12 May 2005) and Decision of the ad hoc Committee on the Application for Annulment of the Argentine Republic (25 September 2007).
Enron Corporation and Ponderosa Assets, L.P. v Argentine Republic, ICSID Case No ARB/01/3, Award (22 May 2007) and Decision on the Application for Annulment of the Argentine Republic (30 July 2010).
Gabčikovo-Nagymaros Project (Hungary v Slovakia) (Judgment) [1997] ICJ Rep 7.
Legal Consequences of the Construction of a Wall in the Occupied Palestinian Territory (Advisory Opinion) [2004] ICJ Rep 136.
LG&E Energy Corp, LG&E Capital Corp, and LG&E International, Inc v Argentine Republic, ICSID Case No ARB/02/1, Decision on Liability, 3 October 2006.
Rainbow Warrior (New Zealand v France) (1990), 20 RIAA p. 217.
Sempra Energy International v The Argentine Republic, ICSID Case No ARB/02/16, Award (28 September 2007) and Decision on the Argentine Republic's Application for Annulment of the Award (29 June 2010).
Suez, Sociedad General de Aguas de Barcelona S.A., and InterAguas Servicios Integrales del Agua S.A. v The Argentine Republic, ICSID Case No ARB/03/17, Decision in Liability (30 July 2010) and Decision on Annulment, 14 December 2018.
Unión Fenosa Gas, S.A. v Arab Republic of Egypt, ICSID Case No ARB/14/4, Award, 31 August 2018.
Urbaser S.A. and Consorcio de Aguas Bilbao Bizkaia, Bilbao Biskaia Ur Partzuergoa v The Argentine Republic, ICSID Case No ARB/07/26, Award, 8 December 2016.

Article 26 of the ARSIWA

Compliance with peremptory norms

Federica Paddeu

Nothing in this chapter precludes the wrongfulness of any act of a State which is not in conformity with an obligation arising under a peremptory norm of general international law.

A. Introduction	1	C. Application in international investment law	5
B. Application in general international law	2	D. Conclusion: Alignment of general international law and international investment law	9

A. Introduction

Article 26 provides that the defences in the law of responsibility cannot be invoked in respect of conduct in breach of peremptory rules.[1] This rule is the extension to the law of responsibility[2] of the principle enshrined in Articles 53 and 64 of the Vienna Convention on the Law of Treaties.[3] If States cannot, by agreement, set aside the application of peremptory rules, it must follow that they cannot do so unilaterally—including by relying on a defence in the law of responsibility. **1**

B. Application in general international law

States may not rely on defences to justify or excuse conduct incompatible with a peremptory rule of international law. While there is no authoritative list of rules recognized as peremptory, the following are usually accepted as belonging to this category: the right to self-determination and the prohibitions of aggression, genocide, slavery, racial **2**

---

[1] See, in general, M Ménard, 'Compliance with Peremptory Norms' in J Crawford, A Pellet and S Olleson (eds), *The Law of International Responsibility* (OUP 2010) 450–53; J Crawford, *State Responsibility: The General Part* (CUP 2013) 315–18; D Costelloe, *Legal Consequences of Peremptory Norms in International Law* (CUP 2017) 224–28.

[2] ILC, 'Draft Articles on Responsibility of States for Internationally Wrongful Acts, with Commentaries' YILC 2001, Vol II, Part Two, 31, Article 26 para 1 (hereafter ARSIWA Commentaries).

[3] Vienna Convention on the Law of Treaties (adopted 23 May 1969, entered into force 27 January 1980) 1155 UNTS 331 (VCLT).

discrimination, crimes against humanity, and torture.[4] Thus, a State taking countermeasures may not derogate from such rules: for example, 'a genocide cannot justify a counter-genocide'.[5] Likewise, state of necessity may not justify or excuse non-compliance with the prohibition of torture.

3   Article 26 applies to all defences, and to all peremptory rules. This said, Article 26 does not exclude that, in some circumstances, the facts that give rise to a defence may be relevant for the application of a primary rule. The Commentary gives the example of consent to the prohibition of force. In this case—and in analogous cases—consent would not operate as a defence, but rather as an element of the rule in question (i.e. as a negative rule-element, intrinsic to the definition of the obligation).[6] Likewise, Article 26 extends to both justifications and excuses—albeit for different analytical reasons.[7]

4   There are, to date, no cases by inter-State courts or tribunals interpreting or applying Article 26.

C. Application in international investment law

5   Article 26 was referred to in *CMS*, in relation to the defence of necessity. In this case, the tribunal said that 'it does not appear, however, that the essential interest of the international community as a whole was affected in any relevant way, nor that a peremptory norm of international law might have been compromised, a situation governed by Article 26 of the Articles.'[8]

6   It was subsequently applied by at least two investment tribunals, in disputes arising out of Zimbabwe's Fast Track Land Reformation Programme (FTLRP). The FTLRP had been enacted by the Mugabe Government for the redistribution of land held mostly by white settlers among Zimbabwe's population. After some delays, and in response to protests and land occupation, the Government began seizing land without compensation, including the applicants' property. Zimbabwe sought to defend its actions on the basis of necessity, arguing that the FTLRP was the 'only way' to safeguard the State from the threat posed by the protests and 'land invasions'.

7   In both cases, the tribunal dismissed the necessity defence for a variety of reasons, among others on the basis of Article 26. The tribunals found that the FTLRP was an 'unjustified policy that discriminated against the landowners on the basis of their skin-color and foreign ancestral heritage' in breach of the *erga omnes* obligation against racial discrimination. Zimbabwe's actions thus 'impaired an essential interest of the international community as a whole', failing to meet the requirement in Article 25(1)(b) of the defence.[9] At the same time, the tribunals noted that 'Zimbabwe's violation of its obligation *erga omnes* means that it has

---

[4] ARSIWA Commentaries (n 2) Article 26 para 5.
[5] ibid para 3. Referring to *Application of the Convention on the Prevention and Punishment of the Crime of Genocide, Counter-Claims, Order of 17 December 1997* [1997] ICJ Rep 243, para 35 ('in no case could one breach of the Convention serve as an excuse for another'). In respect of countermeasures, Article 50(1)(d) specifically states that countermeasures 'shall not affect' obligations arising under peremptory rules.
[6] See in this Commentary: Federica Paddeu, 'Article 20 of the ARSIWA'.
[7] See F Paddeu, 'Humanitarian Intervention and the Law of State Responsibility' (2021) 32 EJIL 649.
[8] *CMS Gas Transmission Company v Argentine Republic*, ICSID Case ARB/01/8, Award, 12 May 2005, para 325.
[9] *Border Timbers et al v Republic of Zimbabwe*, ICSID Case No ARB/10/25, Award, 28 July 2015, para 656 (hereafter *Border Timbers*). See, in almost identical terms, *von Pezold et al v Republic of Zimbabwe*, ICSID Case No ARB/10/15, Award, 28 July 2015, para 657 (hereafter *von Pezold*).

breached ILC Article 26 and is therefore precluded from raising the necessity defence in relation to any events upon which the FTLRP policy touches'.[10]

These two awards confuse the concepts of *erga omnes* obligations and peremptory rules. As explained by the International Law Commission (ILC), peremptory character concerns the 'scope and priority to be given to a certain number of fundamental obligations', whereas *erga omnes* character concerns the question of standing and who has legal interest in their compliance—or who is entitled to invoke responsibility for their breach.[11] But the relation between the two concepts is notoriously complex and uncertain.[12] It seems well accepted that peremptory rules entail *erga omnes* obligations,[13] though it remains unclear whether there can be *erga omnes* obligations that are not also peremptory.[14] In these two decisions, the outcome is most likely correct as it seems accepted that the prohibition against racial discrimination is peremptory and, moreover, that it gives rise to *erga omnes* obligations.[15] But given the uncertainty concerning the relation between these two concepts, tribunals applying Article 26 ought to clearly determine whether the rule in question is indeed a peremptory one and not rely simply on its *erga omnes* character.

D. Conclusion: Alignment of general international law and international investment law

There are no decisions on Article 26 from interstate courts or tribunals. Nevertheless, the principle it expresses is clear and well-accepted.

The few investment tribunals which have interpreted and applied this rule have done so in a manner consistent with general international law, despite some conceptual inaccuracy.

There is no good reason, in this area of international law, for international investment law to deviate from general international law. More so, to the extent any such deviation involves a derogation from a peremptory rule of international law, it would be impermissible and invalid.

---

[10] *Border Timbers* (n 9) para 656. Similarly, *von Pezold* (n 9) para 657.
[11] ARSIWA Commentaries (n 2) Chapter III of Part II, para 7.
[12] The literature on the topic is extensive. See, among others, G Gaja, '*Jus Cogens* Beyond the Vienna Convention' (1981) 172 Recueil 271 (hereafter Gaja, '*Jus Cogens*'); B Simma, 'From Bilateralism to Community Interest in International Law' (1994) 250 Recueil 217, 294–301 (hereafter Simma, 'From Bilateralism to Community Interest'); CJ Tams, *Enforcing Obligations Erga Omnes in International Law*, ch 4 (CUP 2005) (hereafter Tams, *Enforcing*); J Crawford, 'Multilateral Rights and Obligations in International Law' (2006) 319 Recueil 325; E de Wet, '*Jus Cogens* and Obligations *Erga Omnes*' in D Shelton (ed), *Oxford Handbook of International Human Righs Law* (OUP 2013) 541ff; J Crawford, 'Chance, Order, Change: The Course of International Law' (2013) 365 Recueil 9, paras 325–44; MM Bradley, '*Jus Cogens*' Preferred Sister: Obligations *Erga Omnes* and the International Court of Justice—Fifty Years after the *Barcelona Traction* Case' in D Tladi (ed), *Peremptory Norms of General International Law (Jus Cogens): Disquisitions and Disputations* (Brill/Nijhoff 2021).
[13] See, most recently, draft Conclusion 17 of the ILC's Draft Conclusions on Peremptory Norms of General International Law (*jus cogens*), adopted on first reading, at: Report of the International Law Commission, Seventy-First Session, General Assembly Official Records (A/74/10) (2019), 145. In the literature see, among others, Tams, *Enforcing* (n 12) 139–51; F Bordin, 'State Responsibility in Advisory Proceedings: Thoughts on Judicial Propriety and Multilateralism in the *Chagos* Opinion' in T Burri and J Trinidad (eds), *Decolonization and the International Court of Justice: New Directions from the Chagos Advisory Opinion* (CUP 2021) 105–10.
[14] On which see Gaja, '*Jus Cogens*' (n 12) 281; Simma, 'From Bilateralism to Community Interest' (n 12) 300; Tams, *Enforcing* (n 12) 151–54.
[15] It is listed as an example of an *erga omnes* obligation in *Barcelona Traction, Light and Power Company, Limited* (Judgment) [1970] ICJ Rep 3, para 34; and in ARSIWA Commentaries (n 2) Article 48 para 9 (citing *Barcelona Traction*). It is also listed as an example of a peremptory rule ibid, Article 26 para 5; and ibid, Article 40 para 4.

Selected literature

Costelloe D, *Legal Consequences of Peremptory Norms in International Law* (CUP 2017).
Crawford J, *State Responsibility: The General Part* (CUP 2013).
Ménard M, 'Compliance with Peremptory Norms' in Crawford J, Pellet A and Olleson S (eds), *The Law of International Responsibility* (OUP 2010).

Selected decisions

Border Timbers et al v Republic of Zimbabwe, ICSID Case No ARB/10/25, Award, 28 July 2015.
CMS Gas Transmission Company v Argentine Republic, ICSID Case ARB/01/8, Award, 12 May 2005.
von Pezold et al v Republic of Zimbabwe, ICSID Case No ARB/10/15, Award, 28 July 2015.

Article 27 of the ARSIWA

Consequences of invoking a circumstance precluding wrongfulness

Federica Paddeu

The invocation of a circumstance precluding wrongfulness in accordance with this chapter is without prejudice to:

(a) compliance with the obligation in question, if and to the extent that the circumstance precluding wrongfulness no longer exists;

(b) the question of compensation for any material loss caused by the act in question.

A. Introduction	1	D. Conclusion: Some difficulties resulting from uncertainty at general international law	21
B. Application in general international law	2		
C. Application in international investment law	15		

A. Introduction

Article 27 deals with two consequences of the invocation of defences: (i) return to compliance with the underlying obligation, the status and existence of which is not as such affected by the invocation of a defence; and (ii) the question of any potential compensation for material loss caused by the invocation of the defence. These two consequences are distinct and independent from one another.

B. Application in general international law

<u>Return to compliance:</u> The savings clause in paragraph (a) of Article 27 is a logical consequence of the effect of defences as 'shields'[1] and not 'swords': the defences in the law of responsibility do not affect the continued existence of the underlying obligations, in principle at least.[2] Defences permit temporary non-performance (as justifications) or set aside any potential legal consequences of non-performance (as excuses) for as long as the circumstances

---

[1] ILC, 'Draft Articles on Responsibility of States for Internationally Wrongful Acts, with Commentaries' YILC 2001, Vol II, Part Two, 31, Chapter V of Part I, para 1 (hereafter ARSIWA Commentaries).

[2] See, by reference to treaty obligations, *Rainbow Warrior (New Zealand v France)* (1990) XX RIAA 215, para 75; *Gabčíkovo-Nagymaros Project (Hungary/Slovakia)* [1997] ICJ Rep 7, para 47 (hereafter *Gabčíkovo-Nagymaros*).

enlivening the defences last. This implication of the effect of defences is well accepted in international practice. In *Gabčíkovo-Nagymaros*, the International Court of Justice (ICJ) held that '[a]s soon as the state of necessity ceases to exist, the duty to comply with treaty obligations revives'.[3] According to the International Law Commission (ILC), the reference to 'compliance with the obligation in question' includes the obligation to cease the wrongful act if it is continuing.[4]

3 It is possible that the circumstances giving rise to the defence lead to the termination of the relevant obligation. For example, an obligation to return a work of art is terminated if it was destroyed by an irresistible and unforeseen event, such as an earthquake.

4 Article 27(a) also indicates that a State must return to compliance 'to the extent that' the circumstances triggering the defence cease to exist. This allows for a partial performance of the obligation in 'situations in which the conditions preventing compliance gradually lessen'.[5] This proviso raises two interesting questions, for the most part underexplored in practice and scholarship.

5 First is the termination of defences.[6] For some defences there will be a clear-cut moment when the facts giving rise to it disappear. For example, where the State expressly withdraws its consent to the specific conduct in a statement. Similarly, countermeasures must be terminated 'as soon as' the target State complies with its obligations.[7] Partial performance is likely to be irrelevant in these circumstances. In others, the transition will be more difficult: for example, when does the grave and imminent peril to an essential interest disappear? Or when does a material impossibility become a mere difficulty of performance? The boundary may not always be clear, and the question of partial performance—to the extent permitted by the lessening or gradual disappearance of the facts giving rise to the defence—may arise.

6 Second is the effect of partial performance. If the conduct is only partially covered by a defence, does this mean that defences in the law of responsibility can be partial? It seems plausible that excuses could operate as partial defences, precluding some but not other consequences of wrongfulness (eg precluding compensation but not satisfaction). But it is not clear that justifications could operate partially in international law. In domestic systems, partial justifications reduce the gravity of the offence: in English law, for example, a partial defence of diminished responsibility turns a conviction for murder into voluntary manslaughter. But wrongfulness in international law is not scalar in this way, conduct is either in breach of an obligation (in which case it is wrongful) or it is not (in which case it is lawful/permissible). It is thus difficult to conceptualize the effect of a partial justification on the qualification of the relevant conduct. Some support for this view can be found in the Commentary to Article 12, indicating that 'a breach may exist even if the act of the State is only partly contrary to an international obligation incumbent upon it'.[8] This said, partial performance may be significant as it may reduce the extent of the compensation due for any material loss caused.

---

[3] *Gabčíkovo-Nagymaros* (n 2) para 101.
[4] ARSIWA Commentaries (n 1) Article 27 para 3.
[5] ibid para 2.
[6] For some observations on this question, see F Paddeu and M Waibel, 'The Final Act: Exploring the End of Pandemics' (2020) 114 AJIL 698; F Paddeu and M Waibel, 'Necessity 20 Years On: The Limits of Article 25 ARSIWA' (2022) 37 ICSID Rev 160, 182–83 (hereafter Paddeu and Waibel, 'Necessity 20 Years On').
[7] Article 53 of the ARSIWA.
[8] ARSIWA Commentaries (n 1) Article 12 para 2.

Compensation: Paragraph (b) refers to the possibility of an obligation to pay compensation for material loss caused by the act taken under cover of one of the defences ('duty of compensation'). This is another saving clause as it was 'not possible to specify in general terms when compensation is payable'.[9] It is, in principle, applicable to all of the six defences recognized in the Articles.[10]

The duty of compensation referred to in this provision is distinct from compensation as a form of reparation.[11] 'Material loss' in Article 27(b) concerns damage, but 'is narrower than the concept of damage elsewhere in the [A]rticles': it concerns 'only the adjustment of losses that may occur when a party relies' on a defence.[12] It does not include moral damage,[13] and it likely also excludes lost profits (which are compensable under Article 36). Crucially, 'material' here does not refer to the importance or extent of the damage: there is no evidence from the drafting of this provision that 'material' was intended as a threshold below which losses could not be recovered.

There are two main difficulties with this duty. First, it is not clear in which circumstances it applies. The ILC Commentary provides little guidance in this respect. It suggests a rationale based on moral hazard: without such a duty, 'the State whose conduct would otherwise be unlawful might seek to shift the burden of the defence of its own interests or concerns onto an innocent third State'.[14] And then adds that it is for the two relevant States to agree 'on the possibility and extent of compensation payable in a given case'.[15] Second, the legal basis of this duty is unclear. The ILC considered,[16] but rejected,[17] the possibility that this might be a form of liability arising from lawful acts.

For some scholars, the distinction between justifications and excuses can address both of these difficulties.[18] Justifications render conduct lawful, whereas excuses do not affect the illegality of the conduct. The duty, in their view, would arise only for excuses, and would have its legal basis in the wrongfulness of the conduct. But the matter is more complex than this.[19]

First, if the duty were grounded on the wrongfulness of conduct, then it would presumably be part of the obligation to make reparation. As such, excuses would operate only partially to preclude some but not all of the consequences of the wrongful act. This solution would elide the duty of compensation and the obligation to make reparation under Part Two of the Articles,[20] which the ILC sought to distinguish.

Second, it is not clear that all excuses generate a duty of compensation. Crawford, for example, suggested that no such duty should exist in the case of *force majeure* as in these

---

[9] ibid Article 27 para 1.
[10] ibid para 6.
[11] ibid Article 12 para 4.
[12] ibid.
[13] J Crawford, *State Responsibility: The General Part* (CUP 2013) 318 (hereafter Crawford, *General Part*).
[14] ARSIWA Commentaries (n 1) Article 27 para 5.
[15] ibid para 6.
[16] See comments from Quentin-Baxter, 1615th Meeting, YILC 1980, Vol I, 168, para 16; Barboza, 1617th Meeting, YILC 1980, Vol I, 176, para 27.
[17] ILC, 'Report of the Commission on the Work of its Fifty-First Session' YILC 1999, Vol II, Part Two, 85, para 406.
[18] For example, T Christakis, 'Les "circonstances excluant l'illicéité": une illusion optique?' in O Corten and others (eds), *Droit du pouvoir, pouvoir du droit: Mélanges offerts à Jean Salmon* (Bruylant 2007) 235–40.
[19] F Paddeu, *Justification and Excuse in International Law: Concept and Theory of General Defences* (CUP 2018) 77–94.
[20] ARSIWA Commentaries (n 1) Article 27 para 4.

situations it was materially impossible for the invoking State to act in any other way: losses in this case should lie where they fall.[21] Thus, simply to rely on the concept of excuses to determine the circumstances in which the duty arises is insufficient.

13 Third, this solution does not address the key question whether compensation should be due *even* if the conduct is permitted under one of the defences. This is most relevant with respect to the defence of necessity, which is invoked by States as, and is formulated following the logic of, justification.[22]

14 There is relatively little practice on the duty referred to in Article 27(b), and the practice that exists is mostly linked to invocations of necessity. For example, in *Gabčíkovo-Nagymaros* the Court 'pointed out' that Hungary had 'expressly acknowledged' that the plea of necessity 'would not exempt it from its duty to compensate its partner'.[23] Nevertheless, the practice is equivocal and has given rise to contradictory assessments as to the existence of this duty in the academic literature.[24]

C. Application in international investment law

15 Return to compliance: Investor–State tribunals have on occasion referred to Article 27(a), endorsing the basic principle that defences are temporary and States must resume compliance as soon as the conditions giving rise to it come to an end.[25] Some tribunals noted the difficulties relating to the question of partial performance as the facts giving rise to the defence gradually lessen, without addressing it.[26]

16 This question is likely to be relevant in investment disputes relating to the Covid-19 pandemic-management measures. Throughout the period of the pandemic, States have imposed restrictions and then lessened them, only to re-impose them again at a later time, in response to, among others, the evolution of the virus, the spread of infection and the degree of immunity within their population, and the capability of their health services. When the

---

[21] Crawford, *General Part* (n 13) 319. Similarly (though more tentatively): C Binder and P Janig, 'Investment Agreements and Financial Crises' in M Krajewski and RT Hoffmann (eds), *Research Handbook on Foreign Direct Investment* (Edward Elgar Publishing 2019) 129–33 (hereafter Binder and Janig, 'Investment Agreements and Financial Crises').

[22] See in this Commentary: Federica Paddeu and Michael Waibel, 'Article 25: Necessity'.

[23] *Gabčíkovo-Nagymaros* (n 2) para 48.

[24] Arguing the practice supports a customary duty of compensation in cases of necessity: A Reinisch and C Binder, 'Debts and State of Necessity' in JP Bohoslavsky and JL Černič (eds), *Making Sovereign Financing and Human Rights work* (Hart Publishing 2014) 125–26; G Bücheler, *Proportionality in Investor-State Arbitration* (OUP 2015) 243, 290–96; Binder and Janig, 'Investment Agreements and Financial Crises' (n 21) 677–78. For the opposite view, see F Franke, 'The Custom of Necessity in Investor-State Arbitrations' in R Hofman and CJ Tams (eds), *International Investment Law and General International Law* (Nomos 2011) 156–57; A Kent and AR Harrington, 'The Plea of Necessity under Customary International Law: A Critical Review in Light of the Argentine Cases' in C Brown and K Miles (eds), *Evolution in Investment Treaty Arbitration* (CUP 2011) 261–63; M Paparinskis, 'Investment Treaty Arbitration and the (New) Law of State Responsibility' (2013) 24 EJIL 617, 633; D Inverso, 'El estado de necesidad como circunstancia que excluye la ilicitud en la responsabilidad internacional de los Estados' (2015) 47 Rev Der Públ 49, 54. See also F Paddeu, 'Investment Tribunals and the Duty of Compensation in Cases of Necessity: A Customary Law Void?' in P Merkouris and others (eds), *Custom and its Interpretation in International Investment Law* (CUP 2023) 151.

[25] In the context of necessity, see *CMS Gas Transmission Company v Argentine Republic*, ICSID Case No ARB/01/8, Award, 12 May 2005, paras 379–80 (hereafter *CMS Award*); *Enron Corporation and Ponderosa Assets LP v Argentine Republic*, ICSID Case No ARB/01/3, Award, 22 May 2007, para 343 (hereafter *Enron*); *Sempra Energy International v Argentine Republic*, ICSID Case No ARB/02/16, Award, 29 September 2007, para 392 (hereafter *Sempra*). Awards concerning other defences have not, however, referred to this Article.

[26] See, eg, *Sempra* (n 25) para 392.

threat posed by the virus had diminished, were States required to gradually lessen their restrictions and, if so, only some of the restrictions? Assuming only some restrictions affected investment treaties, how to assess whether it is those restrictions that ought to be lifted, or lessened? If the State only lessened the stringency of its measures, would such partial performance of obligations be covered by a defence, considering the ILC's statement that partial performance constitutes a breach? There is little guidance on this point in practice and scholarship, as noted earlier. These assessments are likely to be difficult to make,[27] and tribunals may be required, as explained in *Hochtief*,[28] to exercise their judgment in identifying points in time when the conditions enlivening a defence (for example, a situation of necessity or distress; or a situation of material impossibility) were such that a return to compliance—partial or total as the case may be—was possible.

Compensation: There is considerable case-law on the duty of compensation in ISDS. Among States invoking necessity, Argentina[29] and Zimbabwe[30] have denied a duty of compensation. Bolivia has seemingly endorsed it.[31] Tribunals' decisions on this question are, however, inconsistent. **17**

In support of the duty of compensation: Some tribunals have endorsed a duty of compensation in cases of necessity, though on relatively weak grounds. The tribunal in *CMS v Argentina* held that Article 27(b) 'establishe[d] the appropriate rule of international law on this issue' and this reflected a general principle of law—without producing evidence to back this claim.[32] *SAS v Bolivia* simply asserted the existence of duty of compensation in cases of necessity.[33] In *Enron* and *Sempra*, the tribunals held that the question of compensation was to be decided by the parties or, absent their agreement, by the tribunal.[34] Lastly, the *EDF* tribunal interpreted the defence of necessity as implicitly including a duty of compensation.[35] The Annulment Committee agreed, holding that compensation is 'inherent in the very concept of necessity'.[36] In all cases, however, the tribunals' assertions as to this duty have either (i) not been backed by adequate evidence in state practice or (ii) have involved rather unpersuasive reasoning.[37] **18**

Against the existence of the duty of compensation: The *LG&E* tribunal noted that Article 27(b) was a without prejudice clause,[38] and held that no compensation was due since Article XI of the Bilateral Investment Treaty (BIT) (which it interpreted in line with Article 25 of the **19**

---

[27] On which see Paddeu and Waibel, 'Necessity 20 Years On' (n 6).
[28] *Hochtief Aktiengesellschaft v Argentine Republic*, ICSID Case No ARB/07/31, Award, 9 December 2014, paras 293–94.
[29] See, inter alia, *CMS Award* (n 25) para 389; *CMS Gas Transmission Company v Argentine Republic*, ICSID Case No ARB/01/8, Annulment, 25 September 2007, para 139 (hereafter *CMS Annulment*); *Enron* (n 25) paras 344–45; *Sempra* (n 25) paras 393–94; *BG Group Plc v Argentina*, UNCITRAL Award, 24 December 2007, para 398.
[30] *Border Timbers et al v Republic of Zimbabwe*, ICSID Case No ARB/10/25, Award, 28 July 2015, para 615; *von Pezold et al v Republic of Zimbabwe*, ICSID Case No ARB/10/15, Award, 28 July 2015, para 616.
[31] *South American Silver v Bolivia* (2018), PCA Case No 2013-15, Award of 22 November 2018, para 535 (hereafter *South American Silver*).
[32] *CMS Award* (n 25) para 390. The award was subsequently annulled, among others, due to a manifest error of law in relation to Article 27(b): *CMS Annulment* (n 29) paras 146–47.
[33] *South American Silver* (n 31) para 620.
[34] *Enron* (n 25) para 345; *Sempra* (n 25) para 394.
[35] *EDF International SA, SAUR International SA and Leon Participaciones Argentinas SA v Argentine Republic*, ICSID Case No ARB/03/23, Award, 11 June 2012, para 1171.
[36] *EDF International SA, SAUR International SA and Leon Participaciones Argentinas SA v Argentine Republic*, ICSID Case No ARB/03/23, Annulment, 5 February 2016, para 330.
[37] See F Paddeu, 'Investment Tribunals and the Duty of Compensation in Cases of Necessity: A Customary Law Void?' in P Merkouris and others (eds), *Custom and its Interpretation in International Investment Law* (CUP 2023).
[38] *LG&E Energy Corp, LG&E Capital Corp, LG&E International Inc v Argentine Republic*, ICSID Case No ARB/02/1, Liability, 3 October 2006, para 260.

ARSIWA) 'establishes the state of necessity as a ground for exclusion from wrongfulness of an act of the State, and therefore, the State is exempted from liability'.[39] The reasoning here is circular: the question that Article 27(b) raises is precisely whether compensation *is due* even in these cases.

20 *Agnostic positions*: The Annulment Committee in *CMS* noted that Article 27(b) is a without prejudice clause and not a stipulation, and that it did not attempt to 'specify in which circumstances compensation could be due, notwithstanding the state of necessity'.[40] The Annulment Committee in *Sempra*, in addressing the difference between state of necessity and the BIT's non-precluded-measures clause, noted that no compensation was due in the latter case but that the question of compensation 'was not precluded' in the former. The tribunal thus acknowledges the possibility that compensation could be due, without taking sides in the debate.[41]

D. Conclusion: Some difficulties resulting from uncertainty at general international law

21 The clause in Article 27(a) is well accepted in general international law, and investment tribunals have endorsed it. While there are some tricky aspects to the application of this proviso, in particular concerning partial return to compliance, these have not been addressed in general international law or investment law.

22 The clause in Article 27(b) has created more difficulty. As a without prejudice clause, it does not itself stipulate whether compensation is due. Moreover, the ILC left many questions open—in particular, when compensation was due, and what would be its legal basis. There is scant practice in international law on this duty, and the practice that exists relates to the plea of necessity and is quite equivocal. It is thus not surprising that investor–State tribunals have had difficulty in their engagement with Article 27(b), and thus reached contradictory conclusions.

Selected literature

Crawford J, *State Responsibility: The General Part* (CUP 2013).

Forteau M, 'Reparation in the Event of a Circumstance Precluding Wrongfulness' in Crawford J, Pellet A and Olleson S (eds), *The Law of International Responsibility* (OUP 2010).

Paddeu F, 'Investment Tribunals and the Duty of Compensation in Cases of Necessity: A Customary Law Void?' in Merkouris P and others (eds), *Custom and its Interpretation in International Investment Law* (CUP 2023).

Paddeu F, *Justification and Excuse in International Law: Concept and Theory of General Defences* (CUP 2018).

Ripinsky S, 'State of Necessity: Effect on Compensation' (2007) 4(6) TDM 1.

---

[39] ibid para 261.
[40] *CMS Annulment* (n 29) paras 146–47.
[41] *Sempra Energy International v Argentine Republic*, ICSID Case No ARB/02/16, Annulment, 29 June 2010, para 118.

Part Two, Chapters I and II of the ARSIWA

Remedies

Geraldo Vidigal and Stephanie Forrest

A. General provisions	1	4. Conclusion	29
I. Judicial remedies and the consequences of State responsibility [Article 28]	1	II. Compensation [Article 36]	31
		1. Concept	31
II. Prospective elements of responsibility: The continued obligation to perform and the duties of cessation and non-repetition [Articles 29 and 30]	5	2. Valuation	35
		3. Availability and quantification of moral damages	37
		4. Equitable limitations on compensation	47
III. The duty of reparation and the primacy of restitution [Articles 31 and 34]	11	III. Satisfaction [Article 37]	51
		1. Concept	51
B. Modalities of reparation	16	2. Practice	53
I. Restitution [Article 35]	16	C. Specific issues	58
1. Concept	16	I. Interest [Article 38]	58
2. Material impossibility	20	II. Contribution to the injury [Article 39]	64
3. Lack of proportionality	24	D. Conclusion	68

A. General provisions

I. Judicial remedies and the consequences of State responsibility [Article 28]

Article 28: Legal consequences of an internationally wrongful act

The international responsibility of a State which is entailed by an internationally wrongful act in accordance with the provisions of part one involves legal consequences as set out in this part.

This entry covers the first two chapters of Part Two of the International Law Commission's 1
Articles on Responsibility of States for International Wrongful Acts (ARSIWA), devoted to what the International Law Commission (ILC) has referred to as the 'content of the international responsibility of a state'[1] or the 'consequences of an internationally wrongful act'.[2] International courts and tribunals frequently refer to these provisions when determining the

---

[1] ILC, 'Draft Articles on the Responsibility of States for Internationally Wrongful Acts, with Commentaries' YILC 2001, Vol II, Part Two, 31, Part Two (hereafter ARSIWA Commentaries).
[2] ibid Article 28.

appropriate remedies following a finding of breach.[3] While the ILC notes that Part Two 'does not apply to obligations of reparation to the extent that these arise towards or are invoked by a person or entity other than a State',[4] international courts and tribunals have, by and large, treated these articles as authoritative statements of customary international law and applied them outside of the inter-State dispute context as well.[5]

2 The starting point for Part Two is Article 28, which largely reflects the statement by the Permanent Court of International Justice (PCIJ) in *Chorzów Factory* that '[i]t is a principle of international law that the breach of an engagement involves an obligation to make reparation in an adequate form'.[6] Under the ARSIWA, responsibility creates prospective obligations as well as a retrospective duty to make reparation. Prospectively, a State that breaches an international obligation must cease its unlawful conduct and, in certain cases, provide assurances of non-repetition. Retrospectively, the State must provide reparation for injury caused by its violation, in one of three forms: restitution, compensation, or satisfaction.[7]

3 As the present entry will show, there are significant differences between the practice of international courts and tribunals established under general international law and those under investment law when determining the appropriate remedies. This entry explores several of those differences for each modality of reparation, as well as with respect to specific issues, including interest and contribution to injury.

4 This entry also considers one of the most significant discrepancies that has been identified between general international law and investment law, that being the difference in the forms of remedies most commonly ordered. While the ARSIWA dictate that a violation of international law should typically lead to both prospective performance obligations and retrospective reparation obligations, investment tribunals tend to focus only on the retrospective duty of reparation and, in particular, compensation. This entry will explore that discrepancy and consider how, in the absence of express treaty limitations, investment tribunals may resort to general international law, as codified in the ARSIWA, and go beyond awards for compensation to demand cessations of breach and guarantees of non-repetition, award legal or material restitution, or issue declarations of satisfaction.

---

[3] While the Articles do not use the term 'remedies', this term is used interchangeably with 'consequences of internationally wrongful acts' in the official ILC Commentary and in subsequent jurisprudence and scholarship. See, eg, Whaling in the Antarctic (*Australia v Japan: New Zealand intervening*) (Judgment) [2014] ICJ Rep 226, 298 (hereafter *Whaling in the Antarctic*); J Crawford, *State Responsibility—The General Part* (CUP 2013) 506 (hereafter Crawford, *State Responsibility*).

[4] ARSIWA Commentaries (n 1) Article 28 para 2; See also Article 33(2).

[5] See, eg, *ADM v Mexico*, ICSID Case No ARB(AF)/04/5, Award, 21 November 2007, para 177; *Bernhard von Pezold and Others v Republic of Zimbabwe*, ICSID Case No ARB/10/15, Award, 28 July 2015, para 691 (hereafter *von Pezold v Zimbabwe*). For critique of the application of the ILC Articles to a non-inter-State case, see EACJ, *Zziwa v EAC Secretary General*, Judgment, Appeal No 2 of 2017 (EACJ, 25 May 2018), para 42 (hereafter *Zziwa v EAC Secretary General*). See also Z Douglas, 'The Hybrid Foundations of Investment Treaty Arbitration' (2003) 74 BYIL 151, 186–93; M Paparinskis, 'Investment Treaty Arbitration and the (New) Law of State Responsibility' (2013) 24 EJIL 617; R Volterra, 'ILC Articles on State Responsibility and Investor-State Arbitration: Do Investors Have Rights?' (2010) 25 ICSID Rev 218, 222.

[6] Case Concerning the Factory at Chorzów (*Germany v Poland*) (Claim for Indemnity) (Jurisdiction) [1928] PCIJ Rep Series A No 9, 21 (hereafter *Chorzów* Jurisdiction). In *Vinter v United Kingdom*, ECtHR Judge Ziemele in her concurring opinion cited Article 28 to argue that, by stating that a finding of violation 'constitutes just satisfaction', the ECtHR had blurred the 'distinction that one draws between an internationally wrongful act and its consequences'. *Vinter and others v United Kingdom* App Nos 66069/09, 130/10, and 3896/10 [2016] III ECHR 317 (9 July 2013), 51 (Concurring Opinion of Judge Ziemele).

[7] Importantly, the entitlement to adopt countermeasures is not among these automatic consequences of responsibility but arises only where the responsible State has refused to comply with this new set of obligations. See in this Commentary: Martins Paparinskis, 'Articles 49–54 of the ARSIWA'.

II. Prospective elements of responsibility: The continued obligation to perform and the duties of cessation and non-repetition [Articles 29 and 30]

Article 29: Continued duty of performance

The legal consequences of an internationally wrongful act under this part do not affect the continued duty of the responsible State to perform the obligation breached.

Article 30: Cessation and non-repetition

The State responsible for the internationally wrongful act is under an obligation:

(a) to cease that act, if it is continuing;
(b) to offer appropriate assurances and guarantees of non-repetition, if circumstances so require.

Articles 29 and 30 refer to the prospective elements of responsibility, namely, the duties of cessation and non-repetition. Article 29 confirms that a breach does not affect the continuance of the State's duty to respect the violated obligation or connected obligations,[8] while Article 30 codifies the new obligations that arise for a violating State with respect to its future conduct.

The primary obligation that arises for the responsible State is the duty of cessation, requiring the State to put an end to conduct that violates its international obligations. In *Navigational and Related Rights*, the International Court of Justice (ICJ) observed that, following a finding of breach, the 'obligation to cease wrongful conduct derives both from the general obligation of each State to conduct itself in accordance with international law and from the specific obligation upon States parties to disputes before the Court to comply with its judgments'.[9] In some cases, courts have gone one step further and specified the conduct required to ensure cessation.[10]

The second obligation that arises as a consequence of breach, to provide guarantees of non-repetition, has been mentioned as an available remedy by the ICJ but never fleshed out.[11] The Inter-American Court of Human Rights (IACtHR) has filled this gap, giving the obligation content in its orders that responsible States set up specific policies to prevent the recurrence of human rights violations similar to the ones brought before it. As the IACtHR put it in *Gutiérrez Soler*, these are 'positive measures that the State must adopt to prevent repetition of the harmful events such as those that occurred' in the individual case judged.[12]

In the investment context, little attention has been paid to the prospective elements of responsibility in Articles 29 and 30. For example, in *Mobil v Canada*, the tribunal recognized

---

[8] Consequences for the obligation may also arise under the law of treaties. See B Simma and CJ Tams, 'Reacting against Treaty Breaches' in DB Hollis (ed), *The Oxford Guide to Treaties* (OUP 2020).

[9] Dispute regarding Navigational and Related Rights *(Costa Rica v Nicaragua)* (Judgment) [2009] ICJ Rep 213, 267.

[10] Whaling in the Antarctic (n 3) para 247(7); ECtHR, *Assanidze v Georgia (Merits and Just Satisfaction)*, App No 71503/01, 8 April 2004, paras 195–207; ECtHR, *Ivanţoc v Moldova and Russia (Merits and Just Satisfaction)*, App No 23687/05, 4 April 2012, paras 146–56.

[11] LaGrand *(Germany v United States of America)* (Judgment) [2001] ICJ Rep 466, 485 (hereafter *LaGrand*); Avena and Other Mexican Nationals *(Mexico v United States of America)* (Judgment) [2004], ICJ Rep 12, 69 (hereafter *Avena*).

[12] IACtHR, *Gutiérrez-Soler v Colombia* (Merits, Reparation and Costs) Judgment, 12 September 2005, para 63; IACtHR, *Aloeboetoe v Suriname* (Reparation and Costs), 10 September 1993, Series C No 11, paras 96, 99–108.

that Canada was in 'continuing breach resulting in ongoing damage to the Claimants' interests', but inferred from this solely a right of the claimant to file subsequent claims to request reparation by way of compensation.[13] Claimants in investment arbitration typically focus their claims on reparation for injury, possibly because claims are brought most often when there has been a breakdown in relations with the State and the claimant is uninterested in the State's continued performance of breached obligations.[14] Even in the rare circumstance when investors request the return of property or the reversal of administrative acts, these requests are usually framed as requests for restitution—one of the three forms of reparation—rather than cessation of the breach.[15]

9 Moreover, even in circumstances where tribunals conclude that a State's overall policy is in continuing breach of international obligations broader than those owed to a specific investor, they have refrained from requiring the State to put an end to the relevant policy or measure. Instead, they typically limit their remedial order to the request for individual reparation brought by the claimant. This was the case in *von Pezold v Zimbabwe*, in which the tribunal found that Zimbabwe's 'discriminat[ion] against the landowners on the basis of their skin-color and foreign ancestral heritage' amounted to a 'breach of an obligation *erga omnes* by Zimbabwe [...] an impairment to the international community as a whole'.[16] Despite this, the tribunal focused entirely on the requests for individual reparation put forward by the claimant.[17] This may be a consequence of the expansive interpretation of the limitations on investor–State tribunals' remedial jurisdiction where, for example, measures of restitution demanding a State to alter its legislative measures may be seen as an undue interference on State sovereignty.[18]

10 Occasionally, claimants in investment arbitration have requested tribunals consider cessation as a remedy. Absent a treaty or other limitation, investment tribunals are empowered under general international law to affirm a State's duty to cease the unlawful conduct and may even specify what is required for this purpose.[19] This was recognized by the tribunal in *Chevron v Ecuador*. After concluding that a domestic judgment had been tainted by corruption, the tribunal referred to Articles 28–38 in support of its finding that 'the reinstatement of the Claimants' rights under international law requires of the Respondent the immediate suspension of the enforceability of the *Lago Agrio* Judgment'.[20] Other than in highly specific situations, however, investment tribunals are far less likely to order cessation than their counterparts in other international fora, and have occasionally questioned their entitlement to do so.[21]

---

[13] *Mobil Investments Canada Inc and Murphy Oil Corporation v Canada*, ICSID Case No ARB(AF)/07/4, Award, 29 February 2015, para 429 and para 478.
[14] See, referring to attempts at resolving disputes through means other than ISDS, RL Wellhausen, 'International Investment Law and Foreign Direct Reinvestment' (2019) 73 Int Organ 839; L Johns and RL Wellhausen, 'The Price of Doing Business: Why Replaceable Foreign Firms Get Worse Government Treatment' (2021) 33 Econ Politics 209. We thank Michael Waibel for this point.
[15] *Arif v Moldova*, ICSID Case No ARB/11/23, Award, 8 April 2013, paras 570–72 (hereafter *Arif v Moldova*); *Texaco Overseas Petroleum Co v Government of the Libyan Arab Republic* (1979) 53 ILR 389, paras 507–11.
[16] *von Pezold v Zimbabwe* (n 5) para 657.
[17] It should be noted that the SADC tribunal, though addressing the human rights violation directly, adopted the same remedies. See *Campbell and Others v Zimbabwe*, SADCT Case No 2/2007, Judgment, 28 November 2008, para 92.
[18] See Section B.I below.
[19] This is without prejudice to the State's right, explicitly recognized in many investment treaties, to expropriate investments against compensation.
[20] *Chevron Corporation and Texaco Petroleum Company v The Republic of Ecuador* (II), PCA Case No 2009-23, Second Partial Award on Track II, 30 August 2018, paras 9.9, 9.17 (hereafter *Chevron v Ecuador*).
[21] The tribunal in *Glencore v Colombia* set aside the claimant's request for a determination that Colombia was required to 'continue to perform and observe' the investor–State contract, finding that it did not need to address

III. The duty of reparation and the primacy of restitution [Articles 31 and 34]

Article 31: Reparation

1. The responsible State is under an obligation to make full reparation for the injury caused by the internationally wrongful act.
2. Injury includes any damage, whether material or moral, caused by the internationally wrongful act of a State.

Article 34: Forms of reparation

Full reparation for the injury caused by the internationally wrongful act shall take the form of restitution, compensation and satisfaction, either singly or in combination, in accordance with the provisions of this chapter.

International courts and tribunals often refer to the first paragraph of Article 31, usually together with the PCIJ's Judgment in *Chorzów Factory*, as authority for the customary status of the obligation to provide full reparation for injury caused by a breach.[22] Article 31(1) is also invoked as authority for the requirement of a causal relationship between injury and wrongful conduct.[23] Article 31(2) is commonly cited as authority for the obligation to provide reparation for moral damage—an issue examined in detail in Section B.II.3 below.

In the absence of any express treaty provisions addressing compensation and damages, investment tribunals frequently rely on Article 31(1) and adopt the *Chorzów Factory* standard. This approach has been criticized by some commentators, primarily because the rules of inter-State responsibility assume equality between State parties and may not be transposable to investment disputes between a sovereign State and a private party.[24] Despite

---

the 'theoretical question' whether it was 'authorized to issue an order of this type to a sovereign State', see *Glencore International A.G. and C.I. Prodeco S.A. v Republic of Colombia*, ICSID Case No ARB/16/6, Award, 27 August 2019, paras 1665–67 (hereafter *Glencore v Colombia*).

[22] Application of the Convention on the Prevention and Punishment of the Crime of Genocide (*Bosnia and Herzegovina v Serbia and Montenegro*) (Judgment) [2007] ICJ Rep 43, 233 (hereafter *Bosnian Genocide*); ITLOS, *M/G 'Virginia' (Panama/Guinea Bissau)*, Judgment, 14 April 2014, 110, para 430; ITLOS Seabed Disputes Chamber, *Responsibilities and obligations of States with respect to activities in the Area*, Advisory Opinion, 1 February 2011, *ITLOS Reports 2011*, 10, para 194. *Zongo v Burkina Faso*, Judgment on Reparations, 013/2011 (ACtHPR, 5 June 2015), para 21 (hereafter *Zongo v Burkina Faso*); Eritrea–Ethiopia Claims Commission, Eritrea's Damages Claims, *Eritrea v Ethiopia*, Award, 17 August 2009, para 24; Eritrea–Ethiopia Claims Commission, Ethiopia's Damages Claims, *Ethiopia v Eritrea*, Award, 17 August 2009, para 24; *Murphy Exploration & Production Company International v The Republic of Ecuador*, PCA Case No 2012-16, Partial Final Award, 6 May 2016, paras 424–25; *British Caribbean Bank v Belize*, PCA Case No 2010-18, Award, 19 December 2014, para 289; *Chevron v Ecuador* (n 20) para 10.13(vi); *Glencore v Colombia* (n 21) paras 1570–71.

[23] *Hulley v Russia*, PCA Case No AA 226, Final Award, 18 July 2014, para 1774; *Yukos v Russia*, PCA Case No AA 227, Final Award, 18 July 2014, paras 1589 (hereafter *Yukos v Russia*); *Veteran Petroleum v Russia*, PCA Case No AA 228, Final Award, 18 July 2014, paras 1597–99; *Clayton v Canada*, PCA Case No 2009-04, Award on Damages, 10 January 2019, paras 108–10.

[24] See, eg, REM Goodman and Y Parkhomenko, 'Does the Chorzów Factory Standard Apply in Investment Arbitration? A Contextual Reappraisal' (2017) 32 ICSID Rev 304; C Verburg, 'Damages and Reparation in Energy Related Investment Treaty Arbitrations' (2021) 23 ICLR 5. Consider also the statements of the PCIJ in *Chorzów Factory*, observing that the case in question was 'a dispute between governments and nothing but a dispute between governments' and 'the damage suffered by an individual is never identical in kind with that which will be suffered by a State'. See *Chorzów* Jurisdiction (n 6) 26–28.

this, *Chorzów Factory* remains 'the most frequently cited case in investment treaty arbitration',[25] and the *Chorzów Factory* standard is undeniably part and parcel of international investment law.

13 In addition to Article 31(1) and *Chorzów Factory*, investment tribunals often refer to the ICJ's statement in *Bosnian Genocide* that a request for reparation requires a 'sufficiently direct and certain causal nexus between the wrongful act [...] and the injury suffered by the Applicant' in the sense that the injury 'would in fact have been averted if the Respondent had acted in compliance with its legal obligations'.[26] For example, in *Pey Casado Foundation v Chile (Resubmission)*, the tribunal affirmed that the determination of a duty of reparation 'depends upon injury, and that injury in turn depends on causation'.[27] In *Bilcon v Canada*, the tribunal stated that it 'must be convinced that the Investors' alleged injury would, "in all probability", not have occurred if the NAFTA violation had not been committed'.[28]

14 Separately, Article 34 is generally invoked in support of two principles: (i) that injury caused by an internationally wrongful act requires full reparation and (ii) that this reparation may take the three forms established in the Articles—restitution, compensation, and satisfaction—either singly or in combination.[29] Although Article 34 does not set out an order of priority between the three forms, international courts and tribunals have often referred to this provision, in combination with *Chorzów Factory*,[30] to support the view that restitution is the primary form of reparation.

15 This primacy in principle does not necessarily translate into primacy in practice.[31] Like other international courts and tribunals, investment tribunals frequently refer to restitution as the primary remedy in passing, only to find it inappropriate for the case at hand, using the right to restitution instead as a parameter for determining the amount of compensation.[32] The tribunal in *Teinver v Argentina* went so far as to find that it was incumbent on the claimant requesting restitution 'to establish that right in the circumstances of this case and demonstrate that such an award was reasonable and proportionate'.[33]

---

[25] B Sabahi, *Compensation and Restitution in Investor-State Arbitration: Principles and Practice* (OUP 2011) 48 (hereafter Sabahi, *Compensation*). See also TG Nelson, 'A Factory in Chorzow: The Silesian Dispute that Continues to Influence International Law and Expropriation Damages Almost a Century Later' (2014) 1(1) J Damages Int'l Arb 77; J Paulsson, 'Ghosts of Chorzow: Maha Nunez Schultz v Republic of the Americas' in T Weiler (ed), *International Investment Law and Arbitration* (Cameron May Ltd 2009).

[26] *Bosnian Genocide* (n 22) 234.

[27] *Victor Pey Casado and President Allende Foundation v Republic of Chile*, ICSID Case No ARB/98/2204, Award, 13 September 2016, para 204 (hereafter *Pey Casado v Chile*).

[28] *Clayton v Canada*, PCA Case No 2009-04, Award on Damages, 10 January 2019, para 114 (referring to *Chorzów Factory*).

[29] ITLOS, THE M/V 'Saiga' (No 2) Case, *Saint Vincent v Guinea*, Judgment, Case No 2 (ITLOS, 1 July 1999), para 171 (hereafter *Saiga*); *Zongo v Burkina Faso* (n 22); *Zziwa v EAC Secretary General* (n 5) para 40.

[30] *Case Concerning the Factory at Chorzów (Germany v Poland)* (Claim for Indemnity) (Merits) [1928] PCIJ Rep Series A No 12, 47, 48 (hereafter *Chorzów* Merits).

[31] Gray, 'The Different Forms' (n 39) 589.

[32] *Chorzów* Merits (n 30) 47; *Bosnian Genocide* (n 22) 233; ECtHR, *Papamichalopoulos and others v Greece (Article 50)*, App No 14556/89, 31 October 1995, para 36; IACtHR, *Salvador Chiriboga v Ecuador (Reparation and Costs)*, 3 March 2011, para 59; *S.D. Myers, Inc v Canada*, UNCITRAL Arbitration Proceeding, Partial Award, 13 November 2000, paras 311–15; *Metalclad Corporation v United Mexican States*, ICSID Case No ARB(AF)/97/1, Award, 30 August 2000, para 122; *Nykomb Synergetics Technology Holding AB v Republic of Latvia*, SCC, Award, 16 December 2003, para 154.

[33] *Teinver S.A., Transportes de Cercanías S.A. and Autobuses Urbanos del Sur S.A. v Argentine Republic*, ICSID Case No ARB/09/1, Award, 21 July 2017, para 1097 (hereafter *Teinver v Argentina*).

B. Modalities of reparation

I. Restitution [Article 35]

Article 35: Restitution

A State responsible for an internationally wrongful act is under an obligation to make restitution, that is, to re-establish the situation which existed before the wrongful act was committed, provided and to the extent that restitution:
(a) is not materially impossible;
(b) does not involve a burden out of all proportion to the benefit deriving from restitution instead of compensation.

1. Concept

The ARSIWA treat restitution as the primary form of reparation for unlawful acts,[34] unless a rule of *lex specialis* derogates from this primacy.[35] The Commentary contemplates two categories of restitution: (i) 'material', typically involving the return of territory or property unlawfully seized, or release of persons wrongly detained; and (ii) 'juridical', usually requiring the revocation, annulment, or amendment by the responsible State of the legislative or administrative measure which violated international law.[36]

Under Article 35, restitution requires a party in breach 'to re-establish the situation which existed before the wrongful act was committed'. This implies a narrow definition of restitution, focusing on re-establishing the *status quo ante*. The definition of restitution put forward by the PCIJ in *Chorzów Factory* is broader and involves a duty to 'wipe out all the consequences of the illegal act and re-establish the situation which would, in all probability, have existed if that act had not been committed'.[37] For the ILC, the narrow definition 'has the advantage of focusing on the assessment of a factual situation and of not requiring a hypothetical inquiry into what the situation would have been if the wrongful act had not been committed'. At the same time, as the ILC noted, '[r]estitution in this narrow sense may have to be completed by compensation to ensure full reparation for the damage caused'.[38]

Only rarely has the ICJ explicitly referred to a duty of restitution. However, any such order may be seen as superfluous when the duty to reverse unlawful acts (requiring, for example, return of territory or release of imprisoned persons) also arises from declaratory remedies or determinations of cessation. In cases where restitution has been awarded, the ICJ usually adopts a flexible approach and affords the parties considerable deference in determining

---

[34] A distinction must be drawn between lawful and unlawful expropriation. As observed by the PCIJ in *Chorzów Factory*, lawful expropriation is not an unlawful act under international law but an exercise of a State's right to nationalize foreign property (subject to certain conditions, including compensation) and therefore restitution is not the primary remedy in such circumstances (*Chorzów* Merits (n 30) 46).

[35] Some investment treaties include express provisions which prohibit tribunals from awarding any relief other than monetary damages and interest or restitution of property. Under these treaty provisions, even where restitution is awarded by a tribunal, the responsible State reserves the right to pay 'monetary damages and any applicable interest in lieu of restitution'. See, eg, Energy Charter Treaty (adopted 17 December 1994, entered into force 16 April 1998) 2080 UNTS 10 (ECT), Article 26(8); North American Free Trade Agreement (1994) Article 1135.1; CPTPP Article 9.29/USMCA, Article 14.D.13.

[36] ARSIWA Commentaries (n 1) Article 35 para 5; The first Central American Court of Justice determined that, as restitution, the wrongdoing party was required to terminate a treaty that conflicted with the violated treaty, Corte de Justicia Centroamericana, *Anales* (1917) AJIL 696.

[37] *Chorzów* Merits (n 30) 47.9; ARSIWA Commentaries (n 1) Article 31 paras 1–3.

[38] ARSIWA Commentaries (n 1) Article 35 para 2.

the specific modality for achieving restitution.[39] In *Jurisdictional Immunities of the State*, the Court ordered Italy to reverse the effects of the decisions of its domestic courts that violated Germany's jurisdictional immunity. The ICJ held that 'the Respondent has the right to choose the means it considers best suited to achieve the required result'.[40] In other cases, the Court has been more specific. These include *Arrest Warrant*, in which the Court awarded juridical restitution,[41] as well as the 'order' in *Whaling in the Antarctic* 'that Japan shall revoke any extant authorization, permit or licence to kill, take or treat whales [issued unlawfully]'.[42] In the *Wall* Advisory Opinion, the ICJ stated that Israel was obligated, as far as materially possible, 'to return the land, orchards, olive grove and other immovable property seized from any natural of legal person' during the construction of a wall in the Occupied Palestinian Territory.[43]

19 Under investment law, there has been some suggestion that, in the absence of specific provisions allowing an order of restitution, investment tribunals lack the jurisdiction to make such an order, mainly due to the practical difficulties of enforcement or potential infringement on State sovereignty.[44] The majority view is that restitution is, in principle, available.[45]

2. Material impossibility

20 Article 35 describes restitution as the primary remedy, required unless it is either 'materially impossible' or 'a burden out of all proportion to the benefit deriving from restitution instead of compensation'.[46] With regard to the first exception, the ILC Commentary suggests that impossibility arises when performance is materially impossible, such as 'where property to be restored has been permanently lost or destroyed, or has deteriorated to such an extent as to

---

[39] See, for discussion, Crawford, *State Responsibility* (n 3) 515; C Gray, 'The Different Forms of Reparation: Restitution' in J Crawford, A Pellet and S Olleson (eds), *The Law of International Responsibility* (OUP 2010) 593 (hereafter Gray, 'The Different Forms').

[40] *Jurisdictional Immunities of the State (Germany v Italy: Greece intervening)*, (Judgment) [2012] ICJ Rep 99, 434 (hereafter *Jurisdictional Immunities*).

[41] *Arrest Warrant of 11 April 2000 (Democratic Republic of the Congo v Belgium)* (Judgment) [2002] ICJ Rep 3, 32. Belgium was obliged to cancel the arrest warrant issued against the then Foreign Minister of the Democratic Republic of the Congo. In cases of condemnations marked by procedural irregularities, the ICJ found that the appropriate remedy was for the wrongdoing State to provide 'effective review and reconsideration of the conviction and sentence', correcting the relevant irregularities, see *LaGrand* (n 11) para 125; *Avena* (n 11) paras 138–40, 153; *Jadhav (India v Pakistan)* (Judgment) [2019] ICJ Rep 418, 456.

[42] *Whaling in the Antarctic* (n 3) para 247(7); Some commentators have queried whether this order should fall under the heading of legal restitution or cessation, or if there is any material difference between the two. See, eg, J McIntyre, 'The Declaratory Judgement in Recent Jurisprudence of the ICJ: Conflicting Approaches to State Responsibility?' (2016) 29 LJIL 177, 190; F Torres, 'Revisiting the Chorzów Factory Standard of Reparation—Its Relevance in Contemporary International Law and Practice' (2021) 90(2) Nord J Int'l L 190.

[43] Legal Consequences of the Construction of a Wall in the Occupied Palestinian Territory (Advisory Opinion) [2004] ICJ Rep 136, 198.

[44] Z Douglas, 'Other Specific Regimes of Responsibility: Investment Treaty Arbitration and ICSID' in J Crawford, A Pellet and S Olleson (eds), *The Law of International Responsibility* (OUP 2010) 815, 829; A Kulick, *Global Public Interest in International Investment Law* (CUP 2012) 209. See also *Enron Corporation and Ponderosa Assets, LP v Argentine Republic*, ICSID Case No ARB/01/3, Award, 22 May 2007, para 359 (hereafter *Enron v Argentina*); *CME Czech Republic BV v Czech Republic*, UNCITRAL, Final Award, 14 March 2003, para 501 (hereafter *CME v Czech Republic*); *Libyan American Oil Company (LIAMCO) v Libya*, Award (12 April 1977) 62 ILR 140, 196.

[45] See, eg, *LG&E Energy Corp, LG&E Capital Corp and LG&E International Inc v Argentine Republic*, ICSID Case No ARB/02/1, Award, 25 July 2007, para 32 (hereafter *LG&E v Argentina*); *Occidental Petroleum Corp and Occidental Exploration and Production Co v Republic of Ecuador* (II), ICSID Case No ARB/06/11, Decision on Provisional Measures, 17 August 2007, para 75 (hereafter *Occidental* Provisional Measures); *Burlington Resources, Inc v Republic of Ecuador*, ICSID Case No ARB/08/5, Procedural Order No 1, 29 June 2009, para 70. See also HP Aust, 'Investment Protection and Sustainable Development' in S Hindelang and M Krajewski (eds), *Shifting Paradigms in International Investment Law* (OUP 2016) 218.

[46] The phrase 'provided and to the extent that' suggests that restitution may be partial, available 'to the extent that this is neither impossible nor disproportionate'; ARSIWA Commentaries (n 1) Article 35 para 6.

be valueless'.[47] Restitution is not impossible due to legal or practical difficulties, even if these might entail 'special efforts' on the part of the responsible State, since a State may not rely on provisions of its domestic law as justification for avoiding its international obligations.[48] The Commentary also explains that restitution is not appropriate where the benefit to be gained from restitution is 'wholly disproportionate' to the cost to the responsible State.[49] In practice, these limitations operate to materially restrict its application both in general international law and in international investment law.[50]

A number of treaties, including the Energy Charter Treaty[51] and the European Convention on Human Rights,[52] deviate from the position under Article 35 and explicitly foresee that legal obstacles under domestic law may preclude the award of restitution. Legal difficulties were taken into account in *Forests of Central Rhodopia*, where the arbitrator held that restitution was not 'practical' because, among other things, detailed enquiries would be required to determine the condition of the forests, which were not in the same condition as at the time of their taking, and where third parties had acquired rights in since the State's wrongful act.[53] In *Gabčíkovo-Nagymaros Project*, the ICJ held that the 'possible' manner of wiping out the consequences of the wrongful acts of both parties was for them 'to re-establish co-operative administration of what remains of the Project'.[54]

In the context of investment arbitration, tribunals have on several occasions declined to order restitution on the basis that such an order would be 'impossible', while pointing to a lack of practicality rather than material impossibility.[55] In *Bahloul v Tajikistan*, the tribunal was persuaded that restitution was not materially possible, given the length of time that had passed since the breach in question, the lack of cooperation on the part of the respondent State authorities in the arbitration proceedings, and the existence of third-party rights.[56] Similarly, in *Teinver v Argentina*, the tribunal rejected restitution on grounds that the restoration of corporate rights in an expropriated airline was 'neither practical nor practicable' given the claimant's insolvency and the fact that the airlines had been operated by the respondent State for a number of years.[57]

Some investment tribunals have deviated from the rule and exceptions set out in Article 35(a) and refused restitution on grounds that such an order would unduly interfere with State sovereignty. Earlier tribunals have, as in the *LIAMCO* arbitration, held that it 'is impossible to compel a State to make restitution [as] this would constitute in fact an intolerable interference in the internal sovereignty of a State'.[58] Christine Gray has criticized these decisions on the basis that they contradict the rule that restitution operates as an international

---

[47] ARSIWA Commentaries (n 1) Article 35 para 8.
[48] ibid para 8.
[49] ibid para 11.
[50] C Gray, 'The Choice between Restitution and Compensation' (1999) 10 EJIL 413–23.
[51] ECT Article 26(8).
[52] Convention for the Protection of Human Rights and Fundamental Freedoms (adopted 4 November 1950, entered into force 3 September 1953) 213 UNTS 222, Article 41.
[53] *Forests of Central Rhodopia (Merits)* (1933) 3 RIAA 1405, 1432.
[54] Gabčíkovo-Nagymaros Project (*Hungary v Slovakia*) (Judgment) [1997] ICJ Rep 7, para 150.
[55] See, eg, *AGIP S.p.A. v People's Republic of the Congo*, ICSID Case No ARB/77/1, Award, 30 November 1979, paras 86–88 (hereafter *AGIP v Congo*); *CMS Gas Transmission Co v Argentine Republic*, ICSID Case No ARB/01/8, Award, 12 May 2005, para 407 (hereafter *CMS v Argentina*).
[56] *Mohammad Ammar Al-Bahloul v The Republic of Tajikistan*, SCC Case No V (064/2008), Final Award, 8 June 2010, para 63.
[57] *Teinver v Argentina* (n 33) para 1098.
[58] *LIAMCO v Libya*, Award, 12 April 1977, 125 (hereafter *LIAMCO v Libya*); See also *BP v Libya* (1979), 53 ILR at 353; *AGIP v Congo* (n 55); *Amoco International Finance Corporation v Islamic Republic of Iran, National Iranian Oil Company*, IUSCT Case No 56, Partial Award, 14 July 1987, para 178.

obligation, which a State cannot evade by relying on its domestic law.[59] This approach has nevertheless been extended, by a handful of investment tribunals, to unlawful administrative regulations. The tribunal in *LG&E* stated that it '[could] not compel' Argentina to provide juridical restitution, annulling and enacting legislative and administrative measures, 'without a sentiment of undue interference with its sovereignty'.[60] The *CMS* tribunal stated that it was 'utterly unrealistic for the [t]ribunal to order the Respondent to turn back to the regulatory framework existing before the emergency measures were adopted'.[61]

3. Lack of proportionality

24 The second exception in Article 35(b) applies where there is 'a burden out of all proportion to the benefit deriving from restitution instead of compensation'.[62] This was intended to be a narrow exception, where it is proven that a 'grave disproportionality' exists between the burden imposed on the State and the benefit to the injured party. The Commentary to the ILC Articles states that considerations of equity and reasonableness should be taken into account 'with a preference for the position of the injured State in any case where the balancing process does not indicate a clear preference for compensation'.[63]

25 Before the ICJ, the disproportionality of restitution arose in *Jurisdictional Immunities* and in *Pulp Mills*. In *Jurisdictional Immunities*, invoking the proportionality requirement, the Court held that 'the fact that some of the violations may have been committed by judicial organs, and some of the legal decisions in question have become final in Italian domestic law, does not lift the obligation incumbent upon Italy to make restitution'.[64] In *Pulp Mills*, the Court interpreted the proportionality exception as including an appropriateness standard, connecting restitution not only to the burden on the wrongdoing State but also to the nature of the wrong committed. The ICJ held that 'restitution must be appropriate to the injury suffered, taking into account the nature of the wrongful act having caused it'.[65] Since the obligations breached by Uruguay were not substantive, 'ordering the dismantling of the mill would not, in the view of the Court, constitute an appropriate remedy for the breach of procedural obligations'.[66]

26 In the investment context, the disproportionality exception to restitution has been considered in cases concerning breaches of substantive obligations under investment treaties. For example, in *RWE Innogy*, the tribunal considered a request for restitution requiring the respondent State to 'reinstat[e] the legal and regulatory framework' existing prior to the breach.[67] Citing Article 35(b), the tribunal held that such an order would 'involve a burden to the Respondent out of all proportion to the benefit to the Claimants deriving from

---

[59] C Gray, *Judicial Remedies in International Law* (OUP 1987) (hereafter Gray, *Judicial Remedies*).
[60] See, eg, *LG&E v Argentina* (n 45) paras 84–87; See T Ishikawa, 'Restitution as a 'Second Chance' for Investor-State Relations: Restitution and Monetary Damages as Sequential Options' (2016–17) 3 MJDR 154.
[61] *CMS v Argentina* (n 55) para 406.
[62] The phrase 'provided and to the extent that' suggests that restitution may be partial, available 'to the extent that this is neither impossible nor disproportionate'; ARSIWA Commentaries (n 1) Article 35 para 6.
[63] The Commentary goes on to note that 'the balance will invariably favour the injured State in any case where the failure to provide restitution would jeopardize its political independence or economic stability'. ARSIWA Commentaries (n 1) Article 35 para 11.
[64] *Jurisdictional Immunities* (n 40) para 137.
[65] *Pulp Mills on the River Uruguay (Argentina v Uruguay)* (Judgment) [2010] ICJ Rep 14, para 274 (hereafter *Pulp Mills*).
[66] ibid para 275.
[67] *RWE Innogy GmbH and RWE Innogy Aersa S.A.U. v Kingdom of Spain*, ICSID Case No ARB/14/34, Award, 30 December 2019, para 118.

restitution instead of compensation'. This was because the case 'involve[d] State regulation that is generally applicable across a very important sector in Spain', whereas 'the Claimants can very readily be afforded full reparation through compensation'.[68] Similarly, in *Masdar*, the tribunal held that an order to 'reinstate the pre-breach legislative and regulatory framework would involve a disproportionate burden compared to the benefits potentially yielded to the Claimant', pointing to the benefits it would generate for non-protected investors.[69]

Other investment tribunals have interpreted the disproportionality exception more broadly and refused to award restitution where doing so would disproportionately interfere with State sovereignty or otherwise place an undue burden on the respondent State's legislative and regulatory autonomy.[70] In *Occidental (Provisional Measures)*, the tribunal stated that '[t]o impose on a sovereign State reinstatement of a foreign investor in its concession, after a nationalization or termination of a concession license or contract by the State, would constitute a reparation disproportional to its interference with the sovereignty of the State when compared to monetary compensation'.[71] Tribunals adopted a similar approach in awards under the Energy Charter Treaty relating to Spain's abolishment of a regulatory regime for renewable energy installations.[72]

The reasoning in these decisions diverges from the view, prevalent in general international law, that legal or practical difficulties in implementation do not affect the duty of restitution. As one commentator observes, '[f]rom a strict legal perspective, the imposition by a tribunal of a certain obligation as a form of restitution does not impede the sovereignty of states, not only because such power is inherent in the arbitral and judicial functions, but also because restitution in international law is considered to be the primary mode of reparation'.[73] Where the violating measures are generally applicable legislative or regulatory measures, restitution might require the reestablishment of the legislative or regulatory framework prior to the relevant breach, with effects beyond the investment at issue and a corresponding burden for the State to revoke or modify laws and regulations.

4. Conclusion

Restitution in investment law has been strictly limited. To date, it has only been ordered in situations in which the violating measure was specifically targeted at the claimant (e.g. expropriation of certain property) or involved an ongoing relationship between the claimant and the respondent State.[74] Orders for the return of expropriated property and associated permits were issued by the tribunal in *von Pezold et al v Zimbabwe*.[75] In *Arif v Moldova*, the tribunal

---

[68] ibid para 685.
[69] *Masdar Solar & Wind Cooperatief U.A. v Kingdom of Spain*, ICSID Case No ARB/14/1, Award, 16 May 2018, para 562 (hereafter *Masdar v Spain*).
[70] See also *BP Exploration Co (Libya) Ltd v Libya*, Award, 10 October 1973, para 53; *LIAMCO v Libya* (n 58); *AMCO Asia Corp and others v Republic of Indonesia*, ICSID Case No ARB/81/1, Award, 21 November 1984, para 202; *LG&E v Argentina* (n 45) para 87. See also Gray, *Judicial Remedies* (n 59) 188.
[71] *Occidental* Provisional Measures (n 45) para 84.
[72] *Antin Infrastructure Services Luxembourg S.a.r.l. and Antin Energia Termosolar B.V. v The Kingdom of Spain*, ICSID Case No ARB/13/31, Award, 15 June 2018, paras 634–38; *Eiser Infrastructure Limited and Energía Solar Luxembourg S.à r.l. v Kingdom of Spain*, ICSID Case No ARB/13/36, Award, 4 May 2017; *LG&E v Argentina* (n 45); *Masdar v Spain* (n 69) paras 553–63.
[73] E de Brabandere, *Investment Treaty Arbitration as Public International Law: Procedural Aspects and Implications* (CUP 2014) 184–85 (hereafter de Brabander); See also C Schreuer, 'Non-pecuniary Remedies in ICSID' (2004) 20 Arb Intl 325, 331.
[74] See examples in G Vidigal, 'Targeting Compliance: Prospective Remedies in International Law' (2015) 6 JIDS 462–84 (hereafter Vidigal).
[75] *von Pezold v Zimbabwe* (n 5) para 1020.

ordered Moldova to abide by its contractual obligations and permit the claimant to open and operate his duty-free store at Chisinau International Airport, considering restitution to be 'more consistent with the objectives of bilateral investment treaties, as it preserves both the investment and the relationship between the investor and the Host State'.[76] Other orders for restitution have included the restoration of the claimant investor's right to arbitrate[77] and the repayment of an amount unduly paid by the investor.[78] Some of these orders require the State to 'restore' a situation by paying the investor back, or expressly give the State the choice of paying compensation instead of restoring property. These may still be considered restitution in the sense that the State is being directed to do something it might not otherwise do.

30 Investment tribunals have therefore expansively interpreted the exceptions to restitution, the consequence being that restitution is virtually always set aside,[79] deviating from the position under international law that it should be the primary remedy to which there are only limited exceptions. One could attempt to distinguish the cases in which restitution was ordered by investment tribunals on the basis that the order did not impose an 'undue' or 'disproportionate' burden on the State and only involved a specific action taken with respect to a specific investor. In any event, this expansive approach remains in tension with the position under Articles on the Responsibility of States for Internationally Wrongful Acts (ARSIWA) that the mere challenge of implementing an order of restitution under domestic law cannot form the basis of 'material impossibility'.[80]

II. Compensation [Article 36]

Article 36: Compensation

1. The State responsible for an internationally wrongful act is under an obligation to compensate for the damage caused thereby, insofar as such damage is not made good by restitution.
2. The compensation shall cover any financially assessable damage including loss of profits insofar as it is established.

1. Concept

31 Article 36 of ARSIWA provides that a responsible State is under an obligation to compensate for damage caused by an internationally wrongful act, in cases where restitution may be inadequate for full reparation or unavailable due to one of the limitations in Article 35. Compensation, by way of damages, is generally calculated to determine the amount necessary to return the injured party in the position it would have been if the wrongful act had not occurred.[81]

---

[76] *Arif v Moldova* (n 15) para 570.

[77] In *ATA*, the tribunal ordered the Respondent State to terminate local court proceedings and submit the dispute to a new commercial arbitration tribunal, finding that 'the single remedy which can implement the *Chorzów* standard is a restoration of the Claimant's right to arbitration', see *ATA Construction, Industrial and Trading Company v The Hashemite Kingdom of Jordan*, ICSID Case No ARB/08/2, Award, 18 May 2010, para 131.

[78] This order of restitution was supplemented by an order of compensation of interest in order to achieve full reparation, see *Glencore v Colombia* (n 21) paras 1573–78.

[79] For analysis of the exceptions, see Vidigal (n 74).

[80] ARSIWA Commentaries (n 1) Article 35 para 8.

[81] The distinction between 'damages' and 'compensation' has been eroded in the Articles, where the term 'compensation' refers to the obligation to compensate for all damages not made good by restitution. See S Ripinsky and K Williams, *Damages in International Investment Law* (British Institute of International and Comparative Law 2008), 4 (hereafter Ripinsky and Williams).

The standard for compensation is 'financially assessable damage', which is defined by the **32** ILC as any damage capable of being evaluated in financial terms, including loss of profits.[82] International courts and tribunals have the discretion to adopt any of a number of valuation methods to quantify 'financially assessable damage' and calculate the appropriate compensation. A natural consequence of that discretion is the lack of a consistent approach to quantum in both general international law and investment law.[83] The appropriate heads of compensable damage and the principles of valuation to be used to quantify that damage also naturally vary 'depending upon the content of particular primary obligations, an evaluation of the respective behaviour of the parties and, more generally, a concern to reach an equitable and acceptable outcome'.[84]

Given that 'many sovereign interests do not lend themselves to quantification',[85] precedent **33** in general international law relation to compensation has been limited. The PCIJ and ICJ have traditionally only awarded compensation for breaches affecting specific individuals or specific property only.[86] More recently, the ICJ has tackled more complex questions of reparation in *Certain Activities* and *Armed Activities*, where compensation was awarded for damage suffered by entire communities or the environment.[87] In these cases, significant issues of evidence emerged with respect to both the extent of the damage to be quantified, which is not as straightforward as damage caused to specific individuals or property, and to the causal nexus between the wrongful conduct and the damage. In *Armed Activities*, the ICJ had to elaborate on its position on quantification of damage, finding that a State 'that is not in a position to provide direct proof of certain facts' should be allowed 'liberal recourse to inferences of fact and circumstantial evidence'.[88] In *Certain Activities*, the ICJ held that it may 'decide whether there is a sufficient causal nexus between the wrongful act and the injury suffered', and could make 'just and reasonable inference' from the available evidence.[89]

In other international fora, particularly those that regularly deal with injury to specific in- **34** dividuals and property, such as international human rights courts and the International Tribunal for the Law of the Sea (ITLOS), compensation is the most commonly sought form of reparation, resulting in considerable decisions and literature.[90] The present entry considers

---

[82] ARSIWA Commentaries (n 1) Article 36 para 5.
[83] See, eg, Ripinsky and Williams (n 81) 4; ND Rubins and NS Kinsella, *International Investment, Political Risk and Dispute Resolution: A Practitioner's Guide* (Oceana Publications 2005) 258 (hereafter Rubins and Kinsella).
[84] ARSIWA Commentaries (n 1) Article 36 para 7.
[85] J Barker, 'The Different Forms of Reparation: Compensation' in J Crawford, A Pellet and S Olleson (eds), *The Law of International Responsibility* (OUP 2010) 603.
[86] O Schachter, 'Compensation for Expropriation' (1984) 78 AJIL 121; C Gray, 'Is There an International Law of Remedies?' (1985) 56 BYIL 25, 29.
[87] K Kindji and M Faure, 'Assessing Reparation of Environmental Damage by the ICJ: A lost opportunity?' (2019) 57 Quest Int'l L 5.
[88] *Armed Activities on the Territory of the Congo (DRC v Uganda)* (Compensation), 9 February 2022, para 120 (citing Eritrea–Ethiopia Claims Commission) (hereafter *Armed Activities*).
[89] *Certain Activities Carried Out by Nicaragua in the Border Area (Costa Rica v Nicaragua)* (Compensation) [2018] ICJ Rep 15, paras 34–35.
[90] See, for discussion, Crawford, *State Responsibility* (n 3) ch 16; Ripinsky and Williams (n 81); Sabahi, *Compensation* (n 25); I Marboe, *Calculation of Compensation and Damages in International Investment Law* (OUP 2017) (hereafter Marboe, *Calculation*); I Marboe, 'Compensation and Damages in International Law' (2006) 7 JWIT 723; I Marboe, 'Assessing Compensation and Damages in Expropriation versus Non-expropriation Cases' in C Beharry (ed), *Contemporary and Emerging Issues on the Law of Damages and Valuation in International Investment Arbitration* (Brill Nijhoff 2018); I Marboe, *Damages in Investor State-Arbitration: Current Issues and Challenges*, Brill Research Perspectives in International Investment Law and Arbitration (Brill/Nijhoff 2018); RE Walck, 'Methods of Valuing Losses' in M Bungenberg and others (eds), *International Investment Law* (Hart Publishing 2015), 1045–56; D Shelton, *Remedies in International Human Rights Law* (3rd edn, OUP 2015) 315 ff

three discrete topics in which there are apparent differences between courts and tribunals established under general international law as compared to investment law: the approach to the valuation of damages, the availability and quantification of moral damages, and the applicability of equitable limitations on compensation where a State may be unable to pay damages.

2. Valuation

35 The principles of assessment to be applied when quantifying damage vary, depending on the obligation breached and the particular facts of the case. It is therefore difficult to make a direct comparison between the approaches taken to valuation in general international law and in investment law, other than to note that investment tribunals have usually provided more detailed reasoning for how they have applied principles of valuation when determining the amount of compensation.[91] This is a welcome contribution, given the little guidance provided by general international law. As Judge Greenwood has noted, '[w]hat is required is not the selection of an arbitrary figure but the application of principles which at least enable the reader of the judgment to discern the factors which led the Court to fix the sum awarded'.[92] For example, investment tribunals often explain the reasons for the method of valuation chosen, including whether it is a market-, income-, or asset-based approach[93] and specify the valuation date.

36 The reasoning of investment tribunals may be influential for international courts and human rights courts when tackling questions of compensation down the road.[94] For example, investment tribunals have considered various issues that arise when awarding compensation, including the application of the principle in general international law that damages are valued at the date that the injury occurred.[95] When there has been an indirect expropriation resulting from a series of measures (i.e. a 'creeping' expropriation), it may be challenging to determine exactly when the expropriation occurred and when the injury or harm should be measured for the purposes of valuation of damages.[96] There is a growing consensus that, in cases of indirect expropriation, the appropriate date for valuation should be the culmination

---

(hereafter Shelton, *Remedies*); JB Simmons, 'Valuation In Investor-State Arbitration: Toward A More Exact Science' (2012) 30 Berkeley JIL 196.

[91] As observed by one commentator, 'finding common principles in these awards is not always easy either, given the absence of precedent, the variety of factual situations and the sometimes less than detailed reasoning as to how the final figure, often a compromise global figure, is reached' (H Heilbron, 'Assessing Damages in International Arbitration: Practical Considerations' in R Hill and L Newman (eds), *The Leading Arbitrators' Guide to International Arbitration* (JurisNet 2008), 468).

[92] *Ahmadou Sadio Diallo (Republic of Guinea v Democratic Republic of the Congo)* (Compensation) [2012] ICJ Rep 324, Declaration of Judge Greenwood, para 7 (hereafter *Diallo* Compensation).

[93] See Ripinsky and Williams (n 81) 231, 272; Rubins and Kinsella (n 83) 258. See also UNCITRAL, 'Report of Working Group III (Investor-State Dispute Settlement Reform) on the Work of its Thirty-seventh Session (New York, 1–5 April 2019)' (9 April 2019) <https://uncitral.un.org/en/working_groups/3/Investor-State> accessed 3 March 2022.; TW Walde and B Sabahi, 'Compensation, Damages and Valuation in International Investment Law' in P Muchlinski and others (eds), *The Oxford Handbook of International Investment Law* (OUP 2008) 1112–14.

[94] D Pulkowski, 'Remedies for Wrongful Conduct: Lessons from Investment Arbitration' in CJ Tams, S Schill and R Hofmann (eds), *International Investment Law and General International Law* (Edward Elgar Publishing 2023) 276–78 (hereafter Pulkowski, 'Remedies').

[95] Investment tribunals are also required to apply the terms of the applicable investment treaty. Such treaties generally provide that the valuation date in cases of expropriation is the date of expropriation (or immediately before the expropriation becomes public knowledge, whichever is earlier). For example, the ECT provides that compensation for lawful expropriation 'shall amount to the fair market value of the Investment expropriated *at the time immediately before the Expropriation or impending Expropriation became known* in such a way as to affect the value of the Investment'.

[96] Ripinsky and Williams (n 81) 246.

of all expropriatory events rather than the date of the first event, also referred to as the state of 'irreversible deprivation'.[97]

3. Availability and quantification of moral damages

Article 31 of the ILC Articles clarifies that the 'damage' that must be repaired includes 'any damage, whether material or moral, caused by the internationally wrongful act'.[98] The Claims Commission in the *Lusitania* cases noted that non-material damages may be 'very real, and the mere fact that they are difficult to measure or estimate by monetary standards makes them none the less real and affords no reason why the injured person should not be compensated'.[99] The Commentary excludes the recovery of moral damages to a State, but includes moral damages to nationals where a State brings a diplomatic protection claim on their behalf. For such a claim, the Commentary observes that '[m]aterial and moral damage resulting from an internationally wrongful act will normally be financially assessable and hence covered by the remedy of compensation'.[100]

The availability of moral damages was confirmed by the ICJ in the *Diallo* case. The ICJ held that there had been a violation of the claimant's rights under two international human rights instruments and defined the term 'moral damage' as 'harm other than material injury which is suffered by an injured entity or individual'.[101] The Court recognized that '[n]on-material injury to a person which is cognizable under international law may take various forms'.[102]

While the availability of moral damages is well-established, the method of quantification by courts under general international law remains obscure. In *Diallo*, the ICJ noted the lack of a set of principles 'capable of being applied in a consistent and coherent manner, so that the amount awarded can be regarded as just'.[103] The ICJ awarded USD 85,000 to Guinea referring to equity and reasonableness, without detailing its calculation.[104] Moral damages were also awarded by ITLOS in *M/V Saiga (No 2)*, for the detention of captain and crew members, again with little detail as to the specific calculations.[105]

Equitable considerations have influenced the quantification of moral damages before human rights courts. In *Al-Jedda v United Kingdom*, the Grand Chamber of the European Court of Human Rights (ECtHR) stated that, for determining damage, '[i]ts guiding principle is equity, which above all involves flexibility and an objective consideration of what is fair, just and reasonable'.[106] The IACtHR has stated that compensation for non-pecuniary damages may be determined 'in reasonable exercise of its judicial authority and on the

---

[97] *International Technical Products Corporation and ITP Export Corporation v The Government of the Islamic Republic of Iran*, 9 IUSCT 206, Final Award, 28 October 1986, 240. See also *Compagnia del Desarrollo de Santa Elena v Costa Rica*, ICSID Case No ARB/96/1, Final Award, 17 February 2000, paras 76–78; *Azurix v Argentina*, ICSID Case No ARB/01/12, Award, 14 July 2006, para 417 (hereafter *Azurix v Argentina*). The same approach has also been applied in cases involving multiple breaches of investment protection standards other than indirect expropriation. See, eg, *Azurix v Argentina*, para 417; *Enron v Argentina* (n 44) para 405.
[98] ARSIWA Commentaries (n 1) Article 36 para 5.
[99] Opinion in the *Lusitania* cases (*US v Germany*), November 1923, 7 RIAA 32, 32, 42.
[100] ARSIWA Commentaries (n 1) Article 36 para 5.
[101] *Diallo* Compensation (n 92) para 18.
[102] ibid.
[103] ibid.
[104] ibid para 25.
[105] *Saiga* (n 29) paras 175–76.
[106] ECtHR, *Case of Al-Jedda v The United Kingdom* App No 27021/08, 7 July 2011, para 114.

basis of equity'.[107] This approach has been subject to criticism for lack of consistency and reasoning.[108]

41 Moral damages have only been awarded by a handful of investment tribunals.[109] The tribunal in *Desert Line v Yemen* awarded moral damages for the harassment of the claimant's personnel by government authorities. It noted that 'even if investment treaties primarily aim at protecting property and economic values, they do not exclude, as such, that a party may, *in exceptional circumstances*, ask for compensation for moral damages'. The tribunal accepted that the claim relating to 'physical duress exerted on the executives of the Claimant' was justified, but awarded the claimant USD 1,000,000, instead of the requested USD 10,000,000, with no explanation as to how that sum was calculated.[110] Some commentators have criticized this award, on the basis that the claimant's executives did not qualify as investors under the relevant treaty and therefore had no protected interests.[111]

42 Similarly, the tribunal in *Lemire v Ukraine* considered that moral damages were only available in 'exceptional' or 'extraordinary' circumstances. Although it did not see a reason to award 'separate and additional moral damages' in the case, it found that they were due under three conditions: (i) the 'ill-treatment contravenes the norms according to which civilized nations are expected to act', including physical threats, illegal detention, or other analogous situations; (ii) the State's actions 'cause a deterioration of health, stress, anxiety, other mental suffering such as humiliation, shame and degradation, or loss of reputation, credit and social position'; and (iii) the causes and effects of the ill-treatment are 'grave or substantial'.[112]

43 Similar reasoning and outcome appears in the award in *OI European Group BV v Venezuela*. There, the tribunal in *OI European Group BV v Venezuela* rejected the claimant's request for moral damages, in light of the fact that the respondent State's behaviour was considered not 'worthy of an additional compensation for moral damages' because it did not 'amount [...] to physical threats, illegal detention or ill-treatment'.[113]

44 More recently, the majority of the tribunal in *Gente Oil v Ecuador* granted the claimant's request for moral damages for what was deemed to be 'highly reprehensible' conduct of the State in criminal proceedings.[114] Of particular interest is that the claimant investor had claimed non-pecuniary damages allegedly suffered by its officers and shareholders, which

---

[107] IACHR, *Cantoral Benavides v Peru*, Judgment of 3 December 2001 (Reparations and Costs), Series C No 88, para 53.

[108] See, eg, R White, 'Remedies in a Multi-Level Legal Order: The Strasbourg Court and the UK' in C Kilpatrick and others (eds), *The Future of Remedies in Europe* (OUP 2000) 196–98.

[109] See, for discussion, P Dumberry, 'Moral Damages' in M Bungenberg and others (eds), *International Investment Law* (Hart Publishing 2015) 1130–45; W Coriell and S Marchili, 'Unexceptional Circumstances: Moral Damages in International Investment Law' in I Laird and T Weiler (eds), *Investment Treaty Arbitration and International Law* (Juris 2010); L Markert and E Freiburg, 'Moral Damages in International Investment Disputes: on the Search for a Legal Basis and Guiding Principles' (2013) 14(1) JWIT 1; J Wong, 'The Misapprehension of Moral Damages in Investor-State Arbitration' in A Rovine (ed), *Contemporary Issues in International Arbitration and Mediation: the Fordham Papers 2012* (Martinus Nijhoff Publishers 2013) 67.

[110] *Desert Line Projects LLC v Republic of Yemen*, ICSID Case No ARB/05/17, Award, 6 February 2008, paras 289–291 (emphasis added).

[111] I Schwenzer and P Hachem, 'Moral Damages in International Investment Arbitration' in S Kröll and others (eds), *Liber Amicorum Eric Bergsten, International Arbitration and International Commercial Law: Synergy, Convergence and Evolution* (Wolters Kluwer 2011) 422; de Brabander (n 73) 197.

[112] *Joseph Charles Lemire v Ukraine*, ICSID Case No ARB/06/18, Award, 28 March 2011, paras 333, 344.

[113] *OI European Group BV v Bolivarian Republic of Venezuela*, ICSID Case No ARB/11/25, Award, 10 March 2015, paras 910–17.

[114] *Gente Oil Ecuador v Republic of Ecuador*, PCA Case No 2018-12, Award, 24 May 2022, paras 1398–401 (authors' translation).

Ecuador had disputed. It is, however, unclear from the tribunal's reasoning whether it took these damages into account in its final award.

Other investment tribunals explicitly depart from the ILC Articles, requiring 'exceptional' circumstances which drastically narrows the circumstances in which moral damages are compensable. This requirement has been criticized for being 'unknown to general international law', with particular reference to the different approach taken by human rights courts.[115] Other tribunals have considered, in *obiter dicta*, that satisfaction is the more appropriate remedy for moral damages.[116] These decisions sit in conflict with the general principles set out in Part II of the ARISWA, which dictates that moral damages are available, but also raise the question of the extent to which investment commitments, generally considered to be designed to protect economic interests, should provide reparation for the mistreatment of the person of the investor or personnel carrying out activities on behalf of that investor.

As one commentator has rightly noted, 'no common understanding or calculation mechanisms exists in international law that would justify a particular amount of money' for moral damages.[117] Just like under general international law, the practice of tribunals under international investment law lacks a set of principles which are 'capable of being applied in a consistent and coherent manner, so that the amount awarded can be regarded as just'.[118] The circumstances in which moral damages are available under both general international law and international investment law therefore remain unclear.

4. Equitable limitations on compensation

It is not uncommon for courts and tribunals under general international law to refer to equitable considerations when assessing damages, including pecuniary damages. In recent years, it has been suggested that new limitations should be placed on awards of compensation where a State demonstrates a lack of capacity to pay the appropriate compensation, particularly in cases of what one commentator has referred to as 'crippling compensation'.[119] Those who advocate for such a limitation suggest it should be applied in both general international law and investment law.

Unlike Articles 34 and 37, the Commentary to Article 36 does not provide for any qualification on disproportionality or considerations of equity when determining the appropriate amount of compensation.[120] Instead, the Commentary states that any concern 'that the principle of full reparation may lead to disproportionate and even crippling requirements so far as the responsible State is concerned' should be addressed by 'exclud[ing] damage which is indirect or remote'.[121] In the proceedings in *Armed Activities on the Territory of the Congo*

---

[115] RC Stendel, 'Moral Damages as an 'Exceptional' Remedy in International Investment Law—Re-Connecting Practice with General International Law' (2021) 81 ZaöRV/HJIL 937.

[116] *Pey Casado, v Chile*, ICSID Case No ARB/98/2, Decision on Jurisdiction (8 May 2008), para 689. See also TW Wälde and B Sabahi, 'Compensation, Damages and Valuation in International Investment Law' (2007) 4 TDM.

[117] S Weber, 'Demystifying Moral Damages in International Investment Arbitration' (2020) 19(3) LPICT 417–50.

[118] *Diallo* Compensation (n 92) para 7.

[119] See, eg, M Paparinskis, 'Crippling Compensation in the International Law Commission and Investor–State Arbitration' (2021) 37 ICSID Rev/FILJ 289–312.

[120] The 1996 version of the ILC Articles did provide, in Article 42(3), that reparation must not 'result in depriving the population of a State of its own means of subsistence'. The Commentary to the 1996 draft Articles suggested that 'equitable considerations [...] might be taken into account in providing full reparation, particularly in cases involving an author State with limited financial resources'.

[121] ARSIWA Commentaries (n 1) Article 34 para 5.

(DRC v Uganda) before the ICJ, Uganda proposed in its written and oral pleadings that compensation should be limited so as to avoid imposing crippling burdens upon the paying State.[122] Without expressly addressing this argument, the Judgment noted that the Court was satisfied that the amount of damages awarded was within Uganda's capacity to pay.[123]

49 In the investment context, there is a notable dearth of argument by counsel or any decision by a tribunal arguing for a limitation on compensation where damages would have a crippling effect. In his separate opinion in *CME v Czech Republic*, Ian Brownlie expressed the view that '[i]t would be strange indeed, if the outcome of acceptance of a bilateral investment treaty took the form of [such] liabilities' that may subject a State to 'economic ruin'.[124]

50 An exception to the duty of full reparation has yet to be applied in any international fora. James Crawford observed in his role as Special Rapporteur that a rule against 'crippling compensation' would require the victim(s) to bear the loss.[125] He was not persuaded that a rule against 'crippling compensation' could apply in the context of the secondary obligation of reparation, given that it would require the victim(s) to bear the loss. Martins Paparinskis has argued that a State's inability to pay compensation could instead be taken into account within the existing rules relating to circumstances precluding wrongfulness and the general criteria of loss and causation.[126] It is also open to treaty drafters to include such a limitation on compensation in treaties.[127]

III. Satisfaction [Article 37]

Article 37: Satisfaction

1. The State responsible for an internationally wrongful act is under an obligation to give satisfaction for the injury caused by that act insofar as it cannot be made good by restitution or compensation.
2. Satisfaction may consist in an acknowledgement of the breach, an expression of regret, a formal apology or another appropriate modality.
3. Satisfaction shall not be out of proportion to the injury and may not take a form humiliating to the responsible State.

1. Concept

51 Under Article 37, satisfaction is an exceptional remedy, appropriate only insofar as reparation cannot be achieved through restitution or compensation.[128] As the Commentary notes, it is 'a remedy for those injuries not financially assessable which amount to an affront

---

[122] *Armed Activities* (n 88) para 109.
[123] ibid para 407.
[124] *CME v Czech Republic* (n 44) Separate Opinion on the Issues at the Quantum Phase by Arbitrator Brownlie, paras 77–78.
[125] J Crawford, *Third Report on State Responsibility*, 51, paras 162–64. YILC 2000, Vol I, UN Doc A/CN.4/SER.A/1996, 5, paras 17–18, 24, para 49, 174, para 14.
[126] M Paparinskis, 'Crippling Compensation in the International Law Commission and Investor–State Arbitration' (2021) 37 ICSID Rev/FILJ 289.
[127] ibid.
[128] J Crawford, *Brownlie's Principles of Public International Law* (OUP 2012) 574 (hereafter Crawford, *Brownlie's Principles*); J McIntyre, 'Declaratory Judgments of the International Court of Justice' (2013) 25 Hague YIL 107–57.

to the State'.[129] Crawford subsequently defined satisfaction as 'any measure which the responsible state is bound to take under customary international law or under an agreement of the parties to a dispute, apart from restitution and compensation'.[130]

While Article 37 refers to 'an acknowledgement of the breach, an expression of regret, a formal apology or another appropriate modality', adjudicators typically grant satisfaction through declaratory judgments, often when other forms of reparation are unavailable. In *Corfu Channel*, the ICJ found that satisfaction was the appropriate remedy for the breach of Albania's sovereignty rights, where Albania failed to establish that any injury had been caused that required compensation by damages or should be restored by restitution.[131] Similarly, in *Bosnian Genocide*, the ICJ awarded satisfaction on grounds that the necessary causal link for compensation could not be proven.[132]

2. Practice

Despite the subsidiary character ascribed to satisfaction in the ILC Articles, this form of reparation is commonly awarded in inter-State proceedings. In the *Carthage* and *Manouba* cases, the arbitral tribunals noted:

> [F]or the cases in which one Power has failed to comply with its obligations, whether general or specific, vis-à-vis another Power, the establishment of this fact, in particular in an arbitral award, already constitutes a serious sanction ... this sanction is reinforced, where appropriate, by the payment of damages for material losses ...[133]

It is often the case that no specific form of reparation is requested and all that is sought in this respect is a declaration of breach.[134] In other cases, courts have found restitution and compensation inadequate and instead decided to award satisfaction. In *Pulp Mills*, the ICJ held that 'its finding of wrongful conduct by Uruguay in respect of its procedural obligations per se constitutes a measure of satisfaction for Argentina'.[135]

In the investment context, requests for satisfaction are rare, but the few tribunals addressing a request for a declaratory judgment have found them to be 'transposable to the investor-State context'.[136] Claims for satisfaction against a claimant investor are also rare, but are sometimes be successful. In *Cementownia v Turkey*, the tribunal acceded to the respondent's request for satisfaction by 'declar[ing] formally that the Claimant has filed a fraudulent claim against the Republic of Turkey'.[137]

---

[129] ARSIWA Commentaries (n 1) Article 37 para 3. Some commentators have suggested that pecuniary satisfaction should be the *de facto* remedy for moral damages, but this sits in conflict with the position under Article 37 that satisfaction is only available as a remedy where compensation is not appropriate (ie damages cannot be *financially assessed*). See V Stoica, *Remedies before the International Court of Justice: A Systemic Analysis* (CUP 2021) 148–49.
[130] Crawford, *Brownlie's Principles* (n 128) 574.
[131] The United Kingdom was entitled to compensation for the damage to its ships: *Corfu Channel* (*United Kingdom of Great Britain and Northern Ireland v Albania*) (Judgment) [1948] ICJ Rep 15, 36.
[132] *Bosnian Genocide* (n 22) 195.
[133] *Manouba* (France v Italy) (1913) 11 RIAA 463, 475 (authors' translation); *Carthage* (France v Italy) (1913) 11 RIAA 449, 460 (authors' translation).
[134] See, eg, *Dispute over the Status and Use of the Waters of the Silala* (Chile v Bolivia), Judgment, 1 December 2022, para 44.
[135] *Pulp Mills* (n 65) 102.
[136] *Quiborax S.A., Non-Metallic Minerals S.A. v Plurinational State of Bolivia*, ICSID Case No ARB/06/2, Award, 16 September 2015, para 560 (hereafter *Quiborax v Bolivia*).
[137] See, eg, *Cementownia 'Nowa Huta' S.A. v Republic of Turkey (I)*, ICSID Case No ARB(AF)/06/2, Award, 17 September 2009, para 162–63.

56 Less rare are cases of satisfaction awarded to investors. In *Pawlowski v Czech Republic*, the tribunal found that a declaration that the respondent State had committed a breach was an appropriate remedy, 'proportionate to the injury caused' and 'not humiliating to the responsible State'.[138] In *Biwater Gauff v Tanzania*, the tribunal established that the loss and damage claimed by the investor was not caused by the respondent State's violations of the Bilateral Investment Treaty (BIT), so that 'the only appropriate remedies for the Republic's conduct can be declaratory in nature'.[139] And, in *Quiborax v Bolivia*, the respondent requested the tribunal to dismiss the request for satisfaction, arguing that this was 'punitive relief', unavailable to investors.[140] The tribunal agreed that it could not award a form of reparation that was 'punitive in nature', but found that, 'as part of the process of settling the dispute, a declaration can be conceived in a manner that is not punitive'.[141] The conduct of the respondent in the arbitration did not warrant what the tribunal described as a 'declaration of breach of the duty to arbitrate in good faith'.[142] In contrast, in *CMS v Argentina*, the tribunal considered that, since the dispute was 'not a case of reparation due to an injured State, satisfaction can be ruled out at the outset'.[143]

57 Satisfaction is an integral part of public international law. The idea that this remedy is simply not apposite for investment cases is belied by the very existence of requests for satisfaction, by both investors and States. Given how extensively investment tribunals resort to the Articles for their other decisions regarding remedies, it appears incoherent to reject satisfaction outright, based solely on the distinction between inter-State relations, to which Part Two of the ILC Articles apply, and the legal relations arising from breach of international obligations owed to investors. Investment tribunals should give requests for satisfaction serious consideration and examine objectively whether circumstances justify it.

C. Specific Issues

I. Interest [Article 38]

Article 38: Interest

1. Interest on any principal sum due under this chapter shall be payable when necessary in order to ensure full reparation. The interest rate and mode of calculation shall be set so as to achieve that result.
2. Interest runs from the date when the principal sum should have been paid until the date the obligation to pay is fulfilled.

58 As a general principle, the duty or reparation includes any interest necessary to ensure full reparation.[144] Interest is 'not an autonomous form of reparation, nor is it a necessary part of

---

[138] *Pawlowski AG and Project Sever s.r.o. v Czech Republic*, ICSID Case No ARB/17/11, Award, 1 November 2021, paras 738–41.
[139] *Biwater Gauff (Tanzania) Ltd v United Republic of Tanzania*, ICSID Case No ARB/05/22, Award, 24 July 2008, para 807.
[140] *Quiborax v Bolivia* (n 136) para 536.
[141] ibid para 561.
[142] ibid para 594.
[143] *CMS v Argentina* (n 55) para 399.
[144] ARSIWA Commentaries (n 1) Article 38(1); See *McCollough & Company Inc v Ministry of Post, Telegraph and Telephone*, IUSCT Case No 89, Award No 225-89-3, 16 April 1986, para 98 (hereafter *McCollough Case*); Siemens

compensation in every case'.[145] The PCIJ and ICJ have usually awarded interest to account for post-judgment delays in payment. In *S.S. 'Wimbledon'*, the PCIJ awarded simple interest at 6 per cent from the date of the judgment, on the basis that interest was payable 'from the moment when the amount of the sum due has been fixed and the obligation to pay has been established'.[146] The ICJ applied the same rate and principle in *Armed Activities* and *Certain Activities* for post-judgment interest, making specific rulings on interest running from the date of the injury to that of the Judgment.[147] In the *M/V 'Saiga'* case, ITLOS awarded interest at different rates depending on the category of loss.[148]

By contrast, investment tribunals have consistently awarded interest with the aim of placing investors in the position they would have been in had it not been for the breach(es), usually meaning the inclusion of pre-award interest.[149] As the Iran–US Claims Tribunal observed, the purpose of pre-award interest is 'to compensate for the delay with which the payment to the successful party is made'.[150] In *Crystallex v Venezuela*, the tribunal observed that the function of pre-award interest is to 'compensate the injured party for the loss of its ability to benefit from the use of the principal compensation sum from the date it fell due'.[151] The *Crystallex* tribunal awarded pre-award interest under the principle of full reparation, on the grounds that 'in addition to losing its property and other rights, an investor loses the opportunity to invest funds or to pay debts using money to which the investor was rightfully entitled'.[152]

There is significant variance between how international courts and tribunals approach the appropriate rate of interest, the interest period, and whether interest should be simple or compound (and, if compounded, the periodicity of compounding).[153] These differences can result in markedly different outcomes; for example, awarding compound interest, in particular, can significantly impact the amount of an award for damages. Article 38(1)

A.G. v The Argentine Republic, ICSID Case No ARB/02/8, Award, 6 February 2007, para 396; *LG&E v Argentina* (n 45) para 55; *El Paso Energy Limited Company v Argentina*, ICSID Case No ARB/03/15, Award, 27 April 2006, para 747; *ADC Affiliate Limited and ADC & ADMC Management Limited v Republic of Hungary*, ICSID Case No ARB/03/16, Award, 2 October 2006, paras 521–22 (hereafter *ADC v Hungary*); *PSEG v Turkey*, Award, ICSID Case No ARB/02/5, Award, 19 January 2007, para 341; *Vivendi II v Argentina*, ICSID Case No ARB/97/3, Award, 20 August 2007, para 9.2.1; See also Marboe, Calculation (n 90) para 6.09; John Gotanda, *Supplemental Damages in Private International Law* (Kluwer 1997) 13; CH Schreuer and others, *The ICSID Convention: A Commentary* (CUP 2009); P Nevill, 'Awards of Interest by International Courts and Tribunals' (2008) 78 BYIL 255 (hereafter Nevill, 'Awards').

[145] ARSIWA Commentaries (n 1) Article 38 para 1; See also *SGS Société Générale de Surveillance S.A. v The Republic of Paraguay*, ICSID Case No ARB/07/29, Award, 10 February 2012, para 172. See Nevill, 'Awards' (n 144) 255–34.

[146] The interest rate of 6 per cent was deemed fair, given the 'present financial situation of the world and [...] the conditions prevailing for public loans', see SS 'Wimbledon' (*United Kingdom and ors v Germany*) (Judgment) [1923] PCIJ Rep Series A No 1, 32.

[147] See above, n 88 and 89.

[148] *Saiga* (n 29) para 63.

[149] *Ioan Micula, Viorel Micula, S.C. European Food S.A, S.C. Starmill S.R.L. and S.C. Multipack S.R.L. v Romania* [I], ICSID Case No ARB/05/20, Award, 18 April 2014, paras 1265, 127; *Wena Hotels Limited v Arab Republic of Egypt*, ICSID Case No ARB/98/4, Award, 8 December 2000, paras 128–30; *Occidental Petroleum Corporation and Occidental Exploration and Production Company v The Republic of Ecuador*, ICSID Case No ARB/06/11, Award, 2 November 2015, paras 846–47; *Burlington Resources Inc v Republic of Ecuador (formerly Burlington Resources Inc and others v Republic of Ecuador and Empresa Estatal Petróleos del Ecuador (PetroEcuador))*, ICSID Case No ARB/08/5, Decision on Reconsideration, 7 February 2017, para 531

[150] *McCollough Case* (n 144) para 98.

[151] *Crystallex International Corp v Bolivarian Republic of Venezuela*, ICSID Case No ARB(AF)/11/2, Award, 4 April 2016, para 929.

[152] ibid para 932. See also *Kardassopolous v Georgia*, ICSID Case No ARB/05/18, Award, 3 March 2010, para 664.

[153] ARSIWA Commentaries (n 1) Article 38 para 8.

leaves the matter open, linking the issue to the objective of securing full reparation; '[t]he interest rate and mode of calculation shall be set so as to achieve that result'. International courts and tribunals often taking significantly different approaches to these different elements.[154]

61 The Commentary to ARSIWA provides that '[t]he general view of courts and tribunals has been against the award of compound interest, and this is true even of those tribunals which hold claimants to be normally entitled to compensatory interest'.[155] This view, expressed by arbitrator Huber in the *British Claims in the Spanish Zone of Morocco* case,[156] was confirmed by the Iran–US Claims Tribunal.[157] The ILC Commentary at the time also concluded that 'given the present state of international law, it cannot be said that an injured State has any entitlement to compound interest, in the absence of special circumstances which justify some element of compounding as an aspect of full reparation'.[158] This is the approach that international courts generally continue to take,[159] despite some commentators arguing that 'compound interest reasonably incurred by the injured party should be recoverable as an item of damage'.[160]

62 Investment tribunals mostly diverge from general international law in this regard, with most of them awarding interest on a compound basis, on grounds that compound interest best captures the time value of money. Beginning with the award in *Santa Elena*,[161] a number of investment tribunals have granted compound interest, first in cases relating only to expropriation, then for other breaches.[162] The tribunal in *Continental Casualty v Argentina* reasoned that:

> [C]ompound interest reflects economic reality in modern times [...] The time value of money in free market economies is measured in compound interest; simple interest cannot be relied upon to produce full reparation for a claimant's loss occasioned by delay in payment.[163]

63 This is an obvious divergence from the practice under general international law, which tends towards restricting compound interest to special circumstances. However, a minority of

---

[154] MA Maniatis and others, 'An Unexpected Interest in interest' (*GAR* 2015) <http://globalarbitrationreview.com/article/1034451/an-un-expected-interest-in-interest> accessed 23 October 2023; MA Maniatis, F Dorobantu and F Nunez, 'A Framework for Interest Awards in International Arbitration' (2018) 41(4) Fordham Intl L J 821.
[155] ARSIWA Commentaries (n 1) Article 38 para 8.
[156] *Spanish Zone of Morocco Claims (Great Britain v Spain)* (1924) 2 RIAA 615, 650.
[157] *McCollough Case* (n 144); MM Whiteman, *Damages in International Law* (United States Government Printing Office 1937) 1997.
[158] ARSIWA Commentaries (n 1) Article 38 para 9.
[159] See, eg, *Dr Horst Reineccius, Claimant v Bank for International Settlements, Respondent (Claim no 1) First Eagle SoGen Funds, Inc, Claimant v Bank for International Settlements, Respondent (Claim no 2) Pierre Mathieu and la Societe de Concours Hippique de La Chatre v Bank for International Settlements* (2003) PCA Case No 2000-04, para 138(4) (2003) PCA Case No 2000-04, para 138(4); *Saiga* (n 29) para 175; *Duzgit Integrity Arbitration (Malta v São Tomé and Príncipe)*, PCA Case No 2014-07, Award, 5 September 2016, 45; the M/V 'Norstar' Case (*Panama v Italy*) (2019) ITLOS Case No 25, paras 460, 462; M/V 'Virginia G' (Panama/Guinea-Bissau) (2014), ITLOS Case No 19, paras 444–66.
[160] Crawford, *State Responsibility* (n 3) 538. See also FA Mann, *Compound Interest as an Item of Damage in International Law*, Further Studies in International Law (Clarendon Press 1990) 377, 383; JY Gotanda, 'Awarding Interest in International Arbitration' (1996) 90 AJIL 40, 61.
[161] *Compania del Desarrollo de Santa Elena, SA v The Republic of Costa Rica*, ICSID Case No ARB/96/1, Final Award, 17 February 2000, paras 96–106.
[162] See, eg, *Azurix v Argentina* (n 97) para 440; *ADC v Hungary* (n 144) para 522; *BG Group Plc v Argentine Republic*, UNCITRAL, 24 December 2007, paras 454–56.
[163] *Continental Casualty Company v Argentine Republic*, ICSID Case No ARB/03/9, Award, 5 September 2008, para 309.

investment tribunals have rejected requests for compound interest, with several highlighting both the lack of uniform international practice in this regard and the need to be mindful of whether compound interest is called for in the particular circumstances of the case.[164]

II. Contribution to the Injury [Article 39]

Article 39: Contribution to the injury

In the determination of reparation, account shall be taken of the contribution to the injury by wilful or negligent action or omission of the injured State or any person or entity in relation to whom reparation is sought.

Article 39 recognizes that there may be a reduction of reparation in cases where the injured State or a third party contributed to the injury. Since responsibility is tied to causation, it seems logical that damage suffered by a person to which it has itself contributed should not fully engage the responsibility of another.[165] International courts and tribunals have, on occasion, taken into account the contribution of a State or third party to its own injury.[166] **64**

Investment tribunals have taken account of the claimant's contribution to its own injury, often referring expressly to Article 39. As observed by the International Centre for Settlement of Investment Disputes (ICSID) Annulment Committee in *MTD Equity*: **65**

> Part II of the ILC Articles, in which Article 39 is located, is concerned with claims between States, though it includes claims brought on behalf of individuals, e.g., within the framework of diplomatic protection. There is no reason not to apply the same principle of contribution to claims for breach of treaty brought by individuals.[167]

The application of Article 39 in the investment context can have a significant impact on the amount of compensation awarded. For example, in *Copper Mesa Mining v Ecuador*, the tribunal reduced damages by 30 per cent, taking into account the claimant's negligence with respect to violations of Ecuadorian criminal law.[168] Similarly, in *Hulley v Russia*, the claimant's damages were reduced due to its material and significant misconduct which had contributed to the losses it had suffered.[169] **66**

Some investment tribunals have required a showing that the investor's misconduct was 'material and significant' before finding that it contributed to the damage suffered by the **67**

---

[164] *Strabag SE v State of Libya*, ICSID Case No ARB(AF)/15/1, Award, 29 June 2020, paras 962–63; *Burlington Resources Inc v Republic of Ecuador (formerly Burlington Resources Inc and others) v Republic of Ecuador and Empresa Estatal Petróleos del Ecuador (PetroEcuador)*, ICSID Case No ARB/08/5, Decision on Counterclaim, 7 February 2017, paras 1092–95; *Arif v Moldova* (n 15) paras 616–20.

[165] See DM Pusztai, 'Causation in the Law of State Responsibility' (Doctoral thesis, Cambridge 2017) https://doi.org/10.17863/CAM.13857.

[166] See, eg, *LaGrand* (n 11) 486–87 and 508; *M/V 'Virginia G', Judgment*, ITLOS Reports 2014, 4, 211 (Sep Op Judge Paik). See also *Diallo* Compensation (n 92) 337 (finding that, among other things, Guinea had failed to prove the extent to which Mr Diallo, or the DRC, contributed to Mr Diallo's injuries).

[167] *MTD Equity Sdn Bhd and MTD Chile SA v Republic of Chile*, ICSID Case No ARB/01/17, Decision on Annulment, 21 March 2007, para 99.

[168] *Copper Mesa Mining Corporation v Republic of Ecuador*, PCA Case No 2012-2, Award, 15 March 2016, paras 6.91–6.100.

[169] *Hulley Enterprises Limited (Cyprus) v Russia*, PCA Case No 2005-03/AA226, Final Award, 18 July 2014; *Yukos v Russia* (n 23) paras 1594–636.

claimant.[170] This requirement is not provided for in Article 39, which specifies only that a contribution to injury is relevant if it is 'wilful or negligent'. However, the Commentary confirms that the effect that any negligence has on the determination of reparation will be influenced by the degree on which it contributed to the injury.[171]

D. Conclusion

68 When adjudicating on remedies, both international courts operating in the inter-State context and investment tribunals usually take as a starting point either the ARSIWA directly or the jurisprudence and State practice regarding remedies that the ILC sought to codify. Investment tribunals have consistently invoked the ARSIWA, and cited the ILC's Commentary, when exercising their remedial powers and considering the extent of responsibility for breaches of investment obligations.

69 Despite this shared starting point, over time, numerous divergences in the practices under general international law and under investment law have emerged. The most significant divergence identified is in the forms of remedies most commonly ordered. Investment tribunals have traditionally preferred awards of compensation over all other remedies, while courts and tribunals established under general international law are more likely to consider a wider range of the available remedies, including cessation of the unlawful conduct, determinations of material or juridical restitution, and declarations awarding satisfaction.

70 This difference between the practice of international courts and tribunals established under general international law and investment law may be attributed to the fact that remedies other than compensation are rarely sought by claimant investors. It may also be that they are considered too difficult to obtain. In some cases, the limitations on these other remedies are often interpreted more broadly by investment tribunals. In others, tribunals have also introduced new requirements not found in general international law, such as the requirement that restitution should not cause undue interference with State sovereignty.

71 One may think about these divergences between general international law and investment law in two different ways. If investment treaties are designed only to ensure the protection of the commercial interests of foreign investors and to avoid those investors being dependent on the discretion of their home State to provide diplomatic protection, tribunals are simply enforcing this objective by limiting their remedial powers. If one adopts this view, it is not the role of investment tribunals to order States to continue their performance obligations or make symbolic sanctions for misconduct. Their role is to merely to ensure that investors are made financially no worse off than if the State had complied with its obligations, which they can do by issuing awards of compensation for investments that are lost or nullified in value as a result of unlawful conduct on the part of the State.

72 This view, however, seems unnecessarily limited, not only in terms of its depiction of the role of investment tribunals within the broader framework of public international law, but

---

[170] *Occidental Petroleum Corporation and Occidental Exploration and Production Company v Republic of Ecuador*, ICSID Case No ARB/06/111, Award, 5 October 2012, paras 669–87.
[171] ARSIWA Commentaries (n 1) Article 39 para 5.

also in its failure to consider how investment law fits within that framework. Not all investment claims relate to a single undertaking by an investor in a foreign State where that investor has no personal attachment to the host country or interest in a continued relationship with that State. Even investments made solely for financial reasons may not be easily replaceable with an alternative investment in a different market. In circumstances where investors have an interest in their investment in the future and it is possible for the State to restore the investor's rights, tribunals could weigh seriously the different considerations at hand, possibly first awarding restitution and then placing the burden on the State to provide fair compensation if it does not wish to satisfy such an order.[172] Similarly, to the extent that investors or States seek satisfaction from what they believe is non-financial injury caused by misconduct, tribunals should consider this request seriously as it falls within their remedial powers.

More broadly, the lack of attention on the part of investment tribunals to the wider range of remedies available beyond compensation (including the reluctance to award moral damages) indicates a broader disconnect between how some view the role of investment tribunals and the function of law in a well-ordered international society. Investment law is increasingly portrayed by commentators and tribunals alike not as a mere instrument to enforce bilateral commitments by a State towards a foreign investor, but as an instrument to fulfil broader purposes, such as securing compliance with the rule of law and promoting regulatory stability.[173] If one shares this view, it becomes far less obvious that the sole or primary response to treaty violations should be to give the claimant the most efficient instrument to exit the investor–State relationship, fully compensated; instead, the focus should be on what other remedies the breaching State should be subject to. As one commentator noted in the context of human rights, 'settling a dispute in a manner that lessens the likelihood of future conflicts is a value that some international tribunals may consider as important as upholding the international rule of law, and more important than ensuring fulfilment of all claims of reparations'.[174] **73**

While the different objects and purposes of international investment agreements and human rights treaties must be kept in mind, there certainly is scope for investment tribunals to demand, relying on the provisions on remedies of the ARSIWA, that States fulfil their treaty obligations. Clear possibilities in this regard include orders to preserve a particular legislative or regulatory environment, in order to ensure fair and equitable treatment for those within their territory. Enforcing these broader governance commitments—which one might assume is what governments may have in mind when committing to the international investment regime[175]—not only would be conducive to healthy relations with investors but also may contribute to a stable host-State environment and drive investment in the long term.[176] **74**

---

[172] See examples in Vidigal (n 74).
[173] See, eg, *Arif v Moldova* (n 15) para 570. See also Pulkowski, 'Remedies' (n 94) 261.
[174] Shelton, *Remedies* (n 90) 94–95.
[175] T Schultz and C Dupont, 'Investment Arbitration: Promoting the Rule of Law or Over-empowering Investors? A Quantitative Empirical Study' (2014) 25 EJIL 1147.
[176] On this difficult issue, see JW Yackee, 'Bilateral Investment Treaties, Credible Commitment, and the Rule of (International) Law: Do BITs Promote Foreign Direct Investment?' (2008) 42 (4) L & Soc'y Rev 805; J Bonnitcha, LN Skovgaard Poulsen and M Waibel, *The Political Economy of the Investment Treaty Regime* (OUP 2017) 155ff.

Selected literature

Aust HP, 'Investment Protection and Sustainable Development: What Role for the Law of State Responsibility', in Hindelang S and Krajewski M (eds), *Shifting Paradigms in International Investment Law: More Balanced, Less Isolated, Increasingly Diversified* (OUP 2016).

Ishikawa T, 'Restitution as a 'Second Chance' for Investor-State Relations: Restitution and Monetary Damages as Sequential Options' (2016–17) 3 MJDR 154.

Marboe I, *Calculation of Compensation and Damages in International Investment Law* (OUP 2017).

Marboe I, 'Compensation and Damages in International Law' (2006) 7 JWIT 723.

Nevill P, 'Awards of Interest by International Courts and Tribunals' (2008) 78 BYIL 255.

Pulkowski D, 'Remedies for Wrongful Conduct: Lessons from Investment Arbitration' in Tams CJ, Schill S and Hofmann R (eds), *International Investment Law and General International Law* (Brill 2023).

Ripinsky S and Williams K, *Damages in International Investment Law* (British Institute of International and Comparative Law 2008).

Sabahi B, *Compensation and Restitution in Investor-State Arbitration: Principles and Practice* (OUP 2011).

Stoica V, *Remedies before the International Court of Justice: A Systemic Analysis* (CUP 2021).

Vidigal G, 'Targeting Compliance: Prospective Remedies in International Law' (2015) 6 JIDS 462.

Selected decisions

Application of the Convention on the Prevention and Punishment of the Crime of Genocide (Bosnia and Herzegovina v Serbia and Montenegro) (Judgment) [2007] ICJ Rep 43.

Arif v Moldova, Award, ICSID Case No ARB/11/23, 8 April 2013.

Avena and Other Mexican Nationals (Mexico v United States of America) (Judgment) [2004] ICJ Rep 12.

Bernhard von Pezold and Others v Republic of Zimbabwe, ICSID Case No ARB/10/15, Award, 28 July 2015.

Case Concerning the Factory at Chorzów (Germany v Poland) (Claim for Indemnity) (Jurisdiction) (Judgment) [1928] PCIJ Rep Series A No 9.

Case Concerning the Factory at Chorzów (Germany v Poland) (Claim for Indemnity) (Merits) (Judgment) [1928] PCIJ Rep Series A No 12.

Chevron Corporation and Texaco Petroleum Company v The Republic of Ecuador (II), PCA Case No 2009-23, Second Partial Award on Track II, 30 August 2018.

Glencore International A.G. and C.I. Prodeco S.A. v Republic of Colombia, ICSID Case No ARB/16/6, Award, 27 August 2019.

LaGrand (Germany v United States of America) (Judgment) [2001] ICJ Rep 466.

Whaling in the Antarctic (Australia v Japan: New Zealand intervening) (Judgment) [2014] ICJ Rep 226.

Yukos v Russia, PCA Case No AA 227, Final Award, 18 July 2014.

Articles 49–54 of the ARSIWA

Countermeasures

Martins Paparinskis

Article 49. Object and limits of countermeasures

1. An injured State may only take countermeasures against a State which is responsible for an internationally wrongful act in order to induce that State to comply with its obligations under part two.

2. Countermeasures are limited to the non-performance for the time being of international obligations of the State taking the measures towards the responsible State.

3. Countermeasures shall, as far as possible, be taken in such a way as to permit the resumption of performance of the obligations in question.

Article 50. Obligations not affected by countermeasures

1. Countermeasures shall not affect: (a) the obligation to refrain from the threat or use of force as embodied in the Charter of the United Nations; (b) obligations for the protection of fundamental human rights; (c) obligations of a humanitarian character prohibiting reprisals; (d) other obligations under peremptory norms of general international law.

2. A State taking countermeasures is not relieved from fulfilling its obligations: (a) under any dispute settlement procedure applicable between it and the responsible State; (b) to respect the inviolability of diplomatic or consular agents, premises, archives and documents.

Article 51. Proportionality

Countermeasures must be commensurate with the injury suffered, taking into account the gravity of the internationally wrongful act and the rights in question.

Article 52. Conditions relating to resort to countermeasures

1. Before taking countermeasures, an injured State shall: (a) call upon the responsible State, in accordance with article 43, to fulfil its obligations under part two; (b) notify the responsible State of any decision to take countermeasures and offer to negotiate with that State.

2. Notwithstanding paragraph 1 (b), the injured State may take such urgent countermeasures as are necessary to preserve its rights.

3. Countermeasures may not be taken, and if already taken must be suspended without undue delay if: (a) the internationally wrongful act has ceased; and (b) the dispute is pending before a court or tribunal which has the authority to make decisions binding on the parties.

4. Paragraph 3 does not apply if the responsible State fails to implement the dispute settlement procedures in good faith.

Article 53. Termination of countermeasures

Countermeasures shall be terminated as soon as the responsible State has complied with its obligations under part two in relation to the internationally wrongful act.

Article 54. Measures taken by States other than an injured State

This chapter does not prejudice the right of any State, entitled under article 48, paragraph 1, to invoke the responsibility of another State, to take lawful measures against that State to ensure cessation of the breach and reparation in the interest of the injured State or of the beneficiaries of the obligation breached.

A. Introduction	1	2. Can such countermeasures be successfully invoked in practice?	15
B. Application in general international law	2		
C. Application in international investment law	12	3. Are countermeasures enacted in response to a breach and intended to induce compliance?	19
I Articles 52, 53, and 54	12		
II. Article 49	13	III. Article 50	20
1. Are states entitled to take countermeasures to excuse investment treaty breaches?	13	IV. Article 51	21

A. Introduction

1 Under the international law of State responsibility, the wrongfulness of an act of a State not in conformity with an international obligation towards another State is precluded if and to the extent that the act constitutes a countermeasure taken against the latter State.[1] Countermeasures are distinct both from retorsion—'unfriendly' conduct which is not inconsistent with any obligation of the State even though it may be a response to an internationally wrongful act—and the termination or suspension of treaty relations on account of the material breach of a treaty by another State under the law of treaties.[2] Countermeasures simultaneously play the roles of a shield and a sword in the law of State responsibility.[3] As a shield, they are among the circumstances capable of precluding the wrongfulness of an otherwise unlawful act in international law and are sometimes invoked as defences.[4] As a sword, countermeasures are a traditional means of implementing State responsibility by way of decentralized self-help.[5] In order to be justifiable, a countermeasure must meet certain conditions,[6] and a State taking countermeasures acts at its peril if its unilateral assessment of this objective standard turns out not to be well founded.[7] This entry will discuss these

---

[1] ILC, 'Draft Articles on Responsibility of States for Internationally Wrongful Acts, with Commentaries' YILC 2001, Vol II, Part Two, 31, Article 22 (hereafter ARSIWA Commentaries). See further D Alland, 'The Definition of Countermeasures' in J Crawford, A Pellet and S Olleson (eds), *The Law of International Responsibility* (OUP 2010); J Crawford, *State Responsibility: The General Part* (CUP 2013) 684–86 (hereafter Crawford).

[2] ARSIWA Commentaries (n 1) Part III, Chapter II paras 3, 4.

[3] E Stoegher and CJ Tams, 'Swords, Shields and Other Beasts: The Role of Countermeasures in Investment Arbitration' (2022) 37 ICSID Rev 121 (hereafter Stoegher and Tams).

[4] *Appeal relating to the Jurisdiction of the ICAO Council under Article 84 of the Convention on International Civil Aviation (Bahrain, Egypt, Saudi Arabia and United Arab Emirates v Qatar)* [2020] ICJ Rep 81 para 49; ARSIWA Commentaries (n 1) Article 22; F Paddeu, *Justification and Excuse in International Law* (CUP 2018) ch 6. On circumstances precluding wrongfulness, see in this Commentary: Federica Paddeu, entries on Articles 20, 21, 23, 24, 26, and 27 of the ARSIWA, and Federica Paddeu and Michael Waibel, 'Article 25 of the ARSIWA'.

[5] ARSIWA Commentaries (n 1) Part III, Chapter II; cf Institut de droit international, 'Régime des représailles en temps de paix' (1934) 38 AnnIDI 162.

[6] *Gabčíkovo-Nagymaros Project (Hungary/Slovakia)* [1997] ICJ Rep 7 para 83 (hereafter *Gabčíkovo-Nagymaros Project*).

[7] ARSIWA Commentaries (n 1) Article 49 para 3.

standards by reference to the framework set by Article 49–54 of the 2001 International Law Commission's (ILC) articles on responsibility of States for internationally wrongful acts (ARSIWA),[8] dealing first with application in general international law (Section B) and then in international investment law (Section C).

B. Application in general international law

Article 49 of the ARSIWA sets out the object and limits of countermeasures.[9] The limited object and exceptional nature of countermeasures are indicated by the use of the word 'only' in paragraph 1 ('may only take countermeasures')[10] and the cumulative conditions set out in the full provision.

First, countermeasures under Article 49 may only be taken by an injured State[11] (whether countermeasures may be taken by a State other than an injured State will be considered below under Article 54).

Secondly, countermeasures may only be taken against a State which is responsible for an internationally wrongful act.[12] For example, in the case regarding the *Gabčíkovo-Nagymaros Project*, the International Court of Justice (ICJ) found that Slovakia's conduct satisfied this criterion because it was taken in response to Hungary's internationally wrongful acts and was directed against that State.[13] The necessary implication is that countermeasures are relative in effect and not opposable as a circumstance precluding wrongfulness to States other than the author of the internationally wrongful act.[14] That, however, does not mean that countermeasures may not incidentally affect the position of third States or indeed other third parties.[15]

Thirdly, countermeasures may be taken in order to induce the responsible State to comply with its obligations under Part Two of the ARSIWA. The concept of inducement, to be addressed separately, applies to compliance with obligations of the responsible State falling under the rubric of 'content of State responsibility'. In many cases, the focus will be on

---

[8] But note the disagreement on whether the ARSIWA reflect customary law on this topic, particularly on multilateral aspects raised by Article 54 but also more generally, where some actors in some settings have taken the view that the ARSIWA are too flexible and others that they are too restrictive. For the former, eg F Coulée, 'Pratique française du droit international 2001' (2001) 47 AFDI 555, 572–73; G Marston (ed), 'United Kingdom Materials on International Law 2001' (2001) 72 BYBIL 551, 648–50; 'Draft Articles on State Responsibility: Comments of the Government of the United States of America (March 1, 2001)' in SJ Cummins and DP Stewart (eds), *Digest of United States Practice in International Law 2001* (Office of the Legal Adviser United States Department of State 2002) 365–71. For the latter, see the work of the Special Rapporteur on the negative impact of unilateral coercive measures on the enjoyment of human rights and reactions thereto, most recently Report of the Special Rapporteur on the negative impact of unilateral coercive measures on the enjoyment of human rights, 'Secondary sanctions, civil and criminal penalties for circumvention of sanctions regimes and overcompliance with sanctions' (15 July 2022) UN Doc A/HRC/51/33.
[9] See generally Crawford (n 1) 686–88.
[10] ARSIWA Commentaries (n 1) Article 49 para 1.
[11] ibid Article 49(1).
[12] ibid.
[13] *Gabčíkovo-Nagymaros Project* (n 6) para 85. This judgment was handed down before the adoption of the ARSIWA, but the Court referred to the corresponding provisions adopted in the first reading and the ARSIWA were in turn influenced by the judgment.
[14] ARSIWA Commentaries (n 1) Article 49 para 4.
[15] ibid para 5. The Commentary gives the example of such indirect or collateral effect as the case, of possible relevance to investment law, 'if, as a consequence of suspension of a trade agreement, trade with the responsible State is affected and one or more companies lose business or even go bankrupt', ibid. However, a possibly countervailing consideration for investment law is noted earlier in the same paragraph in relation to transit rights of third States: '[i]f they have no individual rights in the matter they cannot complain', ibid (emphasis added).

ensuring cessation of a continuing wrongful act, but countermeasures may also be taken to ensure reparation, particularly compensation.[16] Fourthly, Article 49, paragraph 1, makes the point that countermeasures may only be taken to induce compliance. For example, in the case regarding *Application of the Interim Accord of 13 September 1995*, the ICJ was not persuaded that Greece's wrongful objection to the FYRM's admission to NATO in 2008 was taken for the purpose of achieving the cessation of the latter's wrongful use of certain symbols that had ceased as of 2004.[17] The more general point is that countermeasures are taken as a form of inducement, not punishment.[18]

6 The rest of Article 49 spells out the structural implications of the focus on inducement. According to paragraph 2, countermeasures are limited to the non-performance for the time being of international obligations of the State taking the measure towards the responsible State (distinctly from the termination or suspension of treaty relations under the law of treaties).[19] According to paragraph 3, countermeasures are, as far as possible, to be taken in such a way as to permit the resumption of performance of the obligations in question. The language 'as far as possible' suggests that the duty to choose measures that are reversible is not absolute and gives certain flexibility to the State adopting countermeasures.[20]

7 Article 50 sets out obligations not affected by countermeasures, which, so far as the law of countermeasures is concerned, are sacrosanct.[21] These obligations fall into two basic categories. Paragraph 1 deals with certain obligations which, by reason of their character, must not be the subject of countermeasures at all[22]: (a) the obligation to refrain from the threat or use of force as embodied in the Charter of the United Nations; (b) obligations for the protection of fundamental human rights; (c) obligations of a humanitarian character prohibiting reprisals; and (d) other obligations under peremptory norms of general international law.[23] Paragraph 2 deals with certain obligations relating in particular to the maintenance of channels of communication between the two States concerned, including machinery for the resolution of their disputes[24]: (a) obligations under any dispute settlement procedure applicable between it and the responsible State; and (b) obligations to respect the inviolability of diplomatic or consular agents, premises, archives, and documents.[25] There is ground for reasonable disagreement on whether Article 50 plays an independent legal role or merely conveniently summarizes prohibitions expressed in particular rules having the character of *lex specialis* or *jus cogens*.

8 Article 51 sets out the requirement of proportionality.[26] First, countermeasures must be commensurate with the injury suffered (which provides a measure of assurance inasmuch as disproportionate countermeasures could give rise to responsibility on the part of the State taking

---

[16] ibid para 8. Note that this proviso applies to measures to 'induce *the responsible State* to comply with its obligations under Part Two of the 2001 ILC Articles' (emphasis added) and not all obligations under Part Two, thus would not on its terms apply to obligations of third States under its Chapter III ('Serious breaches of obligations under peremptory norms of general international law').
[17] *Application of the Interim Accord of 13 September 1995 (FYRM v Greece)* [2011] ICJ Rep 644, para 164 (hereafter *Application of the Interim Accord of 13 September 1995*).
[18] ARSIWA Commentaries (n 1) Article 49 para 7.
[19] ibid Part III, Chapter II, para 4.
[20] ibid Article 49 para 9.
[21] ibid Article 50, para 1. See further chapters by Olleson and Borelli, Leben, and Boisson de Chazournes in J Crawford, A Pellet and S Olleson (eds), *The Law of International Responsibility* (OUP 2010), and generally Crawford (n 1) 688–97.
[22] ARSIWA Commentaries (n 1) Article 50 para 2.
[23] ibid Article 50(1).
[24] ibid Article 50 para 2.
[25] ibid Article 50(2).
[26] ibid Article 51 (described as setting out a recognized principle of customary international law in WTO, *US-Definitive Safeguard Measures on Imports of Circular Welded Carbon Quality Line Pipe from Korea*, WT/DS202/

such measures).[27] Secondly, proportionality must be assessed taking into account not only the purely 'quantitative' element of the injury suffered, but also 'qualitative factors' such as the importance of the interests protected by the rule infringed and the seriousness of the breach.[28] For example, in the *Air Services Arbitration* the tribunal held (by majority) that the US measures were in conformity with the principle of proportionality even though they were rather more severe in terms of their economic effect on the French carriers than the initial French action because they were taken in the same field as the initial measures and concerned the same routes.[29] In the *Gabčíkovo-Nagymaros Project* case, the ICJ similarly took into account the quality or character of the rights in question in the field of international watercourses, and concluded that Czechoslovakia's unilateral assumption of a shared resource was not proportionate.[30]

Article 52 sets out conditions relating to resort to countermeasures.[31] First, paragraph 1 sets out the procedural requirement for the injured State, before taking countermeasures, to (a) call upon the responsible State to fulfil its obligations under Part Two of the ARSIWA, and (b) notify the responsible State of any decision to take countermeasures and offer to negotiate with that State.[32] For example, in the *Application of the Interim Accord of 13 September 1995* case, Judge Bennouna noted that '[s]ince Greece never fulfilled [the obligation in Article 52(1)(b)], it cannot, in any case, invoke the right to take countermeasures in the present case.'[33] Secondly (and however), paragraph 2 provides for the right to take such urgent countermeasures as are necessary to preserve its rights, notwithstanding the requirements of notification and offer of negation in paragraph 1(b).[34] Thirdly, paragraph 3 addresses the interaction between countermeasures and international dispute settlement mechanisms. It sets out two cumulative conditions for when countermeasures may not be taken, and if already taken must be suspended without undue delay: (a) the internationally wrongful act has ceased, and (b) the dispute is pending before a court or tribunal which has the authority to make decisions binding on the parties.[35] Finally, paragraph 4 disapplies paragraph 3 if the responsible State fails to implement the dispute settlement procedures in good faith.[36]

Article 53 addresses termination of countermeasures.[37] It provides that countermeasures are to be terminated as soon as the responsible State has complied with its obligations under Part Two of the ARSIWA in relation to the internationally wrongful act.[38] The proposition is implicit in the other articles of this entry, particularly Article 49 and to an extent Article 52, but is made explicit in Article 53.[39]

AB/R, Report of the Appellate Body, 15 February 2022, para 259). See further T Franck, 'On Proportionality of Countermeasures in International Law' (2008) 102 AJIL 715; R O'Keefe, 'Proportionality' in J Crawford, A Pellet and S Olleson (eds), *The Law of International Responsibility* (OUP 2010); Crawford (n 1) 697–99.

[27] ARSIWA Commentaries (n 1) Article 51 para 1.
[28] ibid para 6.
[29] ibid para 2 (citing *Air Services Agreement (US/France)* (1978) 18 RIAA 417, para 83 (hereafter *Air Services Agreement*)).
[30] ibid para 4 (citing *Gabčíkovo-Nagymaros Project* (n 6) paras 85, 87).
[31] See further Y Iwasawa and N Itwatsuki, 'Procedural Conditions' in J Crawford, A Pellet and S Olleson (eds), *The Law of International Responsibility* (OUP 2010) 700–02.
[32] ARSIWA Commentaries (n 1) Article 52(1).
[33] *Application of the Interim Accord of 13 September 1995* (n 17) Declaration of Judge Bennouna 709, 710.
[34] ARSIWA Commentaries (n 1) Article 52(2).
[35] ibid Article 52(3).
[36] ibid Article 52(4).
[37] See further M Kamto, 'Time Factor in the Application of Countermeasures' in J Crawford, A Pellet and S Olleson (eds), *The Law of International Responsibility* (OUP 2010) 702–03.
[38] ARSIWA Commentaries (n 1) Article 53 (described as reflecting the relevant principles of international law in WTO, *US-Continued Suspension of Obligations in the EC-Hormones Disputes*, WT/DS320/AB/R, Report of the Appellate Body, 16 October 2008, para 382).
[39] ibid Article 53 para 2.

11 Article 54 addresses measures taken by States other than an injured State. Unlike other provisions in Chapter II, Article 54 does not purport to set the applicable rule but is a saving clause which reserves the position and leaves the resolution of the matter to the further development of international law.[40] It states that the Chapter does not prejudice the right of any State, entitled under Article 48, paragraph 1, to invoke the responsibility of another State, to take lawful measures against that State to ensure cessation of the breach and reparation in the interest of the injured State or of the beneficiaries of the obligation breached.[41] After the review of the limited and rather embryonic practice on this subject, the ILC concluded that the (then-)current state of international law of countermeasures taken in the general or collective interest since practice was sparse and involved a limited number of States.[42] Nor did the Commission go further in its later work.[43] There is ground for reasonable disagreement on whether contemporary international law permits countermeasures by States other than an injured State.[44]

C. Application in international investment law

I. Articles 52, 53, and 54

12 It is not clear that any significant role in international investment law has so far been played by Articles 52, 53, and 54.[45] The risk of countermeasures may have affected the drafting of certain recent measures, and it is perhaps surprising that the practice of sanctions has not so far lead to adjudicative engagement with the finer print of the ARSIWA,[46] but there is little that one could point to at the time of writing this piece in terms of publicly available State and arbitral practice.

II. Article 49

1. Are states entitled to take countermeasures to excuse investment treaty breaches?

13 The first issue considered by investment arbitration tribunals is whether States are in principle entitled to take countermeasures in breach of obligations expressed in investment treaties.[47] The starting point is that the right to take countermeasures is a dispositive rule

---

[40] ibid Article 54 para 6.
[41] ibid Article 54, see also Article 48(1); *Application of the Convention on the Prevention and Punishment of the Crime of Genocide (The Gambia v Myanmar)* (Preliminary Objections) [2022] ICJ Rep 477, paras 106–14.
[42] ARSIWA Commentaries (n 1) Article 43 paras 3–6.
[43] ILC, 'Articles on Responsibility of International Organizations' YILC 2011, Vol II, Part Two, UN Doc A/CN.4/SER.A/2011/Add.1 (Part 2) 40, Article 57 para 2; by implication ILC, 'Draft Conclusions on Identification and Legal Consequences of Peremptory Norms of General International Law (*jus cogens*) Report of the International Law Commission: Seventy-third Session (18 April–3 June and 4 July–5 August 2022)* UN Doc A/77/10 11, Draft conclusion 19(4).
[44] See the discussion in CJ Tams, *Enforcing Obligations Erga Omnes in International Law* (CUP 2005) ch 6; L-A Sicilianos, 'Countermeasures in Response to Grave Violations of Obligations owed to the International Community as a Whole' in J Crawford, A Pellet and S Olleson (eds), *The Law of International Responsibility* (OUP 2010); Crawford (n 1) 703–07; M Dawidowicz, *Third-Party Countermeasures in International Law* (CUP 2017); T Ruys, 'Immunity, Inviolability and Countermeasures—A Closer Look at Non-UN Targeted Sanctions' in T Ruys, N Angelet and L Ferro (eds), *The Cambridge Handbook of Immunities and International Law* (CUP 2019) 670, 703–04.
[45] The State did not raise the argument of countermeasures in a case where the investors challenged the implementation of non-United Nations sanctions against Iran, *Bank Melli Iran and Bank Saderat Iran v Bahrain*, PCA Case No 2017-25, Award, 9 November 2021.
[46] M Paparinskis, 'Circumstances Precluding Wrongfulness in International Investment Law' (2016) 31 ICSID Rev 484, 497 (hereafter Paparinskis, 'Circumstances Precluding Wrongfulness in International Investment Law').
[47] For the terminology, see Section A. This section draws upon Paparinskis, 'Circumstances Precluding Wrongfulness in International Investment Law' (n 46) 494–97.

and may be superseded by *lex specialis*.[48] Has this taken place in international investment law? The argument in favour of an affirmative answer could be presented in several ways.[49] The first would rely on subject matter: international investment law addresses important and sensitive issues, which would be greatly harmed by arbitrary interferences of States, by reference to interstate disputes. On its own, however, reliance on the content of primary obligations would be insufficient.[50] Secondly, if States owe obligations directly to investors, could they really be permitted to breach them in response to the conduct of other States?[51] This conflates exclusion of secondary rules in principle and the practical limitations of their application to primary rules drafted in a particular manner.[52] Another argument would consider more broadly the field of international investment law and rely on its efficiency and coherence to suggest that the backdrop of general rules on implementation of responsibility must fade in comparison to this special structure.[53] A yet different, or at least differently focused, argument would rely upon the framing of modern investment dispute settlement law around the investor–State axis as excluding the application of remedies and procedures from traditional interstate law.[54]

The *lex specialis* argument was considered in three North American Free Trade Agreement (NAFTA) claims by US investors against Mexico regarding soft drinks decided in the late 2000s. One tribunal rejected it explicitly, one by necessary implication, one did not address it at all,[55] and one arbitrator wrote a short separate opinion, finding countermeasures inapplicable due to a mixture of purposive and procedural arguments.[56] There is something to be said for a generalist preference regarding the question of principle, at least partly because the practicalities for successful invocation may often be insurmountable.[57]

---

[48] ARSIWA Commentaries (n 1) Article 55.
[49] M Paparinskis, 'Investment Arbitration and the Law of Countermeasures' (2008) 79 BYBIL 264, 345–51 (hereafter Paparinskis, 'Investment Arbitration and the Law of Countermeasures').
[50] In one leading modern case, countermeasures were applicable even though 'the network of air services is in fact an extremely sensitive system, disturbances of which can have wide and unforeseeable consequences', *Air Services Agreement* (n 29) para 92. A narrower argument would focus on primary obligations that are explicitly, or by necessary implication, directed at countermeasures as such. Libya engaged in expropriation as an ostensible countermeasure against the UK, *BP v Libya*, Award (10 October 1973), (1979) 53 ILR 297, 329, and the UK BIT practice expresses the first condition of lawfulness of expropriation as 'public purpose related to the internal needs of that Party', eg Agreement between the Government of the United Kingdom of Great Britain and Northern Ireland and the Government of the Arab Republic of Egypt for the Promotion and Protection of Investments (signed 11 June 1975, entered into force 24 February 1976) (UK–Egypt BIT) Article 5(1), which a countermeasure would find hard to satisfy. As a matter of effectiveness of interpretation, it would be odd if a breach of a primary obligation that attaches responsibility to a countermeasure could be excused by relying on a countermeasure.
[51] Z Douglas, 'Specific Regimes of Responsibility: Investment Treaty Arbitration' in J Crawford, A Pellet and S Olleson (eds), *The Law of International Responsibility* (OUP 2010) 803, 820.
[52] K Parlett, 'The Application of the Rules on Countermeasures in Investment Claims' in C Chinkin and F Baetens (eds), *Sovereignty, Statehood and State Responsibility: Essays in Honour of James Crawford* (CUP 2015) 389, 403.
[53] B Simma and D Pulkowski, '*Leges speciales* and Self-Contained Regimes' in J Crawford, A Pellet and S Olleson (eds), *The Law of International Responsibility* (OUP 2010) 139.
[54] ARSIWA Commentaries (n 1) Article 33(2), which provides for a without prejudice rule regarding responsibility accruing to non-State actors, could not be relied upon for making this argument. It applies only to Part Two, and countermeasures are expressed in Parts One and Three of the ARSIWA.
[55] Respectively *Archer Daniels Midlands Company and Tate & Lyle Ingredients Americas, Inc v Mexico*, ICSID Case No ARB(AF)/04/05, Award, 21 November 2007, paras 120–23 (hereafter *Archer Daniels Midlands*); *Corn Products International, Inc v Mexico*, ICSID Case No ARB(AF)/04/01, Decision on Responsibility, 15 January 2008, para 165 (hereafter *Corn Products*); *Cargill, Inc v Mexico*, ICSID Case No ARB(AF)/05/2, Award, 18 September 2009, para 429 (hereafter *Cargill*).
[56] *Corn Products* ibid Separate Opinion of Arbitrator Lowenfeld.
[57] D McRae, 'Countermeasures and Investment Arbitration' in M Kinnear and others (eds), *Building International Investment Law: The First 50 Years of ICSID* (Kluwer Law International 2015) 495, 497.

2. Can such countermeasures be successfully invoked in practice?

15 The second issue addressed by investment arbitration tribunals is whether countermeasures can be successfully invoked in practice to preclude wrongfulness for the breach of investment protection obligations. A starting point for thinking about the practicalities is the position regarding countermeasures and international human rights law—which, for the purposes of State responsibility, is a regime similar to investment law in that it also permits invocation of responsibility by non-State actors on their own account and without the intermediation of any State.[58] The ARSIWA address the issue in Article 50(1)(a), which provides that '[c]ountermeasures shall not affect ... obligations for the protection of fundamental human rights'. The rationale of this proposition is not entirely clear.[59] Is 'fundamental human rights' a normative statement about a particular category of *lex specialis*? Or does it suggest a dichotomy between the application of countermeasures to 'fundamental' and less important human rights? If so, does one draw the line between rights peremptory and dispositive, between customary and treaty, between non-derogable and derogable or in some other way? Or is the point that human rights obligations are structurally *erga omnes*, and countermeasures vis-à-vis a wrongdoing State will not be opposable to other parties to the obligation? Or, finally, should one rather apply the point that countermeasures are opposable only to the wrongdoer so as to protect individual beneficiaries of human rights, akin to third parties under Article 49?[60] Various readings of the rationale of these general rules on countermeasures could have a different impact for investment law.[61]

16 The three NAFTA Tribunals dealing with soft drink claims read the law of responsibility, at least by implication, along the lines of the latter argument, suggested by the Fifth Special Rapporteur on State Responsibility James Crawford in his third report:

> The position with respect to human rights is at one level the same as the position with respect to the rights of third States. Evidently, human rights obligations are not owed to States as the primary beneficiaries, even though States are entitled to invoke those obligations and to ensure respect for them. Thus it is obvious that human rights obligations (whether or not qualified as 'basic' or 'fundamental') may not themselves be subject to countermeasures, ... and that conduct inconsistent with human rights obligations may not be justified or excused except to the extent provided for by the applicable regime of human rights itself.[62]

17 To determine whether '[t]he position with respect to [investor] rights is at one level the same as the position with respect to the rights of third States', the right question to ask is whether primary obligations under investment law are owed to investors. Tribunals in the soft drinks cases answered the interpretative question differently. For (the majority of) one tribunal, Chapter 11 of NAFTA expressed primary obligations only at the interstate level. Therefore, countermeasures could preclude wrongfulness for their breach,[63] provided that other criteria of countermeasures—particularly adoption in response to an alleged breach

---

[58] ARSIWA Commentaries (n 1) Article 33 para 4.
[59] S Borelli and S Olleson, 'Obligations Relating to Human Rights and Humanitarian Law' in J Crawford, A Pellet and S Olleson (eds), *The Law of International Responsibility* (OUP 2010) 1177, 1182–86.
[60] ARSIWA Commentaries (n 1) Article 49(1).
[61] Paparinskis, 'Investment Arbitration and the Law of Countermeasures' (n 49) 317–45.
[62] J Crawford, 'Third Report on State Responsibility' (15 March, 15 June, 10 and 18 July, and 4 August 2000) UN Doc A/CN.4/507, para 349.
[63] *Archer Daniels Midlands* (n 55) paras 161–80.

and proportionality of the measures—have been met.[64] For two tribunals, as well as one arbitrator of the first tribunal writing separately, investors did have rights under NAFTA, and countermeasures regarding their home State could not be opposed to these rights.[65] Consequently, the first, but not the second, position leaves open the possibility of successful invocation of countermeasures, provided that substantive and procedural conditions are complied with.[66]

The manner in which the question posed by Crawford and the soft drinks tribunals focused on non-State entities' rights is criticized by some scholars, who call instead for greater attention for the inter-State relationship that defines the extent and limits of those rights in the first place, arguably including susceptibility to countermeasures.[67] **18**

3. Are countermeasures enacted in response to a breach and intended to induce compliance?

The third question analysed by investment arbitration tribunals is whether countermeasures are enacted in response to a breach and intended to induce compliance. The *ADM v Mexico* tribunal, which (by majority) had found countermeasures opposable to the inter-state investment protection obligations in principle, considered whether Mexico's taxation measures had been enacted in response to the alleged US breaches and had been intended to induce US compliance with its NAFTA obligations concerning access of Mexican sugar to the US Market and concerning US obligations pursuant to NAFTA Chapter Twenty.[68] The tribunal rejected Mexico's argument on the facts because of essential lack of contemporary documents relating to the process of adoption of the challenged regulations that would show the intention to induce the compliance of the United States with its obligations, by contrast with significant evidence confirming the predominant purpose of protection of the domestic sugar industry.[69] The tribunal left open the possibility that the challenged taxation measures could have been adopted for both purposes, i.e. protection of the domestic sugar industry as well as inducing the compliance of the United States, but the evidence showed that 'protection of the sugar industry was the true motive and intent underlying the enactment of the Tax'.[70] This analysis is consistent with general international law. **19**

III. Article 50

Article 50 has not been directly addressed in investment arbitration practice.[71] In *ADM v Mexico*, the tribunal discussed proportionality of the challenged taxation measure and by way of example of a disproportionate countermeasure referred to Iran's conduct at **20**

---

[64] ARSIWA Commentaries (n 1) Article 33 para 4.
[65] *Corn Products* (n 55) paras 161–79; *Cargill* (n 55) paras 420–28; *Archer Daniel Midlands* (n 55) Concurring Opinion of Arbitrator Rovine, 20 September 2007.
[66] ARSIWA Commentaries (n 1) Article 33 para 4.
[67] A Roberts, 'Triangular Treaties: The Extent and Limits of Investment Treaty Rights' (2015) 56 Harvard Intl L J 353, 399–402; Stoegher and Tams (n 3) 134–36.
[68] Accepted as the correct benchmark by Mexico, *Archer Daniel Midlands* (n 55) para 127.
[69] ibid paras 134–51.
[70] ibid para 150.
[71] See discussion of Article 50 by analogy, Paparinskis, 'Investment Arbitration and the Law of Countermeasures' (n 49) 317–51.

issue in the *United States Diplomatic and Consular Staff (US v Iran)* case.[72] That is incorrect: the latter case is not an authority for the (Article 49) proposition that countermeasures must be proportionate but for the (Article 50(2)(b)) proposition that a State taking countermeasures is not relieved from fulfilling its obligations to respect the inviolability of diplomatic or consular agents, premises, archives, and documents.[73] In *Corn Products International, Inc v Mexico*, the tribunal referred to Article 50 to confirm the (correct) proposition that 'countermeasures ... may operate to preclude wrongfulness in respect of one obligation of the State which takes them, while not affecting another obligation of that State.'[74]

IV. Article 51

21 As noted in the previous section, the *ADM v Mexico* tribunal directly discussed proportionality of the challenged taxation measure:

> [T]he test of whether the countermeasure was appropriate to the particular purpose of securing compliance with the NAFTA by the United States, requires a qualitative comparison between all the international obligations involved: Section A of Chapter Eleven, on the one hand; and Annex 703.2.A (regarding access of Mexican sugar to the United States) and the state-to-state dispute resolution provisions of Chapter XX, on the other hand.[75]

It concluded that:

> Any of the obligations allegedly breached by the United States do not involve investment protection standards for private individuals and companies, but only provide inter-state obligations concerning international trade and the settlement of state-to-state disputes. However, the IEPS Amendment resulted in the non-performance by the Respondent of its obligations under Section A. The adoption of the Tax was not proportionate or necessary and reasonably connected to the aim said to be pursued.[76]

22 The tribunal relied on a mix of correct and incorrect authorities to formulate the test of proportionality.[77] The brevity of analysis and looseness of terminology, taken together with conflation of proportionality of the measure with the distinct and anterior determination that it had not been adopted to induce compliance, make it challenging to determine whether the decision was in line with general international law on the issue. If the tribunal meant to suggest that non-reciprocal countermeasures were necessarily or presumptively disproportionate, it was incorrect.[78]

---

[72] *Archer Daniel Midlands* (n 55) para 156 (citing *United States Diplomatic and Consular Staff (US v Iran)* [1980] ICJ Rep 2, paras 80, 81, 83).
[73] ARSIWA Commentaries (n 1) Article 50 para 15.
[74] *Corn Products* (n 55) paras 158, 159.
[75] *Archer Daniel Midlands* (n 55) para 155.
[76] ibid para 158.
[77] ibid para 152 (citing ARSIWA Commentaries (n 1) Article 51), para 154 (citing *Gabčíkovo-Nagymaros Project* (n 6)). On the incorrect authority, see discussion at nn 71 and 72.
[78] ARSIWA Commentaries (n 1) Part III, Chapter II, para 5.

Selected literature

Alland D, 'The Definition of Countermeasures' in Crawford J, Pellet A and Olleson S (eds), *The Law of International Responsibility* (OUP 2010).

Crawford J, Pellet A and Olleson S (eds), *The Law of International Responsibility* (OUP 2010).

Crawford J, *State Responsibility: The General Part* (CUP 2013).

McRae D, 'Countermeasures and Investment Arbitration' in M Kinnear and others (eds), *Building International Investment Law: The First 50 Years of ICSID* (Kluwer Law International 2015).

Paparinskis M, 'Circumstances Precluding Wrongfulness in International Investment Law' (2016) 31 ICSID Rev 484.

Paparinskis M, 'Investment Arbitration and the Law of Countermeasures' (2008) 79 BYBIL 264.

Stoegher E and Tams CJ, 'Swords, Shields and Other Beasts: The Role of Countermeasures in Investment Arbitration' (2022) 37 ICSID Rev 121.

Selected decisions

Application of the Interim Accord of 13 September 1995 (FYRM v Greece) [2011] ICJ Rep 644.

Archer Daniels Midlands Company and Tate & Lyle Ingredients Americas, Inc v Mexico, ICSID Case No ARB(AF)/04/05, Award, 21 November 2007.

Cargill, Inc v Mexico, ICSID Case No ARB(AF)/05/2, Award, 18 September 2009.

Corn Products International, Inc v Mexico, ICSID Case No ARB(AF)/04/01, Decision on Responsibility, 15 January 2008.

Gabčíkovo-Nagymaros Project (Hungary v Slovakia) [1997] ICJ Rep 7.

Article 55 of the ARSIWA

Lex specialis

Fernando Lusa Bordin

These articles do not apply where and to the extent that the conditions for the existence of an internationally wrongful act or the content or implementation of the international responsibility of a State are governed by special rules of international law.

A. *Lex specialis*, international investment law and State responsibility	1	I. Determining the scope of *lex specialis*	8
B. Applying *lex specialis* in investment disputes	6	II. *Lex generalis* in the application of *lex specialis*	11
		C. Conclusion: The impact of investment law on the *lex specialis* principle	18

A. *Lex specialis*, international investment law and State responsibility

1 In the Conclusions of the Work of the Study Group on the Fragmentation of International Law, the International Law Commission (ILC) explains the concept of *lex specialis* as follows:

> The maxim *lex specialis derogat legi generali* is a generally accepted technique of interpretation and conflict resolution in international law. It suggests that whenever two or more norms deal with the same subject matter, priority should be given to the norm that is more specific.[1]

2 The Commission identifies three rationales for *lex specialis*.[2] First, that 'such special law, being more concrete, often takes better account of the particular features of the context in which it is to be applied than any applicable general law'. Second, that the application of more specific rules often leads to 'a more equitable result'. Third, that more specific rules may 'better reflect the intent of the legal subjects'. This reference to the 'intent of the legal subjects' is key to understanding how, in addition to a principle guiding the identification of the applicable law, *lex specialis* also functions as a technique for law-making. As the International

---

[1] ILC, 'Conclusions of the work of the Study Group on the Fragmentation of International Law: Difficulties arising from the Diversification and Expansion of International Law' YILC 2006, Vol II, Part Two, 178 (hereafter ILC Conclusions on Fragmentation).

[2] ibid. For a rich theoretical exploration of the grounds and uses of the *lex specialis* principle, see U Linderfalk, 'Neither Fish, Nor Fowl A New Way to a Fuller Understanding of the lex specialis Principle' (2023) 25 ICLR 426.

Court of Justice explained in *North Sea Continental Shelf*, 'it is well understood that, in practice, rules of international law can, by agreement, be derogated from in particular cases, or as between particular parties'.[3] To return to the language employed by the ILC, 'most of international law is dispositive', and as such 'special law may be used to apply, clarify, update or modify, as well as set aside, general law'.[4]

International investment law provides a neat illustration of the use of treaties[5] to enact a *lex*   3
specialis that modifies the general law. The customary law on the treatment of aliens comprises rules that protect the property of foreigners by establishing an international minimum standard and imposing certain conditions for expropriation.[6] But the thousands of investment agreements that have been concluded since the second half of the twentieth century typically do two things. First, they confirm those default protections, while also clarifying and updating them.[7] Second, they modify and set aside the general law by adding new substantive standards (such as most-favoured nation treatment, national treatment, and umbrella clauses protecting contractual rights) and providing for compulsory forms of dispute settlement (most notably, investment treaty arbitration). So, in the words of the tribunal in *National Grid v Argentina*, 'the pre-eminence of ... lex specialis governing the scope of protection owed to the investor is the main purpose for concluding a bilateral treaty aimed at protecting foreign investments'.[8]

Article 55 of the Articles on the Responsibility of States for Internationally Wrongful Acts   4
(ARSIWA) confirms the applicability of the *lex specialis* principle to the rules governing 'the conditions for the existence of an internationally wrongful act or the content or implementation of the international responsibility of a State'. It is relevant for investment disputes because international investment law is a liability regime, geared towards securing reparation for foreign investors wronged by the States that host them. The most consequential way in which *lex specialis* has displaced the general law of State responsibility in the investment context is the adoption of dispute settlement clauses that allow investors to invoke the responsibility of a host State directly. Under customary international law, individuals lack the procedural capacity to bring international claims, and thus need to rely on their State of nationality to espouse those claims under the rules of diplomatic protection, after local remedies are exhausted. That default regime is set aside by a large number of investment agreements that empower investors to institute arbitral proceedings on the international plane.[9]

Lex specialis that affects other aspects of State responsibility is comparatively rarer. But in-   5
vestment agreements provide some noteworthy examples of special rules of attribution of conduct and special rules on remedies. Article 26(8) of the Energy Charter Treaty, for instance, prescribes that '[a]n award of arbitration concerning a measure of a sub-national government or authority of the disputing Contracting Party shall provide that the Contracting

---

[3] *North Sea Continental Shelf (Germany v Denmark; Germany v Netherlands)* (Judgment) [1969] ICJ Rep 3, para 72.
[4] ILC Conclusions on Fragmentation (n 1) 178.
[5] While the ILC clarifies that '[t]he source of the norm (whether treaty, custom or general principle of law) is not decisive' for the determination of the more specific standard in any given context, it points out that 'in practice, treaties often act as *lex specialis* by reference to the relevant customary law and general principles': ibid.
[6] See, eg, J Crawford, *Brownlie's Principles of Public International Law* (9th edn, OUP 2019) 591.
[7] As the tribunal in *Archer Daniels* observed, 'Section A of Chapter Eleven [of the NAFTA] offers a form of *lex specialis* to supplement the under-developed standards of customary international law relating to the treatment of aliens and property': *Archer Daniels Midland Company and Tate & Lyle Ingredients Americas, Inc v The United Mexican States*, ICSID Case No ARB (AF)/04/5, Award, 2007, para 117 (hereafter *ADM v Mexico*).
[8] *National Grid plc v The Argentine Republic*, UNCITRAL, Award, 2008, para 86.
[9] *ADM v Mexico* (n 7) para 118.

Party may pay monetary damages in lieu of any other remedy granted', thus limiting the competence of investment tribunals to determine the reparation owed to the investor.[10]

B. Applying *lex specialis* in investment disputes

6 While the basic notion of *lex specialis* is straightforward enough, its application can be challenging, especially in the context of State responsibility in investment law. That is because investment treaties adopting special rules are not always clear as to how those special rules relate with the *lex generalis*. Depending on the language employed in the treaty, it may not be evident to what extent the parties intended to deviate from customary international law. As the ILC clarifies in its commentaries to the ARSIWA:

> For the *lex specialis* principle to apply it is not enough that the same subject matter is dealt with by two provisions; there must be some actual inconsistency between them, or else a discernible intention that one provision is to exclude the other. Thus, the question is essentially one of interpretation.[11]

7 Following this logic, those tasked with identifying the applicable law must proceed in two steps. The first is to establish the exact scope of the relevant special rule. The second is to consider the extent to which the *lex generalis* can play a role in the application of the special rule, that is, if it is either applicable alongside the special rule or if it can otherwise inform the interpretation of the special rule.

I. Determining the scope of *lex specialis*

8 Determining the scope of a *lex specialis* is a process of 'legal qualification'[12] to be effected with recourse to appropriate techniques of legal reasoning and interpretation.[13]

9 Investment treaty arbitration provides several illustrations of this form of legal qualification. To mention one, the tribunal in *Adel A Hamadi el Tamimi v Sultanate of Oman* was asked to apply Article 10.1.2 of the US–Oman Free Trade Agreement (FTA), according to which investment protection standards in the treaty 'shall apply to a state enterprise or other person when it exercises any regulatory, administrative, or other governmental authority delegated to it by that Party'. It qualified that provision as a special rule on the attribution to the host State of conduct carried out by State enterprises, excluding from the purview of the treaty cases where those enterprises perform acts that any ordinary private company would be in a position to perform.[14] A similar approach was followed by the tribunal in *Mesa Power v*

---

[10] A couple of examples of treaty provisions creating *lex specialis* regarding attribution of conduct are discussed in Section B.II. below.
[11] ILC, 'Draft Articles on the Responsibility of States for Internationally Wrongful Acts, with commentaries' YILC 2001, Vol II, Part Two, 31, Article 55 para 4 (hereafter ARSIWA Commentaries).
[12] See A Gourgourinis, '*Lex Specialis* in WTO and Investment Protection Law' (2010) 53 GYIL 569, 593 (hereafter Gourgourinis) (defining 'qualification as the intellectual operation of classifying facts and legal norms, as well as their interaction, in the ambit of a particular dispute').
[13] See in this Commentary: Andreas Kulick and Panos Merkouris, 'Article 31 of the VCLT'; Esmé Shirlow and Michael Waibel, 'Article 32 of the VCLT', Peter Tzeng, 'Article 33 of the VCLT'.
[14] *Adel A Hamadi Al Tamimi v Sultanate of Oman*, ICSID Case No ARB/11/33, Award, 3 November 2015, para 321 (hereafter *Adel A Hamadi Al Tamimi v Sultanate of Oman*).

Canada, applying Article 1503(2) of the North American Free Trade Agreement (NAFTA), similar in language to Article 10.1.2 of the US–Oman FTA. The tribunal found that the provision established 'a special regime which distinguishes between a NAFTA Party and its enterprises'.[15]

Determining the scope of a *lex specialis* is not always straightforward, as the contradictory outcomes that the tribunals reached in *British Caribbean Bank Limited v The Government of Belize* and *Vestey Group Limited v Venezuela* show. Both the Belize–UK Bilateral Investment Treaty (BIT) and the UK–Venezuela BIT contained a provision setting out a standard for compensation for the expropriation of foreign investment.[16] But the claimants in both cases sought to persuade the respective tribunals not to rely on that provision on the grounds that it applied to lawful expropriations only, that is, to expropriations conducted in the public interest and respecting due process. To unlawful expropriations, they argued, the potentially more generous principle of full reparation codified in Article 34 ARSIWA should apply instead. The tribunal in *Vestey Group* accepted the argument. Recognizing that States were free to derogate from the 'general framework of responsibility', it nevertheless found that the UK–Venezuela BIT did not 'purport to establish a special regime of reparation for expropriations which are unlawful due to reasons other than the absence of compensation'.[17] That being the case, the principle of 'full reparation under customary international law' remained applicable.[18] But the tribunal in *British Caribbean Bank* rejected the argument. It took the view that the compensation provision, 'being a *lex specialis*', applied to all cases of expropriation because the language that the parties had 'specifically negotiated' established no distinction between lawful and unlawful expropriations.[19] Thus, while the two tribunals agreed on the characterization of the compensation provisions as *lex specialis*, they disagreed on their scope—the extent to which the parties intended to deviate from the customary rules of State responsibility.[20]

II. *Lex generalis* in the application of *lex specialis*

Once the scope of *lex specialis* is ascertained, the question arises of what role, if any, the general law has to play. Recognizing the applicability of a special (treaty) rule often results in the exclusion of the general (customary) rule that would otherwise have governed the factual scenario. As the tribunal in *Adel A Hamadi el Tamimi* held, the special rule of attribution of

---

[15] *Mesa Power Group, LLC v Government of Canada*, UNCITRAL, PCA Case No 2012-17, Award, 24 March 2016, para 362 (hereafter *Mesa Power Group, LLC v Government of Canada*).
[16] Compare Article 5 of the Belize–UK with Article 5 of the UK–Venezuela BIT.
[17] *Vestey Group Ltd v Bolivarian Republic of Venezuela*, ICSID Case No ARB/06/4, Award, 15 April 2016, para 329.
[18] ibid paras 325–31.
[19] *British Caribbean Bank Limited v The Government of Belize*, PCA Case No 2010-18, Award, 19 December 2014, paras 259–62.
[20] A similar example from the trade context is offered by *United States—Definitive Anti-Dumping and Countervailing Duties on Certain Products from China*. The Panel concluded that 'the taxonomy set forth in Article 1.1 of the SCM Agreement [was] at heart [a special] attribution rule' that excluded the application of the rule in Article 5 of the ARSIWA. In contrast, while confirming that 'the treaty being *applied* is the SCM Agreement', the Appellate Body noted that 'the attribution rules of the ILC Articles are to be *taken into account*', and ultimately found that the phrase 'public body' found in the SCM Agreement shared 'certain attributes with the concept of "government"'. Compare the Report of the Panel, WT/DS379/R, 22 October 2010, paras 8.90–8.91 with the Report of the Appellate Body, WT/DS379/AB/R, 11 March 2011, paras 314–22.

conduct in the US–Oman FTA entailed that 'any broader principles of State responsibility under customary international law or as represented in the ILC Articles cannot be directly relevant'.[21] In a similar vein, the tribunal in *Mesa Power* concluded that Article 1503(2) of the NAFTA constituted 'a *lex specialis* that excludes the application of Article 5 of the ILC Articles'.[22] But this rule of thumb needs to be qualified in at least three ways.

12 First, the *lex specialis* principle cannot exclude the application of a *lex generalis* that is hierarchically superior. As the ILC clarifies, 'States cannot, even as between themselves, provide for legal consequences of a breach of their mutual obligations which would authorize acts contrary to peremptory norms of general international law'.[23] The assumption that underlies the operation of the *lex specialis* principle is that the special rule has 'at least the same legal rank' as the general rule.[24]

13 Second, a provision in a treaty may expressly incorporate a rule of customary international law. In the investment context, that is the case with investment agreements comprising a fair and equitable treatment clause and/or a full protection and security clause that make express reference to the international minimum standard.[25] In that scenario, the *lex specialis* and *lex generalis* are applicable in tandem, but there is no real substantive difference between them except insofar as the text of the treaty provision qualifies the customary rule being incorporated.

14 Third, the *lex generalis* may be relevant for the interpretation of the *lex specialis* in accordance with the principle of systemic integration articulated in Article 31(3)(c) of the Vienna Convention on the Law of Treaties (VCLT).[26] As the Iran–US Claims Tribunal observed, when construing the expropriation clause in the 1955 Treaty of Amity, Economic Relations, and Consular Rights:

> As a *lex specialis* in the relations between the two countries, the Treaty supersedes the *lex generalis*, namely customary international law. This does not mean, however, that the latter is irrelevant in the instant Case. On the contrary, the rules of customary law may be useful in order to fill in possible lacunae of the Treaty, to ascertain the meaning of undefined terms in its text or, more generally, to aid interpretation and implementation of its provisions.[27]

15 In a similar vein, the ILC identified a presumption that 'the parties are taken to refer to customary international law and general principles of law for all questions which the treaty does not itself resolve in express terms'.[28] That entails that whenever 'the treaty is silent on the applicable law' the interpreter must 'look for rules developed in another part of international law to resolve the point'.[29] Accordingly, in *ADM v Mexico*, the tribunal observed that even if 'Chapter Eleven of the NAFTA constitutes *lex specialis* in respect of its express content', 'customary

---

[21] *Adel A Hamadi Al Tamimi v Sultanate of Oman* (n 14) para 321. See in this Commentary: Chester Brown, 'Article 4 of the ARSIWA'; Jorge E Viñuales and Oliver Hailes, 'Article 5 of the ARSIWA'; Jonathan Bonnitcha and Alisha Mathew, 'Article 6 of the ARSIWA and Article 7 of the ARIO'; Chester Brown, 'Article 7 of the ARSIWA'; Jorge E Viñuales and Alina Papanastasiou, 'Article 8 of the ARSIWA'.
[22] *Mesa Power Group, LLC v Government of Canada* (n 15) para 362.
[23] ARSIWA Commentaries (n 11) Article 55 para 2.
[24] ibid.
[25] See, eg, Article 9.6 of the 2015 Trans-Pacific Partnership Agreement.
[26] Article 31(3)(c) of the VCLT provides that account shall be taken, in the interpretation of treaty, of 'any relevant rules of international law applicable in the relations between the parties'. See in this Commentary: Andreas Kulick and Panos Merkouris, 'Article 31 of the VCLT'.
[27] *Amoco v Iran*, Case No 56, Chamber 3, Award No 310-65-3, 1987, para 112.
[28] ILC Conclusions on Fragmentation (n 1) 180.
[29] ibid.

international law continues to govern all matters not covered' there.[30] The question the tribunal faced was whether a breach of the BIT by the host State to the detriment of the investor could be excused by countermeasures taken against the home State. The tribunal decided that because 'Chapter Eleven neither provides nor specifically prohibits the use of countermeasures ... the question of whether the countermeasures defence is available to the Respondent is not a question of *lex specialis*, but of customary international law'.[31] Following a similar approach, in *von Pezold v Zimbabwe*, the tribunal ruled that it was entitled to award the remedy of restitution because, among other reasons, neither of the applicable BITs prohibited it.[32]

Like the Iran–US Claims Tribunal, the ILC also accepts that customary rules and general principles of law are relevant when 'the treaty rule is unclear or open-textured' or when 'the terms used in the treaty have a recognized meaning in customary international law or under general principle of law'.[33] That is illustrated by the way the *El Paso* tribunal dealt with claims by an investor who suffered losses as a result of Argentina's economic collapse at the turn of the century. Central to Argentina's legal defence was Article XI of the Argentina–US BIT, which provided that nothing in the treaty would preclude the taking of 'measures necessary for the maintenance of public order, the fulfilment of its obligations with respect to the maintenance or restoration of international peace or security, or the protection of [the parties'] own essential security interests'. The tribunal decided that Article XI had to be 'interpreted taking into account general principles of international law, some of those being embodied in Article 25 [ARSIWA]', in particular the notion that 'necessity may not be invoked by a State as a ground for precluding wrongfulness if ... [the] State has contributed to the situation of necessity'.[34] It thus read that rule into the Argentina–US BIT.[35] **16**

There is a risk, inevitably, that in exploring the synergies between *lex generalis* and *lex specialis* investment tribunals may conflate the two in problematic ways, even exposing the award to annulment challenges. In *Sempra v Argentina*, like in *El Paso v Argentina*, the tribunal was faced with the question of how Article XI of the Argentina–US BIT related to the customary defence of necessity. It acknowledged the relevance of the *lex specialis* principle, accepting that 'a treaty regime specifically dealing with a given matter will prevail over more general rules of customary law'. Yet, it concluded that, because Article XI of the Argentina–US BIT 'did not deal with the legal elements necessary for the legitimate invocation of a state of necessity', those legal elements were to be found 'under customary law'.[36] That led the tribunal to dismiss Argentina's argument on the grounds that the requirement of necessity had not been met and to rule that there was 'no need to undertake a further judicial review under Article XI given that this Article does not set out conditions different from customary law in such regard'.[37] When Argentina later instituted annulment proceedings, the ad hoc **17**

---

[30] *ADM v Mexico* (n 7) para 119.
[31] ibid para 120.
[32] *Bernhard von Pezold and Others v Republic of Zimbabwe*, ICSID Case No ARB/10/15, Award, 28 July 2015, paras 709–17. In considering cases like *Archer Daniels* and *von Pezold*, it is important to recall that the ARSIWA do not purport to deal with the content and implementation of State responsibility towards entities other than States. Yet, investment tribunals often rely on the rules codified in Parts Two and Three of the ARSIWA.
[33] ILC Conclusions on Fragmentation (n 1) 180. Whether that is the case is itself a potentially tricky question of interpretation, as exemplified by the *United States—Definitive Anti-Dumping and Countervailing Duties on Certain Products from China* discussed in note 21 above.
[34] *El Paso Energy International Company v The Argentine Republic*, ICSID Case No ARB/03/15, Award, 31 October 2011, paras 513 and 617. See in this Commentary: Federica Paddeu, 'Article 25 of the ARSIWA'.
[35] *Sempra Energy International v The Argentine Republic*, ICSID Case No ARB/02/16, Award, 2007, para 378.
[36] ibid.
[37] ibid para 388.

committee offered a harsh critique of the tribunal's handling of Article XI. Article XI and the customary defence of necessity, the ad hoc committee explained, had to be distinguished: the former was relevant to determining whether the BIT had been breached to begin with, while the latter was relevant to determining whether the wrongfulness of a breach of the BIT was precluded.[38] The two pleas provided independent reasons why Argentina might not be liable for violating the BIT, which had to be considered in turn. By adopting 'Article 25 of the ILC Articles as the primary law to be applied, rather than Article XI of the BIT'[39]—by conflating *lex generalis* and *lex specialis*, in other words—the tribunal committed 'a fundamental error in identifying and applying the applicable law', which constituted 'an excess of powers within the meaning of the International Centre for Settlement of Investment Disputes (ICSID) Convention'.[40] The award was therefore annulled.

C. Conclusion: The impact of investment law on the *lex specialis* principle

18 In an insightful study published in 2010, Anastasios Gourgourinis suggested that international investment treaty arbitration, together with dispute settlement at the World Trade Organization, contribute to our understanding of the *lex specialis* principle both in quantitative and qualitative terms. Not only do those two systems feature the principle more than any other subfields of international law, they also lend themselves to the sketching of a 'generic operative framework for *lex specialis*', significant also outside the 'particular adjudicative domain of international economic law'.[41] That assessment remains correct, as international investment law has indeed provided a fertile ground for the application of the *lex specialis* principle and for the exploration of the intricate relationship between special (treaty) rules of treaty law and general (customary) rules.

19 The contribution that investment treaty arbitration has been making to the elucidation of *lex specialis* is not so much conceptual as practical. Investment tribunals have remained faithful to the basic tenets articulated in the work of the ILC, but they have had to work out solutions in practice that are valuable both for dealing with future cases and for the drafting of treaty provisions where the scope of *lex specialis* is defined in the first instance.

---

[38] *Sempra Energy International v The Argentine Republic*, ICSID Case No ARB/02/16, Decision on the Argentine Republic's Application for Annulment of the Award, 2010, para 200. A clear explanation of this point is provided by the ad hoc committee in *CMS v Argentina*: 'Article XI is a threshold requirement: if it applies, the substantive obligations under the Treaty do not apply. By contrast, Article 25 is an excuse which is only relevant once it has been decided that there has otherwise been a breach of those substantive obligations ...': *CMS Gas Transmission Company v The Republic of Argentina*, ICSID Case No ARB/01/8, Decision of the ad hoc Committee on the Application for Annulment of the Argentine Republic, 25 September 2007, paras 129–30 (hereafter *CMS v Argentina*, Annulment).

[39] ibid para 208.

[40] ibid paras 208–09. In contrast, the ad hoc committee in *CMS v Argentina* declined to annul the award because, unlike in *Sempra*, the tribunal was found to have applied Article XI, however defectively: *CMS v Argentina*, Annulment (n 38) paras 135–36.

[41] Gourgourinis (n 13) para 580.

Selected literature

Banaszewska DM, 'Lex Specialis' in *Max-Planck Encyclopedia of Public International Law* (2015).

Fragmentation of International Law: Difficulties Arising from the Diversification and Expansion of International Law, Report of the Study Group of the International Law Commission, finalized by Mr Martti Koskenniemi, A/CN.4/L.682 (2006).

Gourgourinis A, '*Lex Specialis* in WTO and Investment Protection Law' (2010) 53 GYIL 569.

ILC, 'Conclusions of the work of the Study Group on the Fragmentation of International Law: Difficulties Arising from the Diversification and Expansion of International Law' YILC 2006, Vol II, Part Two.

Linderfalk U, 'Neither Fish, Nor Fowl A New Way to a Fuller Understanding of the lex specialis Principle' (2023) 25 ICLR 426.

Selected decisions

Archer Daniels Midland Company and Tate & Lyle Ingredients Americas, Inc v The United Mexican States, ICSID Case No ARB (AF)/04/5, Award, 2007.

Sempra Energy International v The Argentine Republic, ICSID Case No ARB/02/16, Decision on the Argentine Republic's Application for Annulment of the Award, 2010.

British Caribbean Bank Limited v The Government of Belize, PCA Case No 2010-18, Award, 2014.

Adel A Hamadi Al Tamimi v Sultanate of Oman, ICSID Case No ARB/11/33, Award, 2015.

Vestey Group Ltd v Bolivarian Republic of Venezuela, ICSID Case No ARB/06/4, Award, 2016.

PART III
STATE SUCCESSION, SOURCES AND STATE IMMUNITY

The procedure for succession to bilateral investment treaties

Arman Sarvarian

A. Introduction	1	C. Devolution agreements	16
B. Verbal agreements	5	I. Concept	16
I. Concept and form	5	II. Effect	17
II. Express agreement	8	D. General declarations	20
III. Implicit agreement	10	E. Agreement by Conduct	24
		F. Conclusion	27

A. Introduction

This entry addresses the procedural rules of general international law by which a State may succeed to a Bilateral Investment Treaty (BIT).[1] This issue affects international investment law in two respects: first, the transfer of rights and obligations in a BIT from a predecessor to a successor,[2] and second, the jurisdiction of an investment arbitral tribunal based on that treaty.[3] The entry does not deal with the specific rules of succession with respect to partial and total succession;[4] rather, it addresses the methods by which a successor may succeed to a BIT.

Whereas succession to treaties has tended to assume pride of place in the study of State succession by international lawyers, financial (i.e. State property and access to international credit) and constitutional (i.e. government administration and continuity of law) matters tend to be more urgent for successors. Unless a core national interest requires the rapid adoption of policy,[5] the question of succession to treaties has often been postponed or

---

[1] Although it is possible for a succession to affect a plurilateral (closed multilateral) treaty containing a chapter on investment, such as the USMCA, this has yet to occur in practice.

[2] In this entry, a State succession is defined as 'a transfer of territorial title from one State to another'. This definition reflects customary international law and differs from Articles 2(1)(b) of the two Vienna Conventions on Succession of States of 1978 and 1983: 'the replacement of one State by another in the responsibility for the international relations of territory'. See further A Sarvarian, *The Law of State Succession: Principles and Practice* (Oxford University Press 2024).

[3] eg, P Dumberry, *A Guide to State Succession in International Investment Law* (Edward Elgar Publishing 2018) 3–186 (hereafter Dumberry).

[4] See in this Commentary: James Devaney and Christian Tams, 'Succession in respect of cession, unification and separation of States'.

[5] eg, 'Problems of State Succession in Africa: Statement of the Prime Minister of Tanganyika', 11(4) ICLQ (1962) 1210–14; M Whiteman, *Digest of International Law*, Vol II (US Department of State 1963) 1000–01 (hereafter Whiteman).

overlooked.[6] Consequently, there can be considerable delay before a successor express its position with respect to the treaties of the predecessor.

3   Although the scope of the entry corresponds to Articles 8, 9, and 24 of the Vienna Convention on the Succession of States with respect to Treaties 1978 (VCSST),[7] the low participation of States in that treaty[8] means that it has never been applied directly to a succession. The only example to date of a succession involving a predecessor that was party to the VCSST is Montenegro in 2006;[9] however, Montenegro did not invoke the procedure prescribed in Article 7 for the retroactive application of the VCSST to its own succession. The only example of successors invoking Article 7 to apply the VCSST to their own successions are Czechia and Slovakia;[10] yet, no counterparty made the requisite declaration of acceptance.[11]

4   The scope for the direct applicability of the VCSST to BITs is limited to a declaration of retroactive application by a successor to its own succession with a corresponding declaration of acceptance of that declaration by the counterparty to the treaty. Successions not regulated by the VCSST are governed by customary international law and general principles of law.[12] Insofar as provisions of the VCSST might reflect customary international law, previous or subsequent State practice and *opīniōnēs juris* must support them.[13] The guiding question for this entry is: how do arbitral tribunals and domestic courts interpret and apply the rules of State succession in investment disputes?

B. Verbal agreements

I. Concept and form

5   Customary international law provides that a successor may succeed to a bilateral treaty by agreement with the counterparty, subject to its eligibility.[14] Neither the successor[15] nor the counterparty[16] is obliged to agree to the succession. Whereas a 'single succession' to one of the two original counterparties is usual, a 'double succession' entailing a succession to each counterparty has also occurred.[17] Agreement on succession to a bilateral treaty may be reached by: (1) an exchange of words with respect to that treaty; (2) an implied application to that treaty of a broader agreement on succession; and (3) actions and

---

[6] eg, UN Doc A/CN.4/263 (29 May 1972), 56. While Mauritius notified the UN Secretary-General of the outcome of its review of multilateral treaties extended to the Colony and signalled its intention to undertake another review of bilateral treaties, there is no published record of it having been completed—ibid 38.

[7] 1946 UNTS 3.

[8] 23 States are party <https://treaties.un.org/Pages/showDetails.aspx?objid=0800000280044a0e&clang=_en> accessed 23 October 2023.

[9] 2390 UNTS (2006) 228, A-33356; *Multilateral Treaties Deposited with the Secretary-General*, UN Doc ST/LEG/SER.E/26 (1 April 2009), Vol I, xxxii (n 1).

[10] 1946 UNTS 4; 2073 UNTS 240–41.

[11] Dumberry (n 3) 48–50; V Mikulka, 'Article 34—Succession d'États en cas de séparation de parties d'un État' in G Distefano, G Gaggioli and A Hêche (eds), *La Convention de Vienne de 1978 sur la succession d'États en matière de traités*, Vol I (Bruylant 2016) 1153–207, 1191–207.

[12] See in this Commentary: Patrick Dumberry, 'Article 38 of the ICJ Statute: Sources'.

[13] eg, UN Doc A/73/10 (2018) 122, Conclusion 11.

[14] eg, 114 ILR 606, 623, 626, 629–33.

[15] eg, UN Doc A/CN.4/229 (28 May 1970), §§84–86, 100, 106–08; UN Doc A/CN.4/253/Add.1 (9 April 1971) para 50.

[16] eg, International Law Association, *The Effect of Independence on Treaties* (London: Stevens and Sons 1965) 115; UN Doc A/CN.4/229 (28 May 1970), §§84–86; UN Doc A/CN.4/253/Add.1 (9 April 1971), para 49.

[17] eg, UN Doc A/CN.4/229 (28 May 1970), paras 36, 111.

omissions whereby the successor and counterparty apply the treaty. Verbal agreements are typically concluded by a written treaty[18] but can also take the form of an oral treaty[19] or a written instrument other than a treaty.[20] A 'meeting of minds' is the key requirement for an agreement.[21]

Article 24 of the VCSST states that succession to a bilateral treaty may be done when the newly independent State and the counterparty 'expressly so agree' or 'by reason of their conduct they are to be considered as having so agreed'.[22] The latter was also described by the International Law Commission (ILC) as 'tacit' agreement,[23] a term that one national court has recently described as 'not entirely helpful'.[24] Whereas Switzerland[25] and Jamaica[26] have considered Article 24 to reflect customary law,[27] it expresses the customary rule only in part: it does not distinguish between an implied agreement, performed verbally, and an agreement reached by actions or omissions. In positing the two forms of agreement disjunctively rather than conjunctively, it overlooks the possibility of agreement being reached by a combination of techniques; for example, an acceptance by conduct of the counterparty of a notification of succession by the successor.[28]

When a successor succeeds to a bilateral treaty concluded by the predecessor and applied to its territory, the treaty is usually duplicated: the treaty between predecessor and the counterparty continues and a clone of it is created between the successor and the counterparty. No treaty relationship results between the predecessor and the successor: amendment or termination of the one treaty, for example, has no effect on the other.[29] The duplicate treaty is interpreted according to the altered parties and circumstances; in the absence of amendment, for example, references to the predecessor are construed as references to the successor. This customary rule is accurately expressed not only for 'newly independent States' but also for other classes of succession by Articles 25 and 26 of the VCSST,[30] though they overlook the rare occurrence of the substitution of the predecessor by the successor in the original treaty.[31]

---

[18] Vienna Convention on the Law of Treaties, 1155 UNTS 331, Article 2(1)(a); Philippe Gautier, 'Article 2 Convention of 1969' in Olivier Corten and Pierre Klein (eds), *The Vienna Convention on the Law of Treaties: A Commentary*, Vol I (OUP 2011) 37–43.

[19] eg, *UN Materials on Succession of States*, UN Doc ST/LEG/SER.B/14 (1967), 211–13 (hereafter *UN Materials*).

[20] eg, *Gold Pool v Kazakhstan*, PCA Case No 2016-23, Award of 30 July 2020 (unpublished) paras 49–50 (hereafter *Gold Pool v Kazakhstan*).

[21] ibid para 71.

[22] VCSST, Article 24(1); Draft Articles on Succession of States in respect of Treaties with commentaries, YILC 1974, Vol II, Part One, 174, 236–41 (hereafter ILC Articles).

[23] ILC Articles (n 22) 239, para 12, 240, para 16

[24] *Gold Pool v Kazakhstan* (n 20) para 3.

[25] 75 ILR 107, 110–12.

[26] 73 ILR 44, 46–48, 53–54; 72 ILR 63, 66–74.

[27] A Distefano, 'Article 24—Conditions requises pour qu'un traité soit considéré comme étant en vigueur dans le cas d'une succession d'États' in G Distefano, G Gaggioli and A Hêche (eds), *La Convention de Vienne de 1978 sur la succession d'États en matière de traités*, Vol I (Bruylant 2016) 833–909, 839–46.

[28] eg, *Extradition of Sacirbegovic*, US Southern District Court for New York (18 January 2005), No 03 Crim Misc 01 Page 19 (SDNY 18 January 2005), 21–25 (hereafter *Sacirbegovic*); *Extradition of Platko*, US Southern District Court for California (26 July 2002), 213 F Supp 2d 1229 (2002), 1232–33 (hereafter *Platko*).

[29] eg, 75 ILR 107, 110–12; 22 AILC (1969–78) 261, 263–64; 96 ILR 105, 107–08; *UN Materials* (n 19) 193–94; *Temple of Preah Vihear (Cambodia v Thailand)(Preliminary Objections)*, Vol I (Pleadings), Preliminary Objections of Thailand (23 May 1960), 145–47, paras 40–41 (hereafter *Preah Vihear*); Pleadings, Oral Arguments, Documents, Vol II, 22, 31–40, 106–09.

[30] VCSST, Articles 25–26; ILC Articles (n 22) 241–44.

[31] eg, UN Doc A/CN.4/253/Add.1 (9 April 1971) para 84.

II. Express agreement

8 An express agreement may be concluded between a successor and a counterparty that specifically refers to a treaty. This could be a succession agreement for a single treaty[32] or a list of treaties that includes the treaty in question.[33] Over the past thirty years, succession agreements have often included a list of treaties that are replaced by new treaties or otherwise declared to have no application between the parties; this might also be accompanied by a list of treaties to which succession is agreed not to apply. Examples include agreements concluded by counterparties with Azerbaijan,[34] North Macedonia,[35] Bosnia,[36] the FRY,[37] and Montenegro.[38]

9 An express agreement not to succeed to a treaty concluded after a decided dispute with respect to the status of that treaty does not impact on that dispute. This issue arose in the set-aside proceedings before the courts of Singapore with respect to the *Sanum v Laos* investor–State arbitration: amidst a lack of evidence concerning the position of China on the extension to Macao of the Chinese–Laotian BIT after the retrocession of Macao by Portugal in 1999, the arbitral tribunal held the general rule of automatic extension in Article 15 of the VCSST to apply as customary international law.[39] After the Award of 13 December 2013, China and Laos agreed on 7 and 19 February 2014 that their treaty did not apply to Macao.[40] On 29 September 2016, the Court of Appeal of Singapore overruled the High Court of Singapore to uphold the Award on Jurisdiction on the ground, *inter alia*, that the 'doctrine of

---

[32] eg, UN Doc A/CN.4/229 (28 May 1970), paras 23, 33, 46; UN Doc A/CN.4/253/Add.1 (9 April 1971), para 105.

[33] eg, Switzerland–Montenegro, Exchange of notes on the maintenance in force of applicable agreements, 29 June and 10 July 2007, Switzerland Treaty Database, No 999932382002, RO 2008 1737 (French, German, Italian); 1046 *Bundesgesetzblatt* (28 December 1994) (German); 2076 UNTS 3.

[34] eg, 2420 UNTS 114.

[35] eg, Netherlands–North Macedonia, Exchange of notes, 's-Gravenhage, 27 June and 11 July 1994, Netherlands Treaty Database, No 011806, (Dutch); France–North Macedonia, Agreement on the succession of Macedonia, Paris, and Skopje, 13 and 14 December 1995, 188 *Journal Officiel de la République Française* (13 August 1996), 12279 (French); Romania–North Macedonia, Protocol on the bilateral legal framework, Skopje, 8 March 1996 (20 July 1998), Romania Treaty Database (Romanian).

[36] eg, Netherlands–Bosnia, Exchange of notes, Sarajevo, 21 September 1995, 29 February 1996 and 25 August 1998, Netherlands Treaty Database, No 011803 (Dutch); France–Bosnia, Agreement on succession, Paris and Sarajevo (3 and 4 December 2003), 26 *Journal Officiel de la République Française* (31 January 2004) 2225 (French); Russia–Bosnia, Agreement on inventory of agreements, 13 March 2002, Russia Treaty Database, No 20020141 (Russian); Spain–Bosnia, Agreement on succession, Madrid and Sarajevo (21 January and 11 February 2004), 68 *Boletín Oficial del Estado* (19 March 2004), 12202 (Spanish).

[37] Netherlands–FRY, Exchange of notes, 's-Gravenhage, 20 August 2002, Netherlands Treaty Database, No 011802; France–FRY, Agreement on the succession of Serbia and Montenegro, Paris, 26 March 2003, 2239 UNTS 325, Article 1, Annex; Switzerland–FRY, Exchange of notes, 18 March 1998, Switzerland Treaty Database, No 99991137 (unpublished, French); Mexico–SFRY, Trade Agreement, Mexico City, 17 March 1950 (25 September 1953), Mexico Treaty Database (Spanish); China–FRY, Agreement on succession, Belgrade, 3 February 2006, 65(2) Службени гласник републике србије (2 June 2009), 235 (Serbo-Croatian); 2420 UNTS 359, Article 1; Portugal–FRY, Agreement on Succession, Lisbon, 3 November 2003, 101 *Diário da República* I-A (29 April 2004) (Portuguese).

[38] Austria–Montenegro, Bilateral agreements in force, *Bundesgesetzblatt* III 124/2007 (23 November 2007) (German); Finland–Montenegro, Agreement on the application of certain treaties, Helsinki, 18 April 2007, 45 *Sähköinen sopimussarja* (2007), 456 (Finnish); UNTS I-54107; Netherlands–Montenegro, Agreement on continued application of treaties, Belgrade and Podgorica, 15 November 2006 and 18 January 2007, Netherlands Treaty Database No 011614; Moldova–Montenegro, Agreement on succession, Chisinau, 10 December 2008 (12 December 2008), Moldova Bilateral Treaty List, 137, No B01846 (Romanian); Italy–Montenegro, Memorandum on Succession, Podgorica (19 October 2012), Italy Treaty Database, No BILMNE005 (Italian).

[39] *Sanum Investments Ltd v Laos*, PCA Case No 2013-13, Jurisdiction, 13 December 2013, paras 18–23, 51–56, 232–36 (hereafter *Sanum v Laos*, PCA Award). See in this Commentary: James G Devaney and Christian J Tams, 'Succession in respect of cession, unification and separation of States'.

[40] *Sanum Investments Ltd v Laos*, Singapore Court of Appeal, Judgment (29 September 2016) [2016] SGCA 57, para 10 (hereafter *Sanum v Laos*, Singapore Court of Appeal).

the critical date'[41] had rendered their 'self-serving' agreement of scant weight due to having being concluded after the dispute had been crystallized by the initiation of the arbitration proceedings on 14 August 2012.[42] China lists the treaty with Laos not to be applicable to Hong Kong or Macao[43] and there is no recorded practice of extension of Chinese bilateral treaties to Hong Kong[44] or Macao.[45]

III. Implicit agreement

A successor and counterparty may implicitly agree to a succession to a bilateral treaty without naming it. The treaty may be implied in a general agreement to succeed to each of the applicable treaties of the predecessor and counterparty without listing them.[46] A counterparty may acquiesce[47] to a notification by the successor of succession to a single treaty[48] or to all of the treaties of the predecessor.[49] The successor and counterparty may agree to perform a particular treaty without expressing their position on its status;[50] they might amend the treaty in doing so.[51] They might annex an incomplete list of treaties to their succession agreement, yet intend the agreement to apply to other treaties that had been applied to the successor.[52] They might agree to settle a dispute on the basis of that treaty.[53] **10**

The question of the effect of a notification by a successor to a counterparty reportedly arose in the investor–State arbitration of *Deripaska v Montenegro*.[54] Vague language was apparently employed by Montenegro in two notes communicated to Russia with respect to its succession to the 1995 Russia–FRY BIT, which were interpreted to be broad statements expressing its general intent regarding treaties in force for the FRY rather than notifications specifically directed to Russia.[55] The arbitral tribunal seemingly held that, even if there were a general rule of unilateral declarations of general intent comprising a legal undertaking to be bound by all of the treaties of a predecessor, which was not the case, succession to bilateral treaties **11**

---

[41] See in this Commentary: Cameron Miles, 'Cross-cutting procedural powers of international courts and tribunals'.
[42] *Sanum v Laos*, Singapore Court of Appeal (n 40) paras 11, 64–70, 100–21.
[43] The China treaty database includes an option to search for bilateral treaties applicable to Hong Kong and Macao; however, such databases are to be treated with caution as evidence.
[44] Hong Kong SAR <https://www.doj.gov.hk/en/external/international_agreements.html> accessed 23 October 2023. See, eg, ILDC 277 (PL 2003), paras F1–F5, H1–H3, A1–A2, A5–A6; 122 ILR 659, 667–68, 672–77; *Edwards v The Queen*, Federal Court of Appeal of Ontario (14 October 2003), [2003] FCA 378, paras 17–28.
[45] Macao SAR <https://www.io.gov.mo/pt/legis/int/> (Portuguese) accessed 23 October 2023.
[46] eg, Germany–Georgia, Agreement on the continued validity of the German–Soviet treaties, Bonn, 19 May and 9 September 1992, II *Bundesgesetzblatt* 1992, 1128 (German).
[47] See in this Commentary: Cameron Miles, 'Cross-cutting procedural powers of international courts and tribunals'.
[48] eg, *UN Materials* (n 19) 229–30.
[49] eg, 603 UNTS 19; ILA Handbook (n) 195; UN Doc A/CN.4/229 (28 May 1970) para 104, *UN Materials* (n 19) 218; United States Department of State, *Treaties in Force* (2021) 94 (hereafter *Treaties in Force*).
[50] eg, Whiteman (n 5) 987.
[51] eg, UN Doc A/CN.4/253/Add.1 (9 April 1971) paras 72–83.
[52] eg, Switzerland–Ukraine, Exchange of notes, 4 August 1997, No 99991057 (unpublished); ILDC 340 (CH 2005) paras H7–H10, A2–A8.
[53] Botswana-Namibia, Special Agreement (15 May 1996) https://www.icj-cij.org/public/files/case-related/98/7185.pdf accessed 23 October 2023, Article 1; [1999] ICJ Rep 1045, para 18.
[54] *Oleg Vladimirovich Deripaska v Montenegro*, PCA Case No 2017-07, Award, 25 October 2019 (unpublished).
[55] The tribunal also drew upon notification procedure for multilateral treaties—V Djanic, 'Revealed: Reasons Surface for Tribunal's Decision that Montenegro was Not Bound by the Russia-Yugoslavia BIT', *Investment Arbitration Reporter* (3 July 2020).

was qualitatively different: unilateral statements not confirmed by the other side were insufficient to continue a bilateral treaty.[56]

12 The arbitral tribunal reportedly rejected the adequacy of the general declarations of succession to the treaties of the State Union of Serbia and Montenegro made by Montenegro in its declaration of independence.[57] While the Award has not yet been published, the question of acquiescence by Russia to the notes communicated by Montenegro appears not to have been argued by the Claimant. Similarly, whether estoppel was applicable to Montenegro in challenging jurisdiction after having communicated its affirmative position to succeed to the treaty in its notes to the UN Member States and to Russia.[58]

13 The question of implied agreement on succession arose in *World Wide Minerals v Kazakhstan* in which an investor–State arbitral tribunal concluded in 2015 that Kazakhstan had succeeded to the 1989 Soviet–Canadian BIT; Canada had intervened to aver that it considered the treaty 'to remain binding on Kazakhstan' and the tribunal 'considered the BIT to be binding on Kazakhstan based on the conduct of both Canada and the new State and their tacit consent for the continuation of the treaty'.[59] In *Gold Pool v Kazakhstan*, another investor–State arbitral tribunal found in 2020 that it lacked jurisdiction *ratione voluntatis* in respect of the claims of another Canadian investor brought pursuant to the same treaty;[60] while Canada again intervened to affirm the continuity of the treaty, the tribunal held there to have been no 'tacit agreement' with Kazakhstan.[61]

14 In 2021, the High Court of England and Wales, exercising its power of *de novo* rehearing, set aside the Award in the *Gold Pool* arbitration.[62] The Court found that Canada and Kazakhstan had implicitly agreed to the succession of Kazakhstan to the treaty in paragraph 3 of a declaration of economic co-operation of 10 July 1992, which agreement was reaffirmed in an exchange of notes of 13 April 1994 and a citation of the treaty in a trade agreement signed on 29 March 1995.[63] While not stated in these verbal agreements, the finding of the Court was based upon contemporaneous evidence of their negotiations.

15 Successors and counterparties have frequently agreed to provisionally continue to apply a bilateral treaty 'pending the conclusion of a new treaty'.[64] In such cases, the question of fact is whether the parties implicitly intended the continuity to be indefinite or conditional on a time-limit, such as the completion of planned succession negotiations.[65] The parties might intend definitive succession even when using qualifying language.[66] Their intention can change over time: for example, they might intend at the point of agreement for it to be

---

[56] ibid.
[57] ibid; H Tuerk, 'Montenegro' in *Max Planck Encyclopedia of Public International Law* (OUP 2015) para 19.
[58] This was the first occasion on which Montenegro had challenged succession to any bilateral investment treaty—ICSID Case No ARB(AF)/12/8, Award, 4 May 2016, paras 4, 77, 90–93, 174–83; ICSID Case No ARB/14/8, Award, 26 July 2016, paras 1, 42, 97–142.
[59] *World Wide Minerals v Kazakhstan (2)*, UNCITRAL, Jurisdiction of 15 October 2015 (unpublished); Dumberry (n 3) 92.
[60] *Gold Pool v Kazakhstan* (n 20).
[61] V Djanić, 'Kazakhstan Fends off Claims by Canadian Gold Miner, as Tribunal Finds it is Not a Successor to USSR BIT', *Investment Arbitration Reporter* (4 August 2020).
[62] [2021] EWHC 3422 (Comm) paras 7–8, 111–14.
[63] ibid paras 33–42, 47–50, 55–60, 69–81, 84–96.
[64] eg, *UN Materials* (n 19) 220–21 (Jamaica); 2207 UNTS 229, Preamble.
[65] eg, 124 UNTS (1952) 188, 251.
[66] eg, UN Doc A/CN.4/253/Add.1 (9 April 1971) para 37.

provisional and subsequently agree to extend the period to enable negotiations[67] or to prolong it indefinitely.[68]

C. Devolution agreements

I. Concept

A devolution agreement between a predecessor and a successor envisages the transfer of rights **16** and obligations with respect to the transferred territory from the former to the latter. It may be enacted by the predecessor prior to the succession through legislation;[69] an agreement concluded between the predecessor and representatives of the transferred territory before the succession;[70] or a treaty between the predecessor and the successor on or after the date of succession.[71] Originating in colonial practice,[72] it encompasses only those treaties that the predecessor had applied to the transferred territory before the date of succession, whether by including the transferred territory when expressing its consent to be bound by that treaty or in subsequently 'extending' to it the territorial scope of its consent.[73]

II. Effect

Article 8 of the VCSST denies constitutive effect to devolution agreements in the ab- **17** sence of express acceptance of counterparties, based on the rule of the law of treaties whereby third States may not be bound without their consent (*res inter alios acta*).[74] Save for protected States and Territories, this provision reflects customary international law: for bilateral treaties, there are many examples of successors with devolution agreements nonetheless concluding succession agreements with counterparties.[75] There are also examples of successors with devolution agreements denying constitutive effect in their subsequent practice[76] or not succeeding to treaties of the predecessors.[77] *Opīniōnēs juris* treating devolution agreements as not constitutive were expressed by Argentina,[78] Côte d'Ivoire,[79]

---

[67] eg, Norway–Montenegro, Agreement on treaty succession, Podgorica, 31 October 2011, Norway Treaty Database, 31-10-2011 No 43 Bilateral (Norwegian).
[68] eg, ILA Handbook (n) 193, 369; Thailand–Malaya, Exchange of notes regarding extradition treaty, Bangkok, 27 October 1959, Thailand Treaty Database.
[69] Indian Independence (International Arrangements) Order 1947, 3 CILC 144; UNGA Resn 392(V), 15 December 1950, 1–2.
[70] eg, 70 UNTS 183, Article 2.
[71] Such treaties are invariably done with retroactive effect, eg Ceylon (1947); Morocco (1956); Ghana (1957); Somalia (1960); Nigeria (1960); Sierra Leone (1961); Trinidad and Tobago (1962); Western Samoa (1962); Jamaica (1962); Malta (1964); The Gambia (1966); Seychelles (1976).
[72] DP O'Connell, *State Succession in International and Municipal Law*, Vol II (CUP 1967) 359.
[73] eg, 69 UNTS (1950) 200, Article 5; 96 ILR 374, 377–78.
[74] VCSST, Article 8(1); VCLT, Article 36; ILC Articles (n 22) 184–87, paras 8–19; A Garrido-Muñoz, 'Article 8— Accords portant dévolution d'obligations ou de droitsconventionnels d'un Etat predecesseur a un Etat successeur' in G Distefano, G Gaggioli and A Hêche (eds), *La Convention de Vienne de 1978 sur la succession d'États en matière de traités*, Vol I (Bruylant 2016) 270–73; P d'Argent, 'Article 36 Vienna Convention' in O Corten and P Klein (eds), *The Vienna Convention on the Law of Treaties: A Commentary*, Vol I (OUP 2011) 929–40.
[75] eg, UN Materials (n 19) 211–13, 220–24.
[76] eg, ibid 189.
[77] eg, ibid 192; 219 UNTS 340, Annex; UNTS I-52765, Article 28(3); Cyprus Treaty List, 96; Norway–Jamaica, Double Taxation Agreement, London, 30 September 1991 (1 October 1992), Norway Treaty Database, 30-09-1991 No 1 Bilateral, Article 30(3) (Norwegian).
[78] UN Materials (n 19) 6–7.
[79] UN Doc A/CN.4/229 (28 May 1970), para 103.

Indonesia,[80] Nigeria,[81] Thailand,[82] and the United Kingdom.[83] While Laos[84] and Myanmar[85] considered their devolution agreements to be constitutive for certain bilateral treaties, they acquiesced to the negative views of counterparties.

18 In *Sanum v Laos*, the devolution agreement between Portugal and China for the retrocession of Macao[86] was invoked by Laos as evidence that the automatic extension of the Chinese–Laotian BIT provided by the 'moving treaty frontiers' rule was displaced due to being 'otherwise established that the application of the treaty to [Macao] would ... radically change the conditions for its operation'.[87] The arbitral tribunal rejected this argument on the ground, *inter alia*, that the devolution agreement lacked binding effected towards third States.[88] Although the High Court of Singapore set aside the award in 2015,[89] the Court of Appeal reversed its judgment in 2016, upholding the arbitral tribunal's conclusions on the customary law of State succession in placing particular weight on the fact that the transfer of Macao was foreseeable at the time that the Joint Declaration was negotiated in 1987 so that China and Laos could have exempted Macao from their BIT when negotiating it in 1993 and then again when reviewing it in 2002.[90] Consequently, they applied the presumption under Article 15 of the VCSST that their treaty would apply to Macao while the Joint Declaration was a bilateral treaty that did not displace the right of third States to rely upon the presumption that Macao would be included in their treaties with China.

19 The effect of devolution agreements was a pertinent issue in the early days of decolonization, particularly for multilateral treaties. By the time of the codification project of the ILC in the 1970s, however, State practice and *opīniōnēs juris* had coalesced around the negative position for both multilateral and bilateral treaties. Although the extended consideration of the issue in *Sanum v Laos* was partially attributable to the verbal structure of Article 15 of the VCSST—the provision around which the question of extension was argued—the conclusion reached by the arbitral tribunal was consistent with the settled position in customary international law concerning the lack of constitutive effect for devolution agreements.

D. General declarations

20 Customary international law permits a successor to notify counterparties and depositaries of its policy concerning succession to treaties by means of a general declaration. This declaration may be one of either provisional continuity or definitive succession to each of the applicable treaties. Though not a requirement, such declarations have typically been made by

---

[80] ibid 37–38, 186.
[81] ibid 181; ICAO, Convention for the Unification of Certain Rules relating to International Carriage by Air, Warsaw, 12 October 1929 (13 February 1933), Status List, n 37.
[82] *Preah Vihear* (n 29), Pleadings, Oral Arguments, Documents (Vol II), 33.
[83] *UN Materials* (n 19) 188–89.
[84] ibid.
[85] ibid 180–81.
[86] UNTS 228, Article VIII.
[87] *Sanum v Laos*, PCA Award (n 39) paras 254–56.
[88] ibid paras 57–268.
[89] *Government of the Lao People's Democratic Republic and Sanum Investments Ltd*, High Court of Singapore (20 January 2015) paras 64–78.
[90] *Sanum v Laos*, Singapore Court of Appeal (n 40) paras 36–122.

means of a letter addressed to the UN Secretary-General with a request that he disseminate it to the Member States. These are addressed to the Secretary-General neither in his capacity as registrar for treaties, nor as depositary, but rather as a convenient intermediary due to his role as the chief administrative officer of the United Nations.[91]

In declarations of provisional continuity, successors stipulate an interim period in which to review the treaties of the predecessor with a view to deciding on succession. There are three variants of this practice: (1) provisional application of treaties based on reciprocity with a view to reaching definitive agreement on succession with counterparties, failing which the treaties automatically terminate on expiry of the time-limit; (2) presumptive succession to the treaties unless notification of termination be tendered; or (3) provisional application pending declaration as to succession or termination.[92] A counterparty may decline to provisionally apply a bilateral treaty,[93] though consent can be attributed by acquiescence[94] to a counterparty that omits to object to the notification of provisional continuity within a reasonable period of time.[95]

A successor may make a general declaration to all UN Member States of definitive succession to all relevant treaties. Such declarations were made for the mergers to form the United Arab Republic, Tanzania, and Yemen.[96] Unlike general declarations of provisional continuity, such declarations contain no qualifier; for example, counterparties (eg France, the Netherlands, and West Germany) accepted the general declaration of succession for Yemen by expressly listing bilateral treaties as continuing in force.[97]

Article 9 of the VCSST states that rights and obligations under treaties in force do not become rights and obligations of the successor or the counterparties 'by reason only of the fact that the successor State has made a unilateral declaration providing for the continuance in force of the treaties in respect of its territory'.[98] The State practice underpinning this provision[99] pertains to declarations of provisional continuity and was intended to operate in conjunction with Articles 27 and 28 on the provisional application of treaties. Article 9 does not accurately express customary international law because it overlooks the existence of State practice by which counterparties have accepted general declarations of definitive succession. The general declarations of the UAR and Tanzania were cited by the ILC in support of Article 31 on presumptive automaticity for a 'uniting of

---

[91] UN Doc A/CN.4/210 and Adds 1 and 2 (18 April, 9 June and 22 July 1969), YILC 1969, Vol II, Part One, 66.
[92] ILC Articles (n 22) 188–90.
[93] eg, MN Leich, *Digest of United States Practice in International Law 1980* (US Government Printing Office 1986) 35.
[94] See in this Commentary: Cameron Miles, 'Cross-cutting procedural powers of international courts and tribunals'.
[95] eg, 603 UNTS 19; ILA Handbook (n) 195; UN Doc A/CN.4/229 (28 May 1970), §104; *UN Materials* (n 19) para 104, 229–30; *Treaties in Force* (n 49) 94, 281–83.
[96] ILC Articles (n 22) 255 (n 15), 256–58 (§§20–23); UN Doc A/CN.4/253 (24 March 1971), para 190; UN Doc A/CN.4/253/Add.1 (9 April 1971) para 168; *Multilateral Treaties* (n 9) l, lii–liii.
[97] A Zimmermann, *Staatennachfolge in völkerrechtliche Verträge* (Springer 2000) 285. While Yemen does not publish a treaty list, those published by seven counterparties include treaties concluded with her predecessors; eg *Treaties in Force* (n 49) 489.
[98] VCSST, Article 9(1).
[99] ILC Articles (n 22) 187–93.

E. Agreement by Conduct

24 Customary international law permits a successor and counterparty to agree on succession to a treaty by conduct. Actions can manifest the consent of both parties to succeed; equally, they can express the consent of one State in tandem with a verbal expression of the other.[101] An agreement might be constituted through actions pursuant to the treaty; for example, by continuing to implement aerial transport[102] or commercial[103] treaties or by granting an extradition request[104] in response to a notification of the successor.[105] An agreement might be concluded when a successor preserves in force legislation implementing a bilateral treaty of the predecessor on which the counterparty relies; for example by adopting corresponding legislation in response.[106]

25 It is a question of fact whether continuing performance of a particular treaty manifest provisional continuity or definitive succession for which subsequent conduct, such as grants of extradition requests, can be decisive, even if a desire be expressed to conclude a replacement treaty.[107] This is a particular factor for treaties involving regular or continuous performance over short periods, such as those concerning aerial transport and border management.[108] Conversely, an interruption of regular performance might[109] or might not[110] be indicative of a definitive position of the State against succession.[111]

26 Although succession by conduct has yet to arise in investor–State arbitration, it has potentially occurred with respect to the acceptance by a counterparty of a general declaration of succession by a successor. Following the general declaration of succession by Yemen to the treaties of North Yemen and South Yemen,[112] an investment in its hydrocarbons sector was made by Hunt Energy, a US company, for the Yemen LNG project launched in 2005 in the Marib governorate (formerly in North Yemen); the BIT between the United States and North

---

[100] ibid 255–57.
[101] UN Doc A/CN.4/229 (28 May 1970) paras 75–80, 132–33.
[102] UN Doc A/CN.4/253 (24 March 1971) paras 26, 29–58, 83, 111–12, 126–28, 133–37, 144–46, 148–49, 155, 159–75; UN Doc A/CN.4/253/Add.1 (9 April 1971) paras 1–10, 65–70, 169–92; *Nigeria's Treaties in Force* (1971, Vol I) 7–11; *Nigeria's Treaties in Force* (1990, Vol I) vi. See also 602 UNTS 25, Article 20; 497 UNTS 311, Article 18; Cyprus Treaty List, 139.
[103] eg UN Doc A/CN.4/253/Add.1 (9 April 1971) paras 66–71 (Morocco), 149–66 (UAR).
[104] eg, 75 ILR 107, 110–12; 22 AILC (1969–78) 261; 3 LRC [1996] 1, 8–10; 33 ILR 313; ILDC 709 (US 2005), paras F1, H1–H2.
[105] eg, *Sacirbegovic* (n 28); *Platko* (n 28).
[106] eg, UN Doc A/CN.4/229 (28 May 1970) para 58; UN Doc A/CN.4/253/Add.1 (9 April 1971) para 56.
[107] eg, *Sabatier v Dabrowski*, US First Circuit Court of Appeals (15 November 1978), 586 F.2d 866 (1978), 868; 75 ILR 107, 110–12.
[108] eg, UN Doc A/CN.4/253 (24 March 1971) paras 6, 71–78; 2175 UNTS 3.
[109] eg, ibid paras 21–24.
[110] eg, ibid paras 116–25.
[111] eg, ibid paras 71–78.
[112] 132.

Yemen was in force before the succession.[113] Although the investment was made by a private person, not the United States, it is likely that the United States had either verbally consented or acquiesced by conduct to the succession of Yemen to the treaty.

F. Conclusion

While the 'contractual' approach of agreement between a successor and counterparty to a succession to a bilateral treaty is a settled rule of customary international law, it remains to be refined. As in other areas of general international law, a key issue is the interpretation of silence: for example, the 'reasonableness' of the time to be allowed to a counterparty to object to a notification of succession by a successor before acquiescing.[114] The scope for a claimant to invoke the general principle of estoppel towards a respondent that has previously adopted an affirmative position on succession to a BIT is also yet to be defined.

As in proceedings before national courts concerning other types of bilateral treaties— notably, extradition proceedings—a critical issue in an investor–State arbitration in which an investor invokes a BIT towards a successor is the solicitation of the position of the counterparty. The inability of Laos to solicit the position of China concerning the applicability of their treaty to Macao until after the award on jurisdiction[115] was rendered crucial to the outcome. Similarly, the position of Russia was reportedly absent from the *Deripaska v Montenegro* arbitration. In contrast, the affirmative position of Canada was known in the *World Wide Minerals* and *Gold Pool* proceedings and the affirmative position of Austria was known in the *EURAM* arbitration.[116]

The provision of its position as well as background evidence by the non-disputing counterparty, whether through intervention or an official opinion, can assist an investor–State arbitral tribunal to decide on a challenge to succession to a BIT.[117] Such official opinions rendered by executive officers of the State ('affidavits' or 'certificates') have been critical to decide on succession to extradition treaties in extradition proceedings; for example, in the courts of Austria,[118] South Africa[119] and the United States.[120] While the principal burden of evidence lies with the disputing parties, greater use of fact-finding powers[121] by investor–State arbitral tribunals to solicit information from non-disputing counterparties would improve the forensic rigour of inquiries into the existence of an agreement to succeed to a BIT.

---

[113] Investment Guarantees Agreement between the United States of America and the Yemen Arab Republic, dated at San'a 22 October and 4 December 1972, TIAS 7586.
[114] eg, the positions of South Sudan and third States with respect to the twenty-seven bilateral investment treaties to which the Sudan was party at the time of her secession remain obscure. The jurisdictional bases of the two completed investor–State arbitrations involving South Sudan appear to have been based on a national investment law and an investment contract—ICSID Case No ARB/12/26, Award of 30 September 2016 (unpublished); PCA Case No 2013/4, Award of 27 January 2015 (unpublished).
[115] *Sanum v Laos*, PCA Award (n 39) paras 8–10.
[116] *EURAM v Slovak Republic*, PCA Case No 2010-17, Jurisdiction, 22 October 2012, paras 40–41, 77–78 (hereafter *EURAM v Slovakia*); 318 Bundesgesetzblatt (28 December 1994), No 1046 (German).
[117] eg *Gold Pool v Kazakhstan* (n 20) paras 36–41; *EURAM v Slovakia* (n 116) para 80.
[118] Case No 2Ob69/92, Supreme Court of Austria (16 December 1992, German).
[119] eg 52 ILR 84, 85–86, 88; 55 ILR 89, 91–93.
[120] eg, 371 F Supp 2d 651 (E.D. Pa. 2005), 658–659; 22 AILC (1969–78) 261; 96 ILR 105, 107–08.
[121] eg, UNCITRAL Arbitration Rules (2013), Article 27(3); ICSID Arbitration Rules (2022), Rule 36(3).

Selected literature

Distefano G, Gaggioli G and Hêche A (eds), *La Convention de Vienne de 1978 sur la succession d'États en matière de traités*, Vol I (Bruylant 2016).

Draft Articles on Succession of States in respect of Treaties with commentaries, YILC 1974, II(1), Yearbook of International Law Commission.

Dumberry P, *A Guide to State Succession in International Investment Law* (Edward Elgar Publishing 2018).

Eisemann P-M and Koskenniemi M (eds), *State Succession: Codification Tested against the Facts* (Brill 2000)

International Law Association, *The Effect of Independence on Treaties* (London: Stevens and Sons 1965).

O'Connell DP, *State Succession in International and Municipal Law*, Vol II (CUP 1967).

Waldock H, 'Fourth Report on succession in respect of treaties', UN Doc A/CN.4/249 (24 June 1971).

Zimmermann A, *Staatennachfolge in völkerrechtliche Verträge* (Springer 2000).

Selected decisions

Gold Pool JV Limited v Republic of Kazakhstan, High Court of Justice (15 December 2021), [2021] EWHC 3422 (Comm).

Sanum Investments Ltd v Laos, PCA Case No 2013-13, Jurisdiction, 13 December 2013.

Sanum Investments Ltd v Laos, Singapore Court of Appeal, Judgment (29 September 2016) [2016] SGCA.

Succession in respect of cession, unification and separation of States

James G Devaney and Christian J Tams

A. Introduction	1	2. Separation and dissolution	21
B. Cession of territory	6	3. Special rules	28
I. The position under general international law	6	II. Investment law practice	31
II. Investment arbitration practice	11	1. Unification, separation, and dissolution	31
III. Assessment as to alignment or deviation	17	III. Assessment as to alignment or deviation	38
C. Unification and separation/dissolution	18	D. Potential of investment arbitration to influence State succession	42
I. The position under general international law	18		
1. Unification	19	E. Conclusions	45

A. Introduction

This entry examines State succession to treaties, a topic that has prompted heated debate among States for decades. While State succession is sometimes regarded as a niche issue, investment tribunals have been confronted with it in a number of recent investment awards and their jurisprudence, as well as the conduct of States in relation to investment agreements, is an important element of international practice. **1**

State succession denotes 'the definitive replacement of one State by another in respect of sovereignty over a given territory'.[1] The legal rules governing consequences of such replacement are at once highly technical (practical matters such as what to do with state property and archives) and fundamental (implying positions on statehood and legal personality).[2] As far as succession to treaties is concerned, States have sought to formulate general rules in a major international treaty, namely, the Vienna Convention on the Law of the Succession of States in respect of Treaties of 23 August 1978 (VCSST).[3] Unlike other Vienna Conventions negotiated by States, the VCSST has only been partially successful as a codification project. Its limitations are evident in the fact that it has so far attracted a relatively small number **2**

---

[1] J Crawford, *Brownlie's Principles of Public International Law* (9th edn, OUP 2019) 409 (hereafter Crawford).
[2] See in this Commentary: Arman Sarvarian, 'The protection of foreign investment in the law of State succession'.
[3] Vienna Convention on Succession of States in respect of Treaties (adopted 23 August 1978, entered into force 6 November 1996) 1946 UNTS 3.

(twenty-three) of State parties,[4] and explained by a number of factors including its prospective application and the controversial nature of some of its central provisions. Moreover, many of its provisions formulate default rules from which States can deviate by agreement.

3 In the absence of a generally accepted treaty framework, questions of State succession typically are governed either by general rules of customary international law, or by special agreements reached by States affected by instances of succession. As indicated below, general rules of customary international law are not always free from ambiguity, not least because questions of State succession have only rarely been addressed in the jurisprudence of international courts or in authoritative international documents that would bring about clarity. This may explain why States have often preferred to determine the fate of particular treaties through special, tailor-made arrangements that state expressly which treaties continue to apply, and which do not. While such tailor-made arrangements may bring clarity to particular situations, they often reflect pragmatic considerations rather than any general rules.

4 All these factors—partially unsuccessful codification, prominence of tailor-made arrangements catering for individual instances, and less-than-clear customary rules—complicate the task of the present entry, as the content of the general international law framework is at times difficult to discern. For reasons of convenience the VCSST's provisions will be taken as the starting point for discussion, and the extent to which the practice of States affected by succession processes has aligned with these provisions made clear throughout.

5 The international law framework is based on a distinction between different forms of State succession. The central distinction is between instances of succession that involve the cession of territory; and those that involve the unification and separation or dissolution of States. As these are governed by different rules, it is necessary to address each in turn separately. Following this separate discussion, we briefly flag special rules governing succession by newly independent States and succession to particular categories of treaties.

B. Cession of territory

I. The position under general international law

6 Not all instances of State succession involve the creation of new States or the disappearance of old ones.[5] Transfer of territory from one State to another, such as in the case of Walvis Bay or Hong Kong, is a prime example of this fact.[6] In such situations, while the territory of the two States involved is altered, each continues with their international legal personality as before.[7]

---

[4] See the information at https://treaties.un.org/Pages/ViewDetails.aspx?src=IND&mtdsg_no=XXIII-2&chapter=23&clang=_en accessed 18 January 2023.
[5] ILC, 'Draft Articles on Succession of States in Respect of Treaties with commentaries' YILC 1974, Vol II, Part One, 208 (addressing 'cases which do not involve a union of States or merger of one State with another, and equally do not involve the emergence of a newly independent State'). See further CJ Tams, 'Ways Out of the Marshland: International Investment Law and the Law of State Succession' in CJ Tams and others (eds), *Investment Law and Public International Law* (Edward Elgar Publishing 2022) 150, 172–74 (hereafter Tams, 'Ways Out of the Marshland').
[6] O Dörr, 'Cession' (2019) MPEPIL, paras 20–22 <https://opil.ouplaw.com/view/10.1093/law:epil/9780199231690/law-9780199231690-e1377> accessed 16 February 2022.
[7] Crawford (n 1) 409.

The legal regime governing State succession in the form of a cession has traditionally been considered to be settled.[8] The VCSST addresses it in Article 15, which reflects a straightforward and intuitive proposition that is generally known as the 'moving treaty frontiers' rule. This mandates that, as a default, treaties follow the changing frontiers: treaties of the predecessor State cease to be in force in respect of the transferred territory, and treaties of the successor State become applicable instead. This is unless the application of the treaty to that territory would be incompatible with the object and purpose of the treaty or would radically change the conditions for its operation, although such exceptions have rarely been discussed.[9]

Article 15 is strengthened by a pre-existing provision of much more successful codification attempt in an adjacent field, Article 29 of the Vienna Convention on the Law of Treaties 1969,[10] which presumes that when a State concludes a treaty then that treaty applies to the entire territory of that State.[11]

It is generally accepted that Article 15 reflects customary international law.[12] State practice prior to the VCSST and since its adoption by and large has followed the moving treaty frontiers rule. Those cases which have slightly deviated from this rule, such as some treaties relating to Hong Kong, have received the explicit or implicit approval of third States.[13] Some recent investment law practice is relevant in this regard and is addressed below.

Transfer of territory, it is important to note in light of recent practice,[14] only implicates the rules of State succession when it is effected in accordance with international law. This excludes, for example, the application of rules of State succession to instances of unlawful annexation of territory: the annexing State's rights and duties are regulated by specific rules of international law such as the law of occupation.[15] Recent attempts to rely on the law of State succession in such situations[16] may in time qualify the hitherto widely accepted distinction

---

[8] A Zimmermann and J Devaney, 'State Succession in Treaties' MPEPIL, para 8 <https://opil-ouplaw-com.ezproxy.lib.gla.ac.uk/view/10.1093/law:epil/9780199231690/law-9780199231690-e1109?rskey=Lpbxwk&result=1&prd=MPIL> accessed 16 January 2023.

[9] A Tanzi and L Iapichino, 'Article 15' in G Distefano and others (eds), *La convention de Vienne de 1978 sur la succession d'États en matière de traités: Commentaire article par article et études thématique* (Bruylant 2016) 543.

[10] Vienna Convention on the Law of Treaties (adopted 23 May 1969, entered into force 27 January 1980) 1155 UNTS 331. Article 29: 'Unless a different intention appears from the treaty or is otherwise established, a treaty is binding upon each party in respect of its entire territory.' The commentary to VCSST draft Article 14 (eventually Article 15) specifically refers to Article 29 VCLT: (n 3) 208.

[11] M Villiger, *Commentary on the 1969 Vienna Convention on the Law of Treaties* (Brill 2009) 392. See also in this Commentary: Emma Lindsay and Philippa Webb, 'Article 29 of the VCLT: Territorial scope'.

[12] Zimmermann and Devaney, 'Succession to Treaties' (n 8) 520; G Hafner and G Novak, 'State Succession in Respect of Treaty Relationships' in D Hollis (ed), *The Oxford Guide to Treaties* (2nd edn, OUP 2020) 397 (hereafter Hafner and Novak); see also *PJSC CB PrivatBank and Finance Company Finilon LLC v Russian Federation*, PCA Case No 2015-21, Interim Award, 27 March 2017, para 170 (hereafter *Privatbank* Interim Award).

[13] Zimmermann and Devaney, 'Succession to Treaties' (n 8) 521.

[14] See, eg, OG Repousis, 'Why Russian Investment Treaties Could Apply to Crimea and What Would this Mean for the Ongoing Russo-Ukrainian Territorial Conflict' (32) 2016 Arb Intl 459; D Costelloe, 'Treaty Succession in Annexed Territory' (2016) 65 ICLQ 343.

[15] See Article 6 (clarifying that the VCSST only applies 'to the effects of a succession of States occurring in conformity with international law and, in particular, the principles of international law embodied in the Charter of the United Nations'), and similarly Article 40 VCSST (n 3). See further Hafner and Novak (n 12) 387; G Gaggioli, 'Article 6' in Distefano and others (n 9) 206; and on the legal regime of annexation Rainer Hofmann, 'Annexation' (*MPEPIL* 2020)<https://opil.ouplaw.com/view/10.1093/law:epil/9780199231690/law-9780199231690-e1376?print=pdf> accessed 16 February 2022.

[16] But note the unusual position taken by tribunals in, eg, the *Privatbank* Interim Award (n 12) where the issue of the legality of annexation of Crimea (see para 144) is sidestepped and the BIT found to apply through either effective control of territory or interpreting Article 29 VCLT as applying to a state's 'entire territory' regardless of

between succession and unlawful territorial changes, but practice to date has not been sufficiently consistent and coherent to do so.[17]

II. Investment arbitration practice

11 In recent times cession of territory has prompted debate among investment practitioners and scholars. This is mainly due to the *Sanum* cases which brought to the fore particular (and controversial) aspects of the general regime of State succession of this type.[18] Central to these cases was the issue of whether the China–Laos Bilateral Investment Treaty (BIT) applied to Macao, an issue which vexed a United Nations Commission on International Trade Law (UNCITRAL) arbitral tribunal,[19] the Singapore High Court,[20] and the Singapore Court of Appeal.[21] Taken together, their decisions provide support for the moving treaty frontiers rule as reflected in Article 15 VCSST. And importantly, they have shone a spotlight on potential exceptions to the rule.

12 An exception might have been called for because Macao's return to China was a cession that on the face of it would seem to diverge from the norm: while China replaced Portugal 'in respect of sovereignty',[22] Macao was given a special status under the joint Chinese–Portuguese Protocol of 1999.[23] The 'one country, two systems' approach taken in this Protocol presented a challenge to legal decision-makers tasked with determining how the moving treaty frontiers rule would apply in this particular context (if at all). In addition, since the China–Laos BIT itself was silent on the matter of State succession, the question also arose as to whether

---

the manner in which it came to exercise control over it. See further the positions taken in *Oschadbank v Russia*, PCA Case No 2016-14, Award, 26 November 2018 and *PJSC Ukrnafta v The Russian Federation*, PCA Case No 2015-34, Press Release of the Final Awards, 24 April 2019; see J Braun, 'Uncovered: Tribunal in Previously-Unseen Award Against Russia Upheld Jurisdiction over Crimea-Related Claims, and Awarded over 1.3 Billion USD in Compensation' (*Investment Arbitration Reporter*, 13 April 2021) <https://www.iareporter.com/articles/uncovered-tribunal-in-previously-unseen-award-against-russia-upheld-jurisdiction-over-crimea-related-claims-and-awarded-over-1-3-billion-usd-in-compensation/> accessed 19 December 2022. Similarly, the tribunal in *Everest Estate v Russia* on 20 March 2017 in a jurisdictional decision considered that *de facto* control of territory sufficient for the purposes of applicability of the BIT, see J Hepburn, 'Investigation: Full Jurisdictional Reasoning Comes to Light in Crimea-Related BIT Arbitration vs. Russia' (*Investment Arbitration Reporter*, 9 November 2017) <https://www.iareporter.com/articles/full-jurisdictional-reasoning-comes-to-light-in-crimea-related-arbitration-everest-estate-v-russia/> accessed 19 December 2022. While none of these tribunals (as far as we are aware from the parts that have been published) addressed the legality of Russia's control over Crimea, they are noteworthy and could suggest an emerging trend, which would not be easy to reconcile with the traditional approach to State succession set out in the text.

[17] See further P Dumberry, 'Requiem for Crimea: Why Tribunals Should Have Declined Jurisdiction over the Claims of Ukrainian Investors against Russia under the Ukraine-Russia BIT' (2018) 9 JIDS 506.

[18] See OG Repousis, 'On Territoriality and International Investment Law: Applying China's Investment Treaties to Hong Kong and Macao' (2015) 37 Mich J Intl L 113; JM Shijian, 'The Dilemma of Applying Bilateral Investment Treaties of China to Hongkong and Macao' (2018) 33 ICSID Rev 125; C Binder, 'Sanum Investments Limited v The Government of the Lao People's Democratic Republic' (2016) 17 JWIT 280 (hereafter Binder).

[19] *Sanum Investments Limited v Lao People's Democratic Republic*, PCA Case No 2013-13, Jurisdiction, 13 December 2013 (hereafter *Sanum* Arbitral Award).

[20] *Government of the Law People's Democratic Republic v Sanum Investment Ltd* [2015] SGHC 15 (hereafter *Sanum* High Court Decision).

[21] *Sanum Investment Ltd v Government of the Law People's Democratic Republic* [2016] SGCA 57 (hereafter *Sanum* Court of Appeal Decision).

[22] See Crawford (n 1).

[23] Joint Declaration on the Question of Macao (China–Portugal) (13 April 1987) 1498 UNTS 228 and Protocol of 1999.

the application of the BIT to Macao would be incompatible with its object and purpose or would radically change the conditions for its operation.[24]

On this issue the three decisions came to different conclusions. The UNCITRAL arbitral tribunal found that the moving treaty frontiers rule was applicable, while the Singapore High Court, relying on *notes verbales* issued by the treaty parties after the award, found that the parties had agreed otherwise.[25] Finally, the Singapore Court of Appeal overturned the decision of the High Court and found that the BIT was indeed applicable, not least because in its view, the *notes verbales* could not be taken into account.[26] In this regard it is not difficult to see why this has been described as 'a textbook example of the difficulties arising from the application of the general international law of State succession to a particular situation'.[27]

The relevance of this investment law practice beyond the particular facts of these cases is threefold.[28] First, all three decisions took the moving treaty frontiers rule, as codified in Article 15 VCSST, as the starting point for their analysis.[29] None of the tribunals considered that investment treaties are subject to a particular or special regime.[30] In that sense, the three *Sanum* decisions provide further support for the moving treaty frontiers rule.

Second, the decisions provide helpful practical indications on a number of relevant legal issues, including most importantly the kinds of facts which might preclude the application of the moving treaty frontiers rule. In assessing whether, exceptionally, the China–Laos BIT should *not* be subject to the moving treaty frontiers rule, the two Singapore courts predictably looked to the Chinese and Laotian *notes verbales* (on whose relevance they disagreed). Beyond that, all three tribunals distinguished the China–Laos BIT from other Chinese BITs which explicitly defined their territorial application; and they seemed to place at least some reliance on the listing practice of international institutions.[31] None of this is as such remarkable; and it certainly is squarely within the four corners of the moving treaty frontiers rule (and its exceptions). But given the dearth of judicial practice assessing potential exceptions to the moving treaty frontiers rule, the three *Sanum* decisions are likely to remain of value.

Finally, investment practice is instructive regarding the normative force that the moving treaty frontiers rule exerts in particular cases. Despite Macao's autonomous status, the UNCITRAL tribunal and the Singapore Court of Appeal considered the moving treaty frontiers rule to apply[32]: even the 'one country, two systems' approach of the China-Portuguese Joint Declaration was not considered enough to support an exception. Seen in that light, at

---

[24] The UNCITRAL tribunal also looked at the matter from the perspective of Article 29 VCLT, with its slightly separate set of exceptions. See in this Commentary: Emma Lindsay and Philippa Webb, 'Article 29 of the VCLT: Territorial Scope'.
[25] *Sanum* High Court Decision (n 20) paras 70, 110–11.
[26] *Sanum* Court of Appeal Decision (n 21) paras 101–21.
[27] Binder (n 18) 290.
[28] *Sanum* Court of Appeal Decision (n 21) para 101 et seq.
[29] *Sanum* Arbitral Award (n 19) paras 278–95; *Sanum* High Court Decision (n 20) paras 61–62; *Sanum* Court of Appeal Decision (n 21) paras 47–50.
[30] Binder (n 18) 293.
[31] Notably, it was considered relevant that a 2001 WTO Report listing the treaties applicable to Macao did not list the China–Laos BIT; *Sanum* Arbitral Award (n 19) paras 243–51; *Sanum* High Court Decision (n 20) paras 83–86 and 107–09; *Sanum* Court of Appeal Decision (n 21) paras 88–89 and 95–99.
[32] See, for example, *Sanum* Arbitral Award (n 19) paras 243–51; *Sanum* High Court Decision (n 20) para 74; *Sanum* Court of Appeal Decision (n 21) paras 72–82.

least when looking at the UNCITRAL award and the Court of Appeal decision, the *Sanum* saga in the final analysis reflects the strength of the moving treaty frontiers rule.

III. Assessment as to alignment or deviation

17 The preceding analysis suggests that investment practice aligns with, and further consolidates, the general regime of State succession applicable to cessions of territory.[33] Investment tribunals and domestic courts assessing investment awards have engaged with a well-settled aspect of the law of State succession. The moving treaty frontiers rule is widely supported in practice and the general regime offers a straightforward default rule that would be very difficult to ignore. The general regime also sets out exceptions to this rule but does not formulate them very clearly, leaving decision-makers a wide degree of discretion. What is more, the relative dearth of prior decisions on the scope of these exceptions meant that investment tribunals could approach their task almost from scratch. The presence of a well-settled rule and generally formulated exception that had hardly been adjudicated before meant that investment practice was always likely to align with the general regime.

C. Unification and separation/dissolution

I. The position under general international law

18 The VCSST attempts to regulate two other types of succession, unification and separation/dissolution. For both unification and separation/dissolution, it sets out ambitious default regimes. The subsequent analysis outlines the VCSST regime and assesses whether it reflects customary international law.

1. Unification

19 From State practice two different types of unification can be discerned, one specifically envisaged in the VCSST (merger) and one not (incorporation). Incorporation refers to the type of situation that materialized when the German Democratic Republic voluntarily gave up its sovereignty to become part of the Federal Republic of Germany on 3 October 1990, something which the drafters of the VCSST had perhaps thought so unlikely so as to not require regulation.[34] This remains the sole post-VCSST example in practice to date.

20 The VCSST did envisage the merger of two States to create a new successor State. This is reflected in Article 31(1) and (2) which provides that the treaties in force for the predecessor States continue to apply to the successor State, but crucially that their application remains limited to the specific part of the territory to which they previously applied. These provisions create what has been called an awkward 'split regime' in accordance with which pre-existing treaty obligations may only apply to part of the successor State's territory.[35] In practice to date, however, this has been a really rather marginal issue with the only clear post-VCSST example being the unification of Yemen in 1990. Although State practice relating to the Yemeni

---

[33] Hafner and Novak (n 12) 397.
[34] D Vagts, 'State Succession: The Codifiers' View' (1993) 33 Va J Int'l L 277 (hereafter Vagts, 'State Succession'); cf A Zimmermann, *Staatennachfolge in völkerrechtliche Verträge* (Springer 2000) 449, 288 (hereafter Zimmermann).
[35] Zimmermann and Devaney, 'Succession to Treaties' (n 8) 523.

unification seems to have accorded with that envisaged in Article 31,[36] such scant practice precludes any serious claim for Article 31 to have achieved customary status.[37]

2. Separation and dissolution

While the unification of States has turned out to be a relatively marginal issue in practice, the VCSST's provisions regarding State succession in the case of a separation and dissolution of existing States have been of greater practical relevance.[38] Article 34 VCSST (complemented by Article 35, which addresses the position of States that continue to exist after the separation of part of their territory) lays down a default rule of 'automatic succession', i.e. a rule to the effect that in situations where part or parts of a territory separate to become one or more successor States, the treaties in force at the date of the succession of States relating to the entire territory of the predecessor State continue in force for the successor State(s). This default rule applies to new States emerging from instances of separation (where the predecessor State continues with a reduced territory) and dissolution (where the predecessor State has completely dissolved). Under the exceptions set out in Article 34, para. 2, and Article 35(a) and (c),[39] the default rule does not apply if the States involved agree otherwise, or if the automatic succession would be incompatible with the object and purpose of the treaty or would radically change the conditions for its operation. However, even with these exceptions, it is of significant ambition and marks the VCSST's strongest endorsement of a position of treaty continuity. It is all the more ambitious as the automatic succession rule is meant to apply to all treaties that were in force at the time of the separation, irrespective of their nature or importance.

At the time of the VCSST's drafting, the automatic succession rule set out in Article 34 did not reflect uniform State practice.[40] Practice since the VCSST's adoption both in relation to instances of separation and dissolution suggests that, while States have recognized the need for treaty stability, Article 34 has not been followed comprehensively.[41] While no case is exactly the same, practice broadly reflects three trends: First, for multilateral treaties, especially those formulating fundamental principles of international relations, there is a clear expectation of continuity. Second, practice generally conforms to these expectations: as noted by the International Law Association (ILA) in 2002, '[d]ans leur grande majorité, les Etats ont appliqué la règle de continuité aux traités multilatéraux auxquels l'Etat prédécesseur était partie'.[42] At the same time, third, this continuity has been achieved by successor States unilaterally declaring their desire to *remain bound* by earlier treaties, or agreeing with treaty partners on the treaties' continued application—which would not be required were succession automatic.

---

[36] ibid.
[37] Zimmermann (n 34) 283–89.
[38] Newly independent States are subject to a special regime briefly set out below.
[39] Article 35(b) adds a further exception for geographically limited agreements that were always intended to apply to the separating territory only.
[40] See the ILC's Commentary (n 5) 260–66.
[41] See, eg, B Stern, 'La succession d'Etats' (1996) 262 Recueil des cours 9, 315; P Dumberry 'An Uncharted Question of State Succession: Are New States Automatically Bound by the BITs Concluded by Predecessor States Before Independence?' (2015) 6 JIDS 74.
[42] International Law Association, Committee on Aspects of the Law of State Succession, *Rapport final sur la succession en matière de traités* (Delhi 2002) https://www.ila-hq.org/en_GB/documents/conference-report-new-delhi-2002 accessed 18 January 2023), 13–14 (hereafter ILA, Rapport final). See further Zimmermann and Devaney, 'Succession to Treaties' (n 8) 533.

23 To illustrate, treaty continuity was generally sought and maintained by the Czech and Slovak Republics during the dissolution of Czechoslovakia.[43] Both States recognized that treaties concluded by their predecessor would continue to apply. However, in practice, such continuity was often affirmed through special agreements with partner States that explicitly provided for continuity. The dissolution of Yugoslavia involved greater problems of succession: as in the case of Czechoslovakia, treaty continuity was argued for, but the successor States to the former Yugoslavia were not consistent in their practice, and the practice of explicit affirmation of treaty continuity remained common.[44] The overall picture remains dominated by treaty stability achieved through State conduct, which in turn has allowed for nuanced and case-specific solutions.

24 The International Court of Justice (ICJ)'s jurisprudence on Article 34 and the issue of automatic succession has been equally ambiguous. In the *Gabčíkovo Nagymaros case*,[45] the Court chose not to pronounce on the customary status of Article 34. Later, in the two *Genocide cases* brought against Serbia and Montenegro (by Bosnia and Herzegovina and Croatia, respectively), it did not uphold the claimants' argument that Serbia and Montenegro had automatically succeeded to the Genocide Convention (to which the former Yugoslavia had been a party).[46] Rather, in the *Croatian Genocide case*, the Court went out of its way to 'construe' a very generally worded proclamation of State continuity, made by representatives of Serbia and Montenegro, as amounting to a declaration to succeed to the Genocide Convention.[47]

25 Other international actors have been more forthright. Human rights treaty bodies (such as the Human Rights Committee) have often made clear that they would expect the successor State to abide by the treaty commitments of the predecessor.[48] For universal human rights agreements in particular, it has been argued that, as '[t]he rights enshrined in [human rights agreements] belong to the people [...], once the people are accorded the protection of the rights [...], such protection devolves with territory and continues to belong to them, notwithstanding [...] State succession'.[49]

26 This statement clearly reflects a trend towards treaty stability. Whether this trend has hardened into a rule of automatic succession, at least for multilateral treaties protecting important interests of the international community, is much discussed.[50] At present, the better view, given the heterogeneity of practice, is that Article 34, even for multilateral treaties, does not reflect customary international law. But the position has remained controversial.

27 In relation to *bilateral* treaties, the case for automatic succession is more difficult to make.[51] Successor States have, almost inevitably, engaged in discussions with treaty partners about

---

[43] For details see Zimmermann (n 34) 335 et seq.

[44] See the comprehensive account provided by Zimmermann (n 34) 308 et seq.

[45] *Gabčíkovo-Nagymaros Project* (Hungary/Slovakia) [1997] ICJ Rep 3, paras 119–21 (where the Court did not find it 'necessary for the purposes of the present case to enter into a discussion of whether or not Article 34 of the 1978 Convention reflects the State of customary international law') (hereafter *Gabčíkovo-Nagymaros*).

[46] See, eg, *Application of the Convention on the Prevention and Punishment of the Crime of Genocide (Bosnia and Herzegovina v Serbia and Montenegro)* [1996] ICJ Rep 595, paras 23 and 34.

[47] *Application of the Convention on the Prevention and Punishment of the Crime of Genocide (Bosnia and Herzegovina v Serbia and Montenegro)* [2008] ICJ Rep 412, paras 98–117.

[48] Human Rights Committee, General Comment No 26, UN Doc A/53/40, 4 (hereafter Human Rights Committee, General Comment No 26).

[49] ibid.

[50] The different views on this matter are reflected in MT Kamminga, 'State Succession in Respect of Human Rights Treaties' (1996) EJIL 7, 469, on the one hand, and A Rasulov 'Revisiting State Succession to Humanitarian Treaties: Is There a Case for Automaticity?' (2003) 14 EJIL 141, on the other hand.

[51] See, eg, B Stern, 'La succession d'Etats' (1996) 262 Recueil des cours 9, 315; P Dumberry 'An Uncharted Question of State Succession: Are New States Automatically Bound by the BITs Concluded by Predecessor States Before Independence?' (2015) 6 JIDS 74.

the fate of particular treaties and agreed on lists of treaties that would (or would not) continue to apply between them. Underlying this is a perception that bilateral treaties would typically reflect interstate bargains, so that a new State would—expressly or by implication, i.e. based on conduct—need to 'accept' this bargain before being bound. Overall, just as with multilateral treaties, practice points towards continuity, but more clearly as in the case of multilateral treaties, it is a continuity affirmed by agreement, not one imposed by a separate rule of general international law. The above-mentioned Report by the ILA captures both aspects when noting, with respect to bilateral treaties, that 'la pratique générale est celle de discussions bilatérales plus ou moins formelles destinées à clarifier la situation. ... ces discussions sont fondées sur l'idée qu'il existe une règle de continuité des traités bilatéraux'.[52]

3. Special rules
The VCSST's general regime, as outlined above, is complemented by special rules addressing particular instances of succession. Two deserve to be mentioned briefly.

First, while emphasizing automatic succession for regular instances of succession in Articles 31 and 34, the VCSST creates special rules for 'newly independent States', i.e. States whose international legal personality has been restored as a result of their emergence from colonization.[53] In accordance with Article 16 VCSST such States—even under the VCSST's preference for automatic continuity—are *not* automatically bound by treaties of their predecessor States. In other words, the VCSST's push for treaty continuity was not meant to burden States emerging from colonial rule prior treaty commitments. The underlying dichotomy—between regular instances of succession, and emergence from colonial rule—has been questioned on principled grounds[54] but resistance to automatic succession, as noted in the preceding paragraphs, has limited the practical relevance of this debate.

Second, quite apart from the type of succession (cession, separation etc.) or the status of the successor State (newly independent or not), there are categories of treaties which are undoubtedly subject to automatic succession, including for newly independent States. These are treaties that relate to boundaries between States, and treaties establishing 'other territorial regimes', which according to Articles 11 and 12 VCSST are not affected by instances of State succession. Practice both prior to and after the adoption of the VCSST confirms the particular character of such 'dispositive' or 'localised' treaties. Reflecting this, the ICJ has emphasized the duty of States to respect pre-existing boundaries in the event of a State succession and confirmed the customary status of Article 12 VCSST safeguarding the continuity of other territorial regimes.[55] While the precise scope of that category may be open to doubt, these pronouncements reflect the international community's overarching interest in the stability of boundaries and other localized regimes.

---

[52] ILA, Rapport final (n 42) 16.
[53] See Part III VCSST (n 3) Articles 16–30.
[54] See, eg, Crawford (n 1) 411–12.
[55] See, eg, *Gabčíkovo-Nagymaros* (n 45) para 123; and further *Case Concerning the Temple of Preah Vihear (Cambodia v Thailand)* [1962] ICJ Rep 6, 34; *Frontier Dispute (Burkina Faso v Mali)* [1986] ICJ Rep 554, paras 25–26.

II. Investment law practice

1. Unification, separation, and dissolution

31 The remarkable growth in the number of BITs from the beginning of the 1990s meant that investment lawyers came face to face with questions of State succession. However, it is only more recently that questions of State succession have become more widely considered, mainly due to a number of high-profile investment disputes.[56] Almost inevitably, the debate has concerned instances of separation and dissolution.

32 With regard to these types of State succession, in line with the general practice outlined above, rather than strictly following the rule of automatic succession as envisaged in Article 34 VCSST successor States and relevant treaty partners have demonstrated a consistent preference of retaining control over the fate of treaties. To this end, States (in line with the general approach to bilateral treaties summarized above[57]) have very often entered into agreements listing treaties that continue to apply after succession (and those which do not). Fully conforming to the trends noted in the ILA's Report cited above, States have usually agreed on the continued application of treaties to successor States, particularly BITs. State practice in relation to the dissolution of Czechoslovakia is an example in this regard, with the Czech Republic as successor State agreeing to the continued application of fourteen of the sixteen of CSSR's BITs, only entering into new agreements with two countries.[58] In numerous arbitral proceedings relating to such situations tribunals have been happy to simply give effect to the intentions of the parties with regard to BITs.[59]

33 In situations where successor States have not managed (or attempted) to clarify their obligations under relevant BITs investors have nevertheless brought claims against successor States under BITs concluded by predecessor States, leaving arbitral tribunals to decide whether such BITs should continue to apply even in the absence of an explicit position. The three most relevant arbitral awards in this regard (to date) are *World Wide Minerals v Kazakhstan*, *Gold Pool v Kazakhstan*, and *Deripaska v Montenegro* which have all engaged with the general (customary) regime of State succession.[60] All of these decisions turned on the question of whether investors, in proceedings against a successor State[61] (Kazakhstan in *World Wide Minerals* and *Gold Pool* and Montenegro in *Deripaska*), could rely on a BIT

---

[56] See, eg, the cases cited in Tams, 'Ways Out of the Marshland' (n 5) 165–68; see further P Dumberry, 'State Succession to BITs: Analysis of Case Law in the Context of Dissolution and Secession' (2018) 34(1) Arb Intl 445–62 (hereafter Dumberry).

[57] See para 27.

[58] CJ Tams 'State Succession to Investment Treaties: Mapping the Issues' (2016) 31 ICSID Rev/FILJ 314, 330 (hereafter Tams, State Succession to Investment Treaties).

[59] eg, *Ronald S Lauder v the Czech Republic*, UNCITRAL, Final Award, 3 September 2001, paras 2 and 10.

[60] *World Wide Minerals Ltd and Mr Paul A Carroll, QC v Kazakhstan*, UNCITRAL, Award, 19 October 2015; *Gold Pool Limited Partnership v Kazakhstan*, PCA Case No 2016-23, Award, 30 July 2020 (hereafter *Gold Pool*); *Oleg Deripaska v the Republic of Montenegro*, PCA Case No 2017-07, Final Award, 15 October 2019. Of note, one of the authors acted as a party-appointed expert in the proceedings in *Deripaska*.

[61] A different scenario is that which arose recently in *Sudapet v South Sudan*, ICSID Case No ARB/12/26, Award, 30 September 2016, para 427 et seq in which an oil company formerly owned by the state of Sudan prior to succession (unsuccessfully) sought to bring a claim against South Sudan as a successor state under the succession agreement signed between Sudan and South Sudan. See further V Djanic, 'Analysis: State Succession Takes Centre-Stage in Arbitration Between Sudan's State-Owned Oil Company and Newly-Independent South Sudan' (*Investment Arbitration Reporter*, 21 October 2021) https://www.iareporter.com/articles/analysis-state-succession-takes-centre-stage-in-arbitration-between-sudans-state-owned-oil-company-and-newly-independent-south-sudan/ accessed 23 October 2023.

concluded between their State of nationality and the predecessor State (the USSR, and Serbia and Montenegro, respectively). Looking at the outcomes, investment practice seems to offer a mixed picture: the tribunal in *World Wide Minerals* considered Kazakhstan to have succeeded to the Canada–USSR BIT, while the tribunal in *Gold Pool* reached the opposite conclusion (but saw its award quashed by the High Court of England and Wales). In *Deripaska*, the tribunal considered Montenegro not to have succeeded to the Russia–Serbia/Montenegro BIT. The fact that none of the awards has been published in full inevitably affects the analysis. Nonetheless, from the summaries that have been made available, it is possible to discern some important information.

The first thing to note is that none of the tribunals held the respective successor States to have automatically succeeded to their predecessors' BITs. According to a publicly available summary, the *Deripaska* tribunal considered that States did not seem to 'proceed from a generally shared expectation of automaticity'.[62] The tribunal in *Gold Pool* obviously shared that view, while the *World Wide Minerals* tribunals considered Kazakhstan and Canada to have *agreed* to keep the old BIT in force. This approach seems in line with the general regime outlined above, which offers limited support for a general doctrine of automatic succession to bilateral treaties.[63] **34**

It is perhaps worth noting that, in pursuing this path, tribunals in the cases decided so far have been unwilling to view BITs as analogies to human rights treaties, for which protection had been said to 'devolv[e] with territory'.[64] Rather, their approach seems to be based on the idea that succession has to be agreed. **35**

Second, tribunals have been serious in exploring contextual factors which could help clarify whether the parties had agreed to keep a BIT in force. Judging from the available summaries, they have looked at a broad range of materials and drawn from it support for or against succession, including the following: (i) treaty databases of an official or private nature, in which a controversial BIT may or may not have been listed;[65] (ii) references to the controversial BIT in subsequent treaties;[66] (iii) unilateral Statements by State parties to the controversial **36**

---

[62] See V Djanic, 'Revealed: Reasons Surface for Tribunal's Decision that Montenegro was Not Bound by the Russia-Yugoslavia BIT' (*Investment Arbitration Reporter*, 3 July 2020) https://www-iareporter-com.ezproxy.lib.gla.ac.uk/articles/revealed-reasons-surface-for-tribunals-decision-that-montenegro-was-not-bound-by-the-russia-yugoslavia-bit, 3accessed 23 October 2023. Most recently, in November 2022 the Svea Court of Appeal declined to set aside the award of the tribunal in *Deripaska* and agreed with its conclusion that there had been no automatic succession of Montenegro to the Russia–Yugoslavia, see Svea Court of Appeal, *Deripaska v Montenegro*, Judgment, 10 November 2022 (Swedish original at https://jusmundi.com/fr/document/decision/sv-oleg-vladimirovich-deripaska-v-montenegro-svea-hovratt-dom-thursday-10th-november-2022). See further *Selmani v Kosovo*, ICC Case No 24443/MHM/HBH, Final Award, 1 August 2022, fn 497 in which the tribunal noted its agreement with the position taken in *Deripaska* that there was no automatic succession to BITs.

[63] By implication, it also suggests that succession depends on agreement (even though it may be implied), and is not automatic; see further Dumberry (n 56); R Pereira Fleury, 'State Succession and BITs: Challenges for Investment Arbitration' (2016) 27 Am Rev Intl Arb 456–57.

[64] Human Rights Committee, General Comment No 26 (n 48). For hints in this direction, see Zimmermann and Devaney, 'Succession to Treaties' (n 8) paras 19–20; Tams, 'State Succession to Investment Treaties' (n 58) 334–36; Vagts, 'State Succession (n 34) 281.

[65] Djanic (n 61) 6–7.

[66] For example, in the context of the *World Wide Minerals* and *Gold Pool* cases, commentators have referred to the Preamble to the 1997 Trade Agreement between the Government of Canada and the Government of the Republic of Kazakhstan, which mentioned the Canada–USSR BIT: see B Huelmo, 'Is Kazakhstan a State Successor to the USSR? A Perspective from Investment Treaty Arbitration' (2018) 36(2) ASA Bull 295, 309; L Eric Peterson, 'After failure of claim under Kazakh statute, Canadian miner hopes that USSR-Canada investment treaty permits arbitration with Kazakhstan', Investment Arbitration Reporter of 18 December 2013, 1 (hereafter Peterson, 'After failure').

BIT;[67] (iv) the practice of the successor State (and its partner) in addressing the fate of other treaties;[68] and (v) statements made in the context of the successor State's move to independence, eg pledges to respect international obligations.[69] In exploring these factors, investment tribunals have concretized the general regime.

37 *Third*, implicit in all this is a focus on succession by conduct, or by tacit agreement. As noted above, the general regime permits agreements on succession to be reached tacitly; but the issue had hardly ever received much attention. The recent investment decisions are serious about exploring this possibility, and their engagement with a wide range of evidentiary materials elucidates the general regime and fleshes out the hitherto abstract general international legal rules.[70] In fact, in a recent UK High Court decision in *Gold Pool* the High Court engaged in extensive analysis of whether Kazakhstan could be taken to have tacitly agreed to the continuation of the USSR–Canada BIT, in order to eventually set aside the award of the arbitral tribunal and to send it back for reconsideration.[71] Citing a 1992 joint political declaration and a diplomatic exchange of notes between Canada and Kazakhstan, the High Court found there was sufficient evidence conclude that these States intended for the Canada-USSR BIT to continue to apply, despite the absence of an express statement to this effect.[72] This highlights the apparent importance to tribunals of engagement with evidentiary material in establishing tacit consent, or agreement based on conduct—an approach preferred to abstract discussions about the existence of a general rule of automatic succession.

III. Assessment as to alignment or deviation

38 As regards new States' succession to BITs, the awards in *World Wide Minerals*, *Gold Pool* and *Deripaska*, as noted above, suggest that successor States do not automatically succeed to bilateral treaties entered into by their predecessors. This is noteworthy because it provides further support for the position that, as far as bilateral treaties are concerned, the principle of automatic succession enunciated in Article 34 VCSST does not reflect a general practice.

39 Investment decisions do not merely follow the general regime, however. They also shape, or at least finetune, it. Their added value lies in exploring issues that had previously not been addressed. Two issues stand out.

---

[67] Luke E Peterson, 'In a Dramatic Holding, UNCITRAL Tribunal Finds that Kazakhstan is Bound by Terms of Former USSR BIT with Canada' (*Investment Arbitration Reporter*, 28 January 2016) https://www.iareporter.com/articles/in-a-dramatic-holding-uncitral-tribunal-finds-that-kazakhstan-is-bound-by-terms-of-former-ussr-bit-with-canada; Vladislav Djanic, 'Revealed' (n 62) 7–8; Vladislav Djanic, 'Kazakhstan Fends Off Claims by Canadian Gold Miner, as Tribunal Finds it is not a Successor to USSR BIT' (*Investment Arbitration Reporter*, 4 August 2020) https://www-iareporter-com.ezproxy.lib.gla.ac.uk/articles/kazakhstan-fends-off-claims-by-canadian-gold-miner-as-tribunal-finds-it-is-not-a-successor-to-ussr-bit) accessed 18 January 2023, 1.

[68] Djanic, 'Revealed' (n 62) 7–8; Peterson, 'After failure' (n 66) 1; as well as Ministry of Justice (Kazakhstan), 'The Republic of Kazakhstan won a multimillion arbitration brought by Canadian company "Gold Pool"' (press release, 3 August 2020) https://www.gov.kz/memleket/entities/adilet/press/news/details/respublika-kazahstan-vyigrala-mnogomilionnyy-arbitrazhnyy-process-protiv-kanadskoy-kompanii-gold-pool-arbitrazhnyy-tribunal-podtverzhdaet-chto-kazahstan-ne-svyazan-sovetskim-soglasheniem?lang=en accessed 18 January 2023. See also *Gold Pool v Kazakhstan* [2021] EWHC 3422 (Comm) para 81.

[69] Djanic, 'Revealed' (n 62) 3.

[70] Tams, 'Ways Out of the Marshland' (n 5) 166–68; MG Kohen and P Dumberry, 'State Succession and State Responsibility in the Context of Investor-State Dispute Settlement' (2022) 37 ICSID Rev 5.

[71] *Gold Pool* (n 60).

[72] ibid para 111 et seq.

40 First, as far as new States' succession to BITs is concerned, arbitral practice could be read as a rediscovery of succession by tacit agreement or conduct. While always recognized in principle, the question of tacit agreement had received limited attention from courts and commentators. The fact-intensive and context-specific approach adopted in recent investment decisions proceeds from the assumption that succession by tacit agreement is more than a theoretical option: in that sense, arbitral practice affirms the position of an earlier generation of commentators who had noted that '[s]o far as the case of bilateral treaties is concerned, ... States can agree, even in the most informal fashion, to keep treaties in force'.[73]

41 Second, above all, investment decisions addressing questions of succession to treaties mark a move towards a more hands-on approach to State succession, in which the focus is on seriously assessing the intention of the parties. Certainly, with respect to instances of separation, tribunals have eschewed engagement with conceptual legal questions in favour of a more focused, case-specific approach. While working from within the general regime, their decisions provide much evidence of how often the abstract rules governing State succession can be applied in concrete cases. This practice fits within the general regime, but it offers the promise of specificity and concreteness.

D. Potential of investment arbitration to influence State succession

42 Overall, investment decisions on questions of State succession do not deviate from the general regime of State succession. However, the relationship between investment practice and the general regime is particular. Given the absence of an overarching, accepted framework, the general regime cannot simply be found by looking at an accepted text (such as the ARSIWA), or a major multilateral treaty (such as the VCLT). The multilateral treaty that does exist (the VCSST) hardly ever applies as treaty, and it is not a reliable guide to customary international law. The general regime is a patchwork of rules, some settled, others the product of responses to an overly ambitious codification project. And this patchwork exists in the shadow of a dominant practice, by States affected by instances of State succession seeking tailor-made solutions.

43 As far as cessions to territory are concerned, few dispute the desirability of the moving treaty frontiers rule. In the regular course of events, it is difficult to see why investment treaties should not be covered by it—they should align with the general rule. The *Sanum case* raised the narrow but crucial question whether treaty frontier should move even where this overrode the 'one country two systems' principle. The general regime does not preclude an exception, but emphasizing the moving treaty frontiers rule, does not encourage it. This to us seems a plausible approach and we see no good reason for why investment law should not align with the general approach.

44 As far as the question of automatic succession is concerned, the VCSST's approach premised on treaty continuity has often been presented as a desirable path towards treaty continuity. Forty-five years after the adoption of the Convention, it seems clear that the ambitious approach informing Article 34 (and Article 31) lacks nuance. States have preferred tailor-made approaches, and for bilateral treaties typically prefer to address matters via negotiations.

---

[73] DP O'Connell, 'Reflections on the State Succession Convention' (1979) 39 ZaöRV 725, 733.

Reliance on negotiated outcomes (affirming that a treaty remains in force, or exceptionally ceases to apply) has significantly reduced the practical relevance of general rules as most issues are addressed by States explicitly (or can be taken to have been addressed based on conduct). All this suggests that investment law broadly aligns with the general approach to succession. Our discussion suggests that it is in seriously engaging with questions of tacit agreement, investment practice and investment awards have contributed to its consolidation.

E. Conclusions

45 This entry has examined State succession in respect of part of a territory, normally termed cession or transfer of territory, and succession in cases of the unification and separation/dissolution of States. It has shown that the question of the alignment of investment practice with the general rules of State succession is complicated by the fact that those general rules, at least as envisaged in the VCSST, are themselves not particularly well-established. While some general rules of State succession are generally accepted and followed in practice (such as the moving treaties frontiers rule reflected in Article 15 VCSST) there appears to be a general trend in international law to seek tailor-made solutions. This trend reflects the desire of states to manage which treaty obligations apply to them; but it is shaped by an overarching expectation of treaty continuity when succession occurs.

46 In light of this general trend a significant degree of alignment can be discerned between investment practice and more general practice relating to the law of State succession. The preceding sections have shown that investment practice has reaffirmed certain general rules (such as that reflected in Article 15 VCSST) and further weakened ambitious attempts to bring about treaty continuity via a general rule (such as that contained in Article 34 VCSST). They also illustrate that investment tribunals and domestic courts assessing awards have gone to great lengths to establish the intentions of the parties, demonstrating a genuine willingness to identify and give effect to such intentions. Seen in this light, investment practice and investment awards align with the general regime. But they do more than that: they complement the often lofty discourse about broad principles with practical guidance on how to establish State preferences from conduct. This is an eminently useful contribution that enhances the regime of State succession to treaties.

Selected literature

Binder C, 'Sanum Investments Limited v The Government of the Lao People's Democratic Republic' (2016) 17 JWIT 280.

Distefano G, Gaggioli G and Hêche A, *La Convention de Vienne de 1978 sur la succession d'États en matière de traités: Commentaire article par article et études thématique* (Bruylant 2016).

Dumberry P, 'An Uncharted Question of State Succession: Are New States Automatically Bound by the BITs Concluded by Predecessor States Before Independence?' (2015) 6 JIDS 74–96.

Dumberry P, *A Guide to State Succession in International Investment Law* (Edward Elgar Publishing 2018).

Hafner G and Novak G, 'State Succession in Respect of Treaty Relationships' in Duncan Hollis (ed), *The Oxford Guide to Treaties* (2nd edn, OUP 2020) 383–413.

Kohen MG and Dumberry P, 'State Succession and State Responsibility in the Context of Investor-State Dispute Settlement' (2022) 37 ICSID Rev 4.

Ministry of Justice (Kazakhstan), 'The Republic of Kazakhstan won a multimillion arbitration brought by Canadian company "Gold Pool"' (Press Release, 3 August 2020) <https://www.gov.kz/memleket/entities/adilet/press/news/details/respublika-kazahstan-vyigrala-mnogomilionnyy-arbitrazhnyy-process-protiv-kanadskoy-kompanii-gold-pool-arbitrazhnyy-tribunal-podtverzhdaet-chto-kazahstan-ne-svyazan-sovetskim-soglasheniem?lang=en> accessed 18 February 2023.

Repousis OG, 'On Territoriality and International Investment Law: Applying China's Investment Treaties to Hong Kong and Macao' (2015) 37 Mich J Intl L 113.

Shijian JM, 'The Dilemma of Applying Bilateral Investment Treaties of China to Hongkong and Macao' (2018) 33 ICSID Rev 125.

Stern B, 'La succession d'Etats' (1996) 262 Recueil des cours 9.

Tams CJ, 'State Succession to Investment Treaties: Mapping the Issues' (2016) 31 ICSID Rev/FILJ 314–43.

Tams CJ, 'Ways Out of the Marshland: International Investment Law and the Law of State Succession' in Tams CJ and others (eds), *Investment Law and Public International Law* (Edward Elgar Publishing 2023).

Zimmermann A, *Staatennachfolge in völkerrechtliche Verträge* (Springer Heidelberg 2000).

Zimmermann A and Devaney J, 'Succession to Treaties and the Inherent Limits of International Law' in Tams CJ, Tzanakopoulos A and Zimmermann A (eds), *Research Handbook on the Law of Treaties* (Edward Elgar Cheltenham 2014) 505–40.

Zimmermann A and Devaney J, State Succession to Treaties, *Max Planck Encyclopedia* (OUP 2019)

Selected decisions

Application of the Convention on the Prevention and Punishment of the Crime of Genocide, Preliminary Objections (Judgment) [1996] ICJ Rep.

Application of the International Convention on the Elimination of All Forms of Racial Discrimination (*Georgia v Russian Federation*) (Order) [2008] ICJ Rep.

Sanum Investments Limited v Lao People's Democratic Republic, PCA Case No 2013-13, Jurisdiction, 13 December 2013.

Oleg Deripaska (Russian Federation) v the Republic of Montenegro, PCA Case No 2017-07.

Case Concerning the Gabčíkovo–Nagymaros Project (*Hungary v Slovakia*) (Judgment) (25 September 1997) [1997] ICJ Rep.

Gold Pool v Kazakhstan [2021] EWHC 3422 (Comm).

Government of the Law People's Democratic Republic v Sanum Investment Ltd [2015] SGHC 15.

Sanum Investment Ltd v Government of the Law People's Democratic Republic [2016] SGCA 57.

The protection of foreign investment in the law of State succession

Arman Sarvarian

A. Introduction	1	C. Concessionary contracts	20
B. International minimum standard		I. Concept	20
of treatment	3	II. Examples from State practice	21
I. Origin and concept	3	1. Israel	21
II. Examples from State practice	5	2. Algeria and the DRC	22
1. Indonesia	6	3. Tanzania	23
2. Madagascar	7	4. India	24
3. Democratic Republic of the Congo	8	5. Yemen	25
4. Algeria	9	III. Crystallization and scope	26
5. Equatorial Guinea	10	D. Foreign bondholders	27
6. Bangladesh	11	I. Concept	27
7. South Sudan	13	II. Assignment and apportionment	
III. Crystallization and scope	15	of State debt	29
		E. Conclusion	33

A. Introduction

1 This entry examines the protection of the proprietary rights of foreign nationals ('aliens')[1] in the law of State succession and its relevance in international investment law.[2] Three substantive issues have typically arisen in practice: first, the recognition by a successor of such proprietary rights; second, the substitution of a successor for the predecessor as party to a concessionary contract; third, the redemption of public debts contracted by the predecessor and held by private creditors. In investment arbitrations concerning the merits of claims by investors against successors asserting rights created prior to the succession, general

---

[1] On the problematic 'doctrine of acquired rights', see, eg, DP O'Connell, *State Succession in Municipal Law and International Law*, Vol I (CUP 1967) (hereafter O'Connell); EH Feilchenfeld, *Public Debts and State Succession* (Macmillan 1931); N Politis, *Les emprunts d'Etat en droit international* (A. Durand et Pedone-Lauriel 1894); FF Schmidt, *Der Übergang des Staatsschulden bei Gebietsabtretungen* (Dissertation,1913); AN Sack, *Les effets des transformations des états sur leurs dettes publiques* (Recueil Sirey 1927); P Lalive, 'The Doctrine of Acquired Rights' in M Bender (ed), *Rights and Duties of Private Investors Abroad* (International and Comparative Law Centre 1965) 145; S Friedmann, *Expropriation in International Law* (The London Institute for World Affairs 1953) 120; CF Amerasinghe, *State Responsibility for Injuries to Aliens* (Clarendon Press 1967) 145; FV García-Amador, *The Changing Law of International Claims* (Oceana Publications 1984) 263; A Reinisch and G Hafner, *Staatensukzession und Schuldenübernahme* (Service-Fachverl 1995).

[2] For the purpose of this entry, a State succession is defined as 'a transfer of territorial title from one State to another'. This definition, which is suggested to reflect customary international law, differs from Articles 2(1)(b) of the two Vienna Conventions on Succession of States of 1978 and 1983: 'the replacement of one State by another in the responsibility for the international relations of territory'.

international law has not featured, even by reference to 'international law' in choice-of-law provisions. Rather, the applicable law has been exclusively the instrument on which the arbitration was based—typically, a bilateral investment treaty.[3] The key issue has concerned jurisdiction: whether the respondent succeeded to an investment treaty concluded between its predecessor and the home State or a treaty between the respondent and the home State extended to the transferred territory.[4]

No general treaty is applicable to this field.[5] Rather, the substantive rules of general international law derive from customary international law[6] and general principles of law.[7] In default of access to investor–State arbitration under a bilateral investment treaty, investment contract, or investment law, general international law governs the treatment of the property of aliens in the territorial jurisdiction of the successor and thus apply in: the national courts of a successor; a claims commission or mixed arbitral tribunal; or interstate dispute settlement by diplomatic protection.[8]

B. International minimum standard of treatment

I. Origin and concept

Rooted in diplomatic protection, the international minimum standard of treatment is a rule of customary international law that obliges States to respect, *inter alia*, property belonging to aliens.[9] While the fair and equitable treatment standard—developed in the latter half of the twentieth century through bilateral investment treaty practice—is based on the minimum standard of treatment, the two are distinct.[10] Although States are entitled to expropriate

---

[3] For example, *Frontier Petroleum Services Ltd v Czech Republic*, PCA Case No 45035, Final Award, 12 November 2010, paras 28, 278–79, 306–07, 729; *InterTrade Holding GmbH (Germany) v Czech Republic*, PCA Case No 2009-12, Final Award, 29 May 2012, 62–76; *Voecklinghaus v Czech Republic*, UNCITRAL, Final Award, 19 September 2011; *Binder v Czech Republic*, UNCITRAL, Final Award, 15 July 2011, paras 165, 351, 372–73, 437–67; *Achmea B.V. (formerly known as 'Eureko B.V.') v Slovak Republic*, PCA Case No 2008-13, Final Award, 7 December 2012, paras 287–95; *MNSS B.V. and Recupero Credito Acciaio N.V. v Montenegro*, ICSID Case No ARB(AF)/12/8, Award, 4 May 2016, paras 230, 323–28; *Sanum Investments Limited v Laos*, UNCITRAL, Award, 6 August 2019, paras 178–250.

[4] One author identified forty-six such arbitrations: P Dumberry, *A Guide to State Succession in International Investment Law* (Edward Elgar Publishing 2018) vi. It is also possible that recent arbitrations have featured succession to State contracts, eg 'Three are in Place to Hear Contract-Based Arbitration Against South Sudan' (*Investment Arbitration Reporter*, 25 March 2021); L Roddy, 'Indian State Energy Company Brings Claim Against Sudan', *GAR* (17 April 2018).

[5] Amidst deep disagreement concerning a controversial report by the Special Rapporteur, Mohammed Bedjaoui, the International Law Commission omitted private property from the scope of its codification project, which focused on State property and debt—UN Doc A/CN.4/216/Rev.1 (18 June 1969) paras 148–56; UN Doc A/7610/Rev.1 (8 August 1969) paras 43–61. Consequently, the Vienna Convention on Succession of States in respect of State Property, Archives and Debts 1983 is irrelevant.

[6] For example, UN Doc A/73/10 (2018) 122, Conclusions 4, 6, 8–9.

[7] For example, UN Doc A/CN.4/732 (5 April 2019) paras 188–253.

[8] Though rare, these classical dispute settlement mechanisms continue to exist alongside the modern system of investment arbitration—*Ahmadou Sadio Diallo Case (Guinea v Democratic Republic of the Congo)* (Preliminary Objections) [2007] ICJ Rep 582, para 88. Recent successors that were largely detached from the system of international investment arbitration at the date of succession include: Namibia (1990), Eritrea (1993), Timor-Leste (2002), and South Sudan (2011).

[9] See in this Commentary Robert Howse, 'The international law minimum standard of treatment'. See also, eg, A de Nanteuil, *International Investment Law* (Edward Elgar Publishing 2021) 13, 94, 284 (hereafter de Nanteuil).

[10] For example, de Nanteuil (n 9) 285–307.

property owned by aliens,[11] they must do so with due process and a public interest and without discrimination towards or among aliens.[12] States are not obliged to compensate the owners before expropriating, though they must accept the obligation to compensate later.[13]

4 The date of crystallization of the minimum standard of treatment as a rule of customary international law is contested, though it is likely to have taken place during the 1930s.[14] However, its applicability to the law of State succession was an open question during decolonization. Whereas the UN General Assembly endorsed the duty to pay 'appropriate compensation' for expropriation in 1962,[15] it reserved the question for State succession.[16]

II. Examples from State practice

5 Though not yet crystallized as customary law in State succession, extensive State practice before and after 1962 saw successors respect the property of aliens validly-acquired before the date of succession. Recognition can be identified in treaties and devolution agreements in which the successor undertook to respect the proprietary rights of nationals of the predecessor, as well as constitutional and other national laws by which the successor guaranteed the proprietary rights of aliens. The most significant examples of State practice concerned measures taken by successors to expropriate the property of aliens by which they either implemented the requirements for lawful expropriation or agreed to repair unlawful expropriations without stipulating an *ex gratia* or 'without prejudice' clause.

1. Indonesia

6 For the secession of Indonesia from the Netherlands in 1949, Indonesia undertook to safeguard proprietary rights, concessions, and licences,[17] though stipulating that 'it shall be borne in mind that the general economic policy to be pursued ... shall in the first place be focused on the economic building up of the Indonesian community as a whole'.[18] In expropriating property belonging to Dutch nationals from 1958 for the purpose of advancing its claim to Irian Barat (West New Guinea), Indonesia legislated for the payment of compensation by a Government-appointed committee.[19] The Netherlands protested the expropriations as pursuant to a political purpose, discriminatory and confiscatory due to the compensation process not having been implemented.[20] In 1969, Indonesia agreed to pay a lump sum in compensation, including in Irian Barat.[21]

---

[11] An expropriation is a deprivation by the State of specific property from an owner, which also embraces nationalization—de Nanteuil (n 9) 310–12; I Marboe, *Calculation of Compensation and Investment Damages in International Law* (OUP 2017) 44–45 (hereafter Marboe).

[12] Marboe (n 11) 45. State practice in international investment treaties is consistent with these criteria; see, eg, de Nanteuil (n 9) 312; D Khachvani, 'Compensation for Unlawful Expropriation: Targeting the Illegality' (2017) 32(2) ICSID Rev 385, 385–87.

[13] Marboe (n 11) 46–65.

[14] M Paparinskis, *The International Minimum Standard and Fair and Equitable Treatment* (2013) 39–64.

[15] UNGA Res 1803(XVII), 14 December 1962, Article 4. On the compromise between the 'Hull formula' and 'no compensation', see Marboe (n 11) 28–29; de Nanteuil (n 9) 317–18.

[16] UNGA Res 1803(XVII), Preamble.

[17] A Peaslee, *Constitutions of Nations*, Vol 2 (Martinus Nijhof 1956) 368, Articles 8, 26(2), 27(1).

[18] 69 UNTS (1950) 200, Union Statute, Appendix, Article 2; Financial and Economic Agreement, Article 6.

[19] (1959) 6 NILR 291, Articles 1–2. See also 28 ILR (1960) 16, 17, 22, 28–29.

[20] ' Netherlands-Indonesia:Netherlands Note of December 18, 1959, Regarding Nationalization of Dutch-Owned Enterprises' (1960) 54 AJIL 484, 485–89.

[21] 1353 UNTS 287, Article X.

2. Madagascar

For the secession of Madagascar from France in 1956, France and Madagascar had agreed to mutual respect for the proprietary rights of their nationals on independence.[22] While Madagascar had affirmed respect for proprietary rights of foreigners in its 1959 constitution, France successfully objected to the suppression of the principle of compensation for French protected persons (*ressortissants*) prescribed by a law on reclamation of unproductive land of 1 October 1962. While Madagascar initially argued that the laws were enacted pursuant to a constitutional duty to develop natural resources, it agreed to pay 'fair and equitable compensation, in accordance with international law' for the nationalization of 'property, securities, rights and interests'.[23]

3. Democratic Republic of the Congo

For the secession of the Democratic Republic of the Congo (DRC) from Belgium in 1960, the DRC undertook to expropriate investments belonging to aliens only in the public interest and pursuant to a national law providing for payment of fair compensation.[24] Three Belgian companies with interlocking boards, termed 'para-statal entities', operated in the key minerals sector.[25] In 1964, the DRC refused to ratify its devolution agreement with Belgium; instead, it expropriated property, including concessions, belonging to the Belgian companies. In a detailed explanatory statement, it averred: the Belgian companies were charter companies, not private companies; the companies had not acquired rights by purchase but rather had received lands for free at the expense of the native population; and its refusal to compensate was based on UN principles on decolonization.[26] The DRC concluded:

> '[T]he Congo Republic wishes to stress that in taking this position it by no means intends to injure in any way the legitimate rights of aliens residing in the country or having capital invested there. The property and rights of aliens will still be safeguarded by the Government. But it intends to put an end to ownership of colonial origin which was exemplified by the substance of Congolese soil at the disposition of the Compagnie du Katanga, the C.S.K., the C.F.L., and the C.N.K.I.'[27]

Following additional expropriations without compensation in 1966,[28] the DRC agreed to compensate the owners in 1965, 1969, and 1973.[29]

4. Algeria

For its secession from France in 1962, Algeria undertook to respect the property of French nationals exercising Algerian civil rights; in particular, 'no dispossession measures [were to] be taken against them without their being granted fair compensation

---

[22] 820 UNTS (1972) 364, Article 11. See also AJ Peaslee and D Peaslee Xydis, *Constitutions of Nations* (Martinus Nijhof Publishers 1965) 453–72 (hereafter Peaslee and Peaslee Xydis). Preamble; D Bardonnet, *La succession d'Etats à Madagascar* (LGDJ 1970) 632–44.

[23] 2179 UNTS 43, Articles 2–3.

[24] Peaslee and Peaslee Xydis (n 22) 98, Articles 43, 46, 195. See also CRISP, *Congo 1965: Political Documents of a Developing Nation* (1967), 252–53 (French); *La Conférence Belgo-Congolaise Economique, Financière et Sociale* (26 April–16 May 1960), 46–47, 54–55 (hereafter *La Conférence Belgo-Congolaise*).

[25] W Radmann, 'The Nationalization of Zaire's Copper: From Union Minière to GECAMINES' (1978) 25(4) Afr Today 25–47, 26–27, 30–31 (hereafter Radmann, 'The Nationalization of Zaire's Copper').

[26] 4(2) ILM (1965) 232, Articles 1–3, Explanatory Statement, paras 16–18.

[27] ibid, Explanatory Statement, para 21.

[28] I *Moniteur Congolais* (15 August 1966) 523, Article 2; 560, Articles 1–2 (French); I *Moniteur Congolais* (1967) 29, Articles 1–2 (French); 6(5) ILM (1967) 915, Articles 1–3.

[29] 4(2) ILM (1965) 239; Radmann, 'The Nationalization of Zaire's Copper' (n 25) 40, 42, 45.

previously agreed upon'.[30] From 1963, Algeria expropriated without compensation agricultural property belonging to French nationals; invoking its devolution agreement as public policy (*ordre public*) the French courts refused to recognize these acts.[31] In January 1963, Algeria conceded that such property was in the legal possession of absent French owners.[32]

5. Equatorial Guinea

10 For the secession of Equatorial Guinea from Spain in 1968, it guaranteed the property of all persons[33] and undertook to respect the concessions awarded by Spain up to the moment of independence and the persons and property of Spanish nationals 'in application of international law'.[34] In consequence of damages to the property of Spanish nationals caused by riots and governmental action from 12 October 1968,[35] Equatorial Guinea undertook on 23 October 1980 to restore farms confiscated from Spanish owners.[36]

6. Bangladesh

11 For the secession of Bangladesh from Pakistan in 1971, Bangladesh expropriated without compensation any industrial or commercial concern whose owner, director, or manager had left Bangladesh or who, in the opinion of the Government, could not in the public interest be allowed to manage it.[37] In awarding disputed assets to Pakistani claimants, the United States rejected these measures as contrary to public policy due to their confiscatory nature.[38] Banks and industrial enterprises were also nationalized with compensation to be awarded according to Government valuation.[39]

12 Whereas provision was made for the restoration of the immovable property of evacuees, the Government was empowered to confiscate the property of persons convicted of, *inter alia*, citizens of a State which at any time after 25 March 1971 was at war with Bangladesh.[40] In 1977, the Supreme Court of Bangladesh held the Government not to have acquired any beneficial interest in property seized, as such properties were to be restored to the owners after the war.[41] In 2013, Bangladesh enacted the Vested Properties Return (Amendment) Act to provide for the restoration of confiscated properties still in her possession.

7. South Sudan

13 For the secession of South Sudan from the Sudan in 2011, the two States signed a treaty in September 2012 that postponed the question of apportionment of the external State debt, though providing that domestic assets and liabilities were to be apportioned in accordance with the 'territorial principle, by which assets and liabilities [having] a domestic connection

---

[30] 1(2) ILM (1962) 214, Ch II(A)(2)(b), Ch II(B)(2)(b); Declaration of Principles concerning Economic and Financial Cooperation, Preamble, para 1.
[31] For example, 47 ILR 60, 61–62, 120, 125–26; 48 ILR 82, 83. *Contra*: 52 ILR 8, 10.
[32] O'Connell (n 1) 295.
[33] First Constitution of Equatorial Guinea, *Boletín oficial de la Guinea Ecuatorial* (24 July 1968), Article 3; 'Transitional Provisions', para 2a (Spanish).
[34] 50 *Boletín Oficial del Estado* (28 February 1972), 3511, Articles III–VI, VIII–XII (Spanish).
[35] Peaslee and Peaslee Xydis (n 22) 176.
[36] 1322 UNTS (1983) 66, Exchange of Letters; Final Act. See also 88 ILR 691, 694, 696.
[37] 24 Dhaka Law Reports (1972), Bangladesh Statutes 1971–72, 8, ss 2, 5–6.
[38] 22 AILC (1969–78) 279, 280–86; 66 ILR 192, 194–96.
[39] 24 Dhaka Law Reports (1972), Bangladesh Statutes 1971–72, 69 (ss 2, 4, 7–8, 32, Schedule), 78 (ss 4–5, 9).
[40] 24 Dhaka Law Reports (1972), Bangladesh Statutes 1971–72, 30 (s 2(c)); 16 (s 2(b), 12).
[41] 30 Dhaka Law Reports (1978) 139, 145, 147, 151–55, 158.

to the territory of Sudan... be allocated along territorial lines and attributed to the respective State'.[42] Neither 'domestic asset' nor 'domestic liability' was defined.[43]

In 2016, an investor–State arbitral tribunal decided a claim brought by an oil company (Sudapet) against South Sudan for direct expropriation and breach of the international minimum standard of treatment on the basis of the pre-independence Southern Sudan Investment Promotion Act.[44] Although the outcome of the arbitration is not published, it is known that the Respondent argued that the assets of Sudapest 'vested in it by operation of law' upon independence, as State property rather than private property.[45] Whether the assets in question qualified as an 'investment' due to the question of its identity as State property was a novel issue.[46] Finding Sudan and South Sudan to have deliberately adopted the territorial principle, drawing 'upon international law and practice, including where relevant the [VCSP]', to encapsulate both immovable and movable property,[47] the arbitral tribunal applied the principle to the interests of Sudapet to classify them as State property.[48]

III. Crystallization and scope

In 1974, the General Assembly resolved that each State has the right: 'To nationalize, expropriate or transfer ownership of foreign property, in which case appropriate compensation should be paid by the State adopting such measures, taking into account its relevant laws and regulations and all circumstances that the State considers pertinent.'[49] Unlike in 1962,[50] the resolution omitted any qualifier with respect to State succession. Although investment arbitral jurisprudence has not followed the linking by the General Assembly of the adequacy of compensation to domestic law,[51] its resolution was an acceptance by States of the duty of successors to compensate in the exercise of their right to expropriate the property of aliens.

In successions taking place after the adoption of the 1974 resolution, successors consistently recognized the proprietary rights of aliens. A rare exception was the expropriation without compensation by South Viet Nam of property belonging to aliens; in 1995, Viet Nam reached

---

[42] 'Agreement between the Republic of the Sudan and the Republic of South Sudan on Certain Economic Matters' (signed 27 September 2012, entered into force 17 October 2012) https://www.peaceagreements.org/view/857/Agreement%20between%20Sudan%20and%20South%20Sudan%20on%20Certain%20Economic%20Matters accessed 4 September 2019, Articles 3.1, 3.2, 6.
[43] ibid Article 4.1.2.
[44] *Sudapet v South Sudan*, ICSID Case No ARB/12/26, Award Excerpts, 30 September 2016, paras 1, 319.
[45] ibid para 320.
[46] ibid para 324. A similar issue apparently arose in an unpublished award—*Haakon Korsguard v Croatia*, UNCITRAL, Award, 7 November 2022, reported in: Vladislav Djanić, 'Croatia Claims Victory in Under-the-Radar Treaty Arbitration' (10 November 2022) <https://www.iareporter.com/articles/croatia-claims-victory-in-under-the-radar-treaty-arbitration/> accessed 23 October 2023. The State Attorney's Office of Croatia announced that the claims of a Canadian national for expropriation due to his inability to register himself in the land registry of Croatia as owner of real estate, purchased from Serbian trading companies in Croatia that had been owned by them as 'social property', accepting its argument that the relevant annex to the 2001 Agreement on Succession Issues was inapplicable with outstanding property issues due to a bilateral settlement between Croatia and Serbia—DORH, 'Uspjeh u arbitražnom sporu—prihvaćene tvrdnje DORH-a i odbijen tužbeni zahtjev radi naknade štete u iznosu od 230 milijuna eura' https://dorh.hr/hr/priopcenja/uspjeh-u-arbitraznom-sporu-prihvacene-tvrdnje-dorh-i-odbijen-tuzbeni-zahtjev-radi.
[47] ibid paras 440–43.
[48] ibid paras 445–541.
[49] UNGA Res 3281 (XXIX), 12 December 1974, Article 2(2)(c).
[50] UNGA Res 1803(XVII), 14 December 1962.
[51] For example, 66 ILR 518, 599–613; 9 *ICSID Reports* 412, para 497; 31 ILM (1992) 1363; Marboe (n 11) 28–29; de Nanteuil (n 9) 317–18.

a lump sum compensation agreement with the United States.[52] State practice and *opīniōnēs juris* are thus general (widespread, representative, and consistent)[53] in evincing the applicability of the international minimum standard to State succession. Subject to national rules on constitutionality and jurisdiction, succession arrangements made by treaty would displace any national law.[54]

17 To benefit from the protection of the customary rule, owners must be private persons at the date of succession: individuals, companies, or other entities. Disputes have tended to concern the definition of 'public' and 'private' property, such as property owned by a State in its private capacity ('patrimonial property')[55] and the assets of 'para-statal' or quasi-governmental entities.[56] While it is clear that its beneficiaries are confined to aliens, persons holding the nationality of the predecessor at the date of succession might not benefit due to their assumption of the nationality of the successor through collective nationalization.[57] It is possible for private persons to opt for the nationality of the predecessor by declaration or conduct: typically, by moving residence or head office.[58]

18 There is no universal definition of 'property' in international law, which is construed loosely to encompass a vast range of rights founded in title, contract, and statute.[59] The national law of the predecessor in force at the time of the creation of the asset is applied to determine whether it qualifies on procedural or substantive grounds. However, this might be displaced by a specific definition adopted in a treaty or resolution.[60]

19 An important issue in modern arbitral jurisprudence on expropriation is the methodology for the valuation of compensation. Two practical differences have been recognized between the duty to compensate for lawful expropriations and the duty to repair for unlawful expropriations: (1) the availability of the remedy of restitution for unlawful expropriations only; and (2) an increase in the value of the expropriated assets between the date of expropriation and the date of award, which may be taken into account for unlawful expropriations only.[61]

---

[52] 34 ILM (1995) 685, Articles 1–3.
[53] ILC Draft Conclusions (n 6) Conclusions 3, 7–9.
[54] For example, 30 ILM (1991) 463, Article 41, Annex III; 94 ILR 42, 48–53, 59–66.
[55] For example, IMF Doc SM/59/57, Supplement 1 (15 October 1959), 2–3; 51(2) AJIL (1957) 460, Article 2; *La Conférence Belgo-Congolaise* (n 24) 42–44; 61 ILR 143, 146–47, 149, 153–54; 94 ILR 135, 178–81, 192–93.
[56] For example, Wolf Radmann, 'The Nationalization of Zaire's Copper', 25(4) Afr Today (1978) 25.
[57] On the nationality-of-claims rule, see UN Doc A/CN.4/506 and Add. 1 (7 March and 20 April 2000) paras 94–120; ILC Draft Articles on Diplomatic Protection with commentaries, YILC 2006, Vol II, Part Two, 29–30, Article 4, 31–33, Article 5(2); CF Amerasinghe, *Diplomatic Protection* (OUP 2008) 91–92, 100–05; Richard B Lillich and Burns H Weston, *International Claims: Their Settlement by Lump Sum Agreements* Vol I (University Press of Virginia 1975) 48–52 (hereafter Lillich and Weston). In a case pending at annulment stage, the arbitral tribunal reportedly declined jurisdiction *ratione personae* with respect to the first Claimant, Mr Edmond Khudyan, on the basis that he had remained an Armenian national after the secession of Armenia from the Soviet Union and so the prohibition of claims by dual nationals under the ICSID Convention applied—*Edmond Khudyan v Armenia*, ICSID Case No ARB/17/36, Award of 15 December 2021 (not published) reported in L Bohmer, 'Analysis: ICSID Tribunal Examines Citizenship of Individual Investor in State Succession Context' (*Investment Arbitration Reporter*, 21 December 2021) <https://www.iareporter.com/articles/analysis-icsid-tribunal-examines-citizenship-of-individual-investor-in-state-succession-context-and-sees-insufficient-proof-that-corporate-co-claimant-made-an-investment/> 23 October 2023.
[58] For example, 2138 UNTS 93, Article 5(9); Civilians Claims: Eritrea's Claims 15, 16, 23, and 27–32, PCA Case No 2001-02, Partial Award, 17 December 2004, paras 48–52.
[59] In lump sum compensation treaties, for example, broad terms such as 'property, rights and interests' have been interpreted to encompass debts and intangible property, such as debts owed to foreign bondholders—Lillich and Weston (n 57) 180–86.
[60] For example, 118 UNTS 115, Annex, Articles 1–2, 4–5; 133, Annex, Articles 1–2; 22 ILR (1955) 103, 106, 108; 25 ILR (1958-I) 13; 2328 UNTS 1, Articles 3–8, 13, 15–16; Exchange of Notes.
[61] Marboe (n 11) 81.

When a claim is pursued by means of diplomatic protection, however, the claiming State may claim for damages owed to itself (eg satisfaction) in addition to those owed to its injured national.[62] In the absence of a universal valuation framework, arbitral tribunals employ a variety of techniques according to the market value, investment value, or replacement value of the expropriated assets.[63]

C. Concessionary contracts

I. Concept

In investment arbitration, claims for contractual damages with respect to concessions concluded by predecessors have been addressed exclusively within the framework of a bilateral investment treaty.[64] While a concession, as a type of 'State contract', is rarely defined in the State practice on succession, one definition refers to a grant of specific rights or assets by a State to a private company or individual in exchange for specific obligations with respect to their improvement, operation, or maintenance.[65] Examples of concessions include: the construction, operation, or maintenance of public utilities (eg railways); the provision of public services (eg security); and the exploitation of natural resources (eg mining). Though contractual in nature, concessions are recognized as 'property' under the international minimum standard of treatment.[66] The most significant instances of modern State practice have featured disputes as to the duty to respect the rights of foreign concessionaries.

II. Examples from State practice

1. Israel

In 1955, Israel considered that, while it had elected to recognize certain classes of rights granted by Mandatory Palestine, it could have lawfully refrained from recognizing a concession to operate kiosks in railway stations, for 'there [was] no accepted rule of international law requiring an ... emancipated State, to recognize, in its domestic legislation, any action performed by the previous authority – including acts creating private rights for the individual'.[67] However, the *opinio juris* of Israel changed in 1958 when, responding to a complaint of Syria at the U.N. Security Council concerning works in the demilitarized zone, it argued that they were done pursuant to a concession granted to the Palestine Electric Corporation in 1926 for the generation of electricity, which was 'a legally established private right, deriving from the period before Israel's establishment ... a right which, according to the principles of international law, any government would be obliged to respect and to uphold'.[68]

---

[62] Marboe (n 11) 87, 315–26; Lillich and Weston (n 57) 106–10. See, however, Ahmadiou Siado Diallo Case *(Guinea v Democratic Republic of the Congo)* (Compensation) [2012] ICJ Rep 324, paras 10, 13, 57–60.
[63] Marboe (n 11) 213–326.
[64] See references in n 3.
[65] UNGA Res 530(VI), Article VIII(1)(a).
[66] For example, 40 ILR 260; 20 ILR 628, 632.
[67] 22 ILR (1955) 113, 119.
[68] UNSC Off Rec 8th year, 633rd meeting, 30 October 1958, 16, para 81. See also UNGA Res 181 (II), 19 November 1947, (1947), Part I(A).

2. Algeria and the DRC

22 In the aforementioned examples of Algeria and the DRC, the successors expropriated concessions belonging to nationals of their predecessors. In 1966, Algeria undertook to compensate mining concessionaires according to the average price of its shares during the two years preceding nationalization to be paid out of the assets of the company.[69] The French courts denied an obligation of France to pay compensation for nationalized concessions, holding these obligations to have transferred to Algeria.[70] The Belgian Congo had agreed with Belgian concessionaires shortly before independence to early termination of their concessions with compensation.[71] Following expropriation of the remaining concessions, the DRC agreed to compensate the concessionaires in 1969 and 1974.[72]

3. Tanzania

23 In 1921, the United Kingdom granted Belgium a perpetual lease for a notional rent with respect to the Belbase installations at the port of Dar-es-Salaam. In 1955, Belgium renewed with the approval of the United Kingdom a concession to operate the facilities awarded to a Belgian company (*Agence Belge de l'Est Africain*) for twenty-five years. In 1962, Tanganyika proposed that the concession be taken over by the East Africa Common Services Organization with compensation awarded for the capital investment in the sites (upon valuation) less amounts already recovered by amortization.[73] Following receipt of notes from the Congo, Rwanda, and Burundi asserting succession to the 1921 treaty, Tanganyika proposed a new arrangement for the port facilities and that the three States determine the apportionment of compensation *inter se*.[74] The concessionaire continued to manage the installations until the expiry of the concession in 1971 whereupon Tanzania concluded a fresh contract with the concessionaire, which ceased to manage the facilities on 1 January 1996 after seventy years in total.[75]

4. India

24 Whereas mining concessions granted by Portugal in perpetuity in Daman, Diu, and Goa prior to the annexation were upheld by India in 1957, the Supreme Court of India denied an obligation in international law to recognize them, holding it to be the prerogative of India to accept them after the incorporation by contract, executive fiat, or legislation.[76] In 1987, India retroactively declared the abolition of such concessions from 20 December 1961 and their conversion into mining leases with cash compensation to the concession-holders.[77]

5. Yemen

25 Following the merger of North Yemen with South Yemen, Yemen replaced North Yemen in a concession granted to a US company in 1985 as well as South Yemen in a concession made

---

[69] 41 ILR 384, 393–94.
[70] 48 ILR 58–60.
[71] 4(2) ILM (1965) 232, Explanatory Statement, paras 16–18; Radmann, 'The Nationalization of Zaire's Copper' (n 25) 26–27, 30–31; *La Conférence Belgo-Congolaise* (n 24) 46–47, 54–55.
[72] N 29. See also Peaslee and Peaslee Xydis (n 22) 98, Articles 43, 46, 195.
[73] O'Connell (n 1) 242.
[74] ibid 243.
[75] L Darcis, 'Les Belbase: une réalisation peu connue de l'expansion belge en Afrique de l'Est' (2007) 53(2) Bull séances 143.
[76] Mines and Minerals (Regulation and Development) Act 1957, para 4; 118 ILR 429, 443–46.
[77] Goa, Daman and Diu Mining Concessions (Abolition and Declaration as Mining Leases) Act 1987 (No 16 of 1987), paras 2, 4–7.

to a Soviet entity in 1986.[78] In a commercial arbitration, Yemen unsuccessfully challenged substitution to a concession granted by North Yemen to a Belgian company in respect of the maintenance of construction and maintenance of a port. The arbitral award, upheld by the Supreme Court of Cyprus, held Yemen to be party to the contract, notwithstanding the improper appointment of counsel by the Yemeni Port Authority in violation of Yemeni law, because it took its burden with its territorial benefit.[79]

III. Crystallization and scope

In rare cases (eg the secession of North Viet Nam in 1946[80]) successors have cancelled concessions and rejected compensation thereafter. Nonetheless, the weight of State practice and *opīniōnēs juris* supports the applicability of the international minimum standard of treatment to concessionary contracts as a form of property with two distinctive features. First, they entail the substitution of the successor for the predecessor as party to the concession by agreement or conduct ('novation') to ensure its performance.[81] Second, damages for breach of contract are generally governed by the national law governing the contract, though it is possible for a choice-of-law clause to refer to 'international law'.[82] Though analogous to full reparation under the law of State responsibility,[83] the valuation methods applied in investment arbitral jurisprudence have been variegated.[84] A successor is not bound by concessions that were granted in violation of the laws of the predecessor or by an unlawful occupier.[85]

D. Foreign bondholders

I. Concept

Although claims by foreign bondholders for the recovery of debts from a successor has yet to arise in investment arbitration, they have frequently been pursued through diplomatic protection. The substantive question arises whether the debt be extinguished, transferred to the successor, or vested in the predecessor. As customary international law regulates the transfer of State property and debt in cases of succession, the claims of private creditors are affected by agreements between the predecessor and successor as well as decisions taken by public creditors (i.e. the IMF, World Bank and states, typically under the auspices of the Paris

---

[78] World Bank, 'The Republic of Yemen: Unlocking the Potential for Economic Growth' (October 2015), paras 222, 227, 244; As-Saruri and Sorkhabi, 'Petroleum Basins of Yemen', 13(2) GEOExPro (2016) <https://www.geoexpro.com/articles/2016/04/petroleum-basins-of-yemen> accessed 23 October 2023.
[79] ICC Case No 7748/BGD/OLG (unpublished) in: Case No 10717, ILDC 630 (CY 2002), paras F1–F4.
[80] North Viet Nam, Law on Land Reform (4 December 1953), Articles 1–2; J Charpentier, 'Pratique française du droit international' (1956) 2(1) AFDI 838–39. One exception was made for the *Société des Charbonnages du Tonkin*—P Brocheux, 'Les relations économiques entre la France et le Vietnam, 1955–1975' (2017) 2 Outre-Mers 193, 194–96, 199–200. France rejected claims for compensation, considering the rights and obligations of French Indochina to have transferred to North Viet Nam—44 ILR 37, 38; 52 ILR 5, 6.
[81] For example, 40 ILR 158, 160.
[82] Marboe (n 11) 32.
[83] ibid 33, 118–21.
[84] ibid 33–34, 100–18.
[85] For example, 14 ILR (1947) 51; 217 UNTS (1955) 223, Article 23(3); Namibia, Constitution (21 March 1990) https://www.namibiahc.org.uk/perch/resources/pdf/namibia-constitution-2015.pdf accessed 23 October 2023, Articles 140, 145; 91 ILR 341, 360, 368–69; [1992] NR 102 (HC), 104–08; UNSC Res 301 (1971), 12; 29 ILM 469, Articles 2, 4; Constitution of the Democratic Republic of Timor-Leste, 22 March 2002 (25 May 2002) http://timor-leste.gov.tl/wp-content/uploads/2010/03/Constitution_RDTL_ENG.pdf accessed 23 October 2023, para 158(3).

Club). In the absence of a willing respondent, private creditors' claims in successions have been typically addressed in national fora and by diplomatic protection; the London Club of commercial creditors is an important forum.

28 Should a creditor pursue the debt through investment arbitration, an important question is whether sovereign debt qualifies as an 'investment'.[86] Most arbitral tribunals have considered promissory notes and sovereign bonds to qualify for the purposes of jurisdiction.[87] The question is complicated by the lack of a settled test for the definition of an 'investment'[88] and the possibility for parties to specify different debt instruments in bilateral investment treaties, contracts, or investment laws. In customary international law, debts owed to private bondholders have qualified as 'property' for the international minimum standard.[89]

II. Assignment and apportionment of State debt

29 Since the Second World War, State practice and *opīniōnēs juris* support the existence of a customary rule that distinguishes between 'total successions' (merger, absorption, or dismemberment) and 'partial successions' (cession or secession). In total successions, the entirety of the State debt transfers with the territories to the successors due to the extinction of the predecessor. Examples include: the 'absorption' of Austria by Germany;[90] the 'absorption' of the Baltic States by the USSR in 1940;[91] the absorption of the Free City of Danzig by Poland;[92] the absorption of East Germany;[93] and the merger of Yemen.[94] In dismemberment, the property and debt of the predecessor are proportionately distributed among the successors, as for Czecho-Slovakia in 1939[95] and 1993[96] and the SFRY.[97]

---

[86] For example, M Waibel, 'Opening Pandora's Box: Sovereign Bonds in International Arbitration' (2007) 101(4) AJIL 711, 729–36; S Pahis, 'BITs & Bonds: The International Law and Economics of Sovereign Debt' (2021) 115(2) AJIL 242, 244–53.

[87] ibid.

[88] For example, U Kriebaum, C Schreuer, R Dolzer, *Principles of International Investment Law* (OUP 2022) 82 et seq.

[89] N 59. Although the VCSSP was adopted by a vote of 54-11-11, the exclusion of debts owed to private creditors from its scope in Article 31 was a major reason for its lack of support from the minority—*Official Records of the United Nations Conference on Succession of States in respect of State Property, Archives and Debts* (Vol I), Doc A/CONF.117/SR.10, paras 62, 65, 72, 80, 100–01.

[90] For example, RE Clute, *The International Legal Status of Austria 1938-1955* (The Hague: Martinus Nijhoff 1962) 91, 93–94, 425 (hereafter *Austria*); II FRUS (1938) 486, 487–92, 501; 39 MNRG 302, Article 4; 337 *Hansard*, Series 5, Col 34; 36 MNRG (1939) 370, Preamble, Article 2 and Annex (§§1–2, 4–5), Article 3; 40 MNRG (1938) 265, Articles 1, 3; RFBPC (1938), 664.

[91] Foreign Compensation Act 1950 (c12), para 3; Foreign Compensation (USSR)(Registration) Order, SI 1959, No 1968; Russia Treaty Database, Nos 1958010 and 1958011 (unpublished, Russian); 638 UNTS (1968) 41, Articles 1, 2, 5(1); 103 RCCFB (1976) 53–54; 67 RCCFB (1940), 55.

[92] 38 MNRG (3rd Series, 1939) 15, Articles I, III, IV (German); 91 RCCFB (1964), 301–02; 103 RCCFB (1976) 12, 19–20, 45–47.

[93] 30 ILM (1991) 463, Article 23.

[94] IMF Doc SM/90/93 (17 May 1990), 40–43; IMF Doc SM/92/53 (12 March 1992), 4, 20–21, 25–28, 32–33, 36–37.

[95] 41 MNRG (1940) 3, Articles 1–3, 9, 11 (German); 39 MNRG (1940) 101, Articles 1, 14 (German).

[96] Coll *Zákony Prolidi* (13 November 1992), Articles 4–5; IMF, Decision No 10248-(92/157), 30 December 1992; IMF Doc EBS/92/218 (21 December 1992); IMF Doc EBS/92/213 (16 December 1992), 7–10.

[97] IMF Press Release No 92/92 (15 December 1992); Mrăk, *Succession of States* (1999), 155–56, 160–64, 177; A Stanič, 'Financial Aspects of State Succession: The Case of Yugoslavia' (2001) 12 EJIL 751, 761–63; 984 F Supp 209 (SDNY 1997); 2262 UNTS 251, Appendix, para 1; Annex C, Articles 3(3), 4(1), 5(2); IMF Doc SM/05/216 (14 June 2005), 26–27, 36, 46–47, 49; Paris Club, Press Release (17 November 2001) https://clubdeparis.org/en/communications/press-release/restructuring-the-debt-of-the-former-federal-republic-of-yugoslavia-17 accessed 23 October 2023; *Kovačić and others v Slovenia* App Nos 44574/98, 45133/98, and 48316/99, ECtHR, Judgment, 3 October 2008, paras 27–163, 255–69; *Slovenia v Croatia* App No 54155/16, ECtHR, Decision, 16 December 2020, paras 12–16, 31, 73–79.

In partial successions, the local credits and debts of a financially autonomous[98] territory **30** transfer to the successor but not the general debt of the predecessor. Examples include: the secession of Guinea;[99] the secession of the DRC;[100] the retrocession of Hong Kong,[101] and the retrocession of Macao.[102] When a territory lacks financial autonomy, a proportionate share of the general debt of the predecessor transfers to the successor. Examples include: the secession of Bangladesh;[103] the various secessions from the USSR;[104] and the secession of Montenegro in 2006.[105] While the European Court of Human Rights appeared to consider the 'equitable proportion principle' to govern the apportionment of debts owed by the successors to the SFRY to private creditors, rather than the 'territoriality principle' invoked by the Respondents (Slovenia and Serbia), the observation was based on a factual finding that the debts in question did not qualify as local debts and the judgment was ultimately decided on a procedural ground (i.e. good faith negotiation on apportionment).[106]

The 'local' character of the debt is usually evident from the identity of the debtor or its in- **31** clusion in the accounts of the local government.[107] Although the European Court of Human Rights appeared to implicitly doubt the customary rule on 'localized debt' in the *Ališić* case, the rule is nonetheless based on considerable State practice and *opīniōnēs juris* (eg Bangladesh, discussed above). It applies whereby a specific debt is assigned to the territory that it primarily benefited.[108] Though more likely to arise in cases of dismemberment, cession, or secession, it can also occur in other types of succession.[109] Debt that is secured ('bonded', 'mortgaged', or 'hypothecated') against property as collateral is attached to that property.[110]

---

[98] For example, L Orlowski, 'Direct Transfers Between the Former Soviet Union Central Budget and the Republics', Kiel Working Paper No 543 (November 1992).
[99] IMF Doc SM/65/105 (30 December 1965) 6-7, 26-28, 32, 49-50; IMF Doc SM/65/105 (30 December 1965) 69, 73-74, 100, 103-05.
[100] 44 ILR 72, 73; 1 *RBDI* (1965) 513-16; 47 ILR 75, 77-78; 48 ILR 20, 21-23, 25.
[101] IMF Doc SM/97/43 (21 May 1997) paras 21-22, 36, 64-76, 78-83.
[102] IMF Doc SM/99/64 (10 March 1999) paras 18-25.
[103] C Rousseau, *Droit International Public*, Vol III (Sirey 1977), 454; B Klein, 'Chronique des faits internationaux' (1975) 79 RGDIP 165; YILC 1981, Vol I, para 15.
[104] For example, 2380 UNTS 69, Articles 1-4; Russia Treaty Database Nos 19930121, 1992038, 19920384, 19920284, 1993010, 1993076, 19930156, 19933038, 19930396, and 19940194 (Russian).
[105] Decree on the promulgation of the Law on the confirmation of the Agreement between the Republic of Serbia and the Republic of Montenegro on regulation of membership in international financial organizations and division of financial rights and liabilities, signed 10 July 2006, 45(6) *Crna Gora* 17, Articles 2, 16 (Montenegrin) (hereinafter Montenegro Decree).
[106] *Ališić and others v Bosnia and Herzegovina, Croatia, Serbia, Slovenia and the Former Yugoslav Republic of Macedonia* App No 60642/08, 16 July 2014, paras 9-11, 60, 98-125. Though not cited by the Court, the notion of 'equitable proportion' appears to be based on Article 41 of the VCSSP, which has not entered into force.
[107] eg, J Charpentier, 'La pratique française de droit international' (1963) 9 AFDI 1021; 41 ILR 20, 21; 73 ILR 32, 34-35; 74 ILR 97, 99.
[108] eg, 71 ILR 53, 55-57; World Bank Archives, Folder 1771155, Memorandum (2 January 1974), paras 4-5; World Bank Archives, Folder ID 1770953, Memorandum (20 June 1974) ; ibid, Memorandum (11 June 1974), ibid paras 3-4; Memorandum (7 June 1974) paras 2, 4; 1127 UNTS 318, Article 1, Annexe; 1059 UNTS (1977) 21, Articles I-II; 1197 UNTS (1980) 187, paras 3-4.
[109] eg, *Yemen v Compagnie d'Enterprises*, ICC Case No 7748/BGD/OLG (unpublished) in: *Yemen v Compagnie d'Enterprises CFE SA*, Supreme Court of Cyprus (28 June 1992), Case No 10717, ILDC 630 (CY 2002) paras F1-F4.
[110] eg, on *Austria* (n 90). On the German Democratic Republic, see 114 RCCFB (1987) 16.

32 These general rules may be displaced by treaty or international resolution,[111] such as for war reparations[112] or economic aid.[113] An important question is the criteria for apportionment of debt, whether between the predecessor and successor in partial successions or among multiple successors in cases of dismemberment. The available information from modern State practice is limited to: the 'I.M.F. key' of contributions to the central budget, gross domestic product, export earnings over a five-year period, population shares and territorial shares;[114] population sizes, import earnings, export earnings, and gross national product;[115] and gross domestic product.[116] While the practice is consistent insofar as apportionment follows relative economic size, the criteria of measurement to be applied can only be determined by agreement or a dispute settlement process between the predecessor and successor.

E. Conclusion

33 There exist rules of general international law, founded in custom and general principles of law deriving from national systems, which investment arbitration tribunals and domestic courts should interpret and apply to disputes concerning the private rights of foreign nationals in State succession. Although the primary function of the international minimum standard of treatment is to be a default rule applicable to foreign nationals in State succession for diplomatic protection, it can also inform the interpretation of a bilateral investment treaty, investment contract, or national investment law. While concessionary contracts qualify as 'property' for the international minimum standard, its special characteristics are the substitution of the successor for the predecessor in the contract and the broader scope for damages claims in comparison with other forms of property.

34 In decolonization, the key debates were whether a duty to compensate aliens for the expropriation of their property applied to successors all and, if so, whether the adequacy of compensation was to be determined in reference to the law of that successor. Today, it is evident that a duty to compensate according to an objective standard of adequacy applies in State succession. In addressing the overarching issue of the size of the compensation to be paid in lawful versus unlawful expropriations, the key questions in modern arbitral jurisprudence are the admissibility of claims (eg on loss of future profits) and the selection of valuation methods for different forms of property.

---

[111] eg, 540 UNTS (1965) 227, Articles 2–12, schs 2–4; Sudan-South Sudan, Agreement on Certain Economic Matters, 27 September 2012 (17 October 2012) https://www.peaceagreements.org/view/857/Agreement%20betw een%20Sudan%20and%20South%20Sudan%20on%20Certain%20Economic%20Matters accessed 23 October 2023, Articles 3.1, 3.2, 6; Paris Club, 'Claims as of 31 December 2020' (15 July 2021) https://clubdeparis.org/sites/default/files/table2020_2.pdf accessed 23 October 2023.
[112] eg, 49 UNTS (1950) 3, Annexe XIV, paras 6–7; IMF Doc SM/94/285 (28 November 1994) 34–35, 61–69.
[113] eg, UNGA Res 388(V)(A), Article X(1)(b); UN Doc A/1726 (14 December 1950) 9; IMF Doc SM/92/173 (4 September 1992) 2, 3, 12; IMF Doc SM/94/105 (28 April 1994) iii, 2a, 14, 34; IMF Doc SM/99/234 (16 September 1999) 6, 14.
[114] eg on the Socialist Federal Republic of Yugoslavia (SFRY)(n 97).
[115] eg T Ushakova, 'Succession of the Republic of Belarus in respect of State Property' (1999) 1 Belarus JILIntlRel, n 4 (Russian).
[116] eg Montenegro Decree (n 105).

Selected literature

Amerasinghe CF, *Diplomatic Protection* (OUP 2008).

Dumberry P, *A Guide to State Succession in International Investment Law* (Edward Elgar Publishing 2018).

García-Amador FV, *The Changing Law of International Claims* (Oceana Publications 1984).

Lillich RB and Weston BH, *International Claims: Their Settlement by Lump Sum Agreements*, Vol I (University Press of Virginia 1975).

Mrak M, 'Succession to the Former Yugoslavia's External Debt: The Case of Slovenia' in Mrak (ed), *Succession of States* (Martinus Nijhoff 1999).

O'Connell DP, *State Succession in Municipal Law and International Law*, Vol I (CUP 1967).

Reinisch A and Hafner G, *Staatensukzession und Schuldenübernahme* (Service-Fachverl 1995).

Torres C, 'Rights of Private Persons on State Succession: An Approach to the Most Recent Cases' in Eisemann PM and Koskenniemi M (eds), *State Succession: Codification Tested Against the Facts* (Springer 2000).

Selected decisions

Ališić and others v Bosnia and Herzegovina, Croatia, Serbia, Slovenia and the Former Yugoslav Republic of Macedonia App No 60642/08, 16 July 2014.

Yemen v Compagnie d'Enterprises, ICC Case No 7748/BGD/OLG (unpublished) in: Case No 10717, ILDC 630 (CY 2002), paras F1–F4.

Sudapet v South Sudan, ICSID Case No ARB/12/26, Award Excerpts, 30 September 2016.

Edmond Khudyan v Armenia, ICSID Case No ARB/17/36, Award, 15 December 2021 (not published).

Haakon Korsguard v Croatia, UNCITRAL, Award, 7 November 2022 (unpublished).

Article 38 of the ICJ Statute

Sources

Patrick Dumberry

1. The Court, whose function is to decide in accordance with international law such disputes as are submitted to it, shall apply:
a. international conventions, whether general or particular, establishing rules expressly recognized by the contesting states;
b. international custom, as evidence of a general practice accepted as law;
c. the general principles of law recognized by civilized nations;
d. subject to the provisions of Article 59, judicial decisions and the teachings of the most highly qualified publicists of the various nations, as subsidiary means for the determination of rules of law.
2. This provision shall not prejudice the power of the Court to decide a case *ex aequo et bono*, if the parties agree thereto.

A. Introduction	1
B. Interaction between the sources	6
I. Custom and treaties	7
II. Custom and general principles	11
III. Judicial decisions and precedents in investment arbitration	12
C. Customary international law	15
I. International courts and investment tribunals have endorsed the 'double requirement'	15
II. Investment tribunals failed to reveal the existence of customary rules	20
III. Types of evidence of State practice relevant for the identification of custom	22
D. General principles of law (GPL)	24
I. Investment tribunals are increasingly referring to GPL	25
1. Tribunals have failed to identify GPL *foro domestico* based on a comparative analysis	27
2. Investment tribunals often do not explain the actual function of GPL	30
3. Investment tribunals have frequently used the concept of 'general principles of law'	33
II. Examples of GPL that investment tribunals have recognized	36
1. *Actori incumbit onus probandi*	37
2. Estoppel	40
3. *Res judicata*	44
4. Abuse of Rights	46
5. Clean Hands	48
E. Conclusion	51

A. Introduction

1 The starting point of the present entry on the 'sources of international law' in international investment law is Article 38(1) of the Statute of the International Court of Justice (ICJ Statute).[1]

---

[1] *Statute of the ICJ*, reprinted in International Court of Justice, Charter of the United Nations, Statute and Rules of Court and other Documents 61 (No 4 1978).

The sources in Article 38 are generally regarded as applicable not only in ICJ cases, but also before other international courts and tribunals (subject to any specific rules contained in such courts' statutes).[2] Investor–State arbitration tribunals frequently refer to this provision as an authoritative statement of the sources of international law.[3] No arbitral tribunal has ever rejected the relevance of Article 38(1) of the ICJ Statute in the field of international investment law.

The first source mentioned in Article 38 is treaties. They will not be examined in this entry.[4] **2** The second source is custom. Article 38 uses the following (rather awkward) wording: 'international custom, as evidence of a general practice accepted as law'. The shortcomings of this formulation are readily apparent.[5] A better definition of custom is the one adopted by International Law Commission (ILC) Special Rapporteur Wood in his Second Report: customary international law 'means those rules of international law that derive from and reflect a general practice accepted as law'.[6] The third source mentioned in Article 38(1) is the 'general principles of law recognized by civilized nations' (GPL).

Treaties, custom, and GPL are the *formal* sources of international law.[7] They are the means for **3** the *creation* of the law that are *directly* applicable by a judge or an arbitrator in the context of a dispute involving questions of international law.[8] Thus, unlike judicial decisions and doctrine, they are not, as stated under Article 38, merely a 'subsidiary means for the determination of rules of law'. However, as Tams mentions, reference to Article 38 can only be the *starting point* of any analysis of the sources of international *investment* law.[9] According to d'Aspremont, 'Article 38 has never been more than a provision that modestly aims to define the law applicable by the ICJ' and it has 'never purported to provide an exhaustive list of the sources of international law'.[10] The sources mentioned in Article 38 are, therefore, not the *only* sources of international law. Similarly, relying on Article 38 *does not* suggest that the sources of investment arbitration are the *same* as those under general international law.[11] For instance, a

---

[2] ILC, 'First Report on Formation and Evidence of Customary International Law', by Michael Wood, Special Rapporteur, ILC Sixty-fifth Session, Geneva, 6 May–7 June and 8 July–9 August 2013, UN Doc A/CN.4/663, 17 May 2013, 14 (hereafter ILC, First Report); ILC, 'Second Report on Identification of Customary International Law', by Michael Wood, Special Rapporteur, ILC, Sixty-sixth Session, Geneva, 5 May–6 June and 7 July–8 August 2014, UN Doc A/CN.4/672, 6 (hereafter ILC, Second Report).

[3] One example is *Merrill & Ring Forestry L.P. v Canada*, UNCITRAL, Award, 31 March 2010, para 184 (hereafter *Merrill & Ring*). See also *Methanex Corporation v United States*, UNCITRAL, Award, 3 August 2005, Part II, Ch B, para 3.

[4] Treaties are examined extensively in Part I of this Commentary.

[5] As rightly noted by M E Villiger, *Customary International Law and Treaties: A Manual on the Theory and Practice of the Interrelation of Sources* (2nd edn, Kluwer 1997) 15 (hereafter Villiger, *Customary International Law*), 'the Court cannot apply a custom, [but] only customary law', and it is in fact the 'general practice accepted as law' which constitutes evidence of a customary rule' not the other way around. See also J Crawford, 'The Identification and Development of Customary International Law', ILA British Branch Conference (2014), 2 (hereafter Crawford, 'Identification'): '[T]his definition is defective in that it puts the elements of customary international law in the wrong order. Evidence is not a constitutive element of customary international law. Rather, evidence is adduced to "prove" its existence.'

[6] ILC, Second Report (n 2) 7.

[7] E de Brabandere, 'Judicial and Arbitral Decisions as a Source of Rights and Obligations' in T Gazzini and E de Brabandere (eds), *International Investment Law: The Sources of Rights and Obligations* (Martinus Nijhoff 2012) 248 (hereafter de Brabandere, 'Judicial and Arbitral Decisions').

[8] P Daillier, M Forteau and A Pellet, *Droit International Public* (LGDJ 2009) 126.

[9] C J Tams, 'The Sources of International Investment Law' in Gazzini and de Brabandere, *International Investment Law* (n 7) 319 (hereafter Tams, 'The Sources').

[10] J d'Aspremont, *Formalism and the Sources of International Law* (OUP 2011) 149.

[11] The question is examined by Tams, 'The Sources' (n 9) 319–21.

comprehensive book addressing the question of the sources of rights and obligations in international investment law includes chapters on State contracts and national laws.[12]

4   Indeed, 'the question of the sources of international law pertains to how international law is made or identified. [...] [This] question [...] has been at the heart of perennial debates among international lawyers and scholars for centuries'.[13] This is undoubtedly true with regard to general public international law; many books and articles have indeed focused on the question of its sources. Yet, the situation is drastically different in the sub-field of international investment law. Only a limited number of books and articles discussing the fundamental question of the sources in international investment law have been published.[14] However, as noted by d'Aspremont, 'international investment law has now reached a stage of its development where the doctrine of sources can no longer be left in limbo and needs to be critically explored' in order for this field of law to 'res[t] on solid bases in terms of sources'.[15]

5   The first section of this entry will examine the complicated question of the interaction between the different sources (Section B), which will be followed by a specific assessment of custom and GPL (Sections C and D). The aim is to determine situations where there is an alignment, or differences, between investment arbitration and international law regarding the importance of these sources and how they have been used by courts and tribunals.

B. Interaction between the sources

6   Article 38 of the ICJ Statute does not formally establish any hierarchical order between the different sources of law. Yet, some sources have clearly played a more important role than others. States have concluded thousands of Bilateral Investment Treaties (BITs) in the 1990s as a result of the perceived lack of established customary principles.[16] As one writer noted, 'for all practical purposes, treaties have become the fundamental sources of international law in the area of foreign investment'.[17] The fact that international investment law is largely based on bilateral treaties is clearly its most distinctive feature when compared to other sub-fields

---

[12] See, for instance, P Dumberry, 'International Investment Contracts' in Gazzini and de Brabandere, *International Investment Law* (n 7).

[13] S Besson and J d'Aspremont, 'The Sources of International Law: An Introduction' in S Besson and J d'Aspremont (eds), *The Oxford Handbook of Sources of International Law* (OUP 2017) 2, 3.

[14] These publications include: Gazzini and de Brabandere, *International Investment Law* (n 7); P Juillard, 'L'évolution des sources du droit des investissements' (1994) 250 RdC 9–216; M Hirsch, 'Sources of International Investment Law', ILA Study Group on the Role of Soft Law Instruments in International Investment Law (2011) (hereafter Hirsch, 'Sources') (also in AK Bjorklund and A Reinisch (eds), *International Investment Law and Soft Law* (Edward Elgar Publishing 2012)); M Paparinskis, 'Investment Protection Law and Sources of Law: A Critical Look' (2009) 103 ASIL Proc 76–79; Tams, 'The Sources' (n 9) 319–32; F Grisel, 'The Sources of Foreign Investment Law' in Z Douglas, J Pauwelyn and J E Viñuales (eds), *The Foundations of International Investment Law: Bringing Theory into Practice* (OUP 2014) (hereafter Grisel, 'The Sources'); J E Viñuales, 'Sources of International Investment Law: Conceptual Foundations of Unruly Practices' in Besson and d'Aspremont, *Oxford Handbook* (n 13) 1069; SW Schill, 'Sources of International Investment Law: Multilarization, Arbitral Precedent, Comparativism, Soft Law', in ibid 1095.

[15] J d'Aspremont, 'International Customary Investment Law: Story of a Paradox' in Gazzini and de Brabandere, *International Investment Law* (n 7) 8. See also the same assessment made in 1989 by S Zamora, 'Is there Customary International Economic Law?' (1989) 32 GYIL 10–11, in the field of international economic law.

[16] On this question, see P Dumberry, *The Formation and Identification of Rules of Customary International Law in International Investment Law* (CUP 2016) 79ff (hereafter Dumberry, *Formation and Identification*).

[17] J W Salacuse, 'The Treatification of International Investment Law: A Victory of Form Over Life? A Crossroads Crossed?' (2006) 3(3) TDM 5; CH Schreuer, L Malintoppi, A Reinisch and A Sinclair, *The ICSID Convention; A Commentary* (2nd edn, CUP 2009) 605 (hereafter Schreuer and others, *The ICSID Convention*); Grisel, 'The Sources' (n 14) 219.

of international law.[18] This aspect has important practical consequences in the relationship between treaties and other sources (a point further examined in the following sections).

I. Custom and treaties

Why is custom relevant today when so many BITs exist? Three basic reasons have been identified by the Iran–US Claims Tribunal in the *Amoco* case: 'the rules of customary law may be useful in order to fill in possible *lacunae* of the treaty, to ascertain the meaning of undefined terms in the text or, more generally, to aid the interpretation and implementation of its provision.'[19] Thus, custom is especially important in the context of BITs which contain explicit references to custom, such as Fair and Equitable Treatment (FET) clauses increasingly linked to the Minimum Standard of Treatment (MST).[20] Several tribunals have also resorted to using custom to fill gaps in BITs.[21] In any event, since international law is the applicable law in the overwhelming majority of arbitration disputes, tribunals will *necessarily* have to take into account relevant rules of 'customary international law'.[22]

While custom and treaties are two distinct sources of international law, they remain, in many ways, 'entangled'.[23] The first form of interaction between them is codification.[24] As the ICJ recognized,[25] a treaty may be evidence of an *already* existing fully-formed customary rule.[26] This is, however, a phenomenon unknown in the field of investment law. All global multilateral attempts at codification have so far failed.[27] Also, States do not consider BITs as

---

[18] Tams, 'The Sources' (n 9) 323.
[19] *Amoco Int'l Fin. Corp v Iran*, Iran–US CT, 14 July 1987, (1990) 83 ILR para 112. See also Schreuer and others, *The ICSID Convention* (n 17) 606.
[20] See, analysis in Dumberry, *Formation and Identification* (n 16) 354ff; Dumberry, 'The 'Minimum Standard of Treatment' in International Investment Law: The Fascinating Story of the Emergence, the Decline and the Recent Resurrection of a Concept' in A Kulick and others (eds), *Custom and International Investment Law* (CUP 2023).
[21] See, inter alia: *Sempra Energy International v Argentina*, ICSID Case No ARB/02/16, Award, 28 September 2007, para 378; *ADC Affiliate Ltd & ADC & ADMC Management Ltd v Hungary*, ICSID Case No ARB/03/16, Award, 2 October 2006, para 483; *Accession Mezzanine Capital L.P. and Danubius Kereskedohaz Vagyonkezelo v Hungary*, ICSID Case No ARB/12/3, Decision on Respondents Objection Under Arbitration Rule 41(5), 16 January 2013, para 68 (hereafter *Accession*); *Archer Daniels Midland Company and Tate and Lyle Ingredients Americas, Inc, v Mexico*, ICSID Case No ARB(AF)/04/05, Award, 21 November 2007, para 122 (hereafter *ADM*).
[22] In fact, there are good reasons (including the application of the principle of systemic integration set out in Article 31(3)(c) of the *Vienna Convention*) to argue in the context of BITs that customary rules should apply to all investment disputes *independently* of the question of the choice of law made by the parties, cf Dumberry, *Formation and Identification* (n 16) 368. On this question, see also, *Cambodia Power Company v Cambodia and Electricité du Cambodge LLC*, ICSID Case No ARB/09/18, Decision on Jurisdiction, 22 March 2011, paras 332–34.
[23] O Schachter, 'Entangled Treaty and Custom' in Y Dinstein (ed), *International Law at a Time of Perplexity: Essays in Honour of Shabtai Rosenne* (Martinus Nijhoff 1989) 717–38; M Mendelson, 'Disentangling Treaty and Customary International Law' (1987) 81 ASIL Proc 157–63.
[24] R Baxter, 'Multilateral Treaties as Evidence of Customary International Law' (1965–66) 41 BYIL 275–300; Villiger, *Customary International Law* (n 5) 63ff; HWA Thirlway, *International Customary Law and Codification* (Sijthoff 1972) chs 6 and 7; TL Meyer, 'Codifying Custom' (2012) 60 UPaLRev 379; ILC, 'Third Report on Identification of Customary International Law', by Michael Wood, Special Rapporteur, ILC, Sixty-seventh Session, Geneva, 4 May–5 June and 6 July–7 August 2014, UN Doc A/CN.4/682, 20 (hereafter ILC, Third Report).
[25] *Continental Shelf (Libya v Malta)* (Judgment) [1985] ICJ Rep 29–30, para 27 (hereafter *Libya v Malta*).
[26] ILA, 'Statement of Principles Applicable to the Formation of General Customary International Law', Final Report of the Committee on the Formation of Customary Law, Conference Report London (2000) 43 (hereafter ILA, Final Report); ILC, 'Formation and Evidence of Customary International Law, Elements in the Previous Work of the ILC that Could be Particularly Relevant to the Topic', Memorandum by the Secretariat, Sixty-fifth Session Geneva, 5 May–7 June and 8 July–9 August 2013, UN Doc A/CN.4/659, 33; R Baxter, 'Treaties and Custom' (1970) 129 RdC 36.
[27] On the question of the 'multilateralization' of this field of law, see SW Schill, *The Multilateralization of International Investment Law* (CUP 2009).

'codifications' of existing practice. This is a first feature where investment arbitration differs from general international law.

9 The second form of interaction between custom and treaty is the fact that one treaty, or patterns of treaties, can contribute to the formation of *new rules* of customary international law.[28] This possibility is recognized in Article 38 of the *Vienna Convention on the Law of Treaties*[29] and by many international courts,[30] including the ICJ.[31] Importantly, it is not the treaty *itself* which leads to the development and formation of new custom, but rather the practice of States *after* the entry into force of the treaty.[32] What matters is the existence of a general, uniform, and consistent practice of *third States* (those that are not parties to the treaty).[33]

10 A number of investment tribunals[34] have recognized that, under some conditions,[35] a series of similarly drafted provisions found in numerous BITs can provide the necessary impulse towards the development of subsequent State practice in line with that provision which will gradually crystallize into a rule of custom. For instance, one question pertains to whether or not the FET standard contained in numerous BITs can be considered to have transformed into a customary rule.[36] Another controversial question which has been discussed in doctrine is whether the thousands of BITs, when *taken together*, represent the 'new' custom in the field of international investment law.[37]

II. Custom and general principles

11 The *Inceysa* tribunal correctly affirmed that 'the general principles of law are an autonomous or direct source of International Law, along with international conventions and custom'.[38] Some authors have, however, emphasized the 'transitory' nature of GPL.[39] They would consist merely of norms, which have not reached the threshold required for the formation of

---

[28] Another closely related phenomenon is the so-called 'crystallisation' of custom. Here, the treaty is *not* the starting point of the eventual formation of a rule. The treaty intervenes later in the process by *boosting* pre-existing State practice and helping the crystallization of a slowly emerging new rule of custom. The ICJ has recognized the phenomenon in *Fisheries Jurisdiction Case (United Kingdom v Iceland)* (Merits) [1974] ICJ Rep, paras 51–52.

[29] On this provision, see Villiger, *Customary International Law* (n 5) 169.

[30] ILC, Third Report (n 24) 24, referring to many examples.

[31] *North Sea Continental Shelf Cases (Federal Republic of German v Denmark; Federal Republic of Germany Netherlands)* (Judgment) [1969] ICJ Rep, paras 63, 71 (hereafter *North Sea Continental Shelf*).

[32] *Libya v Malta* (n 25) 29–30, para 27.

[33] Y Dinstein, 'The Interaction between Customary International Law and Treaties' (2006) 322 Rec des cours 376–77 (hereafter Dinstein, 'Interaction'); Villiger, *Customary International Law* (n 5) 183–84.

[34] For instance, *Pope & Talbot Inc v Canada*, UNCITRAL, Award on Damages, 31 May 2002, para 59 (hereafter *Pope & Talbot*); *Cargill, Inc v Mexico*, ICSID Case No ARB(AF)/05/02, Award, 18 September 2009, para 276 (hereafter *Cargill*).

[35] These conditions are examined by Dumberry, *Formation and Identification* (n 16) 176ff.

[36] P Dumberry, 'Has the Fair and Equitable Treatment Standard become a Rule of Customary International Law?' (2017) 8(1) JIntDispSettl 155–78, arguing that the standard has not become a rule of custom.

[37] P Dumberry, 'Are BITs Representing the "New" Customary International Law in International Investment Law?' (2010) 28 PennStIntlLRev 675; Dumberry, *Formation and Identification* (n 16) 188ff arguing that these treaties do not represent any consistent and uniform State practice and they clearly lack any *opinio juris*.

[38] *Inceysa Vallisoletana S.L. v El Salvador*, Award, ICSID Case No ARB/03/26, 2 August 2006, para 226 (hereafter *Inceysa*). On the relationship between GPL and custom, see ILC, 'Third Report on General Principles of Law', Special Rapporteur Vázquez-Bermúdez, Seventy-third Session Geneva, 18 April–3 June and 4 July–5 August 2022, UN Doc A/CN. 4/753, 18 April 2022, 28ff. The relationship between GPL and treaties is examined in ibid, and below at para 24.

[39] A Pellet, 'Article 38' in A Zimmermann and others (eds), *The Statute of the International Court of Justice: A Commentary* (2nd edn, OUP 2012) 782 (hereafter Pellet, 'Article 38').

customary law (so-called 'inchoate' custom).[40] In fact, some authors believe that GPL is essentially the *same* source as custom.[41] This view is to be rejected, as recognized by investment tribunals,[42] since the express reference to GPL in Article 38 would otherwise be redundant, contrary to the *effet utile* principle.[43] While in both cases, the practice needs to be 'general' and widespread (a point further discussed below), one clear element of distinction between GPL and custom is the obvious fact that States' *opinio juris* is not required for a GPL to emerge *on the international plane*.

III. Judicial decisions and precedents in investment arbitration

Judicial decisions do not *create* law and judges and arbitrators are *not law-makers*.[44] They have no formal role in the creation of customary rules or GPL.[45] Also, awards have no binding effect on other ad hoc investment tribunals, which have no *obligation* to follow them. Yet, scholars,[46] and some tribunals,[47] are nevertheless referring to the existence of a *de facto* practice of precedents in investment arbitration.

What is clear, however, is that arbitral awards cannot be considered as evidence of State practice for the formation of rules of custom.[48] Awards are the product of *tribunals, not States*. But awards are not *irrelevant* to the development of custom. It is undeniable that judicial decisions and awards play an important role regarding the evolution of customary rules. Parties in international proceedings often refer to awards to show the existence of customary rules. As one tribunal noted, 'parties in international proceedings use [arbitral awards] in their pleadings in support of their arguments of what the law is on a specific issue' and that it was 'an efficient manner for a party in a judicial process to show what it believes to be the law'.[49] Awards play an essential role in 'revealing' the existence of custom, i.e. to determine whether such rules exist.[50] A statement by a tribunal on whether or not a rule exists may also have a decisive influence on the *development* of such a rule.[51] As Henckaerts and Doswald-Beck

---

[40] G Gaja, 'General Principles of Law' in *Max Planck Encyclopedia of Public International Law* (2012) para 18; M Virally, 'Le rôle des "principes" dans le développement du droit international' in M Battelli and others (eds), *Recueil d'études de droit international en hommage à Paul Guggenheim* (IUHEI 1968) 533.

[41] A Verdross, 'Les principes généraux du droit dans la jurisprudence internationale' (1935-II) 52 RdC 200–01, examining the position of G Scelle.

[42] *Venezuela Holdings, BV, et al (case formerly known as Mobil Corporation, Venezuela Holdings, BV, et al) v Venezuela*, ICSID Case No ARB/07/27, Annulment, 9 March 2017, paras 154–59; *Infinito Gold Ltd v Costa Rica*, ICSID Case No ARB/14/5, Award, 3 June 2021, para 333 (hereafter *Infinito*).

[43] CT Kotuby Jr and LA Sobota, *General Principles of Law and International Due Process: Principles and Norms Applicable in Transnational Disputes* (OUP 2017) 9 (hereafter Kotuby and Sobota, *General Principles of Law*).

[44] On this question, see de Brabandere, 'Judicial and Arbitral Decisions' (n 7) 257.

[45] ILC, 'Draft conclusions on identification of customary international law', adopted by the ILC at its seventieth session, in 2018, and submitted to the General Assembly as a part of the Commission's report covering the work of that session (A/73/10), YILC 2018, Vol II, Part Two, conclusion no 13(1) (hereafter ILC, 'Draft conclusions').

[46] de Brabandere, 'Judicial and Arbitral Decisions' (n 7) 257. See also D Charlotin, '"Authorities" in International Dispute Settlement: A Data Analysis' (University of Cambridge, PhD 2020) (hereafter Charlotin, 'Authorities').

[47] For instance, *Suez, Sociedad General de Aguas de Barcelona, S.A. and Vivendi Universal, S.A. v Argentina*, ICSID Case No ARB/03/19, Liability, 30 July 2010, para 189.

[48] *Glamis Gold Ltd v United States*, UNCITRAL, Award, 14 May 2009, para 605 (hereafter *Glamis*).

[49] *Railroad Development Corporation (RDC) v Guatemala*, ICSID Case No ARB/07/23, Award, 29 June 2012, para 217.

[50] J Crawford, *Brownlie's Principles of Public International Law* (8th edn, OUP 2012) 19. It should be added that a decision by a tribunal identifying a given rule of custom is, of course, not per se conclusive as to the customary nature of such a rule. The actual weight to be given to such a decision will depend on the authoritative stature of the court which has rendered the decision as well as the quality of the reasoning. See *Cargill* (n 34) para 277.

[51] Pellet, 'Article 38' (n 39) 789; A Roberts, 'Traditional and Modern Approaches to Customary International Law: A Reconciliation' (2001) 95 AJIL 775 (hereafter Roberts, 'Traditional and Modern').

note, 'a finding by an international court that a rule of customary international law exists constitutes persuasive evidence to that effect'.[52] Moreover, once the ICJ has ruled on the custom status of a given rule, its findings will have a long-lasting influence from its use and application by *other* international courts and tribunals.[53] There are indeed many examples of international tribunals simply referring to an ICJ case to demonstrate the customary nature of one rule.[54] Any convincingly argued decision on the existence of a custom rule will also influence the subsequent practice of States.[55]

14 Finally, reference should be made to Article 38(1) of the ICJ Statute instructing the Court to 'apply … the teachings of the most highly qualified publicists'. As a 'subsidiary means for the determination of rules of law', the writings of scholars cannot 'create' international law.[56] While only a few ICJ majority opinions have cited doctrine,[57] scholarly works are often referred to in individual opinions of judges.[58] In contrast, investor–State tribunals often refer to the work of scholars. According to a survey conducted by Fauchald, their work has been used as an interpretive argument in seventy-three of the ninety-eight decisions he examined, making it 'the second most frequently used interpretive argument, second only to ICSID case law'.[59] The evolution and importance of investment arbitration scholarships is an area of growing interest.[60]

C. Customary international law

I. International courts and investment tribunals have endorsed the 'double requirement'

15 Under Article 38(1)b of the ICJ Statute, 'international custom' has two constitutive elements: a 'general practice' that is 'accepted as law'. The former is generally referred to as the 'material' (or 'objective') requirement. The second constitutive element is generally referred to as *opinio juris* or as the 'psychological' (or 'subjective') requirement. This so-called 'double requirement' is one of the most well-established principles of international law.[61] Thus, as

---

[52] J-M. Henckaerts and L Doswald-Beck (eds), *Customary International Humanitarian Law*, Vol I (CUP 2005) xxxviii.
[53] A Alvarez-Jimenez, 'Methods for the Identification of Customary International Law in the International Court of Justice's Jurisprudence: 2000–2009', (2011) 60 ICLQ 683–84.
[54] Crawford, 'Identification' (n 5) 14. See para 20 below.
[55] T Gazzini, 'The Role of Customary International Law in the Field of Foreign Investment' (2007) 8 JWIT 692–93; Roberts, 'Traditional and Modern' (n 51) 775.
[56] J Kammerhofer, 'Law-Making by Scholars' in C Brölmann and Y Radi (eds), *Research Handbook on the Theory and Practice of International Law Making* (Edward Elgar Publishing 2013); M Wood, 'Teachings of the Most Highly Qualified Publicists (Article 38(1) ICJ Statute)' in R Wolfrum (ed), *Max Planck Encyclopedia of Public International Law* (2012) 783–87.
[57] See ST Helmersen, 'Finding "the Most Highly Qualified Publicists": Lessons from the International Court of Justice' (2019) 30(1) EJIL 510, indicating that 'the Court has cited specific works of teachings on a point of law only seven times in five cases'.
[58] ST Helmersen, *The Application of Teachings by the International Court of Justice* (CUP 2021).
[59] OK Fauchald, 'The Legal Reasoning of ICSID Tribunals—An Empirical Analysis' (2008) 19 EJIL 351 (hereafter Fauchald, 'Legal Reasoning'). For a more recent analysis confirming these findings: N Ridi and T Schultz, 'Empirically Mapping Investment Arbitration Scholarship: Networks, Authorities, and the Research Front' in K Fach Gomez (ed), *Private Actors in International Investment Law* (Springer 2020) 227ff.
[60] See, *inter alia*: SW Schill, 'W(h)ither Fragmentation? On the Literature and Sociology of International Investment Law' (2011) 22 EJIL 875; Ridi and Schultz, ibid; T Schultz and N Ridi, 'Arbitration Literature' in T Schultz and F Ortino (eds), *Oxford Handbook of International Arbitration* (OUP 2019); Charlotin, 'Authorities' (n 46).
[61] ILC, First Report (n 2) 22.

explained by ILC Special Rapporteur Wood, the 'double requirement' is 'generally adopted in the practice of States and the decisions of international courts and tribunals, including the [ICJ]'.[62] While a number of writers have rejected this 'traditional' approach and have developed alternative theories on how custom is created,[63] these theories have had limited impact on decisions.[64]

The Permanent Court of International Justice (PCIJ) and the ICJ have consistently held that a customary rule requires the presence of both State practice and *opinio juris*. For instance, in the *Continental Shelf* case, the Court stated that 'it is of course axiomatic that the material of customary international law is to be looked for primarily in the actual practice and *opinio juris* of States'.[65] This double requirement has also been recognized by other international tribunals, such as the International Tribunal for the Law of the Sea,[66] the International Criminal Tribunal for Yugoslavia (ICTY),[67] and the International Criminal Tribunal for Rwanda (ICTR) as well as a number of 'internationalized courts' for Sierra Leone, Cambodia, and Lebanon.[68] The same is true for Panels and the Appellate Body of the World Trade Organization (WTO) as well as a number of regional courts, including the Inter-American Court of Human Rights, the Court of Justice of the European Union, and the European Court of Human Rights.[69]

The 'double requirement' has also been recognized by a number of investor–State arbitration tribunals.[70] With the exception of the *Pope & Talbot* award,[71] whose position has been rejected by the North American Free Trade Agreement (NAFTA) parties in subsequent cases,[72] tribunals have all referred to the importance of demonstrating *opinio juris*.[73]

The author has found no example of State practice, such as pleadings, where a State has rejected the necessity to demonstrate both elements of custom. States also recognize the 'double requirement' in their investment treaties. For instance, in separate BITs entered into by the United States with Rwanda and Uruguay, the parties explain their 'shared understanding, that customary international law [...] results from a general and consistent practice of States that they follow from a sense of legal obligation'.[74] The same 'understanding' is found in the 2012 US Model BIT.[75]

---

[62] ILC, Second Report (n 2) 8. See also ILC, Third Report (n 24) 3, 7; ILC, 'Draft conclusions' (n 45).
[63] See analysis in Dumberry, *Formation and Identification* (n 16) 30ff.
[64] ILC, Second Report (n 2) 11.
[65] *Libya v Malta* (n 25) 13, para 27.
[66] *M/V 'SAIGA' (No 2) (Saint Vincent and the Grenadines v Guinea)* (Judgment) ITLOS Reports 1999, 10, paras 133–34.
[67] However, cases from the chambers of the tribunal have found custom to exist mainly based on *opinio juris*, without requiring evidence of substantive State practice. See, for instance, *Prosecutor v Kupreškić*, ICTY Case No IT-95-16-T (ICTY Trial Chamber), 14 January 2000, para 527.
[68] See the analysis in: ILC, First Report (n 2) 29ff.
[69] ibid 34ff.
[70] See, for instance, *Enron Corporation and Ponderosa Assets LP v Argentina*, ICSID Case No ARB/01/3, Award, 15 May 2007, para 258 (hereafter *Enron*); *UPS v Canada*, UNCITRAL, Jurisdiction, 22 November 2002, para 84 (hereafter *UPS*). Numerous cases are mentioned in Dumberry, *Formation and Identification* (n 16) 36.
[71] *Pope & Talbot* (n 34) para 62.
[72] See, discussion in: *ADF Group Inc v United States*, ICSID Case No ARB(AF)/00/1, Award, 9 January 2003, para 112; *Mondev International Ltd v United States*, ICSID Case No ARB(AF)/99/2, Award, 11 October 2002, para 110 (hereafter *Mondev*).
[73] One example is *UPS* (n 70) para 84.
[74] US–Rwanda BIT, 2008, Annex A; US–Uruguay BIT, 2005, Annex A. See also US–Singapore FTA, 2004, Article 15.5.
[75] US Model BIT, 2012, Annex A.

19 Finally, investment tribunals have also held that a customary rule needs to be proven by the party that alleges it[76] and that a party has the burden to prove any *subsequent changes* in the evolution of custom.[77]

II. Investment tribunals failed to reveal the existence of customary rules

20 Although investment tribunals have held in recent years that a number of rules should be considered as custom,[78] they have generally failed in their task to properly reveal the existence of these rules based on an analysis of the 'double requirement'.[79] A good example is the *Glamis* tribunal which has relied entirely on the findings of previous NAFTA tribunals to 'reveal' the existence of the prohibition of arbitrary conduct as a customary rule.[80] This example is not isolated. A number of other NAFTA tribunals (*Thunderbird*,[81] *Waste Management*,[82] and *Mobil*[83]) have also come to the same conclusion about the customary nature of the prohibition against arbitrary conduct as part of the MST without actually examining State practice and *opinio juris* on the matter. One exception to this line of doctrinally disappointing awards is the *UPS* tribunal which ultimately concluded that there was 'no rule of customary international law prohibiting or regulating anticompetitive behaviour'[84] based on an examination of the 'double requirement'. Tribunals have almost never examined States' *opinio juris*.[85]

21 Instead, investment tribunals consistently rely on the findings of the ICJ or on the reasoning of *other tribunals* when 'revealing' the customary nature of rules. Scholars have long identified similar shortcomings in the decisions of the ICJ, which very rarely contain detailed analysis of the 'double requirement'.[86] In fact, it seems that the 'main method employed by the Court is neither induction nor deduction but, rather, assertion'.[87]

---

[76] *Cargill* (n 34) para 271.
[77] *UPS* (n 70) para 84; *Glamis* (n 48) para 601.
[78] One undeniable rule of custom is the MST, see P Dumberry, *Fair and Equitable Treatment: Its Interaction with the Minimum Standard and its Customary Status* (Brill Research Perspectives in International Investment Law and Arbitration 2018).
[79] The question is examined in detail in Dumberry, *Formation and Identification* (n 16) 47ff.
[80] *Glamis* (n 48) paras 607, 625–26.
[81] *International Thunderbird Gaming Corporation v Mexico*, UNCITRAL, Award, 26 January 2006, para 194.
[82] *Waste Management, Inc v Mexico ('Number 2')*, ICSID Case No ARB(AF)/00/3, Award, 30 April 2004, para 98 (hereafter *Waste Management*).
[83] *Mobil Investments Canada Inc and Murphy Oil Corporation v Canada*, ICSID Case No ARB(AF)/07/4, Liability and on Principles of Quantum, 22 May 2012, para 152 (hereafter *Mobil*).
[84] *UPS* (n 70) para 92
[85] One rare exception is *Mondev* (n 72) para 111, acknowledging that 'letters of submittal' by which the US government introduces draft legislation in Congress should be considered as a manifestation of that State's *opinio juris*.
[86] Crawford, 'Identification' (n 5) 8; A Pellet, 'Shaping the Future of International Law: The Role of the World Court in Law-Making' in MH Arsanjani and others (eds), *Looking to the Future: Essays on International Law in Honor of W. Michael Reisman* (Martinus Nijhoff Publishers 2011) 1076; RH Geiger, 'Customary International Law in the Jurisprudence of the International Court of Justice: A Critical Appraisal' in U Fastenrath and others (eds), *From Bilateralism to Community Interest: Essays in Honour of Judge Bruno Simma* (OUP 2011) 673, 674; O Yasuaki, 'Is the International Court of Justice an Emperor Without Clothes?' (2002) 81 IntlLegTheory 16.
[87] S Talmon, 'Determining Customary International Law: The ICJ's Methodology between Induction, Deduction and Assertion' (2015) 26(2) EJIL 417–43. For a rebuttal, see O Sender and M Wood, 'The International Court of Justice and Customary International Law: A Reply to Stefan Talmon' EJIL Talks!, 30 November 2015.

III. Types of evidence of State practice relevant for the identification of custom

ICJ decisions have explained that there are three basic requirements for the practice of States to be considered as relevant in the process of identifying customary norms: the practice needs to be uniform and consistent, extensive and representative, and must have taken place during a certain period of time.[88] There are different 'manifestations', or types of evidence, of State practice that are relevant for the creation of custom in both general international law and investor–State arbitration. Treaties can represent persuasive and authoritative evidence of a 'manifestation' of State practice necessary for the creation of custom norms.[89] Investment tribunals have recognized this phenomenon.[90] While it is generally acknowledged that the practice of the executive, legislative, and judicial organs of the State can be considered, depending on a number of circumstances, as State practice relevant to the formation of customary rules,[91] few investment tribunals have examined the issue.[92]

22

As recognized by international tribunals,[93] 'statements' made by States are another type of evidence of State practice.[94] The same conclusion has also been reached by a number of investment tribunals.[95] Not all statements should be treated equally in terms of the extent to which they truly represent State practice. The weight to be given to a statement will depend on 'who is making the statement, when, where and in what set of circumstances'.[96] Importantly, the statements that are considered as an important source of State practice in the field of investment arbitration are not exactly the same as those in general international law. Investment tribunals have recognized the following types of statements as relevant: State pleadings in arbitration proceedings;[97] interventions by non-disputing treaty parties during arbitration proceedings;[98] official statements made by parties to a treaty;[99] joint statements by State parties to a treaty on matters of interpretation;[100] and Model BITs[101] adopted by States.[102] On the contrary, some statements that are important in international law are less relevant in investor–State arbitration: States' official manuals, official legal advisers' opinions, diplomatic statements or correspondence, policy statements, and statements made in the context of the work of international organizations.[103] Such statements are often not

23

---

[88] ILA, Final Report (n 26) 14, 15; ILC, First Report (n 2) 20; ILC, Second Report (n 2) 19; ILC, 'Draft conclusions' (n 45) Conclusion 7(1). On this question, see Dumberry, *Formation and Identification* (n 16) 128ff.
[89] ILC, Third Report (n 24) 17.
[90] *Mondev* (n 72) paras 117, 125; *Cargill* (n 34) para 276.
[91] ILA, Final Report (n 26) 17; ILC, Second Report (n 2); ILC, 'Draft conclusions' (n 45) Conclusion no 6.
[92] One example is *UPS* (n 70) paras 85–88, examining domestic legislation.
[93] *Nuclear Tests Case (Australia & New Zealand v France)* (Judgment) [1974] ICJ Rep 457, para 49; *Jurisdictional Immunities of the State (Germany v Italy: Greece intervening)* (Judgment) [2012] ICJ Rep, para 55.
[94] See Dumberry, *Formation and Identification* (n 16) 205ff.
[95] *Glamis* (n 48) para 603; *Cargill* (n 34) para 275; *Industria Nacional de Alimentos, S.A. and Indalsa Perú, S.A. v Peru*, ICSID Case No ARB/03/4, Annulment Proceeding, 5 September 2007, Dissenting Opinion of Sir Franklin Berman, para 9 (hereafter *Industria Nacional*); *Enron* (n 70) Decision on the Argentine Republic's Request for a Continued Stay of Enforcement of the Award (Rule 54 of the ICSID Arbitration Rules), 7 October 2008, para 85.
[96] Dinstein, 'Interaction' (n 33).
[97] *Glamis* (n 48) para 603; *Cargill* (n 34) para 275.
[98] *ADM* (n 21) para 176.
[99] *Mondev* (n 72) para 111; *Generation Ukraine Inc v Ukraine*, Final Award, 16 September 2003, paras 15.4–15.6. Other cases are examined in Dumberry, *Formation and Identification* (n 16) 237ff.
[100] *Yaung Chi Oo Trading Pte. Ltd v Myanmar*, ASEAN Case No ARB/01/1, Award, 31 March 2003, para 74.
[101] *Glamis* (n 48) para 603.
[102] For a detailed analysis of each type of statements and the relative weight that should be given to them depending on different circumstances, see Dumberry, *Formation and Identification* (n 16) 220ff.
[103] Dumberry, ibid 217ff.

publicly available in arbitration proceedings. This is an area where investment arbitration differs from general international law.

D. General principles of law (GPL)

24 Scholars discussing GPL in international investment law and arbitration[104] generally consider the concept of 'GPL' to encompass two phenomena: general principles existing under the domestic laws of States and general principles emerging in international law.[105] General principles serve two main functions: they have a gap-filling role when other sources of international law do not provide any solution to a given problem and they can be used as a source of interpretation for uncertain and ambiguous treaty terms.[106] These issues are discussed in the next sections.

I. Investment tribunals are increasingly referring to GPL

25 While there is no hierarchy between the different sources of law, it remains that GPL have only played a secondary role in the development of international law. It is often said that they have a *subsidiary* character.[107] Thus, it has been noted that the PCIJ has not once applied a GPL to solve a dispute,[108] that the ICJ never 'concluded positively to the existence of such principles in a case',[109] and that it only made limited use of GPL[110] without explaining its actual meaning[111] or function in international law.[112] Yet, it should be added that the Court

---

[104] See T Gazzini, 'General Principles of Law in the Field of Foreign Investment' (2009) 10 JWTI 103 (hereafter Gazzini, 'General Principl); SW Schill, 'General Principles of International Law and International Investment Law' in Gazzini and de Brabandere, *International Investment Law* (n 7) 133 (hereafter Schill, 'General Principles'); Hirsch, 'Sources' (n 14); MD Nolan and FG Sourgens, 'Issues of Proof of General Principles of Law in International Arbitration' (2009) 3(4–5) World Arb & Med Rev 505; Kotuby and Sobota, *General Principles of Law* (n 43); A Gattini, A Tanzi and F Fontanelli (eds), *General Principles of Law and International Investment Arbitration* (Brill 2018) (hereafter Gattini and others (eds), *General Principles*). Moreover, M Andenas and others (eds), *General Principles and the Coherence of International Law* (Brill 2019) contain four chapters focusing on investment arbitration (hereafter Andenas and others (eds), General Principles). See also P Dumberry, *A Guide to General Principles of Law in International Investment Law* (OUP 2020) (hereafter Dumberry, *A Guide to General Principles*).
[105] ibid 26ff. Some writers also support other conceptions based on natural law.
[106] ibid 49ff, also examining whether GPL can be used to correct existing unsatisfactory law and further develop international law (65ff).
[107] Pellet, 'Article 38' (n 39) 780.
[108] J Lammers, 'General Principles of Law Recognized by Civilized Nations' in F Kalshoven and others (eds), *Essays in the Development of the International Legal Order: In Memory of Haro F. Van Panhuys* (Springer 1980) 70–71; S Besson, 'General Principles in International Law—Whose Principles?' in S Besson and P Pichonnaz (eds), *Les principles en droit européen-Principles in European Law* (Schulthess 2011) 19–64, 39 (hereafter Besson, 'General Principles').
[109] Besson, ibid 39.
[110] Only four times according to Pellet, 'Article 38' (n 39) 766. See also ILC, 'First Report on General Principles of Law', Special Rapporteur Vázquez-Bermúdez, Seventy-first Session (Geneva, 29 April–7 June and 8 July–9 August 2019), para 129, indicating that the Court 'appears to have applied general principles of law' in seven cases (hereafter ILC, 'First Report on General Principles').
[111] Besson, 'General Principles' (n 108) 40; P d'Argent, 'Les principes généraux à la Cour internationale de Justice' in Besson and Pichonnaz (eds), *Les principes* (n 108) 110ff.
[112] MC Bassiouni, 'A Functional Approach to General Principles of International Law' (1990) 11 MichJIntl L 768 (hereafter Bassiouni, 'A Functional Approach'); F Raimondo, *General Principles of Law in the Decisions of International Criminal Courts and Tribunals*, PhD thesis, Amsterdam Center for International Law, 2007 (also published with Martinus Nijhoff 2008) 37–38.

has increasingly referred to GPL in recent years[113] and that individual judges have been more active in analysing them in their opinions in a number of cases.[114]

It is often asserted by writers that investment tribunals have only made limited use of GPL **26** since the 'treatification' of investment arbitration.[115] However, on closer inspection, tribunals actually refer to GPL more often than it is believed. On the one hand, many tribunals have considered GPL to essentially be a reference to principles existing in *foro domestico*.[116] On the other hand, several awards have concluded that principles, such as *actori incumbit onus probandi*, estoppel, *res judicata*, and abuse of rights, are general principles of *international* law.[117] Yet, it must be added that in many other awards it is often unclear which types of general principles tribunals have in mind.[118] They often do not explain *where* the principles they mention are emerging from (i.e. from which legal order: domestic or international).[119] Similarly, while a number of tribunals have referred to *foro domestico* principles, or have used other expressions to the same effect, a closer examination of their reasoning shows that what they really had in mind was general principles of *international* law. For instance, the *Mobil v Venezuela* award, which examined the principle of abuse of rights, started its analysis with this observation: 'in all systems of law, whether domestic or international, there are concepts framed in order to avoid misuse of the law', including good faith and abuse of rights.[120] The tribunal then referred to the way these concepts are embedded in public international law,[121] but did not engage in any discussion as to whether the principle of abuse of rights was found in domestic laws. In contrast, several awards have referred to some principles, such as *res judicata*, estoppel, etc., as being *both* GPL *foro domestico* and general principles of international law, simultaneously. These awards will be examined below.

---

[113] Examples include: *Questions of the Delimitation of the Continental Shelf between Nicaragua and Colombia beyond 200 nautical miles from the Nicaraguan Coast (Nicaragua v Colombia)* (Preliminary Objections) [2016] ICJ Rep 12, para 58 (hereafter *Questions of the Delimitation of the Continental Shelf*); *Maritime Delimitation in the Caribbean Sea and Pacific Ocean and Land Boundary in the Northern Part of the Isla Portillos (Costa Rica v Nicaragua)* (Judgment) [2018] ICJ Rep, para 68 (hereafter *Maritime Delimitation in the Caribbean Sea*). On this question, see M Dordeska, *General Principles of Law Recognized by Civilized Nations (1922–2018)* (Brill Nijhoff 2020); Imogen Saunders, *General Principles as a Source of International Law* (Hart Publishing 2021).

[114] See *North Sea Continental Shelf* (n 31), separate Opinion of Judge Ammoun, para 38. Another example is: *Pulp Mills on the River Uruguay (Argentina v Uruguay)* (Judgment) [2010] ICJ Rep, Separate Opinion of Judge Cançado Trindade, para 20.

[115] Hirsch, 'Sources' (n 14) 26; Tams, 'The Sources' (n 9) 324. *Contra*: Schreuer and others, *The ICSID Convention* (n 17) 606.

[116] *Inceysa* (n 38) para 227; *Total v Argentina*, ICSID Case No ARB/04/1, Liability, 21 December 2010, paras 128ff (hereafter *Total*); *El Paso Energy International Company v Argentina*, ICSID Case No ARB/03/15, Award, 31 October 2011, para 622 (hereafter *El Paso*).

[117] For an analysis: P Dumberry, 'The Emergence of the Concept of 'General Principle of International Law' in Investment Arbitration Case Law' (2020) 11 JIntlDispSettl 194–216 (hereafter Dumberry, 'Emergence').

[118] The *Yukos* award (*Hulley Enterprises (Cyprus) Limited v Russia*, PCA Case No AA 226 (UNCITRAL), Final Award, 18 July 2014, dealing with the doctrine of clean hands, is a good example of such confusion (hereafter *Hulley*). See Dumberry, *A Guide to General Principles* (n 104) 219–21; P Dumberry, 'State of Confusion: The Doctrine of "Clean Hands" in Investment Arbitration After the Yukos Award' (2016) 17 JWIT 229 (hereafter Dumberry, 'State of Confusion'). See also *South American Silver Limited v Bolivia*, PCA Case No 2013–15, Award, 22 November 2018, paras 440–44, 445–46, using confusing terminology by referring to different expressions (hereafter *South American Silver Limited*).

[119] Examples include *Marvin Feldman v Mexico*, ICSID Case No ARB(AF)/99/1, Award, 16 December 2002, Dissenting opinion of Covarrubias Bravo, 9 (hereafter *Feldman*); *Liman Caspian Oil BV v Kazakhstan*, Award, ICSID Case No ARB/07/14, 22 June 2010, para 164.

[120] *Mobil Corporation, Venezuela Holdings, BV and Others v Venezuela*, ICSID Case No ARB/07/27, Jurisdiction, 10 June 2010, para 169.

[121] It examined decisions of the PCIJ, the ICJ, the Appellate Body of the WTO, ICSID tribunals, and the European Court of Justice (ECJ, now CJEU).

1. Tribunals have failed to identify GPL *foro domestico* based on a comparative analysis

27 One notable feature of decisions is the failure of both the ICJ and investment tribunals to identify GPL *foro domestico* based on a comparative analysis.[122] The first step of such an analysis requires the identification of a given principle in a large number of representative domestic legal orders covering the principal legal systems and traditions of the World.[123] The ICJ has never used a comparative analysis in practice.[124] However, a few judges have done so in their individual opinions,[125] and a few States have also used such a method in their pleadings.[126]

28 Only a few investment tribunals have concretely examined States' domestic legal orders to assess the GPL status of a given principle.[127] Yet, none of them have really adopted a comparative methodology.[128] One illustration is the *Total* award, which examined the concept of legitimate expectations based on what it described as a 'comparative analysis'.[129] The tribunal explained that 'while the scope and legal basis of the principle varies, it has been recognized lately both in civil law and in common law jurisdictions within well-defined limits'.[130] Based on two books dealing with the concept, the tribunal explained the German origin of the notion and the fact that it was widely used in Germany and in common law countries (it also cited English law cases).[131] It also mentioned an Argentinian case as an illustration of the use of the concept in civil law countries. The tribunal then proceeded to explain the content of the notion as existing in 'domestic legal systems' based on other articles and books dealing with the notion, as well as how it had been interpreted by the European Court of Human Rights[132] and in Europe.[133] A similar approach was adopted in the *Crystallex* award. Based on the *Total* award, the tribunal explained that the concept of legitimate expectations 'has its origins in principles of domestic administrative law in various legal systems, and

---

[122] Dumberry, *A Guide to General Principles* (n 104) 93ff.

[123] On this question see ILC, 'Second Report on General Principles of Law', Special Rapporteur Vázquez-Bermúdez, Seventy-second Session Geneva, 27 April–5 June and 6 July–7 August 2019, UN Doc A/CN.4/741, 9 April 2020, para 23ff (hereafter ILC, 'Second Report on General Principles'). The other steps (the distillation of the essence of the principle and the adaptation and transposition of the principle into the international legal order) are examined in ibid, paras 73ff. See also Dumberry, *A Guide to General Principles* (n 104) 93ff.

[124] Pellet, 'Article 38' (n 39) 771; ILA, 'The Use of Domestic Law Principles in the Development of International Law', Report of the Sidney Conference (2018) 10 (hereafter ILA, 'The Use of Domestic Law').

[125] eg, *North Sea Continental Shelf* (n 31), separate Opinion of Judge Ammoun, para 38, examining the question of the equitable delimitation of the continental shelf based on the principle of equity found in the legal orders of Western Europe and Latin America, common law, Muslim law, Chinese law, Soviet law, Hindu law and the laws of other African and Asian countries. See also *Oil Platforms (Iran v US)* (Judgment) [2003] ICJ Rep 161, 324, separate opinion of Judge Simma, paras 66–74, undertaking a comparative law analysis of the solutions found under the domestic legal orders of a few States (United States, Canada, France, Switzerland, and Germany) with regard to the question of 'multiple tortfeasors'.

[126] One example is *Right of Passage Over Indian Territory (Portugal v India)* (Judgment) [1960] ICJ Rep 6, 11–12, Reply by Portugal, referring to sixty-four domestic laws regarding the question of right of access to enclave piece of land.

[127] One example is *Amco Asia Corp et al v Indonesia*, ICSID Case No ARB/81/1, Award on the Merits, 21 November 1984, paras 266–67, concluding that *damnum emergens* and *lucrum cessans* were both principles 'common to the main systems of municipal law, and therefore a general principle of law which many considered as a source of international law' (hereafter *Amco*).

[128] V Vadi, *Analogies in International Investment Law and Arbitration* (CUP 2015) 236. See also Fauchald, 'Legal Reasoning' (n 59) 326.

[129] *Total* (n 116) paras 128ff. 'Comparative analysis' is the title of the section dealing with the issue.

[130] ibid para 128.

[131] ibid para 128, n 135.

[132] ibid para 129.

[133] ibid para 130.

finds increasing recognition both in civil and common law countries'.[134] The tribunal did not undertake any comparative assessment, but, importantly, added that the concept was part of Venezuelan law (the law of the host State).[135] The same type of reasoning was also followed by the *Gold Reserve* tribunal, citing the works of scholars and a few cases for the proposition that the concept of legitimate expectations was part of German, French, English, and EU law and was 'also found in Latin American countries', including Venezuela (the host State).[136]

Hence, these tribunals did not adopt a truly comparative methodology.[137] They have essentially relied upon the work of authors which had previously made such comparative analysis[138] and their analysis was limited to only a few laws in Europe and that of the host State.[139]

2. Investment tribunals often do not explain the actual function of GPL

Investment tribunals rarely explain *why* they are referring to a given principle and almost never mention the actual function played by a given principle in their awards. The gap-filling function of GPL has, however, been mentioned by some tribunals both implicitly[140] and explicitly.[141] One illustration of the latter situation is the *Churchill* tribunal which mentioned that since 'neither the ICSID Convention nor the BITs contain substantive provisions addressing the consequences of unlawful conduct by a claimant or its business associate during the performance of an investment', it decided to 'have recourse to principles of international law to determine the consequences of the forgeries' which it had previously established.[142] One of these 'principles' examined was the concept of abuse of rights.

A number of tribunals have also used GPL as a source of interpretation for uncertain and ambiguous treaty terms.[143] One example often cited by scholars is the use of GPL in the interpretation of the FET standard.[144] It has been referred to by authors as 'the perfect laboratory' for the use of GPL by tribunals.[145] A good example is the *Total* tribunal indicating that 'in order to elucidate the content of the [FET] treatment required by Article 3 in conformity with international law, a tribunal is directed to look not just to the BIT in isolation or the decisions of other arbitral tribunals in investment disputes interpreting and applying similarly worded investment protection treaties, but rather to the content of international law more generally'.[146]

---

[134] *Crystallex International Corporation v Venezuela*, ICSID Case No ARB(AF)/11/2, Award, 6 April 2016, para 543.
[135] ibid.
[136] See *Gold Reserve v Venezuela*, ICSID Case No ARB 09/1, Award, 22 September 2014, para 576.
[137] In fact, none of the tribunals has explicitly taken position as to whether or not the concept of legitimate expectations should be considered as a GPL.
[138] D Peat, 'International Investment Law and the Public Law Analogy: The Fallacies of the General Principles Method' (2018) 9 JIDS 665. On this point, T Wongkaew, *Protection of Legitimate Expectations in Investment Treaty Arbitration* (CUP 2019) 19–20; Dumberry, *A Guide to General Principles* (n 104) 333–36.
[139] In any event, their reasoning is much more convincing than that of the recent *South American Silver Limited* award (n 118) paras 445–46, in which the tribunal rejected, without any justification, Bolivia's claim that the 'clean hands doctrine' is a GPL. The tribunal was unable to cite a single domestic law of civil or common law tradition where the doctrine is not present and did not even bother to assess whether the concept exists under the laws of Bolivia.
[140] *Niko Resources (Bangladesh) Ltd v People's Republic of Bangladesh, et al*, ICSID Case No ARB/10/11 and ICSID Case No ARB/10/18, Jurisdiction, 19 August 2013, para 373 (hereafter *Niko Resources*); *Middle East Cement Shipping and Handling Co SA v Egypt*, ICSID Case No ARB/99/6, Award, 12 April 2002, para 167.
[141] *M Meerapfel Söhne AG v Central African Republic*, ICSID Case No ARB/07/10, Award, 12 May 2012, para 291; *Accession* (n 21) para 68.
[142] *Churchill Mining PLC and Planet Mining Pty Ltd v Indonesia*, ICSID Case No ARB/12/14 and 12/40, Award, 6 December 2016, para 488 (hereafter *Churchill*).
[143] *Enron* (n 70) para 257.
[144] Schill, 'General Principles' (n 104) 157ff.
[145] Gazzini, 'General Principles of Law' (n 104) 116. See also M Potestà, 'Legitimate Expectations in Investment Treaty Law: Understanding the Roots and the Limits of a Controversial Concept' (2013) 28 ICSID Rev 92.
[146] *Total* (n 116) para 126. See also *Merrill & Ring* (n 3) paras 186–87.

Specifically, the tribunal explained that it would interpret the FET treatment by 'looking also at general principles and public international law in a non-BIT context'.[147] As mentioned above, the tribunal conducted a 'comparative analysis of the protection of legitimate expectations in domestic jurisdictions'.[148]

32 Finally, a few investment tribunals have also used GPL simply to confirm a conclusion already established based on other sources.[149]

3. Investment tribunals have frequently used the concept of 'general principles of law'

33 For the majority of scholars,[150] a number of judges,[151] the International Law Association (ILA),[152] and the ILC,[153] Article 38 of the ICJ Statute refers not only to *foro domestico* principles, but also includes those principles existing under international law. They are referred to as 'general principles *of international law*'[154] (in French 'principes généraux *du droit*'[155]). Similarly, the recent *Infinito Gold* award recognized that 'it is now widely accepted that GPL include both general principles that emanate from domestic laws [...] as well as general principles of international law that have emerged directly on the international plane'.[156]

34 These general principles of international law 'stem from regular sources of international law such as general treaties and customary international law'.[157] In a ground-breaking article Bassiouni submits that 'foreign policies, bilateral and multilateral treaties, international pronouncements, collective declarations, writings of scholars, international decisions, and international customs, even when unperfected, are valid areas of inquiry from which to determine the existence of "principles" within the international context'.[158] In his First Report, ILC Special Rapporteur Vázquez-Bermúdez noted that 'the existence of a category of general principles of law that find their origin in the international legal system is corroborated by the practice of States and the decisions of international courts and tribunals'.[159] This position has been recently endorsed by the *Infinito Gold* award, noting that GPL is 'a more flexible concept' when compared to custom and that 'they may emerge in a number of ways (including from treaties, decisions of international courts and tribunals, and custom)'.[160]

---

[147] *Total* (n 116) para 127.
[148] ibid paras 111, 128ff.
[149] eg *Amco* (n 127) paras 177–78, 181–83, 244, 245ff, 248ff; *El Paso* (n 116) paras 617, 621, 624.
[150] See many writers mentioned in Dumberry, *A Guide to General Principles* (n 104) 35ff.
[151] *South West Africa Cases (Ethiopia v South Africa; Liberia v South Africa)* (Judgment) [1966] ICJ Rep, dissenting opinion of Judge Tanaka, 295.
[152] ILA, 'The Use of Domestic Law' (n 124) 16.
[153] ILC, 'First Report on General Principles' (n 110) 22, Draft conclusion 3.
[154] Bassiouni, 'A Functional Approach' (n 112) 770. It should be added that ILC, 'First Report on General Principles' (n 110) paras 231ff used a different expression: 'General principles of law formed within the international legal system'.
[155] P-M. Dupuy and Y Kerbrat, *Droit International Public* (12th edn, Dalloz 2016) 376.
[156] *Infinito* (n 42) para 332. On this question, see also Separate Opinion on Jurisdiction and on the Merits, by B Stern, paras 75ff.
[157] Besson, 'General Principles' (n 108) 33.
[158] Bassiouni, 'A Functional Approach' (n 112) 789.
[159] ILC, 'First Report on General Principles' (n 110) para 235, referring to several cases. In ILC, 'Second Report on General Principles' (n 123) paras 121ff, he further explains that 'the essential condition for their existence is that of recognition, which, as for the first category, must be wide and representative, reflecting a common understanding of the community of nations. In the present context, recognition can be considered to take three different forms. First, a principle may be widely recognized in treaties and other international instruments. Second, a principle may underlie general rules of conventional or customary international law. Finally, a principle may be inherent in the basic features and fundamental requirements of the international legal system'.
[160] *Infinito* (n 42) para 333 (citing Dumberry, *A Guide to General Principles* (n 104)).

Contrary to international tribunals, many investment awards have explicitly, and sometimes **35** implicitly, recognized concepts (including estoppel, *res judicata*, abuse of rights, unjust enrichment, clean hands) as 'general principles of international law'.[161] While these awards (further examined below) have not explained in great detail the nature, origin, and meaning of this specific type of general principles, the international law material they have referred to in support of their findings leaves no doubt that they considered them to be grounded in international law. These tribunals have correctly used the above-stated—admittedly loose—methodology required to show the existence of any such general principle on the international plane.

II. Examples of GPL that investment tribunals have recognized

This section examines a selection of the GPL most relevant in international investment law **36** and arbitration.[162]

1. *Actori incumbit onus probandi*

The principle whereby each party in arbitration proceedings has the burden of proving the **37** facts upon which it relies (*actori incumbit onus probandi*) has been recognized by many authors as a GPL.[163] It has also been recognized by international tribunals, including the Appellate Body of the WTO,[164] the PCIJ,[165] and the ICJ.[166] In fact, the ICJ expressly recognized this concept as a 'general principle of law'[167] and as a 'well-established general principle'.[168]

The Appellate Body of the WTO explained the scope of 'the rule that the party who asserts **38** a fact, whether the claimant or the respondent, is responsible for providing proof thereof' and that 'the burden of proof rests upon the party, whether complaining or defending, who asserts the affirmative of a particular claim or defence'.[169] It also added that 'if that party adduces evidence sufficient to raise a presumption that what is claimed is true, the burden then shifts to the other party, who will fail unless it adduces sufficient evidence to rebut the

---

[161] See Dumberry, 'Emergence' (n 117) examining several awards.
[162] This entry only examines those general principles that have been most frequently mentioned in awards (and by scholars), according to searches of all publically available investor–State arbitration cases using the term 'general principle of law' and other expressions to the same effect as conducted in Dumberry, *A Guide to General Principles* (n 104) . Other principles are mentioned in ibid, 138ff, including *lis pendens*, unjust enrichment, etc. All concepts examined in this section are 'procedural' principles, except for the clean hands doctrine, which can be considered as 'substantive'. The concept of 'unjust enrichment' is examined in this Commentary by Kathleen Claussen.
[163] See numerous writers mentioned in Dumberry, *A Guide to General Principles* (n 104) 151.
[164] Appellate Body Report, *United States—Measures Affecting Imports of Woven Wool Shirts and Blouses from India*, 25 April 1997, WT/DS33/AB/R, at 14 (hereafter *Measures Affecting Imports of Woven Wool Shirts*).
[165] *The Mavrommatis Jerusalem Concessions*, Judgment, PCIJ Ser A No 5; *Legal Status of Eastern Greenland*, Judgment, PCIJ Ser A/B No 53, 49.
[166] See, for instance, *Military and Paramilitary Activities in and against Nicaragua (Nicaragua v United States of America)*, Merits (Judgment) [1986] ICJ Rep 437, para 101 (hereafter *Nicaragua case*); *Application of the Convention on the Prevention and Punishment of the Crime of Genocide (Bosnia and Herzegovina v Serbia and Montenegro)* (Judgment) [2007] ICJ Rep 75, para 204 (hereafter *Genocide case*).
[167] *Sovereignty over Pedra Branca/Pulau Batu Puteh, Middle Rocks and South Ledge (Malaysia/Singapore)*, 23 May 2008 (Judgment) [2008] ICJ Rep 12, para 45.
[168] *Dispute regarding Navigational and Related Rights (Costa Rica v Nicaragua)* (Judgment) [2009] ICJ Rep 213, para 101.
[169] *Measures Affecting Imports of Woven Wool Shirts* (n 164) 14.

presumption'.[170] Investment tribunals have interpreted and applied the principle in the same way.[171] Some of them have also highlighted that while the 'legal' burden of proof 'never shifts', the 'evidential' burden of proof 'can shift from one party to another, depending upon the state of the evidence'.[172]

39 The reasoning of a number of investment tribunals suggests that they consider the concept as a general principle of *international* law. Thus, some awards simply noted that the principle existed under 'international law',[173] or used other expressions to the same effect.[174] Other tribunals have referred to the existence of this 'well-established rule', or 'practice', and only cited international law authorities in support of this affirmation.[175] The *Salini* award is a good example.[176] It should be added that other awards have mentioned the existence of the principle under both domestic law and international law.[177]

2. Estoppel

40 The principle of estoppel imposes limits on what the parties are allowed to argue during the arbitration proceedings. It is important to distinguish between two distinct notions of estoppel.[178] First, an extensive definition of the doctrine covers very general propositions, based on good faith, such as *non licet venire contra factum proprium* or *allegans contraria non audiendus est*.[179] In the past, this broad conception of the doctrine has been adopted by international tribunals and in a number of separate opinions of ICJ judges.[180] Some investment tribunals have followed this approach. One example is the *Chevron* award mentioning that 'no party to this arbitration can "have it both ways" or "blow hot and cold", to affirm a thing at one time and to deny that same thing at another time according to the mere exigencies of the moment'.[181] Second, there also exists a much more restrictive and technical conception of estoppel, which originated from common law. This is the conception which has been most often applied in recent years by scholars and by judicial bodies.[182] Under this conception, the basic elements required for the principle to apply can be summarized as follows:

1. State A has voluntarily and unconditionally made an authorized statement of fact (or conduct) which is clear and unambiguous;

---

[170] ibid.
[171] Feldman (n 119) para 177.
[172] *Mercer International Inc v Canada*, ICSID Case No ARB(AF)I121(3), Award, 6 March 2018, para 7.14; *Apotex Holdings Inc & Apotex Inc v United States*, ICSID Case No ARB(AF)/12/1, Award, 25 August 2014, para 8.6 (hereafter *Apotex*).
[173] One example is *National Gas S.A.E. v Egypt*, ICSID Case No ARB/11/7, Award, 3 April 2014, para 118.
[174] *Waguih Elie George Siag and Clorinda Vecchi v Egypt*, ICSID Case No ARB/05/15, Award, 1 June 2009, para 315.
[175] Many examples are cited in Dumberry, *A Guide to General Principles* (n 104) 153.
[176] *Salini Costruttori S.P.A. and Italstrade S.P.A. v Jordan*, ICSID Case No ARB/02/13, Award, 31 January 2006, paras 70–73.
[177] For instance, *Tradex Hellas SA v Albania*, ICSID Case No ARB/94/2, Award, 29 April 1999, paras 73–75. Other examples are cited in Dumberry, *A Guide to General Principles* (n 104) 154–55.
[178] T Cottier and J Müller, 'Estoppel' in *Max Planck Encyclopedia of Public International Law* (2012) para 2 (hereafter Cottier and Müller, 'Estoppel').
[179] See B Cheng, *General Principles of Law as Applied by International Courts and Tribunals* (Stevens 1953) 141ff (hereafter Cheng, *General Principles*).
[180] Cottier and Müller, 'Estoppel' (n 178) paras 2, 8, referring to several cases.
[181] *Chevron Corporation and Texaco Petroleum Corporation v Ecuador*, PCA Case No 2009-23 (UCNITRAL), Second Partial Award on Track II, 30 August 2018, para 7.106 (hereafter *Chevron Corporation*).
[182] See, for instance, *Case concerning the Temple of Preah Vihear (Cambodia v Thailand)* (Merits) [1962] ICJ Rep 101, Dissenting Opinion of Judge Spender, paras 143–44 (hereafter *Temple of Preah Vihear*).

2. Another State (State B) has relied in good faith on such statement (or conduct) by State A; and
3. Reliance on that statement by State B was to its own detriment, or it resulted in an advantage for the party making the statement (State A).[183]

Kulick's comprehensive analysis of investment arbitration decisions up until 2014 shows that **41** all tribunals/arbitrators that have adopted the restrictive view of the concept have ultimately rejected the estoppel claim. In contrast, the argument was successful in half of the cases where they adopted a broad conception.[184] Thus, a number of tribunals that have adopted a broad approach seem to have 'accepted mere inconsistent behaviour as being sufficient, without requiring a showing of detrimental reliance or discussing whether there was a clear and unequivocal representation'.[185] Investment tribunals that have adopted a restrictive conception of estoppel have systematically relied on the three above-mentioned conditions to apply the principle[186] and have referred to international decisions material.[187] On the contrary, tribunals which have adopted a broad approach to estoppel have not cited any authorities in support of their position.[188]

International tribunals usually do not take any position regarding the GPL status of estoppel. **42** The reasoning of some tribunals and judges suggest that they believe, at the very least, that estoppel applies under 'international law'.[189] The Iran–US Claims Tribunal[190] and the individual opinions of ICJ Judges Alfaro[191] and Ammoun[192] have been more explicit in their recognition of the GPL character of the concept. More recently, the *Chagos* tribunal did not hesitate to qualify estoppel as a GPL,[193] adding that 'estoppel in international law differs from "complicated classifications, modalities, species, sub-species and procedural features" of its municipal law counterpart [...] but its frequent invocation in international proceedings has added definition to the scope of the principle'.[194] This award has been interpreted in a recent ILA Report as meaning that the principle which 'might have originally emerged from domestic law', has now become a 'principle of international law that has its own terminology and distinctions that are no longer dependent upon domestic law'.[195]

---

[183] This definition (in Dumberry, *A Guide to General Principles* (n 104) 158) is based on the following sources: *Temple of Preah Vihear* (n 182), Dissenting Opinion of Judge Spender, paras 143–44; DW Bowett, 'Estoppel Before International Tribunals and its Relation to Acquiescence' (1957) 33 BYIL 201–02; A Kulick, 'About the Order of Cart and Horse, Among Other Things: Estoppel in the Jurisprudence of International Investment Arbitration Tribunals' (2016) 27(1) EJIL 109.
[184] Kulick, ibid 114.
[185] ibid 117–18.
[186] ibid 116, citing several cases.
[187] ibid 120.
[188] ibid 117, citing many cases. Kulick goes further, suggesting that a tribunal's choice of one approach or the other may have, in fact, been dictated by the outcome of the case, ibid 120.
[189] For instance: *Dispute Concerning Delimitation of the Maritime Boundary between Bangladesh and Myanmar in the Bay of Bengal (Bangladesh/Myanmar)*, ITLOC Case No 16, Judgment, 14 March 2012, para 124.
[190] *American Bell International Inc v The Islamic Republic of Iran, the Ministry of Defense of the Islamic Republic of Iran, the Ministry of Post, Telegraph and Telephone of the Islamic Republic of Iran and the Telecommunications Company of Iran*, IUSCT Case No 48, Award No 255-48-3, 19 September 1986, para 16.
[191] *Temple of Preah Vihear* (n 182), Separate opinion of Judge Alfaro, 101, 139, 43.
[192] *North Sea Continental Shelf* (n 31), separate opinion of Judge Ammoun, 101, 100, 120–21.
[193] *Chagos Marine Protected Area (Mauritius v United Kingdom)*, Award, PCA Case No 2011-03, 18 March 2015, para 435.
[194] ibid para 436.
[195] ILA, 'The Use of Domestic Law' (n 124) para 61. See also Dumberry, *A Guide to General Principles* (n 104) 166.

43 A number of investment tribunals have expressly stated that estoppel is a GPL.[196] Because BITs do not contain any reference to this principle, it can be assumed that tribunals have used estoppel to fill a gap. While some tribunals have considered the notion as a GPL grounded in domestic law,[197] the reasoning of other awards suggests that they viewed estoppel as a general principle of *international* law.[198] However, it seems that the only tribunal which explicitly referred to a 'general principle of international law' is the recent *Chevron* award.[199]

3. *Res judicata*

44 The principle of *res judicata* stands for two connected purposes, often described as the 'positive' and the 'negative' effect of the doctrine.[200] First, the goal of *res judicata* is to end litigation in order to preserve the general stability of legal relations between parties. Second, it follows that once a tribunal has rendered a verdict, this decision has a binding force between the parties to the dispute (but not for third parties). Consequently, the parties to such a dispute cannot re-litigate the same case again. The definition and scope of the principle of *res judicata* is examined in another entry.[201] The principle is widely recognized as a GPL by international scholars[202] and courts and tribunals, including the PCIJ,[203] the European Court of Justice (ECJ),[204] and the Iran–US Claims Tribunal.[205] Notably, in two recent cases, the ICJ explicitly recognized the doctrine as a 'general principle of law'.[206]

45 *Res judicata* has also been applied by numerous investment tribunals.[207] In fact, several tribunals have explicitly recognized the principle as a GPL,[208] or used expressions to the same

---

[196] *Pan American Energy LLC and BP Argentina Exploration Company v Argentina*, ICSID Case No ARB/03/13, Preliminary Objections, 27 July 2006, para 159 (hereafter *Pan American*); *Canfor Corporation and others v United States*, UNCITRAL, Order of the Consolidation Tribunal, 7 September 2005, para 168 (hereafter *Canfor*); *Desert Line Projects LLC v Yemen*, ICSID ARB/05/17, Award, 6 February 2008, para 207; *Chevron Corporation* (n 181) para 7.99; *Hesham Talaat M. Al-Warraq v Indonesia*, Arbitration under the Agreement on Promotion, Protection and Guarantee of Investments among Member States of the Organisation of the Islamic Conference, Final Award, 15 December 2014, para 224 (hereafter *Al-Warraq*).
[197] *Amco* (n 127) Jurisdiction, 25 September 1983, para 47.1ff.
[198] See *Pan American* (n 196) para 159. See also Dumberry, *A Guide to General Principles* (n 104) 166ff examining several awards. Other awards mention the existence of the doctrine in 'international law' without however citing any authority: *Petrobart Limited v Kyrgyz Republic*, SCC Case No 126/2003, Award, 29 March 2005, para VIII.5.2 (hereafter *Petrobart*).
[199] *Chevron Corporation* (n 181) para 7.99.
[200] *Genocide case* (n 166) para 116.
[201] See entry by Cameron Miles.
[202] See Dumberry, *A Guide to General Principles* (n 104) 174ff; CN Brower and PF Henin, 'Res Judicata' in M Kinnear and others (eds), *Building International Investment Law: The First 50 Years of ICSID* (Kluwer Law International 2015); P Janig and A Reinisch, 'General Principles and the Coherence of International Investment Law: of Res Judicata, Lis Pendens and the Value of Precedents' in Andenas and others (eds), *General Principles* (n 104); A Sheppard, 'Res Judicata and Estoppel' in BM Cremades and JDM Lew (eds), *Parallel State and Arbitral Procedures in International Arbitration* (ICC Publications 2005); C Kotuby and J Egerton-Vernon, 'The Adoption by International Tribunals of a Substantive/Transactional Approach to Res Judicata—A New Paradigm in International Dispute Resolution' (2015) 30(3) ICSID Rev; J Magnaye and A Reinisch, 'Revisiting Res Judicata and Lis Pendens in Investor-State Arbitration' (2016) 15(2) LPICT; A Reinisch, 'The Use and Limits of *Res Judicata* and *Lis Pendens* as Procedural Tools to Avoid Conflicting Dispute Settlement Outcomes' (2004) 3 LPICT.
[203] *Polish Postal Service in Danzig* Case, PCIJ Ser B, No 11, Advisory Opinion, 16 May 1925, 30.
[204] See numerous cases in S Schaffstein, *The Doctrine of Res Judicata Before International Commercial Arbitral Tribunals* (OUP 2016) 74.
[205] *Islamic Republic of Iran v United States*, Iran–US CTR, Award No 601-A3/A8/A9/A14/B61-FT, Partial Award, 17 July 2009, para 114.
[206] *Questions of the Delimitation of the Continental Shelf* (n 113) para 58; *Maritime Delimitation in the Caribbean Sea* (n 113) para 68.
[207] Many cases are mentioned in Dumberry, *A Guide to General Principles* (n 104) 177ff.
[208] *Waste Management* (n 82), Decision as to Mexico's Preliminary Objection, 26 June 2002, paras 39–47; *Amco* (n 127), Resubmitted Case, Jurisdiction, 10 May 1988, (1993) 1 ICSID Rep 543, 549; *Ampal-American*

effect. While the reasoning of some tribunals suggests that they believe that the principle is grounded in domestic law,[209] other awards seem to have viewed the notion as a general principle of *international* law. This is the case of those awards which have actually explicitly used this expression,[210] or used wording to the same effect,[211] and those which held that the concept applies on the international plane.[212] Some awards have mentioned that the principle exists under both domestic and international law.[213] The *Mobil* award is interesting in this respect.[214] The tribunal started its analysis by mentioning the existence of the principle as a GPL grounded in domestic law, but then added that 'whatever its origins, it is now an established principle of international law'.[215] The rest of the sources mentioned by the tribunal shows that it actually considered it as a general principle of *international* law.[216] Given the fact that the BITs in these cases did not refer to this principle, it can be assumed that tribunals have used it to fill gaps.

4. Abuse of rights

The definition and scope of the principle of abuse of rights is examined in another entry of this book.[217] There is widespread support among scholars for the idea that the concept is a GPL.[218] Abuse of rights has been referred to as a GPL by one judge in his separate opinion in an International Tribunal for the Law of the Sea (ITLOS) case.[219] Additionally, the WTO Appellate Body has frequently referred to the principle[220] and has expressly recognized its GPL status in one case.[221]

Investment tribunals commonly use the expression 'abuse of process'. The *Churchill* tribunal noted that the concept of 'abuse of process' was 'a variation of the prohibition of abuse of rights and, like the latter, an emanation of the principle of good faith'.[222] The notion of 'abuse of process' is indeed one application of the prohibition of abuse of rights in the specific context of arbitral or court proceedings.[223] One of the most comprehensive analyses of

---

Israel Corporation and others v Egypt, ICSID Case No ARB/12/11, Liability and Heads of Loss, 21 February 2017, para 262.

[209] See Dumberry, *A Guide to General Principles* (n 104) 178, mentioning many cases.
[210] *Chevron Corporation* (n 181) para 272.
[211] *Petrobart* (n 198) para VIII.4.3; *Industria Nacional* (n 95) para 86.
[212] *Apotex* (n 172) para 7.11.
[213] *Industria Nacional* (n 95) para 86.
[214] *Mobil* (n 83) paras 187ff.
[215] ibid para 187.
[216] The same can be said about *Waste Management* (n 82) paras 39–47, where the tribunal only referred to international law authorities in support of its claim that the principle is a general principle.
[217] See entry by Regis Bismuth.
[218] See Dumberry, *A Guide to General Principles* (n 104) 267, citing numerous authorities.
[219] *The M/V 'Norstar' Case (Panama v Italy)*, ITLOS Case no 25, Preliminary Objections, 4 November 2016, Separate opinion of Judge Lucky, para 74.
[220] AR Ziegler and J Baumgartner, 'Good Faith as a General Principle of (International) Law' in AD Mitchell, M Sornarajah and T Voon (eds), *Good Faith and International Economic Law* (OUP 2015) 33, citing several cases (hereafter Ziegler and Baumgartner, 'Good Faith').
[221] *US: Import Prohibition of Certain Shrimp and Shrimp Products*, Appellate Body, 12 October 1998, (1999) 38 ILM 118, 165, paras 158–59.
[222] *Churchill* (n 142) para 492.
[223] A Llamzon and A Sinclair, 'Investor Wrongdoing in Investment Arbitration: Standards Governing Issues of Corruption, Fraud, Misrepresentation and Other Investor Misconduct' in A Jan van den Berg (ed), *Legitimacy: Myths, Realities, Challenges* (18 ICCA Congress Kluwer 2015) 456 (hereafter Llamzon and Sinclair, 'Investor Wrongdoing'); C Brown, 'The Relevance of the Doctrine of Abuse of Process in International Adjudication' (2011) 8(2) TDM 6–7.

the principle was undertaken by the *Mobil v Venezuela* tribunal.[224] While it did not formally adopt a position as to the status of abuse of rights, it considered that the principle existed 'under general international law'.[225] Many tribunals seem to consider the principle as a general principle of *international* law.[226] Others have considered the doctrine as both a GPL *foro domestico* and a general principle of international law.[227]

5. Clean hands

48 The clean hands doctrine is sometimes expressed in a number of Latin maxims, including *ex delicto non orituractio* ('an unlawful act cannot serve as the basis of an action at law') and *ex turpi causa non oritur* ('an action cannot arise from a dishonourable cause'). In simple terms, it means that 'if some form of illegal or improper conduct is found on the part of the investor, his or her hands will be "unclean", his claims will be barred and any loss suffered will lie where it falls'.[228] As rightly acknowledged by the *Yukos* tribunal, the status of the clean hands principle is 'controversial' in international law.[229] Thus, in the context of State responsibility, the ILC Special Rapporteur James Crawford explained that 'if it exist[s] at all', the doctrine would operate as a ground of inadmissibility rather than as a circumstance precluding wrongfulness or responsibility.[230] International tribunals have been reluctant to recognize the existence of the doctrine. In a 2007 Permanent Court of Arbitration (PCA) arbitration between Guyana and Suriname, the tribunal underlined that the clean hands doctrine had been inconsistently applied by tribunals.[231] While this is true, it remains that there is some support for the principle in older international law cases[232] and by several ICJ judges in their dissenting opinions.[233] The doctrine has been invoked by States in many ICJ cases, but the Court never took position on the matter.[234] In this context, it seems that one can agree with the conclusion reached recently by the *Churchill Mining* tribunal, which noted that the doctrine of 'unclean hands' had 'found expression at the international level, although its status and exact contours are subject to debate and have been approached differently by

---

[224] *Mobil* (n 120) paras 169ff (The name of the case was later changed to *Venezuela Holdings B.V. and others v Venezuela*).

[225] ibid para 177.

[226] *The Renco Group, Inc v Peru*, ICSID Case No UNCT/13/1, Partial Award on Jurisdiction, 15 July 2016, para 175. See also different expressions used by other tribunals: *Saipem S.P.A. v Bangladesh*, ICSID Case No ARB/05/07, Jurisdiction and Award, 30 June 2009, paras 160–61; *Abaclat and Others v Argentina*, ICSID Case No ARB/07/5, Decision on Jurisdiction and Admissibility, 4 August 2011, para 646; *Canfor* (n 196) para 137; *Antin Infrastructure Services Luxembourg S.à.r.l. and Antin Energia Termosolar B.V. v Spain*, ICSID Case No ARB/13/31, Award, 15 June 2018, para 316. See also the implicit recognition in: *Churchill* (n 142) para 488.

[227] *Orascom v Algeria*, ICSID Case No ARB/12/36, Award, 31 May 2017, para 541; *Unión Fenosa Gas, S.A. v Egypt*, Award, ICSID Case No ARB/14/4, 31 August 2018, para 6.79.

[228] A Llamzon, 'Yukos Universal Limited (Isle of Man) v The Russian Federation: The State of the 'Unclean Hands' Doctrine in International Investment Law: Yukos as Both Omega and Alpha' (2015) 30(2) ICSID Rev 316. See also Cheng, *General Principles* (n 179); G Fitzmaurice, 'The General Principles of International Law Considered from the Standpoint of the Rule of Law' (1958) 92 RdC 119.

[229] *Hulley* (n 118) paras 1358–59.

[230] ILC, 'Second Report on State Responsibility by Mr James Crawford, Special Rapporteur', 30 April 1999, A/CN.4/498/Add.2, para 334 YILC 1999, Vol II, Part One, 83, 333, 336. See also J Crawford, *The International Law Commission's Articles on State Responsibility: Introduction, Text and Commentaries* (CUP 2002) 162.

[231] *Guyana v Suriname*, arbitral tribunal constituted under Annex VII of the United Nations Convention on the Law of the Sea (UNCLOS), Award, 17 September 2007, paras 418, 421.

[232] Some have argued that this is the case for *The Diversion of Water from the Meuse (Netherlands v Belgium)*, PCIJ Ser A/B, No 70, opinion of Judge Hudson, 77, 87, and dissenting opinion of Judge Anzilotti, 50.

[233] For instance, *Nicaragua case* (n 166) dissenting opinion of Judge Schwebel, paras 240, 268–72.

[234] For a recent example, *Certain Iranian Assets (Islamic Republic of Iran v United States of America)* (Preliminary Objections) [2019] ICJ Rep 92, paras 117, 121.

international tribunals'.[235] Consequently, the status of the doctrine has been described by many as 'unsettled' in international law.[236]

In recent years, a number of authors have openly supported the application of the doctrine **49** of clean hands in the field of investment arbitration to operate as a bar to the admissibility of claims submitted by investors that have committed violations of host States' laws.[237] Many investment tribunals, as recognized by the recent *Littop* award,[238] have indeed concretely applied the doctrine of clean hands to decide cases.[239] Arguably, the inclusion of a provision in an investment treaty to the effect that protected investments are only those made 'in accordance with the law' in BITs is a manifestation of the doctrine of clean hands.[240] In the *Inceysa* award the tribunal stated that a 'foreign investor cannot seek to benefit from an investment effectuated by means of one or several illegal acts and, consequently, enjoy the protection granted by the host State, such as access to international arbitration to resolve disputes, because it is evident that its act had a fraudulent origin and, as provided by the legal maxim, "nobody can benefit from his own fraud"'.[241] In line with these considerations, many other tribunals have concluded that there exists an implicit legality requirement even in the absence of such a clause in the instrument.[242] The reasoning of the *Niko* tribunal suggests that it viewed the doctrine as a valid ground of defence in arbitration proceedings since it actually applied the doctrine to the facts of the case.[243] Similarly, in the *Al-Warraq* case, the tribunal explained that the Claimant's conduct 'falls within the scope of application of the "clean hands" doctrine, and therefore cannot benefit from the protection afforded by the OIC Agreement'[244] and 'renders the Claimant's claim inadmissible'.[245] The same may be said about the *Rusoro* award.[246]

---

[235] *Churchill* (n 142) para 493. See *Glencore Finance (Bermuda) Limited v Bolivia*, PCA Case No 2016-39, Procedural Order No 2: Decision on Bifurcation, 31 January 2018, para 46, where the tribunal agreed with the statement made by the *Churchill* tribunal.

[236] Llamzon and Sinclair, 'Investor Wrongdoing' (n 223) 510. See also Ziegler and Baumgartner, 'Good Faith' (n 220) 29; A Tanzi, 'The Relevance of the Foreign Investor's Good Faith' in Gattini and others (eds), *General Principles* (n 104) 207.

[237] R Kreindler, 'Corruption in International Investment Arbitration: Jurisdiction and the Unclean Hands Doctrine' in K Hober and others (eds), *Between East and West: Essays in Honour of Ulf Franke* (Juris Publishing 2010) 309 (hereafter Kreindler, 'Corruption'); R Moloo and A Khachaturian, 'The Compliance with the Law Requirement in International Law' (2010) 34 Fordham ILJ 1485–86 (hereafter Moloo and Khachaturian, 'The Compliance'); AK Bjorklund and L Vanhonnaeker, 'Yukos: The Clean Hands Doctrine Revisited' (2015) 9(2) Diritti umani e diritto internazionale 367–68 (hereafter Bjorklund and Vanhonnaeker, 'Yukos'). *Contra*: O Pomson, 'The Clean Hands Doctrine in the Yukos Awards: A Response to Patrick Dumberry' (2017) 18(4) JWIT 724ff (hereafter Pomson).

[238] *Littop Enterprises Limited, Bridgemont Ventures Limited and Bordo Management Limited v Ukraine*, SCC Case No V 2015/092, Final Award, 4 February 2021, paras 439ff (hereafter *Littop*).

[239] R Moloo, 'A Comment on the Clean Hands Doctrine in International Law' (2011) 8(1) TDM 7 (hereafter Moloo, 'A Comment').

[240] ibid 6–7; Moloo and Khachaturian, 'The Compliance' (n 237) 1485; Llamzon and Sinclair, 'Investor Wrongdoing' (n 223) 509; Bjorklund and Vanhonnaeker, 'Yukos' (n 237) 367, 369; Mariano De Alba Uribe, 'Drawing the Line: Addressing Allegations of Unclean Hands in Investment Arbitration' (2005) 12 Brazilian JIL 324. *Contra*: Caroline Le Moullec, 'The Clean Hands Doctrine: A Tool for Accountability of Investor Conduct and Inadmissibility of Investment Claims' (2018) 84(1) Arbitration 24, 29; Pomson (n 237) 724–25.

[241] *Inceysa* (n 38) para 242.

[242] See, for instance, *Plama Consortium Limited v Bulgaria*, ICSID Case No ARB/03/24, Jurisdiction, 8 February 2005; *Phoenix Action, Ltd v Czech Republic*, ICSID Case No ARB/06/5, Award, 15 April 2009, para 101. Many other cases are mentioned in: P Dumberry, 'The Clean Hands Doctrine as a General Principle of International Law' (2020) 21(4) JWIT 489–527 (hereafter Dumberry, 'The Clean Hands Doctrine').

[243] See *Niko Resources* (n 140) paras 480–82.

[244] *Al-Warraq* (n 196) para 647.

[245] ibid para 646. It may be that the tribunal's observations on the clean hands doctrine was simply an *obiter* since it had *already* decided that the claimant could not benefit from the protection offered under the Agreement by virtue of the application of Article 9.

[246] *Rusoro Mining Ltd v Venezuela*, ICSID Case No ARB(AF)/12/5, Award, 22 August 2016, para 482, indicating, rather vaguely, and in the form of an *obiter*, that 'it is undisputed that claimants with "dirty hands" have no standing in investment arbitration'.

50 One can agree with Moloo that even if 'historical application of the clean hands doctrine has been inconsistent, and as such, inconclusive', it remains 'that recent decisions in the investment arbitration context suggest that the doctrine has a place in international law'.[247] Bjorklund and Vanhonnaeker came to the conclusion that 'the doctrine has been indeed recognized and applied in numerous instances by international tribunals',[248] and that, in the context of investor–State arbitration, 'the issue is not so much whether the doctrine should apply but rather on what basis it will be invoked'.[249] In the author's view, the doctrine should be recognized as a 'general principle of *international* law'.[250] While this position has been rejected by the *Yukos*[251] and *South American Silver*[252] tribunals, more recently the *Littop* award recognized the doctrine as a general principle of international law.[253]

E. Conclusion

51 There are many situations where there is an alignment between investment arbitration and the practice of other international courts and tribunals regarding custom. Thus, judicial bodies have considered that two basic requirements, State practice and *opinio juris*, are necessary to conclude the existence of a customary rule. Yet, investment awards and other international judicial decisions have also both generally failed to properly reveal the existence of customary rules. While this feature is regrettable, it may be explained by the simple fact that the parties in their pleadings and tribunals and courts in their awards may not have the time nor the resources to undertake such an exercise. On the other hand, investment arbitration has deviated from the general practice regarding custom with respect to some other aspects. Thus, while judicial bodies in both investment arbitration and beyond have held that 'statements' can be evidence of State practice for the purpose of custom formation, the type of statements that investment awards have considered and applied are not exactly the same as those dominant otherwise in general international law practice.

52 Furthermore, international decisions and investment awards have both generally failed to explain the meaning or function of GPL in international law. However, in recent years, investment tribunals have been increasingly referring to such principles in their awards. Yet, no investment tribunal has so far undertaken any truly comprehensive comparative analysis of the most representative domestic legal systems of the world to identify GPL *foro domestico*. The reason is simple: this is a rather complicated and very time-consuming exercise.

53 One of the most interesting features of investment arbitration is that many awards have explicitly (and sometimes implicitly) recognized concepts as 'general principles of international

---

[247] Moloo, 'A Comment' (n 239) 10.
[248] Bjorklund and Vanhonnaeker, 'Yukos' (n 237) 367. It should be noted, however, that not everyone shares this position. See Llamzon and Sinclair, 'Investor Wrongdoing' (n 223) 513.
[249] Bjorklund and Vanhonnaeker, 'Yukos' (n 237) 367–68.
[250] Dumberry, 'The Clean Hands Doctrine' (n 242); Kreindler, 'Corruption' (n 237) 317–19. Contra: J. Ancelin, 'A propos de la "théorie des mains propres": Observations sur les sentences arbitrales Yukos de la Cour Permanente d'Arbitrage du 18 juillet 2014' (2015) 61 AFDI 837–38; Llamzon and Sinclair, 'Investor Wrongdoing' (n 223) 516–17.
[251] *Hulley* (n 118) paras 1358–59. For a critical analysis: Dumberry, 'State of Confusion' (n 118).
[252] *South American Silver Limited* award (n 118) paras 445–46.
[253] *Littop* (n 238) paras 438–39.

law' based on the loose methodology required to show the existence of any such principles on the international plane. They have, thus, referred to State practice, arbitral awards, and other international decisions, as well as the works of scholars to show that these principles have been frequently and consistently recognized and applied by States and tribunals. This flexible methodology is clearly one reason why the concept of 'general principle of international law' is particularly relevant and useful in the specific context of international investment law. The use of this methodology is a perfectly legitimate and reasonable path which should be more frequently used by tribunals in the future. Arbitrators should indeed be encouraged to use all available tools to solve legal disputes. GPL, including general principles of international law, can be used by tribunals to improve the outcome of decision-making by achieving a better balance between investors' rights and States' public interests. For instance, abuse of rights and the clean hands doctrine can be used by tribunals to limit access to international arbitration to foreign investors who adopt a certain standard of behaviour. They allow tribunals to impose some obligations on foreign investors in the context of investment arbitration. GPL can therefore be helpful to recalibrate international investment law in reaction to the current backlash against the legitimacy of the system perceived by some as inherently favourable to the interests of foreign corporations.

Selected literature

Al Faruque A, 'Creating Customary International Law through Bilateral Investment Treaties: A Critical Appraisal' (2004) 44 Indian JIL 292–318.

Alvarez JE, 'A BIT on Custom' (2009) 42 NYUJIntlL&Pol 17–80.

Andenas M, Fitzmaurice M, Tanzi A and Wouters J (eds), *General Principles and the Coherence of International Law* (Brill 2019).

Congyan C, 'International Investment Treaties and the Formation, Application and Transformation of Customary International Law Rules' (2008) 7 Chinese JIL 659–79.

d'Aspremont J, 'International Customary Investment Law: Story of a Paradox' in Gazzini T and de Brabandere E (eds), *International Investment Law. The Sources of Rights and Obligations* (Brill 2012).

Dumberry P, *A Guide to General Principles of Law in International Investment Law* (OUP 2020).

Dumberry P, *The Formation and Identification of Rules of Customary International Law in International Investment Law* (CUP 2016).

Gattini A, Tanzi A and Fontanelli F (eds), *General Principles of Law and International Investment Arbitration* (Brill 2018).

Gazzini T, 'General Principles of Law in the Field of Foreign Investment' (2009) 10 JWIT 103–19.

Gazzini T, 'The Role of Customary International Law in the Field of Foreign Investment' (2007) 8 JWIT 691–716.

Hirsch M, 'Sources of International Investment Law', ILA Study Group on the Role of Soft Law Instruments in International Investment Law (2011).

Kotuby Charles T Jr and Sobota Luke A, *General Principles of Law and International Due Process: Principles and Norms Applicable in Transnational Disputes* (OUP 2017).

Kulick A, 'About the Order of Cart and Horse, Among Other Things: Estoppel in the Jurisprudence of International Investment Arbitration Tribunals' (2016) 27(1) EJIL 107–28.

Nolan MD and Sourgens FG, 'Issues of Proof of General Principles of Law in International Arbitration' (2009) 3(4–5) World Arb & Med Rev 505–33.

Schill SW, 'General Principles of International Law and International Investment Law' in Gazzini T and de Brabandere E (eds), *International Investment Law. The Sources of Rights and Obligations* (Brill 2012).

Selected decisions

Churchill Mining PLC and Planet Mining Pty Ltd v Indonesia, ICSID Case No ARB/12/14 and 12/40, Award, 6 December 2016.
Crystallex International Corporation v Venezuela, ICSID Case No ARB(AF)/11/2, Award, 6 April 2016.
Glamis Gold Ltd v United States, UNCITRAL, Award, 14 May 2009.
Gold Reserve v Venezuela, ICSID Case No ARB 09/1, Award, 22 September 2014.
Hulley Enterprises (Cyprus) Limited v Russia, UNCITRAL, PCA Case No AA 226, Final Award, 18 July 2014.
Infinito Gold Ltd v Costa Rica, ICSID Case No ARB/14/5, Award, 3 June 2021.
Mobil Corporation, Venezuela Holdings, BV and Others v Venezuela, Decision on Jurisdiction, ICSID Case No ARB/07/27, 10 June 2010.
South American Silver Limited v Bolivia, PCA Case No 2013-15, Award, 22 November 2018.
Total v Argentina, ICSID Case No ARB/04/1, Liability, 21 December 2010.
UPS v Canada, UNCITRAL, Jurisdiction, 22 November 2002.

State Immunity in investment arbitration

August Reinisch

A. Introduction	1	1. Expropriation and sovereign taking vs. commercial breach of contract	21
B. The development of customary international law principles concerning State immunity	4	2. Sovereign vs. commercial breach in the context of fair and equitable treatment	26
C. State immunity principles before investment tribunals	9	3. Attribution	27
I. False friends—immunity from jurisdiction vs. immunity from liability	9	III. State immunity as a factor in requiring security for a stay of the enforcement of an award during annulment proceedings	35
II. State immunity principles as guidance for other legal issues	20	D. Conclusion	43

A. Introduction

A State's immunity from jurisdiction, usually invoked before foreign domestic courts, is not an issue before international arbitral panels since investment arbitration is predicated upon the consent of the parties and arbitral tribunals are not national courts. In investment dispute settlement, State immunity is primarily a post-arbitral phenomenon. It arises when successful investors try to enforce an arbitral award and seek assets that are exempt from enforcement immunity.[1] As made explicit in Article 55 of the International Centre for Settlement of Investment Disputes (ICSID) Convention,[2] and as implicit in the New York Convention regime,[3] the enforcement obligations of the Contracting Parties to these treaties do not override their customary international law duties to accord other States immunity from execution/enforcement measures.

This clearly distinguishes the issue of State immunity from other topics in this volume, pertaining to matters of State responsibility or the law of treaties, which are frequently addressed

---

[1] See in detail AK Bjorklund, 'State Immunity and the Enforcement of Investor–State Arbitral Awards' in C Binder and others (eds), *International Investment Law for the 21st Century: Essays in Honour of Christoph Schreuer* (OUP 2009) 302–21 (hereafter Bjorklund, 'State Immunity'); A Reinisch, 'Enforcement of Investment Treaty Awards' in Katia Yannaca-Small (ed), *Arbitration under International Investment Agreements* (2nd edn, OUP 2018) 797–822; C Schreuer and others, *The ICSID Convention: A Commentary* (2nd edn, CUP 2009) 1151 et seq.

[2] Convention on the Settlement of Investment Disputes between States and Nationals of Other States, 18 March 1965, 575 UNTS 159.

[3] New York Convention on the Recognition and Enforcement of Foreign Arbitral Awards, 10 June 1958, 330 UNTS 38.

by investment tribunals. As a result, only few arbitral awards directly discuss the issue of State immunity. Still, arbitral tribunals have opined on immunity in a number of cases. Particular caution is required though since the use of the term 'immunity' in some investment awards may differ from what international law normally considers to be immunity from the jurisdiction of national courts or from enforcement measures by national bodies.

3 Rules on State immunity applicable in the investment context are of a customary character. They have primarily developed as national court practice while international courts and tribunals only rarely address immunity issues. The entry will thus start with a brief overview of the development of the principles of State immunity by national courts and then consider to what extent they have been confirmed by the International Court of Justice (ICJ) and other international courts and tribunals. It will then analyse the limited instances where investment tribunals have interpreted (and in fact rarely applied) State immunity principles in investment disputes. This will also include an assessment whether investment arbitration practice aligns with or deviates from customary international law principles of State immunity, including an inquiry into possible reasons and justifications for such deviations, if any.

B. The development of customary international law principles concerning State immunity

4 State immunity, requiring the exemption of States from the jurisdiction of foreign national courts or from enforcement measures by national bodies of other States, has developed significantly over the last 150 years.[4] Based on the notion of sovereign equality, it derives its justification from the idea that no sovereign should sit in judgment over another sovereign (*par in parem non habet iurisdictionem/imperium*).[5] Historically, this was initially interpreted to mean that national courts should always abstain from exercising jurisdiction over foreign States or taking enforcement measures concerning their assets. Such absolute immunity was gradually eroded by the jurisprudence of various national courts since the late nineteenth century. Courts started to grant immunity to foreign States only where they acted as sovereigns/*iure imperii*, as opposed to States acting as merchants in a commercial or *iure gestionis* capacity.

5 In order to distinguish between sovereign/*iure imperii* and commercial/*iure gestionis* activities, most courts rely on the nature and no longer on the purpose of an activity.[6] With a slight time lag the initial absolute immunity in regard to enforcement or execution measures was also eroded. Courts started to exempt only foreign State assets which served sovereign

---

[4] See C Schreuer, *State Immunity: Some Recent Developments* (Grotius 1988); EK Bankas, *The State Immunity Controversy in International Law: Private Suits against Sovereign States in Domestic Courts* (Springer 2005); X Yang, *State Immunity in International Law* (CUP 2012); H Fox and P Webb, *The Law of State Immunity* (3rd edn, OUP 2013) (hereafter Fox and Webb, *State Immunity*).

[5] *Jurisdictional Immunities of the State (Germany v Italy: Greece intervening)* (Judgment) [2012] ICJ Rep 99, 123, para 57 ('The Court considers that the rule of State immunity occupies an important place in international law and international relations. It derives from the principle of sovereign equality of States, ...'). See also Explanatory Report to the European Convention on State Immunity, ETS No 74, para 1 http://conventions.coe.int/Treaty/EN/Reports/Html/074.htm accessed 16 October 2023.

[6] See, eg, R van Alebeek and R Pavoni, 'Immunities of States and their Officials' in A Nollkaemper and A Reinisch (eds), *International Law in Domestic Courts: A Casebook* (OUP 2018) 100, 112 ('the practice of a large number of states which are firmly anchored to the "nature test" '); E Chukwuemeke Okeke, *Jurisdictional Immunities of States and International Organizations* (OUP 2018) 105; M Shaw, *International Law* (9th edn, CUP 2021) 611.

purposes from measures of constraint, implying that there may be limited enforcement measures taken against assets serving non-governmental purposes.[7] In this context, the purpose assets are serving remains relevant. By the mid-twentieth century many national courts have endorsed such developments to an extent that the former absolute immunity could no longer be regarded as reflecting customary international law.[8] Rather, focusing on the nature of the underlying State activity as either sovereign or commercial/*iure gestionis*, the principle of restrictive immunity was adopted by many national courts and codified in specific State immunity legislation in many countries.[9]

When the International Law Commission (ILC) undertook to codify the customary international law in this area, it also started from the premise of a restrictive immunity enjoyed by States and their assets, while recognizing that a limited number of States still considered absolute immunity to be the norm.[10] The resulting 2004 United Nations Convention on Jurisdictional Immunities of States and Their Property[11] thus provides for jurisdictional immunity of foreign States except for commercial activities,[12] tortious acts in the forum state,[13] and employment contracts.[14] In regard to enforcement measures, the Convention exempts from immunity 'property [...] specifically in use or intended for use by the State for other than government non-commercial purposes',[15] i.e. assets serving non-sovereign purposes. In addition, Article 21 UN Convention lists diplomatic, military, central bank, and cultural assets as types of property which should be normally regarded as serving governmental purposes and would thus enjoy immunity from enforcement measures.[16]

While the 2004 Convention has not yet entered into force because the required number of ratifications has not been attained, its provisions have been widely regarded as reflecting customary international law.[17]

---

[7] See also A Reinisch, 'European Court Practice Concerning State Immunity from Enforcement Measures' (2006) 17 EJIL 803; Fox and Webb, State Immunity (n 4) 479; see generally, in particular for earlier practice, J Crawford, 'Execution of Judgments and Foreign Sovereign Immunity' (1981) 75 AJIL 820.

[8] See, eg, OGH 1 Ob 171/50 (*Dralle v Republic of Czechoslovakia*) 10 May 1950, SZ 1950 No 23/143, 304–32; 17 ILR 155, 163 ('[...] it can no longer be said that by international law so-called *acta gestionis* are exempt from municipal jurisdiction'); BVerfGE 2 BvM 1/62 (*Empire of Iran Case*) 30 April 1963, 45 ILR 57; *Philippine Admiral (Owners) v Wallem Shipping (Hong Kong) Ltd and Another*, 5 November 1975, 64 ILR 90; *Trendtex Trading Corporation v Central Bank of Nigeria*, 13 January 1977, 64 ILR 111.

[9] See, eg, US Foreign Sovereign Immunities Act 1976, 28 USC §§ 1330, 1602–11, 15 ILM 1388 (1976); UK State Immunity Act 1978, 17 ILM 1123 (1978); Canada State Immunity Act 1982, 21 ILM 798 (1982); Australia Foreign States Immunities Act 1985, 25 ILM 715 (1986).

[10] Draft Articles on Jurisdictional Immunities of States and Their Property YILC 1991, Vol II, Part Two, 13. See also C Kessedjian and C Schreuer, 'Le Projet d'Articles de la Commission du Droit International des Nations Unies sur les immunités des Etats' (1992) 96 RGDIP 299; B Heß, 'The International Law Commission's Draft Convention on Jurisdictional Immunities of States and Their Property' (1993) 4 EJIL 269.

[11] United Nations Convention on Jurisdictional Immunities of States and Their Property, adopted by the UN General Assembly on 2 December 2004, UN, GAOR, 59th Session, Supp No 22 (A/59/22), 44 ILM 803 (2005); see also G Hafner and U Köhler, 'The United Nations Convention on Jurisdictional Immunities of States and Their Property' (2004) 35 NYIL 3; DP Stewart, 'The UN Convention on Jurisdictional Immunities of States and Their Property' (2005) 99 AJIL 194; R O'Keefe and CJ Tams (eds), *The United Nations Convention on Jurisdictional Immunities of States and Their Property—A Commentary* (OUP 2013).

[12] Article 10 (Commercial transactions) UN Convention (n 11).

[13] Article 12 (Personal injuries and damage to property) UN Convention (n 11).

[14] Article 11 (Contracts of employment) UN Convention (n 11).

[15] Article 19(c) UN Convention (n 11).

[16] Article 21 (Specific categories of property) UN Convention (n 11).

[17] E Chukwuemeke Okeke, *Jurisdictional Immunities of States and International Organizations* (OUP 2018) 48 ('In sum, the Convention is in some aspects declaratory of customary international law [...]'); see also J Crawford, *Brownlie's Principles of Public International Law* (9th edn, OUP 2019) 473 ('the UN Convention has been understood by several courts to reflect an international consensus on state immunity'); *García de Borrisow v Embassy of Lebanon, Decision on Admissibility*, Case No 32096, ILDC 1009 (CO 2007), 13 December 2007, Colombia; Supreme Court of Justice, para 26; see also *Wallishauser v Austria*, ECtHR, 17 July 2012, No 156/04, para 30 ('State immunity

8 Significantly, also the ICJ has regarded restrictive immunity to reflect customary international law when it was called upon to decide a dispute between Germany and Italy concerning the correct application of State immunity principles. In the *Jurisdictional Immunities Case*, the ICJ noted 'that many States (including both Germany and Italy) now distinguish between *acta jure gestionis*, in respect of which they have limited the immunity which they claim for themselves and which they accord to others, and *acta jure imperii*',[18] and that '[b]oth Parties agree that States are generally entitled to immunity in respect of *acta jure imperii*'.[19] In regard to enforcement immunity, the Court endorsed the three exceptions codified in Article 19 of the 2004 UN Convention.[20]

C. State immunity principles before investment tribunals

I. False friends—immunity from jurisdiction vs. immunity from liability

9 As already mentioned, the usage of the term 'immunity' by investment tribunals may sometimes not conform to its meaning in public international law, i.e. an exemption from or procedural bar to the adjudicatory or enforcement power of national courts or authorities. Rather, it has at times been used to refer to an exemption from liability, something that in general international law is closer to the concept of privilege than that of immunity.[21] The use of the term 'immunity' in investment arbitration may be a 'false friend'.[22] Nevertheless, even false friends may bring benefits to the extent they offer solutions based on analogy. As Cordero-Moss has justly remarked the 'classification of a principle or rule under a certain area of the law does not necessarily prevent adopting the principle or rule in another area'.[23]

10 A good example is the North American Free Trade Agreement (NAFTA) award in *Mondev v USA*.[24] The investor considered that the so-called 'statutory immunity' from suit for intentional torts given to public authorities constituted a failure to provide full protection and security to investments and thus contravened Article 1105(1) NAFTA. Specifically,

---

from jurisdiction is governed by customary international law, the codification of which is enshrined in the United Nations Convention on Jurisdictional Immunities of States and their Property of 2 December 2004 ("the 2004 Convention"); *Case of Oleynikov v Russia*, ECtHR, 14 March 2013, No 36703/04, para 66 ('the International Law Commission's 1991 Draft Articles, as now enshrined in the 2004 Convention, apply under customary international law, even if the State in question has not ratified that convention, provided it has not opposed it either').

[18] *Jurisdictional Immunities of the State (Germany v Italy: Greece intervening)* (Judgment) [2012] ICJ Rep 99, 124, para 59.

[19] ibid 125, para 61.

[20] ibid 148, para 118 ('[...] it suffices for the Court to find that there is at least one condition that has to be satisfied before any measure of constraint may be taken against property belonging to a foreign State: that the property in question must be in use for an activity not pursuing government non-commercial purposes, or that the State which owns the property has expressly consented to the taking of a measure of constraint, or that that State has allocated the property in question for the satisfaction of a judicial claim').

[21] See HG Schermers and NM Blokker, *International Institutional Law: Unity within Diversity* (Brill 6th edn, 2018) 268 (suggesting to 'use the word "privilege" for all cases in which local legislation is not, or is differently, applicable, and the word "immunity" for the immunity from jurisdiction').

[22] In linguistics, and also in comparative law, similar expressions that have a markedly different meaning are sometimes referred to as 'false friends' or '*faux amis*'.

[23] See G Cordero-Moss, 'Commercial Arbitration and Investment Arbitration: Fertile Soil for False Friends?' in C Binder and others (eds), *International Investment Law for the 21st Century. Essays in Honour of Christoph Schreuer* (OUP 2009) 782, 792.

[24] *Mondev International Ltd v United States of America*, ICSID Case No ARB(AF)/99/2 (NAFTA), Final Award, 11 October 2002.

the claimant complained about a US court decision holding the Boston Redevelopment Authority immune from liability for interference with contractual relations by reason of a Massachusetts statute.[25]

The *Mondev* tribunal rightly pointed out that this 'statutory immunity' under Massachusetts law did not really raise a State immunity issue. Rather, there was a 'closer analogy with certain decisions concerning statutory immunities of State agencies before their own courts'.[26]

The tribunal was not persuaded:

'[…] that the doctrine of foreign State immunity presents any useful analogy to the present situation. That immunity is concerned not with the position of State agencies before their own courts, but before the courts of third States, where considerations of interstate relations and the proper allocation of jurisdictional competence are raised.'[27]

This correctly reflects the notion that the international law concept of State immunity applies only to sovereign States before foreign national courts and not to the exemption from liability under the applicable domestic law. The tribunal concluded that the extension to a statutory authority of a limited immunity from suit for interference with contractual relations did not amount to a breach of Article 1105(1).[28]

Still, the *Mondev* tribunal seems to have been tempted to seek guidance by the false friend, or rather analogy, of immunity: when it discussed the non-availability of a legal remedy against certain types of State action, it also recurred to contemporary jurisprudence of the European Court of Human Rights (ECtHR) concerning immunity from suit.[29] It considered that it was 'well established that foreign States and their agencies may claim immunities in respect of conduct in the exercise of governmental authority, even if such conduct is or would otherwise be civilly wrongful'.[30] As already mentioned though, the tribunal eventually rightly dismissed the analogy to foreign State immunity and considered that the ECtHR's case-law 'concerning statutory immunities of State agencies before their own courts' is more relevant to assess whether such immunities would be incompatible with the right of access to court enshrined in Article 6(1) of the European Convention on Human Rights,[31] because they effectively exclude access to the courts in the determination of civil rights. Ultimately, though,

---

[25] Under para 10(c) of the Massachusetts Tort Claims Act (PL 258), a public employer which is not an 'independent body politic and corporate' is immune from 'any claim arising out of an intentional tort, including assault, battery, false imprisonment, false arrest, intentional mental distress, malicious prosecution, malicious abuse of process, libel, slander, misrepresentation, deceit, invasion of privacy, interference with advantageous relations or interference with contractual relations'.
[26] ibid para 143.
[27] ibid para 142.
[28] ibid para 154.
[29] The *Mondev* tribunal specifically referred to *Al-Adsani v United Kingdom* App No 35763/97, (2002) 34 EHRR 11; *McElhinney v Ireland* App No 31253/96, (2002) 34 EHRR 13; *Fogarty v United Kingdom* App No 37112/97, (2002) 34 EHRR 12.
[30] *Mondev International Ltd v United States of America*, ICSID Case No ARB(AF)/99/2 (NAFTA), Final Award, 11 October 2002, para 141.
[31] Article 6(1) European Convention for the Protection of Human Rights and Fundamental Freedoms (adopted 4 November 1950, entered into force 3 September 1953) 213 UNTS 221 (In the determination of his civil rights and obligations or of any criminal charge against him, everyone is entitled to a fair and public hearing within a reasonable time by an independent and impartial tribunal established by law.) See *Golder v United Kingdom*, ECtHR, App No 4451/70, 21 February 1975 [1975] ECHR 1, para 36 ('Article 6 para. 1 (Art. 6-1) secures to everyone the right to have any claim relating to his civil rights and obligations brought before a court or tribunal. In this way the Article embodies the "right to a court", of which the right of access, that is the right to institute proceedings before courts in civil matters, constitutes one aspect only').

the *Mondev* tribunal considered that the ECtHR jurisprudence was not unequivocal and, in any event, specific to a different region.

15 In the context of the *Mondev* scenario, it is interesting to note that true State immunity decisions by national courts appear not to have given rise to investment claims so far. However, the possibility exists. In fact, if the courts of a host State uphold another State's jurisdictional immunity, this could be regarded not only as a violation of the obligation to provide access to court under human-rights instruments, but also as a breach of the obligation to afford fair and equitable treatment, which includes the obligation to afford access to justice,[32] or of the obligation to provide full protection and security. It has been rightly pointed out that the absence of such cases may result from the fact that investors are protected in their relations with host States where they have made investments and will usually have disputes with these States before arbitral tribunals and not with third States which may be afforded immunity by the courts of the host States.[33]

16 A second example of an investment tribunal using the term 'immunity' in the sense of an exemption from liability can be seen in the jurisdictional decision of *Saipem v Bangladesh*. There, the issue was whether the specific formulation of the applicable Bilateral Investment Treaty (BIT)'s expropriation clause[34] could be read as providing for 'an exclusion of the consent to arbitrate with respect to judicial acts'.[35] The *Saipem* tribunal denied this by holding that the provision 'cannot be understood as creating immunity in favour of the judiciary power'.[36] The issue thus did not concern immunity in a technical sense. Rather, the question was whether a limited scope of consent to arbitration might be understood as preventing the tribunal from assessing the acts of the judiciary. The tribunal rejected this claim and interpreted the BIT provision as relating only to the traditional question whether an expropriation could be regarded as lawful.[37] In other words, it did not immunize judicial acts from scrutiny and it reserved its power to assess whether acts of the judiciary may have constituted expropriation.

17 Another misleading use of the notion of (State) immunity appears in a number of investment awards where tribunals characterize a State's consent to the jurisdiction of an arbitral tribunal as a 'waiver of immunity'.

---

[32] See, eg, *Robert Azinian, Kenneth Davitian, & Ellen Baca v The United Mexican States*, ICSID Case No ARB (AF)/97/2, Award, 1 November 1999, para 102 ('[a] denial of justice could be pleaded if the relevant courts refuse to entertain a suit [...]'); *Iberdrola Energía S.A. v Republic of Guatemala*, ICSID Case No ARB/09/5, Award, 17 August 2012, para 432 ('[...] under international law a denial of justice could constitute: (i) the unjustified refusal of a tribunal to hear a matter within its competence or any other State action having the effect of preventing access to justice; [...]').

[33] See S Schill, 'International Investment Law and the Law of State Immunity: Antagonists or Two Sides of the Same Coin?' in R Hofmann and C Tams (eds), *International Investment Law and General International Law* (Nomos 2011) 231–75, 252.

[34] Article 5(1)(1) Italy–Bangladesh BIT ('The investments to which this Agreement relates shall not be subject to any measure which might limit permanently or temporarily their joined rights of ownership, possession, control or enjoyment, save where specifically provided by law and by judgments or orders issued by Courts or Tribunals having jurisdiction').

[35] *Saipem S.p.A. v The People's Republic of Bangladesh*, ICSID Case No ARB/05/07, Jurisdiction and Recommendation on Provisional Measures, 21 March 2007, para 136.

[36] ibid para 137.

[37] ibid. ('This provision merely affirms the principle that, "in order to escape being considered an internationally wrongful act, a State measure limiting or excluding an investor's rights of ownership, control or enjoyment can only be considered legal if it has been adopted by law or by a judicial decision"').

For instance, in *SPP v Egypt*, an early ICSID tribunal accepted the respondent's view 'that consent by a State to the jurisdiction of an international tribunal involves a waiver of sovereign immunity'.[38] More recent tribunals have used similar language when referring to a State's consent to jurisdiction. An example is the award in *Tulip v Turkey*, where the tribunal not only held that 'consent is the cornerstone of all international treaty commitments and that here the provisions of the BIT qualify the state sovereignty of Turkey',[39] but also added that the applicable BIT's article providing for arbitration under the ICSID Convention was 'a specific and qualified derogation to Turkey's sovereign immunity'.[40] Similarly, the tribunal in *Mamidoil v Albania* thought that 'States accept arbitration and accept to waive part of their immunity from jurisdiction to encourage and protect investments in international conventions'.[41]

From a public international law perspective, though, the question of consent to arbitration before an international tribunal is separate from the issue of immunity from the jurisdiction of foreign national courts. Immunity is a consequence of sovereign equality and aims at preventing that the courts of one State sit in judgment, or exercise jurisdiction, over another State. This rationale does not apply where a State accepts the jurisdiction of an international court or tribunal, which elevates disputes to the international plane and is premised on the sovereign equality of the disputing States. This being said, one has to acknowledge that States are generally not subject to the jurisdiction of any international dispute settlement mechanism absent their consent. Thus, one may—in a very loose sense—speak of the 'waiver' of the freedom not to be sued before any international court or tribunal, but not of a waiver of immunity.

II. State immunity principles as guidance for other legal issues

While State immunity does not arise before investment tribunals, State immunity principles have sometimes been used in order to address related issues. In particular, the distinction between sovereign and commercial acts, highly relevant for the scope of restrictive State immunity, has been discussed by arbitral panels in a range of cases. The qualification of State acts as sovereign, non-commercial acts has played a crucial role in regard to a number of legal problems, in particular concerning the attribution of conduct, the question of a taking/expropriation of contractual rights and the issue of sovereign as opposed to commercial breach of obligations more broadly.

1. Expropriation and sovereign taking vs. commercial breach of contract

In *Siemens v Argentina*,[42] an ICSID tribunal concluded that a series of governmental measures interfering with the investor's contract to provide an integrated identity card system for the host state amounted to a 'creeping expropriation'. Argentina argued that its measures,

---

[38] *Southern Pacific Properties (Middle East) Limited v Arab Republic of Egypt*, ICSID Case No ARB/84/3, Jurisdiction, 14 April 1988, para 118.
[39] *Tulip Real Estate and Development Netherlands B.V. v Republic of Turkey*, ICSID Case No ARB/11/28, Bifurcated Jurisdictional Issue, 5 March 2013, para 44.
[40] ibid. Subsequently, at para 135, the *Tulip* tribunal opined that 'jurisdiction under a BIT constitutes a qualified waiver of State sovereignty'.
[41] *Mamidoil Jetoil Greek Petroleum Products Societe Anonyme S.A. v Republic of Albania*, ICSID Case No ARB/11/24, Award, 30 March 2015, para 359.
[42] *Siemens A.G. v The Argentine Republic*, ICSID Case No ARB/02/08, Award, 6 February 2007.

including the termination of a contract under the 2000 Emergency Law, could not be regarded as 'an exercise of its police powers as a State'.[43] However, the tribunal rejected 'Argentina's view of when a State acts *iure imperii*' as 'exceedingly narrow'.[44] The tribunal explained:

> 'The distinction between acts *iure imperii* and *iure gestionis* has its origins in the area of immunity of the State under international law and it differentiates between acts of a commercial nature and those which pertain to the powers of a State acting as such. Usually States have been restrictive in their understanding of which activities would not be covered by their immunity in judicial proceedings before the courts of another State. Here we have the reverse situation where the State party posits a wide content of the notion of *iure gestionis*'.[45]

22 It then relied on the jurisprudence of other tribunals[46] to consider that

> '[i]n applying this distinction in the realm of investor-State arbitration [...] for the behaviour of the State as party to a contract to be considered a breach of an investment treaty, such behaviour must be beyond that which an ordinary contracting party could adopt and involve State interference with the operation of the contract'.[47]

23 In the tribunal's view, Argentina had acted on the basis of its governmental powers, rather than as a contracting party. This ultimately led to a finding of expropriation.[48]

24 The *Siemens* tribunal only touched upon State immunity in order to explain the origin of the distinction between sovereign and commercial acts which, in this case, was relevant to determine whether there was a commercial breach of contract or a governmental interference with a contract.

25 Other tribunals have been cautious in relying on the State immunity-inspired distinction in cases of governmental breaches of contracts.[49]

2. Sovereign vs. commercial breach in the context of fair and equitable treatment

26 A number of investment tribunals have relied upon the same distinction between sovereign and commercial acts in order to determine whether host State acts breached the obligation to accord fair and equitable treatment. Although not expressly referring to State immunity, some tribunals clearly opine that contractual breaches can constitute fair and equitable treatment (FET) violations only if they involve sovereign acts or the exercise of '*puissance publique*'.[50]

---

[43] ibid para 246.
[44] ibid.
[45] ibid para 247.
[46] *Consortium R.F.C.C. v Kingdom of Morocco*, ICSID Case No ARB/00/6, Award, 22 December 2003, para 65; *Waste Management, Inc v United Mexican States*, ARB(AF)/00/3, Award, 30 April 2004, paras 172 et seq; *SGS Société Générale de Surveillance S.A. v The Republic of Philippines*, ICSID Case No ARB/02/6, Objections to Jurisdiction, 29 January 2004, para 161.
[47] *Siemens A.G. v The Argentine Republic*, ICSID Case No ARB/02/08, Award, 6 February 2007, para 248.
[48] ibid para 271.
[49] See, eg, *United Utilities (Tallinn) B.V. and Aktsiaselts Tallinna Vesi v Republic of Estonia*, ICSID Case No ARB/14/24, Award, 21 June 2019, para 589.
[50] *Impregilo S.p.A. v Islamic Republic of Pakistan*, ICSID Case No ARB/03/3, Jurisdiction, 22 April 2005, para 268; *Bureau Veritas, Inspection, Valuation, Assessment and Control, BIVAC B.V. v The Republic of Paraguay*, ICSID Case No ARB/07/9, Further Decision on Objections to Jurisdiction, 9 October 2012, paras 246, 247; *Duke Energy Electroquil Partners & Electroquil S.A. v Republic of Ecuador*, ICSID Case No ARB/04/19, Award, 18 August 2008, para 345; *Burlington Resources Inc v Republic of Ecuador (formerly Burlington Resources Inc and others v Republic*

3. Attribution

27 Another area where the distinction between sovereign/governmental and commercial/private acts is relevant concerns issues of attribution for purposes of State responsibility.[51] As explained in other entries of this book, in addition to acts of State organs,[52] acts of other entities may be attributed to States if they are 'empowered to exercise elements of governmental authority' and are acting 'in that capacity', as expressed in Article 5 ARSIWA (Articles on the Responsibility of States for Internationally Wrongful Acts).[53]

28 While all acts of State organs are attributed to a State, regardless of whether the 'conduct of a State organ may be classified as "commercial" or as *acta iure gestionis*',[54] only governmental acts of other, non-State entities may be attributed. Thus, the question whether certain activities can be qualified as governmental as opposed to merely commercial or private has attracted some attention by investment tribunals. Following the general rule as stated in the ARSIWA, investment tribunals have largely acknowledged that the distinction between sovereign/governmental and commercial/private activities is irrelevant for purposes of attribution of acts of State organs.[55]

29 However, investment tribunals have turned to such immunity concepts for guidance in regard to attributing acts of other, i.e. non-State entities 'exercising elements of governmental authority'.

30 A good example is provided by the United Nations Commission on International Trade Law (UNCITRAL) award in *Paushok v Mongolia*.[56] There, the tribunal touched upon State immunity when assessing attribution questions. Specifically, it had to determine whether acts of MongolBank, Mongolia's central bank, could be attributed to the host State. While the tribunal ultimately left it open whether MongolBank should be regarded as a State organ or a non-State entity exercising governmental authority, it found that in a number of respects it had acted '*de jure imperii*' and thus concluded that 'even if MongolBank were not to be considered an organ of the State but merely an entity exercising elements of governmental authority, Claimants would be entitled to pursue their claim against Respondent in connection with the actions mentioned above'.[57]

---

of Ecuador and Empresa Estatal Petróleos del Ecuador (PetroEcuador)), ICSID Case No ARB/08/5, Jurisdiction, 14 June 2010, para 204.

[51] Articles on State Responsibility, Report of the International Law Commission on the Work of Its Fifty-third Session, UN GAOR, 56th Session, Supp No 10, 43, UN Doc A/56/10 (2001) (hereafter ARSIWA).

[52] Article 4 ARSIWA (n 51). See in this Commentary: Chester Brown, 'Article 4 of the ARSIWA: Conduct of organs of a State'.

[53] Article 5 ARSIWA (n 51) ('The conduct of a person or entity which is not an organ of the State under article 4 but which is empowered by the law of that State to exercise elements of the governmental authority shall be considered an act of the State under international law, provided the person or entity is acting in that capacity in the particular instance'). See in this Commentary: Jorge E Viñuales and Oliver Hailes, 'Article 5 of the ARSIWA: Conduct of empowered entities'.

[54] ARSIWA Commentary to Article 4 para 6.

[55] For instance, in *F-W Oil Interests, Inc v Republic of Trinidad & Tobago*, ICSID Case No ARB/01/14, Award, 3 March 2006, a tribunal referred to the ILC Commentary on Article 4 ARSIWA confirming that the nature of the activities of State organs was irrelevant for attribution purposes. ibid para 200 ('[...], in seeking to bolster its argument by drawing on the distinction between commercial and sovereign activities that underlies the law on State immunity, the Respondent is guilty of introducing an element foreign to the quite different context of State responsibility—as the ILC has, once again, been at pains to point out (eg, para (6) of the Commentary to Article 4)'). See already *Noble Ventures, Inc v Romania*, an ICSID Case No ARB/01/11, Award, 12 October 2005, para 82.

[56] *Sergei Paushok, CJSC Golden East Company, CJSC Vostokneftegaz Company v The Government of Mongolia*, UNCITRAL, Jurisdiction and Liability, 28 April 2011.

[57] ibid para 592.

31 In order to arrive at this conclusion, the tribunal relied on the distinction between *iure imperii* and *iure gestionis* acts used in the law of State immunity, partly even invoking relevant domestic cases on State immunity. The tribunal specifically held that in 'case of other entities exercising elements of governmental authority as described in Article 5 of the ILC Articles, [...] the liability of the State is engaged only if they act *jure imperii* and not *jure gestionis*'.[58]

32 One of the reasons why the tribunal was hesitant to regard MongolBank as a State organ was the well-known English *Trendtex* case[59] in which the Court of Appeal had held that the Nigerian Central Bank was not a State organ. Turning to a possible attribution of MongolBank's acts pursuant to Article 5 of the ILC Articles, the *Paushok* tribunal then relied on another English case, *KOO Golden East Mongolia and Bank of Nova Scotia and others*,[60] in which the Court of Appeal had to address the question 'whether MongolBank [had] entered into the contract (with the Bank of Nova Scotia) in the exercise of sovereign authority'.[61] It concluded that since 'the purpose of the transactions including the refining of the gold and the placing of a quantity of refined gold on the unallocated account of the bank was for the purposes of increasing Mongolia's currency reserves [...] that was an exercise of sovereign authority within the meaning of the 1978 Act (State Immunity)'.[62]

33 The *Paushok* tribunal, noting the similarities of the activities complained of in its case, also concluded that 'MongolBank acted *de jure imperii*, if not in entering into the SCSA, at least when it exported GEM's gold for refining and deposited it or its value in an unallocated account in England "with the purposes of increasing the country's reserves". Those actions were *de jure imperii* and went beyond a mere contractual relationship.'[63]

34 One may critically note though that when applying the distinction between *iure imperii* and *iure gestionis* acts both the UK court as well as the *Paushok* tribunal appeared to stress the purpose of the act and not its nature, which is no longer the prevailing criterion in State immunity law.

III. State immunity as a factor in requiring security for a stay of the enforcement of an award during annulment proceedings

35 Immunity from jurisdiction is usually not an issue in investor–State dispute settlement since the agreement to investment arbitration provides an alternative forum to State courts. Because States have specifically consented to such arbitration they cannot invoke immunity before investment tribunals. However, immunity from enforcement measures remains highly relevant in the post-arbitration phase when it comes to the potential need to seek measures of constraint directed against assets of a State unwilling to comply with an award.[64]

---

[58] ibid para 580.
[59] *Trendtex Trading Corporation v Central Bank of Nigeria* (1977) 2 WLR 356.
[60] *KOO Golden East Mongolia and Bank of Nova Scotia and others*, (2007) EWCA Civ 1443.
[61] ibid para 40.
[62] ibid para 42.
[63] *Sergei Paushok, CJSC Golden East Company, CJSC Vostokneftegaz Company v The Government of Mongolia*, UNCITRAL, Jurisdiction and Liability, 28 April 2011, para 592.
[64] Bjorklund, 'State Immunity' (n 1) 302–21; A Reinisch, 'Enforcement of Investment Treaty Awards' in K Yannaca-Small (ed), *Arbitration under International Investment Agreements* (2nd edn, OUP 2018) 797–822; C Schreuer and others, *The ICSID Convention: A Commentary* (2nd edn, CUP 2009) 1151; Phoebe D Winch, 'State Immunity and the Execution of Investment Arbitration Awards' in C Titi (ed), *European Yearbook of International Economic Law—Special Issue: Public Actors in International Investment Law* (Springer 2021) 57.

As such enforcement measures are decided by national courts or enforcement authorities, investment tribunals play no direct role here. Whether or not to permit enforcement measures to satisfy an investment award and, most importantly, against which kinds of State assets is a question for national courts and enforcement authorities.

36 Nevertheless, in a number of instances, ICSID ad hoc committees have referred to enforcement immunity as a factor when assessing whether or not to grant a stay of enforcement.[65] The special scrutiny system of the ICSID Convention removes any challenge or set-aside power of ICSID awards from national courts and bestows it exclusively upon ad hoc committees under the ICSID annulment process.[66] Such committees may grant a stay of enforcement of the challenged award during the pendency of an annulment application.[67]

37 While the Convention is silent on the matter, annulment committees have held that they have the power to condition a stay of enforcement upon some form of security for the eventual enforcement of an award.[68] In early annulment proceedings, ad hoc committees have in fact routinely conditioned stays of enforcement upon the posting of security.[69] Nevertheless, annulment committees have voiced discomfort over the fact that requiring the posting of full security for a challenged award would put award creditors in a better position than they would otherwise be, since it would convert the obligation in Article 53 ICSID Convention into a financial guarantee and avoid the 'reservation' of sovereign immunity in Article 55.

38 According to the ad hoc committee in *CMS v Argentina*,

> '[...] the provision of a bank guarantee puts a claimant in a better position that it would be if annulment had not been sought, since it converts the undertaking of compliance under Article 53 of the Convention into a financial guarantee and avoids any issue of sovereign immunity from execution, which is expressly reserved by Article 55 of the Convention.'[70]

39 In fact, Article 53 of the Convention obliges States to comply with an award, while Article 55 clarifies that the obligation of all Convention parties to enforce an award like a final domestic court judgment, does not alter the applicable rules on enforcement/execution immunity. In other words, while all States party to the ICSID Convention are under an obligation to

---

[65] See *Albaniabeg Ambient Sh.p.k, M. Angelo Novelli and Costruzioni S.r.l. v Republic of Albania*, ICSID Case No ARB/14/26, Decision on the Applicant's Request for the Continuation of the Provisional Stay of Enforcement of the Award, 10 August 2021, para 101 ('the relevant factors in the discretionary criteria include the risk of non-recoupment from the Respondent should the Annulment Application be successful, including problems arising from immunity from execution, and the prospect of prompt enforcement of the award if it is upheld. [...]').

[66] See, eg, K Yannaca-Small, 'Annulment of ICSID Awards: Is it Enough or is Appeal around the Corner?' in K Yannaca-Small (ed), *Arbitration Under International Investment Agreements: A Guide to the Key Issues* (2nd edn, OUP 2018) 727–58.

[67] See Article 52(5) ICSID Convention.

[68] See, eg, *Standard Chartered Bank (Hong Kong) Limited v Tanzania Electric Supply Company Limited*, ICSID Case No ARB/10/20, Applicant Request for a Continued Stay on Enforcement of the Award, 12 April 2017, para 85; *Perenco Ecuador Limited v Republic of Ecuador*, ICSID Case No ARB/08/6, Stay of Enforcement of the Award, 21 February 2020, para 79.

[69] See C Schreuer and others, *The ICSID Convention. A Commentary* (2nd edn, CUP 2009) 1075 et seq.

[70] *CMS Gas Transmission Company v The Republic of Argentina*, ICSID Case No ARB/01/8, Decision on the Argentine Republic's Request for a Continued Stay of Enforcement of the Award, 1 September 2006, para 39. See also *MTD Equity Sdn. Bhd. and MTD Chile S.A. v Republic of Chile*, ICSID Case No ARB/01/7, Respondent's Request for a Continued Stay of Execution, 1 June 2005, para 26; see also *Víctor Pey Casado and President Allende Foundation v Republic of Chile I*, ICSID Case No ARB/98/2, Decision on the Republic of Chile's Application for a Stay of Enforcement of the Award, 5 May 2010, para 34.

recognize and enforce an ICSID award, they may still apply the rules on enforcement/execution immunity that may exempt certain types of assets from enforcement measures. It is thus true that the provision of financial security, eg in the form of a bank guarantee, as a condition for a stay of enforcement of an award will put an investor in a better position since, if the award is not annulled, it will have an immediate financial asset to satisfy its award; without such security, it would have to pursue enforcement measures before domestic courts in States where the applicable immunity rules may otherwise exempt a number of foreign State assets from enforcement measures. However, views are divided on whether the advantage for investors resulting from a security-conditioned stay would make it too onerous for States to seek annulment. This may largely depend upon whether one emphasizes Article 53 or Article 55: Should the obligation of award debtors to comply with an award pursuant to Article 53 ICSID Convention prevail? Or does the possibility to invoke enforcement immunity before national courts of other ICSID parties pursuant to Article 55 ICSID Convention legitimately limit the obligation under Article 53?

40 Some ICSID annulment committees have taken the former approach. For instance, the committee in *MINE v Guinea*[71] held:

> 'It should be clearly understood ... that State immunity may well afford a legal defense to forcible execution, but it provides neither argument nor excuse for failing to comply with an award. In fact, the issue of State immunity from forcible execution of an award will typically arise if the State party refuses to comply with its treaty obligations. Non-compliance by a State constitutes a violation by that State of its international obligations and will attract its own sanctions'.[72]

41 The same idea was highlighted by the ad hoc committee in *Enron v Argentina*, which quoted the above excerpt from *MINE* and added that '[t]his passage appears to manifest an understanding that where an award creditor has to resort to measures under Article 54, a course of action which may give rise to issues of State immunity under Article 55, there will have been a failure by the award debtor to comply with its obligations under Article 53'.[73]

42 In contrast, the latter approach, emphasizing Article 55, seems to be the premise of the annulment committee in *Tethyan v Pakistan*, when it considered that '[r]equiring a blanket waiver of immunity is a proposition that arguably could encroach upon Pakistan's rights under Article 55 of the ICSID Convention'.[74]

---

[71] *Maritime International Nominees Establishment ('MINE') v Republic of Guinea*, ICSID Case No ARB/84/4, Interim Order No 1 on Guinea's Application for Stay of Enforcement of the Award, 12 August 1988.
[72] ibid para 25. See also *CDC Group plc v Republic of the Seychelles*, ICSID Case No ARB/02/14, Decision on Whether or Not to Continue Stay and Order, 14 July 2004, para 19 ('[...] while the Convention preserves sovereign immunity it expressly obligates the award-debtor nonetheless to pay the award and, in default of meeting such obligation, subjects the defaulting state to the jurisdiction of the International Court of Justice').
[73] *Enron v Argentina*, ICSID Case No ARB/01/3, Decision on the Argentine Republic's Request for a Continued Stay of Enforcement of the Award (Rule 54 of the ICSID Arbitration Rules), 7 October 2008, para 76.
[74] *Tethyan Copper Company Pty Limited v Islamic Republic of Pakistan*, ICSID Case No ARB/12/1, Stay of Enforcement of the Award, 17 September 2020, para 204.

D. Conclusion

State immunity does not figure prominently in investment arbitration because States can invoke immunity only before the courts of other States. Investment arbitration as an alternative to litigation before national courts is based on the consent of the parties, including State parties, and does not raise immunity issues, although States and tribunals sometimes misleadingly portray their consent to arbitration as a 'waiver' of immunity.

Nevertheless, investment tribunals have used and relied upon concepts that derive from the law of State immunity in a number of situations. Most prominent are cases when tribunals had to determine whether certain acts allegedly in violation of investment treaty standards could be attributed to host States. Since some attribution rules codified in the ARSIWA rely on the concept of the exercise of governmental authority, tribunals have partly relied on the distinction between sovereign and non-sovereign (i.e. *iure imperii* and *iure gestionis*) acts developed in the context of State immunity. The same distinction has been applied by some tribunals in order to determine whether contractual interferences amount to an expropriation or a violation of fair and equitable treatment or merely constitute a commercial breach of contract.

Finally, the fact that States benefit from immunity from enforcement measures even in cases where they have to abide by an unfavourable investment award has been taken into account by a number of ad hoc committees when considering whether to make a stay of enforcement dependent upon the provision of financial security by award debtors.

In all these situations, investment tribunals did not have much opportunity to ponder State immunity problems in detail. Rather, they have relied on the very basic backbone of the modern and currently prevailing restrictive theory of immunity, according to which only *iure imperii* or sovereign governmental acts merit immunity. This has reduced the risk that such general international law concepts receive a distorted interpretation by investment tribunals. Conversely, there is no indication that the limited invocation of State immunity concepts by investment tribunals has influenced general international law and dispute settlement practice.

Selected literature

Bankas EK, *The State Immunity Controversy in International Law: Private Suits against Sovereign States in Domestic Courts* (Springer 2005).

Bjorklund AK, 'State Immunity and the Enforcement of Investor–State Arbitral Awards' in Binder C and others (eds), *International Investment Law for the 21st Century: Essays in Honour of Christoph Schreuer* (OUP 2009).

Chukwuemeke Okeke E, *Jurisdictional Immunities of States and International Organizations* (OUP 2018).

Fox H and Webb P, *The Law of State Immunity* (3rd edn, OUP 2013).

Hafner G and Köhler U, 'The United Nations Convention on Jurisdictional Immunities of States and Their Property' (2004) 35 NYIL 3.

O'Keefe R and Tams CJ (eds), *The United Nations Convention on Jurisdictional Immunities of States and Their Property—A Commentary* (OUP 2013).

Reinisch A, 'European Court Practice Concerning State Immunity from Enforcement Measures' (2006) 17 EJIL 803.

Schreuer C, *State Immunity: Some Recent Developments* (Grotius 1988).

Stewart DP, 'The UN Convention on Jurisdictional Immunities of States and Their Property' (2005) 99 AJIL 194.

van Alebeek R and Pavoni R, 'Immunities of States and their Officials' in Nollkaemper A and Reinisch A (eds), *International Law in Domestic Courts: A Casebook* (OUP 2018).

Yang X, *State Immunity in International Law* (CUP 2012).

Selected decisions

CMS Gas Transmission Company v The Republic of Argentina, ICSID Case No ARB/01/8, Decision on the Argentine Republic's Request for a Continued Stay of Enforcement of the Award, 1 September 2006.

García de Borrisow v Embassy of Lebanon, Admissibility, Case No 32096, ILDC 1009 (CO 2007), 13 December 2007.

Jurisdictional Immunities of the State (Germany v Italy: Greece intervening) (Judgment) [2012] ICJ Rep 99.

Mamidoil Jetoil Greek Petroleum Products Societe Anonyme S.A. v Republic of Albania, ICSID Case No ARB/11/24, Award, 30 March 2015.

Maritime International Nominees Establishment ('MINE') v Republic of Guinea, ICSID Case No ARB/84/4, Interim Order No 1 on Guinea's Application for Stay of Enforcement of the Award, 12 August 1988.

Saipem S.p.A. v The People's Republic of Bangladesh, ICSID Case No ARB/05/07, Jurisdiction and Recommendation on Provisional Measures, 21 March 2007.

Sergei Paushok, CJSC Golden East Company, CJSC Vostokneftegaz Company v The Government of Mongolia, UNCITRAL, Jurisdiction and Liability, 28 April 2011.

Siemens A.G. v The Argentine Republic, ICSID Case No ARB/02/08, Award, 6 February 2007.

Southern Pacific Properties (Middle East) Limited v Arab Republic of Egypt, ICSID Case No ARB/84/3, Jurisdiction, 14 April 1988.

Tethyan Copper Company Pty Limited v Islamic Republic of Pakistan, ICSID Case No ARB/12/1, Stay of Enforcement of the Award, 17 September 2020.

Tulip Real Estate and Development Netherlands B.V. v Republic of Turkey, ICSID Case No ARB/11/28, Bifurcated Jurisdictional Issue, 5 March 2013.

PART IV
SUBSTANTIVE AND PROCEDURAL ASPECTS OF GENERAL INTERNATIONAL LAW IN INTERNATIONAL INVESTMENT LAW

Cross-cutting substantive aspects
NAFTA standards in light of the decisions of international courts and tribunals

Jingyuan Zhou and Sergio Puig

A. Introduction — 1	3. NAFTA cases interpreting national treatment — 22
B. Interpretation of substantive standards of treatment — 7	III. Interpretation of expropriation — 27
I. Interpretation of MFN — 8	1. ICJ cases interpreting expropriation — 28
1. ICJ cases interpreting MFN — 9	2. Influence over the development of interpretation of the ILC and the Iran–US Claims Tribunal — 32
2. Influence over the development of MFN interpretation of the International Law Commission — 13	3. NAFTA cases interpreting expropriation — 34
3. NAFTA cases interpreting MFN — 14	IV. Interpretation of FET/MST — 39
II. Interpretation of national treatment — 19	1. ICJ cases interpreting FET/MST — 39
1. ICJ case interpreting national treatment — 20	2. NAFTA cases interpreting FET/MST — 42
2. Influence over the development of national treatment interpretation of the General Agreement on Tariffs and Trade (GATT) and the World Trade Organization (WTO) — 21	C. Evaluation — 44
	I. Divergence/misalignment — 47
	II. Convergence/Alignment — 52
	D. Conclusion — 56

A. Introduction

Investor–State dispute settlement (ISDS) cases under international investment agreements (IIAs) continue to be filed despite growing concerns over the legitimacy of international courts and tribunals. Among other criticism, one that is often made against ISDS decisions, is that 'incorrect' treaty interpretations are not uncommon. In this context, tribunals are expected to interpret investment treaties within the larger context of international law. Yet, in practice, some tribunals have shown their limited understanding of treaty interpretation, of the applicable jurisprudence of the International Court of Justice (ICJ), and of public international law more generally. **1**

Part of the problem, however, is that ISDS lacks a hierarchical institution to allow ad hoc tribunals dealing with complex disputes advanced by investors based on different treaties to identify better analyses. In fact, in the current ISDS reform process under United Nations Commission on International Trade Law (UNCITRAL), proponents of change argue that an Appeals Mechanism (AM) may invite tribunals to identify key aspects more precisely and analyse the particular features of a treaty within a larger context of international law. **2**

This assertion has been adopted without a deep analysis of the current influence that public international law and its institutions already exert over other international tribunals.[1] Hence, this entry aims at identifying how the practice of the ICJ has influenced ISDS in general.

3 But we do not just stop there. There is another side of the puzzle, this is, to what extent does the ICJ's prominence actually matters for ISDS tribunals. Thus, this entry also seeks to make an assessment over two related questions: (1) is ISDS practice align with ICJ's interpretations and (2) what institutional factors might explain any misalignments. It does so by comparing the practice of the ICJ on core substantive standards that are also contained in IIAs with the practice of ISDS tribunals adjudicating disputes under a particular treaty text—in this case, the North American Free Trade Agreement (NAFTA). Of course, the primary forum that develops these substantive standards remains ISDS, where tribunals are regularly asked to determine the scope and extent of treaty provisions that protect foreign investors. Yet, understanding this cross-fertilization is also important.

4 As the entry explains, part of the limits this cross-fertilization and the different evolutionary trajectories is that the dispute settlement bodies differ in their institutional set-up. The ICJ is the 'principal judicial organ' of the United Nations[2] and has jurisdiction (albeit limited) over '[a]ll Members of the United Nations'.[3] As of 31 December 2022, the ICJ has issued judgments in 141 contentious cases that emerged from disputes between states in multiple contexts.[4] On the other hand, the Investment Chapter ('Chapter Eleven') of the NAFTA,[5] now replaced by the United States–Mexico–Canada Agreement,[6] has had a significant influence over the development and understanding of international investment law beyond its geographical boundary. Chapter Eleven provides for national treatment,[7] most-favoured-nation treatment (MFN),[8] minimum standard of treatment (MST),[9] and just compensation upon expropriation obligations.[10] As of 31 December 2021, investors have initiated seventy-six cases under the agreement, winning eleven; states prevailed in

---

[1] RY Jennings, 'The United Nations at Fifty—The International Court of Justice after Fifty Years' (1995) 89 AJIL 493.
[2] United Nations Charter Article 7; the Statute of International Court of Justice Statute Article 1 (hereafter 'the ICJ Statute').
[3] Article 93 of the UN Charter.
[4] Contentious Cases, International Court of Justice, https://www.icj-cij.org/en/contentious-cases accessed 8 February 2023. The ICJ also issues advisory opinions pursuant to Article 65 of the ICJ Statute.
[5] North American Free Trade Agreement between the Government of the United States of America, the Government of Canada, and the Government of the United Mexican States, 17 December 1992, 32 ILM 612 (hereafter 'NAFTA').
[6] Agreement between the United States of America, the United Mexican States, and Canada, 30 November 2018, Office of the US Trade Representative (hereafter 'USMCA'). USMCA eliminates ISDS claims between the United States and Canada (except for Legacy Investment Claims and Pending Claims) and constrains ISDS claims between Mexico and the United States to areas of oil and gas, power, infrastructure, telecommunications, and transport. Annex 14-E, para 2(a)1.
[7] Article 1102 (n 5) (requiring Member States to accord to investors and investments of investors of another party no less favourable than it accords, in like circumstances, to its own investors and investments of its own investors with respect to the establishment, acquisition, expansion, management, conduct, operation, and sale or other disposition of investments).
[8] Article 1103 (n 5) (requiring Member States to accord investors and investment of investors of another party no less favourable than that it accords, in like circumstances, to investors and investments of investors of any other party or a non-party with respect to the establishment, acquisition, expansion, management, conduct, operation, and sale or other disposition of investments).
[9] Article 1105 (n 5) (requiring Member States to accord to investments of investors of another party treatment in accordance with international law, including fair and equitable treatment and full protection and security).
[10] Article 1110 (n 5).

twenty-eight arbitrations; and the remaining arbitrations were settled, discontinued, or withdrawn.[11]

The entry chooses NAFTA—the first free trade agreement to include ISDS—as the primary comparator of the ICJ decisions for three reasons: (1) its over-a-quarter-century of history provides an opportunity to examine the evolution of practices in treaty interpretation over-time; (2) the highly institutionalized system of arbitration under the NAFTA offers insights into how arbitrators interpret a given treaty between a stable set of parties in a more controlled way; and (3) its systemic impact over IIAs in North America and widespread spill over on IIAs concluded by other countries and areas of general public international laws.[12] Thus, NAFTA's unique place in ISDS jurisprudence, we believe, warrants a greater attention.[13]

This entry proceeds as follows. Part B examines interpretation on MFN, national treatment, expropriation, and MST, all of which are substantive standards of treatment provided in IIAs, including NAFTA. It reviews both the ICJ and NAFTA decisions on these substantive standards, and the broader context of general international law within which the ICJ and NAFTA interact and operate. The analysis of NAFTA focuses on whether Chapter Eleven tribunals have referenced relevant ICJ judgments, and if so, whether these tribunals affirm and adopt them or adapt and differentiate them. Part C proceeds with assessing and explaining the findings, which is then followed by a short Conclusion.

B. Interpretation of substantive standards of treatment

This section describes the interpretation of substantive standards of treatment by the ICJ and by NAFTA Chapter Eleven tribunals. For each substantive standard of treatment, this section proceeds with a tripartite analytical framework. It first analyses ICJ jurisprudence, then assesses its influence over the development of international law-making and interpretation, and lastly examines awards and rationale of the most relevant NAFTA Chapter Eleven cases.

---

[11] Investment Dispute Settlement Navigator, Investment Policy Hub, United Nations Conference on Trade and Development (accessed 31 December 2021). The eleven cases are *Metalclad Corp v Mexico*, ICSID Case No ARB(AF)/97/1; *Marvin Roy Feldman Karpa v United Mexican States*, ICSID Case No ARB(AF)/99/1; *Corn Products International, Inc v United Mexican States*, ICSID Case No ARB(AF)/04/1; *Archer Daniels Midland Co and Tate & Lyle Ingredients Americas, Inc v United Mexican States*, ICSID Case No ARB(AF)/04/5; *Cargill, Inc v United Mexican States*, ICSID Case No ARB(AF)/05/2; *Mobil Investments Canada Inc and Murphy Oil Corporation v Government of Canada*, ICSID Case No ARB(AF)/07/4; *S.D. Myers v Government of Canada*, UNCITRAL (NAFTA); *Pope & Talbot, Inc v Government of Canada*, UNCITRAL (NAFTA); *Clayton and Bilcon of Delaware Inc v Government of Canada*, PCA Case No 2009-04; *Windstream Energy LLC v Government of Canada*, UNCITRAL (NAFTA); and *Lion Mexico Consolidated L.P. v United Mexican States*, ICSID Case No ARB(AF)/15/2. In context, between 1987 and 2020, a total of 1,104 cases have been initiated. *Investor-State Dispute Settlement Cases: Facts and Figures 2020*, IIA Issue Note, Issue 4, United Nations Conference on Trade and Development (September 2021).

[12] For instance, NAFTA Parties and their investors utilize parallel arbitration/litigation proceedings to extract favourable treaty interpretations through ISDS and other adjudicatory mechanism such as the World Trade Organization's dispute settlement mechanism, thus enriching the understanding of obligations. High-profile parallel proceedings include the trio of *Cargill, Inc v United Mexican States*, ICSID Case No ARB(AF)/05/2 (NAFTA), Award, 18 September 2009 (hereafter 'Cargill Award'); *Archer Daniels Midland Co and Tate & Lyle Ingredients Americas, Inc v United Mexican States*, ICSID Case No ARB(AF)/04/5 (NAFTA), Award (Redacted Version), 21 November 2007; and *Corn Products International, Inc v United Mexican States*, ICSID Case No ARB(AF)/04/1 (NAFTA), Award, 18 August 2009, and the softwood lumber dispute comprising *Tembec Inc et al v United States of America*, UNCITRAL (NAFTA); *Canfor Corp v United States of America*, UNCITRAL (NAFTA); and *Terminal Forest Products Ltd v United States of America*, UNCITRAL (NAFTA).

[13] For instance, commentators have observed that '[m]any if not most national treatment cases have arisen under NAFTA Chapter 11'. A Bjorklund, 'The National Treatment Obligation' in K Yannaca-Small (ed), *Arbitration Under International Investment Agreements: A Guide to the Key Issues* (2nd edn, OUP 2018).

I. Interpretation of MFN

8 MFN is often considered the 'cornerstone of all modern commercial treaties'.[14] Generally, the standard aims at 'establish[ing] a fundamental equality without discrimination among all of the countries concerned'.[15]

1. ICJ cases interpreting MFN

9 The ICJ has dealt with MFN in, at least, three cases: (1) *Anglo–Iranian Oil Co. (UK v Iran)*,[16] (2) *Rights of Nationals of the United States of America in Morocco (Fr v US)*,[17] and (3) *Ambatielos Claim (Greece v UK)*.[18]

10 In *Anglo–Iranian Oil Co. (UK v Iran)*,[19] the ICJ delineated the analytical framework for a successful MFN claim, which requires the identification of (1) the basic treaty containing the MFN clause and then (2) the third-party treaties under which the benefits are sought.[20] Importantly, the basic treaty must contemplate entitlements later sought,[21] because '[a] third-party treaty, independent of and isolated from the basic treaty, cannot produce any legal effect' beyond the parties.[22] While the majority was silent on whether MFN clauses can extend to future rights ('rights *in futuro*'), a question often relevant for ISDS tribunals, the dissents confirmed that MFN clauses are capable of extending into future rights.[23]

11 In *Rights of Nationals of the United States of America in Morocco*, the Court reasoned that to 'import' privileges in the third-party treaty through MFN, continued effectiveness of the third-party treaty through which benefits are claimed at the time of invocation must be shown.[24] The ICJ rejected the argument that once privileges were in existence when

---

[14] SK Hornbeck, 'The Most-Favored-Nation Clause' (1909) 3 AJIL 395, 395.
[15] *Rights of Nationals of the United States of America in Morocco (Fr v US)* [1952] ICJ Rep 176, 192 (hereafter *Rights of US Nationals*).
[16] *Anglo–Iranian Oil Co (UK v Iran)* (Judgment on Jurisdiction) [1952] ICJ Rep 93.
[17] *Rights of US Nationals* (n 15).
[18] *Ambatielos Claim (Greece v UK)* 12 RIAA 83 (Comm'n Arb 1956). The arbitral award came after the ICJ ordered the United Kingdom to submit the dispute to arbitration in *Ambatielos Case (Greece v UK)* (Merits: Obligation to Arbitrate) [1953] ICJ Rep 10.
[19] *Anglo–Iranian Oil Co (UK v Iran)* (Jurisdiction) [1952] ICJ Rep 93, 108–09. One example of the MFN clause the United Kingdom relied on reads:

> 'The High Contracting Parties engage that, in the establishment and recognition of Consuls-General, Consuls, Vice-Consuls, and Consular Agents, each shall be placed in the dominions of the other on the footing of the most-favoured nation; and that the treatment of their respective subjects, and their trade, shall also, in every respect, be placed on the footing of the treatment of the subjects and commerce of the most-favoured nation.'

Consequently, the ICJ rejected United Kingdom's invocation of MFN and declined jurisdiction.
[20] ibid 109 (stating that '[t]he treaty containing the most-favoured-nation clause is the basic treaty upon which the United Kingdom must rely').
[21] ibid 109–110.
[22] ibid 109.
[23] Dissenting Opinion of Judge Hackworth, ibid 140–41. Dissenting Opinion of Judge Levi Carneiro, ibid 157–58, para 9.
[24] *Rights of US Nationals* (n 15). The MFN clause at issue reads:

> Art. 14. The commerce with the United States, shall be on the same footing as is the commerce with Spain, or as that with the most favoured nation for the time being; [...]
> Art. 24. [...] And it is further declared, that whatever indulgence, in trade or otherwise, shall be granted to any of the Christian Powers, the citizens of the United States shall be equally entitled to them.
> *Rights of US Nationals* (n 15) [1952] ICJ Pleadings, Vol I, 511, 513.

the MFN clause became effective, such privileges 'would be incorporated permanently by reference and enjoyed and exercised even after the abrogation of the treaty provisions from which they had been derived'.[25] As we will see, this issue has been less debated by ISDS tribunals.

Finally, in the much cited *Ambatielos Claim*, the decision reasoned that under the principle **12** of *ejusdem generis*, MFN can be extended to the administration of justice so long as the 'matter[] belong[s] to the same category of subject as that to which the clause itself relates'.[26] Finding the phrase 'all matters relating to commerce and navigation' was flexible enough to include administration of justice, which 'naturally' belonged to the protection of rights of traders as 'matters relating to commerce and navigation',[27] the ICJ in *Ambatielos Claim* held that MFN clause did apply. Less well known is that the Court also concluded that the principle of *ejusdem generis* cannot be used to incorporate principles of international law.[28] The first aspect of the decision has been often debated in ISDS while the second in very few instances.

2. Influence over the development of MFN interpretation of the International Law Commission

While 'there is no such thing as *the* most-favoured-nation clause: every treaty requires inde- **13** pendent examination',[29] ICJ's analysis of MFN has influenced the work of the International Law Commission (ILC). In the Commentaries of the 1978 Draft Articles on Most-Favoured-Nation Clauses,[30] the ILC explicitly references *Anglo–Iranian Oil Co.* for the source and scope of MFN,[31] *Ambatielos* and *Anglo–Iranian Oil Co.* for the scope of rights[32] and acquisition of rights,[33] and *Rights of US Nationals in Morocco* for the termination and suspension of rights under MFN.[34] The ILC continued to rely on ICJ's MFN interpretations to analyse and develop the understanding of MFN in contemporary context.[35] The ILC's MFN Commentaries remain the main source of inspiration for ISDS tribunals when addressing MFN issues.

---

[25] *Rights of US Nationals* (n 15) (Judgment) 190–92. The ICJ consequently rejected the United States' attempt to import the more favourable rights—broader consular jurisdiction—from third-party treaties that were ineffective at the time of dispute.

[26] *Ambatielos Claim* (*Greece v UK*) 12 RIAA 83, 106–07 (Comm'n Arb 1956). The arbitral award came after the ICJ ordered the United Kingdom to submit the dispute to arbitration in *Ambatielos Case* (*Greece v UK*) (Merits: Obligation to Arbitrate) [1953] ICJ Rep 19. The MFN clause at issue reads:

'The Contracting Parties agree that, in all matters relating to commerce and navigation, any privilege, favour or immunity whatever which either Contracting Party has actually granted or may hereafter grant to the subjects or citizens of any other State shall be extended immediately and unconditionally to the subjects or citizens of the other Contracting Party; it being their intention that the trade and navigation of each country shall be placed, in all respects, by the other on the footing of the most favoured nation.'

[27] ibid.

[28] ibid 108. The Commission provided another reason for the exclusion of the inclusion of the principles of international law to the MFN coverage based on the wording and the object of the Anglo–Bolivian Treaty, which Greece relied on. ibid 109.

[29] AD McNair, *The Law of Treaties* (OUP 1938) 285.

[30] Draft Articles on Most-Favoured-Nation Clauses with Commentaries, YILC 1978, Vol II, Part Two.

[31] ibid Article 8.

[32] ibid Article 9.

[33] ibid Article 10.

[34] ibid Article 21.

[35] ILC, Final Report of the Study Group on the Most-Favored-Nation Clause, para 15, 80, UN Doc A/70/10, Annex (2015).

3. NAFTA cases interpreting MFN

14 NAFTA grants MFN status to business actors.[36] Article 1103 requires NAFTA Parties to accord investments of investors of another party and investors of another party treatment 'no less favourable than it accords, in like circumstances', to investors and investments of any other party or a non-party with respect to the establishment, acquisition, expansion, management, conduct, operation, and sale or other disposition of investments.

15 To date, NAFTA tribunals have yet to find breaches of MFN obligations.[37] The review conducted for this entry shows NAFTA tribunals usually dispense of MFN claims on technical grounds: Claimants either failed to prove the existence of more favourable *substantive treatment* or failed to show they were accorded less favourable treatment *in like circumstance*.

16 In assessing the existence of more favourable *substantive treatment*, NAFTA tribunals rejected investors' repeated claims that Article 1103 can be used to import and expand substantive treatment into NAFTA, especially when MFN is invoked to circumvent the conditions of Article 1105 on MST.[38] The *Apotex* tribunal further stated, 'whether the NAFTA Parties are correct [regarding their interpretation of Article 1103] will have to await the decision of another NAFTA tribunal'.[39]

17 Also, the identification of an appropriate comparator is considered key to 'like circumstances' determination. For instance, the *Cargill* tribunal dismissed the MFN claim after finding the claimant failed to show an appropriate comparator.[40] Similar dismissals based on claimant's inability to prove they are 'in like circumstances' with their comparators can be found in *Grand River Enterprises Six Nations, Ltd., et al. v United States of America*,[41] *Apotex Holdings Inc. and Apotex Inc. v United States of America*,[42] *Vento Motorcycles, Inc. v United Mexican States*,[43] and *Mercer International Inc. v Government of Canada*.[44]

18 Finally, NAFTA tribunals often fail to rule on MFN based on judicial economy.[45] In *Methanex*, the tribunal did not address MFN despite strong opposition from both the United States and Canada on using Article 1103 as a choice-of-law clause to import obligations not found in the specific provisions of NAFTA.[46] Notably, none of these NAFTA awards referenced ICJ MFN judgments explicitly.

---

[36] Article 102 of NAFTA.
[37] The rarity of finding MFN violations is also the case in investor–State arbitration more generally, see J Bonnitcha, L Poulsen and M Waibel, *The Political Economy of the Investment Treaty Regime* (OUP 2017) 94.
[38] *ADF Group Inc v United States of America*, ICSID Case No ARB(AF)/00/1, Award (9 January 2003) para 194.
[39] *Apotex Holdings Inc and Apotex Inc v United States of America*, ICSID Case No ARB(AF)/12/1, Award (25 August 2014) para 9.71.
[40] *Cargill* Award (n 12) paras 233–34.
[41] UNCITRAL, Award (12 January 2011) paras 156–72.
[42] ICSID Case No ARB(AF)/12/1, Award (25 August 2014) paras 8.59–8.77.
[43] ICSID Case No ARB(AF)/17/3, Award (6 July 2020) paras 241, 265 (stating that 'the Tribunal rejects all claims that the Respondent breached NAFTA Articles 1102(1) or 1103(1) for failure to accord to Vento treatment no less favourable than that it accorded to Mexican investors or to investors of a non-NAFTA Party').
[44] ICSID Case No ARB(AF)/12/3, Award (6 March 2018) para 7.45 (stating that 'Whilst ostensibly comparators, none were "in like circumstances" for the purposes of NAFTA Articles 1102 and 1103; and their different treatment can best be explained on the basis of their individual circumstances').
[45] See, eg, *Chemtura Corporation v Government of Canada*, UNCITRAL, Award (2 August 2010) paras 235–36.
[46] *Methanex Corporation v United States of America*, UNCITRAL, Response of Respondent United States of America to Methanex's Submission Concerning the NAFTA Free Trade Commission's July 31, 2001, Interpretation, at 9, 11 (26 October 2001). Third-Party Submission of Canada Pursuant to NAFTA Article 1128, para 11 (8 February 2002).

II. Interpretation of national treatment

National treatment is included in most IIAs[47] and aims at 'prevent[ing] protectionist measures whereby host States tend to favour their own investors to the detriment of foreign ones'.[48]

1. ICJ case interpreting national treatment

The ICJ interpreted a national treatment provision in, at least, one case: the famous *ELSI Elettronica Sicula SpA (United States of America v Italy)* (*ELSI*),[49] shedding light on issues of the burden of proof and discriminatory intent. The ICJ placed the burden of proof in showing 'the local law, either in its terms or its application, has treated [nationals of the complaining state] less well than [the host state's] nationals'[50] on the complaining state. Because the United States failed to demonstrate that the wholly-owned Italian subsidiary of an American company was treated differently than its Italian counterparts, the ICJ declined to find a breach of national treatment.[51] Notably, discriminatory intent was not requirement in finding a violation of national treatment; instead, the ICJ emphasized the conduct and circumstances surrounding the measure.[52]

2. Influence over the development of national treatment interpretation of the General Agreement on Tariffs and Trade (GATT) and the World Trade Organization (WTO)

The ICJ's brief and unremarkable pronouncement on national treatment in *ELSI* has left an open canvass for interpretation of other tribunals, most notably, at the GATT/WTO forum. Guided by the fundamental purpose to avoid trade protectionism,[53] GATT/WTO's national treatment analysis focuses on the overall assessment of competitive relationship and centres around conditions of competition and the determination of 'like products'[54] and 'like services'.[55] Where differential treatments are found, GATT/WTO tribunals might also assess if discrimination exists 'so as to afford protection to domestic production'.[56] The GATT/WTO's emphasis on the holistic review of conduct and surrounding conditions, in which discriminatory intent plays a part but is not determinative, nevertheless echoes with ICJ'S *ELSI* analysis.

3. NAFTA cases interpreting national treatment

Article 1102 requires governments to accord treatment to foreign investments and investors 'no less favourable' than accorded to its own investors and investments 'in like circumstances'.

---

[47] United Nations Conference on Trade and Development (UNCTAD), *National Treatment* (1999), UNCTAD/ITE/IIT/11 (Vol IV) 15–24.
[48] A Reinisch, 'National Treatment' in M Bungenberg, et al (eds), *International Investment Law: A Handbook* (Nomos 2015) 848 (hereafter Reinisch, 'National Treatment').
[49] [1989] ICJ Rep 56.
[50] ibid 64.
[51] ibid 61–62.
[52] ibid.
[53] *Japan—Taxes on Alcoholic Beverages*, WT/DS11/AB/R (4 October 1996).
[54] Article III, GATT. *Japan—Taxes on Alcoholic Beverages*, WT/DS11/AB/R (4 October 1996) 18–30; *European Communities—Measures Affecting Asbestos and Asbestos-Containing Products*, WT/DS135/AB/R (12 March 2001) paras 96–98.
[55] *EC—Bananas III*, Panel Report, para 7.322. *China—Electronic Payment Services*, Panel Report, para 7.700–7.702.
[56] Article III:1, GATT. *Chile—Taxes on Alcoholic Beverages*, WT/DS110/AB/R (13 December 1999) para 71.

It effectively bans favourable treatment to 'national champions'.[57] To date, Chapter Eleven tribunals have found six breaches of national treatment obligation.[58]

23 Like the technical approach adopted in MFN interpretation, NAFTA tribunals dispose of national treatment claims by looking at (1) whether the claimant proves itself or its investments were accorded less favourable treatment in like circumstances compared to identified comparators and (2) whether the differential treatment was the result of nationality. Interpreting the 'nationality' element, the *Feldman* tribunal presumed that the discriminatory treatment was 'a result of the [c]laimant's nationality ... in the absence of any evidence to the contrary'.[59]

24 NAFTA tribunals' interpretation of 'like circumstances' evolved overtime. After initially looking to GATT/WTO 'like products' interpretations,[60] more recent NAFTA tribunals questioned and refused such an analogy. The *Methanex* tribunal rejected the relevance of GATT's 'like products' interpretation on the basis that NAFTA Article 1102 made no reference to 'any like, directly competitive or substitutable goods' as was provided in GATT Article III.[61] Subsequent cases, *inter alia*, *Cargill v Mexico*,[62] *Merrill & Ring v Canada*,[63] and *Bilcon v Canada*[64] all similarly challenged the GATT/WTO analogy. As the *Bilcon* tribunal stated, '[']like circumstances['] is not restricted as it is in some other trade-liberalizing agreements, such as those that refer to [']like products['].'[65] Instead, 'a Tribunal must also take into account the objects of NAFTA, which include according to Article 102(1)(c) [']to increase substantially investment opportunities in the territories of the Parties['].'[66]

25 Therefore, NAFTA tribunals have held that 'like circumstances' should not only include business conditions, but also the regulatory framework and environment that governs the sector,[67] a position proffered by NAFTA State Parties, especially the United States. However, NAFTA tribunals employ different approaches when weighing regulatory framework and

---

[57] Article 1102(3) requires NAFTA parties to accord treatment 'no less favourable than the most favourable treatment accorded, in like circumstances, by that state or provinces to investors, and to investments of investors, of the Party of which it forms a part'. See also *United Postal Service of America Inc v Government of Canada*, ICSID Case No UNCT/02/1, Separate Statement of Dean Ronald A Cass (Award on the Merits) (24 May 2007) 22, para 61.

[58] *S.D. Myers, Inc v Canada*, UNCITRAL (NAFTA), Final Award (30 December 2002) (hereafter 'S.D. Myers Award'); *Marvin Roy Feldman Karpa v Mexico*, ICSID Case No ARB(AF)/99/1 (NAFTA), Award on Merits (16 December 2002) (hereafter '*Feldman* Award'); *Corn Products International, Inc v United Mexican States*, ICSID Case No ARB(AF)/04/1 (NAFTA), Award (18 August 2009) (hereafter '*Corn Products* Award'); *Archer Daniels Midland Company and Tate & Lyle Ingredients Americas, Inc v Mexico*, ICSID Case No ARB(AF)/04/5 (NAFTA), Award (Redacted Version) (21 November 2007) (hereafter '*ADM* Award'); *Cargill* Award (n 12); *Bilcon of Delaware Inc v Canada*, UNCITRAL (NAFTA), PCA Case No 2009-04, Jurisdiction and Liability (17 March 2015) (hereafter '*Bilcon* Award').

[59] *Feldman* Award (n 58) paras 181–84.

[60] *S.D. Myers* Award (n 58). *Pope & Talbot, Inc v Government of Canada*, UNCITRAL (NAFTA), Final Award, Award in Respect of Costs (26 November 2002) (hereafter *Pope & Talbot*).

[61] *Methanex Corp v United States of America*, UNICTRAL, Award (3 August 2005) Pt II, Ch B, paras, 6, 29, 30, 37 (hereafter *Methanex*).

[62] *Cargill* Award (n 12).

[63] *Merrill & Ring Forestry L.P. v Canada*, ICSID Case No UNCT/07/1, Award (31 March 2010) (hereafter *Merrill & Ring*).

[64] *Bilcon of Delaware Inc v Canada*, UNCITRAL (NAFTA), PCA Case No 2009-04, Jurisdiction and Liability (17 March 2015).

[65] ibid para 692.

[66] ibid.

[67] See *Loewen Grp, Inc v United States*, ICSID Case No ARB(AF)/98/3, Counter-Memorial of the United States of America, 118–21 (30 March 2001); *United Parcel Service of America Inc v Canada*, UNCITRAL (NAFTA), Canada's Counter Memorial (Merit Phase, paras 597–605 (22 June 2005); *Methanex* (n 61); *Bilcon* Award (n 58).

public policy in interpreting 'less favourable treatment' and 'in like circumstances'.[68] In one line of reasoning, tribunals in *S.D. Myers, Feldman, Pope & Talbot*, and *Bilcon* considered public policy as an exception. Namely, once the claimant has established the existence of differential treatment, the tribunal then determines whether states sufficiently justified legitimate public policy differences. In other words, tribunals there placed the burden of proof of the existence of reasonable nexus between the policy justification and differential treatment on the states. On the other hand, tribunals in *ADF, GAMI, Loewen, Methanex, Archer Daniels*, and *Corn Products* would reverse the order and only consider whether the treatment was less favourable after concluding claimants were in like circumstances with comparators.

Regardless of the aforementioned different approaches, identifying an appropriate comparator, i.e. the domestic investments/investors, is essential. However, NAFTA tribunals differ on whether the domestic investments/investors must be in a direct competitive relationship or operating in the same or similar sector with the claimant. Some tribunals have adopted a restrictive view. For instance, the *UPS* tribunal rejected the national treatment claim because it found that UPS failed to prove the *importation of goods as mail and by courier* were appropriate comparators, and thus, failed to prove the 'like circumstances' requirement.[69] On the other spectrum, the *Bilcon* tribunal found the domestic investors' oil and gas projects, while broader in scope than the quarry project at issue in the case, were appropriate comparators.[70]

III. Interpretation of expropriation

Expropriation clauses under international treaties require governments not to expropriate or nationalize protected property rights of the national of the other treaty party unless certain prescribed requirements are met—notably, the payment of compensation.[71]

1. ICJ cases interpreting expropriation

The ICJ has interpreted expropriation clauses in, a least, four cases. One of the most often-cited decisions, *Factory at Chorzow (Ger. v Pol.)* articulates standards for damages/compensation when an expropriation had occurred.[72] The Permanent Court of International Justice (PCIJ) (the predecessor of the ICJ) distinguished lawful takings from unlawful expropriations and assigned different financial consequences accordingly. For lawful expropriation, reparation must be made through 'payment of fair compensation' or 'the just price of what was expropriated' at the time of the expropriation. That is, the 'value of the undertaking at the moment of dispossession, plus interest to the day of payment'.[73] In contrast, when the expropriation is unlawful, 'international law provides for *restitutio in integrum* or, if impossible, its monetary equivalent at the time of the judgment'. Moreover, 'injury result[ing] from

---

[68] S Puig and M Kinnear, 'NAFTA Chapter Eleven at Fifteen: Contributions to a Systemic Approach in Investment Arbitration' (2010) 25 ICSID Rev/FILJ 225, 242. Reinisch, 'National Treatment' (n 48) 852–53.
[69] *United Parcel Service of America Inc v Government of Canada*, ICSID Case No UNCT/02/1, Award on Merits (24 May 2007) paras 102–20.
[70] *Bilcon* Award (n 58) para 696–716.
[71] UNCTAD, *Expropriation* (UNCTAD Series on Issues in International Investment Agreements II) UNCTAD/DIAE/IA/2011/7.
[72] *Case concerning certain German interests in Polish Upper Silesia (Factory at Chorzow) (Germany v Poland)* (Judgment) PCIJ Series A No 7.
[73] ibid.

third parties from the unlawful act should be excluded from the damage to be estimated'.[74] With respect to the types of interests that can be expropriated, the PCIJ found the right to manage the factory and the remuneration fixed by the contract for the management and for the use of patents and licences are vested rights that can be and were expropriated.[75]

29 In *Oscar Chinn Case (UK v Belgium)* the PCIJ concluded that 'genuine vested rights' can be the object of expropriation claims.[76] However, neither '[f]avourable business conditions and goodwill [because they] are transient circumstances, subject to inevitable change',[77] nor 'the possession of customers and the possibility of making a profit',[78] are genuine vested interests. The PCIJ thus rejected the United Kingdom's expropriation claim after concluding that expropriation cannot be found for changes of general economic conditions.

30 In the above-mentioned *ELSI* case, the ICJ concluded ELSI's status of insolvency before and at the time of expropriation prevented a finding of expropriation. The chamber reasoned this because it was the company's financial status that deprived its shareholder of the right and not the challenged measures.[79] Therefore, the chamber implied that a 'but for' causation is required in expropriation claims.

31 A relevant issue for ISDS is that expropriation claims concerning a corporate entity differ from claims for expropriating shareholders' rights in the corporation. This was perhaps the most relevant finding in *Barcelona Traction, Light and Power Co. Ltd. (Belgium v Spain)*. According to the Court, a *de facto* expropriation could only occur when the company was 'entirely deprived of means for pursuing its corporate objects',[80] such as 'a total loss of assets'.[81] Thus, the damages to the company are different from those of the shareholders.[82] 'The damage to the company is that it is destroyed; the damage to the shareholders is that they are injured in respect of their property through the destruction of the investment.'[83]

2. Influence over the development of interpretation of the ILC and the Iran–US Claims Tribunal

32 The ICJ's interpretation on expropriation has had huge influence on the works of ILC and the Iran–US Claims Tribunal, and continues to influence subsequent ISDS cases. In its 2001 Articles on the Responsibility of States for Internationally Wrongful Acts, the ILC cemented the *Factory at Chorzow*'s importance in reparation (Article 31), forms of reparation (Article 34), restitution (Article 35), and compensation (Article 36).[84]

---

[74] ibid 31.
[75] ibid 44. The PCIJ reached this conclusion despite a prior arbitral award issued by the Permanent Court of Arbitration that concluded that contractual rights can be protected rights for expropriation and the cancellation of existing contracts amounted to a *de facto* expropriation. *Norwegian Shipowners' Claims (Norway v USA)*, Permanent Court of Arbitration, Award of 13 October 1922, 1 RIAA 325.
[76] *Oscar Chinn Case (UK v Belgium)* (Judgment) PCIJ Ser A/B No 6.
[77] ibid 88.
[78] ibid.
[79] [1989] ICJ Rep 81, para 135.
[80] *Barcelona Traction, Light and Power Co Ltd (Belgium v Spain)* (hereafter *Barcelona Traction*) (Separate opinion Judge Gros) [1970] ICJ Rep 3, 277, para 15 (concerning shareholders' expropriation claim; the majority of the ICJ rejected Belgium's expropriation claim filed under diplomatic protection for lack of jurisdiction).
[81] ibid 274.
[82] ibid 277, para 15.
[83] ibid.
[84] Draft Articles on Responsibility of States for Internationally Wrongful Acts, with commentaries (2001), YILC 2001, Vol II, Part Two.

Building on the ICJ jurisprudence, the Iran–US Claims Tribunal[85] substantially developed   33
the definition of expropriation, the assessment of damages, and the evaluation of expropriated property.[86] It elaborated on incremental measures and other circumstances giving rise to indirect expropriation[87] and reaffirmed the *Factory at Chorzow*'s 'lawful/unlawful' distinction when calculating damages.[88]

3. NAFTA cases interpreting expropriation

Article 1110 bans NAFTA parties from directly or indirectly nationalizing or expropriating   34
the investments of an investor of another party in its territory or taking measures tantamount to nationalization or expropriation of such investments except for a public purpose, on a non-discriminatory basis, in accordance with due process of law and Article 1105(1), and on fair, prompt, and adequate compensation. Where an expropriation has taken place, Article 1110 mandates the payment of compensation equivalent to the fair market value of the expropriated investment immediately before the expropriation took place.

NAFTA tribunals have thus far found states liable for expropriation in only one case,   35
Metalclad Corp. v Mexico.[89] The *Metalclad* tribunal interpreted 'tantamount to expropriation' to include 'covert or incidental interference with the use of property which has the effect of depriving the owner, in whole or in significant part, of the use or reasonably-to-be-expected economic benefit of property even if not necessarily to the obvious benefit of the host State'.[90] Such strenuous interpretation was criticized as 'extremely broad'[91] and subsequent tribunals did not adopt this standard.

Nevertheless, NAFTA tribunals have made other important findings regarding this standard.   36
'Vested interests' that can be expropriated have been interpreted more broadly than in the ICJ jurisprudence. The *Pope & Talbot* tribunal held that 'the Investor's access to the US market is a property interest subject to protection under Article 1110'.[92] *Merrill & Ring* further concluded that market access can be expropriated as long as it is shown 'to be an actual and demonstrable entitlement of the investor to a certain benefit under an existing contract or other legal instrument'.[93] The *Methanex* tribunal similarly concluded that 'goodwill and market share may [...] figure in the valuation'.[94]

Despite the expansive scope of interests capable of being protected from expropriation,   37
NAFTA tribunals recognize that NAFTA is 'not insurance policies'.[95] This means that in general

---

[85] The tribunal was established in 1981 pursuant to the Algiers Declarations of 19 January 1981, reprinted in 20 ILM 224 (1981), 75 AJIL 418 (1981).
[86] For a more detailed recounting of the Iran–US Claims Tribunal jurisprudence on expropriation, see George H Aldrich, 'What Constitutes a Compensable Taking of Property? The Decisions of the Iran-United States Claims Tribunal' (1994) 88 AJIL 585.
[87] *Tippets, Abbett, McCarthy, Stratton v TAMS-AFFA Consulting Engineers of Iran*, Award No 141-7-2, reprinted in 6 Iran–United States CTR 219 (1984). See also *Sedco, Inc v Nat'l Iranian Oil Co*, 9 Iran–US CTR 248 (1986). *Phillips Petroleum Co v Islamic Republic of Iran*, at 115, *Starrett Housing Corp v Islamic Republic of Iran*, 4 Iran–US CTR 122 (1983) 156–57.
[88] *Amoco Int'l Finance Corp v Iran*, 15 Iran–US CTR 189 (1987) para 191.
[89] *Metalclad Corp v Mexico*, ICSID Case No ARB(AF)/97/1, Award (30 August 2000).
[90] ibid para 103.
[91] *Mexico v Metalclad Corp*, 2001 BCSC 664, Reasons for Judgment (2 May 2001) para 99.
[92] *Pope & Talbot*, Interim Award, 2000, para 96. See also *S.D. Myers*, Partial Award, 2000, para 281 (considering market share as vested interests, thus capable of being expropriated).
[93] *Merrill & Ring* (n 63) paras 142–44.
[94] *Methanex* (n 61), Part IV—Ch D, para 17 (citing *Pope & Talbot* affirmatively).
[95] *International Thunderbird Gaming Corp v United Mexican States*, UNCITRAL, Award (26 January 2006) para 433 (hereafter *Thunderbird* Award).

'[r]egulatory conduct by public authorities is unlikely to be the subject of legitimate complaint under Article 1110 of the NAFTA'. However, *Waste Management II* concluded that an outright repudiation, such as a decree or executive act that leads to breach of contract by executive actions may constitute indirect expropriation.[96] The bottom line seems to be that when regulatory or indirect taking is at issue, the existence of severe economic impact is the main issue.[97]

38   Overall, NAFTA tribunals developed a multi-factor test—now widely-used—to determine whether an expropriation has occurred based upon ICJ and Iran–US Claims Tribunal judgments.[98] Also, NAFTA tribunals very often have relied on *Factory at Chorzow* when determining the amount of compensation for expropriation.[99] In part as a result of NAFTA Chapter Eleven the rationale of the ICJ cases has made it to other cases.[100] For example, the *Saluka* tribunal relied on *Methanex* in holding that regulatory expropriation does not occur where a state 'adopts general regulations that are "commonly accepted as within the police power of States"'.[101]

IV. Interpretation of FET/MST

1. ICJ cases interpreting FET/MST

39   The ICJ in, at least, three cases interpreted the Fair and Equitable Treatment/Minimum Standard of Treatment (FET/MST). In *ELSI*, the decision dealt with the exhaustion of local remedies requirement and arbitrariness determination which might be relevant for FET/MST analysis.[102] The ICJ reasoned that the exhaustion requirement is met as long as the 'essence of the claim has been brought before the competent tribunals and pursued as far as permitted by local law and procedures, and without success'.[103] With respect to 'arbitrariness', the ICJ interpret it as a 'wilful disregard of due process of law ... which shocks, or at least surprises, a sense of judicial propriety'.[104] This case and reasoning has had an important impact on ISDS.

40   Recent ICJ decision have clarified the *ELSI* decision. The ICJ in *Case Concerning Ahmadou Sadio Diallo (Guinea v Democratic Republic of the Congo)* confirmed that the exhaustion requirement

---

[96] Para 103 (stating that 'the outright refusal by a State to honour a money order or similar instruments payable under its own law may well constitute either expropriation or at least a measure tantamount to an expropriation of the value of the order').
[97] *Glamis Gold, Ltd v United States of America*, ICSID Case No ARB(AF)/97/1 (NAFTA), Award (8 June 2009) para 355.
[98] *Fireman's Fund Insurance Co v Mexico*, ICSID Case No ARB(AF)/02/1, Award (17 July 2006) para 176 (internal citation omitted). But cf *Pope & Talbot*, at para 104 (stating that the Iran–United States Claims Tribunal's interpretation of expropriation was not relevant to the interpretation of 'tantamount to expropriation' under Article 1110 because the '[Iran-U.S. Claims Tribunal's] mandate expressly extend[ed] beyond expropriation to include "other measures affecting property rights"'). For a response and critic, see Maurizio Brunetti, 'The Iran-United States Claims Tribunal, NAFTA Chapter 11, and the Doctrine of Indirect Expropriation' (2001) 2 Chi J Int'l L 203. The Metalclad tribunal cited both *Chorzow Factory* and *Phelps Dodge Corp v Iran*, the famous PCIJ and Iran–US Claims Tribunal cases to determine fair market value.
[99] *S.D. Myers*, Award (n 58).
[100] *CMS Gas Transmission Co v The Argentine Republic*, ICSID Case No ARB/01/8, Award (12 May 2005) para 262.
[101] *Saluka Investments B.V. v The Czech Republic*, UNCITRAL, Partial Award (17 March 2006) para 262.
[102] *ELSI Elettronica Sicula SpA (United States of America v Italy)* [1989] ICJ Rep 56, para 54.
[103] ibid para 59.
[104] ibid para 128. Dissenting Judge Schwebel appears to differentiate treaty-based arbitrariness (merits) from customary international law-based arbitrariness (procedure). For a detailed discussion, in Jerrod Hepburn's Denial of Justice entry.

extends to administrative remedies if '[administrative remedies] are aimed at vindicating a right and not at obtaining a favour'.[105]

In *Barcelona Traction*, while the ICJ rejected Belgium's denial of justice claim for lack of jurisdiction,[106] Judge Tanaka separately set forth considerations for denial of justice claims. According to Judge Tanaka, denial of justice claims require 'corruption, threats, unwarrantable delay, flagrant abuse of judicial procedure, a judgment dictated by the executive, or so manifestly unjust that no court which was both competent and honest could have given it'.[107]

2. NAFTA cases interpreting FET/MST

Article 1105 requires NAFTA parties to 'accord investments of investors of another Party treatment in accordance with international law, including fair and equitable treatment and full protection and security'. The interpretive note issued by the NAFTA Free Trade Commission (FTC Note)[108] clarifies that Article 1105 reflects the customary international law minimum standard and does not require treatment in addition to or beyond which is required by customary international law.[109] This topic is addressed elsewhere in this volume.[110] However, it is worth pointing out that NAFTA's concept of FET/MST, which references customary international law, does not necessarily apply to other IIAs with different formulations.[111]

NAFTA tribunals are divided on the precise scope of customary international law on arbitrariness as an element of FET/MST despite articulations in *ELSI* (the 'wilful disregard' standard) and *Neer* (the 'outrageous, bad faith, and wilful neglect standard').[112] Through the years, NAFTA jurisprudence developed two standards—one with a lower threshold favoured by the investor, and one with a higher threshold that follows the 'wilful' standard more closely.[113]

---

[105] Ahmadou Sadio Diallo (*Republic of Guinea v Democratic Republic of the Congo*) (Preliminary Objections) [2007] ICJ Rep 582, paras 23, 47.
[106] ibid at (stating that for diplomatic protection, 'it is only if they [shareholders] became deprived of all such possibility that an independent right of action for them and their government could arise').
[107] *Barcelona Traction* (n 80) (Separate Opinion of Judge Tanaka) 154–60. Based on the standard, Judge Tanaka concluded Belgium's denial of justice claim was unfounded.
[108] NAFTA Free Trade Commission, Notes of Interpretation of Certain Chapter 11 Provisions (31 July 2001) http://www.international.gc.ca/trade-agreements-accords-commerciaux/disp-diff/NAFTA-Interpr.aspx?lang=en 23 October 2023 (hereafter 'FTC Notes') (addressing *Pope & Talbot*'s problematic 'additive test').
[109] An interpretation of MFN that was not well accepted by NAFTA State Parties is found in *Pope & Talbot*, where the tribunal concluded that Article 1105 supplied an 'autonomous' standard of FET that is additive to what was required under customary international law. *Pope & Talbot Inc v Canada*, UNCITRAL (NAFTA), Award on the Merits Phase 2 (10 April 2001) para 110.
[110] See in this Commentary: Rob Howse, 'The international law minimum standard of treatment'.
[111] See C Schreuer, 'Fair and Equitable Treatment in Arbitral Practice' (2005) 6 JWIT 357, 360, 363, 364 (stating that 'In the context of Article 1105(1) NAFTA the concept of fair and equitable treatment is equivalent to the minimum standard of treatment under customary international law. This however, does not necessarily apply to other treaties, although some treaties outside of the North American context contain a similar language referring to custom. "As a matter of textual interpretation, it is inherently implausible that a treaty would use an expression such as "fair and equitable treatment" to denote a well-known concept such as the "minimum standard of treatment in customary international law". If the parties to a treaty want to refer to customary international law, it must be presumed that they will refer to it as such rather than using a different expression." Thus, it seems that the fair and equitable treatment standard contained in BITS represents an autonomous concept, which may overlap with (or even be identical to) the customary MST, depending on the wording of a particular treaty').
[112] *LFH Neer and Pauline Neer (USA) v United Mexican States*, 4 Rep Int'l Arb Awards 60 (1926), United Nations, Reports of International Arbitral Awards, 1926, IV, 60ff (stating that 'outrage, to bad faith, to wilful neglect of duty, or to an insufficiency of governmental action so far short of international standards').
[113] *Merrill & Ring* (n 63) 182–208.

For instance, tribunals in *Lion Mexico*,[114] *Mondev*,[115] *Loewen*,[116] *S.D. Myers*,[117] *Thunderbird*,[118] and *Mercer*[119] all applied *ELSI*'s 'wilful disregard' standard, with refinements tailored to the investment context. Specifically, the *Lion Mexico* tribunal examined *ELSI* for both arbitrariness determination ('wilful disregard' standard) and the exhaustion of local remedies requirement, and invoked the *Ambatielos* decision on access to courts in making a finding of violation under denial of justice claim under NAFTA.[120] In contrast, the *Merrill & Ring* tribunal refused to apply *ELSI* because it 'deal[s] with situations concerning due process of law, denial of justice and physical mistreatment, and only marginally with matters relating to business, trade or investments'.[121]

C. Evaluation

44 This section now turns to the two questions posited at the beginning of the entry, namely: (1) to what extent does investment arbitration practice align with ICJ's interpretations? and (2) what institutional factors might explain any misalignments? On the outset, it is worth keeping in mind that both the ICJ and NAFTA Chapter Eleven tribunals (as well as other ISDS arbitral tribunals) are guided by the interpretive rubrics of the Vienna Convention on the Law of Treaties (VCLT). Articles 31 and 32 of the VCLT require tribunals to give the term its 'ordinary meaning ... in their context and in the light of its object and purpose'.[122]

45 Yet, the examination of the above description sees both convergence/alignment and divergence/misalignment in the interpretation of the substantive standards of treatment by the ICJ and ISDS arbitral tribunals under NAFTA. At a very high level, convergence/alignment manifests itself mostly in the interpretation of expropriation and MST/FET, whereas divergence/misalignment is primarily observed in national treatment and MFN.

46 We believe that there are, at least, five reasons for these different trajectories, which we briefly discuss: (1) the focus and scope of the subject matter of disputes, (2) different treaty texts and textual ambiguity of IIAs, (3) the institutional structure of NAFTA, (4) the fact-specific nature required by the substantive standards of treatment, and (5) the evolution of jurisprudence and State practices. Nevertheless, it is worth pointing out that NAFTA arbitral tribunals, as an example of ISDS, largely have employed the general interpretive frameworks developed by the ICJ as we now explain.

I. Divergence/misalignment

47 The different focus and scope of the underlying treaties and institutional design of dispute settlement mechanisms may be an important cause for the misalignment. For instance, in

---

[114] *Lion Mexico Consolidated L.P. v United Mexican States*, ICSID Case No ARB(AF)/15/2, Award (20 September 2021).
[115] *Mondev International Ltd v United States of America*, ICSID Case No ARB(AF)/99/2, Award (11 October 2002).
[116] *Loewen Group Inc and Raymond, L. Loewen v Untied States of America*, ICSID Case No ARB(AF)/98/3, Award, 26 June 2003, para 131 (stating 'Nevertheless the Tribunal did not find it necessary to go beyond the formulation by the International Court of Justice *in Eletrronica Sicula SpA (ELSI) (United States v Italy)* [1989] ICJ Rep 15 at 76').
[117] *S.D. Myers, Inc. v. Government of Canada*, UNCITRAL (NAFTA), Partial Award (Merits) (13 November 2000) para 263.
[118] *Thunderbird* Award (n 95) paras 194, 197 (citing ELSI affirmatively).
[119] *Mercer International Inc v Government of Canada*, ICSID Case No ARB(AF)/12/3, Award (6 March 2018) para 7.78 (citing *ELSI* affirmatively).
[120] *Lion Mexico Consolidated v Mexico*, Award (n 114) paras 225, 289–99, 371, 395, 544.
[121] *Merrill & Ring* (n 63) para 197.
[122] Article 31 of the VCLT.

the bilateral treaties of Friendship, Commerce and Navigation (FCN) containing national treatment and MFN the focus of the ICJ interpretations was trade and shipping matters. In comparison, NAFTA specifically aims at 'increas[ing] substantially investment opportunities' through the application of national treatment and MFN.[123] Hence, ISDS arbitral tribunals interpreting investment-promotion IIAs tend to focus specifically on investment protection, emphasizing the private investors' economic interests.

Different treaty texts and framing of national treatment and MFN provisions is another crucial factor for misalignment. For example, the treaties underlying the three ICJ MFN cases were written in broad and general terms without any limitation to 'like circumstances'. In contrast, NAFTA Article 1103 expressly bars less favourable treatment in 'like circumstances' pre- and post-establishment. It is also unclear whether the phrase 'like circumstances' is in essence an expression of the principle of *ejusdem generis* articulated in *Ambatielos*. Therefore, the term 'like circumstances' leaves room for ISDS tribunals to exercise some discretion. As the review conducted for the entry shows, in some cases, 'like circumstances' have been restricted to specific business fields,[124] in others extended to include broader business activities and sectors,[125] while still others covered regulatory framework and policy objectives.[126]

The structure of NAFTA Chapter Eleven, in particular, the lack of general exception provisions, *inter alia*, for the protection of health, safety, and environment in Chapter Eleven may also cause the divergence in interpreting national treatment and MFN. This lack of exception may in turn have prompted NAFTA tribunals to consider the 'public policy' justification under other terms of the legal obligations when the situation calls on governments to regulate the investor/investment.

The fact-specific nature required by national treatment and MFN claims further contributes to the divergence. The claimant's ability to present sufficient evidence to satisfy the burden of proof for national treatment and MFN violations regardless of the sequencing in determining 'like circumstances' and 'public policy' also affect the outcome of interpretation.

Finally, the evolution of jurisprudence and State practices may have played a role as well. For instances, the ICJ majority in *Anglo–Iranian Oil Co.* was silent on whether MFN encompasses future rights when jurisprudence on that issue was scarce. Nowadays, with the 1,190 known treaty-based ISDS cases,[127] it is more or less accepted that future rights are indeed covered unless otherwise expressly indicated by states.[128] Similarly, due to the scarcity of ICJ's elaboration on national treatment, much interpretative room has been left to the arbitrators.

II. Convergence/alignment

Interpretations of expropriation and MST/FET nevertheless converge between the ICJ and NAFTA Chapter Eleven cases perhaps because both standards of treatment tend to reflect customary international law. To recount, Article 1105 of NAFTA and the FTC Note explicitly limit the scope of MST/FET to what is prescribed in customary international law. Thus, NAFTA tribunals are bound by customary international law on MST/FET, with the evidentiary burden of proof of the exact content and scope resting with the claimants. Article 1110

---

[123] Article 102 of NAFTA.
[124] See, eg, *S.D. Myers,* Award (n 58).
[125] See, eg, *Bilcon,* Award (n 58).
[126] See, eg, *Pope & Talbot* (n 60).
[127] UNCTAD Investment Policy Hub <https://investmentpolicy.unctad.org/investment-dispute-settlement?id=42&name=china&role=respondent> accessed 23 October 2023.
[128] UNCTAD Series on International Investment Agreement II, 19.

prescribes conditions for direct and indirect expropriation and sets forth the standard for compensation that is often link to customary international law.

53 This reliance on customary international law partially explains the convergence between the ICJ and NAFTA tribunals. The reliance on *Factory at Chorzow* and *Barcelona Traction* in the pleadings and arguments of the parties has cemented those judgments' central role in investment arbitration.

54 The joint interpretations by the Parties to the treaty and clarifying substantive standards of treatment in new ones might have drawn ISDS tribunals closer to ICJ jurisprudence. The unique third-party submission mechanism provided in Article 1128 allows State parties to submit their positions on treaty interpretation, establishing a better understanding of the terms. In this process, the crystallization of customary international law is also later reflected in subsequent US Model Bilateral Investment Treaties (BITs). This feedback loop might help to keep tribunals in bound with the contents of established customary international law, of which the ICJ's jurisprudence is a critical part of its foundation.

55 Nevertheless, convergence might be also the result of less formal inter-judicial dialogue.[129] Arbitrators are increasingly aware of, thanks in no small part to research done by academics and practitioners, of the multiple decisions issued by NAFTA and other ISDS tribunals.

D. Conclusion

56 The twenty-five years (plus) of experience of NAFTA ISDS adjudication and interpretation have provided great insights into the systemic influence—and cross-influences—of the ICJ on other international adjudicatory bodies, including ISDS tribunals. Convergence/alignment is found more often in the interpretation of expropriation and MST/FET, whereas divergence/misalignment primarily falls in national treatment and MFN. This entry proffers five reasons that may have contributed to the misalignments: (1) the focus and scope of the subject matter of disputes, (2) the treaty texts and textual ambiguity of IIAs, (3) the institutional structure of NAFTA, (4) the fact-specific nature of the inquiry to find a violation of substantive standards of treatment, and (5) the evolution of jurisprudence and State practices. Nevertheless, NAFTA tribunals have made the ICJ jurisprudence relevant for ISDS in general.

Selected literature

Address by HE Judge Gilbert Guillaume, President of the International Court of Justice, to the United Nations General Assembly (26 October 2000).

Aldrich GH, 'What Constitutes a Compensable Taking of Property? The Decisions of the Iran-United States Claims Tribunal' (1994) 88 AJIL 585.

Bjorklund AK, 'The National Treatment Obligation' in Yannaca-Small K (ed), *Arbitration Under International Investment Agreements (2nd Edition): A Guide to the Key Issues* (OUP 2018) 538.

---

[129] Address by HE Judge Gilbert Guillaume, President of the International Court of Justice, to the United Nations General Assembly (26 October 2000), <https://www.icj-cij.org/public/files/press-releases/9/2999.pdf> accessed 23 October 2023 (warning against the risks of non-cohesive application of international law by different international tribunals).

Bonnitcha J, Poulsen L and Waibel M, *The Political Economy of the Investment Treaty Regime* (OUP 2017).

Brunetti M, 'The Iran-United States Claims Tribunal, NAFTA Chapter 11, and the Doctrine of Indirect Expropriation' (2001) 2 Chi J Intl L 203.

Draft Articles on Most-Favoured-Nation Clauses with Commentaries (1978), YILC 1978, Vol II, Part Two.

Draft articles on Responsibility of States for Internationally Wrongful Acts, with commentaries (2001), YILC 2001, Vol II, Part Two.

Hornbeck SK, 'The Most-Favored-Nation Clause' (1909) 3 AJIL 395.

International Law Commission, Final Report of the Study Group on the Most-Favored-Nation Clause, UN Doc A/70/10, Annex (2015).

Investor-State Dispute Settlement Cases: Facts and Figures 2020, IIA Issue Note, Issue 4, United Nations Conference on Trade and Development (September 2021).

Jennings RY, 'The United Nations at Fifty—The International Court of Justice after Fifty Years' (1995) 89 AJIL 493.

McNair AD, *The Law of Treaties, British Practice and Opinion* (CUP 1938).

Puig S and Kinnear M, 'NAFTA Chapter Eleven at Fifteen: Contributions to a Systemic Approach in Investment Arbitration' (2010) 25 ICSID Rev/FILJ 225.

Reinisch A, 'National Treatment' in Bungenberg M, Griebel J, Hobe S and Reinisch A (eds), *International Investment Law: A Handbook* (Nomos/Hart 2015) 848.

Schreuer C, 'Fair and Equitable Treatment in Arbitral Practice' (2005) 6 JWIT 357.

United Nations Conference on Trade and Development (UNCTAD), *Expropriation* (2011) (UNCTAD Series on Issues in International Investment Agreements II) UNCTAD/DIAE/IA/2011/7.

United Nations Conference on Trade and Development (UNCTAD), *National Treatment* (1999), UNCTAD/ITE/IIT /11 (Vol IV).

Selected decisions

ADF Group Inc v United States of America, ICSID Case No ARB(AF)/00/1, Award (9 January 2003).

Ambatielos Claim (*Greece v UK*), 12 RIAA 83 (Comm'n Arb 1956).

Amoco Int'l Finance Corp v Islamic Republic of Iran, 15 IUSCTR 189 (1987).

Anglo-Iranian Oil Co (*UK v Iran*) (Judgment on Jurisdiction) [1952] ICJ Rep 93.

Apotex Holdings Inc and Apotex Inc v United States of America, ICSID Case No ARB(AF)/12/1, Award (25 August 2014).

Archer Daniels Midland Co and Tate & Lyle Ingredients Americas, Inc v United Mexican States, ICSID Case No ARB(AF)/04/5, Award (21 November 2007).

Barcelona Traction, Light and Power Co Ltd (*Belgium v Spain*) [1970] ICJ Rep 3.

Cargill, Inc v United Mexican States, ICSID Case No ARB(AF)/05/2, Award (18 September 2009).

Case Concerning Ahmadou Sadio Diallo (*Guinea v Democratic Republic of the Congo*) [2007] ICJ Rep 4.

Case concerning certain German interests in Polish Upper Silesia (Factory at Chorzow) (*Ger v Pol*) [1926] PCIJ Ser A No 7.

Chemtura Corporation v Government of Canada, PCA Case No 2008-01 (NAFTA), Award (2 August 2010).

Chile—Taxes on Alcoholic Beverages (13 December 1999) WT/DS110/AB/R.

China—Certain Measures Affecting Electronic Payment Services (16 July 2012) WT/DS413/R.

Clayton and Bilcon of Delaware Inc v Government of Canada, PCA Case No 2009-04, Award (02 August 2010).

CMS Gas Transmission Co v The Argentine Republic, ICSID Case No ARB/01/8, Award (12 May 2005).

Corn Products International, Inc v United Mexican States, ICSID Case No ARB(AF)/04/1, Award (18 August 2009).

ELSI Elettronica Sicula SpA (United States of America v Italy) [1989] ICJ Rep 56.
European Communities—Measures Affecting Asbestos and Asbestos-Containing Products (12 March 2001) WT/DS135/AB/R.
European Communities—Regime for the Importation, Sale and Distribution of Bananas (22 May 1997) WT/DS27/R.
Fireman's Fund Insurance Co v Mexico, ICSID Case No ARB(AF)/02/1, Award (17 July 2006).
Glamis Gold, Ltd v United States of America, ICSID Case No ARB(AF)/97/1 (NAFTA), Award (8 June 2009).
Grand River Enterprises Six Nations, Ltd, et al v United States of America, UNCITRAL (NAFTA), Award (12 January 2011).
International Thunderbird Gaming Corp v United Mexican States, ICSID Case No ARB(AF)/99/2 (NAFTA), Award (26 January 2006).
Japan—Taxes on Alcoholic Beverages, (4 October 1996) WT/DS11/AB/R.
Lion Mexico Consolidated L.P. v United Mexican States, ICSID Case No ARB(AF)/15/2, Award (20 September 2021)
Loewen Grp, Inc v United States of America, ICSID Case No ARB(AF)/98/3, Award (26 June 2003).
Marvin Roy Feldman Karpa v United Mexican States, ICSID Case No ARB(AF)/99/1, Award (16 December 2002).
Mercer International Inc v Government of Canada, ICSID Case No ARB(AF)/12/3, Award (6 March 2018).
Merrill & Ring Forestry L.P. v Government of Canada, ICSID Case No UNCT/07/1, Award (31 March 2010).
Metalclad Corp v Mexico, ICSID Case No ARB(AF)/97/1, Award (30 August 2000).
Methanex Corporation v United States of America, UNCITRAL, Partial Award (7 August 2002).
Mobil Investments Canada Inc and Murphy Oil Corporation v Government of Canada, ICSID Case No ARB(AF)/07/4, Award (20 February 2015).
Mondev International Ltd v United States of America, ICSID Case No ARB(AF)/99/2, Award (11 October 2002).
Oscar Chinn Case (UK v Belgium) [1934] PCIJ Ser A/B No 63.
Phillips Petroleum Co v Islamic Republic of Iran, 21 IUSCTR 79 (1989).
Pope & Talbot, Inc v Government of Canada, UNCITRAL (NAFTA)
Interim Award (26 June 2000).
Award on the Merits of Phase 2 (10 April 2001).
Award in Respect of Damages (31 May 2002).
Award in Respect of Costs (26 November 2002).
Rights of Nationals of the United States of America in Morocco (Fr v US) [1952] ICJ Rep 176, 192.
S.D. Myers v Government of Canada, UNCITRAL (NAFTA), Final Award (30 December 2002).
Saluka Investments B.V. v The Czech Republic, UNCITRAL, Partial Award (17 March 2006).
Sedco, Inc v Nat'l Iranian Oil Co, 9 Iran-US CTR 248 (1986).
Starrett Housing Corp v Islamic Republic of Iran, 4 IUSCTR 122 (1983).
Tippets, Abbett, McCarthy, Stratton v TAMS-AFFA Consulting Engineers of Iran, 6 IUSCTR 219 (1984).
United Postal Service of America Inc v Government of Canada, ICSID Case No UNCT/02/1, Separate Statement of Dean Ronald A. Cass (Award on the Merits) (24 May 2007).
Vento Motorcycles, Inc v United Mexican States, ICSID Case No ARB(AF)/17/3, Award (6 July 2020).
Windstream Energy LLC v Government of Canada, PCA Case No. 2013-22 (NAFTA), Award (27 September 2016).

Denial of justice

Jarrod Hepburn

A. Introduction	1	II. International investment law	29
B. Content	4	E. Temporal jurisdiction	35
I. General international law	4	I. General international law	35
II. International investment law	15	II. International investment law	38
C. Judicial finality	22	F. Remedy	39
I. General international law	22	I. General international law	39
II. International investment law	24	II. International investment law	42
D. Standing	27	G. Conclusion	44
I. General international law	27		

A. Introduction

Denial of justice is a long-established rule of customary international law relating to deficiencies suffered by aliens in the domestic administration of justice within a state. On typical accounts of the rule, denial of justice arises when judges in a local court are corrupt, biased, or unreasonably slow; when the executive branch interferes in domestic judicial proceedings or fails to comply with judgments; or when the legislature bars access to local courts or grants overly wide immunities to local authorities, preventing valid claims by aliens.[1] Examples of these situations abound, in cases stretching back at least to the mid-1800s.[2]

At least five questions can be asked about denial of justice:[3]

(a) What is the **content** of the rule? In particular, can a denial of justice result from a domestic judicial process the outcome of which is substantively unjust?

(b) Does a claim for denial of justice require the substantive exhaustion of local remedies (today often labelled the rule of '**judicial finality**')? In particular, can a denial of justice

---

[1] C Focarelli, 'Denial of Justice', *Max Planck Encyclopedia of Public International Law* [11]–[28] (hereafter Focarelli).
[2] See, eg, J Paulsson, *Denial of Justice in International Law* (CUP 2005) xvii–xxii (hereafter Paulsson).
[3] Several further complex questions—such as whether domestic courts can violate rules of international law other than denial of justice (addressed in cases such as *Eli Lilly v Canada* and *Manchester v Poland*), and whether denial of justice protects *international* adjudication as well as domestic adjudication—are beyond the scope of this entry. On the latter, see J Hepburn, 'The International Extension of Denial of Justice' (2022) 85 MLR 1357.

result from a domestic administrative process for which a domestic judicial appeal remains possible?
   (c) Who has **standing** to claim a denial of justice? In particular, does the party alleging the denial of justice need to be the same as the party that suffered the denial of justice? What if the latter party is a national of the Respondent State?
   (d) When does **temporal jurisdiction** arise over a denial of justice claim? If a denial of justice arises during unsuccessful local judicial efforts to remedy an earlier wrong, is this a separate breach or a continuation of the earlier wrong?
   (e) What is the **remedy** for denial of justice?

3 Sections B–F of this entry aim to identify how international courts generally, and investment tribunals specifically, have answered each of these five questions. Section G then considers the alignment of these two bodies of judicial practice.

B. Content

I. General international law

4 The International Court of Justice (ICJ) has said relatively little about the content of denial of justice. The most relevant judgment is *Barcelona Traction*, where Belgium's central claim was that the Barcelona Traction company had suffered a denial of justice in Spanish courts. As is well-known, the Court rejected the admissibility of the claim, finding that the company was incorporated in Canada and was therefore a Canadian national, and that Belgium did not have standing to claim on behalf of it, despite the Belgian nationality of the company's shareholders.

5 In the course of dismissing the claim, the Court observed that states owed some obligations *erga omnes*, meaning that any state (including Belgium) could claim for Spain's breach of such obligations regardless of the nationality of the victims.[4] The Court located these obligations either in custom or in 'universal or near-universal treaties'.[5] For the Court, these *erga omnes* obligations included 'the basic rights of the human person'.[6] Later in its judgment, the Court appeared to indicate that those basic rights in turn included 'protection against denial of justice'.[7] However, the Court concluded that the relevant obligations at issue in Belgium's claims—presumably, customary obligations on denial of justice—were not owed *erga omnes* but were owed only to the home state of the nationals in question.[8] Since Belgium was not the home state of the relevant national, it was unable to claim. It is unclear how to reconcile the Court's apparent findings both that customary denial of justice was an *erga omnes* obligation (breach of which presumably could be invoked by Belgium) and that customary denial of justice was not an *erga omnes* obligation but was owed by Spain only to Canada.[9]

---

[4] *Barcelona Traction (Belgium v Spain)* (Judgment) [1970] ICJ Rep 3, 32, para 33.
[5] ibid para 34.
[6] ibid.
[7] ibid para 91. Presumably, the Court specifically mentioned denial of justice here because it was the central claim discussed in the parties' pleadings, although the judgment does not clarify this.
[8] ibid para 35.
[9] Tams suggests that, given its eventual conclusion, the Court implicitly did *not* consider denial of justice to be within the notion of basic human rights owed *erga omnes*, despite the text at ibid para 91: C Tams, *Enforcing Obligations* Erga Omnes *in International Law* (CUP 2005) 138; see also ibid, 176–79 for other controversies over these parts of the judgment. Alternatively, in declaring that human rights included protection against denial of justice, the Court may have meant only that human rights obligations offered protections targeting the fact

In any event, regardless of the nature of the denial of justice obligation, the Court's judg- **6**
ment in *Barcelona Traction* gives no insight into the content of the obligation. The separate
opinion of Judge Tanaka does, however, discuss denial of justice in more detail. Judge Tanaka
first noted the multiple meanings of the phrase 'denial of justice' used historically, ranging
from a narrow view, prohibiting only refusal of access to local courts, to a much broader
view, encompassing essentially any international wrong.[10] Judge Tanaka preferred a middle-
ground definition offered by Waldock: denial of justice included 'corruption, threats, unwarrantable delay, flagrant abuse of judicial procedure, a judgment dictated by the executive,
or [a judgment which was] so manifestly unjust that no court which was both competent
and honest could have given it', adding that 'no merely erroneous or even unjust judgment
of a court will constitute a denial of justice'.[11] Tanaka confirmed again later in his opinion
that a high threshold was required for denial of justice arising via judicial conduct, and that
states did not breach the obligation merely by issuing incorrect decisions under local law.[12]
Tanaka also clarified, though, that denial of justice could arise through the conduct of any
State organ, not only judicial organs.[13]

Denial of justice was also tangentially relevant in the *ELSI* case at the ICJ, brought by the **7**
United States against Italy. There was no claim for breach of customary denial of justice in
the case, nor did the claimant rely on a provision of the treaty underpinning the case that
granted access to justice in local courts for foreign nationals.[14] The United States did present
a claim that a sixteen-month delay in local administrative proceedings violated a treaty provision granting 'full protection and security', describing this breach as a 'denial of procedural
justice'. However, the Court rejected this claim on the merits, finding that the delay did not
breach the international minimum standard (to which the treaty clause on 'full protection
and security' was taken to refer).[15]

Nevertheless, the Court in *ELSI* set out the well-known definition of arbitrariness, in the **8**
course of interpreting another treaty provision prohibiting arbitrary measures. For the
Court, arbitrariness was 'not so much something opposed to a rule of law, as something opposed to the rule of law'; it was 'a wilful disregard of due process of law, an act which shocks,
or at least surprises, a sense of juridical propriety'.[16] Concepts of arbitrariness are often central to denial of justice claims, meaning that the *ELSI* judgment might be taken to illuminate
that aspect of denial of justice. (Indeed, *ELSI* has sometimes been cited by investment tribunals in denial of justice analyses.)[17]

---

scenarios that underpin typical claims of denials of justice. In this case, the Court would not have been declaring
that customary denial of justice was an obligation *erga omnes*. However, this view requires assuming that the Court
used the phrase 'denial of justice' at para 91 in a very loose or colloquial manner, which seems inconsistent with it
being the claimant's central claim.

[10] On the differing meanings of 'denial of justice' over time, see C Amerasinghe, *Local Remedies in International Law* (2nd edn, CUP 2004) 84–92; M Sattorova, 'Denial of Justice Disguised? Investment Arbitration and the Protection of Foreign Investors from Judicial Misconduct' (2012) 61 ICLQ 223, 223–25.
[11] *Barcelona Traction (Belgium v Spain)* (Separate Opinion of Judge Tanaka) [1970] ICJ Rep 114, 144.
[12] ibid 153.
[13] ibid.
[14] *Elettronica Sicula SpA (ELSI) (United States v Italy)* (Judgment) [1989] ICJ Rep 15, paras 102, 110.
[15] ibid para 110.
[16] ibid para 128.
[17] See, eg, *Chevron Corporation v Ecuador*, PCA Case No 2009-23, Second Partial Award on Track II (30 August 2018) para 8.38 (hereafter *Chevron*); *Dan Cake SA v Hungary*, ICSID Case No ARB/12/9, Jurisdiction and Liability, 24 August 2015, para 146 even describes *ELSI* as defining denial of justice (hereafter *Dan Cake*).

9 Judge Oda's separate opinion in *ELSI* noted briefly that the claimant could have argued a denial of justice if the judgment of the highest Italian court had been 'manifestly unjust', but he saw no evidence of that on the facts.[18] Judge Schwebel's dissenting opinion, meanwhile, suggested that there was no denial of justice in the Italian courts even though the local court process produced an overall outcome that was arbitrary (and therefore in violation of the treaty provision on arbitrary measures).[19] Judge Schwebel thus appeared to contrast the treaty provision, which he viewed as an obligation of result,[20] with customary denial of justice, which was presumably viewed as an obligation of conduct. On this view, contrary to Judge Oda's view, a domestic court decision that is manifestly unjust in its outcome would seemingly not constitute a denial of justice.

10 Apart from *Barcelona Traction* and (perhaps) *ELSI*, decisions of the ICJ have not otherwise addressed denial of justice. The Permanent Court of International Justice (PCIJ), meanwhile, offered brief relevant examinations. In *Lotus*, the PCIJ described denial of justice as relating to 'the manner in which the [domestic] proceedings ... were conducted'.[21] The Court also accepted the possibility that errors in a domestic court judgment could generate a denial of justice, although without specifying what nature of error (or level of egregiousness) was required.[22] In *Phosphates in Morocco*, the PCIJ appeared to accept that refusal of access to court could constitute denial of justice, although it declined jurisdiction over the denial of justice claim.[23]

11 Otherwise, numerous other international courts and tribunals—mostly the various mixed claims commissions of the early twentieth century—have directly considered and developed the content of the customary rule on denial of justice. The resulting case-law is extensive and cannot be described in full here. However, it is usually analysed into a number of categories: refusal of access to court, delay, due process failings, manifestly unjust judgments, and refusal to enforce judgments.[24] As perhaps reflected in the separate opinions of Judges Oda and Schwebel in *ELSI*, most legal debate in these tribunals centred on the question of whether manifestly unjust judgments could constitute denial of justice. Positions ranged from rejecting any possibility of denial of justice arising from the content of a judgment, through re-framing substantive failings in a judgment as procedural failings, to accepting substantive denial of justice (for instance where the judgment displayed an 'obvious juridical contradiction', in the *Martini* case).[25]

12 Lastly, international courts and tribunals have at times addressed concepts related to denial of justice, if not in the context of the customary rule itself. In the *Application for Review of Judgment No 158 of the United Nations Administrative Tribunal* advisory opinion, for example, the ICJ interpreted the phrase 'failure of justice' in the statute of the United Nations

---

[18] *Elettronica Sicula SpA (ELSI) (United States v Italy)* (Separate Opinion of Judge Oda) [1989] ICJ Rep 83, 92–93.
[19] *Elettronica Sicula SpA (ELSI) (United States v Italy)* (Dissenting Opinion of Judge Schwebel) [1989] ICJ Rep 94, 115.
[20] ibid 117.
[21] *SS Lotus (France v Turkey)* (Judgment) PCIJ Rep Series A No 10, 13.
[22] ibid 24.
[23] *Phosphates in Morocco (Italy v France)* (Judgment) PCIJ Rep Series A/B No 74, 28 (hereafter *Phosphates in Morocco*).
[24] For example, Paulsson (n 2) 204–06; M Paparinskis, *The International Minimum Standard and Fair and Equitable Treatment* (OUP 2013) 189 (hereafter Paparinskis); Focarelli (n 1). Paulsson suggests, however, that no 'definitive list of instances' of denial of justice is possible to draw up: Paulsson (n 2) 205.
[25] See Paparinskis (n 24) 195–97; *Martini (Italy v Venezuela)* (1930) 2 RIAA 975, 1000 (hereafter *Martini*).

Administrative Tribunal (UNAT). The Court defined this phrase in opposition to a 'fair hearing', which covered 'the right to an independent and impartial tribunal established by law; the right to have the case heard and determined within a reasonable time; the right to a reasonable opportunity to present the case to the tribunal and to comment upon the opponent's case; the right to equality in the proceedings vis-à-vis the opponent; and the right to a reasoned decision'.[26]

Similarly, the *Ambatielos* arbitration of 1956 involved the interpretation of a treaty clause guaranteeing nationals 'free access to the Courts of Justice' in each State party.[27] For the tribunal, the crux of this clause was non-discrimination: a foreign national was to be granted 'full freedom to appear before the courts for the protection or defence of his rights, whether as plaintiff or defendant; to bring any action provided or authorised by law; to deliver any pleading by way of defence, set off or counterclaim; to engage Counsel; to adduce evidence, whether documentary or oral or of any other kind; to apply for bail; to lodge appeals and, in short, to use the Courts fully and to avail himself of any procedural remedies or guarantees provided by the law of the land in order that justice may be administered on a footing of equality with nationals of the country'.[28]

Human rights courts have interpreted treaty-based guarantees of fair trial, which some scholars have linked to customary denial of justice.[29] Those courts have defined the content of fair trial in broadly similar terms to denial of justice as elaborated above, although with similar debates over whether a substantively unfair judgment breaches the right of fair trial.[30] The UN Human Rights Committee, for instance, has stated that it will not substantively review a domestic criminal court's evaluation of facts and evidence unless this evaluation was 'clearly arbitrary or amounted to a manifest error or denial of justice',[31] while the European Court of Human Rights has sometimes appeared to suggest that substantively unfair criminal judgments would breach the right to fair trial.[32]

II. International investment law

Most investment treaties do not contain any reference to 'denial of justice'. Instead, denial of justice is universally taken to form part of treaty clauses on fair and equitable treatment (FET).[33] This is arguably a curious position, given the centrality of the 'ordinary meaning' of

---

[26] *Application for Review of Judgment No 158 of the United Nations Administrative Tribunal*, (Advisory Opinion) [1973] ICJ Rep 166, para 92.
[27] Despite the treaty rule, Paparinskis (n 24) 195 nevertheless connects *Ambatielos* directly to customary denial of justice.
[28] *Ambatielos (Greece v United Kingdom)* Award, 6 March 1956, 12 RIAA 83, 111.
[29] See, eg, C McLachlan, L Shore and M Weiniger, *International Investment Arbitration: Substantive Principles* (2nd edn, OUP 2017) para 7.110 (hereafter McLachlan, Shore and Weiniger) and the discussion in Paparinskis (n 24) 197–200.
[30] Paparinskis (n 24) 200–04, 215–16.
[31] Human Rights Committee, 'General Comment No 32: Article 14: Right to Equality before Courts and Tribunals and to a Fair Trial', UN Doc CCPR/C/GC/32 (2007), para 26. See, eg, A Clooney and P Webb, *The Right to a Fair Trial in International Law* (OUP 2021) 125.
[32] L Loucaides, 'Questions of Fair Trial under the European Convention on Human Rights' (2003) 3 HRLR 27, 31–33.
[33] See, eg, R Dolzer and C Schreuer, *Principles of International Investment Law* (OUP 2008) 142; A Reinisch and C Schreuer, *International Protection of Investments: The Substantive Standards* (CUP 2020) 379, 381; *Jan de Nul NV v Egypt*, ICSID Case No ARB/04/13, Award, 6 November 2008, para 188; *Jan Oostergetel v Slovakia*, UNCITRAL, Award, 23 April 2012, para 272; *Manchester Securities Corporation v Poland*, UNCITRAL, Award, 7 December 2018, paras 405–07 (hereafter *Manchester*).

text in prevailing approaches to treaty interpretation. However, it may be explained by the contingent history of claims for denial of justice, and for breach of FET, in investment treaty arbitration.

16 Denial of justice first appeared as a distinct claim in investment treaty arbitration in the 2002 *Mondev v USA* case, which was brought under North American Free Trade Agreement (NAFTA). The claimant primarily alleged a breach of NAFTA Article 1105(1) arising because of certain decisions of the US courts.[34] Article 1105(1) requires NAFTA states to accord 'treatment in accordance with international law', including FET. For the tribunal, there was no question that denial of justice—i.e. the customary international law rule on denial of justice—was part of the 'international law' referred to in Article 1105(1).[35] For the content of the customary rule, the *Mondev* tribunal cited an earlier NAFTA award in *Azinian v Mexico*, as well as citing the discussion of arbitrariness in *ELSI*, which the tribunal found 'useful also in the context of denial of justice'.[36]

17 The earlier *Azinian* case did not directly involve denial of justice; the claimants' pleadings in that case specifically indicated that they were not alleging any denial of justice.[37] However, the claim did relate to conduct of the Mexican courts, which had annulled a concession contract. In the claimants' view, this annulment amounted to an expropriation in breach of NAFTA Article 1110. In its defence pleadings, Mexico cited Judge Tanaka's opinion in *Barcelona Traction* for the principle that international courts could not review the contents of domestic court decisions unless those decisions amounted to a denial of justice.[38] Since there was no evidence (nor any claim) of denial of justice here, Mexico said, the claimants' complaint over the domestic courts' conduct could not succeed.[39] The tribunal (chaired by Paulsson) broadly agreed, supported by a quotation from Jiménez de Aréchaga, in turn referring to customary denial of justice.[40] The *Azinian* tribunal then set out a definition of denial of justice, identifying four categories: refusal of access, delay, failures of due process, and 'clear and malicious misapplication of the law'.[41] Although the tribunal cited no references for this definition, Mexico's pleadings had relied on a definition of customary denial of justice from Freeman identifying the first three categories, which likely inspired the tribunal's own definition.[42] The fourth category, furthermore, may map onto a comment from the Jiménez de Aréchaga source cited by the tribunal, which identifies 'certain exceptional and well-defined circumstances' in which 'a State is responsible for a judicial decision contrary to municipal law'.[43]

18 Given these references to Freeman, Jiménez de Aréchaga and Tanaka, it is clear that the *Azinian* tribunal was discussing the notion of denial of justice as understood in customary

---

[34] *Mondev International Ltd v USA*, ICSID Case No ARB(AF)/99/2, Award, 11 October 2002, para 92 (hereafter *Mondev*).
[35] ibid para 96.
[36] ibid paras 126–27.
[37] *Robert Azinian v Mexico*, ICSID Case No ARB(AF)/97/2, Claimants' Reply to Counter Memorial, 19 January 1999, 77.
[38] *Robert Azinian v Mexico*, ICSID Case No ARB(AF)/97/2, Counter Memorial, 5 October 1998, para 233 (hereafter *Azinian*, Counter Memorial).
[39] ibid para 237.
[40] *Robert Azinian v Mexico* ICSID Case No ARB(AF)/97/2, Award, 1 November 1999, para 98 (hereafter *Azinian*, Award).
[41] ibid paras 102–03.
[42] *Azinian*, Counter Memorial (n 38) para 237.
[43] See *Azinian*, Award (n 40) para 98.

international law. In turn, the *Mondev* tribunal's reliance on the definition in *Azinian* solidified the reference to custom for the understanding of denial of justice under NAFTA Article 1105(1). These two cases were cited again in several other early NAFTA claims relating to denial of justice, including *Loewen v USA* in 2003 and *Waste Management v Mexico* in 2004.[44] A link was thus established between customary denial of justice and NAFTA Article 1105(1).

Importantly, though, even when claimants began invoking the FET clause in Bilateral **19** Investment Treaties (BITs) that did not explicitly limit FET to (customary) international law standards, this customary understanding of denial of justice was nevertheless carried across by tribunals.[45] *Genin v Estonia* is (possibly) the first example of this, in a decision rendered even before *Mondev*. The *Genin* claimant alleged (among other claims) that the revocation of their banking licence breached various provisions of the US–Estonia BIT.[46] As well, the claimant alleged that subsequent domestic court proceedings challenging the licence revocation were a 'travesty of justice', violating the BIT's provisions on FET, arbitrary measures and 'effective means', among others.[47] In response, Estonia noted that local courts were accessible to the claimant, that those courts were impartial, and that any delays were caused by the claimant itself, meaning that there were 'no grounds for a "denial of justice" claim'.[48] Thus, although it appears that the claimant did not directly refer to any denial of justice,[49] the respondent interpreted the claims in that way. The *Genin* tribunal held that Estonia had not committed a denial of justice.[50] The tribunal did not offer any clear definition of denial of justice, nor did it clarify whether it was referring to international law or domestic law for its understanding of this concept.[51] (The tribunal had earlier held that Estonian law applied to the merits of the dispute, although it added that Estonian law was no different to international law on the relevant issues.)[52] This leaves possible conclusions from the *Genin* award somewhat unclear. Nevertheless, the general context of the award does suggest that the tribunal connected the customary international law understanding of denial of justice to the treaty provision on FET.

A much clearer and more recent example is *Chevron v Ecuador II*, where the tribunal held **20** that both the investment treaty and custom 'provide similar protections against denial of justice', and that 'references ... to denial of justice under the FET standard should be understood ... as referring also to denial of justice under customary international law'.[53] The *Iberdrola* tribunal similarly held that 'it cannot be deduced from the text of [the FET clause] that the signatory States set, regarding the standard of denial of justice, "broader" parameters for [denial of justice] than those of customary international law'.[54]

---

[44] *The Loewen Group Inc v USA*, ICSID Case No ARB(AF)/98/3, Award, 26 June 2003, para 133 (hereafter *Loewen*); *Waste Management Inc v Mexico*, ICSID Case No ARB(AF)/00/3, Award, 30 April 2004, para 130.
[45] *Chevron* (n 17) paras 7.12, 8.24; *Liman Caspian Oil BV v Kazakhstan*, ICSID Case No ARB/07/14, Award, 22 June 2010, paras 263, 268; *Iberdrola Energia SA v Guatemala*, ICSID Case No ARB/09/5, Award, 17 August 2012, paras 423–27 (hereafter *Iberdrola*); B Demirkol, 'Exhaustion of Local Remedies and Wrongful Judicial Acts other than Denial of Justice' (2019) 2 TDM; McLachlan, Shore and Weiniger (n 29) 305–07; Paulsson (n 2) ch 5.
[46] *Alex Genin v Estonia*, ICSID Case No ARB/99/2, Award, 25 June 2001, para 91 (hereafter *Genin*).
[47] ibid para 94.
[48] ibid paras 167, 191, 230, 302.
[49] The claimant's full pleadings are not publicly available.
[50] *Genin* (n 46) para 357.
[51] The tribunal did cite *ELSI*, however, in its later discussion of the BIT's arbitrary measures clause: ibid para 371.
[52] ibid para 350.
[53] *Chevron* (n 17) paras 7.12–7.13.
[54] *Iberdrola* (n 45) para 426.

21 One tribunal—in *Merck v Ecuador*—has, however, suggested that the content of treaty-based denial of justice is different to the content of customary denial of justice. The still-unpublished *Merck* award reportedly indicated that denial of justice under a treaty might carry a lower threshold for breach than its customary equivalent, where the treaty did not limit FET to custom.[55]

C. Judicial finality

I. General international law

22 Decisions of the mixed claims commissions and the Iran–US Claims Tribunal, as well as statements and pleadings of states, International Law Commission (ILC) materials, and other writers, have emphasized the judicial finality rule as an aspect of customary denial of justice.[56] The well-understood exceptions to the procedural rule on exhaustion of local remedies have also been transposed without difficulty as exceptions to the substantive judicial finality rule.[57]

23 In *Amco Asia v Indonesia*, the tribunal found that an administrative body could commit a denial of justice (and that this had occurred on the facts in issue).[58] Paulsson criticizes this finding on the grounds that it undermines the judicial finality rule; 'responsibility for denial of justice occurs only when the system as a whole has been tested'.[59] However, the *Amco* tribunal may have used the phrase 'denial of justice' in a broader or colloquial sense, rather than specifically referring to customary denial of justice as examined in this entry.[60] It is thus not clear that *Amco* represents a standard view among international courts and tribunals that administrative bodies can commit customary denials of justice.

II. International investment law

24 Since the *Loewen* case,[61] investment tribunals have uniformly accepted that claimants must substantively exhaust local remedies if they wish to succeed in a denial of justice claim.[62] While the earlier *Mondev* tribunal questioned the judicial finality rule, it did not need to answer the question, since the claimants had exhausted local remedies in any event.[63] The *Chevron v Ecuador* tribunal likely provides an accurate summary of the current position: 'it is well settled that a claimant asserting a claim for denial of justice committed by a State's

---

[55] D Charlotin and L Peterson, 'The Merck Award (Part Two): On the Merits, Ecuador Found Liable for Denial of Justice After Foreign Investor is Ordered to Pay "Wholly Disproportionate Sum" Without Court Engaging in Objective Analysis or Calculation' (*IAReporter*, 27 March 2018) <bit.ly/2SefF2V> accessed 17 October 2023 (hereafter Charlotin and Peterson).
[56] See, eg, Paparinskis (n 24) 182 and the materials described in *Loewen* (n 44) paras 149–56.
[57] Paparinskis (n 24) 184–86.
[58] *Amco Asia Corporation v Indonesia*, ICSID Case No ARB/81/1, Award, 31 May 1990, para 137 (hereafter *Amco Asia*). The *Amco* case was heard by an ICSID tribunal and is sometimes considered part of the investment treaty jurisprudence but was not brought under an investment treaty.
[59] Paulsson (n 2) 125.
[60] *Amco Asia Corporation v Indonesia*, ICSID Case No ARB/81/1, Annulment Decision, 17 December 1992, paras 7.42–7.47; Paparinskis (n 24) 209.
[61] *Loewen* (n 44) paras 142–56.
[62] McLachlan, Shore and Weiniger (n 29) para 7.140; A Newcombe and L Paradell, *Law and Practice of Investment Treaties: Standards of Treatment* (Kluwer 2009) 241.
[63] *Mondev* (n 34) paras 1, 96.

judicial system must satisfy ... a requirement as to the exhaustion of local remedies or, as now better expressed, a substantive rule of judicial finality'.[64]

Investment tribunals have applied the judicial finality rule on the grounds that the content **25** of denial of justice under investment treaties is provided by customary international law (as explained above), and that customary denial of justice includes this rule.[65] In *Manchester v Poland*, however, arbitrator Brower suggested that the substance of the judicial finality rule might differ between treaty-based and customary denial of justice.[66] Brower indicated that case-law on the point was 'unclear', but did not identify the relevant cases. While the *Rompetrol v Romania* tribunal has been described as 'distanc[ing] the treaty obligations from [the] criteria of denial of justice set out in customary law',[67] that tribunal only observed that claims under an investment treaty did not attract the same *procedural* requirements (including exhaustion of local remedies) as claims under custom.[68] Ultimately, as suggested in Section B.II above, it seems unlikely that the substantive elements of the primary rule on denial of justice differ depending on whether the rule is found in a treaty or in customary international law (unless specified otherwise in the treaty).[69]

Lastly, the *Thunderbird v Mexico* tribunal appeared to suggest that a denial of justice could **26** arise from administrative proceedings, even before any appeal of the administrative decision to a judicial authority.[70] This would align with the position of the *Amco* tribunal, discussed in Section C.I above, and would similarly suggest that judicial finality is not required in at least some situations. However, as with *Amco*, it has been suggested that the *Thunderbird* tribunal was not strictly referring to the obligation of denial of justice but was using the phrase more loosely to mean something like 'breaches of due process'.[71] Meanwhile, in *Corona Materials v Dominican Republic*, the relevant investment treaty (like several other recent investment treaties) prohibited denial of justice in criminal or civil proceedings or 'administrative adjudicatory proceedings'. On its face, this provision appears to suggest that denial of justice is possible in administrative proceedings even before seeking any judicial remedy. However, even in the presence of this treaty text, the tribunal reiterated the position that denial of justice arises only when the entire judicial system has been tested. Since the claimant had failed to pursue any judicial remedy for the failure of an administrative agency to decide its request for more than five years, there was no denial of justice.[72] Given this finding, the judicial finality rule seems well entrenched in investment tribunal practice.[73]

---

[64] *Chevron* (n 17) para 7.117.
[65] See the review of custom in *Loewen* (n 44) paras 149–56.
[66] *Manchester* (n 33) fn 745.
[67] M Paparinskis, '*Franck Charles Arif v Republic of Moldova*: Courts Behaving Nicely and What to Do About It' (2016) 31 ICSID Rev 122, 126–27.
[68] *The Rompetrol Group NV v Romania*, ICSID Case No ARB/06/3, Award, 6 May 2013, para 160 (hereafter *Rompetrol*).
[69] Paparinskis (n 67) 125–26; *Corona Materials LLC v Dominican Republic*, ICSID Case No ARB(AF)/14/3, Submission of the United States of America (11 March 2016) para 13. See also F Balcerzak and J Hepburn, '*Manchester Securities v Poland*: Denial of Justice in the European Union' (2020) 35 ICSID Rev 478, 487.
[70] *International Thunderbird Gaming Corporation v Mexico*, UNCITRAL, Arbitral Award, 26 January 2006, paras 197–201.
[71] Paparinskis (n 24) 209.
[72] *Corona Materials LLC v Dominican Republic*, ICSID Case No ARB(AF)/14/3, Award on the Respondent's Expedited Preliminary Objections in Accordance with Article 10.20.5 of the DR–CAFTA, 31 May 2016, paras 243, 254, 264 (hereafter *Corona Materials*).
[73] cf J Crook, '*Denial of Justice in International Law*. By Jan Paulsson. Cambridge, New York: Cambridge University Press, 2005' (2006) 100 AJIL 742, 745–46, who criticizes the rule for 'potentially making it difficult ever to establish such a claim absent truly exceptional circumstances'.

D. Standing

I. General international law

27 Claims of denial of justice might involve certain questions of standing. In particular, adjudicators might need to consider whether a claimant has standing to claim in relation to a denial of justice suffered in local courts by another entity (typically a local subsidiary of the foreign claimant), and, if so, whether a foreign claimant has standing to claim in relation to a denial of justice suffered by a local entity that would not typically be owed obligations under customary international law.

28 Unlike in investment arbitration practice (see Section D.II below), these questions of standing do not appear to have arisen in other international courts or tribunals.[74] Perhaps unsurprisingly, claimants in the pre-World War Two arbitrations appear to have been the foreign nationals who themselves suffered the denial of justice, under diplomatic protection by their home states. In the 2013 decision in the investment treaty case *Arif v Moldova*, the tribunal found no international case-law 'where a party to an international arbitration claiming denial of justice is legally distinct from the party in the incriminated local court proceedings'.[75]

II. International investment law

29 Investment tribunals have considered two principal questions of standing relevant to denial of justice claims: whether the claimant must be the party that suffered the denial of justice in local courts, and whether the protection of the denial of justice obligation is restricted to foreign claimants.

30 In *Arif v Moldova*, the tribunal held that a claim for denial of justice under customary international law was only open to a party who had directly participated in the impugned local court proceedings.[76] Since the party to the relevant local proceedings in the case was not the claimant but his wholly-owned company, the tribunal rejected his claim on this basis. However, the tribunal observed that the treaty's FET obligation was owed to 'investments' of investors. Since this FET obligation itself included the concept of denial of justice, the tribunal proceeded to hear a claim that the claimant's investment, his company, had suffered a denial of justice.[77] The tribunal thus established a distinction between claims for customary denial of justice, which must be brought by the party in the affected local proceedings,[78] and

---

[74] Of course, the denial of justice claim in *Barcelona Traction* was dismissed on a question of standing, as explained above, but the relevant issue of standing there was not any of the ones discussed here.

[75] *Franck Arif v Moldova*, ICSID Case No ARB/11/23, Award, 8 April 2013, para 426 (hereafter *Arif*). Although not clear, the tribunal's inquiry was presumably not limited to investment treaty claims. The tribunal may even have intended to *exclude* investment treaty claims, or otherwise it may have overlooked *Mondev* (n 34), where the Canadian claimant complained (on its own behalf, under NAFTA Article 1116: see para 86) of a denial of justice allegedly suffered in the United States by its US subsidiary, or also *LLC AMTO v Ukraine*, SCC Case No 080/2005, Final Award, 26 March 2008 (hereafter *AMTO v Ukraine*).

[76] *Arif* (n 75) para 435. See also *Bridgestone Licensing Services Inc v Panama*, ICSID Case No ARB/16/34, Award, 14 August 2020, para 165 (hereafter *Bridgestone*).

[77] *Arif* (n 75) para 438; *Bridgestone* (n 76) para 166.

[78] Or, presumably, their home state, via diplomatic protection.

claims for treaty-based denial of justice, which may be brought by a shareholder of the party in the affected local proceedings.

Although without referring to *Arif*, the *Krederi v Ukraine* tribunal appeared to doubt this distinction, musing whether a denial of justice allegedly committed against a subsidiary of the claimant could amount to a treaty-based denial of justice (ie a breach of FET) against the claimant itself.[79] However, the tribunal ultimately found that no denial of justice had occurred, meaning that it had no reason to clarify the distinction. **31**

Apart from the distinction based on the affected party, another point affecting standing is that the customary obligation on denial of justice is owed only to aliens, not to locals.[80] The *Arif* tribunal could thus have dismissed the foreign claimant's customary denial of justice claim for a second reason: while Moldova did owe customary obligations to the foreign claimant, the mistreated party was his locally incorporated company, to which Moldova owed no customary obligations.[81] **32**

These questions of standing arise when claimants seek to bring claims of breach of customary obligations in proceedings commenced under an investment treaty (for instance, under clauses allowing arbitration of 'any dispute relating to investments', as in *Arif*).[82] Other questions of standing can arise when claimants allege breaches of treaty-based denial of justice (via the FET clause). In these situations, the particular treaty text may raise different issues of standing compared to denial of justice claims under custom. **33**

For instance, in submissions in NAFTA cases, the United States has observed that the denial of justice obligation under NAFTA Article 1105(1) is expressed to apply only to investments, not to investors. For the United States, this means that an investor–claimant can only succeed by demonstrating that its investment (rather than itself) suffered a denial of justice.[83] The treaty text thus essentially *prevents* the affected party in the local proceedings from being the claimant in the international proceedings, the reverse of the situation under custom. As well, given that 'investments' under NAFTA are often locally incorporated enterprises, it may be possible that a NAFTA tribunal finds that a respondent state has committed a denial of justice in relation to its own national,[84] a situation which could not arise in a claim under custom.[85] Indeed, this was essentially the situation in *Loewen v USA*, where the party in the relevant Mississippi litigation was a US subsidiary of the Canadian corporate claimant.[86] **34**

---

[79] *Krederi Ltd v Ukraine*, ICSID Case No ARB/14/17, Award, 2 July 2018, para 494 (hereafter *Krederi v Ukraine*).
[80] See *Rompetrol* (n 68) paras 165–66.
[81] Paparinskis (n 67) 126.
[82] Article 7(1) France–Moldova BIT.
[83] See, eg, *Lion Mexico Consolidated LP v Mexico*, ICSID Case No ARB(AF)/15/2, Submission of the United States of America, 21 June 2019, para 10. Ukraine raised a similar objection in *AMTO v Ukraine*: (n 75) para 28. However, the *Lion* tribunal disagreed: *Lion Mexico Consolidated LP v Mexico*, ICSID Case No ARB(AF)/15/2, Award, 20 September 2021, paras 356–58 (hereafter *Lion v Mexico*).
[84] Even if responsibility for that breach is being invoked by a non-national, the investor–claimant.
[85] Ukraine objected in *AMTO* that the claimant's investment, a Ukrainian company, was not protected by treaty clauses on denial of justice since that protection was only owed to aliens: (n 75) para 28. While that objection might be valid in a claim for customary denial of justice, as discussed in relation to *Arif* above, it is not clear that it would succeed in a claim for treaty-based denial of justice, where the treaty text offers protection against denial of justice to 'investments', which may be national entities of the Respondent State. The *AMTO* tribunal seemed to ignore the issue, instead finding that there was no denial of justice: (n 75) para 84.
[86] *Loewen* (n 44) para 3. However, the Canadian claimant was also a party to the Mississippi litigation.

E. Temporal jurisdiction

I. General international law

35 Questions of temporal jurisdiction arise in relation to denial of justice largely because the alleged denial of justice may often be suffered by aliens while pursuing domestic remedies for some earlier alleged wrong. Given the time difference (which may be extensive) between the earlier wrong and the domestic judicial proceedings, the relevant court's or tribunal's temporal jurisdiction may have commenced or concluded in the interim.

36 In *Phosphates in Morocco* before the PCIJ, Italy alleged that its national had suffered a denial of justice due to 'obstacles placed in the way of a petition' to local authorities. The petition sought to complain about an earlier alleged interference with mining rights. The earlier interference was outside the PCIJ's temporal jurisdiction, but the events underpinning the denial of justice claim were within temporal jurisdiction. The PCIJ's jurisdiction to hear the claim then depended on whether the later alleged denial of justice was (as Italy argued) a separate claim in itself, or was merely the continuation of the earlier dispute.

37 The Court rejected Italy's argument, finding that the denial of justice 'cannot be separated from' the earlier interference because 'the Court could not regard the denial of justice as established unless it had first satisfied itself as to the existence of the rights of the private citizens alleged to have been refused judicial protection'.[87] The Court thus declined temporal jurisdiction. However, commentators suggest that customary denials of justice in general constitute separate breaches by a state regardless of any earlier wrongful acts, and that the *Phosphates* finding is limited to the situation described (ie where the denial of justice hinges on the existence of domestic rights, determination of which is outside jurisdiction).[88]

II. International investment law

38 In the limited experience to date, investment tribunals appear to have followed the customary law position in relation to temporal jurisdiction for denial of justice claims. In *Corona Materials v Dominican Republic*, state authorities had refused to grant an environmental licence. The claimant sought reconsideration of this refusal, but the authorities failed to decide the reconsideration request for more than five years. The earlier refusal was outside temporal jurisdiction, but the claimant argued that the later failure to decide constituted a denial of justice that was within temporal jurisdiction. The tribunal disagreed, finding that the failure to decide was 'nothing but an implicit confirmation of its previous decision' that did not 'produce any separate effects on [the claimant's] investment other than those that were already produced by the initial decision'.[89] This result parallels the outcome in *Phosphates of Morocco* (discussed in Section E.I above), and the tribunal could perhaps be viewed as adopting similar reasoning: the state's refusal of access to court could only be wrongful if the claimant had any rights to pursue in court. However, the parties did not cite *Phosphates* in their pleadings, and the tribunal did not discuss the PCIJ judgment. Furthermore, the claimant had presented its case as a 'unified' set of claims pertaining to a 'single, uninterrupted event',[90] making the tribunal's task somewhat easier.

---

[87] *Phosphates in Morocco* (n 23) 28–29.
[88] Paparinskis (n 24) 187.
[89] *Corona Materials* (n 72) paras 211–12.
[90] ibid paras 206, 208.

F. Remedy

I. General international law

The ICJ has not yet considered the question of the appropriate remedy for denial of justice. Meanwhile, other international courts and tribunals agree on the basic principle as encapsulated in the *Chorzow Factory* case: the goal of the remedy is to extinguish the consequences of the denial of justice and restore the *status quo*. Problems arise, however, in applying this basic principle to the varying fact patterns of denial of justice claims.[91]

Non-monetary orders have featured in some cases. In situations where obligations have wrongfully been imposed on a claimant as a result of a denial of justice, as in the *Martini* case, the international tribunal has ordered the obligations to be annulled.[92] This could be viewed as an order of cessation of wrongful conduct.[93] In other cases, monetary compensation has been ordered. Such orders are sometimes simple to determine, such as in the situation of a judgment corruptly transferring the claimant's property to the judge,[94] where the compensation will be for the value of the property,[95] or the situation of failure to enforce a monetary judgment, where the compensation order will be for the judgment amount owed.[96] In other situations, the exact consequences of the denial of justice—and thus the compensation due—are more difficult to determine.

A question arises here whether compensation is due for pure procedural harms, i.e. in situations where the substantive outcome might have been the same even if the domestic proceedings had not been tainted by a denial of justice. On this question, several approaches are possible, all arguably within the broad *Chorzow Factory* principle.[97] First, tribunals might consider that they have no power to determine the outcome of domestic proceedings in the absence of a denial of justice, and might thus award no compensation, finding any loss unproven. The European Court of Human Rights has often taken this approach in analogous claims for breach of Article 6(1) of the European Convention, on the right to a fair hearing.[98] Second, tribunals might simply award full compensation for the loss suffered as a result of the substantive outcome of the tainted proceedings, disregarding whether the loss was truly caused by the denial of justice. This was seemingly the approach of the *Amco Asia v Indonesia* tribunal.[99] Third, tribunals might assess the foreigner's chance of success in an untainted local proceeding and apply this probability to the loss suffered from the tainted substantive outcome. Fourth, tribunals might step into the shoes of the domestic courts and resolve the dispute under domestic law themselves. This last approach is perhaps most in conformity with the *Chorzow Factory* principle but may be perceived as most intrusive upon domestic sovereignty.

---

[91] Paulsson (n 2) 208, 226.
[92] *Martini* (n 25) 975.
[93] Draft Articles on the Responsibility of States for Internationally Wrongful Acts, YILC 2001, Vol II, Part Two, Article 30.
[94] *Cotesworth and Powell (Great Britain v Colombia)* (1875) 2 Moore Intl Arbitrations 2050.
[95] See *Smith v Marianao* (1930) 24 AJIL 384 or *de Sabla (US v Panama)* (1933) 6 RIAA 358 for other instances of loss of property due to denial of justice.
[96] See, eg, *Montano (Peru v US)* (1863) 2 Moore Intl Arbitrations 1630 or *Idler (US v Venezuela)* 4 Moore Intl Arbitrations 3491, or *Fabiani (France v Venezuela)* 4 Moore Intl Arbitrations 4878 where the failure to enforce led to various other adverse consequences compensated as indirect losses.
[97] See B Demirkol, *Judicial Acts and Investment Treaty Arbitration* (CUP 2018) Ch 4 (hereafter Demirkol).
[98] However, the *lex specialis* reference in Article 41 of the European Convention on Human Rights to 'just satisfaction' might complicate a comparison here.
[99] *Amco Asia* (n 58) para 178; Demirkol (n 97) 128–29, Paulsson (n 2) 222.

II. International investment law

42 Relatively few claims for denial of justice have succeeded before investment treaty tribunals, making it difficult to give a general picture of tribunals' approaches to remedies. In *Flughafen v Venezuela*, a denial of justice claim succeeded, but the tribunal also found an expropriation, leading the damages to be calculated on the basis of a discounted cash-flow model as typically used in expropriation analyses.[100] In *Energoalians v Moldova*, the claim succeeded, but the tribunal's reasoning was highly opaque, and other breaches were also found, making the tribunal's damages analysis of little assistance.[101] Claims also succeeded in *Dan Cake v Hungary*, *Merck v Ecuador*, and *Chevron v Ecuador II*, but the damages awards are still unpublished in the first two cases and still pending in *Chevron*.[102] In two other cases of successful denial of justice claims, *Al-Warraq v Indonesia* and *Pey Casado v Chile*, tribunals found that the investors had not proven that any loss was actually suffered due to the denial of justice (rather than other causes), and so no compensation was awarded.[103]

43 *Manchester v Poland* and *Lion v Mexico* provide two of the few examples of an investment treaty tribunal awarding damages directly for a denial of justice. In both cases, the tribunals agreed with the basic principle on damages adopted by other international tribunals as set out in *Chorzow Factory*.[104] Applying this principle, the *Manchester* tribunal adopted the fourth approach to remedies outlined in Section F.I above; the tribunal determined what compensation the claimant would have received in a domestic bankruptcy process if the Polish courts had not improperly invalidated the claimant's rights.[105] The *Lion* tribunal, meanwhile, effectively adopted the third approach, determining the value of certain mortgage interests lost due to the denial of justice but then discounting this value by 30 per cent to account for the uncertainties involved in pursuing domestic foreclosure proceedings to seize and re-sell the mortgaged properties.[106]

G. Conclusion

44 As the previous sections have demonstrated, investment tribunals have aligned strongly with the customary notion of denial of justice elaborated by the ICJ and other international courts and tribunals. The alignment is particularly clear in relation to the content of denial of justice, the judicial finality rule, questions of temporal jurisdiction, and the remedies for denial of justice. This has been justified by interpretive approaches linking the text of investment treaties to customary standards of protection including denial of justice. Investment tribunals have diverged, however, on questions of standing, driven by *lex specialis* rules in investment treaties lessening the relevance of the customary position.

---

[100] *Flughafen Zürich AG v Venezuela*, ICSID Case No ARB/10/19, Award, 18 November 2014, paras 509, 721, 978.
[101] *Energoalians Ltd v Moldova*, UNCITRAL, Arbitral Award, 23 October 2013, paras 356, 381.
[102] *Dan Cake* (n 17) para 146; Charlotin and Peterson (n 55); *Chevron* (n 17) para 8.77.
[103] Both cases carry complications: the *Al-Warraq* merits and damages discussion was rendered *obiter* by the tribunal's finding that the entire claim was inadmissible due to investor misconduct, and the *Pey Casado* finding (by a resubmission tribunal) came after the original tribunal's award of USD 10 million in damages for denial of justice was annulled for failing to distinguish damages for expropriation from damages for denial of justice.
[104] *Manchester* (n 33) para 503; *Lion v Mexico* (n 83) para 621.
[105] *Manchester* (n 33) paras 506–18.
[106] *Lion v Mexico* (n 83) paras 761–74.

On content, investment tribunals have 'largely endorsed the customary international law **45** principles concerning denial of justice'.[107] To the extent that legal tests applied in particular cases might differ, this is potentially due to the fact that the customary position is not necessarily clear itself—for instance, on whether manifestly or substantively unjust domestic judgments amount to denial of justice.[108] To the extent that outcomes might differ, this is potentially due to differing assessments by adjudicators of how the relevant facts fit the broad legal tests, ie whether a delay is sufficiently long, whether due process was afforded, or whether a domestic judgment is unjust (manifestly or otherwise).

On judicial finality, investment tribunals have adhered to the rule even when treaty text **46** might appear to suggest otherwise, as in the *Corona Materials* case.[109] On temporal jurisdiction, *Corona Materials* also provides some evidence that investment tribunals have followed the customary law position adopted in other international courts, although the evidence is somewhat unclear as discussed in Section E.

On remedies, although there is little evidence to date (as noted in Section F), it appears that **47** investment arbitration practice aligns with the practice of other international courts and tribunals. Investment tribunals routinely accept the basic principle on damages followed by other international tribunals, and they have applied this principle in at least two denial of justice cases to date, *Manchester v Poland* and *Lion v Mexico*. Even if different tribunals might adopt the different approaches outlined in Section F.I, it is arguable that all of the approaches represent applications of the basic principle in different ways, making it difficult to criticize such choices from a doctrinal perspective. To the extent that other tribunals award non-monetary remedies for denial of justice, investment tribunal practice might be expected to diverge from this practice where the terms of the relevant investment treaty limit awards to monetary compensation. In *Chevron v Ecuador II*, for instance, the investment tribunal found that it had no power to declare void a domestic decision tainted by denial of justice. However, the tribunal imposed a non-monetary interim measure, ordering Ecuador to refrain from enforcing the decision against the investor and to take steps to ensure that third parties did not enforce the decision either, in Ecuador or elsewhere.[110] This interim measure is not yet a final order on remedies from the *Chevron* tribunal.

On questions of standing, meanwhile, investment tribunals have deviated from the position **48** of other tribunals. As described in Section D, investment tribunals have permitted claimants to claim for treaty-based denials of justice in circumstances where another international tribunal would likely have denied standing for an equivalent claim under customary denial of justice.[111] In other situations, such as where the treaty obligation applies to 'investments' rather than 'investors', the proper claimant in a treaty-based claim and a customary claim may need to differ.

The basic reason for the large degree of alignment is likely that investment tribunals have **49** consciously connected the treaty-based obligation on denial of justice with the customary obligation, making it natural to draw on the interpretation and application of the latter

---

[107] *Krederi v Ukraine* (n 79) para 443; see also McLachlan, Shore and Weiniger (n 29) para 7.107.
[108] See, eg, the debate in *Lion v Mexico* (n 83) paras 211–19, and a differing conclusion in *Infinito Gold Ltd v Costa Rica*, ICSID Case No ARB/14/5, Award, 3 June 2021, para 445.
[109] *Corona Materials* (n 72). See Section C.II above.
[110] *Chevron* (n 17) paras 9.14, 10.13.
[111] Even setting aside the likely context of diplomatic protection, in a claim before other international courts or tribunals.

obligation by other international courts and tribunals. Where investment tribunals have deviated or might in future deviate (on remedies or standing), this is driven by treaty text binding the arbitrators.[112] Such deviation seems readily justifiable as giving effect to the express intentions of the treaty parties, departing from the customary position.

50 Whether it is justifiable for investment tribunals otherwise to align with custom when interpreting and applying a treaty-based obligation on denial of justice, meanwhile, depends largely on the correctness of tribunals' frequent findings that FET clauses incorporate the customary rule on denial of justice.[113] These findings are likely justifiable where tribunals find that the FET clause reflects the customary minimum standard. But even investment tribunals that otherwise treat FET clauses as 'autonomous' and unconnected to custom have nevertheless referred to custom for the denial of justice component of FET.[114] This would presumably need to be justified from the perspective of treaty interpretation.

Selected literature

Balcerzak F and Hepburn J, '*Manchester Securities v Poland*: Denial of Justice in the European Union' (2020) 35 ICSID Rev 478.

Demirkol B, *Judicial Acts and Investment Treaty Arbitration* (CUP 2018).

Focarelli C, 'Denial of Justice' in *Max Planck Encyclopedia of Public International Law* (2020).

Paparinskis M, *The International Minimum Standard and Fair and Equitable Treatment* (OUP 2013).

Paulsson J, *Denial of Justice in International Law* (CUP 2005).

Sattorova M, 'Denial of Justice Disguised? Investment Arbitration and the Protection of Foreign Investors from Judicial Misconduct' (2012) 61 ICLQ 223.

Selected decisions

Chevron Corporation v Ecuador, PCA Case No 2009-23, Second Partial Award on Track II (30 August 2018).

Franck Arif v Moldova, ICSID Case No ARB/11/23, Award (8 April 2013).

Lion Mexico Consolidated LP v Mexico, ICSID Case No ARB(AF)/15/2, Award (20 September 2021).

Manchester Securities Corporation v Poland, UNCITRAL, Award (7 December 2018).

Mondev International Ltd v USA, ICSID Case No ARB(AF)/99/2, Award (11 October 2002).

The Loewen Group Inc v USA, ICSID Case No ARB(AF)/98/3, Award (26 June 2003).

---

[112] See *Bridgestone* (n 76) para 174.

[113] Others have offered extensive views on the correctness of the link between FET and custom: see, eg, Paparinskis (n 24).

[114] See, eg, *Liman Caspian Oil BV v Kazakhstan*, ICSID Case No ARB/07/14, Award, 22 June 2010, paras 263, 268; *Iberdrola* (n 45) paras 423–27.

The international law minimum standard of treatment

*Robert Howse**

A. Introduction	1	E. The NAFTA: A turning point?	34
B. The emergence of the international minimum standard and the historical evolution of its content	4	I. The NAFTA Commission interpretation	36
		II. The *Pope* tribunal's response to the NAFTA Commission 1105 interpretation	41
I. The origins	4	III. *Neer* sightedness and the MST: *Glamis Gold*	44
II. Early formulations of the content of the international law minimum standard	8	IV. *Bilcon v Canada*: An example of the post-*Glamis* debate over the MST	47
III. Failed codification and the shift to treaty law	15	V. The USMCA revision of NAFTA: The disappearance of *Neer*	51
C. Content and contours	22	F. Conclusion: The emerging predominance of treaty-based international standards for the treatment of aliens	53
D. The application of the MST in investment law	24		

A. Introduction

The responsibility of States for their conduct toward aliens present on their territory is a longstanding feature of customary international law. Such responsibility was originally understood as responsibility to the State of which the alien is a national, the concept of diplomatic protection. The customary international law standard of treatment is the notion that there are certain fundamental norms of justice that determine this responsibility, and these must not be violated regardless of the application of the State's internal laws to the alien. As Miles explains, the claim that such a standard exists arose in the context of colonial powers seeking to protect their citizens and corporations engaged in commerce in places thought to lack 'civilized' internal legal systems.[1] Counter to the notion of a minimum standard is

---

* I disclose as a matter of scholarly integrity that I participated in some of the disputes discussed in this entry, either as an expert witness or as a consultant to the investor's legal counsel. I am indebted to Donald Donovan, with whom I teach international investment law and arbitration at NYU law school, for our ongoing debates about the investment regime and general international law and above all to Barry Appleton, with whom I have been engaged on these issues since the very first NAFTA cases.

[1] K Miles, *The Origins of International Investment Law: Empire, Environment and the Safeguarding of Capital* (CUP 2013) 49–52.

the Calvo doctrine through which Latin American nations responded to legal colonialism: aliens should be entitled to non-discriminatory treatment under internal law, and no more. They should not enjoy as aliens legal protections and rights that nationals of the host state do not have.

2 Despite successive efforts, the substantive content of the customary minimum standard has never been codified. Through the New International Economic Order (NIEO) developing countries sought to balance the protection of aliens' property under the minimum standard with recognition of the sovereign right to natural resources and the international legality of nationalization. The global South largely lost the battle to allow standards of compensation for taking of property that reflected not just the market value but the development needs and priorities of those countries. Sornarajah explains: 'Customary law, as conceived by the developed states, was assailed at a more global level during the articulation of the NIEO [footnote omitted] and the doctrine of permanent sovereignty over natural resources. The emphasis in the conflict was largely on the standard of compensation, with the developing states advancing "appropriate compensation" as the new standard, and the developed states adhering to the Hull formula of :prompt, adequate and effective" compensation'.[2]

3 By the 1960s, the global North was moving toward bilateral treaties as a means of protecting the economic activities of their nationals in the developing world. At first, these typically took the form of treaties of Friendship, Commerce, and Navigation (FCN) and then Bilateral Investment Treaties (BITs).[3] While establishing primary obligations to protect nationals engaged in commercial activity on the territory of another treaty party, these agreements sometimes referred back to general international law or customary international law to interpret or define the content of the primary obligations (especially fair and equitable treatment). Thus, within the treaty-based regime of investor protection the minimum standard of treatment (MST) acquired a sort of half-life, the most significant instance being the North American Free Trade Agreement (NAFTA). An authoritative interpretation of the NAFTA by the treaty parties established the international law standard of treatment as the *ceiling* for the treatment required under the NAFTA's fair and equitable treatment clause (Article 1105). The successor treaty to NAFTA, the United States Mexico Canada Agreement (USMCA) largely dispensed with Fair and Equitable Treatment, limiting most kinds of investor claims to violations of National Treatment and situations of direct expropriation. At the same time, as will be discussed, very recent treaty developments reflect a tendency (including by one of the USMCA parties, Canada) to seek a detailed codification of the content of the minimum standard.

B. The emergence of the international minimum standard and the historical evolution of its content

I. The origins

4 The minimum standard first arose in the context of gunboat diplomacy, as a justification for use of force against a country based on the purportedly outrageous treatment of a national

---

[2] MJ Sornarajah, *Resistance and Change in the International Law of Foreign Investment* (CUP 2015) 192.
[3] See D Lustig, *Veiled Power: International Law and the Private Corporation, 1886-1981* (OUP 2020) Ch 7. 'From the NIEO to the International Investment Law Regime: The Rise of the Multinational Corporation as a Subject of Regulatory Concern in International Law'.

by the other state. Under the leadership of Argentine Foreign Minister Luis Maria Drago, Latin American-focused resistance to gunboat diplomacy led to the 1907 Hague Convention favouring peaceful settlement of such disputes, including those involving contract claims of aliens. The minimum standard became thereafter inseparable from the notion of diplomatic protection or espousal through means such as good offices, mediation, arbitration, claims commissions, and international adjudication.[4] The underlying theory of international responsibility remained that of repairing a moral injury to the state whose national was mistreated. Yet increasingly claims commissions and other third-party dispute settlement entities determined compensation in light of the harm suffered by the alien, not the dignitary offense to the state of which they were a national.

One safeguard against legal colonialism under diplomatic protection was the requirement of exhaustion of local remedies—the home state could only espouse the claim of its national once that national had exhausted all reasonably available avenues of domestic recourse. The treaty regime for investor protection would typically (though in not all cases) dispense with this local remedies requirement to allow the aggrieved alien to bring a claim before an international arbitration tribunal without having first to have recourse to the domestic legal system of the host state.

With the rise of such investor–State Dispute Settlement (ISDS) from the 1990s onwards, claims of protection were increasingly brought by private parties directly and not through State-to-State proceedings. Diplomatic protection fell into disuse as a vehicle for guarding the commercial interests of the global North. Through international institutions such as the World Bank, developing states were encouraged to buy into the investment protection regime, including ISDS.[5] Indeed, under the International Centre for Settlement of Investment Disputes (ICSID) (Washington) Convention, to bring an ICSID case requires the claimant to renounce diplomatic protection.

As for diplomatic protection outside the investment context, claimants and tribunals relied less and less on the MST concept and increasingly on treaty-based primary obligations in a range of regional and multilateral human rights conventions.[6] The most prominent recent case, in the International Court of Justice (ICJ), *Diallo*, is a spectacular example. The mistreatment by the DRC of a Guinean businessman was entirely decided on by the application of human rights treaty provisions.[7] Guinea had also pleaded violation of 'the principle that aliens should be treated in accordance with "a minimum standard of civilization" the obligation to respect the freedom and property of aliens, [and] the right of aliens accused of an offence to a fair trial on adversarial principles by an impartial court'. The sole response of the ICJ was the *obiter dictum* that 'there is no doubt that the prohibition on inhuman and degrading treatment is among the rules of general international law which are binding on States in all circumstances, even apart from treaty commitments'.[8] It is questionable whether

---

[4] M Paul Friedman and T Long, 'Soft Balancing in the Americas: Latin American Opposition to U.S. Intervention, 1898–1936' (2015) 40 Int Secur 120–56.

[5] See generally, T St John, *The Rise of Investor-State Arbitration: Politics, Law and Unintended Consequences* (OUP 2018) and L Poulsen, *Bounded Rationality and Economic Diplomacy: The Politics of Investment Treaties in Developing Countries* (CUP 2015).

[6] See D Leys, 'Diplomatic Protection and Individual Rights: A Complementary Approach' (2016) 57 HarvIntlLJ (Online Vol).

[7] *Case Concerning Ahmadou Sadio Diallo (Republic of Guinea v Democratic Republic of the Congo)* (Judgment on compensation) [2012] ICJ Rep 324 (hereafter *Diallo*).

[8] ibid para 87.

even here the ICJ was alluding to the MST as opposed to a human rights norm that it deemed to have become custom (if not *ius cogens*).

II. Early formulations of the content of the international law minimum standard

8 It is best to begin with two formulations of the international law MST cited pervasively by disputing parties, tribunals, and academic commentators. The first comes from the 1926 *Neer* arbitration in the US Mexico Claims Commission: 'the treatment of an alien, in order to constitute an international delinquency, should amount to an outrage, to bad faith, to willful neglect of duty, or to an insufficiency of government action so far short of international standards that every reasonable and impartial man would readily recognize its insufficiency. Whether the insufficiency proceeds from deficient execution of an intelligent law or from the fact that the laws of the country do not empower the authorities to measure up to the international standards is immaterial'.[9]

9 The second articulation occurs more than a half century later, by a chamber of the ICJ in the *ELSI* case (applying an FCN treaty between the United States and Italy): 'arbitrariness is not so much something opposed to a rule of law, as something opposed to the rule of law. This idea was expressed by the Court in the Asylum case, when it spoke of "arbitrary action" being "substituted for the rule of law" ... It is a willful disregard of due process of law, an act which shocks, or at least surprises, a sense of judicial propriety.'[10]

10 Both of these formulations state the test for whether conduct is wrongful in terms of the reaction of a supposedly objective and impartial observer. In the case of *Neer*, that observer is any 'reasonable and impartial man' and in *ELSI* someone with 'a sense of judicial propriety'. However, there is a significant difference between the *Neer* approach and that in *ELSI*. In *Neer*, the tribunal distinguishes between international standards as such and those cases where violation of such standards are sufficiently grave to rise to the level of 'international delinquency' under the law of diplomatic protection, i.e. conduct that is sufficiently serious to amount to an international wrong against the *state* of which the alien is a national. In fact, the *Neer* tribunal itself did not articulate the content of the international standards. It did not need to, because based on the evidence as the tribunal saw it, the conduct toward the alien was not so deficient as to amount to the kind of outrage that would constitute an international wrong toward the alien's home state.

11 When one thinks of the Calvo-type objection to the international minimum standard, it is understandable that the *Neer* tribunal sought to limit those instances where a shortfall in terms of international standards would be a basis for a State-to-State dispute. There are legitimate sovereignty concerns about converting the operation of a country's domestic legal system into the subject matter of a dispute with another state. At the same time, the requirement of exhaustion of domestic remedies, articulated as finality in the case of denial of justice, is a further protection against the cavalier elevation of (non-discriminatory) operation of a sovereign State's legal system into an interstate dispute.[11]

---

[9] *LFH Neer and Pauline Neer (United States v Mexico)* (1926) 4 RIAA 60, para 4.
[10] *Elettronica Sicula S.p.A. (ELSI) (US v Italy)* [1989] ICJ Rep 15, para 29 (hereafter *ELSI*).
[11] The discussion of the development of the minimum standard in the shadow of the Calvo doctrine in M Paparinskis, *The Minimum Standard and Fair and Equitable Treatment* (OUP 2013) Chs 1 and 2 (hereafter Paparinskis).

The influence of human rights on diplomatic protection, and the focus of investment or economic treaties on impacts on the alien's property and business activity, has each in its own way made the harm suffered by the alien the central concern. Today a state could bring a claim of diplomatic protection against any state that violates the international legal rights of its national without having to establish that the conduct is so egregious as to constitute a dignitary injury to the home state itself.

In *Diallo*, the ICJ pointed out: 'Owing to the substantive development of international law over recent decades in respect of the rights it accords to individuals, the scope *ratione materiae* of diplomatic protection, originally limited to alleged violations of the minimum standard of treatment of aliens, has subsequently widened to include, *inter alia*, internationally guaranteed human rights.'[12] Indeed, the Draft International Law Commission (ILC) Articles on Diplomatic Protection in its definition of diplomatic protection refers only to injury to natural or legal persons of the home state.[13] The definition is silent about injury to the home state. In the *Avena* case the ICJ distinguished between a claim of diplomatic protection based solely on injury to the claimant State's national, and, on the other hand a claim that the state '*has itself suffered, directly and through its nationals*', an injury.[14]

In sum, under contemporary customary international law, diplomatic protection may be invoked where the rights of a national under international law are violated, even if the violation is not of such a kind as to constitute an injury to the state itself. In such cases, the *Avena* court stressed, the rule of exhaustion of domestic remedies still fully applies.

III. Failed codification and the shift to treaty law

Contrasting with the emergence of human rights law, where treaty-based international standards emerged for the treatment of natural (and to some degree legal) persons, in the domains of diplomatic protection and international economic law there was a failure to codify the content of the customary MST. Nevertheless, from even before *Neer*, one can discern from various primary sources as well as academic commentary certain broadly shared understandings of the core of this content, at least: Denial of justice in judicial and administrative proceedings.[15]

At the same time, it is widely accepted that mere breach of or a departure from domestic law does not violate the minimum standard. Sometimes the stand is framed in terms of non-discrimination against aliens, sometimes as the duty to provide 'reasonable' protection, or even due diligence. Expropriation is illegal unless for a public purpose, non-discriminatory, in accord with due process of law, and accompanied by prompt and effective compensation. In some relatively early sources, arbitrariness is also evoked as a violation of the minimum standard, as well as inhuman and degrading treatment that would now be recognized as in violation of treaty-based human rights (arbitrary detention, torture, seizure, search or destruction of property without rule of law or due process).[16]

---

[12] *Diallo* (n 7) para 38.
[13] *Draft Articles on Diplomatic Protection with Commentaries*, YILC 2006, Vol II, Part Two, Article 1.
[14] *Avena and Other Mexican Nationals (Mex v US)* (Judgment) [2004] ICJ Rep 1, para 38 (emphasis added).
[15] See in this Commentary: Jarrod Hepburn, 'Denial of justice'.
[16] See Paparinskis (n 11) Ch 3 'Development of the International Minimum Standard (1940s)'.

17 The various elements set out above come into play in the efforts to codify the minimum standard, especially in the context of protection of economic activity and property at the beginning of the 1960s. While none of these individual efforts was successful on its own terms, they brought to light considerable common ground on the content of the minimum standard. At the same time, there was evident disagreement between developed countries and the global South, most notably on the standard of compensation for otherwise legal expropriation, and to some extent on the question of exhaustion of domestic remedies, the extent of deference to domestic legal and administrative authorities.

18 The 1961 Harvard Draft Convention on the Responsibility of States for Injury to the Economic Interests of Aliens (Harvard Draft)[17] included norms on detention and treatment under detention, due process rights, access to justice, prohibitions on the destruction of or harm to property, and expropriation. On the last, the Harvard Draft reflects the common recitation of customary international law that expropriation is illegal unless for a public purpose, non-discriminatory, in accord with due process of law, and accompanied by effective, prompt compensation reflective of fair market value. At the same time, the Harvard draft exempted from the compensation requirement takings in the exercise of the State's normal police powers, 'inter alia for the maintenance of public order, health or morality...'.

19 Contemporary to the Harvard draft are the revised draft ILC Articles on Responsibility of the State for Injuries caused in its Territory to the Person or Property of Aliens (revised ILC draft). The latter incorporates human rights norms. Article 1 provides: 'aliens enjoy the same rights and the same legal guarantees as nationals, but these rights and guarantees shall in no case be less than the human rights and fundamental freedoms recognized and defined in contemporary international instruments.'[18]

20 The revised ILC draft reflected the concerns of developing countries on expropriation and nationalization as an economic development strategy. It stipulated that 'in the case of nationalization or expropriation measures that are of a general nature and which are not directed against a particular person or against particular persons',[19] the host state would responsible only where the taking was discriminatory and/or not in the public interest.

21 The Abs-Shawcross draft Convention[20] was deliberated in the Organization for Economic Co-operation and Development (OECD) (with some consultative involvement of developing nations). The draft Convention contained a fair and equitable treatment (FET) obligation with language similar to that which would appear in many early era BITs. The compensation requirement for expropriation was expressed in terms of 'just and effective' and 'adequate' compensation. The use of the words 'just' and 'adequate' seems to reflect consideration of developing countries' concerns about the Hull Formula, i.e. the requirement to pay full market value compensation regardless of the country's economic needs and development policies.

---

[17] LB Sohn and RR Baxter, 'Responsibility of States for Injuries to the Economic Interests of Aliens: II. Draft Convention on the International Responsibility of States for Injuries to Aliens' (1961) 55(3) AJIL 545–584.
[18] 'Addendum: Responsibility of the State for Injuries caused in its territory to the person or property of aliens: Revised Draft', Sixth Report, YILC 1961, Vol 2, Part One, 1–54, UN Doc A/CN.4/134 and Add 1 (1961).
[19] ibid Article 9.2.
[20] H Abs and H Shawcross, 'Draft Convention on Investments Abroad' in 'The Proposed Convention to Protect Private Foreign Investment: A Round Table'" (1960) 1 J Pub L (presently Emory L J) 115–18.

C. Content and contours

In thinking about these three largely contemporaneous codification efforts together, one can 22 identify a core of sorts that clearly establishes State responsibility for arbitrary and discriminatory conduct toward aliens, including the taking of property in an arbitrary and discriminatory manner. Similarly, denial of justice and serious breaches of due process and rule of law more generally seem included albeit in somewhat different language in each codification effort.[21] The lack of general acceptance of the Hull Formula, and variations in approaches to the question of how or whether non-discriminatory, non-arbitrary takings in the public interest should be compensated is notable.

An area of common ground between the three drafts is that they all lack any reference to 23 subjective tests such as those in *Neer* and *ELSI* ('shocking', 'surprising' etc.). Second, while some of the provisions that appear to codify the minimum standard incorporate a notion of gravity (the ILC revised draft refers to 'manifest' injustice or arbitrariness), none imposes a condition that conduct be seen as outrageous or shocking in order to engage State responsibility. A third area of common ground is the obligation to fulfil certain kinds of commitments made by the host state to the alien. The Harvard draft prohibits 'arbitrary' violations of contracts and 'concessions', with an extensive definition of what is 'arbitrary' in Article 12. The Abs-Shawcross draft includes the obligation to 'ensure the observance of any undertakings, which it may have given in relation to investments made by nations of any other Party', Article 2. The ILC revised draft provides: 'the State is responsible for the non-performance of obligations stipulated in a contract entered into with an alien or in a concession granted to him, if the non-performance is not justified on grounds of public interest or of the economic necessity of the State, or [in the case of] denial of justice.'

D. The application of the MST in investment law

As Dumberry notes, only a minority of BITs and other international investment agreements 24 (IIAs) refer to the customary international law MST explicitly.[22] Instead, more typically, these instruments incorporate as conventional obligations elements of the MST, typically through provisions on Fair and Equitable Treatment (sometimes explicitly referring to Denial of Justice, sometimes not) and expropriation (usually adopting the Hull formula for compensation). Often 'Full Protection and Security' (FPS) is explicitly added to FET. In the case of FET and FPS there is no reason to assume, i.e. in the absence of specific language in the treaty, that these have broader or different coverage than the customary international law MST. Nor is the opposite assumption justified, namely, that the parties intended to limit FET and FPS to the MST.

With respect to police protection, the tribunal in *AAPL v Sri Lanka* noted: 'the addition of 25 words like "constant" or "full" to strengthen the required standards of protection could justifiably indicate the Parties' intention to require within their treat relationship a standard of "due diligence" higher than the "minimum standard" of general international law. But the nature of both the obligation and ensuing responsibility remains unchanged, since the

---

[21] See in this Commentary: Jarrod Hepburn, 'Denial of justice'.
[22] P Dumberry, *The Fair and Equitable Treatment Standard: A Guide to NAFTA Case Law on Article 1105* (Kluwer Law International 2013) Ch 1.

added words "constant" or "full" are by themselves not sufficient to establish that the Parties intended to transform their mutual obligation into a "strict liability".[23]

26 Some later tribunals employed 'due diligence' as a subjective standard unconnected to international law governing the particular kinds of actions or omissions of state actors (for instance, destruction by armed forces or parastatal militias of the investor's property). They have turned FPS into something more akin to an absolute liability regime, or de facto political risk insurance. The legitimacy issues here are not dissimilar to those that arise from tribunals reading regulatory stabilization into FET under the guiles of protection of the investor's 'expectations'.[24]

27 Where FET provisions do not explicitly refer to the MST, often ISDS tribunals have felt free to interpret these clauses as providing a level of protection beyond the customary international law MST. In these cases, the FET provision in the treaty is often described as 'autonomous'. In the *Certain Iranian Assets* case, the ICJ took the view that the MST could be ignored in cases where the FET provision in a treaty does not refer to it.[25] Justification for such an approach may be found in the notion that BITs and other IIAs have the aim (often stated in their preambles) of encouraging economic activity between the parties and creating a favourable environment for cross-border investment: thus, one would expect more fulsome protection than that contemplated in the customary international law of protection of aliens.

28 However, such teleological interpretation, while broadly compatible with the approach in Article 31 of the Vienna Convention on the Law of Treaties (VCLT), may be too simplistic.[26] The efforts at codification of the MST discussed above took into account, and were to some extent driven by, concerns with protection of economic activity and investments explicitly. But, in the ways outlined above, these initiatives did not simply jettison concern for state sovereignty, concerns of the global South about economic imperialism, or the legitimate role of states in regulating for the public interest. Moreover, Article 31 of the VCLT, while referring to the preamble of a treaty, and its object and purpose, also requires, according to its paragraph (3)(c), that the treaty interpreter take into account any relevant rules of international law applicable between the parties—and this would certainly include the customary international law MST, where interpreting the FET and FPS provisions of an IIA.

29 Thus, however the FET and/or FPS clause is drafted in the treaty, it cannot be read properly as simply autonomous from the MST *as a rule of custom*. In the *Philip Morris v Uruguay* award, the tribunal invoked Article 31(3)(c) VCLT to consider the State's police powers under the MST in order to interpret the BIT provision on expropriation. The

---

[23] *Asian Agric Prods Ltd v Republic of Sri Lanka*, ICSID Case No ARB/87/3 (15 June 1990) para 4, 4 ICSID Rep 296, para 50.
[24] See R Howse and AR Yacoub, 'Litigating Terror in The Sinai After The Egyptian Spring Revolution: Should States Be Liable to Foreign Investors for Failure to Prevent Terrorist Attacks?' (2022) 43 MichJIntlL 595.
[25] 'Article IV, paragraph 1, neither refers to the "customary minimum standard of treatment", nor employs other formulations sometimes associated with that standard, such as "required by international law". Accordingly, there is no need to examine the content of the customary minimum standard of treatment. The Court will focus on Article IV, paragraph 1, of the Treaty and apply it to the present case.' International Court of Justice, *Certain Iranian Assets (Iran v United States)*, Judgment, 30 March 2023, para 141 (not yet published in the ICJ Reports).
[26] cf M Waibel, 'International Investment Law and Treaty Interpretation' in R Hofmann and CJ Tams (eds), *International Investment Law and General International Law: From Clinical Isolation to Systemic Integration?* (Nomos 2011) 39.

tribunal noted that 'the police powers doctrine was propounded much earlier than its recognition by investment treaty decisions'.[27] The tribunal went as far back as the 1903 *Bischoff* case in the sources it cited to establish that customary international law allows the state the sovereign right to take regulatory action that mounts to a taking when exercising its police powers in a reasonable non-discriminatory manner without having to pay compensation. The tribunal noted: 'it is an accepted principle of customary international law that where economic injury results from a bona fide non-discriminatory regulation within the police power of the State, compensation is not required'.[28] It is notable that Judge Charlesworth, in her separate opinion in *Certain Iranian Assets*, approved of the *Phillip Morris* tribunal's use of the customary MST jurisprudence in the *interpretation* of treaty norms.[29]

As mentioned, some tribunals have taken their 'autonomous' readings of FET so far as to construct an obligation of regulatory stabilization, the notion that the expectations of the investor based on the legal and regulatory framework at the time the investment was made are protected by FET. This raises serious legitimacy issues from the perspective of democratic governance, at least where the expectations are not grounded (reasonable reliance) on specific commitments or undertakings to the investor. Thus, other tribunals have required evidence of representations or undertakings, especially ones made to induce the investment in the first place.

The difference in approach is illustrated by the *Charanne*[30] and *Eiser*[31] awards, respectively, under the Energy Charter Treaty, where the claimants were challenging Spain's measures altering the kind of level of subsidization in its incentive scheme for renewably generated electricity. In the NAFTA *Bilcon* award,[32] to be discussed further below, the tribunal majority accepted that some investor expectations were in fact protected under the customary international law MST, where the host state made specific statements indicated that the investment was generally suitable under its laws and policies and encouraging the investor in question to proceed. Apart from reliance interests arising from specific representations and undertakings, regulatory stabilization is clearly additive to the customary international law MST.

Determining whether treaty provisions in a BIT or other IIA reflect an intent by the parties to contract out of custom *inter se* poses a particular interpretive challenge. In *ELSI*, the ICJ Chamber opined: 'the Chamber finds itself unable to accept that an important principle of customary international law should be held to have been tacitly dispensed with, in the absence of any words making clear an intention to do so.'[33] In the *Bear Creek v Peru* case, the

---

[27] *Philip Morris Brands Sarl, Philip Morris Products S.A. and Abal Hermanos S.A. v Oriental Republic of Uruguay*, ICSID Case No. ARB/10/7, Award, 8 July 2016, para 292.
[28] ibid para 293.
[29] 'I note that international jurisprudence tends to recognize that the domestic regulator is vested with a measure of discretion in this connection. In the case of *Philip Morris v. Uruguay*, for example, the tribunal's finding that the impugned measures were adopted in good faith, directed at the legitimate public welfare aim of public health protection and capable of contributing to its achievement, was sufficient to defeat a claim of unlawful expropriation.' International Court of Justice, *Certain Iranian Assets (Iran v United States)*, Judgment of the Court, 30 March 2023, Separate Opinion of Judge Charlesworth, para 4 (not yet published in the ICJ Reports).
[30] *Charanne and Construction Investments v Spain*, SCC Case No V 062/2012, Award, 21 January 2016.
[31] *Eiser Infrastructure Limited and Energía Solar Luxembourg S.à r.l. v Kingdom of Spain*, ICSID Case No ARB/13/36, 4 May 2017.
[32] *Bilcon of Delaware et al v Government of Canada*, PCA Case No 2009-04, Jurisdiction and Liability, 17 March 2015.
[33] *ELSI* (n 10) para 50.

tribunal determined that 'in view of the very detailed provisions of the FTA regarding expropriation ... and regarding exceptions the interpretation of the FTA must lead to the conclusions that no other exceptions from general international law or otherwise can be considered applicable in this case. There is, thus, no need to enter into the discussion between the Parties regarding the jurisprudence concerning any police power exception for measures addressed to investments.'[34]

33 In fact, in Annex 812.1, cited by the tribunal, the parties had elaborated what is recognizable as their own version of police powers under the customary international law MST: 'Except in rare circumstances, such as when a measures or series of measures is so severe in the light of its purpose that it cannot be reasonably viewed as having been adopted and applied in good faith, non-discriminatory measures of a Party that are designed and applied to protect legitimate public welfare objectives, such as health, safety and the environment, do not constitute indirect expropriation.'[35]

E. The NAFTA: A turning point?

34 Article 1105 of the NAFTA links the content of the FET and FPS obligations to international law, without specifically referring to the MST, or custom. Thus, Article 1105(1) provides: '[e]ach Party shall accord to investments of investors of another Party treatment in accordance with international law, including fair and equitable treatment and full protection and security.' On its face, this provision incorporates norms of international law even beyond those associated with FET and FPS—note the expression 'including' that suggests the relevant international law encompasses FET and FPS but reaches beyond. This might extend, for example, to human rights norms or aspects of international economic law (eg the multilateral trading order General Agreement on Tariffs and Trade (GATT)/World Trade Organization (WTO)) that have not attained the status of custom but are to be found in treaties by which all three NAFTA parties are bound.

35 In an early NAFTA investment dispute, *Pope & Talbot v Canada*,[36] the tribunal held that the content of FET in Article 1105 incorporated fairness elements in contemporaneous or earlier BITs where the FET provisions were not explicitly linked either to international law in general or the MST in particular. Thus, the *Pope* tribunal sought to harmonize FET in the NAFTA with 'autonomous' FET clauses in other treaties. In other words, for the tribunal the relevant 'international law' benchmark was to be found in other bilateral agreements containing FET provisions that themselves do *not* reference international law. Among the doubtful features of this approach is that the BITs in question quite obviously did not give rise to norms of international binding on all the parties to NAFTA, unlike the case, for instance, of the WTO Agreements, or the UN Covenant on Civil and Political Rights, to name two kinds of multilateral treaties that might be relevant to the standards of treatment with respect to investors and investments.

---

[34] *Bear Creek Mining v Peru*, ICSID Case No. ARB/14/21, Award, 30 November 2017, paras 473–74.
[35] Free Trade Agreement between Canada and the Republic of Peru (2008), Annex 812.1.
[36] *Pope & Talbot v Canada*, UNCITRAL, Final Merits Award, 10 April 2001.

I. The NAFTA Commission interpretation

In reaction to the *Pope* tribunal's apparent conversion of Article 1105 into an 'autonomous' FET clause, Canada obtained the agreement of the other NAFTA parties to an authoritative interpretation that Article 1105 did not require 'treatment in addition to or beyond that which is required by the customary international law minimum standard of treatment' and, moreover, that 'a determination that there has been a breach of another provisions of the NAFTA, or a separate international agreement, does not establish there has been a breach of Article 1105(1)'.[37]

The above interpretation was issued before the *Pope & Talbot* arbitration was concluded, i.e. prior to the damages phase.

Complicated issues arose as to whether its retroactive application would be appropriate, perhaps leading to a modification of the award on the merits. The interpretation was issued by the NAFTA partners in the guise of the NAFTA Commission, which is provided under the NAFTA with authority to issue binding interpretations but not to agree amendments (which require other procedures). Pairing down the reference to international law, without qualification, in the text of Article 1105 to the customary international law MST arguably went beyond the limits of interpretation, subtracting from the content of the obligations in the treaty text. According to Canada, moreover, the interpretation had the effect of precluding the use of any other international law sources to elaborate the obligations in Article 1105, which would at the limit involve displacing Article 31(3)(c) VCLT. Even if the borderline between 'interpretation' and 'amendment' is not entirely stable or clear, it is certainly not plausible that the NAFTA parties would have given themselves authority, through an *interpretation*, to contract out of customary rules of treaty interpretation as reflected in Article 31 VCLT.

The only real basis for regarding the NAFTA Commission statement on Article 1105 as legitimately an exercise of the Commission's power to make authoritative interpretation is the heading of Article 1105 as a whole, which is 'Minimum Standard of Treatment'. Yet the use of the expression 'Minimum Standard of Treatment' here in the heading may simply be a means of setting off the obligation in Article 1105 from the National Treatment and most-favoured-nation (MFN) (non-discrimination) obligation elsewhere in Chapter 11 of the NAFTA. The concept of 'minimum standard' as discussed earlier in this contribution is that of a level of treatment required by international law regardless of whether the alien is being treated as well as similarly situated nationals (non-discrimination).

The idea of an absolute minimum contrasts with relative standards of treatment, those of non-discrimination, where the benchmark for the required treatment is how nationals, or in the case of MFN, aliens of a different nationality, are treated. Minimum here does not mean *minimal*. It simply reflects the intention that, while the relative standards of non-discrimination may well require treatment that *exceeds* international standards, depending on how others are being treated (nationals, aliens of a different nationality), the international

---

[37] Notes of Interpretation of Certain Chapter 11 Provisions (NAFTA Free Trade Commission, 31 July 2001), <https://perma.cc/FU9G-HXCB> accessed 23 October 2023. See A Roberts, 'Power and Persuasion in Investment Treaty Interpretation: The Dual Role of States' (2010) 104 AJIL 179.

standards still apply even where treatment *below* those standards would not violate non-discrimination obligations—eg a situation where the treatment of both the alien *and* the host country's nationals does not meet international standards. It is exactly this that is captured by the notion of a 'minimum' standard.

40 Further, the fact that the concept of an international law MST emerged in the context of diplomatic protection of aliens does not justify identifying its substantive content or scope with the *original customary law* of diplomatic protection. All relevant international standards that states must adhere to regardless of their domestic legal systems fall under the concept of the international law minimum standard. Indeed, in *Diallo*, as we have seen, the ICJ observed that diplomatic protection now encompasses treaty-based international human rights standards binding on the host state.

II. The *Pope* tribunal's response to the NAFTA Commission 1105 interpretation

41 In *obiter dicta*,[38] the *Pope* tribunal suggested it was inclined to the view that the NAFTA Commission statement was an improper attempt at amendment of NAFTA in the guise of an interpretation. In its *ratio*, however, the tribunal managed to avoid relying on that point of view, and indeed to avoid the question of retroactivity altogether. The *Pope* arbitrators did this by holding that the interpretation would not affect their original findings on Article 1105 in the award on merits, since the customary international law standard of treatment *had itself evolved* to merge with the 'additive' standard that the tribunal had articulated in its original merits award. The *Pope* tribunal regarded the proliferation of BITs with autonomous FET clauses as evidence of evolving custom, as well tribunal rulings impugning conduct that would not necessarily be shocking or egregious under the *Neer* standard.

42 This might seem like a dubious artifice to avoid the intended effect of the NAFTA Commission interpretation. As Campbell McLachlan notes: 'Standard approaches to the formation of custom would give a largely negative account of the potential contribution of bilateral treaties.' McLachlan cites the Report of the International Law Association Committee on the Formation of Customary (General) International Law. In the case of BITs, the Report notes, to establish that they are reflective of evolved custom would require one to 'demonstrate a widespread acceptance of the rules set out in these treaties outside of the treaty framework'.[39]

43 A further difficulty in resorting to BITs as evidence of expanded custom is that in a significant range of more recent treaties FET clauses or related provisions of the treaty have limited or restricted the content of FET in various ways. This has indeed been in response to expansive readings of the earlier 'autonomous' clauses. In some instances, discussed later in this entry, the drafters abandoned FET altogether, or replaced it by an exhaustive listing of the *content* of FET in the treaty text.

---

[38] *Pope & Talbot, Inc v Canada*, UNCITRAL, Award in Respect of Damages, 31 May 2002.
[39] C McLachlan, 'Investment Treaties and General International law' (2008) 57(2) ICLQ 361, 392.

III. *Neer* sightedness and the MST: *Glamis Gold*

44 The idea of an evolving customary international law MST has been taken up by numerous NAFTA tribunals subsequent to *Pope*. This does not mean, however, that these tribunals have tended to equate evolved custom with the most expansive interpretations of 'autonomous' FET clauses in BITs. On the other hand, a few tribunals, beginning with *Glamis Gold*,[40] agreed with the view presented by Canada in *Pope*, and held that the customary international law MST, within the meaning of the NAFTA Commission interpretation, has apparently not evolved since *Neer*.

45 The basic conceit is that the claimant has not born the burden to prove through State practice and *opinio juris* the evolution of a different or more expansive customary international standard than that in *Neer*. Ironically, the so-called '*Neer* standard' is a bare declaration by the tribunal of what is required for conduct to constitute an 'international delinquency' under the traditional customary law of diplomatic protection. In *Neer*, there was no analysis of State practice or *opinio juris*. To the contrary, well prior to the rise of BITs and IIAs with FET clauses there are clear indications that a threshold of shocking or egregious conduct was never really adopted as a requirement for State responsibility with respect to the treatment of aliens. For instance, as noted above, *none* of the codification exercises in the 1960s adopts such a threshold for 'international delinquency'.

46 In *Glamis*, the tribunal further muddied the waters by suggesting that, over time, what was shocking and outrageous to a reasonable objective person—or to a judicial sensibility— could itself evolve. This provides even greater discretion to arbitrators than Canada's initial conception of *Neer* as reflecting frozen State practice as to what *kind* of conduct is wrongful under the customary international law MST.

IV. *Bilcon v Canada*: An example of the post-*Glamis* debate over the MST

47 The Bilcon merits award is an example of the direction that the debate over Glamis Gold and the role of Neer has taken in the NAFTA jurisprudence.[41] Two of the three arbitrators, Bruno Simma and Donald McRae, are eminent public international lawyers. The majority opinion (Simma and the third arbitrator, Canadian public law scholar Bryan Schwartz) and the dissent by McRae join issue on the question of the threshold of gravity required to justify international responsibility for a departure from the domestic rule of law. Common ground between the majority and the dissent is that the content of the MST was not frozen with Neer or that era's jurisprudence on diplomatic protection of aliens. Indeed, both the majority and the dissent appear to endorse the formulation of the MST in the *Waste Management* Award:

'the [MST] of fair and equitable treatment is infringed by conduct attributable to the State and harmful to the claimant if the conduct is arbitrary, grossly unfair, unjust or idiosyncratic, is discriminatory and exposes the claimant to sectional or racial prejudice, or involves a lack of due process leading to an outcome which offends judicial propriety-as might be the case

---

[40] *Glamis Gold, Ltd v United States of America*, UNCITRAL (NAFTA), Award, 8 June 2009.
[41] *Bilcon v Government of Canada*, UNCITRAL, Jurisdiction and Liability, 17 March 2015, paras 98–99.

with a manifest failure of natural justice in judicial proceedings or a complete lack of transparency and candor in an administration process.'

48 For the majority there are systemic (Calvo-type) legitimacy considerations that justify a deferential approach to domestic legal and regulatory processes:

> The Tribunal agrees that international responsibility and dispute resolution, in the investor context, is not supposed to be the continuation of domestic politics and litigation by other means. Modern regulatory and social welfare states tackle complex problems. Not all situations can be addressed in advance by the laws that are enacted. Room must be left for judgment to be used to interpret legal standards and apply them to the facts… The imprudent exercise of discretion or even outright mistakes do not, as a rule, lead to a breach of the international minimum standard [in the absence of bad faith].[42]

49 Additionally, the tribunal noted: 'domestic authorities may also enjoy distinctive kinds of legitimacy, such as being elected or accountable to elective authorities.'[43] Nevertheless, for the majority, deference is not absolute. There can be departures from appropriate standards of justice or due process in the domestic legal and administrative system that are sufficiently grave or severe to justify an arbitral tribunal holding the state responsible as in violation of the customary international law MST—these are denoted by qualifiers such as 'grossly' and 'complete lack of' in the *Waste Management* award.

50 For McRae, the dissenting arbitrator, there is an additional element of deference[44]: a departure from, or failure to apply, domestic legal standards cannot constitute a violation of the customary international law MST no matter how serious or egregious, at least provided that there remains some kind of recourse in the domestic legal system to correct the errors or misconduct in question. This seems the equivalent of writing into the NAFTA a requirement of exhaustion of local remedies. Of course, such a requirement continues to exist in diplomatic protection, as illustrated by the *Diallo* decision. In fact, in the successor agreement to NAFTA, the USMCA, the NAFTA parties introduced a time-limited (thirty months) rule of exhaustion of local remedies before bringing an ISDS claim.

V. The USMCA revision of NAFTA: The disappearance of *Neer*

51 While in *Bilcon*, despite this divergence on deference between the majority and dissent, the entire tribunal rejected the *Neer* standard as the appropriate contemporary benchmark for the MST. In the USMCA revision of NAFTA the insistence by Canadian (and US) officials on the correctness of *Neer* was dealt a further blow. In the end, the States parties made no reference to it in the USMCA articulation of customary international law. To the contrary, Annex 14-A of the USMCA, which sets out, the parties' understanding of customary international law that determines the MST, refers to the applicability of 'all customary international law principles that protect the investments of aliens'.

52 As opposed to limiting custom to that which was formed or applied in the early twentieth century era of diplomatic protection (*Neer*), this provision opens up the content of the

---

[42] ibid para 437.
[43] ibid para 439.
[44] See generally on the concept of deference in international adjudication, the excellent work E Shirlow, *Judging at the Interface: Deference to State Decision-Making Authority in International Adjudication* (CUP 2001).

customary international law MST to all international norms that currently have the status of custom, and are relevant to the protection of aliens in the investment context. This would include, arguably, at least some human rights norms. At the same time, in the USMCA the parties affirmed that 'customary international law results from a general and consistent practice of states that they follow from a sense of legal obligation'. While here stating how customary norms *originate*—'results from'—this formulation is far from fully endorsing the *Glamis Gold* nostrum that in each and every case it is necessary to retrace historically the State practice and *opinio juris* out of which the relevant customary principles have emerged, much less that there is a burden of proof on the claimant.

F. Conclusion: The Emerging predominance of treaty-based international standards for the treatment of aliens

Canada, in its response to the merits award in *Pope*, led the charge as it were in cutting FET down to size by circumscribing it as the customary international law MST, which brings to life this concept in the investment context. By contrast, as exemplified by *Diallo* in the evolution of diplomatic protection, State responsibility for the treatment of aliens was increasingly based on conventional law, in particular human rights and related (consular rights) conventions.

Significantly, in much of its most recent investment treaty practice, Canada has reversed course and taken the approach of stating exhaustively in the treaty text itself the content of FET.[45]

This is clearly reflected in the EU–Canada Comprehensive Economic and Trade Agreement (CETA),[46] where Canada and the EU made no use of the concept of a customary international law MST in their articulation of FET but rather defined its content thus:

> A Party breaches the obligation of fair and equitable treatment … if a measure or series of measures constitutes: denial of justice in criminal, civil or administrative proceedings; fundamental breach of due process, including a fundamental breach of transparency, in judicial and administrative proceedings; manifest arbitrariness, targeted discrimination on manifestly wrongly grounds, such as gender, race or religious belief; abusive treatment of investors, such as coercion, duress and harassment (…).

There is moreover a provision that *requires* regular review of this content by the CETA parties, reflecting a strongly evolutionary concept of FET.

In Canada's 2021 model Foreign Investment Protection Agreement (FIPA)[47] the customary international law MST is still mentioned but there is an exhaustive list that defines the content of FET, regardless of the MST:

> (a) denial of justice in criminal, civil, or administrative proceedings; (b) fundamental breach of due process in judicial and administrative proceedings; (c) manifest arbitrariness;

---

[45] This may be a reflection of a recent trend of states attempting to guard against arbitrator discretion that threatens regulatory autonomy through attempt to draft more precise and bounded treaty norms around general concepts like FET, or to substitute for them. See, eg, C Henckels, 'Protecting Regulatory Autonomy through Greater Precision in Investment Treaties: The TPP, CETA, and TTIP' (2016) 19 JIEL 27 and W Alschner, *Investment Arbitration and State Driven Reform: New Treaties, Old Outcomes* (OUP 2022).
[46] Comprehensive Trade and Economic Agreement between Canada and the European Union (2016).
[47] Government of Canada, 'Canada's 2021 Investment Protection and Promotion Agreement (FIPA) Model' <https://www.international.gc.ca/trade-commerce/trade-agreements-accords-commerciaux/agr-acc/fipa-apie/index.aspx?lang=eng> accessed 23 October 2023.

(d) targeted discrimination on manifestly wrongful grounds such as gender, race, or religious beliefs; (e) abusive treatment of investors, such as physical coercion, duress, and harassment; or (f) a failure to provide full protection and security.

58 It is evident that, in this emerging treaty-based approach to defining international standards for treatment of investors and investments, the normative content overlaps considerably with that of contemporary regional and multilateral human rights instruments. To this extent, the Calvo-type concerns about an absolute standard of protection for aliens that the host state's own states nationals do not enjoy should be lessened. Because under human rights instruments with parallel or overlapping norms, states are internationally responsible for breaches toward their own nationals as well as aliens. This leaves the question, raised by the opinion of dissenting arbitrator Professor McRae in *Bilcon*, of why, if exhaustion of local remedies remains the rule in the context of diplomatic protection (and largely so in human rights) it should also not be a more common practice in the context of investment agreements.

Selected literature

Dumberry P, *The Fair and Equitable Treatment Standard: A Guide to NAFTA Case Law on Article 1105* (Kluwer Law International 2013).

McLachlan C, 'Investment Treaties and General International law' (2008) 57(2) ICLQ 361.

Paparinskis M, *The Minimum Standard and Fair and Equitable Treatment* (OUP 2013).

Shirlow E, *Judging at the Interface: Deference to State Decision-Making Authority in International Adjudication* (CUP 2001).

Sohn LB and Baxter RR, 'Responsibility of States for Injuries to the Economic Interests of Aliens: II. Draft Convention on the International Responsibility of States for Injuries to Aliens' (1961) 55 (3) AJIL 545–584.

Waibel M, 'International Investment Law and Treaty Interpretation' in Hofmann R and Tams CJ (eds), *International Investment Law and General International Law: From Clinical Isolation to Systemic Integration?* (Nomos 2011).

Selected decisions

Bilcon of Delaware et al v Government of Canada, Jurisdiction and Liability, PCA Case No 2009-04 (17 March 2015).

Bilcon v Government of Canada, UNCITRAL, Jurisdiction and Liability (17 March 2015).

Case Concerning Ahmadou Sadio Diallo (Republic of Guinea v Democratic Republic of the Congo) Judgment on compensation, 19 June 2012.

Elettronica Sicula S.p.A. (ELSI) (US v Italy) [1989] ICJ Rep 15.

Pope & Talbot v Canada, UNCITRAL, Final Merits Award (10 April 2001).

Pope & Talbot, Inc v Canada, UNCITRAL, Award in Respect of Damages (31 May 2002).

Cross-cutting procedural powers of international courts and tribunals

Cameron Miles

A. Introduction	1	II. Domestic law	48
B. Jurisdiction and admissibility	4	E. Rules of evidence	52
I. Jurisdiction *pro tem*	10	I. Burden of proof	53
II. Incidental jurisdiction	14	II. Standard of proof	56
III. Existence of a dispute and negotiation requirements	19	F. Counterclaims	59
		G. Costs	66
IV. Alternative forum for settlement of the dispute	25	H. Judgments and awards	69
		I. Res judicata	71
V. Extinctive prescription	29	II. Interpretation	77
VI. The *Monetary Gold* principle	32	III. Revision	83
C. Provisional measures	36	I. Conclusion	91
D. Applicable law	41		
I. Precedent	43		

A. Introduction

International procedure does not always fit easily within general international law. Although a treaty provision or procedural rule may grant an international court or tribunal (ICT) the power to do something, articulation and application of that power are left to the ICT itself. These questions are not governed by general international law (in the sense of being rooted firmly in the sources of international law) but by the scope of the parties' consent to dispute settlement. Consent is the source of international jurisdiction as a matter of general international law[1] and international investment law[2] (IIL).

But that is not to say that the scope of the parties' consent is immediately obvious. On one level, they have consented to the exercise of the *express* procedural powers set out in an ICT's constitutive instrument (eg the ICJ Statute,[3] the ICSID Convention,[4] or the applicable

---

[1] *Status of the Eastern Carelia* (Advisory Opinion) PCIJ Series B No 5, 27.
[2] *ST-AD GmbH v Bulgaria*, PCA Case No 2011-06, Jurisdiction, 18 July 2013, paras 336–37.
[3] Statute of the International Court of Justice, 24 October 1945, 33 UNTS 993.
[4] Convention on the Settlement of Investment Disputes between States and Nationals of Other States, 18 March 1965, 575 UNTS 159.

investment treaty) or procedural rules (eg the ICJ Rules,[5] the ICSID Rules,[6] the ICSID Additional Facility Rules,[7] or the 1976 or 2010 UNCITRAL Rules[8]). But on another level, they have consented to a dispute settlement process designed to produce an effective outcome. This includes the exercise of those *inherent* powers necessary for an ICT to function as such—even where those powers have not been spelled out in the relevant constitutive or procedural instruments. These will be determined by the character of the ICT. IIL tribunals are usually given jurisdiction to ascertain their inherent powers expressly.[9]

3 Despite their formal separation, ICTs confronted with the same procedural problems will often talk to each other to develop solutions. This process of cross-fertilization produced a 'common law of international adjudication'.[10] This entry introduces the reader to some of the procedural institutions of that common law—driven by the practice of the Permanent Court of International Justice (PCIJ) and the International Court of Justice (ICJ)—and compares their application in IIL. It addresses them in the order in which they would appear in the course of an international dispute, starting with preliminary objections and ending with *res judicata* and its implications.

B. Jurisdiction and admissibility

4 All ICTs have the inherent power to determine the scope of their jurisdiction and the circumstances of its exercise: *compétence de la competence*. This has been recognized since the nineteenth century,[11] and is stated in constitutive and procedural instruments.[12] If a respondent objects to the jurisdiction of an ICT, or the admissibility of a claim or issue, that objection will be decided by the ICT using its *compétence de la compétence*.

5 Jurisdiction and admissibility are the main techniques by which ICTs structure and police their adjudicative functions. The distinction between the two concepts is notoriously slippery, but at a high level the difference is clear enough: jurisdiction refers to the *scope* of the ICT's adjudicative power, admissibility to its *exercise*.[13]

6 As jurisdiction is rooted in party consent, its parameters are governed by the instrument(s) by which the parties agree to settle their dispute. For the ICJ, this is set out in Articles 36(1) and (2) of its Statute, which allow seisin of the Court in a variety of ways. Conversely, the jurisdictional foundation of an IIL tribunal is relatively consistent, comprising the dispute settlement clause of a bilateral or multilateral investment treaty[14] (respectively, BIT or MIT) combined as required with Article 25 of the ICSID Convention. But the overarching

---

[5] Rules of Court, 14 April 1978.
[6] ICSID Arbitration Rules, 1 July 2022.
[7] Rules Governing the Additional Facility for the Administration of Proceedings by the Secretariat of the International Centre for Settlement of Investment Disputes: Schedule C—Arbitration Rules, 10 April 2006.
[8] UNCITRAL Arbitration Rules, 15 December 1976, revised 6 December 2010.
[9] ICSID Convention, Article 44; 1976 UNCITRAL Rules, Article 15(1); 2010 UNCITRAL Rules, Article 17(1).
[10] C Brown, *A Common Law of International Adjudication* (OUP 2007) 4–6 (hereafter Brown, *Common Law*).
[11] See, eg, *Alabama Claims (US/GB)* (1871) XXIX RIAA 125, 129; *Rio Grande Irrigation and Land Company Ltd (GB) v US* (1923) 6 RIAA 131, 135–36.
[12] See, eg, ICJ Statute, Article 36(6); ICSID Convention, Article 41(1); 1976 UNCITRAL Rules, Article 21(1); 2010 UNCITRAL Rules, Article 23(1).
[13] Z Douglas, *The International Law of Investment Claims* (CUP 2009) 301–12 (hereafter Douglas, *Investment Claims*).
[14] Also possible is jurisdiction by investment contract, investment legislation or *forum prorogatum*.

principle is the same: the dispute settlement clause must be opposable between the claimant and the respondent, and the former must meet any preconditions to arbitration set out therein. The claimant must also meet the requirements of Article 25.

Admissibility is more instrumentalist. Rather than focusing on the ICT, it aims at a claim or counterclaim so as 'to allow the translation of general judicial policies relating to justice, fairness, legality, legitimacy and effectiveness to specific cases'.[15] As such, it constitutes 'a legally appropriate method to decline jurisdiction'.[16] For this reason, objections to admissibility are ordinarily not grounded in an ICT's constituent instrument, and the ICT will have more control over whether to allow or refuse the objection.

Early decisions doubted whether admissibility could be transposed to the IIL context. In *Methanex v US*, a tribunal operating under the North American Free Trade Agreement[17] (NAFTA) held that the 1976 United Nations Commission on International Trade Law (UNCITRAL) Rules did not allow it to rule on admissibility objections and that no inherent power to that effect could be inferred.[18] Under this approach, admissibility objections were elided with the merits. But tribunals today accept admissibility as a valid category of preliminary objection.[19]

The distinction between jurisdiction and admissibility is also of practical importance. An ICT has an obligation to satisfy itself of its jurisdiction, irrespective of whether any objection is made.[20] By contrast, admissibility objections may be waived and defects, in certain cases, remedied post-seisin.[21] Furthermore, the ICT must address the question of its jurisdiction first and if it finds it lacking, take the matter no further.[22] This distinction has additional importance in the IIL context, where a tribunal's decisions on jurisdiction—but not admissibility—can be reviewed by a supervisory body.[23]

I. Jurisdiction *pro tem*

The ICJ Statute includes no mechanism for the summary dismissal of claims that are *ex facie* bad, in that they lack a foundation in the law that the Court must apply. The ICJ's response to this has been to develop an analogue that assesses its jurisdiction over the substantive dispute *pro tem*. The modern test was developed in *Oil Platforms*. Iran alleged that the destruction by

---

[15] Y Shany, 'Jurisdiction and Admissibility' in CPR Romano, KJ Alter and Y Shany (eds), *The Oxford Handbook of International Adjudication* (OUP 2014) 779, 804. Further: *Oil Platforms (Iran v US)*, Judgment [2003] ICJ Rep 161, para 29 (hereafter *Oil Platforms*, Judgment).
[16] Y Shany, *Jurisdiction and Admissibility before International Courts* (CUP 2016) 52.
[17] North American Free Trade Agreement, 17 December 1992, 32 ILM 289, Ch 11.
[18] *Methanex Corporation v US*, UNCITRAL/NAFTA, Partial Award, 7 August 2002, paras 123–26. See also *CMS Gas Transmission Company v Argentina*, ICSID Case No ARB/01/8, Jurisdiction, 17 July 2003, para 41.
[19] See, eg, *Orascom TMT Investments Sàrl v Algeria*, ICSID Case No ARB/12/35, Annulment, 17 September 2020, para 254; *Mathias Kruck & Ors v Spain*, ICSID Case No ARB/15/23, Jurisdiction and Admissibility, 19 April 2021, para 192. But cf *Nissan Motor Co Ltd v India*, PCA Case No 2017-37, Jurisdiction, 29 April 2019, para 275 (hereafter *Nissan v India*, Jurisdiction).
[20] *Jurisdiction of the ICAO Council (India v Pakistan)*, Judgment [1972] ICJ Rep 46, para 13; *Jürgen Wirtgen & Ors v Czech Republic*, PCA Case No 2014-03, Award, 11 October 2017, para 250.
[21] *SGS Société Générale de Surveillance SA v Philippines*, ICSID Case No ARB/02/6, Jurisdiction, 29 January 2004, paras 157, 174–76 (hereafter *SGS v Philippines*, Jurisdiction).
[22] *Application of the Convention on the Prevention and Punishment of the Crime of Genocide (Croatia v Serbia)* (Preliminary Objections) [2008] ICJ Rep 412, para 120 (hereafter *Croatian Genocide*, Preliminary Objections).
[23] *PAO Tatneft v Ukraine* [2018] 1 WLR 5947, paras 82–102. See also *Swissbourgh Diamond Mines (Pty) Limited & Ors v Lesotho* [2019] 1 SLR 263, paras 205–09.

the United States of Iranian oil production facilities in the Persian Gulf breached the Treaty of Amity[24] between the two states. The United States objected to the Court's jurisdiction on the basis that Iran's claim was not a dispute as to the 'interpretation or application' of the Treaty, as required by Article XXI(2). The Court held that to determine this objection, it needed to:

> [A]scertain whether the violations of the Treaty [...] pleaded by Iran do or do not fall within the provisions of the Treaty and whether, as a consequence, the dispute is one which the Court has jurisdiction *ratione materiae* to entertain, pursuant to Article XXI, paragraph 2.[25]

11 Judge Higgins' separate opinion elaborated:

> The only way in which, in the present case, it can be determined whether the claims of Iran are sufficiently plausibly based upon the [Treaty] is to accept *pro tem* the facts as alleged by Iran to be true and in that light to interpret Articles I, IV and X for jurisdictional purposes—that is to say, to see if on the basis of Iran's claims of fact there could occur a violation of one or more of them.[26]

12 The *pro tem* test allows the ICJ to exclude hopeless cases without engaging with the facts or deciding legally controversial questions. Some commentators argue that its obduracy has led to inconsistent application,[27] advocating a return to the pre-*Oil Platforms* position.[28]

13 Given the extent to which their remit revolves around interpretation and application of treaties, IIL tribunals have adopted the ICJ's formulation of jurisdiction *pro tem*. The test's utility has, however, been reduced as advances in treaty drafting[29] and procedural rules[30] have provided bespoke tools to deal with ill-founded claims. Nevertheless, jurisdiction *pro tem* is frequently invoked[31] and supplemented by discussion of Judge Higgins' separate opinion.[32] IIL tribunals have been careful to keep the test within its proper limits.[33]

---

[24] Treaty of Amity, Economic Relations and Consular Rights, 15 August 1955, 24 UNTS 93.
[25] *Oil Platforms (Iran v US)* (Preliminary Objection) [1996] ICJ Rep 803, para 13 (hereafter *Oil Platforms*, Preliminary Objection).
[26] *Oil Platforms*, Preliminary Objection (n 25) paras 32–33 (Separate Opinion of Judge Higgins).
[27] M Dimetto, '"To Fall, or Not to Fall, That Is the (Preliminary) Question": Disputes, Compromissory Clauses and Swinging Jurisdictional Tests at the ICJ' (2022) 21 LPICT 5, 26–34.
[28] See, eg, *Mavrommatis Palestine Concessions (Greece v GB)*, Judgment (1925) PCIJ Series A No 2, 16, 23–29 (hereafter *Mavrommatis Palestine Concessions*, Judgment); *Ambatielos (Greece v UK)*, Judgment [1953] ICJ Rep 10, paras 18–19.
[29] Most notably the procedure set out in (*inter alia*) the 2012 US Model BIT, Article 28(4): L Caplan and J Sharpe, 'United States' in C Brown (ed), *Commentaries on Selected Model Investment Treaties* (OUP 2013) 755, 834–35. On the scope of the procedure, see *The Renco Group Inc v Peru (I)*, ICSID Case No UNCT/13/1, Preliminary Objections (18 December 2014) paras 165–257.
[30] Most notably the procedure in the ICSID Rules, Rule 41 (Rule 41(5) in the previous edition of the ICSID Rules): M Potestà, 'Preliminary Objections to Dismiss Claims that are Manifestly Without Legal Merit under Rule 41(5) of the ICSID Arbitration Rules' in C Baltag (ed), *ICSID Convention after 50 Years: Unsettled Issues* (Kluwer 2016) 249. On the scope of the procedure, see *Trans-Global Petroleum Inc v Jordan*, ICSID Case No ARB/07/25, Rule 41(5), 12 May 2008, paras 72–105.
[31] For a summary of the decisions, see *Resolute Forest Products Inc v Canada*, PCA Case No 2016-13, Jurisdiction and Admissibility, 30 January 2018, paras 298–311.
[32] *AES Solar & Ors (PV Investors) v Spain*, PCA Case No 2012-14, Jurisdiction, 14 October 2014, para 230.
[33] *Casinos Austria International GmbH & Casinos Austria Aktiengesellschaft v Argentina*, ICSID Case No ARB/14/32, Jurisdiction, 29 June 2018, paras 213, 262.

II. Incidental jurisdiction

Related to the concept of jurisdiction *pro tem*—which is concerned with the 'core' jurisdiction *ratione materiae* of an ICT—is incidental jurisdiction. An ICT will usually be authorized to address some legal issues, but not others. But to answer an authorized question, an ICT will often need to consider matters external to that mandate. Those may be dealt with as part of its incidental jurisdiction.

Under the orthodox approach to incidental jurisdiction, the jurisdiction is engaged only where determination of an external issue is necessarily antecedent to a question within an ICT's jurisdiction,[34] unless otherwise excluded.[35] In *Certain German Interests*, Germany challenged certain Polish laws under the Convention concerning Upper Silesia.[36] Those laws invoked Article 256 of the Treaty of Versailles,[37] which was referred to in the Convention. Poland protested that interpretation of the Treaty of Versailles was beyond the scope of the Court's jurisdiction. The PCIJ disagreed:

> It is true that the application of the Convention is hardly possible without giving an interpretation of Article 256 of the Treaty of Versailles […]. But these matters then constitute merely questions preliminary or incidental to the application of the Convention. Now the interpretation of other international agreements is indisputably within the competence of the Court if such interpretation must be regarded as incidental to a decision on a point in regard to which it does have jurisdiction […][38]

Incidental jurisdiction in the interstate context was consistent until tribunals operating under Annex VII of the UN Convention on the Law of the Sea[39] (UNCLOS) began to expand its parameters. For those tribunals, whether an external issue was within their jurisdiction was determined by 'characterisation' of the dispute and assessment of its relative 'weight', viz. whether the dispute was concerned primarily with the interpretation or application of UNCLOS or the external issue. The former was deemed to be within the tribunal's jurisdiction, the latter outside it.[40] Under this approach, the external issue was fair game if answering it gave a 'complete' answer to a dispute within jurisdiction, even if the external issue arose only after those issues within that jurisdiction had been resolved.[41] The ICJ has not adopted a similar approach and has confined itself to considering whether the claimant's claims concern interpretation or application of the treaty on which its jurisdiction is founded.[42]

---

[34] *Mavrommatis Palestine Concessions*, Judgment (n 28) 28.
[35] *Aegean Sea Continental Shelf (Greece v Turkey)*, Judgment [1978] ICJ Rep 3, para 83.
[36] German–Polish Convention concerning Upper Silesia, 15 May 1922, 1922 *Reichsgesetzblatt* II.
[37] Treaty of Versailles, 28 June 1919, 225 CTS 188.
[38] *Certain German Interests in Polish Upper Silesia (Germany v Poland)*, Preliminary Objections (1925) PCIJ Ser A No 6, 18 (hereafter *Certain German Interests*, Preliminary Objections). Further: B Cheng, *General Principles of Law as Applied by International Courts and Tribunals* (reissue, CUP 1994) 266–67 (hereafter Cheng, *General Principles*).
[39] United Nations Convention on the Law of the Sea, 10 December 1982, 1833 UNTS 3.
[40] *Chagos Marine Protected Area Arbitration (Mauritius v UK)*, Award (2015) XXXI RIAA 359, paras 207–12, 229–30; *South China Sea Arbitration (Philippines v China)*, Jurisdiction and Admissibility (2015) XXXIII RIAA 1, paras 150–53 (hereafter *South China Sea*, Jurisdiction and Admissibility); *Coastal State Rights in the Black Sea, Sea of Azov and Kerch Strait (Ukraine v Russia)*, Preliminary Objections (2020) 191 ILR 1, paras 151–166, 191–197 (hereafter *Coastal State Rights*, Preliminary Objections); *The 'Enrica Lexie' Incident (Italy v India)*, Award (2020) 115 ILM 185, paras 231–44, 808, 1094.B.2.
[41] This approach has been criticized as unprincipled: C Harris, 'Claims with an Ulterior Purpose: Characterising Disputes Concerning the "Interpretation or Application" of a Treaty' (2019) 18 LPICT 279, 286–98.
[42] *Question of the Delimitation of the Continental Shelf Between Nicaragua and Colombia Beyond 200 Nautical Miles from the Nicaraguan Coast (Nicaragua v Colombia)*, Preliminary Objections [2016] ICJ Rep 100, para 114

17 In IIL, the orthodox approach to incidental jurisdiction has prevailed for those tribunals whose jurisdiction *ratione materiae* is confined to disputes arising out of a respondent's breach of an investment treaty.[43] Nevertheless, those tribunals will engage their incidental jurisdiction in every case. This is because there is no international law of property,[44] such that determination of whether the claimant owns an asset capable of constituting an investment requires application of the respondent's property law[45]—outside the terms of the investment treaty. The same analysis may be relevant to substantive questions of treaty breach, eg expropriation of domestic property[46] or violation of an observance of obligations clause.[47]

18 Incidental jurisdiction also arises when considering countermeasures in an IIL context. In *Archer Daniels v Mexico*, a tribunal was required to consider Mexico's defence that its imposition of tariffs on US-manufactured soft drinks was a lawful countermeasure. Resolution of that defence would have required the tribunal to determine whether the United States had breached provisions of NAFTA outside its jurisdiction under NAFTA Article 1116. The tribunal held that it had no jurisdiction to decide whether the United States had committed a wrongful act that justified a countermeasure.[48] But its analysis elided the US's claims before the tribunal with Mexico's defence. Given that former's claims concerned the interpretation and application of instruments over which the tribunal had jurisdiction, the tribunal also had jurisdiction to decide any defences raised in response to those claims, including countermeasures.[49]

III. Existence of a dispute and negotiation requirements

19 ICTs do not decide questions in a vacuum: their contentious jurisdiction can only be invoked with respect to a 'dispute'. For the ICJ, this is made clear in Article 38(1) of its Statute, providing that the Court's function 'is to decide in accordance with international law such disputes as are submitted to it'. It is also spelled out in many of the treaties that bestow jurisdiction on the Court in accordance with Article 36(1). Thus, Article 22 of the International Convention on the Elimination of All Forms of Racial Discrimination (ICERD) provides:

(hereafter *Delimitation Beyond 200 Nautical Miles*, Preliminary Objections); *Jurisdiction of the ICAO Council under Article 84 of the Convention on Civil Aviation (Bahrain, Egypt, Saudi Arabia & UAE v Qatar)*, Judgment [2020] ICJ Rep 81, para 43 (hereafter *Convention on Civil Aviation*, Judgment); *Jurisdiction of the ICAO Council under Article II, Section 2, of the 1944 International Air Services Agreement (Bahrain, Egypt, Saudi Arabia & UAE v Qatar)*, Judgment [2020] ICJ Rep 172, para 43; *Alleged Violations of the 1955 Treaty of Amity, Economic Relations and Consular Rights (Iran v US)*, ICJ General List No 175, Preliminary Objections (3 February 2021) para 51.

[43] R Radovic, 'Incidental Jurisdiction in Investment Treaty Arbitration and the Question of Party Consent' (2022) 116 AJIL Unbound 181.

[44] On the wider implications of this, see Z Douglas, 'Property, Investment and the Scope of Investment Protection Obligations' in Z Douglas, J Pauwelyn and J Viñuales (eds), *The Foundations of International Investment Law: Bringing Theory into Practice* (OUP 2014) 363.

[45] *Yukos Capital SARL v Russia*, PCA Case No 2013-31, Interim Award, 18 January 2017, paras 446–55.

[46] *Emmis International Holding BV & Ors v Hungary*, ICSID Case No ARB/12/2, Award, 16 April 2014, paras 158–192 (hereafter *Emmis v Hungary*, Award).

[47] *PSEG Global Inc & Anor v Turkey*, ICSID Case No ARB/02/5, Award, 19 January 2007, paras 263–71; *Ioan Micula & Ors v Romania (I)*, ICSID Case No ARB/05/20, Award, 11 December 2013, 416–59.

[48] *Archer Daniels Midland Co v United Mexican States*, ICSID Case No ARB(AF)/04/05, Award, 21 November 2007 para 131.

[49] *Convention on Civil Aviation*, Judgment (n 42) para 49; *International Air Services Agreement*, Judgment (n 42) para 49.

Any dispute between two or more States Parties with respect to the interpretation or application of this Convention, which is not settled by negotiation or by the procedures expressly provided for in this Convention, shall, at the request of any of the parties to the dispute, be referred to the International Court of Justice for decision, unless the disputants agree to another mode of settlement.[50]

The jurisdiction of an IIL tribunal is often conditioned similarly. Article 25(1) of the ICSID **20** Convention provides that ICSID tribunals have jurisdiction 'over any legal dispute arising directly out of an investment'. Many investment treaties also require the existence of a dispute.[51] As most IIL cases will be preceded by disagreement between an investor and the host state combined with an investor's notification of intent to commence arbitration, there is usually little doubt that a dispute is on foot between the parties.[52]

In *Mavrommatis Palestine Concessions*, the PCIJ defined a dispute as 'a disagreement on a **21** point of law or fact, or a conflict of legal views or interests between two persons'.[53] This formula has survived, with discrete elaborations, for nearly a century. A dispute 'is a matter for objective determination'[54] such that it is 'not sufficient for one party to assert [that one exists]',[55] and will arise at the point at which 'the claim of one party is positively opposed by the other'.[56] In providing substantive content to the term, IIL tribunals have reached for the ICJ's definition.[57] But a more recent addition in the *Nuclear Arms and Disarmament* cases—that a dispute will only be deemed to arise once the respondent is aware (or could not have been unaware) that its position is opposed by the claimant[58]— is unprincipled, contrary to the Court's practice,[59] and unlikely to play a role in future

---

[50] International Convention on the Elimination of All Forms of Racial Discrimination, 21 December 1965, 660 UNTS 1, Article 22.

[51] See, eg, Energy Charter Treaty, 17 December 1994, 2080 UNTS 100, Article 26(1).

[52] Although cf *Ping An Life Insurance Company of China Limited & Anor v Belgium*, ICSID Case No ARB/12/29, Award, 30 April 2015, paras 203–33 (hereafter *Ping An v Belgium*, Award).

[53] *Mavrommatis Palestine Concessions*, Judgment (n 28) 11. Further: C Tomuschat, 'Article 36' in A Zimmermann and CJ Tams (eds), *The Statute of the International Court of Justice: A Commentary* (3rd edn, OUP 2019) 712, paras 8–10; R Jennings, 'Reflections on the Term "Dispute"' in R St John Macdonald (ed), *Essays in Honour of Wang Tieya* (Brill 1994) 401; C Schreuer, 'What is a Legal Dispute?' in I Buffard and others (eds), *International Law between Universalism and Fragmentation: Festschrift in Honour of Gerhard Hafner* (Brill 2008) 959.

[54] *Interpretation of Peace Treaties with Bulgaria, Hungary and Romania*, First Phase [1950] ICJ Rep 65, 71 (hereafter *Interpretation of Peace Treaties*, Advisory Opinion).

[55] *Nuclear Tests (Australia v France)*, Judgment [1974] ICJ Rep 253, para 55; *Nuclear Tests (NZ v France)*, Judgment [1974] ICJ Rep 457, para 58.

[56] *South West Africa Cases (Ethiopia v South Africa; Liberia v South Africa)*, Preliminary Objections [1962] ICJ Rep 319, 328. Further: *Northern Cameroons (Cameroon v United Kingdom)*, Preliminary Objections [1963] ICJ Rep 15, para 27.

[57] See, eg, *Tokios Tokelés v Ukraine*, ICSID Case No ARB/02/18, Jurisdiction, 29 April 2004, para 106; *El Paso Energy International Company v Argentina*, ICSID Case No ARB/03/15, Jurisdiction, 27 April 2006, para 61; *Magyar Farming Company Ltd & Ors v Hungary*, ICSID Case No ARB/17/27, Award, 13 November 2019, para 277. See also *South Korea v Dayyani & Ors* [2020] Bus LR 884, para 84. But cf A Kulick, 'Let's (Not) (Dis)Agree to Disagree!? Some Thoughts on the "Dispute" Requirement in International Adjudication' (2020) 19 LPICT 79, 101–03.

[58] See, eg, *Obligations concerning Negotiations relating to Cessation of the Nuclear Arms Race and to Nuclear Disarmament (Marshall Islands v United Kingdom)*, Preliminary Objections [2016] ICJ Rep 833, paras 26–58 (hereafter *Nuclear Arms and Disarmament*, Preliminary Objections). The Court's avoidance of these cases likely stems from its aversion to dealing with nuclear weapons, creating a situation of *de facto* non-justiciability: M Casas, 'Functional Justiciability and the Existence of a Dispute: A Means of Jurisdictional Avoidance?' (2019) 10 JIDS 599.

[59] Under which limited technical defects in seizing the Court could be remedied by the time at which it decided its jurisdiction: *Nuclear Arms and Disarmament*, Preliminary Objections (n 58) paras 9–40 (Judge Robinson, diss); ibid paras 3–19 (Judge Crawford, diss). Further: *Mavrommatis Palestine Concessions*, Judgment (n 28) 34; *Croatian Genocide*, Preliminary Objections (n 22) paras 81, 85.

cases (whether before the ICJ or IIL tribunals), at least in the formalistic sense in which it debuted.[60]

22 In certain cases, the requirement of a dispute may be paired with a further requirement that the claimant attempt to negotiate with the respondent before seising the Court. In *Georgia v Russia*, the Court interpreted the words '[a]ny dispute [...] which is not settled by negotiation or by the procedures expressly provided for in this Convention' in ICERD Article 22 as establishing a barrier to Georgia's claim and dismissed it, as Georgia had not made genuine efforts to engage Russia in dialogue.[61] The ICJ's formalism confirmed such requirements as preconditions to its jurisdiction,[62] which is 'based on the consent of the parties and is confined to the extent accepted by them', such that '[w]hen that consent is expressed in a compromissory clause in an international agreement, any conditions to which its consent is subject must be regarded as constituting the limits thereto'.[63] But this formalism is not unlimited. While the Court will insist that negotiations are commenced, if they fail or are futile,[64] the Court may be approached.[65] Subsequent claimants invoking ICERD have been careful to meet these preconditions.[66]

23 Many investment treaties contain similar negotiation requirements. Article 8(3) of the UK–Tanzania BIT provides that:

> If any such dispute should arise and agreement cannot be reached within six months between the parties to this dispute through the pursuit of local remedies or otherwise, then [...] either party may institute proceedings [before ICSID].[67]

24 Provisions like this one are jurisdictional, as a number of IIL tribunals have held while adopting the ICJ's approach of not requiring compliance where negotiations are or would be futile.[68] But other tribunals have considered compliance with them optional, on the basis that 'properly construed [they are] procedural and directory in nature', and that their strict

---

[60] See now *Application of the Convention on the Prevention and Punishment of the Crime of Genocide (Gambia v Myanmar)*, Preliminary Objections [2022] ICJ Rep 477, paras 51–77.
[61] *Application of the International Convention on the Elimination of All Forms of Racial Discrimination (Georgia v Russia)*, Preliminary Objections [2011] ICJ Rep 70, paras 115–85 (hereafter *Georgia v Russia*, Preliminary Objections).
[62] *Mavrommatis Palestine Concessions*, Judgment (n 28) 13.
[63] *Armed Activities on the Territory of the Congo (New Application: 2002) (DRC v Rwanda)*, Jurisdiction and Admissibility [2006] ICJ Rep 6, para 88.
[64] *United States Diplomatic and Consular Staff in Tehran (US v Iran)*, Judgment [1980] ICJ Rep 3, para 51 (hereafter *US Diplomatic and Consular Staff*, Judgment).
[65] This is a corollary of the obligation to negotiate, not a selective disapplication of that obligation: *Georgia v Russia*, Preliminary Objections (n 61) paras 157–61.
[66] *Application of the International Convention for the Suppression of the Financing of Terrorism and of the International Convention for the Elimination of All Forms of Racial Discrimination (Ukraine v Russia)*, Preliminary Objections [2019] ICJ Rep 558, paras 98–121.
[67] Agreement between the Government of the United Kingdom of Great Britain and Northern Ireland and the Government of the United Republic of Tanzania for the Promotion and Protection of Investments, 7 January 1994, [1996] UKTS 90, Art. 8(3).
[68] See, eg, *Wintershall Aktiengesellschaft v Argentina*, ICSID Case No ARB/04/14, Award, 8 December 2008, paras 69, 133–56; *Urbaser SA & Ors v Argentina*, ICSID Case No ARB/07/26, Jurisdiction, 19 December 2012, para 128; *Tulip Real Estate Investment and Development Netherlands BV v Turkey*, ICSID Case No ARB/11/28, Jurisdiction, 5 March 2013, para 71; *Supervision y Control SA v Costa Rica*, ICSID Case No ARB/12/4, Award, 18 January 2017, paras 340–341; *A11Y LTD v Czech Republic*, ICSID Case No UNCT/15/1, Jurisdiction, 9 February 2017, para 139; *Louis Dreyfus Armateurs SAS v India*, PCA Case No 2014-26, Jurisdiction, 22 December 2015, paras 94–98; *Almasryia for Operating & Maintaining Touristic Construction Co LLC v Kuwait*, ICSID Case No ARB/18/2, Rule 41(5), 1 November 2019, para 40.

application 'would not have been contemplated in the framing [of such provisions]'.[69] Put another way, negotiation requirements give rise to admissibility objections at best. This approach makes no sense and is unprincipled. Just because a requirement is procedural does not mean it cannot condition jurisdiction, and the 'if/then' conditionality used in such provisions indicates that this is precisely what the treaty parties intended. To find otherwise is to ignore the role of state consent in jurisdiction.

IV. Alternative forum for settlement of the dispute

The proliferation of ICTs since the end of the Cold War has created a network of dispute settlement bodies of overlapping jurisdiction. The question therefore arises as to what a particular ICT should do when seised of a dispute that could have been brought elsewhere. For the ICJ, this is usually a problem for somebody else. If there is a valid basis for the Court's jurisdiction in a particular case, the Court will exercise it, unless the parties have indicated that they want the dispute resolved elsewhere, in which case the claim is inadmissible:[70] the Court will not exercise jurisdiction where the claimant attempts to repudiate the parties' prior arrangement.

Other ICTs are willing to surrender jurisdiction in less extreme cases. In *Southern Bluefin Tuna*, an Annex VII tribunal interpreted the alternative dispute settlement regime created by the parties under the Convention for the Conservation of Southern Bluefin Tuna[71] as overriding the dispute settlement provisions of UNCLOS. Even though the two mechanisms engaged different treaty provisions, the tribunal declined jurisdiction.[72] Its convoluted reasoning was given short shrift by the Annex VII tribunal in *South China Sea*.[73]

These issues may also arise in the IIL context. Overlapping investment treaties may give an investor the right to claim under multiple treaties for the same set of host state acts. Standard practice is for the claimant to either choose one treaty to claim under or invoke multiple treaties while seizing a single tribunal.[74] These instruments are not generally expressed as being exclusive *inter se*, and so the claimant is free to choose the treaty that best meets its needs.

IIL tribunals are more cautious when a claimant and respondent have made other arrangements for settlement of the dispute. In *SGS v Philippines*, the claimant bought a

---

[69] *Biwater Gauff (Tanzania) Limited v Tanzania*, ICSID Case No ARB/05/22, Award, 24 July 2008, para 343. Further: *Ethyl Corporation v Canada*, UNCITRAL, Jurisdiction, 24 June 1998, para 84; *Ronald S Lauder v Czech Republic*, UNCITRAL, Award, 3 September 2001, para 187; *Alps Finance and Trade AG v Slovakia*, UNCITRAL, Award, 5 March 2011, para 200; *Abaclat & Ors v Argentina*, ICSID Case No ARB/07/5, Jurisdiction and Admissibility, 4 August 2011, para 564 (hereafter *Abaclat v Argentina*, Jurisdiction and Admissibility); *Olin Holdings Limited v Libya*, ICC Case No 20355/MCP, Partial Award, 28 June 2016, para 217.
[70] *Rights of Minorities in Upper Silesia (Minority Schools)* (*Germany v Poland*), Judgment (1928) PCIJ Ser A No 15, 28. But cf *Mavrommatis Palestine Concessions*, Judgment (n 28) 32. Further: Y Shany, *The Competing Jurisdictions of International Courts and Tribunals* (OUP 2003) 230–34.
[71] Convention for the Conservation of Southern Bluefin Tuna, 10 May 1993, 1918 UNTS 360.
[72] *Southern Bluefin Tuna (Australia v Japan; NZ v Japan)*, Jurisdiction and Admissibility (2000) XXIII RIAA 1, paras 44–65.
[73] *South China Sea*, Jurisdiction and Admissibility (n 40) [178]. But cf *Coastal State Rights*, Preliminary Objections (n 40) paras 475–87.
[74] This will not be possible where ICSID has jurisdiction under one treaty but not the other and the claimant opts for ICSID arbitration: *Plama Consortium Limited v Bulgaria*, ICSID Case No ARB/03/24, Jurisdiction, 8 February 2005, paras 183–227.

claim under the umbrella clause of the relevant BIT, alleging breach of an agreement for the provision of import services contract with the Philippines. The agreement, however, contained an exclusive jurisdiction agreement stating that all disputes 'in connection with the obligations of either party to [the contract] shall be tried at the Regional Trial Courts of Makati and Manila'. The tribunal held that the claim concerning breach of the contract by the Philippines was inadmissible until the claimant had pursued a remedy before those courts.[75]

V. Extinctive prescription

29 Most legal systems have a doctrine of *laches* under which a party cannot rely on a right or claim having delayed unreasonably in its pursuit. In international law, this finds expression in extinctive prescription, an objection to admissibility invoked consistently since the nineteenth century.[76] The principle was restated by the ICJ in *Phosphate Lands*:

> The Court recognizes that, even in the absence of any applicable treaty provision, delay on the part of the claimant State may render the application inadmissible. It notes, however, that international law does not lay down any specific time limit in that regard. It is therefore for the Court to determine in light of the circumstances of each case whether the passage of time renders the application inadmissible.[77]

30 The doctrine is fact-sensitive, taking account of the time elapsed since the claim arose and any prejudice to the respondent. A key consideration is whether the respondent knew there was a dispute between the parties. In *Phosphate Lands*, Nauru did not bring its claim against Australia for over two decades, but the Court ruled it admissible regardless, as the issue had been raised semi-regularly by Nauru in the intervening period.[78]

31 Extinctive prescription is applicable in the IIL context[79] but has been rendered largely redundant as: (a) the doctrine will take a considerable period of time (i.e. upwards of ten years) to

---

[75] *SGS v Philippines*, Jurisdiction (n 21) paras 136–55. Other tribunals have reached similar conclusions as concerns IIL claims based on contractual breach: *Bureau Veritas, Inspection, Valuation, Assessment and Control, BIVAC BV v Paraguay*, ICSID Case No ARB/07/9, Jurisdiction, 29 May 2009, para 142 (hereafter *BIVAC v Paraguay*, Jurisdiction); *Bosh International Inc & Anor v Ukraine*, ICSID Case No ARB/08/11, Award, 25 October 2012, para 252. But cf *Nissan v India*, Jurisdiction (n 19) paras 274–81.

[76] See, eg, *Gentini (Italy) v Venezuela* (1903) X RIAA 551, 558; *Tagliaferro (Italy) v Venezuela* (1903) X RIAA 592, 593; *Giacopini (Italy) v Venezuela* (1903) X RIAA 594, 595–96; *Spader (US) v Venezuela* (1903–05) IX RIAA 223, 224; *Cayuga Indians (GB) v US* (1926) VI RIAA 173, 189; *Ambatielos (Greece/UK)*, Award (1956) XII RIAA 83, 103–04.

[77] *Certain Phosphate Lands in Nauru (Nauru v Australia)*, Preliminary Objections [1992] ICJ Rep 240, para 32 (hereafter *Phosphate Lands*, Preliminary Objections). See also *LaGrand (Germany v US)*, Judgment [2001] ICJ Rep 466, paras 53–57 (hereafter *LaGrand*, Judgment); *Armed Activities on the Territory of the Congo (DRC v Uganda)*, Judgment [2005] ICJ Rep 168, para 295. In the UNCLOS context, see *The M/V 'Norstar' Case (Panama v Italy)*, Preliminary Objections [2016] ITLOS Rep 44, para 211 (hereafter *Norstar*, Preliminary Objections).

[78] *Phosphate Lands*, Preliminary Objections (n 77) paras 33–36.

[79] See, eg, *Wena Hotels Limited v Egypt*, ICSID Case No ARB/98/4, Award, 8 December 2000, para 106; *William Nagel v Czech Republic*, SCC Case No 049/2002, Award, 9 September 2003, para 128; *Grand River Enterprises Six Nations Ltd & Ors v US*, UNCITRAL/NAFTA, Decision on Jurisdiction, 20 July 2006, para 33; *UAB E energija v Latvia*, ICSID Case No ARB/12/33, Award, 22 December 2017, para 539 (hereafter *UAB v Latvia*, Award); *Webuild SpA v Argentine Republic*, ICSID Case No ARB/15/39, Jurisdiction and Admissibility, 23 February 2018, paras 90–91; *(DS)2 SA, Peter de Sutter & Anor v Madagascar (II)*, ICSID Case No ARB/17/18, Award, 17 April 2020, para 356. But cf *SGS Société Générale de Surveillance SA v Paraguay*, ICSID Case No ARB/07/29, Award, 10 February 2012, para 161 (hereafter *SGS v Paraguay*, Award).

bite on any particular claim; and (b) many investment treaties impose jurisdictional bars for far lesser time spans to which respondents will have first recourse.[80]

VI. The *Monetary Gold* principle

The *Monetary Gold* principle—named after the case in which it debuted[81]—is another corollary of the consent-based character of international jurisdiction,[82] properly considered an objection to admissibility.[83] It provides that an ICT should refuse to exercise its jurisdiction where 'the very subject matter' of its decision would be the rights, obligations, or responsibility of an absent third state.[84]

32

In *Monetary Gold*, the question before the Court was whether Italy was entitled to return of the eponymous gold from the respondents. To decide Italy's claim, it was necessary to determine if Albania—owner of the gold in a previous arbitration—had committed a wrong against Italy, such that Italy was entitled to the gold as an effective set-off. The Court held:

33

> To go into the merits of such questions would be to decide an issue between Italy and Albania. […] The Court cannot decide such a dispute without the consent of Albania. […] To adjudicate upon the international responsibility of Albania without her consent would run counter to a well-established principle of international law embodied in the Court's Statute, namely, that the Court can only exercise jurisdiction over a State with its consent. […] In the present case, Albania's legal interests would not only be affected by a decision, but would form the very subject-matter of the decision. In such a case, the Statute cannot be regarded, by implication, as authorizing proceedings to be continued in the absence of Albania.[85]

The *Monetary Gold* principle will render a claim inadmissible when an ICT is required to pronounce on the non-concurrent[86] rights or liabilities of a third state without its consent.[87] An exception exists where the third state's rights or liabilities have been determined elsewhere, such that they may be 'taken as givens'.[88] In *East Timor*, the ICJ rejected Portugal's argument that

34

---

[80] See, eg, NAFTA, Arts 1116(2), 1117(2). Further: *Mobil Investments Canada Inc v Canada (II)*, ICSID Case No ARB/15/6, Jurisdiction and Admissibility, 13 July 2018, paras 145–74.

[81] *Monetary Gold Removed from Rome in 1943 (Italy v France, GB & US)*, Preliminary Question [1954] ICJ Rep 19 (hereafter *Monetary Gold*, Preliminary Question).

[82] It is also known as the indispensable third-party principle, a term from US civil procedure. It is inapposite in an international context, having crept into the nomenclature via the US pleadings in *Military and Paramilitary Activities*, where it was expressly rejected by the Court: *Military and Paramilitary Activities in and against Nicaragua (Nicaragua v United States of America)*, Preliminary Objections [1984] ICJ Rep 392, para 88 (hereafter *Military and Paramilitary Activities*, Preliminary Objections).

[83] J Crawford, *State Responsibility: The General Part* (CUP 2013) 657–66 (hereafter Crawford, *State Responsibility*). Other commentators treat it as a matter of jurisdiction: H Lauterpacht, *The Development of International Law by the International Court* (CUP 1958) 102–03, 343–44. For a third view, see J McIntyre, 'Rules are Rules: Reconceiving *Monetary Gold* as a Rule of Procedure' (2021) 115 AJIL Unbound 144.

[84] *Monetary Gold*, Preliminary Question (n 81) 32. Further: M Paparinskis, 'Revisiting the Indispensable Third Party Principle' (2020) 103 RDI 49 (hereafter Paparinskis, 'Third Party Principle'). The principle has recently come under sustained attack: Z Mollengarden and N Zamir, 'The *Monetary Gold* Principle: Back to Basics' (2021) 115 AJIL 41. For a crushing retort, see M Paparinskis, 'Long Live *Monetary Gold* *Terms and Conditions Apply' (2021) 115 AJIL Unbound 154.

[85] *Monetary Gold*, Preliminary Question (n 81) 32–33.

[86] In the sense that the principle will not be engaged merely by the prospect that finding the respondent liable will imply a simultaneous finding of third-state liability: *Phosphate Lands*, Preliminary Objections (n 77) paras 50–55.

[87] Crawford, *State Responsibility* (n 83) 668–69.

[88] Paparinskis, 'Third Party Principle' (n 84) 80–81.

certain UN resolutions established Indonesia's annexation of East Timor as unlawful, such that the Court did not need to pronounce on that issue to rule on Portugal's claim.[89] However, the Court hinted that more definitive practice could have achieved Portugal's objective. This suggestion manifested before a Special Chamber of the International Tribunal for the Law of the Sea (ITLOS) in *Maldives/Mauritius*, which relied on the ICJ's finding in the *Chagos Archipelago* advisory opinion that the UK had no sovereignty over the Chagos Archipelago,[90] such that the UK's absence could not obstruct a maritime delimitation in the Indian Ocean.[91] This was a surprising conclusion given that advisory opinions lack *res judicata* effect.[92]

35 The *Monetary Gold* principle has been invoked before IIL tribunals, usually unsuccessfully. The *Chevron v Ecuador* tribunal analysed the principle in a judicial setting but left the question of its applicability open.[93] Belgium raised it in *Ping An v Belgium*, but did not pursue the point.[94] Croatia's attempts to rely on it in *Addiko Bank v Croatia*[95] and *Raiffeisen v Croatia*[96] were dismissed. However, the *Güriş v Syria* tribunal applied it when Syria argued that Turkey's contribution to the Syrian Civil War barred the Turkish claimants from proceeding under the relevant BIT due to unclean hands. The tribunal dismissed the argument on the basis that 'as Turkey is not a party to this arbitration, it is impermissible for the Tribunal to pass judgment on the lawfulness or otherwise of Turkey's conduct'.[97]

C. Provisional measures

36 Provisional measures are orders made by ICTs requiring the parties to a dispute to do (or not do) something so as to preserve the subject matter of the dispute pending resolution. As their name suggests, they are temporary only, and a determination made by a court or tribunal when deciding such relief is not *res judicata*. The capacity to order such measures is an inherent power of all ICTs.[98] Read properly, the authorities reveal two species of order:[99] specific orders for the protection of rights subject to adjudication,[100] and general orders for the non-aggravation of the dispute.[101] This applies equally in the IIL context.[102]

---

[89] On the basis this UN practice was less far-reaching than Portugal suggested, and subsequent State practice inconsistent: *East Timor (Portugal v Australia)*, Judgment [1995] ICJ Rep 90, para 32.
[90] *Legal Consequences of the Separation of the Chagos Archipelago from Mauritius in 1965*, Advisory Opinion [2019] ICJ Rep 95, paras 170–82.
[91] *Delimitation of the Maritime Boundary between Mauritius and the Maldives in the Indian Ocean (Maldives/Mauritius)*, Preliminary Objections (2021) 60 ILM 969, paras 167–248. For other UNCLOS practice, see *South China Sea*, Jurisdiction and Admissibility (n 40) paras 180–88; *Norstar*, Preliminary Objections (n 77) paras 171–75. See elsewhere *Lance Larsen v Hawaii*, Award (2001) 119 ILR 566, paras 11.8–11.24.
[92] *Interpretation of Peace Treaties*, Advisory Opinion (n 54) 71.
[93] *Chevron Corporation & Anor v Ecuador (II)*, PCA Case No 2009-23, Third Interim Award, 27 February 2012, paras 4.60–4.71.
[94] *Ping An v Belgium*, Award (n 52) paras 127–28, 238.
[95] *Addiko Bank AG & Anor v Croatia*, ICSID Case No ARB/17/37, Intra-EU Objection, 12 June 2020, para 306.
[96] *Raiffeisen Bank International AG & Anor v Croatia (I)*, ICSID Case No ARB/17/34, Jurisdiction, 30 September 2020, paras 294–97.
[97] *Güriş İnşaat ve Mühendislik Anonim Şirketi & Ors v Syria*, ICC Case No 21845/ZF/AYZ, Award, 31 August 2020, para 224.
[98] C Miles, *Provisional Measures before International Courts and Tribunals* (CUP 2017) 136–43.
[99] ibid 1–3.
[100] See, eg, *Fisheries Jurisdiction (UK v Iceland)*, Interim Protection [1972] ICJ Rep 12, para 21; *Fisheries Jurisdiction (FRG v Iceland)*, Interim Protection [1972] ICJ Rep 30, para 22.
[101] See, eg, *Electricity Company of Sofia and Bulgaria (Belgium v Bulgaria)*, Interim Measures (1939) PCIJ Series A/B No 79, 199.
[102] *Biwater Gauff (Tanzania) Ltd v Tanzania*, ICSID Case No ARB/05/22, Procedural Order No 3, 29 September 2006, para 135.

An ICT's jurisdiction to order provisional measures is usually set out in its constitutive instrument **37** or procedural rules.[103] Given the imprecision with which the power is framed in some of these provisions, it is left to the ICTs applying them to develop their own practice. In this, the ICJ looms large, either through adoption of its thinking on provisional measures, or because its understanding of its jurisdiction has shaped the drafting of later treaties and rules. The result is an approach to provisional measures across ICTs that is broadly uniform in two respects: (a) the preconditions for the ordering of provisional measures; and (b) their binding effect on the parties to the dispute.

Five preconditions for the award of provisional measures have emerged from the practice **38** of the ICJ. First, where a party applies for measures before the ICT has affirmed its jurisdiction, the ICT must be satisfied that it possesses *prima facie* jurisdiction over the dispute.[104] Second, it must be satisfied that the rights that the measures protect are connected to those which will be adjudicated in the final judgment or award.[105] Third, it must be satisfied that the party seeking the measures has a plausible case on the merits—in that it can plausibly establish that the rights underpinning the claim exist in law and have been breached in fact by the respondent.[106] Fourth, it must be satisfied that there is a risk of 'irreparable' (read: serious or significant) prejudice to the applicant's rights if measures are not awarded.[107] Fifth, it must

---

[103] ICJ Statute, Art. 41; UNCLOS, Art. 290; ICSID Convention, Art. 47; 1976 UNCITRAL Rules, Art. 26; 2010 UNCITRAL Arbitration Rules, Art. 26.

[104] See, eg, before the PCIJ/ICJ: *Military and Paramilitary Activities in and against Nicaragua* (*Nicaragua v US*), Provisional Measures [1984] ICJ Rep 169, para 24; *Application of the International Convention on the Elimination of All Forms of Racial Discrimination* (*Georgia v Russia*), Provisional Measures [2008] ICJ Rep 353, para 85; *Alleged Violations of the 1955 Treaty of Amity, Economic Relations and Consular Rights* (*Iran v US*), Provisional Measures [2018] ICJ Rep 623, para 24 (hereafter *Treaty of Amity*, Provisional Measures). See, eg, before IIL tribunals: *Sergei Paushok & Ors v Mongolia*, UNCITRAL, Interim Measures, 2 September 2008, para 47 (hereafter *Paushok v Mongolia*, Interim Measures); *Perenco Ecuador Limited v Ecuador*, ICSID Case No ARB/08/6, Provisional Measures, 8 May 2009, para 39 (hereafter *Perenco v Ecuador*, Provisional Measures); *Churchill Mining PLC v Indonesia*, ICSID Case No ARB/12/13, Procedural Order No 3, 3 March 2013, para 36; *Uniper SE & Ors v Netherlands*, ICSID Case No ARB/21/22, Procedural Order No 2, 9 May 2022, para 59. The ICJ has also confirmed that it may examine the *prima facie* admissibility of the claim: *Application of the Convention on the Prevention and Punishment of the Crime of Genocide* (*Gambia v Myanmar*), Provisional Measures [2020] ICJ Rep 3, para 42.

[105] See, eg, before the PCIJ/ICJ: *Legal Status of the South-Eastern Territory of Greenland* (*Norway v Denmark*), Interim Measures (1932) PCIJ Series A/B No 48, 284; *Arbitral Award of 31 July 1989* (*Guinea-Bissau v Senegal*), Provisional Measures [1990] ICJ Rep 64, [26]. But cf *Allegations of Genocide under the Convention on the Prevention and Punishment of the Crime of Genocide* (*Ukraine v Russia*), ICJ General List No 182, Provisional Measures, 16 March 2022, paras 61–64, which arguably renders the requirement redundant. Further: A Kulick, 'Provisional Measures after *Ukraine v Russia* (2022)' (2022) 13 JIDS 323, 333–35. See, eg, before IIL tribunals: *Paushok v Mongolia*, Interim Measures (n 104) paras 76–77; *Plama Consortium Limited v Bulgaria*, ICSID Case No ARB/03/24, Provisional Measures, 6 September 2005 [40]; *Quiborax SA & Ors v Bolivia*, ICSID Case No ARB/06/2, Provisional Measures, 26 February 2010, paras 78, 116–24.

[106] See, eg, before the PCIJ/ICJ: *Application of the International Convention for the Suppression of the Financing of Terrorism and of the International Convention on the Elimination of All Forms of Racial Discrimination* (*Ukraine v Russia*), Provisional Measures [2017] ICJ Rep 104, paras 63–68; *Application of the Convention on the Prevention and Punishment of the Crime of Genocide* (*Gambia v Myanmar*), Provisional Measures [2020] ICJ Rep 3, paras 45–56 (hereafter, *Rohingya Genocide*, Provisional Measures). See, eg, before IIL tribunals: *Paushok v Mongolia*, Interim Measures (n 104) para 55; *PNG Sustainable Development Program Ltd v PNG*, ICSID Case No ARB/33/13, Provisional Measures, 21 January 2015, para 120 (hereafter *PNGSDP v PNG*, Provisional Measures). Further: C Miles, 'Provisional Measures and the "New" Plausibility in the Jurisprudence of the International Court of Justice' (2017) 88 BYIL 1.

[107] Before the PCIJ/ICJ: *Treaty of Amity*, Provisional Measures (n 104) para 77; *Rohingya Genocide*, Provisional Measures (n 106) para 64; *Denunciation of the Treaty of 2 November 1865 between China and Belgium* (*Belgium v China*), Order (1927) PCIJ Series A No 8, 7. Before IIL tribunals see, eg, *Perenco v Ecuador*, Provisional Measures (n 104) para 43; *Paushok v Mongolia*, Interim Measures (n 104) paras 63–69; *PNGSDP v PNG*, Provisional Measures (n 106) [109]; *CEMEX Caracas Investments BV & Anor v Venezuela*, ICSID Case No ARB/08/15, Provisional Measures, 3 March 2010, paras 37–56.

be satisfied that the measures are urgently required—in that the prejudice identified may materialize prior to the final judgment or award.[108]

39 The ICJ has also been significant in establishing provisional measures ordered by ICTs as binding—despite Article 41(1) of its Statute only allowing the Court to 'indicate' measures which 'ought' to be taken. After ducking the question for some eighty years, the Court was forced to answer it in *LaGrand*, where the United States put a German national to death after the Court ordered under Article 41(1) that his execution be stayed.[109] Germany asked the Court to hold that (a) its provisional measures were binding, and (b) the United States had breached them. The Court duly did.[110]

40 The Court's finding in *LaGrand* impacted the practice concerning Article 47 of the ICSID Convention.[111] In *Pey Casado v Chile*, the tribunal relied on *LaGrand* in holding its provisional measures binding.[112] *LaGrand* was similarly cited in (*inter alia*) *Perenco v Ecuador*[113] and *Quiborax v Bolivia*.[114] The decision and the principle it stands for are today fully integrated into the positive law.[115]

D. Applicable law

41 Any dispute before an ICT must be resolved in accordance with the applicable law. The primacy of party consent is as relevant here as anywhere else: the applicable law is the law selected by the parties, as circumscribed by the jurisdiction of the ICT in question. Thus, UNCLOS Art 293(1) provides that '[a] court or tribunal having jurisdiction under [Part XV, Section 2] shall apply this Convention and other rules of international law not incompatible with this Convention'.[116] Similarly, Article 42(1) of the ICSID Convention provides:

---

[108] Before the PCIJ/ICJ see, eg, *Passage through the Great Belt (Finland v Denmark)*, Provisional Measures [1991] ICJ Rep 12, paras 23–27; *Questions relating to the Seizure and Detention of Certain Documents and Data (Timor-Leste v Australia)*, Provisional Measures [2014] ICJ Rep 147, paras 23–48. Before IIL tribunals see, eg, *Paushok v Mongolia*, Interim Measures (n 104) para 61; *Biwater Gauff (Tanzania) Limited v Tanzania*, ICSID Case No ARB/05/22, Procedural Order No 1, 31 March 2006, para 76; *Occidental Petroleum Corporation & Occidental Exploration and Production Company v Republic of Ecuador (II)*, ICSID Case No ARB/06/11, Decision on Provisional Measures, 17 August 2007, para 69.

[109] *LaGrand (Germany v US)*, Provisional Measures [1999] ICJ Rep 9.

[110] *LaGrand*, Judgment (n 77) para 102. Further: *Treaty of Amity*, Provisional Measures (n 104) para 100; *Rohingya Genocide*, Provisional Measures (n 106) para 84.

[111] The problem does not arise in relation to Article 26 of the 1976 and 2010 UNCITRAL Rules, neither of which gives any doubt that measures ordered under these provisions are binding. The same may be said of UNCLOS Article 290(6).

[112] *Víctor Pey Casado & Anor v Chile (I)*, ICSID Case No ARB/98/2, Provisional Measures, 25 September 2001 [20]–[21]. See also *Emilio Agustín Maffezini v Spain*, ICSID Case No ARB/97/7, Procedural Order No 2, 28 October 1999 [9].

[113] *Perenco v Ecuador*, Provisional Measures (n 104) [75]–[76].

[114] *Quiborax SA & Anor v Bolivia*, ICSID Case No ARB/06/2, Award, 16 September 2015, para 579.

[115] But cf *Fouad Alghanim & Sons Co for General Trading & Contracting WLL & Anor v Jordan*, ICSID Case No ARB/13/38, Dissenting Opinion of Professor Marcelo Kohen, 24 November 2014. Further: T Gazzini and R Kolb, 'Provisional Measures in ICSID Arbitration from "Wonderland's Jurisprudence" to Informal Modification of Treaties' (2017) 16 LPICT 159.

[116] Some UNCLOS dispute settlement bodies have (wrongly) used Article 293(1) to expand their jurisdiction beyond Article 288(1), which limits their jurisdiction to interpretation and application of UNCLOS: *Guyana v Suriname*, Award (2007) XXX RIAA 1, para 406. cf *Access to Information Under Article 9 of the OSPAR Convention (Ireland v UK)*, Award (2003) XXIII RIAA 59, para 85.

The Tribunal shall decide a dispute in accordance with such rules of law as may be agreed by the parties. In the absence of such agreement, the Tribunal shall apply the law of the Contracting State party to the dispute (including its rules on the conflict of laws) and such rules of international law as may be applicable.

42 The interplay between international and domestic law that occurs in every IIL arbitration—as recognized by Article 42(1)—is largely beyond the scope of this entry.[117] It will consider two areas of overlap between the concept of applicable law in IIL and elsewhere in international law.

I. Precedent

43 International law knows no doctrine of binding precedent akin to *stare decisis*. This is reflected in the treatment of an ICT's decisions as a subsidiary means for determination of the law under Article 38(1)(d) of the ICJ Statute. It is further reflected in Article 59 of the Statute, pursuant to which decisions of the Court have no 'binding force except between the parties'. Put another way, '[i]nternational law is not created by an accumulation of opinions and systems; neither is its source a sum total of judgments, even if they agree with each other'.[118]

44 Yes and no. Once states began to design international adjudicative bodies that could hear more than one case, international dispute settlement became a system, with a system's capacity for producing internally consistent results. The result was a type of precedent reflecting the question, '[h]ave we not had this before or something like it?'.[119] This conceptualization is the dominant justification for reliance on precedent by ICTs today. A well-reasoned decision has its own persuasive value, and the more often that reasoning is affirmed, the more persuasive it becomes. Eventually, only radical change in the premise of the decision, or circumstances rendering it distinguishable, will justify departure. This is a *jurisprudence constante*—a settled practice that, all things being equal, should be followed.[120]

45 Whereas the PCIJ and ICJ were historically reluctant to refer to the decisions of other ICTs,[121] the modern Court refers to them with some regularity, particularly where another ICT has subject matter expertise.[122] A similar pattern can be seen in the jurisprudence of ITLOS, which refers to decisions of the ICJ on maritime delimitation.[123]

---

[117] Further: Douglas, *Investment Claims* (n 13) paras 77–271.
[118] *SS Lotus* (*France v Turkey*), Judgment (1927) PCIJ Series A No 10, 43–44 (Judge Weiss, diss).
[119] Lord Wright, 'Precedents' (1943) 8 CLJ 118, 144. Further: H Lauterpacht, 'The So-Called Anglo-American and Continental Schools of Thought in International Law' in E Lauterpacht (ed), *International Law, Being the Collected Papers of Hersch Lauterpacht*, Vol 2 (CUP 1975) 452, 473–74 (hereafter Lauterpacht, 'Anglo-American and Continental Schools').
[120] *US Diplomatic and Consular Staff*, Judgment (n 64) paras 33–37; *Arrest Warrant of 11 April 2000* (*DRC v Belgium*), Judgment [2002] ICJ Rep 3, para 26.
[121] There were rare exceptions: eg, *Polish Postal Service in Danzig*, Advisory Opinion (1925) PCIJ Series B No 11, 30; *Legal Status of Eastern Greenland* (*Denmark v Norway*), Judgment (1931) PCIJ Series A/B 53, 46 (hereafter *Eastern Greenland*, Judgment); *Delimitation of the Maritime Boundary in the Gulf of Maine Area* (*Canada/US*), Judgment [1984] ICJ Rep 246, para 92.
[122] See, eg, *Ahmadou Sadio Diallo* (*Guinea v DRC*), Compensation [2012] ICJ Rep 324, paras 18, 24, 33, 40, 49 (hereafter *Diallo*, Compensation); *Territorial and Maritime Dispute* (*Nicaragua v Colombia*) [2012] ICJ Rep 624, para 178; *Maritime Delimitation in the Indian Ocean* (*Somalia v Kenya*), ICJ General List No 161, Judgment, 12 October 2021, para 124.
[123] See, eg, *Delimitation of the Maritime Boundary between Ghana and Côte d'Ivoire in the Atlantic Ocean* (*Ghana/Côte d'Ivoire*), Judgment [2017] ITLOS Rep 4, paras 212, 215, 226, 262, 285, 393, 409, 452, 453, 470, 471, 475, 533 (hereafter *Ghana/Côte d'Ivoire*, Judgment).

46 Precedent takes on additional importance in the IIL context. IIL's architecture also gives no formal weight to prior decisions: Article 53(1) of the ICSID Convention provides that an award is binding on the parties only. Many investment treaties contain similar provisions.[124] Moreover, given the ad hoc character and horizontal arrangement of IIL tribunals, the authority of prior decisions is essential for systemic stability and predictability. But it is not a guarantee. Many problems confronted by IIL tribunals stem from particular treaty wording, and even where treaty provisions are identical, contextual differences may compel different results.[125] Furthermore, the corpus of IIL awards is now so vast that an authority (seemingly) can be found for almost any proposition, and the parties' pleadings come freighted with endless parallel citations that do not help tribunal find the right answer, and repeat consideration of certain issues gives rise to deep rifts in the caselaw, such that a *jurisprudence constante* on certain matters cannot be observed.

47 As a result, most IIL tribunals adopt an approach of giving due consideration to prior decisions, but not unthinkingly following them,[126] a product of the 'ongoing demand for more consistency within the international investment system, a demand rooted in the need to enhance its legitimacy'.[127] To the extent they are relevant, deference is shown to decisions of the PCIJ and ICJ.[128] Other tribunals have gone further, assuming a 'duty to adopt solutions established in a series of consistent cases'.[129] Caution should here be exercised. The stability that such a duty implies, while laudable, is no substitute for consideration of whether a line of authority is properly reasoned, the basis on which a *jurisprudence constante* accretes.

II. Domestic law

48 ICTs often claim that '[f]rom the standpoint of International Law [...] municipal laws are merely facts'.[130] Reality is more complicated. For many disputes, domestic law is not the applicable law—but where it is considered, the ICT will engage in a process of assessment and

---

[124] See, eg, ECT, Art. 26(8).
[125] See, eg, *Daniel W Kappes & Anor v Guatemala*, ICSID Case No ARB/18/43, Preliminary Objections, 13 March 2020, para 156.
[126] See, eg, *SGS v Philippines*, Jurisdiction (n 21) para 97; *BIVAC v Paraguay*, Jurisdiction (n 75) para 58; *AES Corporation v Argentina*, ICSID Case No ARB/02/17, Jurisdiction, 26 April 2005, para 30; *Fireman's Fund Insurance Company v Mexico*, ICSID Case No ARB(AF)/02/1, Award, 17 July 2006, para 172; *Cargill Incorporated v Poland*, ICSID Case No ARB(AF)/04/2, Award, 29 February 2008, para 224; *Austrian Airlines v Slovakia*, UNCITRAL, Award, 9 October 2009, para 84; *Total SA v Argentina*, ICSID Case No ARB/04/1, Liability, 27 December 2010, para 176; *Tenaris SA & Talta—Trading e Marketing Sociedade Unipessoal Lda v Venezuela (I)*, ICSID Case No ARB/11/26, Annulment, 8 August 2018, para 236; *Ioan Micula & Ors v Romania (II)*, ICSID Case No ARB/14/29, Award, 5 March 2020, para 352; *Infrastructure Services Luxembourg Sàrl & Anor v Spain*, ICSID Case No ARB/13/31, Annulment, 30 July 2021, para 156; *Fernando Fraiz Trapote v Venezuela*, PCA Case No 2019-11, Award, 31 January 2022, para 273.
[127] *Michael Anthony Lee-Chin v Dominican Republic*, ICSID Case No UNCT/18/3, Partial Award, 15 July 2020, para 80.
[128] *Azurix Corp v Argentina*, ICSID Case No ARB/01/12, Award, 14 July 2006, para 390; *Tulip Real Estate and Development Netherlands BV v Turkey*, ICSID Case No ARB/11/28, Bifurcation, 5 March 2013, para 45.
[129] See, eg, *Saipem SpA v Bangladesh*, ICSID Case No ARB/05/7, Award, 30 June 2009, para 90 (hereafter *Saipem v Bangladesh*, Award); *Bayindir Insaat Turizm Ticaret Ve Sanayi AS v Pakistan*, ICSID Case No ARB/03/29, Award, 27 August 2009, para 145; *AWG Group Ltd v Argentina*, UNCITRAL, Liability, 30 July 2010, para 189.
[130] *Certain German Interests*, Preliminary Objections (n 38) 19. See also *Payment of Various Serbian Loans Issued in France (France v Serbia)*, Judgment (1929) PCIJ Series A No 20, 19; 22; *Lighthouses Case between France and Greece (France v Greece)*, Judgment (1934) PCIJ Series A/B No 62, 22 (hereafter *Lighthouses*, Judgment); *Panevezys-Saldutiskis Railway (Estonia v Lithuania)*, Judgment (1939) PCIJ Series A/B No 76, 19.

application that exceeds factual inquiry, while falling short of legal adjudication.[131] The resulting twilight zone has several aspects.[132] While a finding of domestic law may be a critical element of an international law determination,[133] it cannot constitute a *res judicata* in and of itself. The ICT is also not presumed to know domestic law, but may conduct its own research.[134] The ICT further does not have authority to declare a rule of domestic law unconstitutional or invalid.[135] And when called upon to deploy domestic law, it must attempt to apply it as would be done in the state in question, showing due (but not complete) deference to the decisions of domestic courts.[136]

The tenuous claim that ICTs treat questions of domestic law strictly as matters of fact is put under further strain in the IIL context. Given that property rights grounded in a domestic legal order are the basis of every claim, the idea that an IIL tribunal should consider domestic laws as facts is absurd.[137] IIL tribunals have therefore been refreshingly direct in dismissing the domestic law *qua* fact paradigm.[138] **49**

The result of this is that domestic law is often made part of the applicable law of an IIL dispute. The default rule of Article 42 of the ICSID Convention provides that a tribunal 'shall apply the law of the Contracting State party to the dispute'. Many investment treaties contain similar provisions.[139] Furthermore, even if the applicable law clause of the relevant treaty refers to international law exclusively,[140] the intertwining of domestic law property rights with the jurisdictional premise of the tribunal and the merits of the case is such that tribunals acknowledge that domestic law must be applied concurrently with international law.[141] This becomes most acute when dealing with observance of obligations clauses, which require an understanding of domestic law before a breach of the treaty can be determined.[142] But even where domestic law is considered part of the applicable law of the dispute, the principle of deference to domestic courts still applies.[143] **50**

---

[131] An ICT can also consider domestic law as law when asked to do so by the parties: see, eg, *Lighthouses*, Judgment (n 130) 19–20.

[132] J Crawford, *Brownlie's Principles of Public International Law* (9th edn, OUP 2019) 49–50.

[133] See, eg, *Application of the Convention of 1902 Governing the Guardianship of Infants (Netherlands v Sweden)*, Judgment [1958] ICJ Rep 55, 62; *Questions relating to Prosecute or Extradite (Belgium v Senegal)*, Judgment [2012] ICJ Rep 422, paras 75–78.

[134] *Payment in Gold of Brazilian Federal Loans Contracted in France (France v Brazil)*, Judgment (1929) PCIJ Series A No 21 (hereafter *Brazilian Loans*, Judgment); *Nottebohm (Liechtenstein v Guatemala)*, Preliminary Objection [1953] ICJ Rep 11, 36 (Judge Read, diss), 51 (Judge Guggenheim, diss); *US—Countervailing Duties on Certain Corrosion-Resistant Carbon Steel Flat Products from Germany*, WTO Doc WT/DS213/AB/R (Appellate Body Report, 28 November 2002), para 157.

[135] In the sense that an ICT's finding on domestic law will have no effect within the domestic legal order: *Interpretation of the Statute of the Memel Territory*, Advisory Opinion (1932) PCIJ Series A/B No 49, 336.

[136] *Brazilian Loans*, Judgment (n 134) 124.

[137] Douglas, *Investment Claims* (n 13) para 115.

[138] For an early example see *Southern Pacific Properties (Middle East) Limited v Egypt*, ICSID Case No ARB/84/3, Jurisdiction, 14 April 1988, para 58.

[139] See, eg, Agreement between the Government of the United Kingdom of Great Britain and Northern Irelands and the Government of the Republic of Argentina for the Promotion and Protection of Investments, 11 December 1990, [1993] UKTS 41, Art. 8(4). See further *National Grid Plc v Argentina*, UNCITRAL (Award, 3 November 2008), paras 83–85.

[140] See, eg, NAFTA, Art. 1131(1).

[141] See, eg, *MTD Equity Sdn Bhd & Anor v Chile*, ICSID Case No ARB/01/7, Annulment, 21 March 2007, para 72; *Bayview Irrigation District & Ors v Mexico*, ICSID Case No ARB(AF)/05/1, Award, 19 June 2007, para 109–18; *Fraport AG Frankfurt Airport Services Worldwide v Philippines (II)*, ICSID Case No ARB/11/12, Award, 10 December 2014, para 298.

[142] See, eg, *WNC Factoring Ltd v Czech Republic*, PCA Case No 2014-34, Award, 22 February 2017, paras 321–47.

[143] *Emmis v Hungary*, Award (n 46) para 175.

51 The treatment of domestic law *qua* law has consequences within IIL. Unlike questions of fact, which are largely insulated from review, the failure to apply domestic law as the applicable law of dispute will serve as a basis for annulment under Article 52(1)(b) of the ICSID Convention.[144] In non-ICSID cases, an error of domestic law may lead to the award being set aside—*lex arbitri* depending.[145]

E. Rules of evidence

52 International rules on evidence are rudimentary when compared to those in domestic jurisdictions.[146] The different domestic legal traditions on judicial fact-finding necessitate a flexible international system that leaves much to the discretion of the ICT.[147] That system has solidified somewhat in IIL via importation of soft law instruments from international commercial arbitration,[148] although its open character has been largely maintained.[149] In contrast, the jurisprudence of the permanent interstate courts and tribunals such as the ICJ reflects a lesser sophistication, the product of their limited caselaw.

I. Burden of proof

53 The basic burden of proof in international law is encompassed in the maxim *actori incumbit onus probandi*: the party making an allegation must prove it. This was stated in *Island of Palmas*,[150] and despite some uncertainty before the PCIJ and other inter-war tribunals,[151] has been upheld consistently by the ICJ.[152] Precisely who is making an allegation is to be determined pragmatically, with an eye to each party's positive case. Thus, in *Temple of Preah Vihear*, both Cambodia and Thailand based their respective claims to sovereignty over the disputed territory on facts that had to be independently proved: that Cambodia was the claimant did not require it to disprove Thailand's claim.[153] Equally, as the Court made clear in *Oil Platforms*, the party asserting a defence to a positive claim will have the burden of proving on which the defence is grounded.[154]

---

[144] Although simple errors of domestic law will not give rise to an annullable error: *Caratube International Oil Company LLP v Kazakhstan (I)*, ICSID Case No ARB/08/12, Annulment, 21 February 2014, paras 77–81. Similar matters may lead to enforcement of a non-ICSID award being refused under the New York Convention: C Borris and R Henneke, 'Excess of Competence or Jurisdiction, Article V(1)(c)' in R Wolff (ed), *New York Convention: Article-by-Article Commentary* (2nd edn, CH Beck/Hart/Nomos 2019) 321, paras 235–44.

[145] See, eg, Arbitration Act 1996 (Eng), ss 67(1), 69(1).

[146] Especially those within the common law tradition: see, eg, H M Malek (ed), *Phipson on Evidence* (20th edn, Sweet & Maxwell 2021). But cf the developed practice of international criminal tribunals: K Ambos, A Heinze and P Ambach (eds), *Evidence in International Criminal Procedure* (CH Beck/Hart/Nomos 2023).

[147] Lauterpacht, 'Anglo-American and Continental Schools' (n 119) 462–64.

[148] See, eg, *IBA Rules on the Taking of Evidence in International Arbitration* (3rd edn, International Bar Association 2020).

[149] *The Rompetrol Group NV v Romania*, ICSID Case No ARB/06/3, Award, 6 May 2013, para 181 (hereafter *Rompetrol v Romania*, Award); *Georg Gavrilović & Anor v Croatia*, ICSID Case No ARB/12/39, Award, 26 July 2018, para 229 (hereafter *Gavrilović v Croatia*, Award).

[150] *Island of Palmas (Netherlands v US)*, Award (1928) II RIAA 829, 837.

[151] Cheng, *General Principles* (n 38) 326–35.

[152] A Riddell and B Plant, *Evidence before the International Court of Justice* (BIICL 2009) 87–98.

[153] *Temple of Preah Vihear (Cambodia v Thailand)*, Judgment [1962] ICJ Rep 6, 15–16.

[154] *Oil Platforms*, Judgment (n 15) para 57.

The Court has reiterated this position,[155] as have other ICTs.[156] At the same time, it is not absolute, and a party may have to prove a negative in circumstances where it is better placed to evidence a position than the party making the allegation.[157] The burden of proof (or, rather, the burden of evidence[158]) will also shift once the party making the allegation has established it to requisite level. In that case, the other party will need to put on evidence sufficient to disprove the allegation.[159]

IIL tribunals also require each party to prove the positive facts on which its case depends, noting that *actori incumbit onus probandi* 'can be considered a general principle of international procedure—and probably also of virtually all national civil procedural laws— namely that it is the claimant who has the burden of proof […] to establish the claim'.[160] The claimant must also establish the jurisdiction of the tribunal.[161] Conversely, it is for the respondent to establish any positive preliminary objection (eg abuse of process) or defence on the merits (eg necessity) on which it seeks to rely.[162] Likewise, the successful establishment of an allegation by one party may allocate the burden of disproving that allegation to the other party.[163]

---

[155] See, eg, *Military and Paramilitary Activities*, Preliminary Objections (n 82) para 101; *Application of the Convention on the Prevention and Punishment of the Crime of Genocide (Bosnia & Herzegovina v Serbia & Montenegro)*, Judgment [2007] ICJ Rep 43, para 204 (hereafter *Bosnian Genocide*, Judgment); *Sovereignty over Pedra Branca/Pulau Batu Puteh, Middle Rocks and South Ledge (Malaysia/Singapore)*, Judgment [2008] ICJ Rep 12, para 45; *Application of the Convention on the Prevention and Punishment of Genocide (Croatia v Serbia)*, Judgment [2015] ICJ Rep 3, para 172 (hereafter *Croatian Genocide*, Judgment); *Certain Activities carried out by Nicaragua in the Border Area (Costa Rica v Nicaragua)*, Compensation [2018] ICJ Rep 15, para 33 (hereafter *Border Area*, Compensation).

[156] See, eg, *Iran v US (Case A-20)* (1986) 11 Iran–US CTR 271, 274; *US—Measure Affecting Imports of Woven Wool Shirts and Blouses from India*, WTO Doc No WT/DS33/AB/R (Appellate Body Report, 25 April 1997) para 14 (hereafter *US—Wool Shirts and Blouses*, Appellate Body Report); *Aram Sabet & Ors v Iran & Ors*, IUSCT Case Nos 815, 816 and 817, Partial Award, 30 June 1999, para 48; *The M/V 'Norstar' Case (Panama v Italy)*, Judgment [2018–2019] ITLOS Rep 10, para 94 (hereafter *Norstar*, Judgment)

[157] *Ahmadio Sadio Diallo (Guinea v DRC)*, Judgment [2010] ICJ Rep 639, paras 54–55. See also *Border Area*, Compensation (n 155) para 33.

[158] In the sense that the legal burden of proof does not shift, but the party resisting the allegation may adduce evidence to establish that the burden is not met.

[159] *US—Wool Shirts and Blouses*, Appellate Body Report (n 156) para 24; *Reza Said Malek v Iran*, IUSCT Case No 193, Award, 11 August 1992, para 111.

[160] *Tradex Hellas SA v Albania*, ICSID Case No ARB/94/2, Award, 29 April 1999, para 74. See, eg, *Saipem v Bangladesh*, Award (n 129) para 113; *SGS v Paraguay*, Award (n 79) para 79; *Rompetrol v Romania*, Award (n 149) para 179; *Hussein Nauman Soufraki v UAE*, ICSID Case No ARB/02/7, Award, 7 July 2004, para 58; *Waguih Elie George Siag & Anor v Egypt*, ICSID Case No ARB/05/15, Award, 1 June 2009, para 315; *Alpha Projektholding GmbH v Ukraine*, ICSID Case No ARB/07/16, Award, 8 November 2010, para 236 (hereafter *Alpha Projektholding v Ukraine*, Award); *Vito G Gallo v Canada*, PCA Case No 2008-03, Award, 15 September 2011, para 277; *Churchill Mining & Planet Mining Pty Ltd v Republic of Indonesia*, ICSID Case No ARB/12/40 & 12/14, Award, 6 December 2016, para 238 (hereafter *Churchill Mining v Indonesia*, Award).

[161] See, eg, *Emmis v Hungary*, Award (n 46) paras 171–74; *Abaclat v Argentina*, Jurisdiction and Admissibility (n 69) para 678; *Gustav F W Hamester GmbH & Co KG v Ghana*, ICSID Case No ARB/07/24, Award, 18 June 2010, para 143; *National Gas SAE v Egypt*, ICSID Case No ARB/11/7, Award, 3 April 2014, para 118; *Westmoreland Mining Holdings LLC v Canada*, ICSID Case No UNCT/20/3, Award, 31 January 2022, para 193.

[162] See, eg, *Chevron Corporation & Anor v Ecuador (I)*, PCA Case No 2007-02, Interim Award, 1 December 2008, para 139; *Unión Fenosa Gas SA v Egypt*, ICSID Case No ARB/14/4, Award, 31 August 2018, para 8.38 (hereafter *Unión Fenosa v Egypt*, Award); *Michael Ballantine & Anor v Dominican Republic*, PCA Case No 2016-17, Award, 3 September 2019, para 510; *Infracapital F1 Sàrl & Anor v Spain*, ICSID Case No ARB/16/18, Jurisdiction, Liability and Directions on Quantum, 13 September 2021, para 334.

[163] See, eg, *Alpha Projektholding v Ukraine*, Award (n 160) para 236; *Asian Agricultural Products Ltd v Lanka*, ICSID Case No ARB/87/3, Award, 27 June 1990, para 56; *Marvin Roy Feldman Karpa v Mexico*, ICSID Case No ARB(AF)/99/1, Award, 16 December 2002, para 177; *Niko Resources (Bangladesh) Ltd v Bangladesh Oil Gas and Mineral Corporation & Anor*, ICSID Case No ARB/10/18, Corruption Claim, 25 February 2019, paras 787–91. But cf *Rompetrol v Romania*, Award (n 149) para 178; *Apotex Holdings Inc & Anor v US*, ICSID Case No ARB(AF)/12/1, Award, 25 August 2014, para 8.8 (hereafter *Apotex v US*, Award).

II. Standard of proof

56 When it comes to the standard of proof, the picture is less clear. The ICJ often shifts between different standards without justification, or applies a standard without saying what it is.[164] The default position appears to be that a fact need only be proved on the balance of probabilities.[165] With respect to specific issues—eg the existence of a tacit agreement between states—the Court appears to require a higher standard of 'compelling' evidence.[166] And for 'charges of exceptional gravity'—eg the occurrence of genocide—the standard of proof may be commensurate with the nature of the allegation, such that only 'fully conclusive' evidence will do.[167] What the common lawyer sees as a maddening lack of precision, however, is met with equanimity by the civil lawyer, for whom the only standard in a given case is the conviction of the judge.

57 The practice of IIL tribunals also reflects greater consistency than the ICJ when it comes to standard of proof. The default rule is again the balance of probabilities, which is applied to establish a range of essential facts, including those underpinning the tribunal's jurisdiction,[168] breach of treaty by the state,[169] as well as what damage was caused to the claimant and quantification of the same.[170] The requirements of a specific cause of action, moreover, may render the standard more difficult to meet, as is the case for denial of justice, which requires 'clear evidence of an outrageous failure of the judicial system'.[171]

58 IIL tribunals also recognize that extraordinary claims require extraordinary proof. This is particularly so for allegations of fraud, corruption, or bad faith, which will ordinarily require 'clear and convincing' evidence,[172] a standard 'higher than the balance of probabilities but less than the criminal standard of beyond reasonable doubt'.[173] This approach has been criticized, particularly in cases of corruption: corruption is notoriously difficult to prove, and imposing an additional burden on the party alleging it will often put it beyond reach entirely.[174] Some tribunals have agreed, holding that for allegations of corruption (or other illegality)

---

[164] *Oil Platforms*, Judgment (n 15) para 33 (Judge Higgins). cf *Prisoners of War—Eritrea's Claim 17 (Ethiopia/Eritrea)*, Partial Award (2003) XXVI RIAA 23, para 43–53.

[165] See, eg, *Oil Platforms*, Judgment (n 15) [57]; *Land, Island and Maritime Frontier Dispute (El Salvador/Honduras; Nicaragua intervening)*, Judgment [1992] ICJ Rep 351, para 248. See also *Norstar*, Judgment (n 156) paras 410, 448.

[166] *Territorial and Maritime Dispute between Nicaragua and Honduras in the Caribbean Sea (Nicaragua v Honduras)*, Judgment [2007] ICJ Rep 658, para 253; *Obligation to Negotiate Access to the Pacific Ocean (Bolivia v Chile)*, Judgment [2018] ICJ Rep 507, para 97. See also *Ghana/Côte d'Ivoire*, Judgment (n 123) paras 198–208.

[167] *Bosnian Genocide*, Judgment (n 155) para 209; *Croatian Genocide*, Judgment (n 155) paras 177–79; *Corfu Channel (United Kingdom v Albania)*, Judgment [1949] ICJ Rep 14, 18

[168] See, eg, *PNG Sustainable Development Program Ltd v PNG*, ICSID Case No ARB/13/33, Award, 5 May 2015, para 255; *Sergei Viktorovich Pugachev v Russia*, UNCITRAL, Jurisdiction, 18 June 2020, para 256. That said, some tribunals have considered that when dealing with issues of jurisdiction *ratione voluntatis*, the threshold increases such that 'consent [to arbitration] should be expressed in a manner that leaves no doubts': *Brandes Investment Partners LP v Venezuela*, ICSID Case No ARB/08/3, Award, 2 August 2011, para 113.

[169] See, eg, *UAB v Latvia*, Award (n 79) para 830; *Copper Mesa Mining Corporation v Ecuador*, PCA Case No 2012-02, Award, 15 March 2016, para 6.3.

[170] See, eg, *Ioannis Kardassopoulos v Georgia*, ICSID Case No ARB/05/18, Award, 3 March 2010, para 229; *Abed El Jaouni & Imperial Holding SAL v Lebanon*, ICSID Case No ARB/15/3, Award, 14 January 2021, para 60.

[171] *Philip Morris Brand SARL & Ors v Uruguay*, ICSID Case No ARB/10/7, Award, 8 July 2016, para 500.

[172] See, eg, *Karkey Karadeniz Elektrik Uretim AS v Islamic Republic of Pakistan*, ICSID Case No ARB/13/1, Award, 22 August 2017, para 492 (hereafter *Karkey v Pakistan*, Award); *Fraport AG Frankfurt Airport Services Worldwide v Philippines (II)*, ICSID Case No ARB/11/12, Award, 10 December 2014, para 479.

[173] See, eg, *Sanum Investments v Laos (I)*, PCA Case No 2013-13, Award, 6 August 2019, para 108.

[174] See, eg, C Partasides, 'Proving Corruption in International Arbitration: A Balanced Standard for the Real World' (2010) 25 ICSID Rev 47.

the standard of proof remains the balance of probabilities, while at the same time allowing that the allegation is inherently unlikely.[175]

F. Counterclaims

A counterclaim is a claim for relief asserted against an opposing party after the claim proper has been made—especially a respondent's claim in opposition or set-off. It is distinct from a defence on the merits, by which the respondent seeks to have the claim proper dismissed, and instead constitutes 'an autonomous legal act the object of which is to submit a new claim'.[176] But controversy arises with respect to the scope of that autonomy. **59**

The ICJ has developed its jurisprudence on counterclaims through elaboration of its procedural rules and its caselaw. Article 80 of the ICJ Rules distils the Court's practice to its essentials. It sets out two requirements, both of which must be met if the counterclaim is to be admitted: '[t]he Court may entertain a counterclaim only if it comes within the jurisdiction of the Court and is directly connected with the subject-matter of the claim of the other party.' **60**

The first requirement is obvious and proceeds from the consent-based character of international jurisdiction. The mere fact that the claim proper has been brought does not create a free-for-all: the Court must have jurisdiction over the counterclaim independently of the claim. There is no reason of principle, however, to confine the acceptable bases of jurisdiction to those on which the claim is founded, as to do so undermines the counterclaim's autonomy.[177] A more difficult question is the time at which the Court's jurisdiction over the counterclaim is to be assessed—is it at the time that the claim is brought or at the time the counterclaim is filed? In *Sovereign Rights and Maritime Spaces*, the Court opted for the former, holding that Colombia could raise counterclaims against Nicaragua notwithstanding it had denounced the basis of the Court's jurisdiction, the Pact of Bogotá,[178] three years prior. This was said to follow from the fact that counterclaims, while autonomous, are nonetheless closely linked to claims proper such that 'their purpose is to react to them in the same proceedings in respect of which they are incidental'.[179] **61**

The second requirement is one of admissibility. It proceeds from the counterclaim's character as an incidental proceeding and the need to ensure sound administration of justice. A respondent cannot be permitted to hijack the proceedings by counterclaiming for every *inter partes* grievance over which the Court has jurisdiction: it can only react to the claim proper.[180] The requirement of a 'direct connection' has factual and legal elements.[181] So far as the factual connection is concerned, it is sufficient that the counterclaim arises out of (a) the **62**

---

[175] See, eg, *Churchill Mining v Indonesia*, Award (n 160) para 244; *Unión Fenosa v Egypt*, Award (n 162) para 7.52.
[176] *Application of the Convention on the Prevention and Punishment of the Crime of Genocide (Bosnia & Herzegovina v Yugoslavia)*, Counterclaims [1997] ICJ Rep 243, para 27 (hereafter *Bosnian Genocide*, Counterclaims).
[177] R Kolb, *The International Court of Justice* (Hart Publishing 2013) 663–70 (hereafter Kolb, *International Court*). cf C Antonopoulos, *Counterclaims before the International Court of Justice* (TMC Asser 2011) 76–78. The Court's jurisprudence on this subject is equivocal: *Factory at Chorzów (Claim for Indemnity) (Germany v Poland)*, Judgment (1928) PCIJ Ser A No 17, 37–38; cf *Oil Platforms (Iran v US)*, Counterclaim [1998] ICJ Rep 190, para 36 (hereafter *Oil Platforms*, Counterclaim).
[178] American Treaty on Pacific Settlement, 30 April 1948, 30 UNTS 55.
[179] *Alleged Violations of Sovereign Rights and Maritime Spaces in the Caribbean Sea (Nicaragua v Colombia)*, Counterclaims [2017] ICJ Rep 289, para 67 (hereafter *Sovereign Rights and Maritime Spaces*, Counterclaims). But cf ibid paras 21–22 (Judges Tomka, Gaja, Sebutinde, Gevorgian and Judge ad hoc Daudet).
[180] Kolb, *International Court* (n 177) 670–71.
[181] *Bosnian Genocide*, Counterclaims (n 176) para 33.

same geographic and temporal context as the claim, and (b) allegations of similar conduct by the claimant.[182] So far as the legal connection is concerned, this question is related to, but extends beyond, the question of whether claim and counterclaim allege breach of the same legal instrument. Rather, it is concerned with whether they 'pursue the same legal aims'[183] in the sense that each party seeks to hold the other responsible under the same body of law (eg the use of force).[184]

63 The ICJ's formulation of its power to hear and determine counterclaims has influenced other ICTs.[185] The same cannot be said, however, for IIL tribunals—reflecting the different institutional features of this form of dispute settlement, which involves two parties from different legal orders who are not bound by reciprocal obligations. While provisions such as Article 46 of the ICSID Convention allow tribunals to determine counterclaims per se,[186] difficulties arise from the fact that the jurisdiction *ratione materiae* of an IIL tribunal is often confined to the terms of an investment treaty[187] conferring rights on investors but not corresponding obligations. Thus, a respondent that wishes to bring a counterclaim against the investor may be unable to identify a legal basis for the counterclaim that is within the tribunal's substantive jurisdiction.[188]

64 IIL counterclaims are nevertheless possible in limited circumstances. The respondent will be able to raise a counterclaim if the dispute settlement clause of the relevant investment treaty is broadly worded—giving the tribunal jurisdiction over 'any dispute' arising out of an investment,[189] as opposed to claims for breaches of the investment treaty,[190] and further envisaging a situation in what a state (as opposed to only an investor) can submit claims to arbitration.[191] This may allow the respondent to bring a counterclaim for the claimant's breaches of its domestic law. Alternatively, the investment treaty in question may impose positive obligations on investors. Although previously unusual,[192] these are now a familiar part of the IIL landscape.[193] Questions may arise, however, as to whether a regime of investor responsibility has developed so as make these obligations effective in all cases.[194]

---

[182] *Sovereign Rights and Maritime Spaces*, Counterclaims (n 179) [24]. See further *Oil Platforms*, Counterclaim (n 177) [38]; *Armed Activities in the Territory of the Congo (DRC v Uganda)*, Counterclaims [2001] ICJ Rep 660, paras 38–43 (hereafter *Armed Activities*, Counterclaims).
[183] *Bosnian Genocide*, Counterclaims (n 176) para 35; *Oil Platforms*, Counterclaims (n 177) para 38.
[184] Kolb, *International Court* (n 177) 672. See further *Armed Activities*, Counterclaims (n 182) paras 38–43; *Sovereign Rights and Maritime Spaces*, Counterclaims (n 179) paras 36–39.
[185] See, eg, *M/V 'Virginia G' (Panama/Guinea Bissau)*, Order [2012] ITLOS Rep 309, para 37.
[186] See also 1976 UNCITRAL Rules, Art. 19(3); 2010 UNCITRAL Rules, Art. 21(3).
[187] See, eg, NAFTA, Arts 1116, 1117.
[188] A de Nanteuil, 'Counterclaims in Investment Arbitration: Old Questions, New Answers?' (2018) 17 LPICT 374, 376 (hereafter de Nanteuil, 'Old Questions, New Answers').
[189] See, eg, *Saluka Investments BV v Czech Republic*, PCA Case No 2001-04, Counterclaim, 7 May 2004, para 39 (hereafter *Saluka v Czech Republic*, Counterclaim); *Sergei Paushok & Ors v Mongolia*, UNCITRAL, Jurisdiction and Liability, 28 April 2011, para 689; *Metal-Tech Ltd v Republic of Uzbekistan*, ICSID Case No ARB/10/3, Award, 4 October 2013, para 410.
[190] See, eg, *Spyridon Roussalis v Romania*, ICSID Case No ARB/06/1, Award, 7 December 2011, paras 868–77.
[191] *Karkey v Pakistan*, Award (n 172) paras 1101–06.
[192] See, eg, Agreement on Promotion, Protection and Guarantee of Investment Among Member States of the Organisation of the Islamic Conference, 5 June 1981, Art. 9. Further: *Hesham Talaat M Al-Warraq v Republic of Indonesia*, UNCITRAL, Award, 15 December 2014, paras 662–64 (hereafter *Al-Warraq v Indonesia*, Award).
[193] See, eg, Reciprocal Investment Promotion and Protection Agreement between the Government of the Kingdom of Morocco and the Government of the Federal Republic of Nigeria, 3 December 2016, Arts 17–19, 24.
[194] de Nanteuil, 'Old Questions, New Answers' (n 188) 389–92; J Ho, 'The Creation of Elusive Investor Responsibility' (2019) 113 AJIL Unbound 10.

Some IIL tribunals have limited the admissibility of counterclaims by reference to their relationship with claims proper. This has generally been done without reference to the similar test developed by the ICJ. Thus, in *Saluka v Czech Republic*, an UNCITRAL tribunal operating under a BIT referred to the Iran–US Claims tribunal and early ICSID practice and identified 'a general legal principle as to the nature of the close connection which a counterclaim must have with the primary claim if a tribunal with jurisdiction over the primary claim is to have the counterclaim'.[195] It did this notwithstanding that the UNCITRAL Rules—unlike Article 46 of the ICSID Convention—do not require the counterclaim to arise 'directly out of the subject matter of the dispute' that produced the claim proper. The nature of the connection is, however, variable 'since so much will always turn on the particular circumstances of individual cases, including not only their facts but also the relevant treaty and other texts'.[196] Some tribunals have focused on a legal connection, requiring the counterclaim to arise out of the same legal instrument as the claim.[197] Others have looked at the question from both a factual and legal perspective similar to that of the ICJ to ascertain if the claim and counterclaim arise out of the same subject matter.[198]

G. Costs

Cases generally end with a winner and a loser. While costs 'follow the event' in some domestic proceedings, the situation is more open textured for ICTs. Article 64 of the ICJ Statute provides that '[u]nless otherwise decided by the Court, each party shall bear its own costs'. The Court considers this a general principle of law.[199] The international rule is therefore that there will be no order as to costs, although they may be awarded if necessary. This discretion, however, has never been exercised by the ICJ or its predecessor despite repeated requests[200] and the Court's willingness to award compensation elsewhere.[201] The Court's power to award costs therefore seems hypothetical—although it may be that the Court is waiting for an abuse of sufficient gravity to occur before costs are (at last) awarded.[202]

The IIL landscape is different. Most procedural frameworks are neutral on the question of costs, at least so far as those associated with the parties' legal representation are concerned.[203] Costs are requested and contested in nearly every IIL case: hardly surprising in

---

[195] *Saluka v Czech Republic*, Counterclaim (n 189) para 76.
[196] *Saluka v Czech Republic*, Counterclaim (n 189) para 63.
[197] *Tethyan Copper Company Pty Limited v Pakistan*, ICSID Case No ARB/12/1, Jurisdiction and Liability, 10 November 2017 [1414]; *Naturgy Energy Group SA & Anor v Colombia*, ICSID Case No UNCT/18/1, Award, 12 March 2021, para 623.
[198] *Al-Warraq v Indonesia*, Award (n 192) [667]–[668]; *Urbaser SA & Ors v Argentina*, ICSID Case No ARB/07/26, Award, 8 December 2016, para 1151.
[199] *Review of UNAT Judgment No 158*, Advisory Opinion [1973] ICJ Rep 166, para 98.
[200] See, eg, *Eastern Greenland*, Judgment (n 121) 74; *Pajs, Czáky, Esterházy (Hungary v Yugoslavia)*, Judgment (1936) PCIJ Ser A/B No 68, 65; *Interpretation of the Judgment of 11 June 1998 in the Case concerning the Land and Maritime Boundary between Cameroon and Nigeria (Cameroon v Nigeria) (Nigeria v Cameroon)*, Judgment [1999] ICJ Rep 31, para 18.
[201] *Diallo*, Compensation (n 122) paras 58–60.
[202] Kolb, *International Court* (n 177) 1003. But cf *Certain Activities Carried Out by Nicaragua in the Border Area (Costa Rica v Nicaragua)/Construction of a Road in Costa Rica along the San Juan River (Nicaragua v Costa Rica)*, Judgment [2015] ICJ Rep 665, paras 1–9 (Judges Tomka, Greenwood, Sebutinde and Judge ad hoc Dugard).
[203] Which is to say, the vast majority of costs in any given proceeding: ICSID Convention, Article 61(2), 1976 UNCITRAL Rules, Article 40(2). But cf 2010 UNCITRAL Rules, Art. 42(1). Further: M Bradfield and G Verdirame, 'Costs in Investment Treaty Arbitration' in C Giorgetti (ed), *Litigating International Investment Disputes: A Practitioner's Guide* (Brill 2014) 411, 422–25 (hereafter Bradfield and Verdirame, 'Costs').

circumstances where the combined mean costs of the parties in a typical proceeding is over USD 10 million.[204] While the ICJ's approach is still adopted with regularity, particularly where the issues raised by the arbitration are complicated and the losing party has conducted itself professionally,[205] there has been an increasing tendency on the part of IIL tribunals to adopt a costs follow the event approach.[206] This appears to adopt the approach in international commercial arbitration.[207]

68 The upshot of this is that IIL tribunals increasingly award the winning party its costs[208]—with some describing a 'trend' in this respect.[209] But that does not mean that the losing party will be required to pay all of those costs. The prevailing practice of tribunals is to assess the outcome of the proceedings and the parties' conduct holistically, and to give the winning party only a portion of its legal fees and expenses—a process that may result in no costs award.[210]

H. Judgments and awards

69 Every international dispute, unless discontinued, ends with a judgment or award—the purpose of which is to produce a *res judicata* for the parties. Literally 'a thing adjudicated', *res judicata* is a preclusion arising from the final decision of an ICT and confirming its binding character. It is a general principle of law,[211] although aspects of it are often recorded in the constitutive instrument of an ICT through statements as to the mandatory force of decisions.[212]

70 ICTs tend not to be arranged hierarchically, such that there is ordinarily no right of appeal from judgments or awards.[213] Review of a *res judicata* requires a party to return to the ICT that produced the relevant decision. But given the need for certainty that underpins *res judicata* as a doctrine, and ICT's ability to revisit its prior determinations is restrained. Two

---

[204] The combined median cost is less onerous, but still over USD 6 million: M Hodgson, Y Kryvoi and D Hrcka, *2021 Empirical Study: Costs, Damages and Duration in Investor-State Arbitration* (BIICL 2021) fig 3.
[205] See, eg, *Poštová banka as & Istrokapital SE v Hellenic Republic*, ICSID Case No ARB/13/8, Award, 9 April 2015, para 377; *Belenergia SA v Italy*, ICSID Case No ARB/15/40, Award, 6 August 2019, para 647; *Muhammet Çap & Anor v Turkmenistan*, ICSID Case No ARB/12/6, Award, 4 May 2021, para 990.
[206] Bradfield and Verdirame, 'Costs' (n 203) 417–19.
[207] Some tribunals see it as a reflection of principle of full reparation for internationally wrongful acts in the law of State responsibility: *Gemplus SA & Ors v Mexico*, ICSID Case Nos ARB(AF)/04/3 & ARB(AF)/04/4, Award 16 June 2010, para 17.21–17.22.
[208] See, eg, *Karkey v Pakistan*, Award (n 172) para 1060; *Unión Fenosa v Egypt*, Award (n 162) para 12.15; *Adel A Hamadi Al Tamimi v Oman*, ICSID Case No ARB/11/33, Award, 3 November 2015, para 473; *Cortec Mining Kenya Limited & Ors v Kenya*, ICSID Case No ARB/15/29, Award, 22 October 2018, para 388–401; *Stadtwerke München GmbH & Ors v Spain*, ICSID Case No ARB/15/1, Award, 2 December 2019, paras 398–406.
[209] See, eg, *Gavrilović v Croatia*, Award (n 149) para 1316; *Marco Gavazzi & Anor v Romania*, ICSID Case No ARB/12/25, Award, 18 April 2017, para 311; *Blue Bank International & Trust Ltd v Venezuela*, ICSID Case No ARB/12/20, Award, 26 April 2017, para 207.
[210] Bradfield and Verdirame, 'Costs' (n 203) 419–21. See, eg, *Krederi Ltd v Ukraine*, ICSID Case No ARB/14/17, Award, 2 July 2018, para 739.
[211] Brown, *Common Law* (n 10) 155.
[212] See, eg, ICJ Statute, Articles 59–61: *Bosnian Genocide*, Judgment (n 155) para 115.
[213] Though there are exceptions, eg the right of appeal to the PCIJ from decisions of the inter-war Mixed Arbitral Tribunals: *Judgment of the Hungaro-Czechoslovak Mixed Arbitral Tribunal (Peter Pàzmàny University v Czechoslovakia) (Czechoslovakia v Hungary)*, Judgment (1933) PCIJ Series A/B No 61. The ICJ previously possessed more limited review powers over the administrative tribunals of some UN bodies, eg the International Labour Organization: *Judgment No 2867 of the Administrative Tribunal of the International Labour Organization upon a Complaint Filed against the International Fund for Agricultural Development*, Advisory Opinion [2012] ICJ Rep 10, paras 28–32.

widely recognized jurisdictions are here examined: the interpretation jurisdiction, by which the ICT does not formally displace a *res judicata* but instead elaborates on its scope and meaning; and the revision jurisdiction, by which the ICT interrogates the *res judicata* in light of new information and determines whether it can stand.[214] Although often treated compendiously, they are separate procedures with distinct requirements.[215]

I. *Res judicata*

Although *res judicata* as it arises in different systems of domestic law is not a uniform concept,[216] its meaning in international law has been stable for over a century: once an issue between two (or more) parties has been decided by an ICT, it cannot later be reopened between those parties.[217] The rationale for such principle is straightforward, and was distilled by the *Trail Smelter* tribunal: '[i]f it is true that international relations based on law and justice require arbitral or judicial adjudication of international disputes, it is equally true that such adjudication must […] remain unchallenged, if it is to be effective.'[218]   **71**

On this basis, *res judicata* has two effects: a positive one, that a judgment or award is final and binding on the parties and should be implemented, subject to any available appeal or review; and a negative one, that the subject matter of a judgment or award cannot be re-litigated once decided.[219] The latter is also capable of producing a *res judicata* internal to particular proceedings. If, for example, an ICT determines a substantive matter in a decision on jurisdiction, then that decision cannot be re-opened in later in the proceedings.[220]   **72**

The doctrine is subject to two significant limitations. The first is the so-called 'triple identity' test of 'parties, object, cause'[221]: for a particular issue to be precluded by operation of *res judicata*, it must be between the same parties as an earlier decision in which the issue is said to have been decided, consider the same material facts, and have the same broad objective. The ambit of the latter two elements—occasionally collapsed into a single element requiring consideration of the same 'question at issue'[222]—should not be policed fastidiously lest the rule be avoided through artful pleading.   **73**

---

[214] Not examined is the *sui generis* jurisdiction arising under Article 52(1) of the ICSID Convention for annulment of an ICSID award on narrow procedural grounds. Nor is the rectification jurisdiction arising under Article 49(2) of the ICSID Convention, by which an ICSID tribunal may be asked to correct a relatively minor clerical, arithmetical, or similar error. This has been considered an inherent power of ICTs: *Delimitation of the Continental Shelf (UK/France)*, Decision of 14 March 1978 (1978) XVIII RIAA 271, para 36 (hereafter *Anglo-French Continental Shelf*, Decision); *Application for Revision and Interpretation of the Judgment of 24 February 1982 in the Case concerning the* Continental Shelf (Tunisia/Libya) *(Tunisia v Libya)*, Judgment [1985] ICJ Rep 192, para 10.

[215] J Joly Hébert, 'Distinguishing Interpretation and Revision Proceedings at the International Court of Justice' (2020) 19 LPICT 200. That said, the two are not always immediately distinguishable: *Anglo-French Continental Shelf*, Decision (n 214) para 29.

[216] K Hobér, '*Res Judicata* and *Lis Pendens* in International Arbitration' (2014) 336 RdC 106, 126–44, 153–59.

[217] *Company General of the Orinoco (France) v Venezuela* (1905) X RIAA 184, 276. Further: *Barcelona Traction, Light and Power Company, Limited (Belgium v Spain)*, Preliminary Objections [1964] ICJ Rep 6, 20.

[218] *Trail Smelter (US/Canada)* Decision of 11 March 1941 (1941) III RIAA 1938, 1950–51 (hereafter *Trail Smelter*, Decision).

[219] *GPF GP Sàrl v Poland*, SCC Case No 2014/168, Award, 29 April 2020, para 284.

[220] *Bosnian Genocide*, Judgment (n 155) paras 120, 140. But cf *Standard Chartered Bank (Hong Kong) Limited v Tanzania Electric Supply Company Limited*, ICSID Case No ARB/10/20, Award, 12 September 2016, para 315; *Infracapital F1 Sàrl & Anor v Spain*, ICSID Case No ARB/16/18, Reconsideration, 1 February 2022, para 84.

[221] *Trail Smelter*, Decision (n 218) 1952.

[222] See, eg, *China Navigation Co Ltd (GB) v US* (1921) VI RIAA 64, 65.

74 The second is that only those findings recorded by the ICT in the operative part of the decision have preclusive force.[223] This means that 'the binding effect [of the judgment] attaches only to the operative part and not to the statement of reasons'.[224] Again, however, this statement should not be applied strictly, as 'it is almost always necessary to refer to the statement of reasons to understand clearly the operative part and above all to ascertain the *causa petendi*'.[225]

75 Thus, a *res judicata* will be produced not only by the ultimate finding as recorded in the *dispositif*, but all legal and factual determinations necessary to support that finding.[226] From this, it follows that where the ICT (a) does not resolve a particular question (eg where it makes no finding on the merits on the basis that it lacks jurisdiction,[227] or dismisses a particular allegation for lack of evidence[228]), or (b) rests no part of the operative part of its decision on its answer to that question, no *res judicata* will arise.[229]

76 The IIL conception of *res judicata* elaborates discretely on the wider concept. The major constitutive instruments and procedural rules include affirmations of its positive effect,[230] with the negative effect being established as a general principle of law.[231] The injection of corporate groups into the procedural framework has, however, caused some tribunals to widen the entities that might be affected by *res judicata* to the parties and their privies; that is, entities that share a party's interest such that they are indissociable. Thus, in *RSM v Grenada*, the claimants were the shareholders of the claimant in a prior BIT arbitration against the respondent, and were held bound by the decisions of the prior tribunal as a result.[232]

II. Interpretation

77 Interpretation as a jurisdiction involves an ICT revisiting an earlier-pronounced *res judicata* at the request of one or both of the parties in light of a dispute over its meaning. The first recognizable modern examples arose in the nineteenth century.[233] That said, the early record contains a greater number of cases in which interpretation was refused. This was not a reflection of *res judicata*, but of the ad hoc arbitration then-prevalent, pursuant to which an arbitrator was rendered *functus officio* once the award was rendered. The problem was not so much that the arbitrator lacked jurisdiction to interpret the award so much as he lacked jurisdiction to do anything at all.[234]

---

[223] Cheng, *General Principles* (n 38) 348–50.
[224] *Interpretation of Judgments Nos 7 and 8 (Factory at Chorzów) (Germany v Poland)*, Judgment (1927) PCIJ Series A No 13, 24 (hereafter *Chorzów Factory (Interpretation)*, Judgment).
[225] *Chorzów Factory (Interpretation)*, Judgment (n 224) 24 (Judge Anzilotti). See more recently *Bosnian Genocide*, Judgment (n 155) para 126; *Delimitation Beyond 200 Nautical Miles*, Preliminary Objections (n 42) para 59.
[226] *Bosnian Genocide*, Judgment (n 155) para 115. Further: V Lowe, 'Res Judicata and the Rule of Law in International Arbitration' (1996) 8 RADIC 38, 40.
[227] *Trail Smelter*, Decision (n 218) 1953.
[228] *Delimitation Beyond 200 Nautical Miles*, Preliminary Objections (n 42) para 85.
[229] Cheng, *General Principles* (n 38) 350–56.
[230] See, eg, ICSID Convention, Art. 53(1); UNCITRAL Rules 1976, Art. 32(2); UNCITRAL Rules 2010, Art. 34(2). See also New York Convention, Art. III.
[231] See, eg, *Apotex v US*, Award (n 163) para 7.11.
[232] *Rachel S Grynberg & Ors v Grenada*, ICSID Case No ARB/10/6, Award, 10 December 2010, paras 7.1–7.5. See also *Ampal-American Israel Corp & Ors v Egypt*, ICSID Case No ARB/12/11, Liability, 21 February 2017, paras 266–70.
[233] See, eg, *EG Montano (Peru) v US* (1870) II RdAI 583, 601. But cf Brown, *Common Law* (n 10) 165.
[234] K Grzybowski, 'Interpretation of Decisions of International Tribunals' (1941) 35 AJIL 482, 484–85.

To avoid this problem, when dealing with a situation where a tribunal is formed to decide **78** a single dispute, it must be given jurisdiction to interpret its award. Thus, Article 82 of the 1907 Hague Convention provided that '[a]ny dispute arising between the parties as to the interpretation [...] of the Award shall [...] be submitted to the Tribunal which produced it'.[235] Article 50 of the ICSID Convention grants a similar extension to the life of an ICSID tribunal, stating that '[i]f any dispute shall arise between the parties as to the meaning or scope of an award, either party may request interpretation of the award', and that said request 'shall, if possible, be submitted to the Tribunal which rendered the award'. Similar provisions are made in the 1976 and 2010 UNCITRAL Rules.[236] Alternatively, the parties may jointly request that a tribunal be reconstituted to interpret its prior award,[237] or that the matter be submitted to a new tribunal with an interpretive mandate.[238] In the case of a permanent ICT, however, this problem does not arise. Such an ICT has an inherent power to interpret its past decisions where a disputes as to their meaning arise.[239]

The practice of the ICJ provides authoritative guidance as the scope of the interpretation jur- **79** isdiction.[240] Article 60 of the Statute provides that '[i]n the event of dispute as to the meaning or scope of the judgment, the Court shall construe it upon the request of any party'. The Court has interpreted this language strictly, holding that interpretation is confined to the judgment which is in dispute.[241] Thus, in *Avena (Interpretation)*, Mexico's request that the Court pronounce on the domestic enforceability of its prior judgment in that case was ruled inadmissible on the basis that the question was not before the Court in the original proceedings.[242] By contrast, the Court in *Temple (Interpretation)* deemed admissible a request to explain what it meant when it indicated in its original judgment that Thailand was required to withdraw its military and police forces from the 'vicinity' of the eponymous temple. The Court in due course held it had confirmed Cambodian sovereignty over the entire promontory of Preah Vihear and that this constituted the vicinity.[243]

Implicit in the interpretive jurisdiction is the ability for the ICT to identify what has been **80** finally decided in a prior judgment or award.[244] This is more or less coterminous with the *res judicata* that the judgment or award represents.[245] Thus, the Court held in *Temple (Interpretation)* that a request for interpretation 'must relate to the operative clause of the

---

[235] Hague Convention for the Pacific Settlement of International Disputes, 18 October 1907, 205 CTS 233.
[236] 1976 UNCITRAL Rules, Art. 35; 2010 UNCITRAL Rules, Art. 37. See also UNCLOS, Annex VI, Art. 33(3), Annex VII, Art. 12
[237] See, eg, *Interpretation of the Air Transport Services Agreement between the United States of America and France (US/France)*, Decision on Interpretation (1964) XVI RIAA 73, 73–74.
[238] Or occasionally to multiple tribunals: see, eg, *Frontier Case (Argentina/Chile)*, Award (1966) XVI RIAA 109, 174–80; *Delimitation of the Frontier Line between Boundary Post 62 and Mount Fitzroy (Argentina/Chile)*, Award (1994) XXII RIAA 3, paras 61–77.
[239] Brown, *Common Law* (n 10) 162–64. Further: *Crawford & Ors v UN Secretary General*, Award (1955) 1 UNAT Rep 331, 335.
[240] *Anglo-French Continental Shelf*, Decision (n 214) paras 28–29; *Ethiopia-Eritrea Boundary Commission*, Interpretation, Correction and Consultation (2002) XXV RIAA 196, para 16.
[241] *Request for Interpretation of the Judgment of 20 November 1950 in the Asylum Case (Colombia/Peru)* (Colombia/Peru), Judgment [1950] ICJ Rep 395, 403. See also *Chorzów Factory (Interpretation)*, Judgment (n 224) 21.
[242] *Request for Interpretation of the Judgment of 31 March 2004 in the Case concerning Avena and Other Mexican Nationals (Mexico v US)*, Judgment [2009] ICJ Rep 3, para 45.
[243] *Request for Interpretation of the Judgment of 15 June 1962 in the Case concerning* the Temple of Preah Vihear (Cambodia v Thailand), Judgment [2013] ICJ Rep 281, para 108 (hereafter *Temple (Interpretation)*, Judgment).
[244] *Chorzów Factory (Interpretation)*, Judgment (n 224) 11–12; *Temple (Interpretation)*, Judgment (n 243) para 34.
[245] But cf A Kulick, 'Article 60 ICJ Statute, Interpretation Proceedings, and the Competing Concepts of *Res Judicata*' (2015) 28 LJIL 73.

judgment in question and cannot concern the reasons for the judgment except insofar as these are inseparable from the operative clause', with inseparability in this respect referring to those 'essential' findings of law or fact on which the *dispositif* rests.[246]

81 The Court's approach to its interpretation jurisdiction has been influential in the IIL context. In the first request for interpretation under Article 50(1) of the ICSID Convention, the *Wena Hotels v Egypt* tribunal shaped its understanding of its jurisdiction by reference to PCIJ and ICJ decisions—as well as the determinations of the Court of Arbitration in *Anglo-French Continental Shelf*, itself based on ICJ authority.[247] The tribunal held that for an application to be admissible, it had to be directed towards the interpretation of an award and not its expansion,[248] and that it should be limited to the operative part the award and the essential reasoning supporting it.[249] It also added a further requirement that the interpretive dispute that prompted the application 'must at least have some practical relevance to the award's implementation'.[250] This analysis was approved in *ATA v Jordan*,[251] and by tribunals operating under the ICSID Additional Facility Rules.[252]

82 Practice under the UNCITRAL Rules on interpretation is more limited, and less automatically deferential to ICJ authority, but the result is the same.[253] In *Methanex v US*, the tribunal noted that its interpretation jurisdiction was 'limited to an interpretation of the award in the form of clarification; and [...] cannot extend to a request to modify or annul the award or take the form of an appeal or review of the award'.[254]

III. Revision

83 An ICT's revision jurisdiction allows wholescale modification or displacement of a *res judicata* based on the discovery of a new fact after a judgment or award is rendered. Revision is not in any sense a retrial of decided questions, and an error of law, however grave, is not sufficient to invoke it.[255]

84 The early history of the revision jurisdiction parallels that of interpretation: inconsistent practice on whether it was an inherent power of ICTs,[256] followed by the matter being put

---

[246] *Chorzów Factory (Interpretation)*, Judgment (n 224) 20; *Temple (Interpretation)*, Judgment (n 243) para 34. But cf ibid, paras 1–2 (Judges Owada, Bennouna and Gaja).
[247] *Wena Hotels Limited v Egypt*, ICSID Case No ARB/98/4, Interpretation, 31 October 2005 [80]–[126] (hereafter *Wena Hotels v Egypt*, Interpretation).
[248] *Wena Hotels v Egypt*, Interpretation (n 247) paras 82, 106.
[249] ibid para 84.
[250] ibid.
[251] *ATA Construction, Industrial and Trading Company v Jordan*, ICSID Case No ARB/08/2, Interpretation and Provisional Measures, 7 March 2011, para 35.
[252] *David Minnotte & Anor v Poland*, ICSID Case No ARB(AF)/10/1, Interpretation, 22 October 2014, para 11 (hereafter *Minnotte v Poland*, Interpretation). Further: *Marvin Roy Feldman Karpa v Mexico*, ICSID Case No ARB(AF)/99/1, Correction and Interpretation, 13 June 2003 [10].
[253] This is unsurprising given the interpretation jurisprudence of the Iran–US Claims Tribunal, which rejected requests as disguised attempts to reargue the merits: see, eg, *Ford Aerospace & Communications Corp & Ors v Iranian Air Force* (1986) 12 Iran–US CTR 304, 305; *Picker Intl Corp v Iran* (1986) 12 Iran–US CTR 306, 307; *Pepsico Inc v Iran* (1986) 13 Iran–US CTR 328, 329–30; *Paul Donin de Rosiere & Ors v Iran* (1987) 14 Iran–US CTR 100, 101–02; *Norman Gabay v Iran* (1991) 27 Iran–US CTR 194, 195.
[254] *Methanex Corporation v US*, UNCITRAL/NAFTA, Letter on Interpretation, 25 September 2002, para 2.
[255] *Trail Smelter*, Decision (n 218) 1957; *Delimitation of the Frontier Line between Boundary Post 62 and Mount Fitzroy (Argentina/Chile)*, Revision and Interpretation (1995) XXII RIAA 151, para 27.
[256] Particularly that of the Mexican–American Claims Commission: Brown, *Common Law* (n 10) 166–71.

beyond doubt via express grant.[257] Article 51(1) of the ICSID Convention provides that '[e]ither party may request revision of the award […] on the ground of the discovery of some fact or such nature as to decisively affect the award'. No similar provision appears in the 1976 or 2010 UNCITRAL Rules. But the direction of travel is in favour of recognition of revision as an inherent power[258]—provided the ICT is permanent[259] or has jurisdiction over the dispute when the request is made.[260] That said, the institutional features of a particular tribunal may exclude an inherent power to revise its decisions.[261]

As with interpretation, the practice of the ICJ has been determinative in shaping the revision jurisdiction. Article 61(1) of the ICJ Statute sets out the basic parameters of the power: **85**

> An application for revision of a judgment may be made only when it is based upon the discovery of some fact of such a nature as to be a decisive factor, which fact was, when the judgment was given, unknown to the Court and also to the party claiming revision, always provided that such ignorance was not due to negligence.

This language belies several thorny epistemological questions which the Court has tried to answer.[262] The 'fact' on which the request is based must have been extant at the time of judgment, but only 'discovered' after it was handed down.[263] In this sense, what is usually uncovered after the judgment is not the fact itself, but evidence of the fact. Thus, El Salvador's application in *Land, Island and Maritime Frontier Dispute (Revision)* was based in part on a pre-existing fact that was said to be discovered through scientific methods developed after the judgment.[264] The fact must also be 'decisive', in the sense that, if true, it would materially affect the *res judicata* that the revision application seeks to displace.[265] **86**

So far as the level of knowledge required, the Court has not stated this with precision, but it may perhaps be inferred from *Tunisia/Libya (Revision and Interpretation)* that a fact is deemed 'known' by the party seeking revision (and the Court, as required) at the point at which it is established on the evidence available[266]—such that where the fact is particularly grave, the more evidence is required before awareness manifests. With respect to the **87**

---

[257] See, eg, Hague Convention for the Pacific Settlement of International Disputes, 29 July 1899, 187 CTS 410, Art. 55.
[258] Brown, *Common Law* (n 10) 166–71.
[259] *Effect of Awards of Compensation made by the UN Administrative Tribunal*, Advisory Opinion [1954] ICJ Rep 47, 51–53, 55.
[260] *Trail Smelter*, Decision (n 218) 1954.
[261] *Iran v US (Case Nos A3, A8, A9, A14 & B 61)*, IUSCT Case Nos A3, A8, A9, A14, B61 (Decision, 1 July 2011) [64] (hereafter *Case Nos A3, A8, A9, A14, B61*, Decision).
[262] A Zimmermann and R Geiß, 'Article 61' in A Zimmermann and CJ Tams (eds), *The Statute of the International Court of Justice: A Commentary* (3rd edn, OUP 2019) 1651, paras 41–70 (hereafter Zimmermann and Geiß, 'Article 61').
[263] *Application for Revision of the Judgment of 11 July 1996 in the Case concerning* Application of the Convention on the Prevention and Punishment of the Crime of Genocide *(Bosnia and Herzegovina v Yugoslavia), Preliminary Objections (Yugoslavia v Bosnia and Herzegovina)*, Judgment [2003] ICJ Rep 7, para 70. See also *Battus (France) v Bulgaria*, Revision (1929) 9 TAM 284, 284–86.
[264] *Application for Revision of the Judgment of 11 September 1992 in the Case concerning the* Land, Island and Maritime Frontier Dispute (El Salvador/Honduras; Nicaragua intervening) *(El Salvador v Honduras)*, Judgment [2003] ICJ Rep 392, para 26.
[265] *Application for Revision and Interpretation of the Judgment of 24 February 1982 in the Case concerning the* Continental Shelf (Tunisia/Libya) *(Tunisia v Libya)*, Judgment [1985] ICJ Rep 192, [39] (hereafter *Tunisia/Libya (Revision and Interpretation)*, Judgment).
[266] *Tunisia/Libya (Revision and Interpretation)*, Judgment (n 265) para 19.

requirement that the unawareness not be the result of negligence, the party seeking revision is expected to undertake all 'reasonable and appropriate' efforts to uncover the relevant fact prior to judgment.[267] If a reasonably diligent party would have become aware of the fact in the course of preparing its case, this threshold will not be met.[268]

88 If these requirements seem harsh, it is because they reflect the primacy of *res judicata*. The same may be said of the time limits on revision under Articles 61(4) and (5) of the Statute: the application for revision must be made within six months from the discovery of the new fact and within ten years of the date of judgment in any event. Read strictly, if either of these time limits elapse, any request for revision will become inadmissible.

89 As with interpretation, the ICJ's conception of revision has determined IIL's understanding of the subject. This is most apparent in the ICSID context. Article 51(1) of the ICSID Convention is modelled on Article 61(1) of the ICJ Statute and has the same requirements:[269] a newly discovered fact, extant when the award was issued but unknown to the applicant and tribunal, ignorance of which was not the result of the applicant's negligence, and of such a nature as to decisively affect the award.[270] Article 51(2) of the ICSID Convention also imposes time limits on revision, although these are even more restrictive than those contained in the ICJ Statute, requiring that any application be made within ninety days of the discovery of the relevant fact, and within three years of the award in any event. Given this clear debt, it is no surprise that key parts of the discussion in the early authority of *Venezuela Holdings v Venezuela* were driven by the tribunal's consideration of how the ICJ's decision in *Bosnian Genocide (Revision)* applied to the facts of that case.[271]

90 Revision practice in the UNCITRAL context is more limited owing to the lack of an express power to revise in either the 1976 or 2010 UNCITRAL Rules. This silence is exacerbated by the fact that Iran–US Claims Tribunal, as the principal source of practice with respect to the 1976 UNCITRAL Rules in particular, refused to take a firm position on the availability of an implied power of revision,[272] before finally denying its existence.[273] Nonetheless, at least one UNCITRAL tribunal held that that it did have such a power—at least in circumstances where the tribunal was not *functus officio*.[274] Where the tribunal is *functus officio*, the result may be different—as decisions rendered under the ICSID Additional Facility Rules, which do not include an express power of revision, show.[275]

---

[267] ibid para 24.
[268] Zimmermann and Geiß, 'Article 61' (n 262) paras 67–70.
[269] C Schreuer, L Malintoppi, A Reinisch and A Sinclair, *The ICSID Convention: A Commentary* (2nd edn, CUP 2009) 879.
[270] *Venezuela Holdings BV & Ors v Venezuela*, ICSID Case No ARB/07/27, Revision, 12 June 2015, para 3.1.3 (hereafter *Venezuela Holdings v Venezuela*, Revision).
[271] *Venezuela Holdings v Venezuela*, Revision (n 270) paras 3.1.16–3.1.17. Further: *Víctor Pey Casado & Anor v Chile (I)*, ICSID Case No ARB/98/2, Revision, 18 November 2009, paras 30–34; *Burlington Resources Inc v Ecuador*, ICSID Case No ARB/08/5, Award, 7 February 2017, paras 97, 100.
[272] See, eg, *Morris v Iran* (1983) 3 Iran–US CTR 364, 365; *Ram International Industries Inc v Iran* (1993) 29 Iran–US CTR 383, 390.
[273] *Case Nos A3, A8, A9, A14, B61*, Decision (n 261) para 64.
[274] *Antoine Biloune & Anor v Ghana*, Damages and Costs (1990) 95 ILR 211, para 67.
[275] See, eg, *Minnotte v Poland*, Interpretation (n 252) para 12; *Gold Reserve Inc v Venezuela*, ICSID Case No ARB(AF)/09/1, Corrections, 15 December 2014, para 37.

I. Conclusion

IIL tribunals—whether ICSID or otherwise—operate in accordance with a general procedural law rooted in the principle of state consent to international jurisdiction. While the influence of this law on IIL tribunals is not as direct as, say, the law of treaties or the law on State responsibility, it exerts a palpable influence on the way things are done. Its motive force is the practice of the PCIJ and ICJ, in which many of the concepts addressed in this entry were developed over the Court's century of activity. Other tribunals also form part of the picture: the various Claims Commissions of the late nineteenth and early twentieth centuries, the Iran–US Claims Tribunal, ITLOS and UNCLOS Annex VII tribunals, the World Trade Organization (WTO) Dispute Settlement Panels and Appellate Body, and a constellation of ad hoc interstate arbitral tribunals and other bodies. 91

As IIL has grown and matured, its tribunals have begun to develop their own, *sui generis*, practice on matters like counterclaims and on costs. Moreover, through their constituent instruments and procedural rules, they may also be said to have rendered other concepts redundant—such as extinctive prescription—at least in part. All this is not to say, however, that IIL is breaking off from the wider system of international dispute settlement, merely that the institutional features of the ICSID Convention, BITs, and MITs produce bespoke outcomes, as their drafters intended. But the practice of IIL tribunals show that until displaced, the usual rules apply, allowing the decisions of these bodies to, in turn, influence the ocean of principles on which their operation depends. In this sense, the procedural ties that link IIL to general international law are continually renewed and strengthened, to the benefit of international dispute settlement as a whole. 92

Selected literature

Core Sources

Brower CN and Brueschke JD, *The Iran–United States Claims Tribunal* (Martinus Nijhoff Publishers 1998).

Brown C, *A Common Law of International Adjudication* (OUP 2004).

Cheng B, *General Principles of Law as Applied by International Courts and Tribunals* (Stevens & Sons 1953; reissue CUP 1994).

De Brabandere E, *Investment Treaty Arbitration as Public International Law: Procedural Aspects and Implications* (CUP 2014).

Douglas Z, *The International Law of Investment Claims* (CUP 2009).

Lauterpacht E, 'Principles of Procedure in International Litigation' (2011) 345 RdC 387.

Lauterpacht H, *Private Law Sources and Analogies of International Law* (Longmans 1927).

Pellet A, 'The Case Law of the ICJ in Investment Arbitration' (2013) 28 ICSID Rev 223.

Particular Topics

Bjorklund A and Brosseau J, 'Sources of Inherent Powers in International Adjudication' in Franco Ferrari and Friedrich Rosenfeld (eds), *Inherent Powers in International Arbitration* (JurisNet 2018).

Bradfield M and Verdirame G, 'Costs in Investment Treaty Arbitration' in Chiara Giorgetti (ed), *Litigating International Investment Disputes: A Practitioner's Guide* (Brill 2014).

Caron DD and Caplan LM, *The UNCITRAL Arbitration Rules: A Commentary* (2nd edn, OUP 2013).

Commission Jeffrey and Moloo Rahim, *Procedural Issues in International Investment Arbitration* (OUP 2018).

Crawford J, 'Treaty and Contract in Investment Arbitration' (2008) 24 Arb Int 351.

Crawford J, *State Responsibility: The General Part* (CUP 2013).

Douglas Z, 'Can a Doctrine of Precedent be Justified in Investment Treaty Arbitration?' (2010) 25 ICSID Rev/FILJ 104.

Douglas Z, Pauwelyn J and Viñuales J (eds), *The Foundations of International Investment Law: Bringing Theory into Practice* (OUP 2014).

Fouret J, Gerbay R and Alvarez GM (eds), *The ICSID Convention, Regulations and Rules: A Practical Commentary* (Edward Elgar Publishing 2019).

Grzybowski K, 'Interpretation of Decisions of International Tribunals' (1941) 35 AJIL 482.

Harris C, 'Incidental Determinations in Proceedings under Compromissory Clauses' (2021) 70 ICLQ 417.

Hepburn J, *Domestic Law in International Investment Arbitration* (OUP 2017).

Hobér K, 'Extinctive Prescription and Public International Law' in *Essays on International Arbitration* (JurisNet 2006) 153.

Hobér K, '*Res Judicata* and *Lis Pendens* in International Arbitration' (2014) 336 RdC 106.

Jenks CW, 'The Interpretation and Application of Municipal Law by the Permanent Court of International Justice' (1938) 19 BYIL 67.

Joly Hébert J, 'Distinguishing Interpretation and Revision Proceedings at the International Court of Justice' (2020) 19 LPICT 200.

Kaikobad KH, *Interpretation and Revision of International Boundary Decisions* (CUP 2007).

Kinnear M and others (eds), *Building International Investment Law: The First 50 Years of ICSID* (Kluwer 2016).

Kolb R, *The International Court of Justice* (Hart 2013).

Lowe V, '*Res Judicata* and the Rule of Law in International Arbitration' (1996) 8 RADIC 38.

McIntyre J, 'Put on Notice: The Role of the Dispute Requirement in Assessing Jurisdiction and Admissibility before the International Court' (2018) 19 MJIL 546.

Miles C, *Provisional Measures before International Courts and Tribunals* (CUP 2017).

de Nanteuil A, 'Counterclaims in Investment Arbitration: Old Questions, New Answers?' (2018) 17 LPICT 374.

Paparinskis M, 'Revisiting the Indispensable Third Party Principle' (2020) 103 RDI 49.

Paparinskis M, 'Long Live *Monetary Gold* *Terms and Conditions Apply' (2021) 115 AJIL Unbound 154.

Reisman WM, *Nullity and Revision: The Review and Enforcement of International Judgments and Awards* (YUP 1971).

Riddell A and Plant B, *Evidence before the International Court of Justice* (BIICL 2009).

Sasson M, *Substantive Law in Investment Treaty Arbitration: The Unsettled Relationship between International Law and Municipal Law* (2nd edn, Kluwer 2017).

Schreuer C and others, *The ICSID Convention: A Commentary* (2nd edn, CUP 2009).[*]

Shahabuddeen M, *Precedent in the World Court* (CUP 1996).

Shany Y, *The Competing Jurisdictions of International Courts and Tribunals* (OUP 2003).

Shany Y, *Jurisdiction and Admissibility before International Courts* (CUP 2016).

Sheppard A, 'The Jurisdictional Threshold of a *Prima Facie* Case' in Muchlinski PT and others (eds), *The Oxford Handbook of International Investment Law* (OUP 2008) 932.

---

[*] See now SW Schill and others (eds), *Schreuer's Commentary on the ICSID Convention* (3rd edn, CUP 2022), published while this entry was in press.

Sourgens FG et al, *Evidence in International Investment Arbitration* (OUP 2018).
Yannaca-Small K (ed), *Arbitration under International Investment Agreements: A Guide to the Key Issues* (2nd edn, OUP 2018).
Zimmermann A and Tams CJ (eds), *The Statute of the International Court of Justice: A Commentary* (3rd edn, OUP 2019).

Nationality

Chiara Giorgetti

A.	Introduction	1	IV.	Effective nationality in ICSID practice: Article 25 ICSID Convention as *lex specialis*	35
B.	Acquisition and recognition of nationality	5	V.	Exceptions to the effective nationality principle in non-ICSID cases	40
	I. International law generally recognizes domestic regulation of nationality	5	VI.	Continuous nationality rule	41
	1. Definitions of nationality in BITs	9	VII.	Notable exceptions related to nationality of individuals	42
	2. Nationality requirements in the ICSID Convention	14	D.	The nationality of corporations	44
C.	Nationality of individuals in the practice of investment tribunals	15	I.	General principle: The nationality of corporation is regulated domestically	44
	I. Dual nationality and the requirement of a dominant and effective nationality	23	II.	Specific Challenges: nationality of shareholders, piercing the corporate veil and nationality of convenience	46
	II. General practice of the dominant and effective nationality principle in public international law	24	III.	Corporate nationality in the practice of international courts and tribunal	47
	1. The practice of the Iran–US Claims Tribunal	31	IV.	Application of the principles governing corporate nationality in the practice of investment tribunals	51
	2. The practice of the United Nations Claims Commission	32	E.	Conclusions	55
	III. Effective nationality in the practice of investment arbitral tribunals	33			

A. Introduction

1 Nationality provides the foundation for the protection of a person, be it natural or corporate, under international law. As such, it is an essential and also a complex concept. It is essential because it provides the crucial link between the State and physical or juridical persons that ties the substantive principles of international investment law (IIL) to those individuals who can benefit from them, and thus also grants them access to their rights and remedies.[1] It is also a complex concept because it is both a domestic and an international concept and not neatly regulated. International law recognizes the right of a State to enact legislation domestically as to individuals who are entitled to nationality and to regulate those nationals even

---

[1] P Weis, *Nationality and Statelessness in International Law* (2nd edn, Sijthoff & Noordhoff 1979) 65 ('the right of a State to determine who are, and who are not, its nationals is an essential element of its sovereignty'). See K Parlett, *The Individual in the International Legal System* (CUP 2011) and, generally, MN Shaw, *International Law* (9th edn, CUP 2021) 235.

when they are outside of its territory.[2] International law also imposes broad limits to domestic legislation via international treaties, for example on efforts to reduce statelessness or to regulate dual nationalities.[3]

When an individual is harmed due to another State's violation of international law, international law recognizes the right of the State of nationality of the individual to engage in so-called 'diplomatic protection' of nationals and pursue a claim on their behalf. More recently, individuals are also granted direct access to international tribunals to seek redress for international law violations.[4] Under specific treaty regimes, including most Bilateral Investment Treaties (BITs), individuals will be accorded certain rights based on their nationality, so that nationals of one of the contracting (home) State will be given certain protections in the other contracting (host) State.

Nationality is particularly relevant in IIL. When non-national aliens invest in a foreign State, BITs, treaties of friendship, commerce and navigation, and other international agreements afford them certain specific protections.[5] These usually include national treatment, the most-favoured-nation (MFN) standard,[6] and a variety of other rights, including fair and equitable treatment (FET), protection against illegal expropriation, prohibition of arbitrary and discriminatory treatment, and full protection and security.[7] In addition, customary international law also grants aliens a minimum standard of treatment. Conversely, investment treaties might also exclude aliens from engaging in certain specific economic sectors (for example telecommunication or natural resources) and be required to respect local law. Crucially, aliens' protection of their IIL rights largely depends on their nationality. Thus, a State might espouse its national's right against another State in an international forum as a form of diplomatic protection, or, nowadays more frequently, foreign investors may directly exercise their right under international law in an international forum against a host State.[8]

Because of the key role that nationality plays in IIL, the practice of international courts and tribunals on the issue is both frequent and relevant, including on issues such as acquisition and recognition of nationality, dual nationality, and nationality of corporations. Indeed, commentators rightly note that 'the practice on nationality in investment law was shaped by the [nationality] rules of diplomatic protection developed in the practice of international courts and tribunals'.[9]

---

[2] See Convention of Nationality of The Hague Nationality, Art. 1 ('It is for each State to determine under its law who are its nationals. This law shall be recognised by other States in so far as it is consistent with international conventions, international custom, and the principles of law generally recognised with regard to nationality').

[3] See, for example, the 1930 Convention on certain Questions Relating to the Conflict of Nationality Laws, 12 April 1930, 179 LNTS 89; the 1963 Convention on reduction of Cases of Multiple Nationality and Military Obligations, 6 May 1963, ETS No 43 and its protocols; the Council of Europe's European Convention on Nationality, 6 November 1997, 37 ILM 44 (1998). For recent academic works, see ML Siegelberg, *Statelessness: A Modern History* (Harvard University Press 2020); W Hanley, 'Statelessness: An Invisible Theme in the History of International Law' (2014) 25 EJIL 321–27; N Jain, 'Manufacturing Statelessness' (2022) 116 AJIL 237–88

[4] See generally FO Vicuña, 'Changing Approaches to the Nationality of Claims in the Context of Diplomatic Protection and International Dispute Settlement' (2000) 15 ICSID Rev/FILJ 340 and C Baltag, *The Energy Charter Treaty: The Notion of Investor* (Kluwer Law International 2012) (hereafter Baltag).

[5] See generally A Reinisch, *Advanced Introduction to International Investment Law* (Edward Elgar Publishing 2020).

[6] See in this Commentary: Jingyuan Zhou and Sergio Puig, 'Cross-cutting substantive aspects: NAFTA standards in light of the decisions of international courts and tribunals'.

[7] ibid.

[8] See generally JG Olmedo, 'Nationality of Claim: Investment Arbitration' in *Max Planck Encyclopedia of International Procedural Law* (Oxford Public International Law 2019) (hereafter Olmedo).

[9] Baltag (n 4) 74.

B. Acquisition and recognition of nationality

I. International law generally recognizes domestic regulation of nationality

5   Each State generally has the right to regulate how to accord nationality (sometimes also referred to as 'citizenship') domestically.[10] Article 1 of the 1930 Conflict of Nationality Convention specifically states that 'it is for each State to determine under its own law who are its nationals' and that such law 'shall be recognized by other States in so far as it is consistent with international conventions, international custom, and the principles of law generally recognized with regard to nationality'.[11] For example, under the *jus soli* principle, those who are born in the territory of a State can acquire the nationality of that State. Similarly, under the *jus sanguinis* principle, those who are born by parents of a certain nationality acquire their nationality. Nationality can also be acquired by marriage, long-term residency, or can be awarded for special reasons, after military service or after making significant contributions or substantial investment.[12] Domestic legislation also provides for exceptions to these rules, for example most States do not award *jus soli* nationality to children of foreign diplomats. The nationality of a corporation is generally that of the State in which it has been incorporated or where its seat is headquartered.[13]

6   In *Nationality Decrees Issues in Tunis and Morocco*, the Permanent Court of International Justice (PCIJ) confirmed that questions of nationality are 'in principle within this reserved domain'[14] of States, though due consideration should be given to its obligations to other States. The PCIJ reiterated the same concept in *Acquisition of Polish Nationality*, where it stated that Poland's right to decide who should be regarded as its nationals be subject to the obligations it undertook under a specific Treaty (so-called Minorities Treaty).[15]

7   The principle that nationality is regulated domestically had also specifically been confirmed in the *Canevaro Claim*, which was decided by an arbitral tribunal sitting at the Permanent Court of Arbitration (PCA) in 1912 and related to an expropriated sovereign debt.[16] The tribunal rejected a claim by Raphael Canevaro on the grounds that, as a Peruvian national,

---

[10] International Law Commission, Draft Articles on Diplomatic Protection with commentaries, 2006 (A/61/10), Part II, Chapter II, Article 4, para 3 (hereinafter 'ILC Draft Articles on Diplomatic Protection with commentaries').

[11] Convention on Certain Questions Relating to the Conflict of Nationality Laws (12 April 1930, entered into force 1 July 1937) 179 LNTS 89.

[12] O Dörr, 'Nationality' in *Max Planck Encyclopedia of Public International Law* (Oxford Public International Law 2019).

[13] Draft Articles on Diplomatic Protection, Art. 9.

[14] *Nationality Decrees Issues in Tunis and Morocco*, Advisory Opinion, 7 February 1923, PCIJ Series B No 4, 24. The Court also went on to observe that 'it may well happen that, in a matter which, like that of nationality, is not, in principle, regulated by international law, the right of a State to use its discretion is nevertheless restricted by obligations which it may have undertaken towards other States' id.

[15] *Acquisition of Polish Nationality*, Advisory Opinion, 15 September 1923, PCIJ Series B, No 7 at 16, stating that 'Though, generally speaking, it is true that a sovereign State has the right to decide what persons shall be regarded as its nationals, it is no less true that this principle is applicable only subject to the Treaty obligations [of the Minorities Treaty between the Principal Allied and Associated Parties and Poland, signed at Versailles on June 28th 1919]'. Article 3 of the said Treaty provides that 'Poland admits and declared to Polish national ipso facto and without the requirement of any formalities German, Austrian, Hungarian or Russian nationals habitually resident at the date of the coming into force of the present treaty in territory which is or may be recognised as forming part of Poland, bus subject to any provision in the Treaties of Peace with Germany or Austria respectively relating to person who became resident in such territory after a specified date'.

[16] *Canevaro Claim (Italy v Peru)* PCA Case No 1910-01, Award of the Tribunal, 3 May 1912 https://pcacases.com/web/sendAttach/516 accessed 23 October 2023 (hereafter *Canevaro Claim*).

he could not bring an international case against Peru. The tribunal found that both Italy and Peru could properly legislate about his nationality.[17]

Because domestic legislations act separately and do not coordinate, it is possible for a person to be born 'stateless', i.e. without a nationality, or with more than one nationality. These situations, especially the latter one, have resulted in substantial case law in international investment arbitration, as this entry explored in Section C.I below.

1. Definitions of nationality in BITs

Most BITs and regional investment treaties include a definition of nationals to which the treaty terms apply. For example, the 1991 Argentina–US BIT defines a national of a party as 'a natural person who is a national of Party under its applicable law'.[18] The more recent US–Uruguay BIT, which is based on the 2012 Model BIT, is more specific. It defines an investor of 'a Party or state enterprise thereof, or a national or an enterprise of a Party, that attempts to make, is making, or has made an investment in the territory of the other Party'.[19]

BITs often include specific definitions for individual (natural persons) and corporate (legal persons) investors. For example, the Argentina–Italy BIT specifies that

> The term 'investor' includes any natural or legal person of one Contracting Party who has affected or assume the obligation to investments in the territory of the other contracting party.
> - 'natural person' means with regard to either Contracting Party to any natural person having the citizenship of that State in accordance with its laws.
> - 'legal person' means, in relation to each of the Contracting Parties, any entity constituted in accordance with the legislation of one Contracting Party in the territory of that Party and by the latter recognized, such as public entities involved in economic activity, corporations or associations, foundations and irrespective of whether their liabilities are limited or not.[20]

Because, as explained above, nationality rules are regulated domestically, a BIT could include two distinct definitions each applying to one of the signatory parties. Thus, for example, the Argentina–UK BIT defines an investor in respect of the UK as:

---

[17] id 1–2 (unofficial English translation) ('whereas, according to Peruvian legislation (Article 34 of the Constitution), Raphael Canevaro is a Peruvian by birth because he was born on Peruvian territory. As, on the other hand, the Italian legislation (Article 4 of the Civil Code) attributes to him Italian nationality because he was born of an Italian father [...] according to Peruvian legislation (Article 34 of the Constitution) [...] Whereas, under these circumstances, whatever Raphael Canevaro's status may be in Italy with respect to his nationality, the Government of Peru has the right to consider him as a Peruvian citizen and to deny his status as an Italian claimant'). See also *Flegenheimer* Case, Conciliation Commissions Established Pursuant to Article 83 Peace Treaty with Italy, Decision No 182 of 20 September 1958 (exclusive competence of the State in matters of nationality).

[18] Treaty Between United States of America and the Argentine Republic Concerning the Reciprocal Encouragement and Protection of Investment, signed on 14 November 1991 and entered into force on 20 October 1994, Article 1(1)(C).

[19] Treaty Between United States of America and the Oriental Republic of Uruguay Concerning the Reciprocal Encouragement and Protection of Investment, signed on 4 November 2005 and entered into force on 1 November 2006, Article 1 (definitions). The 2012 US Model Bilateral Investment Treaty is available at <https://2009-2017.state.gov/documents/organization/188371> accessed 23 October 2023.

[20] Agreement Between the Argentine Republic and the Italian Republic on Investment Promotion and Protection, signed on 22 May 1990 and entered into force on 14 October 1993, Article 1 (definitions).

(aa) natural persons deriving their status as United Kingdom nationals from the law in force in the United Kingdom; and
(bb) companies, corporations, firms, and associations incorporated or constituted under the law in force in any part of the United Kingdom or in any territory to which this Agreement is extended in accordance with the provisions of Article 12.[21]

12 And in respect of Argentina as:

(aa) any natural person, who is a national of the Republic of Argentina in accordance with its laws on nationality; and
(bb) any legal person constituted according to the laws and regulations of the Republic of Argentina or having its seat in the territory of the Republic of Argentina.[22]

13 Additionally, certain BIT may also include residence or domicile requirements. For example, the Germany–Israel BIT defines an Israeli national as a person having permanent residence in Israel.[23]

2. Nationality requirements in the ICSID Convention

14 Additionally, nationality can also be a personal jurisdiction requirement to access certain forums. Most notably, Article 25 of the International Centre for Settlement of Investment Disputes (ICSID) Convention extends jurisdiction to any legal dispute arising directly out of an investment between a Contracting State 'and a national of another Contracting State' and defines specifically the necessary requirements. Thus, natural persons must have 'the nationality of a Contracting State other than the State party to the dispute on the date on which the parties consented to submit such dispute to conciliation or arbitration as well as on the date on which the request was registered' and must also not have the nationality of the Contracting State party to the dispute on either date. Juridical person must have 'the nationality of a Contracting State other than the State party to the dispute on the date on which the parties consented to submit such dispute to conciliation or arbitration'.[24]

C. Nationality of individuals in the practice of investment tribunals

15 Although nationality provisions are regulated domestically, when questions of nationality reach international tribunals and are often essential to their jurisdictional findings, tribunals routinely address and review the application of domestic rules.[25]

16 For example, in *von Pezold and others v Zimbabwe*, a case arising out of an expropriation of three estates owned by claimants and applying the Switzerland–Zimbabwe and

---

[21] Agreement Between the Government of the United Kingdom of Great Britain and Northern Ireland and the Government of the Republic of Argentina for the Promotion and Protection of Investments, 11 December 1990, Article 1(c), 1765 UNTS 33.
[22] ibid.
[23] Treaty between the Federal Republic of Germany and the State of Israel concerning the Encouragement and Reciprocal Protection of Investments, signed on 24 June 1976, Article 1.
[24] Convention on the Settlement of Investment Disputes between States and Nationals of Other States, Article 25.
[25] See, eg, *Flegenheimer* Case, Conciliation Commissions Established Pursuant to Article 83 Peace Treaty with Italy, Decision No 182 of 20 September 1958 (power of investigation of international tribunals, evidence of nationality).

Germany–Zimbabwe BITs, the von Pezold claimants argued that they were both Swiss and German nationals, save for Rüdiger von Pezold who was only a German national. Responded agreed but also argued that Heinrich and Rüdiger von Pezold also had Zimbabwean nationality which disqualified them from bringing a claim against Zimbabwe. Claimants denied they had Zimbabwean nationality and respondent did not pursue the argument further. The tribunal reviewed the evidence and was satisfied that 'each of the von Pezold Claimants fulfill[ed] the nationality criteria'.[26]

Importantly, international arbitral tribunals confirmed that they assess nationality independently. **17**

In *Champion Trading v Egypt*, for example, an ICSID arbitral tribunal decided on a claim arising out of the enactment of Egyptian laws in the mid-1990s that privatized and liberalized cotton trade, and denied jurisdiction based on an Egypt–US BIT to the three individual claimants because they had unknowingly acquired Egyptian nationality at birth from their Egyptian father and therefore could not bring a case against Egypt.[27] **18**

In *Soufraki v UAE*, the investor relied on the Italy-UAE BIT for certain claims related to a post-concession agreement. The Tribunal, however, denied jurisdiction as the investor had failed to satisfy the nationality requirements, even tough the Claimant's Italian nationality was supported by five nationality certificates issued by several Italian public authorities. The tribunal found that, unknowingly, Claimant had lost Italian nationality by operation of Italian law for lack of required residency.[28] The tribunal held that **19**

> It is accepted within international law that nationality is within the domestic jurisdiction of the State, which settles, by its own legislation, the rules relating to the acquisition (and loss) of its nationality. Article 1(3) of the BIT reflects this rule. But it is no less accepted that when, in international arbitral or judicial proceedings, the nationality of a person is challenged, the international tribunal is competent to pass upon that challenge. It will accord great weight to the nationality law of the State in question and to the interpretation and application of that law by its authorities. But it will in the end decide for itself whether, on the facts and the law before it, the person whose nationality is at issue was or was not a national of the State in question and when, and what follows from that finding. Where, as in the instant case, the jurisdiction of an international tribunal turns on an issue of nationality, the international tribunal is empowered, indeed bound, to decide that issue.[29]

While purporting to apply domestic law to the specific facts of the case following the example of previous tribunals, the extent of the tribunal's review in this case pushes the limits of proper review, as it denied the validity of multiple nationality certificate issued by State's agencies. Indeed, it itself acknowledged the anomaly of the system and recognized that 'Mr. Soufraki, had he been properly advised at the time, easily could have reacquired Italian nationality by a timely application' or could have acted through a corporate vehicle rather than **20**

---

[26] *Von Pezold and others v Zimbabwe*, ICSID Case No ARB/10/15, Award, 28 July 2015, para 204, see also para 204 (where 'the Claimants denied that Heinrich or Rüdiger has ever been a Zimbabwean citizen and explained that the documents relied upon by the Respondent reflected clerical errors made by the accountants who had filed them').
[27] *Champion Trading Company and Ameritrade International, Inc v Arab Republic of Egypt*, ICSID Case No ARB/02/9, Jurisdiction, 21 October 2003, para 36 (hereafter *Champion Trading v Egypt*).
[28] *Hussein Nuaman Soufraki v The United Arab Emirates*, ICSID Case No ARB/02/7, Award, 7 July 2004.
[29] ibid para 55.

as an Individual. But concluded that 'the Tribunal can only take the facts as they are and as it has found them to be'.[30]

21 Similarly, in *Siag v Egypt*, the tribunal found the Claimant had lost Egyptian nationality by operation of Egyptian law and found that it had jurisdiction to hear the claim against Egypt as the Claimant was to be considered a foreign investor.[31] The tribunal held that

> The Tribunal must determine the nationality of the Claimants. Application of international law principles requires an application of the Egyptian nationality laws with reference to international law as may be appropriate in the circumstances. Both Egyptian law and the practice of international tribunals is that the documents referred to by the Respondent evidencing the nationality of the Claimants are prima facie evidence only. While such documents are relevant, they do not alleviate the requirement on the Tribunal to apply the Egyptian nationality law, which is the only means of determining Egyptian nationality.[32]

22 In both cases, the tribunals took it upon themselves to apply domestic law and pushed their review as to how to apply domestic law. Given the facts posture of the cases and the arguments made by the parties, this was necessary. Indeed, the fundamental importance of nationality as key requirement for jurisdiction and the increasing prevalence of dual or multiple nationality will continue to deepen tribunals' review of nationality claims in IIL.

I. Dual nationality and the requirement of a dominant and effective nationality

23 The question of determination of nationality for maintaining an international claim especially in the sphere of investor–State arbitration is critical. The fundamental principle has been that an investor should be a national of a contracting state other than the host State. This principle has historically guided international tribunals and has been expressly articulated in Article 25 of the ICSID Convention.[33]

II. General practice of the dominant and effective nationality principle in public international law

24 The issue is of particularly relevance in situations of dual nationality, which is increasingly common.[34] When confronted by claims from a dual national, general international law

---

[30] ibid para 83 ('It recognizes that Mr. Soufraki, had he been properly advised at the time, easily could have re-acquired Italian nationality by a timely application. It further appreciates that, had Mr. Soufraki contracted with the United Arab Emirates through a corporate vehicle incorporated in Italy, rather than contracting in his personal capacity, no problem of jurisdiction would now arise. But the tribunal can only take the facts as they are and as it has found them to be').

[31] *Waguih Elie George Siag & Clorinda Vecchi v Egypt*, ICSID Case No ARB/05/15, Award, 1 April 2007. See Michael Waibel, 'II. Investment Arbitration: Jurisdiction and Admissibility' in Marc Bungenberg and others (eds), *International Investment Law* (Nomos 2015) .

[32] ibid para 153.

[33] JH Ralston, International Arbitration and Procedure (1910) ('[T]he claim must be founded upon an injury or wrong to a citizen of the claimant government, and that the title to such claim must have remained continuously in the hands of citizens of such government until the time of its presentation for filing before the commission').

[34] PJ Shapiro, 'Multiple Nationality' in *Max Planck Encyclopedia of Public International Law* (OUP 2008) ('Dual nationality was not a pressing issue in a world of low mobility'. [...] 'Recent State practice with respect to multiple nationality points to increased acceptance of the status').

practice by international courts and tribunals has historically rejected claims by claimants who also possessed the nationality of the respondent host State.

For example, in the 1912 *Canevaro Claim*, the arbitral tribunal hearing a claim at the PCA brought by three Italian brothers against Peru denied jurisdiction to one of the claimants because he also had Peruvian nationality.[35] The same principle has been expressed by the Italian–Venezuela Commission in the *Miliani* case, in which the Umpire found that both Italy and Venezuela could properly legislate on the issue of nationality, Claimant could not avail himself of his Italian nationality to sue Venezuela as he also had Venezuelan nationality.[36]

Similarly, in *Reparation for Injuries Suffered in the Service of the United Nations (Advisory Opinion)*, the International Court of Justice (ICJ) referred to the practice of States not excising protection on behalf of its nationals against a State which also regards them as their own national as 'the ordinary practice'.[37]

International courts and tribunals have found the requirement of a 'dominant and effective' nationality, to which *Canevaro* also offers some support, to be helpful to clarify when an individual or a State could properly make a claim against (or bring a claim on behalf of) a State of which they possess nationality. Under this principle, only an individual or a State that could claim a 'dominant and effective' nationality of a State or a 'genuine' link to a State could assert a claim asserting that nationality against another State.[38]

Notably, the principle was applied in 1955 by the ICJ in the *Nottebohm* case (*Liechtenstein v Guatemala*) in which the Court held that Mr. Nottebohm did not have a 'genuine link' with Liechtenstein who therefore could not exercise diplomatic protection on his behalf against Guatemala, in a case of an uncompensated expropriation.[39] The Court held that Liechtenstein's claim was inadmissible because Mr. Nottebohm lacked the required nationality, because it was the bond of nationality between a State and an individual which alone conferred upon the State the right to put forward an international claim on his behalf. As Mr. Nottebohm lacked any 'genuine link' to Liechtenstein, Liechtenstein could not bring a case on his behalf. This case was, however, rightly criticized because it resulted in the unavailability of any international remedy for Mr. Nottebohm, who only had one nationality (Liechtenstein).

The US–Italy Conciliation Commissions in the *Mergé* case offered a more refined analysis. The commission rejected Mrs. Mergé's application against Italy and found that

---

[35] *Canevaro Claim*, see n 16, at 2 (unofficial English translation) ('under these circumstances, whatever Raphael Canevaro's status may be in Italy with respect to his nationality, the Government of Peru has the right to consider him as a Peruvian citizen and to deny his status as an Italian claimant').
[36] *Miliani* Case, Italian–Venezuela Commission, X Reports of International Arbitral Awards 584–91, at 590 (1903) ('while the children of Miliani may with absolute legal propriety be recognized as Italians in Italy, or by Italy in any country other than Venezuela, in this country, and, as a consequence [...] before this tribunal, they must be considered, for the purposes of this litigation, as Venezuelans'). See also *Cases of Dual Nationality*, UK–Italy Mixed Commission, Decision No 22, 8 May 1954 (declining jurisdiction over British claimants who were also Italian nationals).
[37] Reparation for Injuries Suffered in the Service of the United Nations, Advisory Opinion, 11 April 1949, 186.
[38] For an excellent review of the applicable case law, see *Mergé* Case, Italy–US Conciliation Commission, Decision No 55 of 10 June 1955, XIV RIAA, 236, 242–44.
[39] *Nottebohm (Liechtenstein v Guatemala)* (Judgment, Second Phase) [1955] ICJ Rep 4 ('According to the practice of States, to arbitral and judicial decisions and to the opinions of writers, nationality is a legal bond having as its basis a social fact of attachment, a genuine connection of existence, interests and sentiments, together with the existence of reciprocal rights and duties. [...] Conferred by a State, it only entitles that State to exercise protection vis-à-vis another State, if it constitutes a translation into juridical terms of the individual's connection with the State which has made him its national').

she could not be considered 'dominantly' a US national because she had not lived in the United States for many years and 'the family did not have its habitual residence in the United States and the interests and the permanent professional life of the head of the family were not established there'.[40] Indeed, in *Flegenheimer*, the Italy–US Conciliation Commission expressly limited the dominant nationality doctrine to cases involving dual nationals.[41]

30 In *Flegenheimer*, the Commission also confirmed the general principle that a fraudulent acquisition of nationality will not be recognized.[42] The principle also provided the underlining reasoning in the ICJ *Nottebohm* case.

1. The practice of the Iran–US Claims Tribunal

31 The test was also appropriately used by the Iran–US Claims Tribunal (IUSCT).[43] For example, in the precedent-setting decision in Case No. A/18, the IUSCT concluded that the 'dominant and effective nationality' of the claimant would determine jurisdiction. The tribunal examined a claim of a dual US–Iranian national against Iran and examined all relevant factors, including 'habitual residence, center of interests, family ties, participation in public life and other evidence of attachment' to determine the dominant and effective nationality of a dual national. It concluded that as the dominant and effective nationality of the claimant was the US one, the tribunal had jurisdiction over claims against Iran brought by a US–Iranian dual national.[44]

2. The practice of the United Nations Claims Commission

32 How to address claims by dual nationals was also very important to the work of the United Nations Compensation Commission (UNCC), another reparation commission created by the UN Security Council to hear individual, corporate, and sovereign claims arising out of Iraq's invasion of Kuwait in 1990. The specific issue to be resolved was access to the UNCC by Iraqi nationals, who generally were not entitled to bring a claim for compensation. In that specific situation, however, the Governing Council adopted a lenient standard and decided to allow certain claims by dual nationals and only requiring that Iraqi nationals have a 'bona fide' nationality of another State in order to be eligible to submit a claim for compensation.[45]

---

[40] *Mergé* Case, Italy–US Conciliation Commission, Decision No 55, 10 June 1955, XIV RIAA, 236–48, at 248.

[41] See also *Flegenheimer* Case, Conciliation Commissions Established Pursuant to Article 83 Peace Treaty with Italy, Decision No 182 of 20 September 1958 ('But when a person is vested with only one nationality, which is attributed to him or her either jure sanguinis or jure soli, or by a valid naturalization entailing the positive loss of the former nationality, the theory of effective nationality cannot be applied without the risk of causing confusion. It lacks a sufficiently positive basis to be applied to a nationality which finds support in a state law. There does not in fact exist any criterion of proven effectiveness for disclosing the effectiveness of a bond with a political collectivity, the persons by the thousands who, because of the facility of travel in the modern world, possess the positive legal nationality of a State, but live in foreign States where they are domiciled and where their family and business center is located, would be exposed to non-recognition, at the international level, of the nationality with which they are undeniably vested by virtue of the laws of their national State, if this doctrine were to be generalized').

[42] *Flegenheimer*, paras 36–39, see also paras 33–35.

[43] *Iran v US*, Case No A-18, Decision, 6 April 1984, 5 IUCT Rep 251.

[44] ibid para 51.

[45] Governing Council of the United Nations Compensation Commission, Criteria for Expedited Processing of Urgent Claims, 2 August 1991, S/AC.26/1991/1, para 17.

III. Effective nationality in the practice of investment arbitral tribunals

The doctrine of dominant and effective nationality has proven particularly useful in non-ICISD international investment arbitration as a way to determine the nationality of an investor and thus determine treaty eligibility.[46]

33

For example, in *Ballantine v Dominican Republic*, the tribunal used the test of 'dominant and effective nationality' under the Dominican Republic-Central American Free Trade Agreement ('DR-CAFTA').[47] The dispute revolved around the question of whether the Ballantine claimants could demonstrate that their US nationality was 'dominant and effective'. In a majority award, however, the tribunal found that the claimants' 'dominant and effective' nationality was that of the host State (i.e. the Dominican Republic) and therefore concluded that the tribunal lacked jurisdiction to hear the dispute under DR-CAFTA.

34

IV. Effective nationality in ICSID practice: Article 25 ICSID Convention as *lex specialis*

Importantly, however, the dominant and effective nationality doctrine is not applicable in ICSID proceedings, where Article 25 of the ICSID Convention specifically bars claims from individuals holding the nationality of the host State.

35

In *Champion Trading v Egypt*, for example, the ICSID arbitral tribunal denied jurisdiction over three individual claimants under the US–Egypt BIT because of their Egyptian nationality and held that 'the mere fact that this investment in Egypt by the three individual Claimants was done by using, for whatever reason and purpose, exclusively their Egyptian nationality clearly qualifies them as dual nationals within the meaning of the Convention and thereby based on Article 25 (2)(a) excludes them from invoking the Convention'.[48]

36

Similarly, in *Micula v Romania*, the ICSID tribunal applying a Romania–Swedish BIT on issues related to various investments in disfavoured regions of Romania held that a genuine link is not necessary when there is only one nationality and held that 'the regime established under Article 25 of the ICSID Convention does not leave room for a test of dominant or effective nationality'.[49]

37

---

[46] See generally S Trevisanut, 'Nationality Cases before International Courts and Tribunals' in *Max Planck Encyclopedia of Public International Law* (2011).
[47] *Michael Ballantine and Lisa Ballantine v The Dominican Republic*, PCA Case No 2016–17, Final Award, 3 September 2019.
[48] *Champion Trading v Egypt* (n 27) para 63, see more generally paras 59–64.
[49] *Ioan Micula, Viorel Micula, S.C. European Food S.A, S.C. Starmill S.R.L. and S.C. Multipack S.R.L. v Romania* [I], ICSID Case No ARB/05/20, Jurisdiction and Admissibility, 24 September 2006, para 100, see also more generally 98–101. Note that the tribunal also cites *Siag/Vecchi v Egypt* with approval, see para 100 and accompanying n 21 and n 29. See also *Edmond Khudyan and Arin Capital & Investment Corp v Republic of Armenia*, ICSID Case No ARB/17/36 (Tribunal found that Mr Khudyan had dual Armenian–US nationality which barred him from bringing a claim against the host State under ICSID).

38 In *Olguin v Paraguay*, the ICSID arbitral tribunal examined the issue of dual nationality and the irrelevance of genuine link when claimant also possess another nationality not relevant to the specific case. In the case at issue, the Claimant was Peruvian–US dual national and the tribunal applied a Peru–Paraguay BIT.[50]

39 The issue of validity of a renunciation of nationality by a dual national was explored in details in *Victor Pey Casado and President Allende Foundation v Chile*. Mr. Pey Casado had renounced his Chilean nationality when he acquired Spanish nationality. His claim against Chile was based on his Spanish nationality and was brought under the Spanish–Chile BIT. The ICSID tribunal held that Mr. Pey Casado's renunciation was validly made and that he was not a Chilean national at the relevant time and thus 'could not admit the jurisdictional exception' by Chile.[51]

V. Exceptions to the effective nationality principle in non-ICSID cases

40 Note that the inapplicability of the dominant and effective nationality doctrine is not limited to ICSID cases. Non-ICSID tribunals have also found that absent specific treaty requirements, dual nationals might be able to bring a claim. In *Garcıa Armas v Venezuela*, the tribunal applying the Spain–Venezuela BIT under 1976 United Nations Commission on International Trade Law (UNCITRAL) rules at the PCA held that the BIT was *lex specialis* between the parties and that on its face the Treaty did not impose any jurisdictional limitation on dual nationals. It ruled that there was sufficient ground for its jurisdiction because the Spain–Venezuela BIT did not regulate the status of dual nationals, and allowed the two Venezuelan–Spanish investors to sue Venezuela.[52]

VI. Continuous nationality rule

41 The right of an individual or a State to initiate a case against another State derives from the close connection nationals, whether natural persons or juridical entities, have with the state itself. As a rule, therefore, a claimant needs to have the nationality of the State both at the time of the injury which originated the claim and at the date of the presentation of the claim.[53] This continuous nationality rule is intended to avoid an abuse of diplomatic protection. Article 25 of the ICSID Convention provides so specifically.

---

[50] *Eudoro Armando Olguín v Republic of Paraguay*, ICSID Case No ARB/98/5, Award, 26 July 2001, para 62 ('In the case of a dual national's diplomatic protection, either of his mother countries has the capacity to act on his behalf against a third country, and the third country would have no way of invoking rules, on an international scale, that would serve, in the protecting nation's internal laws, to transfer the responsibility for such protection—which is, in any case, not obligatory—to the co-mother country, on account of the person's registered address or other similar factor').

[51] *Pey Casado and Allende Foundation v Chile Víctor Pey Casado and President Allende Foundation v Republic of Chile*, ICSID Case No ARB/98/2, Jurisdiction, 8 May 2002, para 323 (French original).

[52] *Garcıa Armas v Venezuela*, PCA Case No 2013-3, Jurisdiction, 15 December 2014 (original Spanish) 92.

[53] Draft Articles on Diplomatic Protection, Article 5.

VII. Notable exceptions related to nationality of individuals

States can deviate from the generally applicable norms and negotiate alternative arrangements in relation to nationality. For example, Article 1(7) of the Energy Charter Treaty equates nationality to permanent residency and identifies an investor as 'a natural person having the citizenship or nationality of or who is permanently residing in that Contracting Party in accordance with its applicable law'.[54] **42**

Notably, moreover, the Algiers Agreement that established the Eritrea–Ethiopia Claims Commission (EECC) provided that in 'appropriate cases, each party may file claims on behalf of persons of Ethiopian or Eritrean origin who may not be its nationals. Such claims shall be considered by the Commission on the same basis as claims submitted on behalf of that party's nationals.'[55] This allowed Eritrea to file claims on behalf of Ethiopian nationals of Eritrean origin.[56] **43**

D. The nationality of corporations

I. General principle: The nationality of corporation is regulated domestically

Principles of nationality also apply to corporations. Indeed, the nationality of corporations is a complex matter that has been examined at length by international courts and tribunals. **44**

Nationality of a corporation is usually of the State where it is incorporated or where its headquarters is based. As is the case for individuals, it pertains to each State to legislate on the nationality of corporations under their domestic law. This was specifically recognized by the ICJ in *Ahmadou Sadio Diallo*.[57] Here the Court held that 'only the State of nationality may exercise diplomatic protection on behalf of the company when its rights are injured by a wrongful act of another State. In determining whether a company possesses independent and distinct legal personality, international law looks to the rules of the relevant domestic law.'[58] **45**

II. Specific challenges: Nationality of shareholders, piercing the corporate veil and nationality of convenience

The increasing variety of corporate ownership and the internationalization of business practice, however, mean that the reality of the nationality of corporation is more nuanced and, indeed, complex. Issues to be considered are the nationality of the shareholders, piercing the corporate veil and nationality of convenience. **46**

---

[54] Energy Charter Treaty (signed 17 December 1994, entered into force 16 April 1998) 2080 UNTS 100.
[55] Algiers Agreement between Eritrea and Ethiopia, Article 5(9).
[56] *Partial Award, Civilians Claims, Eritrea's Claims 15, 16, 23 & 27–32*, Eritrea–Ethiopia Claims Commission, The Hague, 17 December 2004, paras 18–19.
[57] *Ahmadou Sadio Diallo (Republic of Guinea v Democratic Republic of the Congo)* (Preliminary Objections) [2007] ICJ Rep 582.
[58] ibid 62.

III. Corporate nationality in the practice of international courts and tribunal

47 The ICJ examined the question of nationality of corporations in several instances to establish which State could validly exercise diplomatic protection on behalf of a corporation. In *Barcelona Traction*, a case brought by Belgium against Spain, for example, the Court was asked to decide whether Belgium could exercise diplomatic protection for certain Belgian shareholders, representing about 88 per cent of the shares of Barcelona Traction, a company incorporated in Canada and seeking compensation for damages caused to them by certain acts committed by Spain in violation of international law.[59] The Court reject the claim and, in declining to pierce the corporate veil, found that Belgium did not have legal standing. It held that the genuine link theory could not apply for corporations and that the nationality of corporations must be determined based on the domestic law of the State of incorporation.[60]

48 Generally, the rules that define the nationality of corporations are found in the applicable treaties, and they can go beyond the requirement of the seat of incorporation. Treaty provisions generally reflect domestic preferences, and, as highlighted above for individuals, treaties may contain two different definitions of nationality for corporations. Some treaties, for example, also include a 'control' test to define treaty application. For instance, Article 1 of the 2007 Bahrain–Netherlands BIT define a nationals legal persons incorporated under the law of a Contracting State as well as legal persons 'controlled directly or indirectly, by nationals of a Contracting State'.[61]

49 International courts and tribunals have recognized and applied the relevant provisions as stated. For example, in *Elettronica Sicula SpA*, the ICJ found it had jurisdiction to hear a claim brought by the United States on behalf of two American companies that owned 100 per cent of the shares of a company incorporated in Italy, Elettronica Sicula (ELSI), for an alleged illegal requisition of the company because of the language of the applicable treaty. The Court found that it was 'common ground between the Parties' that the Court had jurisdiction over the case.[62] Indeed, Article III of the applicable 1948 bilateral Treaty of Friendship, Commerce, and Navigation provided that 'nationals, corporations and associations of either High Contracting Party shall be permitted, in conformity with the applicable laws and regulations within the territories of the other High Contracting Party, to organize, control and manage corporations and associations of such other High Contracting Party'.[63]

50 Additional requirements can also be included in treaties. For example, the ICSID Convention includes temporal requirement and under the provision of Article 25 of the ICSID Convention, a juridical person is required to have the nationality of a Contracting State other than the State party to the dispute on the date in which the parties consented to

---

[59] *Barcelona Traction, Light and Power Company, Limited* (*Belgium v Spain*) (New Application: 1962) (Preliminary Objections) [1970] ICJ Rep 3.
[60] ibid para 70.
[61] Agreement on Promotion and Protection of Investments between the Government of the Kingdom of Bahrain and the Government of the Kingdom of the Netherlands (2007), Article 1.
[62] *Elettronica Sicula SpA* (ELSI) (*US v Italy*) (Merits) [1989] ICJ Rep 15, para 48.
[63] ibid para 68.

submit the dispute to arbitration. Contracting States may also agree to provide an exception for companies incorporated in host State but owned by nationals of the Contracting State and consider them under foreign control.[64]

IV. Application of the principles governing corporate nationality in the practice of investment tribunals

International investment tribunals have, along the lines of other international courts and tribunals, generally adopted a strict interpretation of the applicable norms and have commonly declined to pierce the corporate veil.[65] 51

In *Champion Trading v Egypt*, for example, the ICSID tribunal held it had jurisdiction over a claim brought by two US companies incorporated in Delaware against Egypt and owned by dual (US–Egypt) nationals. The tribunal applied the definition of corporation in the applicable BIT and of investor in the ICSID Convention and found that neither 'contained any exclusion of dual nationals as shareholder of companies of the other Contracting State'.[66] 52

To determine the nationality of a corporate investor, arbitral tribunals have relied on the definitions contained in the applicable international instruments, without examining the corporate structure or the nationality of shareholders in more detail. For example, in *Tokios Tokelés v Ukraine*, the tribunal, deciding by majority, held it had jurisdiction over a claim against Ukraine brought by a company incorporated in Lithuania but fully owned by Ukrainian investors.[67] It rejected respondent's argument that the corporation was not a 'genuine entity' of Lithuania and its request to pierce the corporate veil. The arbitrators did not consider they should 'read in the BITs limitations not found in the text nor evident from negotiating history'.[68] 53

Similarly, in *Saluka v Czech Republic*, respondent asserted that claimant did not have any 'real and continuous link' to The Netherlands, the country where it was incorporated. The tribunal expressed 'some sympathy for the argument that a company which has no real connection with a State party to a BIT, and which is in reality a mere shell company controlled by another company which is not constituted under the laws of that State, should not be entitled to invoke the provisions of that treaty'.[69] However, in application of terms in the relevant Netherlands–Czech and Slovak Republic BIT, the tribunal found it could not impose a definition that they had not agreed upon and thus upheld its jurisdiction.[70] The question of change of corporate nationality and when it is potentially abusive was specifically addressed in *Philips Morris Asia v Australia*.[71] Philips Morris Asia brought a case against Australia under 54

---

[64] ICSID Convention, Article 25(2)(b).
[65] See, generally, Olmedo (n 8).
[66] *Champion Trading v Egypt* (n 27) paras 65–71.
[67] *Tokios Tokelés v Ukraine*, ICSID Case No ARB/02/18, Jurisdiction, 29 April 2004. The president of the tribunal took the very unusual step of filing a dissenting opinion.
[68] ibid para 52. Note that tribunals consistently followed this approach, including in the *Yukos v Russian Federation*, a notable case which resulted in an award in favour of claimants for over USD 50 billion. See the three parallel cases: *Veteran Petroleum LTD v Russia*; *Yukos Universal LTD v Russia*; and *Hulley Enterprises LTD v Russia*.
[69] *Saluka Investments BV v The Czech Republic*, PCA Case No 2001-04, Partial Award, 17 March 2006, para 240.
[70] ibid paras 241–42.
[71] *Philip Morris Asia Limited v The Commonwealth of Australia*, PCA Case No 2012-12, Jurisdiction and Admissibility, 17 December 2015.

the Hong Kong–Australia BIT related to Australia's plain packaging measures. Australia argued that the Philips Morris had restructured its investment with the primary motivation of bringing a Treaty claim using an entity from Hong Kong, and the tribunal agreed. It found that 'at the time of the restructuring, the dispute that materialized subsequently was foreseeable to the Claimant' and that such change in corporate structure therefore constituted an abuse of right and denied jurisdiction.[72]

E. Conclusions

55 To conclude, nationality is a fundamental and key principle in international law generally and IIL specifically because it provides foreign investors personal jurisdiction to file claims against host States for violations of the host State's international obligations towards them.

56 The issue of nationality, and more specifically how to attach nationality to a foreign investor, both natural and corporate, has been examined routinely by investment tribunals. This gave rise to a particularly rich practice on the issue of nationality.

57 The practice of international investment tribunals does not significantly deviate from, and rather aligns with, the practice of other international courts and tribunals. Indeed, investment tribunals routinely cite and refer to prior decisions of other international courts and tribunals, such as the ICJ and international claims tribunals, in their examinations of questions related to nationality, including issues related to dual nationality and of continuous nationality.

58 The practice of both international investment tribunals and other international courts and tribunals shows a remarkable difference between the approach they take in assessing nationality for natural and for corporate persons. To wit, international tribunals have been reluctant to pierce the corporate veil of corporations and have accepted their nationality of incorporation without further examining the nationality of shareholders. Conversely, arbitrators have much more thoroughly examined claims of nationality of individuals and have rejected nationality declarations based on their own assessment of domestic nationality provisions.

Selected literature

Baltag C, *The Energy Charter Treaty: The Notion of Investor* (Kluwer Law International 2012).
Baumgartner J, *Treaty Shopping in International Investment Law* (OUP 2016).
Burgstaller M, 'Nationality of Corporate Investors and International Claims against the Investor's Own State' (2006) 7 JWIT 857.
Casey CA, *Nationals Abroad: Globalization, Individual Rights, and the Making of Modern International Law* (CUP 2020), esp ch 6.

---

[72] ibid paras 569 and 585–88 (see also the excellent review of abuse of rights precedent at paras 538–54). On treaty shopping generally, see J Baumgartner, *Treaty Shopping in International Investment Law* (OUP 2016). Note also that the 2018 Dutch Model Bilateral Investment Treaty, Article 1(b)–(c) specifically contains a definition of investor aiming to excluding mailbox companies from the scope of treaty protection—legal persons must have 'substantial business activities' in their home territory.

Dörr O, 'Nationality' in *Max Planck Encyclopedia of Public International Law* (OUP 2019).
Eichberger FB, 'Die Grenzen der Zulässigkeit des "nationality planning" im Investitionsschutzrecht' (2020) 58 Archiv des Völkerrechts 307–36.
Giorgetti C, 'Rethinking the Individual in International Law' (2019) 22 LCLR 1085.
Janig P, 'Cynicism and Nationality Planning in International Investment Law' in Björnstjern B and others (eds), *Cynical International Law? Abuse and Circumvention in Public International and European Law* (Springer Berlin Heidelberg 2021).
Mendelson M, 'The Runaway Train: the "Continuous Nationality Rule" from Panevezys-saludutiskis Railway case to Loewen' in Weiler T (ed), *International Investment Law and Arbitration - Leading Cases from the ICSID, NAFTA, Bilateral Treaties and Customary International Law* (London: Cameron May 2005).
Olmedo JG, 'Nationality of Claim: Investment Arbitration' in *Max Planck Encyclopedia of International Procedural Law* (OUP 2019).
Vicuña FO, 'Changing Approaches to the Nationality of Claims in the Context of Diplomatic Protection and International Dispute Settlement' (2000) 15 ICSID Rev/FILJ 340–361.
Parlett K, *The Individual in the International Legal System* (CUP 2011).
Shapiro PJ, 'Multiple Nationality' in *Max Planck Encyclopedia of Public International Law* (OUP 2008).
de Stefano C, 'Corporate Nationality in International Investment Law: Substance over Formality' (2019) 55 RDIPP 819–55.
Trevisanut S, 'Nationality Cases before International Courts and Tribunals' in *Max Planck Encyclopedia of Public International Law* (OUP 2011).
Vastardis AY, *The Nationality of Corporate Investors Under International Investment Law* (Bloomsbury Publishing 2020).
Weis P, *Nationality and Statelessness in International Law* (2nd edn, Sijthoff & Noordhoff 1979).

Selected decisions

Acquisition of Polish Nationality, Advisory Opinion, PCIJ Series B No 7, 15 September 1923.
Ahmadou Sadio Diallo (*Republic of Guinea v Democratic Republic of the Congo*) (Preliminary Objections) [2007] ICJ Rep 582.
Barcelona Traction, Light and Power Company, Limited (*Belgium v Spain*) (New Application: 1962) (Preliminary Objections) [1970] ICJ Rep 3.
Canevaro Claim (*Italy v Peru*) PCA Case No 1910-01, Award, 3 May 1912.
Champion Trading Company and Ameritrade International, Inc v Arab Republic of Egypt, ICSID Case No ARB/02/9, Jurisdiction, 21 October 2003.
Edmond Khudyan and Arin Capital & Investment Corp v Republic of Armenia, ICSID Case No ARB/17/36, Award, 15 December 2021.
Elettronica Sicula SpA (ELSI) (*US v Italy*) (Merits) [1989] ICJ Rep 15.
Eritrea-Ethiopia Claims Commission, Partial Award, *Civilians Claims, Eritrea's Claims* 15, 16, 23 & 27-32, Eritrea-Ethiopia Claims Commission, The Hague, Partial Award, 17 December 2004, The Hague.
Eudoro Armando Olguín v Republic of Paraguay, ICSID Case No ARB/98/5, Award, 26 July 2001.
García Armas v Venezuela, PCA Case No 2013-3, Jurisdiction, 15 December 2014 (original Spanish).
Governing Council of the United Nations Compensation Commission, Criteria for Expedited Processing of Urgent Claims, 2 August 1991, S/AC.26/1991/1.
Hussein Nuaman Soufraki v The United Arab Emirates, ICSID Case No ARB/02/7, Award, 7 July 2004.
Ioan Micula, Viorel Micula, S.C. European Food S.A, S.C. Starmill S.R.L. and S.C. Multipack S.R.L. v Romania [I], ICSID Case No ARB/05/20, Jurisdiction and Admissibility, 24 September 2006.
Iran v US, IUSCT Case No A-18, Decision, 6 April 1984, 5 IUCT Rep 251.

Mergé Case, Italy-US Conciliation Commission, Decision No 55, 10 June 1955, XIV RIAA, 236.
Miliani Case, Italian-Venezuela Commission, X RIAA 584–91 (1903).
Pey Casado and Allende Foundation v Chile Víctor Pey Casado and President Allende Foundation v Republic of Chile, ICSID Case No ARB/98/2, Jurisdiction, 8 May 2002.
Philip Morris Asia Limited v The Commonwealth of Australia, PCA Case No 2012-12, Jurisdiction and Admissibility, 17 December 2015.
Tokios Tokelés v Ukraine, ICSID Case No ARB/02/18, Jurisdiction, 29 April 2004
Von Pezold and others v Zimbabwe, ICSID Case No ARB/10/15, Award, 28 July 2015.
Waguih Elie George Siag & Clorinda Vecchi v Egypt, ICSID Case No ARB/05/15, Award, 1 April 2007.

Abuse of process

Régis Bismuth

A. Introduction	1	II. Situations of parallel proceedings	22
B. Application in general international law	7	III. Situations of corporate restructuring	24
I. The applicability of the abuse of process doctrine	7	D. Explaining the divergence between general international law and international investment law	28
II. Applicable standards governing abuse of process claims	12	I. A reluctance to rely on the ISDS jurisprudence	29
C. Application in international investment law	18	II. Possible considerations of judicial policy	34
I. Applicability and evidentiary standards	18	E. Conclusion	38

A. Introduction

Abuse of process has become a commonplace allegation in proceedings before international courts and tribunals,[1] particularly in investment arbitration. Whereas the International Court of Justice (ICJ) has so far always rejected claims of abuse of process, they have proven to be successful in some investment cases. Before exploring the differences between Investor–State Dispute Settlement (ISDS) and ICJ cases, it is first necessary to explain what is meant by 'abuse of process' and to discuss its—still controversial—legal status. **1**

The notion of abuse of process can be regarded as a subcategory of the broader doctrine of abuse of rights (*abus de droit*) which refers to the unreasonable exercise of a right 'for an end different from that for which the right was created'[2] and to the injury of another subject.[3] The two pillars on which this doctrine is based (a formal entitlement, and an improper purpose) reflect its social ordering function including in the procedural context of abuse of process. As Kolb's commonly cited definition underscores, abuse of process consists of 'the use of procedural instruments or rights by one or more parties for purposes that are alien to those for which the procedural rights are established'[4] and especially 'for a fraudulent, procrastinatory **2**

---

[1] For an overview of allegations of abuse of process in different interstate adjudicative mechanisms, see, AD Mitchell and T Malone, 'Abuse of Process in Inter-State Dispute Resolution' in H Ruiz Fabri (ed), *Max Planck Encyclopedia of International Procedural Law* (2018) (hereafter Mitchell and Malone).
[2] A Kiss, 'Abuse of Rights', Max Planck Encyclopedia of International Law (2006) para 1.
[3] See also more generally, M Lemey, *L'abus de Droit En Droit International Public* (LGDJ 2021) (hereafter Lemey).
[4] R Kolb, 'General Principles of Procedural Law' in Andreas Zimmermann and others (eds), *The Statute of the International Court of Justice: A Commentary* (3rd edn, OUP 2019) 998 (hereafter Kolb).

or frivolous purpose, for the purpose of causing harm or obtaining an illegitimate advantage, for the purpose of reducing or removing the effectiveness of some other available process or for purposes of pure propaganda'.[5]

3 Even though the ICJ considers that 'a distinction has been drawn between abuse of rights and abuse of process',[6] the expression 'abuse of process' has not been applied in a systemic and rigorous manner. It is thus not surprising that procedural abuses have been labelled, even in the same decision, as 'abuse of rights',[7] 'abuse of procedure',[8] '*détournement de procedure*',[9] or 'abuse of the international investment protection regime'.[10]

4 This lack of terminological rigour echoes to some extent the blurred and even controversial legal status of the abuse of rights doctrine. Leaving aside the scholarly debate as to its contested existence,[11] this doctrine is closely related to other fundamental principles of international law. This is clearly the case for the principle of good faith, but there is a debate as to whether the doctrine of abuse of rights just 'flows' from this principle[12] or is 'supplemental to the principle of good faith' in that 'it provides the threshold at which a lack of good faith gives rise to a violation of international law'.[13] Moreover, the principle of due process or the doctrine of estoppel could be invoked in circumstances that are similar to those potentially giving rise to an abuse of process.[14]

5 Leaving aside the legal nature and pedigree of the abuse of process doctrine, litigants in international dispute settlement mechanisms have raised abuse of process claims that have not been rejected as such by international courts and tribunals.[15] Thus, the question is no longer whether abuse of process can be regarded as a fully fledged and independent general principle,[16] but rather to determine what are its scope and effects, and to understand why the threshold for admitting an abuse also depends on the adjudicative mechanism concerned.[17] In that regard, an apparent difference exists between investment tribunals and other international courts and tribunals, the former having proven to be more inclined to accept abuse of process claims under certain conditions.

6 This entry first examines how the abuse of process doctrine has been applied in general international law (Section B) and then how it has been shaped in investment arbitration

---

[5] ibid 904.
[6] *Immunities and Criminal Proceedings (Equatorial Guinea v France)* (Preliminary Objections) [2018] ICJ Rep 292, 335, para 146 (hereafter ICJ, *Immunities and Criminal Proceedings*).
[7] *Phoenix Action, Ltd v The Czech Republic*, ICSID Case No ARB/06/5, Award, 15 April 2009, para 143 (hereafter *Phoenix*).
[8] ibid para 94.
[9] ibid para 143.
[10] ibid para 151. See also *Mobil Corporation, Venezuela Holdings, B.V., et al v Bolivarian Republic of Venezuela*, ICSID Case No ARB/07/27, Jurisdiction, 10 June 2010, para 169 (hereafter *Mobil Corporation*).
[11] J Paulsson, *The Unruly Notion of Abuse of Rights* (CUP 2020).
[12] Mitchell and Malone (n 1) paras 7–8.
[13] M Byers, 'Abuse of Rights: An Old Principle, a New Age' (2002) 47 McGillLJ 389, 411 (hereafter Byers).
[14] Mitchell and Malone (n 1) paras 9–10.
[15] For an overview of cases in which the doctrine of abuse of process has been applied by courts and tribunals, see Sections B and C.
[16] M Forteau, 'General Principles of International Procedural Law' in Hélène Ruiz Fabri (ed), *Max Planck Encyclopedia of International Procedural Law* (2018) para 36 (pointing out that international courts and tribunals 'identified procedural "principles" without indicating that they constitute, as such, general principles of law in the strict meaning of the term').
[17] M Lemey, 'Incidental Proceedings before the International Court of Justice: The Fine Line between "Litigation Strategy" and "Abuse of Process"' (2021) 20 LPICT 5, 6 (hereafter Lemey).

jurisprudence (Section C). It explains the divergences and the limited judicial dialogue between interstate courts and investment tribunals (Section D).

B. Application in general international law

I. The applicability of the abuse of process doctrine

International courts and tribunals have no express power in their statutory instruments to remedy an abuse of process. The only explicit exceptions are the dispute settlement mechanisms envisaged by the United Nations Convention on the Law of the Sea (UNCLoS) and the European Court of Human Rights (ECtHR). UNCLoS provides that in the context of preliminary proceedings of specific disputes concerning the rights of coastal states, the Court or the tribunal 'shall determine at the request of a party, or may determine *proprio motu*, whether the claim constitutes an abuse of legal process or whether prima facie it is well founded'.[18] Likewise, according to the European Convention on Human Rights (ECHR), the Court shall declare inadmissible any individual application if it considers that it constitutes an 'abuse of the right of individual application'.[19] While not referring explicitly to abuse of procedure, the World Trade Organization (WTO) Dispute Settlement Understanding (DSU) also includes a provision suggesting that the adjudicative system shall not be used for an end different from that for which the right was created when it states that 'all Members will engage in these procedures in good faith in an effort to resolve the dispute'.[20]

The significance of these provisions should not, however, be overstated for two main reasons.

First, international courts and tribunals have considered, even in the absence of any provision on the matter in their statutory instruments, that they had the power to remedy an abuse of process, either on the basis of a general principle or as part of their inherent powers.[21] The ICJ for instance recognized this power implicitly when it considered that the objection to admissibility must be rejected since the defendant's conduct 'does not amount to an abuse of process'[22] without giving, in that case, further details about the applicable standards governing the characterization of such abuse.

Second, even when applying a specific provision explicitly referring to procedural abuse in UNCLoS or in the ECHR, international courts and tribunals have interpreted the idea of abuse of process in light of 'its ordinary sense according to general legal theory—namely, the harmful exercise of a right for purposes other than those for which it is designed'.[23]

Allegations of abuse of process have significantly increased before the ICJ[24] over the last years. Various types of alleged abuses have been raised. For instance: initiating a claim too quickly under the optional clause,[25] using the Court with an artificial request as a means

---

[18] UNCLOS, Article 294(1).
[19] ECHR, Article 35(3)(a).
[20] WTO DSU, Article 3(10).
[21] Mitchell and Malone (n 1) para 18; L Tattersall and A Khan, 'Taking Stock: Abuse of Process within the International Court of Justice' (2020) 19 LPICT 229, 230 (hereafter Tattersall and Khan). On the concept of inherent powers and how they are related to general principles of law, see C Brown, *A Common Law of International Adjudication* (OUP 2007) 67.
[22] *Certain Phosphate Lands in Nauru (Nauru v Australia)* (Preliminary Objections) [1992] ICJ Rep 240, para 38.
[23] ECtHR, *Zhdanov and others v Russia*, No 12200/08, Judgment, 16 July 2019, para 79.
[24] Kolb (n 4) 998–99; Tattersall and Khan (n 21) 231–34.
[25] *Right of Passage over Indian Territory (Portugal v India)* (Preliminary Objections) [1957] ICJ Rep 125, paras 147–48.

of exerting political pressure,[26] or an undue request for provisional measures.[27] However, such claims have proven to be unsuccessful given the very high threshold for characterizing abuse.

II. Applicable standards governing abuse of process claims

12 It is only in recent decisions that the World Court has attempted—probably insufficiently—to make more explicit the standards governing claims of abuse of process. In *Immunities and Criminal Proceedings*, the ICJ clarified for the first time that 'a distinction has been drawn between abuse of rights and abuse of process'[28] to the extent that 'an abuse of process goes to the procedure before a court or tribunal and can be considered at the preliminary phase of these proceedings'.[29] While the issue of the burden of proof does not raise any particular difficulties (it lies with the party making the allegation),[30] the required standard of proof raises more specific concerns.

13 In *Immunities and Criminal Proceedings*, the Court considered that a claimant having established a valid title of jurisdiction should not be barred at the jurisdictional stage 'without clear evidence that its conduct could amount to an abuse of process'[31] and that 'it is only in exceptional circumstances that the Court should reject a claim based on a valid title of jurisdiction on the ground of abuse of process'.[32] Unfortunately, the ICJ had confined itself to noting that 'such evidence has not been presented to the Court' and that it did not 'consider the present case to be one of those circumstances'.[33]

14 So far, the Court's guidance on the abuse of process doctrine 'lacks any real substance'.[34] The ICJ has refrained from specifying evidentiary standards, and many questions remain unanswered. It did not, for instance, indicate whether an abuse of process implies bad faith and how the parties'—predominant or not—motivations should be assessed when instituting proceedings.[35] Eventually, the lack of clarity in the ICJ's jurisprudence on the matter also leads parties to raise this objection more frequently, as could be witnessed over the past few years.[36]

15 No relevant and useful guidance can be found in the context of interstate disputes under UNCLoS. In the *South China Sea Arbitration* case, the arbitral tribunal only briefly stated that an abuse of process can be found 'in only the most blatant cases of abuse or harassment'.[37]

---

[26] *Border and Transborder Armed Actions (Nicaragua v Honduras)* (Jurisdiction and Admissibility) [1988] ICJ Rep 69, para 51.
[27] *Application of the Convention on the Prevention and Punishment of the Crime of Genocide (Bosnia and Herzegovina v Serbia and Montenegro)* (Provisional Measures) [1993] ICJ Rep 325, para 19.
[28] *Immunities and Criminal Proceedings* (n 6) 292, 335, para 146
[29] ibid 336, para 150.
[30] With regard to the abuse of rights doctrine, the PCIJ considered that the 'misuse' of a right 'cannot be presumed, and it rests with the party who states that there has been such misuse to prove his statement'. See *Certain German Interests in Polish Upper Silesia* (Merits) (1926) PCIJ Series A, No 7, 30.
[31] *Immunities and Criminal Proceedings* (n 6) 292, 336, para 150.
[32] ibid.
[33] ibid.
[34] Tattersall and Khan (n 21) 240.
[35] Lemey (n 17) 23–24.
[36] ibid 10.
[37] *The South China Sea Arbitration (The Republic of Philippines v The People's Republic of China)*, PCA Case No 2013-19, Jurisdiction and Admissibility, 29 October 2015, para 128.

In other cases, the UNCLOS tribunals either rejected[38] or made no explicit determination[39] with regard to abuse of process allegations.

The ECtHR has considered that abuse of procedure is an 'exceptional procedural measure'[40]— echoing to some extent the 'exceptional circumstances' standard in the jurisprudence of the ICJ. Such abuse occurred in several instances,[41] for example where the application is knowingly based on untrue facts,[42] where the applicant uses vexatious, insulting, threatening or provocative language,[43] or where the applicant had lodged a succession of ill-founded and querulous complaints, creating unnecessary work which was incompatible with the Court's real functions.[44]

Most of the allegations of abuses before the ECtHR concern what could be labelled as 'procedural misconducts' rather than abuses of a given adjudication mechanism.[45] They differ significantly in nature from those raised before the ICJ and other interstate courts and tribunals. The latter are mainly related to the use of incidental proceedings, the absence of a genuine link between the subject matter of a dispute and the scope of consent to the jurisdiction, the circumvention of specific jurisdictional requirements or situations of forum shopping or parallel proceedings.[46] The Strasbourg Court's jurisprudence is therefore of limited interest to shed light on the commonly accepted standards governing the abuse of process doctrine under general international law. However, investment arbitration has proven to be an interesting laboratory in which arbitral tribunals have had the occasion to refine the doctrine.

C. Application in international investment law

I. Applicability and evidentiary standards

The major instruments governing investment arbitration proceedings do not make explicit reference to the 'abuse of process' or 'abuse of rights' doctrines. This is the case for instance of the International Centre for Settlement of Investment Disputes (ICSID) Convention and its arbitration rules. The doctrine, whatever its label, has thus been applied in investment arbitration without any explicit textual basis, primarily as an expression of the general principle of good faith.[47]

---

[38] See, eg, *Southern Bluefin Tuna (New Zealand–Japan, Australia–Japan)*, Jurisdiction and Admissibility, 4 August 2000, RIAA, Vol XXIII, 1, 46, para 65.
[39] See, eg, *Chagos Marine Protected Area Arbitration (Mauritius v United Kingdom)*, PCA Case No 2011-03, Award, 18 March 2015, paras 198, 219–21.
[40] ECtHR, *Mirolubovs and others v Latvia*, No 798/05, Judgment, 15 September 2009, para 62 (available in French and Russian only).
[41] For an overview, see European Court of Human Rights, *Practical Guide on Admissibility Criteria* (Council of Europe 2022) 52–56.
[42] ECtHR, *Varbanov v Bulgaria*, No 31365/96, Judgment, 5 October 2000, para 36.
[43] ECtHR, *Zhdanov and others v Russia*, Nos 12200/08, 35949/11, and 58282/12, Judgment, 16 July 2019, para 80.
[44] ECtHR, *Petrovic v Serbia*, No 56551/11, Decision, 18 October 2011. See also ECtHR, *Zambrano v France*, No 41994/21, Decision, 21 September 2021, para 36–37.
[45] On this distinction, see H Ascensio, 'Abuse of Process in International Investment Arbitration' (2014) 13 ChinJIntL 763, 767 (hereafter Ascensio).
[46] Lemey (n 17) 11–21; Tattersall and Khan (n 21) 234–52.
[47] *Phoenix* (n 7) para 143; *Abaclat and Others v Argentina*, ICSID Case No ARB/07/5, Jurisdiction and Admissibility, 4 August 2011, para 646; *Pac Rim Cayman LLC v Republic of El Salvador*, ICSID Case No ARB/09/12, Respondent's Jurisdictional Objections, 1 June 2012, para 2.47.

19 The abuse of process objection has been mainly formulated in two different ways.[48] Initially, the doctrine has only been applied to determine the existence of a *bona fide* investor or a *bona fide* investment when assessing the jurisdiction *ratione personae* or *ratione materiae* of the arbitral tribunal pursuant to an investment treaty.[49] It is only subsequently that abuse of process has been treated autonomously 'as a distinct objection,[50] not in relation to the definition of an investment or of an investor.[51] Some tribunals have considered that in the context of an ICSID arbitration, rejecting an application solely on the basis of abuse of process would be a "proposition of a very far-reaching character" which would need "to be backed by some positive authority" in the Convention itself, in its negotiating history, or in the case-law under it.[52] This is perhaps why in recent investment treaty practice, some states have decided to clarify this matter and have included in investment agreements 'abuse of process' as a ground for challenging the admissibility of investors' claims.[53] However, even though the normative basis of abuse of process has been debated,[54] that debate seems now closed in light of the recent decisions.[55]

20 The general evidentiary standards governing abuse of process allegations in investment arbitration do not differ from those of the ICJ decisions. Given the principle of good faith, 'a claimant is not required to prove that its claim is asserted in a non-abusive manner'.[56] A tribunal will not presume an abuse,[57] and therefore the burden of proof lies with the party making the allegation. With regard to the standard of proof, investment tribunals have underlined, even before the World Court in *Immunities and Criminal Proceedings*, that given the seriousness of the allegation, 'the threshold for a finding of abuse of process is high' and that the evidence of abuse will be affirmed only 'in very exceptional circumstances'.[58] An abuse of process does not imply bad faith.[59]

21 Allegations of abuse of process have been raised in investment arbitration for very different reasons, including procedural issues such as: non-payment of securities for costs;[60] frivolous claims and fraudulent conduct;[61] undue requests for disqualification of arbitrators:[62] for

---

[48] J Viñuales, 'Defence Arguments in Investment Arbitration' (2020) 18 ICSID Rep 42.
[49] Ascensio (n 45) 778.
[50] ibid 779.
[51] See, eg, Pac Rim, para 2.1.
[52] *The Rompetrol Group N.V. v Romania*, ICSID Case No ARB/06/3, Respondent's Preliminary Objections on Jurisdiction and Admissibility, 18 April 2008, para 115.
[53] See, eg, Slovakia–United Arab Emirates BIT (2016), art 17(2)(b) (underlining that the investor's claim shall be dismissed if the 'investment has been made through an abuse of process under the Host State's laws and Regulations'); EU–Vietnam Investment Protection Agreement (2019), art 3(27)(2) (referring to a 'conduct amounting to an abuse of process').
[54] JP Gaffney, '"Abuse of Process" in Investment Treaty Arbitration' (2010) 11 JWIT 515, 518.
[55] In this regard, see *Orascom TMT Investments S.à r.l. v People's Democratic Republic of Algeria*, ICSID Case No ARB/12/35, Annulment, 17 September 2020, paras 302–08.
[56] *Chevron Corporation (USA) and Texaco Petroleum Company (USA) v The Republic of Ecuador* (UNCITRAL) PCA Case No 34877, Interim Award, 1 December 2008, para 139.
[57] *Renée Rose Levy and Gremcitel S.A. v Republic of Peru*, ICSID Case No ARB/11/17, Award, 9 January 2015, para 186 (hereafter *Renée Rose Levy and Gremcitel*).
[58] *Renée Rose Levy and Gremcitel* (n 57) para 186. See also *Philip Morris Asia Limited v The Commonwealth of Australia* (UNCITRAL) PCA Case No 2012-12, Jurisdiction and Admissibility, 17 December 2015, para 539 (hereafter *Philip Morris*).
[59] *Philip Morris* (n 58) para 539.
[60] *Sergei Paushok, CJSC Golden East Company and CJSC Vostokneftegaz Company v The Government of Mongolia*, UNCITRAL, Jurisdiction and Liability, 28 April 2011, para 224.
[61] *Europe Cement Investment & Trade S.A. v Republic of Turkey*, ICSID Case No ARB(AF)/07/2, Award, 13 August 2009, para 180; *Cementownia 'Nowa Huta' S.A. v Republic of Turkey*, ICSID Case No ARB(AF)/06/2, Award, 17 September 2009, para 159.
[62] *AS PNB Banka and Others v Republic of Latvia*, ICSID Case No ARB/17/47, Decision on the Proposal to Disqualify Messrs James Spigelman, Peter Tomka, and John M Townsend, 16 June 2020, para 107.

interim measures;[63] for the production of documents;[64] and regarding simultaneous applications for pursuing revision and annulment proceedings in parallel.[65] However, to better shed light on the substance of the doctrine, it is more relevant to focus the analysis on abuses of the investment arbitration system as a whole, and not just situations of procedural misconduct within the arbitral process.[66] In that regard, two types of issues have shaped the doctrine in investment arbitration, namely, first, cases of parallel proceedings and overlapping claims, and, second, cases of corporate restructuring and forum shopping.

II. Situations of parallel proceedings

With regard to parallel proceedings in the context of overlapping claims, *Orascom* is an interesting precedent. The respondent considered that the claim was inadmissible under the doctrine of abuse of process (labelled as 'abuse of rights' in this award) because the investor used his group of companies to introduce several parallel and overlapping arbitration proceedings against the same respondent State at different levels of the chain of companies. The tribunal considered that while 'structuring an investment through several layers of corporate entities in different states is not illegitimate' in itself, an investor who controls several entities in a chain of companies may nonetheless commit an abuse 'if it seeks to impugn the same host state measures and claims for the same harm at various levels of the chain in reliance on several investment treaties concluded by the host state'.[67] In the tribunal's view, this would entail the 'exercise of rights for purposes that are alien to those for which' investment treaties were established and allowing 'such additional protection would give rise to a risk of multiple recoveries and conflicting decisions, not to speak of the waste of resources that multiple proceedings involve'.[68] 22

In *Ampal*, the tribunal had to face a situation with four parallel arbitrations with essentially 'the same factual matrix, the same witnesses and many identical claims'.[69] It considered that the situation may look abusive but noted that only one claim was 'a double pursuit of the same claim in respect of the same interest'[70] and that other claims did not generate a situation of abuse of process since they concerned 'distinct tranches of the same investment'.[71] The development of parallel arbitrations arising out of the same factual matrix is not 'desirable' but it cannot as such be characterized as abusive, all the more when the respondent has declined claimants' offers to consolidate the proceedings.[72] As pointed out in *Orascom*, what matters is mainly to avoid 'claims involving the same economic damage be adjudged twice'.[73] 23

---

[63] *Sergei Viktorovich Pugachev v The Russian Federation* (UNCITRAL) Interim Award, 7 July 2017, para 107.
[64] *Aguas del Tunari v Republic of Bolivia*, ICSID Case No ARB/02/3, Procedural Order No 1, para 14.
[65] *Dan Cake (Portugal) S.A. v Hungary*, ICSID Case No ARB/12/9, Applicant's Request for the Continued Stay of Enforcement of the Award, 25 December 2018, para 58.
[66] Ascensio (n 45) 767. On procedural misconducts, see Abba Kolo, 'Witness Intimidation, Tampering and Other Related Abuses of Process in Investment Arbitration: Possible Remedies Available to the Arbitral Tribunal' (2010) 26 ArbIntl 43.
[67] *Orascom TMT Investments S.à r.l. v People's Democratic Republic of Algeria*, ICSID Case No ARB/12/35, Final Award, 31 May 2017, para 542 (hereafter *Orascom*).
[68] ibid para 543.
[69] *Ampal-American Israel Corporation and others v Arab Republic of Egypt*, ICSID Case No ARB/12/11, Jurisdiction, 1 February 2016, para 328 (hereafter *Ampal*).
[70] ibid para 331.
[71] ibid para 329.
[72] *Ampal* (n 69) para 329. See also *Orascom* (n 67) para 547.
[73] *Orascom* (n 67) para 542, fn 835.

III. Situations of corporate restructuring

24 Situations of abuses of process have mainly concerned cases of corporate restructuring carried out with the purpose of gaining access to the protection granted under an investment treaty. The initial structuring and even the subsequent restructuring of an investment made with the view of obtaining procedural guarantees under an investment agreement do not constitute in themselves abusive conduct. A tribunal stated that 'this was a perfectly legitimate goal as far as it concerned future disputes'.[74] Strategies of treaty shopping, even by incorporating letterbox or shell companies, are thus possible to the extent that they are not prohibited under investment agreements, for instance when they deny the benefit of the treaty protection to investors without substantial business activities in their home State.[75] They are also possible to the extent that they do not constitute an abuse of process, also labelled as an 'abuse of corporate form' or an 'abuse of legal personality'[76] in the decisions.

25 The *Phoenix* tribunal was the first to dismiss a request at the jurisdictional stage because of an abuse of process. It considered that 'a corporation cannot modify the structure of its investment for the sole purpose of gaining access to ICSID jurisdiction, after damages have occurred'.[77] It attempted to unveil 'the true nature of the operation' which was in its view made 'to gain access to ICSID jurisdiction to which the initial investor was not entitled'[78] and the 'unique goal of the "investment" was to transform a pre-existing domestic dispute into an international dispute subject to ICSID arbitration under a bilateral investment treaty'.[79]

26 The criteria for abuse of process have been refined in subsequent decisions. *Philip Morris v Australia* incorporated previous jurisprudential developments.[80] The tribunal found that 'the abuse is subject to an objective test and is seen in the fact that an investor who is not protected by an investment treaty restructures its investment in such a fashion as to fall within the scope of protection of a treaty in view of a specific foreseeable dispute'.[81] Different foreseeability tests have been implemented in the decisions,[82] resting 'between the two extremes [of] ... a very high probability and not merely a possible controversy'.[83] The *Philip Morris* tribunal considered that a dispute is foreseeable 'when there is a reasonable prospect ... that a measure which may give rise to a treaty claim will materialise'.[84] Also, as to the motives behind the restructuring, it is necessary to establish its 'main and determinative'—and not necessarily the sole and exclusive—reason is the intention to bring a claim under the investment agreement.[85]

---

[74] *Mobil Corporation* (n 10) para 204.
[75] H Wehland, 'Forum Shopping: Investment Arbitration' in Hélène Ruiz Fabri (ed), *Max Planck Encyclopedia of International Procedural Law* (2020) paras 29–33.
[76] *Mobil Corporation* (n 10) para 176.
[77] *Phoenix* (n 7) para 92.
[78] ibid para 140.
[79] ibid para 142.
[80] *Inter alia, Tidewater Inc et al v The Bolivarian Republic of Venezuela*, ICSID Case No ARB/10/5, Jurisdiction, 8 February 2013, para 184; *Mobil Corporation* (n 10) para 204; *Renée Rose Levy and Gremcitel* (n 57) para 184; Pac Rim, para 2.99; *Lao Holdings N.V. v Lao People's Democratic Republic*, ICSID Case No ARB(AF)/12/6, Jurisdiction, 20 February 2014, para 70.
[81] *Philip Morris* (n 58) para 539.
[82] For an overview, see Jorun Baumgartner, *Treaty Shopping in International Investment Law* (OUP 2016) 222–27.
[83] *Philip Morris* (n 58) para 554.
[84] ibid para 554.
[85] ibid para 584.

With regard to the chronological sequence of the events, a more recent award contemplated **27**
a different type of abuse of corporate form. The arbitral tribunal admitted that there is an
abuse of process when a shell corporation that did not have any economic and administrative activity (eg, no meetings of the general assembly or board of directors) for years before
the dispute is suddenly reactivated just after the institution of proceedings in order to meet
the nationality requirement of the claim.[86] Cases of abuses of corporate form may therefore
go beyond situations of corporate restructuring.

D. Explaining the divergence between general international law and international investment law

At first glance, there seems to be a convergence as to the main legal standards applicable to **28**
abuse of process allegations in investment arbitration and in other international courts and
tribunals. In both contexts, there is no longer a debate as to the existence and applicability of
the doctrine by international courts and tribunals without any explicit textual basis. In both
contexts, the burden of proof lies with the party making the allegation, the threshold for a
finding of abuse of process is high, and the evidence of abuse will be affirmed only in exceptional circumstances. However, international courts and tribunals, and first and foremost
the ICJ, have proven to implement vague standards in the context of interstate disputes. So
far, the ICJ and International Tribunal for the Law of the Sea (ITLOS) rejected all abuse of
process allegations.

I. A reluctance to rely on the ISDS jurisprudence

There could have been some fruitful interaction and dialogue on the matter between investment tribunals[87] and the ICJ given—perhaps not the similarity but at least—the analogy of **29**
situations where allegations of abuse have been made. Arguably, the divergent orientations
taken by the ICJ and investment tribunals could be explained by the specificity of the disputes and/or by other factors.

Precedents of corporate restructuring in investment arbitration may be compared to the **30**
situation contemplated in *Immunities and Criminal Proceedings*. It is thus not a surprise that
France relied in its pleadings before the ICJ on the approach of investment tribunals.[88] In
both cases, the alleged abusive conduct stems from the transformation of the legal status of
an entity, person, or asset (changing the nationality of a corporation, transforming a private
residence into diplomatic premises, granting someone an eminent political position) to ensure the application of a legal regime (an investment agreement, the 1961 Vienna Convention
on Diplomatic Relations (VCDR), head of State immunity) potentially playing a specific role
at the jurisdictional stage.[89] Investment tribunals underlined that when assessing an abuse
of process allegation, they have 'under general international law as well as under ICSID case

---

[86] *Capital Financial Holdings Luxembourg S.A. v Republic of Cameroon*, ICSID Case No ARB/15/18, Award, 22 June 2017, paras 362–65.
[87] See, C. Ceretelli, 'Abuse of Process: An Impossible Dialogue Between ICJ and ICSID Tribunals?' (2020) 11 JIDS 47 (hereafter Ceretelli).
[88] ICJ, CR 2018/2, 19 February 2018, para 26.
[89] Ceretelli (n 87) 55.

law' to take 'into account all the circumstances of the case'[90] and review for instance the timing of the investment and of the claim, the substance of the transaction, the true nature of the operation and the degree of foreseeability of the governmental action at the time of restructuring.[91] In *Immunities and Criminal Proceedings*, the ICJ refrained from carrying out an extensive examination of all the circumstances but nonetheless considered that there was no 'clear evidence that [Equatorial Guinea's] conduct could amount to an abuse of process'.[92]

31 In my view, the ICJ's stance on the matter relied less on insufficient evidence than on what it considered to be the dual nature, procedural and substantive, of the rights allegedly abused. France's objection has been considered only in relation to the 1961 VCDR[93] which constituted the basis of one of Equatorial Guinea's substantive claims—namely, the legality of granting diplomatic status to a private residence in these particular circumstances. In that regard, the Court considered 'that abuse of rights cannot be invoked as a ground of inadmissibility when the establishment of the right in question is properly a matter for the merits'.[94] In that regard, the issue at stake is at first sight different from the one envisaged in the context of a corporate restructuring since the assessment of the evidence surrounding the restructuring, taken separately, concerns exclusively the effectiveness of a procedural right—gaining access to arbitration—and does not play a role at the merits stage.

32 The World Court, therefore, relies on a stringent procedure/substance divide narrowing the possibility of opening an examination of the abuse of process allegation at the jurisdictional stage. This view has not been shared by all the members of the Court. In a detailed and convincing dissenting opinion, Judge Donoghue, following more the approach of investment tribunals, considered that there was conclusive evidence that the purpose of the sequence of actions taken by the applicant is 'manifest' and that this case 'is such an exceptional circumstance'.[95] She noted eventually that the Court 'should not have allowed itself to be used' by the applicant 'to preserve the integrity of its judicial function'.[96]

33 With regard to parallel proceedings, it has been suggested that the abuse of process doctrine, as implemented by investment tribunals in the context of overlapping claims concerning the same tranche of investment and the same economic damage, should inspire the ICJ to better regulate situations of parallel litigation.[97] The United Arab Emirates (UAE) raised an abuse of process allegation in the context of Qatar's simultaneous proceedings before the Court and the Committee on the Elimination of Racial Discrimination for a violation of the International Convention on the Elimination of All Forms of Racial Discrimination (CERD). The UAE more specifically considered that by prosecuting these two procedures simultaneously and by failing to respect the principle *Electa una via non datur recursus ad alteram*, Qatar was 'abusing the Convention's complaints mechanism process and its rights under the Convention'.[98] The CERD Committee, however, rejected the exception without

---

[90] *Renée Rose Levy and Gremcitel* (n 57) para 186.
[91] *Transglobal Green Energy, LLC and Transglobal Green Energy de Panama, S.A. v The Republic of Panama*, ICSID Case No ARB/13/28, Award, 2 June 2016, para 103.
[92] ICJ, *Immunities and Criminal Proceedings* (n 6) para 150.
[93] The ICJ found that it lacked jurisdiction under the Palermo Convention—*Immunities and Criminal Proceedings* (n 6) para 118.
[94] *Immunities and Criminal Proceedings* (n 6) para 151.
[95] *Immunities and Criminal Proceedings* (n 6) 292, Dissenting Opinion of Judge Donoghue, 387, para 18.
[96] ibid para 19.
[97] Ceretelli (n 87) 60–63.
[98] CERD, Admissibility of the Inter-state communication submitted by Qatar against the United Arab Emirates, CERD/C/99/4, 30 August 2019, para 20.

any reference to the abuse of process doctrine.[99] Likewise, the ICJ rejected the argument at the interim measures stage,[100] and the respondent did not pursue the allegation during the preliminary objections.[101] Qatar's claims have been considered by some authors as an abusive multiplication 'of identical proceedings' entangling the respondent 'in expensive, time-consuming procedures' with a risk of conflicting interpretations of the same treaty.[102] However, it is clear that the ICJ is not ready to use the abuse of process doctrine as a tool to regulate situations of *lis pendens*.

II. Possible considerations of judicial policy

The reluctance of the ICJ and other interstate tribunals to dismiss a claim on the ground of the abuse of process doctrine may be explained by considerations of judicial policy. One must resist the temptation of an idealistic vision of interstate proceedings deprived of any abusive behaviour, procedural harassment, or intent to instrumentalize international justice.[103] This was Judge Donoghue's core argument when she highlighted the necessity to 'preserve the integrity' of the Court's judicial function: 'the Court allows the case to proceed to the merits, as if this is yet another disagreement about the nuances of the régime of diplomatic immunity.'[104] **34**

First, the reluctance to dismiss an abusive claim in interstate proceedings may be explained by the nature of the parties and its impact on the number of proceedings. Investment tribunals and the ECtHR are respectively accessible to a vast number of private claimants whose behaviour may differ in some cases from those of States' representatives.[105] Besides, in *Immunities and Criminal Proceedings*, Equatorial Guinea used that argument to consider that 'cases in the investment field, being cases brought by private persons against States, are inherently very different, and we would say cannot serve as precedents for inter-State proceedings'.[106] Conversely, interstate courts are available to a structurally limited number of claimants and have to adjudicate a limited number of cases compared with the number of ISDS cases introduced each year. If they apply less stringent standards and eventually start dismissing claims on the ground of abuse of process, they also risk having states no longer consent to their jurisdiction.[107] **35**

Second, the reluctance of interstate courts may be due to the pejorative connotation of an abuse of process accusation.[108] Indeed, 'international courts and tribunals have to presume that states act in good faith' and 'to do otherwise would call the honour of states into question'.[109] This is what Equatorial Guinea suggested in *Immunities and Criminal Proceedings* **36**

---

[99] ibid para 51.
[100] Application of the International Convention on the Elimination of All Forms of Racial Discrimination (*Qatar v United Arab Emirates*) (Provisional Measures) [2019] ICJ Rep 361, 369–70, para 25.
[101] Application of the International Convention on the Elimination of All Forms of Racial Discrimination (*Qatar v United Arab Emirates*) (Preliminary Objections) [2021] ICJ Rep 71, 87, para 39.
[102] Ceretelli (n 87) 66.
[103] Lemey (n 17) 288.
[104] *Immunities and Criminal Proceedings* (n 6) 292, Dissenting Opinion of Judge Donoghue, 387, paras 18–19.
[105] Lemey (n 3) 304; Tattersall and Khan (n 21) 253.
[106] ICJ, CR 2018/3, 20 February 2018, para 10.
[107] Lemey (n 3) 305; Mitchell and Malone (n 1) para 21.
[108] Lemey (n 17) 26.
[109] Byers (n 13) 412.

when it stated that 'France once again calls into question the motives of Equatorial Guinea in a manner that is unacceptable in international relations'.[110]

37 Third and lastly, the reluctance of interstate courts, and mainly the ICJ, may also be explained by other extra-legal considerations. The ICJ is not just an adjudicative mechanism, it has also played a significant role in the peaceful settlement of disputes as the principal judicial organ of the United Nations. Upholding a complaint founded on the abuse of process doctrine at the early admissibility stage could not only lead the Court to call into question the honour of the claimant, but also 'risk introducing political and diplomatic factors into the judicial process, impede international relations, and increase the danger of escalation'.[111] Interestingly, one of Nicaragua's counsel in several cases before the ICJ even admitted that even if some of Nicaragua's requests before the World Court 'could ... be seen as unwarranted, not to say abusive, the recourse to the ICJ has been no doubt a means to ease the tension between the two States [in dispute]' and 'the Court has been able to find balanced and appeasing solutions'.[112]

E. Conclusion

38 Over the past years, interstate courts, investment tribunals, and other international adjudicative bodies have contributed to shaping the abuse of process doctrine in general international law. The controversies surrounding its existence as a general principle, its genealogy and its autonomy now have less relevance. The main issue in the current practice of international adjudicative bodies mainly concerns the substance of the doctrine. The threshold for a finding of abuse of process is high and it is only in 'exceptional circumstances' that a court or tribunal will reject a claim on such grounds. However, although investment tribunals had many occasions to refine the evidentiary standards applicable to allegations of abuse of process in cases of abuse of corporate form or of parallel proceedings, interstate courts and tribunals have chosen to use very vague standards, and have refrained from relying on what could have been regarded as instructive and relevant investment arbitration precedents. To date, the ICJ and ITLOS have rejected all abuse of process allegations submitted before them.

39 In this entry, it has been suggested that these variations in the application of the doctrine and the ICJ's reluctance may be explained by various reasons, including the nature of parties, the specificity of interstate proceedings, and the necessity to maintain the accessibility of a courtroom playing an important role in the peaceful settlement of disputes. One may also look at things from a different perspective and attempt to explain why investment tribunals have chosen to adopt more refined standards and uphold abuse of process allegations, most of the time just as an additional ground for inadmissibility. One possible explanation would be envisaging the doctrine as one of many regulation tools to correct the anomalies of—and eventually to sustain—an investment treaty system facing an increasing backlash. As pointed out in *Orascom*, the resort to the abuse of process doctrine 'has allowed tribunals to apply investment treaties in such a manner as to avoid consequences unforeseen by their drafters and at odds with the very purposes underlying the conclusion of those treaties'.[113]

---

[110] ICJ, CR 2018/3, 20 February 2018, para 8.
[111] Byers (n 13) 412.
[112] Alain Pellet, 'Introduction from the Podium' in Edgardo Sobenes Obregon and Benjamin Samson (eds), *Nicaragua Before the International Court of Justice—Impacts on International Law* (Springer 2018) 31.
[113] Orascom (n 67) para 547.

On balance, there are possibly many extra-legal considerations that have also influenced **40** how the abuse of process doctrine has been implemented over the past years, and this may explain its variability depending on the needs and constraints weighing on the adjudicative mechanism at stake.

Selected literature

Ascensio H, 'Abuse of Process in International Investment Arbitration' (2014) 13 ChinJInt L 763–85.

Byers M, 'Abuse of Rights: An Old Principle, a New Age' (2002) 47 McGillLJ 389–431.

Ceretelli C, 'Abuse of Process: An Impossible Dialogue Between ICJ and ICSID Tribunals?' (2020) 11 JIDS 47–68.

Kolb R, 'General Principles of Procedural Law' in Andreas Zimmermann and others (eds), *The Statute of the International Court of Justice: A Commentary* (3rd edn, OUP 2019).

Lemey M, 'Incidental Proceedings before the International Court of Justice: The Fine Line between "Litigation Strategy" and "Abuse of Process"' (2021) 20 LPICT 5–29.

Mitchell AD and Malone T, 'Abuse of Process in Inter-State Dispute Resolution' in Hélène Ruiz Fabri (ed), *Max Planck Encyclopedia of International Procedural Law* (OUP 2018).

Tattersall L and Khan A, 'Taking Stock: Abuse of Process within the International Court of Justice' (2020) 19 LPICT 229–268.

Selected decisions

Ampal-American Israel Corporation and others v Arab Republic of Egypt, ICSID Case No ARB/12/11, Jurisdiction, 1 February 2016.

Immunities and Criminal Proceedings (Equatorial Guinea v France) (Preliminary Objections) [2018] ICJ Rep 292.

Mobil Corporation, Venezuela Holdings, B.V., et al v Bolivarian Republic of Venezuela, ICSID Case No ARB/07/27, Jurisdiction, 10 June 2010.

Orascom TMT Investments S.à r.l. v People's Democratic Republic of Algeria, ICSID Case No ARB/12/35, Final Award, 31 May 2017.

Philip Morris Asia Limited v The Commonwealth of Australia, UNCITRAL, PCA Case No 2012-12, Jurisdiction and Admissibility, 17 December 2015.

Phoenix Action, Ltd v The Czech Republic, ICSID Case No ARB/06/5, Award, 15 April 2009.

Renée Rose Levy and Gremcitel S.A. v Republic of Peru, ICSID Case No ARB/11/17, Award, 9 January 2015.

Unjust enrichment

Kathleen Claussen

A. Introduction	1	D. Application in international investment law	27
B. What is 'unjust enrichment'	3		
C. Application in general international law	12	E. Divergence between general international law and international investment law	37
I. Early decisions: *Chorzów Factory* and *Lena Goldfields* arbitration	14		
II. After *Lena Goldfields*	18	F. Conclusion	44
III. The decisions of the Iran–US Claims Tribunal	22		

A. Introduction

1 The concept of unjust enrichment, where one entity has been enriched at another's expense in a way the law regards as unjust, is well recognized across legal systems. Its appreciation as a legal principle is prevalent enough among domestic legal regimes to warrant its characterization as a general principle of law[1] (see also further below at paragraph 3, with references). The treatment of unjust enrichment in international law, however, is varied. There is little shared understanding of how 'unjust enrichment' operates, as reflected in the decisions of international courts and tribunals. Even within international investment law, there is no consensus as to how tribunals ought to treat claims to unjust enrichment.

2 This entry first explains how actors in international law have identified the principle of unjust enrichment before turning to its use by and at the International Court of Justice (ICJ), as well as by arbitration tribunals, in particular the Iran–US Claims Tribunal. Second, the entry describes how investment tribunals have engaged with claims of unjust enrichment. Finally, the entry analyses how the investment arbitration community has departed from other regimes of international law in its consideration of unjust enrichment. Taken together, this examination of unjust enrichment provides an important illustration of how even a general principle can lead to divergent applications and fragmentation in international law.

---

[1] On general principles of law see also Patrick Dumberry, 'Article 38 of the ICJ Statute: Sources (and select general principles)'.

B. What is 'unjust enrichment'

The concept of 'unjust enrichment' finds its origins in domestic law, like most general principles of international law. Across dozens of jurisdictions with varied legal pedigrees, unjust enrichment is a concept that resonates with courts and with litigants.[2] To provide just one example, the United States Restatement of the Law of Restitution provides that a 'person who has been unjustly enriched at the expense of another is required to make restitution to the other'.[3] Given the common view across certain major legal systems of the world, some commentators consider unjust enrichment to be the epitome of a general principle of law.[4] Influential international law scholars have affirmed this in their writing since the early part of the twentieth century.[5]

Despite this widespread acceptance that something akin to unjust enrichment is a cognizable legal claim, there is no consensus as to its content. While the basic concept may be widely appreciated, the terms that comprise its core remain disputed. To give two examples, out of many more: One legal dictionary refers to receipt of a benefit without restitution 'required by law';[6] further, the presence or absence of a contract between the parties is a point of notable inconsistency.[7]

International law scholars have elaborated the contours of the concept. For example, one writes of the 'enrichment of one party to the detriment of the other as a consequence of the same act or event without justification for the enrichment and no other remedy available to the injured party to seek compensation from the party enriched'.[8]

Note that this articulation highlights three important elements: first, that unjust enrichment has implications for both parties—enrichment of one at the detriment of the other; second, that these conditions must be met without a just cause; and third, that recovering for unjust enrichment cannot be achieved through an ordinary contract claim. But these elements are largely implied.

While the circumstances in any given case may merit a finding of unjust enrichment across diverse jurisdictions, it is less well substantiated that there is a general principle.[9] To the extent one could identify a generally accepted principle it is with respect to the identification

---

[2] Christina Binder has done much of this investigation. She refers to the United States, United Kingdom, France, and Germany, among others. See C Binder, 'Unjust Enrichment as a General Principle of Law' in A Gattini and others (eds), *General Principles of Law and International Investment Arbitration* (Brill Nijhoff 2018) 269–89 (hereafter Binder, 'Unjust Enrichment'). See also DC Dicke, 'Unjust Enrichment and Compensation' in DC Dicke (ed), *Foreign Investment in the Present and a New International Economic Order* (Fribourg University Press 1987).

[3] Restatement (First) of Restitution, § 1.

[4] See, eg, Binder, 'Unjust Enrichment' (n 2) 274, 278.

[5] See, eg, Lord McNair, 'The Seizure of Property and Enterprises,' (1959) 6 NILR 218, 240; M Whiteman, *Damages in International Law* (Washington: United States Government Printing Office 1943).

[6] Wex Legal Dictionary, Legal Information Institute <https://www.law.cornell.edu/wex/unjust_enrichment> accessed 23 October 2023.

[7] ibid.

[8] Binder, 'Unjust Enrichment' (n 2) 269.

[9] Interestingly, the concept was discussed in the International Law Commission's early efforts to codify the law of State responsibility. Oliver Hailes presents the complicated history of this discussion. O Hailes, 'Unjust enrichment in investor–State arbitration: A principled limit on compensation for future income from fossil fuels' (2022) 13 RECIEL 1 (hereafter Hailes, 'Unjust enrichment').

of circumstances giving rise to unjust enrichment in which the party harmed has some right to relief.[10]

8 The decisions separate the cause from the remedy without clear definition on the latter, complicating its classification as a general principle. Most commentators (and to some degree, tribunals) do not discuss the general requirements for relief. Rather, they engage in diverse discussions as to the implications of such a factual finding of unjust enrichment.

9 There is even less commonality with respect to the principle's operation or application. Some scholars consider unjust enrichment to be a primary rule of international law; others consider it to be a secondary rule.[11] The distinction is also made among adjudicatory bodies. Courts and tribunals have permitted claims of unjust enrichment as an alternate claim to relief for breach of an agreement where the harms are difficult to demonstrate. Adjudicators also have accepted claims to unjust enrichment as standalone claims or causes of actions on their own.

10 Among the additional challenges in deciphering the content of a principle of unjust enrichment is tracking all the iterations of the concept and terminologies used. Some jurisdictions refer to 'unjustified enrichment' but it not clear whether those jurisdictions are using that term entirely interchangeably with 'unjust enrichment' as used elsewhere.[12] As noted above, any study of the principle is made more difficult by the fact that the term 'unjust enrichment', or variations on it, is used to refer both to the facts upon which the claim is based as well as the amount according to which the respondent was unjustly enriched.

11 A final, related complexity in understanding unjust enrichment concerns its indiscriminate deployment. Claims to unjust enrichment may be advocated by both claimants and respondents, as defences, as ancillary or supplemental claims, or as merits claims, among other possibilities. These disparate dispositions are discussed further in Section C.

C. Application in general international law

12 Although unjust enrichment is widely accepted as a general principle of law, it is not widely discussed among international courts and tribunals. The ICJ has never rendered a judgment or other decision concerning unjust enrichment, although its predecessor court did. The principle was raised by at least one of the parties in a reasonably significant way in three ICJ disputes.[13] For different reasons in each instance, the Court did not decide the issue in

---

[10] Black's Law Dictionary refers to unjust enrichment as 'the area of law dealing with unjustifiable benefits' without specifying the legal elements. Unjust Enrichment Definition, Black's Law Dictionary (9th edn, 2009), available at Westlaw.

[11] Compare Binder, 'Unjust Enrichment' (n 2) to B Juratowitch and J Schaerf who argue that unjust enrichment is a primary rule of international law. Ana Vorhyzek concludes likewise that unjust enrichment may be a 'cause of action'. A Vohryzek, 'Unjust Enrichment Unjustly Ignored: Opportunities and Pitfalls in Bringing Unjust Enrichment Claims under ICSID' (2009) 31 LoyLAIntl&CompLRev 501, 502 (hereafter Vohryzek, 'Opportunities'). H Dagan treats it as 'an applicable measure of recovery'. H Dagan, *Unjust Enrichment: A Study of Private Law and Public Values* (CUP 1997) 132 (hereafter Dagan, *Study*).

[12] CH Schreuer, 'Unjustified Enrichment in International Law' (1974) 22 AmJCompL 281.

[13] See, eg, *Territorial and Maritime Dispute (Nicaragua v Colombia)*, ICJ, Reply of Nicaragua (18 September 2009); *Certain Property (Liechtenstein v Germany)*, ICJ, Memorial of Lichtenstein (28 March 2002); *Ambatielos (Greece v United Kingdom)*, ICJ, Rejoinder Submitted by the Government of the United Kingdom (3 January 1953). In several other disputes, the issue has come up in a less significant way.

its final judgment. The ICJ's recent relative silence on the question sets 'unjust enrichment' apart from several of the other principles discussed in this volume.

The Permanent Court of International Justice (PCIJ) elaborated the principle in one of its most important decisions, and arbitration tribunals have been active in deciding questions about unjust enrichment before and after the PCIJ.[14] This section highlights the major court and State-to-State arbitral decisions in international law that have applied this general principle of international law, confirming its relevance.

I. Early decisions: *Chorzów Factory* and *Lena Goldfields* arbitration

The principle was elaborated early in the twentieth century in the *Factory at Chorzów* case at the PCIJ in 1928.[15] This case, well-known in public international law, also provides much of the groundwork for later investment law in its discussion of expropriation, and that is not a coincidence. In the investment decisions of the early twenty-first century, unjust enrichment claims often appear alongside expropriation claims where they appear at all.

In the *Chorzów* dispute, Germany sued Poland for expropriating a German investor's factory after the First World War. Poland operated and developed the factory from the time of its seizure until the conclusion of the case, when the PCIJ found that Poland's actions constituted an illegal expropriation. Although the relevant law prescribed restitution as the remedy, the PCIJ articulated several different options for calculation of the award. Noting that when a party violates international law, reparations or restitutions must be awarded to 'wipe out all consequences' of the unlawful act, the PCIJ considered multiple possible calculations as articulated by an expert.[16] Scholars have differed on the reading of the Court's menu of damages options, and the case later settled. However, one interpretation of the Court's discussion is that it was effectively awarding Germany the amount by which Poland was enriched.[17] Some investment tribunals have relied on this reading to decide unjust enrichment claims.

Shortly after the *Chorzów* case, the tribunal in the *Lena Goldfields* arbitration in 1930[18] had occasion to consider the principle once again, and to do so in greater detail—so much so that it has been referred to as the 'fountainhead of all unjust enrichment claims' in investment disputes.[19] In this case, the tribunal found that the USSR breached a contract in such a manner as to exempt the claimant from further obligations and as to merit damages. Rather than calculate damages on the contract, however, the tribunal elected to base its award on an unjust enrichment principle.[20]

---

[14] Hailes acknowledges arbitrations involving governments as early as the late nineteenth century confronting the question. Hailes, 'Unjust enrichment' (n 9) 5–6.
[15] *Factory at Chorzów (Germany v Poland)* (Merits) (1928) PCIJ Series A No 17, 47.
[16] ibid 47.
[17] Vohryzek, 'Opportunities' (n 11) 522–27.
[18] *Lena Goldfields Co Ltd v The Government of USSR*, Award, 3 September 1930, The Times 7; ibid [1929–30] 5 AnnDig 3 (hereafter *Lena Goldfields*). Text of the Award in English may also be found in the Appendix to A Nussbaum, 'Arbitration Between the Lena Goldfields Ltd. and the Soviet Government' (1950) 36 CornellLRev 31.
[19] Vohryzek, 'Opportunities' (n 11) 520.
[20] *Lena Goldfields* (n 18) para 25.

17 According to the *Lena Goldfields* tribunal, unjust enrichment 'arises where the defendant has in his possession money or money's worth of the plaintiff's to which he has no just right'.[21] The tribunal went on to analyse whether the respondent's enrichment had a just cause. Finding none, the tribunal concluded:

> In consequence Lena is entitled to be relieved from the burden of further obligations thereunder and to be compensated in money for the value of the benefits of which it had been wrongfully deprived. On ordinary legal principles this constitutes a right of action for damages, but the Court prefers to base its award on the principle of 'unjust enrichment', although in its opinion the money result is the same.[22]

II. After *Lena Goldfields*

18 Among the difficulties arising in determining whether a party has been unjustly enriched is to define under what circumstances enrichment is regarded as unjust or unjustified, or whether there is a just cause. This issue has arisen particularly in the consideration of obligations for successor States in respect of the debt of their predecessor States, given the lapse the legal relationship between the prior parties created by supervening events.[23]

19 This issue came up many years after *Lena Goldfields* in the 1950s, in the *Lighthouses Arbitration*.[24] A French company held a lighthouse concession from the Ottoman government in territory ceded to Greece. The tribunal was called upon to decide the pecuniary claims of the company against Greece and to make an assessment of the redemption value of the lighthouses concession. The tribunal dismissed an ancillary unjust enrichment claim for the repair of the lighthouse, concluding that there was a just cause for the enrichment: the repair of the lighthouse was part of the normal obligations under the concession contract.

20 A second common issue seen in these milestone cases is that of calculating the damages associated with unjust enrichment, or otherwise accommodating an unjust enrichment claim in the remedy devised by the tribunal. Another twenty years after the *Lighthouses Arbitration*, the arbitrator in the case between the Libyan American Oil Company (LIAMCO) and Libya evaluated an unjust enrichment theory in his calculation of damages together with the other claims in the case. Ultimately, the arbitrator balanced the two parties' claims to award what he called 'equitable compensation'.[25]

21 As can be seen from this short history, the principle did not receive considerable attention among tribunals until the creation of the Iran–US Claims Tribunal (IUSCT), which has the most developed jurisprudence among international tribunals on this question.

---

[21] ibid para 23.
[22] ibid para 25.
[23] M Waibel, 'Decolonization and Sovereign Debt: A Quagmire' in JH Flores Zendejas and P Penet (eds), *Sovereign Debt Diplomacies* (OUP 2021).
[24] *Lighthouses Arbitration (France v Greece)*, Award, 24 July 1956, 12 RIAA 155, 209.
[25] *Libyan American Oil Company v The Government of the Libyan Arab Republic*, Award, 12 April 1977.

III. The decisions of the Iran–US Claims Tribunal

The leading case at the IUSCT is *Sea-Land Service, Inc. v The Islamic Republic of Iran* in 1984.[26] This case concerned a claim regarding a containerized cargo facility in Iran. Sea-Land claimed its rights of use were deprived by Iran and that this constituted unjust enrichment, meriting compensation. The IUSCT agreed with the claimant, finding that it ought to be compensated for assets left in Iran that were retained and therefore a benefit to Iran. In its elaboration, the tribunal remarked on the boundaries of the principle. It noted that unjust enrichment compensation does not extend so far as loss of unpaid debts, freight charges, termination expenses, or other future profits.[27] Rather, the tribunal found that, in that instance, it must award damages based on a monetary value representing the extent to which Iran was enriched by its early acquisition of the cargo facility. The tribunal limited the claimant's relief to the value of the early acquisition of the cargo facility.

Additional rulings on unjust enrichment would follow at the IUSCT with the tribunal carving out its exceptions and requirements for purposes of the claims before it. In a 1986 case,[28] the tribunal dismissed a claim of unjust enrichment based on lease agreements of marine transport equipment between Flexi-Van Leasing, Inc. and Iran. Much like in the earlier arbitrations outside IUSCT, Flexi-Van presented its unjust enrichment claim as an alternative ground for relief, alleging that the government of Iran was unjustly enriched through the retention of Flexi Van's equipment. Consistent with its prior practice of applying unjust enrichment only as a last resort, the tribunal dismissed the claim.[29]

Another important milestone in the IUSCT series was the 1987 case, *Schlegel Corporation v National Iranian Copper Industries Company*.[30] Until that case, the IUSCT had consistently adopted the view that it would not entertain an unjust enrichment claim if the parties had a valid contract.[31] Despite these prior rulings, Schlegel prevailed on a claim based on unjust enrichment. The tribunal found that the National Iranian Copper Industries Company (NICIC) did not satisfy its contractual obligations in good faith, and that Schlegel made reasonable efforts to recover its detriment to no avail. According to the tribunal, Schlegel effectively showed that NICIC had been unjustly enriched since both the enrichment of the NICIC and detriment of Schlegel arose out of the same act or event.[32]

Finally, in a non-contract case involving Lockheed Martin and Iran,[33] the tribunal introduced an idea of contributory negligence without using that terminology. The tribunal evaluated an unjust enrichment claim by Lockheed and concluded that Lockheed did not suffer any detriment due to the actions of the Iranian Air Force but rather by its own actions. Lockheed had continued to provide service without arranging proper payment to its own

---

[26] *Sea-Land Service, Inc v The Islamic Republic of Iran*, IUSCT Case No 33, Award No 135-33-1, 22 June 1984.
[27] ibid para 68.
[28] *Flexi-Van Leasing, Inc v The Government of the Islamic Republic of Iran*, IUSCT Case No 36, Award No 259-36-1, 13 October 1986.
[29] *Consortium for International Development ('CID') v Iran*, 26 IUSCT Rep (Grotius Cambridge 1992) 244, 251.
[30] *Schlegel Corporation v National Iranian Copper Industries Company*, IUSCT Case No 834, Award, 27 March 1987.
[31] 4 Iran–US Claims Tribunal Reports (Grotius Cambridge 1985) 212, 220–21, 231–32; see also *TCSB Inc v Iran*, 5 IUSCT Rep (Grotius Cambridge 1985) 160, 171–72.
[32] ibid para 16.
[33] *Lockheed Corporation v The Government of Iran, The Ministry of War & The Iranian Air Force*, IUSCT Case No 829, Award No 367-829-2, 9 June 1988.

detriment. Thus, the tribunal concluded, Lockheed had assumed the risk of non-payment without appropriate mitigation.

26 Commentators have sought to distil the primary features that stand out from the early arbitrations and the IUSCT decisions, including those not mentioned here.[34] Those discussions coalesce around four points: first, that there is an enrichment of one party to the detriment of the other. Second, that there is an absence of a justification for the enrichment and the impoverishment. Third, the respondent is the enriched entity. And, fourth, there is an absence of a remedy provided by law. These cases and common features become important for several international investment arbitrations that would follow them, as detailed in the next section.

D. Application in international investment law

27 At least ten investment arbitration tribunals have considered claims of unjust enrichment.[35] The results of their findings are mixed with respect to the elements they consider and their treatment of those elements on the merits or in damages calculations. For example, some tribunals have addressed a claim to unjust enrichment in a separate order or decision, apart from the merits decision, while others have considered the claim but only as a remedy of last resort. Already in the early 2000s, scholars raised concerns about this unsystematic and disjointed approach to unjust enrichment claims in investment arbitration.[36] One trend stands out, however: Tribunals have rarely reached unjust enrichment claims and even more rarely have they awarded damages under an unjust enrichment theory. This section discusses some of these illustrative cases.

28 In one of the earliest International Centre for Settlement of Investment Disputes (ICSID) cases in 1993, an ICSID tribunal rejected a claim to unjust enrichment following respondent Indonesia's revocation of claimant Amco's investment licence on the basis that other claims substantiated the relief Amco sought, and thus the tribunal found it need not reach the unjust enrichment claim.[37] In addition to its unjust enrichment argument, Amco also claimed expropriation and breach of contract. The tribunal concluded that Indonesia was liable under the other two theories (expropriation and breach of contract) and thus did not engage in a discussion on the unjust enrichment claim. While this conclusion might have closed off any consideration of unjust enrichment in the damages calculation as well, the tribunal invoked *Chorzów Factory* and considered Indonesia's potential enrichment to approximate Amco's sustained damage, leading at least one commentator to conclude that unjust enrichment played somewhat of a backdoor role in the case.[38]

29 At least six other cases in which unjust enrichment was expressly raised by the parties did not result in any damages awarded under an unjust enrichment theory.

---

[34] Binder, 'Unjust Enrichment' (n 2) 271. See also C Binder and C Schreuer, 'Unjust Enrichment', Max Planck Encyclopedia of Public International Law (August 2013) (hereafter Binder and Schreuer, 'Unjust Enrichment').
[35] In this entry, I highlight some of the most significant decisions on the matter. While these decisions focus on claims of unjust enrichment against States, some commentators have argued that they also operate against investors as a limit on compensation. See Hailes, 'Unjust enrichment' (n 9).
[36] See, eg, Vohryzek, 'Opportunities' (n 11).
[37] *Amco Asia Corp. & Others v Indonesia*, ICSID Case No ARB/81/1, 5 June 1993, Vol 1, 569, 38–50 (1993).
[38] Vohryzek, 'Opportunities' (n 11) 528–29. Ultimately, the tribunal concluded that Indonesia was not enriched.

Zhinvali Development Ltd. v Republic of Georgia (2003)[39]: The tribunal in this dispute was called upon to decide an issue of liability on four possible grounds: breach of preliminary contract, breach of contract, promissory estoppel, and unjust enrichment. The tribunal declined to exercise jurisdiction over all four of the claimant's claims and thus did not rule on the unjust enrichment claim. In dicta, the tribunal noted that evidence as to the calculation of the 'market value' of its contributions is essential for an unjust enrichment claim because the quantum of damages relates to the benefit received by the enriched party. In a separate opinion, one arbitrator concluded that there was liability on all of these grounds, but that the breach of contract was the most conclusive ground and basis for liability and recovery.[40] 30

Azurix Corp. v Argentine Republic (2006)[41]: In this case, the tribunal did not pursue the claimant's alternative theory of compensation based on unjust enrichment as it found a remedy based on the fair market value of the investment. 31

Saluka v Czech Republic (2006)[42]: In this United Nations Commission on International Trade Law (UNCITRAL) case, the tribunal held that the unjust enrichment claim failed because there was no enrichment to the Czech Republic to the detriment of Saluka. Taking a narrower view on the concept of unjust enrichment, the tribunal found that Saluka's argument stretched the principle of unjust enrichment beyond its proper scope by extending State responsibility for wrongful acts to minority shareholder States. According to the tribunal, the State was 'an accessory to an unjustified transfer' between other parties, and that could not serve as a basis for unjust enrichment. 32

ADC v Hungary (2006)[43]: The claimants sought damages under an unjust enrichment 'approach' of nearly USD 100 million. The tribunal decided that the claimants had not substantiated their claim with sufficient facts or law. 33

Churchill Mining v Indonesia (2016)[44]: The tribunal rejected the claimants' unjust enrichment theory on the basis that that claim, like the others before the tribunal, was inadmissible. The claims were based on forged documents which led the tribunal to find that the claimants could not benefit from protection. 34

CMC v Mozambique (2019)[45]: The claimants in this case argued that they were entitled to damages, in the alternative, because Mozambique was unjustly enriched. The tribunal, having found no breach under the bilateral investment treaty, concluded that any claim that claimants had falling outside the treaty needed to be pursued under the dispute resolution provisions of the governing contract. 35

Exceptionally, in *Occidental Petroleum v Ecuador* (2012), an ICSID tribunal considered unjust enrichment as ground for relief. The tribunal split over the issue of damages where 36

---

[39] *Zhinvali Development Ltd v Republic of Georgia*, ICSID Case No ARB/00/1, Award, 24 January 2003.
[40] *Zhinvali Development Ltd v Republic of Georgia*, ICSID Case No ARB/00/1, Separate Opinion of Andrew J Jacovides, 24 January 2003, para 23.
[41] *Azurix Corp. v Argentine Republic*, ICSID Case No ARB/01/12, Award, 14 July 2006, 123–57.
[42] *Saluka Investments BV (The Netherlands) v the Czech Republic*, Partial Award, 17 March 2006, 67, 92–93, 101
[43] *ADC Affiliate Ltd and ADC and ADMC Management Ltd v Republic of Hungary*, ICSID Case No ARB/03/16, Award, 2 October 2006.
[44] *Churchill Mining PLC and Planet Mining Pty Ltd v Republic of Indonesia*, ICSID Case No ARB/12/14 and 12/40, Award, 6 December 2016. See also IA Sutalaksana, A–A Chandrawulanet and P Amalia, 'The Implementation of Unjust Enrichment in Investment Arbitration: Case Study Churchill Mining PLC v. the Government of the Republic of Indonesia' (2019) 18(5) SEAJBEL 102–107.
[45] *CMC Muratori Cementisti CMC Di Ravenna SOC. Coop. v Republic of Mozambique*, ICSID Case No ARB/17/23, Award, 24 October 2019, 176.

Ecuador terminated an American oil company's contract.[46] Both parties presented competing arguments and allegations of unjust enrichment. Ecuador argued that that claimants were compensated for the full fair market value after being paid 40 per cent interest in the economic rights in question. Even though the tribunal agreed that the claimant company breached the relevant contract, it found that Ecuador's response to the breach was disproportionate and that Ecuador would be unjustly enriched if it only compensated 60 per cent of a fully unlawful taking. The dissenting arbitrator disputed the scope of the tribunal's application of unjust enrichment and found that, properly applied, the unjust enrichment principle would not warrant any compensation.[47]

E. Divergence between general international law and international investment law

37 The treatment of unjust enrichment by investment arbitration tribunals deviates from that of the ICJ simply by the fact that the issue arises frequently in the former.[48] That claims for unjust enrichment would be more prevalent among private actors as compared to conflicts between States ought not be surprising. The contract-styled environment that forms the foundation of international investment law lends itself to the entertainment of unjust enrichment claims more often than public international law disputes between States given that in the private context claims for expropriation do not arise, for example.

38 But the lack of treatment of unjust enrichment in State-to-State cases makes it difficult to assess whether investment law is special in its treatment.[49] The comparator set is particularly limited.

39 The IUSCT decisions are perhaps both a more appropriate comparator and one that provides some substantive content, although that too is limited. Given the tribunal's unique origin and pathology, at least one commentator has thought of IUSCT jurisprudence as lex specialis.[50] Moreover, there is no clear pattern of divergence in the investment law jurisprudence as compared to the IUSCT analyses as they still vary considerably in their postures.

40 Thus, one cannot conclude that international investment law treats unjust enrichment differently than it would be treated in general international law—apart from its increased appearance. Indeed, as discussed above, some investment tribunals have drawn from the PCIJ *Chorzów Factory* case to inform their understanding, even if they do not say so expressly.

41 At the least, the reliance on unjust enrichment by parties in investment law and at the IUSCT suggests that the concept is one of contract and of private law rather than one that is widely adopted as related to State responsibility and internationally wrongful acts.[51] Such a

---

[46] *Occidental Petroleum Corporation and Occidental Exploration and Production Company v Republic of Ecuador*, ICSID Case No ARB/06/11, Award, 5 October 2012.
[47] *Occidental Petroleum Corporation and Occidental Exploration and Production Company v Republic of Ecuador*, ICSID Case No ARB/06/11, Dissenting Opinion of Professor Brigitte Stern, 5 October 2012.
[48] DR Bishop, J Crawford and WM Reisman (eds) *Foreign Investment Disputes: Cases, Materials and Commentary* (2nd edn, Kluwer Law International 2014).
[49] M Sornarajah, *The International Law on Foreign Investment* (2nd edn, CUP 2004) 444–45.
[50] Dagan, *Study* (n 11) 159 (pointing to a treaty clause that governs compensation and that supersedes customary international law).
[51] But see discussion above at note 9 concerning the International Law Commission's treatment of unjust enrichment.

characterization accords with the diverse use of the principle as primary, secondary, or alternative claim for damages.

In Investor–State Dispute Settlement (ISDS) cases, the few tribunals that have addressed the topic have reached it at several different stages under a range of circumstances. Parties have deployed the principle as compensation, to offset loss, or for equitable balancing.[52] But given the rare occasions that tribunals engage with the principle, there appears to be some reluctance to use it as a basis for liability or for recovery.

Yet, as one commentator has noted, some tribunals appear to rely on an idea of unjust enrichment even if not naming it as such.[53] Another scholar has pointed to tribunal discussions of 'full compensation' or 'equitable compensation' as using the same notion.[54] These implicit uses are foreseeable given how counsel likewise use the principle loosely.

F. Conclusion

What do these observations mean for our understanding of unjust enrichment in international law? First, studying unjust enrichment reprises an old debate about the threshold level of acceptance for a general principle and its application across different legal regimes. In fact, this discussion may provide more conclusions for the idea of the general principle than it does for the content of unjust enrichment as a legal construct or for its significance to investment law. More research is needed, including through conversations with counsel, as to their choices to rely on unjust enrichment in certain types of cases.

Similarly, reviewing the presence and absence of unjust enrichment in these institutions contributes to the longstanding conversation on fragmentation. Even if one concludes there is a general principle of unjust enrichment that is common to many bodies of law, the decisions discussed here indicate that they find greater salience in contract disputes involving private parties. This review also highlights the possibility of demonstrating the presence of a general principle within a specialized area of law and then generalizing it to public international law in later decisions.

Further, and related to the prior points, this analysis of unjust enrichment in these many contexts may suggest that it is worth reconsidering what is meant by 'general' in our references to 'general principles' of law. One could refer to 'general' in two senses: first, 'general' could mean widespread use, but a principle may not be general without a certain degree of frequency. Likewise, the specificity of content and the forms of operation may also be relevant to the establishment of a general principle. One that may be generalized at its most general level may not be useful as a legal construct on the one hand, but on the other it could be helpful to find commonality across legal systems or even within the same system, even if only broadly so.

Although unjust enrichment is found in many legal systems, there is little shared understanding of how 'unjust enrichment' operates in international law. This entry has explained how investment tribunals rarely have considered claims of unjust enrichment, and that when

---

[52] Binder and Schreuer, 'Unjust Enrichment' (n 34) paras 13–16.
[53] Vohryzek, 'Opportunities' (n 11) 538.
[54] Dagan, *Study* (n 11) 158–59.

the claim has arisen, they have not awarded relief. Nevertheless, unjust enrichment claims are made more frequently in investment law than at the ICJ. In light of the diversity in its appearance and treatment, this examination of unjust enrichment has demonstrated how a principle as widely accepted as unjust enrichment can lead to little common ground in international courts and tribunals.

Selected literature

Binder C and Schreuer C, 'Unjust Enrichment', Max Planck Encyclopedia of Public International Law (2013).

Binder C, 'Unjust Enrichment as a General Principle of Law' in Gattini A and others (eds), *General Principles of Law and International Investment Arbitration* (Brill Nijhoff 2018) 269–89.

Dagan H, *Unjust Enrichment: A Study of Private Law and Public Values* (CUP 1997).

Dicke DC, 'Unjust Enrichment and Compensation' in Dicke DC (ed), *Foreign Investment in the Present and a New International Economic Order* (Fribourg University Press 1987).

Francioni F, 'Compensation for Nationalisation of Foreign Property: The borderland between law and equity' (1975) 24 ICLQ 255–83.

Fombad CM, 'The Principle of Unjust Enrichment in International Law' (1997) 30 CILSA 120–30.

Hailes O, 'Unjust enrichment in investor–State arbitration: A principled limit on compensation for future income from fossil fuels' (2022) 13(1) RECIEL 358–70.

Johnston D and Zimmermann R, *Unjustified Enrichment: Key Issues in Comparative Perspective* (CUP 2002).

Juratowitch B and Shaerf J, 'Unjust Enrichment as a Primary Rule of International Law' in Mads A and others (eds), *General Principles and the Coherence of International Law* (Brill 2019).

Schreuer CH, 'Unjustified Enrichment in International Law' (1974) 22 AmJCompL 281.

Vohryzek A, 'Unjust Enrichment Unjustly Ignored: Opportunities and Pitfalls in Bringing Unjust Enrichment Claims under ICSID' (2009) 31 LoyLAIntl&CompLRev 501.

Waibel M, 'Decolonization and Sovereign Debt: A Quagmire' in Flores Zendejas JH and Penet P (eds), *Sovereign Debt Diplomacies* (OUP 2021).

Selected decisions

Amco Asia Corp. & Others v. Indonesia, ICSID Case No ARB/81/1, Vol 1, 569, 38–50 (5 June 1993).

Azurix Corp v Argentine Republic, ICSID Case No ARB/01/12, Award, 14 July 2006.

Factory at Chorzów (Germany v Poland), PCIJ Series A No 17, Judgment on the Merits, 13 September 1928.

Sea-Land Service, Inc v The Islamic Republic of Iran, IUSCT Case No 33, Award No 135-33-1, 22 June 1984.

Zhinvali Development Ltd v Republic of Georgia, ICSID Case No ARB/00/1, Separate Opinion, 24 January 2003.

Index

For the benefit of digital users, indexed terms that span two pages (e.g., 52–53) may, on occasion, appear on only one of those pages.

Abs-Shawcross draft Convention 544, 545
abuse of process 605–17
   abuse of rights 483–84, 605–6, 608, 614
   admissibility 610, 611, 616
   alignment 613
   applicability of doctrine 607–8, 609–11
   burden of proof 608, 610, 613
   consent to the jurisdiction 609
   corporate form, abuse of 613, 616
   corporate restructuring 610–11, 612–14
   definition 605–6, 607
   deviation 613–16
   due process 606
   estoppel 606
   evidentiary standards 608, 610, 613, 614, 616
   exceptional circumstances standard 609, 614, 616
   good faith 606, 607, 608, 609–10, 615–16
   inherent powers 607
   judicial policy 615–16
   jurisdiction 608, 610, 612, 613–14
   overlapping cases 610–11
   parallel proceedings 609, 610–11, 614–15, 616
   procedure 605–6, 607, 609, 610–11, 612, 614–15
   provisional measures 607–8, 610–11, 614–15
   standard of proof 608
   standards 608–9, 610
abuse of rights 483, 609
   abuse of process 483–84, 605–6, 608, 614
   definition 483, 605–6
   general principle of law, as 18, 475, 483–84
   good faith 18, 483–84
   pacta sunt servanda 66, 70
   procedure 4–5, 6, 18
access to local courts 523, 525, 526, 527, 528, 529
acte jure imperii (sovereign or public powers) versus *acte jure gestionis* (commercial conduct) distinction
   attribution 303, 306–7, 497–98
   conduct of empowered entities 265–66, 269, 275–77, 303
   organs of the State, conduct of 253, 262
   non-State entities, governmental acts of other 497–98
   State immunity 490–91, 492, 495–98, 501
admissibility
   abuse of process 610, 611, 616
   counterclaims 575–76, 577
   international courts and tribunals, cross-cutting procedural powers of 556, 557, 563

Ago, Roberto 299–300, 343–44
amendment and modification of multilateral treaties (Articles 40–41 VCLT) 9–10, 182–86
   customary international law 177, 182–83
   deviation 212
   European Union 184–86, 212
   fundamental change of circumstances 233–35, 240–43
   intention 185–86
   interpretation 212
   object and purpose 185–86
   procedural mechanisms 182–83
   renegotiation/adaptation clauses 240–41, 242–43
   subsequent practice 212
   transparency 184
amendment and modification of treaties *see also* amendment and modification of multilateral treaties (Articles 40–41 VCLT); amendment of bilateral treaties, general rule (Article 39 VCLT)
   general rule and amendment of bilateral treaties 178–82
   interpretation 134–36, 144, 549, 550
   partial amendment 203, 204
   subsequent agreements 134–35
   subsequent practice 134–36, 144
amendment of bilateral treaties, general rule (Article 39 VCLT) 178–82
   customary international law 177, 178–79, 180
   decentralization 180
   default rule 178–79
   dispute resolution mechanisms, access to 181–82
   due process 181–82
   formal modifications 179
   informal modification 179
   interpretation 179–82
      amendment, dividing line from 179
      notes and statements 180–82
      subsequent practice 179–81
   non-retroactivity 181–82
   procedural mechanisms 178
   subsequent agreements 180
   subsequent practice 179–81
   UNCTAD International Investment Agreements Mapping Project 178–79
   USMCA, replacement of NAFTA with 178–79
annexation 102, 103, 437–38
annexes 39, 40, 41–42, 125

applicable law 17–18, 568–72
  clauses 79–80
  consent 568
  international courts and tribunals, cross-cutting procedural powers of 568–72
  internal law 79–80, 570–72
  jurisdiction 568
  observance of treaties 79–80
  precedent 569–70
  State succession 450–51
armed conflicts 211, 336–37
Articles on the Responsibility of States for Internationally Wrongful Acts (ARSIWA) 11–14
  breach consisting of a composite act 325–30
  compensation 19–20
  compliance with peremptory norms 365–68
  conduct of empowered entities 264–79
  conduct of organs placed at disposal of a State by another State 280–87
  consent 331–35
  contribution to the injury 397–98
  customary international law 11–12, 13–14, 19–20, 143
  distress (Article 24) 348–52
  excess of authority or contravention of instructions (Article 7) 288–97
  extension in time of the breach of an international obligation (Article 14) 318–24
  force majeure (Article 23) 13, 341–47
  interest (Article 38) 394–97
  international obligation in force for a State (Article 13) 313–17
  intertemporal aspects of responsibility 12–13
  lex specialis (Article 55) 11, 412–19
  necessity (Article 25) 353–64
  organs of a State, conduct of 249–63
  prospective elements of responsibility (Articles 29 and 30) 377–78
  remedies 13–14, 379–80
  reparation and primacy of restitution (Articles 31 and 34) 379–80
  restitution (Article 35)
    juridical restitution 381–82, 383–84, 398
    material restitution 381, 382–84, 386, 398
    primacy of restitution (Articles 31 and 34) 379–80
  savings clause 11
  self-defence (Article 21) 336–40
  supervening impossibility of performance 206–7
  wrongfulness, circumstances precluding 13, 369–74
attribution 11–12, *see also* attribution of conduct of empowered entities (Article 5 ARSIWA); attribution of conduct instructed, directed or controlled by a State (Article 8 ARSIWA); attribution of conduct of organs of a State (Article 4 ARSIWA); attribution of conduct of organs placed at disposal of a State by another State (Article 6 ARSIWA and Article 7 ARIO)

acte jure imperii versus *acte jure gestionis*
  distinction 497–98
  conduct of empowered entities 264–78, 303, 497–98, 501
  customary international law 6–7, 12
  disposal of a State by another State, conduct of organs placed at 280–87
  excess of authority or contravention of instructions 288–96
  lex specialis 413–16
  non-State entities, governmental acts of other 497–98
  organs of the State, conduct of 249–51, 253, 256–58, 259–63
  State immunity 495, 497–98, 501
  territorial scope 100
attribution of conduct of empowered entities (Article 5 ARSIWA) 264–79
  acte jure imperii versus *acte jure gestionis*
    distinction 265–66, 269, 275–77, 303, 497–98, 501
  complete dependence test 269
  content of empowerment 272–73, 274–75, 277–78
  core components through investment arbitration, clarifying 272–78
  customary international law 264–65, 268–69, 270, 272–73, 277–78
  delegation, mode of 275, 276
  effective control 303–4
  empowered entities, definition of 265
  exercise of empowerment 276–78
  form of empowerment 273–74, 277–78
  functional test 269–70, 274–75
  internal laws, empowerment through 273–74
  lex specialis 271
  private contractor test 275
  private military and security companies 264–65
  private or independent entities exercising elements of government authority 264–78
  privatization 264–65, 266–67, 272–73
  public body, definition of 271–72
  regional government 274
  special attribution rules 271–72
  State organs, exclusion of 268–72
    de facto 268–69, 270, 272
    de jure 268–69
  structural test 269–70
  supervision, level of 275
  two-step test 272–73, 277–78
  umbrella clauses 277
attribution of conduct instructed, directed or controlled by a State (Article 8 ARSIWA) 298–312
  agency 301–2
  analytical distinctions 301–4
  appointments by the State 299–300
  companies/corporations 298–99, 304
  control-based rule 299–301, 303–4
  control, definition of 305–7

effective control 300–1, 303–4, 305–7, 310
  general and specific rules 309–10
  instructions, directions, or control of the State 303–4, 305–9
  overall control 300, 305
customary international law 298–99
deviation 311
effective control 300–1, 303–4, 305–7, 310
factual relationships between persons or entities and State 298–99, 306
general and specific rules 309–10
individuals 298–99, 302–3, 304
instructions, directions, or control of the State 303–4, 305–9
internal law 301–2
interpretation 299
legal persons 304
lex specialis 309, 310–11
natural persons 304
overall control 300, 305
persons or a group of persons 304
primary obligations 301, 302
private entities 298–99, 300, 302–3, 304
scholarship 299
scope and operation 301–4
time of wrongful act, requirements must be met at the 304
trade unions 302–3
umbrella clauses 301–2
violations of international law 301
attribution of conduct of organs of a State (Article 4 ARSIWA) 249–63
acte jure imperii versus *acte jure gestionis* distinction 253, 262
branches or sub-branches of government 252–53
complete dependence test 255, 256, 257, 303
conflation of tests 259–60
contractual liability, issues of 260–61, 262–63
customary international law 249–50
de facto organs 254–57, 259, 262–63, 303
doctrinal issues in investment arbitration 257–62
domestic law to determine status of organs, reliance on 258–59, 262–63
effective control 303–4
federal subdivisions, irrelevance of 253–54
interpretation 262–63
lex specialis 257, 261
local subdivisions, irrelevance of 253–54, 262
rank, irrelevance of 253
regional subdivisions, irrelevance of 253–54, 262
residual, rules as 257, 261–63
State organ, definition and scope of 252–57
attribution of conduct of organs placed at disposal of a State by another State (Article 6 ARSIWA and Article 7 ARIO) 280–87
attribution 280–87
customary international law 280–82
ECHR's doctrine of equivalent protection 284
effective command 283–84, 286

European Union 281, 284–87
factual approach 281, 287
international organizations 280–87
interpretation 281–86
legal approach 281, 287
multinational peacekeeping forces 281, 282–84
opinio juris 280–81
paramilitary groups 281
sovereign debt restructuring arrangements 281
State aid 284–85, 286
ultimate authority 282–83
authority *see* excess of authority or contravention of instructions (Article 7 ARSIWA)
awards *see* judgments and awards

bias 523, 526–27
bilateral investment treaties (BITs) *see also* amendment of bilateral treaties, general rule (Article 39 VCLT); succession to BITs
amendment and modification 184–85
cession 438–39
clean hands principle 485
competence to conclude treaties, provisions of internal law regarding 188
concessionary contracts 457
contextual interpretation 127
customary international law 466–68, 471, 473–74, 546–47
  fair and equitable treatment (FET) standard 546–47, 550, 551
  NAFTA 548, 550–51
dictionaries, use of 126
diplomatic or consular relations, severance of 208
estoppel 482
European Union 9–10, 197–200, 218
  consent, termination by 197–200
  implied by conclusion of a later treaty, suspension of termination 203, 204
  invalidity of treaties 187, 210
  successive treaties relating to the same subject matter 114–15, 118
  suspension 210, 219–24
  termination 195, 197–200, 210, 219–24
  withdrawal 210
expropriation 415
fair and equitable treatment (FET) standard 467, 468, 546–47, 550, 551
foreign bondholders 460
gap-filling 467
general principles of law 477–78
implied by conclusion of a later treaty, suspension of termination 203, 204
international courts and tribunals, cross-cutting procedural powers of 562–64, 566
interpretation 179–82, 187
  contextual interpretation 127
  dictionaries, use of 126
  languages 171–73
  State succession 462

INDEX

bilateral investment treaties (BITs) (*cont.*)
    subsequent practice 131, 133–34
    supplementary means 162
    third-parties 127, 144
  invalidity of treaties 187, 211
  jus cogens 192
  languages, interpretation of treaties authenticated in two or more 171–73
  lex specialis 415, 416–18
  minimum standard of treatment (MST) 451–52, 467, 540, 544, 545, 546, 547–48
    autonomous FET clauses 546–47, 550, 551
    customary international law 550
    NAFTA 546–47, 548, 550–51
  nationality 589, 591–92, 598, 600, 601–2
  necessity 358, 360–61, 417–18
  non-retroactivity of treaties 48, 95–96, 97
  notification or deposit of instruments, consent to be bound through 49–50
  object and purpose 358
  provisional application 55
  res judicata 482–83
  reservations 36
  self-defence 336–37
  separation/dissolution of States 442–43
  State immunity 494, 495
  subsequent practice 131, 133–34
  supervening impossibility of performance 206–7
  suspension 202, 211, 218, 219–24
  termination
    consent, by 197–200
    later treaties, conclusion of 218, 219–24
    procedure 211
    terms of the treaty, by 194–96
    unilateral 194–96
  territorial scope 101, 103, 104
  third-parties 127, 144
  Trade and Cooperation Agreement (TCA) and UK BITs, conflict between 218
  withdrawal 211
  wrongfulness, consequences of invoking a circumstance precluding 373–74
BITs *see* bilateral investment treaties (BITs)
bondholders *see* foreign bondholders
breach consisting of a composite act (Article 15 ARSIWA) 325–30
  alignment 329–30
  cessation, obligation of 327
  compensation 327, 329
  connecting factors 326, 328
  continuing acts 325, 327
  customary international law 326
  denial of justice 327–28
  entry into force, conduct predating 325, 329
  expropriation 327–28
  fair and equitable treatment (DET) standard 327–28
  human rights 327
  intention 326, 328

  limitation periods 329
  policies or plans 326
  practice, definition of 327
  systematic obligations, breach of 326–27, 330
  temporal jurisdiction 327, 328, 329
breach, termination or suspension as a consequence of (Article 60 VCLT) 205–6
  background and status 225–27
  compensation 225–26
  countermeasures 225–26, 229
  customary international law 205–6, 225–26
  flexibility 226–27
  general principles of law, as 228
  interpretation 230
  lex specialis rule 230
  material breach 193–94, 205–6, 225–26, 228–31
    definition 227
    international investment agreements (IIAs), of 230
  non-compliance with arbitration awards 230–31
  object and purpose 205, 227, 228–29, 230–31
  relevance for international investment practice 229–31
  reparations 225–26
  reprisals 205
  repudiation 227, 228, 229
  scholarship 226–27
  State responsibility 206
Brexit 193, 199, 209–10
burden of proof 572–73
  abuse of process 608, 610, 613
  actori incumbit onus probandi maxim 475, 479–80, 572, 573
  consent 332
  corruption of a representative of a State 212
  customary international law 472
  evidential burden 479–80
  fair and equitable treatment (FET) standard 519–20
  interpretation 131
  jurisdiction 573
  legal burden 479–80
  minimum standard of treatment (MST) 519–20
  most favoured nation treatment (MFN) standard 519
  national treatment (NT) standard 511, 512–13, 519
  necessity 358, 360
  wrongfulness, consequences of invoking a circumstance precluding 371

Calvo doctrine 539–40, 542, 554
cessation
  composite act, breach consisting of a 327
  continuous breaches 321, 323
  countermeasures 403–4, 406
  denial of justice 535
  judicial remedies 376, 398
  prospective elements of responsibility 377–78
cession/secession 15, 460–61
  alignment 440

INDEX 633

foreign bondholders 460–61
moving treaty frontiers rule 437, 438–40
object and purpose 437, 438–39
occupation, laws of 437
radical change of conditions 437
succession to treaties 436–40, 448
unlawful annexation 437–38
unlawful territorial changes 437–38
claims commission 451, 526, 530, 540–41, 585
clean hands principle 190, 484–86
colonialism 91, 106, 429, 443, 453, 462, 539–40, 541
companies *see* corporations
compensation *see also* compensation (Article 36 ARSIWA); damages; expropriation, just compensation for (NAFTA)
breach, termination or suspension as a consequence of 225–26
composite act, breach consisting of a 327, 329
concessionary contracts 458, 459
contribution to the injury 397–98
countermeasures 403–4
customary international law 13–14, 19–20
denial of justice 535, 536, 537
equitable compensation 622, 627
judicial remedies 376
minimum standard of treatment (MST) 540–41, 543–45
reparations 19–20, 379–80
satisfaction 380, 392–93
unavailability or inadequacy 392–93
unjust enrichment 622, 627
wrongfulness, consequences of invoking a circumstance precluding 369, 370, 371–72, 373–74
compensation (Article 36 ARSIWA) 13, 19–20, 386–92, 398
calculation 386–89
causal link 387, 391–92
compound interest 19–20
concept 386–88
crippling compensation/inability to pay 391–92
diplomatic protection claims 389
equitable considerations 389–90, 391–92
evidence 387
expropriation 388–89
financially assessable damage, definition of 387
full reparation, exception to principle of 392
human rights 387–88, 389–90, 391
interpretation 514
limitations 392
loss of profits 387
moral damages 19–20, 389–91, 399
proportionality 391–92
restitution 398–99
valuation, principles of 387–89
compétence de la competence 556
competence to conclude treaties, provisions of internal law regarding (Article 46 VCLT) 187–89

allocation of competence 189
customary international law 187
due diligence 188
European Union 188–89, 212
fundamental importance, rules of internal law must be of 187–88
invalidity of treaties 186–87
manifest, definition of 187–88, 189, 212
temporal limitation 189
compliance with peremptory norms (Article 26 ARSIWA) 365–68
alignment 367
consent 366
countermeasures 365–66
erga omnes obligations 367
essential interests 366
justifications and excuses 365–66
necessity 366–67
composite acts 94, 96, 97, 317, 325, *see also* breach consisting of a composite act (Article 15 ARSIWA)
concessionary contracts 450–51, 457–59, 462
examples 457
expropriation, compensation for 458
minimum standard of treatment (MST) 462
opinio juris 457
property, qualifying as 457, 462
State succession 450–51, 457–59, 462
substitute of successors for predecessors as parties to 450–51, 462
conduct *see also* attribution of conduct of empowered entities (Article 5 ARSIWA); attribution of conduct instructed, directed or controlled by a State (Article 8 ARSIWA); attribution of conduct of organs of a State (Article 4 ARSIWA); attribution of conduct of organs placed at disposal of a State by another State (Article 6 ARSIWA and Article 7 ARIO)
corruption of a representative of a State 190
disposal of a State by another State, conduct of organs placed at 280–87
empowered entities 264–79
organs of a State 249–63
conflict rules
consent 331
internal law and observance of treaties 76–77, 79–80, 82–83
interpretation 7–8
procedure/substance 7–8
successive treaties 111, 113–17, 118, 214–24
Trade and Cooperation Agreement (TCA) and UK BITs, conflict between 218
consent *see also* consent (Article 20 ARSIWA)
abuse of process 609
applicable law 568
counterclaims 575
entry into force 46, 48–50
fundamental change of circumstances 207, 234, 238–39, 240–42

consent (*cont.*)
  implied by conclusion of a later treaty, suspension of termination 203
  international courts and tribunals, cross-cutting procedural powers of 555–57, 585
  invalidity of treaties 186
  jus cogens 366
  nationality of corporations 600–1
  non-retroactivity of treaties 94–95
  notification or deposit of instruments, consent to be bound through 46, 48–50
  object and purpose of a treaty prior to its entry into force, obligation not to defeat the 23
  procedure for invalidity, termination, withdrawal or suspension 208, 211
  provisional application 59
  State immunity 489, 494, 495
  succession to treaties 111–12, 428, 429, 431–33
  suspension of treaties 193, 201, 215
  temporal jurisdiction 187
  termination of treaties 193, 195–200, 215
  wrongfulness, consequences of invoking a circumstance precluding 370
consent (Article 20 ARSIWA) 331–35
  acquiescence or waiver 332
  agreement, consent by way of 331
  alignment 334–35
  authority 332–33, 334–35
  countermeasures 334
  burden of proof 332
  conflicts of norms 331
  continuing acts 332
  defects, freedom from 332, 333
  defence, as a 332, 333, 334–35
  error, fraud, corruption, or coercion 333
  express consent 333
  extraterritorial jurisdiction 331
  form 333
  host States, non-performance by 334
  implied consent 333
  informal or tacit agreements 333
  negative rule-element approach 332
  non-performance of obligations 331–35
  non-retroactivity of treaties 46–47
  non-State actors 333
  remedies 334
  termination or withdrawal 333
  underlying obligations distinguished, consent to 331
  validity of consent 332, 333, 334–35
consequences of invoking a circumstance precluding wrongfulness (Article 27 ARSIWA) 13, 369–74
  BITs 373–74
  burden of proof 371
  compensation for material loss 369, 370, 371–72, 373–74
  compliance, return to 369–70, 372–73, 374
  consent, withdrawal of 370
  countermeasures 370
  essential interests 370
  force majeure 371–72
  justifications and excuses 369–70, 371–72
  loss of profits 371
  moral damage 371
  necessity 373–74
  non-performance, legal consequences of 369–70
  partial performance 370, 372–73
  reparations 371
  temporary non-performance 369–70
  termination of obligations 370
continuing acts
  completed acts with continuing consequences 92
  composite act, breach consisting of a 325, 327
  consent 332
  definition 91
  examples 91–92
  extension in time of the breach of an international obligation 318, 319–24, 325
  international obligation in force for a State 317, 325
  investigate, failure to 93
  non-retroactivity of treaties 85, 91–94, 96–97
  temporal jurisdiction 93
contra proferentem **rule** 123, 130
contribution to the injury (Article 39 ARSIWA) 397–98
control
  attribution 299–301, 303–4, 305–9
  control, definition of 305–7
  general and specific rules 309–10
  effective control 300–1, 303–4, 305–7, 310
  instructions, directions, or control of the State 303–4, 305–9
  overall control 300, 305
convergence *see* alignment
Cordero-Moss, G 492
corporations *see also* **nationality of corporations**
  abuse of process 610–11, 612–13, 616
  attribution 298–99, 304
  corporate form, abuse of 613, 616
  restructuring 610–11, 612–14
corruption 378, 523, 525, 574–75, *see also* **corruption of a representative of a State (Article 50 VCLT)**
corruption of a representative of a State (Article 50 VCLT) 190–91
  burden of proof 212
  causal link 190, 212
  circumstantial evidence 191
  clean hands principle 190
  concealment 191
  consent to be bound, vitiation of 190
  customary international law 190
  interpretation 212
  invalidity of treaties 190–91
  procurement contracts 190
  standard of proof 191, 212
  substantial gravity, acts of 190

costs 577–78, 585
  follow the event 577–78
  general principles of law 577
  legal representation 577–78
counterclaims 575–77, 585
  admissibility 575–76, 577
  consent to jurisdiction 575
  definition 575
  direct connection requirement 575–76
  jurisdiction 575–77
countermeasures 403–10
  breach, termination or suspension as a consequence of 225–26, 229
  cessation 403–4, 406
  channels of communication, maintenance of 404
  compensation 403–4
  conditions relating to resort to countermeasures 401, 403
  consent 334
  customary international law 13
  defences 402–3
  diplomatic or consular agents, premises, archives, and documents, obligations to respect the inviolability of 404, 409–10
  erga omnes obligations 408
  good faith 405
  human rights 404, 408
  inducement, concept of 403–4, 409, 410
  injured State, countermeasures may only be taken by the 403
  internationally wrongful acts, only against States responsible for 403, 406–7
  jus cogens 365–66, 404
  lex specialis 404, 406–8
  objects and limits 401, 403–4, 406–9
  obligations not affected by countermeasures 401
  practice, whether countermeasures can be successfully invoked in 408–9
  primary rules 406–7
  procedural requirements 405, 408–9
  proportionality 401, 408–10
  reparations 403–4, 406
  reprisals, humanitarian obligations prohibiting 404
  resumption of performance, permitting the 404
  retorsion, distinguished from 402–3
  secondary rules 406–7
  self-defence 339
  shield and a sword, as a 402–3
  States other than injured States, by 402
  substantive conditions 408–9
  suspension 402–3, 405
  termination 401, 402–3, 405
  third States, effect on 403, 408–9
  threat or use of force, obligation from the 404
  wrongfulness, circumstances precluding 13, 370
Covid-19 345–46, 351, 372–73
Crawford, James 13–14, 251, 260, 267, 275, 290, 300–1, 326, 327–28, 332–33, 343, 356, 371–72, 392–93, 408, 409, 484–85

customary international law 5–8, 11–12, 465–74, *see also opinio juris*
  acceptance 4–5
  accepted as law as a constitutive element 470–71
  amendment and modification of treaties 177, 178–322
  Article 38 ICJ Statute 465–74
  attribution 6–7, 12
  BITs 15–16, 466–68
    double requirement 471
    evolved custom 550
    succession 424–25, 430, 431–32, 433
  breach, termination or suspension as a consequence of 205–6, 225–26
  burden of proof 472
  cession 437
  changes, proof of 472
  codification 85, 467–68
  compensation 13–14, 19–20
  competence to conclude treaties, provisions of internal law regarding 187
  composite act, breach consisting of a 326
  conduct of empowered entities 264–65, 268–70, 272–73, 277–78
  conflicts of law 7–8
  corruption of a representative of a State 190
  countermeasures 13
  crystallization 468
  definition 465
  denial of justice 17, 523, 524–27, 528–30, 536–38
  devolution agreements 430
  diplomatic protection 543, 551, 552–53
  disposal of a State by another State, conduct of organs placed at 280–82
  distress 348
  double requirement 15–16, 470–72
  effectiveness, principle of 143
  entry into force 46–47
  erga omnes obligations 47, 107, 367, 378, 408, 524
  excess of authority or contravention of instructions 289, 296
  exhaustion of local remedies 519–20
  expropriation 415, 416, 456, 519–20
  extension in time of the breach of an international obligation 318
  fair and equitable treatment (FET) standard 517–18, 519–20
  force majeure 341, 344
  foreign bondholders 459–60, 461
  gap-filling 15–16
  general principles of law 478
  general rule and amendment of bilateral treaties 177, 178–79, 180
  good faith 6–7
  inchoate custom 468–69
  internal law and observance of treaties 74–75
  international obligation in force for a State 313
  interpretation 8–9, 121–24, 142–44
    languages 166–67

customary international law (*cont.*)
    special regimes 141–42
    supplementary means 146, 148–49
    systemic integration, principle of 136–37, 143
    teleological interpretation 143
invalidity of treaties 186, 209, 211
judicial decisions 469
judicial remedies 375–76
languages, interpretation of treaties authenticated in two or more 166–67
lex specialis 413, 414, 415–16, 417–18
material or objective requirement 470–71
minimum standard of treatment (MST) 539–40, 545, 546–48
    alignment 519–20
    diplomatic protection 543, 551, 552–53
    expropriation 544
    NAFTA 548, 549, 550–53
    origin and concept 451–52
    State practice 452, 551, 552–53
moving treaty frontiers principle 7–8, 14–15
NAFTA standards 520
nationality 590
necessity 13, 353, 358–59, 361, 363
new rules 468
non-retroactivity of treaties 84, 85
object and purpose of a treaty prior to its entry into force, obligation not to defeat the 23–24, 30
objections 5
opinio juris 15–16, 470–71, 472
organs of the State, conduct of 249–50
provisional application 52–53
psychological or subjective requirement 470–71
reparations 379
reservations 34, 40
self-defence 337
source of law, as 1–2, 15–16, 136–37
standing 532–33
State immunity 148–49, 489, 490–92
State practice 15–16, 452, 469–71, 486
    evidence 473–74
    minimum standard of treatment (MST) 551, 552–53
State succession 4–5, 14–15, 451, 462
subsequent practice 469–70
succession to treaties 14–15, 110, 435–36, 447
suspension 193–94, 209, 211, 214–15
systemic integration, principle of 136–37, 143
temporal jurisdiction 193–94
territorial scope 100, 101, 106
textuality, lack of 4–5
treaty law, interaction with 466–70
unification of States 440–41
unjust enrichment 18–19
withdrawal 201, 209, 211

damages *see also* **compensation**
    calculation 622–23, 624–27

    compensation 19–20, 386, 389–91
    concessionary contracts 457, 459, 462
    object and purpose of a treaty prior to its entry into force, obligation not to defeat the 25
    reparations 379–80
    unjust enrichment 622–23, 624–27
declaratory judgments 393–94, 398
delay
    denial of justice 323, 324, 523, 525, 526–27, 528, 537
    extension in time of the breach of an international obligation 323, 324
    interest 394–95, 396
    succession to BITs, procedure for 423–24
decolonization 462
denial of justice 523–38, *see also* **exhaustion of local remedies/judicial finality**
    access to local courts 523, 525, 526, 527, 528, 529
    alignment 537–38
    annulment orders 535
    arbitrariness 525, 528
    bias 523
    cessation orders 535
    compensation 535, 536, 537
    composite act, breach consisting of a 327–28
    content of obligation 523, 524–30
    corruption 523, 525
    customary international law 17, 523, 524–27, 528–30, 536–38
    delay 323, 324, 523, 525, 526–27, 528, 537
    deviation 537–38
    due process 525, 528, 537
    equality of arms 526–27
    erga omnes obligations 524
    exhaustion of local remedies 523–24, 530–31, 536, 537
    expropriation 528, 536
    extension in time of the breach of an international obligation 323, 324
    fair and equitable treatment (FET) standard 517–18, 527–28, 529–30, 538
    human rights 527, 535
    ICJ practice 524–27, 536
        Barcelona Traction 524, 525, 526, 528
        Chorzow Factory case 535, 536
        ELSI case 525–26, 528
        remedies 535, 536
    independent and impartial tribunals 526–27
    interpretation 527–28, 536, 537–38
    judicial independence 523, 525, 526–27
    judicial proceedings 323
    lex specialis 536
    manifestly/substantially unjust judgments 526, 537
    minimum standard of treatment (MST) 517–18, 541, 542, 543–44, 545
    NAFTA 528–29
    non-monetary orders 535
    reasons, duty to provide 526–27

remedies 523–24, 535–36
standard of proof 574
standing 524, 532–33, 536
substance 4–5, 6, 17
temporal jurisdiction 524, 534, 536, 537
developing countries 540, 541, 544
deviation
  abuse of process 613–16
  amendment and modification of treaties 212
  cession 440
  denial of justice 537–38
  extension in time of the breach of an international obligation 324
  force majeure 346
  interest 396–97
  internal law and observance of treaties 82
  interpretation 141–42, 144, 151–54, 518
  invalidity of treaties 212
  judicial remedies 376
  languages, interpretation of treaties authenticated in two or more 168, 169, 170, 174–75
  most-favoured-nation treatment (MFN) standard 518–19, 520
  NAFTA standards 518–19, 520
  non-retroactivity of treaties 98
  obligation not to defeat the object and purpose of a treaty prior to its entry into force 31
  pacta sunt servanda 72
  remedies 398
  succession to treaties 446–47, 448
  supplementary means of interpretation 151–54
  territorial scope 104–7
  unjust enrichment 618, 626–27
devolution agreements 429–30, 452
dictionaries for interpretation, use of 125–26, 144
diplomatic protection
  compensation 389
  customary international law 543, 551, 552–53
  expropriation 17, 456–57
  foreign bondholders 459–60
  human rights 543
  lex specialis 413
  minimum standard of treatment (MST) 539–42, 543
    expropriation 17, 456–57
    NAFTA 550, 551, 552–53, 554
    property 17, 451–52
    State succession 462
  nationality 589, 595, 598, 599, 600
  premises, archives, and documents, obligations to respect the inviolability of 404, 409–10
  severance of diplomatic or consular relations 208
  subject matter jurisdiction 543
  State succession 451, 462
discrimination *see* nationality discrimination
dispute, existence of a 560–62
disputed territories 106–7

dissolution of States *see* separation/dissolution of States
distress (Article 24 ARSIWA) 348–52
  avert the danger, no other reasonable way to 349
  comparable or greater peril, requirement not to create a 349, 350
  conditions 349–50
  customary international law 348
  flexibility 349–50
  good faith 350
  human dimension 348–49
  interpretation 349
  justifications and excuses 350
  life, protection of 348–49
  necessity 349–50, 351–52
  non-contribution to situations 349, 350
  Rainbow Warrior award 349–50, 351
  reasonableness 350, 351, 352
  refuge, right of 348, 351
  serious health risks 349
  special relationships between State organs and individuals in danger 349–50, 351
  threats to life, existence of 349
divergence *see* deviation
domestic law *see* internal law
dualism 76

economic crises 359–61, 362, 363
effective control 11, 102, 104–6
effectiveness, principle of
  Article 38 ICJ Statute 468–69
  attribution 304
  customary international law 143
  good faith 129–30
  interpretation 123, 129–30, 143
  successive treaties relating to the same subject matter, application of 117
ejusdem generis maxim 130, 509, 519
empowered entities *see* conduct of empowered entities (Article 5 ARSIWA)
enforcement of judgments and awards
  arbitral awards 1, 16, 489, 490–91, 492, 498–500, 501
  denial of justice 535
  State immunity 1, 16, 489, 490–91, 492, 498–500, 501
entry into force *see also* entry into force (Article 24 VCLT)
  composite act, breach consisting of a 325, 329
  extension in time of the breach of an international obligation 318, 321, 322–23
  international obligation in force for a State 315–17
  non-retroactivity of treaties 84–98
  object and purpose of a treaty prior to its entry into force, obligation not to defeat the 23–31
  provisional application 52, 54, 56, 60–61
  successive treaties 111–12, 316

entry into force (Article 24 VCLT) 45–51
  BITs 46, 48, 49–50
  consent to be bound 46
    acceptance 46, 48–50
    accession 46, 48–50
    approval 46, 48–50
    exchange of instruments constituting a treaty 46
    non-retroactivity of treaties 46–47
    notification or deposit of instruments 46, 48–50
    object and purpose of treaties 46–47
    particular point in time, at a (Article 16 VCLT) 46
    ratification 46, 48–50
    signature, expressed by 46
  customary international law 45, 46–47
  general principle of law, as 45
  ICJ Statute 46
  non-retroactivity of treaties (Article 28 VCLT) 46–48, 50
  notification or deposit of instruments, consent to be bound through 46, 48–50
  object and purpose of treaties 46–47
  provisional application of treaties 46–47
erga omnes **obligations** 47, 107, 367, 378, 408, 524
estoppel
  abuse of process 606
  common law 480
  detrimental reliance 481
  gap-filling 482
  general principles of law 475, 480–82
  good faith 481
  succession to BITs, procedure for 433
European Union
  amendment and modification of treaties 184–86, 212
  BITs
    conflicts 218
    consent, termination by 197–200
    implied by conclusion of a later treaty, suspension of termination 203, 204
    invalidity of treaties 187, 210
    successive treaties relating to the same subject matter 114–15, 118
    suspension 210, 219–24
    termination 195, 197–200, 210, 219–24
    VCLT 9–10
    withdrawal 210
  Brexit 193, 199, 209–10
  competence to conclude treaties, provisions of internal law regarding 188–89, 212
  disposal of a State by another State, conduct of organs placed at 281, 284–87
  interpretation 136, 137, 139
  invalidity of treaties 187, 209–10
  primacy of EU law 221
  provisional application of treaties 62
  State succession 216–17
  successive treaties relating to the same subject matter 114–15, 116, 117, 118
  suspension 209–10, 216–17, 219–24

termination
  consent, by 197–200
  later treaty, implied by a 216–17, 219–24
  procedure 209–10
Termination Treaty 197–200, 203, 223
territorial scope 106
Trade and Cooperation Agreement (TCA) and UK BITs, conflict between 218
withdrawal 209–10
evidence, rules of 572–75, *see also* **burden of proof; standard of proof**
  abuse of process 608, 610, 613, 614, 616
  compensation 387
  international courts and tribunals, cross-cutting procedural powers of 572–75
  subsequent agreements 131–32
  subsequent practice 132–34
excess of authority or contravention of instructions (Article 7 ARSIWA) 288–97
  attribution 288–96
  customary international law 289, 296
  doctrinal issues 291–96
  effective control 291
  government authority, exercise of elements of 288–96
  internal law, characterization of acts under 288–89
  irrelevance of breach of international obligations 296
  official capacity, acting in an 288, 291–93
  scope of application 291
  systematic or recurrent conduct 291
  ultra vires 288–96
exhaustion of local remedies/judicial finality 530–31
  administrative bodies 530, 531
  customary international law 530–31
  denial of justice 523–24, 530–31, 536, 537
  due process 531
  exceptions 530
  fair and equitable treatment (FET) standard 516–18
  minimum standard of treatment (MST) 516–18, 541, 542, 543, 544, 552
expropriation *see also* **expropriation, just compensation for (NAFTA)**
  Barcelona Traction, Light and Power Co Ltd (Belgium v Spain) 514, 520
  BITs 415
  compensation
    cash-flow model 536
    concessionary contracts 458
    Hull formula 540, 544–45
    just and effective 544
    lawful versus unlawful 462
    minimum standard of treatment (MST) 451–57, 540, 543–45
    prompt and effective 543
    State succession 462
  concessionary contracts 458
  creeping 322, 327–28, 495–96
  customary international law 415, 416, 456
  de facto 320, 322

de jure 322
denial of justice 528, 536
developing countries 544
diplomatic protection 456–57
due process 451–52, 543
ELSI Elettronica Sicula SpA (US v Italy) 514
Factory at Chorzow (Germany v Poland) 513–14, 515, 516, 520
ex gratia or without prejudice clause 452
extension in time of the breach of an international obligation 320, 322
fair and equitable treatment (FET) standard 501
Hull formula 540, 544–45
indirect 388–89, 548
internal law and observance of treaties 77, 81
interpretation 546–48
irreversible deprivation, state of 388–89
lex specialis 415, 416
minimum standard of treatment (MST) 17, 540, 544–45
　compensation 451–57, 540, 543–45
　interpretation 546–48
　nationality 589
opinio juris 455–56
Oscar ChinnCase (UK v Belgium) 514
property, definition of 456
public interest 451–52
restitution 385–86, 456–57
scope 455–57
sovereign taking versus commercial breach of contract 495–96
State immunity 494, 495–96, 501
State succession 462
unjust enrichment 621, 624, 626
valuation 456–57, 462
expropriation, just compensation for (NAFTA) 506–7, 513–16
alignment 518, 519–20
but for causation 514
customary international law 519–20
de facto expropriation 514
due process 515
expropriation, definition of 515
genuine vested rights 514
indirect expropriation 515–16, 519–20
interpretation 513–16, 518, 520
　ICJ cases 513–15, 516, 520
　NAFTA cases 515–16, 520
Iran-US Claims Tribunal, influence of ICJ on works of 514–15
lawful/unlawful distinction 513–14, 515
Metalclad Corp v Mexico 515
multi-factor test 516
regulatory expropriation 515–16
restitution 513–14
shareholders' rights 514
standards 513–14
tantamount to expropriation 515
vested interests 515

extension in time of the breach of an international obligation (Article 14 ARSIWA) 318–24
alignment 324
background or context 318, 325
cessation, orders of 321, 323
continuous breaches 318, 319–24, 325
customary international law 318
delay 323, 324
denial of justice claims 323, 324
deviation 324
disappearances, investigations of forced 321
entry into force, conduct preceding 318, 321, 322–23
examples of non-continuing breaches 319
expropriation 320, 322
human rights 320, 321, 324
instantaneous breaches 318, 319–20, 321, 322, 323
limitation periods 321, 324
omissions 319
property, right to 320, 324
remedies 321, 323
temporal jurisdiction 320, 322–23
extinctive prescription 564–65, 585
extradition 432, 433

fair and equitable treatment (FET) standard/minimum standard of treatment (MST) 506–7, 516–18
Barcelona Traction 517
burden of proof 519–20
Case Concerning Ahmadou Sadio Diallo (Guinea v DRC) 516–17, 550, 552, 553
composite act, breach consisting of a 327–28
customary international law 517–18, 519–20
denial of justice 517–18, 527–28, 529–30, 538, 545
due process 516, 517–18
ELSI Elettronica Sicula SpA (US v Italy) 516–18
exhaustion of local remedies 516–18
expropriation 501
full protection and security (FPS) standard 545–47
interpretation 477–78, 516–18
　ICJ cases 516–17
　NAFTA cases 517–18
lex specialis 416
Lion Mexico case 517–18
minimum standard of treatment (MST) 17, 451–52, 540, 544, 545–47, 553–54
NAFTA 506–7, 516–18, 519–20
nationality 589
object and purpose of a treaty prior to its entry into force, obligation not to defeat the 30
outrageous, bad faith, and wilful neglect standard 517–18
regulatory stabilization, obligation of 547
standing 532–33
State immunity 496
wilful disregard standard 517–18

fair hearing, right to a 527, 535, 541–42
FET *see* fair and equitable treatment (FET) standard
finality *see* exhaustion of local remedies/judicial
    finality; *res judicata*
Fiore's Draft Code 1918 121–22
Fitzmaurice, Gerald 75–76
force majeure (Article 23 ARSIWA) 341–47
  actual impossibility 342
  assumption of risk 341, 345–46
  beyond the control of the State 341, 342
  causal link 342, 344–45
  conditions 341
  contract law 344, 345
  contributed to the situation, State must not
      have 341, 344
  customary international law 341, 344
  deviation from GIL 346
  force, definition of 342
  foreseeability 342, 345, 346
  general principles of law 13
  impossibility
    absolute 342–44, 346
    material 341, 342–45, 346
    relative 343
  interpretation 346
  irresistible force 342
  justifications and excuses 344
  material impossibility 341, 342–45, 346
  necessity, defence of 346
  non-contribution, requirement of 342, 344, 345
  objectivity 343–44
  probability of events, degree of 342
  subjectivity 343–44
  triggering events 341, 342, 344–45
  wrongfulness, circumstances precluding 13, 371–72
foreign bondholders 459–62
  assignment and apportionment of State debt 460–62
  cession or secession 460–61
  customary international law 459–60, 461
  diplomatic protection 459–60
  local character of debt 461
  merger, absorption, or dismemberment 460, 462
  minimum standard of treatment (MST) 460
  opinio juris 460, 461
  partial successions 460–61, 462
  State succession 459–62
  total successions 460
foro domestico, failure to identify 475, 476–77, 483–84
forum shopping 609, 610–11
fragmentation 1–2, 43–44, 618, 627
full protection and security (FPS) standard
  fair and equitable treatment (FET) standard 545–47
  lex specialis 416
  minimum standard of treatment (MST) 545–47
  nationality 589
  State immunity 492–93
functus officio 580, 584
fundamental change of circumstances (Article 62
    VCLT) 193–94, 207–8

  boundaries, treaty establishing 207
  breach by parties invoking change of
      circumstances 207
  codification 237
  coherence, clarity, and consistency 239
  consent to be bound 207, 234, 238–39, 240–42
  customary international law 207, 234–35
  economic emergency measures 207–8
  existing circumstances, non-correspondence
      with 235–37
  foreseeability 207–8
  historical background 234
  hostilities, outbreak of 207
  intention 237, 238–39, 240–41
  interpretation 234, 236, 237–38, 239, 240
  modification of treaties 233–35, 240–43
  pacta sunt servanda 233–34, 244
  public interest 240
  renegotiation/adaptation clauses 240–41, 242–43
  shared expectations, breach of 237–39
  stability and security 233–34, 238–39, 244
  stabilization clauses 240–42
  State interests 240
  State practice 234–35, 236, 240, 243, 244
  suspension 233–34, 244
  termination 233–35, 237, 239–40, 244
  threshold 207–8
  VCLT 11
  vital State interests 239

gap-filling 7–8, 19, 474, 477, 482–83
general principles of law (GPL) 465–66, 468–69, 474–87
  abuse of rights 475, 483–84
  actori incumbit onus probandi 475, 479–80
  breach, termination or suspension as a
      consequence of 228
  clean hands principle 484–86
  corruption of a representative of a State 190
  costs 577
  customary international law 5, 6, 478
  definition 486
  estoppel 475, 480–82
  force majeure 13
  foro domestico, failure to identify GPL 475, 476–77, 483–84
  functions 474–75, 477–78
  gap-filling role 474, 477, 482–83
  good faith 475
  Article 38 ICJ Statute 465–66, 468–69, 474–87
  international obligation in force for a State 313
  interpretation 122, 474, 477–78
  invalidity of treaties 186
  nationality 590, 599
  non-retroactivity of treaties 46–47, 84
  public interest 486–87
  res judicata 475, 482–83, 580
  scholarship 474, 482
  sources of law 1–2, 15–16, 136–37, 474–75

State succession 451, 462
subsidiary character 474–75
succession to treaties 424
unjust enrichment 18–19, 618–20, 621, 627
genocide
composite act, breach consisting of a 326
Genocide Convention 35, 47, 442
non-retroactivity 87–88
supplementary means of interpretation 148–49, 155
territorial scope 101
travaux préparatoires 148–49
jus cogens 365–66
non-retroactivity of treaties 87–88
reservations 35
territorial scope 101
good faith
abuse of process 606, 607, 608, 609–10, 615–16
abuse of rights 18, 483–84
competence to conclude treaties, provisions of internal law regarding 188
countermeasures 405
customary international law 6–7
distress 350
effectiveness, principle of 129–30
general principles of law 475
human rights 69
interpretation 128–30, 147–48
invalidity of treaties 187, 209
non-retroactivity 30
object and purpose of a treaty prior to its entry into force, obligation not to defeat the 25, 28, 29–30
customary international law 23–24
pacta sunt servanda 24
proof 31
retroactivity 30*pacta sunt servanda* 9–10, 65–69, 70–71, 72
autonomous obligation, as 68, 71, 72
object and purpose 24
presumption 70
procedures for invalidity, termination, withdrawal from or suspension 209
reasonableness 129
reservations 41
standard of proof 574–75
supplementary means of interpretation 147–48
termination or suspension treaties 209
withdrawal of treaties 209

Hart, HLA 5–6
heard, right to be 526–27
Huber, Max 84
human rights 19
compensation 387–88, 389–90, 391
composite act, breach consisting of a 327
conduct of empowered entities 272
countermeasures 404, 408
denial of justice 526–27, 535

diplomatic protection 17, 543
disposal of a State by another State, conduct of organs placed at 282–84, 287
extension in time of the breach of an international obligation 320, 321, 324
fair hearing, right to a 527, 535
general rule and amendment of bilateral treaties 179
good faith 71
heard, right to be 526–27
jus cogens 192
life, right to 321
minimum standard of treatment (MST) 541–42, 543, 544, 554
diplomatic protection 17, 543
NAFTA 548, 550, 553
nationality 18
necessity 359
non-retroactivity of treaties 88–91, 92, 93
pacta sunt servanda 69
prospective elements of responsibility 377
remedies 399
reservations 43–44
restitution 383
self-defence 336–37
separation/dissolution of States 442
subsequent practice 132
succession to treaties 445
territorial scope 101–3, 104–7

ILC Articles *see* **Articles on the Responsibility of States for Internationally Wrongful Acts (ARSIWA)**
immunities 523, *see also* **State immunity**
impossibility *see* **supervening impossibility of performance (Article 61 VCLT)**
independence of the judiciary 523, 525, 526–27
instructions *see* **excess of authority or contravention of instructions (Article 7 ARSIWA)**
integration *see* **systemic integration, principle of**
intention
amendment and modification of treaties 185–86
composite act, breach consisting of a 326, 328
fundamental change of circumstances 237, 238–39, 240–41
implied by conclusion of a later treaty, suspension of termination 202
interpretation 85, 125, 127, 140–41
lex specialis 412–13
non-retroactivity of treaties 85, 86
procedures for invalidity, termination, withdrawal from or suspension 210, 211
reservations 40, 41, 43
succession to treaties 110–11, 448
supplementary means of interpretation 160–64
suspension of treaties 201, 216, 217–18, 219–20
termination of treaties 216, 217–18, 219–20
territorial scope 102–3, 104, 105
withdrawal 201

642 INDEX

interest (Article 38 ARSIWA) 394–97
  compound interest 19–20, 395–97
  date of judgment 394–95
  delays 394–95, 396
  deviation 396–97
  full reparation, principle of 395–96
  international courts and tribunals 394–96
  judicial remedies 376
  pre-award interest 395
  simple interest 394–96
interim remedies *see* **provisional measures**
internal law *see also* **internal law and observance of treaties (Article 27 VCLT)**
  applicable law 570–72
  attribution 301–2
  competence to conclude treaties, provisions of internal law regarding 187–89
  conduct of empowered entities 273–74
  errors of domestic law, setting side awards due to 572
  invalidity of treaties 186
  minimum standard of treatment (MST) 539–40, 543
  nationality 589, 599, 600
  provisional application 56–60
  res judicata 570–71
  restitution 382–84
  State succession 451
internal law and observance of treaties (Article 27 VCLT) 10–11, 74–83
  administrative acts 75–77
  alignment 82
  applicable law clauses and hierarchy of sources 79–80
  ARSIWA 74, 78–79
  binding forces over treaties 76–77
  coherence 82
  competence to conclude treaties (Article 46 VCLT) 74
  conflict rules 76–77, 79–80, 82–83
  constitutions 74–75, 76
  customary international law 74–75
  deviation 82
  domestic courts, decisions of 76–77
  expropriation, unlawful 77, 81
  hierarchy of sources within the applicable law clause, establishing the 79–80
  internal law, definition of 76
  interpretation 75–76, 77, 80, 82
  investment arbitration 77–82
  monist states 76
  organs and officials, extension to the actions of State 78–79
  pacta sunt servanda 75, 76–77
  predictability 82
  primacy of international law 75–77, 79–80, 82–83
  procedural standards 77
  property rights 81–82
  provisional application 59–60

renvoi to domestic law 76, 81–82
standards of investment protection 77
subsequent to entry into force, enactment of laws 76
termination 75
International Court of Justice (ICJ) Statute 464–88
  BITs 466–68
  customary international law 465–74
  deviation 466
  effectiveness, principle of 468–69
  entry into force 46
  general principles of law 465–66, 468–69, 474–87
  interaction between sources 466–70
  interpretation 467, 470
  opinio juris 468–69, 486
  precedents 469–70, 486
  provisional measures 568
  sources of law 15–16, 464–70
  third States, general, uniform, and consistent practice of 468
  treaty law 465–70
international courts and tribunals (ICTs), cross-cutting procedural powers of 555–87
  admissibility 556, 557, 563
  alternative forums for the settlement of disputes 563–64
  applicable law 568–72
  BITs
    exclusive jurisdiction clauses 563–64
    Monetary Gold principle 566
    negotiation requirements 562–63
  common law of international adjudication 556
  consent 555–57, 585
  constitutive instruments 555–56, 557, 585
  costs 577–78, 585
  counterclaims 575–77, 585
  countermeasures 560
  cross-fertilization 556
  dispute, existence of a 560–62
  evidence, rules of 572–75
  express powers, consent to 555–56
  extinctive prescription 564–65, 585
  ICJ, practice of 556, 557–58, 575–78
    burden of proof 572–73
    dispute, existence of a 560–62
    evidence, rules of 572, 574
    extinctive prescription 564
    incidental jurisdiction 559
    interpretation 581–82
    jurisdiction 556–58, 559, 562–63, 565–66, 585
    Monetary Gold principle 565–66
    negotiation requirements 562–63
    Oil Platforms case 557–58
    precedent 569–70
    provisional measures 567–68
    revision of judgments and awards 582–84
    standard of proof 574
    Statute 556–58, 560, 569, 583, 584

INDEX 643

inherent powers 555–56
interpretation 559–60
judgments and awards 578–84
jurisdiction 555–63
  admissibility distinguished 556, 557
  consent 555–57, 585
  declining 557, 563, 565–66
  definition 556
  exclusive jurisdiction clauses 563–64
  incidental 559–60
  Monetary Gold principle 565–66
  overlapping 563
  pro tem 557–59
Monetary Gold principle 565–66
negotiation requirements 562–63
PCIJ, practice of 556, 561–62
  burden of proof 572
  Certain German Interests decision 559
  dispute, existence of a 561–62
  jurisdiction 559, 561–62, 585
  precedent 569–70
provisional measures 566–68
res judicata 565–66, 578–84
rules of procedure/procedural instruments 555–56, 585
third states, rights or obligations of absent 565–66
international humanitarian law (IHL) 336–37
international minimum standard (IMS) *see* **minimum standard of treatment (MST)**
international obligation in force for a State (Article 13 ARSIWA) 313–17
alignment 317
continuing and composite acts 317, 325
customary international law 313
entry into force 315–17
evolutionary interpretation 314
general principle of law, as 313
non-retroactivity, principle of 313–17
State conduct 314, 316
successive investment treaties 316
sunset clauses 315
temporal jurisdiction 314, 315–17
termination of obligations 313–14, 315
interpretation *see also* **treaty interpretation, general rule (Article 31 VCLT); supplementary means of interpretation (Article 32 VCLT)**
alignment 7–8, 518
amendment and modification of treaties 179–82, 212, 549, 550
attribution 299
BITs 179–82, 462
  contextual interpretation 127
  dictionaries, use of 126
  languages 171–73
  subsequent practice 131, 133–34
  supplementary means 162
  third-parties 127, 144
breach, termination or suspension as a consequence of 230

broad language 8–9
compensation 514
conflicts 7–8
corruption of a representative of a State 212
customary international law 8–9
denial of justice 527–28, 536, 537–38
deviation 518
disposal of a State by another State, conduct of organs placed at 281–84
distress 349
evolutionary interpretation 314
expropriation 513–16, 518, 520, 546–48
fair and equitable treatment (FET) standard 477–78, 516–18
force majeure 346
fundamental change of circumstances 234, 236, 237–38, 239, 240
general principles of law 474, 477–78
internal law and observance of treaties 75–76, 77, 80, 82
international courts and tribunals, cross-cutting procedural powers of 559–60
judgments and awards 578–79, 580–82
jus cogens 192–93
languages, interpretation of treaties authenticated in two or more 166–76
minimum standard of treatment (MST) 17, 462, 540, 546–48, 549
most-favoured-nation treatment (MFN) standard 508–10, 518
NAFTA standards 505, 506, 507, 520
  expropriation, just compensation for 513–16, 518
  fair and equitable treatment (FET) standard 516–18
  minimum standard of treatment (MST) 516–18
  most-favoured-nation treatment (MFN) standard 508–10, 518
  national treatment (NT) standard 511–13, 518
  substantive standards of treatment 507–18
national treatment (NT) standard 511–13, 518
necessity 13, 361
non-retroactivity of treaties 48, 85
object and purpose of a treaty prior to its entry into force, obligation not to defeat the 24, 27–31
ordinary meaning 105, 518, 527–28
organs of the State, conduct of 262–63
res judicata 578–79, 580–82
reservations 35, 36, 37–38, 40–42, 43
restitution 514
State immunity 490
State succession 462
subsequent practice 19–20, 212
succession to treaties 109–10, 111–13, 115–18, 425, 427–28, 433
termination and suspension of the operation of a treaty implied by conclusion of a

later treaty 217–18
  territorial scope 101–4, 105–6, 107
  vagueness 8–9
  VCLT 7–9, 19–20, 518, 549
Interpretation of Treaties 1933 121–22
invalidity of treaties 9–10, 186–87
  absolute validity 187
  competence to conclude treaties, provisions of
      internal law regarding 186–87
  consent, defects to 186
  corruption of a representative of a State (Article 50
      VCLT) 190–91
  customary international law 186
  deviation 212
  domestic law, violations of 186
  general principles of law 186
  good faith 187
  grounds, list of 186–87
  imperfect consent 186
  improper substance 186
  jus cogens 187, 191–93
  manifest invalidity 187
  presumption of validity 186
  procedure 208–11
  relative invalidity or voidability 187
  reservations 35, 40, 43
  successive treaties relating to the same subject
      matter 109–10
  void agreements 186, 187

judges *see* **judiciary**
judgments and awards 578–84, *see also* **enforcement
      of judgments and awards**
  appeals 578–79
  binding character 578
  constitutive instruments 578
  declaratory judgments 393–94, 398
  interpretation 578–79, 580–82
  res judicata 578–84
  revision 582–84
**judicial remedies and consequences of State
      responsibility (Article 28
      ARSIWA)** 375–23
  cessation of unlawful conduct 376, 398
  compensation 376
  contribution to injury 376
  customary international law 375–76
  deviation 376
  forms of remedies 376
  interest 376
  non-repetition, assurances of 376
  prospective obligations 376
  reparations 375–76
  restitution 376
  retrospective duty to make
      reparations 376
  satisfaction, declarations of 376
judiciary
  denial of justice 523, 525, 526–27

  dialogue 520
  independence 523, 525, 526–27
  judicial acts 322
  judicial economy principle 510
  judicial finality 523–24, 530–31, 536
  judicial policy 615–16
jurisdiction *see also* **temporal jurisdiction; territorial
      scope (Article 29 VCLT)**
  abuse of process 608, 610, 612, 613–14
  applicable law 568
  burden of proof 573
  clauses 104–5
  counterclaims 575–77
  extraterritoriality 331
  international courts and tribunals,
      cross-cutting procedural
      powers of 555–64, 565–66, 585
  nationality 592, 593–94, 595, 596, 597, 598,
      600, 601–2
  non-retroactivity of treaties 85–98
  provisional measures 567–68
  revision of judgments and awards 582–83
  self-defence 339
  standard of proof 574
  State immunity 491–95
  State succession 450–51
  succession to treaties 423
jus cogens
  Article 53 VCLT 191–93
  automatic termination 187
  BITs 192
  compliance with peremptory
      norms 365–68
  conflicts 7–8
  countermeasures 404
  human rights 192
  interpretation 192–93
  invalidity of treaties 191–93
  lex specialis 416
  successive treaties relating to the same subject
      matter 111
  territorial scope 107
justifications and excuses
  distress 350
  force majeure 344
  jus cogens 365–66
  necessity 354
  wrongfulness, consequences of invoking a
      circumstance precluding 369–70, 371–72

**languages, interpretation of treaties authenticated in
      two or more (Article 33 VCLT)** 166–76
  BITs 171–73
  common meaning rule 167–75
  customary international law 166–67
  deviation 168, 169, 170, 174–75
  discretion 167
  object and purpose 167, 168, 169–70, 171,
      172, 174–75

INDEX 645

ordinary meaning 170–71
restrictive or limited interpretation 167
subjectivity 167
legal reasoning, techniques of 414
legitimate expectations 73, 476–78
lex specialis 11, 406–8, *see also lex specialis* (Article 55 ARSIWA)
   attribution 309, 310–11
   breach, termination or suspension as a consequence of 230
   conduct of empowered entities 271
   conflicts 7–8
   countermeasures 404, 406–8
   denial of justice 536
   interpretation 416
   organs of the State, conduct of 257, 261
   secondary rules 7–8
   unjust enrichment 626
lex specialis (Article 55 ARSIWA) 412–19
   application in investment disputes 414–18
   attribution, special rules on 413–16
   BITs 415, 416–18
   customary international law 44, 414, 415–16, 417–18
   definition 412, 418
   diplomatic protection 413
   dispute resolution clauses 413
   expropriation 415, 416
   fair and equitable treatment (FET) clauses 416
   full protection and security clauses 416
   intention 412–13
   international courts and tribunals 418
   interpretation 412, 414, 417
   jus cogens 416
   legal reasoning, techniques of 414
   lex generalis 414, 415–18
   necessity 417–18
   rationales 412–13
   remedies, special rules on 413–14
   reparations 413–14, 415
   same subject matter 412
   scope, determining the 414–15
   specific norms, priority given to more 412
   systemic integration, principle of 416
limitation periods
   composite act, breach consisting of a 329
   continuous breaches 321–416
   extension in time of the breach of an international obligation 321, 324
   extinctive prescription 564–65, 585
   judicial proceedings 321
   revision of judgments and awards 584
locus standi see standing

McNair, Arnold 75–76
MFN see most-favoured-nation treatment (MFN) standard (NAFTA)
minimum standard of treatment (MST) 1, 17, 539–54, *see also*

minimum standard of treatment (MST) (NAFTA)
   alignment 519–20
   arbitrariness 542, 543, 545
   bilateral treaties 540, 544, 545, 546–48
   BITs 451–52, 540, 544, 545, 546–48
   codification 543–45
   compensation 540–41, 543–45
   concessionary contracts 462
   content and contours 545
   customary international law 540, 544, 545, 546–48
      colonialism 539–40
      denial of justice 543
      diplomatic protection 543
      fair and equitable treatment (FET) standard 553
      State succession 451–52
   default rule 462
   denial of justice 541, 542, 543–44, 545
   detention and treatment in detention 544
   developing countries 540, 541, 544
   devolution agreements 452
   diplomatic protection 17, 539–42, 543
      customary international law 543
      human rights 543
      State succession 451–52, 456–57, 462
   due diligence 543, 545–46
   due process 543, 545
   early formulations 542–43
   economic imperialism 546
   emergence of standard 540–45
   exhaustion of local remedies 541, 542, 543, 544
   expropriation 17, 455–57, 544
      compensation 451–57, 540, 543–45
      direct 540
      due process 451–52, 543
      ex gratia or without prejudice clause 452
      indirect 548
      interpretation 546–48
      scope 455–57
      State succession 451–57
      valuation, types of 456–57
   fair and equitable treatment (FET) standard 17, 540, 544, 545–47, 553–54
      denial of justice 545
      full protection and security (FPS) standard 545–47
      regulatory stabilization, obligation of 547
      State succession 451–52
   fair hearing, right to a 541–42
   full protection and security (FPS) standard 545–47
   gunboat diplomacy 540–41
   historical evolution 540–45
   Hull formula of prompt, adequate and effective compensation 540, 544–45
   human rights 17, 541–42, 543, 544, 554
   ICJ practice 541–43, 546, 547–48
      ELSI 542, 545
      Neer approach 542, 543, 545
   inducement 547
   internal law 539–40, 543

minimum standard of treatment (MST) (NAFTA) (cont.)
  interpretation 462, 540, 546–48
  national treatment (NT) standard 540
  nationality discrimination 539–40, 543, 544, 545, 548, 554
  nationalization 540, 544
  natural resources, permanent sovereignty over 540
  objective and impartial observers 542
  origins 451–52, 540–42
  police powers 545–46, 548
  property rights 17, 539–54
  rule of law 542, 545
  scope 455–57
  State succession 451–57, 462
  strict liability 545–46
  subjective test 545
  substance 4–5, 6
  treaty law 543–44
minimum standard of treatment (MST) (NAFTA) 506–7, 516–18, 547, 548–53
  absolute minimum 549–50
  amendment of NAFTA 549, 550
  Barcelona Traction 517
  Bilcon v Canada award 551–52, 554
  BITs 546–47, 548, 550–51
  burden of proof 519–20
  Case Concerning Ahmadou Sadio Diallo (Guinea v DRC) 516–17, 550, 552, 553
  customary international law 549, 550–53
    alignment 519–20
    evolved 550–51
    fair and equitable treatment (FET) standard 517–18, 548
  denial of justice 517–18
  diplomatic protection 550, 551, 552–53, 554
  due process 516, 517–18
  ELSI Elettronica Sicula SpA (US v Italy) 516–18
  exhaustion of local remedies 516–18, 552
  fair and equitable treatment (FET) standard 540, 548–49, 553
  full protection and security (FPS) standard 548
  Glamis Gold award 551–53
  human rights 548, 550, 553
  ICJ's practice on adjudicating on standards 506–7, 516–18, 519–20
  interpretation 549–53
  legitimacy 552
  Lion Mexico case 517–18
  minimum, meaning of 549–50
  most-favoured nation (MFN) standard 549–50
  national treatment (NT) standard 549
  nationality discrimination 549–50
  Neer standard 551, 552–53
  opinio juris 551, 552–53
  outrageous, bad faith, and wilful neglect standard 517–18
  Pope & Talbot v Canada award 548–49, 550, 553
  relative standards of treatment 549–50
  retroactivity 549, 550
  USMCA revision 540, 552–53
  wilful disregard standard 517–18
modification of treaties *see* amendment and modification of treaties; amendment and modification of multilateral treaties (Articles 40–41 VCLT)
monism 76
moral damage 19–20, 371, 379, 387–88, 389–91, 399
most-favoured-nation treatment (MFN) standard (NAFTA) 506–7, 508–10
  Ambatielos Claim (Greece v UK) 509, 519
  Anglo-Indian Oil Co (UK v Iran) 508, 509, 519
  burden of proof 519
  comparators 510
  deviation 518–19, 520
  ejusdem generis, principle of 509, 519
  future rights 508, 519
  interpretation 508–10
    ICJ cases 508–10, 518
    NAFTA cases 510, 518, 520
  judicial economy principle 510
  like circumstances determination 510, 519
  minimum standard of treatment (MST) 549–50
  NAFTA standards 506–7, 508–10
    deviation 518–19, 520
    interpretation 518, 520
  nationality 589
  public policy 519
  Rights of Nationals of USA in Morocco (France v US) 508–9
  substantive treatment, proof of more favourable 510
  third-party treaties 508–9
moving treaty frontiers principle
  cession 437, 438–40
  customary international law 7–8
  exceptions 438–40, 447–48
  succession to treaties 14–15, 430, 437–40, 447–48
  State succession 14–15
MST *see* minimum standard of treatment (MST)
multinational peacekeeping forces 281, 282–84
mutual termination/termination by consent (Article 54b VCLT) 196–200
  acquired rights, doctrine of 199
  BITs 196–200
  consent of third States 199
  customary international law 198–99
  due process 199–200
  EU Termination Agreement 197–200
  non-retrospectivity 198–200
  sunset clauses 196–98, 200
  survival clauses 196–97
  two-step approach 196–97, 198

NAFTA *see also* expropriation, just compensation for (NAFTA); minimum standard of treatment (MST) (NAFTA); NAFTA standards
  amendment of treaties 135, 144

Annexes 39, 40, 41, 42
denial of justice 528–29
fair and equitable treatment (FET) standard 506–7, 516–18
general rule and amendment of bilateral treaties 180–81
internal law and observance of treaties 78
interpretation 42, 180–81
jus cogens 192–93
minimum standard of treatment (MST) 506–7, 516–18
most-favoured-nation treatment (MFN) standard 506–7, 508–10
reservations 37, 38–41, 42
standing 533
NAFTA standards 505–22
alignment 506, 518, 519–20
cross-fertilization 506–7
customary international law 520
development of IIL 506–7
deviation 518–19, 520
different treaty texts 518, 519, 520
evolution of jurisprudence 518
expropriation, just compensation for 506–7, 513–16, 518, 519–20
fair and equitable treatment (FET) standard 516–18, 519–20
institutional factors 518–19, 520
interpretation 505, 506, 507, 516–18, 520
  expropriation, just compensation for 513–16, 518
  fair and equitable treatment (FET) standard 516–18
  minimum standard of treatment (MST) 516–18
  most-favoured-nation treatment (MFN) standard 508–10, 518
  national treatment (NT) standard 511–13, 518
  ordinary meaning 518
  substantive standards of treatment 507–18
judicial dialogue 520
legitimacy 505
minimum standard of treatment (MST) 506–7, 516–18, 519–20
most-favoured-nation treatment (MFN) standard 506–7, 508–10
  deviation 518–19, 520
  interpretation 518, 520
national treatment (NT) standard 506–7, 511–13, 518–19, 520
public policy 519
subject matter of disputes 518
substantive standards of treatment 507–18
textual ambiguity of IIAs 518
USMCA, replacement of NAFTA with 506–7
national champions 511–12
national treatment (NT) standard 506–7, 511–13
business conditions 512–13
burden of proof 511, 512–13, 519
comparators 512–13
discriminatory intent 511

ELSI Elettronica Sicula SpA (US v Italy) 511
GATT, influence on 511, 512
  interpretation 511–13
  ICJ case 511–13, 518
  NAFTA cases 511–13
like circumstances determination 511–13
like products determination 511, 512
minimum standard of treatment (MST) 540, 549
NAFTA standards standard 506–7, 511–13, 518–19, 520
national champions 511–12
nationality element 512
protectionism 511
public policy 512–13
nationality 588–604, *see also* **nationality discrimination; nationality of corporations**
acquisition and recognition 590–92
birth, nationality by 590
BITs 589, 591–92, 598
Conflict of Nationality Convention 1930 590
continuous nationality rule 598, 602
customary international law 590
definition 18
diplomatic protection 589, 595, 598
domestic regulation, recognition of 588–89, 590–91
domicile 592
dominant and effective nationality principle 594–98
dual or multiple nationality 594–95, 596, 598, 602
exceptions 599
expropriation 589
fair and equitable treatment (FET) standard 589
fraud 596
full protection and security (FPS) standard 589
general principles of law 590
human rights 18
individuals 18, 589, 591, 592–99
international courts and tribunals 589, 595, 602
jurisdiction 592, 593–94, 595, 596, 597, 598, 602
legal persons 591, 592
marriage, by 590
most-favoured-nation (MFN) standard 589
national treatment (NT) standard 589
natural persons 591, 592, 602
parents, nationality of 590
procedure 4–5, 6, 18
residence 590, 592, 593
special reasons, acquisition for 590
statelessness at birth 591
treaty shopping/nationality planning 18
nationality discrimination
exceeding international standards 549–50
expropriation 451–52
jus cogens 192–93
minimum standard of treatment (MST) 539–40, 543, 544, 545, 548, 554, 589
most-favoured-nation (MFN) treatment 508
national treatment (NT) standard 511
reservations 36

nationality of corporations 18, 591, 599–602
  BITs 592, 600, 601–2
  control test 600
  convenience, nationality of 599
  diplomatic protection 599, 600
  general principles of law 599
  genuine link theory 600
  internal law 599, 600
  jurisdiction 600, 601–2
  legal personality 599
  piercing the corporate veil 599, 600, 601–2
  place of incorporation 590, 599
  seat 590, 599, 600
  shareholders 599, 600, 601, 602
  standing 600
nationalization 540, 544
natural resources CC08P37, 540
necessity
  BITs 417–18
  customary international law 13
  distress 349–50, 351–52
  force majeure 346
  interpretation 13
  jus cogens 366–67
  lex specialis 417–18
  wrongfulness, circumstances precluding 13, 373–74
necessity (Article 25 ARSIWA) 353–64
  alignment 362–63
  BITs 358, 360–61
  burden of proof 358, 360
  causal link 361–62, 363
    endogenous factors 361–62
    exogenous factors 361–62
  conditions 354, 358, 360–61
  customary international law 353, 358–59, 361, 363
  domestic courts 357–58
  economic crises 359–61, 362, 363
  essential interests 354, 355–56, 358, 363
    definition 359–60
    exception clauses in treaties 358–59
    identification and weighing 354, 355–56, 358
    interests impaired 356, 360
    interests safeguarded 355–56
    weighing, definition of 356, 360
  exception clauses in treaties 358–59
  exclusion by relevant primary rule 354, 355
  flexibility 358, 360–61
  grave and imminent peril 354, 355
  human rights 359
  interpretation 361
  justifications and excuses 354
  lesser-evils based justification 353
  margin of appreciation 358, 359–60
  military necessity 355
  non-contribution to situations of necessity 354, 357, 358, 361–62, 363
  object and purpose 358
  objectivity 355, 359
  only way standard 354, 356, 358, 360–61, 363
  reasonableness 356
  strict defence, as 354, 356
New International Economic Order (NIEO) 540
non-repetition, duty of 377–78
non-retroactivity of treaties *see also* non-retroactivity of treaties (Article 28 VCLT)
  general rule and amendment of bilateral treaties 181–82
  international obligation in force for a State 313–17
  minimum standard of treatment (MST) 549, 550
  object and purpose of a treaty prior to its entry into force, obligation not to defeat the 30
  provisional application 56
  succession to BITs, procedure for 424
  termination by consent 198–200
  VCLT 10
non-retroactivity of treaties (Article 28 VCLT) 84–99
  acts occurring before entry into force 86–91, 95–97
  alignment 97
  BITs 46, 95–96, 97
  composite acts 94, 96, 97
  consent to be bound 46–47
  continuing acts 85, 91–94, 96–97
  customary international law 84, 85
  declarations 89, 90, 94–95
  default rules 47
  deviation 98
  disputes arising before entry into force 94–95, 97–98
  entry into force 46–48, 50, 84–98
    composite acts 94
    definition 94
    disputes arising 94–95, 97–98
    jurisdiction to consider acts occurring 86–91, 95–97
  exceptions 85
  flexibility 48
  general principle of law, as 84
  Genocide Convention 47, 87–88
  interpretation 48, 85
  jurisdiction 85–98
  object and purpose of treaties 46–47
  objective intention of the State parties 85, 86
  primary obligations 85, 86, 91, 98
  ratione temporis jurisdiction 88–89, 92, 94, 96, 98
  reciprocal consent of parties 94–95
  substantive obligations 95–96
North American Free Trade Agreement *see* NAFTA
notification or deposit of instruments, consent to be bound through 46, 48–50

object and purpose of a treaty prior to its entry into force, obligation not to defeat the (Article 18 VCLT) 23–31
  alignment 31
  consent to be bound, expression of 23

constitutional courts 28, 29
customary international law 23–24, 30
damages 25
deviation 31
domestic court/tribunal decisions 25, 27–29, 31
draft of article 25–26
fair and equitable treatment (FET) standard 30
good faith 23–24, 25, 28, 29–30
   legal obligations 25
   proof 31
   retroactivity 30
imperative rules 30–31
inconsistency of conduct 27, 28
interpretation 24, 27–31
knowledge, actual or constructive 26
languages, interpretation of treaties authenticated in two or more 167, 168, 169–70, 171, 172, 174–75
legal obligations 25
moral obligations 25
negative duty, as 26
object and purpose, definition of 26
objectivity 25–26, 29–30
origins 24–25
pacta sunt servanda 24
proof 30–31
qualifying acts 26
regional court decisions 27, 29
retroactivity 30
signed but not ratified, where treaty has been 23, 27, 28
State immunity 28–29
status quo, preserving the 26
supreme courts 28
travaux préparatoires 25
object and purpose of treaties *see also* **object and purpose of a treaty prior to its entry into force, obligation not to defeat the (Article 18 VCLT)**
amendment and modification of treaties 185–86
BITs 358
breach, termination or suspension as a consequence of 205, 227, 228–29, 230–31
cession 437, 438–39
context 126
entry into force 46–47
interpretation 121, 124–25, 126, 127–28, 129–30, 140–41
   ordinary meaning 125, 128
   special meaning 140–41
   supplementary means 147–49, 159
   text 127–28
   whole of the treaty 128
necessity 358
non-retroactivity of treaties 46–47
ordinary meaning 125, 128
pacta sunt servanda 65, 67, 68, 70
preambles 128
reservations 35, 37–38, 41, 42–44

separation/dissolution of States 441
special meaning 140–41
successive treaties relating to the same subject matter 117
supplementary means of interpretation 147–49, 159
observance of treaties *see* **internal law and observance of treaties (Article 27 VCLT)**
occupation 106–7, 437
opinio juris
   Article 38 ICJ Statute 468–69, 486
   concessionary contracts 457
   customary international law 470–71, 472
   disposal of a State by another State, conduct of organs placed at 280–81
   expropriation 455–56
   foreign bondholders 460, 461
   interpretation 142–43
   minimum standard of treatment (MST) 551, 552–53
   succession to BITs, procedure for 424, 429–30

pacta sunt servanda **(Article 26 VCLT)** 64–73
abuse of legal rights 66, 70
alignment 72
declarations 65
definition 64
deviation 72
flexibility 72
fundamental change of circumstances 233–36, 244
good faith 10–11, 65, 66–69, 70–72
   autonomous obligation, as 68, 71, 72
   human rights courts and tribunals 69
   presumption 70
human rights 69
internal law and observance of treaties 75, 76–77
interpretation 71, 72, 140
legitimate expectations 68–69
literal application and purpose, conflict between 65–66
object and purpose of treaties, parties must not frustrate the 24, 65, 67, 68, 70
primacy of terms of treaties 68
procedural obligations 66
provisional application 57
substantive obligations 67
systemic integration, principle of 140
parallel conduct 133–34
parallel proceedings 609, 610–11, 614–15, 616
peremptory norms *see* ***jus cogens***
performance *see* **supervening impossibility of performance (Article 61 VCLT)**
piercing the corporate veil 599, 600, 601–2
preambles, interpretation of 125, 126, 128
precedent 569–70
   Article 38 ICJ Statute 469–70, 486, 569
   persuasive value 569
   sources of law 15–16
primacy of international law 75–77, 79–80, 82–83

primary rules 16–17, 19
  conflicts 7–8
  customary international law 6
  definition of 5–6
  general principles of law 6
  procedure 6, 7–8, 16–17
  secondary rules 5–6
procedure *see also* **international courts and tribunals (ICTs), cross-cutting procedural powers of; procedures for invalidity, termination, withdrawal from or suspension (Articles 65–68 VCLT)**
  abuse of process 605–6, 607, 609, 610–11, 612, 614–15
  abuse of rights 4–5, 6, 18
  amendment and modification of treaties 182–83
  applicable law 17–18
  arbitrators, role, functions, and qualifications of 17–18
  BITs, succession to 423–34
  compétence de la competence 556
  conflicts 7–8
  countermeasures 405, 408–9
  general rule and amendment of bilateral treaties 178
  internal law and observance of treaties 77
  nationality 4–5, 6, 18
  non-investment considerations 17–18
  pacta sunt servanda 66
  primary rules 6, 7–8, 16–17
  provisional measures 567
  rules of procedure/procedural instruments 585
  substance/procedure divide 614
  succession to BITs, procedure for 423–34
  transparency 17–18
  unjust enrichment 4–5, 6, 18–19
procedures for invalidity, termination, withdrawal from or suspension (Articles 65–68 VCLT) 208–11
  armed conflicts, effect of 211
  automatic termination 211
  BITs 210, 211
  conditions 209
  consent to be bound 208, 211
  customary international law 209, 211
  European Union 209–10
  good faith 209
  implied termination 210–11
  intention 210, 211
  legal certainty 210
  notification of claims 208, 209–11
  progressive development of law 209, 211
  revocation of notifications and instruments 209–11
procurement contracts 190
property rights 17, 81–82, 450–63, 539–54
proportionality
  compensation 391–92
  countermeasures 401, 408–10

  restitution 382–83, 384–85, 386
  satisfaction 394
prospective elements of responsibility (Articles 29 and 30 ARSIWA) 377–78
  cessation, duty of 377–78
  continued obligation to perform 377–78
  corruption 378
  erga omnes obligations 378
  human rights 377
  non-repetition, duty of 377–78
  reparations 377–78
  restitution 377–78
protectionism 511
provisional application of treaties (Article 25 VCLT) 52–63
  all-or-nothing approach 60
  alternative approach 60
  BITs 55
  consent to be bound 59
  consistency 53–54, 56–57, 58–59, 60
  customary international law 52–53
  declarations 54–55, 57–58, 59, 60
  domestic law, impact of 56–60
  Energy Charter Treaty (ECT) 53–55, 56–60
    declarations 54–55, 57–58, 59, 60
    entry into force 61
    limitation clause 58, 60
    notification of intention not to become a party 61
    ratification 61
    survival clause 54
    termination 61
    territorial scope 61
  entry into force 46–47, 52, 54, 56, 60–61
  European Union's provisional application of mixed agreements 62
  internal law and observation of treaties 59–60
  nature of agreement 54–55
  non-ratification 60–61
  pacta sunt servanda 57
  piecemeal approach 60
  ratification 60–61
  resolutions 55
  retroactive effect 56
provisional measures 566–68
  abuse of process 607–8, 610–11, 614–15
  adjudication, protection of rights subject to 566
  binding effect 567, 568
  constitutive instruments 567
  general non-aggravation orders 566
  irreparable prejudice, risk of 567–68
  jurisdiction 567–68
  merits, requirement for a plausible case on the 567–68
  preconditions 567–68
  procedural rules 567
  res judicata 566
  urgency 567–68
public interest 240, 486–87

reasons, duty to provide 526–27, 580, 581–82
rebus sic stantibus principle *see* fundamental change of circumstances (Article 62 VCLT)
remedies *see also* compensation; damages; exhaustion of local remedies/judicial finality;
provisional measures; remedies (ARSIWA)
   Chorzów Factory principle 13–14
   compensation 13–14
   consent 334
   customary international law 13–14
   denial of justice 524, 535–36
   extension in time of the breach of an international obligation 321, 323
   failure to remedy or redress unlawful acts 320
   reparations 13–14
remedies (ARSIWA) 398–99
   compensation 19–20
   deviation 398
   human rights 399
   judicial remedies and consequences of State responsibility (Article 28 ARSIWA) 375–23
   lex specialis 413–14
   limits 398
   reparations 379–80
   rule of law 399
   special rules 413–14
renegotiation/adaptation clauses 240–41, 242–43
renvoi 76, 81–82, 334–35
reparation
   ARSIWA Articles 31 and 34 379–80
   breach, termination or suspension as a consequence of 225–26
   causal link 379, 380
   compensation 379–80
   countermeasures 403–4, 406
   customary international law 379
   full reparation, principle of 392, 395–96
   judicial remedies 375–76
   lex specialis 413–14, 415
   prospective elements of responsibility 377–78
   retrospective duty 376
   satisfaction 380, 392–94, 398–99
   wrongfulness, consequences of invoking a circumstance precluding 371
reprisals 205, 404
res judicata 578–84
   BITs 482–83
   definition 578
   functus officio 580
   gap-filling 482–83
   general principles of law 475, 482–83, 580
   internal law 570–71
   interpretation 578–79, 580–82
   limitations 579
   negative effect 482, 579, 580

   operative part of decisions 580, 581–82
   positive effect 482, 579, 580
   provisional measures 566
   reasons, statements of 580, 581–82
   revision 582–84
   triple identity test of parties, objects, causes 579
reservations (Articles 19-23 VCLT) 33–44
   alternative flexibility devices 34–35, 36, 37, 40, 42–44
   Annexes 39, 40, 41–42
   asymmetric commitments 42–43
   authorized reservations 37–38, 39, 41–44
   BITs 36
   customary international law 34, 40
   entry into force 39
   exceptions
      devising 36–42
      modification 43
   flexibility 34–35, 42–44
   fragmentation 43–44
   genuine reservations, mechanisms as constituting 37
   good faith interpretation 41
   human rights 43–44
   intent 40, 41, 43
   interpretation 35, 36, 37–38, 40–42, 43, 157
   investment decisions 40–42
   legal certainty 43
   liberalization 36, 37, 38, 39, 42–43
   multilateral treaties 35, 36–43
   NAFTA 37, 38–41
      Annexes 39, 40, 41, 42
      interpretation 42
      non-conforming measures 38, 39, 40
      Schedules 39, 40
      unilateral nature of reservations 41
   non-conforming measures 38, 39, 40
   object and purpose of the treaty 35, 37–38, 41, 42–44
   objections 43
   objectivity 35
   phasing out commitments 43
   presumption in favour of reservations 35
   ratchet effect 43
   reciprocity principle 39, 42–43
   reservation, definition of 34
   Reservations to the Genocide Convention (ICJ) 35
   rollback regular negotiations 43
   Schedules 39, 40
   specified reservations 37–38, 39, 40, 42–44
   subjectivity 35
   uniformity 35
   USMCA 37, 38–40
      Annexes 39, 40
      non-conforming measures 38, 40
      Schedules 39
   validity 35, 40, 43
   withdrawal 37–38, 43

restitution *see also* restitution (Article 35 ARSIWA)
  judicial remedies 376
  legal 376
  material 376
  prospective elements of responsibility 377–78
  satisfaction 392–93
  unavailability or inadequacy 392–93
  unjust enrichment 619, 621
restitution (Article 35 ARSIWA) 381–86
  concept 381–82
  definition 381
  expropriation 385–86
  internal law to avoid international obligations, states may not rely on 382–84
  interpretation 514
  juridical restitution 381–82, 383–84, 398
  material impossibility 382–84, 386
  material restitution 381, 382–84, 386, 398
  primary form of reparation, as 381, 382–83, 386
  proportionality 382–83, 384–85, 386
  reasonableness 384
  State sovereignty 382, 383–84, 385, 398
  status quo, re-establishing the 381
retroactivity *see* non-retroactivity of treaties; non-retroactivity of treaties (Article 28 VCLT)
revision of judgments and awards 582–84
  decisive factors, discovery of 583–84
  errors of law 582
  functus officio 584
  implied powers 584
  inherent powers 582–83
  jurisdiction 582–83
  knowledge, level of 583–84
  res judicata 582, 583, 584
  time limits 584
rule of law 399, 525, 542, 545

same subject matter, treaties relating to the *see* successive treaties relating to the same subject matter, application of
satisfaction (Article 37 ARSIWA) 392–94, 398–99
  causal link 393
  compensation, unavailability or inadequacy of 392–93
  concept 392–93
  customary international law 392–93
  declaratory judgments 393–94, 398
  definition 392–93
  practice 393–94
  proportionality 394
  restitution, unavailability or inadequacy of 392–93
Schedules 39, 40
secession *see* cession/secession
secondary rules 5–8, 16–17, 19
  definition 5–6
  primary rules, application of 5–6
  sources, law of 6
self-defence (Article 21 ARSIWA) 336–40
  alignment 339–40
  aviation treaties 336–37
  collateral violations 338
  commercial obligations under bilateral treaties 336–37
  countermeasures 339
  customary international law 337
  formal state of war, decline in importance of 337
  human rights 336–37
  international humanitarian law 336–37
  inter-State defence, as 338–39
  jurisdiction 339
  justification 336–39
  non-intervention 336–37, 338
  peacefully, obligation to settle disputes 336–37
  private actors' rights 339
  territorial sovereignty 336–37, 338
  total restraint, obligations of 336–37
separation/dissolution of States 441–43
  automatic succession, default rule of 441–43
  continuity 441–43
  customary international law 442
  default regimes 440, 441
  Genocide Convention 442
  human rights 442
  object and purpose 441
  stability of treaties 442
  succession to treaties 436, 440, 441–43, 448
  VCSST 440, 441–43
sources of law
  arbitration 15–16
  customary international law 1–2, 15–16, 136–37, 465–70
  doctrine 15–16
  general principles of law 1–2, 15–16, 136–37, 474–75
  hierarchy 79–80, 474–75
  ICJ Statute 15–16, 464–70
  interaction between sources 466–70
  interpretation 121–24, 136–37
  judicial decisions 15–16
  precedent 15–16
  secondary rules 6
  systemic integration, principle of 136–37
  treaty law 1–2, 15–16, 136–37
stabilization clauses 240–42
standard of proof 574–75, *see also* burden of proof
  abuse of process 608
  balance of probabilities 574–75
  corruption of a representative of a State 190
  denial of justice 574
  fraud, corruption, or bad faith 574–75
  jurisdiction 574
standards *see* fair and equitable treatment (FET) standard; full protection and security (FPS) standard; minimum standard of treatment (MST); most-favoured-nation treatment (MFN) standard (NAFTA); national treatment (NT) standard

INDEX

standing 532–33
  customary international law 532–33
  denial of justice 524, 532–33, 536
  fair and equitable treatment (FET) standard 532–33
  foreign claimants 532, 533
  local courts 532–33
  nationality of corporations 600
State immunity 489–502
  absolute immunity 490–91
  acte jure imperii versus *acte jure gestionis* distinction 490–91, 492, 495–98, 501
  attribution 495, 497–98, 501
  BITs 494, 495
  consent 489, 494, 495
  customary international law 489, 490–92
  definition 492, 494
  domestic courts 489–91, 498–99, 501
  enforcement of arbitral awards 1, 16, 489, 490–91, 492, 498–500, 501
  expropriation 494, 495–96, 501
  fair and equitable treatment (FET) standard 496
  foreign domestic courts 489
  full protection and security (FPS) standard 492–93
  guidance for other legal issues 495–500
  human rights 493–94
  international courts and tribunals 490, 492, 493–94, 495
  interpretation 490
  jurisdictional immunities 491–95
  liability, immunity from 492–95
  New York Convention 1958 489
  object and purpose of a treaty prior to its entry into force, obligation not to defeat the 28–29
  restrictive immunity 490–92, 495, 501
  sovereign equality, principle of 490, 495
  sovereign taking versus commercial breach of contract 495–96
  statutory immunity 492–93
  stay of proceedings during annulment proceedings, security for 498–500, 501
  waiver 494–95, 500, 501
State responsibility *see* Articles on the Responsibility of States for Internationally Wrongful Acts (ARSIWA)
State sovereignty 382, 383–84, 385, 398
State succession 14–15, *see also* succession to treaties; Vienna Convention on Succession of States in Respect of Treaties (VCSST)
  applicable law 450–51
  concessionary contracts 450–51, 457–59, 462
  customary international law 4–5, 451, 462
  diplomatic protection 451–52
  domestic courts 451, 462
  enforcement of arbitral awards 1
  expropriation, compensation for 462
  foreign bondholders 459–62
  general principles of law 451, 462
  internal laws 451
  interpretation 462
  jurisdiction 450–51
  minimum standard of treatment (MST) 451–57, 462
  partial successions 460–61, 462
  property and debts 15, 450–63
  protection of foreign investment 450–63
  recognition of proprietary rights 450–51
  redemption of public debts held by private creditors 450–51
  termination and suspension of the operation of a treaty implied by conclusion of a later treaty 216–17
  total successions 460
  treaties, in respect of 14–15
  unjust enrichment 622
statelessness 588–89, 591
subsequent agreements, interpretation of 121, 130–32
  agreements concluded after conclusion, binding nature of 131
  conduct after conclusion of the treaty 130–31
  evidence 131–32
  formalities 133, 135
  joint conduct 131–32, 133
  modification of treaties 134–35
  requirements 131–32
  subsequent practice 134
  tacit agreement 134–35
subsequent practice
  agreement and form 132–33
  amendment and modification of treaties 134–36, 144, 212
  common understandings 134
  conclusion, binding nature of agreements concluded after 131
  conduct after conclusion of the treaty 130–31
  customary international law 469–70
  evidence 132–34
  evolutionary interpretation 130–31
  flexible approach 132–33
  form and agreement 132–33
  formalities 133
  general rule and amendment of bilateral treaties 179–80
  informal modification 179
  interpretation 19–20, 121, 130–36, 144, 179–81
  parallel conduct 133–34
  requirements 131–34
  restrictive approach 133–34, 136
  subsequent agreements 134
  uniform and consistent practice 132
succession *see* State succession; succession to BITs; succession to treaties
succession to BITs 423–34, 444–48
  acquiescence 427, 428, 429–30, 431, 433
  conduct 432–33
  consent to be bound 428, 429, 431–33
  critical date, doctrine of the 426–27

succession to BITs (*cont.*)
  customary international law 424, 430, 433
  declarations 428, 432–33
    general 430–32
    provisional continuity, of 430–31
    UN Secretary-General, to 430–31
  delay 423–24
  devolution agreements 429–30
  domestic courts 424, 426–27, 428, 433
  double succession 424–25
  estoppel 433
  European Union 114–15, 118
  express agreements 426–27
  implicit agreements 427–29
  interpretation 425, 427–28, 433
  moving treaty frontiers rule 430
  notification 427–28, 433
  opinio juris 424, 429–30
  partial succession 423
  presumptive succession 431
  procedure 423–34
  provisional continuity, declarations of 430–32
  retroactive application 424
  same subject matter 114–16, 118
  silence, interpretation of 433
  single succession 424–25
  total succession 423
  transfer of rights and obligations 423, 429
  verbal agreements 424–29
succession to treaties 435–49
  alignment 446–47, 448
  automatic succession, default rule of 441–46
  BITs 423–34, 444–48
  cession of territory 436–40, 448
  conduct of States in relation to investment agreements 435
  continuity 441–43, 448
  customary international law 436, 447
  default rules 435–36
  deviation 446–47, 448
  forms of succession 436
  human rights 445
  intention 448
  international courts and tribunals 436, 443
  moving treaty frontiers rule 437, 438–40, 447–48
  opinio juris 424, 429–30
  procedure 369–434
  separation/dissolution of States 436, 440, 441–43, 448
  special rules 443
  territorial scope 106–7
  unification of States 436, 440–41, 448
  VCSST 435, 436, 440–43, 448
successive treaties relating to the same subject matter (Article 30 VCLT) 109–18
  adoption of treaty, date of 111–12
  BITs 114–16, 118
  conclusion, definition of 111–12
  conflicts 111, 113–17, 118
  consent, date of expression of 111–12
  customary international law 110
  date of becoming party to treaties 110
  default rules 110, 115–16
  earlier treaties
    all parties, where later treaty does not include 111, 114
    suspension or termination 111
    which treaty is earlier or later in time 111–12, 116–17
  effectiveness, principle of 117
  elements 110–13
  entry into force, date of 111–12
  European Union 114–15, 116, 117, 118
  incompatibility 113, 114–15, 116–17
  intention 110–11
  interpretation 109–10, 111–13, 115–18
  jus cogens 111
  lex posterior principle 110–11, 112–13, 114
  non-investment disputes 114
  object and purpose of treaties 117
  party, definition of 110
  relating to the same subject matter, definition of 116–18
  same subject matter, definition of 112–13, 116
  State responsibility 109–10, 111
  suspension of earlier treaties 111
  termination 109–10, 111, 214–15, 216, 217, 218–21
  threshold 110
  travaux préparatoires 113
  validity 109–10
  which treaty is earlier or later in time 111–12, 116–17
supervening impossibility of performance (Article 61 VCLT) 193–94, 206–7
  ARSIWA 206–7
  BITs 206–7
  countermeasures 206–7
  customary international law 207
  destruction of objects 343–44
  disappearance or destruction of subject matter 206
  force majeure 206–7, 342, 343
  necessity 206–7
  State responsibility 206–7
  temporary impossibility 206
  travaux préparatoires 343
supplementary means of interpretation (Article 32 VCLT) 146–65
  alignment 153–54, 163–64
  ambiguous or obscure meanings 147–48, 149–53, 163
  BITs 162
  circumstances of conclusion of treaties 154–55
  contextual interpretation 147–48, 150, 151
  customary international law 146, 148–49
  definition 154–55
  deviation 151–54
  domestic courts 146–47, 154–55

INDEX 655

flexibility 147–48, 154, 157–58, 159, 164
general rule of interpretation 149–50, 152–54, 164
Genocide Convention 148–49, 155
good faith 147–48
intention 160–64
manifestly absurd or unreasonable results 147–48, 149–51, 153
object and purpose 147–49, 159
ordinary meaning 147–48, 152–53
qualitative criteria 147, 159–60, 162–63
relevance 147, 162, 163
reservations 157
State-to-State disputes 154
subjectivity 147–48
textual interpretation 148–49, 150, 151
travaux préparatoires 148–49, 150–53, 154–57, 163–64
triggers 147–49, 151, 153, 164
what constitutes supplementary means 154–64
when recourse can be had to supplementary matters 147–54
suspension of a treaty (Articles 57 and 58 VCLT) 201–2
BITs 202
consent of parties 201
customary international law 202
flexibility 202
intention 201
inter se suspension 202
multilateral parties 201
renegotiation of treaties 202
unilateral suspension 202
suspension of treaties *see* termination and suspension of investment treaties; termination and suspension of the operation of a treaty implied by conclusion of a later treaty (Article 59 VCLT)
systemic integration, principle of
applicability 137–38
customary international law 136–37, 143
interpretation 121, 122–23, 136–40, 143–44
intertemporality 140
lex specialis 416
parties 139–40
relevance 138–39, 140
rules 136–37, 138–40

temporal jurisdiction
aliens 534
competence to conclude treaties, provisions of internal law regarding 189
composite act, breach consisting of a 327, 329
customary international law 534
denial of justice 524, 534, 536, 537
extension in time of the breach of an international obligation 320, 322–23
international courts and tribunals 534
international obligation in force for a State 314, 315–17

interpretation 130
Islands of Palmas rule 12–13
non-retroactivity of treaties 10, 88–89, 92, 94, 96, 98
termination and suspension of the operation of a treaty implied by conclusion of a later treaty 216, 218
termination and suspension of treaties 9–10, 193–211, *see also* **termination and suspension of the operation of a treaty implied by conclusion of a later treaty (Article 59 VCLT)**
automatic termination 187, 211
breach, as a consequence of 205–6
consent of parties 193
customary international law 193–94
declaring invalid, terminating, withdrawing from or suspending operation of treaties, instruments for 209
default rules 193–94
diplomatic or consular relations, severance of (Article 63 VCLT) 208
fundamental change of circumstances 193–94, 207–8, 233–35, 237, 239–40, 244
implied by conclusion of a later treaty 202–4
internal law and observance of treaties 75
international obligation in force for a State 313–14, 315
mutual termination/termination by consent 196–200
notification in writing 209
primacy of treaty language 193
procedure 208
provisional application 54–55, 60–62
revocation of notifications and instruments provided for in Articles 65 and 67 209–11
supervening impossibility of performance 193–94, 206–7
suspension of a treaty 201–2
unilateral termination 194–96
withdrawal 200–1, 208–11
termination and suspension of the operation of a treaty implied by conclusion of a later treaty (Article 59 VCLT) 178, 202–4, 214–24
abrogation 216
alignment 223
automatic suspension/termination 216
BITs 218, 219–23
compatibility clauses 217
conditions 215–18
conflicts between successive treaties 214–24
consent of parties 203, 215
customary international law 203, 214–15
default rule, as 215, 222–23
duration of the treaties 218
entry into force of later treaties 218
European Union 216–17, 219–24
flexibility 215

treaty (Article 59 VCLT) (*cont.*)
  intention 202, 216, 217–18, 219–20
  interpretation 217–18
  intra-EU arbitration objections 219–24
  mutual termination/termination by consent 215
  notification procedure 212
  partial amendment 203, 204
  partial termination or suspension 218–19
  parties 216
  retrospective aspects of termination 212
  revival of earlier treaties 218
  same subject matter 193–94, 202, 214–15, 217, 219–20
  special regimes 218–19
  State succession 216–17
  subject matter and content 214–15, 216, 217, 219–20
  subjectivity 217
  successive treaties relating to the same subject matter 109–10, 111
  tacit abrogation 216, 217–18, 223
  temporal circumstances 216, 218
  Trade and Cooperation Agreement (TCA) and UK BITs, conflict between 218
  travaux préparatoires 221
  which treaty preceded the other 218
territorial scope (Article 29 VCLT) 100–8
  alignment or deviation 104–7
    justifications 106–7
    reasons 105–6
  annexation 102, 103
  application 101–4
  attribution 100
  BITs 101, 103, 104
  colonial clauses 106
  customary international law 100, 101, 106
  de facto control 103
  dependent territories, provisional application to 100
  deviation or alignment 104–7
  disputed territories 11, 106–7
  effective control 11, 102, 104–6
  entire territory, treaties as binding in respect of 101–2, 103–4
  erga omnes norms 107
  European Union 106
  exceptions 100, 102–3, 104
  federal clauses 106
  general rule 100, 101–2, 104
  Genocide Convention 101
  human rights 101–3, 104–7
  intention is established, where a different 102–3, 104, 105
  international courts and tribunals 101–3, 104–7
  interpretation 101–4, 105–6, 107
  jurisdiction clauses 104–5
  jus cogens 107
  metropolitan territories and non-metropolitan territories, distinction between 106
  natural resources 107
  occupation, unlawful 106–7
  overseas territories 105, 106
  sovereignty 11, 106–7
  succession to treaties 100, 437
  territory, definition of 106–7
  unilateral declarations 102
  use of force 107
territorial sovereignty 336–37, 338
textual analysis 125, 127–28, 129–30, 140–41
transparency 17–18, 37, 184
travaux préparatoires
  international organizations, documents prepared by 155
  interpretation 140–41, 148–49, 150–64
  object and purpose of a treaty prior to its entry into force, obligation not to defeat the 25
  successive treaties relating to the same subject matter 113
  supervening impossibility of performance 343
  termination and suspension of the operation of a treaty implied by conclusion of a later treaty 221
treaty interpretation, general rule (Article 31 VCLT) 120–45
  agreements concluded after conclusion, binding nature of 131
  annexes 125
  applicability 137–38
  BITs 126, 127, 131, 133–34, 144
  canons of interpretation 121, 124–28, 142
    context 122–23, 124–25, 129–30, 140–41, 144
    good faith 128
    hierarchy 124–25
    maxims distinguished 121
    object and purpose 121, 124–25, 129–30, 140–41
    ordinary meaning 122–23, 124–26, 140–41
  codification 121–22, 142–43
  consistency 142
  contemporaneity, principle of 123, 130, 140
  contextual interpretation 122–23, 124–25, 126–27, 144
    extrinsic documents 126–27
    in dubio pro investore interpretive rule 129–30
    object and purpose 126
    ordinary meaning 125, 126
    preambles 125, 126
    punctuation and syntax 126
    sentences, structure of 126
    special meaning 140–41
  contra proferentem rule 123, 130
  customary international law 121–24, 142–44
  default rules 122–23
  deviation 141–42, 144
  dictionaries 125–26, 144
  doctrine 124–42
  drafting VCLT 121–23
  effectiveness, principle of 123, 129–30, 143

ejusdem generis maxim 130
European Union 136, 137, 139
evolutive interpretation 123, 130
expressio unius est exclusion alterius
  maxim 130
extrinsic documents 126–27
flexibility 138–39, 144
general principles 122
genesis of VCLT 121–23
good faith 128–30
in claris non fit interpretario principle 122–23
in dubio mitius principle 123, 129–30
in dubio pro investore interpretive rule 129–30, 144
in pari materia principle 122–23
integral approach 124–25
intention 125, 127, 140–41
interaction of elements 124–25
international organizations, participation of 137
intertemporality 140
lex specialis 416
literal meaning 125
maxims of interpretation 122, 123, 128–30, 142, 144
  definition 121
  subsequent agreements 134–35
  subsequent practice 134–36
modification of treaties 134–36, 144
object and purpose 121, 124–25, 127–28, 129–30
  context 126
  special meaning 140–41
  whole of the treaty 128
ordinary meaning 122–23, 124–26
  dictionaries 125–26, 144
  literal meaning distinguished 125
  object and purpose 125, 128
  special meaning 126, 140–41
  systemic integration, principle of 136
  textual analysis 125, 129–30
pacta sunt servanda 140
parties 139–40
practice 124–42
preambles 125, 126, 128
principles 123–24
pro proferentem principle 123
punctuation and syntax 126
relevance of rules 138–39, 140
rules 136–37, 138–40
scope of interpretation 134–36
sentences, structure of 126
singular, rule as 124–25
sources of law 121–24, 136–37
special meaning 126, 140–41
special regimes or one unitary regime 141–42
subsequent agreements 121, 130–32
  agreements concluded after conclusion, binding nature of 131
  conduct after conclusion of the treaty 130–31
  evidence 131–32
  evolutionary interpretation 130–31
  formalities 133, 135
  joint conduct 131–32, 133
  modification of treaties 134–35
  requirements 131–32
  subsequent practice 134
  tacit agreement 134–35
subsequent practice 121, 130–31
  agreement and form 132–33
  common understandings 134
  conclusion, binding nature of agreements concluded after 131
  conduct after conclusion of the treaty 130–31
  evidence 132–34
  evolutionary interpretation 130–31
  flexible approach 132–33
  form and agreement 132–33
  formalities 133
  investment arbitration 132–33
  modification of treaties 134–36, 144
  parallel conduct 133–34
  requirements 131–34
  restrictive approach 133–34, 136
  subsequent agreements 134
  uniform and consistent practice 132
supplementary means 136–38
systemic integration, principle of 121, 122–23, 136–40, 144
teleological interpretation 143
temporal dimension 130
textual analysis 125, 127–28, 129–30, 140–41
title 126, 128
travaux préparatoires 140–41
treaty law 141–42
uniformity 141–42, 144
treaty law 1–2, 8–11, *see also pacta sunt servanda* (Article 26 VCLT); Vienna Convention on the Law of Treaties (VCLT)
  arbitration 8
  customary international law 5, 466–70
  general principles of law 5
  interpretation 141–42
  invalidity of investment treaties 186–87
  investment treaty, definition of 8
  minimum standard of treatment (MST) 543–44
  outward-flowing interaction 20
  secondary rules 6
  source of law, as 1–2, 15–16, 136–37
treaty shopping 18, 612

UNCTAD International Investment Agreements Mapping Project 178–79
unification of States 444–46
  customary international law 440–41
  default regimes 440
  incorporation 440
  merger 440–41
  succession to treaties 436, 440–41, 448

unilateral termination/termination by the terms of the treaty (Article 54a VCLT) 194–96
   BITs 194–96
   consent to arbitration 195–96
   customary international law 194
   re-negotiation of investment treaties 195
   withdrawal 194
United Nations (UN) Charter 111, 336–37
unjust enrichment 618–28
   Chorzów Factory case 621, 626
   contributory negligence 623–24
   customary international law 18–19
   damages, calculation of 622–23, 624–27
   definition 618, 619
   deviation 618, 626–27
   early decisions 621–22
   equitable compensation 622, 627
   expropriation 621, 624, 626
   fragmentation 618, 627
   general principle of law, as 18–19, 618–20, 621, 627
   government contracts 18–19
   indiscriminate deployment of concept 620
   just cause 622, 624
   Lena Goldfields case 621–22
   lex specialis 626
   Lighthouses Arbitration 622
   primary rule, as 620, 626–27
   procedure 4–5, 6, 18–19
   restitution 619, 621
   Sea-Land Service, Inc v Iran 623–24
   secondary rule, as 620, 626–27
   successor States 622

validity of treaties *see* invalidity of investment treaties
VCLT *see* Vienna Convention on the Law of Treaties (VCLT)
VCSST *see* Vienna Convention on Succession of States in Respect of Treaties (VCSST)
Vienna Convention on Succession of States in respect of State Property, Archives and Debts (VCSSPAD) 15
Vienna Convention on Succession of States in Respect of Treaties (VCSST) 14–15, 430
   BITs 424–25
   cession 15, 437, 439
   continuity principle 15, 443
   customary international law 14–15, 424, 437, 443
   devolution agreements 429–30
   general principles of law 424
   limitations 435
   moving treaty-frontiers principle 14–15
   multilateral treaties 15
   retroactive application 424
   separation/dissolution of States 440, 441–43
   special rules 443
   succession to BITs, procedure for 424–25
   transfers of territories 14–15
   unification of States 440–41

universal succession, principle of 15
verbal agreements 425
Vienna Convention on the Law of Treaties (VCLT)
   amendment and modification (Articles 40–41) 9–10, 182–86
   bilateral treaties 9–10
   competence to conclude treaties, provisions of internal law regarding (Article 46) 187–89
   corruption of a representative of a State (Article 50) 190–91
   customary international law 5, 8, 424
   diplomatic or consular relations, severance of (Article 63 VCLT) 208
   drafting 121–23
   entry into force (Article 24) 45–51
   fundamental change of circumstances (Article 62) 193–94, 207–8, 233–44
   general rule and amendment of bilateral treaties (Article 39) 178–82
   ICJ 468
   instruments for declaring invalid, terminating, withdrawing from or suspending operation of treaties (Article 67) 209
   internal law and observance of treaties (Article 27) 74–83
   internal law to justify failure to perform treaty obligations, States may not use 10–11
   international obligation in force for a State 313
   interpretation 7–9, 19–20, 518, 549
      amendment of bilateral treaties (Article 39) 178–82
      general rule of interpretation (Article 31) 120–45
      minimum standard of treatment (MST) 546–47
      supplementary means (Article 32) 146–65
   intertemporal aspects 10
   invalidity 9–10
   jus cogens (Article 53) 191–93
   languages, interpretation of treaties authenticated in two or more (Article 33) 176
   mutual termination/termination by consent (Article 54b) 196–200
   NAFTA standards standard 518
   non-retroactivity of treaties (Article 28) 84–99
   number of State parties 8
   obligation not to defeat the object and purpose of a treaty prior to its entry into force (Article 18) 23–31
   pacta sunt servanda 10–11, 64–73
   procedures for invalidity, termination, withdrawal from or suspension (Articles 65–68) 208–11
   provisional application (Article 25) 52–63
   rebus sic stantibus 11
   reservations (Articles 19–23 VCLT) 9–10, 33–44
   retroactivity 10
   State succession 4–5

successive treaties relating to the same subject matter, application of 9–10, 109–18
supervening impossibility of performance (Article 61) 193–94, 206–7
supplementary means of interpretation (Article 32) 146–65
suspension 9–10, 202–4
  breach 205–6
  declarations, instruments for 209
  implied by conclusion of a later treaty 178, 202–4
termination 9–10, 205–6
  breach 205–6
  declarations, instruments for 209
  implied by conclusion of a later treaty (Article 59) 178, 202–4
  mutual termination/termination by consent (Article 54b VCLT) 196–200
territorial scope (Article 29) 11, 100–8
unilateral termination/termination by the terms of the treaty (Article 54a) 194–96
withdrawal declarations, instruments for 209
withdrawal in the absence of treaty provisions or consent (Article 56)

Waldock, Humphrey 147–48, 167, 169, 525
withdrawal
  absence of treaty provisions or consent (Article 56 VCLT) 200–1
  declarations, instruments for 209
  denunciation 193–94, 200–1
  implied 193–94
  intention 201
  reservations 37–38, 43
  unilateral withdrawal 193, 194
Wood, Michael 465, 470–71
wrongfulness, circumstances precluding *see* consequences of invoking a circumstance precluding wrongfulness (Article 27 ARSIWA)